Managing Human Resources

Managing Human Resources

Fifth Edition

Luis R. Gómez-Mejía
Arizona State University

David B. Balkin
University of Colorado, Boulder

Robert L. Cardy
Chair of the Department of Management
University of Texas at San Antonio

PEARSON

Prentice Hall

Upper Saddle River, New Jersey 07458

Library of Congress Cataloging-in-Publication Data

Gomez-Mejia, Luis R.
  Managing human resources / Luis R. Gómez-Mejía, David B. Balkin, Robert L.
Cardy.—5th ed.
    p. cm.
  Includes bibliographical references and index.
  ISBN 0-13-187067-x (alk. paper)
    1. Personnel management. I. Balkin, David B., 1948-II. Cardy, Robert L., 1955-III.
Title.

HF5549.G64 2006
658.3—dc22   2006043202

Senior Acquisitions Editor: David Parker
VP/Editorial Director: Jeff Shelstad
Product Development Manager: Ashley Santora
Director of Development: Steve Deitmer
Development Editor: Elisa Adams
Editorial Assitant: Stephanie Kamens
Product Development Manger, Media: Nancy Welcher
Marketing Manager: Anne Howard
Marketing Assistant: Susan Osterlitz
Associate Director, Production Editorial: Judy Leale
Managing Editor: Renata Butera
Production Editor: Suzanne Grappi
Permissions Coordinator: Charles Morris
Associate Director, Manufacturing: Vinnie Scelta
Manufacturing Buyer: Indira Gutierrez
Design/Composition Manager: Christy Mahon
Composition Liaison: Nancy Thompson
Art Director: Pat Smythe
Interior Design: Judy Allan
Cover Design: Ray Cruz
Director, Image Resource Center: Melinda Reo
Manager, Rights and Permissions: Zina Arabia
Manager: Visual Research: Beth Brenzel
Image Permission Coordinator: Robert Farrell
Photo Researcher: Teri Stratford
Composition: Laserwords Private Limited
Full-Service Project Management: Jennifer Welsch/BookMasters, Inc.
Printer/Binder: Quebecor World–Dubuque
Typeface: 10/12 Berkeley

Credits and acknowledgments borrowed from other sources and reproduced, with permission, in this textbook appear
on appropriate page within text and on page 618.

Pearson Education LTD.   Pearson Education Australia PTY, Limited
Pearson Education Singapore, Pte. Ltd   Pearson Education North Asia Ltd
Pearson Education, Canada, Ltd   Pearson Educación de Mexico, S.A. de C.V.
Pearson Education–Japan   Pearson Education Malaysia, Pte. Ltd.

10 9 8 7 6 5 4 3 2
ISBN: 0-13-187067-x

To my wife Ana, my two sons Vince and Alex,
and my daughter Dulce
—L.G.M.

To my parents, Daniel and Jeanne
—D.B.B.

To my parents, Ralph and Dorothy; my wife, Laurel;
and my two daughters, Lara and Emery
—R.L.C.

Brief Contents

Contents

Managing Human Resources, Fifth Edition, prepares ALL FUTURE managers with a business understanding of the need for human resource management skills. Since the first edition of *Managing Human Resources* was published, the general management perspective has become much more prevalent among practicing managers. Recent environmental and organizational forces have contributed greatly to this trend. Organizations are becoming flatter. Technology such as the Internet fosters communication among all levels of personnel, and managers are expected to be generalists with a broad set of skills, including human resource management (HRM) skills. At the same time, fewer firms have a highly centralized, powerful human resource (HR) department that acts as monitor, decision maker, and controller of HR practices throughout the organization.

Most employees are now being asked to make difficult choices regarding benefit plans and often participate in HR decisions concerning recruitment and selection of new applicants, performance appraisals of peers and team members, enforcement of ethical policies, and the like. We believe that the "nonfunctional" HR approach used in this book makes HR relevant to anyone who has to deal with HR issues, including those who do not hold the title of managers.

Manager's Notebooks

The Manager's Notebook provides exposure to a variety of issues that managers confront daily, from providing feedback during an appraisal session to preparing employees for a layoff. Manager's Notebooks are divided into four categories:

- **Customer-Driven HR** demonstrates how managers and employees can benefit by approaching employees as internal customers.
- **Ethics** focuses on HR-specific ethics issues that challenge managers and employees.
- **Emerging Trends** presents new developments in HRM practice that are likely to require increased attention in the near future.
- **Global** focuses on HR practices in different countries and offers lessons that can be applied to diverse work contexts within the United States and elsewhere.

"You Manage It!" Discussion Cases

In an effort to make the theory of the Manager's Notebooks come to life, we provide case studies at the end of each chapter to support each of the Manager's Notebooks themes. For each case, we've included critical thinking questions, team exercises, and experiential exercises. These cases are organized as follows:

- **Emerging Trends** cases illustrate an HR-related issue that is likely to require increased attention in the future.
- **Customer-Driven HR** cases illustrate how HRM can add value to an organization by taking a customer-oriented perspective.
- **Ethics** cases illustrate how managing people can involve tough, real-life choices regarding the "right" actions that should be taken.

■ **Global** cases draw students' attention outside of the boundaries of the United States and illustrate that HR issues may be international in scope.

New to the Fifth Edition

Chapter 1, "Meeting Present and Emerging Strategic Human Resource Challenges," has been substantially revised to include some of the most recent environmental, organizational, and individual trends affecting HR practices. New topics include disaster preparedness, data security, ethical breaches, international brain drain, intellectual property, industrial metamorphosis, and research on "HR best practices" associated with high-performing firms. Most of the issues covered in the prior edition, such as globalization and rapid change, have been updated with new material.

Chapter 2, "Managing Work Flows and Conducting Job Analysis," has expanded coverage on virtual teams, part-time work, college interns, and an international comparison of the length of the work week. A discussion of offshore outsourcing to India and China have been added to this chapter.

Chapter 3, "Understanding Equal Opportunity and the Legal Environment," contains new EEOC rules pertaining to people with intellectual disabilities and the use of English-only rules at companies. Expanded coverage on gender discrimination and sexual harassment has also been added to this chapter.

Chapter 4, "Managing Diversity," has been thoroughly updated to include expanded treatment of people with disabilities, older workers, women, legal and undocumented immigrants, and people with different sexual orientations. A new category has been added concerning religious beliefs. The revised chapter examines issues to consider in diversity training and when conducting diversity audits. New cases have been added to deal with the most current diversity issues.

Chapter 5, "Recruiting and Selecting Employees," has expanded coverage on international issues, such as labor-shortage problems in China, temporary workers, and the recruitment of nontraditional labor. A new case addresses managing the supply and demand for labor from a supply chain perspective. Other new cases challenge students to consider recruiting and retaining female employees and reducing turnover while maximizing performance.

Chapter 6, "Managing Employee Separations, Downsizing, and Outplacement," has expanded coverage of the calculation and cause of turnover rates and considers the increase in turnover in Hong Kong. Layoffs, such as the recent GM layoff, are considered. Maintaining morale and performance following a layoff as well as understanding survivor anxiety are topics included in this edition. New cases in this chapter include consideration of the concept of employment-at-will and the effectiveness of retraining.

Chapter 7, "Appraising and Managing Performance," now includes coverage of the concept of competencies and presents examples of performance competencies. The global use of 360 degree appraisal is considered as a tool to instill a common set of values across cultures. The chapter also includes case exercises on the provocative issues of forced ranking (also termed "rank and yank") and cultural competency.

Chapter 8, "Training the Workforce," has expanded coverage on the link between training and profitability. In addition, there is expanded coverage of the use and effectiveness of online training, training to increase team performance, and ethics training. New case exercises lead students to consider training in global organizations, ethics training, and evaluating the behavioral impact of training.

Chapter 9, "Developing Careers," has expanded coverage of the issue of career advancement of women and expands consideration of the glass ceiling to other countries. The chapter now includes a self-assessment of career anchors and explores the implications of career anchors for effective personnel management. The topics of succession planning and mentoring receive increased attention. New case exercises address topics such as career self-assessment and career anchors.

Chapter 10, "Managing Compensation," provides new material on pay dispersion when there is high performance variance, cutbacks in compensation entitlements, "add ons" or "pay caps" that are renegotiable on an individual basis, new tax regulations for expensing stock options, new regulations concerning overtime pay, nonmonetary rewards, and compensation of knowledge workers.

Chapter 11, "Rewarding Performance," includes treatment of several new contemporary topics in pay for performance, such as the role of incentives in prompting unethical behaviors; team-based incentives and team-building exercises; linking incentives to a customer driven organizational strategy; firm reactions to the expensing of stock options; new SEC rules requiring detailed disclosure of CEO pay, including perks; and the Sabanes-Oxley Act. This chapter also revisits the age-old question: Does money motivate?

Chapter 12, "Designing and Administering Benefits," has expanded coverage on Social Security, including the use of cost-of-living increases for retirement benefits and the new prescription drug coverage under Medicare. New provisions to HIPAA that protect the privacy of employees medical information are explained. Recent developments in benefits added to the text include health savings accounts (HSAs) and the use of automatic enrollment for 401(K) retirement plans.

Chapter 13, "Developing Employee Relations," has increased emphasis on developing employee relations through technology, such as the online distribution of the employee handbook, and the appropriateness of e-mail for sending messages high in emotional content. Expanded coverage is given to patterns of informal communication that occur between employees and the use of employee assistance programs (EAPs) to resolve employee problems that occur away from the workplace but that affect job performance.

Chapter 14, "Respecting Employee Rights and Managing Discipline," includes new coverage of workplace bullying, a form of harassment that makes some workers dread going to their place of employment. New expanded coverage of workplace smoking policies, employee drug testing, electronic monitoring of employees, and the Sarbanes-Oxley law protection of whistleblowers has been added to the text.

Chapter 15, "Working with Organized Labor," includes expanded coverage on integrative bargaining tactics, how to bargain in good faith, the employer's use of the lockout to achieve its bargaining goals, and recent developments that have resulted in a reduction in the number of unions belonging to the AFL-CIO.

Chapter 16, "Managing Workplace Safety and Health," includes expanded consideration of the reduction of injury rates and costs. Expanded coverage of OSHA penalties and the management of these fines through negotiation is provided. Workplace fatality rates have been updated and workplace violence and wellness programs now receive expanded coverage. New case exercises include real-life issues, including workplace bullying, the danger posted by beryllium in the workplace, and the increasing importance of workers' mental health.

Chapter 17, "International HRM Challenges," now covers several new topics, including the **rise of outsourcing**; hiring and training of employees to monitor cyberspace; cultural intelligence; global compensation surveys; and payment of bribes overseas. More detailed coverage of HR policies for expatriates has also been added.

Faculty Resources

Instructor's Resource Center

Register. Redeem. Login.

www.prenhall.com/irc is where instructors can access a variety of print, media, and presentation resources available with this text in downloadable, digital format. For most texts, resources are also available for course management platforms such as Blackboard, WebCT, and Course Compass.

It gets better. Once you register, you will not have additional forms to fill out, or multiple usernames and passwords to remember to access new titles and/or editions. As a registered faculty member, you can login directly to download resource files, and receive immediate access and instructions for installing Course Management content to your campus server.

Need help? Our dedicated Technical Support team is ready to assist instructors with questions about the media supplements that accompany this text. Visit: *http://247.prenhall.com/* for answers to frequently asked questions and toll-free user support phone numbers. The following supplements are available to adopting instructors.

> **For detailed descriptions of all of the supplements listed below, please visit:** *www.prenhall.com/irc*

Instructor's Resource Center (IRC) on CD-ROM ISBN: 0-13-187069-6
Printed Instructor's Manual ISBN: 0-13-187068-8
Printed Test Item File ISBN: 0-13-187075-0
TestGen test generating software Visit the IRC (both online and on CD-Rom) for this text.
PowerPoints Visit the IRC (both online and on CD-Rom) for this text.
NEW! ABC News Videos on DVD ISBN: 0-13-187074-2

Student Resources

Student PowerPoint package located at *www.prenhall.com/gomez*

VangoNotes.com

Study on the go with VangoNotes—chapter reviews from your text in downloadable mp3 format. Now wherever you are—whatever you're doing—you can study by listening to the following for each chapter of your textbook:

- **Big Ideas:** Your "need to know" for each chapter
- **Practice Test:** A gut check for the Big Ideas—tells you if you need to keep studying
- **Key Terms:** Audio "flashcards" to help you review key concepts and terms
- **Rapid Review:** A quick drill session—use it right before your test

VangoNotes are **flexible**; download all the material directly to your player, or only the chapters you need. And they're **efficient**. Use them in your car, at the gym, walking to class, wherever. So get yours today. And get studying.

SafariX eTextbooks Online

The Largest eTextbook Store on the Internet!

Developed for students looking to save money on required or recommended textbooks, SafariX eTextbooks Online saves students up to 50 percent off the suggested list price of the print text. Students simply select their eText by title or author and purchase immediate access to the content for the duration of the course using any major credit card. With a SafariX eText, students can search for specific keywords or page numbers, make notes online, print out reading assignments that incorporate lecture notes, and bookmark important passages for later review. For more information, or to purchase a SafariX eTextbook, visit *www.safarix.com*.

Feedback

The author and product team would appreciate hearing from you! Let us know what you think about this textbook by writing to *college_marketing@prenhall.com* Please include "Feedback about Gomez-Mejia 5e" in the subject line.

If you have questions related to this product, please contact our customer service department online at *www.247.prenhall.com*

The contributions of many people made this book possible. The support and contributions of David Parker, Jeff Shelstad, Ashley Santora, Stephanie Kamens, and Elisa Adams made a tremendous difference.

The production and manufacturing teams at Prentice Hall also deserve special mention. Production Editor Suzanne Grappi handled the details, scheduling, and management of this project with grace and aplomb. Many thanks also to Renata Butera, Arnold Vila, and Vincent Scelta. Kudos to Permissions Supervisor Charles Morris and Photo Researcher Elaine Soares. Without their assistance, many visuals and text items would never have made their way into this book.

Our experience in working with everyone at Prentice Hall has been superb. Everyone at PH approached this book with commitment and enthusiasm. We were partners with the PH staff and feel that we are part of a high-performance team. We appreciate the commitment they displayed and would like to thank them for the experience.

We would also like to thank the many colleagues who reviewed the manuscript and offered valuable feedback. Their comments were pivotal in the development of the text:

Uzo Anakwe	Pace University	David Kaplan	James Madison University
Kamala Arogyaswamy	University of South Dakota	Tim Keaveny	Marquette University
Kristen Backhaus	SUNY New Paltz	Donald Knight	University of Maryland
Trevor Bain	University of Alabama	Anachai Kongchan	Chulalongkor University
Murray Barrick	University of Iowa	Lewis Lash	Barry University
Richard Bartlett	Muskingum Tech College	Helen Lavan	DePaul University
Deborah Bishop	Saginaw Valley State University	Stan Malos	San Jose State University
Jim Brakefield	Western Illinois University	Candice Miller	Brigham Young University—Idaho
Larry Brandt	Nova Southeastern University	Joe Mosca	Monmouth University
Mark Butler	San Diego State University	Paul Muchinsky	University of North Carolina at Greensboro
Steve Childers	East Carolina University	Smita Oxford	Mary Washington College
Denise Daniels	Seattle Pacific University	Steve Painchaud	Southern New Hampshire University
Kermit Davis	Auburn University	Elaine Potoker	Maine Maritime Academy
Kerry Davis	Auburn University	Dr. Jim Sethi	University of Montana-Western
Michelle Dean	University of North Texas	Marcia Simmering	Louisiana Tech University
Rebby Diehl	Salt Lake Community College	Janice Smith	North Carolina A&T
Cathy DuBois	Kent State University	Howard Stager	Buffalo State College
Rebecca Ellis	California Polytechnic State University	Cynthia Sutton	Indiana University
Debbie Goodwin	Lewis-Clark State College	Thomas Tang	Middle Tennessee State University
Anne Fiedler	Barry University	Tom Taveggia	University of Arizona
Hugh Findley	Troy State University	David Wade	Northern Illinois University
David Foote	Middle Tennessee State University	Edward Ward	St. Cloud State
David A. Hofmann	Michigan State University	Sandy Wayne	University of Illinois at Chicago
Harry Hollis	Belmont University	Les Wiletzky	Hawaii Pacific University
Deb Humphreys	California Polytechnic State University	Carol Young	Wittenberg University

Finally, this book would not have been possible without the indulgence of family and friends. We sincerely appreciate the patience and tolerance that were extended to us as we wrote the fifth edition.

Luis R. Gómez-Mejia
David B. Balkin
Robert L. Cardy

Luis R. Gómez-Mejía holds the Horace Steel chair in the W. P. Carey College of Business at Arizona State University. He received his Ph.D. and M.A. in industrial relations from the University of Minnesota and a "Summa Cum Laude" B.A. in economics from the University of Minnesota. Prior to entering academia, Professor Gómez-Mejía worked for eight years in human resources for the City of Minneapolis and Control Data Corporation. He has served as consultant to numerous organizations since then. Prior to joining ASU, he taught at the University of Colorado and the University of Florida. He has served two terms on the editorial board of the *Academy of Management Journal* and is editor and cofounder of the *Journal of High Technology Management Research*. He is president and founder of the Iberoamerican Academy of Management and was past president of the Human Resource Division of the

Academy of Management. He has published over 120 articles appearing in the most prestigious management journals, including the *Academy of Management Journal, Administrative Science Quarterly, Strategic Management Journal, Industrial Relations,* and *Personnel Psychology.* He has also written and edited a dozen management books published by McGraw-Hill, Prentice Hall, Southwestern Press, JAI Press, and Grid. He was ranked one of the top nine in research productivity based on the number of publications in the *Academy of Management Journal.* He has received numerous awards, including "best article" in the *Academy of Management Journal* (1992), Council of 100 Distinguished Scholars at Arizona State University (1994), "Hall of Fame" of the Academy of Management (2000), the "Outstanding Service, Leadership, and Commitment" award by the Management Doctoral Student Association (2002), the "Outstanding Alumni Achievement Award" by University of Minnesota (2004), and Regents Professor by Arizona State University (2004). Professor Gómez-Mejía's research focuses on macro HR issues, international HR practices, and compensation.

David B. Balkin Is Professor of Management in the College of Business Administration at the University of Colorado at Boulder. He received his Ph.D. in industrial relations from the University of Minnesota. Prior to joining the University of Colorado, he served on the faculties of Louisiana State University and Northeastern University. He has published over 35 articles appearing in such journals as the *Academy of*

Management Journal, Strategic Management Journal, Industrial Relations, Personnel Psychology, Journal of Labor Research, and *Academy of Management Executive.* One of his publications (coauthored with Luis R. Gómez-Mejía) was selected as the best article published in 1992 in the *Academy of Management Journal.* Professor Balkin has written or edited three books on HRM topics. He has consulted for a number of organizations, including U.S. West, Baxter Healthcare, Hydro Quebec, and The Commonwealth of Massachusetts. Professor Balkin's research focuses on the interaction between business strategy and HR policies, and the design and implementation of reward systems.

Robert L. Cardy Is Chair of the Department of Management at The University of Texas at San Antonio. He received his Ph.D. in industrial/organizational psychology from Virginia Tech in 1982. He is an ad hoc reviewer for a variety of journals, including the *Academy of Management Journal* and the *Academy of Management Review.* He is editor and cofounder of the *Journal of Quality Management.* Professor Cardy has been recognized for his research, teaching, and service. He was ranked in the

top 20 in research productivity for the decade 1980–89 based on the number of publications in the *Journal of Applied Psychology.* He was doctoral coordinator in ASU's management department for five years and received a University Mentor Award in 1993 for his work with doctoral students. He authors a regular column on current issues in HRM and received an Academy of Management certificate for outstanding service as a columnist for the HR division newsletter. Professor Cardy was a 1992 recipient of a certificate for significant contributions to the quality of life for students at ASU. His research focuses on performance appraisal and effective HRM practices in a quality-oriented organizational environment.

Managing Human Resources

Meeting Present and Emerging Strategic Human Resource Challenges

Challenges

After reading this chapter, you should be able to deal more effectively with the following challenges:

1 **Explain** how a firm's human resources influence its performance.

2 **Describe** how firms can use HR initiatives to cope with workplace changes and trends such as a more diverse workforce, the global economy, downsizing, and new legislation.

3 **Distinguish** between the role of the HR department and the role of the firm's managers in utilizing human resources effectively.

4 **Formulate** and implement HR strategies that can help the firm achieve a sustained competitive advantage.

5 **Identify** HR strategies that fit corporate and business unit strategies.

6 **Indicate** "HR Best Practices" associated with high-performing firms.

James Roberts is understandably bitter about the realignment of America's steel industry. "It's hardly fair; hardly right," said Mr. Roberts, a 68-year-old retiree from the Bethlehem Steel plant in Steelton, Pennsylvania, who lost his health-care coverage and a third of his pension as the company sank into bankruptcy in the early 2000s.

But for Jerry Ernest, a 54-year-old maintenance technician at a former Bethlehem plant, the company's subsequent reorganization and reemergence as part of the global giant Mittal Steel was not quite as bad. The money is better, thanks in part to generous bonuses and performance incentives. "I'm in my golden period," Mr. Ernest said. "I'm doing better at this mill than I've ever done."

What was once Bethlehem Steel is more competitive now than it has been in a long while, combusting cheap foreign steel as a larger company with a leaner workforce and more pricing power. To arrive at this stage, Bethlehem trimmed its workforce to 8,200, down from 11,500 three years ago, and cast off many of its roughly 70,000 retirees from the company's pension plan. Layers of management were eliminated, giving workers much more autonomy to do their jobs. Variable "one-time" bonuses have supplanted the salary increases of a bygone era.[1]

Bethlehem's story illustrates the changing landscape in human resource management. According to one observer, the company "abandoned the part of industrial America's social contract that implied that if workers gave the company decades of hot and dirty factory work, the company would, in return, provide generously for them in old age."[2] Numerous organizations are rescinding pension plans, health-care benefits, assured salaries, and job security. These include most major airlines (such as Delta, Northwest, United, and U.S. Airways), Polaroid, Delphi Corporation (the largest autoparts maker), and General Motors, among many others.[3] For example, Delphi Corporation has proposed to cut average employee wages from $25 to $9 dollars an hour during 2007–2010. Little job security now exists in the private sector, with the U.S. economy creating and destroying more than 30 million jobs a year.[4] And more companies (including such American icons as Wal-Mart, General Motors and Chrysler) are demanding that employees take more control of their health-care spending (and offering high-deductible insurance plans coupled with health savings accounts).[5]

On the plus side, employees probably have more options than ever before to find the best match for their talents without being wedded to a particular organization. They are being given increasing responsibility and autonomy with less need for close supervision. And rewards are now more closely tied to performance than ever before, with the percentage of variable pay (such as bonuses and incentives) more than doubling during the past 10 years.[6] Most importantly, in the long run (as the case of Bethlehem suggests), the only way a company can share greater economic gains with employees is to become more competitive and generate more wealth.

For many employees who are dissatisfied with a corporate setting or face the possibility of being laid off, entrepreneurship represents a way out. Seventy percent of *Inc. Magazine*'s 500 firms were started by entrepreneurs who got their original idea while working for other employers.[7] A 2005 study by the highly respected Kauffman Foundation reports that, on average, an astonishing 550,000 new businesses are launched in the United States each month.[8]

In the highly competitive world of work just described, which the *Wall Street Journal* has labeled "the jungle,"[9] human resource management is relevant not just for people who plan to work in a human resource department. To be successful, employees are being asked to manage time effectively, to plan their career, to keep on learning, to monitor the pulse of the labor market and be ready to change employers on short notice, to negotiate compensation packages, to invest wisely for their retirement, to work with people from diverse backgrounds, to participate in the selection and appraisal of peers, to be on the alert for sexual harassment and discriminatory practices, to report unethical or illegal practices, and the like.

This book is written with the idea that most employees are likely to have some human resource responsibility, either for themselves or for those around them. Hence, it is important to learn how to operate effectively in this environment even if you never intend to work in a human resource department or become a human resource management specialist. We also believe that each manager is a human resources manager. Thus, we offer helpful guidelines and information that managers—from supervisors to top executives—can apply to everyday situations. For instance, we examine how to hire and retain the best people, reward employees fairly, train and develop employees, and use a diverse workforce to gain a competitive advantage.

THE MANAGERIAL PERSPECTIVE

This book is about the people who work in an organization and their relationship with that organization. Different terms are used to describe these people: *employees, associates* (at Wal-Mart, for instance), *personnel, human resources.* None of these terms is better than the others, and they often are used

Businesses are finding innovative ways to retain employees who must work harder than ever to keep their firms competitive. Architectural firm Gould Evans Goodman has a "nap tent" for workers to use whenever they need to catch up on sleep. Other businesses offer employees benefits such as on-site yoga classes, sculpting lessons, and concierge services.

interchangeably. The term we have chosen for the title of this text, and which we will use throughout, is **human resources (HR)**.* It has gained widespread acceptance over the last decade, because it expresses the belief that workers are a valuable and sometimes irreplaceable resource. Effective human resource management (HRM) is a major component of any manager's job.

A **human resource strategy** refers to a firm's deliberate use of human resources to help it gain or maintain an edge against its competitors in the marketplace.[10] It is the grand plan or general approach an organization adopts to ensure that it effectively uses its people to accomplish its mission. A **human resource tactic** is a particular policy or program that helps to advance a firm's strategic goal. Strategy precedes and is more important than tactics.

In this chapter, we focus on the general framework within which specific HR activities and programs fit. With the help of the company's human resources department, managers implement the chosen HR strategies.[11] In subsequent chapters, we move from the general to the specific and examine in detail the spectrum of HR strategies (for example, those regarding work design, staffing, performance appraisal, career planning, and compensation).[12]

Human resources (HR)
People who work in an organization. Also called *personnel.*

Human resource strategy
A firm's deliberate use of human resources to help it gain or maintain an edge against its competitors in the marketplace. The grand plan or general approach an organization adopts to ensure that it effectively uses its people to accomplish its mission.

Human resource tactic
A particular HR policy or program that helps to advance a firm's strategic goal.

Human Resource Management: The Challenges

Managers are people who are in charge of others and are responsible for the timely and correct execution of actions that promote their units' successful performance. In this book, we use the term *unit* broadly; it may refer to a work team, department, business unit, division, or corporation.

All employees (including managers) can be differentiated as line or staff. **Line employees** are directly involved in producing the company's good(s) or delivering the service(s). A *line manager* manages line employees. **Staff employees** are those who support the line function. For example, people who work in the HR department are considered staff employees because their job is to provide supporting services for line employees. Employees may also be differentiated

Manager
A person who is in charge of others and is responsible for the timely and correct execution of actions that promote his or her unit's success.

Line employee
An employee involved directly in producing the company's good(s) or delivering the service(s).

*All terms in boldface also appear in the Key Terms list at the end of the chapter.

Staff employee
An employee who supports line employees.

according to how much responsibility they have. *Senior employees* are those who have been with the company longer and have more responsibility than *junior employees*. *Exempt employees* (sometimes called *salaried employees*) are those who do not receive extra pay for overtime work (beyond 40 hours per week). *Nonexempt employees* do receive overtime compensation. This text is written primarily to help students who intend to be managers deal effectively with the challenges of managing people.

Figure 1.1 summarizes the major HR challenges facing today's managers. Firms that deal with these challenges effectively are likely to outperform those that do not. These challenges may be categorized according to their primary focus: the environment, the organization, or the individual.

Environmental Challenges

Environmental challenges
Forces external to a firm that affect the firm's performance but are beyond the control of management.

Environmental challenges are the forces external to the firm. They influence organizational performance but are largely beyond management's control. Managers, therefore, need to monitor the external environment constantly for opportunities and threats. They must also maintain the flexibility to react quickly to challenges. One common and effective method for monitoring the environment is to read the business press, including *BusinessWeek, Fortune,* and the *Wall Street Journal.* (The Appendix at the end of this book provides an annotated listing of both general business publications and more specialized publications on HR management and related topics.)

Seven important environmental challenges today are rapid change, the rise of the Internet, workforce diversity, globalization, legislation, evolving work and family roles, skill shortages and the rise of the service sector.

Rapid Change
Many organizations face a volatile environment in which change is nearly constant.[13] For this reason IBM's CEO, Sam Palmisano, tells his managers that he doesn't believe in forecasts longer than one week.[14] If they are to survive and prosper, they need to adapt to change quickly

Key HR Challenges for Today's Managers

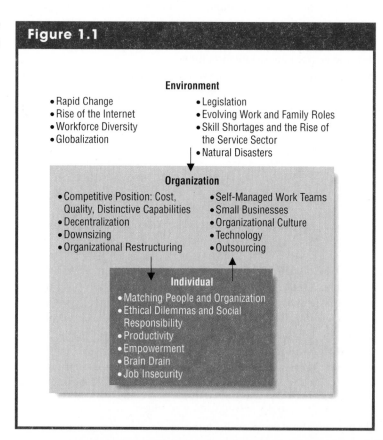

Figure 1.1

Environment
- Rapid Change
- Rise of the Internet
- Workforce Diversity
- Globalization
- Legislation
- Evolving Work and Family Roles
- Skill Shortages and the Rise of the Service Sector
- Natural Disasters

Organization
- Competitive Position: Cost, Quality, Distinctive Capabilities
- Decentralization
- Downsizing
- Organizational Restructuring
- Self-Managed Work Teams
- Small Businesses
- Organizational Culture
- Technology
- Outsourcing

Individual
- Matching People and Organization
- Ethical Dilemmas and Social Responsibility
- Productivity
- Empowerment
- Brain Drain
- Job Insecurity

and effectively. Human resources are almost always at the heart of an effective response system.[15] Here are a few examples of how HR policies can help or hinder a firm grappling with external change:

A Question of Ethics

How much responsibility does an organization have to shield its employees from the effects of rapid change in the environment? What risks does this type of "shock absorber" approach to management entail?

- **New company town** As firms experience high pressure to become more productive and deal with very short product life cycles (often measured in months), Americans are working longer, harder, and faster.[16] As a result, the line between home and work is blurred for many employees. To deal with this phenomenon, observes sociologist Helen Mederer at University of Rhode Island, "companies are taking the best aspects of home and incorporating them into work."[17]

  A 2005 survey of 975 employers by consulting firm Hewitt Associates found that an increasing number of companies are providing "home at work" benefits. These include dry cleaner/laundry service, company store, take-home meals, concierge service, oil changes/autocare, hair salon, and pet care.[18]

  According to a report in the *New York Times:*[19]

  > . . . things like nap rooms and massage recliners may sound out of place to some in a working environment. But such perks can boost productivity when there are older workers with sore backs, or young parents with sometimes sleepless nights. Musical performance, too, may seem at first like an unnecessary distraction. But companies trying them say that they can be done simply and inexpensively, and that they produce better morale, increased motivation and less stress.

- **Dealing with stress** Rapid change and work overload can put employees under a great deal of stress. In 2003, the Bureau of Labor Statistics reported that 50 percent of the 19.8 million Americans who say they work at home at least once a week aren't compensated for it. In other words, millions of employees must work at home just in order to catch up.[20]

  Unless the organization develops support mechanisms to keep stress manageable, both the firm and employees may pay a heavy price.[21] In some extreme cases, workplace violence may result. In 2005, the Center for Disease Control called workplace violence a "national epidemic"; the most recent figures indicate that U.S. employees at work were the victims of 18,104 injuries from assault and 609 homicides.[22] Typically, however, the observed results of poorly handled stress are more subtle yet still highly destructive, costing the company money. According to some estimates, stress-related ailments cost companies about $200 billion a year in increased absenteeism, tardiness, and the loss of talented workers.[23] One recent survey reports that 67 percent of employees categorize their work-related stress as high.[24] Many firms, including Microsoft, Sysco Food Services, Apple, IBM, General Motors, Google, Chrysler, Johnson & Johnson, Coors Brewing Co., CitiGroup Inc., Texas Instruments, and Hughes Aircraft, among others, have introduced stress-control programs in recent years.[25]

Throughout this book we emphasize how HR practices can enable a firm to respond quickly and effectively to external changes. Two chapters (Chapter 13 on employee relations and Chapter 16 on managing workplace safety and health) specifically deal with issues related to employee stress.

The Internet Revolution

The dramatic growth of the Internet in recent years probably represents the single most important environmental trend affecting organizations and their human resource practices. In the mid-1990s, the term *Web economy* had not yet been coined.[26] Now, almost all firms use the Internet as part of their normal business practices. The Internet is having pervasive impact on how organizations manage their human resources, as the following examples show:

- **Necessitating greater written communication skills** Companies have discovered that Internet technology creates a high demand for workers who can deal effectively with e-mail messages.[27] This skill is key if companies want to keep fickle Internet customers loyal, making them less likely to go to a competitor by simply tapping a few keystrokes.

  E-mail writing may also involve legal issues. For instance, an employee's e-mail response to a customer complaint may be legally binding on the firm, and there is the "written" record to prove it.

And, although English is the main language of the Internet, almost half of Internet communication takes place in foreign languages and only 7 percent of users on a global basis are native English speakers.[28] Major multimillion-dollar blunders due to language problems have already been documented, such as the case of Juan Pablo Davila, a commodity trader in Chile. He typed the word "buy" on the computer by mistake instead of "sell." To rectify his mistake, he started a frenzy of buying and selling, losing 0.5 percent of his country's GNP. His name became [an Internet-related] verb, "davilar," meaning "to screw up royally."[29]

- **Dealing with information overflow** Although executives spend on average four hours a day receiving, checking, preparing, and sending e-mails, they are still spending 130 minutes a day in formal and informal face-to-face meetings. According to Neil Flett, CEO of a large communication consulting firm, "While some have seen e-mail as a time-saving device, e-mail appears to be adding to the time spent communicating in business, not reducing time."[30]

  According to some estimates, almost a third of e-mails received by employees were not directly relevant to their jobs, and considering that employees are now receiving an average of 30 e-mails each day, this may translate into as much as one hour a day of lost productivity.[31]

- **Breaking down labor market barriers** More than ever before, the Internet is creating an open labor market where information about prospective employees and firms is available on a global basis and may be obtained quickly and inexpensively.[32] *Monster.com*, for instance, posted 50 million resumes in the fall of 2005.[33] Thousands of specialized search engines (such as *Indeed.com, Simplyhired.com, Workzoo.com,* and *Jobsearch.org*) now scan both well-known and obscure employment boards on the job seeker's behalf.[34]

- **Using online learning** Corporate training has always been dominated by in-house traditional "paper-and-pencil" training programs. Over the last few years, however, there has been a tremendous migration from classroom learning to online learning.[35] For example, 99 percent of employees at Mayo Clinic opted for online training to learn about new rules on health-care privacy (even though the clinic gave them the option to attend a traditional classroom seminar on company time covering the same material).[36]

- **Enabling HR to focus on management** The Internet allows firms to handle many operational HR details much more quickly and efficiently. According to Philip Fauver, president and CEO of Employease Inc., the Internet is "the enabler."[37] For a flat fee of about $5 to $6 per employee, Employease manages HR information for 700 small to midsize companies. One of its clients is Amerisure Insurance Cos., in Farmington Hills, Michigan. According to Derick Adams, Amerisure's HR vice president, the Internet allowed his 14-member HR department to devote more attention to important managerial challenges. For instance, Adams notes that his department was able to "develop a variable pay plan after handing off the department's data entry work to Employease."[38]

Workforce Diversity

Managers across the United States are confronted daily with the increasing diversity of the workforce. In 2006, approximately 33 percent of the U.S. workforce was made up of African Americans (12%), Asian Americans (4.7%), Latinos (14%), and other minorities (2%).[39] In many large urban centers, such as Miami, Los Angeles, and New York, the workforce is already at least half composed of minorities. The influx of women workers is another major change in the composition of the U.S. workforce. Women with children under age 6 are now the fastest-growing segment of the workforce. Currently, more than 76 percent of employed men have employed wives. This compares with 54 percent in 1980.[40]

These trends are likely to accelerate in the future. By 2050, the U.S. population is expected to increase by 50 percent, with nearly half the population consisting of minority groups. Nonwhite immigrants, mostly Hispanics, will account for 60 percent of the population growth. Despite fears that immigrants are not assimilating, children of immigrants actually do better than children of natives in the same socioeconomic class.[41]

Furthermore, never before in history has such a large-scale mixing of the races occurred, due to a sharp rise in the rate of intermarriage.[42] "One day race will not be needed because it will be obsolete," notes Candy Mills, a magazine editor in Los Angeles, who is black. Candy is married to a French-Hungarian with whom she has a child. Speaking of her family, she says, "We are what America will look like in maybe 100 years."[43] The U.S. Census Bureau has acknowledged this reality, incorporating "mixed" categories for future population censuses.

All these trends present both a significant challenge and a real opportunity for managers.[44] Firms that formulate and implement HR strategies that capitalize on employee diversity are more likely to survive and prosper. Chapter 4 is devoted exclusively to the topic of managing employee diversity. This issue is also discussed in several other chapters throughout this book.

Globalization

One of the most dramatic challenges facing U.S. firms as they enter the second decade of the twenty-first century is how to compete against foreign firms, both domestically and abroad. The Internet is fueling globalization, and most large firms are actively involved in manufacturing overseas, international joint ventures, or collaboration with foreign firms on specific projects.

The implications of a global economy for HRM are many. Here are a few examples:

- **Worldwide company culture** Some firms try to develop a global company identity to smooth over cultural differences between domestic employees and those in international operations. Minimizing these differences increases cooperation and can have a strong impact on the bottom line. For instance, the head of human resources at the European division of Colgate Palmolive notes, "We try to build a common corporate culture. We want them all to be Colgaters."[45]

- **Worldwide recruiting** Some firms recruit workers globally, particularly in the high-technology area, where specialized knowledge and expertise are not limited by national boundaries.[46] For instance, Unisys (an e-business solutions company whose 37,000 employees help customers in 100 countries apply information technology) recruits between 5,000 and 7,000 people a year, 50 percent of whom are information technology (IT) professionals. In the words of one Unisys executive: "If we were looking for someone to run a practice in Europe, we would not hold the search to a single country. We would be looking across borders to try to find the best person."[47]

  Global recruitment, however, is no panacea, because good employees everywhere are in high demand, and there may not be as much information available to make the appropriate selection decision.[48] Kevin Barnes, technical director for Store Perform, with facilities in Bangalore, India, notes that "top Indian engineers are world-class, but most are taken. Anyone in India who can spell *Java* already has a job." And the labor market attracts legions of unqualified candidates, Barnes says, making it harder to distinguish good from mediocre performers.[49]

- **Industrial metamorphosis** The proportion of the American labor force in manufacturing has dropped to less than 10 percent from 25 percent about 30 years ago. Similar drops have been experienced in several European countries, including England, Germany, and France. "It has happened because rich-world companies have replaced workers with new technology to boost productivity and shifted production from labor-intensive products such as textiles to higher-tech, higher value-added, sectors such as pharmaceuticals. Within firms, low-skilled jobs have moved offshore."[50] Labor unions have lost much of their influence.[51] For instance, during 2005–2006 Volkswagen in Germany demanded—and won—three rounds of wage concessions from labor unions, partly by threatening to move car production to Portugal, where hourly wages are less than a third of those in Germany.

- **Global alliances** International alliances with foreign firms require a highly trained and devoted staff. For instance, Philips (a Dutch lighting and electronics firm) became the largest lighting manufacturer in the world by establishing a joint venture with AT&T and making several key acquisitions, including Magnavox, parts of GE Sylvania, and the largest lighting company in France.[52]

- **A virtual workforce** Because of restrictive U.S. immigration quotas,[53] U.S. firms are tapping skilled foreign labor but not moving those workers to the United States. The Internet is making this possible with little additional expense. For example, Microsoft Corp. and Real Networks Inc. use a Bangalore, India, company, Adite Corp., to handle customer e-mails.[54] In addition, many "virtual" expatriates work abroad but live at home. "Virtual expatriation arises when someone takes an assignment to manage an operation or area abroad without being located permanently in that country. . . . Communications technology [allows them] to stay in touch with far-flung troops. . . . The virtual expat is a new breed of manager that is multiplying."[55]

An entire chapter of this book (Chapter 17) is devoted to the HR issues firms face as they expand overseas. We also include international examples throughout the book to illustrate how firms in other countries manage their human resources.

Legislation

Much of the growth in the HR function over the past three decades may be attributed to its crucial role in keeping the company out of trouble with the law.[56] Most firms are deeply concerned with potential liability resulting from personnel decisions that may violate laws enacted by the U.S. Congress, state legislatures, or local governments.[57] Discrimination charges filed by older employees, minorities, and the disabled, for instance, have been on the rise for years. In some cases, such as charges of sex discrimination by Hispanic and Asian women, the increase has exceeded 65 percent in the past 15 years.[58]

One legal area growing in importance is alleged misuse of "proprietary company information" by ex-employees. Pitney Bowes, the world's largest maker of postage meters and other mailing equipment, recently sued eight ex-employees who opened a small competing firm called Nexxpost. According to Pitney Bowes' spokesperson:

> The company invests a great deal of time and money in areas of developing our intellectual property, in marketing and training our sales force. We must protect our investment, which also includes our customer lists, information about consumer preferences as well as pricing. All that has a significant competitive value. When a former employee wants to challenge us, we take that breach very seriously and do what we need to do to protect it.[59]

Operating within the legal framework requires keeping track of the external legal environment and developing internal systems (for example, supervisory training and grievance procedures) to ensure compliance and minimize complaints. Many firms are now developing formal policies on sexual harrassment and establishing internal administrative channels to deal with alleged incidents before employees feel the need to file a lawsuit. In a country where mass litigation is on the rise,[60] these efforts may well be worth the time and money.

Legislation may differentiate between public- and private-sector organizations. (*Public sector* is another term for governmental agencies; *private sector* refers to all other types of organizations.) For instance, affirmative action requirements (see Chapter 3) are typically limited to public organizations and to organizations that do contract work for them. However, much legislation applies to both public- and private-sector organizations. In fact, it is difficult to think of any HR practices that are *not* influenced by government regulations. For this reason, each chapter of this book addresses pertinent legal issues, and an entire chapter (Chapter 3) provides an overall framework that consolidates the main legal issues and concerns facing employers today.

Evolving Work and Family Roles

The proportion of *dual-career* families, in which both wife and husband (or both members of a couple) work, is increasing every year. More companies are introducing "family-friendly" programs that give them a competitive advantage in the labor market.[61] These programs are HR tactics that companies use to hire and retain the best-qualified employees, male or female. Through the Office of Personnel Management, the federal government provides technical assistance to organizations that wish to implement family-friendly policies. On its 2006 Web page (*www.opm.gov*), for instance, the office makes available numerous publications on such issues as adoption benefits, child care, elder-care resources, parenting support, and telework.

Family-friendly policies are discussed in detail in Chapter 12 under the heading "Employee Services." Special issues that women confront in the workplace are discussed in Chapter 4.

Skill Shortages and the Rise of the Service Sector

As noted earlier, U.S. manufacturing has dropped dramatically in terms of the percentage of employees who work in the sector. Most employment growth has taken place in the service industry. The categories with the fastest growth are expected to be professional specialties (27%) and technical occupations (22%). The fastest-growing occupations demand at least two years of college training.[62] Expansion of service-sector employment is linked to a number of factors, including changes in consumer tastes and preferences, legal and regulatory changes, advances in science and technology that have eliminated many manufacturing jobs, and changes in the way businesses are organized and managed.

Unfortunately, many available workers will be too unskilled to fill those jobs. Even now, many companies complain that the supply of skilled labor is dwindling and that they must provide their employees with basic training to make up for the shortcomings of the public education system.[63] For example, 84 percent of the 23,000 people applying for entry-level jobs at Bell Atlantic Telephone (formerly NYNEX) failed the qualifying test.[64] Chemical Bank reported that it had to interview 40 applicants to find one proficient teller.[65] David Hearns, former chairman and CEO of Xerox, laments that "the American workforce is running out of qualified people."[66]

To rectify these shortcomings, companies spend at least $55 billion a year on a wide variety of training programs. This is in addition to the $24 billion spent on training programs by the federal government each year.[67] On the employee-selection side, an increasing number of organizations are relying on job simulations to test for the "soft skills" needed to succeed in a service environment [such as sound judgment in ambiguous situations, the ability to relate to diverse groups of people, and effective handling of angry or dissatisfied customers (see Manager's Notebook: Customer-Driven HR, "Job Simulations to Hire Employees")].

A Question of Ethics

What is the ethical responsibility of an employer to employees who lack basic literacy and numeracy skills? Should companies be required by law to provide training opportunities for such employees, as some have proposed?

Customer-Driven HR

MANAGER'S NOTEBOOK

Job Simulations to Hire Employees

While reality television takes the "show me" job interview to extremes, ordinary employers use more modest simulations to hire everyone from customer-service representatives to firefighters to chief executives. Many employers now believe that work simulations are a more reliable predictor of job performance than traditional screening methods. Fear of lawsuits has made employee references virtually useless, and savvy job candidates easily can bluff their way through the familiar interview questions, which are posted online along with the "right" answers. Simulations can better capture the "soft skills" needed to succeed in a service society.

Central Pierce Fire & Rescue near Tacoma, Washington, relies on simulations to fill openings in its 180-person workforce. Potential mechanics, secretaries, firefighters, and computer-support people are put through a battery of tests to measure job skills, ethics, attitudes, and patience. Karen Johnson, HR manager, said that role-playing and other exercises reveal qualities about candidates that may otherwise be hidden. Because firefighters spend more time dealing with the public than fighting fires, they're tested on both technical skills and on how they deal with irate or troubled citizens.

"There are definitely people who shine," Johnson said, "but you'll find that some people don't know how to react when someone's yelling at them. We've had a couple candidates throw (the role-player) out the door. As you can imagine," she added, "they don't score highly."

Simulations for top jobs often will include a lifelike office with ringing phones, pinging e-mail messages, and a subordinate standing in the doorway with an urgent question. The candidate's response can demonstrate whether the person is a delegator, a micromanager, a leader, or a bully.

Source: Adapted with permission from Holt, S. (2005). More job simulations: Candidates tested for abilities, reactions. *Seattle Times,* D-1.

The skill shortage is likely to remain a major challenge for U.S. firms. During 2007–2009, New York is expected to become the first state in the nation to issue a "work readiness" credential to high school students who pass a voluntary test measuring their ability to succeed in entry-level jobs. "Employers have complained for years that too many students leave high school without basic skills, despite the battery of exams—considered among the most stringent in the nation—that New York requires for graduation."[68] The proposed test would cover "soft skills," including the ability to communicate, follow directions, negotiate and make basic decisions, in 10 broad areas. Chapter 8 focuses directly on training; Chapters 5 (staffing), 7 (appraising employee performance), and 9 (career development) discuss issues related to the skills and knowledge required to succeed on the job.

Natural Disasters

A stream of recent disasters, including the tsunami that killed over 250,000 people in Asia in early 2005 and a string of devastating hurricanes, most notably Katrina, which destroyed most of the city of New Orleans in August 2005, have increased awareness among HR professionals of the importance of having plans to deal with such catastrophes. A survey conducted by Mercer Human Resource Consulting indicated that almost 3 million employees were affected in one way or another by Katrina.[69] Employers had to suddenly deal with HR issues that they had given little thought to before. These included deciding whether to keep paying employees who were unreachable and unable to report to work: paying for a variety of living expenses for displaced staffers in temporary living quarters, providing telecommuting equipment for employees working from hotels, awarding hazardous duty pay, hiring temporary employees (many of whom were undocumented workers) to fill the manpower void, and preventing the loss of key talent to competitors outside the disaster area.[70] Time Warner Inc. waived medical deductibles and supported out-of-network medical coverage for affected Katrina families. Wal-Mart, with more than 34,000 employees displaced by Katrina, guaranteed them work in any other U.S. Wal-Mart store and created an "Associate Disaster Relief Fund" for employees whose homes were flooded or destroyed.[71] Surprisingly, even after Katrina, almost half of firms don't have HR policies to deal with major disasters.[72] But this is likely to change as new potential threats (such as avian flu, major earthquakes, chemical contamination, and more hurricanes) loom on the horizon,[73] along with terrorism fears, which we discuss later.

Organizational Challenges

Organizational challenges
Concerns or problems internal to a firm; often a by-product of environmental forces.

Organizational challenges are concerns or problems internal to a firm. Effective managers spot organizational issues and deal with them before they become major problems. One of the themes of this text is *proactivity:* the need for firms to take action before problems get out of hand. This can be done only by managers who are well informed about important HR issues and organizational challenges.

Competitive Position: Cost, Quality, or Distinctive Capabilities

Human resources represent the single most important cost in many organizations. Organizational labor costs range from 36 percent in capital-intensive firms like commercial airlines to 80 percent in labor-intensive firms like the U.S. Postal Service. How effectively a company uses its human resources can have a dramatic effect on its ability to compete (or survive) in an increasingly competitive environment.

HR policies can affect an organization's competitive position by controlling costs, improving quality, and creating distinctive capabilities.

- **Controlling costs** A compensation system that uses innovative reward strategies to control labor costs can help the organization grow, as we discuss in Chapters 10 and 11. Other ways to keep labor costs under control include making better employee selection decisions (Chapter 5); training employees to make them more efficient and productive (Chapter 8); attaining harmonious labor relations (Chapter 15); effectively managing health and safety issues in the workplace (Chapter 16); and reducing the time and resources needed to design, produce, and deliver quality products or services (Chapter 2).

Total quality management (TQM)
An organizationwide approach to improving the quality of all the processes that lead to a final product or service.

- **Improving quality** Many companies have implemented **total quality management (TQM)** initiatives, designed to improve the quality of all the processes that lead to a final product or service. Continuing evidence shows that firms that effectively implement quality programs tend to outperform those that don't.[74]

- **Creating distinctive capabilities** The third way to gain a competitive advantage is to use people with distinctive capabilities to create unsurpassed competence in a particular area (for example, 3M's competence in adhesives, Carlson Corporation's leading presence in the travel business, and Xerox's dominance of the photocopier market). Chapter 5 (which discusses the recruitment and selection of employees), Chapter 8 (training), and Chapter 9 (the long-term grooming of employees within the firm) are particularly relevant.

Decentralization

Organizations commonly centralize major functions, such as HR, marketing, and production, in a single location that serves as the firm's command center. Multiple layers of management execute orders issued at the top and employees move up the ranks over time in what some have called the *internal labor market*.[75] However, the traditional topdown form of organization is being replaced by **decentralization**, which transfers responsibility and decision-making authority from a central office to people and locations closer to the situation that demands attention. The Internet helps companies to decentralize even faster by improving the communication flow among the workforce, reducing the need to rely on the traditional organizational pyramid.[76]

    The need for maintaining or creating organizational flexibility in HR strategies is addressed in several chapters of this book, including those dealing with work flows (Chapter 2), compensation (Chapters 10 and 11), training (Chapter 8), staffing (Chapter 5), and globalization (Chapter 17).

Downsizing

Periodic reductions in a company's workforce to improve its bottom line—often called **downsizing**—are becoming standard business practice, even among firms that were once legendary for their "no layoff" policies, such as IBM, Kodak, and Xerox.[77] Although U.S. firms traditionally were far more willing to resort to layoffs as a cost-cutting measure than companies in other industrialized nations, globalization is quickly closing the gap. During 2005–2006, for instance, Japanese firms once legendary for their tight job security (such as Sony and Hitachi) have eliminated thousands of jobs.[78] In recent years, German companies, ranging from electronic giant Siemens to chip maker Infineron Technologies to Commerzbank, have announced thousands of layoffs. Countries such as France, where authorities have repeatedly blocked management efforts to cut costs via layoffs, often find that these well-intentioned efforts are counterproductive, leading to a wave of bankruptcies. This was the fate of appliance maker Moulinex, once considered an icon of French industry, which shut its doors in 2002, with almost 9,000 employees losing their jobs as a result.[79]

    Globalization makes it increasingly difficult to resist pressures to downsize when survival is threatened. Many European and Asian firms are now hiring top executives who are experienced in the implementation of such policies. For instance, Wolfang Bernhard was recruited as CEO by Volkswagen. He came from Chrysler where he and his former boss, Dieter Zetsche, cut 26,000 jobs and closed 6 factories. Bernhard repeated his feat by implementing tough cost-cutting measures at Volkswagen during 2005–2006. In his words, "when you have been through this before, you know how it works; you can see how to make it work."[80] Mr. Zetsche also returned to Germany as CEO of his parent company, DaimlerChrysler. One of his first acts was to announce 8,500 job cuts at Daimler's Mercedes-Benz factories in Germany during 2006–2008.[81]

    Chapter 6 is devoted to downsizing and how to manage the process effectively. Other relevant chapters include those on benefits (Chapter 12), the legal environment (Chapter 3), labor relations (Chapter 15), and employee relations and communications (Chapter 13).

Organizational Restructuring

The past two decades have witnessed a dramatic transformation in how firms are structured. Tall organizations that had many management levels are becoming flatter as companies reduce the number of people between the chief executive officer (CEO) and the lowest-ranking employee in an effort to become more competitive. Mergers and acquisitions have been going on for decades. Often mergers fail because the cultures and HR systems of the firms involved do not coalesce.[82] A newer and rapidly growing form of interorganizational bonding comes in the form of joint ventures, alliances, and collaborations among firms that remain independent, yet work together on specific products to spread costs and risks.

    To be successful, organizational restructuring requires effective management of human resources.[83] For instance, flattening the organization requires careful examination of staffing demands, work flows, communication channels, training needs, and so on. Likewise, mergers and

Decentralization
Transferring responsibility and decision-making authority from a central office to people and locations closer to the situation that demands attention.

Downsizing
A reduction in a company's workforce to improve its bottom line.

other forms of interorganizational relations require the successful blending of dissimilar organizational structures, management practices, technical expertise, and so forth.[84] Chapter 2 deals specifically with these issues. Other chapters that focus on related issues are Chapter 5 (staffing), Chapter 8 (training), Chapter 9 (career development), and Chapter 17 (international management).

Self-Managed Work Teams

The traditional system in which individual employees report to a single boss (who oversees a group of three to seven subordinates) is being replaced in some organizations by the self-managed team system. Employees are assigned to a group of peers and, together, they are responsible for a particular area or task. It has been estimated that 40 percent of U.S. workers are operating in some kind of team environment.[85]

According to two experts on self-managed work teams, "Today's competitive environment demands intense improvement in productivity, quality, and response time. Teams can deliver this improvement. Bosses can't. . . . Just as dinosaurs once ruled the earth and later faded into extinction, the days of bosses may be numbered."[86]

Very few rigorous scientific studies have been done on the effectiveness of self-managed work teams. However, case studies do suggest that many firms that use teams enjoy impressive payoffs. For example, company officials at General Motors' Fitzgerald Battery Plant, which is organized in teams, reported cost savings of 30 to 40 percent over traditionally organized plants. At FedEx, a thousand clerical workers, divided into teams of 5 to 10 people, helped the company reduce service problems by 13 percent.[87]

HR issues concerning self-managed work teams are discussed in detail in Chapter 2 (work flows), Chapter 10 (compensation), and Chapter 11 (rewarding performance).

The Growth of Small Businesses

According to the U.S. Small Business Administration (SBA), the precise definition of a small business depends on the industry in which it operates. For instance, to be considered "small" by the SBA, a manufacturing company may have a maximum of 500 to 1,500 employees (depending on the type of manufacturing). In wholesaling, a company is considered small if the number of its employees does not exceed 100.[88]

An increasing percentage of the 14 million businesses in the United States can be considered small.[89] One study using tax returns as its source of data found that 99.8 percent of U.S. businesses have fewer than 100 employees and approximately 90 percent have fewer than 20 employees.[90] Another study reports that approximately 85 percent of these firms are family owned.[91] A 2005 study found that Latinos and immigrants have substantially higher entrepreneurship rates than U.S. natives, and that African Americans increasingly are becoming entrepreneurs.[92]

Unfortunately, small businesses face a high risk of failure. According to some estimates, 40 percent of them fail in the first year, 60 percent fail before the start of the third year, and only 10 percent survive a decade.[93] To survive and prosper, a small business must manage its human resources effectively. For instance, a mediocre performance by one person in a 10-employee firm can mean the difference between making a profit and losing money.

Organizational Culture

Organizational culture
The basic assumptions and beliefs shared by members of an organization. These beliefs operate unconsciously and define in a basic taken-for-granted fashion an organization's view of itself and its environment.

The term **organizational culture** refers to the basic assumptions and beliefs shared by members of an organization. These beliefs operate unconsciously and define in a basic "taken for granted" fashion an organization's view of itself and its environment.[94] The key elements of organizational culture are:[95]

- *Observed behavioral regularities* when people interact, such as the language used and the rituals surrounding deference and demeanor
- The *norms* that evolve in working groups, such as the norm of a fair day's work for a fair day's pay
- The *dominant values espoused* by an organization, such as product quality or low prices
- The *philosophy* that guides an organization's policy toward employees and customers
- The *rules of the game* for getting along in the organization—"the ropes" that a newcomer must learn to become an accepted member
- The *feeling or climate* that is conveyed in an organization by the physical layout and the way in which members of the organization interact with one another, customers, and outsiders

Firms that make cultural adjustments to keep up with environmental changes are likely to outperform those whose culture is rigid and unresponsive to external jolts. Campbell's Soup Co.'s problems in the 2000s are often attributed to norms and values that have not kept up with rapidly changing consumer tastes. "It's definitely a risk-averse, control-oriented culture. It's all about two things: financial control and how much they can squeeze out of a tomato. Campbell needs to reward risk-taking, remove organizational roadblocks, and summon up the courage to move bold initiatives from proposal to execution quickly and regularly."[96]

Changing an entrenched organizational culture is not easy. For example, Carleton S. Fiorina, an outsider with nontechnical background, was brought into Hewlett-Packard (HP) as CEO in 1999 in order to overhaul the company.[97] Yet she was fired just six years later because her marketing focus, aggressiveness, autocratic style, flair for public drama, and what many thought was an overblown ego alienated key HP's employees, managers, and members of the board of directors.

Technology

Although technology is rapidly changing in many areas, such as robotics, one area in particular is revolutionizing human resources: information technology.[98] The *telematics technologies*—a broad array of tools including computers, networking programs, telecommunications, and fax machines—are now available and affordable to businesses of every size, even one-person companies. These technologies, coupled with the rise of the Internet, have had many effects on them, specifically:

- **The rise of telecommuting** Because technology makes information easy to store, retrieve, and analyze, the number of company employees working at home (*telecommuters*) at least part-time has been increasing by 15 percent annually. Because telecommuting arrangements are expected to continue growing in the future, they raise many important issues such as performance monitoring and career planning. A 2005 survey uncovered that almost half of offsite employees believe that people who work on site get more recognition than those who work offsite. And more telecommuters than onsite employees reported that "they would be very extremely likely to leave their current company if they found a similar job and compensation elsewhere."[99]

- **The ethics of proper data use** Data control, accuracy, right to privacy, and ethics are at the core of a growing controversy brought about by the new information technologies, particularly the Internet.[100] Personal computers now make it possible to access huge databases containing information on credit files, work history, driving records, health reports, criminal convictions, and family makeup. One Web site, for example, promises that in exchange for a $7 fee, it will scan "over two million records to create a single report on an individual."[101] A critical observer notes: "The worst thing about this information blitzkrieg is that even though errors abound, what's said about us by computers is usually considered accurate, and significant decisions are made based on this information. Often those affected are unaware of the process and are given no chance to offer explanations."[102]

- **Electronic monitoring** Many companies are using sophisticated software that monitors when, how, and why workers are using the Internet. (See Manager's Notebook: Emerging Trends, "Snooping E-Mail by Software Is Now a Workplace Norm.")

Emerging Trends

MANAGER'S NOTEBOOK

Snooping E-Mail by Software Is Now a Workplace Norm

It still isn't known how the e-mail that cost Harry Stonecipher his job as chief executive at Boeing Co. was intercepted or by whom. Boeing directors ousted the CEO in 2005 after they learned about an e-mail he had sent to a female employee with whom he was having an affair.

Every employee should realize by now how completely nonprivate their office e-mail is. In a 2005 survey of 840 U.S. companies by the American Management Association, 60 percent said they now use some type of software to monitor their employees' incoming and outgoing e-mail, up from 47 percent in 2001. Other workplace privacy experts place the current percentage even higher.

In most states, companies don't have to tell employees their e-mail is being monitored. Only Connecticut and Delaware have laws requiring companies to notify employees that they are being monitored, says Jeremy Gruber, legal director at the National Workrights Institute, a Princeton, New Jersey, workplace privacy advocacy organization.

Elsewhere, companies are free to monitor at will all e-mail sent and received using company equipment or company e-mail accounts, says Gruber, adding that he doesn't know of a single case where an employee has successfully challenged workplace e-mail monitoring. As an employee, "you have no rights whatsoever," says Gruber.

Companies are also increasingly hiring staffers to read individual outgoing e-mail messages, says Jonathan Penn, an analyst at Forrester Research. Of the companies that already use software to scan e-mails, 31 percent have hired employees to physically monitor e-mails, according to a study the firm conducted. The practice was especially common at companies with more than 20,000 employees, Mr. Penn says.

Source: Adapted from Tam, P. W., White, E., Wingfield, N., and Maher, K. (2005, March 9). Snooping e-mail by software is now a workplace norm. *Wall Street Journal,* B-1.

According to Clares Voice, a Dallas-based messaging security company, "We look at every piece of mail while it is in motion."[103] E-mail messages are now used as evidence for all sorts of legal cases concerning age discrimination, sexual harassment, price fixing, and the like.[104] "Some 70 percent of the evidence that we routinely deal with is in the form of electronic communication," says Garry G. Mathiason, a senior partner at Littler Mendelson, a prestigious legal firm in San Francisco.[105]

■ **Medical testing** Genetic testing, high-tech imaging, and DNA analysis may soon be available to aid in making employment decisions. As noted in a 2005 report concerning the potential use of brain scans as a selection tool, "It used to be an art to find out which job candidate would make the ideal manager. It may soon be cutting-edge technology."[106] Firms' decisions about how to harness the new information (to screen applicants, establish health insurance premiums, decide who should be laid off and the like) are full of ethical implications. IBM seems to be on the forefront, announcing in 2006 that it will not use genetic data for employment decisions. This is one area where the legal system is still far behind technical advances.

■ **An increase in egalitarianism** Because information is now available both instantaneously and broadly, organizational structures are becoming more *egalitarian,* meaning that power and authority are spread more evenly among all employees. Groupware networks, which enable hundreds of workers to share information simultaneously, can give office workers intelligence previously available only to their bosses.[107] They also enable the rank-and-file to join in online discussions with senior executives. In these kinds of interactions people are judged more by what they say than by their rank on the corporate ladder.[108]

The challenges and implications of rapidly changing technologies—especially information technologies—for human resources are discussed in every chapter of this book.

Internal Security

The September 11, 2001, terrorist attacks engendered a U.S. collective obsession with security. Many consulting firms are now focusing their attention on how to detect potential security problems, and a wide range of firms and industry groups, from trucking associations to sporting-event organizers, have made security screening a top priority.[109] For example, anyone can purchase a software package for $39.77 at Sam's Club that promises "to make better hiring decisions [and] conduct background checks quickly and easily!"[110] Choice Point began selling background checks recently via Yahoo!'s Hot Jobs site. Entersert, a security firm, is also launching a "user friendly employee background security check" at *CareerBuilding.com*. Apart from background checks, HR departments are increasingly involved in beefing security details by scanning employees' eyes and fingerprints for positive identification, hiring armed guards to patrol facilities, identifying employees who might pose a violence threat, and even spotting potential spies.[111]

Although few would question that security checks are necessary, one concern from a human resource perspective is to ensure that applicants' and employers' rights are not violated and that due process is followed whenever suspected problems are identified. For example, should a person convicted of a drunken driving violation 15 years ago be denied a job as a flight attendant? How about people whose past reveals some facts that may be warning signals, depending on the bias of the evaluator (for instance, graduation from a Middle Eastern university, frequent job changes, multiple divorces, and the like)? Health sites offer tools used by medical pros and companies to track data, including test results from HIV and cancer exams.[112] Should firms use this type of information as part of their selection process?

According to one study conducted by a computer-based, security-service firm, Automatic Data Accessing, more than 40 percent of résumés misrepresent education or employment history. But "how employers respond when they find an employee has fibbed varies depending on company policies, the worker's value, and the organizational culture. Many companies say they are willing to overlook some degree of inaccuracy."[113] In other words, how security-related information is used is a matter of interpretation, perhaps except in the most grievous cases. Chapter 14, "Respecting Employee Rights and Managing Discipline," deals with these and related issues.

Data Security

Numerous cases of unauthorized access to private data have been revealed since the last edition of this book, in some situations leading to widespread identity fraud. During a six-month period in 2005 alone, the Privacy Rights Clearinghouse, a consumer advocacy group in San Diego, counted over 80 major data breaches involving the personal information of more than 50 million people.[114] In one case, CardSystems (a credit card processor), left the account information of more than 40 million shareholders exposed to fraud.[115] Well-known organizations subject to serious data breaches during 2004–2007 include Lexis/Nexis Group, Choice Point, Bank of America, the United States Airforce, and even the FBI.[116] Data security is not just a concern for specialized computer experts; it should also involve HR policies to determine who has access to sensitive information and monitoring systems to prevent abuses by managers and employees.

Outsourcing

Many large firms now shift work once performed internally to outside suppliers and contractors, a process called **outsourcing**. The motivation is simple: Outsourcing saves money. The *Wall Street Journal* reports that more than 40 percent of *Fortune* 500 companies have outsourced some department or service—everything from HR administration to computer systems.[117] A 2005 survey conducted by the Worldatwork Association (which has more than 10,000 members in responsible HR positions) found that the following HR practices are now completely or partially outsourced by a large proportion of participating firms: health and welfare (79%), pension plans (90%), payroll (62%), training (50%), and recruitment and selection (32%).[118]

Outsourcing creates several HR challenges for firms. Although it often helps companies slash costs, employees may face layoffs when their jobs are farmed out to the lowest bidder. For instance, UPS subcontracted 5,000 jobs at its 65 customer service centers.[119] In addition, customer dissatisfaction can result if subcontractors are not carefully watched and evaluated. For instance, a group of former employees at now-liquidated Skillset Software Inc. filed suit against its outside HR provider, TriNet Group Inc., for negligence in handling their claim. Part of the problem is that these HR providers often don't provide enough access and human interaction (many rely extensively on the Web) to handle employee concerns and complaints.[120] Subcontractors may take on more work than they can handle,[121] and small businesses may not receive the best available service and support. Finally, when subcontracting HR activities such as training, staffing and compensation, data security issues become paramount. The organization would have to trust that the subcontractor can effectively protect personal data (such as Social Security numbers, marital status, income level, performance problems, bank accounts) from misuse by insiders or outsiders. Outsourcing that includes a foreign location (which is increasingly common) further complicates the data security issue.

We discuss outsourcing and its challenges for HRM throughout this book. Chapter 2 discusses subcontracting within the context of downsizing, and Chapter 15, on labor relations, discusses how outsourcing affects unions.

Outsourcing
Subcontracting work to an outside company that specializes in and is more efficient at doing that kind of work.

Individual Challenges

Individual challenges
Human resource issues that
address the decisions most
pertinent to individual
employees.

Human resource issues at the individual level address the decisions most pertinent to specific employees. These **individual challenges** almost always reflect what is happening in the larger organization. For instance, technology affects individual productivity; it also has ethical ramifications in terms of how information is used to make HR decisions (for example, use of credit or medical history data to decide whom to hire). How the company treats its individual employees is also likely to affect the organizational challenges we discussed earlier. For example, if many key employees leave the firm to join competitors, the organization's competitive position is affected. In other words, there is a two-way relationship between organizational and individual challenges. This is unlike the relationship between environmental and organizational challenges, in which the relationship goes only one way (see Figure 1.1); few organizations can have much impact on the environment. The most important individual challenges today are matching people and organizations, ethics and social responsibility, productivity, empowerment, brain drain, and job security.

Matching People and Organizations

Research suggests that HR strategies contribute to firm performance most when the firm uses these strategies to attract and retain the type of employee who best fits the firm's culture and overall business objectives. For example, one study showed that fast-growth firms perform better with managers who have a strong marketing and sales background, who are willing to take risks, and who have a high tolerance for ambiguity. However, these managerial traits actually reduce the performance of mature firms that have an established product and are more interested in maintaining (rather than expanding) their market share.[122]

Chapter 5 deals specifically with the attempt to achieve the right fit between employees and the organization to enhance performance.

Ethics and Social Responsibility

In the last edition of this book, we discussed the well-publicized scandals at Enron, Worldcom, Tyco, and Global Crossings in which corruption apparently became a way of life at the top. Since 2004, we can scarcely read any business periodical without being bombarded by multiple cases of egregious unethical behaviors across a wide variety of organizations. These include, for example, American International Group (or AIG, one of the largest insurance companies, which artificially inflated its reserves by $500 million);[123] Time Warner (accused of fraudulent accounting);[124] Bank of America (forced to pay $1 billion in fines for ethical lapses);[125] CitiGroup (several officers are being tried for alleged money laundering);[126] Boeing (where top executives were sentenced in an Air Force procument scandal involving millions of dollars);[127] Choice Point (one of the largest credit reporting agencies, which allegedly kept hidden for a month information about an identity theft ring's access to personal data on about 145,000 people, providing sufficient time for top executives to dump their Choice Point stock);[128] Stratton Veterans Affairs Medical Center (at which certain employees posing as doctors conducted unauthorized clinical research on cancer patients, leading to death in some cases);[129] State University of New York at Albany (whose president, Karen R. Hitchcock, was forced to resign after accusations that she hired a contractor who promised to fund an endowed university professorship just for her);[130] and the famous Getty Museum in Los Angeles (which is beset by charges of stolen antiquities and profligate executive perks).[131]

Similar ethical breaches have been documented abroad during the past three years. For instance, executives at the Dutch supermarket chain AholdNv are being tried for overstating earnings by more than $800 million;[132] Mitsubishi Motors in Japan confessed that it had been hiding reports on vehicle defects from safety officials since 1980;[133] and in a 500-page report the United Nations revealed that more than half of 4,500 companies from over 60 countries paid $1.8 billion in illegal surcharges and kickbacks to Saddam Hussein during a 10-year period.[134]

We can safely assume that reported cases of unethical behavior represent only the tip of the iceberg.[135]

In response to these concerns, people's fears that their employers will behave unethically are increasing,[136] so much so that many firms and professional organizations have created codes of ethics outlining principles and standards of personal conduct for their members. Unfortunately, these codes often do not meet employees' expectations of ethical employer behavior. In a poll of *Harvard Business Review* readers, almost half the respondents indicated their belief that managers do not consistently make ethical decisions.[137]

The widespread perceptions of unethical behavior may be attributed to the fact that managerial decisions are rarely clear-cut. Except in a few blatant cases (such as willful misrepresentation), what is ethical or unethical is open to debate. Even the most detailed codes of ethics are still general enough to allow much room for managerial discretion. In fact, many of the executives convicted of illegal activities thought they were just buying time to turn the company around or that subordinates were too zealous in implementing "revenue enhancing" directives.[138] Perhaps even more so than in other business areas, many specific decisions related to the management of human resources are subject to judgment calls. Often these judgment calls constitute a Catch-22 because none of the alternatives is desirable.[139]

Some companies are using the Web to infuse employees and managers with ethical values. For instance, many of Lockheed Martin's 160,000 employees are required to take a step-by-step online training program on ethics.[140] CitiGroup started an online ethics training program that is mandatory for all of its 300,000 employees.[141] Other companies are using more traditional training methods to implement so called "zero-tolerance policies." For instance, at Goldman Sachs, the chief executive (Henry M. Paulson Junior at the time of this writing) has been moderating seminars on various business judgments and ethical issues with all the bank's managing directors.[142]

A company that exercises *social responsibility* attempts to balance its commitments—not only to its investors, but also to its employees, its customers, other businesses, and the community or communities in which it operates. For example, McDonald's established Ronald McDonald houses years ago to provide lodging for families of sick children hospitalized away from home. Sears and General Electric support artists and performers, and many local merchants support local children's sports teams. Philip Morris is trying to turn around its "ugly duckling" image by entering the business of treating smoke-related illnesses and supporting research projects on lung-disease prevention.[143]

An entire chapter of this book is devoted to employee rights and responsibilities (Chapter 13); each chapter includes (at selected points) pertinent ethical questions for which there are no absolute answers. Most chapters also include a Manager's Notebook dealing with ethical issues related to the specific topic of that chapter. See the accompanying box for this chapter.

Productivity

Most experts agree that productivity gains from technology have altered the economic playing field since the mid-1990s, allowing for continued economic growth, low unemployment, and low inflation. **Productivity** is a measure of how much value individual employees add to the goods or services that the organization produces. The greater the output per individual, the higher the organization's productivity. For instance, U.S. workers produce a pair of shoes in 24 minutes, whereas Chinese workers take three hours.[144] In a "knowledge-based economy" driven by technology, the success of organizations will depend more and more on the value of intangible human capital. This capital may be "the creativity of their designers (Intel Corp. comes to mind), the proficiency of their software architects (as at Sun Microsystems Inc.), the knowledge of marketers (Procter & Gamble Co., for instance), and even the strength of the internal culture (as in the case of Southwest Airlines)."[145] From an HR perspective, employee productivity is affected by ability, motivation, and quality of work life.

Productivity
A measure of how much value individual employees add to the goods or services that the organization produces.

Ethics

MANAGER'S
NOTEBOOK

How and Why We Lie at the Office: From Pilfered Pens to Padded Accounts

Rank-and-file employees are lying more often at work. Calling in sick has hit a five-year high, and three-fifths of those who call aren't sick at all but are tending to personal needs or just feel entitled to a day off, says a survey of 305 employers by CCH Inc. In a separate survey of 1,316 workers by

Ethics in the Workplace

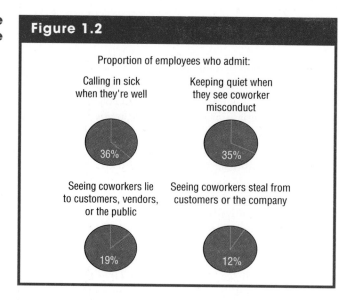

Figure 1.2

Proportion of employees who admit:

Calling in sick when they're well

36%

Keeping quiet when they see coworker misconduct

35%

Seeing coworkers lie to customers, vendors, or the public

19%

Seeing coworkers steal from customers or the company

12%

Kronos Inc., a labor-management and consulting concern, more than one-third of workers admit to having lied about their need for sick days (see Figure 1.2).

Groups that track federal family-leave use say more employees are stretching the reasons for taking time off, even claiming that a common cold warrants a medical leave. In another indicator, job applicants reporting false academic credentials have hit a three-year high, with 12 percent of resumes containing at least some phony information, according to the Liars Index, a survey by recruiting firm Jude M. Werra & Associates.

One factor behind this trend may be stresses brought on by accelerating corporate change. Evidence indicates that misconduct increases in companies where mergers, acquisitions, and restructurings are underway. In other cases, employee dishonesty is a sign policies are outdated. One health-care company in the Northeast prohibited employees from using personal software on company computers, says Lee Essrig of the Ethics Officer Association, Waltham, Massachusetts. But the company shifted gears after realizing that time-pressed workers were secretly installing personal-banking and calendar software on laptops.

Amid a lack of strong policies and an abundance of bad examples at the top, everything from regularly calling in "sick" to stretching revenue forecasts has become more acceptable.

What if the truth will do so much career damage that a face-saving lie seems better? A Newport Beach, California, HR director says her boss is so demanding that she lies to protect family time, fabricating work-related reasons for missing staff meetings, taking time off, or refusing business trips.

"Am I proud of it? No," she writes in an e-mail. "But it helps my BP maintain the illusion that everyone is as dedicated—that is, as much of a workaholic—as he is."

Source: Adapted with permission from Shellenberger, S. (2005). How and why we lie at the office: From pilfered pens to padded accounts. *Wall Street Journal,* D-1.

Ability
Competence in performing a job.

Employee **ability**, competence in performing a job, can be improved through a hiring and placement process that selects the best individuals for the job;[146] Chapter 5 specifically deals with this process. It can also be improved through training and career development programs designed to sharpen employees' skills and prepare them for additional responsibilities; Chapters 8 and 9 discuss these issues.

Motivation
A person's desire to do the best possible job or to exert the maximum effort to perform assigned tasks.

Motivation refers to a person's desire to do the best possible job or to exert the maximum effort to perform assigned tasks. Motivation energizes, directs, and sustains human behavior. Several key factors affecting employee motivation are discussed in this book, including work design (Chapter 2), matching of employee and job requirements (Chapter 5), rewards (Chapters 11 and 13), and due process (Chapter 14).

Quality of work life
A measure of how safe and satisfied employees feel with their jobs.

A growing number of companies recognize that employees are more likely to choose a firm and stay there if they believe that it offers a high **quality of work life**. A high quality of work life is related to job satisfaction, which in turn is a strong predictor of absenteeism and turnover.[147] A firm's investments in improving the quality of work life also pay off in the form of better customer service.[148] We discuss issues covering job design and their effects on employee attitudes and behavior in Chapter 2.

Empowerment

Many firms have reduced employee dependence on superiors and placed more emphasis on individual control over (and responsibility for) the work that needs to be done. This process has been labeled **empowerment** because it transfers direction from an external source (normally the immediate supervisor) to an internal source (the individual's own desire to do well). In essence, the process of empowerment entails providing workers with the skills and authority to make decisions that would traditionally be made by managers. The goal of empowerment is an organization consisting of enthusiastic, committed people who perform their work ably because they believe in it and enjoy doing it (*internal control*). This situation is in stark contrast to an organization that gets people to work as an act of compliance to avoid punishment (for example, being fired) or to qualify for a paycheck (*external control*).

> **Empowerment**
> Providing workers with the skills and authority to make decisions that would traditionally be made by managers.

Empowerment can encourage employees to be creative and to take risks, which are key components that can give a firm a competitive edge in a fast-changing environment. Empowering employees is "the hardest thing to do because it means giving up control," says Lee Fielder, retired president of Kelly Springfield Tire Co., a unit of Goodyear. "But [according to Fielder], managers who try to tell employees what and how to do every little thing will end up with only mediocre people, because the talented ones won't submit to control."[149] To encourage risk taking, General Electric past CEO Jack Welch exhorted his managers and employees to "shake it, shake it, break it."[150]

HR issues related to internal and external control of behavior are explicitly discussed in Chapter 2 (work flows).

Brain Drain

With organizational success more and more dependent on knowledge held by specific employees, companies are becoming more susceptible to **brain drain**—the loss of intellectual property that results when competitors lure away key employees. Important industries such as semiconductors and electronics also suffer from high employee turnover as key employees, leave to start their own businesses. This brain drain can negatively affect innovation and cause major delays in the introduction of new products.[151]

> **Brain drain**
> The loss of high-talent key personnel to competitors or start-up ventures.

At a national level, brain drain has been a major problem for developing countries, because the best educated tend to leave. Universities and R&D labs in the United States are full of faculty and graduate students from China, India, and other emerging economies. In some of the poorest countries, like Haiti, more than three-fourths of college-educated individuals have emigrated. According to the National Academy of Engineering, in 2005 more than half of engineers with advanced degrees in the United States were foreign born, as were over one-third of Nobel-award winners during the past 15 years.[152] At Microsoft, more than 20 percent of employees are from India. This dependence on foreign talent places the United States in a vulnerable position, particularly as giants such as China and India keep growing in strides.[153] (For a related story, see Manager's Notebook: Global, "Erosion of the U.S. Competitive Edge in Science.")

Global   **MANAGER'S NOTEBOOK**

Erosion of the U.S. Competitive Edge in Science

A 20-member panel composed of Nobel Laureates, university presidents, corporate chairmen, and former president appointees recently concluded that the United States is quickly falling behind other countries in the training of scientists and engineers. Furthermore, the cost of hiring top-level scientific talent is much higher in the United States, inducing American firms to move R&D facilities overseas.

One of the panel's recommendations is to have international students in the United States who receive doctorates in science, technology, engineering, or math get automatic one-year visa extensions that allow them to seek employment. If these students receive job offers and pass a security-screening test, they would automatically get U.S. work permits and expedited residence status.

The panel cited many examples demonstrating that the United States was falling behind:

- Last year, more than 600,000 engineers graduated from institutions of higher education in China, compared to 350,000 in India and 70,000 in the United States.
- Recently, American 12th graders performed below the international average for 21 countries on general knowledge in math and science.
- The cost of employing one chemist or engineer in the United States is equal to the cost of about 5 in China and 11 in India.
- Chemical companies last year shut 70 facilities in the United States and marked 40 for closure. Of 120 large chemical plants under construction globally, one is in the United States and 50 are in China.
- China has devoted $1 billion between 2006 and 2009 to hire some of the best Chinese-speaking scientists who are currently working in U.S. universities and R&D labs.

"Thanks to globalization," the report said, "workers in virtually every sector must now face competitors who live just a mouse-click away in Ireland, Finland, China, India, or dozens of other nations whose economies are growing."

Source: Adapted with permission from Broad, J. (2005, October 13). Top advisory panel warns of an erosion of the U.S. competitive edge in science. *New York Times*, A-16. For a full report see *www.nationalacademies.org.*

Brain drain and measures for dealing with it effectively are discussed in several chapters of this book, particularly in Chapter 3 (equal opportunity and the legal environment), Chapter 4 (managing diversity), Chapter 6 (employee separations and outplacement), and Chapter 11 (rewarding performance).

Job Insecurity

As noted in the introduction, most workers cannot count on a steady job and regular promotions. Companies argue that regardless of how well the firm is doing, layoffs have become essential in an age of cutthroat competition. For employees, however, chronic job insecurity is a major source of stress and can lead to lower performance and productivity. Reed Moskowitz, founder of a stress disorder center at New York University, notes that workers' mental health has taken a turn for the worse because "nobody feels secure any more."[154]

Many workers still belong to unions, and job security is now a top union priority.

We discuss the challenges of laying off employees and making the remaining employees feel secure and valued in Chapter 6. We discuss employee stress (and ways to relieve it) in Chapter 16. We explore union–management relations in Chapter 15.

Planning and Implementing Strategic HR Policies

To be successful, firms must closely align their HR strategies and programs (tactics) with environmental opportunities, business strategies, and the organization's unique characteristics and distinctive competence.

Strategic human resource (HR) planning
The process of formulating HR strategies and establishing programs or tactics to implement them.

The Benefits of Strategic HR Planning

The process of formulating HR strategies and establishing programs or tactics to implement them is called **strategic human resource (HR) planning**. When done correctly, strategic HR planning provides many direct and indirect benefits for the company.

Encouragement of Proactive Rather Than Reactive Behavior

Being *proactive* means looking ahead and developing a vision of where the company wants to be and how it can use human resources to get there. In contrast, being *reactive* means responding to problems as they come up. Companies that are reactive may lose sight of the long-term direction of their business; proactive companies are better prepared for the future. For instance, as bankruptcies have soared in the 2000s, companies need to hold their key talent tightly, perhaps offering special inducements for star performers to persevere through hard times "even though it may seem counterintuitive to continue spending money on employee compensation when the firm can't pay its bills."[155]

Explicit Communication of Company Goals

Strategic HR planning can help a firm develop a focused set of strategic objectives that capitalizes on its special talents and know-how.

For instance, 3M has had an explicit strategy of competing through innovation, with the goal of having at least 25 percent of revenues generated from products introduced during the past five years. To achieve this goal, 3M's human resource strategy may be summarized as "Hire top-notch scientists in every field, give each an ample endowment, then stand back and let them do their thing. The anything goes approach has yielded thousands of new products over the decades, from sand-paper and magnetic audio tape to Post-it notes and thinsulate insulation."[156] One hundred years after its foundation, 3M clearly expresses the philosophy that guides its HR practices: "The spirit of innovation. That's 3M. Our unstoppable commitment to innovation, creating new technologies and products, places us exactly where our customer need us. . . . Every day, 3M people find new ways to make amazing things happen."

Stimulation of Critical Thinking and Ongoing Examination of Assumptions

Managers often depend on their personal views and experiences to solve problems and make business decisions. The assumptions on which they make their decisions can lead to success if they are appropriate to the environment in which the business operates. However, serious problems can arise when these assumptions no longer hold. For instance, in the 1980s IBM deemphasized sales of its personal computer because IBM managers were afraid that PC growth would decrease the profitability of the firm's highly profitable mainframe products. This decision allowed competitors to move aggressively into the PC market, eventually devastating IBM.[157]

Strategic HR planning can stimulate critical thinking and the development of new initiatives only if it is a continuing and flexible process rather than a rigid procedure with a discrete beginning and a specific deadline for completion. This is why many firms have formed an executive committee, which includes an HR professional and the CEO, to discuss strategic issues on an ongoing basis and periodically modify the company's overall HR strategies and programs.

Identification of Gaps between Current Situation and Future Vision

Strategic HR planning can help a firm identify the difference between "where we are today" and "where we want to be." Despite a $1 billion budget and a staff of 7,000, 3M's vaunted laboratory was not able in recent years to deliver fast growth, partly because some of the R&D lacked focus and money wasn't always wisely spent. To speed up growth, 3M announced a series of performance objectives for individual business chiefs who had before enjoyed much free rein. In addition, 3M introduced specially trained "black belts" to root out inefficiencies in departments from R&D to sales.[158]

Encouragement of Line Managers' Participation

For HR strategy to be effective, line managers at all levels must buy into it. If they do not, it is likely to fail. For example, a large cosmetics manufacturing plant decided to introduce a reward program in which work teams would receive a large bonus for turning out high-quality products. The bonus was part of a strategic plan to foster greater cooperation among employees. But the plan, which had been developed by top executives in consultation with the HR department, backfired when managers and supervisors began hunting for individual employees responsible for errors. The plan was eventually dropped.

Identification of HR Constraints and Opportunities

When overall business strategy planning is done in combination with HR strategic planning, firms can identify the potential problems and opportunities with respect to the people expected to implement the business strategy.

A cornerstone of Motorola's business strategy is to identify, encourage, and financially support new-product ventures. To implement this strategy, Motorola relies on in-house venture teams, normally composed of five to six employees, one each from research and development (R&D), marketing, sales, manufacturing, engineering, and finance. Positions are broadly defined to allow all employees to use their creativity and to serve as champions of new ideas.

Creation of Common Bonds

A substantial amount of research shows that, in the long run, organizations that have a strong sense of "who we are" tend to outperform those that do not. A strategic HR plan that reinforces, adjusts, or redirects the organization's present culture can foster values such as a customer focus, innovation, fast growth, and cooperation.

The Challenges of Strategic HR Planning

In developing an effective HR strategy, the organization faces several important challenges.

Maintaining a Competitive Advantage

Any competitive advantage enjoyed by an organization tends to be short-lived because other companies are likely to imitate it. This is as true for HR advantages as for technological and marketing advantages. For example, many high-tech firms have "borrowed" reward programs for key scientists and engineers from other successful high-tech firms.

The challenge from an HR perspective is to develop strategies that offer the firm a sustained competitive advantage. For instance, a company may develop programs that maximize present employees' potential through carefully developed career ladders (see Chapter 9) while at the same time rewarding them generously with company stock with strings attached (for example, a provision that they will forfeit the stock if they quit before a certain date).

Reinforcing Overall Business Strategy

Developing HR strategies to support the firm's overall business strategy is a challenge for several reasons. First, top management may not always be able to enunciate clearly the firm's overall business strategy. Second, there may be much uncertainty or disagreement concerning which HR strategies should be used to support the overall business strategy. In other words, it is seldom obvious how particular HR strategies will contribute to the achievement of organizational strategies. Third, large corporations may have different business units, each with its own business strategies. Ideally, each unit should be able to formulate the HR strategy that fits its business strategy best. For instance, a division that produces high-tech equipment may decide to pay its engineering staff well above average to attract and retain the best people, while the consumer products division may decide to pay its engineers an average wage. Such differentials may cause problems if the engineers from the two divisions have contact with each other. Thus, diverse HR strategies may spur feelings of inequity and resentment.

Avoiding Excessive Concentration on Day-to-Day Problems

Some managers are so busy putting out fires that they have no time to focus on the long term. Nonetheless, a successful HR strategy demands a vision tied to the long-term direction of the business. Thus, a major challenge of strategic HR planning is prodding people into stepping back and considering the big picture.

In many small companies, staffs are so absorbed in growing the business today that they seldom pause to look at the big picture for tomorrow. Also, strategic HR planning in small companies is often synonymous with the whims of the company owner or founder, who may not take the time to formalize his or her plans.

Developing HR Strategies Suited to Unique Organizational Features

No two firms are exactly alike. Firms differ in history, culture, leadership style, technology, and so on. The chances are high that any ambitious HR strategy or program that is not molded to organizational characteristics will fail.[159] And therein lies one of the central challenges in formulating HR strategies: creating a vision of the organization of the future that does not provoke a destructive clash with the organization of the present.

Coping with the Environment

Just as no two firms are exactly alike, no two firms operate in an identical environment. Some must deal with rapid change, as in the computer industry; others operate in a relatively stable market, as in the market for food processors. Some face a virtually guaranteed demand for their products or services (for example, medical providers); others must deal with turbulent demand (for example, fashion designers). Even within a very narrowly defined industry, some firms may be competing in a market where customer service is the key (IBM's traditional competitive advantage), while others are competing in a market driven by cost considerations (the competitive advantage offered by the many firms producing IBM clones). A major challenge in developing HR strategies is crafting strategies that will work in the firm's unique environment to give it a sustainable competitive advantage.

Securing Management Commitment

HR strategies that originate in the HR department will have little chance of succeeding unless managers at all levels—including top executives—support them completely. To ensure managers' commitment, HR professionals must work closely with them when formulating policies.

Translating the Strategic Plan into Action

The acid test of any strategic plan is whether or not it makes a difference in practice. If the plan does not affect practice, employees and managers will regard it as all talk and no action.

Cynicism is practically guaranteed when a firm experiences frequent turnover at the top, with each new wave of high-level managers introducing their own freshly minted strategic plan. Perhaps the greatest challenge in strategic HR planning lies not in the formulation of strategy, but rather in the development of an appropriate set of programs that will make the strategy work.

Combining Intended and Emergent Strategies

Debate continues over whether strategies are *intended* or *emergent*—that is, whether they are proactive, rational, deliberate plans designed to attain predetermined objectives (intended) or general "fuzzy" patterns collectively molded by the interplay of power, politics, improvisation,

Bausch & Lomb's mission statement outlines a forward-thinking company vision.

negotiation, and personalities within the organization (emergent).[160] Most people agree that organizations have intended *and* emergent strategies, that both are necessary, and that the challenge is to combine the best aspects of the two.

Intended strategies can provide a sense of purpose and a guide for the allocation of resources. They are also useful for recognizing environmental opportunities and threats and mobilizing top management to respond appropriately. On the downside, intended strategies may lead to a top-down strategic approach that squashes creativity and widespread involvement.

Emergent strategies also have their advantages and disadvantages. Among their benefits: (1) They involve everyone in the organization, which fosters grass-roots support; (2) they develop gradually out of the organization's experiences and, thus, can be less upsetting than intended strategies; and (3) they are more pragmatic than intended strategies because they evolve to deal with specific problems or issues facing the firm. On the negative side, emergent strategies may lack strong leadership and fail to infuse the organization with a creative vision.[161]

Combining intended and emergent strategies effectively requires that managers blend the benefits of formal planning (to provide strong guidance and direction in setting priorities) with the untidy realities of dispersed employees who, through their unplanned activities, formulate emergent strategies throughout the firm.

Accommodating Change

Strategic HR plans must be flexible enough to accommodate change.[162] A firm with an inflexible strategic plan may find itself unable to respond to changes quickly because it is so committed to a particular course of action. This may lead the organization to continue devoting resources to an activity of questionable value simply because so much has been invested in it already.[163] The challenge is to create a strategic vision and develop the plans to achieve it while staying flexible enough to adapt to change.

Strategic HR Choices

Strategic HR choices
The options available to a firm in designing its human resources system.

A firm's **strategic HR choices** are the options it has available in designing its human resources system. Figure 1.3 shows a sampling of strategic HR choices. Here keep three things in mind. First, the list is not exhaustive. Second, many different HR programs or practices may be used separately or together to implement each of these choices. For example, if a firm chooses to base pay on performance, it can use many different programs to implement this decision, including cash awards, lump-sum annual bonuses, raises based on supervisory appraisals, and an employee-of-the-month award. Third, the strategic HR choices listed in Figure 1.3 represent two opposite poles on a continuum. Very few organizations fall at these extremes. Some organizations will be closer to the right end, some closer to the left end, and others closer to the middle.

A brief description of the strategic HR choices shown in Figure 1.3 follows. We will examine these choices and provide examples of companies' strategic decisions in these areas in later chapters.

Work Flows

Work flows refer to the ways tasks are organized to meet production or service goals. Organizations face several choices in what they emphasize as they structure work flows (Chapter 2). They can emphasize:

- Efficiency (getting work done at minimum cost) or innovation (encouraging creativity, exploration, and new ways of doing things, even though this may increase production costs)
- Control (establishing predetermined procedures) or flexibility (allowing room for exceptions and personal judgment)
- Explicit job descriptions (in which each job's duties and requirements are carefully spelled out) or broad job classes (in which employees perform multiple tasks and are expected to fill different jobs as needed)
- Detailed work planning (in which processes, objectives, and schedules are laid out well in advance) or loose work planning (in which activities and schedules may be modified on relatively short notice, depending on changing needs)

Figure 1.3

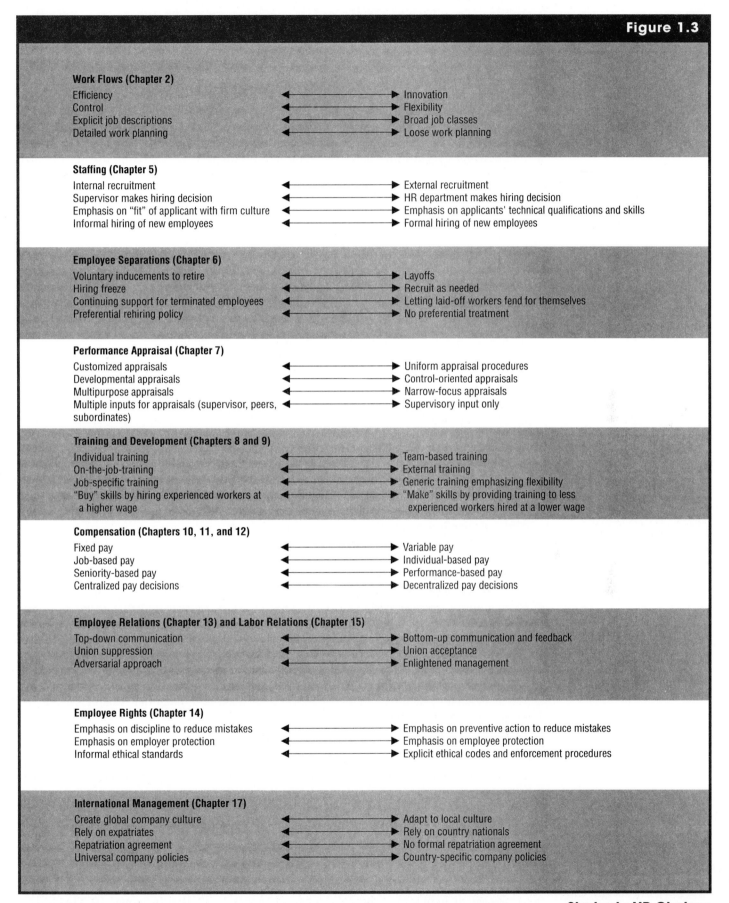

Work Flows (Chapter 2)

Efficiency   ◄────────► Innovation
Control   ◄────────► Flexibility
Explicit job descriptions   ◄────────► Broad job classes
Detailed work planning   ◄────────► Loose work planning

Staffing (Chapter 5)

Internal recruitment   ◄────────► External recruitment
Supervisor makes hiring decision   ◄────────► HR department makes hiring decision
Emphasis on "fit" of applicant with firm culture   ◄────────► Emphasis on applicants' technical qualifications and skills
Informal hiring of new employees   ◄────────► Formal hiring of new employees

Employee Separations (Chapter 6)

Voluntary inducements to retire   ◄────────► Layoffs
Hiring freeze   ◄────────► Recruit as needed
Continuing support for terminated employees   ◄────────► Letting laid-off workers fend for themselves
Preferential rehiring policy   ◄────────► No preferential treatment

Performance Appraisal (Chapter 7)

Customized appraisals   ◄────────► Uniform appraisal procedures
Developmental appraisals   ◄────────► Control-oriented appraisals
Multipurpose appraisals   ◄────────► Narrow-focus appraisals
Multiple inputs for appraisals (supervisor, peers,   ◄────────► Supervisory input only
subordinates)

Training and Development (Chapters 8 and 9)

Individual training   ◄────────► Team-based training
On-the-job-training   ◄────────► External training
Job-specific training   ◄────────► Generic training emphasizing flexibility
"Buy" skills by hiring experienced workers at   ◄────────► "Make" skills by providing training to less
  a higher wage   experienced workers hired at a lower wage

Compensation (Chapters 10, 11, and 12)

Fixed pay   ◄────────► Variable pay
Job-based pay   ◄────────► Individual-based pay
Seniority-based pay   ◄────────► Performance-based pay
Centralized pay decisions   ◄────────► Decentralized pay decisions

Employee Relations (Chapter 13) and Labor Relations (Chapter 15)

Top-down communication   ◄────────► Bottom-up communication and feedback
Union suppression   ◄────────► Union acceptance
Adversarial approach   ◄────────► Enlightened management

Employee Rights (Chapter 14)

Emphasis on discipline to reduce mistakes   ◄────────► Emphasis on preventive action to reduce mistakes
Emphasis on employer protection   ◄────────► Emphasis on employee protection
Informal ethical standards   ◄────────► Explicit ethical codes and enforcement procedures

International Management (Chapter 17)

Create global company culture   ◄────────► Adapt to local culture
Rely on expatriates   ◄────────► Rely on country nationals
Repatriation agreement   ◄────────► No formal repatriation agreement
Universal company policies   ◄────────► Country-specific company policies

Strategic HR Choices

Staffing

Staffing encompasses the HR activities designed to secure the right employees at the right place at the right time (Chapter 5). Organizations face several strategic HR choices in recruiting, selecting, and socializing employees—all part of the staffing process. These include:

- Promoting from within (*internal* recruitment) versus hiring from the outside (*external* recruitment)
- Empowering immediate supervisors to make hiring decisions versus centralizing these decisions in the HR department
- Emphasizing a good fit between the applicant and the firm versus hiring the most knowledgeable individual regardless of interpersonal considerations
- Hiring new workers informally or choosing a more formal and systematic approach to hiring

Employee Separations

Employee separations occur when employees leave the firm, either voluntarily or involuntarily (Chapter 6). Some strategic HR choices available to the firm for handling employee separations are:

- Use of voluntary inducements (such as early retirement packages) to downsize a workforce versus use of layoffs
- Imposing a hiring freeze to avoid laying off current employees versus recruiting employees as needed, even if doing so means laying off current employees
- Providing continuing support to terminated employees (perhaps by offering them assistance in securing another job) versus leaving laid-off employees to fend for themselves
- Making a commitment to rehire terminated employees if conditions improve versus avoiding any type of preferential hiring treatment for ex-employees

Performance Appraisal

Managers assess how well employees are carrying out their assigned duties by conducting performance appraisals (Chapter 7). Some strategic HR choices concerning employee appraisals are:

- Developing an appraisal system that is customized to the needs of various employee groups (for example, by designing a different appraisal form for each job family) versus using a standardized appraisal system throughout the organization
- Using the appraisal data as a developmental tool to help employees improve their performance versus using appraisals as a control mechanism to weed out low producers
- Designing the appraisal system with multiple objectives in mind (such as training, promotion, and selection decisions) versus designing it for a narrow purpose (such as pay decisions only)
- Developing an appraisal system that encourages the active participation of multiple employee groups (for example, supervisor, peers, and subordinates) versus developing one that asks solely for the input of each employee's supervisor

Training and Career Development

Training and career development activities are designed to help an organization meet its skill requirements and to help its employees realize their maximum potential (Chapters 8 and 9). Some of the strategic HR choices pertaining to these activities are:

- Choosing whether to provide training to individuals or to teams of employees who may come from diverse areas of the firm
- Deciding whether to teach required skills on the job or rely on external sources for training
- Choosing whether to emphasize job-specific training or generic training
- Deciding whether to hire at a high wage people from outside the firm who already have the required talents ("buy skills") or to invest resources in training the firm's own lower-wage employees in the necessary skills ("make skills")

Compensation

Compensation is the payment that employees receive in exchange for their labor. U.S. organizations vary widely in how they choose to compensate their employees (Chapters 10, 11, and 12). Some of the strategic HR choices related to pay are:

- Providing employees with a fixed salary and benefits package that changes little from year to year (and, therefore, involves minimal risk) versus paying employees a variable amount subject to change
- Paying employees on the basis of the job they hold versus paying them for their individual contributions to the firm
- Rewarding employees for the time they have spent with the firm versus rewarding them for performance
- Centralizing pay decisions in a single location (such as the HR department) versus empowering the supervisor or work team to make pay decisions

Employee Rights

Employee rights concern the relationship between the organization and individual employees (Chapter 14). Some of the strategic choices that the firm needs to make in this area are:

- Emphasizing discipline as the mechanism for controlling employee behavior versus proactively encouraging appropriate behavior in the first place
- Developing policies that emphasize protecting the employer's interests versus policies that emphasize protecting the employees' interests
- Relying on informal ethical standards versus developing explicit standards and procedures to enforce those standards

Employee and Labor Relations

Employee and labor relations (Chapters 13 and 15) refer to the interaction between workers (either as individuals or as represented by a union) and management. Some of the strategic HR choices facing the firm in these areas are:

- Relying on "top-down" communication channels from managers to subordinates versus encouraging "bottom-up" feedback from employees to managers
- Actively trying to avoid or suppress union-organizing activity versus accepting unions as representatives of employees' interests
- Adopting an adversarial approach to dealing with employees versus responding to employees' needs so that the incentive for unionization is removed (enlightened management)

International Management

Firms that operate outside domestic boundaries face a set of strategic HR options regarding how to manage human resources on a global basis (Chapter 17). Some of the key strategic HR choices involved in international management are:

- Creating a common company culture to reduce intercountry cultural differences versus allowing foreign subsidiaries to adapt to the local culture
- Sending expatriates (domestic employees) abroad to manage foreign subsidiaries versus hiring local people to manage them
- Establishing a repatriation agreement with each employee going abroad (carefully stipulating what the expatriate can expect upon return in terms of career advancement, compensation, and the like) versus avoiding any type of commitment to expatriates
- Establishing company policies that must be followed in all subsidiaries versus decentralizing policy formulation so that each local office can develop its own policies

Selecting HR Strategies to Increase Firm Performance

No HR strategy is "good" or "bad" in and of itself. Rather, an HR strategy's effect on firm performance is always dependent on how well it fits with other factors. This fact leads to a simple yet powerful prediction for HR strategies that has been widely supported by research: Fit leads to better performance, and lack of fit creates inconsistencies that reduce performance.[164] *Fit* refers to the compatibility between HR strategies and other important aspects of the organization.

Figure 1.4 depicts the key factors that firms should consider in determining which HR strategies will have a positive impact on firm performance: organizational strategies, environment, organizational characteristics, and organizational capabilities. As the figure shows, the relative contribution of an HR strategy to firm performance increases:

- The better the match between the HR strategy and the firm's overall organizational strategies
- The more the HR strategy is attuned to the environment in which the firm is operating
- The more closely the HR strategy is molded to unique organizational features
- The better the HR strategy enables the firm to capitalize on its distinctive competencies
- The more the HR strategies are mutually consistent or reinforce one another

Fit with Organizational Strategies

A corporation may have multiple businesses that are very similar to or completely different from one another. **Corporate strategy** refers to the mix of businesses a corporation decides to hold and the flow of resources among those businesses. The main strategic business decisions at the corporate level concern acquisition, divestment, diversification, and growth. **Business unit strategies** refer to the formulation and implementation of strategies by firms that are relatively autonomous, even if they are part of a larger corporation. For instance, until fairly recently, AT&T as a corporate entity owned hundreds of largely independent firms, including perfume makers and Hostess Twinkies, each with its own business strategy.[165] Similarly, diversified giant DuPont combines businesses such as drugs, agriculture, and chemicals under one roof.[166] In firms that produce a single product or highly related products or services, the business and corporate strategies are identical. For companies that have distinct corporate and business unit strategies, it is important to examine each in terms of its fit with HR strategies.

Corporate Strategies

There are two major types of corporate strategies and matching HR strategies. Corporations adopting an *evolutionary business strategy* engage in aggressive acquisitions of new businesses, even if these are totally unrelated to one another.[167]

In evolutionary firms, the management of change is crucial to survival. Entrepreneurship is encouraged and control is deemphasized because each unit is relatively autonomous. HR strategies that foster flexibility, quick response, entrepreneurship, risk sharing, and decentralization are particularly appropriate. Because the evolutionary corporation is not committed to a particular business or industry, it may hire workers from the external market as needed and lay them off to reduce costs if necessary, with no promise of rehiring them. These HR strategies are appropriate because they "fit" with the organizational reality that change is the only constant.

Corporate strategy
The mix of businesses a corporation decides to hold and the flow of resources among those businesses.

Business unit strategy
The formulation and implementation of strategies by a firm that is relatively autonomous, even if it is part of a larger corporation.

A Question of Ethics

The dark side of strategic planning is that workers are sometimes thought of as numbers on a page or dollars in a budget rather than as flesh-and-blood human beings. When divisions are spun off or merged, individual employees are dramatically affected. What responsibility does the employer have toward its employees in situations like these?

Effective HR Strategy Formulation and Implementation

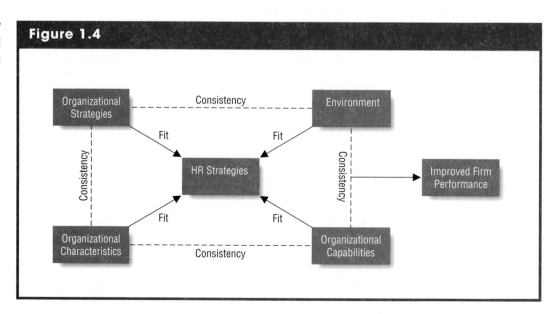

Figure 1.4

At the other end of the spectrum, corporations adopting a *steady-state strategy* are very choosy about how they grow. They avoid acquiring firms outside their industry or even companies within the industry that are very different from them. Top managers exercise a great deal of direct control over the company, and internal development of new products and technologies and interunit coordination are very important.[168] This is the case at Rubbermaid, a company known for producing such mundane products as trash cans and dustpans. Yet, Rubbermaid's record for innovation is anything but mundane. The company brings out new products at the rate of one a day.[169] The HR strategies most appropriate to steady-state firms emphasize efficiency, detailed work planning, internal grooming of employees for promotion and long-term career development, centralization, and a paternalistic attitude.

Porter's Business Unit Strategies

Two well-known business unit strategies were formulated by Porter[170] and Miles and Snow[171] to analyze which HR strategies represent the best fit with a firm's business strategy.

Porter has identified three types of business unit strategies that help a firm cope with competitive forces and outperform other firms in the industry. For each of these strategies, outlined in Figure 1.5, a certain set of HR strategies would fit best.[172]

The *overall cost leadership strategy* is aimed at gaining a competitive advantage through lower costs. Cost leadership requires aggressive construction of efficient plant facilities (which requires sustained capital investment), intense supervision of labor, vigorous pursuit of cost reductions, and tight control of distribution costs and overhead. Firms that have successfully pursued a low-cost leadership strategy include Briggs & Stratton, Emerson Electric, Texas Instruments, Black & Decker, and DuPont.[173]

Low-cost firms tend to emphasize structured tasks and responsibilities, products designed for easy manufacture, and the need to predict costs with minimal margin of error. The HR strategies that fit a low-cost orientation emphasize efficient, low-cost production; reinforce adherence to rational, highly structured procedures to minimize uncertainty; and discourage creativity and innovation (which may lead to costly experimentation and mistakes).

		Figure 1.5
Business Strategy	**Common Organizational Characteristics**	**HR Strategies**
Overall Cost Leadership	■ Sustained capital investment and access to capital ■ Intense supervision of labor ■ Tight cost control requiring frequent, detailed control reports ■ Low-cost distribution system ■ Structured organization and responsibilities ■ Products designed for ease in manufacture	■ Efficient production ■ Explicit job descriptions ■ Detailed work planning ■ Emphasis on technical qualifications and skills ■ Emphasis on job-specific training ■ Emphasis on job-based pay ■ Use of performance appraisal as a control device
Differentiation	■ Strong marketing abilities ■ Product engineering ■ Strong capability in basic research ■ Corporate reputation for quality or technological leadership ■ Amenities to attract highly skilled labor, scientists, or creative people	■ Emphasis on innovation and flexibility ■ Broad job classes ■ Loose work planning ■ External recruitment ■ Team-based training ■ Emphasis on individual-based pay ■ Use of performance appraisal as developmental tool
Focus	Combination of cost-leadership and differentiation strategy directed at a particular strategic target	Combination of HR strategies above

Source: Common organizational characteristics: Porter, M. E. (1980). *Competitive Strategy,* 40–41. New York: Free Press.

Selected HR Strategies That Fit Porter's Three Major Types of Business Strategies

A firm with a *differentiation business strategy* attempts to achieve a competitive advantage by creating a product or service that is perceived as unique. Some common characteristics of such firms are strong marketing abilities, an emphasis on product engineering and basic research, a corporate reputation for quality products, and amenities that are attractive to highly skilled labor. Approaches to differentiating can take many forms; among them are design or brand image (Fieldcrest in top-of-the-line towels and linens; Mercedes-Benz in automobiles); technology (Hyster in lift trucks; Fisher in stereo components; Coleman in camping equipment); features (Jenn-Air in electric ranges); customer service (IBM in computers); and dealer networks (Caterpillar Tractor in construction equipment).

Differentiation provides a competitive advantage because of the brand loyalty it fosters. This enables the differentiator to enjoy higher profit margins, which in turn allow it to invest in extensive research, experimentation with new ideas and product designs, catering to the needs of different customers, and supporting creative initiatives by managers and employees.

HR strategies that fit a differentiation strategy emphasize innovation, flexibility, renewal of the workforce by attracting new talent from other firms, opportunities for mavericks, and reinforcement (rather than discouragement) of creative flair.

The *focus strategy* relies on both a low-cost position and differentiation, with the objective of serving a narrow target market better than other firms. The firm seeks to achieve differentiation either from better meeting the needs of the particular target, or from lowering costs in serving this target, or both.[174] Firms that have used this strategy successfully include Illinois Tool Works (in the specialty market for fasteners), Gymboree (a national franchise providing creative activities and accessories for children under the age of 5), Fort Howard Paper (manufacturer of specialized industrial grade papers), and Porter Paint (producer of paints for professional house-painters).

The HR strategies likely to fit the focus strategy best would be somewhere in the middle of those described for low-cost producers and differentiators. At Illinois Tool Works (ITW), for instance, the chairman stresses working hand-in-hand with customers both to find out what they want and to learn how ITW can help them lower their operating costs. HR strategies reflect this focus by boosting efficiency to hold costs down. ITW's business is decentralized into 200 fairly small operating units, headed by managers whose pay is largely tied to sales and profits at their individual operations. The company's workers are nonunion, which helps to hold costs down. To keep ITW's products geared to customer needs, management puts heavy emphasis on R&D. ITW's R&D spending of almost $40 million a year keeps creativity high; ITW holds over 4,000 active patents.[175]

Miles and Snow's Business Strategies

Miles and Snow created another well-known classification of business unit strategies.[176] They characterize successful businesses as adopting either a defender or a prospector strategy.

Defenders are conservative business units that prefer to maintain a secure position in relatively stable product or service areas instead of looking to expand into uncharted territory. Defenders tend to be highly formalized and to emphasize cost control, and to operate in a stable environment. Many defenders develop an elaborate internal system for promoting, transferring, and rewarding workers that is relatively isolated from the uncertainties of the external labor market. In exchange for a long-term commitment to the firm, employees are rewarded with job security and the expectation of upward mobility through the ranks.

The HR strategies that best fit defenders' needs, categorized according to six major strategic HR choices we saw in Figure 1.3 earlier, are summarized in Figure 1.6. These strategies include work flows emphasizing managerial control and reliability, staffing and employee separation policies designed to foster long-term employee attachment to the firm, performance appraisals focused on managerial control and hierarchy, structured training programs, and compensation policies that emphasize job security.

Unlike defenders, whose success comes primarily from efficiently serving a stable market, *prospectors* emphasize growth and innovation, development of new products, and an eagerness to be the first in new-product or market areas, even if some of these efforts fail.[177] The prospector's strategy is associated with flexible and decentralized organizational structures, complex products (such as computers and pharmaceuticals), and unstable environments that change rapidly.

Strategic HR Area	Defender Strategy	Prospector Strategy
Work Flows	■ Efficient production ■ Control emphasis ■ Explicit job descriptions ■ Detailed work planning	■ Innovation ■ Flexibility ■ Broad job classes ■ Loose work planning
Staffing	■ Internal recruitment ■ HR department makes selection decision ■ Emphasis on technical qualifications and skills ■ Formal hiring and socialization process	■ External recruitment ■ Coworkers help make selection decision ■ Emphasis on fit of applicant with culture ■ Informal hiring and socialization process of new employees
Employee Separations	■ Voluntary inducements to leave ■ Hiring freeze ■ Continuing concern for terminated employee ■ Preferential rehiring policy	■ Layoffs ■ Recruit as needed ■ Individual on his or her own ■ No preferential treatment for laid-off workers
Performance Appraisal	■ Uniform appraisal procedures ■ Used as control device ■ Narrow focus ■ High dependence on superior	■ Customized appraisals ■ Used as developmental tool ■ Multipurpose appraisals ■ Multiple inputs for appraisals
Training	■ Individual training ■ On-the-job training ■ Job-specific training ■ "Make" skills	■ Team-based or cross-functional training ■ External training ■ Generic training emphasizing flexibility ■ "Buy" skills
Compensation	■ Fixed pay ■ Job-based pay ■ Seniority-based pay ■ Centralized pay decisions	■ Variable pay ■ Individual-based pay ■ Performance-based pay ■ Decentralized pay decisions

Source: Gómez-Mejía, L. R. (2006). Compensation strategies and Miles and Snow's business strategy taxonomy. Unpublished report. Management Department, Arizona State University.

Selected HR Strategies That Fit Miles and Snow's Two Major Types of Business Strategies

The HR strategies that match the strategic orientation of prospectors, also summarized in Figure 1.6, include work flows that foster creativity and adaptability; staffing and employee separation policies that focus on the external labor market; customized, participative employee appraisals used for multiple purposes (including employee development); training strategies targeting broad skills; and a decentralized compensation system that rewards risk taking and performance. Exhibit 1.1, "Lincoln Electric and Hewlett-Packard: Defender and Prospector," on page 32 discusses how these two firms have successfully used HR strategies to support their opposite business strategies.

Fit with the Environment

In addition to reinforcing overall organizational strategies, HR strategies should help the organization better exploit environmental opportunities or cope with the unique environmental forces that affect it. We can examine the environment in terms of four major dimensions: (1) *degree of uncertainty* (how much accurate information is available to make appropriate business decisions); (2) *volatility* (how often the environment changes); (3) *magnitude of change* (how drastic

EXHIBIT 1.1

Lincoln Electric and Hewlett-Packard: Defender and Prospector

To get a better idea of what it means for a company to be a defender or a prospector, let us look at the activities of two companies: Ohio-based Lincoln Electric, a manufacturer of electrical products; and Hewlett-Packard, the Palo Alto, California, electronics manufacturer that put Silicon Valley on the high-tech map.

Lincoln Electric

Lincoln Electric is a classic defender. It has carved out a niche in the electrical products industry (the manufacture of electric arc-welding generators, welding equipment, and supplies) and has "defended" it for over 70 years through continuous efforts to improve production processes and product quality, cut costs, lower prices, and provide outstanding customer service. Lincoln is best known for its incentive system, which rewards high-quantity, high-quality output with wages and bonuses that average over *twice* the national average for comparable work classifications. Lincoln's HR strategies fit with the company's strategy because Lincoln has created a secure market share with moderate, steady growth. It relies heavily on internally developed human resources. Employees are carefully selected, placed, and trained, and they are expected to be with the company for much, if not all, of their careers.

The appropriate role for the HR department at Lincoln is clear. Selection, placement, appraisal, and long-term training assistance are key services. In addition, the HR department must constantly maintain the fit between job design and the incentive system. Lincoln is a tightly integrated company that requires predictable, planned HR inputs and regular maintenance.

As of 2006, Lincoln Electric still emphasizes cost reductions, high reliability, and a focus on state-of-the-art welding technologies (for instance, through increased use of robotics).

Hewlett-Packard

Hewlett-Packard (HP) began with the notion that high returns were possible from moving products as rapidly as possible from basic design to the market. It is a company well suited to the rapid expansion of a growing industry—a true prospector—with small, changing product divisions as its basic organizational building blocks. (The company has over 60,000 employees in more than 60 divisions or units.) A new-product idea or offshoot is evolved, a self-contained division is created, and a market is pursued as long as HP has a distinctive design or technological advantage. When products reach the stage where successful competition turns primarily on cost, HP may move out of the arena and turn its attention to a new design or an entirely new product.

HR units at both the division and the corporate level have the constant task of starting new groups, and finding and deploying managerial and technical resources. In this setting, HR departments perform an essentially entrepreneurial role, helping to identify and quickly develop (through rapid movement and alternative assignments) crucial human resources. Key human resources are brought in from the outside and invested in myriad units and divisions, as well as developed internally. Thus, the overall HR strategy at Hewlett-Packard can be characterized as acquiring human resources.

As of 2006, HP continues unabated with this HR strategy. In fact, its company Web page "jobs at HP" (*www.jobs.hp.com*) is one of the most comprehensive ones around, enabling candidates to search for job opportunities at HP facilities in 178 countries.

Source: Based on Miles, R. E., and Snow, C. C. (1984). Designing strategic human resources systems. *Organizational Dynamics* 13(1), 43–46. © 1984 American Management Association, New York. All rights reserved. Updated information provided by Gómez-Mejía, L. R., Balkin, D. B., and Cardy, R. L.

the changes are); and (4) *complexity* (how many different elements in the environment affect the firm, either individually or together). For example, much of the computer and high-tech industry is very high on all four of these dimensions:

■ **Degree of uncertainty.** Compaq thought consumers would continue to pay a premium price for its high-performance computers. The company was proved wrong in the 1990s as low-cost competitors such as Dell, Packard Bell, and AST quickly cut into Compaq's market.
■ **Volatility.** IBM paid dearly when demand for its mainframe computers declined drastically in the late 1980s and it was caught unprepared.
■ **Magnitude of change.** The advent of each successive new generation of computer microprocessor chips (for example, Intel's 386, 486, Pentium) has almost immediately rendered all previously sold machines obsolete. Polaroid was forced to declare bankruptcy as quick adoption of digital cameras turned its main product (instant photography) obsolete almost overnight.
■ **Complexity.** The number and variety of competitors in the computer industry, both domestically and overseas, have grown dramatically in recent years. The life of a product seldom extends more than three years now, as new innovations drive previous equipment and software out of the market.

As Figure 1.7 on page 33 shows, firms that are high on these four dimensions are more likely to benefit from HR strategies that promote flexibility, adaptiveness, quick response, transferability of skills, the ability to secure external talent as needed, and risk sharing with employees through variable pay.

Conversely, firms facing environments that are low on uncertainty, volatility, magnitude of change, and complexity benefit from HR strategies that allow for an orderly, rational, and routine approach to dealing with a relatively predictable and stable environment. The "old" AT&T

Figure 1.7

Environmental Dimension	Low	High
Degree of Uncertainty	■ Detailed work planning ■ Job-specific training ■ Fixed pay ■ High dependence on superior	■ Loose work planning ■ Generic training ■ Variable pay ■ Multiple inputs for appraisals
Volatility	■ Control emphasis ■ Efficient production ■ Job-specific training ■ Fixed pay	■ Flexibility ■ Innovation ■ Generic training ■ Variable pay
Magnitude of Change	■ Explicit job descriptions ■ Formal hiring and socialization of new employees ■ "Make" skills ■ Uniform appraisal procedures	■ Broad job classes ■ Informal hiring and socialization of new employees ■ "Buy" skills ■ Customized appraisals
Complexity	■ Control emphasis ■ Internal recruitment ■ Centralized pay decisions ■ High dependence on superior	■ Flexibility ■ External recruitment ■ Decentralized pay decisions ■ Multiple inputs for appraisals

Sources: Based on Gómez-Mejía, L. R., Balkin, D. B., and Cardy, R. (2007). *Management.* New York: Irwin/McGraw-Hill; Gómez-Mejía, L. R., and Balkin, D. B. (1992). *Compensation, organizational strategy, and firm performance.* Cincinnati, OH: South-Western; Gómez-Mejía, L. R., Balkin, D. B., and Milkovich, G. T. (1990). Rethinking your rewards for technical employees. *Organizational Dynamics, 18*(4), 62–75; Gómez-Mejía, L. R. (1992). Structure and process of diversification, compensation strategy, and firm performance. *Strategic Management Journal, 13,* 381–397.

Selected HR Strategies for Firms Low and High on Different Environmental Characteristics

(before divestment), much of the airline and trucking industry before deregulation, utilities, and government bureaucracies fall at the low end of the scale on these four dimensions. Figure 1.7 shows that the HR strategies that fit firms operating under these conditions tend to be rather mechanistic: detailed work planning, job-specific training, fixed pay, explicit job descriptions, centralized pay decisions, and the like.

Fit with Organizational Characteristics

To be effective, HR strategies must be tailored to the organization's personality. The features of an organization's personality can be broken down into five major categories.

The Production Process for Converting Inputs into Output
Firms with a relatively routine production process (such as large-volume steel mills, lumber mills, and automobile plants) tend to benefit from HR strategies that emphasize control, such as explicit job descriptions and job-specific training. The opposite is true for firms with nonroutine production processes (such as advertising firms, custom printers, and biotechnology companies). These firms benefit from flexible HR strategies that support organizational adaptability, quick response to change, and creative decision making. These flexible strategies may include broad job classes, loose work planning, and generic training.

The Firm's Market Posture
Firms that experience a high rate of sales growth and engage in product innovation destined for a wide market segment tend to benefit from HR strategies that support growth and entrepreneurial activities. These HR strategies include external recruitment ("buying" skills), decentralized pay decisions, and customized appraisals. The opposite is true for firms with low rates of growth and limited product innovation destined for a narrow market segment. These firms tend to benefit more from HR strategies that emphasize efficiency, control, and firm-specific knowledge. Such strategies include internal recruitment ("making" skills), on-the-job training, and high dependence on superiors.

The Firm's Overall Managerial Philosophy
Companies whose top executives are averse to risk, operate with an autocratic leadership style, establish a strong internal pecking order, and are inwardly rather than outwardly focused may find that certain HR practices match this outlook best. The HR strategies most often used in these kinds of firms include seniority-based pay, formal hiring and socializing of new employees, selection decisions made by the HR department, and use of top-down communication channels. The HR strategies that fit a managerial philosophy high on risk taking, participation, egalitarianism, and an external, proactive environmental orientation include variable pay, giving supervisors a major role in hiring decisions, up-and-down communication channels, and multiple inputs for performance appraisals.

The Firm's Organizational Structure
Some HR strategies fit very well with highly formalized organizations that are divided into functional areas (for example, marketing, finance, production, and so on) and that concentrate decision making at the top. The HR strategies appropriate for this type of firm include a control emphasis, centralized pay decisions, explicit job descriptions, and job-based pay. Firms whose organizational structures are less regimented will benefit from a different set of HR strategies, including informal hiring and socializing of new employees, decentralized pay decisions, broad job classes, and individual-based pay.

The Firm's Organizational Culture
Companies that foster an *entrepreneurial climate* benefit from supporting HR strategies such as loose work planning, informal hiring and socializing of new employees, and variable pay. Firms that discourage entrepreneurship generally prefer a control emphasis, detailed work planning, formal hiring and socializing of new employees, and fixed pay.

A strong emphasis on *moral commitment*—the extent to which a firm tries to foster a long-term emotional attachment between the firm and its employees—is also associated with certain supporting HR strategies. These include an emphasis on preventive versus remedial disciplinary action to handle employee mistakes, employee protection, and explicit ethical codes to monitor and guide behavior. Firms that are low on moral commitment usually rely on an authoritarian relationship between employee and company. HR strategies consistent with this orientation include an emphasis on discipline or punishment to reduce employee mistakes, employment at will (discussed in Chapters 3 and 14), and informal ethical standards.

Fit with Organizational Capabilities

A firm's organizational capabilities include its **distinctive competencies**, those characteristics (such as technical ability, management systems, and reputation) that give the firm a competitive edge. For instance, Mercedes-Benz automobiles are widely regarded as superior because of the quality of their design and engineering. Wal-Mart's phenomenal success has been due, at least in part, to its ability to track products from supplier to customer better than its competitors can.

Distinctive competencies
The characteristics that give a firm a competitive edge.

HR strategies make a greater contribution to firm performance the greater the extent to which (1) they help the company exploit its specific advantages or strengths while avoiding weaknesses, and (2) they assist the firm in better utilizing its own unique blend of human resource skills and assets.

The following examples illustrate how one type of HR strategy—compensation strategy— may be aligned with organizational capabilities.[178]

■ Firms known for excellence in customer service tend to pay their sales force only partially on commission, thereby reducing their sales employees' potential for abrasive behaviors and overselling.
■ Smaller firms can use compensation to their advantage by paying low wages but being generous in stock offerings to employees. This strategy allows them to use more of their scarce cash to fuel future growth.
■ Organizations may take advantage of their unused capacity in their compensation strategies. For example, most private universities offer free tuition to faculty and their immediate family. With average tuition at private colleges exceeding $18,000 a year in 2007, this benefit represents a huge cash savings to faculty members, thereby allowing private universities to attract and retain good faculty with minimal adverse impact on their cost structure.

Choosing Consistent and Appropriate HR Tactics to Implement HR Strategies

Even the best-laid strategic HR plans may fail when specific HR programs are poorly chosen or implemented.[179] In addition to fitting with each of the four factors just described (organizational strategy, environment, organizational characteristics, and organizational capabilities), a firm's HR strategies are more likely to be effective if they reinforce one another rather than work at cross-purposes. For instance, many organizations are currently trying to improve their performance by structuring work in teams. However, these same organizations often continue to use a traditional performance appraisal system in which each employee is evaluated individually. The appraisal system needs to be overhauled to make it consistent with the emphasis on team performance.

Because it is not always possible to know beforehand if an HR program will meet its objectives, a periodic evaluation of HR programs is necessary. Figure 1.8 lists a series of important questions that should be raised to examine the appropriateness of HR programs. These questions should be answered as new programs are being chosen and while they are in effect.

HR Best Practices

Several authors have argued that certain HR practices are associated with sustained high firm performance.[180] Figure 1.9 includes one of the most widely referenced lists of "HR best practices" created by Professor Jeffrey Pfeffer at Stanford University. Debate continues among academics about whether high firm performance leads to given HR practices, or vice versa (that is, whether introducing particular HR practices causes better firm performance).[181] For instance, can firms that are doing well afford to provide higher wages and more job security, or do firms that pay more and have a more stable workforce derive a performance premium

---

Figure 1.8

HR programs that look good on paper may turn out to be disasters when implemented because they conflict too much with company realities. To avoid this kind of unpleasant surprise, it is important to ask the following questions *before* implementing a new HR program.

1. Are the HR Programs Effective Tools for Implementing HR Strategies?
   ✓ Are the proposed HR programs the most appropriate ones for implementing the firm's HR strategies?
   ✓ Has an analysis been done of how each of the past, current, or planned HR programs contributes to or hinders the successful implementation of the firm's HR strategies?
   ✓ Can the proposed HR programs be easily changed or modified to meet new strategic considerations without violating either a "psychological" or a legal contract with employees?
2. Do the HR Programs Meet Resource Constraints?
   ✓ Does the organization have the capacity to implement the proposed HR programs? In other words, are the HR programs realistic?
   ✓ Are the proposed programs going to be introduced at a rate that can be easily absorbed, or will the timing and extent of changes lead to widespread confusion and strong employee resistance?
3. How Will the HR Programs Be Communicated?
   ✓ Are the proposed HR programs well understood by those who will implement them (for example, line supervisors and employees)?
   ✓ Does top management understand how the proposed programs are intended to affect the firm's strategic objectives?
4. Who Will Put the HR Programs in Motion?
   ✓ Is the HR department playing the role of an internal consultant to assist employees and managers responsible for carrying out the proposed HR programs?
   ✓ Is top management visibly and emphatically committed to the proposed programs?

But Will It Work? Questions for Testing the Appropriateness of HR Programs Before Implementation

by following these practices? It is extraordinarily difficult to prove the casual relationship one way or the other, yet it seems reasonable that organizations should consider implementation of those practices associated with the highest-performing firms.

The HR Department and Managers: An Important Partnership

This book takes a managerial approach to human resources and HR strategy. All managers—regardless of their functional area, their position in the hierarchy, and the size of the firm for which they work—must deal effectively with HR issues because these issues are at the heart of being a good manager.

The role of a company's human resources department is to support, not to supplant, managers' HR responsibilities. For instance, the HR department may develop a form to help managers measure the performance of subordinates, but it is the managers who conduct the actual evaluation. Stated another way, the HR department is primarily responsible for helping the firm meet its business objectives by designing HR programs, but managers must carry out these programs. This means that every manager is a human resource manager.

Companies can take certain steps to foster an effective partnership between managers and the HR department.[182] Specifically, companies should:

- Analyze the people side of productivity rather than depend solely on technical solutions to problems. This requires that managers be trained in certain HR skills and that they value human resources as a key element in organizational performance.
- View HR professionals as internal consultants who can provide valuable advice and support that improve the management of operations.
- Instill a shared sense of common fate in the firm rather than a win/lose perspective among individual departments and units.
- Require some managerial experience as part of the training of HR professionals. This requirement should make HR staff more sensitive to and cognizant of the problems managers face.

Figure 1.9

Employment Security
Security of employment signals a long-standing commitment by the organization to its workforce.

Selectivity in Recruiting
Security in employment and reliance on the workforce for competitive success mean that one must be careful to choose the right people, in the right way.

High Wages
If you want to recruit outstanding people, and want them to stay with the organization, paying more is helpful, although not absolutely necessary.

Incentive Pay
There has been a tendency to overuse money in an effort to solve myriad organizational problems. People are motivated by more than money—things like recognition, security, and fair treatment matter a great deal. Nevertheless, if people are responsible for enhanced levels of performance and profitability, they will want to share in the benefits.

Employee Ownership
Employee ownership offers two advantages. First, employees who have ownership interests in the organizations for which they work have less conflict between capital and labor—to some degree they are both capital and labor. Second, ownership makes employees more inclined to take a long-term view of the organization, its strategy, and its investment policies.

Information Sharing
If people are to be a source of competitive advantage, clearly they must have the information necessary to do what is required to be successful.

Participation and Empowerment
High-performing organizations encourage decentralization of decision making and elicit ideas from workers and allow employees greater control over their work processes.

Self-Managed Teams
Teams are effective because of peer monitoring and high expectations of coworkers that induce team members to be more highly motivated to do the best job possible.

Training and Skill Development
High-performance organizations show a greater commitment to training and skill development. Note, however, that this training will produce positive returns only if the trained workers are then permitted to employ their skills.

Cross-Utilization and Cross-Training
Having people do multiple jobs has a number of potential benefits. The most obvious is that doing more things can make work more interesting—variety is one of the core job dimensions that affect how people respond to their work.

Promotion from Within
Promotion from within is a useful adjunct to many of the practices described. It encourages training and skill development because the availability of promotion opportunities within the firm binds workers to employers and vise versa.

Sources: Adapted with permission from Pfeffer, J. (1995). Producing sustainable competitive advantage through the effective management of people. *Academy of Management Executive,* 10, 55–72. For an exhaustive literature review of the relationship between HR practices and firm performance, see Wright, P. M., Gardner, T. M., Moynihan, L. M., & Allen, M. R. (2005). The relationship between HR practices and firm performance: Examining causal order. *Personnel Psychology,* 58, 409–446.

HR Best Practices

- Actively involve top corporate and divisional managers in formulating, implementing, and reviewing all HR plans and strategies in close collaboration with the HR department.
- Require senior HR executives to participate on an equal basis with other key managers from the various functional areas (marketing, finance) in charting the enterprise's strategic direction.

Companies should also periodically conduct an **HR audit** to evaluate how effectively they are using their human resources. The audit, which is typically conducted by the HR department, deals with a broad set of questions, including:

- Is the turnover rate exceptionally low or high?
- Are the people quitting good employees who are frustrated in their present job, or are they marginal performers?

HR audit
A periodic review of the effectiveness with which a company uses its human resources. Frequently includes an evaluation of the HR department itself.

- Is the firm receiving a high return on the money it spends on recruitment, training, and pay-for-performance plans?
- Is the firm complying with government regulations?
- How well is the company managing employee diversity?
- Is the HR department providing the services that line managers need?
- Are HRM policies and procedures helping the firm accomplish its long-term goals?

The HR audit addresses these and other important issues systematically so that effective programs can be maintained and ineffective programs corrected or eliminated.

Specialization in Human Resource Management

Over the past three decades, the size of the typical HR department has increased considerably. This increase reflects both the growth and complexity of government regulations and a greater awareness that HR issues are important to the achievement of business objectives.

Many colleges and universities now offer specialized degrees in human resources at the associate, bachelor's, master's, and doctoral levels. The Society for Human Resource Management (SHRM), which has almost 60,000 members, has set up a certification institute to offer HR professionals the opportunity to be certified officially at the PHR (Professional Human Resources) or SPHR (Senior Professional Human Resources) level. SHRM certification requires a certain amount of experience and mastery of a body of knowledge as indicated by successful completion of a comprehensive examination. (For additional information and application materials, write to the Society at 1800 Duke Street, Alexandria, VA 22314 or visit the Web site at *www.shrm.org.*) Other organizations whose members specialize in a particular area of HRM are WorldatWork (previously the American Compensation Association), the Human Resource Planning Society, and the American Society for Training and Development.[183]

In recent years, the compensation of HR specialists has increased faster than other jobs, and for some HR jobs pay is sharply on the rise, reflecting greater professionalization and increasing awareness by business that a well-managed HR function may help the firm achieve a sustainable competitive advantage. In 2006, experienced HR directors earned approximately $88,000 a year, on average; those with the title of vice president for human resources earned approximately $171,000 a year, on average. These are only averages, however. In some of the largest firms, the top job in this field paid more than $700,000 in 2006. Among the specialized subfields (such as executive trainees, corporate compensation directors, benefit directors, and corporate security managers) average salaries exceed $110,000.[184]

Summary and Conclusions

Human Resource Management: The Challenges

The major HR challenges facing managers today can be divided into three categories: environmental challenges, organizational challenges, and individual challenges.

The environmental challenges are rapid change, rise of the Internet, workforce diversity, economic globalization, legislation, evolving work and family roles, skill shortages, and the rise of the service sector.

The organizational challenges are choosing a competitive position, decentralization, downsizing, organizational restructuring, the rise of self-managed work teams, the increased number of small businesses, organizational culture, advances in technology, and the rise of outsourcing.

The individual challenges involve matching people with the organization, treating employees ethically and engaging in socially responsible behavior, increasing individual productivity, deciding whether to empower employees, taking steps to avoid brain drain, and dealing with issues of job insecurity.

Planning and Implementing Strategic HR Policies

Correctly done, strategic HR planning provides many direct and indirect benefits for a company. These include the encouragement of proactive (rather than reactive) behavior; explicit communication of company goals; stimulation of critical thinking and ongoing examination of assumptions; identification of gaps between the company's current situation and its future vision; the encouragement of line managers' participation in the strategic planning process; the identification of HR constraints and opportunities; and the creation of common bonds within the organization.

In developing an effective HR strategy, an organization faces several challenges. These include putting in place a strategy that creates and maintains a competitive advantage for the company and reinforces the overall business strategy; avoiding excessive concentration on day-to-day problems; developing strategies suited to unique organizational features; coping with the environment in which the business operates; securing management commitment; translating the strategic plan into action; combining intended and emergent strategies; and accommodating change.

A firm's strategic HR choices are the options available to it in designing its human resources systems. Firms must make strategic choices in many HR areas, including work flows, staffing, employee separations, performance appraisal, training and career development, compensation, employee rights, employee and labor relations, and international management.

Selecting HR Strategies to Increase Firm Performance

To be effective, HR strategies must fit with overall organizational strategies, the environment in which the firm is operating, unique organizational characteristics, and organizational capabilities. HR strategies should also be mutually consistent and reinforce one another.

The HR Department and Managers: An Important Partnership

Responsibility for the effective use of human resources lies primarily with managers. Hence, all managers are personnel managers. HR professionals' role is to act as internal consultants or experts, assisting managers to do their jobs better.

Over the past three decades, the size of the typical HR department has increased considerably. This increase reflects both the growth and complexity of government regulations and a greater awareness that HR issues are important to the achievement of business objectives.

Key Terms

ability, 18
brain drain, 19
business unit strategy, 28
corporate strategy, 28
decentralization, 11
distinctive competencies, 34
downsizing, 11
empowerment, 19
environmental challenges, 4

HR audit, 37
human resources (HR), 3
human resource strategy, 3
human resource tactic, 3
individual challenges, 16
line employee, 3
manager, 3
motivation, 18
organizational challenges, 10

organizational culture, 12
outsourcing, 15
productivity, 17
quality of work life, 18
staff employee, 3
strategic HR choices, 24
strategic human resource (HR)
    planning, 20
total quality management (TQM), 10

Discussion Questions

1. Going back to Manager's Notebook, "Snooping E-Mail by Software Is Now a Workplace Norm," what policies should a company have in place to ensure that employees' rights are not violated and that such "snooping" policies are implemented consistently? Should a company have a zero-tolerance policy against personal use of the Internet on company time, or should the policy be flexible? Explain.

2. Which of the environmental, organizational, and individual challenges identified in this chapter will be most important for human resource management in the twenty-first century, in your opinion? Which will be least important? Use your own experiences in your answer.

3. In a recent national survey of HR executives in more than 400 companies, most respondents reported that the priorities of top management at their firms are to counter competition, cut costs, and improve performance. Yet only 12 percent of these HR executives said that their department had a major responsibility for improving productivity, quality, and customer service in their companies. What do you think are some of the reasons for this gap between top management's priorities and the responsibility of the HR department? What are some of the consequences of this gap? Outline several ways in which HR departments can align themselves with their company's strategic goals. How do you think an HR department can gain top management's support for *its* programs and goals?

4. An increasing number of firms discipline employees for smoking and some conduct random testing to check for nicotine use, even if such use takes place on the employee's free time.[185] Do you think a company has the right to monitor and punish employees for behaviors that may increase company costs, even if they are legal and carried out outside normal working hours? Why or why not?

5. Several surveys indicate that unethical behaviors at work are on the rise. Going back to Manager's Notebook, "How and Why We Lie at the Office: From Pilfered Pens to Padded Accounts," do you think this

problem is getting worse? If so, what may be the cause? What can firms do to change this situation? Explain.

6. A study by Professors Judiesch and Lyness of the City University of New York's Baruch College found that adjusting for factors such as age, gender, education, and job factors, employees who take leave under the Family and Medical Leave Act (FMLA) of 1993 were heavily penalized. (The FMLA permits employees to take unpaid leave of up to 12 weeks for family or medical reasons.) Employees who took leave were less likely to be promoted than non-leave takers, received lower job performance ratings for the year in which they took time-off, and received smaller salary increases than their peers with similar low rating.[186] What may account for these findings? Based on your opinion, what does this say in terms of attempts to induce changes in HR practices via government intervention? Explain.

7. 3M's competitive business strategy is based on innovation. 3M requires that at least 25 percent of its annual sales come from products introduced over the previous five years, a goal it often exceeds. Specific HR programs adopted to implement this strategy include the creation of a special fund that allows employees to start new projects or follow up on ideas. 3M's "release time" program, in which workers are given time off during the day to pursue their own interests, is given credit for the creation of new products that management would not have thought of by itself. In addition, 3M's appraisal process encourages risk taking. A senior manager at 3M says, "If you are threatened with dismissal after working on a project that fails, you will never try again." What other types of HR policies might 3M institute to spur product innovation?

8. Many believe that top managers care little about human resources compared to such areas as marketing, finance, production, and engineering. What might account for this perception, and what would you do to change it?

There is a variety of additional material available on the Web site that accompanies this text. You can access this information by visiting the Web site at **www.prenhall.com/gomez**.

YOU MANAGE IT! # Emerging Trends Case 1.1

Are We Becoming a Nation of Workaholics?

The United States has always been known for its ethos of hard work. Today, over 31 percent of college-educated male workers are regularly logging 50 or more hours a week at work, up from 22 percent in 1980. About 40 percent of American adults get fewer than 7 hours of sleep on weekdays, up from 34 percent in 2001. Almost 60 percent of meals are rushed, and 38 percent of lunches are choked down on the run. To avoid wasting time, we're talking on our cell phones while rushing to work, answering e-mails during conference calls, waking up at 4 A.M. to call Europe, and generally multitasking our brains out.

This epidemic of spending long hours at the office—whether physically or remotely—defies historical precedent and common sense. Over the past 25 years, the Information Revolution has increased productivity by almost 70 percent. Because we're producing more in fewer hours, it would seem that such gains would translate into a shorter work week, as they have in the past. However, instead of technology being a time saver, says Warren Bennis, a University of Southern California professor and author of such management classics as *On Becoming a Leader,* "everybody I know is working harder and longer."

The long hours aren't a result of demanding corporations exploiting the powerless. Most of the groggy-eyed are the best educated and best paid—college grads whose wages in real terms have risen by more than 30 percent since the 1980s. This is a change from 25 years ago, when it was the lowest-wage workers who were most likely to put in 50 hours or more a week, according to new research by Peter Kuhn of the University of California at Santa Barbara and Fernando A. Lozano of Pomona College.

Communications seem to absorb more time than ever even though technology (for instance, the Internet and cell phones) has improved dramatically. Twenty-five percent of executives at large companies say their communications—voice mail, e-mail, and meetings—are nearly or completely unmanageable, according to a new McKinsey survey of more than 7,800 managers around the world. Nearly 40 percent of managers say they spend a half to a full day per week on communications that are not valuable. Other surveys echo similar results. "We're making our people compete with sandbags strapped to their legs," says Shoshana Zuboff, a former professor at Harvard Business School.

For instance, in 2006, 44 percent of Intel's staff regularly worked from home.[a] IBM's National Mobility Program offers equipment employees need to work at home, such as laptops, cell phones, and printers. IBM also provides substantial support for work-at-home employees, including telework policies and guidelines, training and responsibility agreements, and extensive use of distant communication technologies, such as using the Internet for meetings, conference calling, and video-conferencing.[b]

Critical Thinking Questions

1. Why do you think most managers and employees report that they are working harder than ever? Are globalization and the Internet part of the problem? Explain.

2. Many employees believe that to receive high performance evaluations, rise above the fray when it comes to promotions, or just keep their jobs during downsizing, it is necessary to put in long hours. For instance, one observer notes that "over the past 15 years, real pay for a 55-hour work week rose by about 14 percent, but pay for a normal 40-hour week hardly budged." Why do you think this is happening? Do you think this is a good or a bad thing? Do you think this trend toward longer hours is likely to increase or decrease in the future? Explain.

3. What can an organization do to avoid employees "working like dogs" past the point where they become ineffective due to stress and fatigue? Explain.

Team Exercise

Class is divided into groups of five. Each team is to provide a list of suggestions as to how an organization can implement the following guidelines to ease time pressures and boost productivity and innovation.

1. **Manage output rather than hours.** Eliminate or reduce low-value activities and meetings. This will allow more

time for innovation and creative thinking. Appraise employees' performance based on demonstrated results rather than on effort.

2. **Manage time effectively.** Conduct internal surveys to understand how people really spend their time, and use that information to eliminate the worst bottlenecks.

3. **Push decision making further down the hierarchy.** Explicitly broaden the range of decisions that lower-level managers and professionals can make without getting approval.

4. **Develop policies for Internet use.** Eliminate or reduce unnecessary electronic interaction, such as reducing the number and size of distribution lists.

Depending on class size, each team will present its recommendations to entire class for approximately 10 minutes, to be followed by open class discussion moderated by instructor.

Experiential Exercise

Each student will interview a manager or an employee (who might be a family member, a friend or an acquaintance) to determine the extent to which the issues raised in this case are represented in his or her organization and what steps, if any, the firm has taken to make employees more productive without working excessive long hours. (Alternatively, if the student has substantial work experience he or she may offer his or her own views based on personal observation.) Instructor will moderate open class discussion based on the findings brought to class by students.

Sources: Adapted with permission from Mandel, M. (2005, October 3). The real reasons you are working so hard. *BusinessWeek,* 60–73; [a]Koeppel, G. (2005, January 26). Telecommuting on the rise. *Arizona Republic,* 3; [b]Offutt, S. (2005, October 5). Best workplaces for commuters. *Workspan,* 45–47.

Emerging Trends Case 1.2   YOU MANAGE IT!

Savviest Job Hunters Research the Cultures of Potential Employers

Harold L. Maurer got a jolt of corporate-culture shock when he joined a Chicago advertising agency a few years ago. The communications executive had spent most of his career in the more traditional world of manufacturing. "Business casual" there meant pressed slacks, a button-down shirt, and a tie. But the ad agency was much more relaxed. His coworkers wore Hawaiian shirts, flip-flops, and shorts to work nearly every day in the summer. To fit in, Maurer dropped his ties and fished a Hawaiian shirt out of his closet. But he never felt at ease wearing super casual clothes to work. "I'm much more comfortable in a more formal environment," the 57-year-old executive says. Maurer spent about two years at

the ad agency. Today, he does marketing work in the Washington, D.C., area, where the office's culture tends to be more traditional.

Corporate-culture clashes are an increasingly common predicament these days. People are switching employers more often, hopping back and forth among companies with radically different attitudes toward everything from dress to management style and conflict resolution. As a result, the ability to gauge a company's culture has become an important skill for job applicants, says Marc Cenedella, president and CEO of *Ladders.com,* an executive job-search service firm based in New York.

Yet many job seekers pay little attention to a prospective employer's culture. Rather than considering how they will mesh with their new colleagues, they focus on their likely duties, salary, and boss. That's a mistake, recruiters and career consultants say. Culture clash is one of the biggest reasons that new hires fail. Even when a cultural mismatch doesn't cost you your job, it can still make your life at the office a struggle.

Critical Thinking Questions

1. How would you go about discovering what the culture of an organization is before you accept a job there? Be specific.
2. What factors affect the extent to which employees adapt or fail to adapt to an organization's culture? Explain.
3. What role should the HR department play in communicating the organization's culture to incoming and prospective employees? Explain.

Team Exercise

Class is divided up into groups of five. Team members are asked to describe the culture of organizations they have worked for or that they are familiar with. Each team is expected to develop a list of similarities and differences across the various organizational cultures represented (or known to the team) and speculate about the role played by HR policies and practices in reinforcing that culture. Instructor will then serve as a moderator in a general class discussion where various teams present their findings.

Experiential Exercise

Each student should list five characteristics of an organizational culture that he or she believes would make him or her feel most comfortable. The list prepared by each student is turned in to the instructor. When class reconvenes, instructor hands out the entire list to the class and uses it to moderate discussion, pointing out what appear to be major differences and similarities in what class members look for in an organizational culture. Instructor may ask students to identify ways in which prospective employees may be selected so that they best fit some of the cultural characteristics identified by class (for instance, interview questions, past experiences, job simulations, and the like). Lastly, instructor may also ask students to go to the Web sites of some of *Fortune's* "Best Places to Work" (listed at *www.fortune.com*) and, based on information provided there, identify firms that appear to exemplify some of the cultural elements discussed in class.

Source: Adapted with permission from White, E. (2005, March 29). Savviest job hunters research the cultures of potential employers. *Wall Street Journal*, B-1.

YOU MANAGE IT! Discussion Case 1.3

Managers and HR Professionals at Sands Corporation: Friends or Foes?

Sands Corporation is a medium-sized company located in the Midwest. It manufactures specialized computer equipment used in cars, serving as a subcontractor to several automobile manufacturers as well as to the military. Federal contracts are an important part of Sands' total sales. In 1965, the firm had 130 employees. At that time, the personnel department had a full-time director (who was a high school graduate) and a part-time clerk. The department was responsible for maintaining files, placing recruitment ads in the newspaper at management's request, processing employment applications and payroll, answering phones, and handling other routine administrative tasks. Managers and supervisors were responsible for most personnel matters, including whom to hire, whom to promote, whom to fire, and whom to train.

Today Sands employs 700 people. Personnel, now called the human resources department, has a full-time director with a master's degree in industrial relations, three specialists (with appropriate college degrees and certifications: one in compensation, one in staffing, and one in training and development), and four personnel assistants. Sands' top management believes that a strong HR department with a highly qualified staff can do a better job of handling most personnel matters than line supervisors can. It is also convinced that a good HR department can keep line managers from inadvertently creating costly legal problems. One of Sands' competitors recently lost a $5 million sex discrimination suit, which has only strengthened Sands' resolve to maintain a strong HR department.

Some of the key responsibilities the company assigns to its HR department are:

- **Hiring** The HR department approves all ads, screens all applicants, tests and interviews candidates, and so forth. Line supervisors are given a limited list of candidates (usually no more than three) per position from which to choose.
- **Workforce diversity** The HR department ensures that the composition of Sands' workforce meets the government's diversity guidelines for federal contractors.
- **Compensation** The HR department sets the pay range for each job based on its own compensation studies and survey data of salaries at similar companies. The department must approve all pay decisions.
- **Employee appraisal** The HR department requires all supervisors to complete annual appraisal forms on their subordinates. The department scrutinizes these appraisals of employees' performance closely; it is not uncommon for

supervisors to be called on the carpet to justify performance ratings that are unusually high or low.

■ **Training** The HR department conducts several training programs for employees, including programs in improving human relations, quality management, and the use of computer packages.

■ **Attitude surveys** The HR department conducts an in-depth attitude survey of all employees each year, asking them how they feel about various facets of their job, such as satisfaction with supervisor and working conditions.

Over the past few weeks several supervisors have complained to top executives that the HR department has taken away many of their management rights. Some of their gripes are:

■ The HR department ranks applicants based on test scores or other formal criteria (for example, years of experience). Often the people they pick do not fit well in the department and/or do not get along with the supervisor and co-workers.

■ Excellent performers are leaving because the HR department will not approve pay raises exceeding a fixed limit for the job title held, even when a person is able to perform duties beyond those specified in the job description.

■ It takes so long to process the paperwork to hire new employees that the unit loses good candidates to competitors.

■ Much of the training required of employees is not focused on the job itself. These "canned" programs waste valuable employee time and provide few benefits to the company.

■ Supervisors are afraid to be truthful in their performance ratings for fear of being investigated by the HR department.

■ Attitude survey data are broken down by department. The HR department then scrutinizes departments with low scores. Some supervisors feel that the attitude survey has become a popularity contest that penalizes managers who are willing to make necessary (but unpopular) decisions.

The HR department director rejects all of these accusations, arguing that supervisors "just want to do things their way, not taking into account what is best for the company."

Critical Thinking Questions

1. What seems to be the main source of conflict between supervisors and the HR department at Sands Corporation? Explain.

2. Do you believe that managers should be given more autonomy to make personnel decisions such as hiring, appraising, and compensating subordinates? If so, what are some potential drawbacks to granting them this authority? Explain.

3. How should Sands' top executives deal with the complaints expressed by supervisors? How should the director of the HR department deal with the situation? Explain.

Team Exercise

The CEO of Sands Corporation has called a meeting of four managers, all of whom have lodged some of the complaints noted in the case, and four members of the HR department (the director and three specialists). The instructor or a student acts as the CEO in that meeting. The exercise is carried out as follows: (a) Each side presents its case, with the CEO acting as moderator. (b) The two groups then try to agree on how Sands' HR department and managers can develop a closer working relationship in the future. The two groups and the CEO may conduct this exercise in separate groups or in front of the classroom.

Experiential Exercise

One student will role-play the HR department director and three students will fill the roles of disgruntled supervisors. The role-play will take place in front of entire class for approximately 10 to 15 minutes. At the end, the instructor will moderate class discussion, focusing on key issues that were raised by students during the role-play.

Managing Work Flows and

Conducting Job Analysis

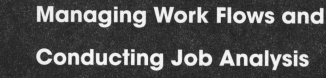
Challenges

After reading this chapter, you should be able to deal more effectively with the following challenges:

1 **Describe** bureaucratic, flat, and boundaryless organizational structures and the business environments in which each is most appropriate.

2 **List** the factors influencing worker motivation that are under managers' control.

3 **Conduct** a job analysis and prepare job descriptions and specifications.

4 **Apply** flexible work designs to situations in which employees have conflicts between work and family, or employers face fluctuating demand for their products.

5 **Develop** policies and procedures to protect human resource information system data so that employees' privacy rights are maintained.

The powerful forces of technology and global competition are forcing managers to rethink all aspects of business. Work is in a state of flux as companies change basic work processes, job requirements and expectations, and organizational structures to focus more on customers' needs.

One important change is the practice of using work teams instead of individual workers as the basic work unit. Today many workers spend much of their time on a team established to satisfy customers' needs. For example:

◾ Southwest Airlines is able to prepare an aircraft from landing to takeoff in 20 minutes by using work teams to unload, service, and load the aircraft. This is one-third the time it takes Southwest's competitors to load and unload their planes and helps explain why Southwest is one of the most profitable airlines.[1]

■ General Motors slashed the development time it takes to produce a full mock-up of a car from 12 weeks to two by using collaborative engineering teams that share design information between auto parts suppliers and engineering units within the company. The time saved frees up workers to think more creatively and come up with three or four more alternative designs per car.[2]

■ General Mills employees observed an Indianapolis-500 pit crew work with incredible speed using a high-performing-team approach. Employees applied these practices to reduce production-line cycle time in a California factory that switched between different products from 4.5 hours to just 12 minutes.[3]

THE MANAGERIAL PERSPECTIVE

This chapter is about managing work, which is a highly dynamic process. Managers design structures to organize work into departments, teams, and jobs so that work is performed efficiently and provides a valuable product or service for a customer. Human resource specialists assist managers by keeping track of and documenting the changes for the content of each job through a process called *job analysis.* In this chapter, we explore why job analysis is important to managers and why it is the bedrock of most human resource programs.

Like work teams, organizations are fundamentally groups of people. The relationships among these people can be structured in different ways. In this chapter, we describe how top managers decide on the most appropriate structure for the organization as a whole and for the flow of work within the organization. Although you may never be asked to redesign your organization, it is likely that your company will eventually undergo structural change, because such change is necessary for survival. It is important that you understand structural issues so that you can see the big picture and take an active role in implementing changes.

Work can be viewed from three different perspectives: the entire organization, work groups, and individual employees. We examine each of these perspectives and their implications for human resource management. We also discuss job analysis (a critical HR activity) and the use of contingent workers and alternative work schedules to create a flexible workforce. An understanding of job analysis gives managers a tool to measure how much and what types of work are necessary to achieve organizational objectives. We conclude the chapter with a discussion of human resource information systems.

Work: The Organizational Perspective

Organizational structure refers to the formal or informal relationships between people in an organization. **Work flow** is the way work is organized to meet the organization's production or service goals. In this section, we discuss the relationship between strategy and organizational structure, the three basic organizational structures, and the uses of work-flow analysis.

Strategy and Organizational Structure

An organization develops a business strategy by establishing a set of long-term goals based on (1) an analysis of environmental opportunities and threats and (2) a realistic appraisal of how the business can deploy its assets to compete most effectively. The business strategy selected by management determines the structure most appropriate to the organization.[4] Whenever management changes its business strategy, it should also reassess its organizational structure.

Organizational structure
The formal or informal relationships between people in an organization.

Work flow
The way work is organized to meet the organization's production or service goals.

Recall from Chapter 1 that a company would select a *defender strategy* when it is competing in a stable market and has a well-established product. For example, a regulated electric utility company might adopt such a strategy. Under a defender strategy, work can be efficiently organized into a structure based on an extensive division of labor, with hierarchies of jobs assigned to functional units such as customer service, power generation, and accounting. Management is centralized and top management has the responsibility for making key decisions. Decisions are implemented from the top down via the chain of command. Workers are told what to do by supervisors, who in turn are handed directions from middle managers, who take orders from the company's top executives.

A company would select a *prospector strategy* when operating in uncertain business environments that require flexibility. Companies that are experiencing rapid growth and launching many new products into a dynamic market are likely to select such a strategy. In companies with a prospector strategy, control is decentralized so that each division has some autonomy to make decisions that affect its customers. Workers who are close to the customer are allowed to respond quickly to customers' needs without having to seek approval from supervisors.

Management selects HR strategies to fit and support its business strategies and organizational structure. Here are some examples of strategic HR choices regarding structure and work flows that companies have made to achieve cost efficiency and product quality.

■ General Electric (GE) signed a 10-year maintenance deal with British Airways to do engine maintenance and overhaul work. The maintenance agreement will help British Airways save costs by outsourcing this work to GE, which builds, designs, and maintains commercial aircraft engines as a core business.[5]
■ Abbey Life Insurance outsourced the claims-adjustment process for its 1.75 million policyholders to Unisys Corp. under a 10-year agreement. Abbey Life saves $80 million over the life of the agreement. Error rates on claims have fallen from 5 to 2 percent, and 95 percent of claims are handled within 6 days, down from 10 days.[6]

Designing the Organization

Designing an organization requires choosing an organizational structure that will help the company achieve its goals most effectively. There are three basic types of organizational structure: bureaucratic, flat, and boundaryless (see Figure 2.1).

Bureaucratic Organization

Bureaucratic organizational structure
A pyramid-shaped organizational structure that consists of hierarchies with many levels of management.

Companies that adopt a defender business strategy are likely to choose the **bureaucratic organizational structure**. This pyramid-shaped structure consists of hierarchies with many levels of management. It uses a top-down or "command-and-control" approach to management in which managers provide considerable direction to and have considerable control over their subordinates. The classic example of a bureaucratic organization is the military, which has a long pecking order of intermediate officers between the generals (who initiate combat orders) and the troops (who do the fighting on the battlefield).

A bureaucratic organization is based on a *functional division of labor*. Employees are divided into divisions based on their function. Thus, production employees are grouped in one division, marketing employees in another, engineering employees in a third, and so on. Rigid boundaries separate the functional units from one another. At a bureaucratic auto parts company, for instance, automotive engineers would develop plans for a new part and then deliver its specifications to the production workers.

Rigid boundaries also separate workers from one another and from their managers because the bureaucratic structure relies on *work specialization*. Narrowly specified job descriptions clearly mark the boundaries of each employee's work. Employees are encouraged to do only the work specified in their job description—no more and no less. They spend most of their time working individually at specialized tasks and usually advance only within one function. For example, employees who begin their career in sales can advance to higher and higher positions in sales or marketing but cannot switch into production or finance.

A Question of Ethics

Implicit in this chapter is the view that organizational change is necessary for survival. However, organizational change often places individual employees under considerable stress, particularly the stress resulting from having to learn new skills and job requirements constantly. Is the organization ethically responsible for protecting employees from these stressful changes?

Figure 2.1

Organizational Structures

Organizational Structure	Characteristics

Bureaucratic

- Top-down management approach
- Many levels of management
- Hierarchical career paths within one function
- Highly specialized jobs
- Narrowly specified job descriptions
- Rigid boundaries between jobs and units
- Employees or individuals working independently

United States Army

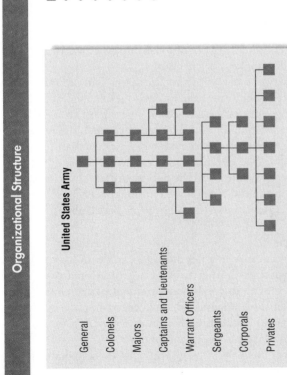

General

Colonels

Majors

Captains and Lieutenants

Warrant Officers

Sergeants

Corporals

Privates

Flat

- Decentralized management approach
- Few levels of management
- Horizontal career paths that cross functions
- Broadly defined jobs
- General job descriptions
- Flexible boundaries between jobs and units
- Emphasis on teams
- Strong focus on the customer

A Typical Law Firm

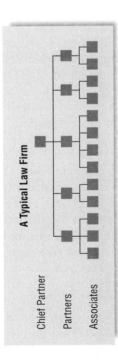

Chief Partner

Partners

Associates

Boundaryless

- Joint ventures with customers, suppliers, and competitors
- Emphasis on teams whose members may cross organizational boundaries
- Shares many characteristics of flat organizational structure

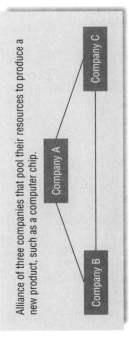

Company A

Company B

Company C

Alliance of three companies that pool their resources to produce a new product, such as a computer chip.

The bureaucratic structure works best in a predictable and stable environment. It is highly centralized and depends on frontline workers performing repetitive tasks according to managers' orders. In a dynamic environment, this structure is less efficient and sometimes disastrous.

Flat Organization

Flat organizational structure
An organizational structure that has only a few levels of management and emphasizes decentralization.

A company that selects the prospector business strategy is likely to choose the **flat organizational structure**. A flat organization has only a few levels of managers and emphasizes a decentralized approach to management. Flat organizations encourage high employee involvement in business decisions. Nucor (a Charlotte, North Carolina, steel company) has a flat organizational structure. Though Nucor has over 5,000 employees, only three levels separate the frontline steel workers from the president of the company. Headquarters staff consists of a mere 30 people in a modest cluster of offices.[7]

Flat organizations are likely to be divided into units or teams that represent different products, services, or customers. The purpose of this structure is to create independent small businesses that can respond rapidly to customers' needs or changes in the business environment. For example, Johnson & Johnson, a manufacturer of health-care products, is organized into more than 200 operating companies that are located in 57 countries. Each operating company behaves like a minibusiness that is responsible for generating profits for the overall company, and employees within each unit feel as if they are working for a small company. The flat organization structure has fostered an entrepreneurial culture that has enabled Johnson & Johnson to innovate; it was the number one pharmaceutical company in *Fortune*'s 2005 Most Admired Companies list.[8]

The flat organizational structure reduces some of the boundaries that isolate employees from one another in bureaucratic organizations. Boundaries between workers at the same level are reduced because employees are likely to be working in teams. In contrast to workers at bureaucratic organizations, employees of a flat organization can cross functional boundaries as they pursue their careers (for instance, starting in sales, moving to finance, and then into production). In addition, job descriptions in flat organizations are more general and encourage employees to develop a broad range of skills (including management skills). Boundaries that separate employees from managers and supervisors also break down in flat organizations, because employees are empowered to make more decisions.

Flat organizational structures can be useful for organizations that are implementing a total quality management (TQM) strategy that emphasizes customer satisfaction. Implementing a TQM strategy may require changing work processes so that customers can receive higher-quality products and better service. For example, an auto insurance company may change its claims adjustment process to speed up reimbursement to customers. Rather than using 25 employees who take 14 days to process a claim, the company may create a claims adjustment team that works closely with the customer to take care of all the paperwork within 3 days.

The flat structure works best in rapidly changing environments because it enables management to create an entrepreneurial culture that fosters employee participation.

Boundaryless Organization

Boundaryless organizational structure
An organizational structure that enables an organization to form relationships with customers, suppliers, and/or competitors, either to pool organizational resources for mutual benefit or to encourage cooperation in an uncertain environment.

A **boundaryless organizational structure** enables an organization to form relationships with customers, suppliers, and/or competitors, either to pool organizational resources for mutual benefit or to encourage cooperation in an uncertain environment. Such relationships often take the form of joint ventures, which let the companies share talented employees, intellectual property (such as a manufacturing process), marketing distribution channels (such as a direct sales force), or financial resources. Boundaryless organizational structures are most often used by companies that select the prospector business strategy and operate in a volatile environment.

Boundaryless organizations share many of the characteristics of flat organizations. They break down boundaries between the organization and its suppliers, customers, or competitors. They also strongly emphasize teams, which are likely to include employees representing different companies in the joint venture. For example, a quality expert from an automobile manufacturing company may work closely with employees at one of the company's auto parts suppliers to train them in specific quality management processes.

Companies often use a boundaryless organizational structure when they (1) collaborate with customers or suppliers to provide better-quality products or services; (2) are entering foreign

La Opinion, *a newspaper based in Los Angeles, California, has a flat organizational structure that supports workers who must keep up with the fast pace of the news business. Here graphic designers work together to devise an eye-catching page design.*

markets that have entry barriers to foreign competitors, or (3) need to manage the risk of developing an expensive new technology. The boundaryless organization is appropriate in these situations because it is open to change, it facilitates the formation of joint ventures with foreign companies, and it reduces the financial risk to any one organization. Here are some examples of boundaryless organizational structures:

- Paramount and Twentieth Century Fox film studios collaborated to produce, market, and distribute the expensive and ultimately successful epic movie *Titanic,* which broke box office records around the world in the late 1990s. The collaboration was necessary: The production costs of the movie (over $200 million) were too steep for one film company to risk without putting the studio in financial jeopardy.
- Airbus Industries is a boundaryless organizational design that consists of a partnership of European firms from four countries (France, Germany, England, and Spain) that worked together to market and develop commercial jet aircraft to compete with Boeing and become a leading producer of passenger jets.
- Sun Microsystems, a producer of computer workstations and servers, has formed a partnership with America Online, the largest provider of online services for computers. The partners' goal is to create a combination of services and products that lets companies obtain all their software and online services over the Internet, instead of buying software in boxes. The strength of this partnership could pose a major threat to Microsoft's strong market position.[9]

Work-Flow Analysis

We said earlier that work flow is the way work is organized to meet the organization's production or service goals. Managers need to do **work-flow analysis** to examine how work creates or adds value to the ongoing business processes. (*Processes* are value-adding, value-creating activities such as product development, customer service, and order fulfillment.[10]) Work-flow analysis looks at how work moves from the customer (who initiates the need for work) through the organization (where employees add value to the work in a series of value-creating steps) to the point at which the work leaves the organization as a product or service for the customer.

Each job in the organization should receive work as an input, add value to that work by doing something useful to it, and then move the work on to another worker. Work-flow analysis usually reveals that some steps or jobs can be combined, simplified, or even eliminated. In some

Work-flow analysis
The process of examining how work creates or adds value to the ongoing processes in a business.

cases, it has resulted in the reorganization of work so that teams rather than individual workers are the source of value creation.

Work-flow analysis can be used to tighten the alignment between employees' work and customers' needs. It can also help a company make major performance improvements through another program called *business process reengineering*.

Business Process Reengineering

The term *reengineering* was coined by Michael Hammer and James Champy in their pioneering book *Reengineering the Corporation.* Hammer and Champy emphasize that reengineering should not be confused with restructuring or simply laying off employees in an effort to eliminate layers of management.[11] **Business process reengineering (BPR)** is not a quick fix but rather a fundamental rethinking and radical redesign of business processes to achieve dramatic improvements in cost, quality, service, and speed.[12] Reengineering examines the way a company conducts its business by closely analyzing the core processes involved in producing its product or delivering its service to the customer. By taking advantage of computer technology and different ways of organizing human resources, the company may be able to reinvent itself.[13]

BPR uses work-flow analysis to identify jobs that can be eliminated or recombined to improve company performance. Figure 2.2 shows the steps in processing a loan application at IBM Credit Corporation before and after BPR. Before the BPR effort, work-flow analysis showed that loan applications were processed in a series of five steps by five loan specialists, each of whom did something different to the loan application. The entire process took an average of six days to complete, which gave customers the opportunity to look elsewhere for financing.[14] For much of that time, the application was either in transit between the loan specialists or sitting on someone's desk waiting to be processed.

Using BPR, the jobs of the five loan specialists were reorganized into the job of just one generalist called the *deal structurer.* The deal structurer uses a new software program to print out a standardized loan contract, access different credit checking databases, price the loan, and add boilerplate language to the contract. With the new process, loan applications can be completed in four hours instead of six days.[15]

Critics of reengineering claim that over half of reengineering projects fail to meet their objectives while causing pain to companies and employees in the form of layoffs and disruptions

Business process reengineering (BPR)
A fundamental rethinking and radical redesign of business processes to achieve dramatic improvements in cost, quality, service, and speed.

Processing a Loan Application at IBM Credit Corporation Before and After BPR

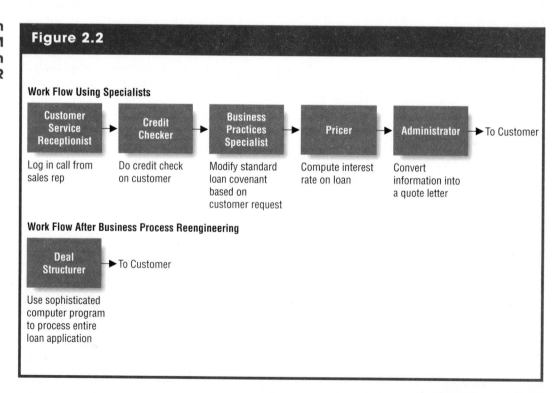

Figure 2.2

Work Flow Using Specialists

| Customer Service Receptionist | Credit Checker | Business Practices Specialist | Pricer | Administrator | → To Customer |

| Log in call from sales rep | Do credit check on customer | Modify standard loan covenant based on customer request | Compute interest rate on loan | Convert information into a quote letter |

Work Flow After Business Process Reengineering

Deal Structurer → To Customer

Use sophisticated computer program to process entire loan application to established work patterns.[16] However, a survey by CSC Index, a leading reengineering consulting firm, reported that reengineering is very popular in both the United States and Europe. The survey of 621 large European and U.S. companies found that 69 percent of U.S. firms and 75 percent of European firms are already engaged in reengineering and over half of the remaining companies are thinking about embarking on a reengineering project.[17]

Work: The Group Perspective

We turn now to an examination of work from the perspective of employee groups. In the flat and boundaryless organizational structures, teamwork is an imperative. Indeed, as we have seen, teams are the basic building blocks of both structures.

What exactly is a team and how does it operate? A **team** is a small number of people with complementary skills who work toward common goals for which they hold themselves mutually accountable.[18] The size of most teams ranges from 6 to 18 employees.[19] Unlike *work groups,* which depend on a supervisor for direction, a team depends on its own members to provide leadership and direction.[20] Teams can also be organized as departments. For example, a company may have a product development team, a manufacturing team, and a sales team.

Several types of teams are used in organizations today. The type that is having the most impact on U.S. companies is the self-managed team.

Team
A small number of people with complementary skills who work toward common goals for which they hold themselves mutually accountable.

Self-Managed Teams

Organizations are implementing self-managed work teams primarily to improve quality and productivity and to reduce operating costs. **Self-managed teams (SMTs)** are responsible for producing an entire product, a component, or an ongoing service. In most cases, SMT members are cross-trained on the different tasks assigned to the team.[21] Some SMTs have members with a set of complex skills—for example, scientists and engineers with training in different disciplines. Members of the SMT have many managerial duties, including work scheduling, selecting work methods, ordering materials, evaluating performance, and disciplining team members.[22]

One company that has switched over to SMTs is the San Diego Zoo. The zoo's employees traditionally had very narrow and well-defined job responsibilities: Keepers did the keeping and gardeners did the gardening. Then the zoo decided to develop bioclimatic zones, in which plants and animals are grouped together in cageless enclosures that resemble their native habitats. Because the zones themselves are interdependent, the employees who manage them must work together. For instance, the humid 3.5-acre Tiger River exhibit is run by a seven-member team of mammal and bird specialists, horticulturists, and maintenance and construction workers.[23]

HRM practices are likely to change in the following ways when SMTs are established:[24]

Self-managed team (SMT)
A team responsible for producing an entire product, a component, or an ongoing service.

- Peers, rather than a supervisor, are likely to evaluate individual employee performance.
- Pay practices are likely to shift from pay based on seniority or individual performance to pay focused on team performance (for example, team bonuses).[25]
- Rather than being based solely on input from managers and HR staff, decisions on new hires may include a decisive amount of input from team members.
- Team leaders are likely to step forward and identify themselves. For example, SEI Investments encourages leaders to emerge on their own initiative in its self-managed teams.[26]

Self-managed teams have made some impressive contributions to the bottom lines of companies that have used them. For instance, after implementing SMTs, Shenandoah Life found it could process 50 percent more applications and customer service requests with 10 percent fewer employees.[27] Xerox plants using SMTs are 30 percent more productive than Xerox plants organized without them.[28] Boeing used SMTs to reduce the number of engineering problems in the development of the new 777 passenger jet by more than half.[29] For a look at how self-managed teams work at Lucent Technologies, a manufacturer of telecommunications products, see Exhibit 2.1.

EXHIBIT 2.1

Lynn Mercer's Teams at Lucent

Lynn Mercer is the cellular-phone factory manager at Lucent Technologies. She is dedicated to the concept of self-managed teams and has worked hard to make them succeed. The teams in her operation decide how the work should be done, what improvements are needed, and who should perform them. She notes that she just sets the mission of the factory, and the rest is up to the teams. Lucent's teams elect their own leaders and are exceptionally flexible so they can adapt to the ever-changing needs of the cellular-phone industry. Mercer wants this flexibility because team members truly understand their customers' needs.

Mercer explains that, although all instructions are still written down in her team-managed factory, every individual can make online changes to a procedure if the individual's team agrees. Not only do teams have the power to change procedures, others can also learn from them and do not have to reinvent the wheel. Team members learn many different tasks and skills and how to perform them well. The results have been remarkable. Mercer's factory has not missed a deadline in over two years, and labor costs remain a very low percentage of total costs.

Sources: Vanguri, R. (2004). Wireless provisioning service solution and deployment—A real-life experience in global project management. *Bell Labs Technical Journal,* 9(4), 35–48; Nahavandi, A. (2000). *The art and science of leadership* (2nd ed.). Upper Saddle River, NJ: Prentice Hall, 163. Adapted from T. Pezinger Jr. (March 7, 1997). How Lynn Mercer manages a factory that manages itself, *Wall Street Journal,* B1.

Because team members often initially lack the skills necessary for the team to function successfully, it may take several years for an SMT to become fully operational.[30] A company can hasten this evolution by using its HR department to train employees in the skills required of team members. Three areas are important:[31]

1. **Technical skills** Team members must be cross-trained in new technical skills so that they can rotate among jobs as necessary. Team members who are cross-trained give the team greater flexibility and allow it to operate efficiently with fewer workers.
2. **Administrative skills** Teams do much of the work done by supervisors in organizations that don't have teams. Therefore, team members need training in such management/administrative skills as budgeting, scheduling, monitoring and evaluating peers, and interviewing job applicants.
3. **Interpersonal skills** Team members need good communication skills to form an effective team. They must be able to express themselves effectively in order to share information, deal with conflict, and give feedback to one another.[32]

Other Types of Teams

Problem-solving team
A team consisting of volunteers from a unit or department who meet one or two hours per week to discuss quality improvement, cost reduction, or improvement in the work environment.

Special-purpose team
A team or task force consisting of workers who span functional or organizational boundaries and whose purpose is to examine complex issues.

In addition to the SMT, businesses use other types of teams: the problem-solving team, the special-purpose team, and the virtual team.[33] The **problem-solving team** consists of volunteers from a unit or department who meet one or two hours per week to discuss quality improvement, cost reduction, or improvement in the work environment. The formation of problem-solving teams does not affect an organization's structure because these teams exist for only a limited period; they are usually disbanded after they have achieved their objectives. Google, the Internet search company, uses innovation teams, a type of problem-solving team, to encourage technical staff to work on personal research projects that interest them. The company hopes that some of the innovations the teams develop will turn into breakaway technological innovations.[34]

The **special-purpose team** or *task force* consists of members who span functional or organizational boundaries and whose purpose is to examine complex issues—for example, introducing a new technology, improving the quality of a work process that spans several functional units, or encouraging cooperation between labor and management in a unionized setting. An example of a special-purpose team is the quality of work life (QWL) program, which consists of team members (including union representatives and managers) who collaborate on making improvements in all aspects of work life, including product quality. The QWL program at Ford and General Motors has focused on improving product quality, whereas the QWL program between the United Steel Workers of America and the major steel companies has concentrated on developing new ways to improve employee morale and working conditions.[35]

For more on problem-solving teams, refer to the Manager's Notebook titled "Tips on Managing Problem-Solving Teams."

Customer-Driven HR

Tips on Managing Problem-Solving Teams

Managers should be able to use problem-solving teams consisting of employees with cross-functional skills to solve challenging organizational issues. In designing and managing such teams, the following are some important points to consider:

- If the team is expected to implement new ideas, include members from different levels of the organization. Creating a team with members from different levels (frontline employees and supervisors, for example) can also foster cooperation and reduce barriers between employees and managers.
- Monitor the team to ensure that the free exchange of ideas and creativity is not stifled if managers and employees are on the same team.
- Select members for their expertise and diverse perspectives but also for their ability to compromise and solve problems collaboratively.
- Allow the team enough time to complete its task. The more complex the problem, and the more creative the solution needs to be, the more large blocks of time the members will need.
- Coordinate with other managers to free up time for the members.
- Provide clear goals and guidelines on what you expect the team to do. Tell them what they can and cannot address.
- Schedule periodic team meetings to reinforce the process of solving problems collectively. Such meetings can be used to evaluate the effectiveness of the team.

Source: Kepcher, C. (2005, February). Collegial teams. *Leadership Excellence*, 7–8; Nahavandi, A., and Malekzadeh, A. R. (1999). *Organizational behavior*. Upper Saddle River, NJ: Prentice Hall, 276.

The **virtual team** uses interactive computer technologies such as the Internet, groupware (software that permits people at different computer workstations to collaborate on a project simultaneously), and computer-based videoconferencing to work together despite being separated by physical distance.[36] Virtual teams are similar to problem-solving teams because they do not require full-time commitment from team members. The difference is that virtual team members interact with each other electronically, rather than face-to-face.[37]

Because of their part-time nature and flexibility in accommodating distance, virtual teams allow organizations to tap individuals who might not be otherwise available. For example, a management consulting firm working on a project out of its San Francisco office for a local bank include financial specialists from its New York and Chicago offices on the project team. This type of team also makes it possible for companies to cross organizational boundaries by linking customers, suppliers, and business partners in a collaborative effort that can increase the quality and speed with which the new product or service is brought to market. In writing this textbook, the authors (university professors) formed a virtual team with the publishing company's editors and also with the design specialists who created the graphics and visual images for the text.

One of the best practices that has emerged from research on virtual teams is the use of a virtual work space, which is essentially a Web site that only team members have access to, where

Virtual team
A team that relies on interactive technology to work together when separated by physical distance.

the team is reminded of its decisions, rationales, and commitments.[38] The virtual team work space has a homepage with links to other "walls," each of which is devoted to a specific aspect of the team project. One wall, for example, contains information about all the people on the virtual team, including contact information and profiles of their expertise and accomplishments. Another wall displays information about teleconference meetings, such as when they are being held, who is supposed to attend, the agendas, and the meeting minutes, that can be shared with team members. Shell Chemicals, for example, has had success with the use of a virtual work space on a company-wide project to develop a new cash-based approach to financial management.[39]

Work: The Individual Perspective

The third and final perspective from which we will examine work flows and structure is that of the individual employee and job. We look first at the various theories of what motivates employees to achieve higher levels of performance and then at different ways jobs can be designed to maximize employee productivity. In the next section, we look at job analysis, the gathering and organization of information concerning the tasks and duties of specific jobs. The section concludes with a discussion of job descriptions, which are one of the primary results of job analysis.

Motivating Employees

Motivation
That which energizes, directs, and sustains human behavior. In HRM, a person's desire to do the best possible job or to exert the maximum effort to perform assigned tasks.

Motivation can be defined as that which energizes, directs, and sustains human behavior.[40] In HRM, the term refers to a person's desire to do the best possible job or to exert the maximum effort to perform assigned tasks. An important feature of motivation is that it is behavior directed toward a goal.

Motivation theory seeks to explain why employees are more motivated by and satisfied with one type of work than another. It is essential that managers have a basic understanding of work motivation because highly motivated employees are more likely to produce a superior-quality product or service than employees who lack motivation.

Two-Factor Theory

The *two-factor theory of motivation,* developed by Frederick Herzberg, attempts to identify and explain the factors that employees find satisfying and dissatisfying about their jobs.[41] The first set of factors, called *motivators,* are internal job factors that lead to job satisfaction and higher motivation. In the absence of motivators, employees will probably not be satisfied with their work or motivated to perform up to their potential. Some examples of motivators are the work itself, achievement, recognition, responsibility, and opportunities for advancement.

Notice that salary is not included in the motivator list. Herzberg contends that pay belongs among the second set of factors, which he calls *hygiene* or *maintenance factors.* Hygiene factors are external to the job; they are located in the work environment. The absence of a hygiene factor can lead to active dissatisfaction and demotivation and, in extreme situations, to avoidance of the work altogether. Hygiene factors include the following:

- Company policies
- Working conditions
- Job security
- Salary
- Employee benefits
- Relationships with supervisors and managers
- Relationships with coworkers
- Relationships with subordinates

According to Herzberg, if management provides the appropriate hygiene factors, employees will not be dissatisfied with their jobs, but neither will they be motivated to perform at their full potential. To motivate workers, management must provide some motivators.

Two-factor theory has two implications for job design: (1) Jobs should be designed to provide as many motivators as possible, and (2) making (external) changes in hygiene factors such as pay or working conditions is not likely to sustain improvements in employee motivation over the long run unless (internal) changes are also made in the work itself.

Work Adjustment Theory

Every worker has unique needs and abilities. *Work adjustment theory* suggests that employees' motivation levels and job satisfaction depend on the fit between their needs and abilities and the characteristics of the job and the organization.[42] A poor fit between individual characteristics and the work environment may lead to reduced levels of motivation. Work adjustment theory proposes that:

- A job design that one employee finds challenging and motivating may not motivate another employee. For example, a mentally disabled employee may find a repetitive job at a fast-food restaurant highly motivating and challenging, but a college graduate may find the same job boring.
- Not all employees want to be involved in decision making. Employees with low needs for involvement may fit poorly on a self-managed team because they may resist managing other team members and taking responsibility for team decisions.

Goal-Setting Theory

Goal-setting theory, developed by Edwin Locke, suggests that employees' goals help to explain motivation and job performance.[43] The reasoning is as follows: Because motivation is goal-directed behavior, goals that are clear and challenging will result in higher levels of employee motivation than goals that are ambiguous and easy.

Because it suggests that managers can increase employee motivation by managing the goal-setting process, goal-setting theory has some important implications for managers:[44]

- Employees will be more motivated to perform when they have clear and specific goals. A store manager whose specific goal is to "increase store profitability by 20 percent in the next six months" will exert more effort than one who is told to "do the best you can" to increase profits.
- Employees will be more motivated to accomplish difficult goals than easy goals. Of course, the goals must be attainable; otherwise the employee is likely to become frustrated. For example, an inexperienced computer programmer may promise to deliver a program in an unrealistic amount of time. The programmer's manager may work with her to establish a more realistic, yet still challenging, deadline for delivering the program.
- In many (but not all) cases, goals that employees participate in creating for themselves are more motivating than goals that are simply assigned by managers. Managers may establish mutually agreed-upon goals with employees through a management by objectives (MBO) approach (discussed in Chapter 7) or by creating self-managed teams that take responsibility for establishing their own goals.
- Employees who receive frequent feedback on their progress toward reaching their goals sustain higher levels of motivation and performance than employees who receive sporadic or no feedback. For example, a restaurant manager can motivate servers to provide better service by soliciting customer feedback on service quality and then communicating this information to employees.

Job Characteristics Theory

Developed by Richard Hackman and Greg Oldham, *job characteristics theory* states that employees will be more motivated to work and more satisfied with their jobs to the extent that jobs contain certain core characteristics.[45] These core job characteristics create the conditions that allow employees to experience critical psychological states that are related to beneficial work outcomes, including high work motivation. The strength of the linkage among job characteristics, psychological states, and work outcomes is determined by the intensity of the individual employee's need for growth (that is, how important the employee considers growth and development on the job).

There are five core job characteristics that activate three critical psychological states. The core job characteristics are:[46]

1. **Skill variety** The degree to which the job requires the person to do different things and involves the use of a number of different skills, abilities, and talents.
2. **Task identity** The degree to which a person can do the job from beginning to end with a visible outcome.
3. **Task significance** The degree to which the job has a significant impact on others—both inside and outside the organization.
4. **Autonomy** The amount of freedom, independence, and discretion the employee has in areas such as scheduling the work, making decisions, and determining how to do the job.
5. **Feedback** The degree to which the job provides the employee with clear and direct information about job outcomes and performance.

The three critical psychological states affected by the core job characteristics are:[47]

1. **Experienced meaningfulness** The extent to which the employee experiences the work as important, valuable, and worthwhile.
2. **Experienced responsibility** The degree to which the employee feels personally responsible or accountable for the results of the work.
3. **Knowledge of results** The degree to which the employee understands on a regular basis how effectively he or she is performing the job.

Skill variety, task identity, and task significance are all linked to experienced meaningfulness of work, as Figure 2.3 shows. Autonomy is related to experienced responsibility and feedback to knowledge of results.

A job with characteristics that enable an employee to experience all three critical psychological states provides internal rewards that sustain motivation.[48] These rewards come from having a job where the person can learn (knowledge of results) that he or she has performed well on a task (experienced responsibility) that he or she cares about (experienced meaningfulness).[49] In addition, this situation results in certain outcomes that are beneficial to the employer:

The Job Characteristics Theory of Work Motivation

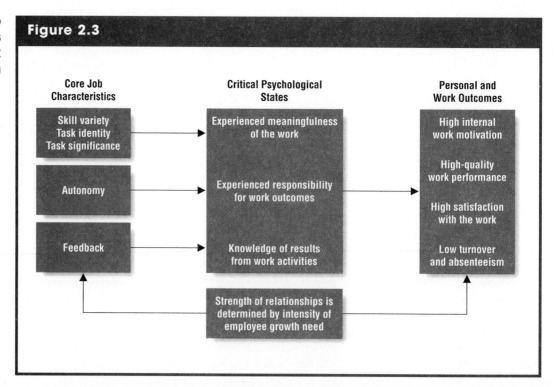

Figure 2.3

Core Job Characteristics	Critical Psychological States	Personal and Work Outcomes
Skill variety / Task identity / Task significance	Experienced meaningfulness of the work	High internal work motivation
Autonomy	Experienced responsibility for work outcomes	High-quality work performance
Feedback	Knowledge of results from work activities	High satisfaction with the work / Low turnover and absenteeism

Strength of relationships is determined by intensity of employee growth need high-quality performance, higher employee satisfaction, and lower turnover and absenteeism. Job characteristics theory maintains that jobs can be designed to contain the characteristics that employees find rewarding and motivating.

Designing Jobs and Conducting Job Analysis

All the theories of employee motivation suggest that jobs can be designed to increase motivation and performance. **Job design** is the process of organizing work into the tasks required to perform a specific job.

Job Design

There are three important influences on job design. One is work-flow analysis, which (you will recall) seeks to ensure that each job in the organization receives work as an input, adds value to that work, and then passes it on to another worker. The other two influences are business strategy and the organizational structure that best fits that strategy. For example, an emphasis on highly specialized jobs could be expected in a bureaucratic organizational structure because work in bureaucratic organizations is built around the division of labor.

We will examine five approaches to job design: work simplification, job enlargement, job rotation, job enrichment, and team-based job design.

Work Simplification

Work simplification assumes that work can be broken down into simple, repetitive tasks that maximize efficiency. This approach to job design assigns most of the thinking aspects of work (such as planning and organizing) to managers and supervisors, while giving the employee a narrowly defined task to perform. Work simplification can utilize labor effectively to produce a large amount of a standardized product. The automobile assembly line, where workers engage in highly mechanical and repetitive tasks, exemplifies the work simplification approach.

Although work simplification can be efficient in a stable environment, it is less effective in a changing environment where customers demand custom-built products of high quality. Moreover, work simplification often leads to high levels of employee turnover and low levels of employee satisfaction. (In fact, where work simplification is used, employees may feel the need to form unions to gain some control over their work.) Finally, higher-level professionals subjected to work simplification may become so specialized in what they do that they cannot see how their job affects the organization's overall product or service. The result can be employees doing work that has no value to the customer. Many professional employees in highly specialized jobs became casualties of corporate restructurings over the last decade because organizations discovered such work did not provide value to consumers.

Work simplification is not to be confused with *work elimination*. Companies trying to eliminate work challenge every task and every step within a task to see if there is a better way to get the work done. Even if parts of the work cannot be eliminated, some aspect of the job may be simplified or combined with another job. Oryx—a Dallas, Texas–based oil and gas producer— saved $70 million in operating costs in one year after it set up teams to take a fresh look at its operations. The teams discovered many procedures, reviews, reports, and approvals that had little to do with Oryx's business and could easily be eliminated. Work elimination is similar to BPR, though it differs in that work elimination typically focuses on particular jobs and processes rather than on overhauling the entire company.[50]

Job Enlargement and Job Rotation

Job enlargement and job rotation are used to redesign jobs to reduce fatigue and boredom among workers performing simplified and highly specialized work. **Job enlargement** expands a job's duties. For example, auto workers whose specialized job is to install carpets on the car floor may have their job enlarged to include the extra duties of installing the car's seats and instrument panel.[51]

Job rotation rotates workers among different narrowly defined tasks without disrupting the flow of work. On an auto assembly line, for example, a worker whose job is installing carpets

Job design
The process of organizing work into the tasks required to perform a specific job.

Job enlargement
The process of expanding a job's duties.

Job rotation
The process of rotating workers among different narrowly defined tasks without disrupting the flow of work.

would be rotated periodically to a second workstation where she would install only seats in the car. At a later time period she might be rotated to a third workstation, where her job would be to install only the car's instrument panels. During the course of a day on the assembly line, the worker might be shifted at two-hour intervals among all three workstations.

Both job enlargement and job rotation have limitations because these approaches focus mainly on eliminating the demotivating aspects of work and, thus, improve only one of the five core job characteristics that motivate workers (skill variety).

Job Enrichment

Job enrichment
The process of putting specialized tasks back together so that one person is responsible for producing a whole product or an entire service.

Job enrichment is an approach to job design that directly applies job characteristics theory (see Figure 2.3) to make jobs more interesting and to improve employee motivation. **Job enrichment** puts specialized tasks back together so that one person is responsible for producing a whole product or an entire service.[52]

Job enrichment expands both the horizontal and the vertical dimensions of a job. Instead of people working on an assembly line at one or more stations, the entire assembly line process is abandoned to enable each worker to assemble an entire product, such as a kitchen appliance or radio.[53] For example, at Motorola's Communications Division, individual employees are now responsible for assembling, testing, and packaging the company's pocket radio-paging devices. Previously, these products were made on an assembly line that broke the work down into 100 different steps and used as many workers.[54]

Job enrichment gives employees more opportunities for autonomy and feedback. It also gives them more responsibilities that require decision making, such as scheduling work, determining work methods, and judging quality.[55] However, the successful implementation of job enrichment is limited by the production technology available and the capabilities of the employees who produce the product or service. Some products are highly complex and require too many steps for one individual to produce them efficiently. Other products require the application of so many different skills that it is not feasible to train employees in all of them. For example, it could take an employee a lifetime to master all the skills necessary to assemble a Boeing 777 aircraft.

Team-Based Job Designs

Team-based job designs focus on giving a team, rather than an individual, a whole and meaningful piece of work to do.[56] Team members are empowered to decide among themselves how to accomplish the work.[57] They are cross-trained in different skills, then rotated to do different tasks within the team. Team-based job designs match best with flat and boundaryless organizational structures.

One company that emphasizes team-based job design is GM's Saturn division, located in Spring Hill, Tennessee. The process of assembling the Saturn car is accomplished by self-managed teams of 8 to 15 workers. Each team takes responsibility for managing itself. It interviews and hires new team members, manages its own budget, and receives reports on the amount of waste it generates so that it can develop plans to utilize its materials more effectively.[58]

Job Analysis

Job analysis
The systematic process of collecting information used to make decisions about jobs. Job analysis identifies the tasks, duties, and responsibilities of a particular job.

After a work-flow analysis has been done and jobs have been designed, the employer needs to define and communicate job expectations for individual employees. This is best done through **job analysis**, which is the systematic gathering and organization of information concerning jobs. Job analysis puts a job under the microscope to reveal important details about it. Specifically, it identifies the tasks, duties, and responsibilities of a particular job.

- A *task* is a basic element of work that is a logical and necessary step in performing a job duty.
- A *duty* consists of one or more tasks that constitute a significant activity performed in a job.
- A *responsibility* is one or several duties that identify and describe the major purpose or reason for the job's existence.

Thus, for the job of administrative assistant, a task might be completing a travel authorization form, which is part of the duty to keep track of the department's travel expenses, which is part of the responsibility to manage the departmental budget.

Job analysis provides information to answer the following questions: Where does the work come from? What machines and special equipment must be used? What knowledge, skills, and abilities (KSAs) does the job holder need to perform the job? How much supervision is necessary? Under what working conditions should this job be performed? What are the performance expectations for this job? On whom must the job holders depend to perform this job? With whom must they interact? Job analysis can answer these questions, thereby giving managers valuable information that can help them develop more effective HRM policies and programs, as described in the remaining chapters of this text.

Who Performs Job Analysis?

Depending on the technique selected, job analysis is performed either by a member of the HR department or by the *job incumbent* (the person who is currently assigned to the job in question). In some businesses a manager may perform the job analysis.

Methods of Gathering Job Information

Companies use several methods to gather job information: interviews, observation, diaries, and questionnaires. Factors such as cost and job complexity will influence the choice of method.

- **Interviews** The interviewer (usually a member of the HR department) interviews a representative sample of job incumbents using a structured interview. The structured interview includes a series of job-related questions that is presented to each interviewee in the same order.
- **Observation** An individual observes the job incumbent actually performing the job and records the core job characteristics from observation. This method is used in cases where the job is fairly routine and the observer can identify the job essentials in a reasonable amount of time. The job analyst may videotape the job incumbent in order to study the job in greater detail.
- **Diaries** Several job incumbents may be asked to keep diaries or logs of their daily job activities and record the amount of time spent on each activity. By analyzing these diaries over a representative period of time (perhaps several weeks), a job analyst is able to capture the job's essential characteristics.
- **Questionnaires** The job incumbent fills out a questionnaire that asks a series of questions about the job's knowledge, skill, and ability requirements, duties, and responsibilities. Each question is associated with a quantitative scale that measures the importance of the job factor or the frequency with which it occurs. A computer can then tally the scores on the questionnaires and create a printout summarizing the job's characteristics. The computerized method of gathering job information with questionnaires is the most expensive method.

The Uses of Job Analysis

Job analysis measures job content and the relative importance of different job duties and responsibilities. Having this information helps companies comply with government regulations and defend their actions from legal challenges that allege unfairness or discrimination. As we will see in Chapter 3, the generic defense against a charge of discrimination is that the contested decision (to hire, to give a raise, to terminate) was made for job-related reasons. Job analysis provides the documentation for such a defense. For instance:

- A company may be able to defend its policy of requiring sales representatives to have a valid driver's license if it can show via job analysis that driving is an essential activity in the sales rep's job. Otherwise, under the Americans with Disabilities Act (see Chapter 3), the employer may be asked to make a reasonable accommodation for a blind job applicant who asserts his rights to be considered for the job.
- The owner of a fast-food restaurant who pays an assistant manager a weekly salary (without any overtime pay) may be able to defend herself from charges of an overtime pay violation with a job analysis proving that the assistant manager job is exempt from the overtime provisions of the Fair Labor Standards Act (see Chapter 10). The owner can prove this by showing that most of the job duties and responsibilities entail supervising and directing others rather than preparing food and providing service to customers.

In addition to establishing job relatedness for legal purposes, job analysis is also useful for the following HR activities:

- **Recruitment** Job analysis can help the HR department generate a higher-quality pool of job applicants by making it easy to describe a job in newspaper ads that can be targeted to qualified job applicants. Job analysis also helps college recruiters screen job applicants because it tells them what tasks, duties, and responsibilities the job entails.
- **Selection** Job analysis can be used to determine whether an applicant for a specific job should be required to take a personality test or some other kind of test. For example, a personality test that measures extroversion (the degree to which someone is talkative, sociable, active, aggressive, or excitable) may be justified for selecting a life insurance sales representative. (Such a job is likely to emphasize customer contact, which includes making "cold calls" on potential new accounts.) Job analysis may also reveal that the personality test measuring extroversion has a weak relationship to the job content of other jobs (for example, lab technician) and should not be used as part of the selection process for those jobs.
- **Performance appraisal** The performance standards used to judge employee performance for purposes of promotion, rewards, discipline, or layoff should be job related. Under federal law, a company is required to defend its appraisal system against lawsuits and prove the job relatedness of the performance criteria used in the appraisal.
- **Compensation** Job analysis information can be used to compare the relative worth of each job's contributions to the company's overall performance. The value of each job's contribution is an important determinant of the job's pay level. In a typical pay structure, jobs that require mastery of more complex skills or that have greater levels of responsibility pay more than jobs that require only basic skills or have low amounts of responsibility.
- **Training and career development** Job analysis is an important input for determining training needs. By comparing the knowledge, skills, and abilities that employees bring to the job with those that are identified by job analysis, managers can identify their employees' skill gaps. Training programs can then be put in place to improve job performance.

The Techniques of Job Analysis

Figure 2.4 lists eight major techniques of job analysis. Detailed descriptions of these techniques are beyond the scope of this book. However, we briefly describe four of them—task inventory analysis, the critical incident technique, the position analysis questionnaire, and functional job analysis—to give you a sense of what job analysis entails. For a set of general guidelines on conducting a job analysis effectively, see the Manager's Notebook titled "Guidelines for Conducting a Job Analysis."

Knowledge, skills, and abilities (KSAs)
The knowledge, skills, and abilities needed to perform a job successfully.

Task Inventory Analysis. *Task inventory analysis* is actually a collection of methods that are offshoots of the U.S. Air Force task inventory method.[59] The technique is used to determine the **knowledge, skills, and abilities (KSAs)** needed to perform a job successfully. The analysis has three steps: (1) interview, (2) survey, and (3) generation of a task by KSA matrix.

The interview step focuses on developing lists of tasks that are part of the job. Interviews are conducted both with workers who currently hold the job and with their managers. The goal of the interviews is to generate specific descriptions of individual tasks that can be used in the task inventory survey.

The survey step involves generating and administering a survey consisting of task statements and rating scales. The survey might ask respondents—the current job holders—to rate each task on importance, frequency, and training time needed. Whether the survey is sent to a sample of the workers or to all of them will depend on the number of workers and the economic constraints on the job analysis.

The final step is the creation of a task by KSA matrix, which is used to rate the extent to which a variety of KSAs are important for the successful completion of each task. An abbreviated example of a KSA rating matrix is presented in Figure 2.5 on page 62. Ratings in the matrix are usually determined by subject matter experts, who might include supervisors, managers, consultants, and job incumbents.

Task inventory analysis has two major advantages. First, it is a systematic means for analyzing the tasks in a particular situation. Second, it uses a tailor-made questionnaire rather than

Figure 2.4

Technique	Employee Group Focused On	Data-Collection Method	Analysis Results	Description
1. Task Inventory Analysis	Any—large number of workers needed	Questionnaire	Rating of tasks	Tasks are rated by job incumbent,* supervisor, or job analyst. Ratings may be on characteristics such as importance of task and time spent doing it.
2. Critical Incident Technique	Any	Interview	Behavioral description	Behavioral incidents representing poor through excellent performance are generated for each dimension of the job.
3. Position Analysis Questionnaire (PAQ)	Any	Questionnaire	Rating of 194 job elements	Elements are rated on six scales (for example, extent of use, importance to job). Ratings are analyzed by computer.
4. Functional Job Analysis (FJA)	Any	Group interview/ questionnaire	Rating of how job incumbent relates to people, data, and things	Originally designed to improve counseling and placement of people registered at local state employment offices. Task statements are generated and then presented to job incumbents to rate on such dimensions as frequency and importance.
5. Methods Analysis (Motion Study)	Manufacturing	Observation	Time per unit of work	Systematic means for determining the standard time for various work tasks. Based on observation and timing of work tasks.
6. Guidelines-Oriented Job Analysis	Any	Interview	Skills and knowledge required	Job incumbents identify duties as well as knowledge, skills, physical abilities, and other characteristics needed to perform the job.
7. Management Position Description Questionnaire (MPDQ)	Managerial	Questionnaire	Checklist of 197 items	Managers check items descriptive of their responsibilities.
8. Hay Plan	Managerial	Interview	Impact of job on organization	Managers are interviewed regarding such issues as their responsibilities and accountabilities. Responses are analyzed according to four dimensions: objectives, dimensions, nature and scope, accountability.

*The term *job incumbent* refers to the person currently filling a particular job.

The Techniques of Job Analysis

an already prepared stock questionnaire. Managers can use the technique to develop job descriptions and performance appraisal forms, as well as to develop or identify appropriate selection tests.

Critical Incident Technique.   The *critical incident technique (CIT)* is used to develop behavioral descriptions of a job.[60] In CIT, supervisors and workers generate behavioral incidents of job performance. The technique uses the following four steps: (1) generate dimensions, (2) generate incidents, (3) retranslate, and (4) assign effectiveness values. In the generating dimensions step, supervisors and workers identify the major dimensions of a job. "Dimensions" are simply aspects of performance. For example, interacting with customers, ordering stock, and balancing the cash drawer are the major dimensions of a retail job. Once they have agreed on the

Figure 2.5

Rating Scale Importance of characteristics for successful performance of task				
1 Very Low	2 Low	3 Medium	4 High	5 Very High

Job Task	Mathematical Reasoning	Analytical Ability	Ability to Follow Directions	Memory	Comprehension—Oral	Comprehension—Written	Expression—Oral	Expression—Written	Problem-Solving Ability	Clerical Accuracy
1. Reviews production schedules to determine correct job sequencing										
2. Identifies problem jobs and takes corrective action										
3. Determines need for and provides special work orders										
4. Maintains log book and makes required assignments										
5. Negotiates with foremen to determine critical dates for emergency situations										
6. Analyzes material availability and performs order maintenance										
7. Prepares job packets										
8. Maintains customer order file										
9. Negotiates with Purchasing to ensure material availability										
10. Determines product availability for future customer orders										
11. Determines promise dates and provides to customer										
12. Determines adequacy of materials given document forecast										

Worker Characteristics

Sample Task by KSA Matrix

job's major dimensions, supervisors and workers generate "critical incidents" of behavior that represent high, moderate, and low levels of performance on each dimension. An example of a critical incident of high performance on the dimension "interacting with customers" might be:

When a customer complained to the clerk that she could not find a particular item, seeing no one else was in line, this clerk walked with the customer back to the shelves to find the item.

An example of low performance on the same dimension might be:

When a customer handed the clerk a large number of coupons, the clerk complained out loud to the bagger that he hated dealing with coupons.

The last two steps, retranslation and assigning effectiveness values, involve making sure that the critical incidents generated in the first two steps are commonly viewed the same way by other employees.

The CIT provides a detailed behavioral description of jobs. It is often used as a basis for performance appraisal systems and training programs, as well as to develop behaviorally based selection interview questions. The appendix to Chapter 7 gives you the opportunity to develop critical incidents.

Position Analysis Questionnaire (PAQ).   The PAQ is a job analysis questionnaire that contains 194 different items. Using a five-point scale, the PAQ seeks to determine the degree to which the different items, or job elements, are involved in performing a particular job.[61] The 194 items are organized into six sections:

1. **Information input** Where and how a worker gets information needed to perform the job.
2. **Mental processes** The reasoning, decision-making, planning, and information-processing activities involved in performing the job.
3. **Work output** The physical activities, tools, and devices used by the worker to perform the job.
4. **Relationships with other persons** The relationships with other people required in performing the job.
5. **Job context** The physical and social contexts in which the work is performed.
6. **Other characteristics** The other activities, conditions, and characteristics relevant to the job.

Customer-Driven HR

MANAGER'S NOTEBOOK

Guidelines for Conducting a Job Analysis

Conducting a job analysis requires managers to take five steps:

1. **Determine the desired applications of the job analysis.** For example, if used as a basis for performance appraisal, job analysis should collect data that are representative of differing levels of job performance. If used as a basis for determining training needs, then job analysis should collect information on the necessary knowledge, skills, and abilities that lead to effective job performance.
2. **Select the jobs to be analyzed.** Factors that make specific jobs appropriate for job analysis include the stability or obsolescence of job content (rapidly changing jobs require more frequent job analysis). Entry-level jobs (which require selection tools that determine who gets hired and who gets rejected) are also analyzed regularly.
3. **Gather the job information.** Within budget constraints, collect the desired information using the most appropriate job-analysis technique.
4. **Verify the accuracy of the job information.** Both the job incumbents and their immediate supervisors should review the job information to ensure that it is representative of the actual job.
5. **Document the job analysis by writing a job description.** Document the job-analysis information in a job description that summarizes the job's essential duties and responsibilities, as well as the knowledge, skills, and abilities necessary for the job. This document allows managers to compare different jobs on various dimensions and is an important part of many HR programs.

Source: Adapted from Gatewood, R. D., and Feild, H. S. (2001). *Human resource selection* (5th ed.) Fort Worth, TX: Harcourt College Publishers.

A computer analyzes the completed PAQ and generates a score for the job and a profile of its characteristics.

Functional Job Analysis.   Functional job analysis, a technique used in the public sector, can be done by either interview or questionnaire.[62] This technique collects information on the following aspects of the job:[63]

1. What the job incumbent does to people, data, and things.
2. The methods and techniques the job incumbent uses to perform the job.
3. The machines, tools, and equipment used by the job incumbent.
4. The materials, projects, or services produced by the job incumbent.

The results of functional job analyses are published by the U.S. federal government in the *Dictionary of Occupational Titles (DOT)*.[64] The DOT contains standard and comprehensive descriptions of about 20,000 jobs and has helped to bring about more uniformity in the job titles used in different sections of the country. The DOT listings also facilitate the exchange of statistical information about jobs.

Job Analysis and the Legal Environment

Because job analysis can be the basis on which a firm wins or loses a lawsuit over how it selects or appraises employees, it is important that organizations carefully document their job-analysis efforts.

There are two important questions regarding job analysis. First: Which job analysis method is best? Although there are many job-analysis techniques, there is no clear choice as to which is best. Some, like task inventory analysis and Guidelines-Oriented Job Analysis, were developed to satisfy legal requirements, but there is no legal basis to prefer one to another. The *Uniform Guidelines* published by the Equal Employment Opportunity Commission state that a job analysis should be done, but do not specify a preferred technique.

As a general rule, the more concrete and observable the information, the better. Thus, job-analysis approaches that provide specific task or behavioral statements, such as task inventory analysis or CIT, may be preferable. CIT can be very expensive because of the time commitment required of supervisors and workers.

Given the lack of a single best technique, the choice of job-analysis technique should, within economic constraints, be guided by the purpose of the analysis. For example, if the major purpose for the analysis is the redesign of jobs, then an analysis focusing on tasks would probably be best. But if the major purpose is the development of a training program, a behaviorally focused technique would probably be best.

Job Analysis and Organizational Flexibility

The second question regarding job analysis is: How does detailed job-analysis information fit into today's organizations, which need to be flexible and innovative to remain competitive?

Whatever technique is used, job analysis is a static view of the job as it currently exists, and a static view of jobs is at odds with current organizational trends emphasizing flexibility and innovativeness. For instance, America West Airlines attempts to keep labor costs down by having employees do a variety of tasks. The same person may be a flight attendant, ticket agent, and baggage handler all in the same week. And almost all jobs today are affected by the constant advances in information and communication technologies. Such factors can render even the most thorough job analysis virtually useless after a very short time.

In an organizational environment of change and innovation, it is better to focus job analyses on *worker* characteristics than on *job* characteristics. The required tasks in jobs may change, but such employee characteristics as innovativeness, team orientation, interpersonal skills, and communication skills will likely remain critical to organizational success. Unfortunately, most job-analysis techniques are not focused on discovering worker characteristics unless the characteristics are directly related to the immediate tasks. But, because the importance of fit with the organization is being increasingly recognized as a factor that should be considered in selection,[65] job analysis may become more focused on underlying employee factors.[66] Sun Microsystems, Toyota (USA), and AFG Industries are some of the organizations that have expanded job analysis to emphasize fit between prospective employees and the organization.

Job Descriptions

A **job description** is a summary statement of the information collected in the job-analysis process. It is a written document that identifies, defines, and describes a job in terms of its duties, responsibilities, working conditions, and specifications. There are two types of job descriptions: specific job descriptions and general job descriptions.

A *specific job description* is a detailed summary of a job's tasks, duties, and responsibilities. This type of job description is associated with work flow strategies that emphasize efficiency, control, and detailed work planning. It fits best with a bureaucratic organizational structure with well-defined boundaries that separate functions and the different levels of management. Figure 2.6 shows an example of a specific job description for the job of service and safety supervisor. Note that this job description closely specifies the work that is unique to a person who will supervise *safety* employees. The specific job knowledge of safety regulations and Red Cross first-aid procedures included in this job description make it inappropriate for any other type of supervisor (for example, a supervisor at a local supermarket).

The *general job description,* which is fairly new on the scene, is associated with work flow strategies that emphasize innovation, flexibility, and loose work planning. This type of job description fits best with a flat or boundaryless organizational structure in which there are few boundaries between functions and levels of management.[67]

Only the most generic duties, responsibilities, and skills for a position are documented in the general job description.[68] Figure 2.7 on page 67 shows a general job description for the job of "supervisor." Note that all the job duties and responsibilities in Figure 2.7 apply to the job of *any* supervisor—one who supervises accountants, engineers, or even the safety employees managed by the service and safety supervisor in Figure 2.6.

The driving force behind a move toward general job descriptions may be a TQM program or BPR.[69] For example, the Arizona Public Service (APS), a public utility, moved toward general job descriptions after discovering that it had 1,000 specific job descriptions for its 3,600 workers.[70] This massive number of specific job descriptions erected false barriers among work functions, choked off change, and prevented APS from providing high levels of customer service. By using general job descriptions, APS was able to reduce the number of its job descriptions to 450.

An even more impressive application of general job descriptions is seen at Nissan, the Japanese auto manufacturer. Nissan has only one general job description for all its hourly wage production employees.[71] By comparison, some of the divisions of General Motors have hundreds of specific job descriptions for their hourly production workforce. This fact is partially explained by the vigilance of the United Auto Workers' Union (UAW) in defending the rights of its members to work in specific jobs.

Elements of a Job Description

Job descriptions have four key elements: identification information, job summary, job duties and responsibilities, and job specifications and minimum qualifications.[72] Figures 2.6 and 2.7 show how this information is organized on the job description.

To comply with federal law, it is important that job descriptions document only the essential aspects of a job. Otherwise, qualified women, minorities, and persons with disabilities may be unintentionally discriminated against for not meeting specified job requirements. For example, a valid driver's license should not be put in the job description if the job can be modified so that it can be performed by a person with physical disabilities without a driver's license.

Identification Information.   The first part of the job description identifies the job title, location, and source of job-analysis information; who wrote the job description; the dates of the job analysis and the verification of the job description; and whether the job is exempt from the overtime provision of the Fair Labor Standards Act or subject to overtime pay rates. To be certain that the identification information ensures equal employment opportunities, HR staff should:

- Make sure the job titles do not refer to a specific gender. For example, use the job title "sales representative" rather than "salesman."
- Make sure job descriptions are updated regularly so that the date on the job description is current. Job descriptions more than two years old have low credibility and may provide flawed information.

Job description
A written document that identifies, describes, and defines a job in terms of its duties, responsibilities, working conditions, and specifications.

Figure 2.6

Job Title: Service and Safety Supervisor

DIVISION: Plastics
DEPARTMENT: Manufacturing
SOURCE(S): John Doe   WAGE CATEGORY: Exempt
JOB ANALYST: John Smith   VERIFIED BY: Bill Johnson
DATE ANALYZED: 12/26/06   DATE VERIFIED: 1/5/07

Job Summary

The SERVICE AND SAFETY SUPERVISOR works under the direction of the IMPREGNATING & LAMINATING MANAGER: **schedules** labor pool employees; **supervises** the work of gardeners, cleaners, waste disposal, and plant security personnel; **coordinates** plant safety programs; **maintains** daily records on personnel, equipment, and scrap.

Job Duties and Responsibilities

1. **Schedules** labor employees to provide relief personnel for all manufacturing departments; **prepares** assignment schedules and **assigns** individuals to departments based on routine as well as special needs in order to maintain adequate labor levels through the plant; **notifies** Industrial Relations Department weekly about vacation and layoff status of labor pool employees, contractual disputes, and other employment-related developments.
2. **Supervises** the work of gardeners, cleaners, waste disposal, and plant security personnel; **plans** yard, cleanup, and security activities based on weekly determination of needs; **assigns** tasks and responsibilities to employees on a daily basis; **monitors** progress or status of assigned tasks; **disciplines** employees.
3. **Coordinates** plant safety programs; **teaches** basic first-aid procedures to security, supervisory, and lease personnel in order to maintain adequate coverage of medical emergencies; **trains** employees in fire fighting and hazardous materials handling procedures; **verifies** plant compliance with new or changing OSHA regulations; **represents** division during company-wide safety programs and meetings.
4. **Maintains** daily records on personnel, equipment, and scrap; **reports** amount of waste and scrap to cost accounting department; **updates** personnel records as necessary; **reviews** maintenance checklists for towmotors.
5. **Performs** other miscellaneous duties as assigned.

Job Requirements

1. Ability to apply basic principles and techniques of supervision.
   a. Knowledge of principles and techniques of supervision.
   b. Ability to plan and organize the activities of others.
   c. Ability to get ideas accepted and to guide a group or individual to accomplish the task.
   d. Ability to modify leadership style and management approach to reach goal.
2. Ability to express ideas clearly both in written and oral communications.
3. Knowledge of current Red Cross first-aid operations.
4. Knowledge of OSHA regulations as they affect plant operations.
5. Knowledge of labor pool jobs, company policies, and labor contracts.

Minimum Qualifications

Twelve years of general education or equivalent; one year supervisory experience; and first-aid instructor's certification.

OR

Substitute 45 hours classroom supervisory training for supervisory experience.

Source: Jones, M. A. (1984, May). Job descriptions made easy. *Personnel Journal.* Copyright May 1984. Reprinted with the permission of *Personnel Journal.* ACC Communications, Inc., Costa Mesa, California; all rights reserved.

Example of a Specific Job Description

■ Ensure that the supervisor of the job incumbent(s) verifies the job description. This is a good way to ensure that the job description does not misrepresent the actual job duties and responsibilities. (A manager who is familiar with the job may also be used to verify the description.)

Job Summary.   The job summary is a short statement that summarizes the job's duties, responsibilities, and place in the organizational structure.

Figure 2.7

Job Title: Supervisor

DIVISION: Plastics
DEPARTMENT: Manufacturing
SOURCE(S): John Doe, S. Lee   WAGE CATEGORY: Exempt
JOB ANALYST: John Smith   VERIFIED BY: Bill Johnson
DATE ANALYZED: 12/26/06   DATE VERIFIED: 1/5/07

Job Summary

The SUPERVISOR works under the direction of the MANAGER: **plans** goals; **supervises** the work of employees; **develops** employees with feedback and coaching; **maintains** accurate records; **coordinates** with others to achieve optimal use of organizational resources.

Job Duties and Responsibilities

1. **Plans** goals and allocates resources to achieve them; **monitors** progress toward objectives and adjusts plans as necessary to reach them; **allocates** and **schedules** resources to assure their availability according to priority.
2. **Supervises** the work of employees; **provides** clear instructions and explanations to employees when giving assignments; **schedules** and assigns work among employees for maximum efficiency; **monitors** employees' performance in order to achieve assigned objectives.
3. **Develops** employees through direct performance feedback and job coaching; **conducts** performance appraisals with each employee on a regular basis; **provides** employees with praise and recognition when performance is excellent; **corrects** employees promptly when their performance fails to meet expected performance levels.
4. **Maintains** accurate records and documents actions; **processes** paper work on a timely basis, and with close attention to details; **documents** important aspects of decisions and actions.
5. **Coordinates** with others to achieve the optimal use of organizational resources; **maintains** good working relationships with colleagues in other organizational units; **represents** others in unit during division or corporatewide meetings.

Job Requirements

1. Ability to apply basic principles and techniques of supervision.
   a. Knowledge of principles and techniques of supervision.
   b. Ability to plan and organize the activities of others.
   c. Ability to get ideas accepted and to guide a group or individual to accomplish the task.
   d. Ability to modify leadership style and management approach to reach goal.
2. Ability to express ideas clearly in both written and oral communications.

Minimum Qualifications

Twelve years of general education or equivalent; and one year supervisory experience.

OR

Substitute 45 hours classroom supervisory training for supervisory experience.

Example of a General Job Description

Job Duties and Responsibilities.   Job duties and responsibilities explain what is done on the job, how it is done, and why it is done.[73]

Each job description typically lists the job's three to five most important responsibilities. Each responsibility statement begins with an action verb. For example, the job of supervisor in Figure 2.7 has five responsibilities that start with the following action verbs: plans, supervises, develops, maintains, and coordinates. Each responsibility is associated with one or more job duties, which also start with action verbs. For example, the supervisor job in Figure 2.7 has two job duties associated with the responsibility of "plans goals": (1) monitors progress toward objectives, and (2) allocates and schedules resources. The job duties and responsibilities statement is probably the most important section of the job description because it influences all the other parts of the job description. Therefore, it must be comprehensive and accurate.

Job specifications
The worker characteristics needed to perform a job successfully.

Job Specifications and Minimum Qualifications   The **job specifications** section lists the worker characteristics (KSAs) needed to perform a job successfully. The KSAs represent the things that an employee who has mastered the job can do.

When documenting KSAs it is important to list only those that are related to successful job performance. For example, a current computer programmer may have mastered some programming languages that are not necessary for job performance. These should not be included in the job description.

The *minimum qualifications* are the basic standards a job applicant must have achieved to be considered for the job. These can be used to screen job applicants during the recruiting and selection process. Here are some things to watch for when documenting minimum qualifications:

- A college degree should be a minimum qualification only if it is related to the successful performance of the job. For example, a bachelor's degree may be a minimum qualification for an accountant in a major accounting firm, but it is not likely to be necessary for the job of shift supervisor in a fast-food restaurant.
- Work experience qualifications should be carefully specified so that they do not discriminate against minorities or persons with disabilities. For example, the job description in Figure 2.7 provides for a substitute of 45 classroom hours of supervisory training for the one year of work experience minimum qualification. This provision allows people who have been excluded from employment opportunities in the past to be considered for the position. This flexibility allows the company to consider diverse job applicants, who are less likely to meet the work experience qualification.

The Flexible Workforce

We have seen how organizations can be structured and jobs designed to maximize flexibility. In this section, we examine two additional strategies for ensuring flexibility: contingent workers and flexible work schedules.

Contingent Workers

Core workers
An organization's full-time employees.

Contingent workers
Workers hired to deal with temporary increases in an organization's workload or to do work that is not part of its core set of capabilities.

There are two types of workers: core workers and contingent workers. A company's **core workers** have full-time jobs and enjoy privileges not available to contingent workers. Many core workers expect a long-term relationship with the employer that includes a career in the organization, a full array of benefits, and job security. In contrast, the jobs of **contingent workers** are based on the employer's convenience and efficiency needs. Firms hire contingent workers to help them deal with temporary increases in their workload or to do work that is not part of their core set of capabilities. When the business cycle moves into a downturn, the contingent workers are the first employees to be discharged. They thus provide a buffer zone of protection for the core workers. For example, in some large Japanese corporations core workers' jobs are protected by a large contingent workforce that can be rapidly downsized when business conditions change.

Contingent workers include temporary employees, part-time employees, outsourced subcontractors, contract workers, and college interns. According to the U.S. Bureau of Labor Statistics in the United States, contingent workers made up 24 percent of the total labor force in 2001. This number includes approximately 22 million part-time employees, 9 million contract workers, and 1.2 million temporary employees. The jobs held by contingent workers are diverse, ranging from secretaries, security guards, sales clerks, and assembly-line workers to doctors, college professors, engineers, managers, and even chief executives.

Temporary Employees

Temporary employment agencies provide companies with *temporary employees* (or "temps") for short-term work assignments. Temps work for the temporary employment agency and are simply reassigned to another employer when their current job ends. Manpower, the largest of the 7,000 U.S. temporary employment agencies, is also the nation's largest private employer, with almost 750,000 people on its payroll.[74]

Temporary employees provide employers with two major benefits:

- Temps on average receive less compensation than core workers. They are not likely to receive health insurance, retirement, or vacation benefits from the company that uses their services. A majority of temporary employees do not receive these benefits from the temporary agency because they must meet a minimum service requirement of several months or longer of continuous employment with the agency to qualify for the benefits. For example, as layoffs mounted in the 1990s, the total payroll for professionals and managers employed by temporary firms more than tripled.[75] However, many managers working at temp jobs earn 50 percent less than they earned as core workers.[76]

- Temporary employees may be highly motivated workers since many employers choose full-time employees from the ranks of the top-performing temps. Because temps can be screened for long-term career potential in an actual work setting and be easily dismissed if the company determines that they have low potential, hiring temps helps employers reduce the risk of selecting employees who prove to be a poor fit.

Employers should understand the legal limits of using a temporary worker on a long-term basis. Several thousand Microsoft temps who held long-term positions but were employed through a temporary agency ("Permatemps") filed a class action lawsuit, claiming that Microsoft treated them as full-time workers in every way except in terms of compensation and benefits. A federal court of appeals ruled that workers who were on Microsoft's payroll for more than a few months—even if placed by temporary agencies—should be considered common-law employees who are entitled to the same benefits that permanent employees receive.[77]

Temporary employees are being used with increasing regularity throughout the world. In France, one in five workers is on a temporary or part-time contract, and in Britain more than 25 percent of the workforce is part-time. Almost 33 percent of new jobs created in Spain were for temporary workers.[78]

Day laborers sign up at Labor Ready in Chicago, a temporary agency specializing in unskilled labor for unpleasant tasks such as ditch-digging or industrial cleanup.

Part-Time Employees

Part-time employees work fewer hours than full-time core employees and receive far fewer employee benefits, thus providing substantial savings to employers. Traditionally, part-timers have been employed by service businesses that have a high variance in demand between peak and off-peak times. For example, restaurants and markets hire many part-time employees to provide service to customers during peak hours (usually evenings and weekends).

Companies are finding many new applications for part-time workers. For example, UPS has created 25-hour-per-week part-time jobs for shipping clerks and supervisors who sort packages at its distribution centers. Companies that downsize their workforces to reduce payroll costs have been known to restructure full-time core jobs into part-time positions.

Job sharing

A work arrangement in which two or more employees divide a job's responsibilities, hours, and benefits among themselves.

In a special type of part-time employment called **job sharing**, a full-time job is divided between two or more people to create two part-time jobs. During a down-scaling of its workforce, DuPont used job sharing between employees in its management, research, and secretarial areas to avoid layoffs.[79]

Companies are increasingly using part-time work as a way to reverse the "brain drain" of highly skilled female professionals who need greater work–life balance to provide more time for their family. Johnson & Johnson, the large health-care products company, allows professional women with substantial work experience to take a reduced-hour option so the company won't lose them. Pfizer, the pharmaceutical giant, offers part-time work to its pharmaceutical sales professionals who are highly trained in product knowledge and have developed valuable relationships with doctors who are their clients. Sales representatives choosing the part-time option work 60 percent of the hours of full-time employees and can structure their working day around children's school hours. Ninety-three percent of those selecting part-time work at Pfizer are working mothers, and these individuals remain eligible for promotion and may return to full-time status at their discretion.[80]

Outsourcing/Subcontracting

As we saw in Chapter 1, outsourcing (sometimes called *subcontracting*) is the process by which employers transfer routine or peripheral work to another organization that specializes in that work and can perform it more efficiently. Employers that outsource some of their nonessential work gain improved quality and cost savings. Outsourcing agreements may result in a long-term relationship between an employer and the subcontractor, though it is the employer who has the flexibility to renew or end the relationship at its convenience.[81]

Outsourcing is the wave of the future as more and more companies look to the "virtual corporation" as an organizational model.[82] A *virtual company* consists of a small core of permanent employees and a constantly shifting workforce of contingent employees.

A Question of Ethics

Many employees and union representatives complain bitterly about the practice of outsourcing work, particularly to foreign countries. Part of the complaint is that companies do this to avoid paying fair wages and providing employee benefits that U.S. workers expect. Is this an ethical issue? If so, on what basis should companies make outsourcing decisions?

Consistent with the outsourcing trend, human resource activities are being outsourced by organizations. For example, payroll, benefits, training, and recruiting are often outsourced to external service providers.[83] Previously these outsourced activities were performed in-house. In fact, human resource outsourcing is a fast-growing $80 billion industry, and total annual industry revenues recently increased 33 percent.[84] Although outsourcing routine human resource activities such as payroll produces efficiencies, the outsourcing of critical HR systems such as training or performance evaluation may lead to a loss of control over important systems or a loss of opportunity to learn from one's best human resource practices that could achieve fundamental improvements in other human resource activities.

Establishing the right relationship with service vendors is very important for companies that decide to outsource. Although some companies view their outsourced vendors as strategic partners, others caution that, ultimately, company and vendor do not have identical interests. For example, UOP, an Illinois-based engineering firm that develops technology used to build oil refineries, sued Andersen Consulting, the information-technology firm UOP had hired to streamline and improve some of its work processes. UOP sued for $100 million in damages, alleging breach of contract. UOP's president and CEO claimed that "the difference between what Andersen promised us . . . and what it actually delivered is staggering."[85] The lesson is that it pays to communicate clearly and specifically with vendors from the beginning.[86]

One company that relies on outsourcing as a source of competitive advantage is Benetton, the Italian multinational corporation that makes clothing sold in 110 countries. Benetton views itself as a "clothing services" company rather than as a retailer or manufacturer.[87] The company outsources a large amount of clothes manufacturing to local suppliers but makes sure to provide its subcontractors with the clothes-making skills that Benetton views as crucial to maintaining quality and cost efficiency.[88]

The Manager's Notebook, "Advantages and Disadvantages of Outsourcing an HR Activity," provides some useful information on factors to consider before outsourcing.

Emerging Trends

MANAGER'S NOTEBOOK

Advantages and Disadvantages of Outsourcing an HR Activity

Outsourcing an HR activity to a firm that specializes in providing an HR service to customers has both advantages and disadvantages. Here are some important factors to consider:

Outsourcing Advantages

■ An outsourcing firm can provide better-quality people and the most current practices and information pertaining to an activity or task. Because the HR activity is the core mission of the outsourcing firm, it can specialize in doing it very well. For example, a firm that specializes in training employees on the use of word processing software is likely to be able to train employees to use the most recent upgrades on the software that contains the newest features and applications.

■ Outsourcing certain tasks can result in a reduction in administrative costs because the outsourcer can do the task more efficiently and gain economies of scale by virtue of having a large network of customers.

■ Outsourcing specific activities and employees that do not fit with company culture may be useful to preserve a strong culture or employee morale. An example is outsourcing the benefits administration activity at a law firm, where the law-firm culture is shared by people who are trained as attorneys.

Outsourcing Disadvantages

■ Deploying an HR activity to an outsourcing firm may lead to losing control of an important activity, which can be a costly problem. For example, by outsourcing employee recruiting to an external recruiting firm, the client company may experience missed deadlines on time-sensitive projects if the recruiting firm has other more important clients to serve.

■ Outsourcing an HR activity may result in losing the opportunity to gain knowledge and information that could benefit other company processes and activities. For example, outsourcing executive training and development to a company that provides a standardized training package can result in a lost opportunity to learn about the unique aspects of a firm's way of shaping leadership with respect to its own culture.

Source: Smith, S. (2005, May 9). Look before you leap into HR outsourcing. *Canadian HR Reporter,* 13; Kaplan, J. (2002, January 14). The realities of outsourcing. *Network World,* 33; and Baron, J., and Kreps, D. (1999). *Strategic human resources: Frameworks for general managers.* New York: John Wiley & Sons.

Offshore Outsourcing.   The spectacular economic growth of China and India during the first decade of the twenty-first century has created lucrative opportunities for companies in North America, Europe, and Asia to take advantage of the professional skills and low labor costs provided by outsource firms in those two countries.[89] The labor cost savings these offshore outsource firms can offer are impressive. For example, an information technology (IT) professional with three to five years of work experience would earn an annual salary of around $26,000 in India compared to about $75,000 in the United States. A call-center employee in India would earn around $2,000 a year, compared to $20,000 in Britain.[90] *Offshore outsourcing,* sometimes referred to as *offshoring,* refers to the use of international outsource providers to gain competitive advantage in the market.[91]

Offshore outsource providers in India are particularly competitive in offering services such as call centers, IT consulting, and software development. For example, Indian call-center providers handle customer-service calls and process insurance claims, loans, travel bookings, and credit-card bills.[92]

China has developed a high level of expertise in manufacturing. Chinese outsource firms manufacture a broad range of products for clients, from consumer electronics, such as television sets and DVDs, to memory chips, to consumer goods, such as microwave ovens, dishwashers, and toys for children, as well as autos and trucks. Currently, a large portion of the inventory of the goods sold in Wal-Mart, the world's largest retail store, comes from Chinese suppliers who partner with Wal-Mart. Additional information on offshore outsourcing can be found in Chapter 17 ("International HRM Challenge").

Contract Workers

Contract workers are employees who develop work relationships directly with an employer (instead of with a subcontractor through an outsourcing arrangement) for a specific piece of work or time period.[93] They are likely to be self-employed, supply their own tools, and determine their hours of employment. Sometimes contract workers are called *consultants* or *freelancers.*

Many professionals with specialized skills become contract workers.[94] Hospitals use contract workers as emergency room physicians. Universities use them as adjunct professors to teach basic courses. Qwest, one of the Baby Bell telecommunications companies, uses contract workers for many of its HR jobs. Small business also are likely to use contract workers. When things get too busy for its 30 full-time employees, Ippolita, a New York City jewelry manufacturer, brings in a small army of freelancers—fashion experts, sculptors of miniature models, designers, and marketers. The biggest challenge is managing the relationship between freelancers and full-time employees. Management has found it very beneficial to have written job descriptions for both full-time employees and contract workers so that everyone knows his or her specific assignment.[95]

Contract workers can often be more productive and efficient than in-house employees because freelancers' time is usually not taken up with the inevitable company bureaucracy and meetings. They can also give companies a fresh outsider's perspective. However, it is not always easy to motivate a freelancer for whom you are one of several clients, each with urgent projects and pressing deadlines.

College Interns

One of the newest developments in the contingency work area is the use of *college interns,* college students who work on full-time or part-time assignments of short duration (usually for one academic semester or summer) to obtain work experience. Some interns are paid, some are not. Employers use interns to provide support to professional staff. Sometimes interns work a trial run for consideration as a potential core employee after graduation from college. Large companies that use college interns include IBM and General Electric (which have internships for electrical engineers), the Big Four accounting firms (which use interns on auditing engagements with clients), and Procter & Gamble (which uses interns in its sales and marketing areas).

College interns are also used extensively by small companies that want to attract employees who will grow with the company. For instance, at Seal Press, a small publishing company in Seattle, Washington, a woman who started as a marketing intern went on to become marketing assistant and is now marketing director. Editorial interns log in and read unsolicited manuscripts, write detailed reader's reports, and sometimes attend staff meetings. Because the work is challenging, there is a long waiting list of applicants.

Flexible Work Schedules

Flexible work schedules alter the scheduling of work while leaving intact the job design and the employment relationship. Employers may get higher levels of productivity and job satisfaction.[96] Employees may feel that they are trusted by management, which can improve the quality of employee relations (see Chapter 13).[97] Employees with flexible work schedules may also experience less stress by avoiding rush hour traffic.

The three most common types of flexible work schedules are flexible work hours, compressed workweeks, and telecommuting.

Flexible Work Hours

Flexible work hours give employees control over the starting and ending times of their daily work schedules. Employees are required to put in a full 40-hour workweek at their onsite workstation, but have some control over the hours when they perform the work. **Flexible work hours** divide work schedules into **core time**, when all employees are expected to be at work, and *flexible time* (**flextime**), when employees can choose to organize work routines around personal activities.

Hewlett-Packard's policy gives workers the flexibility to arrive at work between 6:30 A.M. and 8:30 A.M. and leave after they put in eight hours of work. Hewlett-Packard's core hours are between 8:30 A.M. and 2:30 P.M.[98] Meetings and team activities take place in this core time.

Compressed Workweeks

Compressed workweeks alter the number of workdays per week by increasing the length of the workday to 10 or more hours. One type of compressed workweek schedule consists of four 10-hour workdays. Another consists of four 12-hour workdays in a four days on/four days off schedule. This schedule gives workers two four-day blocks of time off every 16 days.[99]

Compressed workweeks create less potential for disruptions to businesses that provide 24-hour-per-day services, such as hospitals and police forces. They also lower absenteeism and tardiness at companies with work sites in remote locations that require long commutes to work (for example, off-shore oil drilling platforms).

Their major advantage is that they give employees three- or four-day weekends to spend with their families or engage in personal interests. However, employees who work a compressed workweek may experience increased levels of stress and fatigue.[100]

Figure 2.8 shows the length of the workweek for full-time employment in different countries. Notice that the workweek ranges from 35 hours in France to 48 hours in Hong Kong.

Telecommuting

Personal computers, modems, fax machines, e-mail, and the Internet (which connects computers in an international network) have created the opportunity for millions of people in the United States to work from a home office or **telecommute**.[101] Telecommuting allows employees to cultivate tailored lifestyles while working a full-time job.[102]

Flexible work hours
A work arrangement that gives employees control over the starting and ending times of their daily work schedules.

Core time
Time when all employees are expected to be at work. Part of a flexible work hours arrangement.

Flextime
Time during which employees can choose not to be at work. Part of a flexible work hours arrangement.

Telecommuting
A work arrangement that allows employees to work in their homes full-time, maintaining their connection to the office through phone, fax, and computer.

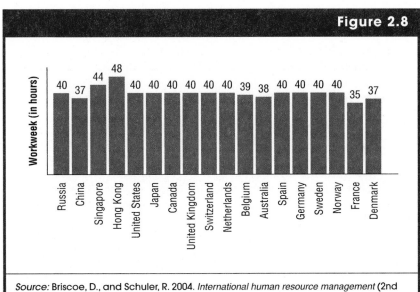

Figure 2.8

The Length of the Workweek in Selected Countries

Source: Briscoe, D., and Schuler, R. 2004. *International human resource management* (2nd ed.). New York: Routledge.

Jill Smith telecommutes from her home as a reservation agent for JetBlue Airways.

Telecommuting gives employers the flexibility to hire talented employees who might not otherwise be able to offer their services. Employers also save on office space costs with telecommuting. However, telecommuting does present several challenges to managers. We discuss these in detail in Chapter 13.

Recently, France passed a 35-hour workweek employment law to offer employees a better balance between work and family life. The Manager's Notebook titled "France Establishes a 35-hour Workweek" describes the French experience with a shortened workweek.

MANAGER'S NOTEBOOK

Global

France Establishes a 35-Hour Workweek

In 2000, France implemented a 35-hour workweek that was designed to create an incentive for employers to create more jobs for the unemployed. The new employment law resulted in a 4-hour reduction in the weekly hours that full-time employees were required to work. The new law also required that French companies pay 39 hours of wages for 35 hours of work, meaning that employees would not be penalized with a reduction in pay when the 35-hour workweek was put into practice. The economic logic of this law was controversial, because it assumed there was a fixed amount of work available to French employees, and that reducing the length of the workweek would make additional work hours available to share with those who had difficulty finding jobs. The law offered employees greater flexibility to balance work and their private lives. However, it also made businesses view France as being less competitive internationally, because French working hours were some of the shortest in the world.

Therefore, in 2005, despite the popularity of the 35-hour workweek with some sectors of the workforce, French lawmakers voted to overhaul the 35-hour workweek and give employers the flexibility to allow employees to work up to the 48 hours per week permitted under European Union legal guidelines. One reason was that the unemployment rate in France remained high, at around 10 percent during the five years of the 35-hour workweek, challenging the assumption that employers have a fixed amount of labor to allocate to the workforce. The French experiment with the 35-hour workweek suggests that in the global economy employers have other choices than to use domestic employees to fill jobs; they may decide to employ international employees by outsourcing to low-cost countries. Therefore, the economic shock of the 35-hour workweek in France may have provided an incentive for some employers to find lower-cost substitutes for domestic employees rather than offer more jobs to French workers.

Sources: Bennhold, K. (2005, March 23). France votes to overhaul 35-hour workweek. *International Herald Tribune,* 3; Smith, C. (2003, January 10). Shortend workweek shortens French tempers. *New York Times,* A3; *The Economist* (2002, June 15). France's 35-hour work-week is fine, so long as it is voluntary, 78.

Human Resource Information Systems

Human resource information systems (HRIS) are systems used to collect, record, store, analyze, and retrieve data concerning an organization's human resources.[103] Most of today's HRIS are computerized; we will briefly explore two relevant issues: the applications of HRIS and the management of security and privacy issues related to HRIS.

Human resource information system (HRIS)
A system used to collect, record, store, analyze, and retrieve data concerning an organization's human resources.

HRIS Applications

A computerized HRIS contains computer hardware and software applications that work together to help managers make HR decisions.[104] The software may be a custom-designed program or an off-the-shelf (prepackaged) applications program.

Figure 2.9 shows some HRIS software applications currently available to business. These include:

- An *employee information program* sets up a database that provides basic employee information: name, sex, address, phone number, date of birth, race, marital status, job title, and salary. Other applications programs can access the data in the employee information database for more specialized HR uses.

Figure 2.9

Selected Human Resource Information Systems Applications

Applicant tracking	Health and safety	Pension and retirement
Basic employee information	Health insurance utilization	Performance management
Benefits administration	Hiring procedures	Short- and long-term
Bonus and incentive	HR planning and forecasting	disabilities
management	Job descriptions/analysis	Skills inventory
Career development/	Job evaluation	Succession planning
planning	Job posting	Time and attendance
Compensation budgeting	Labor relations planning	Travel costs
EEO/AA compliance	Payroll	Turnover analysis
Employment history		
Goal-setting system		

Source: Dzamba, A. (2001, January). What are your peers doing to boost HRIS performance? *HR Focus,* 5–6; Kavanagh, M., Gueutal, H., and Tannenbaum, S. (1990). *Human resource information systems: Development and application,* 50. Boston: PWS-Kent. Reproduced with the permission of South-Western College Publishing. Copyright 1990 by PWS-Kent. All rights reserved.

- An *applicant tracking program* can automate some of the labor-intensive activities associated with recruiting job applicants. These include storing job applicant information so that multiple users can access it and evaluate the applicant, scheduling interviews with different managers, updating the personal status of the job applicant, generating correspondence (for example, a job offer or a rejection letter), and producing the necessary equal employment opportunity (EEO) records required by the government.
- A *skills inventory* keeps track of the supply of job skills in the employer's workforce and searches for matches between skill supply and the organization's demand for job skills.
- A *payroll applications program* computes gross pay, federal taxes, state taxes, Social Security, other taxes, and net pay. It can also be programmed to make other deductions from the paycheck for such items as employee contributions to health insurance, employee contributions to a tax-deferred retirement plan, and union dues.
- A *benefits application program* can automate benefits record-keeping, administer various benefit programs, or provide advice about benefit choices. Benefits software can also provide an annual benefits statement for each employee.
- An *employee time management program* tracks the way each employee uses time on the job. The program monitors employee attendance, absenteeism, and tardiness.[105]

HRIS Security and Privacy

The HR department must develop policies and guidelines to protect the integrity and security of the HRIS. Unauthorized users of HRIS can create havoc. In one case, an executive who worked for a brokerage house tapped into her company's HRIS to get employee names and addresses for her husband, a life insurance agent who used the information to mail solicitations to his wife's colleagues. The solicited employees brought a million-dollar class-action suit against the company for invasion of privacy.[106] In another case, a computer programmer tapped into a computer company's HRIS, detected the salaries of a number of employees (including top managers and executives), and disclosed this information to other employees. The situation became very disruptive when angry employees demanded to know why large pay discrepancies existed.[107]

To maintain the security and privacy of HRIS records, companies should:

- Limit access to the HRIS by controlling access to the computer and its data files and locking the areas where they are stored and encrypting the data.
- Permit limited access to different portions of the database with the use of passwords and special codes.
- Grant permission to access employee information only on a need-to-know basis.
- Develop policies and guidelines that govern the utilization of employee information and notify employees how this policy works.
- Allow employees to verify and correct their personal records.

Summary and Conclusions

Work: The Organizational Perspective

A firm's business strategy determines how it structures its work. Under a defender strategy, work can be efficiently organized into a functional structure based on division of labor, with hierarchies of jobs assigned to functional units. Under a prospector strategy, decentralization and a low division of labor are more appropriate. The bureaucratic organizational structure is likely to be most effective when an organization is operating in a stable environment. The flat and the boundaryless organizational structures are more likely to be effective when organizations operate in uncertain environments that require flexibility.

Work-flow analysis examines how work creates or adds value to ongoing business processes. It helps managers determine if work is being accomplished as efficiently as possible. Work-flow analysis can be very useful in TQM programs and business process reengineering.

Work: The Group Perspective

Flat and boundaryless organizational structures are likely to emphasize the use of self-managed teams (SMTs), small work units (between 6 and 18 employees) that are responsible for producing an entire product, a component, or an ongoing service. Businesses also use two other types of team designs.

Problem-solving teams consist of volunteers from a unit or department who meet one or two hours per week to discuss quality improvement, cost reduction, or improvement in the work environment. Special-purpose teams consist of members who span functional or organizational boundaries and whose purpose is to examine complex issues. Virtual teams allow geographically separated employees to collaborate together on projects or special problems by interacting on the computer or via other technology.

Work: The Individual Perspective

Motivation theory seeks to explain how different job designs can affect employee motivation. Four important work motivation theories are the two-factor, work adjustment, goal-setting, and job characteristics theories.

Designing Jobs and Conducting Job Analysis

Job design is the process of organizing work into the tasks required to perform a specific job. Different approaches to job design are work simplification, job enlargement, job rotation, job enrichment, and team-based job designs.

Job analysis is the systematic process of gathering and organizing information concerning the tasks, duties, and responsibilities of jobs. It is the basic building block of many important HR activities. Job analysis can be used for purposes of legal compliance, recruitment, selection, performance appraisal, compensation, and training and career development. Given the lack of a single best job-analysis technique, the choice of technique should be guided by the purposes of the analysis.

Job descriptions are statements of a job's essential duties, responsibilities, working conditions, and specifications. They are derived from job analysis. Job descriptions, which can be specific or general, have four elements: identification information, job summary, job duties and responsibilities, and job specifications and minimum qualifications.

The Flexible Workforce

Flexible work designs help managers deal with unexpected jolts in the environment and accommodate the needs of a diverse workforce. To maintain flexibility in the workforce, employers can use contingent workers (temporary employees, part-time employees, outsourced subcontractors, contract workers, and college interns). They can also alter work with flexible work schedules (flexible work hours, compressed workweeks, and telecommuting).

Human Resource Information Systems

Human resource information systems (HRIS) are systems used to collect, record, store, analyze, and retrieve relevant HR data. HRIS data matched with the appropriate computer software have many applications that support HR activities. These include applicant tracking, skills inventories, payroll management, and benefits administration. It is important that the HR department develop policies to protect the security of the HRIS data and the privacy rights of its employees.

Key Terms

boundaryless organizational structure, 48
bureaucratic organizational structure, 46
business process reengineering (BPR), 50
contingent workers, 68
core time, 73
core workers, 68
flat organizational structure, 48
flexible work hours, 73
flextime, 73

human resource information system (HRIS), 75
job analysis, 58
job description, 65
job design, 57
job enlargement, 57
job enrichment, 58
job rotation, 57
job sharing, 70
job specifications, 68
knowledge, skills, and abilities (KSAs), 60

motivation, 54
organizational structure, 45
problem-solving team, 52
self-managed team (SMT) force, 51
special-purpose team, 52
team, 51
telecommuting, 73
virtual team, 53
work flow, 45
work flow analysis, 49

Discussion Questions

1. Are job descriptions really necessary? What would happen if a company decided not to use any job descriptions at all?
2. Are managers likely to question the work commitment of their contingent workers? What might be the consequences for management when the majority of a company's workforce consists of temporary employees and contract workers?
3. What are the drawbacks to using flexible work hours from the organization's perspective? Compressed workweeks? Telecommuting? How should the HR department deal with these challenges?

4. Some management experts do not agree that a virtual team is really a team at all. Based on the definition of a team, what properties of a virtual team satisfy the definition of a team? Do any aspects of a virtual team give rise to doubts over whether it satisfies the definition of a true team? Suppose you needed to organize a virtual team of consultants working in different cities to do an important project for a client. What human resource management practices could you apply that would influence the virtual team members to behave as if they were on a true team, such as a self-managed or problem-solving team?

5. A recent trend more and more companies are embracing is to outsource all or most of their human resource management activities. Do you agree or disagree with this trend? What risks is a company taking when it decides to outsource its entire set of human resource management activities? Try to describe a situation in which it is more beneficial to retain most of the human resource management activities within a company so that HR is provided by the human resource management department.

6. In recent years, there has been an increase in the number of companies that have wrongly classified an "employee" as a "contract worker" and, consequently,

were taken to court by workers who believed they were entitled to certain rights and privileges enjoyed by individuals who were given "employee" status. What are some of the rights and privileges that are given to employees but not to contract workers? What advantages do employers gain with contract workers over regular employees? How could a contract worker prove to the courts that he or she is really an employee and was wrongly classified as a contract worker?

7. What is team-based job design? Would the use of team-based job designs influence the type of job description (specific or general) and the variety of tasks, duties, and responsibilities listed in the written job description?

8. Large U.S. companies such as Accenture, America Online and Dell have outsourced customer-service call centers to India. Customers use these call centers for help when they are having difficulty using the services provided by these companies. Many of the outsourced jobs at the call centers were entry-level jobs that had the potential to lead to higher-skilled jobs at those firms. Can you think of any ethical employment issues that managers who use offshore outsource suppliers in India or other low-labor-cost countries should be concerned about? If so, what are those issues?

There is a variety of additional material available on the Web site that accompanies this text. You can access this information by visiting the Web site at **www.prenhall.com/gomez.**

YOU MANAGE IT!   # Emerging Trends Case 2.1

Are American Employees Overworking?

As the boundaries between office hours and off-duty hours continue to blur, one in three American employees reports being chronically overworked, according to *Overwork in America*, a report issued by the nonprofit Families and Work Institute. The report indicated that the very factors giving companies a competitive edge—technology, multitasking, and globalization—may be undermining their workers' physical and emotional well-being. In addition, the report notes that one in three workers forfeit some of their paid vacation time, and two in five work while on vacation, in part because they cannot escape their demanding jobs.

"Technology has made staying in touch instantly much more available. That creates the expectation of an instant response," said Ellen Galinsky, president of the institute. "How many

times have you seen people at parties with their BlackBerry? Or sitting in church with their BlackBerry?" It is likely that these people are often answering their work e-mails.

A year and a half ago, when Albert So was principal engineer at a Silicon Valley–based game developer that had 15 employees, he routinely skipped dinner and did not get home in time to tuck his newborn son into bed. His boss called him at home on nights and weekends, urging him to drop what he was doing, including his father's birthday celebration, and fix a glitch. He didn't have to leave the house to comply, but he said, "that hid the problem." Albert So is happier now that he works elsewhere. But others remain miserable. Employees who toil without enough downtime to rest and recover make more mistakes, exhibit poorer health, and show more symptoms of clinical depression, the study reports.

Although rank-and-file employees may not have much choice, executives may also succumb to work overload, even though they may deny it. Rand Morimoto, president of Convergent Computing in Oakland, California, spends more than 100 hours a week bolstering the image of his Internet security company, which has 65 employees. Even though he receives 30 vacation days a year, he uses only five of them—for Christmas and a few other special occasions. "The tough part about vacation is I work twice as many hours before I leave on vacation to prepare to go," he said. "And then when I get back, I work twice as many hours to catch up."

Despite Morimoto's nonstop schedule, he does not consider himself overworked. "I work for myself, and I choose to work as hard as I do," he said. "In this economy, you've got to work hard to keep your job."

Critical Thinking Questions

1. Why should employers be concerned when employees overwork? Shouldn't companies encourage their employees to overwork?

2. The case suggests that technology makes employees easier to contact away from the job so that the boundaries between work and leisure time are less defined. Why can't employees just decide to not answer the e-mail on the BlackBerry or voice mail on their mobile phone until the next day when they arrive at work?

Team Exercise

Form a small group with several of your class members and develop some "best practices" that will reduce the need for employees to feel compelled to overwork, so that they can maintain a healthy balance between their personal life and work life. Here are some possible areas to explore when developing a list of best practices: (1) using technology; (2) adapting flexible work schedules; (3) educating employees about healthy lifestyles; and (4) dealing with expectations concerning employees' off-duty hours. Be prepared to present your best practices to other members of your class.

Experiential Exercise

In this exercise, you need to gather some background information from other students to determine whether they appear to be overworked. Interview some classmates and friends about their work schedules. Find out how many hours per week they: (1) attend classes; (2) study; (3) work at part-time jobs; (4) answer e-mails and other communications from classmates. What conclusions can you draw? Are students at your university or college overworked? When is a student's work schedule unbalanced? What do you recommend to students to attain a healthy balance in their lives?

Source: Wong, N. (2005, March 16). Overworked—and angry about it. *www.siliconvalley.com/mld/siliconvalley/business/columnists/.*

Customer-Driven HR Case 2.2 — YOU MANAGE IT!

Employees Write Their Own Job Titles for Customers

The breaking down of hierarchies and barriers within companies due to the Internet and the need to become more customer focused has influenced the practice of using job titles. The latest idea is to give two job titles to an employee: One job title reflects the employee's internal role within the company and the second job title is a customer-focused one. The customer-focused job title is descriptive and individualistic and lets employees have fun and creativity with designing their job title. Here are some creative examples of customer-focused job titles:

- **Chief Talent Scout:** Xcelerate, a Fort Lauderdale, Florida–based company uses this title for the person in charge of recruiting.
- **Director of Privacy:** This title is used at DoubleClick, an Internet services company, for the person responsible to protect customers' privacy as well as the company's own intellectual property such as copyrighted software code.

- **Director of Consumer Delight & Loyalty:** San Francisco–based Relect.com uses this title for the employee who is responsible for marketing new products and services.
- **Senior Vice President of Great People:** This title has been used in several firms for the top executive responsible for human resources.
- **Sultan of Sound Bites:** This title has been used in a large public company to communicate information to members of the investment community regarding company performance and future business prospects.

Critical Thinking Questions

1. How important are job titles? What would happen if there were no job titles? What would happen if everyone in a company had the same job title, such as "associate"? Some companies actually have such a policy.

2. What problems do you foresee when a company adopts a policy of customer-focused job titles and lets employees develop their own unique titles? How should the process of developing customer-focused job titles be managed?

Team Exercise

Assume you are the manager of engineering at this telecommunications company and a group of engineers is requesting that you allow them to use customer-focused job titles. Some examples of the titles that they have proposed include "thought leader," "czar of debugging," and "inventor extraordinaire." Discuss this proposal with your team members and develop an approach to deal with this employee request. Determine first whether you will encourage or discourage employees to use customer-focused job titles and explain the basis for your decision. Next, decide what guidelines you will use to manage the adoption of job titles if you have decided that it makes sense to use customer-focused job titles.

Experiential Exercise

Think of a job or internship you hold or have held. Develop a customer-focused job title for this job or internship. Try to come up with a unique and creative job title that describes what value you gave to the customers for the work you performed. The customers could be internal (managers or employees), external (clients of the company), or both. Next, find a partner and exchange the customer-focused job titles for your respective jobs. Take turns and tell your partner what the customer-based job title means to you and vice versa. What does the customer-based job title that you used say about your experience on the job or internship? What does it say about your partner's work experience? What do you think think would happen if organizations used customer-based job titles for all their jobs?

Source: Conlin, M. (2000, August 28). Write your own job title. *Business-Week*, 148.

YOU MANAGE IT!   # Global Case 2.3

The Dilemma of Offshore Outsourcing

When Michael Calderone started his online coffee business in 2002, an in-house customer-service department was not feasible. He had no experience running a call center, and his start-up company, SmilesCoffee.com, based in Henderson, Nevada, could not afford one. So Calderone decided to outsource a call center.

An experience with a local outsource call center in Utah was a disaster. SmilesCoffee's selling point is freshness. Beans are shipped 95 percent roasted, and customers complete the process in their microwave ovens, which makes for an extra-tasty brew. However, sometimes new customers find the process confusing and need some hand-holding. Customers had difficulty getting through to the outsource call center and when they did make contact some of the information they received from the service representatives was inaccurate.

Calderone found another outsource provider—one in the Phillipines. Now, nine dedicated and friendly representatives assist SmilesCoffee customers with roasting issues, shipping questions, and account information. Better still, the improved service comes at a lower cost. The call center in the Phillipines pays representatives about $3,600 a year, a fraction of what call-center employees cost in Utah. Despite his success with the Phillipines' call center, Calderone has mixed feelings about using offshore labor. But he knows that if SmilesCoffee is to remain competitives, he probably has little choice.

Offshore outsourcing is a trend that affects both large and small businesses in the United States and other developed countries. In 2004, the last two Levi Strauss manufacturing plants in the United States closed their doors. The bulk of the company's jeans will be manufactured by suppliers in 50 other countries in Asia and the Caribbean. It is the end of an era for an America icon—Levi jeans have been manufactured in the United States since 1873.

India is without a doubt the world's largest destination for offshore outsourcing services for companies with head offices in North America, Europe, and Asia. India's business process outsourcing industry, which includes call centers, accounted for $3.6 billion in sales in 2003 and is forecasted to become a $21 billion to $24 billion industry by 2008. The most obvious benefits of offshore outsourcing are signficiant savings and often improved quality.

Critical Thinking Questions

1. What are the disadvantages to the employer of offshore outsourcing?
2. Why do you think Michael Calderone had mixed feelings about using an offshore outsource company in the Phillipines?

Team Exercise

Form a small group of four or five students and discuss the ethical issues related to Michael Calderone's decision to use an offshore call center in the Phillipines. Compare Calderone's choice to Levi Strauss' decision to outsource all its jeans manufacturing facilities outside the United States. Should it matter if a company is large or small when it decides to outsource jobs and opportunities to another country that offers much lower wages? Should any other factors influence the offshore outsource decision? Be prepared to present your findings to the class.

Experiential Exercise

Find a partner to enact the following role-play situation related to an outsourcing decision. One role is that of the owner of a small company. The other role is that of a call-center service employee who works at the owner's firm. The business owner has scheduled a meeting with the call-center employee to inform him or her that all call-center jobs are going to be outsourced to a firm in India. The business owner tries to present a rationale for the outsourcing of the jobs and hopes that the call-center employee will understand why his or her job will be eliminated. The call-center employee reacts to this decision of having his or her job eliminated. Both role players should enact their roles according to the way they would interpret the situation if it happened to them. The role-play should continue for about five minutes before stopping or end earlier if a resolution is reached. The partners should be prepared to report back to the class about what they learned about offshore outsourcing from the role-play experience.

Sources: Wahlgren, E. (2004, April). The outsourcing dilemma. *Inc. Magazine*, 41–42; Doh, J. (2005). Offshore outsourcing: Implications for international business and strategic management theory and practice. *Journal of Management Studies*, 695–704; Strankowski, D. (2004, March/April). 1-800-Offshoring: White-collar outsourcing wave crashes hard on foreign shores. *Colorado Company*, 58–59; *The Economist* (2004, November 13). A world of work: A survey of outsourcing, 10.

Customer-Driven HR Case 2.4 — YOU MANAGE IT!

Writing a Job Description

Job descriptions are useful tools that document job content and can aid decisions for recruitment, staffing, training, compensation, and human resource planning. The purpose of this skill-building activity is to give you some experience writing a job description. In preparation, carefully read the section in this chapter titled "Job Descriptions" and refer to the figures in that section that provide examples of a specific job description and a general job description.

Next, select a job and write a job description. Ideally, your job description should be based on a job you are familiar with—one at which you are currently employed or recently experienced is the best candidate for this exercise. It could be a part-time or full-time job. If you have no work experience to draw from for this exercise, then ask a friend or relative to provide detailed information about his or her job.

Once you have chosen the job for this exercise you are ready to begin.

Critical Thinking Questions

1. What do you see as the main differences between a specific job description and a general job description?
2. Suppose several people are employed in the same job as the one for which you are writing a job description. Would it be necessary to write a different job description for each person who works in the same job?

3. Carefully follow the format for the "Specific Job Description" provided in Figure 2.6 when writing the job description for the job you selected. Make sure that you include in your job description the following elements: (1) job title and identification information, (2) job summary, (3) job duties and responsibilities, (4) job requirements, and (5) minimum qualifications. Check your work to make sure the style of your job description matches the example in the text as closely as possible.

Team Exercise

Work with a partner or a small group of three to four people and exchange job descriptions with a partner or group member. Read each other's job descriptions and make suggestions for improvements based on the example provided in the text. Take turns discussing the suggested revisions with your partner or group so that each person receives some feedback on his or her job description. Make revisions to your job description as needed to improve it. It is normal for a job description to go through several revisions before the document is finished. Now examine the job description you just wrote and revised. Discuss with your partner or group how this job description could be applied to making decisions in the organization that offers the job. Next, discuss what additional steps would be needed to finalize the job description before it could actually be used as a basis for employment decisions in a company.

Experiential Exercise

The purpose of this experiential exercise is to learn how managers actually use job descriptions in their organizations. First, you will need to get the names and contact information for three to five managers you know from your work experience or from personal contacts. Or, ask a professor or someone in the career development office at your school for a few names of managers. You can contact the managers in person, by e-mail, or on the telephone. Ask each what uses they have for job descriptions in their organizations. Also, ask the manager how important job descriptions are for making human resource decisions in their organization—and follow up one more time by asking them to explain why they think they are important (or not). Record the responses and summarize your findings. Be prepared to share your findings with other members of the class. Did you find a diversity of opinion from the managers about how they use job descriptions and how important they find them to be? If you found a diverse set of responses, what do you think accounted for this variety of opinions?

Understanding Equal Opportunity and the Legal Environment

Challenges

After reading this chapter, you should be able to deal more effectively with the following challenges:

1 **Explain** why compliance with HR law is an important part of doing business.

2 **Follow** changes in HR law, regulation, and court decisions.

3 **Manage** within equal employment opportunity laws and understand the rationale and requirements of affirmative action.

4 **Make** managerial decisions that will avoid legal liability.

5 **Know** when to seek the advice of legal counsel on HRM matters.

Which Company Would You Rather Work For?

Company A

An employee at a large, Silicon Valley computer systems company has filed a sexual harassment lawsuit against her boss claiming he repeatedly harassed her and withheld a pay raise because she would not accept his romantic advances. The lawsuit claims that the woman in the lawsuit was harassed by her boss at various locations and through e-mail messages. When she resisted, her boss allegedly said she was performing her work poorly and threatened her with termination. When she complained to the HR department, the company's staff failed to adequately investigate her claims and did little to help her.[1]

Company B

A female employee of a convention services firm was subjected to a company vice president's crude sexual comments and gestures. When she asked the vice president to stop the offensive behavior, he retaliated and profanely criticized her work. After the female employee reported this harassment to the director of human resources, an investigation followed and the director found the complaint valid. The firm gave the vice president a written reprimand and suspended him without pay for 7 days. The employer promised the female employee she would never have to work with the vice president again and offered to pay for counseling she might need related to the incident.[2]

THE MANAGERIAL PERSPECTIVE

Managers must understand the legal issues that affect the practice of HRM because many of their decisions are constrained to some extent by law. They should consider legal issues when making the following decisions:

- Which employees to hire
- How to compensate employees
- What benefits to offer
- How to accommodate employees with dependents
- How and when to fire employees

Legal constraints on HR practices have become increasingly more complex, in large part because of new employment laws and recent court decisions that interpret existing laws. The new employment laws mainly affect people with disabilities and those who seek a medical leave of absence from work. The court decisions relate to numerous issues such as worker safety and sexual harassment. Changes in the law have made HR decisions more difficult and risky—thereby increasing the cost of poor decisions.

HR managers consult and advise managers about the legal aspects of a personnel decision. Legal concerns are not the only priority in employment decisions but are heavily considered along with other factors such as timeliness, product quality, and economic efficiency. The dynamism of the legal environment means that managers must seek the advice of HR specialists who, in turn, add value to management decisions with their expertise in employment laws and regulations.

In this chapter, we examine the various aspects of HR law and regulation. First, we look at why managers must understand the HR legal environment. Next we explore several challenges that managers face when they try to comply with the law. Then we discuss *equal employment opportunity (EEO)* law, the enforcement mechanisms in place to ensure compliance, and several other laws that affect HRM. Finally, we describe ways for the effective manager to avoid potential legal pitfalls.

We need to start with a caveat. As with any legal issue you face, you should seek the advice of a qualified attorney to grapple with specific legal questions or problems relating to HRM. There are many lawyers who specialize in labor and employment law. However, you should not feel that you cannot make *any* decisions without specific legal counsel, and it is a mistake to let legal considerations become so important that you end up making poor business decisions. One goal of this chapter is to give you enough information to know when you need to seek legal counsel.

Why Understanding the Legal Environment Is Important

Understanding and complying with HR law is important for three reasons. It helps you do the right thing, realize the limitations of your firm's HR and legal departments, and minimize your firm's potential liability.

Doing the Right Thing

First and foremost, compliance with the law is important because it is the right thing to do. Although you may disagree with the specific applications of some of the laws we discuss, the primary requirement of all these laws is to mandate good management practice. The earliest of the EEO laws requires that male and female employees who do the same job for the same organization receive the same pay. This is the right thing to do. The most recent EEO law requires that applicants or employees who are able to perform a job should not be discriminated against because of a disability. This, too, is the right thing to do.

Operating within these laws has benefits beyond simple legal compliance. Compensation practices that discriminate against women not only create potential legal liability but also lead to poor employee morale and low job satisfaction, which can in turn lead to poor job performance. Discriminating against qualified employees with disabilities makes no sense; in discriminating, the organization hurts itself by not hiring and retaining the best employees. McDonald's has taken the lead in hiring youth with learning disabilities. This is socially responsible and has created a positive impression among many customers.[3]

Realizing the Limitations of the HR and Legal Departments

A firm's HR department has considerable responsibilities with respect to HR law. These include keeping records, writing and implementing good HR policies, and monitoring the firm's HR decisions. However, if managers make poor decisions, the HR department will not always be able to resolve the situation. For instance, if a manager gives a poor employee an excellent performance rating, the HR department cannot undo the damage and provide the documentation necessary to support a decision to terminate the employee.

Nor can a firm's legal department magically solve problems created by managers. One of the key functions of legal counsel, whether internal or external, is to try to limit damage after it has occurred. Managers should work to prevent the damage from happening in the first place.

Members of the HR department support managers who have to make HR decisions with legal implications. HR staff may monitor managers' decisions or act as consultants. For example:

■ A supervisor wants to discharge an employee for unexcused absences and consults the HR department to determine whether there is enough evidence to discharge this person for "just cause." The HR department can help the manager and the company avoid a lawsuit for "wrongful discharge."
■ A manager receives a phone call from a company that is inquiring about the qualification of a former employee. The manager is not sure how much information in the former employee's work history to reveal, so she seeks the HR department's advice. HR can help the manager and the company avoid a lawsuit for defamation (damage to an employee's reputation as a result of giving out false information to a third party).

Limiting Potential Liability

Considerable financial liabilities can occur when HR laws are broken or perceived to be broken. Typical court awards to victims of age, sex, race, or disability discrimination range from $50,000 to $300,000, depending on the size of the employer. Nonetheless, individual awards can actually be much larger. In 2001, the U.S. federal appeals court upheld a jury verdict awarding Troy Swinton $1.03 million for punitive damages, back wages, and emotional stress for racial discrimination suffered at U.S. Mat in Woodinville, Washington. The only African American of 140 employees, Swinton was subjected to a regular stream of racial "jokes" and slurs during his six months of employment.[4]

Organizations may also face a public relations nightmare when discrimination charges are publicized. In highly publicized cases in the early 1990s, several individual store managers and employees of Denny's restaurant chain were alleged to have discriminated against African American customers. Not only did the company subsequently have to pay $46 million to African American patrons and $8.7 million in legal fees to settle these complaints, but the company's image with customers was damaged as well.[5] In recent years, though, Denny's has made major strides: As of 2005, minorities owned 45 percent of Denny's 1,011 franchised restaurants. African Americans owned 33, Hispanics owned 66, and Asians owned 354. In 1993, only one franchised restaurant was owned by an African American. Further, *Fortune* has consistently recognized Denny's at the top ranks of its survey of "America's 50 Best Companies for Minorities." Denny's was ranked number one in 2000 and 2001, number three in 2002, and number five in 2004.[6]

A lawsuit that has not yet been resolved could include the claims of 1.6 million women who have worked at Wal-Mart since 1998. The lawsuit alleges that women have been underpaid and underpromoted relative to their male peers. The settlement in the lawsuit could cost Wal-Mart billions of dollars. At present, the company is fighting these allegations.[7]

Challenges to Legal Compliance

Several challenges confront managers attempting to comply with HR law. These include a dynamic legal landscape, the complexity of regulations, conflicting strategies for fair employment, and unintended consequences.

A Dynamic Legal Landscape

A quick scan of the Appendix to this chapter clearly demonstrates that many laws affect the practice of HRM. Several have been passed in the last decade.

The opinions handed down in court cases add to this dynamic environment. For example, in 1971 the Supreme Court handed down a landmark civil rights decision in a case titled *Griggs v. Duke Power.*[8] Among other things, this decision placed a heavy burden of proof on the employer in an employment discrimination case. Normally, a Supreme Court decision sets a precedent that the Court is then very reluctant to overturn. However, in a 1989 case, the Court revised the standard it had set in *Griggs,* making it more difficult for an employee to win a discrimination case.[9] Then, in 1991, Congress passed a lengthy amendment to the Civil Rights Act of 1964 (discussed later in this chapter) that returned to the burden-of-proof standard established in the *Griggs* decision.

These rapid changes are not limited to issues of courtroom procedure. Sexual harassment regulations were adopted by the Equal Employment Opportunity Commission (EEOC) in the early 1980s and accepted by the Supreme Court in 1986. Since then, companies, lawyers, and judges have been attempting to figure out just what they mean and require. Opinions on these issues vary widely, which means that different courts have made differing decisions about what constitutes sexual harassment. Until the Supreme Court makes several more rulings, or Congress clarifies the underlying law, managers will need to pay close attention to the unfolding developments.

The Complexity of Laws

HR law, like most other types of law, is very complex. Each individual law is accompanied by a set of regulations that can be lengthy. For instance, the Americans with Disabilities Act (1990) is spelled out in a technical manual that is several hundred pages long. To make matters even more complex, one analysis has concluded that there may be as many as 1,000 different disabilities affecting over 43 million Americans.[10] It is very difficult for an expert in HR law, much less a manager, to understand all the possible implications of a particular law.

Nonetheless, the gist of most HR law is fairly straightforward. Managers should be able to understand the basic intention of all such laws without too much difficulty and can easily obtain the working knowledge they need to comply with those laws in the vast majority of situations.

Conflicting Strategies for Fair Employment

Society at large, political representatives, government employees, and judges all have different views regarding the best ways to achieve equitable HR laws. One of the major debates in this area centers on the competing strategies used to further the goal of **fair employment**—the situation in which employment decisions are not affected by illegal discrimination. The plain language of most civil rights law prohibits employers from making decisions about employees (hiring, performance appraisal, compensation, and so on) on the basis of race, sex, or age. Thus, one strategy to reach the goal of fair employment is for employment decisions to be made without regard to these characteristics. A second strategy, **affirmative action**, aims to accomplish the goal of fair employment by urging employers to hire certain groups of people who were discriminated against in the past. Thus, affirmative action programs require that employment decisions be made, at least in part, on the basis of characteristics such as race, sex, or age. Obviously, there is a conflict between these two strategies—one proposing that only "blind" hiring practices are fair, the other proposing that fairness requires organizations to make an effort to employ certain categories of people (Figure 3.1).

While the battle resulting from these competing strategies is being played out throughout society, the main legal struggle has occurred in the Supreme Court. Based on a series of Supreme Court decisions, the following conclusions seem warranted:

- The affirmative action strategy has been upheld. Specifically, employers are permitted to base employment decisions, in part, on a person's race, sex, age, and certain other characteristics.
- To be permissible, the employment decision cannot be made solely on the basis of these characteristics. Further, the people considered for the position should be "essentially equally qualified" on job-relevant characteristics before these other characteristics are permitted to play a role in the employment decision.
- The one situation in which affirmative action is not permitted is during layoffs. For instance, a white teacher should not be laid off to save the job of a Latino teacher, even if this means that minorities will be underrepresented in the postlayoff workforce.
- Courts may order an affirmative action program with specific quotas when an organization has a history of blatant discrimination.

Fair employment
The goal of EEO legislation and regulation: a situation in which employment decisions are not affected by illegal discrimination.

Affirmative action
A strategy intended to achieve fair employment by urging employers to hire certain groups of people who were discriminated against in the past.

A Question of Ethics

Is it ethical to refuse to give preferential treatment to minorities and women, who have been widely discriminated against in the past?

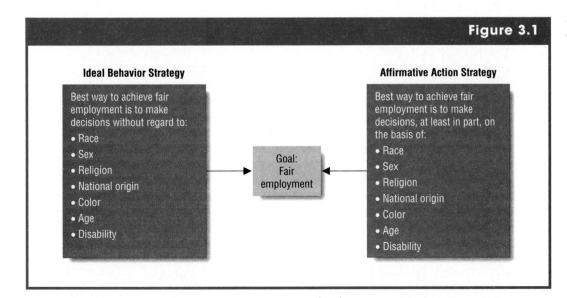

Figure 3.1

Competing Strategies for Fair Employment

Unintended Consequences

It is very common for a law, a government program, or an organizational policy to have numerous unanticipated consequences, some of which turn out to be negative. HR law is certainly not immune to this phenomenon. For example, the Americans with Disabilities Act (ADA) was primarily intended to increase the possibility of employment for people with physical and/or mental disabilities. However, since the law has gone into effect, job applicants have filed relatively few ADA complaints. Rather, current employees injured on the job have filed the majority of complaints. Traditionally, state workers' compensation laws (see Chapter 12) regulate the benefits given to employees injured on the job, including income continuation. Nobody intended the ADA to become a national workers' compensation law, but that appears to be just what is happening. The challenge to managers is to anticipate and deal with both the intended and unintended consequences of law.

Equal Employment Opportunity Laws

The laws that affect HR issues can be divided into two broad categories: (1) equal employment opportunity laws and (2) everything else. We will spend the bulk of this chapter on the EEO laws because these are the ones that most affect a manager's day-to-day behavior. In addition, the EEO laws cut across almost every other issue that we discuss in this text. The other laws tend to be more specifically focused, and we discuss them in the context in which they apply. For instance, we discuss the laws governing union activities in Chapter 15 and the Occupational Safety and Health Act (OSHA) in Chapter 16.

The major EEO laws are the Equal Pay Act of 1963, Title VII of the Civil Rights Act of 1964, the Age Discrimination in Employment Act of 1967, and the Americans with Disabilities Act of 1990. The Civil Rights Act of 1964 has been amended through the years, most recently in 1991. The theme that ties these laws together is simple: Employment decisions should not be based on characteristics such as race, sex, age, or disability.

The Equal Pay Act of 1963

Equal Pay Act (1963)
The law that requires the same pay for men and women who do the same job in the same organization.

The first of the civil rights laws was the **Equal Pay Act**, which became law in 1963. It requires that men and women who do the same job in the same organization should receive the same pay. "Same pay" means that no difference is acceptable.

Determining whether two employees are doing the same job can be difficult. The law specifies that jobs are the same if they are equal in terms of skill, effort, responsibility, and working conditions. Thus, it is permissible to pay one employee more than another if the first employee has significant extra job duties, such as supervisory responsibility. Pay can also be different for different work shifts. The law also specifies that equal pay is required only for jobs held in the same geographical region. This allows an organization to make allowances for the local cost of living and the fact that it might be harder to find qualified employees in some areas.

The law contains several explicit exceptions. First, it does not prohibit the use of a merit pay plan. That is, an employer can pay a man more if he is doing a better job than his female co-worker. In addition, companies are permitted to pay for differences in quantity and quality of production. Seniority plans also are exempted; a company that ties pay rates to seniority can pay a man more if he has been with the company longer than a female employee. Finally, the law indicates that any factor other than sex may be used to justify different pay rates.[11]

When the Equal Pay Act was passed, the average female employee earned only about 59 cents for each dollar earned by the average male worker. While this gap has narrowed in the intervening years, to about 77 cents in 2004,[12] this average differential remains troubling, and in some jobs it is much higher. For instance, 30-year-old male sales representatives earned $60,000 in 2001, whereas their female counterparts in sales, doing the same amount and same kind of work, earned only $36,000 at the same age.[13] Some states, such as Washington and Illinois, have responded to this issue by requiring that civil service employers pay equally for work of comparable worth.[14]

Understanding equal pay and comparable worth requires more knowledge of compensation decisions, so we will return to these issues in Chapter 10.

Title VII of the Civil Rights Act of 1964

Although not the oldest of the civil rights laws, **Title VII of the Civil Rights Act of 1964** is universally seen as the most important passed to date. This law was enacted in the midst of the seething civil rights conflicts of the 1960s, one year after the civil rights march on Washington at which Dr. Martin Luther King, Jr., delivered his "I Have a Dream" speech.

Before passage of the Civil Rights Act of 1964, open and explicit discrimination based on race, particularly against African Americans, was widespread. *Jim Crow laws* legalized racial segregation in many southern states. The act itself had several sections, or titles, all of which aim to prohibit discrimination in various parts of society. For instance, Title IX applies to educational institutions. Title VII applies to employers that have 15 or more employees, as well as to employment agencies and labor unions.

General Provisions

Title VII prohibits employers from basing employment decisions on a person's race, color, religion, sex, or national origin. The heart of the law, Section 703(a), is reprinted in Figure 3.2. Note that employment decisions include "compensation, terms, conditions, or privileges of employment."

Title VII clearly covers persons of any race, any color, any religion, both sexes, and any national origin. However, as court cases and regulations have grown up around this law, so has the legal theory of a **protected class**. This theory states that groups of people who suffered discrimination in the past require, and should be given, special protection by the judicial system. Under Title VII, the protected classes are African Americans, Asian Americans, Latinos, Native Americans, and women. While it is not impossible for a nonprotected-class plaintiff to win a Title VII case, it is highly unusual.

Discrimination Defined

Despite the negative connotation the word has acquired, **discrimination** simply means making distinctions—in the HR context, distinctions among people. Therefore, even the most progressive companies are constantly discriminating when they decide who should be promoted, who should receive a merit raise, and who should be laid off. What Title VII prohibits is making discriminations among people based on their race, color, religion, sex, or national origin. Specifically, it makes two types of discrimination illegal.

The first type of discrimination, **disparate treatment**, occurs when an employer treats an employee differently because of his or her protected-class status. Disparate treatment is the kind of treatment that you probably first think of when considering discrimination. For instance, Robert Frazier, who is a bricklayer's assistant and an African American, was fired after quarreling with a white bricklayer. However, Frazier's employer did not discipline the white bricklayer at all, even though he had injured Frazier by throwing a broken brick at him. A federal court judge ruled that Frazier had been treated more harshly because of his race and, thus, suffered from disparate treatment discrimination.[15]

Title VII
Section of the Civil Rights Act of 1964 that applies to employment decisions; mandates that employment decisions not be based on race, color, religion, sex, or national origin.

Protected class
A group of people who suffered discrimination in the past and who are given special protection by the judicial system.

Discrimination
The making of distinctions. In HR context, the making of distinctions among people.

Disparate treatment
Discrimination that occurs when individuals are treated differently because of their membership in a protected class.

Figure 3.2

Title VII of the Civil Rights Act of 1964

Section 703. (a) It shall be an unlawful employment practice for an employer—

(1) to fail or refuse to hire or to discharge any individual, or otherwise to discriminate against any individual with respect to his compensation, terms, conditions, or privileges of employment, because of such individual's race, color, religion, sex, or national origin; or

(2) to limit, segregate, or classify his employees or applicants for employment in any way which would deprive or tend to deprive any individual of employment opportunities or otherwise adversely affect his status as an employee, because of such individual's race, color, religion, sex, or national origin.

Adverse impact
Discrimination that occurs when the equal application of an employment standard has an unequal effect on one or more protected classes. Also called *disparate impact.*

The second type of discrimination, **adverse impact** (also called *disparate impact*), occurs when the same standard is applied to all applicants or employees, but that standard affects a protected class more negatively (adversely). For example, most police departments around the United States have dropped the requirement that officers be of a minimum height because the equal application of that standard has an adverse impact on women, Latinos, and Asian Americans (that is, any given height standard will rule out more women than men, and more Latinos and Asian Americans than African Americans and nonminority individuals). Figure 3.3 summarizes the distinctions between disparate treatment and adverse impact.

The adverse impact definition of discrimination was confirmed in a very important 1971 Supreme Court case that we have already discussed, *Griggs v. Duke Power.*[16] Griggs was an African American employee of the Duke Power Company in North Carolina. He and other African American employees were refused promotions because Duke Power, on the day that Title VII took effect, had implemented promotion standards that included a high school diploma and passing scores on two tests, one of general intellectual ability and one of mechanical ability. The Supreme Court ruled that such standards, even though applied equally to all employees, were discriminatory because (1) they had an adverse impact on a protected class (in this case, African Americans) and (2) Duke Power was unable to show that the standards were related to subsequent job performance.

Griggs v. Duke Power has some important implications. Under the *Griggs* ruling, courts may find that a company is acting in a discriminatory manner even though it works hard to ensure that its HR decision processes are applied equally to all employees. If the outcome is such that a protected class suffers from adverse impact, then the organization may be required to demonstrate that the standards used in the decision process were related to the job. In October 1993, Domino's Pizza lost a case in which it attempted to defend a "no-beard policy." The appellate court ruled that the policy had an adverse effect on African Americans because almost half of male African Americans suffer from a genetic condition that makes shaving very painful or impossible. Almost no white men suffer from this malady. Therefore, African Americans are more adversely affected by this requirement than whites are.[17] Domino's could have won this case if it had shown that not having a beard was necessary for good job performance. It could not, so the court ruled the no-beard policy a violation of Title VII.

In an earlier (1975) case, *Albemarle Paper Company v. Moody,* the Supreme Court established procedures to help employers determine when it is appropriate to use employment tests as a basis for hiring or promoting employees. The Court ruled that employers can use an employment test only when they can demonstrate that the test is a valid predictor of job performance. Thus, *Albemarle* places the burden of proof on the employer to prove that a contested test (for example, a test that has an adverse impact on a protected class) or other selection tool is a valid predictor of job success.[18]

Two Kinds of Discrimination

Figure 3.3

Disparate Treatment	Adverse Impact
Direct discrimination	Indirect discrimination
Unequal treatment	Unequal consequences or results
Decision rules with a racial/sexual premise or cause	Decision rules with racial/sexual consequences or results
Intentional discrimination	Unintentional discrimination
Prejudiced actions	Neutral actions
Different standards for different groups	Same standards, but different consequences for different groups

Source: Adapted from Ledvinka, J., and Scarpello, V. G. (1991). *Federal regulation of personnel and human resource management* (2nd ed.). Boston: PWS-Kent. Reproduced with the permission of South-Western College Publishing. Copyright 1991 by PWS-Kent. All rights reserved.

Defense of Discrimination Charges

When a discrimination case makes it to court, it is the responsibility of the plaintiff (the person bringing the complaint) to show reasonable evidence that discrimination has occurred. The legal term for this type of evidence is *prima facie,* which means "on its face." In a disparate treatment lawsuit, to establish a prima facie case the plaintiff only needs to show that the organization did not hire her (or him), that she appeared to be qualified for the job, and that the company continued to try to hire someone else for the position after rejecting her. This set of requirements, which originated from a court case brought against the McDonnell-Douglas Corporation, is often called the *McDonnell-Douglas test.*[19] In an adverse impact lawsuit, the plaintiff only needs to show that a restricted policy is in effect—that is, that a disproportionate number of protected-class individuals were affected by the employment decisions.

One important EEOC provision for establishing a prima facie case that an HR practice is discriminatory and has an adverse impact is the **four-fifths rule**. The four-fifths rule comes from the EEOC's *Uniform Guidelines on Employee Selection Procedures,* an important document that informs employers how to establish selection procedures that are valid and, therefore, legal.[20]

The four-fifths rule compares the hiring rates of protected classes to those of majority groups (such as white men) in the organization. It assumes that an HR practice has an adverse impact if the hiring rate of a protected class is less than four-fifths the hiring rate of a majority group. For example, assume that an accounting firm hires 50 percent of all its white male job applicants for entry-level accounting positions. Also assume that only 25 percent of all African American male job applicants are hired for the same job. Applying the four-fifths rule, there is prima facie evidence that the accounting firm has discriminatory hiring practices because 50 percent $\times$ 4/5 = 40 percent, and 40 percent exceeds the 25 percent hiring rate for African American men.

Once the plaintiff has established a prima facie case, the burden of proof switches to the organization. In other words, the employer is then placed in a position of proving that illegal discrimination did not occur. This can be very tough to prove. Suppose that a sales manager interviews two applicants for a sales position, a man and a woman. Their qualifications look very much the same on paper. However, in the interview the man seems to be more motivated. He is hired, and the rejected female applicant files a disparate treatment discrimination suit. She can, almost automatically, establish a prima facie case (she was qualified, she was not hired, the company did hire someone else). Now the sales manager has to prove that the decision was based on a judgment about the applicant's motivation, not on the applicant's sex.

Although these cases can be difficult, employers do win their share of them. There are four basic defenses that an employer can use:

- **Job relatedness.** The employer has to show that the decision was made for job-related reasons. This is much easier to do if the employer has written documentation to support and explain the decision. In our example, the manager will be asked to give specific job-related reasons for the decision to hire the man for the sales job. As we noted in Chapter 2, job descriptions are particularly useful for documenting the job-related reasons for any particular HR decision.
- **Bona fide occupational qualification.** A **bona fide occupational qualification (BFOQ)** is a characteristic that must be present in all employees for a particular job. For instance, a film director is permitted to consider only females for parts that call for an actress.
- **Seniority.** Employment decisions that are made in the context of a formal seniority system are permitted, even if they discriminate against certain protected-class individuals. However this defense requires the seniority system to be well established and applied universally, not just in some circumstances.
- **Business necessity.** The employer can use the business necessity defense when the employment practice is necessary for the safe and efficient operation of the organization and there is an overriding business purpose for the discriminatory practice. For example, an employee drug test may adversely impact a disadvantaged minority group, but the need for safety (to protect other employees and customers) may justify the drug-testing procedure.

Of these four defenses, the job-relatedness defense is the most common because of the strict limitations courts have placed on the BFOQ, seniority, and business necessity defenses.

When an employer requires employees to speak only English at all times on the job, this *speak-English-only rule* may violate EEOC law, unless the employer can show that the rule is

Four-fifths rule
An EEOC provision for establishing a prima facie case that an HR practice is discriminatory and has an adverse impact. A practice has an adverse impact if the hiring rate of a protected class is less than four-fifths the hiring rate of a majority group.

Bona fide occupational qualification (BFOQ)
A characteristic that must be present in all employees for a particular job.

necessary for conducting business.[21] Similarly an employer may not deny an individual an employment opportunity, such as a job or promotion, if the individual speaks with an accent, unless the employer can show that speaking with an accent has a detrimental effect on job performance.

Title VII and Pregnancy

In 1978, Congress amended Title VII to state explicitly that women are protected from discrimination based either on their ability to become pregnant or on their actual pregnancy. The *Pregnancy Discrimination Act of 1978* requires employers to treat an employee who is pregnant in the same way as any other employee who has a medical condition.[22] For instance, an employer cannot deny sick leave for pregnancy-related illnesses such as morning sickness if the employer allows sick leave for other medical conditions such as nausea-related illnesses. The law also states that a company cannot design an employee health benefit plan that provides no coverage for pregnancy. These are strict requirements, as evidenced by the following cases.

In one case that applied the Pregnancy Discrimination Act, a woman who worked at the U.S. Postal Service (USPS) claimed she was subjected to pregnancy discrimination when she was not reappointed after she had served a one-year appointment. The USPS cited her absences from work and that she was considered a high-risk pregnancy and should be doing only light-duty work. However, the EEOC found the complainant was treated less favorably than comparative employees based on her pregnancy. The basis of the EEOC's ruling was that the law requires the employer to treat pregnant employees just as it treats other employees with temporary impairments.[23]

A female police officer in Pinellas Park, Florida, claimed she experienced pregnancy discrimination when she was demoted to dispatcher after becoming pregnant and requesting light duty. She showed evidence that her male supervisor informed her that he was forced to hire women, and he specifically gave women the least desirable shifts and days off to punish them if they became pregnant. The city settled in favor of the complainant and reinstated her as police officer.[24]

Sexual Harassment

The Title VII prohibition of sex-based discrimination has also been interpreted to prohibit sexual harassment. In contrast to protection for pregnancy, sexual harassment protection was not an amendment to the law but rather a 1980 EEOC interpretation of the law.[25] The EEOC's definition of sexual harassment is given in Figure 3.4. Also shown in the figure is the definition of

EEOC Definitions of Harassment

Figure 3.4

1980 Definition of Sexual Harassment

Unwelcome sexual advances, requests for sexual favors, and other verbal or physical conduct of a sexual nature constitute sexual harassment when:

1. submission to such conduct is made either explicitly or implicitly a term or condition of an individual's employment;
2. submission to or rejection of such conduct by an individual is used as a basis for employment decisions affecting such individual; or
3. such conduct has the purpose or effect of unreasonably interfering with an individual's work performance or creating an intimidating, hostile, or offensive working environment.

1993 Definition of Harassment

Unlawful harassment is verbal or physical conduct that denigrates or shows hostility or aversion toward an individual because of his or her race, color, religion, gender, national origin, age or disability, or that of his/her relatives, friends, or associates, and that:

1. has the purpose or effect of creating an intimidating, hostile, or offensive working environment;
2. has the purpose or effect of unreasonably interfering with an individual's work performance; or
3. otherwise adversely affects an individual's employment opportunities.

U.S. law requires employers to treat pregnant employees in the same way as any other employees with a medical condition. In addition, the Family and Medical Leave Act of 1993 requires certain employers to provide up to 12 weeks' unpaid leave to eligible employees who adopt a child or need to care for a sick parent, child, or spouse.

general harassment that the EEOC issued in 1993. The majority of harassment cases filed to date have dealt with sexual harassment, but this may change in the future.[26] Courts appear to be extending sexual harassment definitions to other protected classes, such as race, age, and disability.

There are two broad categories of sexual harassment. The first, **quid pro quo sexual harassment**, covers the first two parts of the EEOC's definitions. It occurs when sexual activity is demanded in return for getting or keeping a job or job-related benefit.[27] For instance, a buyer for the University of Massachusetts Medical Center was awarded $1 million in 1994 after she testified that her supervisor had forced her to engage in sex once or twice a week over a 20-month period as a condition of keeping her job.[28]

The second category, **hostile work environment sexual harassment**, occurs when the behavior of coworkers, supervisors, customers, or anyone else in the work setting is sexual in nature and the employee perceives the behavior as offensive and undesirable.[29] Consider this example from a Supreme Court case decided in 1993.[30]

Teresa Harris was a manager at Forklift Systems, Inc., an equipment rental firm in Nashville, Tennessee. Her boss was Charles Hardy, the company president. Throughout the two and one-half years that Harris worked at Forklift, Hardy made such comments to her as "You're a woman, what do you know?" and "We need a man as the rental manager." He suggested in front of other employees that the two of them "go to the Holiday Inn to negotiate her raise." When Harris asked Hardy to stop, he expressed surprise at her annoyance but did not apologize. Less than one month later, after Harris had negotiated a deal with a customer, Hardy asked her in front of other employees, "What did you do, promise the guy . . . some [sex] Saturday night?" Harris quit her job at the end of that month.

Quid pro quo sexual harassment
Harassment that occurs when sexual activity is required in return for getting or keeping a job or job-related benefit.

Hostile work environment sexual harassment
Harassment that occurs when the behavior of anyone in the work setting is sexual in nature and is perceived by an employee as offensive and undesirable.

Do You Have a Hostile Work Environment?

Figure 3.5

The Supreme Court listed these questions to help judges and juries decide whether verbal and other nonphysical behavior of a sexual nature create a hostile work environment.

- How frequent is the discriminatory conduct?
- How severe is the discriminatory conduct?
- Is the conduct physically threatening or humiliating?
- Does the conduct interfere with the employee's work performance?

The issue the Court had to decide was whether Hardy violated the sexual harassment regulations based on Title VII. Lower courts had held that Hardy's behavior was certainly objectionable, but that Harris had not suffered serious psychological harm and that Hardy had not created a hostile work environment. The Supreme Court disagreed, holding that the behavior only needed to be such that a "reasonable person" would find it to create a hostile or abusive work environment. Figure 3.5 lists the tests that the Supreme Court said should be considered by judges and juries in deciding whether certain conduct creates a "hostile work environment" and is thus prohibited by Title VII.

Some cases of sexual harassment have involved groups of employees who have lodged hostile work environment claims. In 1998 Mitsubishi Motor Manufacturing of America paid out $34 million to settle a sexual harassment case brought by the EEOC on behalf of more than 300 female employees. Among their complaints were being groped, gestured to, urged to reveal their sexual preferences, and exposed to sexually explicit pictures.[31] In 1999, Ford Motor Company achieved a settlement with women in two Chicago area factories in regard to their sexual harassment complaints. The female employees claimed there existed a long-term pattern of groping, name-calling, and partying with strippers and prostitutes. The carmaker agreed to set aside $7.5 million to compensate victims of harassment and $10 million more to provide diversity training to managers and male workers.[32] Mitsubishi had changed its image as a leader in corporate forgiveness of sexual harassment in 1998 to a model corporate citizen four years later in 2002. Mitsubishi made improvements that included a zero tolerance policy for sexual harassment and provided training for all employees about the illegality of harassment and how to investigate complaints when they arise.[33]

Sexual harassment cases are not only expensive, but they also can be highly disruptive to business and political organizations. Consider the disruption to the executive branch of the U.S. government when Paula Jones sued President Clinton for sexual harassment. She alleged that the president made an unwanted sexual advance toward her in 1991 while he was the governor of Arkansas and she was a state employee. In 1999 President Clinton paid $850,000 to settle the suit.[34]

Although most sexual harassment cases involve women as victims, the number of cases in which men are the victims is increasing.[35] In 1995, a federal judge awarded a man $237,257 for being sexually harassed by a female supervisor at a Domino's Pizza restaurant. The female supervisor made unwelcome sexual advances to the male subordinate, creating a hostile work environment. When the man threatened to report the supervisor's inappropriate conduct to top management, he was fired.[36]

Courts also consider same-sex harassment improper work-related behavior. Joseph Oncale, an oil-rig worker who alleged that fellow male workers physically and verbally abused him with sexual taunts and threats, was allowed to bring a sexual harassment lawsuit against his employer. Despite arguments to the contrary, a court reviewing the *Oncale* case ruled in 1998 that same-sex harassment, not just that between the sexes, can be the basis for a sexual harassment lawsuit.[37]

As Figure 3.6 indicates, sexual harassment is a major EEO issue for employers. A recent Harris survey found that 31 percent of women reported that they had been sexually harassed in the workplace.[38] According to the EEOC, plaintiffs filed 13,136 cases of sexual harassment with federal and state agencies in 2004 (Figure 3.6). Men filed approximately 15 percent of those cases.

The Manager's Notebook titled "Reducing Potential Liability for Sexual Harassment" spells out some ways to prevent or correct instances of sexual harassment.

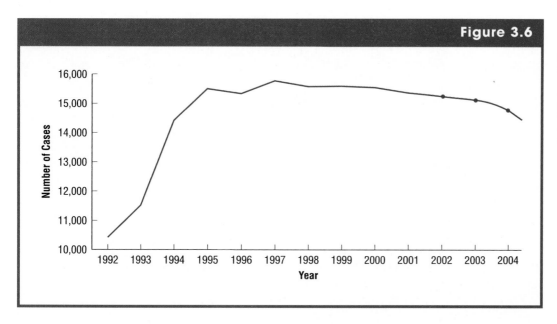

Figure 3.6

Number of Sexual Harassment Charges in the United States from 1992 to 2004

Source: The U.S. Equal Employment Opportunity Commission (2005). *http://www.eeoc.gov/stats/harass.html.*

Customer-Driven HR

MANAGER'S NOTEBOOK

Reducing Potential Liability for Sexual Harassment

To reduce the potential liability of a sexual harassment suit, managers should:

- Establish a written policy prohibiting harassment.
- Communicate the policy and train employees in what constitutes harassment.
- Establish an effective complaint procedure.
- Quickly investigate all claims.
- Take remedial action to correct past harassment.
- Make sure that the complainant does not end up in a less desirable position if he or she needs to be transferred.
- Follow up to prevent continuation of harassment.

Source: Commerce Clearing House. (1991). *Sexual harassment manual for managers and supervisors.* Chicago: Commerce Clearing House.

Recent U.S. Supreme Court sexual harassment rulings directly affect employer liability in sexual harassment cases. First, an employer may be held liable for the actions of supervisors toward their subordinate employees even if the offense is not reported to top management. Second, the Supreme Court has established an employer defense against sexual harassment claims. The employer must prove two items: (1) It exercised reasonable care to prevent and correct sexual harassment problems in a timely manner[39], and (2) The plaintiff failed to use the internal procedures for reporting sexual harassment.[40]

If the employee reasonably believes that reporting the offensive conduct is not a viable option, then the employer cannot take advantage of the defense. The internal procedures, then, must consist of fair investigations.[41] The Manager's Notebook entitled "How to Handle a Sexual Harassment Investigation" provides some guidelines.

Female employees at two Ford plants claimed groping and name-calling created a hostile environment. The suit resulted in a large settlement to compensate the victims of sexual harassment.

Customer-Driven HR

How to Handle a Sexual Harassment Investigation

Failure to investigate a sexual harassment complaint can result in an employer liability if the case goes to court. Here are some guidelines for conducting an investigation into sexual harassment:

- **Timeliness.** Managers should respond quickly, within 24 to 48 hours of a complaint of sexual harassment. Reacting later than that risks a charge of negligence.
- **Documentation.** Managers should ask open-ended questions to get as much detail as possible about the harassment. Notes taken during the interview should be rewritten or typed after the meeting is concluded. The manager should write the report based on notes from the interview with the complainant.
- **Employee agreement.** After documenting the facts in the report, the manager should go over the events with the complainant and document the employee's agreement with the report.
- **Resolution.** Managers should ask what end result the employee is seeking. Those with a genuine complaint usually say they want the harassment to stop. Those with a personal vendetta are often looking to have the alleged perpetrator fired.
- **Findings of fact.** The manager should interview witnesses who can corroborate or discredit the allegations of sexual harassment. The manager should then interview the alleged harasser. The accused should have the opportunity to defend himself or herself. A "findings of fact" document should be recorded to represent all the facts in the complaint; when this document is completed, the investigation is considered completed.
- **Remedy.** The employer is obligated only to take steps reasonably likely to stop the harassment and has the right to determine an appropriate course of action. An effective sexual harassment policy gives managers the flexibility to choose from a range of various sanctions, from a written warning to the harasser to stop, to a transfer or demotion, to termination of the harasser.

Source: Covey, A. (2001, July). How to handle harassment complaints. *HR Focus,* 5–6; Segal, J. (2001, October). HR as judge, jury, prosecutor and defender. *HRMagazine,* 141–154.

To safeguard against sexual harassment claims, experts recommend that employers develop a zero-tolerance sexual harassment policy, successfully communicate the policy to employees, and ensure that victims can report abuses without fear of retaliation.[42]

The Civil Rights Act of 1991

In 1991, believing that the Supreme Court was beginning to water down Title VII, Congress passed a comprehensive set of amendments to it. Together, these amendments are known as the *Civil Rights Act of 1991*. Although the legal aspects of these amendments are fairly technical, their impact on many organizations is very real. Among the most important effects of the 1991 amendment are:

- **Burden of proof.** As we noted earlier, the employer bears the burden of proof in a discrimination case. Once the applicant or employee files a discrimination case and shows some justification for it, the organization has to defend itself by proving that it had a good job-related reason for the decision it made. This standard was originally established in the *Griggs v. Duke Power* decision in 1971. Then a 1989 Supreme Court case, *Wards Cove Packing Co. v. Antonio,* had the effect of placing more of the burden of proof on the plaintiff.[43] The 1991 law reinstates the *Griggs* standard.
- **Quotas.** To avoid adverse impact, many organizations (including the Department of Labor) had developed a policy of adjusting scores on employment tests so that a certain percentage of protected-class applicants would be hired. The 1991 law amending Title VII prohibits **quotas**, which are employer adjustments of hiring decisions to ensure that a certain number of people from a certain protected class are hired. Thus, quotas, which had received mixed reviews in Supreme Court decisions before 1991, are now explicitly forbidden. Employers that have an affirmative action program giving preference to protected-class candidates have to walk a very fine line between "giving preference" (which is permissible) and "meeting a quota" (which is forbidden).
- **Damages and jury trials.** The original Title VII law allowed successful plaintiffs to collect only back pay awards. However, racial minorities were also able to use an 1866 law to collect punitive and/or compensatory damages. **Punitive damages** are fines awarded to a plaintiff to punish the defendant. **Compensatory damages** are fines awarded to a plaintiff to compensate for the financial or psychological harm the plaintiff has suffered as a result of the discrimination. The 1991 law extended the possibility of collecting punitive and compensatory damages to persons claiming sex, religious, or disability-based discrimination. Such damages are capped at $50,000 to $300,000, depending on the size of the employer.[44] In addition, the law allows plaintiffs to request a trial by jury.

Some believe that by expressly forbidding quotas, the Civil Rights Act of 1991 has prohibited a very useful mechanism for reducing discrimination in employment decisions. Many organizations had found that the best way to prevent adverse impact was to use a combination of quotas and cognitive ability testing. That is, the employer would select a certain percentage of applicants from various groups, and then choose the highest performers on cognitive ability tests from each group. This employment strategy resulted in both the maintenance of a high-quality workforce and greater participation of minorities in that workforce. Yet, by outlawing quotas, the Civil Rights Act of 1991 has prohibited this option.[45]

Executive Order 11246

Executive orders are policies that the president establishes for the federal government and organizations that contract with the federal government. Executive Order 11246 (as amended by Executive Order 11375), issued by President Johnson in 1965, is *not* part of Title VII. It does, however, prohibit discrimination against the same categories of people that Title VII protects. In addition, it goes beyond the Title VII requirement of no discrimination by requiring covered organizations (firms with government contracts over $50,000 and 50 or more employees) to develop affirmative action programs to promote the employment of protected-class members.

Quotas
Employer adjustments of hiring decisions to ensure that a certain number of people from a certain protected class are hired.

Punitive damages
Fines awarded to a plaintiff in order to punish the defendant.

Compensatory damages
Fines awarded to a plaintiff to compensate for the financial or psychological harm the plaintiff has suffered.

Executive order
A presidential directive that has the force of law. In HR context, a policy with which all federal agencies and organizations doing business with the federal government must comply.

For instance, government contractors such as Northrop Grumman and Lockheed Martin are required to have active affirmative action programs.

The Age Discrimination in Employment Act of 1967

Age Discrimination in Employment Act (1967)
The law prohibiting discrimination against people who are 40 or older.

The **Age Discrimination in Employment Act (ADEA)** prohibits discrimination against people who are 40 or older. When first enacted in 1967, it protected people aged 40 to 65. Subsequently, it was amended to raise the age to 70, and in 1986 the upper age limit was removed entirely.

The majority of ADEA complaints are filed by employees who have been terminated. For instance, a 57-year-old computerized-control salesman for GE Fanuc Automation was the only employee terminated during a "reduction in force"; he was replaced by six younger sales representatives. He brought a lawsuit, claiming that he was fired because of his age, and a Detroit jury awarded him $1.1 million in damages and lost wages and benefits.[46] Employers can also lose lawsuits as a result of ill-informed workplace humor. Employers have lost several age discrimination cases because terminated employees had evidence that supervisors had told jokes about old age.[47]

An important amendment to the ADEA is the *Older Workers Protection Act (OWPA)* of 1990, which makes it illegal for employers to discriminate in providing benefits to employees based on age. For example, it would be illegal for employers to provide disability benefits only to employees who are age 60 or less or to require older disabled employees to take early retirement. Another OWPA provision makes it more difficult for firms to ask older workers in downsizing and layoff situations to sign waivers in which they give up their right to any future age-discrimination claims in exchange for a payment.[48]

The Americans with Disabilities Act of 1990

Americans with Disabilities Act (1990)
The law forbidding employment discrimination against people with disabilities who are able to perform the essential functions of the job with or without reasonable accommodation.

The most recent of the major EEO laws is the **Americans with Disabilities Act (ADA)**. Signed into law in 1990 and gradually implemented since then, ADA has three major sections. Title I contains the employment provisions; Titles II and III concern the operation of state and local governments and places of public accommodation such as hotels, restaurants, and grocery stores. The employment provisions began to be enforced for the approximately 264,000 U.S. employers with 25 or more employees on July 26, 1992, and for the approximately 666,000 U.S. employers with 15 or more employees on July 26, 1994.[49]

The central requirement of Title I of the ADA is as follows:

> Employment discrimination is prohibited against *individuals with disabilities* who are able to perform the *essential functions* of the job with or without *reasonable accommodation*.

Three parts of this requirement need definition.

Individuals with Disabilities

Individuals with disabilities
Persons who have a physical or mental impairment that substantially affects one or more major life activities.

For the purposes of ADA, **individuals with disabilities** are people who have a physical or mental impairment that substantially affects one or more major life activities. Some examples of major life activities are:[50]

- Walking
- Speaking
- Breathing
- Performing manual tasks

- Sitting
- Lifting
- Seeing
- Hearing

- Learning
- Caring for oneself
- Working
- Reading

Obviously, persons who are blind, hearing impaired, or wheelchair bound are individuals with disabilities. But the category also includes people who have a controlled impairment. For instance, a person with epilepsy is disabled even if the epilepsy is controlled through medication. The impairment must be physical or mental and not due to environmental, cultural, or economic disadvantages. For example, a person who has difficulty reading due to dyslexia is considered disabled, but a person who cannot read because he or she dropped out of school is not. Persons with communicable diseases, including those who are HIV-positive (infected with the virus that causes AIDS), are included in the definition of individuals with disabilities.

ADA coverage is extended only to people with disabilities that impair a major life activity. It does not provide remedies to people with disabilities that impair only a work activity. This limitation of ADA coverage was decided in a 2002 Supreme Court decision when an employee at a Toyota plant in Kentucky, whose carpal tunnel syndrome restricted her ability to use pneumatic tools at work, sought a remedy under the ADA. It was denied by the court.[51]

In addition, the ADA protects persons who are *perceived* to be disabled. For instance, an employee might suffer a heart attack. When he tries to return to work, his boss may be scared that the workload will be "too much" and refuse to let him come back. The employer would be in violation of the ADA because he perceives the employee as disabled and is discriminating against him on the basis of that perception.

Two particular classes of people are explicitly *not* considered disabled: individuals whose current use of alcohol is affecting their job performance and those who use illegal drugs (whether they are addicted or not). However, those who are recovering from their former use of either alcohol or drugs are covered by ADA.

A 1999 Supreme Court decision clarified who is entitled to ADA protection. The court ruled that a person is not considered disabled under the ADA if his or her impairment is corrected and does not substantially limit a major life activity. For example, it held that two female job applicants for a pilot position with United Airlines could not claim ADA protection for the disability of poor eyesight. The women's uncorrected eyesight was below United's 20/100 uncorrected vision requirement for pilots; their corrected vision with glasses was 20/20. The court found that because the women's vision could be corrected with glasses they were not disabled under the terms of the act and denied them a remedy.[52] This decision is likely to affect ADA coverage of other impairments that can be corrected, such as hearing loss, high blood pressure, or asthma.

Intellectual Disabilities.   In 2005, the EEOC provided guidelines to address challenges faced by employers in hiring, accommodating, and preventing harassment of employees with intellectual disabilities. The EEOC estimates that within the United States about 2.5 million individuals have *intellectual disabilities* that occur when: (1) the person's intellectual function level (IQ) is below 70–75; (2) the person has significant limitations in adaptive skill areas as expressed in conceptual, social, and practical adaptive skills; and (3) the disability originated before the age of 18. *Adaptive skills* are the basic skills needed for everyday life. They include communication, self-care, home living, social skills, leisure, health and safety, self-direction, functional academics (reading, writing, basic math), and work.[53]

Not everyone with an intellectual impairment is covered by the ADA. An individual's intellectual impairment must substantially limit one or more major life activities, such as walking, seeing, hearing, thinking, speaking, learning, concentrating, performing manual tasks, caring for oneself, and working. The following is an example of someone who has an intellectual impairment that would be covered under the ADA.

> Bob has an intellectual impairment and is capable of living on his own but requires frequent assistance from family, friends, and neighbors with cleaning his apartment, grocery shopping, getting to doctors' appointments, and cooking. He is unable to read at a higher level than the third grade, and so needs someone to read his mail and help him pay bills. Bob is substantially limited in caring for himself and therefore has a disability that qualifies for ADA coverage.

Essential Functions

The EEOC separates job duties and tasks into two categories: essential and marginal. **Essential functions** are job duties that every employee must do or must be able to do to be an effective employee. *Marginal functions* are job duties that are required of only some employees or are not critical to job performance. The following examples illustrate the difference between essential and marginal functions:

Essential functions
Job duties that each person in a certain position must do or must be able to do to be an effective employee.

- A company advertises a position for a "floating" supervisor to substitute when regular supervisors on the day, night, and graveyard shifts are absent. The ability to work any time of the day or night is an essential job function.

■ A company wishes to expand its business with Japan. In addition to sales experience, it requires all new hires to speak fluent Japanese. This language skill is an essential job function.

■ In any job requiring computer use, it is essential that the employee have the ability to access, input, or retrieve information from the computer terminal. However, it may not be essential that the employee be capable of manually entering or visually retrieving information because technology exists for voice recognition input and auditory output.

■ A group of chemists working together in a lab may occasionally need to answer the telephone. This is considered a marginal job duty because if not every one of the chemists can answer the phone the other chemists can do so.

ADA requires that employers make decisions about applicants with disabilities solely on the basis of their ability to perform essential job functions.

Reasonable Accommodation

Organizations are required to take some reasonable action to allow disabled employees to work for them. The major aspects of this requirement are:

Reasonable accommodation
An action taken to accommodate the known disabilities of applicants or employees so that disabled persons enjoy equal employment opportunity.

■ Employers must make **reasonable accommodation** for the known disabilities of applicants or employees so that disabled people enjoy equal employment opportunity.[54] For example, an applicant who uses a wheelchair may need accommodation if the interviewing site is not wheelchair accessible.

■ Employers cannot deny a disabled person employment to avoid providing the reasonable accommodation, unless providing the accommodation would cause an "undue hardship." Undue hardship is a highly subjective determination, based on the cost of the accommodation and the employer's resources. For instance, an accommodation routinely provided by large employers (such as specialized computer equipment) may not be required of small employers because the small employers do not have the large employer's financial resources.

■ No accommodation is required if the individual is not otherwise qualified for the position.

■ It is usually the obligation of the disabled individual to request the accommodation.

■ If the cost of the accommodation would create an undue hardship for the employer, the disabled individual should be given the option of providing the accommodation. For instance, if a visually impaired person applies for a computer operator position in a small company that cannot afford to accommodate the applicant, then the applicant should be given the option to provide the accommodating technology. (Note, though, that the President's Committee on Employment of People with Disabilities reports that 20 percent of accommodations do not cost anything at all, and less than 4 percent cost more than $5,000.[55]).

A wide variety of accommodations is possible, and they can come from some surprising sources. For example, Kreonite, Inc., a small family-owned business of about 250 employees that manufactures specialized photographic film, has been committed to employing persons with disabilities and has several employees who are deaf. Kreonite turned to a local not-for-profit training center for someone to teach sign language to its hearing employees. The training was free, and 30 Kreonite employees volunteered to attend.[56]

Some additional examples of potential reasonable accommodations that the EEOC has suggested are reassigning marginal job duties, modifying work schedules, modifying examinations or training materials, providing qualified readers and interpreters, and permitting use of paid or unpaid leave for treatment.[57]

As we noted earlier in the chapter, the main focus of the ADA and its accompanying regulations is the hiring process. However, the majority of complaints filed so far involves situations in which current employees have become disabled on the job. According to the EEOC, the total number of disability cases filed under the ADA in 2004 was 15,346. The two largest categories of cases were emotional and psychiatric impairments and back injuries, both of which are difficult to diagnose and treat.[58] Managers need to be prepared to deal with a set of issues not anticipated by the lawmakers and regulators who created and passed the ADA.

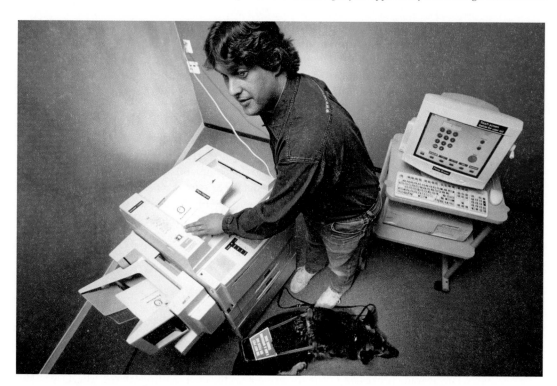

David Redman, a blind office worker, uses a braille-labeled copy machine that his employer purchased in order to provide a reasonable accommodation for him under the ADA.

The Vocational Rehabilitation Act of 1973

The *Vocational Rehabilitation Act* is the precursor to the ADA. However, this act applied only to the federal government and its contractors. Like Executive Order 11246, the Vocational Rehabilitation Act not only prohibits discrimination (in this case, on the basis of disability) but also requires that the covered organizations have an affirmative action plan to promote the employment of disabled individuals. Familiarity with this law is useful to organizations attempting to comply with the ADA because it has led to over 20 years' worth of court and regulatory decisions based on the same central prohibition against disability-based discrimination.

The Vietnam Era Veterans Readjustment Act of 1974

One additional EEO law deserves brief mention. The *Vietnam Era Veterans Readjustment Act of 1974* prohibits discrimination against Vietnam-era veterans (those who served in the military between August 5, 1964, and May 7, 1975) by federal contractors. It also requires federal contractors to take affirmative action to hire Vietnam-era veterans.

EEO Enforcement and Compliance

The enforcement of EEO laws is the responsibility of the executive branch of government, which is headed by the president. In this section we describe the regulatory agencies that enforce the various EEO laws, as well as some of the plans that have been used to comply with affirmative action requirements.

Regulatory Agencies

Two agencies are primarily responsible for the enforcement of EEO law: the Equal Employment Opportunity Commission (EEOC) and the Office of Federal Contract Compliance Programs (OFCCP).

Equal Employment Opportunity Commission (EEOC)

The federal agency responsible for enforcing EEO laws.

Equal Employment Opportunity Commission (EEOC)

The **Equal Employment Opportunity Commission (EEOC)**, which was created by Title VII, has three major functions. The first is processing discrimination complaints. The second is issuing written regulations. The third is information gathering and dissemination.[59]

In processing discrimination complaints, the EEOC follows a three-step process:

- **Investigation.** An applicant or employee who thinks that he or she has been discriminated against begins the process by filing a complaint with the EEOC. The EEOC then notifies the company that a complaint has been filed, and the company becomes responsible for ensuring that any records relating to the complaint are kept safe. The EEOC usually finds itself with a backlog, so it may take up to two years to begin investigating the complaint. In 2004, 79,432 cases were filed with the EEOC, compared to 62,100 in 1990.

    Of the 79,432 total charges filed with the EEOC in 2004, the common types of discrimination of all filings were:[60]

    - Race: 27,696 or 34.9%
    - Sex/Gender: 24,249 or 30.5%
    - Age: 17,837 or 22.5%
    - Disability: 15,346 or 19.4%
    - National Origin: 8,361 or 10.5%
    - Religion: 2,466 or 3.1%
    - Equal Pay: 1,011 or 1.3%

    The average processing time for private sector charge filings at the EEOC was 165 days in 2004, which is an improvement of 5 days over the previous year.

    After conducting the investigation, the EEOC determines whether it is likely that the company did in fact violate one or more EEO laws. Complainants are always free to file a lawsuit, but the courts are unlikely to rule in their favor without the EEOC's backing.

- **Conciliation.** If the EEOC finds that an EEO law was probably violated, it attempts to resolve the case through conciliation. **Conciliation** consists of negotiation among the three parties involved: the complainant, the employer, and the EEOC. The goal of conciliation is to reach a fair settlement while avoiding a trial.

- **Litigation.** If conciliation is not possible, the EEOC can choose between two courses of action. The EEOC does not have the power to compel an employer to pay compensation or any other kind of damages; this can be done only as the result of a court's decision. Because pursuing a lawsuit is very expensive, the EEOC takes this course of action only in a relatively small percentage of cases. If the EEOC chooses not to pursue the case, it issues a right-to-sue letter to the complainant, who is then free to pursue court action with the blessing (if not the financial or legal support) of the EEOC.

Conciliation

An attempt to reach a negotiated settlement between the employer and an employee or applicant in an EEO case.

In addition to resolving complaints, the EEOC is responsible for issuing regulations and guidelines. These documents put "meat on the bones" of the individual laws. For instance, when the EEOC decided that sexual harassment was prohibited by Title VII, it issued regulations defining what sexual harassment is (see Figure 3.4) and what it expects employers to do in response to employee complaints of harassment. Similarly, when the ADA was signed into law in 1990, the EEOC was given the responsibility of issuing regulations that would inform employers exactly what they would (and would not) be expected to do to comply with the law. The EEOC Web site (*www.EEOC.gov*) also provides a list of its regulations. Figure 3.7 lists some of the most prominent EEOC regulations.

The EEOC also gathers information to monitor the hiring practices of organizations. It does this by requiring organizations with 100 or more employees to file an annual report (EEO-1) indicating the number of women and minorities who hold jobs in nine different job categories. The EEOC examines this information to identify patterns of discrimination that may exist in organizations.

Finally, the EEOC disseminates posters to employers. These posters explain to workers how to protect themselves from employment discrimination and how to file a complaint. The EEOC requires employers to display the posters in a prominent place (such as the company cafeteria).

Figure 3.7

Sex discrimination guidelines	Affirmative action guidelines
Questions and answers on pregnancy disability and reproductive hazards	EEO in the federal government
	Equal Pay Act interpretations
Religious discrimination guidelines	Policy statement on maternity benefits
National origin discrimination guidelines	Policy statement on relationship of Title VII to 1986 Immigration Reform and Control Act
Interpretations of the Age Discrimination in Employment Act	
	Policy statement on reproductive and fetal hazards
Employee selection guidelines	Policy statement on religious accommodation under Title VII
Questions and answers on employee selection guidelines	Disability discrimination guidelines
Sexual harassment guidelines	
Record keeping and reports	

Principal EEOC Regulations

Office of Federal Contract Compliance Programs (OFCCP)

The **Office of Federal Contract Compliance Programs (OFCCP)** is responsible for enforcing the laws and executive orders that apply to the federal government and its contractors. Specifically, it enforces Executive Order 11246 and the Vocational Rehabilitation Act, which both go beyond prohibiting discrimination to requiring affirmative action programs by covered employers.

Many of the regulations written by the OFCCP are very similar to those issued by the EEOC. However, there are two major differences between the enforcement activities of the two agencies. First, in contrast to the EEOC, the OFCCP actively monitors compliance with its regulations. That is, it does not wait for an employee or applicant to file a complaint. Rather, it requires covered employers to submit annual reports on the state of their affirmative action program. Second, unlike the EEOC, the OFCCP has considerable enforcement power. Being a government contractor is considered a privilege, not a right. The OFCCP can take away that privilege if it determines that an employer is not complying with the law. It can also levy fines and other forms of punishment.

Office of Federal Contract Compliance Programs (OFCCP)
The federal agency responsible for monitoring and enforcing the laws and executive orders that apply to the federal government and its contractors.

Affirmative Action Plans

An affirmative action plan is required of all government agencies and businesses that do a significant amount of work for the government. There are three steps to developing an affirmative action plan: conducting a utilization analysis, establishing goals and timetables, and determining action options.

Utilization Analysis

The first step in developing an affirmative action plan is conducting a *utilization analysis* to describe the organization's current work force relative to the pool of qualified workers in the labor force. There are two parts to conducting this analysis. The first involves determining the demographic composition of the current work force by dividing all the jobs in the organization into classifications. For instance, all management jobs are placed in one classification, all clerical and secretarial jobs in a second, all sales positions in a third, and so on. The percentage of persons from each protected class working in each of these classifications is then determined.

The second part is determining the percentage of those same protected classes in the available labor market. In gathering this information, organizations need to consider the eight different pieces of information listed in Figure 3.8. For instance, what percentage of qualified and available managers are women? What percentage are African Americans? What percentage are

Figure 3.8

Determine the percentage of protected-class members for each of the following groups of people:

■ Local population
■ Local unemployed workers
■ Local labor force
■ Qualified workers in the local labor market
■ Qualified workers in the labor market from which you recruit
■ Current employees who might be promoted into the job classification
■ Graduates of local education and training programs that prepare people for this job classification
■ Participants in training programs sponsored by the employer

Components of an Eight-Factor Availability Analysis

Asian Americans? The OFCCP offers guidelines for determining these figures. If the available figures are significantly higher than the currently employed in any category, the protected groups are said to be underutilized in that job category.

Goals and Timetables

The second step is setting goals and timetables for correcting underutilization. The OFCCP explicitly requires that rigid numerical quotas *not* be set. Rather, the employer should take into consideration the size of the underutilization, how fast the workforce turns over, and whether the workforce is growing or contracting. Another consideration in setting goals and timetables is the types of actions the employer intends to take.

Action Plans

The final step in developing an affirmative action plan is deciding exactly what affirmative actions to take. The OFCCP suggests the following guidelines:

■ Recruiting protected-class members.
■ Redesigning jobs so that the underrepresented workers are more likely to be qualified.
■ Providing specialized training sessions for underprepared applicants.
■ Removing any unnecessary barriers to employment. For instance, a company located in an area not served by public transportation might consider providing van service from certain areas so that potential applicants who do not have reliable transportation can become employees.

The central concern for organizations is determining how much (if any) preference they should give to applicants who belong to an underutilized protected class. For instance, a few years ago there was a job opening in the transportation department of Santa Clara County, California. After going through the normal selection process, the candidates for promotion were ranked according to their performance on tests and in interviews. County rules allowed any of the top seven candidates to be chosen. The supervisors were poised to choose the employee ranked second—Paul Johnson, a white man. Diane Joyce, a white woman who was ranked fourth, called the county's affirmative action officer and ended up with the job.

Johnson filed suit. His argument was straightforward: Title VII prohibits discrimination based on sex, and he did not get the job because he is a man. This is a classic case of alleged **reverse discrimination**, discrimination that occurs as the result of an attempt to recruit and hire more people from the protected classes. In this case, the job classification to which the person was to be promoted had 238 positions, none of which were held by women. Johnson pursued his case all the way to the U.S. Supreme Court. In 1987 the Court ruled that Santa Clara County's decision was permissible.[61]

The Supreme Court has decided over a dozen reverse discrimination cases since the first one in 1977.[62] Although the Court has favored the affirmative action strategy side of the tension outlined in Figure 3.1, almost all these cases were decided by 6–3 or 5–4 margins. Because

Reverse discrimination
Discrimination against a nonprotected-class member resulting from attempts to recruit and hire members of protected classes.

new justices are added to the Supreme Court fairly regularly, the way these kinds of cases will be decided in the future is very much an open question.

The United States is not the only country with affirmative action. Other countries have created similar policies to provide employment or educational opportunities for disadvantaged groups. For example, India has tried to improve the status of the untouchables, the lowest caste in its society, by providing them with preferential treatment in employment and education. This policy has had mixed results because it has enraged some members of the higher castes. Malaysia has favored the Islamic Malays over the Chinese (who on average are wealthier and more highly educated than the Malays) for jobs and higher education opportunities. Significant numbers of Chinese Malaysians have responded to this policy by emigrating to Asia and North America.[63] Other countries have disadvantaged groups in their population but have decided not to create employment policies favorable to these groups. For example, France has a large population of Algerians who have been historically disadvantaged, but it has avoided remedying the high Algerian unemployment rate with a policy similar to affirmative action in the United States. In Great Britain, the government's Commission for Racial Equality concluded that most British firms do little to ensure equal employment opportunity beyond giving verbal support to the idea.[64]

Other Important Laws

We have concentrated on equal employment opportunity laws in this chapter because they have a broad effect on almost all HR issues and are highly likely to influence managers' behavior. The other HR laws, listed in the Appendix to this chapter and discussed elsewhere in the book, are much more narrowly focused. These include laws that affect compensation and benefit plans (state workers' compensation laws, the Social Security Act, the Fair Labor Standards Act, the Employee Retirement and Income Security Act, the Consolidated Omnibus Budget Reconciliation Act, and the Family and Medical Leave Act), union–management relations (the Wagner Act, the Taft-Hartley Act, and the Landrum-Griffin Act), safety and health issues (the Occupational Safety and Health Act), and layoffs (the Worker Adjustment and Retraining Act).

Four laws deserve brief mention. The *Immigration Reform and Control Act of 1986* was intended to reduce the inflow of illegal immigrants to the United States. The law has one provision that affects employers. To discourage the hiring of illegal immigrants, the law mandates that employers hire only people who can document that they are legally permitted to work in the United States. The Employment Eligibility Verification (I-9) form specifies which documents employers need to see from new employees. It appears that the major impact of the Immigration Reform and Control Act has been the creation of a market for fake documents.

The *Immigration Act of 1990* was legislated to make it easier for skilled immigrants to enter the United States. This law represents a modification of previous U.S. immigration policy, which favored immigrants who either (1) had family members who are U.S. citizens or (2) were leaving a country that was assigned a large quota of immigrants to the United States based on historical trends.[65]

The *Drug-Free Workplace Act of 1988* requires that government contractors try to ensure that their workplaces are free from drug use. Employers are required to prevent the use of illegal drugs at their work sites and to educate their employees about the hazards of drug use. Although the law does not mandate drug testing, it—along with other more narrowly focused laws and regulations—has led to a general acceptance of drug testing, both of current employees and applicants, across the United States.[66] About 98 percent of *Fortune* 200 companies now conduct some form of drug testing.[67]

The *Uniformed Services Employment and Reemployment Rights Act of 1994* protects the rights of people who take short leaves from a private-sector employer to perform military service (such as reserve duty). The law protects these employees' seniority rights and benefits. It also protects them from employer discrimination in hiring, promotion, or layoff decisions. Some employers have been giving military reservists returning from combat duty in Iraq perks and benefits that exceed what is legally required, as described in the Manager's Notebook titled "Military Reservists Returning from Iraq Are Finding their Skills in High Demand."

A Question of Ethics

Is it ethical for a U.S. employer to require all employees to speak only English at the workplace?

Marine Corps Major Keith Canevaro, a military reservist, will soon be back as a program manager in telecommunications products at Cisco Systems after leading a Marine Corps unit.

Emerging Trends

Military Reservists Returning from Iraq Are Finding Their Skills in High Demand

Reservists make up 40 percent of active duty troops serving in Iraq—the largest number of reservists to see combat since World War II. Their average age is 32, 4 years older than the average soldier.

Employers are finding that reservists return from duty in Iraq with seasoned management, people, and communication skills. They also return with leadership skills that have been honed in combat. Army Major David Wood, a 41-year-old reservist, commanded a helicopter squadron in Iraq and Afghanistan. Wood says his soldiers always seemed more enthusiastic about a mission when they knew a senior officer was taking part. Back home, as a vice president at Jay Group, a packaging company in Pennsylvania, Wood says he now often goes down to the plant floor to pack and ship products alongside workers. "You can't be what we call a coffee-cup commander," Wood says. "You have to be on the field, leading from the front."

Recognizing the value of skills obtained in the context of military combat, employers are going out of their way to recruit and retain reservists. Although employers are required by law to give returning reservists back their jobs with the same responsibility and pay, some employers go even further than the law requires, offering them such perks as continued pay and benefits while on military duty. Here are a few examples:

- Adolph Coors makes up the difference between a reservist's regular salary and military pay for up to one year of active duty. An internal volunteer organization works with reservists' families, boxing and shipping donated items to the troops.
- American Express provides full pay and benefits for up to five years as well as cash contributions to the employee's retirement plan.
- General Electric pays one month of full salary and makes up the difference in pay for up to three years. GE has a military recruiting division and leadership programs for military members transitioning to the corporate world.

Source: Palmeri, C. (2004, December 13). Served in Iraq? Come work for us. *BusinessWeek*, 78–80.

Avoiding Pitfalls in EEO

The great majority of employees and job applicants in the United States fall into one or more protected classes. This means that almost any decision made by a manager that affects a worker's employment status can be challenged in a court of law. In most cases, sound management practices will not only help managers avoid EEO lawsuits but will also contribute to the organization's bottom line. Five specific management practices are recommended: providing training, establishing a complaint resolution process, documenting decisions, being honest, and asking applicants only for needed information.

Provide Training

One of the best ways to avoid EEO problems is to provide training. Two types of training are appropriate. First, the HR department should provide supervisors, managers, and executives with regular updates on EEO and other labor issues, because this area of law is in a constant state of flux.[68] The Supreme Court regularly decides cases that affect HR practice. Although managers can try to read periodicals or search the Web to obtain current information, most find their everyday demands too taxing to allow time for this. Regular, focused training sessions conducted by the HR department are the most efficient method of communicating this information to managers.

Second, employers should focus on communicating to employees their commitment to a discrimination-free work environment. For instance, all employees need to be instructed in what sexual harassment is, how to stop it before it becomes a problem, and what to do if it does become a problem. Honeywell has a council of employees with disabilities, one function of which is to promote awareness of disability issues throughout the company.[69]

Establish a Complaint Resolution Process

Every organization should establish a process for the internal resolution of EEO and other types of employee complaints. It is much less expensive to resolve these concerns if the EEOC, OFCCP, and legal counsel are not involved. More important, employee morale and satisfaction can be improved when employees are able to pass along their concerns to upper-level management. (We describe complaint resolution systems in detail in Chapters 13 and 15.)

Once in place, the complaint resolution process should be followed correctly. AT&T avoided liability in a sexual harassment case because it was able to show that it had acted promptly to remedy the problem once management had been informed of it.[70] Exhibit 3.1, "Alternative Dispute Resolution Methods at Marriott and the EEOC," describes how Marriott and the EEOC have taken the lead in experimenting with new ways to resolve employee EEO complaints.

Alternative Dispute Resolution Methods at Marriott and the EEOC   **EXHIBIT 3.1**

Ron Wilensky, vice president for employee relations for Marriott International, was not satisfied with the company's "Guarantee of Fair Treatment" program, which instructed employees with complaints to go first to their immediate supervisor, then to the supervisor's manager, and so on up the ladder if necessary. Based on his experience with three *Fortune* 500 companies that had similar policies, he estimated that 75 percent of employees bypass such a policy and consult an attorney. To verify his hunch, he established a committee to examine employee satisfaction with the Guarantee of Fair Treatment. The results indicated that employees did not trust the policy. Instead, they wanted a system that would give those with grievances a chance to air their concerns before impartial listeners and have those concerns addressed promptly—without fear of retribution.

To give employees what they want, Wilensky and his committee have been experimenting with three dispute resolution systems.

(continued)

1. **Mutual agreement through mediation** A neutral person, typically an expert in dispute resolution, meets with both parties to the conflict and tries to arrange a negotiated settlement. Because 80 to 90 percent of litigation is settled out of court anyway, the goal is to reduce attorney fees and other associated costs.

2. **A helping hot line** Wilensky found that it was difficult to track employee grievances across so many different geographical locations, so Marriott uses a toll-free 800-number hot line at 300 of its food service locations. Available 24 hours a day, 7 days per week, the hotline is intended to be used only to report cases of perceived wrongful discharge, discrimination, and harassment. Marriott promises to initiate an investigation within three days of receiving the complaint.

3. **A panel of peers** In 50 Marriott locations, employees have an opportunity to air their grievance before a panel of their peers. The panel is chosen at random from a group of specially trained volunteers. The panel has the authority to make final, binding decisions on all grievances brought before it.[A]

The EEOC also uses alternative dispute resolution systems. It relies on mediation to achieve faster resolution of its large backlog of cases. The EEOC chairwoman, Ida L. Castro, recently made a strong commitment to use mediation by increasing the mediation budget by $13 million in 1999 to expand the use of mediation in each EEOC district office.[B]

Source: [A]Wilensky, R., and Jones, K. M. (1994, March). Quick response key to resolving complaints. *HRMagazine*, 42–47. Reprinted with the permission of *HRMagazine*, published by the Society for Human Resource Management, Alexandria, VA; [B]Leonard, B. (1999, February). A new era at the EEOC. *HRMagazine*, 54–62.

Document Decisions

Financial transactions and decisions need to be well documented so they can be audited and summarized, problem areas identified, and solutions implemented.[71] The same rationale applies to decisions made about employees. The nature of any HR decision, and the rationale for it, should be clearly documented. Both the EEOC and OFCCP have certain reporting requirements. Employers that have a sound human resource information system in place do not find it difficult to comply with these requirements.

Be Honest

Typically, applicants and employees will not file an EEO complaint unless they think they have been mistreated. Perceptions of mistreatment often result from situations in which employees' or applicants' expectations have not been met. Imagine the following scenario: A 50-year-old employee has consistently received excellent performance evaluations over a 20-year period. He is then abruptly terminated by his manager for poor work performance. This employee is likely to file a lawsuit because over time he has developed the expectation that he is a valued employee, and he now believes that the only possible reason for his termination is his age. Although it may be painful in the short term, providing honest feedback to employees is a good management practice that may reduce legal problems in the long run.

Ask Only for Information You Need to Know

Companies should ask only for information that is related to job performance. For instance, you should not ask about an applicant's religious affiliation, although you may ask whether a person can work on specific days of the week. Similarly, you can ask whether the applicant is capable of performing the essential physical aspects of the job (preferably specifically listed), but asking general questions about health would probably be interpreted as a violation of the ADA. Figure 3.9 gives examples of appropriate and inappropriate questions to ask on an application form or during an interview.

Figure 3.9

Subject of Question	Examples of Acceptable Questions	Examples of Unacceptable Questions	Comments
Name	"What is your name?" "Have you worked for this company under another name?"	"What was your maiden name?"	Questions about an applicant's name that may indicate marital status or national origin should be avoided.
Age	"Are you at least 18 years old?" "Upon employment, all employees must submit legal proof of age. Can you furnish proof of age?"	"What is your date of birth?" "What is your age?"	A request for age-related data may discourage older workers from applying.
Race, Ethnicity, and Physical Characteristics	"After employment, the company must have a photograph of all employees. If employed, can you furnish a photograph?" "Do you read, speak, or write a foreign language?"	"What is your race?" "What are your height and weight?" "Would you please submit a photograph with your application for identification purposes?" "What language do you commonly use?"	Information relative to physical characteristics may be associated with sexual or racial group membership.
Religion	A statement may be made by the employer of the days, hours, and shifts worked.	"What is your religious faith?" "Does your religion keep you from working on weekends?"	Questions that determine applicants' availability have an exclusionary effect because of some people's religious practices.
Gender, Marital Status, and Family	"If you are a minor, please list the name and address of a parent or guardian." "Please provide the name, address, and telephone number of someone who should be contacted in case of an emergency."	"What is your sex?" "Describe your current marital status." "List the number and ages of your children." "If you have children, please describe the provisions you have made for child care." "With whom do you reside?"	Direct or indirect questions about marital status, children, pregnancy, and childbearing plans frequently discriminate against women and may be a violation of Title VII.
Physical Conditions	"Are you willing to take a physical exam if the nature of the job for which you are applying requires one?"	"Do you have any physical disabilities, defects, or handicaps?" "How would you describe your general physical health?" "When was your last physical exam?"	A blanket policy excluding the disabled is discriminatory. Where physical condition is a requirement for employment, employers should be able to document the business necessity for questions on the application form relating to physical condition.

Examples of Acceptable and Unacceptable Questions Asked on Application Forms or During Interviews

Figure 3.9 (Continued)

Subject of Question	Examples of Acceptable Questions	Examples of Unacceptable Questions	Comments
Military Service	"Please list any specific educational or job experiences you may have acquired during military service that you believe would be useful in the job for which you are applying."	"Please list the dates and type of discharge you may have received from military service."	Minority service members have a higher percentage of undesirable military discharges. A policy of rejecting those with less than an honorable discharge may be discriminatory.
Hobbies, Clubs, and Organizations	"Do you have any hobbies that are related to the job for which you are making application?" "Please list any clubs or organizations in which you are a member that relate to the job for which you are applying."	"Please list any hobbies you may have." "Please list all clubs and other organizations in which you are a member."	If questions on club/organization memberships are asked, a statement should be added that applicants may omit those organizations associated with age, race, sex, or religion.
Credit Rating	None.	"Do you own your own car?" "Do you own or rent your residence?"	Use of credit rating questions tends to have an adverse impact on minority group applicants and has been found unlawful. Unless shown to be job related, questions on car ownership, home ownership, length of residence, garnishments of wages, etc., may violate Title VII.
Arrest Record	"Have you ever been convicted of a crime related to the job you will be expected to perform?" Example: A conviction of embezzlement is related to the job of bank loan officer.	"Have you ever been arrested for a crime?"	Asking if an applicant has ever been arrested violates the applicant's Title VII rights because such questions adversely affect minority applicants.

Source: Adapted from Gatewood, R. D., and Feild, H. S. (2001). *Human resource selection,* 5th ed. Fort Worth, TX: Harcourt College Publishers. Copyright © 2001 by the Harcourt College Publishers, reproduced by permission of the publisher and Bland, T., and Stalcup, S. (1999, March). Build a legal employment application. *HRMagazine,* 129–133.

The EEOC rules that affect the type of information asked during the employment-application process do not apply to employment decisions made outside the United States. As described in the Manager's Notebook titled "Outside the United States the Rules for Providing Résumé Information Are More Permissive," European employers can ask job applicants to provide more personal information than would be possible within the United States.

Global

Outside the United States the Rules for Providing Résumé Information Are More Permissive

Whereas EEOC laws place restrictions on using certain kinds of information such as age, marital status, and gender within a résumé, such limitations do not apply outside the United States. Such restrictions prevent employers from using inappropriate information that can result in a lawsuit by an employee who may allege that he or she was discriminated against in an employment decision. In Europe, however, many employers expect an employee to provide date of birth, gender, nationality, and a photograph as part of the employment-application process. Some European employers also expect an employee to list the number of spoken languages and the level of competence in each. For example, in Switzerland, where three languages are officially recognized—German, French, and Italian—employers need to know which languages an applicant has mastered.

Although the rules that govern the type of specific employee background information expected do vary between some European countries, none of the countries follow the same rules as the United States, because there is no European equivalent to the EEOC laws. Currently the European Union is trying to standardize the type of information permitted to be disclosed within a résumé in any project that it sponsors.

Source: Fuller, T. (2004, December 1). Defining a standard in résumés. *International Herald Tribune*, 11.

Summary and Conclusions

Why Understanding the Legal Environment Is Important

Understanding and complying with human resource law is important because (1) it is the right thing to do, (2) it helps you realize the limitations of your firm's HR and legal departments, and (3) it helps you minimize your firm's potential liability.

Challenges to Legal Compliance

HR law is challenging for four reasons. Laws, regulations, and court decisions are all part of a dynamic legal landscape. The laws and regulations are complex. The strategies for fair employment required by the laws and regulations sometime compete with, rather than reinforce, one another. And laws often have unanticipated or unintended consequences.

Equal Employment Opportunity Laws

The following are the most important EEO laws: (1) Equal Pay Act of 1963—prohibits discrimination in pay between men and women performing the same job in the same organization. (2) Title VII of the Civil Rights Act of 1964—prohibits employers from basing employment decisions on a person's race, color, religion, sex, or national origin. It has been amended or interpreted to prohibit discrimination based on pregnancy (the Pregnancy Discrimination Act of 1978) and sexual harassment. Most recently, it has been amended by the Civil Rights Act of 1991, which places the burden of proof in a discrimination case squarely on the

defendant (employer), prohibits the use of quotas, and allows for punitive and compensatory damages as well as jury trials. Executive Order 11246 prohibits discrimination against the same categories of people that Title VII protects but also requires that government agencies and contractors take affirmative action to promote the employment of persons in protected classes. (3) Age Discrimination in Employment Act of 1967—prohibits discrimination against employees who are 40 years old or older. (4) Americans with Disabilities Act of 1990—prohibits discrimination against individuals with disabilities who can perform the essential functions of a job with or without reasonable accommodation. The Vocational Rehabilitation Act of 1973, the precursor to ADA, applied only to government agencies and contractors. (5) Vietnam Era Veterans Readjustment Act of 1974—prohibits discrimination against Vietnam-era veterans by federal contractors and requires federal contractors to take affirmative action to hire Vietnam-era veterans.

EEO Enforcement and Compliance

Two main agencies are responsible for enforcing EEO laws. The Equal Employment Opportunity Commission (EEOC) enforces EEO laws. It processes discrimination complaints, issues written regulations, and gathers and disseminates information. The Office of Federal Contract Compliance Programs (OFCCP) enforces the laws and executive orders that apply to the federal government and its contractors. The OFCCP also monitors the quality and effectiveness of affirmative action plans.

Other Important Laws

The Immigration Reform and Control Act of 1986 requires employers to document the legal work status of their employees. The Immigration Act of 1990 makes it easier for skilled immigrants to enter the United States. The Drug-Free Workplace Act of 1988 requires that government contractors try to ensure that their workplaces are free of drug use. The Uniformed Services Employment and Reemployment Act of 1994 protects the rights of private sector employees who take short leaves to perform military service.

Avoiding Pitfalls in EEO

Employers can avoid many pitfalls associated with HR law by engaging in sound management practices. Among the most important of these practices are training, establishing an employee complaint resolution system, documenting decisions, communicating honestly with employees, and asking job applicants only for information the employer needs to know.

Key Terms

adverse impact, 90
affirmative action, 87
Age Discrimination in Employment Act (1967), 98
Americans with Disabilities Act (1990), 98
bona fide occupational qualification (BFOQ), 91
compensatory damages, 97
conciliation, 102
discrimination, 89

disparate treatment, 89
Equal Employment Opportunity Commission (EEOC), 102
Equal Pay Act (1963), 88
essential functions, 99
executive order, 97
fair employment, 87
four-fifths rule, 91
hostile work environment sexual harassment, 93
individuals with disabilities, 98

Office of Federal Contract Compliance Programs (OFCCP), 103
protected class, 89
punitive damages, 97
quid pro quo sexual harassment, 93
quotas, 97
reasonable accommodation, 100
reverse discrimination, 104
Title VII (Civil Rights Act of 1964), 89

Discussion Questions

1. Explain why HR decisions are heavily regulated. Based on your analysis of current social forces, what new laws or regulations do you think will be passed or issued in the next few years?

2. You own a small construction business. One of your workers is 55 years old and had heart bypass surgery about six months ago. He wants to come back to work, but you are concerned that he will not be able to handle the job's physical tasks. What should you do? What are you prohibited from doing? What laws apply in this case?

3. What is adverse impact? How does it differ from adverse treatment?

4. Should employers have a policy that prevents employees from dating each other? Would such a policy be legal? Would it be ethical?

5. How can an individual show prima facie evidence for adverse impact discrimination? How would an employer defend itself from this evidence?

6. What are bona fide occupational qualifications (BFOQ)? What is a business necessity? Can race be a BFOQ? Can it be a business necessity? Why or why not?

7. Many companies in the United States have recently put an end to the practice of giving an annual employee Christmas party due to complaints by employees with non-Christian religious backgrounds or spiritual values who claimed the Christmas party was a discriminatory employment practice. These employees argued that the employer who celebrated by paying for an employee Christmas party favored Christianity over other religions and belief systems. Do you think non-Christian employees are treated illegally or unethically when the employer decides to give a Christmas party for all the employees? Why? What reasonable accommodation could an employer make to satisfy both the Christian and non-Christian employees?

8. Kate has severe diabetes that seriously limits her ability to eat. Even when taking insulin to help manage her diabetes, Kate must test her blood sugar several times a day and strictly monitor the availability of food, the time she eats, and the type and quantity of food she eats to avoid serious medical consequences. Does Kate have a disability under the ADA? Explain your answer.

There is a variety of additional material available on the Web site that accompanies this text. You can access this information by visiting the Web site at **www.prenhall.com/gomez**.

Emerging Trends Case 3.1   YOU MANAGE IT!

The Importance of Tolerance in the Workplace

The EEOC has reported a significant increase in the number of charges of alleged discrimination based on religion and/or national origin. Many of the charges have been filed by individuals who are perceived to be Muslim, Arab, South Asian, or Sikh. These charges commonly allege harassment and discharge.

Title VII of the Civil Rights Act of 1964 prohibits workplace discrimination based on religion, ethnicity, country of origin, race, and color. Such discrimination is prohibited in any aspect of employment, including recruitment, hiring, promotion, benefits, training, job duties, and termination. Workplace harassment is also prohibited by Title VII. In addition, an employer must provide a reasonable accommodation for religious practices unless doing so would result in undue hardship.

Read the following situations regarding hiring and employment decisions and answer the questions that follow:

Incident 1: Wearing a Head Scarf on a Temporary Assignment

Susan is an experienced clerical worker who wears a hijab (head scarf) in conformance with her Muslim beliefs. ABC Temps places Susan in a long-term assignment with one of its clients. The client contacts ABC and requests that it instruct Susan to remove her hijab while working at the front desk, or ABC must provide a person who does not need to wear the hijab at work, effectively displacing Susan from her job. According to the client, Susan's religious attire violates the firm's dress code and presents the "wrong image" because it is a very conservative firm. Should ABC comply with its client's request?

Incident 2: Is It Harassment or Joking?

Muhammad, who is Arab American, works for Friendly Motors, a large used car business. Muhammad meets with his manager and complains that Bill, one of his coworkers, regularly calls him names like "the ayatollah," "the local terrorist," and "camel jockey," and has intentionally embarrassed him in front of customers by claiming he is incompetent.

When confronted with these allegations, Bill claimed he was just joking with Muhammad, that he dubs coworkers with names such as "shorty," "dude," and "stinky," and has never had any complaints from them. Instead they are amused by Bill's colorful names. How should the manager deal with this situation?

Critical Thinking Questions

1. In incident 1, does it make a difference whether ABC Temps or the client asks Susan to remove her head scarf? What should ABC Temps do if the client refuses to withdraw its request that Susan not wear the head scarf at its office?

2. In incident 2, should the manager accept Bill's defense, that he was only joking and that Muhammad needs to lighten up and learn to appreciate the American sense of humor, where nicknames are part of having fun at the workplace? When does a joke stop being funny and turn into a case of harassment?

Team Exercise

Assume you are a manager in a company and you noticed a significant increase in complaints by Arab and Muslim employees that they are being harassed and shunned by the other employees. With three or four of your fellow classmates develop an approach to deal with this pattern of hostile employee behavior toward Arab and Muslim employees. Should harassment be treated as a "special case" as a consequence of the U.S. president's war on terrorism, or should it be treated as any other instance of harassment? Make sure you are able to defend your approach.

Experiential Exercise

With a partner, enact a 5-minute role-play situation based on incident 2. Assume that Bill and Muhammad have been asked by their manager to have a meeting to try to work out their differences and better understand each other. Let Bill begin the role-play by attempting to explain his joking behavior and use of nicknames to Muhammad. Muhammad listens to Bill and then in turn tries to explain why he finds the nicknames disrespectful and a form of harassment. Afterwards the role players should discuss any conclusions that can be drawn from this experience. Who is right, Bill or Muhammad? Is Bill being culturally insensitive? Is Muhammad misinterpreting Bill's gesture of friendliness with a nickname, due to his lack of understanding of American culture? (For example, President Bush gives nicknames to many of his associates.) The partners in the role-play should be prepared to share their answers with the class.

Source: The U.S. Equal Employment Opportunity Commission (2002, May 14). Questions and answers about employer responsibilities concerning the employment of Muslims, Arabs, South Asians, and Sikhs. *www.eeoc. gov/facts/backlash-employer.html; HR Focus.* (2001, November). The growing importance of tolerance in the workplace, 3–5.

YOU MANAGE IT!

Global Case 3.2

"Positive Discrimination" in India Stirs Up Controversy

A form of affirmative action has been used in India since the 1950s to provide public-sector jobs and places in schools and colleges for disadvantaged members of Indian society, which include the lowest caste members, called *dalits* or *untouchables,* and other lower-ranked members of India's caste system. In India, affirmative action is called "positive discrimination" and is implemented by means of quotas for jobs and school admissions. These quotas were formalized such that 15 percent of positions are reserved for dalits and an additional 7.5 percent for "scheduled tribes." Attempts to extend this to cover 25 percent of the population deemed "other backward castes" ran into furious opposition in the early 1990s. Until recently, private businesses were regarded as exempt from affirmative action. However, in 2005, with a boom in the private sector, Indian politicians have been discussing extending positive discrimination rules to private sector firms.

Businesses in India strongly oppose these compulsory quotas. They fear such rules will weaken the competitive advantages that have allowed them to prosper globally in recent years. The government of Maharashtra, India's richest state, has already drafted legislation that would "reserve" more than half the jobs in some companies for scheduled tribes, dalits, and "other backward castes." In response, some businesses have threatened to leave the state if the law is ever implemented.

Many analysts agree that in the public sector the practice of reserving jobs for individuals in lower castes has been widely abused; some local officials have even sold fraudulent caste certificates. Despite the abuse, politicians in India recognize that positive discrimination in the private sector is a vote winner, and some politicians may use this issue to gain votes and power.

Critical Thinking Questions

1. How does affirmative action in India differ from that in the United States? Why do you think affirmative action in India is called "positive discrimination"?

2. In the United States, many large, private firms such as IBM, Xerox and PepsiCo are supporters of affirmative action. What benefits do these firms derive from affirmative action, as practiced in the United States? Assuming that these firms have business units in India, do you think they would support positve discrimination in India if a law extended it to private companies? Why or why not?

Team Exercise

Form a group of four or five students and gather data on the practice of affirmative action in other countries. You can use a computer-based search engine to find articles on this topic with search words such as "affirmative action," "positive discrimination," and the name of a specific country. Compare the practice of affirmative action in each country with how it is practiced in the United States. What is unique about affirmative action in the United States? Are there other countries that use the term "positive discrimination" besides India? Which ones? What disadvantaged groups are the beneficiaries of affirmative action outside the United States? Let each group member become an "expert" on a country that uses affirmative action or positive discrimination to increase oppportunity for disadvantaged groups within that country. Be prepared to share your findings with the class.

Experiential Exercise

Most institutions of higher education receive money from the federal government for research and other activities. Their eligibility depends on their implementing affirmative action policies.

Interview some undergraduate and graduate students and faculty about their opinions of affirmative action. Try to do five interviews that sample these three groups, such as with students in other classes that you do not know very well, faculty you have taken classes from, or faculty that your advisor may be able to suggest to you. If you do not know any graduate students, you can go to one of the graduate programs on campus, such as the law or medical school, and ask a student there whether he or she would mind being interviewed by you.

Ask your interviewees a few questions about the perceived advantages and disadvantages of having an affirmative action policy for hiring and college admissions decisions at your school.

After reviewing the notes from your interviews, draw some conclusions about affirmative action within the context of higher education. Were there any surprises? What aspects, if any, did your interviewees find controversial? What would happen if affirmative action no longer were used in schools? How has the data you gathered influenced your own opinion about affirmative action?

Source: The Economist. (2004, November 13). Job-preferment in India: A backward cast of mind?, 47.

Emerging Trends Case 3.3   YOU MANAGE IT!

Are Women Breaking Through the Glass Ceiling?

"Glass ceiling" refers to invisible or artificial barriers that prevent women and people of color from advancing above a certain level in an organization. In the United States, women represent 30 percent of all managers but less than 5 percent of executives.

The glass ceiling does not represent a typical form of discrimination that consists of entry barriers to women and minorities within organizations. Rather, it represents a subtle form of discrimination that includes gender stereotypes, lack of opportunities for women to gain job experiences necessary for advancement, and lack of top-management commitment to providing resources to promote initiatives that support an environment for women to advance to the top executive ranks.

As an invisible barrier, the glass ceiling is difficult to crash through legislation. Informal networking and mentoring are often mentioned as ways of increasing opportunities for women to become executives. However, cross-gender relationships between a male mentor and a female employee may be discouraged by the sexual tensions that arise in such relationships, because they can become close, blurring the distinction between their professional and personal lives. In some instances, a mentoring relationship with a younger female may threaten the established male with the potential for a career-wrecking allegation of sexual harassment in which the woman is viewed as the victim, because she ranks lower in the hierarchy. Although same-gender female mentoring relationships are less likely to be as problematic as the cross-gender ones, they depend on the availability of senior female executives willing and able to nurture high-potential women.

Despite the glass ceiling, by 2005 the number of women who achieved the position of chief executive officer (CEO) or chairman of a major *Fortune* 500 corporation in the United States was much greater than the number of women who were top executives in large corporations in 1997. Here are some women executives who have clearly broken through the glass ceiling, as of 2005:

- Andrea Jung, CEO of Avon, a large cosmetics firm
- Charlotte Beers, chairman of J. Walter Thompson, one of the world's largest advertising firms

- Patricia Russo, CEO of Lucent Technologies
- Anne Mulcahy, CEO and chairman of Xerox
- Oprah Winfrey, chairman of Harpo Entertainment Group
- Marjorie Scardino, CEO of Pearson

Critical Thinking Questions

1. Go to the Web sites of Avon (*www.Avon.com*), Lucent Technologies (*www.lucent.com*), and Xerox (*www.xerox.com*) and explore those sites to learn more about the women who are either the CEO or chairperson at these companies. Several of the Web sites have a "biography of executives" feature to click on to learn more about the CEO and other top executives. Another possibility is to use a search engine such as Yahoo! and search on the company name and name of the CEO or chairperson to gather some background on the careers of executive women. Based on the information you gather, develop a rationale to explain how these women overcame the "glass ceiling" and attained the top executive role in a major U.S. corporation.

2. Some male senior executives avoid becoming mentors to younger women because of their fear of possible sexual harassment claims against them (as retribution for a romantic relationship that ends badly) or office gossip suggesting the mentoring pair are having a romance. Do you think it is reasonable for male executives to have fears about what could evolve or be suggested about professional relationships with female managers? How could a woman seeking a mentor go about cultivating a mentoring relationship with a male senior executive, being aware that some men have reservations about establishing close professional relationships with women due to office gossip or the possibility of a romantic relationship that results in the male having to defend himself against charges of sexual harassment?

Team Exercise

With a team of four or five students, develop an HR plan to break down some of the glass ceiling barriers in an organization that is male dominated at the upper ranks. Some examples of male-dominated industries include high technology

(Intel, Texas Instruments, and Cisco Systems, for example), defense (Boeing, Lockheed Martin, and General Dynamics, for example), and energy (Exxon, BP-Amoco, and Chevron, for example). Think of specific HR activities that could "add value" to the firm by breaking down barriers to women who are seeking to become executives in the organization. Some HR functions that could provide fruitful sources include training, recruitment and selection, compensation, benefits, work systems, HR planning, performance appraisal, employee relations, and discipline. Be prepared to present and defend your plan to other members of your class.

Experiential Exercise

Some women avoid the glass ceiling by becoming entrepreneurs. Contact three female entrepreneurs or business owners and ask them some questions that pertain to owning their own business. Start with your own network of family and friends and the entrepreneurship center at the business school at your university or a professor who teaches entrepreneurship. You could also contact the Chamber of Commerce in your city.

Here are some questions to pose in your interviews: Why did you decide to start your own business? What have you learned from the experience of being an entrepreneur? When is the best time in one's career to start a business? Why do you think there is a growing trend among professional women to start their own businesses? Now that more women are becoming CEOs of large corporations, do you think there are fewer obstacles for women to advance to the top of organizations?

After you complete your interviews, summarize the results. What seem to be the key advantages of being a business owner? Do you think that male entrepreneurs would provide the same answers to your questions? Did any of the women you spoke with bring up gender issues related to their former employer as motivations for their career change? Be prepared to share your findings with other members of the class.

Sources: Morris, B. (2005, January 10). How corporate America is betraying women. *Fortune,* 64–74; Bell, M., McLaughlin, M., and Sequeira, J. (2002, April). Discrimination, harassment, and the glass ceiling: Women executives as change agents. *Journal of Business Ethics,* 65–76; and Haben, M. (2001, April/May). Shattering the glass ceiling. *Executive Speeches,* 4–10.

Appendix to Chapter 3

Human Resource Legislation Discussed in This Text

The laws are listed in chronological order.

Law	Year	Description	Chapter(s)
Workers' Compensation Laws	Various	State-by-state laws that establish insurance plans to compensate employees injured on the job	12, 15, 16
Social Security Act	1935	Payroll tax to fund retirement benefits, disability and unemployment insurance	12
Wagner Act	1935	Legitimized labor unions and established the National Labor Relations Board	14, 15
Fair Labor Standards Act	1938	Established minimum wage and overtime pay	10, 15
Taft-Hartley Act	1947	Provided some protections for employers and limited union power; permitted states to enact right-to-work laws	15
Landrum-Griffin Act	1959	Protects union members' right to participate in union affairs	15
Equal Pay Act	1963	Prohibits unequal pay for same job	3, 10
Title VII of Civil Rights Act	1964	Prohibits employment decisions based on race, color, religion, sex, and national origin	3, 4, 5, 7, 14, 16, 17
Executive Order 11246	1965	Same as Title VII; also requires affirmative action	3
Age Discrimination in Employment Act	1967	Prohibits employment decisions based on age when person is 40 or older	3, 5
Occupational Safety and Health Act	1970	Establishes safety and health standards for organizations to protect employees	14, 16
Employee Retirement Income Security Act (ERISA)	1974	Regulates the financial stability of employee benefit and pension plans	12, 16
Job Training Partnership Act	1982	Provides block money grants to states, which pass them on to local governments and private entities that provide on-the-job training	8
Vietnam-Era Veterans Readjustment Act	1974	Prohibits federal contractors from discriminating against Vietnam-era veterans and encourages affirmative action plans to hire Vietnam veterans	3
Pregnancy Discrimination Act	1978	Prohibits employers from discriminating against pregnant women	3, 16
Consolidated Omnibus Budget Reconciliation Act (COBRA)	1985	Requires continued health insurance coverage (paid by employee) following termination	12
Immigration Reform and Control Act	1986	Prohibits discrimination based on citizenship status; employers required to document employees' legal work status	3, 17
Worker Adjustment and Retraining Act (WARN)	1988	Employers required to notify workers of impending layoffs	6
Drug-Free Workplace Act	1988	Covered employers must implement certain policies to restrict employee drug use	3, 16
Americans with Disabilities Act (ADA)	1990	Prohibits discrimination based on disability	3, 4, 5, 14, 16
Civil Rights Act	1991	Amends Title VII; prohibits quotas, allows for monetary punitive damages	3, 5
Family and Medical Leave Act	1993	Employers must provide unpaid leave for childbirth, adoption, illness	12, 15
Uniformed Services Employment and Reemployment Rights Act	1994	Employers must not discriminate against individuals who take leave from work to fulfill military service obligations	3
Health Insurance Portability and Accountability Act	1996	Employees are allowed to transfer their coverage of existing illnesses to new employer's insurance plan	12

Laws discussed briefly:

Byrnes Antistrikebreaking Act—Chapter 15
Coal Mine Health and Safety Act—Chapters 4, 16
Employee Polygraph Protection Act—Chapter 5
Immigration Act of 1990—Chapter 3
Norris-LaGuardia Act—Chapter 15
Older Workers Protection Act of 1990—Chapter 3
Railway Labor Act—Chapter 15

Managing Diversity

After reading this chapter, you should be able to deal more effectively with the following challenges:

1 **Link** affirmative action programs to employee diversity programs to ensure that the two support each other.

2 **Identify** the forces that contribute to the successful management of diversity within the firm.

3 **Reduce** potential conflict among employees resulting from cultural clashes and misunderstandings.

4 **Draw** a profile of employee groups that are less likely to be part of the corporate mainstream and develop policies specifically targeted to these groups' needs.

5 **Implement** HR systems that assist the firm in successfully managing diversity.

The second-grade school teacher posed a simple problem to the class: "There are four blackbirds sitting in a tree. You take a slingshot and shoot one of them. How many are left?"

"Three," answered the seven-year-old European with certainty. "One subtracted from four leaves three."

"Zero," answered the seven-year-old African with equal certainty. "If you shoot one bird, the others will fly away."

Which child answered correctly? Clearly, the answer depends on your cultural point of view. For the first child, the birds in the problem represented a hypothetical situation that required a literal answer. For the second child, the birds in the problem had a relationship to known behavior that could be expected to occur.[1]

THE MANAGERIAL PERSPECTIVE

To succeed as a manager in the twenty-first century, you must work effectively with people who are different from you. The labor force is becoming more diverse in terms of ethnicity, race, sex, sexual orientation, disability, and other cultural factors. The managerial challenge is learning how to take advantage of this diversity while fostering cooperation and cohesiveness among dissimilar employees. The HR department may help you meet this challenge by developing training programs, offering assistance and advice, establishing fair selection procedures, and the like. But in the end, the line manager is the person who interacts face-to-face with diverse employees on a daily basis. In this chapter, we explore diversity issues that affect managers and the skills needed to make employee diversity a source of competitive advantage.

The blackbird story clearly illustrates one of the most important truths of HRM: People with different life experiences may interpret reality very differently. By the time people enter an organization, their *cognitive structure*—the way they perceive and respond to the world around them—has been largely determined. This cognitive structure is shaped both by unique personal experiences (with family, peers, school system) and by the socializing influences of the person's culture, and it operates both at home and in the workplace.

What Is Diversity?

Although definitions vary, **diversity** simply refers to human characteristics that make people different from one another. The English language has well over 23,000 words to describe personality[2] (such as "outgoing," "intelligent," "friendly," "loyal," "paranoid," and "nerdy"). The sources of individual variation are complex, but they can generally be grouped into two categories: those over which people have little or no control and those over which they have some control.[3]

Individual characteristics over which a person has little or no control include biologically determined characteristics such as race, sex, age, and certain physical attributes, as well as the family and society into which he or she is born. These factors exert a powerful influence on individual identity and directly affect how a person relates to other people.

In the second category are characteristics that people can adopt, drop, or modify during their lives through conscious choice and deliberate efforts. These include work background, income, marital status, military experience, political beliefs, geographic location, and education.

It is important to keep in mind the distinction between the sources of diversity and the diversity itself. Without this distinction, stereotyping tends to occur. Essentially, *stereotyping* is assuming that group averages or tendencies are true for each and every member of that group. For instance, employees who have had significant military experience are generally more accepting of an authoritarian management style than those who have not had such experience. However, if you conclude that *all* veterans favor authoritarian leadership, you will be wrong. Although veterans *on average* are more accepting of authority, there may be, as Figure 4.1 shows, very wide differences among veterans on this score. True, veterans *on the whole* show this characteristic to a greater degree than nonveterans, but the differences *within* each group are far greater than the average difference between groups. In fact, many veterans develop a distaste for authoritarian management *because* of their military experience, and many nonveterans prefer an authoritarian leadership style.

If you take this example and substitute any two groups (male-female, young-old, and so on) and any individual characteristic (aggressiveness, flexibility, amount of education), you will find in the vast majority of cases that the principle illustrated by Figure 4.1 holds true. In fact, it is very difficult to identify individual characteristics that do *not* have a substantial overlap between two groups. The main point of this discussion is to emphasize that while employees are diverse, a relatively small amount of this diversity is explained by their group membership.

Diversity
Human characteristics that make people different from one another.

Group Versus Individual Differences on Acceptance of Authoritarian Leadership

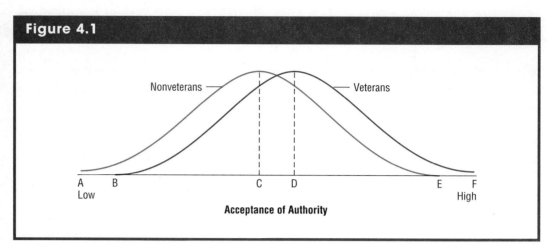

Figure 4.1

Nonveterans — *Veterans*

A   B   C   D   E   F
Low   High

Acceptance of Authority

Why Manage Employee Diversity?

To survive and prosper in an increasingly heterogeneous society, organizations must capitalize on employee diversity as a source of competitive advantage. For example, Computer Associates International hires software developers from many nationalities, filling jobs where there is an extreme shortage of personnel.[4] Because many of these employees are non-English speakers, Computer Associates offers free courses in English as a second language.[5] Avon Products provides another example of how firms capitalize on diversity. Avon uses its diversity to create a competitive advantage, using feedback from its workforce to adapt to women's changing needs quickly and effectively. The input of Avon's minority employees—almost one-third of its workforce—helped the firm find a successful niche in an industry that tends to ignore the beauty needs of women of color.[6] ATT provides formal recognition and support to employee networks formed around a characteristic of diversity (such as the Asian Pacific Islanders' Business Resource Group) if the networks present a business plan to management showing their value to the company.[7]

Affirmative Action Versus Managing Employee Diversity

Many people perceive *management of diversity* as a new label for affirmative action. In reality, these are two very distinct concepts.[8] *Affirmative action* first emerged from government pressures on business to provide greater opportunities for women and minorities. **Management of diversity**, in contrast, recognizes that traditional firms, where white men are the majority, are becoming a thing of the past. There is a growing awareness that a key factor in corporate performance is how well *nontraditional employees* such as women and minorities can be fully integrated and work effectively with one another and with their white male counterparts. For this reason, many organizations (such as the Society for Human Resource Management, Microsoft, Texas Instruments, and Computer Sciences Corporation) specify diversity as the ability to effectively use the talents of people from various backgrounds, experiences, and perspectives.[9]

Management of diversity
The set of activities involved in integrating nontraditional employees (women and minorities) into the workforce and using their diversity to the firm's competitive advantage.

Demographic Trends

In the next decade or so, we will see a dramatic growth rate in people aged 55 or older (46.6%). Asian Americans, Hispanic Americans, and other ethnic minorities have shown very rapid growth rates since 1990, and these are projected to continue at a fast pace into the end of the decade. In 2006, approximately 14 percent of the U.S. population was considered Hispanic, surpassing the percentage of African Americans (12.0%), Asian Americans (4.7%), and other minority groups (2.0%). Both groups have registered increases in workforce participation in recent years, and these are also expected to continue. White Americans still make up a substantial majority of the population in the year 2006 (68%) but less of a majority than in 1990 (79.1%). At current growth rates, in 25 years or so White Americans will be a minority (less than 50% of the total U.S. population). Women's labor force participation rates (currently 47 versus 53% for males) are expected to keep rising and men's to go on declining.

Avon's global workforce and leadership consist mainly of women. It has more female managers than any other Fortune 500 company, including the president of its U.S. Product Marketing Group, Andrea Jung.

Note that the data previously described is national. If we focus on the larger metropolitan areas, where most business takes place, the changes have been even more dramatic. Of the top 25 markets, "minorities" now make up a majority of the population in 18.[10] Most corporations are located within or near these metropolitan areas and are highly dependent on the local non-white labor supply to meet their needs.[11] In some states—most notably California, where non-whites account for more than half the population—the future is already here.

Of the more than 20 million jobs projected to be created over the next decade, 75 percent will be filled by women and minorities. This means that firms must actively compete to attract and retain educated and talented workers from those groups: Most large corporations across different industries are eagerly trying to create receptive environments for nontraditional employees. For instance, Lucent Technologies, Chase Manhattan, Marriott International, FedEx, Xerox, Sun Microsystems, Colgate, Palmolive, Merck, and DuPont, among others, have at least one minority member on their board of directors and close to one-fifth of officials and managers who are minority group members.[12] Together, these demographic changes make it imperative that employers plan for the central role that diversity management will play in the twenty-first century. At IBM, diversity permeates every facet of management and technical operations. During 2004–2005, for instance, IBM received 110 awards for its diversity initiatives, from a broad spectrum of prestigious organizations and publications.[13] These include the Top Ten Best Companies for Asian Americans by *Asian Enterprise* magazine, the National Society of Black Engineers Employer of Choice, Top Employer for Minority MBA Graduates by *Fortune*, Number One Among *Fortune* 100 companies for Hispanics by the Hispanic Association on Corporate Responsibility, and The Freedom to Compete Award for Innovation and Dedication to Recruiting Underrepresented University Minorities, Women, and Persons with Disabilities by the U.S. Equal Employment Opportunity Commission. Members of IBM's Worldwide Executive Council guide specific corporatewide diversity initiatives. The council is held accountable for recruiting, retaining, and advancing all talent and, most important, linking IBM's diversity initiatives to the global marketplace.[14]

Diversity as an Asset

Employee diversity can improve organizational functioning by stimulating greater creativity, better problem solving, and greater system flexibility.[15] Rosabeth Kanter, a well-known business consultant based at Harvard University, notes that most innovative firms purposely establish heterogeneous work groups "to create a marketplace of ideas, recognizing that a multiplicity of points of views need to be brought to bear on a problem."[16]

- **Greater creativity** Employee diversity can stimulate consideration of less obvious alternatives. Consider the following true story:

  > A Hispanic man and a white woman were members of a task force advising the CEO on a planned organizational downsizing. These two people suggested that the recommendation of the task force majority to lay off 10 percent of the workforce would devastate morale. Upon further consideration, the CEO decided not to lay off employees and opted instead for a plan proposed by these two dissenters. The plan proposed to reduce labor costs by offering early retirement, unpaid vacations, and stock in the firm to employees in exchange for a 5-percent salary cut. Most employees reacted very positively to the plan, with many reporting that it increased their loyalty and commitment to the firm.[17]

- **Better problem solving** Homogeneous groups are prone to a phenomenon called *groupthink*, in which all members quickly converge on a mistaken solution because they share the same mind-set and view the problem through the lens of conformity.[18] In a heterogeneous group with a broader and richer reservoir of experiences and cultural perspectives, the potential for groupthink shrinks.
- **Greater system flexibility** In today's rapidly changing business environments, flexibility is an important characteristic of successful firms. If properly managed, employee diversity can infuse more flexibility into the firm. The existence of diversity at different levels generates more openness to new ideas in general and greater tolerance for different ways of doing things.
- **Better information** A more diverse workforce provides the organization with a broader scope of information and set of skills that may be applied to a variety of situations. For example, see the Manager's Notebook, "Police Comb Their Ranks for Foreign-Language Speakers to Keep Tabs on Possible Plots."

Marketing Concerns

Most successful firms realize that effective management of a diverse workforce can lead to better marketing strategies for a multicultural, multiethnic population. For example:

- Colgate acquires the top spot in the oral care market with Total toothpaste, which was designed by a team led by older scientists intent on developing a toothpaste for a maturing population. They discovered Triclosan (an ingredient in Total), a broad-spectrum antibiotic used to fight gingivitis, a bleeding gum disease that people are prone to as they age.[19]
- The appearance of more women online is a boom for e-commerce. Women directly influence more than 80 percent of all retail spending, according to BIGreseach LLC, a market-research firm in Worthington, Ohio. When New York–based Bluefly Inc., a retailer of upscale closeout clothing, was launched in mid-1998, the e-commerce market was still a predominantly male place, and an apparel start-up looked like a sure loser. But the company looked ahead to the day the Internet would attract more women. "We went after this particular category based on the expected shifts," says Jonathan Morris, executive vice president. "We think that's one of the reasons that we're still here, after the dot.com bust."[20]

Challenges in Managing Employee Diversity

Although employee diversity offers opportunities that can enhance organizational performance, it also presents managers with a new set of challenges. In other words, greater employee diversity by itself does not ensure positive outcomes. A number of researchers have attempted to quantify the effects of diversity.[21] These challenges include appropriately valuing employee diversity, balancing individual needs with group fairness, dealing with resistance to change, ensuring group cohesiveness and open communication, avoiding employee resentment and backlash, retaining valued performers, and maximizing opportunity for all.

Customer-Driven HR

Police Comb Their Ranks for Foreign-Language Speakers to Keep Tabs on Possible Plots

Andy Sipowicz, the gruff New York detective on the TV series "NYPD Blue," was known for being a xenophobe. The real New York Police Department (NYPD), though, is reaching out to immigrants to prevent terrorism.

At a time when federal agencies have a backlog of untranslated documents and data from the war against terror, the NYPD has developed a foreign-language program through which undercover officers get intelligence on potential terror plots, as well as translate news events and documents from countries thousands of miles away. The Pentagon's Defense Intelligence Agency, recognizing the NYPD's expertise, has borrowed 17 officers fluent in Arabic to help with translation and interpretation.

The NYPD decided to "put diversity to work" by scouring the files of the department's nearly 50,000 employees, approaching those who had indicated that they had language skills and asking whether they would voluntarily be tested by Berlitz International Inc., the language instruction and translation company. So far, 470 employees, mainly police officers, have passed tests in more than 45 languages considered critical, including Arabic, Urdu, Hindi, Pashto, Farsi, Dari, and Punjabi.

The program doesn't include the more than 10,000 other department members who speak Italian or Spanish. A recent report by the U.S. Justice Department's inspector general said that federal agencies, such as the FBI, had thousands of hours of untranslated communications, and the NYPD program might serve as a model to decrease this backlog.

Source: Adapted with permission from Fields, G. (2005, March 2). New York teaches lesson on fighting terror. *Wall Street Journal,* A-4.

Valuing Employee Diversity

The debate over how to deal with diversity has become highly charged and politicized. Those who oppose diversity argue that the United States is losing the common ground necessary to a viable society, while those who advocate diversity argue that assimilation wrongly assumes a hierarchy of skills and behaviors with white men at the top and women and minorities below them. Organizations often find themselves attacked from both sides and frustrated in their attempts to manage employee diversity effectively. As one divisional manager of a major corporation says:

> I feel like as a company we are walking on eggshells all the time. No matter what we do someone will find it offensive. If we use the term "diversity" some people accuse us of trying to enforce political correctness. If we don't openly celebrate diversity, others will accuse us of being sexists and racists. This is a no-win proposition.[22]

Nonetheless, prejudice is still alive and well, so businesses and the people in them need to make progress to truly value the contributions of women and minorities. For instance, an analysis of Equal Employment Opportunity Commission data by Rutgers University Law School shows that although discrimination has fallen overall, employees in some regions are still highly biased. The researchers report that in Washington State, for example, 25 percent of employers with more than 50 workers still intentionally discriminate against women. And, in Georgia,

Wal-Mart's workforce is an outgrowth of its customer orientation. Its workforce, a reflection of its diverse customer base, helps Wal-Mart to address minority customers' needs more effectively than its competitors can.

almost 40 percent of larger employers discriminate racially, whereas 30 percent display a bias against women.[23]

Individual Versus Group Fairness

Universal concept of management
The management concept holding that all management practices should be standardized.

Cultural relativity concept of management
The management concept holding that management practices should be molded to the different sets of values, beliefs, attitudes, and behaviors exhibited by a diverse workforce.

The extent to which a **universal concept of management**, which leads to standardized management practices, should be replaced by a **cultural relativity concept of management**, which calls for molding management practices to the workforce's different sets of values, beliefs, attitudes, and patterns of behaviors, is an extraordinarily complex question. The proponents of universalism believe that fitting management practices to a diverse workforce sows the seeds for a permanent culture clash in which perceived inequities lead to intense workplace conflict. For instance, when the Lotus software company extended benefits coverage to homosexual couples, unmarried heterosexual employees living with a partner felt that they had been unfairly left out. Conversely, the proponents of relativity argue that failure to adapt HR practices to the needs of a diverse population may alienate much of the workforce and reduce their potential contributions.

Resistance to Change

Although employee diversity is a fact of life, the dominant groups in organizations are still composed of white men. Some argue that a long-established corporate culture is very resistant to change and that this resistance is a major roadblock for women and minorities seeking to survive and prosper in a corporate setting.

Group Cohesiveness and Interpersonal Conflict

Although employee diversity can lead to greater creativity and better problem solving, it can also lead to open conflict and chaos if there is mistrust and lack of respect among groups. This means that as organizations become more diverse, they face greater risks that employees will not work together effectively. Interpersonal friction rather than cooperation may become the norm.

Segmented Communication Networks

Shared experiences are often strongly reinforced by *segmented communication channels* in the workplace. One study found that most communication within organizations occurs between members of the same sex and race. This was found to be true across all professional categories, even at the top, where the number of women and minorities is very small.[24]

The presence of segmented communication poses three major problems to businesses. First, the organization cannot fully capitalize on the perspectives of diverse employees if they remain confined to their own groups. Second, segmented communication makes it more difficult to establish common ground across various groups.[25] Third, women and minorities often miss opportunities or are unintentionally penalized for not being part of the mainstream communication networks.

Resentment

Equal employment opportunity (EEO) was imposed by government rather than self-initiated. In the vast majority of U.S. organizations, it was a forced change rather than a voluntary one. One side effect of forced compliance has been the reinforcement of a belief among some managers and mainstream employees that organizations have to compromise their standards to comply with EEO laws. Some have seen EEO laws as legislating a "forced diversity" that favors political solutions over performance and/or competence.

Given this background, it is perhaps not surprising that twice as many white men as women and minorities feel that promotions received by the latter groups can be attributed to affirmative action.[26] This belief presents two problems. First, women and minorities in positions of authority and responsibility may not be taken as seriously as white men are. Second, the belief that white men are getting the short end of the stick may provoke some of them to vent their frustration against those employees (women and minorities) whom they believe are getting an unfair advantage.

It is important that managers deal with these issues because affirmative action is here to stay. By 2006, polls confirmed that big business's commitment to affirmative action continues to be strong, even though most firms now prefer to use the term "diversity."[27]

Backlash

Some white men feel that they have been made the scapegoats for society's ills and that they have to defend themselves against encroachments by those using their gender or ethnicity to lay claim to organizational resources (such as promotions, salaries, and job security). Thus, whereas women and minorities may view a firm's "cultural diversity policy" as a commitment to improving their chances for advancement, white men may see it as a threat. Clearly, firms face a major challenge in trying to grapple with this backlash—which may be unwarranted, because white men still enjoy considerable advantages.[28]

Retention

The main complaint among female and minority employees is that they lack career growth opportunities. The perception that their upward mobility is thwarted grows stronger at higher levels as women and minorities bump up against the **glass ceiling**, an invisible barrier in the organization that prevents them from rising to any higher position. Lower job satisfaction translates into higher resignation rates, with a resulting loss of valuable talent and greater training costs because of high turnover.

Competition for Opportunities

As minorities grow both proportionately and absolutely in the U.S. population, competition for jobs and opportunities is likely to become much stronger. Already there are rising tensions among minorities jockeying for advancement. Employers are being put into the uncomfortable position of having to decide which minority is most deserving.[29] Consider these examples:

■ "Blacks have been too successful at the expense of everyone else," grumbles Peter Rogbal, a Mexican American captain in the San Francisco Fire Department. "Other groups have been ignored to placate the black community."

A Question of Ethics

Many managers and executives use golfing as an opportunity to combine business and pleasure. How could this practice damage an organization's diversity efforts? Are there any recreational activities that could enhance diversity efforts?

Glass ceiling
The intangible barrier in an organization that prevents female and minority employees from rising to positions above a certain level.

A Question of Ethics

What ethical problems might arise from giving preferential treatment to certain employees based on their group membership?

- One diversity expert notes that "African-Americans, who suffered tremendously for their political gains, worry that Hispanics will stomp on them during their climb to greater power. Latinos wonder whether blacks will make room."[30]
- African Americans fear that newly arrived blacks from places such as Nigeria, Ethiopia, Somalia, Ghana, and Kenya will take away job opportunities from U.S.–born blacks. In the words of Columbia University historian Eric Fosner, "Historically, every immigrant group has jumped over American-born blacks. The final irony would be if African immigrants did, too."[31]

There are no fail-proof techniques for effectively handling these challenges. There is, however, one principle that managers should always keep in mind: Treat employees as individuals, not as members of a group. Many of these challenges then become much more manageable.

Diversity in Organizations

The elements of diversity—such as race, ethnicity, and sex—tend to have a profound impact on how people relate to one another. In this section, we discuss (in alphabetical order) the groups that are most likely to be "left out" of the corporate mainstream. Of course, one individual may belong to several of these groups. For this reason, the Census Bureau in 2000 allowed Americans to classify themselves into multiple racial categories. Nevertheless, the distinction between white versus black, Asian, or Hispanic still lingers in the United States, whether or not a person has mixed ancestry or how an individual chooses to classify himself or herself.

African Americans

African Americans constitute approximately 12 percent of the U.S. workforce. Since the passage of the Civil Rights Act of 1964, the number of African American officials, managers, technicians, and skilled craftspeople has tripled while the number in clerical positions has quadrupled and the number in professional jobs has doubled.[32] However, a significant percentage of African Americans (perhaps as high as 15%) are among the "hardcore" unemployed.

African Americans face two major problems in organizations. First, explicit, intentional racism still exists some 40 plus years after the first civil rights victories.[33] African Americans are not the only group to suffer from blatant racism, but it is safe to say that they are the group that suffers the most. The persistence of the Ku Klux Klan and other white supremacy organizations serves as a constant reminder, to both African Americans and U.S. society as a whole, that the struggle for civil rights is not over. Managers need to be careful to reassure their African American employees, and the entire organization, that racist views will not be tolerated in the workplace.

The second problem African Americans face as a group is less educational preparation than whites.[34] This is not an issue unique to blacks. Both blacks and Hispanics showed approximately half the college graduation rate of whites. Because of the increasing importance of technology and information in the U.S. economy, the discrepancy between the wage rates of college-educated and non-college-educated workers is growing. Therefore, the differential in educational preparation between African Americans (and Hispanic Americans) and whites puts the former at a major disadvantage in the labor market.

There is, however, reason for optimism A recent analysis of 291 metropolitan areas indicated that all but 19 of these areas were more integrated than in 1990. Most recent census figures indicate a record-low black poverty rate (22% versus 36% 20 years earlier) and a record-high black median household income ($30,000, about 20% higher than 20 years earlier, controlling for inflation). During the past three decades, black household incomes have increased almost twice as fast as whites' incomes. Controlling for inflation, among married-couple households, some 51 percent of African Americans had incomes of $50,000 or more. In 1980, barely one of two blacks over age 25 held a high school diploma. In 2005, nearly four of five, or just under 80 percent had a high school diploma; and for blacks in the 25–29 age group, it was

86 percent, which was the same as for whites. And in less than 20 years, the number of black college graduates has doubled.[35] African Americans' share of management jobs has increased at least fivefold since 1966.[36]

One interesting trend since 1990 is the relatively large number of blacks from Africa and the Caribbean settling in the United States. Currently, the proportion of blacks who are foreign born is 7.3 percent, but this figure is almost 70 percent higher than in 1990. In some large eastern cities the numbers are more dramatic. For instance, in New York about one in three blacks are foreign born. For the first time (as per 2005 figures), more blacks are now coming to the United States from Africa than during the slave trade. According to a recent report by the *New York Times,* "New arrivals are redefining what it means to be African American. The steady decline in the percentage of African Americans with ancestors who suffered directly through the middle passage and Jim Crow is also shaping the debate over affirmative action, diversity programs, and other initiatives intended to redress the legacy of slavery."[37]

Asian Americans

Americans of Asian descent constitute approximately 4.7 percent of the U.S. workforce. Their representation in the labor force increased by approximately 60 percent from 1990 to 2006 and is projected to increase by another 20 percent by 2010. Just as the term "Hispanics" applies to a range of people, "Asian Americans" include a wide variety of races, ethnic groups, and nationalities (for instance, Japanese, Chinese, Koreans, Indians, and Pakistanis).[38] Although Asian Americans have done well in technical fields and are very well represented in institutions of higher education, they are underrepresented in top corporate positions. Employer discrimination probably accounts for this to some extent, for Asian Americans are often stereotyped as being too cautious and reserved to lead.[39] They also suffer from the belief held in some quarters that, because of their educational attainments, they are an advantaged group and, therefore, do not deserve special consideration in hiring and promotion decisions. As a result, they are less likely to benefit from programs intended to improve the employment conditions of women and other minorities. Finally, one survey found that 40 percent of African Americans and Hispanic Americans and 27 percent of whites saw Asian Americans as "unscrupulous, crafty, and devious in business."[40] For all these reasons, some Asian Americans are relegated to technical and support positions that require minimal interpersonal interactions and offer limited opportunities for advancement.

John Yang, a vice president at Hewlett-Packard, notes that although Asians are well represented in the high-technology industry, they seldom make it to the upper echelons. Those Asians who are at the top rung of high-tech companies often started their own companies, like Charles Wang, founder and ex-CEO of New York's Computer Associates.[41]

Most Asian immigrants to the United States today are from the Philippines, Indonesia, Sri Lanka, and Thailand. At least half of these immigrants are women, many of whom end up working for very low wages in high-pressure industries like the garment business.[42] Since the terrorist attacks of September 11, 2001, South Asian Americans, including Indian Americans and Pakistani Americans and especially Sikh Americans, have reported several hundred cases of harassment and discrimination at work.[43]

People with Disabilities

There are approximately 43 million people with disabilities in the United States, 15 million of whom are actively employed and 6 million of whom subsist on Social Security payments and disability insurance.[44] At least 3.7 million people with severe disabilities are at work.[45] The remainder are either unemployed (presumably supported by their families) or under working age. People who are physically disabled face four main problems at work.

First, social acceptance of disabilities has not advanced much since the dark ages.[46] Many people still view people with disabilities with suspicion, even scorn, feeling that those who are physically impaired should stay away from the work world and let "normal" people assume their duties. At a more subtle level, coworkers may not befriend employees with disabilities because they simply do not know how to relate to them. Even extroverts can suddenly become shy in front of a person with a disability.

Second, people with disabilities are often seen as being less capable than others. This misconception persists even though people who are legally blind and deaf can perform many tasks just as well as those with normal sight and hearing, and modern technology allows many paralyzed people to run computers.

Third, many employers are afraid to hire people with disabilities or put them in responsible positions for fear that they may quit when work pressures mount. This myth persists despite the fact that absenteeism and turnover among such employees are only a fraction of those of other employees. For instance, Marriott International reports that turnover among employees with disabilities is only 8 percent annually, compared to 105 percent for workers in general.[47] Pizza Hut has also found a huge difference in turnover rates: 20 percent for employees with disabilities versus more than 200 percent for employees without disabilities.[48]

Fourth, many employers have overestimated the costs of accommodating employees with disabilities ever since the passage of the Americans with Disabilities Act in 1990. In fact, employers have found that accommodations are usually simple and cheap, costing on average between $200 and $500 across different firms.[49] For instance, Griener Engineering, Inc., in Irving, Texas, installed a lighter-weight door on the women's restroom and raised a drafting table by putting bricks under its legs.

The U.S. Supreme Court has established a clear distinction between a physical impairment and a disability under the Americans with Disabilites Act (ADA). For example, Ella Williams, an assembly-line worker at a Toyota plant, was unable to work with power tools after she developed crippling pain in her wrists, neck, and shoulders from repetitive motions. The Sixth Circuit Court of Appeals in Cincinnati said her injury was akin to having "damaged or deformed limbs," and it ruled Toyota should have accommodated her by giving her work as an inspector. Toyota appealed the decision to the U.S. Supreme Court. Citing the so-called "toothbrush test," the Supreme Court ruled that to be disabled a worker must have difficulties in doing everyday tasks. According to Justice O'Connor, "Even after [Williams's] condition worsened, she could still brush her teeth, wash her face, bathe, tend her flower garden, fix breakfast, do laundry and pick up around the house." This suggests that Williams did not have a true disability but rather a physical impairment. Thus, she was not entitled to the antidiscrimination protection of ADA.[50]

The Supreme Court is likely to settle more of those issues in upcoming years as it grapples with a sensible interpretation of the ADA.[51] In doing so, it needs to balance concerns of disabled employees, costs to the employer, and subtle forms of discrimination that may ensue if organizations believe that hiring people with disabilities may leave them more exposed to legal challenges, which would discourage their recruitment.

Many companies overestimate the costs of accommodating employees with disabilities. Studies indicate that accommodation costs an average of $200 to $500—costs that are often outweighed by the lower absenteeism and turnover rates of workers with disabilities.

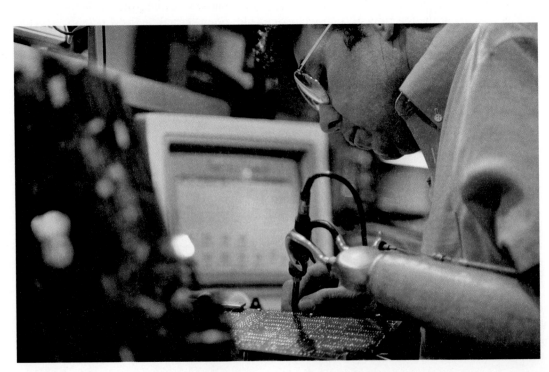

The Foreign Born

Approximately 11 percent of the U.S. population is foreign born, although in some areas, such as California, southern Texas, southern Florida, and in New York City, the proportion reaches close to one-fourth of the population.[52] Reliable statistics are hard to find, because of illegal immigration and census undercounts (fearing legal reprisal, many undocumented workers wish to remain incognito), but at least 30 million immigrants have come to the United States over the past 30 years.[53] In addition, half a million foreign students on temporary visas are attending U.S. universities at any one time, spending about $11 billion a year on tuition and living expenses.[54] Many of these people remain in the United States after obtaining their degrees. Regardless of their parents' legal status, all children born in the United States are automatically U.S. citizens under the U.S. Constitution.

American children of undocumented immigrants born in the United States face an uncertain future.[55] As noted by one analyst, "As the government steps up its enforcement of immigration laws, the fate of American children is often an afterthought."[56] According to Census Bureau figures released in 2005 (which many believe are underestimates), there are about 11 million undocumented immigrants in the United States, compared with 8.4 million in 2000 and 3.5 million in 1990. Mexicans account for about 57 percent of undocumented immigrants, with an additional 24 percent coming from elsewhere in Latin America.[57] A high proportion of these undocumented workers are of childbearing age. This means that a growing percentage of young Americans are raised by parents with few legal rights and who could be subject to immediate deportation.

Partly because of security concerns after September 11 and partly because of a growing belief that our "borders are out of control," public policy has tended toward tightening immigration laws, making it more difficult, for instance, for illegal aliens to obtain a driver's license or limiting the annual cap for low-skilled nonagricultural workers to 66,000 a year.[58] The number of deportations has increased almost 50 percent from 2001 to 2006, although the total number of deportees (about 160,000 annually) is a tiny percentage of the total number of undocumented workers.[59] Despite these restrictions, it appears that undocumented workers (those that, by definition, cannot achieve legal status) will continue to enter the United States as long as there is demand for their services. In the past, obtaining a "green card" (legal permanent residency) has been an arduous process, and for unskilled workers, a nearly impossible dream. At the time of this writing there are many proposals at the highest levels of government to deal with the de-facto reality of the many millions of undocumented employees and their families who live and work in the United States. Clearly, this issue will loom large in public debate for years to come, not only in the United States, but in many countries around the world. Nevertheless, it is fair to say that (perhaps because of its long history of experience of assimilating newcomers) the United States continues to be a leader in weaving new (both legal and illegal) immigrants into the fabric of society.

Homosexuals

Although early research dating from the 1940s suggested that about 10 percent of the population is gay, there is considerable debate about the true percentage, with estimates ranging from 1 to 2 percent to 10 percent.[60] In recent years, gay advocacy groups have become very outspoken about their rights, arguing that sexual preference should not be a criterion for personnel-related decisions. But open homosexuality is still taboo in many workplaces.

Gays have little legal protection at present. No federal law prevents overt discrimination against homosexuals, and only six states (Connecticut, Massachusetts, Minnesota, New Jersey, Wisconsin, and Hawaii) have such antidiscrimination laws on their books. Currently, the U.S. military has a controversial "don't ask, don't tell" policy that prevents gay soldiers from openly discussing their sexual orientation but also prohibits inquiries about the sexual orientation of new or current enlistees. Many other organizations have explicit or implicit policies against the hiring or retention of homosexuals, even if they do not discuss their homosexuality.

Homosexuals face three key problems in the workplace.[61] The first is outright refusal to hire or retain homosexual employees (which is not illegal in most states). The second is intolerance from workers or managers in companies that do not have explicit policies forbidding discrimination against gays. Third, AIDS has added fear to prejudice. These problems have a chilling effect that causes many gay people to stay in the closet for fear of being fired or ostracized at work.

A recent Congressional study concluded that the military has spent more than $200 million to recruit and train personnel to replace more than 10,000 troops discharged for being openly gay in the last decade.[62] Most European countries had similar "don't ask, don't tell" laws until the 1990s, when these were abolished by the European court for violating European human rights laws. Apparently, the worst fears of top European military commanders of widespread disruption by lifting the homosexual ban have not materialized (see the Manager's Notebook, "Growing Tolerance for Global Diversity in Sexual Orientation Where You Least Expect: The Military").

MANAGER'S NOTEBOOK

Global

Growing Tolerance for Global Diversity in Sexual Orientation Where You Least Expect: The Military

The British military had agonized for years over the issue, and always concluded that allowing gays and lesbians to serve would prove prohibitively disruptive and ruin discipline and cohension. But after a European court ruled in 1999 that Britain's ban on gays in the military violated European human rights laws, Britain had little choice but to reverse its policy. Beginning in 2000, the military said gays would no longer be prohibited from serving. It also stopped monitoring its recruits' sex lives, saying that as long as it did not intrude into the workplace, sexuality should not be an issue one way or another.

Gay men and women in the British services have lived and fought in Iraq alongside heterosexuals without problems, according to military officials. "I would say that before the European court ruling, it was difficult to see this policy happening or working," said Lt. Cmdr. Craig Jones, a gay naval officer who often speaks publicly, with the navy's approval, on gay rights issues.

"People were quite hot under the collar about it; the admirals, generals and air marshals were really concerned," he added. "I'm quite sure that these folks look now and think, 'what was all that fuss about?' "

Source: Adapted with permission from Lyall, A. (2005, February 22). New course by Royal Navy: A campaign to recruit gays. *New York Times*, A-1.

Latinos (Hispanic Americans)

People from Latin America have traditionally used cultural self-definition to distinguish their cultural identity from that of non-Latino North Americans. The label *Hispanic*, the official label used by the U.S. government, is "essentially a term of convenience for administrative agencies and researchers."[63]

Latinos include people of European descent (there are at least 70 million of them in Latin America) and African descent (there are at least 25 million living in the Spanish-speaking Antilles and the Caribbean basin), as well as Latin Indians (who make up a very large proportion of the Mexican and Andean population), Asians (there are probably 10 million Asians of Hispanic descent), and a very large number of people of mixed origin.

There are at least 35 million Latinos in the United States, with more estimates as high as 45 million.[64] Latino immigrants have birth rates twice as high as those of the rest of the U.S. population. Between 2006 and 2020, Latinos are expected to account for about half the growth of the U.S. labor force.[65] According to most recent estimates (2006), Hispanic represent 14 percent of the U.S. population; approximately 8 percent are native born and 6 percent foreign born.[66] Many Latinos are professionals and entrepreneurs; others are unskilled laborers and farmers. At the high end of the scale are upper- and middle-class Cubans who came to the United States in the aftermath of the 1959 Cuban Revolution; on the low end are migrant workers.[67]

Latinos face a number of problems in the U.S. workplace. One is language.[68] Second, cultural clashes may occur because of value differences. Some Latinos see non-Latino North Americans as unemotional, insensitive, self-centered, rigid, and ambitious. Meanwhile, non-Latinos often complain that with Latinos "punctuality, absenteeism, planning, and scheduling can be a lot more loose than one would expect."[69]

Third, Latinos of African or Latin American Indian descent (many of whom migrate to the United States because of their extreme poverty at home) often face an additional hurdle: racial discrimination because of their skin color.

These challenges do not negate the noteworthy progress that Latinos have made in recent years. The largest 500 Latino-owned firms in the United States export more than $1 billion worth of goods each year, generating many U.S. jobs in the process.[70] Almost a quarter of the *Fortune* 1000 firms have some Latino senior executives, with 70 serving as executive officer. Latinos occupy 181 board seats in these companies, double the 1993 number. Hispanic middle-class households (those earning $40,000 to $140,000 annually) have grown 71 percent during the past 20 years, with 13 percent of Latino families reporting incomes of more than $75,000. Total Hispanic purchasing power has reached nearly $500 billion. The proportion of college graduates is now 20 percent, an increase of 43 percent over two decades.[71]

To quell the fears of those who believe Latinos do not assimilate as well as prior European immigrants did, the evidence shows that the first generation is mostly bilingual and English becomes dominant in the second generation.[72] Furthermore, most Latinos do not live in densely packed, highly homogeneous, Spanish-language communities. Rather, most live in neighborhoods with non-Hispanic majorities.[73]

Older Workers

The U.S. workforce is getting older. The average U.S. worker is 38, expected to reach close to 42 by the year 2010, and 45 percent of employees are currently over the age of 40. Older workers face several important challenges in the workplace. First, the United States is a youth-oriented culture that has not yet come to terms with its changing demographics.[74] Starting around the age of 40, but particularly after the age of 50, employees encounter a number of sterotypes that may block their career advancement. Partly because of this reason, the number of age bias claims against private sector employers filed with the Equal Employment Opportunity Commission has recently reached 22 percent of all discrimination claims in a given year.[75] In 2005, the U.S. Supreme Court opened a new door for older workers to sue for age discrimination. The Court ruled that workers over 40 years old could bring charges when the firm's action has a "disparate negative impact" on their age group; they do not have to meet the tougher standard of proving that the employer actually intended to discriminate.[76] Apart from legal considerations, one of the growing ethical issues in human resource management is the extent to which older workers have become easy targets for efforts to reduce salary and health insurance costs.

Among the most common negative assumptions about older workers are that they are less motivated to work hard, are "dead wood," are resistant to change and cannot learn new methods, and they are "fire proof."[77]

These negative characterizations are not supported by research. In fact, one of the most stunning economic achievements in U.S. business in the last decade—the turnaround of manufacturing productivity and growth—has been accomplished at plants staffed predominantly by older assembly-line workers.[78] Furthermore, some recent surveys show that the absenteeism rate for those 55 and over (4.2 days per year) was almost identical to the absenteeism rate of other age groups (3.9).[79] Recent studies also show that older workers are just as committed to their jobs as younger workers.[80] Many successful companies have implemented programs to use the knowledge and wisdom of older workers to mentor employees. In the words of an HR consultant, "These companies are striking gold in a silver mine by leveraging senior workers as knowledge champions."[81]

Second, *generational conflict* may arise. Older workers sometimes feel that their position and status are threatened by "young bucks" eager to push "over-the-hill" employees out of the way. This tension can negatively affect the cohesiveness of teams and work units. It can also sour the relationship between boss and subordinate.

Third, even if in good health, this group is more susceptible to physical problems. Often older workers are forced to step down from their jobs because the firm cannot and/or will not find appropriate opportunities for them to use their seasoned judgment, knowledge, and ability to serve as mentors for new workers. Although an illegal practice that is difficult to prove in court, older workers are often targeted for layoffs because they earn more money.[82]

Religious Minorities

Although the Jewish population as a percentage of the total population has remained relatively stable in both the United States and Europe, other non-Christian minorities have grown rapidly. In the United States, approximately 4 million Americans profess Islamic, Hindu, Taoist, or other non-Christian beliefs. In Western Europe, the Muslim population represents the largest minority group, hovering somewhere between 6 and 15 percent of the population in such countries as France, Holland, Spain, Germany, and the United Kingdom.

The tragic events of September 11 in New York and Washington, D.C., and later the bombings in Madrid and London, have severely tested tolerance toward people of certain religious backgrounds. A recent survey by the Society for Human Resource Management revealed that so-called "ethnic religions" such as Islam now come just after race and gender in U.S. perceptions of "otherness."[83] In Europe, with a much higher Muslim representation and a short history of immigration, blaming Arab minorities for crime, unemployment, and government budget deficits has become commonplace.[84]

In Europe, most Arab immigrants fill unskilled jobs in construction, agriculture, and manufacturing, whereas in the United States people of Arab descent tend to be better educated and wealthier than other Americans.[85] Arabs are nearly twice as likely as the typical U.S. resident to have a college degree, with a median household income $2,300 higher than the average American family. Forty-two percent of Arab Americans work in management jobs, versus 34 percent of the rest of the population. Unfortunately, as noted by Helen Sanhan, executive director of the Arab-American Institute Foundation, "usually the Arab community is only covered in the media in a negative sense."[86]

Security fears due to terrorist threats in the United States and Europe have led to many complaints of "racial profiling" and discrimination by people of Arab descent, as well as those who may be mistaken for Muslims, such as some people of East Indian background. Many firms on both sides of the Atlantic are now grappling with policies to cover such issues as permissible garments at work, religious holidays, potential harassment or ridicule based on one's faith, and the display of religious symbols on company premises.[87]

Women

The projected participation rate for women in the workforce is expected to reach 48 percent by 2010.[88] Unfortunately, women's earnings have not mirrored their rising participation trend. After falling to a low of 59 percent of male earnings in 1975, the female-to-male earnings ratio rose slowly and is now approximately 73 percent, just 10 points above its level in 1920, when only 20 percent of women were in the labor force.[89]

There may be reason for optimism, however. Women's share of top-management jobs has increased at least threefold during the last three decades.[90] Recent examples of women moving to the top include the appointment of Patricia Russo as CEO of Kodak, Carole Black as CEO of Lifetime Entertainment Services, Ann Mulcahy as CEO of Xerox, Margaret Whitman as CEO of eBay, and Abigail Johnson as CEO of Fidelity.[91] And 55 percent of employed women bring in half or more of their total household income.[92]

Gender differences in educational achievement are quickly being erased. Over the past generation, the percentage of bachelor's, master's, and doctorates in the hard sciences going to women has soared (see the Manager's Notebook, "Women Are Moving into Fields Previously the Province of Men"). Recipients of professional degrees (medicine, business, and law) are now almost equally divided by gender.

Emerging Trends

Women Are Moving into Fields Previously the Province of Men

Until the last 30 or so years, few women studied the sciences, so there was little mystery about why most people in those professions were men. Over the past generation, however, a truly stunning change has occurred. As an illustration of the gains by women in historically male disciplines, consider how the percentages of women receiving university degrees in the sciences increased during past three decades.

Bachelor's Degrees	Female Recipients as a Percentage 30 Years Ago	Female Recipients as a Percentage 2005
Engineering	0.8	18.9
Physics	6.7	22.6
Geology	11.0	44.7
Computer science	13.6	27.6
Chemistry	18.4	48.4
Biological sciences	29.1	60.8
Mathematics	37.8	46.7
Health sciences	77.1	85.5

Master's Degrees	Female Recipients as a Percentage 30 Years Ago	Female Recipients as a Percentage 2005
Engineering	1.1	21.4
Physics	6.9	20.9
Geology	9.7	39.7
Computer science	10.3	33.2
Chemistry	21.4	45.6
Biological sciences	33.6	57.8
Mathematics	27.1	42.4
Health sciences	55.4	77.5

Doctorates	Female Recipients as a Percentage 30 Years Ago	Female Recipients as a Percentage 2005
Engineering	0.6	17.3
Physics	2.9	15.5
Geology	3.4	28.5
Computer science	2.3	22.8
Chemistry	8.0	33.9
Biological sciences	16.3	44.3
Mathematics	7.6	29.0
Health sciences	16.5	63.3

Gains for women are evident in many other occupations that require higher education. In the early 1970s, women received less than 10 percent of all graduate degrees in law, medicine, dentistry, and veterinary medicine and less than 20 percent in pharmacy. However, today women earn about two-thirds of the degrees in veterinary medicine and pharmacy. They are approaching 50 percent in law, and they have topped 40 percent in medicine. More than one-third of new dentists are women.

Likewise, women's share of master's degrees from business schools rose from 3.6 in 1970 to 41.0 percent in 2005. Women have also greatly expanded their presence in the social sciences, including economics, political science, and sociology. Overall, women earned 46.3 percent of the doctorates in the mid-2000s up from 13.3 percent three decades ago.

Source: Adapted with permission from Cox, M. W., and Alm, R. (2005, February 28). Scientists are made, not born. *New York Times,* A10.

Still, there is no doubt that most women still earn considerably less than their male counterparts. Other than overt sex discrimination (which is, of course, illegal), several factors may account for the earnings differential between women and men and women's lack of upward mobility. These include biological constraints and social roles, a male-dominated corporate culture, exclusionary networks, and sexual harassment.

Biological Constraints and Social Roles

After three decades of feminism, women continue to encounter a fairly rigid set of expectations regarding their roles and behavior that extend far beyond biological constraints. Women are still primarily responsible for taking care of the children and performing most household duties. A study conducted in the late 1990s estimates that full-time working women still spend three times the amount of time spent by men on household duties.[93]

Perhaps reflecting these societal norms, only a tiny proportion of companies provide day care and other support options (such as job sharing and reduced work hours for employees with young children). For this reason, many talented and highly educated women are forced to curtail their career aspirations and/or quit the organization in their late 20s or early to mid-30s—crucial years in one's career—if they wish to have a family. Practically all male top managers are married and have children, whereas the majority of women who make it to the top are single and childless.

A Male-Dominated Corporate Culture

Most sex differences are not related to performance, particularly in white-collar occupations, where sheer physical strength is seldom required.

A number of studies have shown that men tend to emerge in leadership positions in U.S. culture because they are more likely than women to exhibit traits believed to "go hand-in-hand" with positions of authority. These include (1) more aggressive behaviors and tendencies; (2) initiation of more verbal interactions; (3) focusing of remarks on "output" (as opposed to "process") issues; (4) less willingness to reveal information and expose vulnerability; (5) a greater task (as opposed to social) orientation; and (6) less sensitivity, which presumably enables them to make tough choices quickly.[94] Thus, cultural expectations may create a self-fulfilling prophecy, with individuals exhibiting the "female traits" of focusing on process, social orientation, and so on more likely to be relegated to operational and subordinate roles.

Exclusionary Networks

Old boys' network
An informal social and business network of high-level male executives that typically excludes women and minorities. Access to the old boys' network is often an important factor in career advancement.

Many women are hindered by lack of access to the **old boys' network**, the informal relationships formed between male managers and executives. Because most high-level positions are filled by men, women are often left out of the conversations that help men get ahead.[95]

Sexual Harassment

Women have to confront sexual harassment to a much greater extent than men do. For instance, a group of 23 women at Salomon Smith Barney's branch office in Garden City, New York, alleged that the branch office had a "boom-boom-boom" room in the basement where male brokers and managers gathered to engage in fraternity-house antics that their female coworkers found offensive and harassing.[96] A few years after this case was settled, another group of women filed suit against Smith Barney in 2005, charging that a sexist culture permeates the company. In a recent case involving Wal-Mart, which is still pending, a 10-year employee, 36-year-old Kim Miller, claims her male supervisors referred to her as "bitch" and talked about which female customers they would like to get into bed. The sexual talk allegedly turned toward her and included offers to get her pregnant.[97] Approximately one in five civil suits now concerns harassment or discrimination, compared with one in 20 fifteen years ago. Sexual harassment litigation is also occurring in Europe.[98] Currently, more than 100 insurance firms in the United States offer employment practice liability insurance, which covers employers' legal costs, damages, and settlements in lawsuits for discrimination and harassment.[99]

Businesses have been getting tougher on this issue by crafting stronger sexual harassment policies and setting up intensive seminars for employees. These educational efforts are particularly important because men and women often have different notions of what kind of behavior constitutes sexual harassment.

Improving the Management of Diversity

Organizations that have made the greatest strides in successfully managing diversity tend to share a number of characteristics. These factors are a commitment from top management to valuing diversity, diversity training programs, employee support groups, accommodation of family needs, senior mentoring and apprenticeship programs, communication standards, organized special activities, diversity audits, and a policy of holding management responsible for the effectiveness of diversity efforts.

In recent years, *Fortune* has published a list of the "50 Best Companies for Asians, Blacks, and Hispanics."[100] The judges consider many of the factors just mentioned. Here is a sample of some effective diversity practices enacted by the top companies:

- McDonalds makes a concerted effort to purchase from minorities, who now represent half of its vendors.
- Nordstrom weighs minority retention rates as a key factor in manager performance evaluations. The company also has an outreach program to involve minority-owned firms in new store construction.
- General Motors has held a Diversity Immersion Day, attended by 300 high-ranking executives.

Top-Management Commitment to Valuing Diversity

It is unlikely that division managers, middle managers, supervisors, and others in positions of authority will become champions of diversity unless they believe that the chief executive officer and those reporting to the CEO are totally committed to valuing diversity. Xerox, DuPont, Corning, Procter & Gamble, Avon, the *Miami Herald,* Digital Equipment Corporation, U.S. West, and other pacesetters in the successful management of diversity all have CEOs who are fully dedicated to putting this ideal into practice. For example, Avon has established a multicultural participation council (which includes the CEO) that meets regularly. Similarly, in a startling 10-page color brochure, the CEO of Corning announced that management of diversity is one of Corning's three top priorities, alongside total quality management and a higher return to shareholders.[101]

Diversity Training Programs

Supervisors need to learn new skills that will enable them to manage and motivate a diverse workforce. Ortho-McNeil Pharmaceutical, Hewlett-Packard, Wells Fargo, Kaiser Permanente, Microsoft, and other companies have developed extensive in-house **diversity training programs** that provide awareness training and workshops to educate managers and employees on specific cultural and sex differences and how to respond to these in the workplace.[102]

Much experimentation in this type of training is occurring around the United States.[103] DuPont has sponsored an all-expense-paid conference for African American managers to discuss the problems they encounter and how they can contribute more to the firm. AT&T has offered seminars designed to help straight employees feel comfortable working alongside openly gay employees and to eliminate offensive jokes and insults from the workplace.[104] Corning has introduced a mandatory four-day awareness training program for some 7,000 salaried employees— a day and a half for gender awareness, two and a half days for ethnic awareness.[105]

According to the Society for Human Resource Management (SHRM), diversity training "is a fundamental component of a diversity initiative and represents an opportunity for the organization to inform and educate senior management and staff about diversity."[106] SHRM suggests that effective diversity training programs need to confront complex issues that have more to do with human behavior than with race, gender, age, and the like (see Figure 4.2, "Issues to Consider in Diversity Training"). However, this report also notes that frequently these programs fall short of expectations. Several factors undermine the effectiveness of these programs.[107]

First, the training may have come at a time when employees were preoccupied with more urgent priorities (such as downsizing, increased work level, or launching a new product under tight deadlines). Second, if employees perceive that external forces such as a court order or a politician's decree have prompted the training, they may resist. Third, if the training poses some

Diversity training programs
Programs that provide diversity awareness training and educate employees on specific cultural and sex differences and how to respond to these in the workplace.

Figure 4.2

- Diversity is about each person coming to terms with his or her attitudes, beliefs, and expectations about others and gaining comfort with differentness.
- Diversity is big enough to include everyone: young and old, homeless and affluent, immigrant and native, white and black and goes beyond race and gender.
- No one is or should be the target for blame for current or past inequities. All human beings have been socialized to behave in certain ways, and all of us are at times both perpetrators and victims of discrimination and stereotypes.
- Human beings are ethnocentric—they see the world through their own narrow view and judge the world by what is familiar to them.
- The human species resists change. This makes the constant adaptation required for diversity difficult for people already overwhelmed by staggering transitions in today's organizations.
- Human beings find comfort and trust in likeness. There is a tendency to seek the company of those most similar to ourselves.
- It is difficult for people to share power; history shows that it is rarely done voluntarily and without a reason that will somehow benefit those dominating the pool of wealth.

Source: Society for Human Resource Management (2006). HR resources. *www.shrm.org/diversity.*

Issues to Consider in Diversity Training

as perpetrators and others as victims, those who feel blamed may be defensive. And fourth, if diversity is seen as the domain of a few groups (people of color and women, for example), everyone else may feel left out and view the initiative as being for others, not for them.

To avoid these four problems, SHRM provides recommendations including holding focus groups with people who may find fault with the training; creating a diversity council that represents a cross section of employees with a wide range of views and attitudes; and exploring ways to deliver the training that do not use a typical classroom format (such as one-on-one coaching to help managers deal with diversity challenges or interventions at team meetings on request).[108]

Support Groups

Some employees perceive corporate life as insensitive to their culture and background, perhaps downright hostile. The perception of an attitude that says "You don't belong here" or "You are here because we need to comply with government regulations" is largely responsible for the high turnover of minorities in many corporations.

Support group
A group established by an employer to provide a nurturing climate for employees who would otherwise feel isolated or alienated.

To counteract these feelings of alienation, top management at many firms (such as FedEx, Bank of America, Allstate Insurance, DuPont, Marriott and Ryder) has been setting up **support groups**. These groups are designed to provide a nurturing climate for diverse employees who would otherwise feel shut out. Microsoft, for instance, lists the following employee resource groups on its Web page: Blacks at Microsoft, Arabs at Microsoft, German Speakers at Microsoft, Attention Deficit Disorder at Microsoft, Dads at Microsoft, Working Parents at Microsoft, U.S. Military Veterans at Microsoft, and at least 30 others. As you can see, these groups are truly diverse and are not restricted to traditional categories of gender, race, or age.

A Question of Ethics

To what extent should employers be responsible for the appropriate care of their employees' children?

Accommodation of Family Needs

Firms can dramatically cut the turnover rate of their female employees if they are willing to help them handle a family and career simultaneously. Employers can use the following options to assist women in this endeavor. Unfortunately, most organizations do not yet offer these services.[109]

Day Care

Although the number of U.S. firms providing day-care support is increasing, most firms do not see day care as the company's responsibility.[110] The U.S. government has a "hands off" policy on day care. This is in sharp contrast with most other industrialized countries, where the government takes an active role in the provision of day care. (For more details, see Exhibit 4.1.)

EXHIBIT 4.1

What European Countries Do for Mum, Maman, Mütter, and More . . .

When it comes to creating a family-friendly workplace, more than an ocean separates U.S. and European companies. Unlike the United States, many European countries have provisions for maternity leave, child care, and flexible schedules—and they've had them in place for years. For example:

- Germany adopted its maternity leave law back in 1878. German women receive six weeks' prenatal leave at full pay and eight weeks postnatal leave, also at full pay. After mothers return to work, they get time off to breastfeed. In addition, there is a three-year parental leave for all working parents, both male and female.
- Sweden was the first nation to broaden extended postnatal maternity leave to "parental leave," for either the mother or the father, or for both alternately. Today Swedish parents are guaranteed a one-year leave of absence after childbirth. The first half is reserved for the mother, who receives 90 percent of her salary from social security.
- Denmark, with the highest level of publicly funded services in Europe, offers women 18 weeks' maternity leave, four weeks before the birth and 14 weeks afterward. Men can take 10 days' leave after their baby is born, and parental leave policy allows either the mother or the father to take an additional 10 weeks off after the birth.
- France leads the pack in day-care support. In addition to getting at least 16 weeks' maternity leave at 84 percent of their salaries, working mothers can bring their children to state-run day-care centers called *crèches,* which are open 11 hours a day and cost between $3.00 and $17.50 daily.
- Some European companies, such as National Westminster Bank (NWB) in London, have career break policies that allow employees to take a multiyear leave after the birth of a child. During that period the employee remains in contact with the company, fills in for vacationing employees, and participates in training. At NWB, career breaks of six months to seven years are available to staff at all grades.

"What we tend to find in Europe," says a coordinator of Daycare Trust in London, "is that the more government involvement there is in these issues, the more likely there is to be involvement by employers." In the United States it is up to individual companies to provide family-friendly programs. This creates some pockets of work-family innovation, but there is no national trend toward providing these kinds of services.

Alternative Work Patterns

Employers like Quaker Oats, IBM, Ciba-Geigy, and Pacific Telesis Group have been willing to experiment with new ways to help women balance career goals and mothering, and thereby have retained the services of many of their top performers.[111] As we saw in Chapter 2, these programs come in a variety of forms, including flexible work hours, flextime, and telecommuting. One type of program that is becoming more common is job sharing, where two people divvy up what normally is one person's full-time job. A survey of more than 1,000 companies by consulting firm Hewitt Associates found that 28 percent of the organizations offer job sharing, up from 12 percent in 1990.[112] Another option is extended leave. A rare benefit, **extended leave** allows employees to take a sabbatical from the office, sometimes up to three years, with benefits and the guarantee of a comparable job on return. Some companies require leave-takers to be on call for part-time work during their sabbatical.[113]

Extended leave
A benefit that allows an employee to take a long-term leave from the office, while retaining benefits and the guarantee of a comparable job on return.

Senior Mentoring Programs

Some companies encourage **senior mentoring programs**, in which senior managers identify promising women and minority employees and play an important role in nurturing their career progress.[114] At Marriott, for instance, newly hired employees with disabilities are paired with Marriott managers who serve as their coaches. Honeywell and 3M team up experienced executives

Senior mentoring program
A support program in which senior managers identify promising women and minority employees and play an important role in nurturing their career progress.

with young women and minorities to give them advice on career strategies and corporate politics, as do Xerox and DQE Corporation, a Pittsburgh utilities firm.[115]

Apprenticeships

Apprenticeship
A program in which promising prospective employees are groomed before they are actually hired on a permanent basis.

Apprenticeships are similar to senior mentoring programs, except that promising prospective employees are groomed before they are actually hired on a permanent basis. As with senior mentoring, company managers are encouraged to become actively involved in apprenticeship programs. For example, Sears has established an apprenticeship program that gives students hands-on training in skills like basic electronics and appliance repair. The best students are hired for ten hours a week to work at a Sears Service Center. This on-the-job training is integrated into the school curriculum, and the most talented students are hired upon completion of the program.

Communication Standards

Certain styles of communication may be offensive to women and minority employees. Examples are the use of "he" when referring to managers and "she" when referring to secretaries, inadequately representing or ignoring minorities in annual reports, failure to alphabetize ethnic groups' titles (Asian, Latino, etc.), and using terms, such as *protected classes* and *alien*, that may have a precise legal meaning but are offensive to those being described. To avoid these problems, organizations should set *communication standards* that take into account the sensitivities of a diverse employee population.

Diversity Audits

Diversity audit
A review of the effectiveness of an organization's diversity management program.

Often the roots of an employee diversity problem (such as high turnover of minority employees) are not immediately evident. In these instances, research in the form of a **diversity audit** may be necessary to uncover possible sources of bias. Unfortunately, some companies are reluctant to do an official diversity audit for fear that the information uncovered may later be used in a suit against the company. The case of Johnson & Johnson (J&J), the large drug-manufacturing firm, represents a recent case in point. A voluntary diversity audit by J&J (written in a formal, confidential document) expressed concerns about inadequate tracking of promotions, unequal salaries, and insufficient outreach to recruit women and minorities. The diversity report ended up being used as an unintended legal weapon against J&J when it was uncovered four years later and submitted to a federal court in New Jersey by several African American and Hispanic American employees who argued that "executives knew years ago that they were missing targets for promoting such employees and did little to solve the problem". A company spokesman, Marc Monseau, emphasized that the diversity audit report "should be considered in the larger context of continual self-examination at Johnson & Johnson. We engage in critical self-analysis because we are always looking to improve our process and our performance. That reaches to all aspects of our business, including diversity."[116] At this writing, the lawsuit is still pending.

Management Responsibility and Accountability

Management of diversity will not be a high priority and a formal business objective unless managers and supervisors are held accountable for implementing diversity management and rewarded for doing so successfully. At the very minimum, successful diversity management should be one of the factors in the performance appraisal system for those in positions of authority. For instance, at Garrett Company, a manufacturer of jet engines, bonus pay is tied to a supervisor's record on managing diversity.

Some Warnings

Two potential pitfalls must be avoided if diversity management programs are to be successful. These are (1) avoiding the appearance of "white male bashing" and (2) avoiding the promotion of stereotypes.

Avoiding the Appearance of "White Male Bashing"

Disproving the accusation that managing diversity is just another catchphrase for providing opportunities for women and minorities *at the expense of white men* is crucial to the successful management of diversity programs. Otherwise, these programs are likely to engender resentment, heighten anxieties, and inflame the prejudices of those who feel threatened. Management should continually emphasize the positive aspects of capitalizing on employee diversity by framing it as something that (1) must be done to gain a competitive advantage and (2) is in the best interests of all employees. Training programs, if properly designed, may be used as efficient vehicles to convey these messages. Another approach is to use rewards. For instance, Whirlpool distributed an extra $2,700 to each employee in its Benton Harbor, Michigan, plant in a single year in response to productivity and quality improvements. The plant has a significant minority population, and the group incentive induced all employees to work closely together in what they saw as a win-win effort.[117]

Ideally organizations should adopt an inclusive definition of diversity that addresses all kinds of differences among employees, including (but not limited to) race and gender. A broad definition of diversity will invite participation and decrease resistance.

Avoiding the Promotion of Stereotypes

As we discussed earlier, an inherent danger in diversity programs is inadvertent reinforcement of the notion that one can draw conclusions about a particular person based simply on his or her group characteristics. Remember, differences between individuals *within* any given group are almost always greater than the "average" or typical differences *between* any two groups. **Cultural determinism**—promoting the idea that one can infer an individual's motivations, interests, values, and behavioral traits based on that individual's group memberships—robs employees of their individuality and creates a divisive mind-set of "them versus us."

Unfortunately, cultural awareness programs and other diversity training activities tend (unintentionally) to overdramatize diversity. This may lead participants to hold assumptions regarding groups that are totally incorrect (and most likely offensive) when applied to specific employees.[118] Some organizations have begun to use the term *inclusiveness training* to promote the idea that such training is intended to unite people rather than treat them as members of a particular class.

Cultural determinism
The idea that one can successfully infer an individual's motivations, interests, values, and behavioral traits based on that individual's group memberships.

Summary and Conclusions

What Is Diversity?
Diversity refers to human characteristics that make people different from one another. Today's labor force is highly diverse. If effectively managed, this diversity can provide the organization with a powerful competitive edge because it stimulates creativity, enhances problem solving by offering broader perspectives, and infuses flexibility into the firm.

Challenges in Managing Employee Diversity
An organization confronts significant challenges in making employee diversity work to its advantage. These include (1) genuinely valuing employee diversity, (2) balancing individual needs with group fairness, (3) coping with resistance to change, (4) promoting group cohesiveness, (5) ensuring open communication, (6) retaining valued performers, and (7) managing competition for opportunities.

Diversity in Organizations
Some groups are likely to be left out of the corporate mainstream. African Americans still face a certain amount of stream.

explicit racism and tend to be less educationally prepared for the workplace. Asian Americans confront two stereotypes—one saying they are too cautious and reserved to lead, and another saying they are unscrupulous in business—as well as the feeling that they are too educated to merit special consideration as a minority. Full social acceptance is still denied to people with disabilities, who are often incorrectly perceived as being less capable than others, more prone to quit their jobs under pressure, and costly to accommodate in the workplace.

Foreign-born workers face language and cultural barriers and sometimes ethnic/racial prejudice. They are often resented by Americans of all races, who believe they are taking their jobs.

Homosexuals sometimes face outright discrimination (the refusal to hire or retain them as employees) and ostracism from coworkers or managers. Latinos face language and cultural difficulties and, in some cases, racial discrimination.

Older workers encounter negative stereotypes about their abilities, energy, and adaptability, as well as some physical problems and resentment from younger workers. Women often fare badly in male-dominated corporate cultures that display masculine leadership biases and have old boys' networks that exclude women. They are also subject to sexual harassment to a much greater degree than men.

Improving the Management of Diversity
Organizations that have capitalized the most on their diverse human resources to gain a competitive advantage tend to have top management committed to valuing diversity; solid, ongoing diversity training programs; support groups that nurture non-traditional employees; and policies that accommodate employees'

family needs. They also have senior mentoring and apprenticeship programs to encourage employees' career progress, set communication standards that discourage discrimination, use diversity audits to uncover bias, and hold their managers responsible for effectively implementing diversity policies.

Some Warnings
There are two pitfalls in diversity management programs that managers must be careful to avoid: (1) giving the appearance of "white male bashing" and (2) unintentionally promoting stereotypes.

Key Terms

apprenticeship, 138
cultural determinism, 139
cultural relativity concept of
    management, 124
diversity, 119

diversity audit, 138
diversity training programs, 135
extended leave, 137
glass ceiling, 125
management of diversity, 120

old boys' network, 134
senior mentoring program, 137
support group, 136
universal concept of management, 124

Discussion Questions

1. Why do many firms wait until being faced with a legal suit to respond to diversity issues rather than handling them proactively?

2. For 20 years (since passage of the Immigration and Control Act of 1986) it has been a crime to hire illegal aliens. On paper, employers can be fined $10,000 for every illegal alien they hire, and repeat offenders can be sent to jail. Yet, actual implementation of the law is practically nonexistent (the most recent statistics show that only 13 fines were issued to employers for immigration law violations).[119] Why do you think the employment laws concerning recruitment of undocumented workers are not being enforced? Some people equate these immigration laws to the federal "dry laws" of the early 1930s (which prohibited alcohol usage, yet were widely disregarded). Do you agree? What proposals, if any, would you make to remedy this legal incongruency (that is, laws that are not applied in practice)? Explain.

3. Women and ethnic minorities are often lumped together as a single class. What do these two groups have in common? How do they differ? Explain.

4. According to Laura D'Andrea Tyson, Dean of the College of Business at London Business School, in both the United States and Europe women often choose to opt out of high-powered jobs. In her words: "The opt-out hypothesis could explain why, according to a recent U.S. survey, 1 in 3 women with an MBA is not working full-time, versus 1 in 20 men with the same degree. Today, many companies are recruiting female MBA graduates in nearly equal numbers to male MBA grads, but they're finding

that a substantial percentage of their female recruits drop out within three to five years. The vexing problem for businesses is not finding female talent but retraining it."[120] In your opinion, how large is the opt-out phenomenon, what are its causes, and what can companies do to retain talented women?

5. Some people still believe that the best way—and perhaps the only fair way—to manage is to treat all employees equally regardless of their sex, race, ethnicity, physical impairment, and other personal characteristics. Do you agree? Explain.

6. When a long-time contract employee for Pacific Gas & Electric in Tracy, California, was the first in his unit to be laid off, he claimed that the others—an African American woman and a man of Indian descent—had been kept on (even though they were less qualified than he was) because PG&E was intent on creating a more diverse workplace. What can companies do to keep white males from feeling victimized by diversity efforts and training programs instead of valued as "diverse" employees in their own right?

7. Many U.S. computer companies fear that if they do not hire foreign talent, then competitors in other countries will. What is your position on this? Explain.

8. Doug Dokolosky, a former IBM executive who specializes in coaching women, argues that "to reach the top requires sacrifice and long hours. If that is your ambition, forget things like balancing work and family. . . ." Do you think most U.S. firms just pay lip service to family accommodation policies? Can you think of any noteworthy exceptions?

There is a variety of additional material available on the Web site that accompanies this text. You can access this information by visiting the Web site at **www.prenhall.com/gomez**.

Discussion Case 4.1   YOU MANAGE IT!

Making Time for a Baby

At age 20, the risk of miscarriage is about 9 percent; it doubles by age 35, then doubles again by the time a woman reaches her early forties. As many women have become dedicated to their careers—putting off having children to focus on their work—there has been a 100 percent rise in the past 20 years of childless women ages 40 to 44. Economist Sylvia Ann Hewlett states in her book, *Creating a Life: Professional Women and the Quest for Children* (Talk Miramax Books), that many ambitious young women who hope to have kids are heading down a bad piece of road if they think they can spend a decade establishing their careers and wait until 35 or beyond to establish their families.

Hewlett argues that many women have embraced a "male model" of single-minded career focus, and the result is "an epidemic of childlessness" among professional women. She conducted a national survey of 1,647 "high-achieving women," made up of 1,168 who earn in the top 10 percent of income of their age group or hold degrees in law or medicine and another 479 who are highly educated but are no longer in the workforce. What she learned shocked her. She found that 42 percent of high-achieving women in corporate America—companies with 5,000 or more employees—were still childless after age 40. That ratio was 49 percent of women who earn $100,000 or more. Many other women were able to have only one child because they started their families too late. "They've been making a lot of money," says Dr. David Adamson, a leading fertility specialist at Stanford University, "but it won't buy back the time."

Hewlett argues that many women did not actually choose to be childless. When she asked women to recall their intentions at the time they were finishing college, Hewlett found that only 14 percent said that they definitely did not want to have children.

For most women whom Hewlett interviewed, childlessness was what one called "a creeping non-choice." Time passes, work is relentless. The travel, the hours—relationships are hard to sustain. By the time a woman marries and feels settled enough in her career to think of starting a family, it may often be too late. "They go to a doctor, take a blood test and are told the game is over before it even begins," says I.A.'s Madsen. "They are shocked, devastated and angry." Women generally know their fertility declines with age; they just don't realize how much and how fast.

According to Hewlett, "In just 30 years we've gone from fearing our fertility to squandering it—and very unwittingly."

A few years later after the publication of Hewlett's book, Lawrence H. Summer, President of Harvard University, created a furor in 2005 by arguing that bias could not entirely explain the lack of gender diversity in the sciences. According to him, "what is behind all of this (disparity in representation by gender) is the general clash between people's (read women) legitimate family desires and employers' current desire for high power and high intensity." He made other remarks that high power and high intensity are innate or intrinsic to males (for whom presumably family life is less important), and hence gender discrimination by employers is a lesser factor in explaining the shortage of women in certain occupations. Summer resigned in 2006 under intense pressure by faculty and students at Harvard.

Critical Thinking Questions

1. Hewlett suggests a problem for women in their twenties: The best years for having children coincide with the best years for establishing a career. How do you think women should handle this situation? What role should men play when their partners face this predicament? Explain.

2. Some people believe that organizations should share some of the responsibility for childbearing, which is absolutely necessary for a society's self-preservation. Concepts such as the "mommy track," "baby paid sabbatical," and "child care at work" have been proposed as ways that firms can fulfill this responsibility. Do you agree? Do you think firms would offer such programs voluntarily without government mandate? Explain.

3. Many managers look negatively at a "résumé gap"—the duration of time a person is not in the workforce. Although few managers would admit it, they might not hire a woman of childbearing age or promote her to a more responsible position for fear that she might become pregnant. How can a firm deal with these potential biases? Explain.

Team Exercise

Assume that top executives of a high-technology firm would like to offer women more opportunities to balance career and family. These executives believe that attracting and retaining talented women will give the firm a competitive advantage.

Students divide into groups of six, preferably three males and three females, to role-play this situation and develop some recommendations for top management. Instructor may play the role of CEO.

Experiential Exercise

One student will role-play Sylvia Ann Hewlett; one to three students will role-play a hypothetical 22-year-old female student who has recently graduated from college with a degree in business administration. Both sides will exchange views as to what recent female graduates should do in the next 20 years to balance family and work life. The role-play should last approximately 15 minutes. At the end of the role-play, the entire class will discuss the issues raised by both sides, with the instructor serving as a moderator.

Source: Adapted with permission from Horowitz, J. M., Rawe, J., and Song, S. (2002, April 15). Making time for a baby. *Time,* 49—58. For articles regarding Summer's remarks, see Tyson, L. D. (2005, March 28). What Larry Summers got right. *BusinessWeek,* 24; Atlas, J. (2005, February 27). The battle behind the battle at Harvard. *New York Times,* A14; Healy, P. D., and Riner, S. (2005, February 18). Furor lingers as Harvard chief gives detail of talk on women. *New York Times,* A1; Riner, S. (2005, March 16). Professors, in close vote, censure Harvard leader. *New York Times,* A11.

YOU MANAGE IT! Emerging Trends Case 4.2

How Old Is Too Old to Fly an Airliner?

How old is too old to be flying hundreds of passengers has long been a difficult question. Older pilots may run a greater risk of experiencing sudden incapacitation, slower reactions, or declining mental faculties. Although medical studies have not yet provided a clear-cut answer, many show that skills do deteriorate with aging.

In the United States, commercial airline pilots must leave the cockpit before they hit age 60. But that may change. Travelers may start seeing older captains in the cockpit over the next few years. Other nations are already moving in this direction (or have already done so), and in Congress lawmakers have introduced legislation that would bump up the mandatory retirement age. Even the Airline Pilots Association, which in the past has successfully blocked attempts to raise the age, now says that it is studying whether a change makes sense. It's a thorny issue. Gray-haired pilots have the advantage of extensive and wide-ranging experience at the controls, enabling them to make smart, well-informed decisions, which is just what travelers want if a plane runs into trouble. Consider that in 1989 United Airlines Captain David Cronin flew a Boeing 747 back to Honolulu after a large section of the fuselage blew out, sucking nine passengers to their deaths. Two of four engines quit and wing flaps were damaged, but Captain Cronin's flying skills saved 327 passengers. Then, within a month, he was deemed too old to fly. That same year, Captain Al Haynes guided a crippled United DC-10 to Sioux City, Iowa, using different thrust from right and left engines to steer the plane when hydraulic systems failed. It was a remarkable feat of airmanship, and 184 people survived Flight 232. Two years later, Capt. Haynes had to retire.

The Federal Aviation Administration (FAA) has adopted a stance that retirement at age 60 has proven to be a safe standard and that changing the age might risk safety. "To date, we have not seen any research that reassures us raising the retirement age would maintain safety or raise it," FAA spokeswoman Alison Duquette says. One big driver for the proposed change is money. Pensions at several airlines have been cut drastically, some even canceled, so many pilots would now like to be able to work longer. As it is, they have to retire five years before they can collect full Social Security.

Critical Thinking Questions

1. What do you think is creating the push toward raising pilots' retirement age past 60? What do you think will be the reaction of younger pilots, prospective pilots, and airline management to this proposal? Explain you answer.

2. If you were planning a trip and had the choice of flying several airlines at roughly the same price, would you care if some airlines allowed pilots over 60 to command the plane? Explain your rationale.

3. Think of three or four other occupations that may have a mandatory retirement age below the traditional age of 65. What do they all have in common? How would the ones you have mentioned differ from the case of pilots? Explain.

Team Exercise

The class divides into groups of three to five students. Some teams are given the assignment of justifying a mandatory retirement age for pilots at 60; other teams are asked to argue in favor of a higher retirement age. Both the "pro" and "against" teams should present their recommendations with the instructor acting as a moderator. At the end of the discussion, the instructor may take a straw vote as to which side had more persuasive arguments and provide his or her own views on the issue.

Experiential Exercise

Two or three students are asked to role-play a passenger plane captain nearing age 60 who is in good health who wants to work past the mandatory retirement age. Students role-playing the captain should make a plea to an FAA official to push the mandatory retirement age to at least 65. One student will role-play the FAA official. The role-play should last approximately 15 minutes. The class will then discuss the issues raised during the role-play, with the instructor serving as mediator

Source: Adapted with permission from McCartney, S. (2005, February 22). How old is too old to fly an airliner? *Wall Street Journal*, D4.

Discussion Case 4.3 — YOU MANAGE IT!

Conflict at Northern Sigma

Northern Sigma, a hypothetical high-technology firm headquartered in New York, develops and manufactures advanced electronic equipment. The company has 20 plants around the United States and 22,000 employees, 3,000 of whom work at a single site in Chicago that is responsible for research and development. About half of the employees at that facility are scientists and engineers. The other half are support personnel, managers, and market research personnel. Corporate executives are strongly committed to hiring women and minorities throughout the entire organization, but particularly at the Chicago site. The company has adopted this policy for two reasons: Women and minorities are severely underrepresented in the Chicago plant (making up only about 13 percent of the workforce), and it is becoming increasingly difficult to find top-notch talent in the dwindling applicant pool of white men.

Phillip Wagner is the general manager of the Chicago plant. In his most recent performance evaluation he was severely criticized for not doing enough to retain women and minorities. For the past two years, the turnover rate for these groups has been three times higher than that for other employees. Corporate executives estimate that this high turnover rate is costing at least $1 million a year in training costs, lost production time, recruitment expenses, and so forth. In addition, more than 70 charges of discrimination have been filed with the EEOC during the past three years alone—a much higher number of complaints than would be expected given the plant's size and demographic composition.

Under pressure from headquarters, Wagner has targeted the turnover and discrimination problems as among his highest priorities for this year. As a first step, he has hired a consulting team to interview a representative sample of employees to find out (1) why the turnover rate among women and minorities is so high and (2) what is prompting so many complaints from people in these groups. The interviews were conducted in separate groups of 15 people each. Each group consisted either of white men or a mix of women and minorities. A summary of the report prepared by the consultants follows.

Women and Minority Groups

A large proportion of women and minority employees expressed strong dissatisfaction with the company. Many felt they had been misled when they accepted employment at Northern Sigma. Among their most common complaints:

- Being left out of important task forces.
- Personal input not requested very often—and when requested, suggestions and ideas generally ignored.
- Contributions not taken very seriously by peers in team or group projects.
- Need to be 10 times better than white male counterparts to be promoted.
- A threatening, negative environment that discourages open discussion of alternatives.
- Frequent use of demeaning ethnic- or gender-related jokes.

White Male Groups

Most white men, particularly supervisors, strongly insisted that they were interested solely in performance and that neither race nor sex had anything to do with how they treated their staff members or fellow employees. They often used such terms as equality, fairness, competence, and color-blindness to describe their criteria for promotions, assignments, selection for team projects, and task force membership. Many of these men felt that, rather than being penalized, women and minorities were given "every conceivable break."

The consulting team asked this group of white men specific questions concerning particular problems they may have encountered at work with women and the three largest minority groups in the plant (African Americans, Asian Americans, and Latinos). The most common comments regarding the white men's encounters with each of these groups and with women follow.

African Americans

- Frequently overreact.
- Expect special treatment because of their race.
- Unwilling to blend in with the work group, even when white colleagues try to make them feel comfortable.

Asian Americans

- Very smart with numbers, but have problems verbalizing ideas.
- Stoic and cautious; will not challenge another person even when that person is blatantly wrong.

■ Prone to express agreement or commitment to an idea or course of action, yet are uncommitted to it in their hearts.

Latinos

■ More concerned with their extended family than with work.

■ Often have a difficult time handling structured tasks as employees, yet become dogmatic and authoritarian in supervisory positions.

■ Have a difficult time at work dealing with women whom they expect to be submissive and passive.

■ Very lax about punctuality and schedules.

Women

■ Most are not very committed to work and are inclined to quit when things don't go their way.

■ Often more focused on interpersonal relationships than on work performance.

■ Respond too emotionally when frustrated by minor problems, thus unsuited for more responsibility.

■ Tend to misinterpret chivalry as sexual overtures.

■ Cannot keep things confidential and enjoy gossip.

Phillip Wagner was shocked at many of these comments. He had always thought of his plant as a friendly, easygoing, open-minded, liberal, intellectual place because it has a highly educated workforce (most employees have college degrees, and a significant proportion have advanced graduate degrees). He is now trying to figure out what to do next.

Critical Thinking Questions

1. What consequences are likely to result from the problems at the Northern Sigma plant? Explain your answer.
2. Should Wagner be held responsible for these problems? Explain.
3. What specific recommendations would you offer Wagner to improve the management of diversity at the Chicago plant?

Team Exercise

The class divides into groups of three to five students. Each group should discuss what recommendations it would make to Wagner. After 10 to 15 minutes, each group should present its recommendations to the class. How different are the recommendations from group to group? What principles from the chapter were you able to apply to this problem?

Experiential Exercise

One to three students will role-play a consultant brought in to interview Phillip Wagner (played by another student) and ask why these diversity problems have emerged at Northern Sigma. Based on the reasons provided by Wagner during the role-play interview, the consultants will offer recommendations to help resolve the problems. The role-play should last approximately 15 minutes, after which the class will discuss the issues raised, mediated by instructor.

YOU MANAGE IT!   # Global Case 4.4

Reverse Discrimination or a Case of Cultural Misunderstanding?

Marubeni America Corp., the New York subsidiary of a large Japanese trading company, was looking to hire a salesperson for its textile unit. The company's vice president told the human resources division in an e-mail that he'd prefer an Asian man for the job, because "once [Americans] reach high income, all of a sudden [they] stop working." The e-mail was cited as one of the more egregious examples of alleged reverse discrimination in an unusual lawsuit filed against the company.

"This is sort of a novel issue to us. We tend to see more of a reverse of this," said Sarah Crawford, an employment discrimination expert at the nonprofit, nonpartisan Lawyers Committee for Civil Rights Under Law. "From what I've seen, it's a growing concern, because of the increasing presence of multinational corporations in this country."

Though the Marubeni case isn't unprecedented, the e-mails and other evidence cited in the filing offer a rare inside look at

the employment practices of an overseas firm operating in the United States. The plaintiffs—two Caucasian executives—accuse the defendants of discriminating against Americans, non-Asian minorities, and women. The suit alleges that non-Asians are paid less and hired and promoted less frequently than Asians. According to the suit, the 200-worker company has no African Americans or females and just one Hispanic among its 121 top officers and managers, and just three black employees. The suit also claims that weekly meetings were conducted in Japanese, effectively excluding non-Japanese-speaking employees, and that some executives frequently used racial and ethnic slurs. The suit also alleges that the company violated immigration laws, committed accounting fraud, and allowed executives to abuse their expense accounts.

The suit was brought by Kevin Long, a senior human resources employee, and Ludvic Presto, the company's top internal auditor, both of whom were placed on paid administrative leave—a move their lawyers say was retaliation for complaining about discrimination. The two men are asking for a minimum of $4 million each in severance payments, plus pension and other benefits, and $55 million in damages and legal costs. Two female human resource workers filed similar complaints with the EEOC.

Critical Thinking Questions

1. What would you do if you were asked to investigate whether the allegations in the case are true? Explain.
2. If you were the top Japanese executive of the trading company, what steps would you take to prevent the actual or purported behaviors taking place at the U.S. subsidiary (Marubeni America Corp.)? Explain.
3. What diversity practices would you put in place to prevent the kinds of behaviors alleged in this case? Explain.

Team Exercise

The Japanese trading company has appointed you to a commission responsible for investigating allegations that managers at its U.S. subsidiary have engaged in employment practices that are inconsistent with legal and cultural norms in the United States.

The class is divided into groups of five students, each of which is asked to develop a set of procedures to investigate such allegations and hopefully prevent them from arising again in the future.

Experiential Exercise

In a role-playing exercise, one of the students is asked to be the CEO of a Japanese firm planning to open a subsidiary in the United States. This CEO had heard of the problems faced by Marubeni America Corp. Three students will be asked to serve as the American advisor to the Japanese CEO and provide a clear set of guidelines to avoid the types of problems that are alleged in the case. Students will role-play this scenario for approximately 15 minutes in front of the class, to be followed by a class discussion of the issues raised, mediated by the instructor.

Source: Adapted with permission from Scannell, K. (2005, January 20). Lawsuit charges U.S. unit of Japanese company with bias. *Wall Street Journal*, B1.

Recruiting and Selecting Employees

Challenges

After reading this chapter, you should be able to deal more effectively with the following challenges:

1 **Understand** approaches to matching labor supply and demand.

2 **Weigh** the advantages and disadvantages of internal and external recruiting.

3 **Distinguish** among the major selection methods and use the most legally defensible of them.

4 **Make** staffing decisions that maximize the hiring and promotion of the best people.

5 **Understand** the legal constraints on the hiring process.

Specialty Cabinets Company had rapidly expanded from a two-person operation to a small business with 28 employees. This thriving business catered to those who needed high-end cabinet work in custom-built homes or office buildings. Specialty had been able to attract highly trained carpenters; however, the company's president realized that Specialty needed to hire an additional manager. She gave George Zoran, a senior supervisor with strong interpersonal skills, the responsibility for hiring the new manager.

George posted the opening on the company bulletin board and put an ad online and in the "Help Wanted" section of the local newspaper and soon received numerous applications.

George was particularly impressed with one candidate, Tim Wells. Tim had never worked in carpentry, but George thought Tim seemed personable and had sufficient managerial experience and ambition to handle the job. Interestingly, George also learned that Tim was the son of an old school friend. He thoroughly enjoyed telling Tim about hunting trips he had taken with Tim's father.

On the next round of interviews, George took Tim on a tour of the business operation and offered him the position. George was confident that Tim would be a great addition to the company. Unfortunately, his expectations proved overly optimistic.

Other workers complained about Tim's lack of woodworking experience. They also complained that Tim did not ask for their opinion when he should have. For instance, Tim did not have the knowledge to plan schedules that ensured project deadlines would be met and he did not ask for advice. As a result, his employees recently had to work long hours over a holiday weekend to meet a critical deadline. The workers wondered why George had hired Tim, and Tim wondered why George had led him to believe he could succeed in the job.

THE MANAGERIAL PERSPECTIVE

Although HR managers may be responsible for designing employee recruitment and selection systems in many firms, all managers need to understand and use these systems. After all, attracting and hiring the right kind and level of talent are critical elements of business effectiveness. Stocking a company with top talent has been described as the single most important job of management.[1] The ability to attract and hire effective employees is also a key element of a successful management career. As the Specialty Cabinets example demonstrates, managers may be in charge of recruiting or have a key role in the process. If they do not attract and hire the right people, managers can hurt the organization.

The focus of this chapter is on understanding and conducting effective recruitment and selection. As you think back to the situation at Specialty Cabinets, consider these important questions:

- Who should make the hiring decision?
- What characteristics should a firm look at when deciding whom to hire, and how should those characteristics be measured?
- Should managers consider how a potential employee "fits" with the firm's culture in addition to that employee's skill level?

In this chapter, we explore how managers plan recruitment efforts effectively by assessing the supply of and demand for human resources. Then we examine the hiring process in detail, the challenges managers face in hiring and promoting, and recommendations for dealing with those challenges. Finally, we evaluate specific methods for making hiring decisions and the legal issues that affect hiring decisions.

Human Resource Supply and Demand

Labor supply is the availability of workers who possess the required skills that an employer might need. **Labor demand** is the number of workers an organization needs. Estimating future labor supply and demand and taking steps to balance the two require planning.

Human resource planning (HRP) is the process an organization uses to ensure that it has the right amount and the right kinds of people to deliver a particular level of output or services in the future. Firms that do not conduct HRP may not be able to meet their future labor needs (a labor shortage) or may have to resort to layoffs (in the case of a labor surplus).

Failure to plan can lead to significant financial costs. For instance, firms that lay off large numbers of employees are required to pay higher taxes to the unemployment insurance system, whereas firms that ask their employees to work overtime are required to pay them a wage premium. In addition, firms sometimes need to do HRP to satisfy legally mandated affirmative action programs (see Chapter 4). In large organizations HRP is usually done centrally by specially trained HR staff.

Labor supply
The availability of workers with the required skills to meet the firm's labor demand.

Labor demand
How many workers the organization will need in the future.

**Human Resource
Planning**

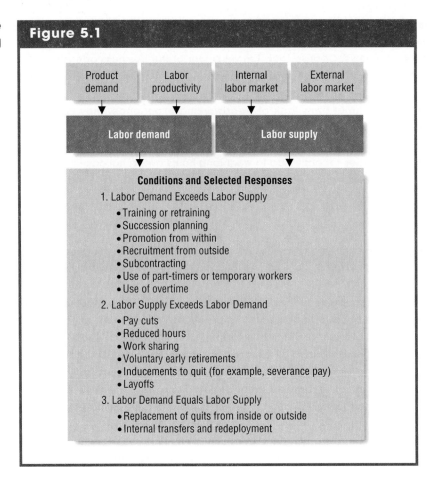

Figure 5.1

Product demand | Labor productivity | Internal labor market | External labor market

Labor demand | Labor supply

Conditions and Selected Responses

1. Labor Demand Exceeds Labor Supply
   - Training or retraining
   - Succession planning
   - Promotion from within
   - Recruitment from outside
   - Subcontracting
   - Use of part-timers or temporary workers
   - Use of overtime
2. Labor Supply Exceeds Labor Demand
   - Pay cuts
   - Reduced hours
   - Work sharing
   - Voluntary early retirements
   - Inducements to quit (for example, severance pay)
   - Layoffs
3. Labor Demand Equals Labor Supply
   - Replacement of quits from inside or outside
   - Internal transfers and redeployment

Human resource planning (HRP)

The process an organization uses to ensure that it has the right amount and the right kind of people to deliver a particular level of output or services in the future.

Figure 5.1 summarizes the HRP process. The first HRP activity entails forecasting labor demand. Labor demand is likely to increase as demand for the firm's product or services increases and to decrease as labor productivity increases (because more output can be produced with fewer workers, usually because of the introduction of new technology).

The second part of the HRP process entails estimating labor supply. The labor supply may come from existing employees (the *internal* labor market) or from outside the organization (the *external* labor market).

After estimating labor demand and supply for a future period, a firm faces one of three conditions, each of which requires a different set of responses. In the first scenario, the firm will need more workers than will be available. A variety of approaches can then be used to increase the labor supply available to a specific firm. These include training or retraining existing workers, grooming current employees to take over vacant positions (*succession planning*), promoting from within, recruiting new employees from outside the firm, subcontracting part of the work to other firms, hiring part-timers or temporary workers, and paying overtime to existing employees.

A labor shortage can be a long-term affair that affects many companies. As described in the Manager's Notebook, "Labor Shortage? In China?" a labor shortage can affect an entire country.

**MANAGER'S
NOTEBOOK** Global

Labor Shortage? In China?

China has a population of over 1 billion, yet Chinese employers can't recruit enough workers. Many people consider China's labor supply to be inexhaustible, but demand is starting to outstrip supply, even for factory and manual workers. The supply of labor for skilled jobs is even tighter.

Many business plans that include outsourcing to China or expanding into China do not take into account the difficulty and cost of recruiting and retaining Chinese labor. It is important to recognize these costs and realize that China is no longer the land of cheap and endless labor. The following are some of the effects of the Chinese labor shortage:

■ Recruitment and retention are at the top of agendas for companies in China.

■ The labor turnover rate in China is increasing and stands at over 11 percent, an increase of approximately 8 percent in three years.

■ Pay and benefit levels are quickly rising.

■ Incentives are becoming commonplace. For example, company cars are being offered by approximately 33 percent of multinational companies doing business in China. Other common perks include mobile phones, free meals, and extra holidays.

Sources: The Economist. (2005, April 16). China's people problem: Human resources, Business section; Yang, D. L. (2005). China's looming labor shortage. *Far Eastern Economic Review, 168,* 19–24.

In the second scenario, labor supply is expected to exceed labor demand. This excess means that the firm will have more employees than it needs. Firms may use a variety of measures to deal with this situation. These include pay cuts, reducing the number of hours worked, and work sharing (all of which may save jobs). In addition, the firm may eliminate positions through a combination of tactics, including early retirement incentives, severance pay, and outright layoffs. (We discuss these issues in detail in Chapter 6 and 13.) If the labor surplus is expected to be modest, the firm may be better off reducing the number of hours worked instead of terminating employees. Under federal law, the latter option would force the firm to pay more into the unemployment compensation insurance program. Furthermore, reducing hours worked rather than laying off workers can avoid additional recruiting and training costs when the demand for labor increases.[2]

In the third scenario, labor demand is expected to match labor supply. The organization can deal with this situation by replacing employees who quit with people promoted from inside the business or hired from the outside. The firm may also transfer or re-deploy employees internally, with training and career development programs designed to support these moves.

A Simplified Example of Forecasting Labor Demand and Supply

Figure 5.2 shows how a large national hotel chain with 25 units forecasts its labor demand for 16 key jobs two years ahead. Column A indicates the number of employees who currently hold each of these jobs. Column B calculates the present ratio of employees to hotels—that is, the number of current employees divided by the current number of hotels (25). The hotel chain expects to add seven additional hotels by the year 2008 (for a total of 32). In column C, the expected number of employees for each job in 2008 is calculated by multiplying the current ratio of employees to hotels (column B) by 32. For instance, in 2005 there were 9 resident managers for 25 hotels, or a ratio of 0.36 (9 ÷ 25). When the number of hotels expands to 32 in 2008, it is forecasted that 12 resident managers will be needed (0.36 × 32 = 11.52, or 12.0 after rounding).

The same hotel chain's labor supply prediction is found in columns A to D of Figure 5.3. on page 151. Column A shows the percentage of employees in each of the 16 key jobs who left the firm during the past two years (2003 to 2005). Multiplying this percentage by the number of present employees in each of these key jobs produces an estimate of how many current employees will have quit by 2008. For example, 38 percent of general managers quit between 2003 and 2005. Because there are now 25 employees holding this job, it is forecasted that by 2008, 10 of them will have left the firm (0.38 × 25 = 9.5, rounded to 10).

The projected turnover for each job is shown in column C. This means that by 2008, 15 of the current general managers (25 minus 10; see column D) will still be working for the company.

Example of Predicting Labor Demand for a Hotel Chain with 25 Hotels

Figure 5.2			
	A Number of Employees (2005)	**B** Ratio of Employees/Hotels (Calculated as Column A ÷ 25)	**C** Projected 2006 Labor Demand for 32 Hotels (Calculated as Column B × 32)*
Key Positions			
General Manager	25	1.00	32
Resident Manager	9	.36	12
Food/Beverage Director	23	.92	29
Controller	25	1.00	32
Assistant Controller	14	.56	18
Chief Engineer	24	.96	31
Director of Sales	25	1.00	32
Sales Manager	45	1.80	58
Convention Manager	14	.56	18
Catering Director	19	.76	24
Banquet Manager	19	.76	24
Personnel Director	15	.60	19
Restaurant Manager	49	1.96	63
Executive Chef	24	.96	31
Sous Chef	24	.96	31
Executive Housekeeper	25	1.00	32
Total	379		486

*These figures are rounded.

Because the projected labor demand for general managers in 2008 is 32 (see Figure 5.2), 17 new general managers (32 minus 15) will have to be hired by 2008.

In the past, many firms avoided HRP, simply because their staffs were too swamped with everyday paperwork to manage the planning process effectively. For example, FedEx used to rely on a 20-page employment application. Imagine the labor and paper this process required when FedEx hires 25,000 new hourly workers each year. These excesses ended when FedEx moved to a paperless Web-based system that immediately caught errors as a job candidate was completing the employment application form and reduced by more than 50 percent the time needed to complete the application form and recruiters to examine it.[3] Furthermore, the Web-based job application system was integrated with the human resource information system (HRIS) so that human resource supply and demand data could be automatically updated. Many software companies, such as PeopleSoft, Lawson, SAP, and Oracle, now offer powerful computer-based HRP programs.[4]

Forecasting Techniques

Two basic categories of forecasting techniques are quantitative and qualitative. The example described in Figure 5.2 is a highly simplified version of a *quantitative technique.* A variety of mathematically sophisticated quantitative techniques has been developed to estimate labor demand and supply.[5]

Although used more often, quantitative forecasting models have two main limitations. First, most rely heavily on past data or previous relationships between staffing levels and other variables, such as output or revenues. Relationships that held in the past may not hold in the future, and it may be better to change previous staffing practices than to perpetuate them.

Second, most of these forecasting techniques were created during the 1950s, 1960s, and early 1970s and were appropriate for the large firms of that era, which had stable environments

		Supply Analysis			Supply-Demand Comparison	
	A	**B**	**C**	**D**	**E**	**F**
	% Quit* **(1998–2000)**	**Number of Present Employees (See Figure 5.2, Column A)**	**Projected Turnover by 2006 (Column A × Column B)**	**Employees Left by 2006 (Column B − Column C)**	**Projected Labor Demand in 2006 (See Figure 5.2, Column C)**	**Projected New Hires in 2006 (Column E − Column D)**
Key Positions						
General Manager	38	25	10	15	32	17
Resident Manager	77	9	7	2	12	10
Food/Beverage Director	47	23	11	12	29	17
Controller	85	25	21	4	32	28
Assistant Controller	66	14	9	5	18	13
Chief Engineer	81	24	16	8	31	23
Director of Sales	34	25	9	16	32	16
Sales Manager	68	45	30	15	58	43
Convention Manager	90	14	13	1	18	17
Catering Director	74	19	14	5	24	19
Banquet Manager	60	19	12	7	24	17
Personnel Director	43	15	6	9	19	10
Restaurant Manager	89	49	44	5	63	58
Executive Chef	70	24	17	7	31	24
Sous Chef	92	24	22	2	31	29
Executive Housekeeper	63	25	16	9	32	23
Total Employees		379	257	122	486	364

*These figures are rounded.

Example of Predicting Labor Supply and Required New Hires for a Hotel Chain

and workforces. They are less appropriate today, when firms are struggling with destabilizing forces such as rapid technological change and intense global competition.

Unlike quantitative techniques, *qualitative techniques* rely on experts' qualitative judgments or subjective estimates of labor demand or supply. The experts may include top managers, whose involvement in and support of the HRP process is a worthwhile objective in itself. One advantage of qualitative techniques is that they are flexible enough to incorporate whatever factors or conditions the expert feels should be considered. However, a potential drawback of these techniques is that subjective judgments may be less accurate or lead to rougher estimates than those obtained through quantitative methods.

For those interested in learning more about quantitative and qualitative forecasting, Figure 5.4 outlines some important techniques and their main advantages and disadvantages.

As described earlier, forecasting supply and demand is often approached as a separate and fairly specialized function. Further, in some ways it is similar to taking a snapshot of the past to predict the future. A drawback of this approach is the rate of change in many of today's workplaces. Labor supply and demand may shift frequently due to changes in projects, products, technology, competition, and so on. What is needed is a real-time approach for forecasting supply and demand that can provide continuous updates. You Manage It! Emerging Trends Case 5.1 at the end of this chapter asks you to consider just such an approach.

Methods of Forecasting Demand

Figure 5.4

Quantitative Techniques
- **Regression analysis** Statistically identifies historical predictors of workplace size. Future demand for human resources is predicted using an equation.
- **Ratio analysis** Examines historical ratios involving workforce size (such as number of customers relative to number of employees) and uses ratios to predict future demand for human resources.

Judgmental Techniques
Information is collected and subjectively weighed to forecast the demand for human resources.
- **Top-down approach** Prediction made by top management.
- **Bottom-up approach** Lower-level managers each make their own initial estimates, which are then consolidated, and the process continues up through higher levels of management. Top management makes final estimates.

Methods of Forecasting Supply
Quantitative Techniques
- **Markov analysis** Estimates the internal supply of labor by turning movement of labor into transition probabilities.

Judgmental Techniques
- **Executive reviews** Top management makes judgments about who should be promoted, reassigned, or let go. The process can clarify where there may be surpluses or shortages of managers.
- **Succession planning** Identifies workers who are ready or will soon be qualified to replace current managers. Can highlight development needs and areas where there may be a shortage of management-level labor.
- **Vacancy analysis** Judgments are made about likely employee movements. Shortages or surpluses of labor can be anticipated by comparing these judgments to estimates of demand.

Source: Adapted from Heneman, H. G., and Heneman, R. L. (1994). *Staffing organizations.* Middleton, WI: Mendata House.

The Hiring Process

Once the firm has determined its staffing needs, it needs to hire the best employees to fill the available positions. As Figure 5.5 shows, the hiring process has three components: recruitment, selection, and socialization.

Recruitment
The process of generating a pool of qualified candidates for a particular job; the first step in the hiring process.

Recruitment is the process of generating a pool of qualified candidates for a particular job. The firm must announce the job's availability to the market (inside and outside the organization) and attract qualified candidates to apply.

Selection
The process of making a "hire" or "no hire" decision regarding each applicant for a job; the second step in the hiring process.

Selection is the process of making a "hire" or "no hire" decision regarding each applicant for a job. The process typically involves determining the characteristics required for effective job performance and then measuring applicants on those characteristics, which are typically based on a job analysis (see Chapter 2). Depending on applicants' scores on various tests and/or the impressions they have made in interviews, managers determine who will be offered a job. This selection process often relies on *cut scores*; applicants who score below these levels are considered unacceptable.

Socialization
The process of orienting new employees to the organization or the unit in which they will be working; the third step in the hiring process.

The staffing process is not, and should not be, complete once applicants are hired or promoted. To retain and maximize the human resources who were so carefully selected, organizations must pay careful attention to socializing them. **Socialization** orients new employees to the organization and to the units in which they will be working. Socialization can make the difference between a new worker's feeling like an outsider and feeling like a member of the team. We discuss the socialization process in more detail in Chapter 8.

Challenges in the Hiring Process

It has been estimated that above-average employees are worth about 40 percent of their salary more to the organization than average employees.[6] Thus, an above-average new hire in a sales job with a $40,000 salary would be worth $16,000 more to the organization than an average employee hired for the same position. Over 10 years, the above-average employee's added value to the company would total $160,000!

Poor hiring decisions are likely to cause problems from day one.[7] Unqualified or unmotivated workers will probably require closer supervision and direction. They may require additional training yet never reach the required level of performance. They may also give customers inaccurate information or give customers a reason to do business with competitors.

Just how costly is employee turnover? A recent estimate provided by the Coca-Cola Research Council is that it costs $4,000 to replace an hourly retail worker.[8] As the level and salary of a worker goes up, so does this cost. The following list describes the major categories of costs, which can add up to a significant sum.[9] Some may be difficult to estimate, but they are real costs just the same. For example, what is the cost of a disruption to peers and to the work process when someone quits? How much productivity was lost before the worker decided to quit?

Figure 5.5

Recruitment → Selection → Socialization

The Hiring Process

Major Turnover Costs[10]

Separation: Exit interview, paperwork processing
Recruitment: Advertising, recruiter fees
Selection: Pre-employment testing, interviewing
Hiring: Orientation, training
Productivity: Vacancy cost, disruption

Getting and keeping the best not only makes sense in terms of treatment of employees as customers of the management process, but it also makes economic sense.

It is essential that line managers and possibly other line workers be involved in the hiring process. Although the HR department has an active role to play in recruiting, selecting, and socializing new employees, line personnel will actively be supervising the new hires, and these managers often have job-related insights that members of the HR department may lack.

The hiring process is fraught with challenges. The most important of these are:

■ Determining which personal characteristics are most important to performance.
■ Measuring those characteristics.
■ Evaluating applicants' motivation levels.
■ Deciding who should make the selection decision.

We'll look at each of these next.

Determining Characteristics Important to Performance

For several reasons, the characteristics a person needs to perform a job effectively are not necessarily obvious. First, the job itself is very often a moving target. For instance, the knowledge, skills, and abilities (KSAs—see Chapter 2) necessary for a good computer programmer right now are certainly going to change as hardware and software continue evolving. Second, the organization's culture may need to be taken into account. Outback Steakhouse, Inc., includes a comprehensive personality assessment as part of its employee selection process.[11] The focus on fit between the applicant and the culture of the organization results in similar employee attitude and customer service across the Outback restaurants. Outback enjoys the lowest turnover rate in its industry, approximately 2 percent per year.[12]

Third, different people in the organization often want different characteristics in a new hire. Upper-level managers may want the new manager of an engineering group to be financially astute, whereas the engineers in the group may want a manager with technical expertise.

Measuring Characteristics That Determine Performance

Suppose mathematical ability is considered critical for job performance. You cannot infer from looking at someone what level of mathematical ability he or she possesses. Rather, you must administer some test of mathematical ability. Some tests are better than others at predicting job performance, and they can vary widely in cost.

The Motivation Factor

Most of the measures used in hiring decisions focus on *ability* rather than *motivation*. There are countless tests of mathematical ability, verbal ability, and mechanical ability. But, as the following equation makes clear, motivation is also critical to performance:

$$\text{Performance} = \text{Ability} \times \text{Motivation}$$

This equation shows that a high ability level can yield poor job performance if it is combined with low motivation. Likewise, a high level of motivation cannot offset a lack of ability. (We will discuss another influence on performance, system factors, in Chapter 7.) The performance equation makes conceptual sense, and recent empirical work supports the importance of both ability and motivation in determining performance. For instance, the early career success of M.B.A. graduates has been found to be a function of both ability and motivation levels.[13]

Unfortunately, motivation is very difficult to measure. Many employers try to assess motivation during the employment interview, but (as we will see later in this chapter) there are numerous problems with this method. In addition, motivation seems to be much more dependent on context than ability is. If you are a typical student, your motivation to work hard in a class depends to a large extent on whether you like the course content, how much you like and respect your instructor, and how grades are determined. Your academic ability is fairly stable from course to course, but your motivation level is much more variable. Work situations are just as variable: How much you like your job responsibilities, how well you get along with your boss, and how you are compensated all affect your level of effort.

Who Should Make the Decision?

There are two good reasons for letting the HR department run the staffing process. The first (and more important) is that the organization must ensure that its employment practices comply with the legal requirements described in Chapter 3, and making HR staff responsible for all hiring decisions can help avoid problems in this area. The second reason is convenience. Since the HR staff is usually responsible for processing initial contacts with applicants and is often the repository of information about applicants, many organizations find it easier to let the HR department follow through and make hiring decisions.

However, this system leaves the line personnel out of a process that is critical to the operation's effectiveness. If an organization decides to involve line employees in hiring decisions, which ones should it consult? The first, and most obvious, are the managers who will be supervising the new hire. The second group consists of the new hire's coworkers. The third group, where applicable, is the new hire's subordinates. As we saw in the Specialty Cabinets Company example that opened this chapter, these groups do not necessarily share the same view of what characteristics are important in the new employee.

Meeting the Challenges of Effective Staffing

Each step of the staffing process—recruitment, selection, and socialization—must be managed carefully. We discuss the first two of these three steps next.

Recruitment

The recruitment process is really a sales activity. A qualified job candidate is your customer when you are trying to sell the job to him or her. Some keys to successfully approaching recruitment as a sales activity are presented in the Manager's Notebook, "Making the Sale with a Customer-Driven Approach to Recruitment."

Customer-Driven HR

Making the Sale with a Customer-Driven Approach to Recruitment

Like the purchase of a product or service, recruitment requires candidates to make a buy decision about your job opening. Recruitment is your opportunity to sell the organization and the job, maybe even the community, to the job candidates. Treating the applicants as customers will help to maximize the chances that they will buy into and choose your job and organization.

Following are key questions that can help you to take a more customer-oriented approach to recruitment. They need to be answered by everyone involved in the recruiting process.

Preparation

- Why do you work for your organization?
- What are the advantages of working here?
- What are the best things about working for this organization?
- What are the career opportunities here?
- What gets recognized and rewarded?
- What are the positives about living in the community?

Process

- Do you treat applicants as your customers?
- Are interviews scheduled around the applicant's preferences?
- Would applicants describe their visit as positive and pleasant or as a series of hoops to jump through?
- Do you welcome each applicant?
- Are applicants treated as guests or as widgets to be processed?
- Are assessments, such as testing or interviews, explained so that applicants understand the purpose and the reason the assessments are needed?
- Are there interview expenses that aren't paid for because you want to reduce costs?

Encounter

- What are the most important things the applicant is looking for in a job?
- What are the most important things the applicant is looking for in an organization?
- What are the most important things the applicant is looking for in a community?
- If the applicant could change something about his or her current job, what would it be?

Once you understand the applicant's needs and preferences based on answers to questions such as these, think about how those needs and preferences can be met. To effectively respond to each applicant's needs and preferences requires in-depth understanding of what the job, organization, and community have to offer.

By perceiving themselves as customers throughout the recruitment process, even applicants who are not hired will nevertheless have a positive impression of the organization. They may become customers of the organization's products or services as well as recommend the organization to others as a potential employer. Positive impressions can be the direct result of a customer approach to recruitment.

Source: Partially adapted with permission from Bozell, J. (2002). Cut to the chase. *Nursing Management, 33,* 39–40.

Sources of Recruiting

A great number of recruitment sources are available to organizations.[14] The most prominent are:

- **Current employees.** Many companies have a policy of informing current employees about job openings before trying to recruit from other sources. Internal job postings give current employees the opportunity to move into the firm's more desirable jobs. However, an internal promotion automatically creates another job opening that has to be filled.

- **Referrals from current employees.** Studies have shown that employees who were hired through referrals from current employees tended to stay with the organization longer and displayed greater loyalty and job satisfaction than employees who were recruited by other means.[15] Red Lobster, the seafood restaurant chain, rewards any employee whose referral results in a successful managerial hire with $1,000 in gift certificates.[16] Some hospitals facing labor shortages are using employee referral incentives as a cost-effective recruiting tool.[17] For example, George Washington University Hospital awards $5,000 to employees who refer registered nurses. The referring employee receives $1,500 after the new nurse completes three months of employment and another $3,500 after the nurse's first-year anniversary. Employee referrals can be an effective recruitment tool, because employees have a good sense of what it takes to be a successful worker and member of the organization. However, to the extent current employees tend to refer people who are demographically similar to themselves, it can create equal employment opportunity (EEO) problems.

- **Former employees.** A firm may decide to recruit employees who previously worked for the organization. Typically, these are people who were laid off, although they may also have worked seasonally (during summer vacations or tax season, for example). Forming an online alumni network could be a simple and cost-effective way to maintain a hiring pool of competitive candidates.[18] Furthermore, a network of former employees can be a source of employee referrals because they are familiar with the company, its culture, and its values.

- **Former military.** Since the war on terror began, employers have had the option to hire discharged soldiers. This is more than patriotism. As presented in the Manager's Notebook, "Going Military," organizations see real performance benefits from hiring former military.

MANAGER'S NOTEBOOK

Emerging Trends

Going Military

A number of organizations are actively recruiting former soldiers. It may be a patriotic thing to do, but these organizations see a military background as a very positive qualification that often includes leadership skills, reliability, discipline, problem-solving abilities and manager's experience.

Approximately 5,000 companies are registered with the Marines for Life program, designed to help discharged soldiers find civilian work. The Big Three automakers currently employ 47,000 military veterans, and approximately 250,000 military personnel transition into the private sector every year. Maytag Corp. aggressively recruits recently discharged soldiers for repair technician positions. Toyota North America has a former military recruitment program that it calls "Hire a Hero." Home Depot is, perhaps, the most widely recognized recruiter of former military personnel. The Home Depot recruitment program is entitled "Operation Career Front," and the organization hired 10,000 veterans in 2003 and 13,000 in 2004.

Home Depot is a major employer of former military personnel.

Source: Booe, M. (2005, January 1). Reporting to the depot: Home Depot prizes the skills and leadership abilities former military personnel bring to the company. *Workforce Management*, 27; Pitt, D. (2005, January 3). Former GIs recruited: Companies offer jobs to ex-soldiers. *Arizona Republic*, D2.

- **Print and radio advertisements.** Advertisements can be used both for local recruitment efforts (newspapers) and for targeted regional, national, or international searches (trade or professional publications). For instance, clinical psychologists often find jobs through listings in the American Psychological Association's monthly newsletter.
- **Internet advertising and career sites.** Employers are increasingly turning to the Web as a recruitment tool because online ads are relatively cheap, are more dynamic, and can often produce faster results than newspaper help-wanted ads.

The Web is not only an economical, efficient means to recruit, but it is also a convenient tool for job seekers. Thousands of career Web sites exist and almost all are free to people searching for jobs. One of the best known sites is Monster.com. Job seekers can search for jobs by industry, geographic location, and in some cases, by job description. The common practice of going through the Sunday help-wanted ads with a highlighter in hand is rapidly becoming a thing of the past. Figure 5.6 lists some sites that might be helpful to you when looking for a job.

- **Employment agencies.** Many organizations use external contractors to recruit and screen applicants for a position. Typically, the employment agency is paid a fee based on the salary offered to the new employee. Agencies can be particularly effective when the firm is looking for an employee with a specialized skill.
- **Temporary workers.** According to the U.S. Bureau of Labor Statistics, in March 2005 approximately 2.4 million workers were employed in temporary or contract positions.[19] Demand for temporary workers is predicted to increase.[20] Temporary workers provide employers the

Figure 5.6	
www.careerbuilder.com	Access to more than 2 million job postings on various Web sites
www.ajb.dni.us	The job bank of the Department of Labor
www.careermosaic.com	Job postings and industry information such as professional association listings
www.careerpath.com	Weekly listings from approximately 90 newspapers and from employer Web sites
www.monster.com	Popular Web site for job postings and résumés

flexibility to quickly meet fluctuating demands. Bringing in temporary workers enables employers to bypass the time-consuming hiring process of job interviews and background checks. As presented in the Manager's Notebook, "Evaluation Hiring: Try 'Em Before You Buy 'Em," temporary labor can also be used in a tryout period to see if workers would be suitable for permanent employment. Some companies are also finding that the older children of employees can be a great source for temporary workers.[21] Bryer's Ice Cream, for example, hires college-bound children of its employees to help out over the summer. If the students work for the full 10 weeks without an accident and no more than one day of absence, they get a bonus—approximately $1,500 in scholarship money paid directly to their colleges.

In addition to providing flexibility, the increase in the demand for temporary workers may also be due to employers using temporary workers as a way to avoid paying benefits. However, this practice can lead to abuse, unfair treatment, and, as we saw in Chapter 3, potential legal liability. Surveys find that over half of temporary workers would prefer the job security and benefits that come with a permanent job.[22] However, after proving their value to the organization as temporary workers, many are hired as permanent employees.

MANAGER'S NOTEBOOK

Ethics

Evaluation Hiring: Try 'Em Before You Buy 'Em

A new wrinkle in temporary labor is *evaluation hiring*. With evaluation hiring, a job candidate is hired by a staffing firm but put to work at another company. After a set period of time (usually 90 days), the company decides whether to hire the worker as a permanent employee. The company can realize several benefits:

- The staffing firm handles recruitment and pays salary and benefits.
- The company can make a better determination of who will best fit in an organization than with just an interview and test.
- The tryout period helps employers avoid making bad hiring decisions.

  However, evaluation hiring raises several ethical issues:

- Is not knowing whether you have a permanent job for 90 days fair?
- What if the tryout period were extended to two years, instead of 90 days; would this still be a fair situation? (Honda, for example, guarantees a job interview after a two-year evaluation period).
- Given that an alternative might be to hire workers on only a temporary basis (to cover, for example, periods of peak demand), is evaluation hiring the more ethical choice?

Source: Matthews, T. (2005, May 13). Once around the block: Employment agency lets companies 'test drive' prospective workers. *The Columbus Dispatch,* Business section, 1.

- **College recruiting.** Your school probably has a job placement office that helps students make contacts with employers. Students whose majors are accounting, engineering, computer programming, and information systems at the undergraduate level and those with graduate degrees in business and law are often considered the most desirable candidates because of the applied training they have received.

  You might think that college recruiting may change in its nature and shift from face-to-face meetings to Web-based interactions. For example, Hewlett-Packard has a Web site specifically focused on college recruiting at *www.jobs.hp.com*. However, savvy organizations recognize that the Internet cannot do the entire recruiting job.[23] There is value in interacting with college students, developing relationships, and generating interest in the college pool of candidates. Company visits to college campuses, job fairs, and various relationships such as internships are likely to continue for the long term.

- **Customers.** An innovative recruitment source is the organization's customers, who are already familiar with the organization and what it offers.[24] Customers can be more valuable than simply as buyers and consumers of a product or service.[25] These people, who must be happy with the organization's product or service because they have remained customers, may bring more enthusiasm to the workplace than other applicants and, as the recipients of the firm's product or service, may have valuable insights into how the organization could be improved.

Finding qualified and motivated employees is a key concern for small businesses, with two-thirds of small businesses reporting they have difficulty finding the qualified employees.[26] Bad hires can be catastrophic for small businesses, which do not have the luxury of reassigning workers who are not well suited for their positions.[27]

How do employers evaluate the effectiveness of different recruitment sources? One way is to look at how long employees recruited from different sources stay with the company. Studies show that employees who know more about the organization and have realistic expectations about the job tend to stay longer than other applicants.[28] Current employees, employee referrals, and former employees are likely to turn up applicants with realistic expectations of the job.

Another way of evaluating recruitment sources is by their cost. There are substantial cost differences between advertising and using cash awards to encourage employee referrals, and between hiring locally and hiring beyond the local area (which entails relocating the new employee).

Comparing the effectiveness of various recruiting sources is easier with the use of a simple spreadsheet. As shown in Figure 5.7, the spreadsheet could have recruiting sources in the rows and effectiveness measures (say, on a scale of 1 to 10) in the columns. The columns might track various outcomes from each of the recruitment sources, such as number of employment offers, number of acceptances, turnover at one year, and employee performance ratings at one year.

Figure 5.7

Source	Number of Employment Offers	Number of Acceptances	Total Cost	Turnover After 1 Year	Average Performance Rating at 1 Year
Referrals					
Print ads					
Internet ads and career sites					
Agencies					
College recruitment					
Customers					

Example Criteria for Assessing Effectiveness of Recruitment Sources

Nontraditional Recruiting

Recruiting new workers is a central concern for managers in U.S. organizations when unemployment rates are low. Regardless of current conditions, a long-term perspective leads to the expectation of a labor shortage because the baby boomer generation is nearing retirement and relatively fewer young people are entering the workforce.[29] Furthermore, even in times of high employment and a general labor surplus, there can be shortages of works with particular skills or in particular areas.

When faced with a labor shortage, companies spend more to advertise job openings via radio, the Web, billboards, television, and print media and at job fairs. Many firms also use employment agencies and employee leasing firms to recruit and select new hires. In addition, many companies recruit from nontraditional labor pools and use innovative methods to attract new employees.

Nontraditional labor pools can include prisoners, welfare recipients, senior citizens, and workers from foreign countries. An innovative and inspiring example of an organization that embraces a nontraditional labor pool is Greyston Bakery in Yonkers, New York (see *www.greystonbakery.com*). Greyston, a gourmet bakery, has supplied cakes and tarts to the White House and bakes the brownies and blondies used in Ben & Jerry's ice cream and yogurt. Greyston produces all these products with employees who had been chronically unemployed. Greyston Bakery is committed to giving people opportunities—people who may be homeless or drug addicts. Currently, the bakery employs 55 people and annually generates more than $3.5 million in revenues. Its choice of a nontraditional labor pool helps people get off the streets and into the workforce.

The partnership between Binding Together, a program run by a nonprofit group, and the Darvin Group, a New York printing company, helps nontraditional employees succeed.[30] Like Greyston Bakery, Binding Together provides vocational training for homeless adults and people with a history of substance abuse. Darvin actively recruits people who have graduated from the Binding Together program. In fact, 50 percent of its production staff—from machine operators to managers—are program graduates.

External Versus Internal Candidates

Hiring externally gives the firm the advantage of fresh perspectives and different approaches. Sometimes it also makes economic sense to search for external specialists rather than bear the expense of training current workers in a new process or technology.

On the downside, current employees may see externally recruited workers as "rookies" and, therefore, discount their ideas and perspectives, limiting their impact. Another disadvantage is

Greyston Bakery, a successful gourmet bakery, provides employment for people who would be considered unemployable.

that it may take weeks before a new recruit has learned the job. Bringing in someone from the outside can also cause difficulties if current workers resent the recruit for filling a job they feel should have gone to a qualified internal worker.

Internal recruiting, usually in the form of promotions and transfers, also has its advantages and disadvantages. On the positive side, it is usually less costly than external recruiting. It provides a clear signal to the current workforce that the organization offers opportunities for advancement. And internal recruits are already familiar with the organization's policies, procedures, and customs.

MetLife, for example, uses its intranet for its internal recruitment program. The program, Careers in Motion, enables managers to post job openings and allows employees to search for MetLife openings across the country. Employees can access the job opportunities posted privately and at any time.[31]

One drawback of internal recruiting is that it reduces the likelihood of introducing innovation and new perspectives. Another is that workers being promoted into higher-level jobs may be undercut in their authority if, for example, former coworkers expect special treatment from a supervisor or manager who used to be a colleague.

Recruiting Protected Classes

An integral part of many organizations' recruitment efforts, both externally and internally, is attracting women, minorities, people with disabilities, and other employees in the protected classes. Although the Equal Employment Opportunity Commission guidelines stipulate only that government employers and government contractors must have written affirmative action policies, many private sector employers believe that such policies make good business sense for them. It stands to reason, for instance, that newspapers with diverse readerships would want to increase the diversity of their editorial and reporting staffs.

A good rule of thumb is to target potential recruits through media or recruitment methods that focus on minorities. For example, recruitment efforts could include black colleges and Hispanic organizations.[32] When a company puts too much emphasis on hiring of minorities in ads, candidates may feel resentful or believe they are being hired simply to fill a quota. Recruitment experts say that minority candidates should be addressed the same way all candidates are.[33] Home Depot, Inc., the largest U.S. home improvement store, is partnering with four Hispanic organizations in order to recruit more Spanish-speaking employees.[34] The recruiting effort is part of Home Depot's strategy to improve service for Hispanic customers.

Planning the Recruitment Effort

To be effective, recruitment should be tied to HRP.[35] As we saw earlier in this chapter, HRP compares present workforce capabilities with future demands. The analysis might indicate, for example, a need for 10 more staff personnel given the firm's expansion plans and anticipated market conditions. This information should play a key role in determining the level of the recruitment effort.

How many candidates should the recruitment effort attempt to attract for each job opening? The answer depends on *yield ratios,* which relate recruiting input to recruiting output. For example, if the firm finds that it has to make two job offers to get one acceptance, this offer-to-acceptance ratio indicates that approximately 200 offers will have to be extended to have 100 accepted. Perhaps the interview-to-offer ratio has been 3:1. This ratio indicates that the firm will have to conduct at least 600 interviews to make 200 offers. Other ratios to consider are the number of invitations-to-interview ratio and the number of advertisements or contacts-to-applicant ratio.

Planning Your Job Search

The flip side of recruitment is the job search process in which people search for the right employer. Are you looking for your first job or a change in your career? In addition to the online sources listed in Figure 5.6, a place to start your job search is the local library. Figure 5.8 lists and briefly describes some of the major sources of information to help formulate your search. In addition, online and CD-ROM searches are available at many libraries.

Sample Library Job Search Sources

Figure 5.8	
Source	**Description**
The Career Guide: Dun's Employment Opportunities Directory	Lists companies by geographic area, industry, and disciplines hired; lists educational and experience requirements
Standard & Poor's Register of Corporations, Directors and Executives	Lists more than 50,000 corporations, most privately owned
Moody's Investment Services Manuals	Presents information from company reports and other sources
The Dictionary of Occupational Titles	Provides information on job responsibilities and required education and experience levels

Source: Walberg, M. (1995, March 20). Job hunters find library offers company data, search assistance. *Arizona Republic*, E5.

Selection

Selection determines the overall quality of an organization's human resources. Consider what happens when the wrong person is hired or promoted. How do you, as a customer, like being served by someone who is slow and inept? How would you, as a line supervisor, like to deal with the problems caused by a worker who cannot perform necessary tasks on a production line? Hiring the wrong person can also cause friction among staff as other workers become resentful of having to pick up the slack for inept employees. Inappropriate hires may even lead better employees to seek employment elsewhere. We've seen that all these effects have economic ramifications.

In fact, the economic value of good selection procedures is higher than most people realize. For example, the federal government's use of ability testing for entry-level jobs has been estimated to save the government over $15 billion per year.[36] This amazing figure is derived from the cumulative effects of modest job performance increases by people hired because they scored better than average on the selection test. Continually hiring people who perform, say, 20 percent above average can make a tremendous difference to an organization that hires many workers.

A variety of tools can be used in the selection process. Before we consider these techniques, though, you should be aware of two concepts important for selection tools: reliability and validity.

Reliability and Validity

Reliability
Consistency of measurement, usually across time but also across judges.

Reliability refers to consistency of measurement, usually across time, but also across judges. If a measure produces perfectly consistent results, that measure is perfectly reliable. For example, if you take a math test every week for five weeks and always obtain the same score, then that measure of your mathematical skill level would be considered to be perfectly reliable. Likewise, if five different interviewers all judged you to have the same level of social skill, the interjudge reliability would be perfect.

However, perfect reliability is rarely if ever achieved. Measurement almost always involves some error and that error is "noise," or unreliability. The greater the amount of noise in a measure, the harder it is to determine the true signal that the measure is trying to detect. Reliability is an index of how much error has influenced the measures.

The error with which something is measured can be broken down into two types: deficiency error and contamination error.[37] *Deficiency error* occurs when a component of the domain being measured is not included in the measure. Not including subtraction questions in a test of basic math skills would yield a deficient measure: one that does not capture the true level of basic math skill.

Contamination error occurs when a measure includes unwanted influences. For example, an interviewer may be under undue time pressure from other job duties and not take the time to accurately assess a job candidate. Or, an interviewer might rate an average job candidate lower than average because of the contrast with an outstanding candidate who preceded him.

Validity is the extent to which the technique measures the intended knowledge, skill, or ability. In the selection context, this means that validity is the extent to which scores on a test or interview correspond to actual job performance. A technique that is not valid is useless and may even present legal problems. When discrimination in hiring practices is charged, the critical evidence will be the job relatedness (validity) of the selection technique.[38] Documentation of validity is critical.

There are typically two basic strategies for demonstrating the validity of selection methods: content and empirical. A *content validity* strategy assesses the degree to which the content of the selection method (say, an interview or a test) is representative of job content. For instance, applicants for the job of commercial airline pilot are required to take a series of exams administered by the Federal Aviation Administration. These exams assess whether the candidates have the necessary knowledge to pilot safely and effectively. However, passing these tests does not guarantee that the applicant has the other abilities necessary to perform well in the cockpit.

An *empirical validity* strategy demonstrates the relationship between the selection method and job performance. Scores on the selection method (say, interview judgments or test scores) are compared to ratings of job performance. If applicants who receive higher scores on the selection method also turn out to be better job performers, then empirical validity has been established.

There are two types of empirical (also known as criterion-related) validity: concurrent and predictive.[39] **Concurrent validity** indicates the extent to which scores on a selection measure are related to job performance levels, when both are measured at roughly the same time. To illustrate, say that a company develops a test to use for hiring additional workers. To see how well the test might indicate job performance levels, the company gives the test to its current workforce. The company then correlates the test scores with the performance appraisal scores that supervisors just completed. The correlation between the test scores and job performance scores indicates the concurrent validity of the test because both the test and job performance scores were measured concurrently in time.

Predictive validity indicates the extent to which scores on a selection measure correlate with future job performance. For example, the company gives the test to all applicants and then checks their job performance level 12 months later. The correlation between the test scores and job performance in this case indicates the predictive validity of the test because the selection measure preceded the assessment of job performance.

Even if empirical validity is the goal when developing or choosing a selection measure, all measures should have content validity.[40] That is, what is being measured to assist in making the hiring decision should be job related. The starting point for establishing job-related content is a job analysis (see Chapter 2). However, content validity does not necessarily guarantee empirical validity. For instance, a measure that is content valid but so difficult that no one can earn a passing score will probably not be found to have empirical validity. Further, if empirical validity is assessed, the two forms, concurrent and predictive, each have their advantages and disadvantages.

Concurrent validation can be done relatively quickly and easily. However, the validity found with the concurrent approach may not be a good estimate of how valid a measure may be when used for assessing job applicants. To illustrate, current workers may not be representative of job applicants in that they may be older and tend to be white and male. We see, then, that concurrent validity may not be a good estimate of how valid a selection measure might be in practice.

In contrast, predictive validation most closely matches the hiring problem of trying to predict who will develop into the best performers for the organization. However, determining the predictive validity of a measure requires a fairly large number of people, at least 30, for whom both selection and job performance scores are available. Further predictive validity cannot be determined until job performance is measured, perhaps 6 to 12 months later.

Validity
The extent to which the technique measures the intended knowledge, skill, or ability. In the selection context, it is the extent to which scores on a test or interview correspond to actual job performance.

Concurrent validity
Extent of correlation between selection and performance scores, when measured at the same time

Predictive validity
Extent to which selection scores correlate with performance scores, when performance is measured later in time.

Selection methods can be reliable but not valid; however, selection methods that are not reliable cannot be valid. This fact has a great deal of practical significance. Whether someone has an M.B.A. or not can be measured with perfect reliability. But if having an M.B.A. is not associated with improved job performance, attainment of an M.B.A. is not a valid selection criterion for that job. It seems clear that more highly motivated applicants make better employees, but if the selection method used to measure motivation is full of errors (not reliable), then it cannot be a valid indicator of job performance.

Selection Tools as Predictors of Job Performance

A Question of Ethics

Suppose you are asked to write a recommendation letter for a friend whom you like but consider unreliable. Would it be ethical for you to write a positive reference even though you anticipate that your friend will not be a good employee? If not, would it be ethical for you to agree to write the letter knowing that you will not be very positive in your assessment of your friend's abilities?

In this section we look at the most commonly used methods of selection, in no particular order. Each approach has its limitations as well as its advantages.

Letters of Recommendation

In general, letters of recommendation are not highly related to job performance because most are highly positive.[41] This does not mean that *all* letters of recommendation are poor indicators of performance, however. A poor letter of recommendation may be very predictive and should not be ignored.

A content approach to considering letters of recommendation can increase the validity of this selection tool. This approach focuses on the content of the letters rather than on the extent of their positivity.[42] Assessment is done in terms of the traits the letter writer attributes to the job candidate.[43] For example, two candidates may be given equally positive letters, but the first candidate's letter may describe a detail-oriented person, whereas the second candidate's letter describes someone who is outgoing and helpful. The job to be filled may require one type of person rather than the other. For example, a job in customer relations requires an outgoing and helpful person, whereas clerical work requires someone who is good at details.

A more proactive approach to increasing the validity and usefulness of letters as well as verbal references (see "Reference Checks," p. 171) is to focus the reference on key job competencies. Rather than asking a reference broad questions, such as "Tell me what you think of this job candidate?" ask the reference about the applicant's specific skill in areas relevant to the job opening.[44]

Application Forms

Organizations often use application forms as screening devices to determine whether a candidate satisfies minimum job specifications, particularly for entry-level jobs. The forms typically ask for information regarding past jobs and present employment status.

A recent variation on the traditional application form is the *biodata form*.[45] This is essentially a more detailed version of the application form in which applicants respond to a series of questions about their background, experiences, and preferences. Responses to these questions are then scored. For instance, candidates might be asked how willing they are to travel on the job, what leisure activities they prefer, and how much experience they have had with computers. As with any selection tool, the biodata most relevant to the job should be identified through job analysis before the application form is created. Biodata have moderate validity in predicting job performance.

Ability Tests

Various tests measure a wide range of abilities, from verbal and qualitative skills to perceptual speed. *Cognitive ability tests* measure a candidate's capability in a certain area, such as math, and are valid predictors of job performance when the abilities tested are based on a job analysis.

A number of studies have examined the validity of *general cognitive ability* (g) as a predictor of job performance. General cognitive ability is typically measured by summing the scores on tests of verbal and quantitative ability. Essentially, g measures general intelligence. A higher level of g indicates a person who can learn more and faster and who can adapt quickly to changing conditions. People with higher levels of g have been found to be better job performers, at least in part because few jobs are static today.[46]

Some more specific tests measure physical or mechanical abilities. For example, the *physical ability tests* used by police and fire departments measure strength and endurance. The results of these tests are considered indicators of how productively and safely a person could perform a job's physical tasks. However, companies can often get a more direct measure of applicants' performance ability by observing how well they perform on actual job tasks. These types of direct performance tests, called *work sample tests,* ask applicants to perform the exact same tasks that they will be performing on the job. For example, one of Levi Strauss's work sample tests asks applicants for maintenance and repair positions to disassemble and reassemble a sewing machine component.[47] Work sample tests typically have high reliability and validity, the essential ingredients for an effective and legal selection tool.[48]

Work sample tests are widely viewed as fair and valid measures of job performance, as long as the work samples adequately capture the variety and complexity of tasks in the actual job. Work sample tests scores have even been used as criteria for assessing the validity of general mental ability selection measures.[49] However, physical ability measures have been found to screen out more women and minorities than white men. Physical preparation before the testing has been found to reduce this adverse impact significantly.[50]

Another form of ability, emotional intelligence, has become popular to measure. Emotional intelligence has been variously defined by researchers,[51] but can probably be fairly described as the ability to perceive and manage emotions in the self and in others.[52] Although the concept is popular, its validity has yet to be proven convincingly.[53] For instance, one study found no correlation between a measure of emotional intelligence and grade point average. However, a measure of general cognitive ability and personality measures were found to be correlated with grade point average. Similar findings for work performance has led researchers to question whether emotional intelligence really adds to our ability to predict performance beyond measures of general intelligence and ability.[54]

Personality Tests

Personality tests assess *traits,* individual workers' characteristics that tend to be consistent and enduring. Personality tests were widely used to make employee selection decisions in the 1940s and 1950s,[55] but then fell out of favor as predictors of job-related behaviors.[56] The arguments against using personality tests revolve around questions of reliability and validity. It has been argued that traits are subjective and unreliable,[57] unrelated to job performance,[58] and not legally acceptable.[59] Today, however, approximately 30 percent of companies use personality testing as part of their selection process.[60]

Many traits can be measured in a variety of ways, and this lack of consistency produces problems with reliability and validity. However, recent research on personality measurement has demonstrated that personality can be reliably measured[61] and summarized as being composed of five dimensions.[62] The "big five" factors, now widely accepted in the field of personality psychology, follow:[63]

- **Extroversion.** The degree to which someone is talkative, sociable, active, aggressive, and excitable.
- **Agreeableness.** The degree to which someone is trusting, amiable, generous, tolerant, honest, cooperative, and flexible.
- **Conscientiousness.** The degree to which someone is dependable and organized and conforms and perseveres on tasks.
- **Emotional stability.** The degree to which someone is secure, calm, independent, and autonomous.
- **Openness to experience.** The degree to which someone is intellectual, philosophical, insightful, creative, artistic, and curious.

Of the five factors, conscientiousness appears to be most related to job performance.[64] It is hard to imagine a measure of job performance that would not require dependability or an organization that would not benefit from employing conscientious workers. Conscientiousness is thus the most generally valid personality predictor of job performance. Conscientiousness has also been found to be related to safety at work.[65] For example, people with low levels of conscientiousness tend to ignore safety rules and regulations and, thus, tend to have more accidents and injuries then people with higher levels of conscientiousness.

The validity of the other personality factors seems to be more job specific, which bring us to two warnings about personality tests. First, whether personality characteristics are valid predictors of job performance depends on both the job and the criteria used to measure job performance. A job analysis should be done first to identify the personality factors that enhance job performance. Second, personality may play little or no role in predicting performance on certain measures, such as the number of pieces produced on a factory line (which may depend largely on such factors as speed of the production line). However, personality factors may play a critical role in jobs that are less regimented and demand teamwork and flexibility. Clearly, then, selection procedures should take both personality and the work situation into account.[66] Some types of people may be better suited for some work situations than for others. Exhibit 5.1 highlights an individual characteristic that may make an important difference in an international setting. Recent studies have found that personality can be an accurate predictor of the performance of not only job candidates[67] but also college students.[68]

Honesty Tests

The typical business organization loses approximately 6 percent of its annual revenue due to employee theft.[69] Survey findings indicate that employee theft accounts for almost half of all inventory shrinkage, with an annual cost of nearly $16 billion.[70] Given this context, it is little wonder that employers want to make sure they are hiring honest workers. The polygraph test measures the interviewee's pulse, breathing rate, and galvanic skin response (perspiration) while he or she is asked a series of questions. The theory is that these physiological measures will

---

EXHIBIT 5.1

Staffing International Positions—A Learning Opportunity

The global economy has forced managers to deal with other countries' cultures and business practices. For individuals, the most extreme cultural adaptation is an assignment to live and work in another country. But what determines how successful these people will be in their adopted setting and culture? Even organizations experienced with international assignments do not have stellar records in terms of effectively selecting or preparing expatriates (those who live and work in a foreign country). However, there seems to be some consensus among managers concerning what it takes to achieve business objectives in an international context: adaptability. Fortunately, learning orientation is an indicator of someone's adaptability and can be both measured and developed.

Learning orientation is based on a belief that personal characteristics can be developed and improved. For a person with a high learning orientation level, performance of a task is an opportunity to learn and improve, not an indicator of the level of his or her ability. A learning orientation would be indicated by someone who strongly agrees with a statement such as "I am willing to select a challenging work assignment that I can learn a lot from" and strongly disagrees with a statement such as "It is more satisfying to work at things I do well than to struggle with those that might be beyond my abilities."

Learning orientation is critical for an expatriate manager. Working in another culture will result in a host of experiences that may not go well on the first try. However, accomplishing organizational goals within the social, legal, and market conditions of another country requires the manager to gradually increase understanding and appreciation of the new environment. Initial difficulties must be embraced as learning opportunities. If the manager withdraws from situations after initial problems, neither learning nor success is likely to occur.

A number of studies demonstrate the importance of a learning orientation in a domestic organizational environment, but there is good reason to believe that it is at least as important in an international context. The degree of learning orientation can be fairly easy and inexpensively measured with questionnaires and situational exercises. Use of learning orientation could give an expatriate manager program a competitive edge.

Source: Porter, G., and Tansky, J. W. (1999). Expatriate success may depend on a "learning orientation": Considerations for selection and training. *Human Resource Management, 8,* 47–60.

change when the interviewee is not telling the truth. However, the passage of the federal Employee Polygraph Protection Act in 1988 has eliminated the use of polygraph tests by most employers.

Honesty or integrity tests are designed to identify job applicants who are likely to engage in theft and other undesirable behavior. Integrity tests can now be administered in a variety of forms, including paper and pencil, via telephone, and via the Internet, among others. The typical test measures attitudes toward honesty, particularly whether the applicant believes that dishonest behavior is normal and not criminal.[71] For example, the test might measure the applicant's tolerance for theft by other people and the extent to which the applicant believes most people steal regularly.

A study by independent researchers appears to confirm the validity of honesty testing.[72] It found that those who scored more poorly on the honesty test were more likely to steal from their employer. A recent study reported by one of the major honesty test publishers supports the validity of the measure. Specifically, a retailer began using an integrity test in 600 of its 1,900 locations. Within one year there was a 35 percent drop in the rate of inventory shrinkage in the stores using the test while there was a 10 percent rise in the shrinkage rates in the stores not using the tests.[73]

Nevertheless, honesty tests are controversial. Most of the arguments against integrity testing center on the issue of false-positive results: people who are honest but score poorly on the tests. Typically, at least 40 percent of the test takers receive failing marks.[74] To see how you might score on such a test, answer the sample honesty test questions in the Manager's Notebook, "Your Answers Could Win—or Cost—You Your Job."

Ethics

MANAGER'S NOTEBOOK

Your Answers Could Win—or Cost—You Your Job

The following are typical questions used in integrity tests prepared by the Chicago-based test publisher Reid Psychological Systems.

- Do you believe a person who writes a check for which he knows there is no money in the bank should be refused a job in which honesty is important?
- Do you think a person should be fired by a company if it is found that he helped the employees cheat the company out of overtime once in a while?
- If you found $100 that was lost by a bank truck on the street yesterday, would you turn the money over to the bank, even though you knew for sure that there was no reward?
- Do you think it is all right for one employee to give another employee a discount even though the company does not allow it?
- Do you believe that an employee who regularly borrows small amounts of money from the place where he works without permission, but always pays it back, is honest?
- Do you think that the way a company is run is more responsible for employee theft than the attitudes and tendencies of employees themselves?
- On the 20th of each month, an old employee took company money to pay on his mortgage. On the 30th of each month—payday—he paid it back. After 15 years the man finally was seen by his boss putting the money back. No shortage was found, but the boss fired him anyway. Do you think the boss was right?
- Would you ever consider buying something from somebody if you knew the item had been stolen?

Source: Adapted from Budman, M. (1993, November–December). Your answers could win—or cost—you your job. *Across the Board,* 35.

Interviews

Although the job interview is probably the most common selection tool, it has often been criticized for its poor reliability and low validity.[75] Countless studies have found that interviewers do not agree with one another on candidate assessments. Other criticisms include human judgment limitations and interviewer biases. For example, one early study found that most interviewers make decisions about candidates in the first two or three minutes of the interview.[76] Snap decisions can adversely affect an interview's validity because they are made based on limited information. More recent research, however, indicates that interviewers may not make such hasty decisions.[77]

Another criticism is that traditional interviews are conducted in such a way that the interview experience is very different from interviewee to interviewee. For instance, it is very common for the interviewer to open with the following question: "Tell me about yourself." The interview then proceeds in a haphazard fashion depending on the applicant's answer to that first question. Essentially, each applicant experiences a different selection method.

Dissatisfaction with the traditional unstructured interview has led to an alternative approach called the structured interview.[78] The **structured interview** is based directly on a thorough job analysis. It applies a series of job-related questions with predetermined answers consistently across all interviews for a particular job.[79]

Figure 5.9 gives examples of the three types of questions commonly used in structured interviews:[80]

- **Situational questions** try to elicit from candidates how they would respond to particular work situations. These questions can be developed from the critical incident technique of job analysis: Supervisors and workers rewrite critical incidents of behavior as situational interview questions, then generate and score possible answers as a benchmark.[81]
- **Job knowledge questions** assess whether candidates have the basic knowledge needed to perform the job.
- **Worker requirements questions** assess candidates' willingness to perform under prevailing job conditions.

Structured interviews are valid predictors of job performance.[82] First, the content of a structured interview is, by design, limited to job-related factors. Second, the questions asked are consistent across all interviewees. Third, all responses are scored the same way. Finally, because a panel of interviewers is typically involved in conducting the structured interview, the impact of individual interviewers' idiosyncrasies and biases is limited.

Structured interviews have been used very successfully at numerous companies. Interviewing panels range from two to six members and typically include an HR professional, the hiring manager, and the person who will be the candidate's manager. The panels often also include key people from other departments who have to work very closely with the new hire.

The usual practice is to interview all candidates over a one- or two-day period. This makes it easier to recall interviewee responses and compare them equitably. Immediately after an

Structured interview
Job interview based on a thorough job analysis, applying job-related questions with predetermined answers consistently across all interviews for a job.

Examples of Structured Interview Questions

Figure 5.9	
Type	**Example**
Situational	You are packing things into your car and getting ready for your family vacation when you realize that you promised to meet a client this morning. You did not pencil the meeting into your calendar and it slipped your mind until just now. What do you do?
Job knowledge	What is the correct procedure for determining the appropriate oven temperature when running a new batch of steel?
Worker requirements	Some periods are extremely busy in our business. What are your feelings about working overtime?

In a structured interview process, a panel of interviewers asks each potential candidate the same job-related questions. The results of this type of interview are valid predictors of job performance.

interview, panel members rate the interviewee using a one- to two-page sheet that lists important job dimensions along with a five-point rating scale. After each interviewer has rated the candidate, one member of the panel—usually either the HR professional or the hiring manager—facilitates a discussion in which the panel arrives at a group rating for the candidate. After all applicants have been interviewed, the panel creates a rank order of acceptable job candidates.[83]

If the structured interview is so effective, why is the traditional interview much more popular? One reason is that many equate the panel format of structured interviews with a stress test. Another is that organizations find the traditional interview quite useful, probably because it serves more functions than just selection.[84] For example, it can be an effective public relations tool in which the interviewer gives a positive impression of the organization. Even a candidate who is not hired may retain this positive impression. In addition, the unstructured interview may be a valid predictor of the degree to which a candidate will fit with the organization.

Finally, unstructured interviews may be better than structured interviews for screening out unsuitable applicants.[85] Many times a candidate who seemed "fine" on paper reveals some disturbing qualities during an unstructured interview (Figure 5.10).

Whether employers choose to use structured or unstructured interviews, they need to make sure their interview questions are not illegal. Companies that ask job applicants certain questions (for example, their race, creed, sex, national origin, marital status, or number of children) either on application forms or in the interview process run the risk of being sued.

To operate within the limits of the law, interviewers should remember the nine don'ts of interviewing:[86]

1. Don't ask applicants if they have children, plan to have children, or what child-care arrangements they have made.
2. Don't ask an applicant's age.
3. Don't ask whether the candidate has a physical or mental disability that would interfere with doing the job. The law allows employers to explore the subject of disabilities only *after* making a job offer that is conditioned on satisfactory completion of a required physical, medical, or job skills test.
4. Don't ask for such identifying characteristics as height or weight on an application.
5. Don't ask a female candidate for her maiden name. Some employers have asked this to ascertain marital status, another topic that is off limits in interviewing both men and women.
6. Don't ask applicants about their citizenship.
7. Don't ask applicants about their arrest records. You are, however, allowed to ask whether the candidate has ever been convicted of a crime.

Unusual Job Interview Behaviors

Figure 5.10

The impression you make through your behavior at a job interview is critical to your being favorably considered for the job. No matter how stellar your résumé, inappropriate behavior during the interview can ruin your chances for a job offer. The following are some real situations that indicate how unusual (even bizarre) the behavior of some job seekers can be.

- The applicant wore a Walkman and said she could listen to me and the music at the same time.

- A balding candidate abruptly excused himself and returned to the office a few minutes later wearing a hairpiece.

- The applicant asked to see the interviewer's résumé to determine if the interviewer was qualified to judge his capabilities for the job.

- The interviewee announced she hadn't had lunch and proceeded to eat a hamburger and french fries in the interviewer's office—wiping the ketchup on her sleeve.

- When I asked the candidate about his hobbies, he stood up and started tap dancing around my office.

- After arriving for a morning interview, the candidate asked to use the employer's phone. She called her current employer, faked a coughing fit, and called in sick to her boss.

- In response to the interviewer's offer to answer questions, a job seeker replied, "What happens if I wake up in the morning and don't feel like going to work?"

- A candidate interrupted a discussion of work hours and the office environment to say that he would take the job only if he could move his desk to the courtyard outside.

- Asked what he would like to do in his next position, a candidate replied, "I'll tell you what I don't want to be doing—sitting in boring meetings, doing grunt work, and having to be nice to people all day long."

- Question: "Why do you want this job?" Answer: "I've got a big house, a big car, and a big credit card balance. Pay me and I'll be happy."

8. Don't ask if a candidate smokes. Because there are numerous state and local ordinances that restrict smoking in certain buildings, a more appropriate question is whether the applicant is aware of these regulations and is willing to comply with them.

9. Don't ask a job candidate if he or she has AIDS or is HIV-positive.

The key point to remember is not to ask questions that are peripheral to the work itself. Rather, interviewers should stay focused on the objective of hiring someone who is qualified to perform the tasks required by the job.

Assessment Centers

Assessment center
A set of simulated tasks or exercises that candidates (usually for managerial positions) are asked to perform.

An **assessment center** is a set of simulated tasks or exercises that candidates (usually for managerial positions) are asked to perform. Observers rate performance on these simulations and make inferences regarding each candidate's managerial skills and abilities. Many organizations use assessment centers for external recruitment and for internal promotion.[87] Responses to a European survey indicated that over half of larger organizations (more than 1,000 employees) use assessment centers.[88]

Although expensive, the assessment center appears to be a valid predictor of managerial job performance.[89] Assessment centers also appear to be an effective technique for judging key leadership competencies.[90] Assessment centers may be well worth the price when the costs of poor hiring or promotion decisions are high.[91] However, given a tight budget, the cost of an assessment center can be prohibitive. For example, the State of Maryland used to require the use of assessment centers in hiring public school principals, but that requirement was dropped because the expense of $1,200 to $1,500 per candidate became too onerous.[92]

Assessment centers are usually conducted off premises, last from one to three days, and may include up to six candidates at a time. Most assessment centers evaluate each candidate's abilities in four areas: organizing, planning, decision making, and leadership. However, there is considerable variability in what exercises an assessment center includes, how these are conducted, and how they are scored.[93] Candidates who can put an activity behind them and focus on the next challenge are likely to perform better in the assessment center.[94] In addition, candidates who are not too dominant or too timid but who can effectively interact with others are likely to perform better.

The *in-basket exercise* is probably the exercise most widely associated with assessment centers. It includes the kinds of problems, messages, reports, and so on that might be found in a manager's in-basket. The candidates are asked to deal with these issues as they see fit, and then are assessed on how well they prioritized the issues, how creative and responsive they were in dealing with each one, the quality of their decisions, and other factors. Performance on an in-basket exercise can be highly revealing. Often it points up the skills of a candidate who might otherwise have appeared average.[95]

Drug Tests

Preemployment drug testing typically requires job applicants to undergo urinalysis as part of routine selection procedures. Applicants whose test results are positive are usually eliminated from further consideration. Alternatively, they may be given the option of taking another test at their own expense if they challenge the test's outcome.[96]

The purpose of preemployment drug testing is to avoid hiring people who may become problem workers. The number of employees who test positive and the number of employers who conduct drug testing has declined. In 1988, the percentage of U.S. workers testing positive for illegal drugs was 13.6 percent. It has steadily decreased, and the percentage positive in 2004 was 4.5 percent.[97] A recent American Management Association study found that 62 percent of companies test for illegal drugs, down from 81 percent in 1996.[98]

Do drug test results correlate to an applicant's later job performance? The answer is yes. In one study done by the U.S. Postal Service, urine samples were taken from more than 5,000 job applicants, but the results were not used in hiring. Six months to one year later, it was found that the applicants who had positive tests were absent 41 percent more often and fired 38 percent more often than those who did not. It appears that drug testing is a valid predictor of job performance.[99]

Reference Checks

One of the best methods of predicting the future success of prospective employees is to look at their past employment record. Fear of defamation suits has often caused companies to not provide job-related information about former employees. However, checking employees' references is an employer's best tactic for avoiding negligent hiring suits, in which the employer is held liable for injuries inflicted by an employee while on the job. What should companies do?

Courts in almost every state have held that employers—both former and prospective—have a "qualified privilege" to discuss an employee's past performance. But to enjoy that privilege, a company must follow three rules. First, it must determine that the inquirer has a job-related need to know. Second, the former employer must release only truthful information. Third, EEO-related information (such as an employee's race or age) should not be released.[100]

Background Checks

Background checks can be distinguished from reference checks and can include, depending on the job opening, criminal-background checks, verifications of academic achievements, driving histories, immigration status checks, and Social Security checks. A primary motivation for organizations to conduct background checks was to avoid a lawsuit charging negligent hiring. However, after the terrorist attack of September 11, 2001, organizations are broadening their screening efforts out of a concern for security. The Patriot Act, passed in November 2001, requires background checks on people who work with certain toxins and bans felons and illegal aliens, among others, from working with these materials.[101] The need for background checks is also underscored by the frequency with which misinformation is submitted on job application forms. HireRight, a company that conducts background checks, has estimated that 34 percent of application forms contain outright lies concerning work experience, education, and required skills. HireRight also finds that about 9 percent of applicants falsify college degrees and list jobs and employers that don't exist.[102]

A Question of Ethics

Some experts contend that urinalysis is an invasion of privacy and, therefore, should be prohibited unless there is reasonable cause to suspect an employee of drug use. Is it ethical for companies to insist that applicants undergo urinalysis? Suppose a company that wants to save on health insurance costs decides to test the cholesterol levels of all job applicants to eliminate those susceptible to heart attacks. Would this practice be ethical? Would it be legal?

Handwriting Analysis

Graphology, the study of handwriting for the purpose of measuring personality or other individual traits, is routinely used to screen job applicants in Europe, the birthplace of the technique. Analysis looks at over 300 aspects of handwriting, including the slope of the letters, the height at which the letter *t* is crossed, and the pressure of the writing. Although graphology is not as widely used in the United States as it is in Europe, it is estimated that over 3,000 U.S. organizations use the procedure as part of their screening process. Furthermore, the covert and occasional use of graphology may be even more widespread and may be growing.[103] The important question, of course, is whether handwriting is a valid predictor of job performance. Research on this issue indicates that the answer is no.

One study collected handwriting samples from 115 real estate associates and gave them to 20 graphologists, who scored each sample on a variety of traits, such as confidence, sales drive, and decision making.[104] Later, these results were compared with the subject's actual performance ratings as well as with objective performance measures such as total sales volume. There was a fair amount of consistency across graphologists' judgments of the handwriting samples (reliability). However, none of the judgments made by the graphologists correlated with any of the performance measures, so graphology cannot be considered a valid measure. This conclusion is echoed by other research on graphology.[105] Thus, it should not be used as an employment screening device, and you should be wary when you see graphology touted as a valuable selection tool in magazines and other popular press outlets.[106]

Combining Predictors

Organizations often use multiple methods to collect information about applicants. For instance, managers may be selected on the basis of past performance ratings, an assessment center evaluation, and an interview with the manager to whom they will be reporting.

How should these pieces of information be combined to make an effective selection decision? There are three basic strategies. The first requires making a preliminary selection decision after completion of each method. This approach is called *multiple-hurdle strategy*, because an applicant has to clear each hurdle before moving on to the next one. Those who do not clear the hurdle are eliminated from further consideration.

Both the remaining approaches require collecting all the information before making any decision; the difference is in how that information is combined. In a *clinical strategy*, the decision maker subjectively evaluates all the information and comes to an overall judgment. In a *statistical strategy*, the various pieces of information are combined according to a mathematical formula, and the job goes to the candidate with the highest score.

The multiple-hurdle strategy is often the choice when a large number of applicants must be considered. Usually, the procedure is to use the less-expensive methods first to screen out clearly unqualified applicants. Research studies indicate that a statistical strategy is generally more reliable and valid than a clinical strategy,[107] but many people—and probably most organizations—prefer a clinical strategy.

Selection and the Person/Organization Fit

Many companies have successfully used the various selection tools to hire above-average employees who have made a significant contribution to the firm's bottom line.[108] However, the traditional approach to selection may not be sufficient for a growing number of organizations. In many companies, activities and decisions are decentralized, and workers find themselves working in cross-functional teams.[109] In these situations, candidates' job skills (as measured by selection tests) may not be as important as their ability to perform effectively in an empowered and high-involvement environment.

For this reason, some companies have been searching for a way to measure the degree of "fit" between job candidates and the organization.[110] However, there are at least two concerns regarding measures of fit in the selection process. First, it is not clear that an organization could defend a discrimination lawsuit by pointing to "lack of fit" instead of "lack of job-specific skills." Second, most research has validated selection methods by using supervisor evaluations of job performance on specific job-relevant characteristics. Thus, although we know which selection tools predict job-specific performance, we do not know how well they predict organizational fit.

Reactions to Selection Devices

Over the last several pages, we have discussed how well the various selection tools predict job performance. Next, we consider reactions to selection tools. How do applicants and managers respond to the selection methods we have discussed? The answer is clearly important, because these responses may be the determining factor in a decision to file a lawsuit.

1. **Applicant reactions to selection devices.** Applicants are a major customer of selection systems; they want and may demand fair selection devices. Moreover, applicants' reactions to selection methods can influence their attraction to and opinions of an organization and their decision to accept or reject an offer of employment.[111] Applicants' reactions to selection tools also influence their willingness to purchase the company's products.[112]

   To which selection tests do applicants respond most favorably and least favorably? Some interesting findings have emerged. For example, despite the increasing use of personality assessment devices as predictors, many job applicants believe that personality traits are "fakeable" and not job relevant. In addition, applicants perceive biodata, which have substantial validity, as irrelevant and invasive; they generally respond negatively to cognitive ability measures also. They respond most favorably to job simulations (for example, assessment center exercises) and interviews.

2. **Manager reactions to selection systems.** Managers need selection systems that are quick and easy to administer and that deliver results that are easy to understand. However, very little research has considered manager reactions to selection systems. One study surveyed 635 managers from 38 agencies in state government.[113] The study assessed the managers' perceptions of various factors related to the selection process, including selection methods. These findings were used to revise selection systems and other HR practices in those agencies.

A central issue is the extent to which an organization should balance the traditional measures of reliability and validity with the measures of applicants' and managers' reactions in determining which selection methods to use. Clearly, reliability and validity cannot be jettisoned completely. A reasonable balance between the traditional criteria of reliability and validity and the quality criteria of applicants'/managers' reactions needs to be maintained.

Legal Issues in Staffing

Legal concerns can play an exceptionally important role in staffing, particularly in selection. A number of legal constraints, most notably federal legislation and its definition of illegal discrimination, affect selection.

Discrimination Laws

The Civil Rights Act of 1964 and its extension, the Civil Rights Act of 1991, provide broad prohibition against discrimination based on race, color, sex, religion, and national origin. These laws, which state that such discrimination in *all terms and conditions* of employment is illegal, affect selection as well as many other organizational programs, including performance appraisal and training.

To decrease the chances of lawsuits claiming discrimination, firms should ensure that selection techniques are job related. In other words, the best defense is evidence of the validity of the selection process. For example, if a minority group member turned down for a job claims discrimination, the organization should have ample evidence to document the job relatedness of its selection process. This evidence should include job analysis information and evidence that test scores are valid predictors of performance.

The Age Discrimination in Employment Act of 1967 and the 1978 amendments to the act prohibit discrimination against people aged 40 and older. Again, the organization needs evidence of the validity of the selection process if older applicants are turned away—particularly if comparable but younger applicants are hired.

The Americans with Disabilities Act (ADA) of 1991 extends the Vocational Rehabilitation Act of 1973 and provides legal protection for people with physical or mental disabilities. ADA requires employers to provide reasonable accommodations for people whose disabilities may prevent them from adequately performing essential job functions, unless doing so will create an undue hardship for the organization. Thus, employers need to determine what constitutes a job's essential functions. Although the law does not clearly define "reasonable accommodation," the courts may deem reasonable such actions as modifications in schedules, equipment, and facilities. In terms of selection, ADA prevents employers from asking applicants if they have a disability and prohibits the requirement of medical examinations before making job offers. However, an employer can ask applicants if they can perform a job's essential functions. Also, job offers can be made contingent on the results of a medical examination.

Affirmative Action

Affirmative action must also be considered. Federal Executive Order 11246 requires organizations that are government contractors or subcontractors to have affirmative action programs in place. These programs are designed to eliminate any underutilization that might occur in an organization's employment practices (see Chapter 3). Affirmative action is not the same as the equal employment opportunity required by the Title VII of Civil Rights Act and related legislation. Making job-related selection decisions while not discriminating against subgroups is not the same as setting utilization goals. However, organizations that are not government contractors or subcontractors can lose the privilege of selecting employees solely on the basis of expected job performance if they are found guilty of discrimination. In that case, they can be ordered to put an affirmative action program in place.

Negligent Hiring

The final legal issue in staffing concerns claims of *negligent hiring*. Negligent hiring refers to a situation in which an employer fails to use reasonable care in hiring an employee, who then commits a crime while in his or her position in the organization. Because claims of negligent hiring have increased over the years,[114] managers need to be particularly sensitive to this issue. For example, Avis Rent A Car hired a man without thoroughly checking his background; the man later raped a female coworker. Avis was found guilty of negligent hiring and had to pay damages of $800,000. Had the company carefully checked the information provided in the man's job application, it would have discovered that he was in prison when he claimed he was attending high school and college. Employers are responsible for conducting a sound investigation into applicants' backgrounds. Factors such as gaps in employment or admission of prior criminal convictions should prompt closer investigation. To avoid liability for negligent hiring, employers should:[115]

- Develop clear policies on hiring as well as on disciplining and dismissing employees. The hiring policy should include a thorough background check of applicants, including verification of educational, employment, and residential information.
- Check state laws regarding hiring applicants with criminal records. What is legal in this area varies widely among states.
- Learn as much as possible about applicants' past work-related behavior, including violence, threats, lying, drug or alcohol abuse, carrying of weapons, and other problems. Keep in mind that privacy and discrimination laws prohibit inquiries into an applicant's personal, non-work-related activities. Behavioral problems may be investigated only in the context of their possible effect on job performance.

Summary and Conclusions

Human Resource Supply and Demand

HRP is the process an organization uses to ensure that it has the right amount and right kinds of people to deliver a particular level of output or services at some point in the future. HRP entails using a variety of qualitative or quantitative methods to forecast labor demand and labor supply and then taking actions based on those estimates.

The Hiring Process

The hiring process consists of three activities: recruitment, selection, and orientation.

Challenges in the Hiring Process

The hiring process is filled with challenges. These include (1) determining which characteristics are most important to performance, (2) measuring these characteristics, (3) evaluating applicants' motivation, and (4) deciding who should make hiring decisions.

Meeting the Challenge of Effective Staffing

Because choosing the right person for a job can have a tremendous positive effect on productivity and customer satisfaction, it is important that each step of the hiring process be managed carefully.

The Recruitment Process

Recruiting should focus on attracting qualified candidates, internally and/or externally. Recruiting efforts should be tied to the firm's HRP efforts. To ensure proper fit between hires and their jobs and to avoid legal problems, firms should conduct job analyses.

The Selection Process

Many selection tools are available. These include letters of recommendation, application forms, ability tests, personality tests, psychological tests, interviews, assessment centers, drug tests, honesty tests, reference checks, and handwriting analysis. The best (and most legally defensible) selection tools are both reliable and valid.

Legal Issues in Staffing

Several federal legal issues govern staffing practices. The Civil Rights Act, the Age Discrimination Act, and the Americans with Disabilities Act all prohibit various forms of discrimination. Executive Order 11246 spells out affirmative action policies. Employers must also take steps to protect themselves from negligent hiring litigation.

Key Terms

assessment center, 170	labor supply, 147	selection, 152
concurrent validity, 163	predictive validity, 163	socialization, 152
human resource planning (HRP), 148	recruitment, 152	structured interview, 168
labor demand, 147	reliability, 162	validity, 163

Discussion Questions

1. Smith & Nephew DonJoy, Inc., is a small but fast-growing manufacturer of medical devices in the north end of San Diego County. Because of the recent downsizing of Southern California's aerospace and defense industries, each job opening at DonJoy draws five times more applications than it did just a few years ago. However, selective layoffs made during the downsizings and the need for people to seek new career paths have created a glut of less-than-qualified applicants. What selection tool(s) can DonJoy use to get the most qualified employees from its huge pool of applicants? In general, which selection tool(s) do you think are the best predictors of job performance?

2. Should applicants be selected primarily on the basis of ability or on personality/fit? How can fit be assessed?

3. As of August 1993, the only way for a white man to land a job with the LAPD was to score a perfect 100 on the oral portion of the entrance exam. The lowest eligible score for a Latino man was 96, for an African American man it was 95, and for all female candidates it was 94. This scoring was established when the city agreed to establish goals for recruiting minority and female officers.

   Do you think there are other ways the LAPD can recruit qualified minority and female employees that will not negatively affect white male recruits? Explain. In general, how would you design a selection process to achieve a diverse workforce and hire the most qualified workers?

4. Julie Watkins has worked in her new position writing software documentation for three months. She keeps hearing about how important her job is to the company, but she does not understand how her work contributes to the whole. Her exposure to the company is limited to her department colleagues (other technical writers), the

employee cafeteria, and the payroll office. What could Watkins's company have done to make her see the whole picture and gain an understanding of and commitment to how the company works?

5. Interviewing unqualified applicants can be a frustrating experience and a waste of time for managers, peers, or whoever is responsible for interviewing. How can the HR department minimize or eliminate this problem?

6. You work for a medium-sized, high-tech firm that faces intense competition on a daily basis. Change seems to be the only constant in your workplace, and each worker's responsibilities shift from project to project.

Suppose you have the major responsibility for filling the job openings at your company. How would you go about recruiting and selecting the best people? How would you identify the best people to work in this environment?

There is a variety of additional material available on the Web site that accompanies this text. You can access this information by visiting the Web site at ***www.prenhall.com/gomez***.

YOU MANAGE IT! Emerging Trends Case 5.1

Optimizing the Supply and Demand Match: Putting the Right People with the Right Skills in the Right Place at the Right Time

Matching the supply with the demand for labor has relied on forecasting techniques that examine employer needs and availability of workers. However, workers are not necessarily interchangeable: They bring with them different backgrounds, skills, and interests. Further, the demand for labor with particular skills is shifting all the time. What managers need is a way to allocate labor so that the competencies best match the various demands. Current developments now hold the promise of making this match a reality.

In a new trend, labor is viewed from a supply-chain perspective, in which the demands of various customers, projects, or tasks are matched with workers who have the appropriate skills. For example, the U.S. Department of Defense is working with PeopleSoft (now owned by Oracle) HRM software to develop an integrated system that will cut across all branches of the military. The system will include information about the skills, knowledge, and experiences of all military personnel that the department can immediately access to match available members to various assignments. The plan is to enable the efficient allocation of close to 1.5 million personnel scattered across the world by 2007. The demands of the military can change at a moment's notice, but with the software being developed, the Department of Defense should be able to allocate the best people to the right places or projects at the right time.

IBM is another example of an organization that has developed software to manage the labor supply chain. The IBM system also catalogs employees' competencies and experiences. It has enabled IBM to reduce the average amount of time its consultants spend with their clients by approximately 4 percent, because IBM is now able to assign talent that best matches the

needs of the client. The system has been so successful that IBM is now marketing it to other businesses.

Critical Thinking Questions

1. How does the labor supply chain approach differ from traditional forecasting approaches? Is the labor supply chain preferable? Why or why not?

2. The labor supply chain approach is based on the notion that the best match is of people with the skills and experiences that most closely correspond to the task that needs to be done. Can you think of situations in which this assumption might be false? (For example, might innovation be improved when there is diversity of backgrounds and skill sets that may not best match the tasks?)

Team Exercise

It probably doesn't make sense to use labor supply chain software if you have only a few employees. As a team, identify factors that should drive the decision to use labor supply chain software. (Organization size may be one factor to start with!) Summarize your set of factors for the rest of the class.

Experiential Exercise

The logic of the labor supply chain approach is compelling: Efficiently matching labor skills to demands pays off. However, consider what the labor supply chain approach means to workers. As a unit of labor that has certain qualifications, you could be assigned to any of a variety of places and projects. Depending on the need, you might be part of a virtual or physical team, and you might be temporarily moved to another geographic location, until demands fluctuate again. Do you see a potential problem here? It could take time to learn to effectively work with new people. Moving to a new place can be unsettling. In other words, the human resource is more than a collection of qualifications that can be assigned efficiently. A sense of team, trust, a common culture, interpersonal relations, and so on are all important components of performance.

Divide into teams in favor of and against the use of labor supply chain software. Outline your basic arguments and present them to the class. After the major pros and cons are considered, as a class, identify ways to offset the potential disadvantages of the labor supply chain approach.

Source: Adapted from Malykhina, E. (2005, March 21). Supplying labor to meet demand. *Information Week,* 69–72.

Customer-Driven HR Case 5.2 — YOU MANAGE IT!

Women: Keeping the Supply Lines Open

Women leave the workforce at higher rates than men. In part, this may help explain why only about 2 percent of top CEO positions are held by females. But why do women quit? Further, do they later rejoin the labor force? Can they, after leaving? Let's take a look at these issues.

First, there is little doubt that women are more likely than men to leave the labor force. For example, a recent survey focused on a nationally representative group of women who had either a graduate, professional, or high-honors undergraduate degree. The survey included over 2,400 women. A major finding of the survey was that 24 percent of men had voluntarily left their job whereas nearly 40 percent of women had voluntarily left. These women invested in education that positioned them for successful careers, yet many of them chose to leave the workforce.

Why do women choose to leave the workforce? There is, of course, no single answer. Family and child-care issues certainly can "pull" women away from work. However, a surprising number of women report leaving their jobs due to boredom and frustration. That is, in order to feel challenged and increase their chances for growth and opportunity, women feel that they have to leave their current employer.

The factors that "push" women to leave jobs would seem to be most directly manageable by organizations. GE, for example, has instituted women's networks, coaching and mentoring programs, and family-balance policies. Although it is not possible to draw a conclusion regarding the cause, since instituting these programs GE has its percentage of females in officer positions increase from 9 percent in l997 to a current level of 15 percent.

Critical Thinking Questions

1. Why is the departure of women an issue for organizations?
2. When trying to re-enter the workforce, women often find that they have to take a lower pay rate to "get back in the game." Do you think this is fair? Why or why not?
3. If a lower wage discourages the re-entry of women, what, if anything, can be done about it?

Team Exercise

"Pull" factors are issues or characteristics that draw a woman away from her job responsibilities. "Push" factors are characteristics that repel a woman from her current job responsibilities. Join team members in your class and identify reasons why women leave their jobs. Classify each as a pull or push factor and judge the extent to which each tends to affect women rather than men. (You can use the following rating scale to make these judgments.)

1	2	3	4	5	6	7
Mainly affects men			Affects men and women equally			Mainly affects women

Experiential Exercise

Join team members and research what companies are doing to retain women employees. Classify these management initiatives as addressing either "push" or "pull" factors. Are there approaches that you think would be effective for retaining women but that you did not find being used by organizations? List and describe what you consider to be the best approaches. Be prepared to discuss expected costs and benefits and to justify your recommendations.

Sources: Deutsch, C.H. (2005, May 3). Boredom is the culprit: Exodus of women executives has a cure. *Arizona Republic,* D-4; Hewlett, S. A., and Luce, C. B. (2005). Off-ramps and on-ramps: Keeping talented women on the road to success. *Harvard Business Review, 83,* 43–54.

Put Things in Balance to Keep Employees and Boost Performance

Conflict between work and family commitments is often a source of life and job dissatisfaction and can lead to anxiety, hypertension, and alcohol/substance abuse. It can also create increased tardiness, absenteeism, and turnover. Work–life balance is increasingly seen as a key to keeping valued employees. Work–life balance programs can consist of a variety of options, including flextime arrangements, wellness programs, child-care options, fitness centers, and stress-reduction programs. The goal is to reduce the conflict and stress that can occur between work and life outside work. For instance, offering employees day care for their children can relieve a critical stressor for many employees. Flexible work schedules allow workers to have some control over when they will commit themselves to work-related tasks. Stress-reduction classes and physical fitness facilities help to ensure that break time is really useful and refreshing.

Hard-nosed conventional management would seriously question work–life balance programs. Time away from work would be expected to result only in less work getting done. In addition, investments in non-work-related initiatives, such as a day-care center, would be just a sunk cost. However, current surveys indicate that such initiatives not only reduce work–life stress, but also increase work performance. For example, a compressed workweek at Hewlett-Packard and telecommuting at Illinois Bell were both found to lead to substantial improvements in productivity. When work and life commitments are out of balance, productivity and creativity can drop due to increased stress.

Critical Thinking Questions

1. Do you think work–life balance programs are a cost or an investment? Why? Explain the distinction between these two positions.
2. Do you think work–life programs can increase retention? Why or why not? How could you assess whether such a program were a good investment?

Team Exercise

With team members in your class, identify work–life programs put together by organizations. If possible, use Internet or library resources to identify what organizations are doing in the work–life balance area. Can you find any information about the effectiveness of these programs? Share your findings and any effectiveness data with the rest of the class.

Experiential Exercise

Balance between two competing interests may not capture what is really important to retaining workers and maximizing performance. What may be critical is the match between the values of a worker and the work he or she performs. If the work is not meaningful, no amount of balancing would be expected to increase the satisfaction and happiness of the worker.

As a team, develop a means to assess the work, life, or work–life value orientation of workers. For example, are there survey or interview questions that could be used to assess this value orientation? Identify management policies and programs that you think would be most effective for each of these three basic value orientations. To help get you started, consider the following. Occasionally engaging in activities away from work can recharge people driven by work and be a welcome distraction. Employees whose core values reside in life outside work may view their employment as instrumental in allowing them to do what they want outside work. For the work–life combination category, a management program that emphasizes family involvement and hobby sharing may prove effective.

What programs and policies can your team suggest for each value category? Share and explain your suggestions with the rest of the class.

Sources: Taylor, C. (2005, January). Live in the balance. *Incentive*; Thompson, C. (2005). Work–life: Organizations in denial. *Journal of Employee Assistance, 35*, 7; Krysti, W. (2005, March 14). Life and work in the right measure: Flexibility in the workplace key to keeping staff. *The Daily News* (New Plymouth New Zealand), 8; Michael, N. (2005, February 14). Whatever makes you happy: Success of value-based practices. *The Dominion Post* (Wellington, New Zealand), Business, 4.

Managing with a Shortage

Some jobs aren't glamorous but are critical to our continued survival as communities and as a nation. Unfortunately, not enough workers are being attracted to these jobs.

Consider, for example, the job of vehicle technician. The shortage of technicians is of such concern that the Technical and Maintenance Council of the American Trucking Association has begun a program designed to increase awareness of the need for highly qualified technicians. The program will include a skills competition designed to highlight the diagnostic capabilities of technicians. It will receive national exposure and showcase job opportunities in the industry. However, the industry realizes that it will be a tough battle to counter the perception that trade schools are meant for people who are not "good enough" for college.

A looming shortage of vehicle technicians may not seem like an immediate problem for most of us. Consider, however, if you were a truck driver and couldn't find a technician to fix your rig in a timely fashion or you had to pay an exorbitant repair fee. Or, bring the problem even closer to home. What if you couldn't get your car fixed or had to pay an outlandish repair bill due to a vehicle-technician shortage?

A similar worker shortage story is occurring in the coal mining industry. Coal supplies more than half the United States' energy needs. However, a worker shortage is resulting in decreased mining productivity and is being blamed for record low coal inventories. Worker shortages are greatest in Central Appalachia, and the price of coal from the region has increased from $30 per ton to $50 per ton in two years. Many workers in the coal industry are approaching retirement age. The work can pay well, but it is difficult and not enough young workers are in the pipeline.

Critical Thinking Questions

1. Do you think that the worker shortages, such as those described in this case, are a short-term problem or a long-term problem?
2. Will increased wages solve the shortage problem? Why or why not?

Team Exercise

One coal company is paying electricians (an important job in the coal industry) $27 per hour and $90,000 per year with overtime as a means to attract and retain needed workers. As a team, consider this level of pay and take a position as to whether it is too high for this type of labor. Discuss your position with the rest of the class. Also, identify what else could be done to manage the shortage.

Experiential Exercise

With your teammates, identify steps that could be taken, such as in the vehicle technician and coal mining industries, to alleviate the worker shortage. Be sure to take a multipronged approach. You should consider external activities that could lead to more people pursuing the career. For example, the technician competition is, in large part, a program focused externally at changing awareness and attitudes. You should also include internal activities that are designed to attract and retain workers in the industry. For example, cross-training is being used in the steel industry so that workers are proficient in more than one area, increasing the supply of skilled labor. Present your programs to the rest of the class.

Sources: Dorn, R. (2005). Beating the technician shortage. *Fleet Equipment, 31,* 3; Maher, K. (2005, May 5). Coal companies are slowed by severe shortage of workers: Mines can't boost output, so utilities' low stock piles may lift electricity prices. *Wall Street Journal,* A-2; Maher, K. (2005, May 3). Skills shortage gives training programs new life. *Wall Street Journal,* A-2.

Emerging Trends Case 5.5   YOU MANAGE IT!

Clone or Complement? What to Look for in a Team

In many organizations that have moved to a team structure, the team is the principal unit where work gets done. However, most organizations recruit and hire as though there was one job description and the team didn't exist. The reality is that people have natural strengths or tendencies and, therefore, end up playing different roles on a team. For example, some people are naturally empathetic and focused on interpersonal issues. Others are focused on and most comfortable with technical aspects. Others like the excitement of identifying new concepts and solutions but aren't cut out for dealing with the operational details needed to carry them through. Recent research has found that allowing people to play to their strengths can yield maximum performance and employee satisfaction.

Critical Thinking Questions

1. If there are distinct roles to be played on a team, how would you go about recruiting and hiring for them?
2. The characteristics needed by individual team members depend on the team and the strengths and weaknesses of others who are on the team. In other words, the situation is much more dynamic than assuming that there is one static job with a single set of qualifications. How could you model or include this dynamic and interactive nature in the recruitment and hiring process?

Team Exercise

As a team, identify the roles that you think are important for teams in the workplace.

1. Identify the skills needed to perform each role.
2. In addition to skills, a natural tendency or motivation to perform in a particular type of role can be critical. How could you measure the motivation needed for each role?
3. How could you measure the skills needed for each role?
4. How could you effectively recruit for the various positions or roles?

5. Present your recruitment and selection plan to the rest of the class.

_____

Source: Black, B. (2002). The road to recovery. *Gallup Management Journal, 1,* 10–12.

Managing Employee Separations, Downsizing, and Outplacement

Challenges

After reading this chapter, you should be able to deal more effectively with the following challenges:

1 **Identify** the costs and benefits associated with employee separations.

2 **Understand** the differences between voluntary and involuntary separations.

3 **Avoid** problems in the design of early retirement policies.

4 **Design** HRM policies for downsizing the organization that are alternatives to a layoff; and, when all else fails, develop a layoff program that is effective and fair to the firm's stakeholders.

5 **Understand** the significance and value of outplacement programs.

Place yourself in the following situation:

You're a member of the key management staff at Storage Way, an Internet data storage and restoration service company. A layoff announcement, the fourth in the past 12 months, has just been made by CEO Kim Fennell. The company has been rocked by the sluggish economy and most of its competitors have gone or are going out of business. This fourth layoff will reduce the number of employees at Storage Way another 40 percent and the headcount will dwindle to 38. The vice president of sales and marketing just left the company and some senior staff members also left during the past couple of months. Yet, the CEO is firmly positive about the future of the company. He says there is no cash problem and that despite the layoffs, the company will still be able to service present and future customers.

The layoff looks like its going to hit sales and marketing the hardest, but engineering will also be affected. It is up to you to develop and implement a layoff policy immediately. As you draft the policy, consider the following questions:

- **What criteria should you use to determine who will be laid off?** Should you base the layoff decision on seniority? If so, would the company lose more top-performing employees? But if the layoff is based on merit, do you have an accurate system to measure performance? Will this system be defensible if angry employees challenge it in court?
- **How much notice should be given to employees who will be laid off?** As much as possible? Or would giving advance notification create performance problems as current employees search for new jobs?
- **How will security be provided to our remaining employees and protect the business from sabotage or theft by employees who are losing their jobs?** Should armed guards be hired to escort laid-off employees out of the building? What message would that send to remaining employees and the media?
- **How should news of the layoff be communicated to the employees who will be let go?** Should they be told about the layoff in a memo? Should a general meeting be held? Who should be responsible for telling employees that they have been selected for discharge?
- **When should the media be told about the layoffs?** How can rumors be controlled that may appear in the media? How can investors, distributors, and customers be informed that the layoff will not hurt the company's relationship with them?
- **How will the remaining workforce, the "survivors," feel about working for the company after the layoff?** Will they still be motivated to perform? How can the anger and grief they will be feeling be dealt with?
- **What kinds of services can be provided to laid-off employees to help them find other jobs?** Should a company be retained that can supply these services? Can the laid-off employees be offered benefits for a certain period of time to help ease the pain?

THE MANAGERIAL PERSPECTIVE

As the opening vignette suggests, relationships between employers and employees are constantly subjected to change in today's business environment. Global competition and new technologies such as the Internet have changed the rules of competition, forcing many firms to become increasingly productive with smaller workforces. In addition, in the early 2000s the number of U.S. employees who quit jobs voluntarily increased as employees searched for and found better opportunities in a tight labor market.

Managers must not only develop skills to help an employee who leaves the company voluntarily, but they must also aid employees who have been fired for cause or are being let go for economic reasons. A badly managed ending to the employment relationship can damage a firm's reputation in its industry or community and limit its ability to attract the scarce, talented employees that it may need in the future.

This chapter deals with the sometimes more unpleasant task of managing an organization's outflow of human resources. We explore the process leading up to an employee's exit from the firm and how to manage that process effectively.

What Are Employee Separations?

An **employee separation** occurs when an employee ceases to be a member of an organization.[1] The **turnover rate** is a measure of the rate at which employees leave the firm. Well-managed companies try to monitor their turnover rate and identify and manage causes for turnover. The goal is to minimize turnover and the costs of replacing employees. Replacement costs, particularly for highly skilled position, can be surprisingly high. For example, replacing a U.S. Navy fighter pilot may cost more than $1,000,000.[2] However, multiple turnover rates can be calculated, and it is important to focus on the correct numbers. Exhibit 6.1 presents the basics about calculating turnover rates. An excessively high turnover rate compared to the industry standard is often a symptom of problems within the organization.

Employee separations can and should be managed. Before we discuss the management of separations, however, we examine both the costs and the benefits of separations.

Employee separation
The termination of an employee's membership in an organization.

Turnover rate
The rate of employee separations in an organization.

A Quick Look at the Numbers: A Turnover Rate Primer

EXHIBIT 6.1

Turnover happens in all organizations. The rate of turnover can vary over time and across companies and industries. Before determining whether your turnover rate is high compared to other time periods or to other organizations, be sure you calculate it accurately.

You need the number of employees exiting each month and the average number of employees on staff during each of those months. The following formula calculates this rate:

$$\text{Turnover} = \frac{\text{Number of employees leaving the job}}{\text{Average number of employees during the period}} \times \frac{12}{\text{Number of months in the period}}$$

Let's consider the following situation. Over the course of 6 months, you have had 12 employees leave a department. The average number of employees in the department is 50. Given these numbers, your annualized turnover rate is:

$$12 / 50 \times 12 / 6 = .48$$

Over the 6 months your turnover rate has been 24 percent; however, the formula indicates that this rate is 48 percent on an annual basis.

Knowing the overall turnover rate can provide a rough comparison point. However, breaking the overall rate down into various components can help you to understand the sources for turnover and help to determine whether you have a problem. A helpful way of breaking out the overall rate is to use the categories in Figure 6.1.

Source and Type of Turnover

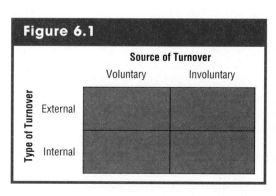

Figure 6.1

(continued)

"Source of turnover" refers to whether the employee decided to leave the organization (voluntary) or management made the decision to end the employment relationship (involuntary). "Type of turnover" can be divided into people who left the organization (external) and employees who left the job but took another position in the organization (internal).

You can calculate turnover rates for each of the four cells in the source-by-type matrix. A high rate of turnover that is voluntary and external could be of particular concern and be symptomatic of organizational problems.

Source: Cleveland, B. (2005, June 1). Tackling turnover. *Call Center,* 16.

The Costs of Employee Separations

By eliminating positions, the company can reduce costs in the long run. However, if not done correctly, layoffs can appear to provide an economic fix in the short term but cause problems for the organization in the long term. Furthermore, even when positions are eliminated, the separation costs can be considerable. For example, as Figure 6.2 shows, from 1993 to 1998 AT&T announced five job cuts to streamline its operations. The separations cost the company billions of dollars. In addition to the monetary cost, AT&T lost talented people, and company morale was crippled. To shore up morale, AT&T executives took a generous approach in its 1998 round of job cuts, offering rich buyout incentives to attract volunteers. As AT&T spokeswoman Adele Ambrose explained, "We wanted to send the right message to our employees, that we need to get cost-competitive but we wanted to be generous to them and express that we care about them."[3]

The cost of turnover can differ across organizations, and some costs associated with turnover can be difficult to estimate. For example, an organization's geographic location may necessitate a particularly high cost of recruiting new employees, which causes the cost of turnover in that organization to be unusually high. The effect of lost talent on sales, on productivity, or on research and development all may be tremendous but difficult to estimate. It is common to estimate the cost of turnover from a conservative 25 percent[4] to 150 percent of the lost employee's annual compensation.[5] Looking at the most conservative end of that range, at an average salary of $30,000, the cost of a turnover would be $6,000. For a company with 1,000 employees and a 20 percent turnover rate, the annual cost of turnover would be at least $1,200,000—not a trivial cost, and it could be much higher depending on the situation. Figure 6.3 presents only some of the costs associated with replacing an employee. The costs can be categorized as *recruitment costs, selection costs, training costs,* and *separation costs.*

Figure 6.2			
Date Announced	**Job-Cut Goal**	**Number of Employees, Jan. 1 of Each Year**	**Charge Taken (in billions)**
Aug. 1993	4,000	313,000	No charge
Feb. 1994	15,000	309,000*	No charge
Sept. 1995	8,500	302,000	$1.6†
Jan. 1996	40,000	301,000	$6.0†
Jan. 1998	18,000	128,000**	$1.0 (estimated)

*Acquired McCaw Cellular Communications in 1993.
**After spinning off Lucent Technologies and NCR in 1997.
†Total charge includes restructuring and consolidation.

Source: Schiesel, S. (1998, February 8). AT&T: A leaner company without a crash diet. *New York Times,* www.nytimes.com/library/financial/Sunday/archive/.

AT&T's Job Cuts: 1993 Through 1998

Figure 6.3

Recruitment Costs	Selection Costs	Training Costs	Separation Costs
■ Advertising	■ Interviewing	■ Orientation	■ Separation pay
■ Campus visits	■ Testing	■ Direct training costs	■ Benefits
■ Recruiter time	■ Reference checks	■ Trainer's time	■ Unemployment Insurance cost
■ Search firm fees	■ Relocation	■ Lost productivity during training	■ Exit Interview
			■ Outplacement
			■ Vacant position

Human Resource Replacement Costs

Recruitment Costs

The costs associated with recruiting a replacement may include advertising the job vacancy and using a professional recruiter to travel to various locations (including college campuses). To fill executive positions or technologically complex openings, it may be necessary to employ a search firm to locate qualified individuals, who most likely are already employed. A search firm typically charges the company a fee of about 30 percent of the employee's annual salary.

Selection Costs

Selection costs are associated with selecting, hiring, and placing a new employee in a job. Interviewing the job applicant includes the costs associated with travel to the interview site and the productivity lost in organizing the interviews and arranging meetings to make selection decisions. For example, a law firm's decision to hire a new associate may require the participation of many junior associates as well as senior partners who may charge clients hundreds of dollars per hour for his or her time.

Other selection costs include testing the employee and conducting reference checks to make sure the applicant's qualifications are legitimate. Finally, the company may have to pay relocation costs, which include the costs of moving the employee's personal property, travel costs, and sometimes even housing costs. Housing costs may include the costs of selling one's previous house and the transaction costs of buying a house in a more expensive market.

Training Costs

Most new employees need some specific training to do their job. Training costs also include the costs associated with an orientation to the company's values and culture. Also important are direct training costs—specifically, the cost of instruction, books, and materials for training courses. The cost of training someone in technical software skills, for instance, can be as high as $30,000 or more.[6] Finally, while new employees are being trained, they are not performing at the level of fully trained employees, so some productivity is lost.

Separation Costs

A company incurs separation costs for all employees who leave, whether or not they will be replaced. The largest separation cost is compensation in terms of pay and benefits. Most companies provide *severance pay* (also called *separation pay*) for laid-off employees. Severance pay may add up to several months' salary for an experienced employee. For example, IBM laid off 170 employees in its San Jose, California, disk drive plant. The affected workers were given 8 to 26 weeks of separation pay, depending on their length of service. However, recent surveys of employers indicate that technical and professional employees receive a median of three weeks' pay and nonexempt employees typically receive two weeks' pay as severance.[7] Nearly 80 percent of 1,000 companies included in one survey reported that they have a severance plan. Although length of service is the main factor in determining the amount of severance pay, many companies also use formulas that take into account factors such as salary, grade level, and title.

Less frequently, employees may continue to receive health benefits until they find a new job. In addition, employers who lay off employees may also see their unemployment insurance rates go up. Companies are penalized with a higher tax if more of their former employees draw benefits from the unemployment insurance fund in the states in which they do business.

Other separation costs are associated with the administration of the separation itself. Administration often includes an **exit interview** to find out the reasons why the employee is leaving (if he or she is leaving voluntarily) or to provide counseling and/or assistance in finding a new job. It is now common practice in larger firms to provide departing employees with **outplacement assistance,** which helps them find a job more rapidly by providing them with training in job-search skills. Finally, employers incur a cost if a position remains vacant and the work does not get done. The result may be a reduction in output or quality of service to the firm's clients or customers.

Who conducts the exit interview? The exiting worker's manager is usually a bad choice, because he or she is often the reason for voluntary separations. The interviewer should have very good communication skills and be in a neutral position regarding the employee's departure. Some organizations are moving to Web-based exit interviews, assuming that people may be more open about their reasons for leaving without a face-to-face interaction.[8] However, some workers may find the human interaction and concern of a skilled interview allows them to open up more than would a Web-based interaction.

The Benefits of Employee Separations

Although many people see separations negatively, they have several benefits. When turnover rates are too low, few new employees will be hired and opportunities for promotion are sharply curtailed. A persistently low turnover rate may have a negative effect on performance if the workforce becomes complacent and fails to generate innovative ideas. As presented in the Manager's Notebook, "Turnover Heating up in Hong Kong: Positive Economic Sign, but Pain for Employers," turnover can even be seen as a positive economic indicator. A certain level of employee separations is a good and necessary part of doing business.

MANAGER'S NOTEBOOK | Global

Turnover Heating up in Hong Kong: Positive Economic Sign, but Pain for Employers

According to Jim Tak-Hing, the human resources director for North Asia for Dairy Farm, employee turnover rate is an immediate and accurate barometer of the Hong Kong economy. During the SARS outbreak in 2003, the turnover rate in Hong Kong was 10 percent. The economy began to pick up, and the rate in 2005 was 15 percent. According to Tak-Hing, workers' priorities are less focused on job security and more on taking some risk and pursuing opportunities. The turnover rate may be a positive sign when considered from the broad perspective of the economy, but what does it mean for employers?

Dairy Farm is grappling with the increasing turnover rate in Hong Kong. Dairy Farm is a large retail operation, with 243 supermarkets and hundreds of smaller retail outlets. With 12,000 workers, its 15 percent turnover rate translates into 900 job openings per year. In order to improve its retention rate, Dairy Farm is looking at more than simply raising pay. The organization is trying to combat turnover with promotion-from-within policies and by developing its workers with various forms of training. Its managers recognize that the increasing turnover rate may be good news for the economy, but it can cause difficulties for individual employers.

Source: Adapted from Metcalfe, T. (2005, February 5). Turn over a new leaf to retain staff: Dairy Farm finds that keeping skilled staff involves more than just boosting salaries. *South China Morning Post,* Human Resources Trends, 4.

Employees may receive some potential benefits from a separation, too. An individual may escape from an unpleasant work situation and eventually find one that is less stressful or more personally and professionally satisfying.

Reduced Labor Costs

An organization can reduce its total labor costs by reducing the size of its workforce. Although separation costs in a layoff can be considerable, the salary savings resulting from the elimination of some jobs can easily outweigh the separation pay and other expenditures associated with the layoff.

Replacement of Poor Performers

An integral part of management is identifying poor performers and helping them improve their performance. If an employee does not respond to coaching or feedback, it may be best to terminate him or her so that a new (and presumably more skilled) employee can be brought in.

Increased Innovation

Separations create advancement opportunities for high-performing individuals. They also open up entry-level positions as employees are promoted from within. An important source of innovation in companies is new people hired from the outside who can offer a fresh perspective.

The Opportunity for Greater Diversity

Separations create opportunities to hire employees from diverse backgrounds and to redistribute the cultural and gender composition of the workforce while maintaining control over hiring practices and complying with the government's Equal Employment Opportunity Commission policies.

Types of Employee Separations

Employee separations can be divided into two categories. Voluntary separations are initiated by the employee. Involuntary separations are initiated by the employer. To protect themselves against legal challenges by former employees, employers must manage involuntary separations very carefully with a well-documented paper trail.

Voluntary Separations

Voluntary separations occur when an employee decides, for personal or professional reasons, to end the relationship with the employer. The decision could be based on the employee's obtaining a better job, changing careers, or wanting more time for family or leisure activities. Alternatively, the decision could be based on the employee's finding the present job unattractive because of poor working conditions, low pay or benefits, a bad relationship with a supervisor, and so on. In most cases, the decision to leave is a combination of having attractive alternatives and being unhappy with aspects of the current job.

Voluntary separation
A separation that occurs when an employee decides, for personal or professional reasons, to end the relationship with the employer.

Voluntary separations can be either *avoidable* or *unavoidable*. Unavoidable voluntary separations result from an employee's life decisions that extend beyond an employer's control, such as a spouse's decision to move to a new area that requires a relocation for the employee. However, recent studies show that approximately 80 percent of voluntary separations are avoidable, and many of those are due to staffing mistakes. By investing in quality HRM recruiting, selection, training, and development programs (see Chapters 5 and 8), companies can avoid a poor match between the employee and the job.[9]

There are two types of voluntary separations: quits and retirements.

Quits

The decision to *quit* depends on (1) the employee's level of dissatisfaction with the job and (2) the number of attractive alternatives the employee has outside the organization.[10] The employee can be dissatisfied with the job itself, the job environment, or both.

In recent years some employers have been using pay incentives to encourage employees to quit voluntarily. Employers use these *voluntary severance plans,* or *buyouts,* to reduce the size of their workforce while avoiding the negative factors associated with a layoff. The pay incentive may amount to a lump-sum cash payment of six months to two years of salary, depending on the employee's tenure with the company and the plan's design. For example, as of 2005 over 180 employees had taken the buyouts offered by the NASA Langley Research Center in Virginia.[11] Faced with budget cuts, the center offered employees incentives, as much as $25,000 for the most experienced, to resign or retire early. Ford Motor Co. was also trying to shed 1,000 salaried workers by offering a voluntary buyout program.[12]

Retirements

A *retirement* differs from a quit in a number of respects. First, a retirement usually occurs at the end of an employee's career. A quit can occur at any time. (In fact, it is in the early stages of one's career that a person is more likely to change jobs.) Second, retirements usually result in the individual's receiving retirement benefits from the organization. These may include a retirement income supplemented with personal savings and Social Security benefits. People who quit do not receive these benefits. Finally, the organization normally plans retirements in advance. HR staff can help employees plan their retirement, and managers can plan in advance to replace retirees by grooming current employees or recruiting new ones. Quits are much more difficult to plan for.

Most employees postpone retirement until they are close to 65 because that is the age at which they are entitled to full Social Security and Medicare benefits from the government (see Chapter 12).[13] Without these benefits, many workers would find it difficult to retire. It is illegal for an employer to force an employee to retire on the basis of age.

Many *Fortune* 500 companies have found *early retirement incentives* to be an effective way to reduce their workforce. These incentives make it financially attractive for senior employees to retire early. Along with buyouts, they are used as alternatives to layoffs because they are seen as a gentler way of downsizing. We discuss the management of early retirements in detail later in this chapter.

Involuntary Separations

Involuntary separation
A separation that occurs when an employer decides to terminate its relationship with an employee due to (1) economic necessity or (2) a poor fit between the employee and the organization.

An **involuntary separation** occurs when management decides to terminate its relationship with an employee due to (1) economic necessity or (2) a poor fit between the employee and the organization. Involuntary separations are the result of very serious and painful decisions that can have a profound effect on the entire organization and especially on the employee who loses his or her job.

Although managers implement the decision to dismiss an employee, the HR staff makes sure that the dismissed employee receives "due process" and that the dismissal is performed within the letter and the spirit of the company's employment policy. Cooperation and teamwork between managers and HR staff are essential to effective management of the dismissal process. HR staff can act as valuable advisers to managers in this arena by helping them avoid mistakes that can lead to claims of wrongful discharge. They can also help protect employees whose rights are violated by managers. There are two types of involuntary separations: discharges and layoffs.

Discharges

A *discharge* takes place when management decides that there is a poor fit between an employee and the organization. The discharge is a result of either poor performance or the employee's failure to change some unacceptable behavior that management has tried repeatedly to correct. Sometimes employees engage in serious misconduct, such as theft or dishonesty, which may result in immediate termination.

Managers who decide to discharge an employee must make sure they follow the company's established discipline procedures. Most nonunion companies and all unionized firms have a *progressive discipline procedure* that allows employees the opportunity to correct their behavior before receiving a more serious punishment. For example, an employee who violates a safety rule may be given a verbal warning, followed by a written warning within a specified period of time. If the employee does not stop breaking the safety rule, the employer may choose to discharge the employee. Managers must document the occurrences of the violation and provide evidence that the employee knew about the rule and was warned that its violation could lead to discharge. In this way, managers can prove that the employee was discharged for just cause. Chapter 14 details the criteria that managers can use to determine whether a discharge meets the standard of just cause.*

An example illustrates how costly discharging an employee can be if handled poorly or without due process. Sandra McHugh won $1.1 million in damages in an age discrimination lawsuit against her employer.[14] McHugh was forced out of her job because of her age—which was 42 at the time.

Layoffs

Layoffs are a means for an organization to cut costs. For example, the massive layoff of 25,000 blue-collar workers by General Motors is estimated to translate into $2.5 billion in annual savings.[15] GM has seen its U.S. market share erode from nearly 50 percent of auto sales in the 1970s down to about 25 percent. The company would like to make as many cuts as possible through buyouts and early retirements, but its goal is to achieve a 22 percent reduction of its workforce by 2008.[16] It is important to understand that GM is engaged in a layoff; it is not discharging workers. A layoff differs from a discharge in several ways. In a layoff, employees lose their jobs because a change in the company's environment or strategy forces it to reduce its workforce. Global competition, reductions in product demand, changing technologies that reduce the need for workers, and mergers and acquisitions are the primary factors behind most layoffs.[17] In contrast, the actions of most discharged employees have usually been a direct cause of their separation. Although we can make these conceptual distinctions between a layoff and a discharge, the GM workers who face being cut simply know that they lost their job, whatever the process is called.

Layoffs have a powerful impact on the organization. They can affect the morale of the organization's remaining employees, who may fear losing their jobs in the future. In addition, layoffs can affect a region's economic vitality, hurting the merchants who depend on the workers' patronage to support their businesses. A 2001 layoff at Dell had a severe impact on a community. Dell fired 1,700 workers in the first major layoff in the company's history.[18] Three months later, another 4,000 jobs were eliminated. Nearly all the cuts were made at Dell's central Texas facility in Round Rock, a city north of Austin. A sales manager at Dell, whose annual salary was greater than $100,000, received less than $1,200 per month in unemployment benefits, and it was four months before he found a job as a waiter. Thousands of laid-off Round Rock workers found it hard to replace their income. The local job market was saturated with thousands of other people who all had similar résumés. The higher end of the Round Rock real estate market is made up

> **A Question of Ethics**
>
> What can a company do to help a community when it decides to close a plant that is important to the community's economic prosperity?

Managers who discharge an employee for a bad cause can cost their company thousands— or even millions—of dollars. Sandra McHugh, who was fired because of her age, won over $1 million in damages.

---

*In some jurisdictions, it is possible for management to discharge an employee based on evidence that does not meet the standard of just cause. However, the authors recommend meeting this standard as a good business practice.

almost entirely of Dell employees. In 2002, the number of homes valued over $250,000 for sale increased tenfold.[19] Even a local deli's sandwich sales decreased by 25 percent. The greater the dependence of a local economy on one employer, the more devastating a layoff can be to that community.

Investors may be affected by layoffs as well. The investment community may interpret a layoff as a signal that the company is having serious problems. This, in turn, may lower the price of the company's stock on the stock market. Finally, layoffs can hurt a company's standing as a good place to work and make it difficult to recruit highly skilled employees who can choose among numerous employers. For example, Northwest and other major airlines used to be perceived as desirable places to work that offered good pay and benefits. However, the airlines are facing great competitive pressures and rising costs. As part of its attempts to cut costs, Northwest has cut more than 14,000 jobs in four years, and more layoffs are expected.[20] The layoffs and the insecurity they produce can influence the industry's ability to attract the best workers.

Layoffs, Downsizing, and Rightsizing

Downsizing

A company strategy to reduce the scale (size) and scope of its business in order to improve the company's financial performance.

Let's clarify the differences between a layoff and downsizing and rightsizing. A company that adopts a **downsizing** strategy reduces the scale (size) and scope of its business to improve its financial performance.[21] When a company decides to downsize, it may choose layoffs as one of several ways of reducing costs or improving profitability.[22] In recent years many firms have done exactly this, but we want to emphasize that companies can take many other measures to increase profitability without resorting to layoffs.[23] We discuss these measures later in this chapter.

Rightsizing

The process of reorganizing a company's employees to improve their efficiency.

Rightsizing means reorganizing a company's employees to improve their efficiency.[24] An organization needs to rightsize when it becomes bloated with too many management layers or bureaucratic work processes that add no value to its product or service. For example, companies that reconfigure their frontline employees into self-managed work teams may find they are overstaffed and need to reduce their headcount to take advantage of the efficiencies provided by the team structure. The result may be layoffs, but layoffs are not always necessary. As with downsizing strategy, management may have several alternatives to layoffs available when it rightsizes its workforce. In the case of the job cuts at GM, the union's perspective is that shrinkage isn't the long-term answer to the company's problems. The United Auto Workers (UAW) contends that what is needed is improvements in product mix and quality.[25] GM's position is that adapting to a smaller market share is simply the reality of the future. In other words, should GM be engaged downsizing or rightsizing? The answer to this question may emerge only after extensive negotiations between GM and the UAW. Whatever the label, the result of downsizing or rightsizing is that people are losing their jobs.

Managing a layoff is an extremely complex process. Before we examine the specifics, however, we'll examine an important alternative: early retirements.

Managing Early Retirements

When a company decides to downsize its operation, its first task is to examine alternatives to layoffs. As we mentioned earlier, one of the most popular of these methods is early retirement. In recent years companies such as IBM, ExxonMobil, DuPont, AT&T, Hewlett-Packard,[26] Bell Atlantic,[27] and GTE[28] have used early retirement to reduce the size of their workforce.

The Features of Early Retirement Policies

Early retirement policies consist of two features: (1) a package of financial incentives that makes it attractive for senior employees to retire earlier than they had planned and (2) an *open window* that restricts eligibility to a fairly short period of time. After the window is closed, the incentives are no longer available.[29]

The financial incentives are usually based on a formula that accelerates senior employees' retirement eligibility and increases their retirement income. It is not unusual for companies to provide a lump-sum payment as an incentive to leave. Many companies also offer the continuation of health benefits so that early retirees enjoy coverage until they are eligible for Medicare at age 65.

However, as companies have opened the early retirement window to more and more employees in recent years, they have had to scale back once-generous severance packages. For instance, when IBM announced its early retirement policy in 1991, it allowed any employee with 30 years of service to retire with full retirement benefits regardless of age. Employees who accepted the offer received a lump sum of one year's salary. By 1993 departing employees got a maximum of 26 weeks' pay plus only six months' paid medical coverage.[30]

Early retirement policies can reduce the size of a company's workforce substantially. For example, a public utility company headquartered in Raleigh, North Carolina, Progress Energy, had a stronger response to an early retirement program than was expected.[31] As a result, the company may have to hire 1,000 people to make up for the shortfall.

Avoiding Problems with Early Retirements

When not properly managed, early retirement policies can cause a host of problems. Too many employees may take early retirement, the wrong employees may leave, and employees may perceive that they are being forced to leave, which may result in age discrimination complaints.

One way to avoid excess resignations is to restrict eligibility to divisions that have redundant employees with high levels of seniority (instead of making the policy available to all employees throughout the corporation). Another way is to ask senior employees how they would respond to a specific early retirement plan. If too many would leave, the incentives could be fine-tuned so that a controlled number of employees take early retirement.

Sometimes the most marketable employees with the best skills can easily find another job and decide to "take the money and run." To avoid this situation and keep its most valuable people, the company can develop provisions to hire back retired employees as temporary consultants until suitable replacements can be promoted, hired, or trained.

Early retirement programs must be managed so that eligible employees do not perceive that they are being forced to retire and consequently file age discrimination charges. Situations that could be interpreted as coercive include the following:

- A longtime employee who has performed satisfactorily over many years suddenly receives an unsatisfactory performance evaluation.

After 13 years as a fuels buyer with BP America, Inc., Ron Colvin started his own business as a chimney sweep. Colvin is happy to be out of corporate life and is making decent money. The only problem: "It gets lonely, working by yourself," he says.

- A manager indicates that senior employees who do not take early retirement may lose their jobs anyway because a layoff is likely in the near future.
- Senior employees notice that their most recent pay raises are quite a bit lower than those of other, younger workers who are not eligible for early retirement.

A former employee who sued IBM for age discrimination was awarded $315,000 in compensatory damages because he convinced the jury that he was forced to take early retirement.[32] The employee introduced evidence showing that his job had been reclassified after he voiced some reservations about taking early retirement. Shortly after that, he claimed, he received a warning that his next performance evaluation would be unsatisfactory.

Managers can avoid lawsuits by following one simple guideline: All managers with senior employees should make certain that they do not treat senior employees any differently than other employees. HR staff members play an important role here by keeping managers aware of the letter and the spirit of the early retirement policy so that they do not (consciously or unconsciously) coerce senior employees during the open window period.

Managing Layoffs

Typically, an organization will institute a layoff when it cannot reduce its labor costs by any other means. Figure 6.4, which presents a model of the layoff decision and its alternatives, shows that managers should first try to reduce their labor costs by using alternatives to layoffs, such as early retirements and other voluntary workforce reductions. After managers make the decision to implement a layoff, they must concern themselves with the outplacement of the former employees.

An important influence on the likelihood of a layoff is the business's HR strategy (see Chapter 1). Companies with a lifelong employment HR strategy are less likely to lay off employees because they have developed alternative policies to protect their permanent employees' job security. The best-known examples of firms with lifelong employment policies are the large Japanese corporations, which employ about one-third of Japanese workers. In the United States a few companies (such as FedEx) have firm no-layoff policies. FedEx has never had a layoff in its U.S. operation, which includes 124,000 employees.[33] Its no-layoff policy means that the organization is committed to preserving jobs and benefits as much as possible. FedEx has dealt with economic recession by relying on **attrition**, which reduces the size of the workforce because departing employees are not replaced, deferring purchases, instituting a hiring freeze, limiting

Attrition
An employment policy designed to reduce the company's workforce by not refilling job vacancies that are created by turnover.

The Layoff Decision and Its Alternatives

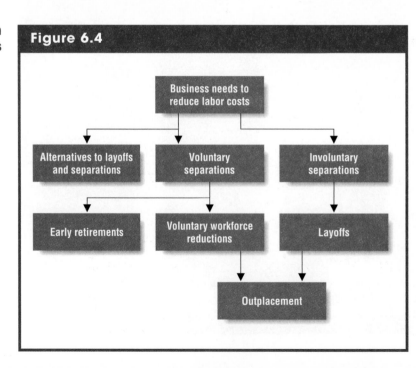

Figure 6.4

employee travel, and deferring bonuses. Most workers, at FedEx or anywhere, would probably agree that these cutbacks are better than losing their jobs. Most firms, however, have market-driven HR strategies that permit layoffs when alternatives are not available.

Alternatives to Layoffs

Most organizations search for alternative cost-reduction methods before turning to layoffs. A recent survey found attrition to be the common strategy.[34] Other approaches include freezing employment, not renewing contract workers, and encouraging employees to take time off voluntarily. Figure 6.5 shows the major alternatives to layoffs. These include employment policies, changes in job design, pay and benefits policies, and training. Managers can use these alternatives both to reduce labor costs and to protect the jobs of full-time employees.

Employment Policies

The first alternatives to layoffs that managers are likely to consider are those that intrude the least on the day-to-day management of the business. These alternatives usually focus on adjustments to employment policies.

The least disruptive way to cut labor costs is through attrition. By not filling job vacancies that are created by turnover, firms can improve the bottom line. After contract negotiations with the UAW, DaimlerChrysler made clear its plan to trim its workforce through attrition and workers who take early retirement packages.[35]

When greater cost reductions are needed, a **hiring freeze** may be implemented. For example, Sacred Heart Medical Center, a leading employer in Spokane, Washington, recently used a temporary hiring freeze to overcome financial difficulties.[36] Temporary employees, part-time employees, student interns, co-ops, and subcontracted employees may also be eliminated to protect the jobs of permanent full-time employees.

Hiring freeze
An employment policy designed to reduce the company's workforce by not hiring any new employees into the company.

Other employment policies aim to decrease the number of hours worked and, therefore, the number of hours for which the company must pay its employees. Workers may be encouraged to take voluntary (unpaid) time off or leaves of absence, or they may be asked to put in a shorter workweek (for example, 35 hours rather than 40).

The strategic application of employment policies to provide job security for a firm's full-time, core employees is called a *rings of defense* approach to job security. Under this approach, headcounts of full-time employees are purposely kept low. An increase in the demand for labor will be satisfied by hiring part-time and temporary employees or subcontracting work to freelancers. For example, Axcelis is a manufacturer of tools used in the semiconductor industry. It has a core of 2,000 full-time permanent workers but uses temporary workers and contract workers as a buffer against changes in market conditions.[37] When faced with a downturn in the market, the company reduced the number of noncore workers from 500 to approximately 50. The advantage of this approach is that it provides some stability and security, at least for the core

Figure 6.5

Employment Policies	Changes in Job Design	Pay and Benefits Policies	Training
■ Reduction through attrition	■ Transfers	■ Pay freeze	■ Retraining
■ Hiring freeze	■ Relocation	■ Cut overtime pay	
■ Cut part-time employees	■ Job sharing	■ Use vacation and leave days	
■ Cut internships or co-ops	■ Demotions	■ Pay cuts	
■ Give subcontracted work to in-house employees		■ Profit sharing or variable pay	
■ Voluntary time off			
■ Leaves of absence			
■ Reduced work hours			

Alternatives to Layoffs

employees. This security can pay off in the form of workers who feel more comfortable and can, therefore, be more innovative—an important competitive characteristic in many industries. However, the increasing use of temporary, or contingent, workers as a strategy to smooth out variations in demand for labor means that more workers are vulnerable and treated as expendable by employers.

Changes in Job Design

Managers can use their human resources more cost-effectively by changing job design and transferring people to different units of the company. Alternatively, they may relocate people to jobs in different parts of the country where the cost of living and salaries are lower. The cost of relocating an employee plus the fact that some employees do not want to move sometimes make this alternative problematic. Another practice, common in unionized companies, allows a senior employee whose job is eliminated to take a job in a different unit of the company from an employee with less seniority. This practice is called *bumping*.

Companies can also use *job sharing* (which we discussed in Chapter 2) when it is possible to reconfigure one job into two part-time jobs. The challenge here is to find two people willing to share the job's hours and pay. Finally, as a last resort, highly paid workers may be demoted to lower-paying jobs.

A Question of Ethics

Is it ethical for top managers to receive cash bonuses while at the same time asking lower-level employees to accept a pay freeze?

Pay and Benefits Policies

As one way of reducing costs, managers can enforce a *pay freeze* during which no wages or salaries are increased. Pay freezes should be done on an across-the-board basis to avoid accusations of discrimination. These policies can be augmented by reductions in overtime pay and policies that ask employees to use up their vacation and leave days. Many state governments have enforced annual pay freezes on their employees. Unfortunately, pay freezes often cause some top-performing, highly marketable employees to leave the company.

A more radical and intrusive pay policy geared toward reducing labor costs is a *pay cut*. This action can be even more demoralizing to the workforce than a pay freeze and should be used only if employees are willing to accept it voluntarily as an alternative to layoffs. Unions in several U.S. industries have accepted wage reductions in return for job security. Comair, a subsidiary of Delta Airlines, recently used both pay freezes and pay cuts in its attempt to remain a competitive regional airline.[38] The airline could not afford to buy the new jets that management said it needed to maintain its competitive position. The union-represented pilots agreed to a pay freeze so that the company could order the new jets. In addition, top company officials took a 10-percent pay cut.

A long-term pay policy that may protect workers from layoffs structures compensation so that profit sharing (the sharing of company profits with employees) or variable pay (pay contingent on meeting performance goals) makes up a significant portion of employees' total compensation (around 15 to 20 percent). When the business cycle hits a low point, the company can save up to about 20 percent of the payroll by not paying out profit sharing or variable pay, but still retain its employees by paying them the salary portion of their total compensation. Few companies in the United States use this approach, but it is very common in Japan.

Training

By retraining employees whose skills have become obsolete, a company may be able to match newly skilled workers with available job vacancies. Without this retraining, the workers might have been laid off. For example, IBM has retrained some of its production workers in computer programming and placed them in jobs requiring this skill.

Implementing a Layoff

Once the layoff decision has been made, managers must implement it carefully. A layoff can be a traumatic event that affects the lives of thousands of people. The key issues that managers must settle are notifying employees, developing layoff criteria, communicating to laid-off employees, coordinating media relations, maintaining security, and reassuring survivors of the layoff.

Notifying Employees

The **Worker Adjustment and Retraining Notification Act (WARN)** requires U.S. employers with 100 or more employees to give 60 days' advance notice to employees who will be laid off as a result of a plant closing or a mass separation of 50 or more workers.[39] This law, passed in 1988, was designed to give workers more time to look for a new job. Employers who do not notify their employees must give them the equivalent of 60 working days of income. Employers who lay off fewer than 50 employees have greater flexibility as to when they can notify the affected employees.

There are several arguments in favor of giving at least several weeks' notice before a layoff. It is socially and professionally correct to extend employees this courtesy. Also, this treatment is reassuring to the employees who will remain with the company. But there are also arguments in favor of giving no notification. If the labor relations climate is poor, there is the potential for theft or sabotage to company equipment. In addition, the productivity of employees who are losing their jobs may decline during the notice period.[40]

The requirements for layoff notification tend to be more restrictive in European countries than in the United States. For example, in Sweden management must give at least 60 days' advance notice in layoffs of five or more workers, while in France as few as two workers must get at least 45 days' notification.[41] Figure 6.6 lists advance notice requirements in several other European nations.

Developing Layoff Criteria

The criteria for dismissal must be clear. When the criteria are clearly laid out, the managers responsible for determining who will be laid off can make consistent, fair decisions. The two most important criteria used as the basis for layoff decisions are seniority and employee performance.

Seniority, the amount of time an employee has been with the firm, is by far the most commonly used layoff criterion. It has two main advantages. First, seniority criteria are easily applied; managers simply examine all employees' dates of hire to determine the seniority of each (in years and days). Second, many employees see the seniority system as fair because (1) managers cannot play "favorites" under a seniority-based decision and (2) the most senior employees have the greatest investment in the company in terms of job rights and privileges (they have accrued more vacation and leave days and have more attractive work schedules, for example).

There are disadvantages to using the "last in, first out" method, however. The firm may lose some top performers, as well as a disproportionate amount of women and minorities—who are more likely to be recent hires in certain jobs. Nonetheless, the courts have upheld seniority as the basis for layoff as long as all employees have equal opportunities to obtain seniority.

Despite efforts to retain senior employees during a layoff, many choose to leave. In the late 1990s, droves of talented senior managers and executives quit their firms because the bull market made them wealthy enough to retire early. To combat this senior "brain drain" trend, Deloitte Consulting launched a Senior Leader's program that allows senior partners in the firm to downshift

Worker Adjustment and Retraining Notification Act (WARN) of 1988
A federal law requiring U.S. employers with 100 or more employees to give 60 days' advance notice to employees who will be laid off as a result of a plant closing or a mass separation of 50 or more workers.

A Question of Ethics

How much notice of a layoff should a company be obligated to give?

Figure 6.6	
Country	**Notice Requirements**
Belgium	30 days
Denmark	30 days
Germany	30 days
Greece	30 days
Ireland	30 days
Italy	22 to 32 days
Luxembourg	60 to 75 days
Netherlands	2 to 6 months
United Kingdom	30 to 90 days (if at least 10 workers are involved)

Source: Ehrenberg, R. G., and Jakubson, G. H. (1988). *Advance notice provisions in plant closing legislation.* Kalamazoo, MI: W. E. Upjohn Institute for Employment Research.

Requirements of Advance Notice for Collective Dismissals in Selected European Countries

from full-time to part-time consulting or mentoring. That way, the firm can retain the talent and knowledge of these highly skilled partners and the employees have the flexibility to pursue other endeavors.[42]

When the workforce is unionized, layoff decisions are usually based on seniority. This provision is written into the labor contract. However, when the workforce is nonunion and especially when cuts must be made in professional and managerial employees, it is not unusual for companies to base layoff decisions on performance criteria or on a combination of performance and seniority. Using performance as the basis for layoffs allows the company to retain its top performers in every work unit and eliminate its weakest performers. Unfortunately, performance levels are not always clearly documented, and the company may be exposed to wrongful discharge litigation if the employee can prove that management discriminated or acted arbitrarily in judging performance. Because of these legal risks, many companies avoid using performance as a basis for layoff.

If a company has taken the time to develop a valid performance appraisal system that accurately measures performance and meets government guidelines, then there is no reason why appraisal data cannot be used as the basis for layoff. For example, IBM used performance as the basis for layoffs of its professional workforce in a 1990s downsizing effort.[43] When using this criterion, managers should take the employee's total performance over a long period of time into account. Managers who focus on one low performance appraisal period and ignore other satisfactory or exceptional performance appraisals could be viewed as acting arbitrarily and unfairly. We discuss this topic in detail in the next chapter.

Communicating to Laid-Off Employees

It is crucial to communicate with the employees who will be laid off as humanely and sensitively as possible. No employee likes being told he or she will be discharged, and the way a manager handles this unpleasant task can affect how the employee and others in the organization accept the decision.

Laid-off employees should first learn of their fate from their supervisor in a face-to-face private discussion. Employees who learn about their dismissal through a less personal form of communication (for example, a peer or a memo) are likely to be hurt and angry. The information session between supervisor and employee should be brief and to the point. The manager should express appreciation for what the employee has contributed, if appropriate, and explain how much severance pay and what benefits will be provided and for how long. This information can be repeated in greater detail at a group meeting of laid-off employees and should be documented in a written pamphlet handed out at the meeting.

The best time to hold the termination session is in the middle of the workweek. It is best to avoid telling workers they are being laid off during their vacation or right before a weekend, when they have large blocks of time on their hands.[44]

One example of how *not* to communicate a layoff is provided by the following example: A petroleum company brought employees together for a rather unsettling meeting. Each employee was given an envelope with the letter *A* or *B* on it. The A's were told to stay put while the B's were ushered into an adjacent room. Then, en masse, the B's were told that they were being laid off.

Coordinating Media Relations

Rumors of an impending layoff can be very dangerous to the workforce's morale as well as to the organization's relationships with customers, suppliers, and the surrounding community. Top managers, working with HR staff members, should develop a plan to provide accurate information about the layoff to external clients (via the media) as well as the workforce (via internal communications).[45] In this way, managers can control and put to rest rumors that may exaggerate the extent of the firm's downsizing efforts. It is also important that direct communication take place with the employees directly affected by the layoff *and* the surviving employees and that all communication be coordinated with press releases to the media. In addition, HR staff must prepare to answer any questions that employees or the media may have regarding outplacement, severance pay, or the continuation of benefits.

Maintaining Security

In some situations, a layoff may threaten company property. Laid-off employees may find themselves rushed out of the building, escorted by armed guards, and their personal belongings delivered to them later in boxes. Although such treatment may seem harsh, it may be necessary in certain industries (such as banking and computer software), where sabotage could result in substantial damage.

For instance, Timothy Lloyd worked for Omega Engineering, Inc., a company that designs and manufactures instruments and process control devices. After he was dismissed but before his last day at the company, Lloyd allegedly set a "program bomb" in the company's computer system. About two weeks after his last day, the bomb deleted key files from Omega's database, resulting in $10 million in damage. Al DiFrancesco, Omega's director of human relations, noted that the company could have avoided the problem with better security, but "hindsight is 20/20. . . ." As a result of the damage, Omega tightened its security policies and procedures to safeguard against disgruntled employees.[46]

In most cases, security precautions are probably not necessary when implementing a layoff, and using armed guards and other heavy-handed tactics will only lead to hard feelings and resentment. Treating laid-off employees with dignity and respect generally reduces the potential for sabotage.

Reassuring Survivors of the Layoff

An organization may lose the cost savings of a layoff if survivor productivity drops as a result of the layoff.[47] Low morale and stress could be made worse if the layoff was not handled well. As presented in the Manager's Notebook, "Survivor Anxiety," survivors of a layoff may face a number of difficulties.

Ethics

MANAGER'S NOTEBOOK

Survivor Anxiety

Even when necessary and handled well, layoffs can leave the company in worse shape than before. The company may be better off financially, but survivors may be looking at other opportunities and leaving their jobs. The following are some of the difficulties faced by layoff survivors that can cause performance and commitment problems:

- **More work.** The company may have cut costs, but the layoff survivors find themselves in the position of having to do more work with the same, or even fewer, resources.
- **Unsettling changes.** Layoffs can alter teams and the way people relate to each other. The workplace and the job may not be the same, and it can take serious adjustment for the survivors to adapt to the new workplace.
- **Self-assessment of contribution.** Survivors may begin to question the degree to which they contribute to the organization. They may question the level of their ability to perform and the extent to which their job is needed in the organization.
- **Guilt.** Survivors often feel concern for their colleagues who were laid off, and concern about whether they can find another job can haunt them. The survivors may also wonder what accounts for their not being laid off. They may wonder if it was luck and not competence.

Source: Adapted from Kennedy, M. M. (2005, May 15). Workplace survivors feel remorse. *Marketing News*, 50.

To cope with these difficulties, the survivors may try to "escape." It is not unusual to see a sharp increase in absenteeism as well as turnover.

Companies can minimize problems in this area by developing special programs for survivors. One simple but critical step is to educate the retained employees about the organization's financial situation.[48] If retained workers understand the economic reasons for the layoff, they may be more likely to blame the bad times on external factors rather than finding some way to blame management. Furthermore, understanding the causes for the layoff may motivate workers to help the organization make it through the rough time. Layoff survivors may also need help keeping a positive work attitude. The Manager's Notebook, "Keeping Up Morale (and Performance)," presents a four-question approach to help managers improve the morale of layoff survivors and end up with engaged and loyal employees.

Customer-Driven HR

Keeping Up Morale (and Performance)

Layoff survivors may face uncertainty, guilt, and an increased workload. These kinds of difficulties can sap the enthusiasm from a workplace and cause a serious downturn in morale. Workers may be less enthusiastic, performance may decrease, and absenteeism may increase. However, managers can take a number of steps to improve the situation. The following are some key questions managers can use to increase morale as well as performance and productivity.

1. **What can you control?** You cannot control the economic issues facing your company. You probably did not control the layoff decision or process. However, you control how you relate to your employees. You control communication with your employees and have the responsibility to create a healthy and engaging workplace.

2. **Do you show appreciation to your employees and make work fun?** Positive comments and compliments can let the workers know that their contributions are still important and appreciated. Adding some fun to work can help layoff survivors adapt and recapture a sense of trust and teamwork.

3. **Are you listening?** It is important for layoff survivors to know that someone is listening to their concerns. A layoff is something they had no control over and may have had no advance warning of. This makes it all the more important to give them a sense of control through input to goal setting and work processes in the new environment.

4. **Are you helping employees see the importance of their work?** Layoff survivors can question the importance of what they do. Perhaps they are the next layoff targets? As a manager, you need to shift people away from that fear and get them to focus on how their efforts make a difference. Remind layoff survivors of their contributions. Even if they are a small piece of a large operation, what they do is still important. Who are their customers? How do they help their customers? Building an understanding of their contributions can give layoff survivors meaning and purpose to their work and ignite their motivation to perform.

Source: Adapted with permission from Marshall, T. (2005, February 1). Management: Morale Maker, Incentive.

Windy City Fieldhouse is a company that organizes team-building events, some of which are specifically designed to boost morale following a layoff.[49] For example, to build comradery and trust among layoff survivors who may be experiencing guilt, the company might use a competitive game called Puzzling Planks. The exercise is a team competition involving a pile of boards that fit together to make three-dimensional figures. The point of the exercise is to get people to again feel their contributions are important and that they are a part of a team and an organization. Other team-building exercises organized by Windy City Fieldhouse might involve more physical exercises, such as obstacle courses.

In addition to such organized events, there are simple suggestions that can help you create a more fun, upbeat, and energetic climate among layoff survivors.[50] For example, host a simple end-of-the-week breakfast—bagels, cream cheese, juice, and coffee should do it. Arrange for a pot-luck luncheon or picnic. Hold a monthly raffle in which a drawing is held for a product, gift certificate, or an afternoon off! Add some games, such as guessing the number of pennies in a jar. The point is to infuse some energy and fun into a workplace that may be suffering from a layoff and to send a message to survivors that management cares about and recognizes them.

Outplacement

As we mentioned at the beginning of this chapter, outplacement is an HR program created to help separated employees deal with the emotional stress of job loss and provide assistance in finding a new job.[51] Outplacement activities are often handled by consulting firms retained by the organization, which pays a fee based on the number of outplaced employees. Companies are often willing to pay for outplacement because it can reduce some of the risks associated with layoffs, such as negative publicity or an increased likelihood that unions will attempt to organize the workforce.[52] Employers who provide outplacement services tend to give the goal of social responsibility a high priority as part of their HR strategy.

The Goals of Outplacement

The goals of an outplacement program reflect the organization's need to control the disruption caused by layoffs and other employee separations. The most important of these goals are (1) reducing the morale problems of employees who are about to be laid off so that they remain productive until they leave the firm, (2) minimizing the amount of litigation initiated by separated employees, and (3) assisting separated employees in finding comparable jobs as quickly as possible.[53]

Outplacement Services

The most common outplacement services are emotional support and job-search assistance. These services are closely tied to the goals of outplacement.

Emotional Support

Outplacement programs usually provide counseling to help employees deal with the emotions associated with job loss—shock, anger, denial, and lowered self-esteem. Because the family may suffer if the breadwinner becomes unemployed, sometimes family members are included in the counseling as well.[54] Counseling also benefits the employer because it helps to defuse some of the hostility that laid-off employees feel toward the company.

Job-Search Assistance

Employees who are outplaced often do not know how to begin the search for a new job. In many cases, these people have not had to look for a job in many years.

An important aspect of this assistance is teaching separated employees the skills they need to find a new job. These skills include résumé writing, interviewing and job-search techniques, career planning, and negotiation skills.[55] Outplaced employees receive instruction in these skills from either a member of the outplacement firm or the HR department. In addition, the former employer sometimes provides administrative support in the form of clerical help, phone answering, access to e-mail, and fax services.[56] These services allow laid-off employees to use computers to prepare résumés, post résumés on the Web or send them via fax and e-mail, and to use copiers to copy résumés.

The use of outplacement has become a global HR management practice. Several large corporations in Great Britain have recently restructured their operations, eliminating thousands of jobs. British Telecom has cut its workforce by 40,000, and Midland Bank has eliminated 10,000 jobs over the past decade.[57] An important part of these downsizing strategies is the use of outplacement services to smooth the affected employees' transition to a new job. Similarly, Japanese corporations use outplacement firms to find jobs for surplus workers.[58]

Summary and Conclusions

What Are Employee Separations?

Employee separations occur when employees cease to be members of an organization. Separations and outplacement can be managed effectively. Managers should plan for the outflow of their human resources with thoughtful policies. Employee separations have both costs and benefits. The costs include (1) recruitment costs, (2) selection costs, (3) training costs, and (4) separation costs. The benefits are (1) reduced labor costs, (2) replacement of poor performers, (3) increased innovation, and (4) the opportunity for greater diversity.

Types of Employee Separations

Employees may leave either voluntarily or involuntarily. Voluntary separations include quits and retirements. Involuntary separations include discharges and layoffs. When an employee is forced to leave involuntarily, a much greater level of documentation is necessary to show that a manager's decision to terminate the employee was fair and consistent.

Managing Early Retirements

When downsizing an organization, managers may elect to use voluntary early retirements as an alternative to layoffs. Early retirement programs must be managed so that eligible employees do not perceive that they are being forced to retire.

Managing Layoffs

Layoffs should be used as a last resort after all other cost-cutting alternatives have been exhausted. Important considerations in developing a layoff policy include (1) notifying employees, (2) developing layoff criteria, (3) communicating to laid-off employees, (4) coordinating media relations, (5) maintaining security, and (6) reassuring survivors of the layoff.

Outplacement

No matter what policy is used to reduce the workforce, it is a good idea for the organization to use outplacement services to help separated employees cope with their emotions and minimize the amount of time they are unemployed.

Key Terms

attrition, 192
downsizing, 190
employee separation, 183
exit interview, 186

hiring freeze, 193
involuntary separation, 188
outplacement assistance, 186
rightsizing, 190

turnover rate, 183
voluntary separation, 187
Worker Adjustment and Retraining
　　Notification Act (WARN), 195

Discussion Questions

1. After eight years as a marketing assistant for the New York office of a large French bank, Sarah Schiffler was told that her job, in a non-revenue-producing department, was being eliminated. Her choices: She could either be laid off (with eight months' severance pay) or stay on and train for the position of credit analyst, a career route she had turned down in the past. Nervous about making mortgage payments on her new condo, Sarah agreed to stay, but after six months of feeling miserable in her new position, she quit. Was her separation from the bank voluntary or involuntary? Can you think of situations in which a voluntary separation is really an involuntary separation? What are the managerial implications of such situations?

2. What are the advantages and disadvantages of using seniority as the basis for layoff? What alternatives to seniority are available as layoff criteria?

3. Would an employer ever want to increase the rate of employee turnover in a company? Why or why not?

4. What advantages might an organization have if it takes a customer-oriented approach to conducting layoffs?

5. In an age when more and more companies are downsizing, an increasingly important concept is "the virtual corporation." The idea is that a company should have a core of owners and managers, but that, to the greatest degree possible, workers should be contingent—temporary, part-time, or on short-term contracts. This gives the corporation maximum flexibility to shift vendors, cut costs, and avoid long-term labor commitments. What are the advantages and disadvantages of the virtual corporation from the point of view of both employers and workers?

6. Under what circumstances might a company's managers prefer to use layoffs instead of early retirements or voluntary severance plans as a way to downsize the workforce?

7. Under what set of conditions should a company lay off employees without giving them advance notice?

8. "The people who actually have the face-to-face contact with the person who is being laid off are not the ones who made the decision. They often did not have any input into which of their people would go," says a technician at a firm that experienced large-scale layoffs. What role should managers—who have the "face-to-face" contact with employees—play in implementing a layoff? Do you think managers and HR staff members always agree on how employee separations should be handled? Why or why not?

9. Managing survivors in a layoff is important. As a manager, what concerns would you have about the surviving workforce after a layoff? How can the HR management staff be of assistance in providing support for the survivors to a layoff?

10. Why should management be concerned with helping employees retire from their organization successfully?

11. Organizations have worked hard to develop teams as a cohesive and effective framework in the workplace. What can a layoff do to this framework and to the sense of cohesiveness? What could you do to manage these problems?

There is a variety of additional material available on the Web site that accompanies this text. You can access this information by visiting the Web site at **www.prenhall.com/gomez**.

Global Case 6.1 — YOU MANAGE IT!

Retraining! Great Concept, but You Have to Execute

Retraining is a compelling avenue for making labor useful again. Workers who may have lost their jobs can improve or change their skill set so that they are more relevant and marketable in the changing workplace. How well does retraining work in practice? Consider the following story about retraining in China.

In an effort to prevent another deadly bird flu outbreak, the Chinese government bought out more than 1,000 poultry workers. The workers were offered two-month retraining courses in occupational areas such as domestic help and gardening, with an allowance of $4,000 a month. One of the displaced poultry farmers was Ms. Lee. She and her husband had started as poultry wholesalers, and with a few partners had built their operation into a multimillion-dollar business. They sold the business in the late 1990s and then operated a small poultry stall until the government buyout.

Ms. Lee decided to take the domestic-helper training, but was disappointed. She claims that the course covered everything that they were supposed to know about cooking in three mornings. Unfortunately, that wasn't much coverage, and Ms. Lee claims that she and her classmates knew more than the instructors. She makes the same observation about other training topics, such as babysitting and housekeeping. Further, the courses have received a poor response from most of the displaced workers; only 45 people attended the retraining (two of those dropped out). Ms. Lee's opinion is that the government acts as if it had gotten rid of workers through the buyout

program. Ms. Lee and her husband have not been able to find work since their poultry business was closed.

Critical Thinking Questions

1. Why do you think the retraining program did not work out for Ms. Lee?
2. Do you think the government should be responsible for retraining, as in this example from China? Why or why not? What are the alternatives?
3. Do you think the ineffectiveness of the retraining could be solved? How?

Team Exercise

As a team, identify major factors that would determine the effectiveness of a retraining effort. For each factor, describe what should be done to maximize the effectiveness of the retraining. For example, your team might identify the content of the training and how it is delivered to be two important factors. Your next task is to describe what should be done with regard to each factor. For each factor, describe how the content should be determined and how it should be delivered.

Experiential Exercise

The intent of retraining is to improve people's skills so they can remain contributing members of the labor force. Join your team members and identify the major factors that determine the effectiveness of retraining. For each factor in your retraining effectiveness "model," identify assessment criteria. That is, identify measures that could be used to evaluate the effectiveness of the retraining. For example, if content is one of your factors, a measure that could be used to judge this factor might be the relevance and quality of the content as judged by the trainees.

Each team identifies measures to assess the effectiveness of each factor in its model and presents the model and effectiveness measures to the rest of the class. As a class, try to build a comprehensive model. Also as a class, address the issue of why having a model and measures may be useful for retraining efforts.

Source: Adapted with permission from Yeung, W. (2005, June 6). Poultry workers blast retraining. _South China Morning Post,_ 1.

YOU MANAGE IT! Ethics Case 6.2

Employment-at-Will: Fair Policy?

As an employee, you have the right to quit your job, right? The policy of employment-at-will (see Chapter 14) gives a similar right to employers to end the employment relationship. The rationale behind employment-at-will is that if an employee can quit at any time and for any reason, so, too, should an employer be free to end the employment relationship at any time and for any reason. A practical implication of this common-law doctrine is that employees can't be sued by employers for leaving, even if their departure disrupts the workplace. Likewise, the employer cannot be held responsible for terminating the employee.

However, there are exceptions to the employment-at-will policy. For example, an employer cannot terminate an employee for refusing to engage in an illegal act or because of the employee's race or gender. Another limitation is that employment-at-will applies only when there is not some sort of agreement, understanding, or contract between the employer and employee about the duration or permanence of employment. For example, an employee who has an employment contract can sue the employer for breach of contract if termination violates the terms of the contract. Likewise, a terminated employee may be able to convince the court that he or she wasn't an at-will employee because of an implied contract formed by statements in the employee handbook. For example, a handbook might offer the positive and supportive statement that as long as you perform, you have a job with the organization. This sort of statement could be viewed as implying permanence of the employment relationship, at least as long as performance is satisfactory.

Critical Thinking Questions

1. Do you agree with the concept of employment-at-will? Why or why not?

2. If you had a choice, would you rather be employed as an at-will employee or have some employment protection? Why?

3. Most workers are not covered by explicit or implicit contracts and are at-will employees. Thus, an employer should be able to terminate these workers at any time and for any reason. A practical reality, however, is that a charge of discrimination as a basis for a termination needs to be defended against. How can an employer defend against a charge that a termination decision was based on discrimination? Does this limit an employer's right to fire-at-will? Explain.

Team Exercise

Exceptions to employment-at-will vary by state. As a team, choose a state and use the Internet to research the exceptions to employment-at-will there. Report your findings to the class. As a class, identify which states seem most and least employer-friendly with regard to these exceptions.

Experiential Exercise

Two small groups will be formed to represent pro and con employment-at-will positions. The two groups should debate the merits of the employment-at-will policy. Each team has five minutes to make its major statement in support or against the policy. Issues that might be considered include ethical treatment, balance of power between employer and employee, and cost of litigation. Each team has an opportunity to rebut and rejoin. The instructor mediates the debate. The major issues and positions will be summarized in the class following the debate.

Sources: Grossenbacher, K. (2005, April 11). What happened to "at will"? _Podium, 26,_ 26; Kight, D. (2005, April 8). Understanding employment-at-will. _Kansas City Daily Record._

Customer-Driven HR Case 6.3 YOU MANAGE IT!

Recognizing the Importance of Workers: Layoffs as a Last Resort

Workers' salaries are a big expense in most organizations. Cutting jobs would seem to be a fiscally rational way to quickly and significantly reduce expenses. Layoffs may appear to make sense in the short term and on paper but not really in the long term. Consider the negative fallout associated with a major layoff of 8,500 workers at Cisco Systems Inc. Following this cost-cutting measure, worker productivity dropped and resulted in sales per employee of $470,000 in October 2001, down from $710,000 a year previously. Some organizations are beginning to realize that layoffs can begin a negative spiral and can bring tremendous costs to the organization, such as lowering morale, productivity, and loyalty, and the possibility of sabotage and loss of customers. These companies are searching for creative but effective alternatives to downsizing. As FedEx spokesperson, Gree Rossiter, has stated, people are what differentiate a company and are simply too important to put at risk.

As an alternative to layoffs, some companies are seeking other ways to cut costs while retaining their most important asset—their employees. For example, job sharing, shortened workweeks, and pay cuts are among the strategies that can be used to stave off or, hopefully, eliminate the need for layoffs. For example, Acxiom Corp., a database and information management company with over 5,000 employees, utilized pay cuts to avoid the need for layoffs. As an initial cost-cutting move, Acxiom imposed a mandatory 5 percent cut in pay for all employees earning less than $25,000. In exchange, employees were given stock options in the amount of salary that had been forfeited. A voluntary pay cut was offered shortly thereafter in which workers could forfeit up to an additional 15 percent of salary in exchange for double that amount in stock options. More than one-third of employees volunteered for the additional pay cut. Axciom estimates that the mandatory and voluntary pay cuts allowed the company to lay off half the number of employees it otherwise would have had to lay off. Axciom did end up laying off 400 workers—7 percent of its workforce. The executive in charge of organizational effectiveness for Axciom, Jeff Standridge, stated, "The intangible benefit is that 85 percent of our employee population became stockholders in the company. They have skin in the game, and now the company's future can be determined by people with a greater stake in the company." When Acxiom expands employment again, it will give preference to the laid-off workers, avoiding some of the costs associated with recruiting and training new employees.

Accenture Ltd., a global information technology consulting company, took a different approach to delay the need for layoffs. The company offered a one-year sabbatical program in which employees would receive 20 percent of their salaries and all of their benefits. Employees can do anything while on a sabbatical—except work for a competitor. The sabbatical program was popular in the United States with 2,200 signing up, filling up all places in the U.S. program so it is now closed.

Accenture has extended the program to employees in the United Kingdom, Sweden, Germany, and Japan. The primary goal of the program is trimming short-term costs while keeping access to talented employees. Unfortunately, Accenture did still have to resort to layoffs, affecting 2,500 employees.

Other companies, such as FedEx and Lincoln Electric, have firm philosophies of no layoffs. Someday layoffs may be needed at these companies, but it would occur only as a last resort. The intent of these companies is to create a deeply loyal and productive workforce.

Critical Thinking Questions

1. In addition to the examples just mentioned, what else could organizations do to avoid or limit layoffs? Generate possibilities by brainstorming, referring to this chapter, as well as by finding additional company examples.
2. Prioritize your alternatives to layoffs. What would you do first, second, and so on?
3. Do you think a sequential strategy could be an effective management tool? Explain.

Team Exercise

With your teammates, discuss steps you would take to avoid layoffs. Putting yourself in the position of managers in an organization, identify how you would get information about these steps out to employees. For example, would you use meetings, newsletters, and so on? Share your alternatives to layoffs and your announcement approach(es) with the rest of the class.

As described in this case, some companies are convinced that layoffs should be avoided. However, layoffs can certainly reduce short-term costs and can be positively responded to by the stock market for publicly traded firms. On the other hand, pursuing alternatives to layoffs is not without its risks. For example, some bitterness was experienced by Acxiom after it laid off workers. How would you, for example, like to take a pay cut and then lose your job?

Experiential Exercise

Form two teams to represent pro- and anti-layoff positions. The two teams will conduct a debate over whether an organization should take steps to avoid layoffs. The pro-layoff team should identify benefits of maintaining unilateral privilege to decide to lay off employees and costs that might be incurred by engaging in alternatives. The anti-layoff team should identify costs associated with layoffs and benefits of alternatives to layoffs. After preparation, each team will have five to seven minutes to present their main arguments. The teams will each have the opportunity to rebut and rejoin. The instructor will moderate the debate and assist the class in identifying major issues and conclusions.

Source: Adapted from King, J. (2002). Working alternatives to job cuts. *Computerworld, 36,* 24–25.

YOU MANAGE IT! # Emerging Trends Case 6.4

Turnover Redux

Turnover can have a crippling effect on organizations. For example, the grocery retailer, Kroger, calculates that its employee turnover rate cost the organization $80 million a couple of years ago. As with other companies, Kroger recognized the cost that turnover can exact and took steps to try to control it. To help reduce its turnover rate, Kroger started a pilot study aimed at hiring workers who would have a lower propensity to quit. Kroger set up kiosks in selected stores where job seekers could fill out an application form electronically. Application could also be made online via the Internet. The pattern of responses to questions on the application was analyzed with a computer model designed to predict the likely retention rate of each applicant. For example, applicants were asked to provide the last name of their supervisor from two jobs ago. The assumption was that if someone can accurately provide this information, he or she is more likely to have stronger ties in the workplace and stay in the job longer. The application system also performed other screening tasks, including background checks.

Kroger has recently committed to expanding the use of this application system to all of its divisions. Although Kroger has not disclosed financial specifics, a return-on-investment within six months for its improved process is a reasonable estimate.

Critical Thinking Questions

1. Kroger's emphasis on the application process focuses on characteristics of workers as an important causal factor in turnover. Do you think that its approach will be effective? Why or why not?
2. Are there system characteristics that might be important determinants of retention and turnover? In other words, what factors about jobs or organizations might be important in determining whether someone decides to quit or stay with an employer?
3. For the system factors you identified in question 2, what would you recommend Kroger do about each? Are there some factors that may be difficult or impossible to change?

Team Exercise

Lowering turnover requires understanding the causes of turnover and then doing something about them. The following simple model can guide your efforts in identifying and managing factors underlying turnover decisions.

As depicted in the model, there are worker characteristics that may be directly related to turnover. Consider the Kroger example. There may be some types of people who just tend to stay longer in a job than others. Likewise, there may be characteristics of the job and organization that are directly linked to turnover decisions. However, in addition to these direct effects, employee characteristics and system characteristics can jointly influence turnover decisions through their degree of fit with each other.

a. As a team, identify worker characteristics and system characteristics that may influence turnover through their degree of fit (or misfit). In addition, identify worker characteristics and system characteristics that may have a direct influence on turnover decisions.
b. Design survey questions or interview questions that could be used to measure each of the characteristics you listed in the preceding question. Determine how you could measure the turnover probability part of the model. (Hint: Consider asking people to judge the extent to which they would like to quit their current job or ask them to consider a time when they did quit a job.)

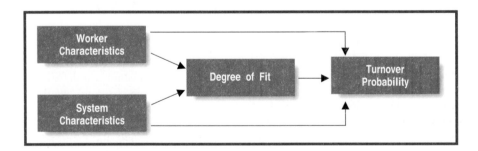

c. How could Kroger use the model and the survey or interview items you generated? Specifically, generate a systematic process for the company to follow to identify causal factors of turnover at Kroger. (Hint: Consider using exit interviews and surveys.) Share your proposed process with the rest of the class.

Experiential Exercise

a. If you have access to an organization, try out your survey or interview items. Consider asking family members, friends, and fellow students to complete the survey or interview. How does your model hold up? For example, did turnover happen or does it seem more likely to occur when worker characteristics and system characteristics are present that you thought should be related to turnover? Does turnover appear more likely when there is poor fit among the worker characteristics and system characteristics? Share your findings with the rest of the class.

b. Kroger seems to be taking the position that worker characteristics may be the most important factor affecting turnover. Divide your team into worker proponents and system proponents and debate which factor is more important and has

a greater impact on turnover decisions. Which would appear to be more easily managed? Is there an advantage to including both factors, as in the model depicted? Is there an advantage to including the factor of fit?

Source: Adapted from Perotta, P. (2002). Kroger is piloting an electronic application. *Supermarket News, 50,* 17+; Business Wire. (2005, February 14). Unicrue identifies grocery industry as leader in workforce selection systems adoption; Business Wire. (2005, May 31). Kroger selects Unicrue as enterprise standard: *Fortune* 21 company to deploy Unicrue's workforce selection and optimization solution across an 20 banners.

Customer-Driven HR Case 6.5 | YOU MANAGE IT!

Layoff and Security

A surprising number of Americans have lost their jobs. In October 2001, 415,000 people were laid off, the largest monthly total in four years. How were those people treated? Surveys indicate that the majority of people are dissatisfied with how their layoff was conducted.[a] This dissatisfaction goes beyond losing a job. It concerns how the layoff was handled. People who have been laid off usually describe it as being made to feel like a criminal.[b] It is little wonder that such feelings occur when standard business practice seems to be to treat laid-off employees as threats. The common layoff procedure involves the following:[c]

1. A brief meeting is held with the employee to tell her of the elimination of her job and to inform her about the existence of benefits and severance, if any. In some companies this meeting is conducted by an HR representative who is not familiar to the worker. In effect, the worker is terminated by a stranger. Simultaneously, the employee's access to the company computer system and e-mail is denied.

2. Immediately upon concluding this brief meeting, the employee is escorted through cleaning out her work space and walked to the door.

The purpose is security. Do some people steal data and sabotage equipment after being terminated? Of course, some do! But the probability isn't high. For example, the director of global staffing at National Semiconductor Corporation estimates that employees informed of being laid off who might pose a security threat are one out of 300 to 400 employees.[d]

Critical Thinking Questions

1. What message is being sent to workers being laid off by following the standard procedure just described?

2. What effect would this standard approach to laying off workers have on the retained workers? A recent survey of such layoff survivors found over 25 percent saying their layoff was handled poorly and nearly 50 percent said they found out about the layoff through informal rumors rather than through official communication.[e] These conditions can make the organization vulnerable to retaliatory theft and sabotage from layoff survivors. Explain how the process by which a layoff is conducted could have these negative effects.

3. It has been recommended that employers should take a more enlightened and customer-oriented approach to laying off workers. For example, it has been suggested that employers establish electronic alumni networks. These networks would allow former workers to keep in touch with the company and with each other.[f] Furthermore, the network could provide a source for new hires that would have limited recruiting and training costs.

   Identify characteristics of a more customer-oriented approach to conducting layoffs. What steps would be involved? Identify major guidelines and characteristics of your proposed process.

Team Exercise

Telling someone his position is being eliminated can be a difficult and emotionally draining task. Role-play laying off a worker with one member of your team taking the role of manager and another member taking the role of worker. Other team members should observe the interaction and provide feedback to the person playing the manager as to how the interaction went and how it might be improved. Conduct the role-play using the standard approach and again using the customer-oriented approach you developed in item 3 of the critical thinking questions. Which approach seemed to work more effectively?

Experiential Exercise

Balancing security concerns with customer-oriented treatment can be difficult. Divide your team in half and debate the advantages and disadvantages of the security-driven standard approach to conducting layoffs with your customer-oriented approach. Share the key advantages and disadvantages with the rest of the class.

Sources: [a]*HR Focus.* (2002, January). If you must lay off workers: Consider the long-term consequences, 79, 8; [b]Jorgenson, B. (2002). Being shown the door: Management must weigh the pros and cons of this touchy layoff procedure. *Electronic Business, 28,* 38; [c]Doler, K. (2002). Layoffs have become a nasty business. *Electronic Business, 28,* 6; [d]Jorgenson (2002); [e]*Security Director's Report.* (2002). Is your corporate climate breeding future thieves? January Newsletter, 6–7, 10–11; [f]*Human Resource Management Report.* (2002). What's your department's policy on rehiring laid-off employees? February Newsletter, *1,* 13–14.

Challenges

After reading this chapter, you should be able to deal more effectively with the following challenges:

1 **Explain** why performance appraisal is important and describe its components.

2 **Discuss** the advantages and disadvantages of different performance rating systems.

3 **Manage** the impact of rating errors and bias on performance appraisals.

4 **Discuss** the potential role of emotion in performance appraisal and how to manage its impact.

5 **Identify** the major legal requirements for appraisal.

6 **Use** performance appraisals to manage and develop employee performance.

The time for the annual performance appraisal was fast approaching at Milo Engineering, and the head of one of the departments was not looking forward to it. All employees submitted an annual report listing their individual activities and accomplishments. The reports were then distributed to all 22 employees in the department. In this way, each employee rated all department employees (except for themselves) on multiple dimensions of job performance.

The department head used the peer ratings as advisory input into his evaluation, but he usually didn't vary that much from the average of the peer judgments. This year, Milo's CEO informed managers that tight budgetary conditions meant there was no money available for merit raises. The department head had actually been relieved to get this bad news. Why? The lack of merit pay meant that the performance ratings wouldn't be that important, and people should not be concerned about them. He didn't realize how wrong he was!

Employees were particularly bitter because the ratings would not result in salary changes. Further, at least one person violated the rules and rated herself quite favorably. In addition, that person and another one gave everyone in the department poor ratings, presumably to make themselves look better by comparison. The department head eliminated the ratings of these two employees. Further, he decided that because merit money was not at stake, instead of having the usual face-to-face meetings, he would simply provide employees a written summary of how peers judged their performance.

After the evaluations were distributed, people in the department were upset. Some people even filed formal grievances over their appraisals, arguing that their peers had evaluated them unfairly and the department head had done nothing to rectify the bias.

The department head concluded that performance appraisal is a losing proposition: Even when it does not matter, people get angry and waste your time with complaints and grievances.

THE MANAGERIAL PERSPECTIVE

The situation at Milo Engineering (a real organization given a fictitious name) illustrates common problems with performance appraisal—the process of assessing employee performance and diagnosing and improving performance problems. Maintaining and improving your performance and the performance of other people in the organization will be an important part of your role as a manager. To conduct this process, you may rely on appraisal forms and systems that are often designed by HR personnel. Although these forms and systems are key elements of the appraisal process, they are only a starting point.

To appraise effectively, you must also spot performance problems, provide constructive feedback, and take action to improve performance. Measuring and managing performance are two of the most difficult issues a manager faces. However, managers must measure performance and provide meaningful feedback to employees if employees are to improve—even if salary dollars are not at stake. We all need, want, and deserve feedback regarding how we are doing in the workplace.

Our first goal in this chapter is to acquaint you with the foundation, design, and implementation of performance measurement systems. Our second is to describe the principles of effective performance management.

What Is Performance Appraisal?

Performance appraisal
The identification, measurement, and management of human performance in organizations.

Performance appraisal, as shown in Figure 7.1, includes the *identification*, *measurement*, and *management* of human performance in organizations.[1]

- **Identification** means determining what areas of work the manager should be examining when measuring performance. Rational and legally defensible identification requires a measurement system based on job analysis, which we explored in Chapter 2. The appraisal system, then, should focus on performance that affects organizational success rather than performance-irrelevant characteristics such as race, age, or sex.
- **Measurement**, the centerpiece of the appraisal system, entails making managerial judgments of how "good" or "bad" employee performance was. Good performance measurement must be consistent throughout the organization. That is, all managers in the organization must maintain comparable rating standards.[2]
- **Management** is the overriding goal of any appraisal system. Appraisal should be more than a past-oriented activity that criticizes or praises workers for their performance in the preceding year. Rather, appraisal must take a future-oriented view of what workers can do to achieve their potential in the organization. This means that managers must provide workers with feedback and coach them to higher levels of performance.

The Uses of Performance Appraisal

Organizations usually conduct appraisals for *administrative* and/or *developmental* purposes.[3] Performance appraisals are used administratively whenever they are the basis for a decision about the employee's work conditions, including promotions, termination, and rewards. Developmental uses of appraisal, which are geared toward improving employees' performance and strengthening their job skills, include providing feedback, counseling employees on effective work behaviors, and offering them training and other learning opportunities.

A recent survey found that over half of senior managers believe that performance appraisal is strategic to their business.[4] If done effectively, performance appraisal can be the key to developing employees and improving their performance. In addition, it provides the criteria against which selection systems are validated and is the typical basis on which personnel decisions, such as terminations, are legally justified. Further, performance appraisal makes the strategy of an organization real. For example, performance measures that assess courtesy and care can make a stated competitive strategy based on customer service very tangible to employees.

Still, many companies struggle to realize the potential in their performance appraisal system. If managers aren't behind the system and see its value, it is little wonder if workers also don't see the value in it. A recent survey found that only 3 of 10 U.S. workers think their performance appraisal process actually improves performance.[5] Many companies conduct performance reviews more than just once a year. In 1997, survey results estimated that 78 percent of organizations conducted performance appraisal once a year.[6] By 2003, that percentage had dropped to 50 percent, and 40 percent of organizations reported that they were beginning to do performance reviews at least twice a year. Merck & Co., Inc., the pharmaceutical firm, has shifted to semiannual performance reviews and employees report getting more and better feedback and more opportunity to improve. Although more frequent formal appraisal can be positive, the practical reality is that informal appraisal, including feedback and discussion with workers, should occur on a continuous basis.

If appraisal is not done well—if, for instance, performance is not measured accurately and feedback is poorly given—the costs of conducting the appraisal may exceed its potential benefits.[7] It makes good business sense to engage in a practice only if the benefits exceed the cost. Some people take the position that performance appraisal should not be done at all.[8] From this perspective, the practice of performance appraisal is staunchly opposed as a hopelessly flawed and demeaning method of trying to improve performance.[9] Thus, performance appraisal should be eliminated as a practice in organizations because of the problems and errors in evaluating performance.[10] The position against doing performance appraisal is based mainly on the quality philosophy[11] that performance is mainly due to the system and that any performance differences among workers are random.

Although there is selected opposition, the vast majority of organizations conduct performance appraisal. Most organizations recognize employees as an important and nonrandom influence on performance. (In order for selection systems to be found valid, employees must have a nontrivial and consistent influence on performance.) However, in order to maintain and improve their performance, employees need assessment and feedback.

Whether the performance is in the workplace, in the classroom, or on a playing field, you have to gauge how you are performing to learn how to improve and, later, to assess whether you have improved. Figure 7.2 lists several reasons, from both the employer's and employee's perspectives, why appraisal is valuable despite the criticisms that have been leveled against it.

In the next two sections, we explain the issues and challenges involved in the first two steps of performance appraisal: identification and measurement. We conclude the chapter by discussing how managers can use the results of appraisal to improve employee performance.

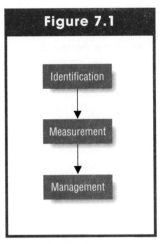

Figure 7.1

Identification

Measurement

Management

A Model of Performance Appraisal

Identifying Performance Dimensions

The first step in the performance appraisal process (see Figure 7.1) is identifying what is to be measured. Consider the following example:

As part of her job as team manager, Nancy has to allocate raises based on performance. She decides to take a participative approach to deciding which aspects, or **dimensions**, determine effective job performance. In a meeting she and her team start generating dimensions of performance. One of the first suggested is the *quality of work* done. However, Nancy realized that some

Dimension
An aspect of performance that determines effective job performance.

Figure 7.2

Employer Perspective

1. Despite imperfect measurement techniques, individual differences in performance can make a difference to company performance.
2. Documentation of performance appraisal and feedback may be needed for legal defense.
3. Appraisal provides a rational basis for constructing a bonus or merit system.
4. Appraisal dimensions and standards can help to implement strategic goals and clarify performance expectations.
5. Providing individual feedback is part of the performance management process.
6. Despite the traditional focus on the individual, appraisal criteria can include teamwork and the teams can be the focus of the appraisal.

Employee Perspective

1. Performance feedback is needed and desired.
2. Improvement in performance requires assessment.
3. Fairness requires that differences in performance levels across workers be measured and have an effect on outcomes.
4. Assessment and recognition of performance levels can motivate workers to improve their performance.

Source: Cardy, R. L., and Carson K. P. (1996). Total quality and the abandonment of performance appraisal: Taking a good thing too far? *Journal of Quality Management*, 193–206.

The Benefits of Performance Appraisal

of the workers she supervises took three times longer than others to complete assignments, so she offered *quantity of work performed* as another dimension. One worker volunteered that how well someone interacted with peers and "customers" inside the organization was pretty important. The team added *interpersonal effectiveness* as another performance dimension.

Raising and considering additional work dimensions might continue until Nancy and her team have identified perhaps six or eight dimensions they think adequately capture performance. The team might also decide to make the dimensions more specific by adding definitions of each and behavioral descriptions of performance levels.

As you have probably realized, the process of identifying performance dimensions is very much like the job-analysis process described in Chapter 2. In fact, job analysis is the mechanism by which performance dimensions should be identified.

Management experts point out that what is measured should be directly tied to what the business is trying to achieve,[12] because measurement should be viewed as a management tool, not a measurement exercise. Many organizations are now identifying performance dimensions based on their strategic objectives. For example, Southwest Washington Medical Center links corporate strategic goals to employee performance goals. This approach makes sure that everyone is working together toward common goals.[13]

An increasingly popular approach to identifying performance dimensions focuses on **competencies**, the observable characteristics people bring with them in order to perform the job successfully.[14] Defining competencies as underlying and unseen characteristics leads to the same difficulties associated with defining and measuring performance as personality traits, as discussed in the following section. The set of competencies associated with a job is often referred to as a **competency model**. An example of a competency model is presented in the Manager's Notebook, "Competencies for Beginning Legal Eagles."

Competencies
Characteristics associated with successful performance.

Competency model
Set of competencies associated with a job.

MANAGER'S NOTEBOOK

Emerging Trends

Competencies for Beginning Legal Eagles

Common competencies that new associates need to exhibit in order to succeed underlie the dynamic work environment of a law firm. Figure 7.3 shows the competencies identified by a law firm as important to the success of new associates. Each abstract, or conceptual, description is followed by behavioral examples illustrating poor and good levels of performance. The law firm is

Figure 7.3

Competency	Behavioral Illustration
Knowledge: Associate has solid grasp of basic legal concepts. Demonstrates intellectual curiosity and commitment to understand. Takes ownership of assignments.	+ Invests time to learn relevant law + Asks informed questions − Counts on others to know law
Skills and Capabilities: Associate demonstrates strong basic skills in written and oral communication, analysis, organization, and problem solving. Seeks out training and work opportunities to improve skills.	+ Produces written work that a partner can send to a client or to the court with limited editing or re-writing − Produces written work that a partner must substantially re-write
Work Management: Associate demonstrates strong work management skills, including time management and timely delivery of product.	+ Submits timesheets daily − Does not deliver work when promised
Character and Commitment: Associate demonstrates ethical integrity and sound judgment. + refers to behaviors indicating strengths − refers to behaviors indicating development needs	+ Protects the confidentiality of client and firm information − Careless with client and firm information

Source: Adapted with permission from Vaaler, B. (2005). Codifying competencies. *Law Firm Partnership & Benefits Report, 10,* 1.

using the competency framework for performance appraisal and also to drive recruitment, training, and promotion. It has already made performance standards clearer to everyone in the organization.

Measuring Performance

To measure employee performance, managers can assign it a number or a label such as "excellent," "good," "average," or "poor."[15]

It is often difficult to quantify performance dimensions. For example, "creativity" may be an important part of the advertising copywriter's job. But how exactly can we measure it—by the number of ads written per year, by the number of ads that win industry awards, or by some other criterion? These are some of the issues that managers face when trying to evaluate an employee's performance.

Measurement Tools

Today managers have a wide array of appraisal formats from which to choose. Here we discuss the formats that are most common and legally defensible. These can be classified in two ways: (1) by the type of judgment that is required (relative or absolute), and (2) by the focus of the measure (trait, behavior, or outcome).

Relative and Absolute Judgments

Appraisal systems based on **relative judgment** ask supervisors to compare an employee's performance to the performance of other employees doing the same job. Providing a *rank order* of workers from best to worst is an example of a relative approach. Another type of relative judgment format classifies employees into groups, such as top third, middle third, and lowest third.

Relative judgment
An appraisal format that asks supervisors to compare an employee's performance to the performance of other employees doing the same job.

Relative rating systems have the advantage of forcing supervisors to differentiate among their workers. Without such a system, many supervisors are inclined to rate everyone the same, which destroys the appraisal system's value. For example, one study that examined the distribution of performance ratings for more than 7,000 managerial and professional employees in two large manufacturing firms found that 95 percent of employees were crowded into just two rating categories.

Most HR specialists believe the disadvantages of relative rating systems outweigh their advantages, however.[16] First, relative judgments (such as ranks) do not make clear how great or small the differences between employees are. Second, such systems do not provide any absolute information, so managers cannot determine how good or poor employees at the extreme rankings are. For example, relative ratings do not reveal whether the top-rated worker in one work team is better or worse than an average worker in another work team. This problem is illustrated in Figure 7.4. Marcos, Jill, and Frank are the highest-ranked performers in their respective work teams. However, Jill, Frank, and Julien are actually the best overall performers.

Third, relative ranking systems force managers to identify differences among workers where none may truly exist.[17] This can cause conflict among workers if and when ratings are disclosed. Finally, relative systems typically require assessment of overall performance. The "big picture" nature of relative ratings makes performance feedback ambiguous and of questionable value to workers who would benefit from specific information about the various dimensions of their performance. For all these reasons, there is a growing trend to use relative rating systems only when there is an administrative need (for example, to make decisions regarding promotions, pay raises, or termination).[18]

Absolute judgment
An appraisal format that asks supervisors to make judgments about an employee's performance based solely on performance standards.

Unlike relative judgment appraisal formats, **absolute judgment** formats ask supervisors to make judgments about an employee's performance based solely on performance standards. Comparisons to the performance of co-workers are not made. Typically, the dimensions of performance deemed relevant for the job are listed on the rating form, and the manager is asked to rate the employee on each dimension. An example of an absolute judgment rating scale is shown in Figure 7.5.

Theoretically, absolute formats allow employees from different work groups, rated by different managers, to be compared to one another. If all employees are excellent workers, they all can receive excellent ratings. Also, because ratings are made on separate dimensions of performance, the feedback to the employee can be more specific and helpful.

Although often preferable to relative systems, absolute rating systems have their drawbacks. One is that all workers in a group can receive the same evaluation if the supervisor is reluctant to differentiate among workers. Another is that different supervisors can have markedly different evaluation standards. For example, a rating of 6 from an "easy" supervisor may actually be lower in value than a rating of 4 from a "tough" supervisor. But when the organization is handing out promotions or pay increases, the worker who received the 6 rating would be rewarded.

Nonetheless, absolute systems do have one distinct advantage: They avoid creating conflict among workers. This, plus the fact that relative systems are generally harder to defend when legal issues arise, may account for the prevalence of absolute systems in U.S. organizations.

It is interesting to note, though, that most people *do* make comparative judgments among both people and things. A political candidate is better or worse than opponents, not good or bad in an absolute sense. If comparative judgments are the common and natural way of making

Rankings and Performance Levels Across Work Teams

Figure 7.4			
Actual	**Ranked Work**	**Ranked Work**	**Ranked Work**
10 (High)		Jill (1)	Frank (1)
9			Julien (2)
8		Tom (2)	Lisa (3)
7	Marcos (1)	Sue (3)	
6	Uma (2)		
5			
4	Joyce (3)	Greg (4)	
3	Bill (4)	Ken (5)	Jolie (4)
2	Richard (5)		Steve (5)
1 (Low)			

Figure 7.5

Sample of Absolute Judgment Rating Scale

PERFORMANCE REVIEW

Three-month (H&S) ☐ Annual (H-Only) ☐
Six-month (H&S) ☐ Special (H&S) ☐
H = Hourly S = Salaried

Employee Name

Social Security # Hourly ☐ Salaried ☐

For probationary employee review: Do you recommend that this employee be retained? Yes ☐ No ☐

Classification/Classification Hire Date

Review period: From__________ To__________

Department/Division

For each applicable performance area, mark the box that most closely reflects the employee's performance.
1 = unacceptable 2 = needs improvement 3 = satisfactory 4 = above average 5 = outstanding

PERFORMANCE AREA	1	2	3	4	5
Ability to make job-related decisions					
Accepts change					
Accepts direction					
Accepts responsibility					
Attendance					
Attitude					
Compliance with rules					
Cooperation					
Cost consciousness					
Dependability					

PERFORMANCE AREA	1	2	3	4	5
Effective under stress					
Initiative					
Knowledge of work					
Leadership					
Operation and care of equipment					
Planning and organizing					
Quality of work					
Quantity of acceptable work					
Safety practices					
SUPERVISOR'S OVERALL APPRAISAL					

For overall appraisals at the 1 or 2 level: Is the employee to remain or be placed on probationary status? Yes ☐ No ☐
If yes, what is the approximate date of next performance review? __________

JOB STRENGTHS AND SUPERIOR PERFORMANCE INCIDENTS:

AREAS FOR IMPROVEMENT:

PROGRESS ACHIEVED IN ATTAINING PREVIOUSLY SET GOALS:

SPECIFIC OBJECTIVES TO BE UNDERTAKEN PRIOR TO NEXT REVIEW FOR IMPROVED WORK PERFORMANCE:

SUPERVISOR COMMENTS:

EMPLOYEE COMMENTS:

Use separate sheet, if necessary, for additional comments by supervisor or employee. Please note on form if separate sheet is used.
Signing a review does not indicate agreement, only acknowledgment of being reviewed.

Employee's Signature Date Rating Supervisor's Signature Social Security # Date

Second Level Supervisor's Signature Date Department Head's Signature Date

judgments, it may be that supervisors can be more accurate when making relative rather than absolute ratings.[19]

Trait, Behavioral, and Outcome Data

In addition to relative and absolute judgments, performance measurement systems can be classified by the type of performance data on which they focus: trait data, behavioral data, or outcome data.

Trait appraisal instrument An appraisal tool that asks a supervisor to make judgments about worker characteristics that tend to be consistent and enduring.

Trait appraisal instruments ask the supervisor to make judgments about *traits,* worker characteristics that tend to be consistent and enduring. Figure 7.6 presents four traits that are typically found on trait-based rating scales: decisiveness, reliability, energy, and loyalty. Although a number of organizations use trait ratings, trait ratings have been criticized for being too ambiguous[20] and for leaving the door open for conscious or unconscious bias. In addition, because of their ambiguous nature trait ratings are less defensible in court than other types of ratings.[21] Definitions of reliability can differ dramatically across supervisors, for example, and the courts seem to be sensitive to the "slippery" nature of traits as criteria. Another difficulty

Sample Trait Scales

Figure 7.6

Rate each worker using the scales below.

Decisiveness

1	2	3	4	5	6	7
Very low			Moderate			Very high

Reliability

1	2	3	4	5	6	7
Very low			Moderate			Very high

Energy

1	2	3	4	5	6	7
Very low			Moderate			Very high

Loyalty

1	2	3	4	5	6	7
Very low			Moderate			Very high

with trait formats is choosing from among the hundreds of possible traits those that should be included in the rating instrument.

Assessment of traits also focuses on the *person* rather than on the *performance,* which can make employees defensive. From the limited research done in this area, it seems that this type of person-focused approach is not conducive to performance development. Measurement approaches that focus more directly on performance, either by evaluating behaviors or results, are generally more acceptable to workers and more effective as development tools.

Despite these problems, trait ratings may be more effective than many believe. After all, traits are simply a shorthand way of describing a person's behavioral tendencies. Thus, trait judgments can be based on behavior, which would make them less error laden than critics suggest. We routinely make trait judgments about others, and it is rare for someone to be described other than through his or her traits. If you doubt this, perform the following experiment:

Let's say a classmate has asked you to describe one of your professors. Also imagine that this professor does magic tricks to maintain class interest and to accentuate lecture points, sparks lively discussion, and is known for wearing outrageous costumes. Would your initial response to your classmate consist of a list of behaviors that you've seen the professor engage in? Not likely! You'd more likely use the words "lively," "wild," "entertaining," "engaging," "crazy"—all trait terms. You might follow up this assessment with some behavioral description, but probably more for the purpose of enjoyable storytelling than anything else. The point is that we routinely make trait judgments about others; they are a powerful way of describing people. Because we do it all the time, we also may be quite good at it. Nonetheless, because traits focus on the person rather than performance many experts do not recommend using trait judgments for feedback purposes. Also, as mentioned earlier, trait judgments can be ambiguous, so they can pose legal defensibility concerns.

Behavioral appraisal instrument

An appraisal tool that asks managers to assess a worker's behaviors.

Behavioral appraisal instruments focus on assessing a worker's behaviors. That is, instead of ranking leadership ability (a trait), the rater is asked to assess whether an employee exhibits certain behaviors (for example, works well with coworkers, comes to meetings on time). In one type of behavioral instrument, Behavioral Observation Scales, supervisors record how frequently the various behaviors listed on the form occurred.[22] However, ratings assessing the value rather than the *frequency* of specific behaviors are more commonly used in organizations. Probably the best-known behavioral scale is the Behaviorally Anchored Rating Scale (BARS). Figure 7.7 is an example of a BARS scale used to rate the effectiveness with which a department manager supervises his or her sales personnel. Behaviorally based rating scales are developed with the *critical incident technique.* We describe the critical incident technique in the Appendix to this chapter.

The main advantage of a behavioral approach is that the performance standards are concrete. Unlike traits, which can have many facets, behaviors across the range of a dimension are included directly on the behavioral scale. This concreteness makes BARS and other behavioral

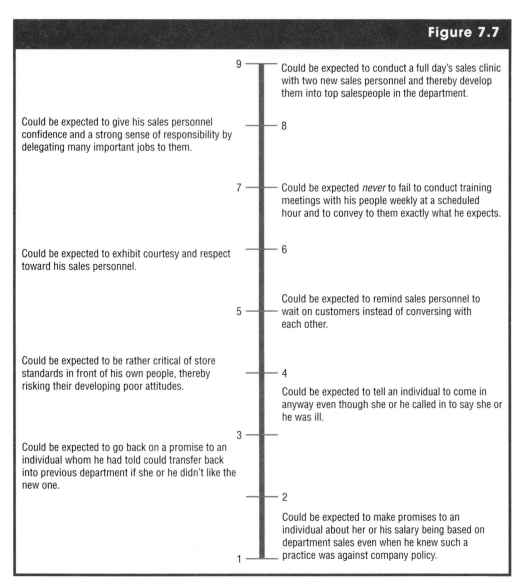

Figure 7.7

9 — Could be expected to conduct a full day's sales clinic with two new sales personnel and thereby develop them into top salespeople in the department.

Could be expected to give his sales personnel confidence and a strong sense of responsibility by delegating many important jobs to them. — 8

7 — Could be expected *never* to fail to conduct training meetings with his people weekly at a scheduled hour and to convey to them exactly what he expects.

— 6

Could be expected to exhibit courtesy and respect toward his sales personnel.

5 — Could be expected to remind sales personnel to wait on customers instead of conversing with each other.

Could be expected to be rather critical of store standards in front of his own people, thereby risking their developing poor attitudes. — 4

Could be expected to tell an individual to come in anyway even though she or he called in to say she or he was ill.

3 —

Could be expected to go back on a promise to an individual whom he had told could transfer back into previous department if she or he didn't like the new one.

— 2

Could be expected to make promises to an individual about her or his salary being based on department sales even when he knew such a practice was against company policy.

1 —

Sample BARS Used to Rate a Sales Manager

Source: Campbell, J. P., Dunnette, M. D., Arvey, R. D., and Hellervik, L. V. (1973). The development and evaluation of behaviorally based rating scales. *Journal of Applied Psychology,* 15–22. © 1973 by the American Psychological Association. Reprinted with permission.

instruments more legally defensible than trait scales, which often use such hard-to-define adjectives as "poor" and "excellent." Behavioral scales also provide employees with specific examples of the types of behaviors to engage in (and to avoid) if they want to do well in the organization, and they encourage supervisors to be specific in their performance feedback. Finally, both workers and supervisors can be involved in the process of generating behavioral scales.[23] This is likely to increase understanding and acceptance of the appraisal system.

Behavioral systems are not without disadvantages, however. Developing them can be very time consuming, easily taking several months. Another disadvantage is their specificity. The points, or *anchors,* on behavioral scales are clear and concrete, but they are only examples of behavior a worker *may* exhibit. Employees may never exhibit some of these anchor behaviors, which can cause difficulty for supervisors at appraisal time. Also, significant organizational changes can invalidate behavioral scales. For example, computerization of operations can dramatically alter the behaviors that workers must exhibit to be successful. Thus, the behaviors painstakingly developed for the appraisal system could become useless or, worse, operate as a drag on organizational change and worker adaptation.

Another potential difficulty is that supervisors may merely translate their trait impressions into behavioral judgments. Thus, although a behavioral approach seems less ambiguous, it may require mental gymnastics that can introduce error into ratings. No research has directly examined this issue, but one study has found a preference among both supervisors and workers for a trait-based system over a behaviorally based system.[24] The "unnaturalness" of a behavioral orientation may underlie this preference. However, it is a valuable skill that can easily be learned.

Outcome appraisal instruments
An appraisal tool that asks managers to assess the results achieved by workers.

Management by objectives (MBO)
A goal-directed approach to performance appraisal in which workers and their supervisors set goals together for the upcoming evaluation period.

Outcome appraisal instruments ask managers to assess the results achieved by workers, such as total sales or number of products produced. The most prevalent outcome approaches are **management by objectives (MBO)**[25] and naturally occurring outcome measures. MBO is a goal-directed approach in which workers and their supervisors set goals together for the upcoming evaluation period. The rating then consists of deciding to what extent the goals have been met. With *naturally occurring outcomes*, the performance measure is not so much discussed and agreed to as it is handed to supervisors and workers. For example, a computerized production system used to manufacture cardboard boxes may automatically generate data regarding the number of pieces produced, the amount of waste, and the defect rate.

The outcome approach provides clear and unambiguous criteria by which worker performance can be judged. It also eliminates subjectivity and the potential for error and bias that goes along with it. In addition, outcome approaches provide increased flexibility. For example, a change in the production system may lead to a new set of outcome measures and, perhaps, a new set of performance standards. With an MBO approach, a worker's objectives can easily be adjusted at the beginning of a new evaluation period if organizational changes call for new emphases. Perhaps the most important thing is that outcomes can easily be tied to strategic objectives.[26]

Are outcome-based systems, then, the answer to the numerous problems with the subjective rating systems discussed earlier? Unfortunately, no. Although objective, outcome measures may give a seriously deficient and distorted view of worker performance levels. Consider an outcome measure defined as follows: "the number of units produced that are within acceptable quality limits." This performance measure may seem fair and acceptable. However, when the machine is not running properly, it can take several hours—sometimes an entire shift—to locate the problem and resolve it. If you were a manager, you would put your best workers on the problem. But consider what would happen to their performance. Your best workers could actually end up looking like the worst workers in terms of the amount of product produced.

This situation actually occurred at a manufacturer of automobile components.[27] To resolve the issue, management concluded that supervisors' subjective performance judgments were superior to objective outcome measures. The subjective ratings differed radically from the outcome measures. But in this case, the subjective ratings were found to be related to workers' scores on job-related tests whereas no such relationship was found for the outcome measures. Clearly, in some situations human judgment is superior to objective measures.

Another potential difficulty with outcome-based performance measures is the development of a "results at any cost" mentality.[28] Using objective measures has the advantage of focusing workers' attention on certain outcomes, but this focus can have negative effects on other facets of performance. For example, an organization may use the number of units produced as a performance measure because it is fairly easy to quantify. Workers concentrating on quantity may neglect quality and follow-up service to the long-term detriment of the organization. Although objective goals and other outcome measures are effective for increasing performance levels, these measures may not reflect the entire spectrum of performance.[29]

Measurement Tools: Summary and Conclusions

Our discussion so far makes it clear that there is no single best appraisal format. Figure 7.8 summarizes the strengths and weaknesses of each approach in the areas of administration, development,

Evaluation of Major Appraisal Formats

Figure 7.8

	CRITERIA		
Appraisal Format	Administrative Use	Developmental Use	Legal Defensibility
Absolute	0	+	0
Relative	++	−	−
Trait	+	−	− −
Behavior	0	+	++
Outcome	0	0	+

− − Very poor − Poor 0 Unclear or mixed + Good ++ Very good and legal defensibility. The choice of appraisal system should rest largely on the appraisal's primary purpose.

For example, say that your main management concern is obtaining desired results. An outcome approach would be best for this purpose. However, when outcomes are not adequately achieved, further evaluation may be needed to diagnose the problem.

Most appraisal systems were developed on the premise that companies could reduce or eliminate rater errors by using the right appraisal format. However, empirical evidence suggests that the type of tool does not make that much difference in the accuracy of ratings.[30]

If formats do not have much impact on ratings, what does? Not surprisingly, it's the person doing the rating. Characteristics such as the rater's intelligence, familiarity with the job,[31] and ability to separate important from unimportant information[32] influence rating quality. Thus, the person doing the rating is an important determinant of the quality of ratings.

Who does the rating is commonly referred to as the *source* of the appraisal. The most common source is the worker's direct supervisor. However, other sources can provide unique and valuable perspectives to the performance appraisal process. Self, peers, subordinates, and even customers are increasingly common sources of appraisal.

Self-review, in which workers rate themselves, allows employees input into the appraisal process and can help them gain insight into the causes of performance problems. For example, there may be a substantial difference in opinion between a supervisor and an employee regarding one area of the employee's evaluation. Communication and possibly investigation are warranted in such a case. In some situations, people can find themselves having to rely on self-appraisal as a guide to managing performance.

In a **peer review,** workers at the same level of the organization rate one another. For instance, peer review played a central role in the appraisal process at Milo Engineering, the business featured in our opening vignette. In a **subordinate review,** workers review their supervisors.

In addition to feedback from within the organization, companies are increasingly looking to customers as a valuable source of appraisal. Traditional top-down appraisal systems may encourage employees to perform only those behaviors that supervisors see or pay attention to. Thus, behaviors that are critical to customer satisfaction may be ignored.[33]

Indeed, customers are often in a better position to evaluate the quality of a company's products or services than supervisors are. Supervisors may have limited information or a limited perspective, while internal and external customers often have a wider focus or greater experience with more parts of the business. Figure 7.9 presents an example of a customer appraisal form.

A Question of Ethics

Is it appropriate for organizations to evaluate and compensate employees according to objective measures of performance, even though performance is at least partially determined by factors beyond their control? Should a salesperson, for instance, be paid completely on commission even in the midst of a recession that makes it practically impossible to sell enough to make a decent living?

Self-review
A performance appraisal system in which workers rate themselves.

Peer review
A performance appraisal system in which workers at the same level in the organization rate one another.

Subordinate review
A performance appraisal system in which workers review their supervisors.

Employees use peer ratings to appraise coworkers. Review by employees familiar with each other's work can result in an accurate assessment of performance.

Figure 7.9

Name: _____

This survey asks your opinion about specific aspects of the products and services you received. Your individual responses will remain confidential and will be compiled with those of other customers to improve customer service. Please use the following scale to indicate the extent to which you agree with the statement. Circle one response for each item.

> 1 = Strongly Disagree
> 2 = Disagree
> 3 = Neutral
> 4 = Agree
> 5 = Strongly Agree
> ? = Unsure

If you feel unable to adequately rate a specific item, please leave it blank.

QUALITY

I had to wait an unreasonable amount of time for my requests to be met ....1 2 3 4 5 ?

The products I have received have met my expectations.....................1 2 3 4 5 ?

My requests were met on or before the agreed upon deadline.................................1 2 3 4 5 ?

The products I have received have generally been error free............1 2 3 4 5 ?

SERVICE/ATTITUDE

When serving me, this person:

Was helpful.......................1 2 3 4 5 ?

Was cooperative in meeting my requests........1 2 3 4 5 ?

Communicated with me to understand my expectations for products..........................1 2 3 4 5 ?

Was uncooperative when I asked for revisions/additional information.......................1 2 3 4 5 ?

Told me when my requests would be filled................................1 2 3 4 5 ?

When necessary, sufficiently explained to me why my expectations could not be met...................................1 2 3 4 5 ?

Kept me informed about the status of my request............................1 2 3 4 5 ?

CUSTOMER SATISFACTION

How would you rate your overall level of satisfaction with the *service* you have received?

> 1 = Very Dissatisfied
> 2 = Dissatisfied
> 3 = Neutral
> 4 = Satisfied
> 5 = Very Satisfied

What specifically could be done to make you more satisfied with the *service*?

_____
_____
_____

How would you rate your overall level of satisfaction with the *products* you have received?

> 1 = Very Dissatisfied
> 2 = Dissatisfied
> 3 = Neutral
> 4 = Satisfied
> 5 = Very Satisfied

What specifically could be done to make you more satisfied with the *products*?

_____
_____
_____

Customer Appraisal Form

Source: Cardy, R. L, and Dobbins, G. H. (1994). *Performance appraisal: Alternative perspectives.* Cincinnati, OH: South-Western.

360° feedback
The combination of peer, subordinate, and self-review.

The combination of peer, subordinate, and self-review and sometimes customer appraisal is termed **360° feedback**. A 360° system can offer a well-rounded picture of an employee's performance, one that is difficult to ignore or discount because it comes from multiple perspectives. Many organizations are now employing technology to make 360° appraisal an efficient and cost-effective system. As illustrated in the Manager's Notebook, "Doin' the Maniac 360°," a 360° system can be used across countries and cultures to instill a common set of values in an organization.

MANAGER'S NOTEBOOK   Global

Doin' the Maniac 360°

Yum Brands, Inc., uses a 360° appraisal system to turn its workers into "customer maniacs." *Customer maniac* is a term coined by Yum management to describe what they are after in employee performance. Yum employs 850,000 workers across its Pizza Hut, Taco Bell, KFC, A&W, and Long John Silver franchises. Yum has 33,000 restaurants that serve 22 million customers around the world each day and plans to open 1,000 restaurants per year, with a strong focus on international expansion. The company currently has 350 restaurants in China.

In order to achieve its goal of turning its workers into customer maniacs, Yum has identified customer-oriented dimensions such as speed, cleanliness, and hospitality.

In order to roll the 360° system out to workers from Beijing to Los Angeles, the company employed a Web-based 360° system that is in the language appropriate for the region. The system collects evaluations and feedback on a worker's performance from peers, managers, subordinates, and customers. The Web-based forms emphasize written feedback to workers, and the focus is on the development of workers into customer maniacs. The system is not currently tied to compensation.

The Yum 360° system is helping make its performance expectations clear to all its employees, no matter where in the world they are. When Yum's CEO, David Novak, asked for performance feedback on his own job performance, 120 employees responded, and the feedback report was 65 pages.

Source: Adapted from Shuit, D. (2005). Former PepsiCo executives do a 360 in managing Yum Brand's workforce. *Workforce Management, 84,* 4.

Challenges to Effective Performance Measurement

How can managers ensure accurate measurement of worker performance? The primary means is to understand the barriers that stand in the way. Managers confront at least five challenges:

- Rater errors and bias
- The influence of liking
- Organizational politics
- Whether to focus on the individual or the group
- Legal issues

Rater Errors and Bias

A **rater error** is an error in performance appraisal that reflects consistent biases on the part of the rater. One of the most prominent rater errors is *halo error,* the tendency to rate similarly across dimensions.[34]

There are at least two causes of halo error:[35] (1) A supervisor may make an overall judgment about a worker and then conform all dimensional ratings to that judgment, and/or (2) a supervisor may make all ratings consistent with the worker's performance level on a dimension that is important to the supervisor. If Nancy rates Luis low on all three performance dimensions (quality of programs written, quantity of programs written, and interpersonal effectiveness) even though his performance on quality and quantity is high, then she has committed a halo error.

Another type of rater error is *restriction of range error,* which occurs when a manager restricts all of his or her ratings to a small portion of the rating scale. Three different forms of range restriction are common: *leniency errors,* or restricting ratings to the high portion of the scale; *central tendency errors,* or using only the middle points of the scale; and *severity errors,* or using only the low portion of the rating scale.

Suppose that you are an HR manager reviewing the performance ratings given by the company's supervisors to their subordinates. The question is: How can you tell how accurate these ratings are? In other words, how can you tell what types of rating error, if any, have colored the ratings? It is very difficult to tell. Let us say that a supervisor has given one of her subordinates the highest possible rating on each of five performance dimensions. There are at least three possible explanations. The employee may actually be very good on one of the dimensions and has been rated very high on all because of this (halo error). Or the rater may only use the top part of the scale (leniency error). Or the employee may be a very good all-around worker (accurate). Although sophisticated statistical techniques have been developed to investigate these possibilities, none is practical for most organizations or managers. Further, current research indicates that "errors" in ratings can sufficiently represent "true" ratee performance levels (the "accurate" possibility presented previously) such that rater errors are *not* good indicators of inaccuracy in rating.[36]

Rater error
An error in performance appraisals that reflects consistent biases on the part of the rater.

Personal bias may also cause errors in evaluation. Consciously or unconsciously, a supervisor may systematically rate certain workers lower or higher than others on the basis of race, national origin, sex, age, or other factors. Conscious bias is extremely difficult, if not impossible, to eliminate. Unconscious bias can be overcome once it is brought to the rater's attention. For example, a supervisor might be unconsciously giving higher evaluations to employees who went to his alma mater. When made aware of this leaning, however, he may correct it.

Blatant, systematic negative biases should be recognized and corrected within the organization. Negative bias became an issue at the U.S. Drug Enforcement Agency (DEA) in the early 1980s when a lawsuit, *Segar v. Civiletti,* established that African American agents were systematically rated lower than white agents and, thus, were less likely to receive promotions and choice job assignments. The DEA failed to provide supervisors with any written instructions on how to evaluate agents' performance, and virtually all the supervisors conducting the evaluations were white.[37]

A major difficulty in performance measurement is ensuring comparability in ratings across raters.[38] **Comparability** refers to the degree to which the performance ratings given by various supervisors in an organization are similar. In essence, the comparability issue is concerned with whether or not supervisors use the same measurement yardsticks. What one supervisor considers excellent performance, another may view as only average.

One of the most effective ways to deal with errors and bias is to develop and communicate evaluation standards via **frame-of-reference (FOR) training**,[39] which uses fictitious behavioral examples of performance that a worker might exhibit.

After rating the performance presented on videotape or paper, the trainees in a typical FOR session are told what their ratings should have been. Discussion of which worker behaviors represent each dimension (and why) follows. This process of rating, feedback, and discussion is succeeded by the presentation of another example. Again, rating, feedback, and discussion follow. The process continues until the appraisers develop a common frame of reference for performance evaluation. In other words, FOR training is all about calibrating everyone to the same performance standards.[40]

FOR training has consistently been found to increase the accuracy of performance ratings.[41] Perhaps even more important, it develops common evaluation standards among supervisors.

The FOR training procedure does have a number of drawbacks, though. One glaring problem is the expense, which can be prohibitive owing to the amount of time and number of people involved. Another drawback is that it can be used only with behaviorally based appraisal systems.

The Influence of Liking

Liking can cause errors in performance appraisals when raters allow their like or dislike of an individual to influence their assessment of that person's performance. Field studies have found rater liking and performance ratings to be substantially correlated.[42] Findings of a correlation might indicate that performance ratings are biased by rater liking. However, good raters may tend to like good performers and dislike poor performers.

The fundamental question, of course, is whether the relationship between liking and performance ratings is appropriate or biased.[43] It is appropriate if supervisors like good performers better than poor performers. It is biased if supervisors like or dislike employees for reasons other than their performance and allow these feelings to contaminate their ratings. It is often very difficult to separate these two possibilities.[44] Nonetheless, most workers appear to believe that their supervisor's liking for them influences the performance ratings they receive.[45] The perception of bias can cause communication problems between workers and supervisors and lower supervisors' effectiveness in managing performance.

Precautions

Given the potentially biasing impact of liking, it is critical that supervisors manage their emotional reactions to workers. They should keep a performance diary of observed behavior for each worker[46] to serve as the basis for evaluation and other managerial actions. An external record of worker behaviors can dramatically reduce error and bias in ratings.

Recordkeeping should be done routinely—for example, daily or weekly. Keeping records of employee performance is a professional habit worth developing, particularly to safeguard against litigation that challenges the fairness of appraisals.[47] To prevent error and bias, the record

---

Comparability
In performance ratings, the degree to which the performance ratings given by various supervisors in an organization are similar.

Frame-of-reference (FOR) training
A type of training that presents supervisors with fictitious examples of worker performance (either in writing or on videotape), asks the supervisors to evaluate the workers in the examples, and then tells them what their ratings should have been.

should reflect what each worker has been doing, not opinions or inferences about the behavior. Further, the record should present a balanced and complete picture by including all performance incidents—positive, negative, or average. A good question to ask yourself is whether someone else reading the record would reach the same conclusion about the level of performance as you have.

In one field study of such recordkeeping, supervisors reported that the task took five minutes or fewer per week.[48] More important, the majority of supervisors reported that they would prefer to continue, rather than discontinue, the recording of behavioral incidents. By compiling a weekly record, they did not have to rely much on general impressions and possibly biased memories when conducting appraisals. In addition, the practice signaled workers that appraisal was not a personality contest. Finally, the diaries provided a legal justification for the appraisal process: The supervisor could cite concrete behavioral examples that justified the rating.

Two warnings are in order here. First, performance diaries are not guarantees against bias due to liking, because supervisors can be biased in the type of incidents they choose to record. However, short of intentional misrepresentation, the keeping of such records should help reduce both actual bias and the perception of bias.

Second, some managers use performance diaries in place of intervention and discussion because it is less uncomfortable, initially, to record a performance problem than to discuss it with the employee. Documenting problems is fine and even useful for creating a legally defensible case if the employee must be terminated. However, it is unfair to keep a secret running list of "offenses" and then suddenly unveil it to the employee when he or she commits an infraction that can't be overlooked. The message for managers is simple: If an employee's behavior warrants discussion, the discussion should take place immediately.[49]

Here's how one company used performance diaries both to aid performance appraisal and to enhance employee coaching:

> In its drive to revamp its performance appraisal system, Azteca Foods, Inc., a 125-employee company, asked its 25 managers to begin keeping a daily log of each employee's performance. Every time an employee did something negative (like arriving late to work or missing an assignment deadline) or something positive (like making a notable contribution) the manager was expected to write it down and give immediate feedback. While this procedure may sound time-consuming, the company found the payback worth the extra effort. At appraisal time managers were able to bring up concrete examples of what an employee did instead of saying "You've done a good (or inadequate) job." The procedure also fosters communication between managers and subordinates and motivates workers to continuously improve performance.[50]

Although liking can be a source of bias in performance appraisals, it can also be the direct result of good performance. Managers tend to like employees who have a positive attitude, who get along well with their coworkers, and who perform consistently well.

Organizational Politics

Thus far we have taken a *rational perspective* on appraisal.[51] In other words, we have assumed that the value of each worker's performance can be estimated. Unlike the rational approach, the *political perspective* assumes that the value of a worker's performance depends on the agenda, or goals, of the supervisor.[52] Consider the following quote from an executive with extensive experience in evaluating his subordinates:

> As a manager, I will use the review process to do what is best for my people and the division. . . . I've got a lot of leeway—call it discretion—to use this process in that manner. . . . I've used it to get my people better raises in lean years, to kick a guy in the pants if he really needed it, to pick up a guy when he was down or even to tell him that he was no longer welcome here. . . . I believe that most of us here at _____ operate this way regarding appraisals.[53]

Let's examine how the rational and the political process differ on various facets of the performance appraisal process.

- The *goal* of appraisal from a rational perspective is accuracy. The goal of appraisal from a political perspective is *utility*, the maximization of benefits over costs given the context and agenda. The value of performance is relative to the political context and the supervisor's goals. For example, a supervisor may give a very poor rating to a worker who seems uncommitted in the hopes of shocking that worker into an acceptable level of performance.
- The rational approach sees supervisors and workers largely as passive agents in the rating process: Supervisors simply notice and evaluate workers' performance. Thus, their accuracy is critical. In contrast, the political approach views both supervisors and workers as motivated participants in the measurement process. Workers actively try to influence their evaluations, either directly or indirectly.

The various persuasion techniques that workers use to alter the supervisor's evaluation are direct forms of influence. For example, just as a student tells a professor that he needs a higher grade to keep his scholarship, a worker might tell her boss that she needs an above-average rating to get a promotion. Indirect influences are behaviors by which workers influence how supervisors notice, interpret, and recall events,[54] ranging from flattery to excuses to apologies. The following quote from a consulting group manager demonstrates how employees in the organization used impression-management tactics:[55]

> Phone calls from customers praising a consultant's performance were rarely received except during the month before appraisals. These phone calls were often instigated by the consultants to highlight their importance.

- From a rational perspective, the *focus* of appraisal is measurement. Supervisors are flesh-and-blood instruments[56] who must be carefully trained to measure performance meaningfully. The evaluations are used in decisions about pay raises, promotions, training, and termination. The political perspective sees the focus of appraisal as management, not accurate measurement. Appraisal is not so much a test that should be fair and accurate as a management tool with which to reward or discipline workers.
- *Assessment criteria*, the standards used to judge worker performance, also differ between the rational and political approaches. The rational approach holds that a worker's performance should be defined as clearly as possible. In the political approach, the definition of what is being assessed is left ambiguous so that it can be bent to the current agenda. Thus, ambiguity ensures the necessary flexibility in the appraisal system.
- Finally, the *decision process* differs between the rational and political approaches. In the rational approach, supervisors make dimensional and overall assessments based on specific behaviors they have observed. For instance, Nancy would rate each programmer on each dimension and then combine all the dimensional ratings into an overall evaluation. In the political approach, appropriate assessment of specifics follows the overall assessment. Thus, Nancy would first decide who in her group should get the highest rating (for whatever reason) and then justify that overall assessment by making appropriate dimensional ratings.

Appraisal in most organizations seems to be a political rather than a rational exercise.[57] It appears to be used as a tool for serving various and changing agendas; accurate assessment is seldom the real goal. But should the rational approach be abandoned because appraisal is typically political? No! Politically driven assessment may be common, but that does not make it the best approach to assessment.

Accuracy may not be the main goal in organizations, but it is the theoretical ideal behind appraisal.[58] Accurate assessment is necessary if feedback, development, and HR decisions are to be based on employees' actual performance levels. Basing feedback and development on managerial agendas is an unjust treatment of human resources. Careers have been ruined, self-esteem lost, and productivity degraded because of the political use of appraisal. In addition to these negative effects, politically driven appraisal is also associated with increased intention of workers to quit their jobs.[59] Such costs are difficult to assess and to ascribe clearly to politics. Nonetheless, they are very real and important for workers.

Individual or Group Focus

If the organization has a team structure, managers need to consider team performance appraisal at two levels: (1) individual contribution to team performance and (2) the performance of the team as a unit.[60] To properly assess individual contributions to team performance, managers and employees must have clear performance criteria relating to traits, behaviors, or outcomes. Behavioral measures are typically most appropriate for assessing individual contributions to team performance because they are more easily observed and understood by team members and others who interact with the team.

The individual contribution measures could be developed with the input of team members. However, a good starting point is the set of competencies for individual contribution to team performance identified in recent research.[61] The following example describes the use of these competencies at Pfizer, a large pharmaceutical company. Peers assess team members online in the finance area of Pfizer.[62]

> The assessment is based on a four-dimensional model of collaboration, communication, self-management, and decision making. Feedback reports are used as a discussion point to improve the functioning of teams. Over time, there has been significant improvement in the average level of ratings given to team members.

The Manager's Notebook, "Measuring the Performance of Teams," presents a seven-step process recommended by management consultant Jack Zigon. Whatever measures are already in existence or are developed for measuring team performance, here are some points to keep in mind:

First, the measurement system needs to be balanced. For example, although financial objectives may be apparent and easy to develop as criteria, these kinds of objectives are measured in such a way that they do not reflect the concerns of customers.

Another point to keep in mind is that outcome measures may need to be complemented with measures of process. For example, achieving a result may be important but so, too, is interpersonal relations. With a balance of measures, it should be clear to team members that achieving outcomes by running roughshod over peers and customers is not acceptable performance.

One more point is that the measures must reflect criteria that the teams can influence.[63]

Emerging Trends

MANAGER'S NOTEBOOK

Measuring the Performance of Teams

1. Review existing measures to make sure the team is aware of the measures and has commitment and responsibility to achieving them.
2. Identify interim checkpoints at which team progress or achievements can be assessed.
3. Identify what the team and team members must do to achieve the desired team-level results.

4. Prioritize team goals according to relative importance.
5. Develop any needed measures of interim and final team and individual performance.
6. Develop team and individual performance standards so that everyone has a clear understanding of performance expectations.
7. Determine how the performance management system will work. Who will be the raters? How will feedback be provided?

Source: Adapted from Denton, K. D. (2001). Better decisions with less information. *Industrial Management, 43,* 21.

Assessing the performance of a team as a unit means that managers must measure performance at the team, not individual, level. Team members may be the best sources for identifying and developing team-level criteria. Going to team members to help develop criteria encourages their participation in selecting measures that they feel they can directly influence.

Two final points: First, experts recommend that individual performance still be assessed, even within a team environment, because U.S. society is so strongly focused on individual performance.[64] Second, there is no consensus as to what type of appraisal instrument should be used for team evaluations. The best approach may include internal and external customers making judgments across both behavioral and outcome criteria.[65]

Legal Issues

The major legal requirements for performance appraisal systems are set forth in Title VII of the Civil Rights Act of 1964, which prohibits discrimination in all terms and conditions of employment (see Chapter 3). This means that performance appraisal must be free of discrimination at both the individual and group levels. Some courts have also held that performance appraisal systems should meet the same *validity* standards as selection tests (see Chapter 5). As with selection tests, *adverse impact* may occur in performance evaluation when members of one group are promoted at a higher rate than members of another group based on their appraisals.

Probably the most significant court test of discrimination in performance appraisal is *Brito v. Zia Company,* a 1973 U.S. Supreme Court case. In essence, the Court determined that appraisal is legally a test and must, therefore, meet all the legal requirements regarding tests in organizations. In practice, however, court decisions since *Brito v. Zia* have employed less stringent criteria when assessing charges of discrimination in appraisal.

Appraisal-related court cases since *Brito v. Zia* suggest that the courts do not wish to rule on whether appraisal systems conform to all accepted professional standards (such as whether employees were allowed to participate in developing the system).[66] Rather, they simply want to determine if discrimination occurred. The essential question is whether individuals who have similar employment situations are treated differently.

The courts look favorably on a system in which a supervisor's manager reviews appraisals to safeguard against the occurrence of individual bias. In addition, the courts take a positive view of feedback and employee counseling to help improve performance problems. A recent analysis of 295 court cases involving performance appraisal found judges' decisions to be favorably influenced by the following additional factors:[67]

- Use of job analysis
- Providing written instructions
- Allowing employees to review appraisal results
- Agreement among multiple raters (if more than one rater was used)
- The presence of rater training

In the extreme, a negative performance appraisal may lead to the dismissal of an employee. Management's right to fire an employee is rooted in a legal doctrine called *employment-at-will.* Employment-at-will is a very complex legal issue that depends on laws and rulings varying from state to state. We discuss employment-at-will fully in Chapter 14. Here, it is enough to say that managers can protect themselves from lawsuits by following good professional practice. If they provide subordinates with honest, accurate, and fair feedback about their performance, and then make decisions consistent with that feedback, they will have nothing to fear from ongoing questions about employment-at-will.

Managing Performance

The effective management of human performance in organizations requires more than formal reporting and annual ratings. A complete appraisal process includes informal day-to-day interactions between managers and workers as well as formal face-to-face interviews. Although the ratings themselves are important, even more critical is what managers do with them. In this section we discuss the third and final component of performance appraisal, performance management.

The Appraisal Interview

Upon completing the performance rating, the supervisor usually conducts an interview with the worker to provide feedback—one of the most important parts of the appraisal process. Many managers dread the performance appraisal, particularly if they do not have good news to impart. The HR department or an external group, such as a management association or consulting group, can help managers by offering training in conducting interviews, providing role-play practice, and offering advice on thorny issues. Figure 7.10 summarizes several communication "microskills" that managers need to effectively conduct an appraisal interview.

Performance reviews are sometimes separated into two sessions: one to discuss performance, the other to discuss salary.[68] (This practice is common in Great Britain, where 85 percent of large companies split the appraisal meeting.) The logic behind this system was based on two assumptions. First, managers cannot simultaneously be both a coach and a judge. Thus, the manager was expected to play the coach role during the performance development meeting and the judge role during the salary meeting. Second, if performance and salary discussions were combined, employees probably would not listen to their performance feedback because their interest would be focused on salary decisions.

However, research has found that discussion of salary in an appraisal session has a *positive* impact on how employees perceive the appraisal's usefulness.[69] Managers who have to justify a low salary increase will probably take time to carefully support their performance assessments, and this more detailed feedback should make the appraisal session more valuable to the employee. Second, feedback, goal setting, and making action plans can become a hollow and meaningless exercise when salary implications are divorced from the session.

In sum, it appears that the best management practice is to combine development and salary discussion into one performance review. Informal performance management throughout the appraisal period requires a combination of judgment and coaching.

Performance Improvement

Because formal appraisal interviews typically are conducted only once a year,[70] they may not always have substantial and lasting impact on worker performance.[71] Much more important than the annual interview is informal day-to-day performance management. Supervisors who manage performance effectively generally share four characteristics. They:

- Explore the causes of performance problems.
- Direct attention to the causes of problems.
- Develop an action plan and empower workers to reach a solution.
- Direct communication at performance and provide effective feedback.[72]

Each of these characteristics is critical to achieving improved and sustained performance levels.

Figure 7.10

Face-to-face communication during the performance appraisal interview can be more effective if managers use "microskills"—communication factors that must be present for effective interpersonal communication. Several examples follow:

Skills	Benefit	Description	Example
Nonverbal Attending	Suggests interest and active listening.	Rater sits with a slight forward, comfortable lean of the upper body, maintains eye contact, and speaks in a steady and soothing voice.	While the ratee is speaking, the rater looks at the person and gently nods head to signal interest.
Open and Closed Questions	Appropriate use of open and closed questions can ensure an effective flow of communication during an interview.	Open questions encourage information sharing and are most appropriate early in an interview or in complex, ambiguous situations.	Open questions start with words like "Could," "Would," "How," "What," or "Why."
		Closed questions evoke short responses and are useful for focusing and clarifying.	Closed questions start with words like "Did," "Is," or "Are."
Paraphrasing	Paraphrasing can clarify and convey to the ratee that you are listening actively.	A paraphrase is a concise statement in your own words of what someone has just said. It should be factual and nonjudgmental.	You might begin by saying "If I have this right . . ." or "What you're saying is . . ." and end with "Is that correct?" or "That's what you are saying?"
Reflection of Feeling	Shows that you are trying to understand the emotional aspect of the workplace. The empathy and sensitivity of such reflection can open up communication and allow the interview to move more meaningfully to task-related issues.	Similar to paraphrase, a reflection of feeling is a factual statement of the emotions you sense the other person is feeling. Be cautious about using this technique insincerely or with those who need professional help.	Start by saying something like "It sounds like you're feeling . . ." End as you would a paraphrase ("Is that right?").
Cultural Sensitivity	Communication is more effective when you are sensitive to the possible influence of cultural differences.	Pay attention to cultural differences that may influence how another person communicates and how you might communicate with others.	When dealing with employees from a culture that is highly formal, avoid addressing them in the workplace by their first names. Doing so may signal disrespect.

Sources: Adapted from Kikoski, J. F. (1998). Effective communication in the performance appraisal interview: Face-to-face communication for public managers in the culturally diverse workplace. *Public Personnel Management, 27,* 491–513; and Ivey, A. B., Ivey, M. B., and Simek-Downing, L. (1987). *Counseling and psychotherapy: Integrating skills, theory, and practice* (2nd ed). Upper Saddle River, NJ: Prentice Hall.

Communication Skills for the Appraisal Interview

Identifying the Causes of Performance Problems

Identifying the causes of performance problems may sound like an easy task, but it is often quite challenging. Performance can be the result of many factors, some of which are beyond the worker's control. In most work situations, though, supervisors tend to blame the worker when they observe poor performance, while workers tend to blame external factors.[73] This tendency is called *actor/observer bias.*[74] The experience of baseball teams provides an analogy. When a team is losing, the players (workers/actors) point to external causes such as injuries, a tough road schedule, or bad weather. The manager (supervisor/observer) blames the players for sloppy execution in the field. And the team's owner and the sportswriters (top management/higher observers) hold the manager responsible for the team's poor performance.

It is important that managers determine the causes of performance deficiencies accurately for three reasons. First, determination of causes can influence how performance is evaluated. For example, a manager is likely to evaluate an episode of poor performance very differently if he thinks it was due to low effort than if he thinks it was due to poor materials. Second, causal determination can be an unspoken and underlying source of conflict between supervisors and their workers. Supervisors often act on what they believe are the causes of performance problems. This is only rational. But when the supervisor's perception significantly differs from the worker's, the difference can cause tension. Third, the cause affects the type of remedy selected; what is thought to be the cause of a performance problem determines what is done about it.

How can the process of determining the causes of performance problems be improved? A starting point is to consider the possible causes consciously and systematically. Traditionally, researchers believed that two primary factors, ability and motivation, determined performance.[75] A major problem with this view is that situational factors external to the worker, such as degree of management support, also affect worker performance.[76]

A more inclusive version of the causes of performance embraces three factors: ability, motivation, and situational factors. The *ability* factor reflects the worker's talents and skills, including characteristics such as intelligence, interpersonal skills, and job knowledge. *Motivation* can be affected by a number of external factors (such as rewards and punishments) but is ultimately an internal decision: It is up to the worker to determine how much effort to exert on any given task. **Situational factors** (or **system factors**) include a wide array of organizational characteristics that can positively or negatively influence performance. System factors include quality of materials, quality of supervisor, and the other factors listed in Figure 7.11.[77]

Situational factors or system factors
A wide array of organizational characteristics that can positively or negatively influence performance.

Performance depends on all three factors. The presence of just one cause is not sufficient for high performance to occur; however, the absence or low value of one factor can result in poor performance. For example, making a strong effort will not result in high performance if the worker has neither the necessary job skills nor adequate support in the workplace. But if the worker doesn't put forth any effort, low performance is inevitable, no matter how good that worker's skills and how much support is provided.

In determining the causes of performance problems, managers should carefully consider situational factors. The factors in Figure 7.11 are only a starting point; they are too generic for use in some situations. Involving workers in creating the lists will both produce examples that supervisors may not have been aware of and send a signal that managers are serious about considering workers' input. The supervisor and worker (or work team) can go over the list together to isolate the causes of any performance difficulties.

Situational constraints/facilitators that managers face can include clerical support, excessive reporting requirements, and the performance of subordinates and coworkers.[78] Only some of these situational factors are under the control of a manager. To determine whether a factor is truly in the person or system category, managers must consider the organizational context.

Managing the Causes of Problems

After supervisor and worker have discussed and agreed on the causes of performance problems, the next step is to take action to control them. Depending on whether the cause of performance

---

Figure 7.11

- Poor coordination of work activities among workers.
- Inadequate information or instructions needed to perform a job.
- Low-quality materials.
- Lack of necessary equipment.
- Inability to obtain raw materials, parts, or supplies.
- Inadequate financial resources.
- Poor supervision.
- Uncooperative co-workers and/or poor relations among people.
- Inadequate training.
- Insufficient time to produce the quantity or quality of work required.
- A poor work environment (for example, cold, hot, noisy, frequent interruptions).
- Equipment breakdown.

Situational (System) Factors to Consider in Determining the Causes of Performance Problems

---

Figure 7.12

Cause	Questions to Ask	Possible Remedies
Ability	Has the worker ever been able to perform adequately? Can others perform the job adequately, but not this worker?	Train Transfer Redesign job Terminate
Effort	Is the worker's performance level declining? Is performance lower on all tasks?	Clarity linkage between performance and rewards Recognize good performance
Situation	Is performance erratic? Are performance problems showing up in all workers, even those who have adequate supplies and equipment?	Streamline work process Clarify needs to suppliers Change suppliers Eliminate conflicting signals or demands Provide adequate tools

Source: Adapted from Schermerhorn, J. R., Gardner, W. I., and Martin, T. N. (1990). Management dialogues: Turning on the marginal performer. *Organizational Dynamics, 18,* 47–59; and Rummler, G. A. (1972). Human performance problems and their solutions. *Human Resource Management, 19,* 2–10.

How to Determine and Remedy Performance Shortfalls

problems is related to ability, effort, or situational characteristics, very different tactics are called for, as Figure 7.12 makes clear. Leaping to a remedy like training (a common reaction) will not fix a problem that is caused by ability and will be a waste of the organization's resources.[79]

Developing an Action Plan and Empowering Workers to Reach a Solution

Effective performance management requires empowering workers to improve their performance. As in a sports team, the supervisor-as-coach assists workers in interpreting and reacting to the work situation. The role is not necessarily one of mentor, friend, or counselor. Rather, it is that of enabler. The supervisor-as-coach works to ensure that the necessary resources are available to workers and helps employees identify an action plan to solve performance problems. For example, the supervisor may suggest ways for the worker to eliminate, avoid, or get around situational obstacles to performance. In addition to creating a supportive, empowered work environment, coach/supervisors clarify performance expectations; provide immediate feedback; and strive to eliminate unnecessary rules, procedures, and other constraints.[80] The most effective performance may result from being specific about desired outcomes but not giving too many details about how the worker should strive to reach these goals.[81] Too much detail may stifle and demoralize an employee. The Manager's Notebook, "Coaching Effectiveness," provides an example assessment of the coaching function.

MANAGER'S NOTEBOOK

Customer-Driven HR

Coaching Effectiveness

When managers are reluctant to be good coaches to their workers, adding to the managers' performance appraisals a measure of how well they are coaching their workers can change all that. Including coaching as a dimension in the appraisal of managers signals the importance that the organization places on coaching and helps assure that it is done as well as possible. Here is an example of the items used by a company to assess how well the coaching function is being carried out. Workers' assessments on these items are used by the company to reward the coaching strengths of managers and to identify areas needing development.

Use the scale below to respond to each of the following items.

1	2	3	4	5
Never	Seldom	Sometimes	Frequently	Always

- My coaching sessions are held every month.
- My coaching sessions are long enough.
- My coach sets challenging but achievable performance goals for me to accomplish.
- My coach sets too many performance goals for me to accomplish.
- My coach shares with me his/her thoughts and feelings, not only facts.
- My coach asks for and appreciates my ideas and suggestions.
- My coaching sessions are stimulating and help me do my job better.
- Because of my coach's position, I would be afraid to question his/her decisions.
- Because of my coach's personality, I would be afraid to question his/her decisions.
- My coach plays favorites when resolving conflicts.
- When my coach delegates work to me, he/she checks and rechecks the smallest details to my frustration and annoyance.
- My coach provides me with the skills and knowledge to be successful.
- My coach is eager to explore my career path in the organization and what I need to do to get there.
- My coach continuously keeps me informed about where the organization is going and keeps me updated on what the other departments and branches are doing.

General Comments:

_____

Source: Adapted with permission from O'Connor, T. J. (2002). Performance management via coaching: Good coaching can help guarantee profitable results and happy employees in an uncertain economy. *Electrical Wholesaling, 83,* 39(3).

Directing Communication at Performance

Communication between supervisor and worker is critical to effective performance management. Exactly what is communicated and how it is communicated can determine whether performance improves or declines.

It is important that communication regarding performance be directed at the performance and not at the person. For example, a worker should not be asked why he is such a jerk! It is usually much more effective to ask the worker why his performance has been ineffective lately. Open-minded communication is more likely to uncover the real reason for a performance problem and thus pave the way for an effective solution.

Summary and Conclusions

What Is Performance Appraisal?

Performance appraisal is the identification, measurement, and management of human performance in organizations. Appraisal should be a future-oriented activity that provides workers with useful feedback and coaches them to higher levels of performance. Appraisal can be used administratively or developmentally.

Identifying Performance Dimensions

Performance appraisal begins by identifying the dimensions of performance that determine effective job performance. Job analysis is the mechanism by which performance dimensions should be identified.

Measuring Performance

The methods used to measure employee performance can be classified in two ways: (1) whether the type of judgment called for is relative or absolute, and (2) whether the measure focuses on traits, behavior, or outcomes. Each measure has its advantages and disadvantages. But it is clear that the overall quality of ratings is much more a function of the rater's motivation and ability than of the type of instrument chosen.

Managers face five challenges in managing performance: rater errors and bias; the influence of liking; organizational politics; whether to focus on the individual or the group; and legal issues (including discrimination and employment at will).

Managing Performance

The primary goal of any appraisal system is performance management. To manage and improve their employees' performance, managers must explore the causes of performance problems, direct manager and employee attention to those causes, develop action plans and empower workers to find solutions, and use performance-focused communication.

Key Terms

absolute judgment, 212
behavioral appraisal instrument, 214
comparability, 220
competencies, 210
competency model, 210
dimension, 210

frame-of-reference (FOR) training, 220
management by objectives (MBO), 216
outcome appraisal instruments, 216
peer review, 217
performance appraisal, 208
rater error, 219

relative judgment, 211
self-review, 217
situational factor or system factors, 227
subordinate review, 217
360° feedback, 218
trait appraisal instrument, 213

Discussion Questions

1. At ARCO Transportation, a $1 billion division of Atlantic Richfield, employees are hired, promoted, and appraised according to how they fulfill the performance dimensions most valued by the company. One of these performance dimensions is "communication"—specifically, "listens and observes attentively, allowing an exchange of information" and "speaks and writes clearly and concisely, with an appropriate awareness of the intended audience." Would you say that ARCO appraises performance based on personality traits, job behavior, or outcome achieved? On which of these three aspects of performance do you think workers should be appraised?

2. Superficially, it seems preferable to use objective performance data (such as productivity figures), when available, rather than subjective supervisory ratings to assess employees. Why might objective data be less effective performance measures than subjective ratings?

3. How important are rating formats to the quality of performance ratings? What is the most important influence on rating quality?

4. What is comparability? How can it be maximized in performance appraisal?

5. "Occasionally an employee comes along who needs to be reminded who the boss is, and the appraisal is an appropriate place for such a reminder." Would the manager quoted here be likely to use a rational or a political approach to appraisal? Contrast the rational and political approaches. To what extent is it possible to separate the two?

6. Do you think performance appraisal should be done? Is it worth the cost?

7. What criteria do you think should be used to measure team performance? What sources should be used for the appraisal? Should individual performance still be measured? Why or why not?

8. You're the owner of a 25-employee company that has just had a fantastic year. Everyone pulled together and worked hard to achieve the boost in company profits. Unfortunately, you need to sink most of those profits into paying your suppliers. All you can afford to give your workers is a 3 percent pay raise across the board. At appraisal time, how would you communicate praise for a job well done coupled with your very limited ability to reward such outstanding performance? Now assume you can afford to hand out some handsome bonuses or raises. What would be the best way to evaluate employees when *everyone* has done exceptional work?

9. Would you design a performance appraisal system based on behaviors, outcomes, or both? Why would you design it in this way?

There is a variety of additional material available on the Web site that accompanies this text. You can access this information by visiting the Web site at ***www.prenhall.com/gomez***.

Ethics Case 7.1 YOU MANAGE IT!

Rank and Yank: Legitimate Performance Improvement Tool or Ruthless and Unethical Management?

Forced ranking is a performance appraisal system popularized by Jack Welch when he was CEO of General Electric. It is a system that has been given the derogatory label of "rank and yank" by its critics. The intent of the forced-ranking system is to improve the performance level of an operation by getting rid of the bottom 10 percent of performers and hiring replacements who will perform at a high level.[a] Ranking judgments can be made in a variety of ways.[b] For example, a forced distribution can pre-assign a set percentage of employees that must be placed into categories such as "most effective," "average," and "needs improvement." Alternatively, a simple ranking of workers from best to worst can be used. Top performers may be rewarded and offered promotion or training. Low performers may be given a warning or terminated.

Forced ranking has been employed by a number of companies, but some legal challenges have been made. For example, Microsoft successfully defended several discrimination suits challenging its use of a forced-ranking system. Conoco used a forced-ranking system and reached an out-of-court settlement in a discrimination lawsuit. Ford Motor Company implemented a forced-ranking system in January 2000 and ended up paying an award of $10.5 million as a result of class action suits charging that the system had a disparate impact on some subgroups of employees. Ford did not admit liability, and although it still places employees into one of three performance categories, it no longer requires a certain percentage of workers to be assigned to each.[c] Overall, however, there have been relatively few legal challenges to the forced-ranking system. It remains a controversial management practice.

Critical Thinking Questions

1. Do you think forced ranking is a good performance management system? Why or why not?
2. Part of the forced-ranking label reflects the intent to force distinctions among worker performance levels. In an absolute-rating system, everyone could be rated "above average." Does this difference between the absolute- and relative-rating approaches mean that the absolute performance judgments are wrong? Explain.
3. As a manager, would you prefer to rely on an absolute performance rating system or a relative system, such as forced ranking? Why?
4. Can you devise an absolute-rating system that would guarantee differentiation among workers? Why or why not?

Team Exercise

As a team, address the effectiveness of the forced-ranking approach for improving the level of performance in an organization. Consider the results of a recent simulation study[d] that used a computer simulation to examine the impact of terminating the lowest-ranked employees on average workforce performance. The computer model found that the system improved the average level of performance, but the effect decreased to a near-zero level within six years.

Address the following issues:

a. Why does the system work? That is, why did the simulation find improved performance?
b. The logic behind the forced-ranking approach and the simulation is that performance in a workplace is normally distributed. Do you think this is an accurate assumption? Why or why not?
c. If performance in a workplace is not normally distributed, do you think a forced-ranking approach would still improve the average level of performance in the organization? Explain.

Share your judgments on these issues with the rest of the class.

Experiential Exercise

Of the companies that are consistent top performers (increased profits by at least 10 percent per year for 10 years), none use a forced-ranking system.[e] Proponents of forced ranking see the system as a means for a quick exchange of personnel in a way that lifts the average performance level of the organization. Critics see the approach as possibly damaging the culture and comradery in an organization and would prefer to keep people and develop their skills.

Select representatives as members of a pro or con forced-ranking team. Each team identifies its assumptions about how performance is distributed in the workplace. They will then offer reasons why they are for or against forced ranking. Some of the issues to be addressed include:

- What is the expected impact of forced ranking on performance in an organization?
- Turnover has costs associated with it (see Chapters 5 and 6). How would these costs affect your position?
- What would be the impact of forced ranking on the organization's culture? What about the culture without the system?
- Is it better to exchange a poor performer or to try to develop and improve that worker?

In a debate-style format, each team makes its presentation of position and rationale and has the opportunity to question and rebut and rejoin the other team. The instructor moderates this process. At the end of the debate, the instructor leads the class in identifying the key reasons for and against the use of forced ranking. Is there a clear consensus in the class for or against the system?

Sources: [a]Beshur, A. (2005, April 4). Survival of the fittest. *Corpus Christi Caller-Times, The Business Leader,* 06. [b]Amalfe, C.A., and Steiner, E.G. (2005). Forced ranking systems: Yesterday's legal target. *New Jersey Law Journal;* [c]Jones, D. (2005, April 2). Thinning the herd: Large companies use some version of forced rankings, also known as rank and yank.

Edmonton Sun (Alberta, Canada), news section 81; [d] Scullen, S.E., Bergey, P.K., and Aiman-Smith, L. (2005). Forced distribution rating systems and the improvement of workforce potential: A baseline simulation. *Personnel Psychology, 58,* 1–32; [e] Marchetti, M. (2005). Letting go of low performers. *Sales and Marketing Management, 157,* 6.

YOU MANAGE IT! Emerging Trends Case 7.2

Cultural Competency

Our population is becoming increasingly diverse. The ability to effectively interact with customers with varying cultural backgrounds can affect sales. For example, some consultants are advising companies that they need to develop cultural competency in order to effectively market and sell to members of different ethnic communities (Zolkos, 2005). Cultural competency means that you not only have knowledge of a culture, but also the skills needed to work with that particular ethnic group and the attitude to do so effectively. The rationale for cultural competency as a key skill goes beyond sales and marketing and includes life and death!

In March 2005, the Governor of New Jersey signed legislation requiring physicians to complete "cultural competency" training. The intent of the training is to provide physicians with a better understanding of health-related cultural beliefs that people bring with them to the doctor's office and how diseases may affect different subgroups. Legislators in Arizona, Illinois, and New York are also considering bills that require cultural-competency training for licensed physicians. The reason is the repeated finding that minority populations receive poorer care. The poorer care may be completely unintentional; it may happen because physicians don't know how to interact with someone from another culture. As a simple example, one doctor has reported that Phillippinos tend to tell a doctor that they feel dizzy when they don't feel good. The doctor, however, should not leap to the conclusion that the patient is suffering from vertigo, because the comment, for people from the Phillipines, is a generic indicator that they don't feel well.

Critical Thinking Questions

1. Is there a distinction between diversity and cultural competency, or are they the same thing? Explain.
2. A possible negative impact of cultural-competency training is the furthering of stereotypes. For example, training content could portray people of certain ethnic backgrounds as acting the same way and lead to overgeneralizations. Do you think the problem could be avoided? How?
3. Do you think that cultural competency should be included as a core competency in most businesses? Why or why not?

Team Exercise

Join your team members to work on operationalizing cultural-competency criteria. Specifically, start by identifying the dimensions of cultural competency. For example, if you think of cultural competency as a general duty or area of responsibility, what aspects make up that area? Perhaps communication is one dimension. In other words, part of cultural competency may be the capability to understand someone's language and to be able to effectively express yourself in that language. Understanding of a culture could be another aspect. Identify as many dimensions as you think are needed to capture the general concept of cultural competency.

Refer to the appendix of this chapter detailing the critical-incident technique. Using the appendix as a guide, generate behavioral examples for each of the cultural-competency dimensions your team identified (see step 2 in the appendix). These "critical incidents" should describe good and poor levels of each cultural competency dimension.

Share your team's dimensions and behavioral examples with the rest of the class. Can a common or core set of dimensions be identified? As a class, address the issue of the utility of these dimensions and the behavioral incidents. Specifically, what could they be used for?

Experiential Exercise

Select representatives as members of a pro or con cultural-competency team. Each team identifies a rationale for their position. This rationale can include, but should not be limited by, the following aspects:

- What is the impetus behind the push for cultural competency?
- What role does cultural competency have in business?
- If it is a competency, should it be measured? How?

■ What about the bottom line? Can a positive return on an investment be expected?

In a debate-style format, each team makes its presentation of position and rationale and has the opportunity to question and rebut and rejoin the other team. The instructor moderates this process. At the end of the debate, the instructor leads the class in identifying the key reasons for and against the use of cultural-competency training. Is there a clear consensus in the class for or against the training?

Source: Pelletier, S. (2005). *N.J. mandates cultural-competency training. Medical Meetings*, 12.

Discussion Case 7.3   YOU MANAGE IT!

How Well Do You Play Your Roles?

In many workplaces today people really do not have a static "job," especially if they work in teams. Traditional appraisal based on job descriptions may be sorely inadequate. People with the same job title could be performing substantially different roles. Further, the roles they play may differ across projects and over time. As a result, important performance issues may not be captured by traditional performance appraisal.

One approach to solving this deficiency is to appraise people on the roles they perform at work. Role-based performance appraisal is used in a handful of companies and initial results indicate that the system captures important aspects of performance that are not measured with a traditional appraisal system. HR personnel and managers developed measures for roles such as "Team Player," "Innovator," and "Job." Brief descriptions of these roles and the types of measures used for each are shown next.

Role	Measure
Team player	Responsive to needs of others in team
	Making sure his or her work group succeeds
Innovator	Creating better processes
	Coming up with new ideas
Job	Quantity of work output
	Quality of work output

Critical Thinking Questions

1. What other roles and additional measures do you think would be useful for role-based appraisal?
2. Rafael wants to put more emphasis on being a team player while Sarah wants to delve into making creative contributions for the coming appraisal period. However, both need to continue to perform their job functions.
   a. Design a system that would allow people choice in what they do and, thus, have flexibility in what they are held accountable for.
   b. Do you think people should be given the chance to place greater or lesser weight on various roles they might play? Why or why not?

3. What advantage might a role-based appraisal system offer to the organization? To the worker?

Team Exercise

The role-based approach seems to capture the reality of many workplaces where workers may shift their responsibilities depending on demands and on who else is available and on the team. However, to be usable, roles need to be operationalized. With your teammates, identify three or more roles in the workplace of your choosing. For each role, generate behavior examples (see step 2 of the appendix in this chapter) that portray good and poor levels of performance in each role. If performance is viewed through a role framework, could your behavioral incidents be used to measure performance? Share your roles and behavioral examples with the rest of the class. Does there seem to be a common set of roles that emerge from the teams?

Experiential Exercise

The role framework allows flexibility in how people apply their skills. For example, people can choose roles that best fit their strengths and interests. Employee should be happier with this arrangement and performance should be maximized, because everyone is not being forced to do the same tasks.

As a team, apply the role framework to the job of professor. It is common to view the job of professor as consisting of three dimensions, or duty areas: research, teaching, and service. (Your instructor can describe each of these dimensions for you.) If you take a role approach to performance of the job of professor, how could that change the "job" of professor? How would it change performance appraisal for professors? Would the change be a good thing? Describe why or why not. Each team should take on the role of consultants who are presenting their recommendations to the dean. As teams, share your description and assessment of the role approach for the job of professor.

Sources: Welbourne, T. M., Johnson, D. E., and Erez. A. (1998). The role-based performance scale: Validity analysis of a theory-based measure. *Academy of Management Journal, 41,* 540–555; Stewart, G. L., Fulmer, I. S., and Barrick, M. R. (2005). An exploration of member roles as a multilevel mechanism for individual traits and team outcomes. *Personnel Psychology, 58,* 343–365.

Customer-Driven HR Case 7.4

Performance Review Software: Making a Difficult Job Easier or Making Things Worse?

Many managers dread appraising the performance of workers and either put it off or do it poorly. However, everyone wants and deserves to know how they are doing. A growing number of companies are offering technology that promises to solve this problem. Software can now not only make the rating task paperless and as easy as point and click, but also generating feedback and performance improvement suggestions can be entirely automated. For example, PerformaWorks is a company that offers a software package, called eWorkbench, that allows 360° appraisal by bosses, peers, subordinates, and even customers.[a] The software is designed to evaluate employees on goals tied to the organization's objectives. The software can calculate the extent to which each employee has contributed to those objectives and, therefore, to the organization's bottom line. The program provides an electronic means for aligning everyone with the same mission and making sure everyone is working toward the same organizational goals. KnowledgePoint is another company that offers an electronic appraisal tool. The KnowledgePoint software is Web based and focuses on goals and competencies that can be generic or customized (see *www.performancereview.com*). In addition, depending on rating levels, the software generates a narrative performance summary to hand to the worker that describes performance levels on competencies or goals and suggests actions the worker should take to improve performance.

Critical Thinking Questions

1. What advantages might there be to using the types of software just described for evaluating the performance of workers? Are there rational advantages, such as speed? What about political advantages, such as a manager being able to blame a poor performance review on the software?

2. What disadvantages might there be to using the electronic approach to performance reviews? Examine this issue from the perspectives of both managers and employees.

3. Some of the major vendors of hosted online performance appraisal systems include KnowledgePoint, Softscape, PerformaWorks, and SuccessFactors.com. These applications can vary in price depending on the number of employees and degree of functionality desired. However, a price of around $100,000 is typical for a midsized firm.[b] The electronic approach offers savings in time and labor. A traditional (paper-based) approach to performance appraisal has been estimated to cost $1,500 per employee,[c] with some of the sources of this cost being time spent

(1) setting goals and objectives, (2) conducting reviews, (3) designing, printing, copying, filing, and distributing appraisal forms, (4) training supervisors to conduct appraisals, and (5) dealing with postappraisal appeals and grievances. An electronic approach might eliminate the costs of designing, printing, and so on, but the approach may not influence the other sources of cost. Do you think the costs of the online performance appraisal systems are worth it? Why? Consider expected costs and benefits to provide a rationale for your answer.

Team Exercise

Examine the steps involved in reviewing performance. Considering these steps as separable parts of a bundle of performance review actions, are there parts that make sense to do electronically and automatically? Are there other parts that shouldn't be done that way? Go back to the lists of advantages and disadvantages you identified in your response to Critical Thinking questions 1 and 2. Examine these advantages and disadvantages to see if some are particularly associated with making certain steps in the review process electronic and automatic. Given the pattern that you find in regard to advantages and disadvantages associated with certain steps, build an electronic performance review system that you think would be maximally effective (for example, work efficiently, be accepted, provide useful information, and so on). What parts would be electronic? What steps would be automated? Which would not? Describe your proposed system and your rationale for it to the rest of the class.

Experiential Exercise

Divide your team into proponents and antagonists in regard to taking an electronic and automated approach to reviewing performance. Debate the merits and drawbacks of the electronic approach. Structure your debate around the perspectives of key constituents (for example, managers, workers, and customers). Also consider a rational versus a political approach in considering the pluses and minuses. Also consider key criteria (such as acceptance of the feedback, ease of use, impact on performance, and so on).

Is there a clear outcome to your debate? Should performance reviews be electronic and automated or not? Describe the outcome of your debate to the rest of the class and explain some of the conclusions that led to this outcome.

Sources: [a]Parker, V. L. (2000, December 31). Software for hard task: Job reviews/Raleigh company sells it. *The News & Observer*, E1; [b]*Managing HR Information Systems.* (2001). Latest software puts performance appraisal online and cuts costs. February Newsletter of the Institute of Management and Administration, 12–14; [c]Dutton, G. (2002). Making reviews more efficient and fair. *Workforce, 80,* 76. *www.performancereview.com.*

Customer-Driven HR Case 7.5

From Formal Appraisal to Informal Feedback and Development: The Power of Coaching

Performance management is often viewed as an annual evaluative snapshot that is linked to an expected sum of money. As such, it has been likened to the task of doing taxes[a]: Nobody looks forward to doing it, filling out the forms is a pain, but we all hope that the result leads to a nice check. Performance management can and should be much more than an exercise linked to compensation. Performance management should focus on improving performance and helping people to develop their maximum potential to perform. One way to achieve this is through coaching workers. For performance potential to be realized, managers need to be more than evaluators and bureaucrats who complete forms. They need to embrace the role of coach.

ABC Electrical Supply (fictitious name, real company) provides an example of an organization that has made coaching a priority and a key part of how performance is managed.[b] ABC used its performance appraisal system as a means to assure that coaching would be taken seriously and done well. Effective coaching is a collaboration between manager and worker in which short- and long-term goals are discussed and set. Then feedback, reviews, and potential solutions are exchanged. In short, coaching involves a partnership focused on performance. Done well, coaching can improve performance, lead to greater learning and understanding, and improve trust and loyalty. ABC considers coaching as a continuing and informal process; the formal coaching program includes a monthly meeting between manager and subordinate. The monthly meetings are focused on sharing business-related information and evaluation of progress on individual performance goals. These performance goals are identified by first considering the overall organizational strategy and related department goals. Individual performance goals are then generated that fit with and contribute to this context. To help make sure that coaching is on track and being done effectively, ABC has workers annually appraise the performance of coaches. The appraisal survey used by ABC is presented in the Manager's Notebook, "Coaching Effectiveness." The assessments provided on this survey are then used with each manager/coach to identify coaching development needs and to reinforce coaching strengths.

Critical Thinking Questions

1. A major difficulty in implementing effective performance coaching programs is the resistance of managers to perform the role of coach. Why do you think managers might be reluctant to take on this role? How would you go about implementing a coaching program that would eliminate or reduce the resistance of managers?

2. An old saying relevant to performance appraisal is "What gets measured gets done." Do you think that the performance coaching program at ABC, or any organization, could work without being made part of the manager's evaluation? Do you think it should be part of the appraisal of managers? Why or why not?

3. How would you handle a manager who doesn't coach very well (for example, the manager has poor interpersonal skills and has difficulty giving effective feedback)?

4. How do you think a manager who believes that performance coaching takes away from more important tasks and is a waste of time should be handled?

Team Exercise

As a team, brainstorm the aspects of coaching that you think are important. You can start by looking at the survey used by ABC Electrical Supply but focus more on the actual coaching sessions. What would you want a coach to do? What should a coach do? Once you have identified these aspects, develop rating scales to use for assessing these aspects. What type of rating scales should be used? Why?

Experiential Exercise

Performance is often a team-level issue, even though it is composed of individual performers. How would you recommend that coaching take place at a team level? Would your rating scales need to be modified for use with a team of workers?

Share your rating scales and recommendations for their use with the rest of the class.

Have someone in your team role-play the part of a worker and someone else play the role of manager/coach. Use the rating scales you developed in the team exercise to rate the coaching performance and to help direct feedback to the person playing this role. Do you think that this process of evaluation and feedback could lead to improved coaching? How would you recommend that your rating scales be used? For example, should observers use the rating scales, or should they be completed by the worker or manager?

Sources: [a]*Pay for Performance Report.* (2002). Performance management: Make it work, make it fun. March Newsletter of the Institute of Management and Administration; [b]O'Connor, T. J. (2002). Performance management via coaching: Good coaching can help guarantee profitable results and happy employees in an uncertain economy. *Electrical Wholesaling, 83,* 39(3).

The Critical-Incident Technique: A Method for Developing a Behaviorally Based Appraisal Instrument

The critical-incident technique (CIT) is one of many types of job-analysis procedures. The CIT is often used because it produces behavioral statements that make explicit to an employee what is required and to a rater what the basis for an evaluation should be.

CIT Steps

The following steps are involved in a complete CIT procedure:

1. **Identify the major dimensions of job performance.**
   This can be done by asking a group of raters and ratees to brainstorm and generate dimensions relevant to job performance. Each person lists, say, three dimensions. The group members then combine their lists and eliminate redundancies.

2. **Generate "critical incidents" of performance.**
   For each dimension, the group members should list as many incidents as they can think of that represent effective, average, and ineffective performance levels. Each person should think back over the past 6 to 12 months for examples of performance-related behaviors that they have witnessed. Each incident should include the surrounding circumstances or situation.

   If you are having trouble generating incidents, you might want to think of the following situation:

   Suppose someone said that person A, whom you feel is the most effective person in the job, is a poor performer. What incidents of person A's behavior would you cite to change the critic's opinion?

   Try to make sure that the incidents you list are observable *behaviors* and not *personality characteristics* (traits).

3. **Double-check that the incidents represent one dimension.**
   This step is called *retranslation*. Here you are trying to make sure there is clear agreement on which incidents represent which performance dimension. If there is substantial disagreement among group members, this incident may need to be clarified. Alternatively, another dimension may need to be added or some dimensions may need to be merged.

In the retranslation process, each person in the group is asked to indicate what dimension each incident represents. If everyone agrees, the group moves on to the next incident. Any incidents on which there is disagreement are put to the side for further examination at the end of the process. At that time they may be discarded or rewritten.

4. **Assign effectiveness to each incident.**
   Effectiveness values are assigned to all the incidents that survived retranslation. How much is incident "A" worth in our organization, on, say, an effectiveness scale of 1 (unacceptable) to 7 (excellent)? All group members should rate each incident. If there is substantial disagreement regarding the value of a certain behavior, that behavior should be discarded.

NOTE: Disagreement on incident values indicates differences in evaluative standards or lack of clarity in organizational policy. Disagreement regarding evaluative standards can be a fundamental problem in appraisal. The CIT procedure can help to reduce these differences.

The chart on the following page shows some CIT worksheets for you to try your hand at. The dimensions included are a subset of those generated in a research project conducted for a hospital that wanted a common evaluation tool for all nonnursing employees.*

The jobs covered ranged from floor sweeper and clerical worker to laboratory technician and social worker. Of course, the behavioral standards for each dimension differed across jobs—an excellent floor sweeper behavior would not be the same as an excellent lab technician behavior. The dimensions included in the worksheets appear fairly generic, though, and are probably applicable to jobs in most organizations. You may want to develop more specific dimensions or other dimensions altogether.

Remember, after generating incidents, your group should determine agreement levels for the dimension and value for each incident. An easy way to do this is for one person to recite an incident and have everyone respond with dimension and value. This process could be informal and verbal or formal and written.

*Goodale, J. G., and Burke, R. J. (1975). Behaviorally based rating scales need not be job specific. *Journal of Applied Psychology, 60,* 389–391.

Critical Incidents Worksheet

Job Title:

Job Dimension: Knowledge of Job—Understanding of the position held and the job's policies, techniques, rules, materials, and manual skills.

Instructions: Provide at least one behavioral statement for each performance level.

1. Needs improvement:
2. Satisfactory:
3. Excellent:
4. Outstanding:

Critical Incidents Worksheet

Job Title:

Job Dimension: Initiative—The enthusiasm to get things done, energy exerted, willingness to accept and perform responsibilities and assignments; seeks better ways to achieve results.

Instructions: Provide at least one behavioral statement for each performance level.

1. Needs improvement:
2. Satisfactory:
3. Excellent:
4. Outstanding:

Critical Incidents Worksheet

Job Title:

Job Dimension: Personal Relations—Attitude and response to supervision, relationships with coworkers, flexibility in working as part of the organization.

Instructions: Provide at least one behavioral statement for each performance level.

1. Needs improvement:
2. Satisfactory:
3. Excellent:
4. Outstanding:

Critical Incidents Worksheet

Job Title:

Job Dimension: Dependability—Attention to responsibility without supervision, meeting of deadlines.

Instructions: Provide at least one behavioral statement for each performance level.

1. Needs improvement:
2. Satisfactory:
3. Excellent:
4. Outstanding:

Training the Workforce

8

Challenges

After reading this chapter, you should be able to deal more effectively with the following challenges:

1 **Determine** when employees need training and the best type of training given a company's circumstances.

2 **Recognize** the characteristics that make training programs successful.

3 **Weigh** the costs and benefits of a computer-based training program.

4 **Design** job aids as complements or alternatives to training.

5 **Understand** how to socialize new employees effectively.

Johnson Controls is a global market leader in automotive systems and facility management and control. The company's automotive business is based in Plymouth, Michigan, and the organization employs more than 57,000 people at 275 facilities around the world. The company's training and development group, the Leadership Institute, sponsors an event that enables workers to learn from each other. The program, called Team Rally, began in 1996 with the participation of 31 North American teams. In 2003, 144 teams in 10 countries competed in 15 semifinal competitions. The 15 teams of 10 plant-floor workers represented 11 countries. The annual Team Rally competition is held at Disney World in Orlando, Florida.

In the Team Rally competition, teams use entertaining skits to demonstrate how they improved operations or service at Johnson Controls. Some teams use parodies of television (*Gilligan's Island*) or movies (*Star Wars*) to entertain and present the teams' project results in improving productivity or quality and decreasing waste. At the 2003 Team Rally competition, a French team created a "Wicked Witch" video to accompany its skit based on the Snow White story. The project portrayed by the French team was estimated to result in savings of $4.14 million over two years. A Slovakian team received a standing ovation for its use of gardening as an analogy as to how it could harvest savings of $726,805 for Johnson Controls in one year. Teams are judged on their results, how efficiently they share improvements with other employee facilities, and other factors.

Although entertaining, the team competition trains employees to use current systems more effectively. The Team Rally program won't work in all situations (for example, when a system is being changed and people need to learn the new skills that will be needed), but it is a powerful tool for training employees on how to improve the use of current systems.

Sources: Adapted from Roznowski, D. (1999, August 19). Johnson Controls employees help to reduce cost, waste, and increase safety, quality through team rally event. *PR Newswire Association, Inc.;* Sawyer, C. A. (2005). Lights! Camera! Quality! At Johnson Controls's annual Team Rally, acting skills are nearly as important as the ability to explain Six Sigma. *Automotive Design and Production, 116,* 56; Winter, D. (2004). Productivity—Not pink slips. *Wards Auto World, 40,* 5.

THE MANAGERIAL PERSPECTIVE

As the opening vignette suggests, successful organizations and managers view employee training as an investment in their people, not an expense. As a manager, you will want your staff to have the best skills and the broadest understanding of the organization and its customers. This chapter examines key training issues and the training process, identifies the major types of training available, and explores how to evaluate the effectiveness of training.

Key Training Issues

Johnson Controls' program illustrates some of the important training issues facing today's organizations. Specifically:

- **How can training keep pace with a changing organizational environment?** Johnson Controls confronts this challenge by taking an empowered approach to training in which teams of employees learn from each other. However, as equipment and techniques change, employees may have to receive training directed by managers (known as a top-down approach to training). Many organizations are turning to computerized options as an efficient means for delivering training. The computerized approach may not be the answer in all situations. For example, in a service-oriented organization, customer service skills training might be most effective if it is conducted face-to-face with people to give the trainee an experience that is much closer to reality.
- **Should training take place in a classroom setting or on the job?** Classroom training may lack realism and not be as effective as training that occurs while on the job. However, on-the-job training can cause slowdowns that decrease production or irritate customers. Johnson Controls trains employees off the job at its Team Rally events, although the training is relevant to the job.
- **How can training be effectively delivered worldwide?** Many of today's organizations conduct operations around the world. Consistent quality of products or service is critical to organizational survival in today's competitive markets. Johnson Controls' Team Rally event involves employees from around the world. Unfortunately, achieving uniformity worldwide can be difficult. Virtual reality (VR) training provides organizations with a realistic and effective training tool that can easily be used worldwide. Solutions for companies that cannot afford VR training might include computer-, teleconference-, or video-based training.

■ **How can training be delivered so that trainees are motivated to learn?** Lectures and workbooks may have outstanding content but be ineffective if they do not engage the trainees or motivate them to learn. The entertaining and competitive format of Johnson Controls' Team Rally event motivates employees to learn performance improvement techniques. Other engaging delivery media might include VR, videos, and multimedia displays.

In this chapter, we distinguish between training and development. Then we discuss the major challenges managers face in trying to improve workers' performance through training. Next we offer some suggestions on managing the three phases of the training process, explore selected types of training, and consider ways to maximize and evaluate training effectiveness. We close with a section on what is arguably the most important training opportunity: the orientation of new employees.

Training Versus Development

Training
The process of providing employees with specific skills or helping them correct deficiencies in their performance.

Development
An effort to provide employees with the abilities the organization will need in the future.

Although training is often used in conjunction with development, the terms are not synonymous. **Training** typically focuses on providing employees with specific skills or helping them correct deficiencies in their performance.[1] For example, new equipment may require workers to learn new ways of doing the job or a worker may have a deficient understanding of a work process. In both cases, training can be used to correct the skill deficit. In contrast, **development** (the subject of Chapter 9) is an effort to provide employees with the abilities the organization will need in the future.

Figure 8.1 summarizes the differences between training and development. In training, the focus is solely on the current job; in development, the focus is on both the current job and jobs that employees will hold in the future. The scope of training is on individual employees, whereas the scope of development is on the entire work group or organization. That is, training is job specific and addresses particular performance deficits or problems. In contrast, development is concerned with the workforce's skills and versatility.[2] Training tends to focus on immediate organizational needs and development tends to focus on long-term requirements. The goal of training is a fairly quick improvement in workers' performance, whereas the goal of development is the overall enrichment of the organization's human resources. Training strongly influences present performance levels, whereas development pays off in terms of more capable and flexible human resources in the long run.

Keep in mind one other distinction between training and development: Training can have a negative connotation. The result is that people might appreciate an opportunity for development but resent being scheduled for training.[3] Why? Training often implies that a person has a skill deficit, so employees may view their selection for training as a negative and embarrassing message rather than an improvement opportunity.

Changing this perception can be difficult. To help make the change, a company can focus on the improvement potential offered through training rather than correction of skill deficit. In other words, the "training" is portrayed as development. Although this tactic muddies the distinction between training and development, the two terms are often used interchangeably in practice. Given the rapid rate of change in many workplaces, training is becoming a necessity. The culture of organizations, then, needs to change so that training is viewed positively.

Training Versus Development

Figure 8.1		
	Training	**Development**
Focus	Current job	Current and future jobs
Scope	Individual employees	Work group or organization
Time Frame	Immediate	Long term
Goal	Fix current skill deficit	Prepare for future work demands

Challenges in Training

The training process brings with it a number of questions that managers must answer. These are:

- Is training the solution to the problem?
- Are the goals of training clear and realistic?
- Is training a good investment?
- Will the training work?

Is Training the Solution?

A fundamental objective of training is the elimination or improvement of performance problems. However, not all performance problems call for training. Performance deficits can have several causes, many of which are beyond the worker's control and would, therefore, not be affected by training.[4] For example, unclear or conflicting requests, morale problems, and poor-quality materials cannot be improved through training.

Are the Goals Clear and Realistic?

To be successful, a training program must have clearly stated and realistic goals. These goals will guide the program's content and determine the criteria by which its effectiveness will be judged. For example, management cannot realistically expect that one training session will make everyone a computer expert. Such an expectation guarantees failure because the goal is unattainable.

Unless the goals are clearly articulated before training programs are set up, the organization is likely to find itself training employees for the wrong reasons and toward the wrong ends. For example, if the goal is to improve specific skills, the training needs to be targeted to those skill areas. Magazine publisher Condé Nast is working to identify and address specific goals for training. However, the director of employee programs at Condé Nast notes: "Prior to last year, we were offering generic training and employees were signing up on a self-selection basis."[5] The director of employee programs believes that goal-driven training teaches skills that are more relevant to workers' jobs. As a result, the company and the employee benefit.

In contrast, the company's training goal may be to provide employees with a broader understanding of the organization. For example, IDG, a highly decentralized publisher with offices around the world, provides three training seminars per year on the interdependent nature of the functions in the organization.[6] Employees selected for the training, mainly those in managerial positions, learn how to interact with other departments more effectively. As these examples show, the training goals should determine the type of training offered—a simple idea worth remembering.

Is Training a Good Investment?

Training can be expensive. Hewlett-Packard, for example, has an annual training budget of $300 million.[7] On average, the amount of money spent by employers on training in 2004 was approximately $820 per employee.[8] In contrast, the average training cost per employer in 2000 was $704.[9] Many companies fervently believe in the importance of training. However, economic conditions can be unstable and budgets limited, making it difficult to deliver needed training. The Manager's Notebook, "Cutting Training Costs but Maintaining Training Effectiveness," offers ways to reduce training costs that don't sacrifice the quality of the training. Although training can be expensive, it can also pay off in more capable and loyal workers. A recent survey in the printing industry found that more profitable companies spend more on training their employees than do less profitable ones.[10] Printing companies in the upper quartile of profitability spent twice as much on employee training than lower-profit companies, with 4.1 percent of the payroll of profit leaders going to training whereas companies in the lower quartile of profitability spent 2 percent of payroll. Interestingly, training was the only expense item on which profit leaders spent more than did less profitable operations. We can't conclude from the survey findings that training caused the higher profitability, but an emphasis on training certainly differentiates more profitable from less profitable companies.

MANAGER'S NOTEBOOK

Emerging Trends

Cutting Training Costs but Maintaining Training Effectiveness

Tight economic conditions can translate into smaller budgets for training in an organization. Doing away with training altogether may mean losing a competitive edge, or worse, losing the business. It isn't easy to maintain effectiveness when budgets are shrunk, but it is possible. Here are some tactics from training professionals to reduce costs.

- **Look inside.** Employees in the organization may be a rich source of training expertise. Furthermore, the relevance of the training can be built in when it comes from someone inside the organization. A director of training and education at a Florida automotive company had to eliminate training or find a low-cost alternative.[a] The 400-employee company now relies entirely on internal expertise for its training resource. Another internal approach to increasing skill levels is to use coaches and mentors—people in supervisory and management roles or people with particular expertise. Thus, training could be done within the top-down hierarchical structure in the organization or could be a peer-based process.
- **Do you need it?** Limit training to what is really needed. Given tighter budgets, a number of companies have shifted from a wide variety of types of training to a couple of key areas.
- **Give training a strategic alignment.** The investment in training will pay off in moving the organization forward to the extent that it is linked with strategy.
- **Consider e-learning.** Organizations might be able to save 50 percent to 70 percent of the cost of training by replacing the traditional instructor-led approach with an e-learning approach.[b] Most of the savings are due to reducing lost work hours and eliminating housing and travel costs.

Sources: [a]Adapted from *Managing Training & Development.* (2002). The five most effective strategies for improving training programs, March Newsletter of the Institute of Management and Administration; [b]Adapted from *Payroll Manager's Report.* (2002). How to train your staff on a smaller training budget. May Newsletter of the Institute of Management and Administration.

It isn't really the cost, per se, that should be the important issue as much as the effectiveness of the investment.

In some cases, training may be appropriate but not cost-effective. Before beginning a training program, managers must weigh the cost of the current problem against the cost of training to eliminate it.

Not conducting training can be a costly choice. A federal appeals court upheld a judgment against an employer because it failed to train its managers in the basic requirements of discrimination law. Phillips Chevrolet, Inc. was found guilty of age discrimination. A general manager who had ultimate hiring authority admitted that he often considered the age of applicants when making hiring decisions and wasn't aware that it was an illegal practice. The courts stated that the failure of the organization to train its managers in the basics of discrimination law was an "extraordinary mistake" and justified the conclusion that the company was recklessly indifferent to antidiscrimination law.[11] The court awarded $50,000 in punitive damages. The company probably realizes now that the cost required to train its managers in discrimination law was little relative to the cost levied against it for not providing that training. Sometimes a company may be legally obligated by the state to invest in training. For example, a recent California law (called AB 1825) requires all supervisors in companies with more than 50 employees to receive two hours of interactive preventive sexual harassment training every two years.[12]

Determining whether training is a good investment requires measuring the training's potential benefits in dollars. Training that focuses on "hard" areas (such as the running and adjustment of machines) that have a fairly direct impact on outcomes (such as productivity) can often be easily translated into a dollar value. Estimating the economic benefits of training in "softer" areas—such as teamwork and diversity training—is much more challenging. However, demonstrating the value of a training investment is important, particularly when budgets are tight. Only approximately 8 percent of organizations collect data and estimate their return on their investments in training.[13] Although not a dollar estimate, whether trainees learn what is covered in the training and then apply the new skills and knowledge back on the job can be indicators of the effectiveness of training. Even learning and application measures of effectiveness are estimated to be conducted by 31 percent and 14 percent of organizations, respectively.[14] Although evaluation may be lacking, the best companies try to maximize return on their training investment by aligning their training with their mission, strategy, and goals.[15] However, only an analysis of costs and benefits will indicate whether a training investment, no matter how well planned and positioned, was worth it or is worth continuing.

Will Training Work?

Designing effective training remains as much an art as a science, because no single type of training has proved most effective overall. For example, an organizational culture that supports change, learning, and improvement can be a more important determinant of a training program's effectiveness than any aspect of the program itself. Participants who view training solely as a day away from work are unlikely to benefit much from the experience. The Manager's Notebook, "Transfer of Training: Moving from Learning to Doing," offers steps you can take to ensure that what you learn in training is applied in your work.

If participants' managers do not endorse the content and purpose of the training, it is unlikely that the training program will have any influence on work processes. Consider the following training success story.

Customer-Driven HR

Transfer of Training: Moving from Learning to Doing

Training is meant to make positive changes in the workplace. For those changes to occur, not only must learning happen, but also the lessons learned need to be transferred to the workplace.

There are many reasons why training may not transfer. For example, upper management may not visibly support the change being promoted by the training. Furthermore, the lessons may be compelling, but the culture of the workplace may work against any changes. There may simply not be enough time to apply the lessons. The work environment may be too chaotic and unstructured for any lessons from training to take hold and make positive changes.

The following suggestions are steps that can be taken to maximize the chances that lessons from training transfer back to the workplace.

- *Be a teacher.* Be a link between the training and people in your area of the workplace. If you teach others what was learned in the training, you will help to spread the training and will practice and reinforce what you learned.
- *Assign yourself homework.* Set specific goals that apply the lessons learned in the training.
- *Develop your own job aids.* Placing a key model, terms, or steps learned in training on a convenient and easily seen spot, such as a tent card on your desk, can help remind you of the core message of the training.

- *Get a training partner.* A partner can help provide support for applying the lessons from training. Overcoming obstacles to transfer of training can be more easily accomplished with a partner than by yourself.
- *Ask for help.* If you need help in transferring the training lessons, you might ask your manager or the HR department for help. Additional materials, follow-up sessions, or other forms of organizational support may be available.

Source: Adapted with permission from Janove, J. W. (2002). Use it or lose it: Training is a waste of time and money if managers don't transfer lessons learned to their daily work lives. *HRMagazine, 47,* 99(4).

The Men's Wearhouse is an off-price retailer of men's business clothing. Despite the increasing size of the service sector (see Chapter 1), management of retail personnel is often poor and turnover is high. Further, training can be nonexistent, and the industry is increasingly competitive. In this context, the Men's Wearhouse has established itself as a quality clothier with a high growth and earnings rate and substantial growth in its stock value. Currently, the company has 22 percent of the U.S. men's suit market, and its profit increased by 18 percent in 2004.[16] Its approach to training differentiates the Men's Wearhouse from its major competitors. The company has constructed a 35,000-square-foot training center and offers programs such as "Suits University" and "Selling Accessories U." Three or four days of training are typically provided each year to both new and seasoned employees.

The company's training investment is substantially greater than that made by others in the industry. However, it seems to pay off well. First, although specific figures aren't available, the employee turnover rate is significantly lower than that of its competitors. Second, the "shrink" (lost inventory due to error or theft) is about one-third of the industry average. Also, the company's decision makers believe that if they create a corporate culture that supports employees, they don't need to spend money on security devices. In fact, the Men's Wearhouse spends nothing on security—no monitors or electronic tagging. Experts claim that the Men's Wearhouse's commitment to training has played a key role in its success.[17]

Finally, training will not work unless it is related to organizational goals. A well-designed training program flows from the company's strategic goals; a poorly designed one has no relationship

The Men's Wearhouse invests time and money to train its employees and the results are positive. The company retains its employees longer, has fewer inventory losses, and has lower security costs than its competitors.

to—or even worse, is at cross-purposes with—those goals. It is the manager's responsibility to ensure that training is linked with organizational goals.

Managing the Training Process

Poor, inappropriate, or inadequate training can be a source of frustration for everyone involved. To maximize the benefits of training, managers must closely monitor the training process.

As Figure 8.2 shows, the training process consists of three phases: (1) needs assessment, (2) development and conduct of training, and (3) evaluation. The *needs assessment phase* involves identifying the problems or needs that the training must address. In the *development and conduct phase,* the most appropriate type of training is designed and offered to the workforce. In the *evaluation phase,* the training program's effectiveness is assessed. In the pages that follow, we provide recommendations for maximizing the effectiveness of each of these phases.

In large organizations, surveys of workers and input of managers are very important for determining what training is needed (phase 1), but the actual training (phase 2) is usually provided by either the organization's own training department or an external resource (such as a consulting firm or a local university). After the training program is complete, managers may become involved to determine whether it has been useful (phase 3). In small businesses, the manager may be responsible for the entire process, although external sources of training may still be used.

The Needs Assessment Phase

The overall purpose of the needs assessment phase is to determine if training is needed, and if so, to provide the information required to design the training program. Needs assessment consists of three levels of analysis: organizational, task, and person.

The Levels of Needs Assessment

Organizational analysis examines broad factors such as the organization's culture, mission, business climate, long- and short-term goals, and structure. Its purpose is to identify both overall organizational needs and the level of support for training. Some of the key issues to be addressed at the organizational level of analysis are the external environment and the organization's goals and values.[18] An analysis of the external environment may indicate a shortage of skilled workers

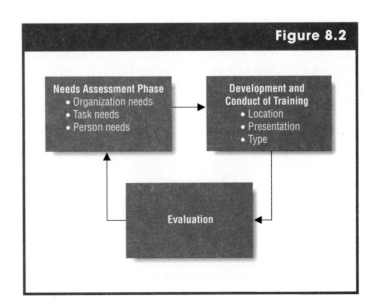

Figure 8.2   **The Training Process**

and changes in technology. Training can help the organization to meet these challenges. The goals of an organization are the targets it is trying to achieve—perhaps increased market share or expansion into a new market. Training may be needed to give employees the skills to achieve the organizational goals. Similarly, values can be the core of how an organization operates. Employees should understand these values and have the skills to work within them. In sum, the organizational level of needs assessment looks at external influences and the direction and principles of the organization to determine whether training is needed.

Task analysis is an examination of the job to be performed. A recent and carefully conducted job analysis should provide all the information needed to understand job requirements. These duties and tasks are used to identify the knowledge, skills, and abilities (KSAs) required to perform the job adequately (see Chapter 2). Then the KSAs are used to determine the kinds of training needed for the job.

Person analysis determines which employees need training by examining how well employees are carrying out the tasks that make up their jobs.[19] Training is often necessary when there is a discrepancy between a worker's performance and the organization's expectations or standards. Often a person analysis entails examining worker performance ratings and then identifying individual workers or groups of workers who are weak in certain skills. The source of most performance ratings is the supervisor, but (as we saw in Chapter 7) a more complete picture of workers' strengths and weaknesses may be obtained by including other sources of appraisal.

As we noted in Chapter 7, performance problems can come from numerous sources, many of which would not be affected by training. The only performance problem that training can address is a deficiency that is under the trainee's control.[20] For example, sales training will improve sales only if poor sales techniques are the source of the problem. If declining sales are due to a poor product, high prices, or a faltering economy, sales training is not going to help.

Training is not the only option available for responding to a worker deficiency. For example, if decision makers determine that the training needed would be too costly, transferring or terminating the deficient workers may be the more cost-effective course. Strict KSA requirements can then be used to select new employees and eliminate the performance gap. The obvious drawbacks of terminating or replacing employees deemed deficient is that these options are likely to harm commitment and morale in the workforce.

Clarifying the Objectives of Training

The assessment phase should provide a set of objectives for any training program that might be developed following the assessment. Each objective should relate to one or more of the KSAs identified in the task analysis and should be challenging, precise, achievable, and understood by all.[21] Pfizer, Inc., for example, gears its training to the competencies it has identified for jobs from entry level to the most senior positions.[22] Similarly, Wyeth, another pharmaceutical company, focuses its training on separate sets of competencies for sales employees and for managers.[23]

Whenever possible, objectives should be stated in behavioral terms and the criteria for judging the training program's effectiveness should flow directly from the behavioral objectives. Suppose the cause of a performance deficiency is poor interpersonal sensitivity. The overall objective of the training program designed to solve this problem, then, would be to increase interpersonal sensitivity. Increasing "interpersonal sensitivity" is a noble training goal, but the term is ambiguous and does not lead to specific content for a training program or to specific criteria by which the training's effectiveness can be judged. Stating this objective in behavioral terms requires determining what an employee will know, do, and not do after training. For example, the employee will greet customers and clients by name, refrain from sexual humor that could be perceived as harassing, and show up for all meetings on time.[24]

Figure 8.3 shows how the overall objective of sensitivity training provides a starting point that can be broken down into dimensions (specific aspects of job performance) for which managers can develop specific behavioral goals. The overall objective in the figure is to increase the interpersonal sensitivity of supervisors in their relations with production employees. First, this overall objective is divided into two dimensions: listening and feedback skills. Then specific behaviors that are part of these dimensions are identified, both to guide the training effort and to help evaluate whether the training has been successful.

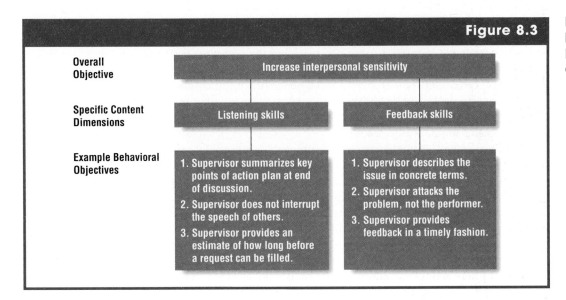

Figure 8.3

The Training and Conduct Phase

The training program that results from assessment should be a direct response to an organizational problem or need. Training approaches vary by location, presentation, and type.

Location Options

Training can be carried out either on the job or off the job. In the very common *on-the-job training (OJT)* approach, the trainee works in the actual work setting, usually under the guidance of an experienced worker, supervisor, or trainer. At the Los Alamos National Laboratory of the U.S. Department of Energy, for instance, training often relies on one-on-one coaching, hands-on demonstrations, and practice. Before setting the training in motion, however, management at this New Mexico–based facility carefully considers the task employees are being trained for, the level of training needed, the number of trainees, and the availability of instructional settings and resources.

Job rotation, apprenticeships, and internships are all forms of OJT.

■ *Job rotation,* as we saw in Chapter 2, allows employees to gain experience in different kinds of narrowly defined jobs in the organization. It is often used to give future managers a broad background.

■ *Apprenticeships,* OJT programs typically associated with the skilled trades, derive from the medieval practice of having the young learn a trade from an experienced worker. In Europe, apprenticeships are still one of the major ways for young men and women to gain entry to skilled jobs. In the United States, apprenticeships are largely confined to adults wanting to work in certain occupations, such as carpentry and plumbing. These apprenticeships generally last four years, and the apprentice's pay starts at about half that of the more experienced "journey workers."

■ Just as apprenticeships are a route to certain skilled blue-collar jobs, *internships* are a route to white-collar or managerial jobs in a variety of fields. Internships are opportunities for students to gain real-world job experience, often during summer vacations from school. Although most internships offer very low or no pay, student interns can often gain college credits and, possibly, the offer of a full-time job after graduation.

OJT has both benefits and drawbacks. This type of training is obviously relevant to the job because the tasks confronted and learned are generated by the job itself. Very little that is learned in the context of OJT would not transfer directly to the job. OJT also spares the organization the expense of taking employees out of the work environment for training and usually the cost of hiring outside trainers, because company employees generally are capable of doing the training.

On the negative side, OJT can prove quite costly to the organization in lost business when on-the-job trainees cause customer frustration. (Have you ever been caught in a checkout line that moves like molasses because a trainee is operating the cash register?) Even if only a handful of customers switch to a competitor because of dissatisfaction with trainee service, the cost to the organization can be substantial. Errors and damage to equipment that occur when a trainee is on the job may also prove costly. Another potential drawback is that trainers might be top-notch in terms of their skills but inadequate at transferring their knowledge to others. In other words, those who can, cannot always teach.

Finally, the quality and content of OJT can vary substantially across organizations. This variability makes it difficult for employers to judge the skill level of a potential worker from another organization. A new worker may claim that he or she received OJT for operating a piece of machinery or conducting a task, but the employer can be left wondering what the worker really learned and what skill level she or he brings to the operation. Consider how Washington State is trying to relieve the problem of variability of OJT.

Washington is home to 1,300 wood products manufacturers, the vast majority of which are small operations—90 percent of these manufacturers employ an average of 16 people. Finding qualified workers is difficult, and the problem is made worse by OJT that can vary substantially in quality and content across employers.

To address this problem, a statewide group of 87 people from industry, schools, and unions formed a team called Washington's Secondary Wood Products Manufacturing Advisory Team (SWPMT). The team wrote skill standards for the wood products industry, identified needed skills (that is, the team did a *task analysis*—see "The Assessment Phase" in this chapter), and then wrote descriptions of the required knowledge and skills. The team's next step is to develop a curriculum and training based on these standards. Thus, a standard training experience will replace the spotty OJT that currently characterizes the industry. Certification based on the skill standards will provide workers with a way to communicate the skills they have achieved and provide employers a way of knowing the skill levels of their workforce.[25]

The work of SWPMT in Washington is linked to the National Skills Standards Board. The goal of the board is to create a national system of skill standards so that businesses can obtain the skilled workforce they need.[26]

Off-the-job training is an effective alternative to OJT. Common examples of off-the-job training are formal courses, simulations, and role-playing exercises in a classroom setting. One advantage of off-the-job training is that it gives employees extended periods of uninterrupted study. Another is that a classroom setting may be more conducive to learning and retention because it avoids the distractions and interruptions that commonly occur in an OJT environment. The big disadvantage of off-the-job training is that what is learned may not transfer back to the job. After all, a classroom is not the workplace, and the situations simulated in the training may not closely match those encountered on the job. Also, if employees view off-the-job training as an opportunity to enjoy some time away from work, not much learning is likely to take place.

Presentation Options

Trainers use a variety of presentation techniques in training sessions. The most common presentation techniques are slides and videotapes, teletraining, computers, simulations, virtual reality, and classroom instruction and role-plays.

Slides and Videotapes. Slides and videotapes can be used either off-the-job or in special media rooms in an organization's facility. Slides and videotapes provide consistent information and, if done well, can be interesting and thought provoking. However, these presentation media do not allow trainees to ask questions or receive further explanation. Many companies prefer to use slides, film, or tapes to supplement a program led by a trainer, who can answer individuals' questions and flesh out explanations when necessary.

Teletraining. A training option that can be useful when trainees are dispersed across various physical locations is teletraining.[27] Satellites are used to beam live training broadcasts to employees at different locations. In addition to the video reception, the satellite link can allow trainees to ask questions of the instructor during the broadcast.

Two disadvantages of teletraining are the need for an expensive satellite connection and the difficulty of scheduling the broadcast so that everyone will be able to attend. A company can solve the scheduling problem by videotaping the presentation and then offering the video-tape to people in locations where schedules conflicted with the live broadcast. The training instructor can be available via phone or computer to respond to questions. This method makes the trainer's expertise available to trainees without requiring him or her to redeliver the entire training program.

Computers. Computer-based training can range from the use of a CD-ROM to training over the Internet. A number of companies are still exploring what type of computer-based training works best for them. However, Web-based training is fast becoming the training method of choice.

Both small and large businesses are finding computer-training to be a cost-effective medium. In particular, if a job requires extensive use of computers, then computer-based training is highly job related and provides for a high degree of transfer of training back to the job. Computers also have the advantage of allowing trainees to learn at a comfortable pace. As a trainer, the computer never becomes tired, bored, or short-tempered. Further, computers can be a multimedia training option in which text can be combined with film, graphics, and audio components.

Using the Internet or company intranet for training, e-learning has been increasing in popularity for obvious reasons. This approach not only offers the content but also administers the training. E-learning also offers a way to standardize training across far-flung employees and centers of operation.[28] Perhaps the most apparent reason is the elimination of travel and lodging costs. A general estimate is that companies can reduce their training costs by 50 to 70 percent by using electronic courses rather than traditional classroom-style training.[29] Since individuals can access training at any time and from any place where an Internet connection is available, it is not surprising that e-learning is a success story at many organizations.

Learnshare is a successful example of collaboration among companies to use e-learning.[30] Members of Learnshare include General Motors Corp., Motorola Inc., Owens-Corning, Deere & Co., and 3M Corp., among others. Some of the companies compete in some areas, but Learnshare enables them to collaborate on meeting their common training needs, sharing courses via the Internet and using their collective strength to leverage discounts from e-learning suppliers.

The wood products industry needs a trained workforce. Washington State's Secondary Wood Products Manufacturing Advisory Team has developed skill standards to help meet this need.

The e-learning market is estimated to account for $18 billion in sales in 2005.[31] The approach can deliver rapid results[32] across geographically dispersed workers. However, it can be more expensive to design good online training than to provide classroom training. One estimate is that 1 hour of classroom time requires 6 design hours, whereas 1 hour of online instruction may require up to 400 hours of design time.[33] In addition, the implementation of electronic training can sometimes pose difficulties. As presented in the Manager's Notebook, "Delivery Glitches Can Kill e-Learning," technical difficulties and end users' skills affect the results.

Customer-Driven HR

Delivery Glitches Can Kill e-Learning

Online training offers many advantages, but unforseen problems can get in the way of smooth and effective delivery and therefore of improved skills and performance. Consider the following examples of real problems:

■ Employees don't know how to log in to the training site or forgot their user name or password.
■ The course doesn't launch when it is clicked.
■ Employees had to attend to another task during training, and when they returned, the place they left off wasn't bookmarked.
■ Employees don't know why they have to take the course for which they have been registered.

These problems seem simple and even silly. However, they can cause e-learning to be a source of frustration rather than real learning.

A first step in avoiding them is to make sure that people understand the purpose of the training and how it is related to the business. Secondly, take a customer perspective to the training delivery. What do employees need to know in order to effectively access the training material? Are there instructions or job aids that would make the training go smoothly for employees? If possible, a pilot program run with a small group of employees can help you uncover unanticipated problems.

Source: Osberg, C. (2004, February). Marketing e-learning. *T&D, 58,* 53–54.

The sophistication of the technology does not make any guarantees about the content of the training. If the content preparation is poor, the training experience will be poor as well. Further, training employees in complex skills or concepts may be best accomplished through interaction with experienced people. Also, in instances when a job's duties do not require the use of a computer, computer-based training may hinder the learning process.[34]

Finally, remember that computer-based training is not an all-or-nothing proposition. For example, a trainer might supplement e-learning with a live workshop to maximize the advantages of each approach.[35] The computerized portion can promote learning by allowing trainees to make mistakes and search for correct choices privately. The workshop can help trainees practice and reinforce their skills through vehicles such as interactive role playing. A number of organizations are successfully taking a blended approach in which e-learning is supplemented with classroom instruction.[36] Caterpillar, for example, has a training program for new manufacturing employees that typically combines e-learning, classroom instruction, and on-the-job training on the assembly line.[37]

Simulation
A device or situation that replicates job demands at an off-the-job site.

Simulations. Particularly effective in training are **simulations**, devices or situations that replicate job demands at an off-the-job site. Organizations often use simulations when the information to be mastered is complex, the equipment used on the job is expensive, and/or the cost of a wrong decision is high. The performance of jobs in the military, law enforcement, and security can sometimes mean life or death. Simulations can be particularly effective at safely training people to handle these situations. Firearms Training Systems Inc. (FATS) provides simulation training for military organizations around the world.[38] The training includes simulated weapons that realistically portray the real things, including recoil. A FATS simulation for training police officers uses a computer and a 10-foot video screen to confront police officers-in-training with the sights and sounds of a number of situations commonly encountered in police work. For example, a dangerous suspect is fleeing on a crowded street. Should the officer shoot at the suspect and risk injuring or killing innocent bystanders? FATS gives police trainees the opportunity to practice making such snap decisions in a safe but realistic setting.

The airline industry has long used simulators to train pilots. Flight simulations often include motion in addition to visual and auditory realism. This aspect substantially increases the cost of the simulation but makes the training even more realistic. The NASA Ames Research Center has, for example, developed a virtual control tower simulator with a price tag of approximately $10 million. Viewers can see any airport in the world outside the control tower's 12 glass windows in a 360-degree view. The tower can simulate any time of day or night, any weather pattern, and the movement of up to 200 aircraft and ground vehicles.

Traditionally, simulators have been considered separate from computer-based training. With advances in multimedia technology, however, the distinctions between these two methods have blurred considerably.

A product called CathSim is an example of the melding of computerized and simulator types of training. The CathSim AccuTouch System gives medical personnel the chance to practice giving shots before giving them to a real patient. The training system combines computer software with tactile-feel robotics so that students, nurses, and doctors can get a realistic experience without practicing on animals or humans.[39] In addition, the CathSim provides trainees with report cards on their effectiveness and allows supervisors to track trainees' progress.

The CathSim works with a PC and includes a small robotic box, called AccuTouch, which is about the size of a paperback book. A computer program allows users to select from a variety of options, such as whether the patient is an elderly woman or a drug user. The program then presents on screen a number of materials and needle sizes to choose from. After that, the trainee inserts a real needle into the AccuTouch box. The box has a rubber-like substance and mimics resistance and other factors of a real patient's arm. If the needle is inserted improperly the computer program may yell "ow" in response.

Air traffic control simulators, though costly, can improve a company's bottom line. Delta's use of an air traffic control simulator to train its personnel has helped the airline save approximately $20 million.

Few studies have been done on the effectiveness of simulations, but the limited data available indicate that this training method does have a positive impact on job performance. For example, one study found that pilots who trained on simulators become proficient at flight maneuvers nearly twice as fast as pilots who trained only in the air.[40] The importance of this difference is underscored by the fact that the cost of simulator training is only about 10 percent of the cost of using the real equipment to train pilots.

Virtual reality (VR)
The use of a number of technologies to replicate the entire real-life working environment in real time.

Virtual Reality. **Virtual reality (VR)** uses a number of technologies to replicate the entire real-life working environment rather than just several aspects of it, as do simulations. VR immerses a participant in a computer-generated virtual environment that changes according to head and body movements.[41] Within these three-dimensional environments, a user can interact with and manipulate objects in real time.

The military uses VR training and continues to invest in the technology. Immersing soldiers in the types of situations they may face on the battlefield can be valuable experience and help them to be better prepared for combat. Additionally, VR may provide a stress inoculation for military personnel and lower their chances of developing psychological problems when placed in actual combat.[42]

VR technology is also being successfully applied in the private sector. For instance, Motorola's Semiconductor Product Sector tested a VR training system developed by Modis Training Technologies.[43] Modis is an Arizona company that specializes in recreating plant floors in VR, complete with production lines and equipment. The test results were positive: Motorola trainees made fewer mistakes and learned faster with the virtual training. The average learning time dropped from 6 weeks to 1.5 weeks. Because a mistake on a semiconductor production line can cost half a million dollars, Motorola's investment in training seems modest compared to the savings.

Tasks that are good candidates for VR training are those that require rehearsal and practice, working from a remote location, or visualizing objects and processes that are not usually accessible. VR training is also excellent for tasks in which there is a high potential for damage to equipment or danger to individuals.

For example, forestry students in Alvdalen, Sweden, practice in a virtual tree harvester before operating the real machine.[44] Researchers found that students who received VR training were more confident and productive when they started operating the real machine. In contrast, students who trained in the real machine (a behemoth that has a 33-foot arm and can carry 90-foot pine trees) were much more nervous and dangerous. A harvesting machine costs approximately $400,000 and damage to it or the environment could be expensive. Wouldn't you rather put in a few hours on the virtual equipment before being responsible for the real thing? Similarly, VR training is becoming the method of choice for training physicians in how to implant carotid stents—devices that hold open the carotid arteries.[45] In the VR training, physicians thread a catheter through an artificial circulatory system and view angiograms of the human mannequin. VR training is being used in more areas of surgery, and the trend will likely continue. So far, two

The CathSim allows medical personnel to practice in a simulation environment rather than on humans or animals.

studies have found that residents trained with VR made fewer errors and had skills similar to those of experienced surgeons. For both the forestry students and medical residents, the improved skills were obtained without putting the environment and individuals at risk.

Classroom Instruction and Role-Plays. Although widely viewed as "boring," classroom instruction can be exciting if other presentation techniques are integrated with the lecture. For example, a videotape could complement the discussion by providing realistic examples of the lecture material. In-class case exercises and role-plays (both of which are found throughout this book) provide an opportunity for trainees to apply what is being taught in the class and transfer that knowledge back to the job. Solving and discussing case problems helps trainees learn technical material and content, and role-plays are an excellent way of applying the interpersonal skills being emphasized in the training. If done well, role-plays give trainees the opportunity to practice the skills they've been studying via books, video, computer, or some other medium.[46]

Types of Training

We focus here on the types of training that are commonly used in today's organizations: skills, retraining, cross-functional, team, creativity, literacy, diversity, crisis, and customer service.

Skills Training. Skills training is probably the most common in organizations. The process is fairly simple: The need or deficit is identified via a thorough assessment. Specific training objectives are generated, and training content is developed to achieve those objectives. The criteria for assessing the training's effectiveness are also based on the objectives identified in the assessment phase.

To understand how skills training programs are developed, let us examine a classic example of skills training. In 1992, 10 percent of all complaints to IBM's CEO centered on the handling of telephone calls. Because customer service is one of IBM's top priorities, the CEO knew he had to take action. He appointed a project team composed of both line managers and trainers to investigate the situation. This arrangement was designed to ensure that line personnel would take the project team's recommendations and actions seriously. (Programs that come out of the "black box" of the HR department are sometimes discounted by line managers.)

The project team did a careful assessment. A survey of IBM customers revealed that 70 percent of customer contact was via telephone.[47] A formal survey of over 10,000 IBM customers revealed that shoddy phone handling was the biggest complaint. As Figure 8.4 shows, customers'

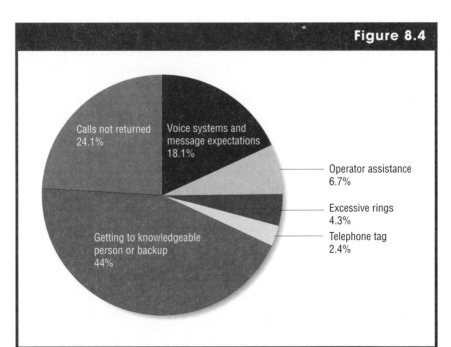

Figure 8.4

Sources of Customer Dissatisfaction with IBM Telephone Service

Source: Estabrooke, R. M., and Fay, N. F. (1992). Answering the call of "tailored training." *Training, 29,* 85–88. Reprinted with permission from the October 1992 issue of *Training.* Copyright 1992. Lakewood Publications, Minneapolis, MN. All rights reserved. Not for resale.

Figure 8.5

Interoffice Memo

Over all, the rating of our telephone service by customers and internal users is poor. Together, we are going to fix this problem, and fix it fast.

IBM Senior Vice President's Memo to All Managers

Source: Estabrooke, R. M., and Fay, N. F. (1992). Answering the call of "tailored training." *Training, 29,* 85–88. Reprinted with permission from the October 1992 issue of *Training.* Copyright 1992. Lakewood Publications. Minneapolis, MN. All rights reserved. Not for resale.

most frequent complaints were that they could not reach a knowledgeable person and that their calls were not being returned. The project team then conducted a survey of IBM employees and found that while more than 75 percent knew how to put a customer on hold, fewer than 5 percent knew how to forward a call. The team also found that most professional employees felt that they did not need telephone skills because calls from customers should be handled by the secretarial staff. Based on these survey results, the team categorized the telephone interaction problem into two broad categories: (1) not using phone features and (2) not treating customers with professional courtesy.

The team presented its findings and recommended a training strategy to senior management. The senior vice president in charge of the team, who agreed that telephone interactions were a problem to be taken seriously, issued the stern memo reprinted in Figure 8.5. Any employee receiving this memo clearly got the message that telephone skills were now a main issue at IBM. The strong support of top management forced line employees to take the issue seriously and helped the project team obtain funds for the training program.

The project team divided employees into two groups on the basis of how often they used the phone system and then tailored the training to each group. The "intensive" group was composed of employees such as secretaries and operators, the "casual" group of engineers, managers, and other professionals. The intensive group was relatively small in number but accounted for most of the phone interaction with customers. It was important that this group be both courteous and well acquainted with the phone system. The casual group needed not only to understand the basics of the phone system but also had to be trained in telephone etiquette.

Training for the intensive user group involved broad-based coverage of expected behaviors and instruction in the phone system's specific operational features. Among the training program's features: a videotape of good and poor role models of phone interaction shown to secretaries and switchboard operators, a computer-based training program that covered details of the phone system as well as courtesy skills, and pamphlets and other reference materials. Depending on their current levels of skill and knowledge, trainees took from three to nine hours to complete the program.

The casual users required a substantially different approach for three reasons. First, they did not need the same level of knowledge as the intensive group because they had much less phone interaction with customers. Second, the cost of intensive training for the approximately 150,000 professional employees who fell into the casual group would be prohibitive. Third, the casual users were not motivated to improve their telephone skills because they did not see a problem in their phone performance. These employees' training package, then, was designed to be brief and entertaining. A videotape shown at departmental meetings provided an overview of the topic. In addition, a brief and humorous audiotape that could be played in the car or on the job emphasized the desired behaviors. An abbreviated version of the computer-based training program focusing on only the key elements of phone operation was included in the casual users' package. Pamphlets and other reference sources were also provided. The project team assumed that most casual users would select the product they preferred and spend perhaps an hour with the material.

Other HR activities focused on motivating employees to solve the phone communication problem. For example, the senior vice president selected telephone effectiveness as one of five key annual performance measures. Additionally, the project team's staff made random calls monthly to assess each business unit's phone effectiveness. Figure 8.6, which can serve as a model for any kind of skill improvement training program, summarizes the process followed by the training project team at IBM.

The program was quite successful. After one year, customer satisfaction with IBM's telephone responsiveness increased by nearly 10 percent. Although the long-term goal is 100 percent satisfaction, a 10 percent increase in the first year of a program is certainly a healthy improvement.

IBM's program offers several lessons:

- In some organizational settings, the most important step in building commitment to training may be the inclusion of people who have a great deal of informal or political power in the organization. If someone is politically strong enough to torpedo an instructional effort, it may be best to include him or her in the program's training design from the outset.

Steps to Skill Improvement at IBM

> **Figure 8.6**
>
> 1. Build in commitment.
>   - Gain support of management.
> 2. Thoroughly analyze the problem.
>   - Is it important?
>   - What is the real problem?
> 3. Gain line support.
> 4. Develop training strategies.
>   - Is there more than one group of employees that needs training?
>   - Design materials appropriate to each group's needs and motivation levels.
> 5. Develop motivational strategies.
>   - Take steps to heighten awareness of issue.
>   - Signal importance of issue through measurement and recognition programs.

- The idea of beginning a training program with assessments at the organizational, task, and person levels may not be realistic. In reality, problems often come suddenly to light in organizations, and something must be done about them quickly if the organization is to remain competitive.

- Multiple forms of a training package may be needed for different groups of trainees. Some employee groups may need detailed knowledge and a high level of skills in a particular area, while others may need only broad familiarity and basic skills. Tailoring the training to each group's skill requirements maximizes the training's effectiveness.

- Providing trainees with materials such as pamphlets and reference guides can help to ensure that the training results in improved performance. These sorts of materials, **job aids**, are external sources of information that workers can access quickly when they need help in making a decision or performing a specific task.[48] Their use is growing rapidly for a few reasons. First, job aids reduce the need to memorize many details and therefore decrease errors and bolster efficiency. Second, although job aids cannot replace formal training programs, they can supplement training and help ensure that the training transfers back to the job. Third, they are relatively inexpensive and can be developed and delivered quickly.

Job aids
External sources of information, such as pamphlets and reference guides, that workers can access quickly when they need help in making a decision or performing a specific task.

Retraining. A subset of skills training, *retraining* gives employees the skills they need to keep pace with their job's changing requirements. For instance, however proficient garment workers may be at a traditional skill such as sewing, they will need retraining when the company invests in computerized sewing equipment. Unfortunately, even though retraining is much cited in the media as an item at the top of the corporate agenda, many companies rush to upgrade their equipment without taking comparable steps to upgrade their employees' skills. They erroneously believe that automation means a lower-skilled workforce when, in fact, it often requires a more highly skilled one.

One company that takes retraining seriously is Nabisco Group Holdings. It gives workers faced with new technology the option of accepting early retirement or receiving retraining. Other significant developments on the retraining front have been spearheaded by creative partnerships between labor unions and employers. For instance, the Garment Industry Development Corporation consolidates union and industry efforts. Its Super Sewer program teaches a worker all the operations necessary to make a garment using computerized pattern making.[49]

Retraining not only gets the presently employed up to speed but also provides training assistance to displaced (laid-off) and unemployed workers. Several government initiatives have provided funding for retraining for displaced workers. *The Job Training Partnership Act (JTPA) of 1982,* the largest single training program financed by the federal government, gives block grants to states, which pass them on to local governments and private entities that provide on-the-job training.

Unfortunately, retraining efforts do not appear to be as effective as some would hope. Government statistics show that only 7 to 12 percent of dislocated workers take advantage of

JTPA retraining programs. Furthermore, not all the people who go through retraining complete the program or benefit from it.[50] Critics also point out that the JTPA's placement rate is a disappointing 50 percent.

Cross-Functional Training.   Traditionally, organizations have developed specialized work functions and detailed job descriptions. However, today's organizations are emphasizing versatility rather than specialization.

Cross-functional training

Training employees to perform operations in areas other than their assigned job.

Cross-functional training teaches employees to perform operations in areas other than their assigned job. For example:

- Job rotation can be used to provide a manager in one functional area with a broader perspective than he or she would otherwise have.
- Departments can trade personnel for periods of time so that each worker or set of workers develops an understanding of the other department's operation.
- **Peer trainers**, high-performing workers who double as internal on-the-job trainers, can be extraordinarily effective in helping employees develop skills in another area of operation.[51]

Peer trainers

High-performing workers who double as internal on-the-job trainers.

Aside from having top-notch skills, peer trainers must be patient and motivated to teach others. An effective way to choose motivated people is simply to ask workers whether they would like to be a peer trainer and then select the best volunteers. Some organizations promote the peer-trainer role as an honor and offer a tangible reward to sweeten the added responsibility. At Walt Disney's parks, peer trainers are paid extra while they are instructing and bear a trainer designation on their name badges as they move around the park. Volunteers at some companies such as national retailer T.J. Maxx undergo a formal training program to become successful peer trainers.

Employees and managers should also be instructed in the importance of such training and the benefits it can provide:

- The more adaptable workers are, the more valuable they become to the organization. Adaptability increases both workers' job security and the organization's "depth on the bench." The analogy to baseball is apt. Suppose a baseball team does not have a trained replacement for a particular player. When that player is injured, the coach has a problem because there is no one on the bench who can effectively play that position. Similarly, an organization is in trouble if a worker who leaves, is promoted, or becomes ill cannot quickly be replaced with someone else who can do the job. Cross-functional training can provide the talent base that ensures operations will continue to run smoothly.
- Versatile employees can better engineer their own career paths.
- When promotions aren't available, broader exposure and responsibility can motivate workers.
- Training coworkers can clarify a worker's own job responsibilities.
- A broader perspective increases workers' understanding of the business as a whole and reduces the need for supervision.[52]
- When workers can fill in for other workers who are absent, it is easier to use flexible scheduling, which is increasingly in demand as more employees want to spend more time with their families.

Employees 50 years or older may be particularly valuable when it comes to cross-functional versatility.[53] Older workers have often already performed a variety of jobs, which will have naturally provided them with a good amount of cross-functional experience. They also tend to have a broader perspective on the organization's operations. For these reasons, older workers are often quick studies in a cross-functional training program and make effective peer trainers.

Team Training.   In the best manufacturing plants, approximately 70 percent of production workers are in self-directed or empowered teams.[54] The team structure offers much promise in terms of performance, but team issues, ranging from personality conflicts to communication problems, can get in the way of teams performing to their potential. A recent survey found only 14.1 percent of companies judged their teaming efforts as "highly effective" and 15 percent as "not effective at all."[55] There certainly appears to be room for improvement in team performance.

Nonetheless, work teams are likely to increase in prevalence and importance. Teams are becoming embedded in how many business operate. Further, many organizations are operating in a global environment, which forces people in far-flung geographic locations to operate as teams. For example, Steelcase, the furniture manufacturer, has a presence on every continent and uses teams with members from different countries to develop new products and processes.[56] For Steelcase, teams are not only a way of life, but they are also a means for survival in a globally competitive market. The team structure is here for the long term, and team training can be the key to unlocking the potential of work teams.

Team training can be divided into two areas based on the two basic team operations: content tasks and group processes.[57] *Content tasks* directly relate to a team's goals—for example, cost control and problem solving. *Group processes* pertain to the way members function as a team—for example, how team members behave toward one another, how they resolve conflicts, and how extensively they participate. Unlike traditional individual training, team training goes beyond the content skills and includes group processes.[58]

Surprisingly, little is known about how to train teams most effectively. The following initial findings can be used to guide team training efforts:

- Team members should be trained in communication skills (both speaking and listening) that encourage respect for all team members.
- Training should emphasize the interdependence of team members.
- Instruction should instill the recognition that team goals and individual goals are not always the same and provide strategies for dealing with conflicts that will inevitably arise between the two.
- Flexibility should be emphasized because teamwork almost always causes unexpected situations.[59]

One type of training that has become increasingly popular for developing teamwork, particularly among managerial and supervisory employees, is outdoor experiential training. Companies such as IBM, General Electric, and DuPont periodically take hundreds of employees out of the office and into the woods in hopes of building teamwork, increasing communication skills, and boosting self-esteem. Many of these experiential training programs resemble Outward Bound, the rigorous outdoor adventure course, although they are less physically demanding.

Group culinary activities are also emerging as an effective way to improve team processes.[60] Culinary team-building programs can be competitive and involve recipe competitions between teams. Or, they can be designed as collaborative efforts, such as when teams need to work together to prepare a multicourse meal. One culinary team-building company assigns teams various dishes to prepare and culinary coaches provide basic instructions. The teams are given 30 minutes to prepare their dish, but after 25 minutes everyone is told to stop and move to the next station on the left! At the new station, no one knows what to do. The team-building company has seen a wide array of responses to this problem, ranging from people just walking away from their stations to leaving one person behind to help the new group through the recipe. The exercise focuses on how teams can better communicate to support each other and improve overall performance. This lesson is certainly pertinent to the workplace, where dynamic changes and unanticipated problems may be encountered at any time.

Creativity Training.   Creativity training is based on the assumption that creativity can be learned. There are several approaches to teaching creativity, all of which attempt to help people solve problems in new ways.[61] One common approach is the use of **brainstorming**, in which participants are given the opportunity to generate ideas as wild as they can come up with, without fear of judgment. Only after a good number of ideas have been generated are they individually submitted to rational judgment in terms of their cost and feasibility. Creativity is generally viewed as having two phases: imaginative and practical.[62] Brainstorming followed by rational consideration of the options it produces satisfies both phases. Figure 8.7 presents some other approaches to increasing creativity.

Because people often find it difficult to break out of their habitual ways of thinking, creativity trainers provide exercises designed to help them see things in a new way. In one innovative program provided by a Dallas–based creativity consultant, half a dozen gifted, outgoing youngsters

Brainstorming
A creativity training technique in which participants are given the opportunity to generate ideas openly, without fear of judgment.

Figure 8.7

Creativity can be learned and developed. The following techniques can be used to improve a trainee's skill in generating innovative ideas and solutions to problems.

1. **Analogies and Metaphors** Drawing comparisons or finding similarities can improve insight into a situation or problem.
2. **Free Association** Freely associating words to describe a problem can lead to unexpected solutions.
3. **Personal Analogy** Trying to see oneself as the problem can lead to fresh perspectives and, possibly, effective solutions.
4. **Mind Mapping** Generating topics and drawing lines to represent the relationships among them can help to identify all the issues and their linkages.

Source: Adapted from Higgins, J. M. (1994). *101 creative problem solving techniques: The handbook of new ideas for business.* Winter Park, FL: New Management Publishing Company.

Techniques to Increase Creativity

from a Dallas school are cloistered with up to 30 top managers in day-long sessions. The adults vent their business problems—and the kids give them advice. The adult participants have found talking to kids about these problems helpful because, as an executive from Texas Utilities Mining put it, "They didn't have any preconceived ideas."[63]

Some companies, such as Pfizer, Inc., and Progressive Corporation, use art as inspiration for problem solving and to spark creativity among employees.[64] Both companies expose employees to art through museum workshops or on-site exhibits. The Boyer Corporation has a company art program designed to get employees thinking about different alternatives and perspectives so they can be more creative in their work.

Skeptics criticize creativity training, saying there is no way to measure its effectiveness. They also say that training in a soft skill like creativity might make people feel good but does not produce any lasting change in their work performance. It is true that documenting the bottom-line results of creativity training is nearly impossible. Yet some companies have found impressive results. For example, Frito-Lay says a cost-management program done in conjunction with creative problem-solving training saved more than $500 million in a five-year period. And when a team of DuPont's top engineers was stumped at why new technology worked in the lab but faltered in a manufacturing plant, creativity trainers came to the rescue. After employees at the plant were trained in creative thinking techniques, the technology worked as planned.

Of course, creativity training is not a magic solution to all problems. No training program is. And while a training program can help stimulate creativity, poor management support or a work climate that doesn't support innovation can limit the impact of creativity training.[65]

Literacy Training.   The abilities to write, speak, and work well with others are critical in today's business environment. Unfortunately, many workers do not meet employer requirements in these areas. For example, although most workplace materials require a tenth- or eleventh-grade reading level, about 20 percent of Americans between the ages of 21 and 25 cannot read at even an eighth-grade level.[66] U.S. companies spend more the $3 billion annually for remedial training for employees.[67]

Literacy
The mastery of basic skills (reading, writing, arithmetic, and their uses in problem solving).

The term **literacy** is generally used to mean the mastery of *basic skills*—that is, the subjects normally taught in public schools (reading, writing, arithmetic, and their uses in problem solving). It is important to distinguish between general literacy and functional literacy. *General literacy* is a person's general skill level, whereas *functional literacy* is a person's skill level in a particular content area. An employee is functionally literate if he or she can read and write well enough to perform important job duties (reading instruction manuals, understanding safety messages, filling out order slips). The most pressing issue for employers is not the general deficiencies in the workforce, but rather their workers' ability to function effectively in their jobs. For example, a generally low level of reading ability may be cause for societal concern, but it is workers' inability to understand safety messages or fill out order slips that is the immediate concern for business. Functional illiteracy can be a serious impediment to an organization's productivity and competitiveness. For instance, the Occupational Safety and Health Administration (see Chapter 16) believes that there is a direct correlation between illiteracy and some workplace accidents.

Functional literacy training programs focus on the basic skills required to perform a job adequately and capitalize on most workers' motivation to get help or advance in a particular job. These programs use materials drawn directly from the job. For example, unlike a reading comprehension course (which teaches general reading skills), functional training teaches employees to comprehend manuals and other reading materials they must use on the job.

Working in concert with unions, government agencies, and schools, companies have devised a number of programs to remedy deficiencies in basic skills. These programs fall into three basic categories:

■ **Company in-house programs** These programs are conducted solely or primarily for company employees. For example, Dofasco, a Canadian steel company, identified employee literacy as a key need in the organization. The company designed custom courses that employees could voluntarily take. During seven years of operation, approximately 600 Dofasco employees have participated in the literacy program, and the company views it as a successful intervention.[68]

■ **Company/local schools programs** Many companies join with a local high school or community college in a partnership in which the companies and/or unions pay for workers to attend classes at local schools. Some companies allow workers up to six hours off per week to attend classes. Sometimes several companies are involved in the partnership, as in the Newark Literacy Campaign, the Alliance for Education in Worcester, Massachusetts, and the Memphis Literacy Coalition.

In Phoenix, the Public Works and Personnel Departments worked with local community colleges and a county literacy volunteer group to develop a curriculum for city employees.[69] The well-received program has been successful despite its relatively low cost, which averages about $2.25 per employee contact hour. More than 950 employees from 13 departments have participated in the program.[70] Gains in literacy help the organization and improve employees' personal and professional quality of life.

■ **Company/local or state government programs** In some areas, local or state government has supplied the major initiative for literacy programs. The South Carolina Institute for Work Force Excellence is one of the most extensive partnership programs between state government and the state's leading employers. In the first year after the South Carolina legislature passed a broad education reform measure, 338 initiative programs enrolling more than 3,000 people were held across the state. A third of the people enrolled work for Springs Industries, Inc., the state's largest employer. Other major participating companies are Campbell Soup, Digital Equipment, and Sun Oil.[71]

A Question of Ethics

Are companies ethically responsible for providing literacy training for workers who lack basic skills? Why or why not?

Diversity Training.   Ensuring that the diverse groups of people working in a company get along and cooperate is vital to organizational success. As we saw in Chapter 4, *diversity training programs* are designed to teach employees about specific cultural and sex differences and how to respond to these in the workplace. Diversity training is particularly important when team structures are used. To be successful, it must include and be sensitive to all groups, including white males who may perceive that the training is directed at or against them.[72] Diversity training that focuses on individual strengths and weaknesses rather than on differences between groups can be a positive experience for all employees. Making the link between diversity and the business is also important. For example, effective organizations are moving their diversity training beyond debunking stereotypes to the need to engage employees from diverse backgrounds.[73] Kodak includes training for all its employees that addresses the importance of diversity for its business.[74] (See Chapter 4 for additional information about diversity training.)

Crisis Training.   Unfortunately, accidents, disasters, and violence are part of life. Events such as plane crashes, chemical spills, and workplace violence can wreak havoc on organizations. Yet many organizations are ill prepared to deal with the tragedies and their aftermath. Consider the criticism leveled against the Federal Emergency Management Agency (FEMA) for its response to the devastation of the New Orleans area due to Hurricane Katrina. The agency was accused of delay and inadequacy and the agency director resigned amid criticisms of how the catastrophe was managed.

In addition to after-the-fact crisis management, *crisis training* can focus on prevention. For example, organizations are becoming increasingly aware of the possibility of workplace violence, such as attacks by disgruntled former employees or violence against spouses. Prevention training often includes seminars on stress management, conflict resolution, and team building.[75]

Ethics Training.   The topic of ethics has become a priority for many organizations (see the Manager's Notebook, "The Golden Expedition"), and ethics training is seen as a key tool to maintain and improve the level of ethics in an organization. The Adolph Coors Co. (now the Molson Coors Brewing Co.) began working on developing a first-rate ethics training program before any of the recent ethics scandals and media attention. It now boasts one of the most comprehensive ethics training programs in the country.

MANAGER'S NOTEBOOK

Ethics

The Golden Expedition

The ethics training program at Coors includes interactive online courses, ethics leadership training, an ethics decision-making aid, highly detailed policies, and a help line. Although the company offers a great deal of details and resources, the goal of the training program is to get people to go beyond the rules and guidelines and to make the ethical principals their own so that they can independently think through situations.

Coors invested $250,000 to develop a Web-based module to ensure that employees have assimilated the ethical principles. The module consists of an ethics expedition in which employees move from a base camp up to the top of a mountain. The training module has four camps, each with its own set of activities that need to be completed before the employee can move to the next level of camp. At the base level, ethics issues consist of black-and-white rules; as the employee progresses up the mountain, the issues become grayer and are based more on values than on rules.

Every new hire must complete the course within 90 days as a condition of employment. The Coors approach provides a model for ethical training.

Source: Adapted from: Greengard, S. (2005). Golden values. *Workforce Management, 84,* 52–53.

Customer Service Training.   Organizations are increasingly recognizing the importance of meeting customers' expectations. In addition to establishing philosophies, standards, and systems that support customer service, companies should provide customer service training to give employees the skills they need to meet and exceed customer expectations. Unfortunately, frontline service employees are often seen as temporary employees who are not worth the investment. However, customer-service skills can determine the very survival of a business. In the restaurant business, service is critical to success, but ratings indicate that it is a weak area. Zagat Survey rates food quality and service at thousands of restaurants and finds that, on average, food is rated higher than service.[76] Zagat reviewers consistently pick service as the thing that irritates them most and that needs the most work. The good news is that customer-service employees are now receiving the largest percentage of training dollars.[77]

Sometimes the market forces a company to realize the importance of customer service. Denny's, the nation's largest family restaurant chain, has been learning the importance of customer service. Denny's was hit with racial bias lawsuits that resulted in a $46 million settlement in 1994. The restaurant chain was found guilty of discrimination by offering poorer and slower service to minority than to majority group members. Thus, Denny's and other family-style restaurants include listening, communicating, and responding to customers as part of their training.[78] Training for customer service may be a way to not only increase profits but also to decrease the chances of a discrimination lawsuit.

The Evaluation Phase

In the evaluation phase of the training process, the effectiveness of the training program is assessed. Companies can measure effectiveness in monetary or nonmonetary terms. Whatever the terms, the training should be judged on how well it addressed the needs it was designed to meet. For example, a business may evaluate a training program designed to increase workers' efficiency by assessing its effects on productivity or costs, but not in terms of employee satisfaction.

All too often the evaluation phase of the training process is neglected. This is tantamount to making an investment without ever determining whether you're receiving an adequate (or any) return on it. Calculating a return on investment can require a study of the costs and benefits of training, and funding such a study can be difficult if funding for the training was barely adequate to begin with. Granted, collecting the necessary data and finding the time to analyze training results may be difficult. But at the very least companies should estimate the costs and benefits of a training program, even if these cannot be directly measured. Without such information, training's financial value cannot be demonstrated, and upper management may feel there is no compelling reason to continue the training effort.

Assessing the effectiveness of training is more than simply estimating financial costs and benefits. A four-level framework for evaluation[79] has been widely accepted in the training area. Level 1 refers to the *reaction* of the trainees, and it may consist of ratings on a satisfaction scale that assess how happy trainees are with the training. Level 2 refers to how much the trainees *learn,* and it may be assessed with a skill exercise. Level 3 refers to the trainees *behavior,* and it may be measured by observers of the work operation. Level 4 refers to the *results,* which are generally assessed through the financial measure of return on investment (ROI). Results, the highest level of measurement, seems to be the most desirable way of assessing the success of a training program. However, other levels of measurement, particularly level 3, behavior, can also be important.

The evaluation process followed by Allied Signal's (now Honeywell) Garrett Engine Division provides an excellent illustration of the application of the four levels of evaluation to measure the effectiveness of training. Personnel responsible for training at Garrett Engine assessed its effectiveness at the four levels presented in Figure 8.8. At level 1, trainees rated the course and instructor at the time of training. At level 2, participants were given an after-training test. The results of these tests were compared against scores on a pretest and against the scores achieved by a group of workers who did not go through the training (the *control group*). At level 3, trainees' use of their new skills and knowledge back on the job were compared against the job performance of the control group. At level 4, the evaluation team examined the critical issue of whether the training made a real difference to the company's bottom line.

In general, the outcomes of the first three levels of measurement were positive. At level 1, trainees gave high ratings to the course and instructor. The test at level 2 indicated that the performance of employees who had received training was higher than that of the employees who

Figure 8.8

Level	Type of Measurement
1	Participants' reaction to the training at the time of the training.
2	Participants' learning of the content of the training.
3	Participants' use of their new skills and knowledge back on the job.
4	Company's return on the training investment.

Source: Pine, J., and Tingley, J. C. (1993). ROI of soft skills training. *Training, 30,* 55–60. Reprinted with permission from the February 1993 issue of *Training.* Copyright 1993. Lakewood Publications, Minneapolis, MN. All rights reserved. Not for resale.

Four Measurement Levels Employed by Garrett Engine Division

had not. The same result was achieved at level 3. Nonetheless, the big question remained: Did the training have a positive dollar impact on the company?

To answer this question, the Garrett training team measured performance before and after training for both trained and untrained groups of maintenance workers in terms of response time to job requests and job-completion time. It was assumed that if the maintenance teams were responding and completing jobs more quickly, the equipment would be down less time and Garrett Engine Division would save money. The maintenance department had already calculated the cost of equipment downtime, and this figure was used to translate downtime into dollar amounts. As Figure 8.9 shows, the after-training downtime for the training group, at $1,156, was $55 less than that for the control group, at $1,211. This $55 value appears to be the monetary benefit of the training experience. Although this may seem like a small amount, it represents the savings *per job,* and the team completed on average 55 jobs per week. The total cost of the team-building training was estimated to be $5,355. A monthly ROI calculation using these figures is presented in Figure 8.10. In the short run, the training certainly appeared to pay off.

Although the financial return on training expenditures is important, it is not always the most appropriate measure of effectiveness. A better measurement might be whether the training resulted in attaining the business goal.[80] In a competitive fight for survival, achieving business goals may be more important than a cost/benefit analysis.

Also, the purpose of evaluation may be more than assessment.[81] For example, measures of training effectiveness might serve as a source of learning and motivation if they are provided as feedback to trainees. A business could use data on behavioral change, for instance, to give workers feedback about their work-related improvements.

Legal Issues and Training

Like all other HRM functions, training is affected by legal regulations. The major requirement here is that employees must have access to training and development programs in a nondiscriminatory fashion. Equal opportunity regulations and antidiscrimination laws apply to the training process, just as they do to all other HR functions.

As we discussed in Chapter 3, determining whether a training program has adverse impact is a primary means of deciding whether a process is discriminatory. If relatively few women and minorities are given training opportunities, it would appear that there is discrimination in terms of development offered to different groups of employees. This situation could trigger an investigation and the company may have to demonstrate that development opportunities are offered on a job-relevant and nondiscriminatory basis.

Performance Levels of Training and Control Groups at Garrett Engine Division

Figure 8.9				
	Response Time	**Completion Time**	**Total Down Time**	**Estimated Cost**
Training Group				
Before training	4.8 hours	13.6 hours	18.4 hours	$1,341
After training	4.1 hours	11.7 hours	15.8 hours	$1,156
Control Group[a]				
Before training	4.4 hours	11.6 hours	16.0 hours	$1,165
After training	4.4 hours	11.7 hours	16.1 hours	$1,211

[a]The control group was not trained. The numbers cited here for the control group were compiled before and after the training group underwent training.

Source: Pine, J., and Tingley, J. C. (1993). ROI of soft skills training. *Training, 30,* 55–60. Reprinted with permission from the February 1993 issue of *Training.* Copyright 1993. Lakewood Publications, Minneapolis, MN. All rights reserved. Not for resale.

Figure 8.10

$$
\begin{array}{rl}
 & \$55 \text{ (average savings per job)} \\
\times & 55 \text{ (jobs per week)} \\
\times & 4 \text{ (number of weeks)} \\
\hline
= & \$12{,}100 \text{ (benefits)} \\
- & \$5{,}355 \text{ (cost of training)} \\
\hline
= & \$6{,}745 \text{ (net benefits)}
\end{array}
$$

$$\frac{6{,}745}{5{,}355} = 1.26 = 126\% \text{ ROI}$$

Source: Pine, J., and Tingley, J. C. (1993). ROI of soft skills training. *Training, 30,* 55–60. Reprinted with permission from the February 1993 issue of *Training.* Copyright 1993. Lakewood Publications, Minneapolis, MN. All rights reserved. Not for resale.

ROI After Four Average Workweeks at Garrett Engine Division

A Special Case: Orientation and Socialization

It is possible, though difficult to prove, that the most important training opportunity occurs when employees start with the firm. At this time managers have the chance to set the tone for new employees through **orientation,** the process of informing new employees about what is expected of them in the job and helping them cope with the stresses of transition. Orientation is an important aspect of the socialization stage of the staffing process as briefly discussed in Chapter 5.

Although many people use the terms *orientation* and *socialization* synonymously, we define socialization as a long-term process with several phases that helps employees acclimate themselves to the new organization, understand its culture and the company's expectations, and settle into the job. We view orientation as a short-term program that informs them about their new position and the company.

The socialization process is often informal and, unfortunately, informal can mean poorly planned and haphazard. A thorough and systematic approach to socializing new employees is necessary if they are to become effective workers. The first step should be an orientation program that helps new employees understand the company's mission and reporting relationships and how things work and why.

Socialization can be divided into three phases: (1) anticipatory, (2) encounter, and (3) settling in.[82] At the *anticipatory stage,* applicants generally have a variety of expectations about the organization and job based on accounts provided by newspapers and other media, word of mouth, public relations, and so on. A number of these expectations may be unrealistic and, if unmet, can lead to dissatisfaction, poor performance, and high turnover.

A **realistic job preview (RJP)** is probably the best method of creating appropriate expectations about the job.[83] As its name indicates, an RJP presents realistic information about the demands of the job, the organization's expectations of the job holder, and the work environment. This presentation may be made either to applicants or to newly selected employees before they start work. For example, a person applying for a job selling life insurance should be told up front about the potentially negative parts of the job, such as the uncertain commission-based income and the need to try to sell insurance to personal acquaintances. Of course, the positive parts of the job, such as personal autonomy and high income potential, should also be mentioned.

RJPs can be presented orally, in written form, on videotape, or, occasionally in a full-blown work sample. For instance, at Toyota USA's Georgetown (Kentucky) plant, job simulations and work samples are used to demonstrate to applicants the repetitive nature of manufacturing work and the need for teamwork. Studies have found RJPs to have beneficial effects on important organizational outcomes such as performance and turnover.[84]

Orientation
The process of informing new employees about what is expected of them in the job and helping them cope with the stresses of transition.

Realistic job preview (RJP)
Realistic information about the demands of the job, the organization's expectations of the job holder, and the work environment.

In the *encounter phase*, the new hire has started work and is facing the reality of the job. Even if an RJP was provided, new hires need information about policies and procedures, reporting relationships, rules, and so on. This type of information is helpful even for new employees who have had substantial experience elsewhere because the organization or work unit often does things somewhat differently than these employees are used to. In addition, providing systematic information about the organization and job can be a very positive signal to new workers that they are valued members of the organization.

During the *settling-in phase*, new workers begin to feel like part of the organization. If the settling in is successful, the worker will feel comfortable with the job and his or her role in the work unit. An *employee mentoring program*, in which an established worker serves as an adviser to the new employee, may help ensure that settling in is a success.[85] (We talk about mentoring programs at length in Chapter 9.) For example, Bojangles', a quick-service restaurant business, has developed a "buddy system" to help orient new employees and reduce employee turnover. The system ensures that each new hire is assigned a mentor who acts as a sounding board and advisor on career issues.[86]

Unfortunately, not all organizations take an active role in orienting new workers. As a new hire, you may find that you have to take the lion's share of the responsibility for socialization yourself. Take a look at Figure 8.11 for ideas on how to do this.

The key point for managers is this: The socialization process may take months, not a day or so. Intracorp, a managed-care and work/life services company, has developed a socialization process called New Directions that recognizes the time it takes to orient employees.[87] The program was implemented to help reduce turnover in the first year of employment.

The New Directions program is divided into four phases.

- **Phase one** acclimates workers by providing expectations and product training.
- **Phase two** is a one-day training session that gives new hires information on the company's history, strategy, policies, and benefits.
- **Phase three** spans he first three months on the job and focuses on training workers about the market, its customers, and business plans.
- **Phase four** carries on through at least six months and consists of interim reviews and feedback.

The program has helped reduce the company's high turnover rate for first-year employees. A number of other companies, such as Texas Instruments, have similar programs.[88]

Figure 8.11

WHAT'S THE PATH TO SUCCESS?
Get to know people in the organization, especially those who can tell you what it takes to succeed. Make it a goal to get to know four new people in the first two weeks on the job.

GET FEEDBACK.
Have a meeting with your boss within the first month to get an informal sense of how you are performing so far.

DO IT.
Pick a reasonable project and complete it within your first two months on the job. Completing the project will not only show initiative, it will probably introduce you to other parts of the organization and further immerse you in the culture.

WHAT DO YOU DO?
Write your own job description within the first two months on the job. Indicate what it is you really do in this job. This description can be used as a way to check with others, including your boss, as to whether that is what you should be doing. At the very least, people may be impressed with your motivation and diligence.

RENEW AND GO FOR IT AGAIN.
Treat months three and four like the first two months on the job. Commit to reenergizing yourself and renewing your enthusiasm for your new job. Get to know even more people, pick another project, and get more feedback!

Source: Adapted from *Detroit News.* (1998, June). Guide gives advice to new hires, L1.

Socialization—Do It Yourself!

Summary and Conclusions

Training Versus Development

Although training and development often go hand in hand and the terms are often used interchangeably, the terms are not synonymous. Training typically focuses on providing employees with specific skills and helping them correct deficiencies in their performance. Development is an effort to provide employees with the abilities that the organization will need in the future.

Challenges in Training

Before embarking on a training program, managers must answer several important questions: (1) Is training the solution to the problem? (2) Are the goals of training clear and realistic? (3) Is training a good investment? (4) Will the training work?

Managing the Training Process

The training process consists of three phases: assessment, development and conduct of training, and evaluation. In the assessment phase, organizational, task, and person needs are identified and the goals of training are clarified. Several options are available during the training phase. Training can take place either on the job or off the job and can be delivered through a variety of techniques (slides and videotapes, teletraining, computers, simulations, virtual reality, classroom instruction, and role-plays). The most appropriate type of training (for example, skills, retraining, cross-functional, team, creativity, literacy, diversity, crisis, or customer service) should be chosen to achieve the stated objectives. In the evaluation phase, the costs and benefits of the training program should be assessed to determine its effectiveness.

A Special Case: Employee Socialization and Orientation

Organizations should pay particular attention to socializing employees. The first step in socializing them is orientation, or informing new employees about what is expected of them in the job and helping them cope with the inevitable stresses of transition. Companies and managers who recognize that socialization is a long-term process and should be carefully planned will benefit from lower turnover.

Key Terms

brainstorming, 257
cross-functional training, 256
development, 240
job aids, 255

literacy, 258
orientation, 263
peer trainers, 256
realistic job preview (RJP), 263

simulation, 250
training, 240
virtual reality (VR), 252

Discussion Questions

1. Performance problems seem all too common in your workplace. People do not seem to be putting forth the needed effort, and interpersonal conflict on the work teams seems to be a constant. Is training the answer? If so, what kind of training should be done? What other actions may be appropriate?

2. How effective do you think training can be in raising employee motivation?

3. Workers who are illiterate suffer from embarrassment and fear. An HR manager notes, "They will ask for directions many times, even though the instruction manual is alongside their machine. . . . Some workers always seem to be having problems with their eyesight or their glasses. . . . The truth is that they simply cannot read." How would you go about identifying workers who should receive literacy training? Discuss the differences between general illiteracy and functional illiteracy and how you would decide which of these issues a training program should address.

4. How important is it that the effectiveness of a training program be measured in dollar terms? Why is it important to measure training effectiveness in the first place?

5. Training provides workers with skills needed in the workplace. However, many organizations have dynamic environments in which change is the norm. How can training requirements be identified when job duties are a moving target?

6. Simuflite, a Texas aviation training company, expected to whip the competition with FasTrak, its computer-based training (CBT) curriculum for corporate pilots. Instead, the new venture sent Simuflite into a nose dive. In traditional ground-school training, pilots ask questions and learn from "war stories" told by classmates and instructors. With FasTrak, they sat in front of a computer for hours absorbing information. Their only interaction was tapping the computer screen to provide answers to questions, and that novelty wore off very quickly. Pilots grew bored with the CBT ground school.

What does Simuflite's experience suggest about the limitations of interactive media and CBT? In what situations is CBT most likely to be beneficial to trainees?

7. According to one survey, trainees list the following as some of the traits of a successful trainer: knowledge of the subject, adaptability, sincerity, and sense of humor. What other traits do you think trainers need to be successful in the training situation?

Taco, Inc., a privately owned manufacturer of pumps and valves, takes a much more qualitative, if not philosophical, approach to measuring training effectiveness. The company offers impressive educational opportunities. More than six dozen courses are offered in an on-site learning center. The facility cost the company $250,000 to build and the education delivery amounts to $300,000

in annual direct expenses and lost productivity. Asked to place a dollar value on the return from the training, the chief executive simply points to the return in the form of employee attitude.

a. What do you think is the best or most appropriate measure of the return on investment for training? Why?

b. In what situations, if any, would a financial measure of return be inappropriate?

c. Evaluate the Taco, Inc., approach to evaluating training effectiveness. Do you agree with its approach?

d. With your partner or team, develop an approach for evaluating the effectiveness of training from a customer perspective. You might want to start with the four levels of measurement presented in this chapter and apply them to a customer perspective.

There is a variety of additional material available on the Web site that accompanies this text. You can access this information by visiting the Web site at **www.prenhall.com/gomez.**

YOU MANAGE IT! Emerging Trends Case 8.1

Training Before Employment: How Honda Keeps Firing on All Cylinders

Honda wanted to build a new factory to manufacture its popular and highly rated Odyssey minivan and engine. What it ended up doing is starting from scratch with workers who did not have any experience in building cars! Yet, within 2 years vehicles were rolling off the line, and within 3 years it is scheduled to go into full production. How did Honda do it? In a word—training.

Honda was approached by many states that wanted to be home to the new factory. Alabama was chosen because of the availability of labor and the state's offer to partner with Honda in recruitment and training. The state of Alabama allocated $30 million for training and the funds paid for a 62,000-square-foot Honda training center in Lincoln, Alabama. The facility has modern classrooms and replicas of Honda equipment. The Alabama operation provided Honda with an opportunity to make a fresh start and build new processes and a new workforce from scratch. However, between December 1999 and April 2002, 1,500 employees had to be found and trained.

A strategy to Honda's successful launch of this new plant was preemployment training. In conjunction with state labor and training agencies, Honda advertised a free training program that was a precondition for applying for a job with the auto manufacturer. Participants were required to have a high school degree or equivalent and two years of work experience. The training involves attending two 1-hour sessions per week for 6 weeks. The first half of the training is classroom

instruction on topics such as math and precision measuring. This initial portion of the training also includes a videotape presentation that conveys the speed and repetitive nature of the manufacturing work. Some people decide the work isn't for them, and Honda has experienced about a 15 percent dropout rate. The final three weeks involves intense hands-on training. Participants are carefully observed by 40 assessors who rate each applicant's speed, accuracy, and ability to follow instructions. Completing the training is not a guarantee of employment—it's only an opportunity to apply for a job. However, the majority of graduates of the training get full-time jobs. Honda views putting in the time and effort by an applicant to complete the program as an indication of his or her commitment level.

The free training offer resulted in 18,000 people responding. In conjunction with state agencies, some applicants were eliminated due to lack of education or experience. The program has been training 340 people every 6 weeks and has graduated over 2,600. There is a backlog of over 1,000 candidates.

Honda considers the plant a success. Honda managers claim they are achieving the same level of performance with a totally inexperienced workforce as Honda operations in which 50 percent of the workforce had auto manufacturing experience. The preemployment training is largely given the credit for the positive results. The training provides skills but also gives people an opportunity to see if they really want to pursue this type of work.

Critical Thinking Questions

1. Do you think it is fair for Honda to offer the training with no guarantee of employment? Why do you think so many people are willing to put in the time and effort needed to complete the preemployment training?

2. Honda focused on classroom and hands-on experiences for its preemployment training approaches at a time when electronic approaches, such as e-learning, were receiving a great deal of attention as the new, effective, and less costly approach to training. Why do you think Honda chose the training approaches it did?

3. Given you had input over how preemployment training was to be delivered, what would you recommend? Specifically, would you recommend an e-learning approach, a more traditional classroom and hands-on approach such as used by Honda, or an approach that blends the two? Identify the characteristics that would drive your recommendation. For example, what characteristics of the work, of the training participants, and of the organization would be important in determining how preemployment training should be delivered? List contingency factors and explain how each factor would suggest a particular approach to delivering preemployment training.

Team Exercise

Honda's assessment of the effectiveness of its preemployment training program seems subjective. As discussed in this chapter, the effectiveness of training can be assessed at a number of levels. Certainly, impact on business results and ROI estimates are important outcomes, but other levels of impact can be important, too.

For each possible level of analysis, identify how you could go about assessing the effectiveness of Honda's preemployment training. What measures or data would you need? Would you use a control group? A before–after comparison? Comparisons with other plants? Share your assessment approaches for each level with the rest of the class.

Experiential Exercise

Divide your team in half with one group responsible for costs and the other group for benefits. Identify the various cost items and benefits that might be involved in a preemployment effort such as Honda's. Estimate the costs and benefits and calculate an ROI for the program. (Note: The assessors involved in Honda's preemployment training are actually part-time state employees, not Honda employees.) Would your ROI calculation be affected by including the assessors on Honda's payroll? What if the facility costs had to be borne by Honda? Would your ROI calculations indicate that Honda would have still pursued this program? Share your estimates and conclusions with the rest of the class.

Source: Adapted from Grossman, R. I. (2002). Made from scratch: When Honda built a plant in Alabama it also built a workforce using local workers who had no experience in making cars. *HRMagazine, 47,* 44(7).

Global Case 8.2   YOU MANAGE IT!

Leading with One Voice: Training in a Global Organization

BP is a global energy company that doubled its size in four years through a series of mergers and acquisitions. Although BP has one name, it is actually comprised of a multitude of nationalities and corporate cultures. It had 35 different leadership development programs taking place around the world. The sheer number of these training programs pointed out a major problem: There was no common understanding, or model, of what it meant to be a leader at BP. How could people have a common understanding and work together toward shared goals without a common approach to how to lead?

Top management at BP decided to address this problem by training first-level leaders (the BP label for first-line supervisors). This is a large and diverse group of more than 10,000 people in every sector of the organization. Although their diversity and geographic dispersion would make the training effort more difficult, this group was too important to BP not to have a common understanding of how to be an effective BP manager.

A leadership training program was developed based on input from first-level leaders across the organization. Finally, BP would have a common management framework across the globe. The course was well received by first-level leaders, with 84 percent reporting satisfaction with the program. (The target satisfaction rate had been set at 80%.) Demand for the program was higher than expected, and additional courses had to be offered.

The team that developed the training realized that it did not have measures with which to demonstrate the value of the training program. The satisfaction surveys given at the end of each course wouldn't answer what the team viewed as the critical issue: What happened when people got back to their jobs after the training was completed? Was the training applied in the workplace?

In order to address whether the training was being transferred back to the job, the team identified behavioral changes that should be evident in leaders who completed the program. These behavioral changes were divided into six categories:

- **Organizational awareness.** Understanding the BP organization and being able to network in it.
- **Communication skills.** Ability to listen and take into account other's viewpoints.
- **Confidence and self-awareness.** Ability to be objective and remain calm under pressure.

- **Management skills.** Problem-solving, prioritizing, delegation, and time-management ability.
- **Leadership skills.** Ability to develop and maintain an effective team, generate commitment and overcome obstacles.
- **Team performance.** Effective team leadership to achieve results.

Using the behavior measures, BP surveyed managers and direct reports of first-level leaders in the first year after the program. Performance on each of the six measures was significantly better for first-level leaders who had taken the training. Another survey the next year again found the same positive results for the training program.

Critical Thinking Questions

1. Referring to Kirkpatrick's four levels of training evaluation discussed in the chapter, what level of evaluation was BP using before it devised the six measures of change?
2. What level of training evaluation is represented in the six measures of change identified by BP? Is this an adequate measure of training effectiveness? Explain.
3. If you oversaw the first-level leader training program at BP, what major steps do you think should be undertaken next? Describe.

Team Exercise

Join your teammates and consider the development of the six change measures. BP employees were asked about areas they thought would be noticeably changed if the leadership training was effective. These behavioral change areas then served as criteria for assessing the effectiveness of the first-level leader training program. Note that these criteria were identified *after* the training program was designed and implemented.

As a team, do you agree with the way the measures were developed? What do you think about identifying effectiveness criteria after a program is developed? Do any of the problems your team sees with the behavioral measures negate the findings that indicate the training was effective? Explain.

As a team, reach a consensus as to whether it would be worthwhile to push for an ROI measure of the effectiveness of the training program. Would an ROI measure be doable and useful?

Share your team's assessments of these issues with the rest of the class. The instructor can lead the class discussion in identifying overall class assessments on these issues.

Experiential Exercise

Assessing the effectiveness of training is an important step in the training process. As identified in the Team Exercise, the behavioral measures may have been developed in a different way. As a team, put yourself in the place of the BP training development team. What criteria would you use to assess the effectiveness of the training program? Describe how your team would recommend these criteria be developed. Specify the process by identifying the steps you would follow and the sources for your information. Share your recommended "model" with the rest of the class. Explain why you think your approach would be an improvement over what BP has done.

Source: Adapted with permission from Brown, J., Eager, R., and Lawrence, P. (2005). BP refines leadership. *T & D, 59,* 3.

YOU MANAGE IT!   Ethics Case 8.3

Ethics Training

Ethics training has gotten a boost from legal guidelines and legislation. The Sarbanes-Oxley Act of 2002 requires publicly traded companies to disclose whether they have a code of ethics. In addition, an amendment to the Federal Sentencing Guidelines for Organization (FSGO) of 1991 that went into effect in late 2004 includes ethics training requirements and emphasizes creation of an ethical culture. The Sarbanes-Oxley Act pertains only to publicly traded companies, and the FSGO is only a set of guidelines, not mandatory requirements. Nonetheless, in light of recent ethics scandals (such as Enron and Worldcom), more companies are implementing ethics training programs.

Just how should an ethics training program be developed and implemented? Here are some basic steps.

1. Set the Standards
   a. What are the standards for ethical behavior in your organization?
   b. What are the goals for the training?
2. Make the Training Mandatory
   The training should apply to everyone in the organization, regardless of their level. No one should be seen as being above the rules.
3. Training Content
   a. *The code of ethics* for the organization should be the centerpiece of the training. Everyone needs to understand the code of ethics and what it means for conducting themselves in the organization.
   b. *Discuss laws* that affect jobs in the organization. Workers need to understand legal limits and requirements.

c. *Include decision-making models* or aids to help people make ethical choices. Texas Instruments, Inc., for example, provides the following set of questions and statements to employees to help them make ethical decisions:

- Is the action legal?
- Is it consistent with our values?
- If you do it, will you feel bad?
- How would it look in the newspaper?
- If you know it's wrong, don't do it!
- If you are not sure, ask, ask, until you get an answer.

d. Provide *ethics resources,* such as where to go if employees have questions or how to report ethics violation.

e. *Role-playing scenarios* can make the training content relevant and meaningful.

Critical Thinking Questions

1. Ethical training seems to be increasing in organizations, perhaps due to new guidelines and legislation. Ethics training programs could, therefore, focus on compliance with legal standards. Do you think this goal is sufficient? Why or why not? What *should* be the goal of ethics training?

2. In larger organizations, ethics training may have to be delivered in various languages and across different countries and cultures. A Web-based approach can efficiently overcome these difficulties. However, some people contend that at least part of ethics training should be face-to-face to maximize the benefits of the training. Do you agree, or do you think ethics training could be just as effective if conducted entirely online?

3. A critical issue in training is the transfer of training, and ethics training is no exception. How could the transfer of ethics training back to the workplace be maximized? Describe the steps or process you would recommend to maximize the transfer of ethics training.

Team Exercise

With your teammates, determine how you think an organization should determine the effectiveness of ethical training. Begin by identifying the objective(s) for ethical training. How could you measure the effectiveness of the ethical training in reaching these objectives? Use the four levels of training effectiveness discussed in this chapter. Can you identify useful measures at each of the four levels? Are there levels that you don't think are important for assessing the effectiveness of ethical training? Why?

Summarize your answers to these issues and present your summary to the rest of the class. As a class, identify the best goals and measures that can be used for ethical training.

Experiential Exercise

Join your teammates and identify a scenario that depicts an ethical situation. The scenario could be an actual situation or one that you construct. Also, the scenario could depict unethical or ethical behavior, or it could depict an ethical dilemma that can be used to discuss various options. Use the scenario your team agrees on as a role-play. Select team members to play the various parts and sketch out what you want to portray in the role-play.

When the teams are ready, present the role-playing scenarios to the class. At the end of the role-play discuss the scenario and what it was meant to portray. As a class, discuss whether role-play scenarios are an effective tool for ethical training. Why might it be important to portray ethical as well as unethical scenarios?

Source: Adapted with permission from Tyler, K. (2005). Do the right thing. *HRMagazine, 50,* 2.

Customer-Driven HR Case 8.4 — YOU MANAGE IT!

Make It Memorable

A professor may have key points to cover in a class, but if he covers them in a boring lecture and puts all the students to sleep, probably not much learning happened in the class. Looking at employees as customers in the training process brings into focus a key issue: What can be done to sell employees on what needs to be learned? How can trainers make sure key points "stick?" If the employees don't see the importance of the training and nothing makes it memorable, how can you possibly expect that the training will have any impact on performance in the workplace?

One approach to increasing the memorability of training is to include a creative component in the training that inspires employees and makes the learning more meaningful. As an example, consider how a physician made a lesson to residents quite memorable. He started by holding up a plastic bag of water with a bar of soap in it. He snipped the corner of the bag, drained the water, and then squeezed out the bar of soap. He told the class how proud he was of the bar of soap and showed it to the class, but he squeezed it a little too hard and it shot out into the class! He acted horrified, but then explained to the class that the lesson they were about to learn was how to deliver a baby, which is as slippery as a bar of soap, without dropping it. The demonstration with the bar of soap was safe, yet it underscored the importance of the topic and likely made the lesson quite memorable.

The slippery-soap demonstration is an example of adding a creative component to training that makes it more memorable. Can you come up with similar memory-enhancing training moments? Following the four principles of creativity can help you to generate these types of training components:

1. **Defer evaluation.** Generate ideas without criticism. Suspend judgment and just focus on coming up with ideas.
2. **Stretch.** Go beyond obvious training ideas. Try to come up with silly or wild possibilities—you can always rule them out later.
3. **Make unusual associations.** Try to make odd connections with your training content. These connections or analogies can make training memorable. The slippery-soap demonstration is an example of an analogy.
4. **Restructure elements.** Think about reordering what will be covered in the training or, maybe, emphasizing or minimizing some topic. This technique may help you to come up with a different, and memorable, way to present the material.

Critical Thinking Questions

1. Is memorability of training important? Why or why not?
2. Have you had a memorable training experience? Describe what made the training memorable.
3. If training isn't memorable, how does that affect the four levels of training effectiveness? Would all of them be decreased, or not necessarily? Explain.

Team Exercise

As a team, identify approaches to improve the perceived importance, and thus the application, of training. Including a creative component in training is one approach to increasing memorablity and learning. However, other approaches can be used to get people to take training seriously and apply what they learn back on the job.

The task for your team is to identify steps that can be taken to increase learning and the impact of training on performance. Adding a creative component to training is one possibility. Can you think of others? Maybe your organization could offer to pay for training only if a post-training test is passed. Maybe it could threaten to *not* pay employees for training if

they don't pass a post-training test. Generate possible alternatives. You can apply the principles of creativity described in this case to help you generate possible tactics.

After you have generated a list of options, trim it down by eliminating any tactics that may be too wild or impractical. Working with your final list, evaluate each option in terms of how customer/employee driven it is. You can use the following scale to assign a number value to each option.

1	2	3	4	5	6	7
Management (Top/Down) Driven			Mixture			Customer/ Employee Driven

Is the extent to which your training options are customer oriented an important consideration? Why or why not? Share your set of options and your judgments about the extent to which each of them is customer driven with the rest of the class. As a class, generate a combined list of training tactics by picking the best from the team presentations. Can the class reach a consensus about the importance of taking a customer orientation in these training tactics?

Experiential Exercise

As a team exercise, generate a creative component for a training program. First, identify a basic training topic, such as a basic skill, literacy, ethics, and so on. Whatever topic your team selects, state it as a problem. For example, you could state the problem as "How can we make people see that ethics is an important issue?" Once you have a "problem" to work on, apply the creativity principles identified in this case and generate a creative training component. Remember, anything is possible. You might use a demonstration, game, role-play, whatever!

Share your creative training component with the rest of the class. As a class, discuss how important adding a creative component can be. Is there a consensus on whether it is worth the effort to include a creative component? What are the benefits?

Source: Adapted with permission from Yelon, S. (2005). The treasure of creative instruction and artful training. *Performance Improvement, 44,* 8–12.

YOU MANAGE IT! # Emerging Trends Case 8.5

Beyond ROI?

The four levels of training effectiveness—reaction, learning, behaviors, results—have been accepted as the training evaluation framework by most training professionals. Because the different measures are categorized into levels, it only seems natural that the top level of results is the measure to strive

toward. Numerous books and articles have been written on calculating the return on investment (ROI) for training programs. However, there is growing recognition that ROI may not be the penultimate measure of training effectiveness.

The ROI of a training program may seem like an important, maybe even mandatory, measure. Certainly, from a business perspective we want to be assured that the financial benefits exceed the costs of a program. However, in many situations ROI estimates for training may not be all that important or useful. Often times, training is a means for a company to achieve a strategy. For example, an organization may decide that having a customer orientation is how it is going to compete in its industry. Employee training may be the critical key for realizing this new strategic advantage. Given this purpose, the ROI of the training may not be useful or of immediate concern. The primary issue would be whether the training increased the customer-service skills of employees. In other words, it is the behavior level of evaluation that is a key concern when the purpose of training is to execute a strategy.[a] If the training delivers the needed behaviors, then the strategy should, in the longer term, provide the bottomline payoff. Whether the training successfully executes the strategy may determine the very survivability of the organization. How much the training costs and its short-term cost-effectiveness may not be concerns of management. What may be critical is determining whether the training is helping the organization to achieve its strategic goals.

Critical Thinking Questions

1. When would the ROI of training be a useful measure? Explain.
2. When would measures of training effectiveness other than ROI be useful? Describe.
3. Behaviors have been described as the forgotten level in the measurement of training effectiveness.[b] Despite the fact that behaviors are the key to executing strategy,[c] measurement of training effectiveness at the behavioral level is not often done. Behaviors occur outside the training program and after it has been delivered. In addition, behaviors can be difficult to measure. Behavioral standards need to be developed and evaluations of these standards need to be collected, perhaps from managers and subordinates. All these reasons can lead managers to ignore the behavioral level of training evaluation.

   What steps would you suggest be taken to ensure that the behavioral level of measurement is conducted? How could you get the support of others to measure behaviors after the training?

Team Exercise

As a team, select a strategy and identify the key behaviors needed to execute that strategy. Further, identify how you would train and then measure those behaviors. For example, your team might select a strategy of customer service, quality, or innovation. For your selected strategy, identify behaviors that would be critical to executing that strategy. What approach would you take to training in order to achieve your strategy? What behaviors would you then measure to determine the effectiveness of the training? How would you make those behavioral measurements? Share your strategy and training and evaluation plans with the rest of the class.

Experiential Exercise

Training effectiveness is commonly measured at the first level of measurement—reaction. For example, most universities assess the effectiveness of classroom instruction with end-of-semester ratings by students. What other measures could be used to assess training effectiveness in a university? With your teammates, consider the evaluation of classroom instruction at a university. Develop measures for levels two and three—learning and behaviors. Can you devise an approach to measure the results level? Would a financial results measure, such as ROI, be feasible? Would it be useful? What level of measures, if any, should be used to assess the effectiveness of the trainer (professor)? Explain.

Share your suggestions with the rest of the class. As a class, combine the suggestions across teams to construct a compilation of suggested measures at each level. Is there a class consensus concerning the feasibility and usefulness of an ROI measure?

Source: [a, b]Kirkpatrick, J. (2005). The missing link. *Leadership Excellence,* 22, 7; [c]Ferrell, D. (2005). What's the ROI of training programs? *Lodging Hospitality, 61,* 46.

Developing Careers

Challenges

After reading this chapter, you should be able to deal more effectively with the following challenges:

1 **Establish** a sound process for helping employees develop their careers.

2 **Understand** how to develop your own career.

3 **Identify** the negative aspects of an overemphasis on career development.

4 **Understand** the importance of dual-career issues in career development.

5 **Develop** a skills inventory and a career path.

6 **Establish** an organizational culture that supports career development.

When his department supervisor retired last year, Steve, an excellent performer, thought he would be promoted into the position. He told Natalie, the unit manager, of his interest, and she assured him that he would be given every consideration. The next thing Steve knew, someone from outside the company had been offered the job.

Steve was disappointed and angry, and the lack of an explanation didn't help. He knew the technical end of the business as well as anyone, and he always achieved his performance objectives. What did he have to do to get into management?

After a couple of weeks of quietly seething, Steve decided to ask Natalie point blank why he had not been offered the supervisor's job. Natalie seemed quite surprised at Steve's eagerness to be promoted. She told him that she hadn't thought his interest in the supervisory position was very strong and that an outsider got the job simply because he had better credentials. She advised Steve to keep trying; sooner or later, something would open up.

Steve was no closer to understanding what he needed to do to get promoted. When he got home that night, he made some phone calls about job openings he had seen advertised. Maybe he could advance faster somewhere else. Even if he didn't leave GCX, he thought, he sure wasn't going to go out of his way for the company anymore. He had some sick days coming and he planned on using them soon.

Allessandra relaxed at home after two long, interesting days. Her company, a large telecommunications firm, had sent her to an assessment center for an evaluation of her strengths and weaknesses as a potential middle-level manager. Currently, she was the head of a sales office located in Des Moines, Iowa, and was responsible for the surrounding metropolitan area.

Her experience at the assessment center could not have been better. After a day and a half of various activities, she had met with the consultants who operate the center. They told her that she definitely had the characteristics her company was looking for in a future manager. She had a few weak areas—most notably, confidence in pushing her ideas in the face of opposition—but she already knew this and was working on overcoming her timidity. They told her that the report she received would also be given to her boss, as well as to the HR manager responsible for management development activities. She knew that although it might take a year or two for a position to become available, she was on her way up.

THE MANAGERIAL PERSPECTIVE

Steve's experience, unfortunately, is much more common than Allessandra's: Workers often have goals and aspirations that their organizations do not know about. Whether these goals are reasonable or unrealistic, lack of progress toward them can have a strongly negative effect on performance.

Giving employees opportunities to grow and develop can ensure that your workforce keeps pace with the demands of the changing business environment. In addition, if you make this kind of investment in your employees, you are more likely to keep workers instead of seeing them lured away by competitors.

The employer and employee often share the responsibility for career development. In your job as a manager, then, you are likely to be partially responsible for your career development and for your workers' career development. As part of that responsibility, you may become involved in a formal or informal mentor relationship. In this chapter we investigate how you can help manage others' career development and your own. First, we define career development. Second, we explore some of the major challenges connected with career development and offer some approaches to help managers avoid problems in this area. We conclude by discussing self-development.

What Is Career Development?

As we noted in Chapter 8, career development is different from training. Career development has a wider focus, longer time frame, and broader scope. The goal of training is improvement in performance; the goal of development is enriched and more capable workers. **Career development** is not a one-shot training program or career-planning workshop. Rather, it is an ongoing organized and formalized effort that recognizes people as a vital organizational resource.[1]

The career development field, though relatively young, has seen tremendous change, largely because career opportunities and paths are less structured and predictable than they were three decades ago.[2] Instead of job security and career-long tenure with one organization, downsizing and technological change now characterize the business world.

Career development
An ongoing and formalized effort that focuses on developing enriched and more capable workers.

Survey results indicate that business realities such as downsizing and rapid change have affected employees' career attitudes.[3] A national survey of more than 1,000 adults found that only 56 percent think long-term career advancement depends on staying with an employer for a long time. An increasing number of workers believe job hopping is an acceptable way to advance their careers. A recent survey of young managers in the hotel industry found learning and growth opportunities to be a key concern.[4] These workers would probably leave their employers if they felt the job did not provide developmental opportunities.

Although many people are concerned about promotion and moving forward in their careers, the Manager's Notebook, "So, You Want to Stay Put?" shows that not everyone has the ambition for increased responsibility.

MANAGER'S NOTEBOOK | Customer-Driven HR

So, You Want to Stay Put?

It is common for today's employees to seek out growth and opportunities for development. But not everyone has upward career movement as a goal. That doesn't mean there is something wrong with them. As in everything, there is variance, and that variance is normal.

Some workers may prefer to stay where they are. Maybe they like their job and their geographic location, and moving ahead might require a move they don't want to make. Some workers just know what they are good at and feel that a promotion would mean their performance and satisfaction would suffer. Some people have experienced something, such as a life-threatening event, that has led them to place a high priority on an acceptable work–life balance. Still others may have come to their own conclusion that the cost of continually climbing the career ladder isn't worth it.

The realization that not everyone has the same career aspirations has some important management implications:

- If someone prefers to stay put, that doesn't mean they don't have ambition. It just means that they have ambitions and priorities that are different from those who want to move up the career ladder.
- You need to know the career aspirations of your workers. Maybe your worries about finding career opportunities for a worker are unfounded and such opportunities could be unwelcome!
- To stay put doesn't mean to be stagnant. Development and learning opportunities can still be important for workers who want to stay put. They can expand their role and contribute in additional ways. For example, they may take on the role of leading a company initiative in addition to their regular job duties.
- Keeping your workers who want to stay put can be very beneficial. These workers may be the best at what they do and don't put pressure on you for continued opportunities and promotions. Don't be put off by their preference to say put—they may be your performance workhorses.

Source: Hube, K. (2004, March 29). Thanks but no thanks: Who doesn't want a promotion? A better job title? Lots of people. *Wall Street Journal,* R.4.

The uncertain business environment and changing employee attitudes hamper career development efforts. Even so, career development remains an important activity. It can play a key role in helping managers recruit and retain the skilled, committed workforce an organization needs to succeed.[5] But it can only do so if it meets the dynamic needs of employers and employees.

In the 1970s, most organizations instituted career development programs to help meet organizational needs (such as preparing employees for anticipated management openings) rather than to meet employees' needs.[6] Today, career development usually tries to meet employee and

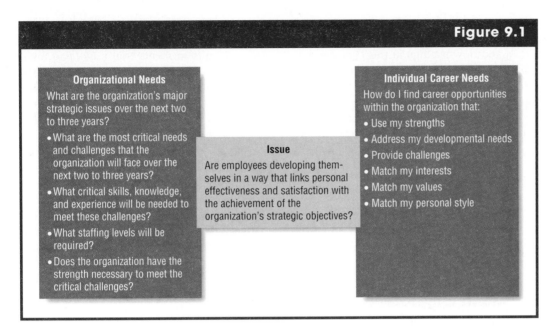

Figure 9.1

Career Development System: Linking Organizational Needs with Individual Career Needs

Source: Gutteridge, T. G., Leibowitz, Z. B., and Shore, J. E. (1993). *Organizational career development: Benchmarks for building a world-class workforce.* Reprinted with permission from *Conceptual Systems,* Silver Springs, MD.

employer needs. Figure 9.1 shows how organizational and individual career needs can be linked to create a successful career development program. Many organizations view career development as a way of preventing job burnout (see Chapter 16), improving the quality of employees' work lives, and meeting affirmative action goals.[7]

This changed emphasis has largely resulted from a combination of competitive pressures (such as downsizing and technological changes) and workers' demands for more opportunities for growth and skill development.[8] These factors have made career development a more difficult endeavor than it used to be. There is no longer a strict hierarchy of jobs from which a career path can easily be constructed. Career development today requires workers' active participation in thinking through the possible directions their careers can take.

An organization must make career development a key business strategy if it intends to survive in an increasingly competitive and global business environment.[9] In the information age, companies will compete more on their workers' knowledge, skill, and innovation levels than on the basis of labor costs or manufacturing capacity.[10] Because career development plays a central role in ensuring a competitive work force, it cannot be a low-priority program offered only during good economic times.

Challenges in Career Development

Although most businesspeople today agree that their organizations should invest in career development, it is not always clear exactly what form this investment should take. Before putting a career development program in place, management needs to consider three major challenges.

Who Will Be Responsible?

The first challenge is deciding who will be ultimately responsible for career development activities. In traditional, bureaucratic organizations development was something done "for" individual employees. For instance, the organization might have an assessment center to identify employees who have the characteristics necessary to hold middle- and upper-management positions. Once identified, these individuals would be groomed through a variety of programs: special project assignments, positions in international divisions, executive training programs, and so on. The individual employee, while certainly not kept in the dark about the company's plans, would not actively participate in the development decisions.

A Question of Ethics

How much responsibility does a company have for managing its employees' careers? Can a company take too much responsibility for employee career development? In what ways might this be harmful to employees?

In contrast, many modern organizations have concluded that employees must take an active role in planning and implementing their own personal development plans. The mergers, acquisitions, and downsizings of the 1980s and 1990s led to layoffs in managerial ranks and managers' realization that they cannot depend on their employers to plan their careers for them. Added to this economic turmoil is the empowerment movement, which shifts decision-making responsibility down through the organizational hierarchy. Both these trends have led companies to encourage their employees to take responsibility for their own development. We will look at strategies for personal development at the end of this chapter.

Career development can occur in many ways in today's organizations. In an increasing number of organizations, career development responsibility is being shifted to the employee. Although an employee empowerment approach to development can be positive, it can be negative if taken too far. Giving employees total responsibility for managing their own careers can create problems in today's flatter organizations, where opportunities to move up through the hierarchy are far fewer than in traditional bureaucratic organizations. Employees need at least general guidance regarding the steps they can take to develop their careers, both within and outside the company.

How Much Emphasis Is Appropriate?

So far, we have presented career development as a positive way for companies to invest in their human resources. However, too great an emphasis on career enhancement can be detrimental to organizational effectiveness.[11] Employees with an extreme careerist orientation can become more concerned about their image than their performance.

It is difficult to pinpoint where an employee's healthy concern for his or her career becomes excessive. However, there are certain warning signs managers should watch for:

- Is the employee more interested in capitalizing on opportunities for advancement than in maintaining adequate performance?
- Does the employee devote more attention to managing the impressions he or she makes on others than to reality?
- Does the employee emphasize networking, flattery, and being seen at social functions over job performance? In the short run, people who engage in these tactics often enjoy advancement. However, sooner or later they run into workplace duties or issues they are not equipped to deal with.

For better or for worse, studies have found that such strategies are effective in helping employees advance through the organization.[12]

Managers should also be aware that a career development program can have serious side effects—including employee dissatisfaction, poor performance, and turnover—if it fosters unrealistic expectations for advancement.

How Will the Needs of a Diverse Workforce Be Met?

To meet the career development needs of today's diverse workforce, companies need to break down the barriers some employees face in achieving advancement. In 1991, the first major government study of the glass ceiling revealed that women and minorities are held back not only from top executive positions, but also from lower-level management positions and directorships. The study revealed that women and minorities are frequently excluded from informal career development activities such as networking, mentoring, and participation in policy-making committees. In addition to outright discrimination, some of the practices that contribute to their exclusion are informal word-of-mouth recruitment, companies' failure to sensitize and instruct managers about equal employment opportunity requirements, lack of mentoring, and the too-swift identification of high-potential employees.[13]

Barriers to the advancement of minorities and women continue to exist nearly 20 years after the initial government study of the glass ceiling. The Office of Federal Contract Compliance Programs (OFCCP) enforces antidiscrimination laws covering federal contractors. The OFCCP began monitoring the pay and promotion practices of companies doing business with the government in 1991. It has found problems in about half of the companies it has audited.[14]

A confidential internal report at Coca-Cola identified barriers to diversity, particularly for African Americans.[15] The report identified not only a glass ceiling wherein few black employees made it to senior levels in the company but also *glass walls*. The notion of glass walls refers to the channeling of minorities and women into non-revenue-generating areas of the organizations. The areas, such as community relations and HR, are less likely than areas such as finance or marketing to lead to senior management positions. Of course, the phenomenon of glass ceilings and walls is not unique to Coca-Cola. For example, as observed by a female president of an insurance company, "It's kind of a male club of senior executives—lots of women in management roles, lots of women running service departments and the like, but not a lot of them in that upper echelon."[16] To improve promotion opportunities, the Coca-Cola report recommends actions such as a mentoring program, a statement of philosophy regarding diversity, and executive accountability for improving diversity.

Interestingly, the glass ceiling phenomenon may account, in part, for the explosive growth in small businesses in the United States. Female-owned businesses are the fastest-growing segment in the U.S. small business sector, and 1 of every 11 women is a business owner.[17] Approximately half of all privately held U.S. companies are owned by women. The glass ceiling has motivated many of these women to choose an entrepreneurial career path.

Evidence suggests that the glass ceiling may be cracking in some industries. For instance, in 1999 Carleton "Carly" Fiorina became the CEO of Hewlett-Packard.[18] Although Fiorina was recently replaced as CEO, she, nonetheless, made it to the top position at HP. After becoming CEO, Fiorina contended that the glass ceiling no longer exists in the information technology industry. She pointed out that the demand for computer scientists, engineers, and programmers is so great that companies cannot afford to be biased against women and minorities. This sentiment is echoed by women in other industries. Jill Campbell, vice president of operations for Cox Communications, says that she never hit a glass ceiling. She largely attributes her successful career at Cox to a mentor who helped guide and support her efforts in the organization.[19] Likewise, a hospital president, Susan Stout Tamme, says that she never experienced a glass ceiling in her health care career.[20]

Although advancement of women in fields such as information technology, health care, and engineering is notable, the glass ceiling still exists over all. Consider this sobering fact: Fewer than 15 percent of *Fortune* 500 officers are women.[21] Even in the health-care arena, where there are many opportunities for advancement, there nevertheless seems to be a glass ceiling. For example, Counsuelo Diaz, CEO of a health-care organization, observes that the health care industry is still largely controlled by men who, perhaps subconsciously, gravitate toward and are most comfortable with candidates who are also white males.[22] In her opinion, women and minorities may have to deal with the glass ceiling for a long time to come.

The glass ceiling is not a problem unique to the United States. The You Manage It! Global Case 9.1, "The Glass Ceiling: More Than a U.S. Issue," at the end of the chapter looks at the glass ceiling in Japan and Sweden.

Another employee group that may need special consideration is **dual-career couples**. Nearly 80 percent of all couples are working couples. The two-income family is replacing the single-income family as the norm.[23] When both members of a couple have career issues at stake, personal lives can complicate and become intertwined with occupational lives. A career opportunity for one member that demands a geographic move can produce a crisis for both the couple and their companies. As described in the Manager's Notebook, "Dual Careers Go International," a geographic move involving a dual-career couple can be difficult when the move is across international boundaries.

Both couples and organizations can take steps to help deal with dual-career issues. Rather than waiting until a crisis point, it is better if the couple resolves competing career issues by planning their careers and discussing how they will proceed if certain options become available. This approach also reduces the possibility of abrupt personnel losses for organizations. Some of the organizational approaches used to deal with the needs of dual-career couples include flexible work schedules, telecommuting (both discussed in Chapter 4), and child-care services (see Chapter 12). These kinds of practices have become more common over the past decade.

Dual-career couple
A couple whose members both have occupational responsibilities and career issues at stake.

Global

Dual Careers Go International

Your best performer just turned down an international assignment because her spouse couldn't obtain a permit to work abroad. Everybody loses in this scenario: It's a lost opportunity for the company, the worker, and even the worker's spouse. One global organization is working toward ending constraints on international mobility.

The Permits Foundation, supported by over 30 multinational companies, including Unilever, British Airways, and BASF, seeks to relax work barriers for expatriate spouses. We may not have yet heard much about the Permits Foundation in the United States, but we soon probably will. The organization's strategic plan is to initially target European countries before focusing on the United States.

Source: Doke, D. (2005, February 22). Global group aims to strike right balance to keep talent. *Personnel Today,* 7.

Some companies have also begun counseling couples in career management. These proactive programs, which work with both the employee and his or her spouse or significant other, have typically been reserved for executives and others who are considered key personnel in the organization.[24] First, each partner individually comes up with his or her goals and action plans. Then the partners are brought together to share their agendas and work through any conflicts. Professional counselors offer possible solutions and alternatives.[25] The result of the process—a joint career plan—is then provided to the organization. Employees and their partners benefit from this approach by formulating a mutually agreeable plan, and the organization benefits by increasing the probability of retaining key employees. Indeed, recent findings underscore the importance of and potential benefits of dual-career counseling and spousal support services.[26] The levels of work stress and job satisfaction experienced by dual-career workers are significantly influenced by the spouse's level of support; over the long term, lack of spousal support can have a negative influence on job performance and even cause a worker to leave his or her job.

Experts strongly recommend counseling and mentoring for dual-career couples facing an overseas assignment, a more common experience than ever before (see Chapter 17).[27] Without an active career support program, the employee may refuse the overseas assignment because of dual-career issues or the expatriate may perform the assignment inadequately. These possibilities cost an organization dearly because high performers are often selected for such duties and the assignment typically involves hefty training, housing, and moving expenses.

Providing career development and support that involves the expatriate spouse or significant other can reduce an organization's risk.[28] For example, an organization may make the transition to a new place and culture easier for the couple by offering the spouse help such as membership in professional organizations, tuition reimbursement, job-search assistance, and transportation to conferences.

Whether at home or on an overseas assignment, a dual-career couple's concerns relating to family issues have been linked to stress, depression, and anxiety for both men and women.[29] At least one member of a dual-career couple may have to spend work time on personal issues and problems. A growing number of companies are going beyond typical family-friendly benefits and offering *work–life programs* as a way to ease the stress of dual-career couples.[30] Worklife programs are outsourced counseling and referral services that may offer assistance ranging from finding child care (offered by companies such as Procter & Gamble and Aetna) to finding a kennel for your pet (Starbucks) or providing a lawyer's advice (U.S. Bancorp).

Meeting the Challenges of Effective Career Development

Creating a development program almost always consists of three phases: the assessment phase, the direction phase, and the development phase (Figure 9.2). Although presented separately in Figure 9.2, the phases of development often blend together in an actual program.

The Assessment Phase

The *assessment phase* of career development includes activities ranging from self-assessment to organizationally provided assessment. The goal of assessment, whether performed by employees themselves or by the organization, is to identify employees' strengths and weaknesses. This kind of clarification helps employees (1) to choose a career that is realistically obtainable and a good fit and (2) to determine the weaknesses they need to overcome to achieve their career goals. Figure 9.3 lists some tools that are commonly used for self-assessment and for organizational assessment.

Self-Assessment

Self-assessment is increasingly important for companies that want to empower their employees to take control of their careers. The major tools used for self-assessment are workbooks and workshops.

In addition to the exercises included in a generic career workbook, tailored workbooks might contain a statement of the organization's policies and procedures regarding career issues as well as descriptions of the career paths and options available in the organization.

Career-planning workshops, which may be led either by the company's HR department or by an external provider such as a consulting firm or local university, give employees information about career options in the organization. They may also be used to give participants feedback on their career aspirations and strategy. Participation in most workshops is voluntary, and some organizations hold these workshops on company time to demonstrate their commitment to their workforce.

Whether done through workbooks or workshops, self-assessment usually means doing skills assessment exercises, completing an interests inventory, and clarifying values.[31]

- As their name implies, *skills assessment exercises* are designed to identify an employee's skills. For example, a workbook exercise might ask the employee to compile a brief list of his or her accomplishments. Once the employee has generated a set of, say, five accomplishments, he or she then identifies the skills involved in making each accomplishment a reality. In a workshop situation, people might share their accomplishments in a group discussion, and then the entire group might help identify the skills underlying the accomplishments.

  Another skills assessment exercise presents employees with a list of skills they must rate on two dimensions: their level of proficiency at that skill and the degree to which they enjoy using it. A total score is then generated for each skill area—for example, by multiplying the proficiency by the preference rating. Figure 9.4 shows an example of this approach to skills assessment. Scores below 6 indicate areas of weakness or dislike, whereas scores of 6 or above indicate areas of strength. The pattern of scores can guide employees regarding the type of career for which they are best suited.

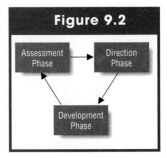

Figure 9.2

The Career Development Process

Figure 9.3	
Self-Assessment	**Organizational Assessment**
Career workbooks	Assessment centers
Career-planning workshops	Psychological testing
	Performance appraisal
	Promotability forecasts
	Succession planning

Common Assessment Tools

Sample Skills Assessment Exercise

Figure 9.4

Use the scales below to rate yourself on each of the following skills. Rate each skill area both for your level of proficiency and for your preference.

Proficiency:

1	2	3
Still learning	OK — competent	Proficient

Preference:

1	2	3
Don't like to use this skill	OK — Don't particularly like or dislike using this skill	Really enjoy using this skill

Skill Area	Proficiency	×	Preference	=	Score
1. Problem solving	_____		_____		_____
2. Team presentation	_____		_____		_____
3. Leadership	_____		_____		_____
4. Inventory	_____		_____		_____
5. Negotiation	_____		_____		_____
6. Conflict management	_____		_____		_____
7. Scheduling	_____		_____		_____
8. Delegation	_____		_____		_____
9. Participative management	_____		_____		_____
10. Feedback	_____		_____		_____
11. Planning	_____		_____		_____
12. Computer	_____		_____		_____

- An *interest inventory* is a measure of a person's occupational interests. Numerous off-the-shelf inventories can give employees insight into what type of career will best fit their interests. One of the best-known inventories is the Strong Vocational Interest Inventory.[32] The interest inventory asks people to indicate how strong or weak an interest they have in activities such as dealing with very old people, making a speech, and raising money for charity. Responses to items on the inventory are then scored to identify the occupations in which the individual has the same interests as the professionals employed in those fields.

- *Values clarification* involves prioritizing personal values. The typical values-clarification exercise presents employees with a list of values and asks them to rate how important each value is to them. For example, employees may be asked to prioritize security, power, money, and family in their lives. Knowing their priority values can help employees make satisfying career choices. The Manager's Notebook, "Anchor Yourself," provides an example of a values-based approach to career development. It presents eight items that describe career "anchors" and identifies implications for effective management for each anchor.

MANAGER'S NOTEBOOK

Ethics

Anchor Yourself

When your career's direction matches what you are really about, the result can be finding meaning and fulfillment in your work. Isn't it only ethical to try to provide the kind of work experience that matches the core values of a worker?

These core values might be considered to be career "anchors" according to Dr. Edgar Schein, an MIT professor who has developed the concept to identify what a worker wants from a career. To determine someone's career anchor, have the person select one of the following eight statements that best describe him or her. Go through the exercise yourself to identify your career anchor:

Career Anchor Assessment

1. I identify with my profession and like to use my skills.
2. I like having a broad overview and enjoy responsibility.
3. I like to work independently.
4. I like it when things are stable and predictable.
5. I like the challenge of starting something new.
6. I want to make the world a better place.
7. I like competition and enjoy solving problems.
8. I want balance in my life.

Even if you determine your workers' career anchors, what can you do about it? The nature of a job should enable a worker to express his or her career anchor. You will probably find that there is enough flexibility in how a job can be structured that you can help a worker to express his or her career anchor. The following list of management implications presents actions that you could take as a manager for each of the eight career anchors.

Basic Management Implications for Each Career Anchor

1. Give the worker opportunity to develop work standards and to mentor others.
2. Give the worker opportunities to lead projects or teams.
3. Ask the worker to take on the role of an internal consultant and tackle a workplace problem.
4. Let the worker know that staying his or her current position is an option.
5. Give this worker new projects and let him or her develop ideas as an internal entrepreneur.
6. Offer this worker some responsibility for a company program, such as diversity, or the opportunity to partner with a local charity.
7. Set stretch goals with the worker and empower him or her to make the decisions needed to get there.
8. Offer this worker flexibility in his or her work schedule and the opportunity to work from home.

Source: Adapted from Kanchier, C. (2006, May 6). What anchors your career? Workplace unhappiness may simply be a matter of a poor personality fit. *Calgary Sun* (Alberta, Canada), News section, 62.

Organizational Assessment

Some of the tools traditionally used by organizations in selection (see Chapter 5) are also valuable for career development. Among these are assessment centers, psychological testing, performance appraisal, promotability forecasts, and succession planning.

■ *Assessment centers* are situational exercises—such as interviews, in-basket exercises, and business games—that are often used to select managerial talent. A developmentally oriented assessment center stresses giving feedback and direction to the worker.[33] The assessment center measures competencies needed for a particular job and provides participants with feedback about their strengths and weaknesses in the competency areas as uncovered in the exercises.

   Like many other tools, assessment centers are being developed in computerized versions.[34] For example, one computerized assessment tool evaluates management skills such as coaching, problem solving, and team building. A variety of scenarios simulate workplace situations in which judgments have to be made about performance, problems need to be solved, and confrontations need to be dealt with. Based on the person's performance in these scenarios, the program provides a development plan for career growth.

   The limited number of studies indicate that assessment centers have significant and positive effects on participants, even months after the assessment center exercise.

■ Some organizations also use *psychological testing* to help employees better understand their skills and interests. Tests that measure personality and attitudes, as well as interest inventories, fall into this category.[35]

■ *Performance appraisal* is another source of valuable career development information. Unfortunately, appraisals are frequently limited to assessment of past performance rather than oriented toward future performance improvements and directions. Future-oriented performance appraisal can give employees important insights into their strengths, their weaknesses, and the career paths available to them. Performance appraisal should be more than simply evaluation; it needs to include learning and lead to improvement in performance and direction for development.[36]

■ **Promotability forecasts** are decisions made by managers regarding the advancement potential of their subordinates. These forecasts allow the organization to identify people who appear to have high advancement potential.[37] The high-potential employees are then given developmental experiences (such as attending an executive training seminar) to help them achieve their advancement potential.

■ **Succession planning** focuses on preparing people to fill executive positions. Formally, succession planning means examining development needs given a firm's strategic plans. That is, the formal approach identifies the organization's future direction and challenges and then derives the competencies new leaders need.[38] Then the organization identifies internal and external target candidates. Once a short list of executives is created, the candidates are researched and tracked using the required competencies as evaluation areas. This tracking and monitoring process continues indefinitely so that an up-to-date list is available when inevitable turnover in leadership occurs. Succession planning is necessary when the organization needs key positions filled without interruption. Without it, the business may sacrifice profitability and stability as the price for not being prepared.

Although the formal approach is advisable, most succession planning is done informally. Informal succession planning means high-level managers identify and develop their own replacements. The employees identified as having upper-management potential may then be given developmental experiences that help prepare them for the executive ranks, such as workshops on the organization's values and mission.

Succession planning can pose difficulties. For example, organizations have been accused of discriminating against women and minorities when filling high-level positions. Rather than outright discrimination, it can be the informality of much succession planning that makes companies unwittingly exclude these groups as candidates. Formal succession planning programs can make the identification of high-potential employees and replacement candidates a more egalitarian procedure.

UPS, the shipping giant, provides an example of an organization that takes succession planning seriously.[39] The UPS program begins with a formal talent identification program.

Promotability forecast
A career development activity in which managers make decisions regarding the advancement potential of subordinates.

Succession planning
A career development activity that focuses on preparing people to fill executive positions.

Some companies ask outside consultants to evaluate their internal candidates for promotion. Here psychologists at the Center for Creative Leadership assess candidates' leadership skills through one-way glass.

Managers identify candidates for advancement, and these suggestions are reviewed by a management development committee that considers the strengths and development needs of each candidate. The development committee is responsible for making sure that the candidates receive the development opportunities they need. Individual members of the management committee identify candidates they think have the possibility of becoming executives in their area. The management committee receives monthly rotating updates on these promising candidates from each of the 12 managers. The UPS program is a formal and ongoing process, not a one-time event. By the time a candidate is moved up to an executive-level position, all the top managers are already aware of the person and what he or she brings to the position.

What employee characteristics and experiences predict success at the managerial and executive levels? A recent study examined the extent to which demographic, human capital, motivational, and organizational variables predict executive career success.[40] The researchers divided career success into objective (for example, pay level) and subjective (for example, job satisfaction) components. The researchers concluded that educational level, quality and prestige of the university, and major were all related to the pay levels of a sample of 1,388 executives. Interestingly, ambition was negatively related to job satisfaction, with the more ambitious executives indicating less satisfaction in their current positions.

Personality characteristics are also a determinant of success in higher-level management jobs. For example, one study examined the effects of both personality and cognitive abilities on the current earnings of managers, and concluded that such characteristics as creativity, sociability, self-reliance, and self-control are strongly related to managers' success as determined by pay level.[41] Recent research suggests that some of the "big five" personality characteristics are related to measures of career success, such as salary, promotions, and career satisfaction.[42] For example, extraversion was positively related to all measures of career success, whereas neuroticism was a negative factor for career satisfaction. Thus, managers should consider these characteristics, as well as level of technical knowledge and motivation, when preparing their promotability forecasts and conducting succession planning.

In small companies, succession planning is crucial because the sudden departure or illness of a key player can cause the business to flounder. Yet just as some people shy away from drafting a will for fear of recognizing their own mortality, some small-business owners shy away from succession planning for fear of recognizing that they will not always be in control of their business. Other small-business owners are too caught up in the daily pressures of running a business to plan for the future.

The Direction Phase

The *direction phase* of career development involves determining the type of career that employees want and the steps they must take to realize their career goals. Appropriate direction requires an accurate understanding of one's current position. Unless the direction phase is based on a thorough assessment of the current situation, the goals and steps identified may be inappropriate. For example, a task force assembled by the Healthcare Financial Management Association reviewed credentials, experience, and other data for more than 5,000 senior finance executives. They also reviewed certification standards and graduate school curricula and worked with two panels of experts. Through this review, the task force developed the competency model shown in Figure 9.5.

The competency model can be most useful for career development by focusing on the type of role the person desires. For example, someone who aspires to be the leader of an enterprise may need to develop the highest competency levels in the area of leading others. Someone aspiring to the role of business advisor might be best served by developing a balanced portfolio of competencies.

The direction phase, represented by the competencies, should be based on a careful assessment of what is needed in the profession. Further, career development direction should not be a stand-alone effort. To be effective, career development must be integrated with other HRM efforts, such as staffing, performance appraisal, and training.

One manager who participated in a study by PricewaterhouseCoopers quoted Mark Twain: "Never try to teach a pig to sing. It wastes your time and annoys the pig."[43] In other words, for

A Competency Growth Model for Healthcare Financial Managers: Basis for Career Development Direction

Figure 9.5

A Healthcare Financial Management Association task force identified behavioral characteristics having to do with the skill, knowledge, social, trait, or motive qualities needed to excel in the profession. These competencies were grouped into the following three components:

COMPONENT 1: UNDERSTANDING THE BUSINESS ENVIRONMENT
Competencies:
1. Strategic thinking—the ability to integrate knowledge of the industry with an understanding of the long range vision of an organization.
2. Systems thinking—an awareness of how one's role fits within an organization and knowing when and how to take actions that support its effectiveness.

COMPONENT 2: MAKING IT HAPPEN
Competencies:
1. Results orientation—the drive to achieve and the ability to diagnose inefficiencies and judge when to take entrepreneurial risks.
2. Collaborative decision making—actions that involve key stakeholders in the decision-making processes.
3. Action orientation—going beyond the minimum role requirements to boldly drive projects and lead the way to improved services, processes, and products.

COMPONENT 3: LEADING OTHERS
Competencies:
1. Championing business thinking—the ability to energize others to understand and achieve business-focused outcomes. Fostering an understanding of issues and challenges through clear articulation and agenda setting.
2. Coaching and mentoring—the ability to release the potential of others by actively promoting responsibility, trust, and recognition.
3. Influence—the ability to communicate a position in a persuasive manner, thus generating support, agreement, or commitment.

Source: **Adapted from** *Healthcare Financial Management.* **(1999). Dynamic healthcare environment demands new career planning tools,** *52,* **70–74.**

your organization's development efforts to be successful, you need to first make sure that you are hiring people who generally match your skill requirements and culture. The two major approaches to career direction are individual counseling and various information services.

Individual Career Counseling

Individual career counseling refers to one-on-one sessions with the goal of helping employees examine their career aspirations.[44] Topics of discussion might include the employee's current job responsibilities, interests, and career objectives. Although career counseling is frequently conducted by managers or HR staff members, some organizations use professional counselors.[45]

The days in which career counseling means face-to-face interaction with a professional counselor or manager may be numbered. Career counseling is now available online at sites such as *www.careerexperience.com* and *www.careerjournal.com*. The Dow Jones' Careerjournal.com site, for example, focuses on executive-level job hunters and offers career counseling and résumé evaluation. The service is not entirely virtual, however. Although material is submitted online, interaction with a career counselor is via phone.

When line managers conduct career counseling sessions, the HR department generally monitors the sessions' effectiveness and provides assistance to the managers in the form of training, suggested counseling formats, and the like. There are several advantages to having managers conduct career counseling sessions with their employees. First, managers are probably more aware of their employees' strengths and weaknesses than anyone else. Second, knowing that managers understand their employees' career development concerns can foster an environment of trust and commitment.

Unfortunately, assigning career counseling responsibility to managers does not guarantee that the task will be carried out carefully. As with performance appraisal and many other important HR activities, managers may treat employee career development simply as a paper-shuffling exercise unless top management signals its strong support for development activities. If managers only go through the motions, there is likely to be a negative impact on employee attitudes, productivity, and profits.

Information Services

As their name suggests, information services provide career development information to employees. Determining what to do with this information is largely the employee's responsibility. This approach makes sense, given the diversity of the interests and aspiration of employees in today's organizations.

The most commonly provided information services are job-posting systems, skills inventories, career paths, and career resource centers.

- **Job-posting systems** are a fairly easy and direct way of providing employees with information on job openings. The jobs available in an organization are announced ("posted") on a bulletin board, in a company newsletter, through a phone recording or computer system, or over a company's intranet. Whatever the medium, all employees have access to the list. All postings should include clear descriptions of both the job's specifications and the criteria that will be used to select among the applicants.

  Job-posting systems have the advantage of reinforcing the notion that the organization promotes from within.[46] This belief not only motivates employees to maintain and improve their performance, but also tends to reduce turnover.

- **Skills inventories** are company-maintained records with information such as employees' abilities, skills, knowledge, and education.[47] The company can use this comprehensive, centralized HR information system to get an overall picture of its workforce's training and development needs, as well as to identify existing talent in one department that may be more productively employed in another.

  Skills inventories can prove valuable for employees as well. Feedback regarding how they stack up against other employees can encourage them to improve their skills or seek out other positions that better match their current skill levels.

- **Career paths** provide valuable information regarding the possible directions and career opportunities available in an organization. A career path presents the steps in a possible career and a plausible timetable for accomplishing them. Just as a variety of paths may lead to the same job, so may starting from the same job lead to very different outcomes. Figure 9.6 provides an example of alternative career paths that a bus person in the hotel business might follow.

  To be realistic, career paths must specify the qualifications necessary to proceed to the next step and the minimum length of time employees must spend at each step to obtain the necessary experience. This information could be generated by computer.

Job-posting system
A system in which an organization announces job openings to all employees on a bulletin board, in a company newsletter, or through a phone recording or computer system.

Skills inventory
A company-maintained record of employees' abilities, skills, knowledge, and education.

Career path
A chart showing the possible directions and career opportunities available in an organization; it presents the steps in a possible career and a plausible timetable for accomplishing them.

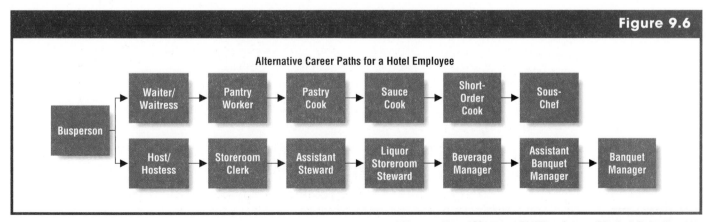

Figure 9.6

Alternative Career Paths for a Hotel Employee

Busperson →
Waiter/Waitress → Pantry Worker → Pastry Cook → Sauce Cook → Short-Order Cook → Sous-Chef

Host/Hostess → Storeroom Clerk → Assistant Steward → Liquor Storeroom Steward → Beverage Manager → Assistant Banquet Manager → Banquet Manager

Alternative Career Paths for a Hotel Employee
This is a generic example of alternative career paths. Actual career paths should specify a time frame for each job.

Figure 9.7 presents examples of two survey forms based on jobs in the hotel industry that might be used to collect career path information. Form A asks employees to indicate how important certain skills are for the performance of their job. The skills included on the form can be determined by examining job-analysis information and by interviewing individual employees. Employee responses can then be used to develop lists of critical and desirable skills for each job.

Form B asks employees to judge the extent to which experience in other jobs in the organization is needed to perform their current job adequately. The lowest-level jobs, which still involve the skill requirements uncovered with the use of Form A, would not require previous job experience within the organization. Higher-level or more complex jobs would likely require more job experience.

Career resource center
A collection of career development materials such as workbooks, tapes, and texts.

■ A **career resource center** is a collection of career development materials such as workbooks, tapes, and texts. These resources might be maintained by the HR department either in its offices or in an area that is readily accessible to employees. Companies with many locations might publicize the availability of these materials and lend them to employees who express interest. Some colleges and universities maintain career resource centers, and many consulting firms (particularly those specializing in employee outplacement) provide career development materials as well. Career resource centers can help people identify for themselves their strengths and weaknesses, career options, and educational and training opportunities.

Figure 9.7

FORM A: SKILL REQUIREMENTS

Instructions: A list of various skills that apply to various jobs is presented below. Use the scale provided to indicate the extent to which each skill is applicable to your current position.

Circle the Most Appropriate Number

Skills	Not applicable	Somewhat desirable useful at times	Very desirable but not essential	Critical— could not perform job without it
1. Determine daily/forecasted production and service equipment requirements.	1	2	3	4
2. Clean guest rooms.	1	2	3	4
3. Set up, break down, and change over function rooms.	1	2	3	4
4. Handle security problems.	1	2	3	4
5. Clean public areas/ restrooms.	1	2	3	4
6. Assist in menu development.	1	2	3	4
7. Register/preregister guests into hotel.	1	2	3	4
8. Participate in the preparation of sauces, soups, stews, and special dishes.	1	2	3	4
9. Prepare and serve salads, fruit cocktails, fruits, juices, and so on.	1	2	3	4
10. Participate in the rating of meats and other dishes.	1	2	3	4
11. Care for, clean, and distribute laundry items.	1	2	3	4

Two Career Path Information Forms

(Continued) **Figure 9.7**

FORM B: EXPERIENCE REQUIREMENTS

Instructions: A list of work experience by job titles is presented below. Use the scale provided to indicate for each item: (a) how important previous experience in this work is for the successful performance of your current job duties; and (b) the amount of experience that constitutes adequate training or exposure so that you are able to function efficiently in your current position.

Circle the Most Appropriate Number

	Importance of Requirement			Minimum Experience				
	Not very important	Very desirable but not essential	Critical—could not perform job without it	0-6 mos	7-11 mos	1-2 yrs	3-5 yrs	6 yrs
Work Experience								
1. *Storeroom Clerk:* Accurately compute daily food costs by assembling food invoices, totaling food requisitions, taking monthly inventory of food storeroom, and so on.	1	2	3	1	2	3	4	5
2. *Liquor Storeroom Steward:* Maintain adequate levels of alcoholic beverages and related supplies; properly receive, store, and issue them to user departments.	1	2	3	1	2	3	4	5
3. *Pantry Worker:* Prepare and serve to waiters salads, fruit cocktails, fruit juices, and so on.	1	2	3	1	2	3	4	5
4. *Pastry Cook:* Prepare mixes for baking cakes, pies, soufflés, and so on.	1	2	3	1	2	3	4	5
5. *Short-Order Cook:* Prepare short-order foods in assigned restaurant areas.	1	2	3	1	2	3	4	5
6. *Sous Chef:* Assist executive chef in all areas of kitchen production; directly supervise the operations of the kitchen in his or her absence.	1	2	3	1	2	3	4	5
7. *Waiter or Waitress:* Take food and beverage orders from customers and serve them in a restaurant or lounge.	1	2	3	1	2	3	4	5
8. *Beverage Manager:* Supervise and schedule personnel as required and maintain budgeted liquor cost and supplies for the lounge and/or banquet functions.	1	2	3	1	2	3	4	5
9. *Assistant Banquet Manager:* Assist in the coordination and successful completion of all banquet functions, such as coordinating staffing requirements, ensuring that function room is properly set and tidied, and keeping banquet manager fully informed of all problems or unusual matters.	1	2	3	1	2	3	4	5

The Development Phase

Meeting the requirements necessary to move up in an organization can require a great deal of growth and self-improvement. The *development phase,* which involves taking actions to create and increase skills to prepare for future job opportunities, is meant to foster this growth and self-improvement. The most common development programs offered by organizations are mentoring, coaching, job rotation, and tuition assistance.

Mentoring

Mentoring
A developmentally oriented relationship between senior and junior colleagues or peers that involves advising, role modeling, sharing contacts, and giving general support.

Mentoring is a developmentally oriented relationship between senior and junior colleagues or peers. Mentoring relationships, which can occur at all levels and in all areas of an organization, generally involve advising, role modeling, sharing contacts, and giving general support. Mentoring can be either voluntary and informal or involuntary and formal. Informal mentoring is generally more effective than mentoring done solely as a formal responsibility,[48] though there are situations in which a formal mentoring program may be the better choice.

Mentoring has been found to make a real difference in careers, with executives who were mentored early in their careers tending to make more money at a younger age and more likely to follow a career plan than those who were not mentored. Research findings support the conclusion that effective mentoring can improve outcomes such as performance levels, promotion rates, upward mobility, income, and job satisfaction.[49] For mentors, particularly those nearing retirement, the mentoring role can offer new challenges and reignite enthusiasm and motivation. A recent survey of mentors found that the supervisors are often considered the most effective mentors.[50] However, survey respondents also view the roles of supervisor and mentor quite differently, with the supervisor focused on results and the mentor on the person. Mentees report that mentors build confidence, stimulate learning, and serve as a role model and sounding board.

The mentoring program at Intel provides an innovative example of matching mentors and mentees.[51] The Intel program matches people by skills and needs, not by position in the organization. The company utilizes interest and e-mail to make global mentor and mentee matches.

Mentoring relationships can be particularly important for minority employees.[52] African American managers, for example, who have had mentors have been found to achieve greater levels of career advancement. The promotion rate for African American women was found in one study to be 70 percent for those with mentors and 50 percent for those without. An effective mentor can help sensitize and educate a mentee about political and cultural issues that might arise that a minority employee may not have had exposure to.

Some organizations are combining job shadowing with mentoring.[53] Job shadowing allows a junior person to observe a more senior employee for a set duration. For example, Edward Jones blends shadowing with mentoring in its GoodKnight Plan. The program pairs a noninvestment representative with a successful veteran for about one year. The new representative is gradually provided the opportunity to take on a percentage of the veteran's accounts before opening his or her office. The company has found the production level of representatives who went through the GoodKnight Plan to be at a level in their first year that isn't reached by representatives who didn't go through the program until their second or third year. Target is another organization blending shadowing with mentoring. Target provides a 15-week Business Analyst Program in which new analysts shadow a mentor. The mentor acclimates the new hires to the Target culture and provides tasks and feedback. By the end of the program, the new analysts can manage their own category of merchandise.

Like women and minorities in large firms, people who work for a small business or are self-employed may find it difficult to find a mentor. These people can benefit from membership in professional and trade associations. This form of "group mentoring" may complement individual mentoring or serve as a substitute for it.

Membership in professional organizations is an effective career development tool. While research is limited, it is clear that association membership provides important networking opportunities, and many a career has been advanced as a result of networking. Even though most professional organizations emphasize the educational content of their functions, the social process and networking opportunities seem to be much more important to members.[54]

Coaching

Employee *coaching* consists of ongoing, sometimes spontaneous, meetings between managers and their employees to discuss the employee's career goals and development. Working with employees to chart and implement their career goals enhances productivity and can spur a manager's own advancement. Then why do so many managers give short shrift to employee coaching? For one thing, in today's flatter organizations managers have more people under their supervision and less time to spend on developing each employee. For another, some managers may view "employee development" as a buzz phrase unless top management clearly and strongly supports it. Finally, managers may be more comfortable working on tasks and believe they lack the skills needed to be an effective coach.[55] Many managers view their role as one of providing answers, pointing out weaknesses, diagnosing problems, and solving them. This role is effective if the purpose is judgment or assessment, but it is not conducive to effective coaching.

Job Rotation

Job rotation assigns employees to various jobs so that they acquire a wider base of skills. Broadened job experience can give workers more flexibility to choose a career path. And, as we discussed in Chapter 8, employees can gain an even wider and more flexible experience base through cross-functional training.

In addition to offering more career options for the employee, job rotation results in a more broadly trained and skilled workforce for the employer. However, job rotation programs have some disadvantages. They do not suit employees who want to maintain a narrow and specialized focus. From the organization's perspective, they can slow down operations as workers learn new skills. While the development benefits of job rotation may be high in the long run, firms should be aware of the short run and intermediate costs. From an employee's perspective, the opportunity of job rotation may be a survival mechanism. Specifically, downsizing in an organization may focus on eliminating an obsolete area. When employees broaden their skills through job rotation, they help ensure their longevity and usefulness to the organization.

Tuition Assistance Programs

Organizations offer *tuition assistance programs* to support their employees' education and development. Tuition and other costs of educational programs (ranging from seminars, workshops, and continuing education programs to degree programs) may be entirely covered, partially covered, or covered contingent upon adequate performance in the program.

A survey of educational reimbursement programs revealed that 43 percent of these plans reimbursed less than 100 percent of tuition. Typically, there is a fixed limit—such as 75 percent of tuition—for all courses. Some companies vary the percentage of tuition funds reimbursed according to the relevance of the course to organizational goals. For instance, a business-book publishing company might encourage its editors to take professional courses related to the business, such as economics and marketing, by reimbursing these courses at 100 percent. However, if editors want to take courses on sign language interpretation, art history, or English literature, the company might reimburse only 50 percent of the tuition.

Self-Development

We conclude this chapter by examining how to manage your personal career.

When an employer does not routinely offer development programs, it is essential that employees work out their own development plan. Employees who neglect to do this risk stagnation and obsolescence. One of the first issues to wrestle with is whether your current job fits with your career plans. The Manager's Notebook, "Career Self-Assessment," presents questions you can use to assess whether your job places you on a career track that is good for you.

Customer-Driven HR

Career Self-Assessment

Career self-assessment has rapidly become the norm in many organizations. But how do you evaluate where you're at in your career? And how can you know if your current job puts you on track for reaching your career goals? The following questions can help you make your own career assessments.

- *Does what you're doing for work resonate with your values?* Use the self-assessment exercise in the Manager's Notebook, "Anchor Yourself." Is your current job a good fit with your career anchor? Or, make a list of your values and judge how well what you are doing at work fits with these values. Are there serious mismatches on values that are most central to you?
- *Do you find your work to be meaningful?* Whatever you do, is it something that you feel makes a positive contribution? For example, does your work allow you to make a positive difference for your customers, organization, or community, and is this effect important to you?
- *How does your organization treat you?* Do you feel you are treated with dignity and respect at work?
- *How do you use your talents at work?* Are you doing what you are good at? Is it what you like to do? Are your contributions appreciated?
- *What is your manager like?* Does your manager support your career growth? Does he or she help your own efforts to develop yourself?
- *What is your life like?* Do you feel in balance? Are you satisfied with the quality of your life? Are there things missing?

Thoughtfully answering the foregoing questions can help you determine if you are on a positive career track or if you need to make some changes. Not every answer can be positive or positive to the maximum degree, but too many negative responses may be a signal that where you are at now isn't contributing to your career.

Source: Adapted with permission from Kaplan-Leiserson, E. (2002). A love match: Do you love your job? Does it love you? *Technology & Development, 56,* 14(2).

Developing your career requires more than just assuring your survival in your organization. Successfully managing your career development means recognizing and developing for yourself the skills needed to advance in today's workplace. The Manager's Notebook, "Guidelines for Today's Leaders," identifies some of the characteristics needed for effective management in today's competitive and dynamic environment. Developing these characteristics in yourself can help you to achieve a positive and rewarding career.

Emerging Trends

Guidelines for Today's Leaders

Today's business environment is more dynamic, competitive, and global than ever before. Success in this environment requires a change in the traditional command-and-control approach to managing. The following points can help guide you to being an effective leader in today's business environment.

- *Take an entrepreneurial perspective.* What are the needs in the marketplace and how can they be better served? Who are your organization's customers and how can you better anticipate their needs? These types of questions direct managers to customer-driven solutions. Being externally driven and looking for solutions rather than complaining about problems will lead to positive things for the organization and for your career.

- *Embrace chaos.* Rather than being a threat, change is now a routine part of the workplace. Effective performance as a leader requires that you be willing to adapt and try new approaches. Decisions need to be viewed as tactical adjustments rather than permanent answers. Given today's fast-paced environment, you have to make the best decisions with the information immediately available and then you need to move forward.

- *Some risk is needed.* Today's effective leaders are not risk averse. However, they also do not act blindly and rashly. The possibility of failure has to be accepted as part of the path to learning and success. However, getting accurate information and attending to details will increase your chances of making the best choices.

- *Breadth is the key.* Adaptability and a customer focus are characteristics highly valued in today's organizations. The ability to partner with others and to come up with ways to get things done may be more important than specialist skills. You can make positive contributions to your organization and career by viewing everything as your job.

- *Soft skills can make or break you.* Strong interpersonal skills are essential for managers to effectively hire, lead, mentor, and retain employees in today's dynamic and team-based workplaces.

Source: Adapted from Kacena, J. F. (2002). New leadership directions. *Journal of Business Strategy, 23,* 21–23; Executive update. (2002), *Technology & Development 56,* 19.

In addition to effective personal characteristics and behaviors, career development can be significantly influenced by situational opportunities. For example, teams, particularly cross-functional or organization-wide teams, can provide a great career development opportunity.[56] Broad teams allow you to gain a wider understanding and perspective of the organization. Furthermore, such teams provide excellent opportunities for adding valuable contacts to your network.

Figure 9.8 lists a set of suggestions to help employees enhance their own development and increase their opportunities for advancement. The *development suggestions* focus on personal growth and direction, whereas the *advancement suggestions* focus on the steps employees can take to improve their promotability in the organization.

Development Suggestions

The development suggestions in Figure 9.8 are based on the assumption that the organization does not offer development programs. However, these suggestions are relevant even when the company provides development activities.

Figure 9.8

Development	Advancement
1. Create your own personal mission statement.	1. Remember that performance in your function is important, but interpersonal performance is critical.
2. Take responsibility for your own direction and growth.	2. Set the right values and priorities.
3. Make enhancement your priority rather than advancement.	3. Provide solutions, not problems.
4. Talk to people in positions to which you aspire and get suggestions on how to proceed.	4. Be a team player.
5. Set reasonable goals.	5. Be customer oriented.
6. Make investment in yourself a priority.	6. Act as if what you're doing makes a difference.

Source: Advancement suggestions adapted from Matejka, K., and Dunsing, R. (1993). Enhancing your advancement in the 1990s. *Management Decision, 31,* 52–54.

Suggestions for Self-Development

1. **Create your own personal mission statement.** Like an organizational mission statement, a *personal mission statement* should indicate the business you would like to be in and the role you would like to play.[57] You should see the statement as changeable over time, not a commandment to which you must blindly adhere regardless of situational or personal factors.

   The process of developing the statement can reveal personal values and preferences you may not have realized you have. Once completed, the mission statement should help you set your strategic direction, clarify your priorities, and avoid investing time and energy in pursuits that are not instrumental to achieving your mission.

2. **Take responsibility for your own direction and growth.** You should not place all your hopes in a company-provided development program. Things change, and steps in a career path can be eliminated as a result of downsizing or reorganizing. Organizations may also eliminate or replace development programs. Such changes could be devastating for people who place their future entirely in the hands of their organization.

3. **Make enhancement, rather than advancement, your priority.** Organizational flattening and downsizing mean that there will be fewer opportunities for advancement in the coming years. Direct upward paths to desired higher-level positions are rare. Enhancing your skills in the short run should lead to advancement in the longer run.

4. **Talk to people in positions to which you aspire and get their suggestions on how to proceed.** People who are currently in the kind of job you desire can give you valuable insight into the job and what you must do to make it to that level. Talking to people is also a good way of networking and keeping your name on people's lips.

5. **Set reasonable goals.** As in any major undertaking, it is best to set reasonable goals along the way to your ultimate goal. Breaking your career aspirations into smaller, more manageable goals can help you take the necessary steps toward accomplishing your ultimate goal. It is important to make these minigoals reasonable and achievable. Expecting too much too soon can lead to disillusionment and frustration.

6. **Make investment in yourself a priority.** When multiple demands are made on your time and attention, it is easy to neglect self-development activities. It is important to remind yourself that these activities are actually investments in yourself and your future, and that no one else is likely to make those investments for you.

Advancement Suggestions

The advancement suggestions in Figure 9.8 focus on the steps you can take to improve your chances of being considered for advancement. The development suggestions are fundamental and provide the necessary base, but the advancement suggestions provide the necessary attitudes and organizational presence.

1. **Remember that performance in your function is important, but interpersonal performance is critical.** Advancing in an organization requires excellent interpersonal skills. The abilities to communicate (both one-on-one and to groups), to collaborate, to listen, to summarize, and to write concise reports and memos are essential to being considered a viable candidate for advancement.

2. **Set the right values and priorities.** Some organizations place a high value on collaboration and teamwork, while others emphasize independence and individual contribution. Aligning your behavior with the organization's values improves your chances for advancement.[58]

3. **Provide solutions, not problems.** Nobody likes to hear complaints. So, rather than voicing complaints and pointing out problems, take some time to think issues through and offer potential solutions. You'll be perceived as a much more valuable member of the organization.

4. **Be a team player.** You should not try to steal the limelight for your work group's accomplishments. Rather, you should try to shine the spotlight on the group's efforts. When you do, you'll be viewed as a facilitator rather than a grandstander. However, you should be sure that those responsible for evaluating your performance know of your personal accomplishments. One way to balance these concerns is to refuse to seek public praise for your performance but not be afraid to call attention to your successes when appropriate.

5. **Be customer oriented.** Always keep in mind that anyone with whom you have an exchange is your "customer." Whether these interactions are internal or external, understanding and satisfying customer needs should be a top priority. When you take a customer-orientation approach to your job, the organization will recognize you as a high-quality representative who can be expected to accomplish things.

6. **Act as if what you are doing makes a difference.** A sure way to be overlooked for advancement is to display an apathetic or negative attitude. Not all tasks or projects to which you are assigned will spur your interest, but if you approach these activities with a positive attitude, others will see you as a contributor and a valuable team player.

Summary and Conclusions

What Is Career Development?
Career development is an ongoing organized and formalized effort that focuses on developing enriched and more capable workers. It has a wider focus, longer time frame, and broader scope than training. Development must be a key business strategy if an organization is to survive in today's increasingly competitive and global business environment.

Challenges in Career Development
Before putting a career development program in place, management needs to determine (1) who will be responsible for development, (2) how much emphasis on development is appropriate, and (3) how the development needs of a diverse workforce (including dual-career couples) will be met.

Meeting the Challenges of Effective Development
Career development is a continuing cycle of three phases: an assessment phase, a direction phase, and a development phase. Each phase is an important part of developing the workforce.

In the assessment phase, employees' skills, interests, and values are identified. These assessments may be carried out by the workers themselves, by the organization, or by both. Self-assessment is often done through career workbooks and career-planning workshops. Organizational assessment is done through assessment centers, psychological testing, performance appraisal, promotability forecasts, and succession planning.

The direction phase involves determining the type of career that employees want and the steps they must take to make their career goals a reality. In this phase workers may receive individual career counseling or information from a variety of sources, including a job-posting system, skills inventories, career paths, and career resource centers.

The development phase involves taking actions to create and increase employees' skills and promotability. The most common development programs are mentoring, coaching, job rotation, and tuition assistance programs.

Self-Development
In situations in which the employer does not routinely offer development programs, employees must take an active role in their own development. To do otherwise is to risk stagnation and obsolescence.

Key Terms

career development, 273
career path, 285
career resource center, 286

dual-career couple, 277
job-posting system, 285
mentoring, 288

promotability forecast, 282
skills inventory, 285
succession planning, 282

Discussion Questions

1. It has been argued that training can lead to turnover, but career development can reduce it. Differentiate between training and career development. Why might training lead to turnover whereas career development might improve retention? Explain.
2. How would you go about retaining and developing older employees who are part of a dual-career couple?
3. Today's organizations are flatter and offer fewer opportunities for advancement. How do you think careers should be developed in this type of organizational environment?
4. What challenges do nontraditional family units pose to company career development plans? How can companies meet these challenges?
5. People who adopt a careerist strategy focus on career advancement through political machinations rather than excellent performance. Experts have pointed out four ways in which workers try to influence their superiors'

opinions of them: favor doing (doing a favor for a superior in hopes that the favor will someday be returned), opinion conformity (agreeing with superiors in order to build trust and a relationship), other enhancement (flattery), and self-presentation (portraying oneself as having very desirable traits and motives).

In what other ways might employees try to influence their superiors' opinions of them? How can managers tell when an employee is sincere? What criteria should be used when deciding which employees to promote?

6. Companies use various tactics to encourage managers to make employee development a top priority. At Honeywell,

for instance, a prestigious award worth $3,000 is given to those managers who contribute strongly to their unit's profitability, who assist the career development of at least three people, and who have excellent records as mentors of diverse employee groups. Winners gain companywide recognition as well as the financial reward. What do you think of this policy of tying financial rewards to people development? What are some other ways companies can hold managers accountable for developing those they supervise?

There is a variety of additional material available on the Web site that accompanies this text. You can access this information by visiting the Web site at ***www.prenhall.com/gomez***.

YOU MANAGE IT!

Global Case 9.1

The Glass Ceiling: More Than a U.S. Issue

The glass ceiling refers to a barrier that prevents people in certain subgroups from advancing to positions of greater power and influence. Although the term is sometimes used to refer to barriers to advancement experienced by any subgroup, the initial meaning of the term and its common usage refers to barriers to the advancement of women. U.S. companies have made progress toward gender equality, but women are still underrepresented in the ranks of top management. The United States is, unfortunately, not alone in wrestling with the glass ceiling.

Consider the rise of women to top-management posts in Japan. Recently, and within a week of each other, both Sanyo Electric Co. and Daiei Inc. (a Japanese retailer) hired women as their CEOs. These events might seem to mark a trend, but they happen to be two isolated examples of women who are at the helm of Japanese firms.[a] Both companies are in deep financial trouble and may be looking for new and different leadership to turn them around.

As in the United States, Japanese firms are aware of the glass ceiling and are committed to doing something about it. For example, Nissan has a target goal of tripling the number of female managers in its ranks to 120. This figure would be 5 percent of its managerial positions; the average percentage of females in management positions in Japan is 2.8 percent.

Sweden is broadly perceived as being progressive and a supporter of gender equality. Unfortunately, Sweden provides another example of a country struggling with a glass ceiling. Women make up 79 percent of Sweden's labor force, but only 3 percent of female employees are managers.[b] A survey

commissioned by the Swedish government found that 42 percent of Swedish companies didn't have a single female on their executive boards. There has been some discussion of legislation requiring gender equality, but most companies are against this approach. However, the majority of Swedish companies conduct gender equality workshops and approximately half view the lack of women at managerial levels as a problem.

Critical Thinking Questions

1. Do you think a glass ceiling exists in the United States and other countries, such as Japan and Sweden? If not, what else, other than discrimination, could account for the under-representation of women in management?
2. In Japan, the glass ceiling may be related to a male-dominant culture. If this is the case, how can the glass ceiling be reduced or eliminated?
3. In Sweden, many women hold positions of power in politics. For example, women hold 11 of 22 cabinet posts. Obviously, the advancement of Swedish women in the corporate world is a different matter. The prevalence of females in top posts in the public sector would seem to argue against a culturally imposed glass ceiling. What else, then, could be preventing the advancement of Swedish women in the private sector?

Team Exercise

As a team, consider the evidence of the limited advancement of women presented in this case. Identify possible causes of the glass ceiling. What steps should be taken to eliminate the glass ceiling? Categorize your suggested actions according to the cause they are trying to remedy and whether they are a short- or long-term solution. Share your plans with the rest of the class.

As a class, identify the best parts from each team's presentation and put together an overall plan. Does the class think that the glass ceiling will be eliminated?

Experiential Exercise

Many believe that the under-representation of women in management is due to unfair discrimination. Thus, legislation forcing fairness (such as gender quotas) is one possible solution. Other people point to the fact that women are more likely to leave the labor force. Some women who have successfully made it to managerial ranks question the existence of a glass ceiling and argue that women need to get tough and leave the belief that they are victims behind.

Select representatives from the class as members who either take the glass ceiling position or do not accept this explanation. Each team should begin by describing its position. The pro-glass-ceiling team should identify what it means by discrimination. Why does glass-ceiling discrimination occur? The anti-glass-ceiling team should identify what accounts for the lower percentage of female managers. If the causative factor isn't discrimination, what other factors may be the cause?

In a debate-style format, each team presents its position and what should be done to solve the problem. Each team has the opportunity to question and rebut and rejoin the other team. The instructor moderates this process. At the end of the debate, the instructor leads the class in discussion of the causes for a barrier to the advancement of women and what actions might be taken to remedy the problem.

Sources: [a]Tashiro, H., and Rowley, I. (2005, May 2). The glass ceiling stays put. *BusinessWeek*, 22; [b]Ritter, K. (2005, April 16). Sex equality hits glass ceiling in Sweden. Associated Press.

Customer-Driven HR Case 9.2   YOU MANAGE IT!

Assess Yourself

The assessment phase of career development has typically been conceived as something the organization does. However, the entire process of career development is increasingly becoming the responsibility of the employee, and assessment is no exception.

Numerous assessment tools are being developed by industries, professional associations, and various companies to help employees in their career development efforts. For example, the accounting profession has developed a Web-based self-assessment tool that includes benchmarks and action plans for career advancement.[a] The entire accounting profession, from students to senior managers, can use the Competency Self-Assessment Tool (CAT). The online assessment includes evaluation of the following competency areas:

- **Personal attributes:** Integrity, ethics, commitment, interpersonal orientation, business writing, speaking, and so on
- **Leadership qualities:** Strategic planning, negotiation, problem solving, decision making
- **Broad business perspective:** Industry practices, organizational understanding
- **Functional specialty:** Technical skills for each practice area

The results of the assessment include a personalized career development plan.

Another example of an online assessment system is the European automotive technician accreditation program.[b] The program was developed by partners such as BMW, DaimlerChrysler, Ford, Hertz, and Toyota and measures knowledge in areas such as air conditioning, braking systems, engine electrical systems, transmission systems, and so on. It allows technicians to assess their skills and plan their development activities. In addition, the program assigns three levels of accreditation: (1) service maintenance technician, (2) diagnostic technician, and (3) master technician. Achieving accreditation requires passing the appropriate knowledge tests as well as demonstrating proficiency on actual tasks as judged by an assessor.

Critical Thinking Questions

1. An effective career development process begins with assessment. The online assessment programs described here put the responsibility for assessment on the employee. Do you agree with this approach or do you think that the employer should be more responsible for the process? Explain.

2. Placing assessment and career planning online makes the process easy and convenient for workers. In short, online career development is customer friendly. However, feedback about competencies and possible career discussions can be sensitive and important issues. Is the online assessment approach sufficient for effective career development or are other approaches needed? If so, describe.

3. Online assessment for particular professions can address fairly specific and relevant competencies. More generic online career development systems are available for business professionals.[c] What are the advantages and disadvantages of occupation- or industry-specific online assessment programs as opposed to more generic online

assessment programs? Are there situations where a generic approach might be most useful? Describe.

Team Exercise

As a team, design a career development process for an organization, paying particular attention to assessment. Your team should consider options for delivery of the program and development of content and make recommendations for delivery and content. Some issues to consider:

■ Should the program be entirely online, face-to-face, or both?
■ How should the competencies be identified? Should the program be an off-the-shelf product or developed in-house?

Present your plan to the class. Include a rationale for each aspect of your plan. As a class, select the best plans. Why are they the best?

Experiential Exercise

Many organizations are implementing online assessment for their career development process. However, some online assessments, such as the automotive technician accreditation system, are supplemented by physical assessment. Select representatives to lead a class discussion on the delivery of career development. Should assessment be entirely online or entirely face-to-face? Should a contingent approach be taken? If so, when should an online approach be used and when should a face-to-face approach be used? The discussion leaders are responsible for leading the discussion and bringing the class to an overall model of how career development should be delivered.

Sources: [a]Feldman, J. (2004). Give your skills a cat scan. *Journal of Accountancy, 198,* 34–39; [b]PR Newswire Europe. (2005, June 15). Motor industry unveils first ever national accreditation for car technicians; [c]PR Newswire US. (2005, January 14). Resume Maker debuts new career software that helps working professionals land jobs they will enjoy! First-ever complete career software offers comprehensive, 5-step job search program.

YOU MANAGE IT!   Ethics Case 9.3

Anchors II

As described in the Manager's Notebook, "Anchor Yourself," employees' career anchors may be motivated by different sets of values. The anchors have important implications for the type of career an individual will find most motivating and satisfying. Review the eight anchors and their implication as presented in the Manager's Notebook on page *281.*

Critical Thinking Questions

1. The concept of career anchors indicates that there is more to career development than having and matching skills to competency requirements. Some managers view development as a moral imperative. That is, business is about making money, but it also should be about helping people to grow and realize their career aspirations. Do you agree? Explain why or why not.
2. Competencies are important to career success, but so, too, are career anchors. These two factors are analogous to ability and motivation being predictors of performance (see Chapter 5). Construct a parallel equation using competencies and anchors as predictors of career success. How is this simple equation useful?

3. In some work environments, career aspirations are ignored and immediate performance is the focus. Do you think this lack of attention to career anchors is an ethical issue? Explain why or why not.

Team Exercise

A key issue in career development has to do with the competencies associated with different paths. Strengths and weaknesses on various competencies can be assessed and then a plan for development can be put into place. Another key issue is the career anchor that employees bring with them. A misfit between an employee's anchor and the company and/or career chosen would likely result in employee dissatisfaction and other difficulties.

As a team, develop a framework or model for how these two sides of career development should be managed. You might label one concern as skills competencies and the other as career anchors/values. Your team could develop a model that uses boxes and arrows to indicate the causes or predictors for the skills side and the anchors side. Your model might take a form similar to the one at the top of page 297.

Given the predictors identified in your model, what are the implications for management? Specifically, if skills are low or

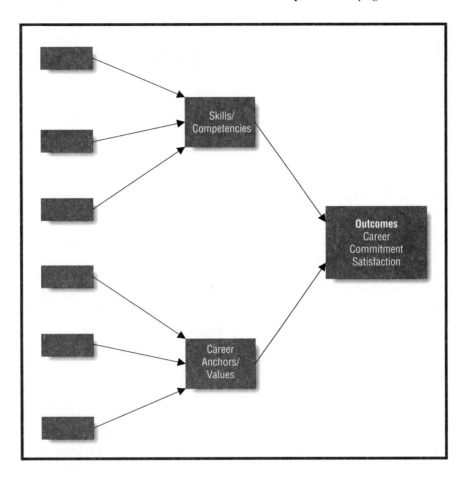

don't match what is needed, what could you, as a manager, do? Likewise, if career anchors don't match, what, if anything, can be done?

Alternatively, your team could develop a 2 × 2 framework using the skill and anchor variables. You can use two levels of each variable: low and high levels of match or fit. Your resulting framework would look something like the following:

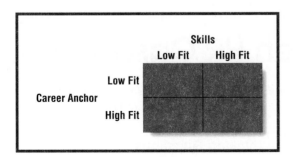

For each cell in the matrix, describe the particular combination of skills and career values. Identify management implications for each of the four cells. For example, what should be done, from a management perspective, in regard to employees whose skills have a high fit but whose career anchors are a misfit?

Experiential Exercise

Use the Manager's Notebook, "Anchor Yourself," to assess your top career anchor(s). What type of career do you think you want to pursue? Does it match with your anchor? Do you think the degree of match is an important consideration? Why or why not?

As a team, select a member to share career anchors and plans. As a class, assess whether there is a high degree of fit with career anchors. What is the consensus of the class regarding the importance of this fit?

YOU MANAGE IT!   Emerging Trends Case 9.4

From Loyalty to Employability: Managing Today's Workforce

Most workplaces used to rely on an unwritten and implicit understanding that loyalty paid off. Workers understood that if they hung in and did a decent job, they could expect steady employment, if not wage increases and promotions. This loyalty concept has largely been swept away by business practices such as downsizing and outsourcing. In the place of loyalty, workers now focus on employability.[a] In other words, workers understand that there is no guarantee of continued employment. Even the most stable job could be swept away in a restructuring and end up as a temporary position. It is only rational then that many of today's workers place great value on maintaining and developing their skills. Loyalty and commitment are no longer relevant issues. Stability may not be possible, but personal growth and learning at work can make the worker more employable. Challenge and growth opportunities can pay off for workers in increased employability.[b]

Critical Thinking Questions

1. As a manager, what could you do to offer "employability" to your workers?
2. By developing workers' employability, employers could lose employees to other job opportunities. Does this mean that employees should not be offered development opportunities?

Team Exercise

Increasing employability sounds fine as a concept, but if it is going to be useful has to be operationalized as a series of concrete steps. As a team, operationalize the concept of employability. Start by defining employability and then identifying steps that managers can follow to increase it. Use the following issues to help you develop your plan:

- What is employability?
- How can managers determine what employees want?
- What can be done if some managers don't support the employability initiative?
- What actions can be taken to increase employability?

Present your plan to the rest of the class. As a class, select the best features and put together one preferred set of steps.

Experiential Exercise

Actively developing workers can lead to fear of losing employees. However, failure to develop employees can also lead to turnover.

Select class members to represent either a pro-employability position or an anti-employability position. Each team needs to identify why employability should or should not be something that management actively supports. Also, each team needs to identify the reasons, including costs and benefits, for supporting or not supporting employability.

In a debate-style format, each team makes its presentation of its position and rationale. Each team has the opportunity to question, rebut, and rejoin the other team. The instructor moderates this process. Is there a clear winning position in this debate?

Sources: [a]White, M. A., and Behr, S. M. (2005). The new employees. *Leadership Excellence*, 22, 9; [b]Witham, G. (2005). Today's young managers want career planning, challenges. *Hotel and Motel Management*, 225, 10.

YOU MANAGE IT!   Customer-Driven HR Case 9.5

Capitalizing on Techno Savvy: Putting Mentoring in Reverse

Jack Welch, former CEO of General Electric, is the person generally credited with introducing formal reverse mentoring. In 1999, Welch ordered 500 of his top managers to find workers who were Internet savvy and to pair with them as mentors. Welch included himself in this effort and committed blocks of time to learn about things such as Internet bookmarks and competitor Web sites. From this beginning, organizations are now expanding the reverse mentoring concept to a variety of topics. An outcome of reverse mentoring may be the growing realization that mentoring is about sharing knowledge and expertise, no matter who has it, so that this knowledge within an organization can be leveraged to full advantage.

Critical Thinking Questions

1. What topics, other than technology, would be appropriate for the reverse mentoring approach?
2. Mentoring and reverse mentoring can be seen as particular directions of knowledge sharing. Would peer-to-peer mentoring be possible? What about customer to employee? Could the traditional concept of mentoring be expanded to something similar to 360° appraisal (see Chapter 7)? If so, how would it change the nature and purpose of mentoring?

Team Exercise

Although reverse mentoring can be a great concept, it can pose problems when trying to put it into operation. For example, the ego of the more experienced manager may get in the way of effectively learning what the less experienced worker has to offer. Likewise, the less experienced worker may need to develop patience and an understanding of what is more or less important in the organizational context.

As a team, confront the reality that reverse mentoring isn't just going to happen. What steps would you recommend that would help assure that reverse mentoring works effectively? For example, would you recommend training? What kind? For whom? Have team members search for examples of reverse mentoring in organizations. How well is the program working and what was done to implement it? Share your recommendations and findings with the rest of the class.

Experiential Exercise

College students often pursue internships at companies. The reverse-mentoring concept leads to the possibility that some companies may learn as much or more from some college students as the students learn from the experience with the company. Explore the possibility of shifting the internship model into a two-way street of information sharing. Select class members to serve as members of three teams who will lead class discussions:

- Team one is responsible for exploring how each side, students and companies, would benefit from this two-way approach.
- Team two is responsible for identifying the types of skills students would need in this approach.
- Team three is responsible for determining how students should be selected for these internship opportunities.

Each team leads a discussion in its area. As a class, determine whether a "two-way internship" looks like a doable and effective approach.

Source: Greengard, S. (2002). Moving forward with reverse mentoring. *Workforce, 81,* 15.

Challenges

After reading this chapter, you should be able to deal more effectively with the following challenges:

1 **Identify** the compensation policies and practices that are most appropriate for a particular firm.

2 **Weigh** the strategic advantages and disadvantages of the different compensation options.

3 **Establish** a job-based compensation scheme that is internally consistent and linked to the labor market.

4 **Understand** the difference between a compensation system in which employees are paid for the skills they use and one in which they are paid for the job they hold.

5 **Make** compensation decisions that comply with the legal framework.

Sigma, Inc., is a medium-sized biotechnology firm specializing in genetic engineering. The firm was founded in 1996 by Dr. Roger Smith, who is still Sigma's chief executive officer and continues to be actively involved in all hiring and pay decisions. He repeatedly tells his line managers that Sigma "will pay whatever it takes to hire the best talent in the market."

During the past year Smith has noticed an erosion in Sigma's "family atmosphere" and an increase in the number of dissatisfied employees. There have been three pay-related complaints during the past week alone, and Smith suspects this is only the tip of the iceberg. The first complaint came from a software developer who has been with Sigma for five years. He is upset that another developer was recently hired at a salary 15 percent higher than his. Smith explained that such starting salaries are necessary to attract top experienced programmers from other firms in a very tight labor market. The second complaint came from a software engineer who feels that

Sigma's best technical people—the lifeblood of a biotechnology firm—are discriminated against in pay because supervisors (who, in his words, are often "failed engineers") receive 30 percent more pay. The third complaint was filed by a head secretary who has been with Sigma from the start. She is angry that janitors are getting more money than she is, and she is not satisfied with Smith's explanation that it is difficult to hire and retain reliable people who are willing to clean up and dispose of dangerous chemicals.

In addition, a 49-year-old engineer who was purportedly terminated for poor performance has just filed an age discrimination suit against the company, arguing that the firm is replacing older, higher-earning employees with Indian employees on temporary visas who are willing to work at much lower wages.

THE MANAGERIAL PERSPECTIVE

Sigma's experience raises several important questions that managers and HR personnel must face in designing and administering compensation programs, such as the following:

■ Who should be responsible for making salary decisions?
■ Should pay be dictated by what other employers are paying?
■ What types of activities should be rewarded with higher salaries?
■ What criteria should be used to determine salaries?
■ Which employee groups should receive special treatment when scarce pay resources are allocated?

The pay system is one of the most important mechanisms that firms and managers can use to attract, retain, and motivate competent employees to perform in ways that support organizational objectives. It also has a direct bearing on the extent to which labor costs detract from or contribute to business objectives and profitability.

In the first part of this chapter, we define the components of compensation and examine the nine criteria used to develop a compensation plan. Then we explore the process of designing a compensation plan and the legal and regulatory influences on compensation.

What Is Compensation?

As Figure 10.1 shows, an employee's **total compensation** has three components. The relative proportion of each (known as the *pay mix*) varies extensively by firm.[1] The first and (in most firms) largest element of total compensation is **base compensation**, the fixed pay an employee receives on a regular basis, either in the form of a salary (for example, a weekly or monthly paycheck) or as an hourly wage. The second component of total compensation is **pay incentives**, programs designed to reward employees for good performance. These incentives come in many forms (including bonuses and profit sharing) and are the focus of Chapter 11. The last component of total compensation is *benefits*, sometimes called *indirect compensation*. Benefits encompass a wide variety of programs (for example, health insurance, vacations, and unemployment compensation), the costs of which approach 42 percent of workers' compensation packages.[2] A special category of benefits called *perquisites,* or perks, is available only to employees with some special status in the organization, usually upper-level managers. Chapter 12 discusses benefit programs in detail.

Compensation is the single most important cost in most firms. Personnel costs are as high as 60 percent of total costs in certain types of manufacturing environments and even higher in some service organizations. This means that the effectiveness with which compensation is allocated can make a significant difference in gaining or losing a competitive edge. Thus, *how much* is paid and *who* gets paid what are crucial strategic issues for the firm.[3]

Total compensation
The package of quantifiable rewards an employee receives for his or her labors. Includes three components: base compensation, pay incentives, and indirect compensation/benefits.

Base compensation
The fixed pay an employee receives on a regular basis, either in the form of a salary or as an hourly wage.

Pay incentive
A program designed to reward employees for good performance.

The Elements of Total Compensation

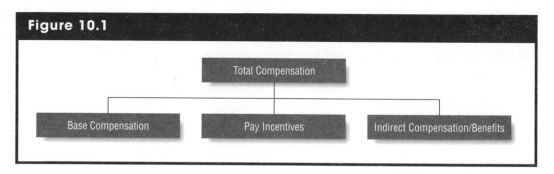

Figure 10.1

Research shows that employees severely undervalue their employer's contributions to indirect compensation or benefits (which is estimated at close to $19,000 per employee, on average, in 2006),[4] and as a result they often take their employer-funded benefits for granted.[5] This situation may be changing as a growing number of companies, including General Motors, IBM, Boeing, Lucent Technologies, and others, are transferring a significant portion of these costs to employees.[6] Firms are also becoming more savvy in explaining to employees how much these benefits cost, and that this leaves them with less money for raises.[7] According to a 2005 survey of 350 large firms, 85 percent are increasing employee communication about the real cost of benefits.[8] This means that employees are more likely to become acutely aware that base compensation, pay incentives, and indirect compensation/benefits are all part of the same pie and that companies cannot increase one piece without reducing the size of the others.

Designing a Compensation System

An employee's paycheck is certainly important for its purchasing power. In most societies, however, a person's earnings also serve as an indicator of power and prestige and are tied to feelings of self-worth. In other words, compensation affects a person economically, sociologically, and psychologically.[9] For this reason, mishandling compensation issues is likely to have a strong negative impact on employees and, ultimately, on the firm's performance.[10]

The wide variety of pay policies and procedures presents managers with a two-pronged challenge: to design a compensation system that (1) enables the firm to achieve its strategic objectives and (2) is molded to the firm's unique characteristics and environment.[11] We discuss the criteria for developing a compensation plan in the sections that follow and summarize these options in Figure 10.2. Although we present each of these as an either/or choice for the sake of simplicity, most firms institute policies that fall somewhere between the two poles.

Internal Versus External Equity

Internal equity
The perceived fairness of the pay structure within a firm.

External equity
The perceived fairness in pay relative to what other employers are paying for the same type of labor.

Fair pay is pay that employees generally view as equitable. There are two forms of pay equity. **Internal equity** refers to the perceived fairness of the pay structure within a firm. **External equity** refers to the perceived fairness of pay relative to what other employers are paying for the same type of labor.

In considering internal versus external equity, managers can use two basic models: the distributive justice model and the labor market model.

The Distributive Justice Model

The *distributive justice model* of pay equity holds that employees exchange their contributions or input to the firm (skills, effort, time, and so forth) for a set of outcomes. Pay is one of the most important of these outcomes, but nonmonetary rewards like a company car may also be significant. This social-psychological perspective suggests that employees are constantly (1) comparing what they bring to the firm to what they receive in return and (2) comparing this input/outcome ratio with that of other employees within the firm. Employees will think they are fairly paid

| Figure 10.2 | The Nine Criteria for Developing a Compensation Plan |

1. **Internal Versus External Equity** Will the compensation plan be perceived as fair within the company, or will it be perceived as fair relative to what other employers are paying for the same type of labor?
2. **Fixed Versus Variable Pay** Will compensation be paid monthly on a fixed basis—through base salaries—or will it fluctuate depending on such preestablished criteria as performance and company profits?
3. **Performance Versus Membership** Will compensation emphasize performance and tie pay to individual or group contributions, or will it emphasize membership in the organization—logging in a prescribed number of hours each week and progressing up the organizational ladder?
4. **Job Versus Individual Pay** Will compensation be based on how the company values a particular job, or will it be based on how much skill and knowledge an employee brings to that job?
5. **Egalitarianism Versus Elitism** Will the compensation plan place most employees under the same compensation system (egalitarianism), or will it establish different plans by organizational level and/or employee group (elitism)?
6. **Below-Market Versus Above-Market Compensation** Will employees be compensated at below-market levels, at market levels, or at above-market levels?
7. **Monetary Versus Nonmonetary Awards** Will the compensation plan emphasize motivating employees through monetary rewards like pay and stock options, or will it stress nonmonetary rewards such as interesting work and job security?
8. **Open Versus Secret Pay** Will employees have access to information about other workers' compensation levels and how compensation decisions are made (open pay), or will this knowledge be withheld from employees (secret pay)?
9. **Centralization Versus Decentralization of Pay Decisions** Will compensation decisions be made in a tightly controlled central location, or will they be delegated to managers of the firm's units?

when the ratio of their inputs and outputs is equivalent to that of other employees whose job demands are similar to their own.

The Labor Market Model

According to the *labor market* model of pay equity, the wage rate for any given occupation is set at the point where the supply of labor equals the demand for labor in the marketplace (W_1 in Figure 10.3). In general, the less employers are willing to pay (low demand for labor) and the lower the pay workers are willing to accept for a given job (high supply of labor), the lower the wage rate for that job.[12]

The actual situation is a great deal more complicated than this basic model suggests. People base their decisions about what jobs they are willing to hold on many more factors than just pay. Moreover, the pay that an employer offers is based on many factors besides the number of available people with the skills and abilities to do the job. A complete exploration of this topic is beyond the scope of this book. However, the basic point of the labor market model is that external equity is achieved when the firm pays its employees the "going rate" for the type of work they do.[13] For a growing number of managerial, professional, and technical occupations, the "going rate" is determined not only by local and domestic factors, but also by global forces.[14]

Balancing Equity

Ideally, a firm should try to establish both internal and external pay equity, but these objectives are often at odds. For instance, universities sometimes pay new assistant professors more than senior faculty who have been with the institution for a decade or more,[15] and firms sometimes pay recent engineering graduates more than engineers who have been on board for many years.[16]

Many firms also have to determine which employee groups' pay will be adjusted upward to meet (or perhaps exceed) market rates. This decision is generally based on each group's relative

The Labor Market Model

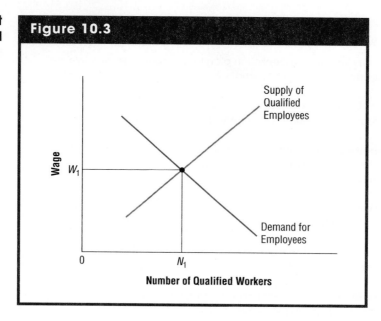

Figure 10.3

Supply of Qualified Employees

Wage

W_1

Demand for Employees

0 N_1

Number of Qualified Workers

Individual equity

The perceived fairness of individual pay decisions.

importance to the firm. For example, marketing employees tend to be paid more in firms that are trying to expand their market share and less in older firms that have a well-established product with high brand recognition.

Once a decision has been made as to which groups will be adjusted upward, one difficult challenge remains: What to do with "superstars." In some cases, these individuals command a much higher salary than the average of those holding the same title. For instance, U.S. universities are expanding their economics departments. This has driven up economics faculty salaries, which average about $140,000 a year, making it one of the highest-paid professions that the government tracks.[17] Yet even at an elite school a top economist can earn more than double the average earnings of his or her peers of the same rank in the same department. Some compensation professionals refer to this type of pay as having **individual equity**, because it is based on the value to the institution of specific people rather than of the job group, position title, or class to which they belong. Individual equity decisions are becoming more important in professions where some key people can make a big difference and where there is high performance variance. These typically include such occupations as top executives, sales, scientists and engineers, software development, and the like.

In general, emphasizing external equity is more appropriate for newer, smaller firms in a rapidly changing market. These firms often have a high need for innovation to remain competitive and are dependent on key individuals to achieve their business objectives.[18]

When faced with choosing between internal and external equity, an increasing number of firms have opted to offer large "sign-on bonuses" to new employees to entice good candidates without disrupting the existing salary schedules. A survey of 348 large and small firms that use sign-on bonuses indicated 80 percent of them use sign-on bonuses for professional staff and executives; 70 percent for midlevel managers and information technology personnel; 60 percent for sales, lower-level managers, and technical staff; and 20 percent for clerical workers. In a sense, the new employee receives a big pay raise "up front"—in many cases 25 percent or more of annual salary—and the company avoids the need to reduce posted salary differentials between junior and senior employees.[19]

Another interesting twist to the balancing equity dilemma in recent years is the practice in which companies facing uncertain financial futures shower "retention bonuses" on key employees. The objective is to retain needed expertise without having to raise the entire salary schedule—which might hasten the firm's demise. For instance, a few years back Kmart spent upward of $92 million in retention bonuses for 9,700 key employees as it filed for bankruptcy protection. Other well-publicized cases of companies that did the same include Enron, Polaroid, Bradlees Inc., and Aerovox, Inc.[20]

Firms can also provide "adds ons" or "caps," which are renegotiable on an individual basis. Going back to the example of economists, one way many universities handle the individual-equity challenge is to base all professors' salaries on a nine-month academic year schedule (usually mid-August to mid-May). Those who are exceptional contributors receive a summer stipend that often adds up to a third of the nine-month salary. They may also receive other perks, such as large travel budgets, research support, secretarial assistance, and the like. These "chairs" or "fellowships," as they usually called, are often renegotiated at certain fixed intervals.

Lastly, a growing number of firms have developed explicit "counteroffer" policies. This means that the organization will match or closely match the compensation offer an employee receives from a competitor, but only if certain criteria are met (for example, the offer comes from a leading-edge company). According to a recent survey, 55 percent of firms make counteroffers, but only for employees who are in key positions and those who are outstanding performers.[21]

Fixed Versus Variable Pay

Firms can choose to pay a high proportion of total compensation in the form of base pay (for example, a predictable monthly paycheck) or in the form of variable pay that fluctuates according to some preestablished criterion. On average, approximately 75 percent of firms offer some form of variable pay.[22]

There is a great deal of variation in the way firms answer the fixed versus variable pay question. On average, 10 percent of an employee's pay in the United States is variable. This compares to 20 percent in Japan. However, the range is huge in both countries—from 0 up to 70 percent. For select employee groups (such as sales), variable pay can be as high as 100 percent.[23] In general, the proportion of variable pay increases as an employee's base pay increases, indicating that those in higher-level positions earn more but their overall compensation is more subject to risk. For employees earning more than $750,000 a year in base pay, variable compensation is close to 90 percent of base pay. For those earning less than $25,000 a year in base pay, this percentage drops to less than 5 percent.[24]

Fixed pay is the rule in the majority of U.S. organizations largely because it reduces the risk to employee and it is easier to administer. However, variable pay can be used advantageously in smaller companies, firms with a product that is not well established, companies with a young professional workforce that is willing to delay immediate gratification in hopes of greater future returns, firms supported by venture capital, organizations going through a prolonged period of cash shortages, and companies that would otherwise have to institute layoffs because their revenues are volatile. The Manager's Notebook, "Compensation Entitlements Are Going out the Window," gives examples of companies' experimenting with compensation.

Emerging Trends

MANAGER'S NOTEBOOK

Compensation Entitlements Are Going out the Window

Not too long ago employers divided pay into fixed (salaries), variable (incentives), and benefits components. Except for incentive pay, which for most employees was a small percentage of their total compensation, workers could count on a promised salary and future benefits as a condition for employment. But even among the oldest and most established firms, salary and benefit entitlements are no longer fixed or secure. A few examples follow.

Reducing Salaries at Auto Companies

General Motors, DaimlerChrysler, and Ford have reduced salaries of nonunion staff, in some departments by as much as 28 percent, in an effort to boost profits. General Motors is trying to replicate Chrysler's feat in negotiating an amendment of its contract that allows the company for the first time to charge UAW workers annual health-care deductibles of $100 to $1,000.[a]

Cutting Dependents' Coverage

More companies are joining the wave of employers cutting health-care costs by reducing the benefits they offer to their retired workers' dependents. In 2005, for instance, IBM employees wouldn't be able to enroll new dependents in the company's health plan beyond those covered on their retirement date. Similarly, Boeing told its nonunion employees who retired in 2005 that they wouldn't be able to seek medical coverage for new dependents after their retirement date. Other companies are going further and making retirees pay for much of their dependents' health coverage. In 2005, for example, Lucent Technologies stopped paying for the cost of medical coverage for dependents of management retirees who retired on or after March 1, 1990, and whose annual salaries were at least $65,000. The salary limit, which went into effect in 2004, was previously $87,000.[b]

Making Wage Concessions at Airlines

United Airlines has cut pilots' pay by 12 percent and flight attendants' by 9.5 percent, in addition to reducing benefits. United has joined the ranks of American Airlines, Continental, Delta, and US Airways, which have all made salary and benefit cuts.[c]

Sources: [a]Adapted with permission from Hawkins, L. (2005, March 21). GM plans to cut salaried staff; overhaul looms. *Wall Street Journal*, A-1; [b]Saranow, J. (2005, March 3). Retirees face more benefit cuts. *Wall Street Journal*, D-2; [c]Maynard, M. (2005, March 1). Continental reaches pacts with unions. *New York Times*, C-7 and *Bloomberg News* (2005, February 1). Cut is forced on mechanics at United Air. Appearing in *New York Times*, C-3.

Apple Computer provides an excellent example of a firm that used variable pay to its own and its employees' advantage. Employees were willing to work for low salaries for several years in exchange for company stock; many who persevered became millionaires after the value of Apple's stock went sky high in the mid-1980s. Software maker Symantec saw its stock increase 150 percent during 2003–2005, and a high percentage of employees received huge gains during this period because they were all eligible for stock options.[25]

As we will discuss in Chapter 11, new tax regulations in effect since fiscal year 2006 are putting a damper on the use of stock options. But this has not stopped firms from experimenting with other types of variable pay. For example, Nordstrom recently gave each employee who worked at least 1,000 hours a year a profit-sharing bonus that was triple what it had been in prior years.[26] Pella, a maker of windows and doors with more than 8,000 employees, has an official policy of giving employees 25 percent of its pretax profits in addition to their normal salaries. Network Appliance, a hardware software provider, gives employees $5,000 to $10,000 for each patent they file.

Not all variable-pay plans work out well for employees, however. Employees at Enron and Global Crossing saw their stockholdings drop from $90 to about 50 cents per share within months, partly due to company mismanagement and partly due to corruption at the top.[27] In fact, by 2006 approximately 10 percent of salaried employees across a wide variety of firms were unpleasantly surprised that the wealth they thought they had accumulated during years of hard work evaporated and in some cases left them with a big tax bill to boot.[28] What is clear, however, is that fixed pay as a percentage of total compensation continues to decline, and firms are asking employees to share more risks with them.[29] Those firms that treat employees fairly and that clearly communicate to them the downside and upside of the compensation risk they face are more likely to prevent a deterioration of morale in spite of the added stress. For example, Emmis Communications, a chain of magazines and radio and TV stations, recently cut pay 10 percent when faced with a profit crunch. Surprisingly, few people left, and employees accepted the bad news as well as could be expected.[30]

Performance Versus Membership

A special case of fixed versus variable compensation requires a choice between performance and membership.[31] A company emphasizes performance when a substantial portion of its employees' pay is tied to individual or group contributions and the amount received can vary significantly from one person or group to another. The most extreme forms of *performance-contingent compensation* are traditional piece-rate plans (pay based on units produced) and sales commissions.

Other performance-contingent plans use awards for cost-saving suggestions, bonuses for perfect attendance, or merit pay based on supervisory appraisals. All these options are provided on top of an individual's base pay (see Chapter 11).

Firms that emphasize *membership-contingent compensation* provide the same or a similar wage to every employee in a given job, as long as the employee achieves at least satisfactory performance. Employees receive a paycheck for logging in a prescribed number of hours of work per week (normally 40). Typically, salary progression occurs by moving up in the organization, not by doing the present job better.

The relative emphasis placed on performance and membership depends largely on the organization's culture and the beliefs of top managers or the company's founder. Most companies that emphasize performance tend to be characterized by fewer management levels, rapid growth, internal competition among people and groups, readily available performance indicators (see Chapter 7), and strong competitive pressures.[32] Regardless of company size, there seems to be a trend not only in the United States, but also in many other countries, away from membership-contingent compensation.[33] Global competition is likely to accelerate this trend as we move into the second decade of the twenty-first century.[34] The Manager's Notebook, "International Convergence in Approaches to Compensation," further discusses this theory.

MANAGER'S NOTEBOOK

International Convergence in Approaches to Compensation

Not long ago, employees of a multinational company were paid one way in the United States, another way in the United Kingdom, and a different way in Japan. Increasingly, these differences are narrowing or disappearing altogether as leading companies take a global approach to designing their pay and benefit plans for employees at all levels, whether they work in Singapore or Sao Paulo. This is one of the chief findings of the annual Worldwide Total Remuneration (WWTR) studies conducted by Towers & Perrin during the past five years, which highlight compensation practices in 25 countries, plus Hong Kong SAR. Companies are discovering that global compensation strategies can achieve cost savings through standardization of programs, tap new financing opportunities available in capital markets, and meet the needs of internationally mobile employees. The WWTR studies indicate that compensation and benefit practices once familiar only to executives are becoming increasingly available to other employees within the organization regardless of country. This trend is evident with two types of variable pay: variable bonus linked to individual performance and long-term incentives (LTI) programs, both of which have grown dramatically in recent years across all 25 countries surveyed (for more on this, see related discussion in Chapter 11). The study cites several factors that are likely to encourage further similarities in global remuneration practices. These factors include greater access to information (particularly through the Web), lower cost of living differences in the European Union, a common currency in the euro zone, more liberal legislation in many countries giving firms greater freedom to set compensation policies, local and regional companies that are beginning to imitate the practices of global companies, and greater mobility across national boundaries.

However, convergence does not mean conformity. Convergence refers to similarity in compensation practices across countries. As the changes just listed evolve globally, they are not expected to eliminate the significant tax, accounting, and legal issues in individual countries. Moreover, each country has its own cultural, historic, and social policies that can influence the relationship between employers and employees.

Source: Towers Perrin Monitor. (2006). Worldwide total remuneration. Available at *www.towers.com.*

Job Versus Individual Pay

Most traditional compensation systems assume that in setting base compensation a firm should evaluate the value or contributions of each job, not how well the employee performs it.[35] This means that the minimum and maximum values of each job are set independently of individual workers, who must be paid somewhere in the range established for that job.

Knowledge-based pay or skill-based pay
A pay system in which employees are paid on the basis of the jobs they can do or talents they have that can be successfully applied to a variety of tasks and situations.

In a **knowledge-based pay or skill-based pay** system, employees are paid on the basis of the jobs they *can* do or the talents they have that can be successfully applied to a variety of tasks and situations.[36] Thus, the more hats an individual can wear, the more pay he or she will receive. Employees' base compensation increases as they become able to perform more duties successfully.

While the traditional job-centered pay system is still predominant, more and more firms are opting for a knowledge-based approach. Proponents argue that knowledge-based pay provides greater motivation for employees, makes it easier to reassign workers to where they are most needed, reduces the costs of turnover and absenteeism because other employees can assume missing employees' duties, and provides managers with much more staffing flexibility. However, critics maintain that a skill-based system may lead to higher labor costs, loss of labor specialization, greater difficulty in selecting applicants because the qualifications are less specific, and a chaotic workplace where "the left hand doesn't know what the right hand is doing."[37]

How, then, should managers approach the job versus individual pay option? A job-based pay policy tends to work best in situations where:

- Technology is stable.
- Jobs do not change often.
- Employees do not need to cover for one another frequently.
- Much training is required to learn a given job.
- Turnover is relatively low.
- Employees are expected to move up through the ranks over time.
- Jobs are fairly standardized within the industry.

The automobile industry fits most of these criteria. Individual-based compensation programs are more suitable when:

- The firm has a relatively educated workforce with both the ability and the willingness to learn different jobs.
- The company's technology and organizational structure change frequently.
- Employee participation and teamwork are encouraged throughout the organization.
- Opportunities for upward mobility are limited.
- Opportunities to learn new skills are present.
- The costs of employee turnover and absenteeism in terms of lost production are high.[38]

Individual-based pay plans are common in manufacturing environments that rely on continuous-process technologies.[39]

Elitism Versus Egalitarianism

Egalitarian pay system
A pay plan in which most employees are part of the same compensation system.

Elitist pay system
A pay plan in which different compensation systems are established for employees or groups at different organizational levels.

Firms must decide whether to place most of their employees under the same compensation plan—an **egalitarian pay system**—or to establish different compensation plans by organizational level and/or employee group—an **elitist pay system**. For example, in some firms only the CEO is eligible for stock options.[40] In other companies even the lowest-paid worker is offered stock options. Some companies offer a wide menu of pay incentives only to specific employee groups[41] (such as salespeople), whereas others make these available to most employees. At Ben & Jerry's Homemade Holdings, Inc., the Vermont-based ice cream company, the compensation system is linked to company prosperity. When the company does well, everyone does well. The profit-sharing plan awards the same percentage to all employees, from the top to the bottom.[42]

Some top executives have recently tried to reinforce an egalitarian perspective by pegging their fortunes to those of employees. For instance, at Synovous, a large financial firm with almost 12,000 employees, executives have forfeited their bonuses in order to provide employees higher pay.[43] At SEI Investments, with close to 2,000 employees, workers own nearly half of SEI stock.

As noted in Figure 10.4, Whole Foods Market limits the maximum compensation anyone can receive (including top executives) to 14 times the average pay of its full-time workers (this ratio often exceeds 300 to 1 across different organizations in the United States). As we will discuss in Chapter 11, these egalitarian policies are probably the exception rather than the norm; pay differentials between upper echelons and lower ranks have steadily increased during the past 20 years.

Most compensation experts would agree that both systems have their advantages and disadvantages. Egalitarianism gives firms more flexibility to deploy employees in different areas without having to change their pay levels. It can also reduce barriers between people who need to work closely together. Elitist pay structures tend to result in a more stable workforce because employees make more money only by moving up through the company.

Elitist compensation systems are more prevalent among older, well-established firms with mature products, a relatively unchanging market share, and limited competition. Egalitarian compensation systems are more common in highly competitive environments, where firms frequently take business risks and try to expand their market share by continually investing in new technologies, ventures, and products.

Below-Market Versus Above-Market Compensation

Employees' pay relative to alternative employment opportunities directly affects the firm's ability to attract workers from other companies. Pay satisfaction is very highly correlated with pay level, and dissatisfaction with pay is one of the most common causes of employee turnover. The decision to pay above market for all employee groups also allows the firm to hire the "cream of the crop,"

Figure 10.4

Company	Number of Employees	% Minorities	% Women	Average Annual Salary	Reward Practices
1. Starbuck's www.starbucks.com	72,185	26%	63%	$44,790	The coffee behemoth is justly famous for its generous benefits. One example: Part-timers and their same- or opposite-sex partners receive comprehensive health coverage. Hypnotherapy? Covered. Naturopathy? Ditto.
2. Valero Energy www.valero.com	15,882	40%	41%	$40,326	This 25-year-old refiner and gas retainer has never laid off an employee. And when it comes to bonuses, the lower levels aren't forgotten: executives receive theirs only if everyone else in the organization does.
3. Whole Foods Market	28,858	44%	43%	$57,157	It's all about equity at this natural-food grocery chain: A wage disclosure report lists everyone's gross pay (execs included), and a salary cap limits compensation to 14 times the average total of all the company's full-times'.
4. Baptist Health South, Fla	10,477	69%	75%	$61,760	Salaries are generous here: Fifty-two of the hospital chain's 2,600 nurses earn more than $100,000. That may explain why nursing turnover at BHSF's 23 facilities is only 9% a year, vs. 19% statewide.
5. Goldman Sachs	11,503	30%	37%	$75,000	Workaholic parents get support at this Wall Street firm. For example, at the on-site children's center, employees get up to 20 days of free backup care for 3- to 6-months-old (in addition to 20 free days available for all kids).

Sample of Best Places to Work and How they Reward Employees

Figure 10.4 (Continued)

Company	Number of Employees	% Minorities	% Women	Average Annual Salary	Reward Practices
6. Four Season Hotels	11,882	64%	44%	$40,402	This luxury chain excels at making employees feel valued. Workers at each hotel select a peer to receive the Employee of the Year Award, which can include an expenses-paid week-long vacation and a $1,000 shopping spree.
7. General Mills	19,019	22%	39%	$39,1165	This food company makes it easy for employees to get smart: It reimburses tuition at 100% up to $6,000 per year, even for new employees. And if the employees leave afterward, they need not repay the money.
8. Medtronic	19,294	25%	46%	$86,280	This medical-device maker gives its people what they crave: creative freedom. All employees can apply to a program that lets them devote 25% of their workday to pursuing tech ideas that fall outside their usual jobs.
9. Vanguard Group	10,231	22%	47%	N.A.	Staffers get the rooms with a view at this big mutual-fund company; officers sit in interior spaces. The firm offers an onsite MBA at all three of its U.S. locations (it's free if your grade average is A or B, and half of if it's a C).
10. Texas Instruments	17,080	34%	26%	$103,907	TI offers a host of in-house services – including a spa and periodic on-site driver's license renewals – and makes parents a priority, with summer camps, a parents' night out, and major baskets for big holidays.
11. Deloitte & Touche	29,541	25%	45%	$63,060	This accounting and consulting firm attracts great hires by creative means. It rewards with cash—and sometimes new cars—employees who refer successful job candidates. Deloitte has awarded nearly $20 million since 1996.
12. FedEx	198,652	40%	28%	$64,948	FedEx kept the faith with employees even after acquiring Kinko's last year. Two of FedEx Express workers' favorite perks: free rides on its airplanes anywhere in the U.S., and a chance to get their kid's name painted on a plane.
13. CDW	3,702	26%	30%	$44,556	Adoptive parents have special benefits at this computer and electronics seller. Agency and placement fees, legal fees, foreign adoption charges, and related travel expenses are reimbursed up to $3,000 per child.
14. SAS Institute	5,062	14%	48%	$89,151	The gym at this software company includes a ten-lane pool, billiards, Ping-Pong tables, volleyball courts, outdoor soccer fields, three tennis courts, and a putting green. Another perk: free restringing for tennis racquets.

Source: Fortune's best companies to work for (2005). See www.fortune.com

minimize voluntary turnover, and create a climate that makes all employees feel they are part of an elite organization.[44] This has traditionally been the choice for "blue-chip" firms such as IBM, Microsoft, and Procter & Gamble. However, few companies can afford such a policy. Instead, most firms recognize the importance of certain groups explicitly by paying them above market and cover these costs by paying other groups below market. For example, many high-tech firms compensate their R&D workers quite well while paying their manufacturing employees below-market wages.

Companies that are trying to grow rapidly in a tight labor market must consider paying above-market wages. For instance, Goldman Sachs increased its workforce by 42 percent within a two-year period in the late 1990s. Its pay is at the top of the scale, with executive secretaries, for example, earning $50,000 a year.[45] Unions, which we discuss in detail in Chapter 15, also contribute to above-market pay. Unionized workers receive approximately 9 to 14 percent higher wages than similar nonunionized workers do.[46]

A recent trend, even among firms that traditionally have paid high wages, is to provide a base salary pegged to the market median, combined with more aggressive incentives. According to one expert, "While it is difficult to cut base salary levels, the salary can be frozen for several years until the competitive market catches up."[47] In the meantime, more incentives are given so that total direct compensation (salary plus incentives) may position the firm at a higher percentile in the relevant labor market.

Monetary Versus Nonmonetary Rewards

One of the oldest debates about compensation concerns monetary versus nonmonetary rewards. Unlike cash or payments that can be converted into cash in the future (such as stocks or a retirement plan), nonmonetary rewards are intangible. Such rewards include interesting work, challenging assignments, and public recognition.[48]

Many surveys have shown that employees rank pay low in importance. For example, a large-scale survey found that only 2 percent of Americans declared that pay is a very important aspect of a job.[49] This finding should be viewed with skepticism, however. Most people may find it culturally desirable to downplay the importance of money. Two well-known commentators say, "pay may rank higher than people care to admit to others—or to themselves. In practice, it appears that good old-fashioned cash is as effective as any reward that has yet been invented."[50]

The relative importance of monetary and nonmonetary rewards is illustrated by an annual study of more than 1,000 large to midsized firms conducted by *Fortune* magazine to identify the 100 best places to work and how they got that way. Figure 10.4 on pages 309–310 lists a sample of 14 such firms and how they reward employees.

One type of nonmonetary reward that is becoming more common falls under the umbrella of "family friendly policies" or "work–life balance programs." It includes flexible work hours, personal time (not to be confused with sick time), fitness centers, day care, backup care when children are sick, and the like. For instance, A.G. Edwards, a brokerage firm with 15,850 employees, provides its employees an indoor walking track, yoga classes, running clubs, and more. First Horizon National (formerly known as First Tennessee), offers its 12,000 employees time off during the school year for parents to visit their children's classrooms.[51]

In general, companies that emphasize monetary rewards want to reinforce individual achievement and responsibility. Those that emphasize nonmonetary rewards prefer to reinforce commitment to the organization. Thus, a greater emphasis on monetary rewards is generally found among firms facing a volatile market with low job security, firms emphasizing sales rather than customer service, and firms trying to foster a competitive internal climate rather than long-term employee commitment. A greater reliance on nonmonetary rewards is usually found in companies with a relatively stable workforce, those that emphasize customer service and loyalty rather than fast sales growth, and those that want to create a more cooperative atmosphere within the firm.[52] Several other recent examples of organizations that emphasize nonmonetary rewards and that tend to fit this profile are described in the Manager's Notebook, "Rewarding Employees with Nonmonetary Compensation." One important issue here is that organizations should be realistic about how employees feel about nonmonetary rewards. In a recent survey of 1,400 firms, the investigators concluded that "when budgets are tight, nonmonetary perks such as time off or a departmental celebration can be valuable tools to acknowledge employee accomplishments. But employees also expect financial compensation for their efforts."[53]

A Question of Ethics

Some people argue that it is wrong for CEOs to earn multimillion-dollar salaries while some of their employees are earning the minimum wage or being laid off. Some suggest that a firm's top earner should earn no more than 20 times what the lowest-ranked employee earns. What do you think?

Emerging Trends

Rewarding Employees with Nonmonetary Compensation

Some firms believe they can attract, retain, and motivate employees better through nonmonetary compensation. However, employees may not always see it that way.

On Campus Fringe Benefits in Lieu of Pay

A video-game programmer curls a dumbbell and checks out his biceps in the mirror. Nearby, two colleagues walk on treadmills, chatting, while another young man levels karate kicks at a boxing bag. These employees of Electronic Arts, the world's largest independent video-game maker, are spending their lunch break in a big, modern company gymnasium that would put many private health clubs to shame. But Electronic Arts, based in Redwood City, California, has become the focal point of a raging debate over whether technology companies are exploiting workers by demanding long hours and "paying" them with on-campus amenities and nonfinancial rewards while skimping on tangible cash payments such as overtime and bonuses.

The debate has called into question the long-standing Silicon Valley compensation formula in which long hours were eased with stock options and bonuses. But with no technology boom to fuel stock prices, and new accounting rules making options much more expensive to grant (more on this on Chapter 11), stock options are no longer the currency that once fueled the Silicon Valley work ethic.[a]

To Keep Employees, Domino's Decides It's Not All About Pay

Turnover is a chronic and costly headache for fast-food businesses, which rely on an army of low-paid workers. Average turnover for most large and midsize companies is about 10 to 15 percent. But at fast-food chains, rates as high as 200 percent a year for hourly workers aren't unusual.

Domino's is willing to try all sorts of tactics to retain hourly employees—except paying them significantly more. "If we had increased everybody's pay 20 percent, could we have moved the needle a little bit to buy a little loyalty? Maybe, but that's not a long-term solution," says Domino's CEO David A. Brandon. He says that although pay is a factor, "you can't overcome a bad culture by paying people a few bucks more."

Domino's has focused its efforts on creating a fun culture, giving each store a friendly feeling. Store managers are selected and trained to make them better communicators and "to treat people respectfully, be polite, and patient." According to a Domino's manager, "it's not the pay that makes employees stick around, it's their relationship with their manager. They can go to McDonald's and make the same or they can go to Pizza Hut," he says. "You've got to make sure they are happy to come to work for you."[b]

Compensating with a Supportive Work Environment

At the average university, only 12 percent of faculty chemists are women and almost one-fourth of the top 50 universities have no women among their full professors of chemistry. But 25 percent of Rutgers's chemistry faculty are women. Rutgers department chair Roger Jones admits that he urges women who are unhappy elsewhere to send him a résumé. His key recruiting pitch isn't about higher salaries, day-care facilities or a relaxed timetable for tenure; it's about the camaraderie that comes with having female peers. "Who wants to be the 'token' woman when you can join a department with numerous women at all ranks?" he asks. Professor Kathryn Uhrich, who spurned Ivy League offers for Rutgers, says that every other chemistry department at which she interviewed had a "binary number" (that's 0 or 1) of female professors. At Rutgers, she says, female scientists know "they're going to be recognized for their science, not anything else."[c]

Sources: [a] Adapted with permission from Richlet, M. (2005, March 9). Changing rules of the game. *New York Times,* C-1; [b] Adapted with permission from White, E. (2005, February 17). To keep employees, Domino's decides it is not all about pay. *Wall Street Journal,* A-1; [c] McGinn, D. (2005, March 14). Gender: Formula for success. *Newsweek,* 10.

Open Versus Secret Pay

Firms vary widely in the extent to which they communicate openly about worker's compensation levels and company compensation practices. At one extreme, some firms require employees to sign an oath that they will not divulge their pay to coworkers; the penalty for breaking the oath is termination. At the other extreme, every employee's pay is a matter of public record (see, for instance, the case of Whole Foods Market in Figure 10.4); in public universities, this information may even be published in the student newspaper. Many organizations are somewhere in between: They do not publish individual data but they do provide information about pay and salary ranges.

Open pay has two advantages over secret pay.[54] First, limiting employees' access to compensation information often leads to greater pay dissatisfaction because employees tend to overestimate the pay of coworkers and superiors. Second, open pay forces managers to be more fair and effective in administering compensation because bad decisions cannot be hidden and good decisions can serve as motivators to the best workers.

But open pay forces managers and supervisors to defend their compensation decisions publicly. Regardless of good-faith attempts to explain these judgments, it may be impossible to satisfy everyone (even those who are doing very well may feel that they should be doing better). To avoid time-consuming and nerve-wracking arguments with employees, managers may eliminate pay differences among subordinates despite differences in performance levels. The result may be turnover of the better performers, who feel underpaid.

Recent research suggests that greater pay openness is more likely to be successful in organizations with extensive employee involvement and an egalitarian culture that engenders trust and commitment.[55] This is so because open pay can foster perceptions of fairness and greater motivation only in a climate that nurtures employee relations. In more competitive climates, it may unleash a destructive cycle of conflict and hostility that is difficult to stop.

Centralization Versus Decentralization of Pay Decisions

In a centralized system, pay decisions are tightly controlled in a central location, normally the HR department at corporate headquarters. In a decentralized system, pay decisions are delegated deep down into the firm, normally to managers of each unit.

Centralized pay is more appropriate when it is cost-effective and efficient to hire compensation specialists who can be located in a single place, and made responsible for salary surveys,

SAS Institute, a business intelligence software company, pays its employees competitive salaries but also emphasizes its nonmonetary rewards, which include day care, a fitness center, an on-site health-care facility, and M&Ms every Wednesday. Its productive workforce is loyal and service oriented.

benefits administration, and recordkeeping.[56] If the organization faces frequent legal challenges, it may also be prudent to centralize major compensation decisions in the hands of professionals.

A centralized system maximizes internal equity, but it does not handle external equity (market) concerns very well. Thus, large and diverse organizations are better served by a decentralized pay system. For example, Mars, Inc., a worldwide leader in the candy market with estimated annual revenues of $11 billion and 30,000 employees, has only two HR people at corporate headquarters. Each Mars unit is responsible for its own pay decisions.[57]

Summary

Compensation is a complex topic that has a significant impact on organizational success. The good news is that there are not as many separate compensation systems as the nine options might suggest. The bad news is that none of these options is a simple either/or decision. Rather, each pair of criteria defines two end points on a continuum, with many possibilities between them.

One final point: Compensation policies that apply to a unionized workforce are subject to negotiation and bargaining. Thus, managers in union shops are often severely restricted in what they can and cannot do with regard to compensation issues.

Compensation Tools

Compensation tools can be grouped into two broad categories depending on the unit of analysis used to make pay decisions: job-based approaches and skill-based approaches.

Job-based approaches include the most traditional and widely used types of compensation programs.[58] These plans assume that work gets done by people who are paid to perform well-defined jobs (for example, secretary, bookkeeper). Each job is designed to accomplish specific tasks (for example, coding, recordkeeping) and is normally performed by several people. Because all jobs are not equally important to the firm and the labor market puts a greater value on some jobs than on others, the compensation system's primary objective is to allocate pay so that the most important jobs pay the most.

A simplified example of a typical job-based pay structure appears in Figure 10.5. It shows the pay structure of a hypothetical large restaurant with 87 employees performing 18 different jobs.

Pay Structure of a Large Restaurant Developed Using a Job-Based Approach

Figure 10.5

	Jobs	Number of Positions	Pay
GRADE 6	Chef	2	$21.50–$32.00/hr.
GRADE 5	Manager	1	$12.50–$22.00/hr.
	Sous-Chef	1	
GRADE 4	Assistant Manager	2	$8.50–$13.00/hr.
	Lead Cook	2	
	Office Manager	1	
GRADE 3	General Cook	5	$7.50–$9.00/hr.
	Short-Order Cook	2	
	Assistant to Lead Cook	2	
	Clerk	1	
GRADE 2	Server	45	$7.00–$8.00/hr.
	Hostess	4	
	Cashier	4	
GRADE 1	Kitchen Helper	2	$6.50–$7.25/hr.
	Dishwasher	3	
	Janitor	2	
	Busser	6	
	Security Guard	2	

These 18 jobs are grouped into six **pay grades**, with pay levels ranging from $6.50 an hour for jobs in the lowest grades to a maximum of $32.00 an hour for the job in the highest grade (chef). Employees are paid within the range established for the grade at which their job is classified. Thus, a dishwasher or a busser would be paid between $6.50 and $7.25 an hour (Grade 1).

The *skill-based approach* is far less common. It assumes that workers should be paid not according to the job they hold, but rather by how flexible or capable they are at performing multiple tasks. Under this type of plan, the greater the variety of job-related skills workers possess, the more they are paid. Figure 10.6 shows a simple example of a skill-based approach that could be used as an alternative to the job-based approach depicted in Figure 10.5. Workers who master the first set of skills (Block 1) receive $7 an hour; those who learn the skills in Block 2 (in addition to those in Block 1) receive $8.50 an hour; those who acquire the skills in Block 3 (in addition to those in Blocks 1 and 2) are paid $11.50 an hour; and so on.

In the sections that follow, we discuss these two major types of compensation programs in greater depth. Because compensation tools and pay plans can be very complex, we avoid many of the operational details, focusing instead on these programs' intended uses and their relative strengths and weaknesses. Excellent sources that provide step-by-step procedures to implement such programs are available elsewhere.[59]

Job-Based Compensation Plans

There are three key components of developing job-based compensation plans: achieving internal equity, achieving external equity, and achieving individual equity. Figure 10.7 summarizes how these are interrelated and the steps involved in each component. The large majority of U.S. firms rely on this or a similar scheme to compensate their workforce.[60]

Achieving Internal Equity: Job Evaluation

Job-based compensation assesses the relative value or contribution of different jobs (*not* individual employees) to an organization. The first part of this process, referred to as **job evaluation**, is

Pay grades
Groups of jobs that are paid within the same pay range.

Job evaluation
The process of evaluating the relative value or contribution of different jobs to an organization.

	Figure 10.6
Skill Block	**Skills**	**Pay**

Skill Block	Skills	Pay
5	■ Create new items for menu ■ Find different uses for leftovers (e.g., hot dishes, buffets) ■ Coordinate and control work of all employees upon manager's absence	$24.00/hr.
4	■ Cook existing menu items following recipe ■ Supervise kitchen help ■ Prepare payroll ■ Ensure quality of food and adherence to standards	$18.00/hr.
3	■ Schedule servers and assign workstations ■ Conduct inventory ■ Organize work flow on restaurant floor	$11.50/hr.
2	■ Greet customers and organize tables ■ Take orders from customers ■ Bring food to tables ■ Assist in kitchen with food preparations ■ Perform security checks ■ Help with delivery	$8.50/hr.
1	■ Use dishwashing equipment ■ Use chemicals/disinfectants to clean premises ■ Use vacuum cleaner, mop, waxer, and other cleaning equipment ■ Clean and set up tables ■ Perform routine kitchen chores (e.g., making coffee)	$7.00/hr.

Pay Schedule of a Large Restaurant Designed Using a Skill-Based Approach

Figure 10.7

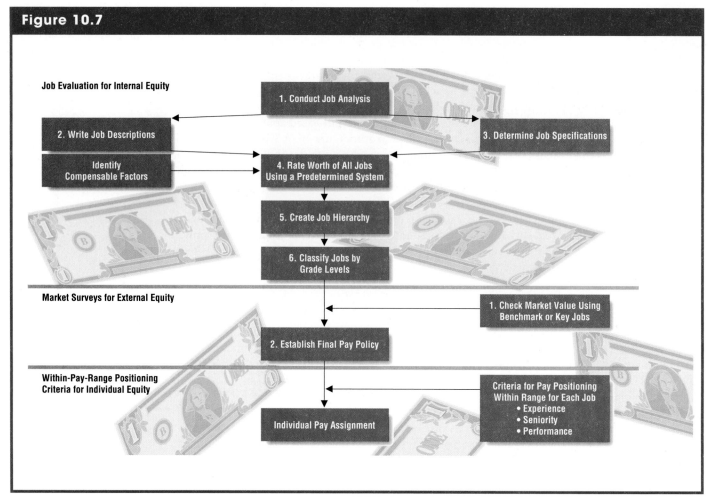

The Key Steps in Creating Job-Based Compensation Plans

composed of six steps intended to provide a rational, orderly, and systematic judgment of how important each job is to the firm. The ultimate goal of job evaluation is to achieve internal equity in the pay structure.

Step 1: Conduct Job Analysis.   As we discussed in Chapter 2, job analysis is the gathering and organization of information concerning the tasks, duties, and responsibilities of specific jobs. In this first step in the job-evaluation process, information is gathered about the duties, tasks, and responsibilities of all jobs being evaluated. Job analysts can use personal interviews with workers, questionnaires completed by employees and/or supervisors, and business records (for example, cost of equipment operated and annual budgets) to study the what, how, and why of various tasks that make up the job. Sample items from a commonly used job analysis questionnaire, the Position Analysis Questionnaire, appear in Figure 10.8. For each question, the job analyst considers what is known about the job and decides which of the five descriptions is most appropriate.

Step 2: Write Job Descriptions.   In the second step in the job-evaluation process, the job-analysis data are boiled down into a written document that identifies, defines, and describes each job in terms of its duties, responsibilities, working conditions, and specifications. This document is called a *job description*. (You will recall this term from Chapter 2.)

Step 3: Determine Job Specifications.   *Job specifications* consist of the worker characteristics that an employee must have to perform the job successfully. These prerequisites are drawn from the job analysis, although in some cases they are legally mandated (for example, plumbers must have a plumbing license). Job specifications are typically very concrete in terms of necessary

Figure 10.8

Mental Processes

Decision Making, Reasoning, and Planning/Scheduling

36. Decision making

Using the response scale below, indicate the level of decision making typically involved in the job; considering the number and complexity of the factors that must be taken into account, the variety of alternatives available, the consequences and importance of the decisions, the background experience, education, and training required, the precedents available for guidance, and other relevant considerations.

Level of Decision

1 *Very limited*
(e.g., decisions such as those in selecting parts in routine assembly, shelving items in a warehouse, cleaning furniture, or handling automatic machines)

2 *Limited*
(e.g., decisions such as those in operating a wood planer, dispatching a taxi, or lubricating an automobile)

3 *Intermediate*
(e.g., decisions such as those in setting up machines for operation, diagnosing mechanical disorders of aircraft, reporting news, or supervising auto service workers)

4 *Substantial*
(e.g., decisions such as those in determining production quotas or making promoting and hiring decisions)

5 *Very substantial*
(e.g., decisions such as those in approving an annual corporate budget, recommending major surgery, or selecting the location for a new plant)

37. Reasoning in problem solving

Using the response scale below, indicate the level of reasoning required in applying knowledge, experience, and judgment to problems.

Level of Reasoning in Problem Solving

1 *Very limited*
(use of common sense to carry out simple or relatively uninvolved instructions, e.g., hand assembler or mixing machine operator)

2 *Limited*
(use of some training and/or experience to select from a limited number of solutions the most appropriate action or procedure in performing the job, e.g., sales clerk, electrician apprentice, or library assistant)

3 *Intermediate*
(use of relevant principles to solve practical problems and to deal with a variety of concrete variables in situations where only limited standardization exists, such as that used by supervisors or technicians)

4 *Substantial*
(use of logic or scientific thinking to define problems, collect information, establish facts, and draw valid conclusions, such as that used by petroleum engineers, personnel directors, or chain store managers)

5 *Very substantial*
(use of logical or scientific thinking to solve a wide range of intellectual and practical problems, such as that used by research chemists, nuclear physicists, corporate presidents, or managers of a large branch or plant)

Source: Purdue Research Foundation, West Lafayette, IN 47907-1650. Used with permission.

Sample Items from Position Analysis Questionnaire

years and type of prior work experience, level and type of education, certificates, vocational training, and so forth. They are usually included on job descriptions.

Step 4: Rate Worth of All Jobs Using a Predetermined System. After job descriptions and job specifications have been finalized, they help determine the relative value or contributions of different jobs to the organization. This job evaluation is normally done by a three- to seven-person committee that may include supervisors, managers, HR department staff, and outside consultants. Several well-known evaluation procedures have evolved over the years, but the *point factor system* is used by the vast majority of firms.[61]

Compensable factors
Work-related criteria that an organization considers most important in assessing the relative value of different jobs.

The point factor system uses **compensable factors** to evaluate jobs. Compensable factors are work-related criteria that the organization considers most important in assessing the relative value of different jobs. One commonly used compensable factor is knowledge. Jobs that require more knowledge (acquired either through formal education or through informal experience) receive a higher rating and, thus, more compensation. Although each firm can determine its own compensable factors, or even create compensable factors suitable to various occupational groups or job families (clerical, technical, managerial, and so on), most firms adopt compensable factors from well-established job-evaluation systems. Two point factor systems that are almost universally accepted are the *Hay Guide Chart Profile Method* and the Management Association of America (MAA) *National Position Evaluation Plan* (formerly known as the NMTA point factor system). The Hay Method, which is summarized in Figure 10.9, uses three compensable factors to evaluate jobs: know-how, problem solving, and accountability. The MAA (NMTA) plan has three separate units: Unit I for hourly blue-collar jobs; Unit II for nonexempt clerical, technical, and service positions; and Unit III for exempt supervisory, professional, and management-level positions. The MAA (NMTA) plan includes 11 factors divided into 4 broad categories (skill, effort, responsibility, and working conditions). The Unit I plan is summarized in Figure 10.10.[62]

In both systems, each compensable factor is assigned a scale of numbers and degrees. The more important factors are given higher point values and the less important factors lower values. For instance, as Figure 10.11 on page 320 shows, the highest possible points under the MAA (NMTA) system are earned for experience, with each degree of experience being worth 22 points. The value of the other two MAA (NMTA) skill factors is 14 points per degree. All other factors are worth either 5 or 10 points per degree.

Hay Compensable Factors

Figure 10.9

Know-How

Know-how is the sum total of every kind of skill, however acquired, necessary for acceptable job performance. This sum total, which comprises the necessary overall "fund of knowledge" an employee needs, has three dimensions:

1 Knowledge of practical procedures, specialized techniques, and learned disciplines.
2 The ability to integrate and harmonize the diversified functions involved in managerial situations (operating, supporting, and administrative). This know-how may be exercised consultatively as well as executively and involves in some combination the areas of organizing, planning, executing, controlling, and evaluating.
3 Active, practicing skills in the area of human relationships.

Problem Solving

Problem solving is the original "self-starting" thinking required by the job for analyzing, evaluating, creating, reasoning, and arriving at conclusions. To the extent that thinking is circumscribed by standards, covered by precedents, or referred to others, problem solving is diminished and the emphasis correspondingly is on know-how.
    Problem solving has two dimensions:

1 The environment in which the thinking takes place.
2 The challenge presented by the thinking to be done.

Accountability

Accountability is the answerability for an action and for the consequences thereof. It is the measured effect of the job on end results. It has three dimensions:

1 Freedom to act—the degree of personal or procedural control and guidance.
2 Job impact on end results.
3 Magnitude—indicated by the general dollar size of the areas(s) most clearly or primarily affected by the job (on an annual basis).

Source: Courtesy of The Hay Group, Boston, MA.

	Figure 10.10

Skill

1. **Knowledge** Measures the level of learning or equivalent formal training applied in a given type of work.
2. **Experience** Measures the amount of time usually needed before being able to perform a job's duties with no more than normal supervision.
3. **Initiative and ingenuity** Indicates the extent to which independent judgment and decision making are exercised on the job.

Effort

4. **Physical demand** Measures how much and how often duties include lifting heavy materials, moving them, and working in difficult positions.
5. **Mental attention or visual demand** Measures how much fatigue occurs from work that is visually or mentally intense, concentrated, and exacting.

Responsibility

6. **Equipment or process** Measures the damage to equipment or process that would probably result from error or carelessness.
7. **Material, product, or service quality** Refers to losses that would likely occur through spoilage, waste, and negligence in processing, inspection, testing, or delivery of service.
8. **Safety of others** Measures the extent to which a job involves protecting others from injury or health hazards.
9. **Work of others or as a member of quality/process team** Refers to the extent of responsibility for assisting, instructing, or directing others or involvement in quality or process teams that impact other operations within the company.

Job Conditions

10. **Working conditions** Measures the degree of exposure to such elements as dust, heat, noise, or fumes.
11. **Hazards** Concerns the risk of injury from materials, tools, equipment, and locations that remains even after protective and safety measures have been taken.

Source: MAA (formerly NMTA) National Position Evaluation Plan.

MAA National Position Evaluation Plan's 11 Compensable Factors (Unit 1—The Manufacturing, Maintenance, Warehousing, Distribution, and Service Positions)

This scale allows the evaluation and compensation committee to assign a number of points to each job on the basis of each factor degree. For example, using the MAA (NMTA) table in Figure 10.11, let us assume that job X is rated at the fifth degree for physical demand (50 points), equipment or process (25 points), material or product (25 points), safety of others (25 points), and work of others (25 points); at the fourth degree for mental or visual demand (20 points), working conditions (40 points), and hazards (20 points); at the second degree for experience (44 points); and at the first degree for knowledge (14 points) and initiative and ingenuity (14 points). The total points for this job across all 11 MAA (NMTA) compensable factors is, thus, 302.

Step 5: Create a Job Hierarchy. The four steps described thus far produce a **job hierarchy,** a listing of jobs in terms of their relative assessed value (from highest to lowest). Figure 10.12 illustrates a job hierarchy for office jobs in a typical large organization. Column 1 of the figure shows the total points assigned to each job in descending order. These range from a high of 300 for customer service representative to a low of 60 for receptionist.

Step 6: Classify Jobs by Grade Levels. For the sake of simplicity, most large organizations classify jobs into grades as the last step in the job-evaluation process. Typically, the job hierarchy is reduced to a manageable number of grade levels, with the assigned points used to determine where to set up dividing lines between grades. For example, column 2 in Figure 10.12 shows

Job hierarchy
A listing of jobs in order of their importance to the organization, from highest to lowest.

Figure 10.11

		POINTS ASSIGNED TO FACTOR DEGREES			
Factor	1st Degree	2nd Degree	3rd Degree	4th Degree	5th Degree
Skill					
1. Knowledge	14	28	42	56	70
2. Experience	22	44	66	88	110
3. Initiative and Ingenuity	14	28	42	56	70
Effort					
4. Physical Demand	10	20	30	40	50
5. Mental or Visual Demand	5	10	15	20	25
Responsibility					
6. Equipment or Process	5	10	15	20	25
7. Material or Product	5	10	15	20	25
8. Safety of Others	5	10	15	20	25
9. Work of Others	5	10	15	20	25
Job Conditions					
10. Working Conditions	10	20	30	40	50
11. Hazards	5	10	15	20	25

Source: MAA (formerly NMTA) National Position Evaluation Plan.

MAA National Position Evaluation Plan: Points Assigned to Factor Degrees

Hierarchy of Clerical Jobs, Pay Grades, and Weekly Pay Range for a Hypothetical Office

Figure 10.12

	1 Points	2 Grade	3 Weekly Pay Range
Customer Service Representative	300	5	$500–$650
Executive Secretary/ Administrative Assistant	298		
Senior Secretary	290		
Secretary	230	4	$450–$550
Senior General Clerk	225		
Credit and Collection Clerk	220		
Accounting Clerk	175	3	$425–$475
General Clerk	170		
Legal Secretary/Assistant	165		
Senior Word Processing Operator	160		
Word Processing Operator	125	2	$390–$430
Purchasing Clerk	120		
Payroll Clerk	120		
Clerk-Typist	115		
File Clerk	95	1	$350–$400
Mail Clerk	80		
Personnel Clerk	80		
Receptionist	60		

how the hierarchy of 18 clerical jobs is divided into five grade levels. All jobs in a given grade are judged to be essentially the same in terms of importance because the points assigned to each are very close in number.

Other job-evaluation systems are the *ranking system* (in which the evaluation committee puts together a hierarchy of job descriptions from highest to lowest based on an overall judgment of value); the *classification system* (in which the committee sorts job descriptions into grades without using a point system, as in the federal civil service job classification system); *factor comparison* (a complex and seldom-used variation of the point and ranking systems); and *policy capturing* (in which mathematical analysis is used to estimate the relative value of each job based on the firm's existing practices).

You should keep two key aspects of our discussion so far in mind. First, job evaluation is performed internally and does not take into account the wage rates in the marketplace or what other firms are doing. Second, job evaluation focuses only on the value of the tasks that make up each job, not the people performing them. The MAA (NMTA) booklet distributed to all employees whose jobs are evaluated under that system makes this very explicit: "The plan does not judge anyone as an individual; it does not rate anyone's ability to perform a job. It [evaluates] each job according to a simple set of [compensable] factors . . . that are applied in exactly the same way to all jobs."[63]

Achieving External Equity: Market Surveys

To achieve external equity, firms often conduct *market surveys*. The purpose of these surveys is to determine the pay ranges for each grade level. An organization may conduct its own salary surveys, but most purchase commercially available surveys. Consulting firms conduct literally hundreds of such surveys each year for almost every type of job and geographical area. CompQuest, for example, is continuously updated by Watson Wyatt Data Services. CompQuest allows users to access online detailed salary and benefits data for almost any imaginable job category for as many as 325 metropolitan areas, every state, and 16 state groups (for a demonstration, go to *www.surveys.com/cq*). Users can create customized reports based on position, job family, geographic area, industry classification, organization size, and the like using simple pull-down menus and point-and-click technology. For additional salary survey sources that are user friendly and instantly available to HR professionals and line managers via the Web, see the Manager's Notebook, "How Much Is a Position Worth in the Marketplace?"

Customer-Driven HR

MANAGER'S NOTEBOOK

How Much Is a Position Worth in the Marketplace?

Salary survey data were commonly obtained by the HR department. But technology is making this process almost obsolete. Line managers can now instantly access salary data analyzed by location, by industry, and by work experience for hundreds of positions. This is possible through online compensation surveys; three of them are Comp Online, Salary Source, and Survey Finder.

Comp Online (*www.towersperrin.com*)

Towers Perrin's Comp Online is a powerful Web-based service that helps managers and HR professionals conduct competitive pay assessments (both domestically and internationally) over the Internet. It allows users to generate custom reports. For example, users can

■ Create their own peer groups of companies by selecting specific companies by name, industry, size, or performance measure.
■ Access new data as it is submitted to the database throughout the year.
■ Customize report formats and content (for example, select preferred percentiles and currencies, show incumbent's data, tailor report titles and labels).

Salary Source (*www.salarysource.com*)

Using Salary Source, a manager can assess the current market value for any of nearly 350 positions from at least three different surveys. Using current market pay movement factors, the data can be adjusted to reflect the current date or any date specified up to 12 months in the future.

Survey Finder (*hrcom.salary.com*)

The Survey Finder enables HR professionals and line managers to search a database of hundreds of up-to-date compensation surveys offered from more than 100 independent vendors, including major human resource consulting firms, compensation consulting firms, survey companies, and industry associations. To make searches easier, the Survey Finder catalogs every survey according to industrial, geographic, and employee population.

Sources: Comp Online™ (*www.towersperrin.com*), Salary Source (*www.salarysource.com*), and Survey Finder (*hrcom.salary.com/surveyfinder*).

Similarly, the federal government regularly conducts salary surveys on a regional and national basis for close to 800 occupations. The results are currently available for free on the Internet (Bureau of Labor Statistics, 2006, National Employment and Wage Estimates by Occupation and Industry, *www.lib.gsu.edu/collections/govdocs/stats.htm*).

Why spend time and money on internal job evaluations when market data can be used to determine the value of jobs? First, most companies have jobs that are unique to the firm and therefore cannot be easily matched to market data.[64] For instance, the job of "administrative assistant" in Company Y may involve supporting top management in important tasks (such as making public appearances for an executive when he or she is not available), whereas in Company Z it may involve only routine clerical duties. Second, the importance of a job can vary from firm to firm. For example, the job of "scientist" in a high-tech firm (where new-product creation is a key to competitive advantage) is usually far more important than in a mature manufacturing company (where scientists are often expected to perform only routine tests).

Using market surveys to link job-evaluation results to external wage/salary data generally requires two steps: benchmarking and establishing a pay policy.

Step 1: Identify Benchmark or Key Jobs.   To link the internal job-evaluation hierarchy or grade-level classification to market salaries, most firms identify **benchmark or key jobs**—that is, jobs that are similar or comparable in content across firms—and check salary surveys to determine how much these key jobs are worth to other employers. The company then sets pay rates for nonkey jobs (for which market data are *not* available) by assigning them the same pay range as key jobs that fall into the same grade level.

An example will help here. Let's say five of the jobs in our office example in Figure 10.12 are identified as key. (These are briefly described in Figure 10.13.) The company purchases a salary survey for office workers in the area showing both average weekly pay and the 25th, 50th, and 75th percentiles in weekly pay for these key jobs. For example, Figure 10.14 shows that 25 percent of the customer service representatives in organizations included in the survey earn $400 per week or less, 50 percent earn $500 or less, and 75 percent earn $650 or less. The average weekly salary in the area for this job is $495. The company uses these market data to assign a pay range for all jobs that were evaluated as being at the same grade level as the key job of customer service representative—in this case, executive secretary and senior secretary. But first it needs to establish a pay policy.

Step 2: Establish a Pay Policy.   Because market wages and salaries vary widely (look again at Figure 10.14), the organization needs to decide whether to lead, lag, or pay the going rate (which is normally defined as the midpoint of the wage/salary distribution in the survey). A firm's **pay policy** is determined by how it chooses to position itself in the pay market. The hypothetical firm shown in Figure 10.12, for example, decided to set a pay policy pegging the minimum pay for each grade to the 50th percentile and the maximum pay to the 75th percentile in the market (see column 3 of Figure 10.12). Some firms use more complex methods to achieve the same objective.

Benchmark or key jobs
A job that is similar or comparable in content across firms.

Pay policy
A firm's decision to pay above, below, or at the market rate for its jobs.

Figure 10.13	**Sample Benchmark Jobs for Office Personnel**

Customer Service Representative Establishes and maintains good customer relations and provides advice and assistance on customer problems.

Credit and Collection Clerk Performs clerical tasks related to credit and collection activities; performs routine credit checks, obtains supplementary information, investigates overdue accounts, follows up by mail and/or telephone to customers on delinquent payments.

Accounting Clerk Performs a variety of routine accounting clerical work such as maintaining journals, subsidiary ledgers, and related reports according to well-defined procedures or detailed instructions.

Word Processing Operator Operates word processing equipment to enter or search, select, and merge text from a storage device or internal memory for continuous or repetitive production of copy.

Clerk-Typist Performs routine clerical and typing work; follows established procedures and detailed written or oral instructions; may operate simple types of office machines and equipment.

Source: AMS Foundation *Office, Secretarial, Professional, Data Processing and Management Salary Report,* AMS Foundation, 550 W. Jackson Blvd., Suite 360, Chicago, IL 60661. See also Salary Wizard (2006). Salary report for administrative support, and clerical job categories. *www.salarywizard.com.*

Figure 10.14 — **Market Salary Data for Selected Benchmark Office Jobs**

	Weekly Pay Percentile			
Benchmark Jobs	**25th**	**50th**	**75th**	**Weekly Pay Average**
1. Customer Service Representative	$400	$500	$650	$495
2. Credit and Collection Clerk	$400	$450	$550	$455
3. Accounting Clerk	$370	$425	$475	$423
4. Word Processing Operator	$380	$390	$430	$394
5. Clerk-Typist	$330	$350	$400	$343

Achieving Individual Equity: Within-Pay-Range Positioning Criteria

After the firm has finalized its pay structure by determining pay ranges for each job, it must perform one last task: Assign each employee a pay rate within the range established for his of her job. Companies frequently use previous experience, seniority, and performance appraisal ratings to determine how much an employee is to be paid within the stipulated range for his or her job. The objective of this last step is to achieve individual equity. Individual equity refers to fairness in pay decisions for employees holding the same job.

Evaluating Job-Based Compensation Plans

Job-based compensation programs are rational, objective, and systematic, all features that minimize employee complaints. They are also relatively easy to set up and administer. However, they have several significant drawbacks:

■ Job-based compensation plans do not take into account the nature of the business and its unique problems. For example, jobs are harder to define and change more rapidly in small, growing companies than in larger, more stable companies (such as those in the insurance industry).

- The process of establishing job-based compensation plans is much more subjective and arbitrary than its proponents suggest.
- Job-based systems are less appropriate at higher levels of an organization, where it is more difficult to separate individual contributions from the job itself. To force people to conform to a narrowly defined job description robs the organization of much-needed creativity.
- As the economy has become more service oriented and the manufacturing sector has continued to shrink, jobs have become more broadly defined. As a result, job descriptions are often awash in generalities. This makes it more difficult to evaluate the relative importance of jobs.
- Job-based compensation plans tend to be bureaucratic, mechanistic, and inflexible. Thus, firms cannot easily adapt their pay structure to a rapidly changing economic environment. In addition, because they rely on fixed salary and benefits associated with each level in the hierarchy, these plans tend to result in layoffs to save on costs during economic downturns. Japanese firms often provide 20 to 30 percent of their employees' pay in variable form and have greater flexibility to absorb the economy's ups and downs.
- The job-evaluation process is biased against those occupations traditionally filled by women (clerical, elementary school teaching, nursing, and the like). Although empirical studies are inconclusive on this issue, critics often use vivid examples to make their point, such as sanitation jobs (garbage collection) in New York City being evaluated higher than teaching jobs.
- Wage and salary data obtained from market surveys are not definitive. After adjusting for job content, company size, firm performance, and geographic location, differences ranging from 35 to 300 percent in the pay of identical jobs within the same industry are not uncommon.[65]
- In determining internal and external equity, it is the employees' perceptions of equity that count, not the assessments of job-evaluation committees and paid consultants. Job-based compensation plans assume that the employer can decide what is equitable for the employee. Because equity is in the eye of the beholder, this approach may simply rationalize an employer's pay practices rather than compensate employees according to their contributions. In a knowledge-based economy, workers, particularly those who work in scientific and technical fields, may compete for work in an open market; hence, they are not tied to a particular organization. They may not want to be constrained by salaries that are set by a job-evaluation procedure. They are more loyal to the profession than to the firm. As a result, they may see themselves as "freelancers" and may resent organizational controls on their earnings.

Despite all these criticisms, job-based compensation plans continue to be widely used, probably because no alternative systems are both cost-efficient and generally applicable.

Suggestions for Practice

Rather than dismissing job-based compensation plans completely, it is more realistic to take steps to reduce the potential problems associated with them:

- **Think strategically in making policy decisions concerning pay.** For example, it may be in the firm's best interests to design a certain number of jobs very broadly and flexibly. The firm may also find it advantageous to pay at the top of the market for critical jobs that are central to its mission and at the low end of the market for jobs it considers less important. In short, the firm's business and HR strategy should drive the use of compensation tools rather than the other way around.
- **Secure employee input.** Employee dissatisfaction will be reduced to the extent that employees have a voice in the design and management of the compensation plan. Computer-assisted job-evaluation systems allow employees to describe their jobs in a way that can be synthesized, displayed, rearranged, and easily compared. This tends to improve the acceptability of job-evaluation results and offers an inexpensive way to update job descriptions regularly.
- **Increase each job's range of pay while expanding its scope of responsibility.** This approach, commonly called **job banding**, entails replacing narrowly defined job descriptions with broader categories (bands) of related jobs.[66] For instance, Fine Products, Inc., a consumer products company, collapsed 13 separate plant, regional, and production manager job titles down to four jobs with increased responsibility. The range between the maximum and the minimum within each band was set at approximately 90 percent (from $28,500 to $54,500 for "Band C," for instance).[67]

Job banding
The practice of replacing narrowly defined job descriptions with broader categories (bands) of related jobs.

Job banding permits employees to receive a substantial pay raise without having to change jobs or get promoted. It has three potential benefits. First, it gives the firm more flexibility because jobs are not narrowly defined. Second, during periods of slow growth, the firm can reward top performers without having to promote them. Third, the firm may save on administrative costs because with banding there are fewer layers of staff and management. However, banding needs to be monitored because managers enjoy substantial discretion in "slotting" an employee within a large allowable salary range. Over time, this flexibility may create unjustifiable salary inequities from one unit to another and from one employee to another.

- **Examine statistical evidence periodically to ensure that the job-evaluation system is doing what it is supposed to.** For instance, high turnover or difficulty in hiring employees in certain job classifications may be a good indicator that job evaluation is not working properly.

- **Expand the proportion of employees' pay that is variable (bonuses, stock plans, and so forth).** Variable-pay programs provide the firm with the flexibility to reduce costs without resorting to layoffs.

- **Develop policies for so-called knowledge workers that specify the types of paid external opportunities they may pursue while still remaining employed by the firm.** For example, many universities stipulate that faculty can devote an average of eight hours per week to consulting activities, although they need to file a report listing the external organizations for which they provide services.

- **Establish dual-career ladders for different types of employees so that moving into management ranks or up the organizational hierarchy is not the only way to receive a substantial increase in pay.** In some situations, such as in a large organization with multiple business units and several layers of management, a tall job hierarchy is appropriate; in others, a relatively flat hierarchy with much room for salary growth (based, for instance, on performance and seniority) makes more sense. Figure 10.15 is an example of a dual-career ladder.

Skill-Based Compensation Plans

Unlike job-based compensation plans, skill-based compensation plans use skills as the basis of pay.[68] All employees start at the same pay rate and advance one pay level for each new skill they master.[69]

	Figure 10.15	
Band	**Managerial**	**Individual Contributor**
13	President	
12	Executive Vice President	Vice President for Research
11	Vice President	Executive Consultant
10	Assistant Vice President	Senior Consultant
9	Director	Consultant
8	Senior Manager	Senior Adviser
7	Manager	Adviser
6		Senior Specialist
5		Specialist
4		Senior Technician
3		Senior Administrative Support, Technician
2		Administrative Support Senior Manufacturing Associate
1		Clerical Support, Manufacturing Associate

Example of a Dual-Career Ladder

Source: LeBlanc, P. Banding the new pay structure for the transformed organization. *Perspectives in Total Compensation,* 3(8). American Compensation Association, Scottsdale, AZ. Used with permission of the author, Peter V. LeBlanc, of Sibson & Company.

Three types of skills may be rewarded. Employees acquire *depth skills* when they learn more about a specialized area or become expert in a given field. They acquire *horizontal* or *breadth skills* when they learn more and more jobs or tasks within the firm and *vertical skills* when they acquire "self-management" abilities, such as scheduling, coordinating, training, and leadership. Skill-based pay has been adopted by a wide range of industries, such as telecommunications (AT&T and Northern Telecom), insurance (Shenandoah Life Insurance), hotels (Embassy Suites), and retailing (Dayton Hudson).[70]

Skill-based pay offers several potential advantages to the firm.[71] First, it creates a more flexible workforce that is not straitjacketed by job descriptions specifying work assignments for a given job title. Second, it promotes cross-training, thus preventing absenteeism and turnover from disrupting the work unit's ability to meet deadlines. Third, it calls for fewer supervisors, so management layers can be cut to produce a leaner organization. Fourth, it increases employees' control over their compensation because they know in advance what it takes to receive a pay raise (learning new skills).

Skill-based pay does pose some risks to the organization and this may help explain why only a relatively small proportion (5 to 7%) of all firms use it.[72] First, it may lead to higher compensation and training costs that are not offset by greater productivity or cost savings. This can happen when many employees master many or all the skills and thus receive a higher wage than they would under a job-based pay rate. Second, unless employees have the opportunity to use all the skills they have acquired, they may become "rusty." Third, when employees hit the top of the pay structure, they may become frustrated and leave the firm because they have no further opportunity to receive a pay raise. Fourth, attaching monetary values to skills can become a guessing game unless external comparable pay data are available. Finally, skill-based pay may become part of the problem it is intended to solve (extensive bureaucracy and inflexibility) if an elaborate and time-consuming process is required to monitor and certify employee skills.

One final observation about skill-based pay: This is the pay system that many new and small businesses use by default. Because flexibility is crucial for continued growth, flexible employees are more highly valued and paid accordingly. When a business is fairly new, of course, there is no formalized system relating specific skills to specific compensation values. However, at some point the company must systematize its compensation structure. It is then that the design issues described earlier become critical.

The Legal Environment and Pay System Governance

Fair Labor Standards Act (FLSA)
The fundamental compensation law in the United States. Requires employers to record earnings and hours worked by all covered employees and to report this information to the U.S. Department of Labor. Defines two categories of employees: exempt and nonexempt.

Exempt employee
An employee who is not covered by the provisions of the Fair Labor Standards Act. Most professional, administrative, executive, and outside sales jobs fall into this category.

Nonexempt employee
An employee who is covered by the provisions of the Fair Labor Standards Act.

The legal framework exerts substantial influence on the design and administration of compensation systems. The key federal laws that govern compensation criteria and procedures are the Fair Labor Standards Act, the Equal Pay Act, and the Internal Revenue Code. In addition to these, each state has its own sets of regulations that complement federal law. Labor laws may also limit managerial discretion in setting pay levels.

The Fair Labor Standards Act

The **Fair Labor Standards Act (FLSA)** of 1938 is the compensation law that affects most pay structures in the United States. To comply with the FLSA, employers must keep accurate records of earnings and hours worked by all covered employees and must report this information to the Wage and Hour Division of the U.S. Department of Labor. Most businesses are covered by the FLSA, except those with only one employee or annual gross sales under $500,000.

The FLSA defines two categories of employees: exempt and nonexempt. **Exempt employees** are not covered by the provisions of the act; **nonexempt employees** are. Exempt categories include professional, administrative, executive, and outside sales jobs. The Department of Labor provides guidelines to determine whether a job is exempt or nonexempt. Managers are often tempted to classify as many jobs as possible as exempt to avoid some of the costs associated with nonexempt status, principally the minimum wage and overtime payments. However, there are heavy penalties for employers who unfairly classify nonexempt jobs as exempt.

Minimum Wages

The federal minimum wage set by the FLSA is currently $5.15 per hour, although in some states and cities it is considerably higher. For instance, in San Francisco it is $8.50 per hour and in California, Alaska, and Connecticut it is $7.15, $6.75, and $7.10, respectively. Minimum wage legislation is controversial. Those in favor believe that it raises the standard of living for the poorest members of society. Those who oppose it argue that it results in higher levels of unemployment and poverty among low-skilled workers because it discourages firms from hiring and/or retaining workers. Opponents also claim that minimum wages encourage U.S. firms to open overseas plants in low-wage countries (such as Mexico and the Philippines), thereby creating more unemployment at home. This debate has not yet been resolved, probably because the minimum wage is set at a much lower level than most U.S. firms are willing to pay. However, the debate is being rekindled by a growing number of local governments passing "living wage" (wage needed to secure a decent standard of living) legislation that sets the minimum wage at a much higher level than the federal minimum of $5.15 per hour. For instance, in 2003 the city of Santa Cruz, California, requires a minimum hourly wage of $12.55 per hour.

Overtime

The FLSA requires that nonexempt employees be paid one and a half times the standard wage for each hour they work over 40 hours a week. This provision was intended to stimulate hiring by making it more costly to expand production using existing employees. In fact, however, many firms would rather pay overtime than incur the costs associated with hiring additional employees (recruitment, training, benefits, and so on).

In the most sweeping revision of overtime pay in 50 years, the Labor Department, as of 2005, requires that employers guarantee overtime for workers who earn up to $23,600 a year, up from the ceiling of $8,660 established in 1975. The change covers manual laborers, other blue-collar workers, and managers who earn $455 a week or less, whether they are paid salary or an hourly wage. Bosses can exempt white-collar workers who make more than $23,600 from overtime pay if they do some "professional, administrative, or executive" duties or are "team leaders," whether or not they supervise workers.[73] These changes are provoking a large number of worker complaints against their employers under the FLSA.

The Equal Pay Act

The Equal Pay Act (EPA) was passed in 1963 as an amendment to the FLSA. As we discussed in Chapter 3, it requires that men and women be paid the same amount of money if they hold similar jobs that are "substantially equal" in terms of skill, effort, responsibility, and working conditions. The EPA includes four exceptions that allow employers to pay one sex more than the other: (1) more seniority; (2) better job performance; (3) greater quantity or quality of production; and (4) certain other factors, such as paying extra compensation to employees for working the night shift. If there is a discrepancy in the average pay of men and women holding similar jobs, managers should ensure that at least one of the four exceptions to the EPA applies to avoid legal costs and back pay to affected employees.

Comparable Worth

Equal pay should not be confused with comparable worth, a much more stringent form of legislation enacted in some countries and used in a few public jurisdictions in the United States. **Comparable worth** calls for comparable pay for jobs that require comparable skills, effort, and responsibility and have comparable working conditions, even if the job content is different. For instance, if a company using the point factor job-evaluation system we described earlier finds that the administrative assistant position (held mostly by women) receives the same number of points as the shift supervisor position (held mostly by men), comparable worth legislation would require paying employees in these jobs equally, even though they might be exercising very different skills and responsibilities.

The considerable controversy surrounding comparable worth legislation centers mainly on how it should be implemented rather than on its main goal of pay equity between the sexes. Supporters of comparable worth legislation favor using job-evaluation tools to advance pay equity, pointing out that many private firms already use this method to set wages. Opponents

Comparable worth
A pay concept or doctrine that calls for comparable pay for jobs that require comparable skills, effort, and responsibility and have comparable working conditions, even if the job content is different.

As more women move into jobs traditionally filled by men, the issue of comparable worth has entered the spotlight.

argue that job evaluations are inherently arbitrary and that they do not take sufficient account of jobs' market value. For example, comparable worth proponents have often said that markets treat nurses unfairly because society links the profession to women's unpaid nurturing role in the family. Despite all the problems with implementation, comparable worth is already being used in many countries, including Britain, Canada, and Australia.[74]

Role of the Office of Federal Contract Compliance (OFCCP)

The OFCCP may evaluate compensation in an effort to monitor compliance with EEO. This agency has extensive powers because it may revoke federal government contracts from employers—a costly loss in revenue for many firms.

During the past 35 years, OFCCP has focused most of its efforts on the implementation of affirmative action plans (see Chapter 3). Recently, however, that emphasis seems to have shifted to more focused investigations of pay disparities by gender and race. Since the last edition of this book, the OFCCP has introduced new standards for systemic compensation discrimination. Starting in 2005, the OFCCP is using a "similarly situated employee" definition for comparative pay purposes by gender and race. An employee would be considered a "similarly situated employee" vis-à-vis another employee if both share much in common in terms of work performed, responsibility level, and the skills and qualifications required for the respective positions. "Legitimate factors" that may allow for a compensation premium among similarly situated employees include higher education, experience, performance, and expensive geographic locations. OFCCP auditors are required to determine whether compensation disparities remain by gender and/or race after taking into account these legitimate factors through a multivariate statistical procedure known as multiple regression.[75] Employers will need to do the necessary research to ensure compliance with these regulations; otherwise, they are exposed to heavy penalties if audited and found guilty of gender and race discrimination.

The Internal Revenue Code

The **Internal Revenue Code (IRC)** affects how much of their earnings employees can keep. It also affects how benefits are treated for tax purposes, as we discuss in Chapter 12. The IRC requires the company to withhold a portion of each employee's income to meet federal tax obligations (and, indirectly, state tax obligations, which in most states are set as a percentage of the federal tax deduction).

Tax laws change from time to time, and these changes affect an employee's take-home pay as well as what forms of compensation can be sheltered from taxes. An employer's failure to take advantage of IRC legislation may result in wasted payroll dollars. For instance, the tax laws currently treat capital gains (profits) on the sale of stock as ordinary income. This reduces the motivational value of stock as a long-term pay incentive because employees bear more risk with stock than with a cash-based form of pay. However, setting the capital gains tax below the tax on ordinary income could make stock more attractive to employees as a pay incentive.

Internal Revenue Code (IRC)
The code of tax laws that affects how much of their earnings employees can keep and how benefits are treated for tax purposes.

Summary and Conclusions

What Is Compensation?

Total compensation has three components: (1) base compensation, the fixed pay received on a regular basis; (2) pay incentives, programs designed to reward good performance; and (3) benefits or indirect compensation, including health insurance, vacations, and perquisites.

Designing a Compensation System

An effective compensation plan enables the firm to achieve its strategic objectives and is suited to the firm's unique characteristics as well as to its environment. The pay options managers need to consider in designing a compensation system are (1) internal versus external equity, (2) fixed versus variable pay, (3) performance versus membership, (4) job versus individual pay, (5) egalitarianism versus elitism, (6) below-market versus above-market compensation, (7) monetary versus nonmonetary rewards, (8) open versus secret pay, and (9) centralization versus decentralization of pay decisions. In all situations, the best choices depend on how well they "fit" with business objectives and the individual organization.

Compensation Tools

There are two broad categories of compensation tools: job-based approaches and skill-based approaches. The typical job-based compensation plan has three components: (1) To achieve internal equity, firms use job evaluation to assess the relative value of jobs throughout the firm. (2) To achieve external equity, they use salary data on benchmark or key jobs obtained from market surveys to set a pay policy. (3) To achieve individual equity, they use a combination of experience, seniority, and performance to establish an individual's position within the pay range for his or her job.

Skill-based compensation systems are more costly and more limited in use. Skill-based pay rewards employees for acquiring depth skills (learning more about a specialized area), horizontal or breadth skills (learning about more areas), and vertical skills (self-management).

The Legal Environment and Pay System Governance

The major federal laws governing compensation practices are the Fair Labor Standards Act (which governs minimum wage and overtime payments and provides guidelines for classifying employees as exempt or nonexempt); the Equal Pay Act (which prohibits pay discrimination based on gender); and the Internal Revenue Code (which specifies how various forms of employee pay are subject to taxation). Some countries and municipalities have comparable worth legislation, which calls for comparable pay for jobs that require comparable skills, effort, and responsibility and have comparable working conditions, even if the job content is different.

Key Terms

base compensation, 301
benchmark or key jobs, 321
comparable worth, 327
compensable factors, 318
egalitarian pay system, 308
elitist pay system, 308
exempt employee, 326
external equity, 302

Fair Labor Standards Act (FLSA), 326
individual equity, 304
internal equity, 302
Internal Revenue Code (IRC), 329
job banding, 324
job evaluation, 315
job hierarchy, 319

knowledge-based pay or skill-based pay, 307
nonexempt employee, 326
pay grades, 315
pay incentive, 301
pay policy, 322
total compensation, 301

Discussion Questions

1. Some companies have a policy of selectively matching external offers to prevent employees from leaving the company. What are the pros and cons of such a policy? Explain.

2. Several companies are moving in the direction of compensating employees with nonmonetary rewards in lieu of higher wages (see the Manager's Notebook, "Rewarding Employees with Nonmonetary Compensation"). Why do you think this is happening? Do you think this is a good thing for companies and employees? Explain.

3. In a feisty response to critics who accuse Wal-Mart of providing poverty-level wages (around $9.68 an hour, on average) and few benefits, Wal-Mart chief executive H. Lee Scott, Jr., said Wal-Mart offered good, stable jobs, noting that when it opens a store, more than 3,000 people often apply for 300 jobs. "It doesn't make sense," Mr. Scott said, "that people would line up for jobs that are worse than they could get elsewhere, with fewer benefits and less opportunities."[76] Based on what you learned in this chapter, do you agree with Mr. Scott's assessment? Explain.

4. One observer argues that external equity should always be the primary concern in compensation, noting that it attracts the best employees and prevents the top performers from leaving. Do you agree?

5. During 2003–2006 many firms laid off thousands of workers, froze employees' pay, and eliminated all bonuses. Yet, many of these firms targeted "key employees" they retained by paying them huge compensation increases, creating large "inequities" within the workforce, even among employees not targeted as key but performing the same job. What are the pros and cons of such a policy? Explain.

6. The United States faces a severe teacher shortage in the hard sciences (biology, chemistry, physics) and mathematics. Many believe it is due to the use of a single salary schedule for all teachers regardless of field, as well as a seniority scale for paying teachers based on how long they have been teaching. Teachers' unions are opposed to any form of "salary discrimination" by field (paying English and history teachers less than biology and chemistry teachers) on the grounds that all teachers perform the same job. Do you agree that all teachers perform the same job regardless of field and, thus, should be subject to the same salary schedule? Explain.

7. As noted in the Manager's Notebook, "Compensation Entitlements Are Going out the Window," fixed or secure pay is becoming rare. What impact do you think this has on employees' outlook? What, if any, are the negative and positive aspects of this trend? Explain.

8. A compensation analyst from a mid-sized oil and gas company rarely has the time to call different survey vendors to discuss discrepancies between pay averages for the same jobs. Instead, he chooses the number with which he is most comfortable based on gut feeling. Because of time pressures, he has to rely on judgment and experience to make a reasonable recommendation as to what is a "competitive offer." Do you think this is a good practice?

There is a variety of additional material available on the Web site that accompanies this text. You can access this information by visiting the Web site at **www.prenhall.com/gomez**.

YOU MANAGE IT! Emerging Trends Case 10.1

A Little Less in the Envelope This Week

A decade or so ago, no other firm treated its employees better than IBM. Big Blue's generous compensation packages offered medical coverage that was virtually free, cushy pensions, and salaries that rose dependably each year. Today those guarantees are gone.

IBM replaced these guaranteed compensation packages with more pay-for-performance plans and leaner benefits. This change began in the early 1990s and became an urgently needed change during the late 1990s' war for talent. A workaholic up-and-comer at IBM in the 1990s could exceed every goal and still wind up with the same raise as the incompetent in the next office. Even worse, fewer than 1,000 employees (in a company with 413,000 employees at the time) had stock options. In a climate that was all about risk and reward, IBM was more about security and one-size-fits-all pay.

So IBM instituted rigorous performance reviews, widened its stock options to 70,000 workers, and made an average of 10 percent of employee pay variable—meaning it could swell or shrink depending on the worker's performance and the company's performance. Benefits were also overhauled. Recently, IBM announced a new pension plan, which saved the company millions but caused anger among employees, many of whom complained of losing as much as half of their benefits. Health coverage cost employees as much as $157 a month. Says IBM engineer Jeff Zitz, who estimates his pension under the new plan could take as much as an 80 percent hit: "Halfway through my career, they changed the deal."

Now, blue-collar and white-collar employees across Corporate America are realizing just how much their deals have changed, too. Nowhere is the shift in risk more painfully obvious, to those affected as well as those who fear being affected in the same way, than at Enron Corp., where employees saw their retirement savings wiped out while executives at the top cashed in.

But you don't have to work at a company that's bankrupt and under siege by federal investigators to feel at least some of the pain. As the examples in the Manager's Notebook, "Compensation Entitlements Are Going out the Window," illustrate, companies as diverse as IBM, General Motors, Lucent Technologies, and others are all moving away from entitlements.

Critical Thinking Questions

1. Not long ago, an ideal job was working in a large corporation that "prided itself on offering employees some insulation from the vagaries of the business cycle with a panoply of benefits and a steady, if slow, climb in pay."[a] Opportunities for these kinds of jobs are fading rapidly. Why do you think this is happening? Explain.

2. "Now, a company's attitude is that you have to take a percent of the risk with them," says Hewitt Associates LLC compensation expert Ken Abosch. "There's no question that most corporations have turned away from fixed forms of compensation in favor of variable forms. There has been an abandonment of entitlement programs."[b] Do you think this is a good trend or a bad trend? Explain.

3. For the past 80 years, job evaluation as a compensation tool was designed to assess the value of each job rather than to evaluate the person doing the job, prompting a flat pay schedule for all incumbents in a particular job. Some

HR experts believe that the emerging trend just discussed has created a new ballgame, where pay inequality has become "normal." Employers are using variable pay to lavish financial resources on their most prized employees, creating a kind of corporate star system. "How do you communicate to a workforce that isn't created equally? How do you treat a workforce in which everyone has a different deal?" asks Jay Schuster of Los Angeles–based compensation consultants Schuster-Zingheim & Associates Inc. If you were asked these questions, how would you answer them? Explain.

Team Exercise

The HR director of a large manufacturing plant has called a meeting of several divisional managers to come up with a plan on how to explain to employees that their annual cash bonus last year (which averaged $10,000) will go down to zero this year. Part of the concern the HR director has is that about 10 percent of employees received huge bonuses this year amounting to 25 percent of base pay, even though the rest received zero bonus. In addition, many employees believe that while they have been penalized by the ups and downs of variable pay, most executives are insulated from risk and some have even received special stipends. Students divide into groups of five to role-play this situation and develop a plan for explaining to employees why this is happening.

Experiential Exercise

One student will role-play a 45-year-old passenger airline pilot whose take-home pay will drop by 15 percent and whose health insurance will increase by 20 percent due to budget cuts. Although making more than six figures a year, the pilot feels that being asked to pay for things that can't be controlled is unfair. Another student will role-play an airline executive who will defend the airline's position. Both sides will role-play in front of the class for approximately 15 minutes. The instructor will then moderate an open class discussion.

Source: Adapted with permission from Conlin, M., and Berner, R. (2002, February 18). A little less in the envelope this week. BusinessWeek, 64–66; a Ibid., p. 65; b Ibid., p. 66. Updated information provided by Gómez-Mejía, L. R., Balkin, D. B., and Cardy, R. L.

Ethics Case 10.2 YOU MANAGE IT!

Conflict of Interest? Compensating Knowledge Workers

The taxpayer-funded National Institutes of Health (NIH) has long been a magnet for some of the world's top scientists, who are drawn to its state-of-the-art laboratories, intellectual freedom, high-powered peers, and good pay. In 2005, the NIH announced a complete ban on private consulting arrangements between scientists and the Institute and pharmaceutical and biotech companies. The reason for this new policy was to prevent conflict of interest: Researchers who accept money from private companies are not as likely to criticize the products of those companies and may even be induced to support the benefits of those products. This was the case, for instance, of

Crestor, a cholesterol-lowering drug from AstraZeneca, which funded the research of Dr. Bryan Brewer, chief of the National Heart, Lung, and Blood Institute's molecular disease branch of NIH. Dr. Brewer wrote an article promoting the benefits of Crestor and failed to mention potentially serious safety problems with the drug. In another case, a senior NIH Alzheimer's researcher received more than $500,000 from Pfizer Inc., which markets a leading drug to treat the disease.

The tight NIH compensation guidelines passed in 2005 mark a reversal of a mid-1990's strategy to loosen NIH ethics rules and put its researchers on par with their peers at universities. That push was led by then-director Harold Varmus, a Nobel laureate, who is now president of Memorial Sloan-Kettering Cancer Center in New York. Under Dr. Varmus, the NIH boosted salaries by putting thousands of its scientists in a special, alternative pay category called Title 42 that allows top employees to earn as much as $200,000 a year, far above U.S. civil-service levels. Dr. Varmus also loosened restrictions on compensation from outside consulting activities, a perk routinely available to university scientists.

The potential competition from academia and private firms, many of which offer more lucrative salaries, may now pose a serious problem to NIH. Some scientists warn that these external organizations can be aggressive in their recruiting. NIH researchers are big draws, whether for their ability to help universities extract grant money from the NIH (about 80% of its budget flows to non-NIH scientists, mostly working at universities) or for the expertise they bring to such companies as Merck, Pfizer, and Johnson & Johnson.

Albert Fornace, a star scientist at the NIH for 27 years, decamped to become a professor at Harvard University's School of Public Health. He says a number of factors prompted his departure, but the new ethics climate was an important consideration. "The ethics rules are irritating. I kind of feel you aren't been treated as an adult, or even trusted," says Dr. Fornace. "I think the NIH is a wonderful place to do research," he adds. "You can do high risk research." He predicts, though, that recruiting and retention problems will mount. "I feel bad about NIH."

Critical Thinking Questions

1. What makes knowledge workers unique in terms of their compensation?

2. How can an organization such as NIH prevent the appearance of ethical lapses without a complete ban on external income?

3. One NIH manager laments that "there is a sense of collective punishment for the wrong doing or dubious behavior of a few. At a subliminal level, that makes them [everyone] feel not only second class, but victimized and scapegoated." Do you think that NIH personnel have to be held to a higher ethical standard with their pay than their counterparts who work elsewhere? And, if so, what would it need to do to prevent large-scale departure of scientists looking for greener pastures?

Team Exercise

Form teams of five. Each team is to develop a proposal to advise NIH of possible problems in recruiting and retaining talent given the new rules. Each team will make recommendations to NIH to prevent these problems, which may include rescinding the rule or modifying it. The instructor will serve as a mediator in the discussion.

Experiential Exercise

Role-play an NIH scientist who has worked with various leading drug manufacturers. You believe that you have always acted ethically and that the compensation you have received has not affected your judgment. Furthermore, you believe that pay at NIH is lower than what you would receive elsewhere and that this additional compensation is necessary "to keep you whole." Another student will role-play an NIH manager who believes that the new rule is necessary to restore public trust in NIH. Role-play will last for approximately 15 minutes. Instructor will then open the issue to the entire class, serving as a mediator.

Source: Adapted with permission from Wysocki, B. (2005, March 3). Some scientists say new ethics rules may damage NIH. *Wall Street Journal*, B-1. For related articles, see Harris, G. (2005, February) and Harris, G. Ethics rules prohibit consulting by agency scientists. *New York Times*, A–18 (2005, February 2).

YOU MANAGE IT!   # Discussion Case 10.3

An Academic Question

Mountain States University is a medium-sized public university with 21,000 students and 1,200 faculty members. The College of Business Administration is the largest one on campus, with 8,000 students and 180 faculty members. For the past few years, the dean has had to deal with a large number of dissatisfied faculty who complain that they are underpaid relative to newly hired faculty. Many of the complainants are senior tenured professors who refuse to engage in committee activities beyond the minimum service requirements and who are seldom in their offices because they feel aggrieved. They teach six hours a week, spend two hours in the office, and then disappear from campus. Recently, the head of the college's faculty council compiled some statistics and sent these to the dean, demanding "prompt action to create more equity in the faculty pay structure." The average salary statistics are shown in the table below.

The dean replied that he has little choice but to make offers to new faculty that are competitive with the market and that the university will not give him enough funds to maintain equitable pay differences between new and current faculty or between higher and lower ranks.

Critical Thinking Questions

1. Based on the data collected by the faculty council, name three compensation problems that exist at Mountain States University.
2. Is the dean's explanation for decreased pay differences by rank and/or seniority justifiable?
3. How would you suggest the dean deal with senior faculty who feel underpaid?

Team Exercise

A group of six faculty members has come to see the dean to express dissatisfaction with pay compression at the college.

All six represent current faculty; two are assistant professors, two are associate professors, and two are full professors. Students divide into groups of seven and role-play this situation as the dean attempts to deal with the pay complaints raised by the faculty. The dean doesn't have the money to correct the pay-compression problem, yet he can't afford to alienate the faculty.

Experiential Exercise

One student will role-play a department chair who has just hired a full professor from another institution at a much higher salary than a full professor who has spent 20 years at the university. Another student will role-play the 20-year veteran who will go to the department chair for explanations. Overall, both professors have approximately the same number of publications in journals of similar quality and their teaching ratings are comparable, but over the past two years the professor who was hired from the outside has published a couple of pieces in a top journal whereas the 20-year veteran has not. Role-play will last for approximately 10 minutes. Open class discussion will follow moderated by the instructor.

	1986		1993	
Rank	New Hires	Current	New Hires	Current
Full professors	$47,000	$42,000	$68,000	$56,000
Associate professors	$39,000	$36,000	$62,000	$51,000
Assistant professors	$34,000	$30,000	$52,000	$48,000
	2000		NOW	
Rank	New Hires	Current	New Hires	Current
Full professors	$79,000	$62,000	$99,935	$76,291
Associate professors	$73,000	$61,000	$92,345	$70,797
Assistant professors	$61,000	$59,000	$80,644	$69,443

Emerging Trends Case 10.4   YOU MANAGE IT!

More Suits for Overtime Pay

Alleged violations of the Fair Labor Standards Act (FLSA) are on the increase. For instance, in a recent year:
- More than 31,000 complaints were registered against employers.

- More than 342,000 employees received back wages.
- Back wages (not including penalties) totaled more than $200 million.
- More than 70 percent of the violations were initiated by an employee complaint.[a]

Let's Take a Look at a Specific Case

Hidetomo Morimoto took a job at a tech company that translates English software into Japanese. With the burst of the tech bubble, he was grateful for the job, even though it paid just $1,800 a month to start. He soon found himself working 60 hours a week, Mr. Morimoto says, and during crunch times often didn't leave till 1:00 A.M. Yet he says he never received any overtime pay.[b]

In May, after he complained in an Internet posting that some employers took advantage of their Japanese staff's strong work ethic, Mr. Morimoto found himself out of work. Now the 31-year-old translator is suing his old employer, demanding the overtime pay he says he should have received. The employer, Pacific Software Publishing Inc. in Bellevue, Washington, maintains it wasn't remiss, because Mr. Morimoto spent all his extra hours in the office on personal matters, not work. It is countersuing, alleging defamation.

Pacific Software Publishing Inc. is not alone. In one suit, several former salesmen last year accused Oracle Corp. of failing to keep accurate time records of their work in order to avoid paying them overtime. A former IBM technician has sued IBM, alleging that managers asked him to manipulate his time cards to reduce overtime pay. The technician, Ray Wheeler, says he was laid off when he complained.

Labor suits for overtime pay such as these are hitting technology outfits in waves, from startups to mature companies. "Wage-and-hour class-action lawsuits have now invaded high-tech in the valley," says Lynne Hermle, an attorney representing several companies.

A result is the kind of wage-and-hour suits previously seen in such old-line industries such as retailing and hotels. "Reality has set in," says Harvey Sohnen, a labor attorney in Orinda, California. He says that "many tech workers are net slaves, putting in unconscionable hours and getting nothing but ashes in their mouth . . . Now they just want to get paid."

Critical Thinking Questions

1. Why do you think there is an increase in the number of cases alleging violations of the FLSA, one of the oldest pieces of legislation governing compensation passed back in the 1930s? Explain.

2. If you were a manager at one of the affected companies, how would you make sure that the company is in compliance with FLSA when dealing with employees such as Mr. Marimoto? Explain.

3. Do you think that workers who complain against employers for FLSA violations may hurt themselves in the market place as other firms may refuse to hire them? If you were in Mr. Marimoto's shoes, what would you have done? Explain.

Team Exercise

According to one observer, not too long ago professional employers "bragged about their long hours and disdained overtime pay as the mark of a clock-watcher."[c] Class is divided into teams of five. Each team is asked to analyze the reasons for what seems to be recent changes in employee attitudes toward overtime pay and their willingness to sue employers for alleged FLSA violations, which until now has been unprecedented among professional employees.

Experiential Exercise

You have been asked by a company to write a section in its employee handbook that specifically outlines the criteria that must be met before employees are eligible for overtime as required by law. The instructor will select some of the best examples produced by class members and distribute them to the class. These will then serve as a rallying point for class discussion.

Sources: [a]Alper, D. E., and Gerard, D. (2005, March). FLSA update. *Workspan,* 38–41; [b]Adapted with permission from Pui-Wing, T., and Wingfield, N. (2005, February 24). As tech matures, workers fill a spate of salary complaints. *Wall Street Journal,* A-1; [c]*Ibid.*

YOU MANAGE IT! | # Emerging Trends Case 10.5

A Challenge at Antle Corporation

Antle Corporation (a fictitious name for a company known to one of this book's authors) is a large electronics and computer firm headquartered on the East Coast. It has more than 100,000 employees. Founded in 1912, Antle was generally regarded as the world's number-one designer and manufacturer of large computer equipment from the late 1940s until the late 1980s. At its peak, its share of the market was estimated at 80 percent.

The compensation system at Antle has evolved through the decades, and top managers as well as employees report high levels of satisfaction with it. The following are the essential elements of the compensation system:

- All jobs are evaluated using a point factor approach once every 10 years, with minor adjustments made in between evaluations to correct inequities.
- The company hires a consulting firm once a year to conduct a salary survey for benchmark jobs. The company's

pay policy is to peg salaries at the 75th percentile of the market.

■ There are 25 grade levels in the company. Employees increase their pay level mainly by moving up the corporate hierarchy over time. The typical employee remains three years in one job before being promoted to a job at the next grade level. All employees are hired at the entry level and are groomed within the company. Although promotions are ostensibly based exclusively on performance, in practice "time on grade" plays an important role in deciding who is ready to move up.

■ Perquisites and special benefits are closely tied to grade level. Stock options, for instance, are available only to employees in grades 17 through 25.

■ Pay and promotion decisions are highly centralized.

■ The only variable compensation comes from a profit-sharing plan under which the company funds a retirement plan for each employee based on the firm's profitability over the preceding year.

■ Although "pay for performance" is the company's official policy, most employees view job security and upward mobility over time as the main rewards offered by the firm.

■ A strict pay-secrecy policy is in force.

For the past 10 years, Antle's market share has been declining at an average rate of 2 percent annually. The board of directors decided to offer early retirement to Antle's chief executive officer, Alan Steven, who had been at the helm for almost 20 years, and replaced him with Peter Merton, who was hired from a smaller but fast-growing competitor. Merton's mandate is to reverse the company's declining market share by fostering growth and enhancing flexibility.

Because labor costs are almost 70 percent of Antle's total costs, one of Merton's first actions was to appoint a committee to examine the firm's compensation practices. The committee included the vice president for human resources, the comptroller, and two external human resource consultants. Four months later, the committee produced a report identifying several key problems with Antle's compensation system and related HRM practices. These problems, according to the report, add to Antle's production costs and reduce the company's flexibility and capacity to respond to market changes. The committee's report presented the following conclusions:

■ The firm has too many management layers. This is expensive and slows communication.

■ Most employees have developed a sense of entitlement; that is, they feel they "deserve" regular raises and promotions. This perception has had a negative effect on motivation.

■ The promotion-from-within policy has meant that once hired, very few employees are terminated, even if they are not performing up to standard. As a result, many employees are trapped at Antle because they cannot earn an equivalent salary at any other company.

■ Jobs are too narrowly defined, increasing labor costs and preventing people from working to their full potential.

■ The company is top heavy with highly paid employees whose best days are over but who are still many years from retirement.

■ The firm's tradition of providing job security is now putting it at a disadvantage because it cannot reduce its labor force to remain competitive.

■ The firm has not been taking advantage of outsourcing to foreign locations in order to preserve employee loyalty. But this means that competitors who are going to places such as China and India enjoy a substantial compensation edge, which improves their bottom line.

After reading the report, Merton is trying to decide what to do about the problems that have been identified.

Critical Thinking Questions

1. Based on what you've read about Antle, do you agree with the problems identified by the committee? If not, what alternative set of problems or issues do you see?
2. What are the pros and cons of Antle's compensation policies? Are they attuned to its new business strategies of fostering growth, increasing market share, and enhancing flexibility to respond to competitors?
3. What recommendations would you offer Alan Merton for redesigning Antel's compensation system?

Team Exercise

Peter Merton has set up a committee composed of the HR director, two general managers, two senior employees, and one external HR consultant. The committee, composed of six students each, will provide recommendations to Merton (played by the instructor) as to what the company should do next to deal with the problems outlined in the report. Depending on the size of the class, several teams (each representing a committee of six) will make a 15-minute presentation. The instructor will then discuss issues raised with the entire class.

Experiential Exercise

Students will assume various roles (HR director, general manager, senior employee and external HR consultant) and each will represent his or her perspective depending on the assigned role. Role-play should last approximately 15 minutes, to be followed by an open class discussion. Roles include Peter Merton (CEO), the HR director, one senior employee with more than 20 years with the company, one union member representing factory workers, and an independent external consultant.

Rewarding Performance

Challenges

After reading this chapter, you should be able to deal more effectively with the following challenges:

1 **Recognize** individual and group contributions to the firm by rewarding high performers.

2 **Develop** pay-for-performance plans that are appropriate for different levels in an organization.

3 **Identify** the potential benefits and drawbacks of different pay-for-performance systems and choose the plan that is most appropriate for a particular firm.

4 **Design** an executive compensation package that motivates executives to make decisions that are in the firm's best interests.

5 **Weigh** the pros and cons of different compensation methods for sales personnel and create an incentive plan that is consistent with the firm's marketing strategy.

6 **Design** an incentive system to reward excellence in customer service.

Century Telephone Company bases its employees' annual pay raises on how well employees perform their job duties. For the past 10 years, these "merit raises" have averaged 4.5 percent of base pay. About two years ago the HR department conducted an employee attitude survey. One of its most striking findings: More than 75 percent of employees felt that pay raises and performance were unrelated. In response, top managers asked the HR staff to determine whether pay raises were indeed based on performance (as required by policy) or on some other unrelated factors. Surprisingly, the data showed that employees were right: Supervisors rated more than 80 percent of their workers as "excellent," and there was only minimal differentiation in the percentage raises received by individual employees.

Top management concluded that supervisors were equalizing performance ratings and raises, sidestepping their responsibility to reward employees on the basis of performance.

To remedy the situation, Century instituted a new procedure a year ago. Under this new system, supervisors must distribute employee performance ratings as follows: excellent (top 15%), very good (next 20%), good (next 20%), satisfactory (next 35%), marginal or unsatisfactory (lowest 10%). Pay raises are pegged to these performance classifications, with employees at the top receiving a 10 percent raise and those at the bottom receiving nothing.

Shortly after the system was put in place, it became obvious that something had gone wrong. A large number of employees could not understand how or why their performance had "dropped" compared to the previous year. Many believed that favoritism played a big role in who received pay increases. Irate employees hounded their supervisors, who in turn complained that increased tension was poisoning interpersonal relationships and interfering with performance.

THE MANAGERIAL PERSPECTIVE

Attempting to motivate employees with pay incentives can backfire, as the experience at Century Telephone (a real company given a fictitious name) shows. Nonetheless, the use of pay incentives is increasing. In 1988, the number of U.S. companies offering pay for performance (chiefly in the form of bonus) to all salaried employees was 47 percent. By 2006, experts estimated that close to 95 percent of U.S. companies do so.[1]

What these numbers do not tell us is the mushrooming of creative incentive plans that are being implemented. For instance, almost all of the publicly traded "Best Companies" in *Fortune*'s list are experimenting with all kinds of monetary and nonmonetary incentives for employees. JM Family Enterprises in Florida offers top performers free haircuts, manicures, and day trips to the Bahamas on the company yacht. Kingston Technology Co., Inc., besides buying free monthly lunches, offers quarterly performance-based bonuses that sometimes exceed the typical employee's full year's salary.[2] At Men's Wearhouse, a clothing company with almost 10,000 employees, executives gave away 113 trips to Hawaii for top performers. After five years, outstanding employees are also eligible for a three-week paid sabbatical.[3]

Kingston Technology Co., Inc., owners John Tu and David Sun believe in creating a work environment that motivates 2,400 employees. To reward top performers, Kingston offers creative incentives, such as free lunches and hefty bonuses.

In this chapter, we discuss the design and implementation of pay-for-performance (incentive) systems. First, we address the major challenges facing managers in their attempts to link pay and performance. Second, we offer a set of general recommendations to deal with these challenges. Third, we describe specific types of pay-for-performance programs and the advantages and disadvantages of each. We conclude with a discussion of unique pay-for-performance plans for two important employee groups, executives and sales personnel.

Pay for Performance: The Challenges

Most workers believe that those who work harder and produce more should be rewarded accordingly. If employees see that pay is not distributed on the basis of merit, they are more likely to lack commitment to the organization, decrease their level of effort, and look for employment opportunities elsewhere.[4]

Pay-for-performance system or incentive system
A system that rewards employees on the assumptions that (1) individual employees and work teams differ in how much they contribute to the firm; (2) the firm's overall performance depends to a large degree on the performance of individuals and groups within the firm; and (3) to attract, retain, and motivate high performers and to be fair to all employees, the firm needs to reward employees on the basis of their relative performance.

Pay-for-performance systems, also called **incentive systems**, reward employee performance on the basis of three assumptions:[5]

1. Individual employees and work teams differ in how much they contribute to the firm—not only in what they do but also in how well they do it.
2. The firm's overall performance depends to a large degree on the performance of individuals and groups within the firm.
3. To attract, retain, and motivate high performers and to be fair to all employees, a company needs to reward employees on the basis of their relative performance.

Before talking about specific types of pay-for-performance plans, we will discuss nine challenges facing organizations that want to adopt an incentive system.

The "Do Only What You Get Paid For" Syndrome

To avoid the charge that pay is distributed on the basis of subjective judgments or favoritism, pay-for-performance systems tend to rely on objective indicators of performance.[6] This may lead some managers to use whatever "objective" data are available to justify pay decisions. Unfortunately, the more closely pay is tied to particular performance indicators, the more employees tend to focus on those indicators and neglect other important job components that are more difficult to measure. Consider the following examples:

■ In some school systems where teachers' pay has been linked to students' scores on standardized tests, teachers spend more time helping students do well on the tests than helping them understand the subject matter. As one expert has noted, "When you interview the teachers, they tell you they would like to teach other things, but they feel they have to teach to the test [because] they are afraid that a poor showing by their pupils will result in negative evaluations for themselves or their schools."[7]
■ Administrators in many colleges and universities rely on student ratings to evaluate faculty performance, even though many people believe that this measure reflects popularity more than quality of instruction.
■ Part of the reason for the scandals associated with Arthur Andersen (one of the five largest accounting firms with 85,000 employees) and subsequent legal problems may have been the way its managers were rewarded for volume of revenues generated through consulting and accounting fees. This may have led managers to poorly monitor their clients (and in some cases approve of outright fraud) for fear of losing lucrative contracts.[8]

Unethical Behaviors

By creating pressure to produce and to "keep score," incentives may induce employees to engage in undesirable behaviors, to cut corners, deceive, misinform, hide negative information, take more credit than they deserve, and the like. Managers may look the other way, because it could be to their advantage to preside over a unit that "meets or exceeds" targets. What starts as a matter of interpretation or perhaps "white lies" may eventually fall into unethical or even illegal terrain. Several examples have recently come to light across a variety of industries; see the Manager's Notebook, "Perverse Incentives." These examples are only the tip of the iceberg; the majority of cases are never reported; hence, it is difficult to know the extent of the problem.

Unfortunately employee cynicism about company ethics and senior leadership are also on the rise. A 2005 survey showed that only 50 percent of employees believed their top executives had high integrity and approximately the same percentage shared similar feelings about the entire organization.[9] As a result, employees may unconsciously blame their employer for questionable behaviors or ethical lapses in order to meet incentive criteria ("they made me do it," "that is the way things get done around here") rather than take full responsibility for their actions.

Negative Effects on the Spirit of Cooperation

The experiences of Century Telephone Company clearly show that pay-for-performance systems may provoke conflict and competition while discouraging cooperation.[10] For instance, employees may withhold information from a colleague if they believe that it will help the other person get ahead. Those who are receiving less than they feel they deserve may try to "get back" at those who are receiving more, perhaps by sabotaging a project or spreading rumors. Internal competition may set off rivalries that lead to quality problems or even cheating.

Lack of Control

Factors beyond an employee's control include the supervisor, performance of other work group members, the quality of the materials the employee is working with, working conditions, the amount of support from management, and environmental factors.[11]

For instance, many medical doctors in group practice now receive a substantial portion of their pay in the form of a bonus. Yet, doctors commonly complain that managed care bureaucrats try to slash revenues as doctors' overhead costs rise. As a result, the managed care system pressures physicians to see more patients in less time. In addition, "[n]urses and pharmacists are allowed to poach on [doctors'] territory."[12] Union membership is soaring among doctors as many see such a situation as demoralizing and inequitable.[13]

Ethics

MANAGER'S NOTEBOOK

Perverse Incentives

Without a firm's intending it, the criteria used to provide a particular incentive may tempt employees to engage in questionable or perhaps even immoral acts and even to cross the line into illegal activities. Some recent examples follow.

Keeping Customers in the Dark

Marsh & McLennan Companies, one of the largest insurance brokers in the United States, received more than $850 million in incentive payments from insurance companies. Insurance brokers at Marsh & McLennan apparently joined in those incentives, which resulted in increased costs to customers. In 2005, some of Marsh & McLennan's brokers pleaded guilty to fraud charges in New York and said the company deliberately worked to keep customers from finding out how the incentive payments worked.[a]

Rental Car Agencies' Insurance Pitches

Car rental companies make a lot of their profits by selling insurance to car renters, an amount that reaches $22 per day on average for most car classes. Dollar and Thrifty, among others, give their employees financial incentives to sell more coverage. Insurance represents about 15 percent of revenues for those two agencies' parent company, Dollar Thrifty Automotive Group Inc. Yet a surprising amount of what the rental car companies push is already covered by credit card companies and the renter's own auto insurance policy. One of the authors of this text had a recent experience at a car rental company. After he told the company employee that he was already covered by MasterCard, the employee responded, "It doesn't matter. If anything happens to the car, we will come after you."[b]

Financial Incentives to Choose More Efficient Medical Care

UnitedHealthcare recently launched a program that enables employers in 13 states to provide financial incentives to employees who choose doctors on a "performance physicians" list. UnitedHealthcare analyzed two years' worth of claims data to identify high-performance physicians—those physicians who provide higher-quality, lower-cost care according to the program's criteria. In areas where the program is in place, on average, about 25 percent of doctors in UnitedHealthcare's network are on the list, the company says. Three large companies—General Motors, DaimlerChrysler AG's Chrysler Group unit, and UPS—have adjusted some of their health benefits so that employees have incentives, such as lower copayments, to go to these doctors. The doctors benefit by having a greater influx of patients covered by insurers. Some physician groups (such as the American Medical Association) see the program as an imprecise money-saving effort that emphasizes cost far more than quality and that limits access to care.[c]

Sources: [a]Adapted with permission from Treaster, J. B. (2005, February 21). Settlement seen for Aon over incentive payments. *New York Times,* B-1; [b]Adapted with permission from Schechner, S. (2005, March 29). Scrutinizing car rental-car agencies' insurance pitches. *Wall Street Journal,* D-8; [c]Rubenstein, S. (2005, March 29). Doctors rap UnitedHealthcare for its new evaluation program. *Wall Street Journal,* D-3.

Difficulties in Measuring Performance

As we saw in Chapter 7, assessing employee performance is one of the thorniest tasks a manager faces, particularly when the assessments are used to dispense rewards.[14] At the employee level, the appraiser must try to untangle individual contributions from those of the work group while avoiding judgments based on a personality bias (being a strict or a lenient rater), likes and dislikes, and political agendas. At the group or team level, the rater must try to isolate the specific contributions of any given team when all teams are interdependent.[15] Appraisers experience the same difficulties in attempting to determine the performance of plants or units that are interrelated among themselves and with corporate headquarters. In short, accurate measures of performance are not easy to achieve, and tying pay to inaccurate measures is likely to create problems.

Psychological Contracts

Once implemented, a pay-for-performance system creates a psychological contract between the employee and the firm.[16] A *psychological contract* is a set of expectations based on prior experience, and it is very resistant to change.

Breaking a psychological contract can have damaging results. For instance, when a computer products manufacturer changed the terms of its pay-for-performance program three times in a two-year period, the result was massive employee protests, the resignation of several key managers, and a general lowering of employee morale.

Two other problems may arise with respect to the psychological contract. First, because employees feel entitled to the reward spelled out in the pay-for-performance plan, it is difficult to change the plan even when conditions call for a change. Second, it is sometimes hard to come up with a formula that is fair to diverse employee groups.

The Credibility Gap

Employees often do not believe that pay-for-performance programs are fair or that they truly reward performance, a phenomenon called the *credibility gap*.[17] Some recent studies indicate that as many as 75 percent of a typical firm's employees question the integrity of pay-for-performance plans.[18] If employees do not consider the system legitimate and acceptable, it may have negative rather than positive effects on their behavior.

In a well-intended attempt by the British government to reward good teaching, "superhead" teachers can earn up to $140,000 a year, a big change from a system where teachers were stuck at the $46,000-a-year level. The bumper pay raises are linked to exam results, lower truancy rates, and improved mathematical and literacy rates. Even though no teacher would receive a pay cut (that is, there is only upside potential to earn more money), teachers' unions have vigorously opposed the program. They argue that teachers cannot always be blamed if pupils do badly and that the bonus received may depend more on luck than performance.[19]

Job Dissatisfaction and Stress

Pay-for-performance systems may lead to greater productivity but lower job satisfaction.[20] Some research suggests that the more pay is tied to performance, the more the work unit begins to unravel and the more unhappy employees become.[21] Exhibit 11.1, "Incentives That Backfired: The Case of Lantech," illustrates how incentives can raise stress along with productivity.

Incentives That Backfired: The Case of Lantech

EXHIBIT 11.1

Lantech, a small manufacturer of machinery in Kentucky, learned through firsthand experience how incentive plans can backfire:

> Incentive pay encourages workers to improve quality, cut costs, and otherwise enhance the corporate good. Right? Well, that's the way it's supposed to work. In the real world, pay for performance can also release passions that turn workers into rival gangs, so greedy for extra dollars they will make another gang's numbers look bad to make their own look good. Such was the experience of Pat Lancaster, the chairman of Lantech. . . . To his dismay, Lancaster discovered that the lust for bonus bucks grew so overheated and so petty that one of his workers tried to stiff a competing division for the toilet paper bill.
>
> "Incentive pay is toxic," says Lancaster, "because it is so open to favoritism and manipulation."
>
> At one point, each of the company's five manufacturing divisions was given a bonus determined by how much profit it made. An individual worker's share of the bonus could amount to as much as 10 percent of his or her regular pay. But the divisions are so interdependent, it was very difficult to sort out which division was entitled to what profits. "That led to so much secrecy, politicking, and sucking noise that you wouldn't believe it," says CEO Jim Lancaster, Pat's son. For example, the division that built standard machines and the one that added custom design features to those machines depended on each other for parts, engineering expertise, and such. So inevitably the groups clashed, each one trying to assign costs to the other and claim credit for revenues.
>
> "I was spending 95 percent of my time in conflict resolution instead of on how to serve our customers," recalls Pat. The divisions wrangled so long over who would get charged for overhead cranes to haul heavy equipment around the factory floor that Lantech couldn't install those useful machines until 1992, several years later than planned. At the end of each month, the divisions would rush to fill orders from other parts of the company. Such behavior created profits for the division filling the order but, unfortunately, generated piles of unnecessary and costly inventory in the receiving division. Some employees even argued over who would have to pay for the toilet paper in the common restrooms.
>
> So Lantech has finally abandoned individual and division performance pay, and relies instead on a profit-sharing system in which all employees get bonuses based on salary. Furious passions have subsided, and the company is doing just fine now, says the senior Lancaster.

Source: Reprinted from Nulty, P. (1995, November 13). Incentive pay can be crippling, *Fortune*, 235.

A Question of Ethics

How much consideration should the organization give to the psychological health of its employees when designing a pay-for-performance system?

Potential Reduction of Intrinsic Drives

Pay-for-performance programs may push employees to the point of doing whatever it takes to get the promised monetary reward and in the process stifle their talents and creativity. Thus, an organization that puts too much emphasis on pay in attempting to influence behaviors may reduce employees' *intrinsic drives*. One expert argues that the more a firm stresses pay as an incentive for high performance, the less likely it is that employees will engage in activities that benefit the organization (such as overtime and extra special service) unless they are promised an explicit reward.[22]

Meeting the Challenges of Pay-for-Performance Systems

Properly designed pay-for-performance systems present managers with an excellent opportunity to align employees' interests with those of the organization. The following recommendations can help to enhance the success of performance programs and avoid the pitfalls we just discussed.

Link Pay and Performance Appropriately

Piece-rate system
A compensation system in which employees are paid per unit produced.

There are few cases in which managers can justify paying workers according to a preestablished formula or measure. Traditional **piece-rate systems**, in which workers are paid per unit produced, represent the tightest link between pay and performance. Many piece-rate systems have been abandoned because they tend to create the kinds of problems discussed earlier, but there are situations in which piece-rate plans are appropriate. The primary requirement is that the employee has complete control over the speed and quality of the work. Interestingly enough, the Internet is creating a new type of piece-rate system in which employees have control over the speed and quality of work. It has allowed many firms, particularly high-tech companies, to have employees work elsewhere (including at home), thereby saving office space, overhead, and supervisory time. Many of the employees work on a contract basis so the company saves on benefits.

Use Pay for Performance as Part of a Broader HRM System

Pay-for-performance programs are not likely to achieve the desired results unless they are accompanied by complementary HRM programs. For instance, performance appraisals and supervisory training usually play a major role in the eventual success or failure of a pay-for-performance plan. As we saw in Chapter 7, performance ratings are often influenced by factors other than performance. Because a defective appraisal process can undermine even the most carefully conceived pay plan, supervisors should be rigorously trained in correct rating practice.

Poor staffing practices can also damage the credibility of a pay-for-performance program. For instance, if employees are hired because of their political connections rather than for their skills and abilities, other employees will get the message that good performance is not that important to the organization.

Employees should also receive training to make them more productive so they are able to earn more. For instance, the U.S. division of Swiss giant Roche, based in Indianapolis, puts all its employees with high leadership potential through a 10-month development program.[23]

Build Employee Trust

Even the best-conceived pay-for-performance program can fail if managers have a poor history of labor relations or if the organization has a cutthroat culture. Under these conditions, employees are likely to attribute rewards not to good performance, but rather to chance or good impression management. If a pay-for-performance program is to have a chance of succeeding, managers need to build employee trust, which may require making major changes in the organization's climate.[24]

Managers should start by answering these questions from their employees' perspective: Does it pay for me to work longer, harder, or smarter? and Does anyone notice my extra efforts?

If the answers are no, managers need to go all out to show that they care about employees and are aware of the work they do. Even more important, they need to keep employees informed and involved when making any changes in management or the compensation plan.[25]

Promote the Belief That Performance Makes a Difference

Because of the problems noted earlier, managers may shy away from using pay to reward performance.[26] However, unless an organization creates an atmosphere in which performance makes a difference, it may end up with a low-achievement organizational culture. In a sense, then, pay-for-performance systems are the lesser of two evils because without them, performance may drop even lower.[27]

Use Multiple Layers of Rewards

Because all pay-for-performance systems have positive and negative features, providing different types of pay incentives for different work situations is likely to produce better results than relying on a single type of pay incentive. With a multiple-layers-of-reward system, the organization can realize the benefits of each incentive plan while minimizing its negative side effects. For instance, at AT&T Credit, variable pay (in the form of bonuses) was based on 12 measures reflecting the performance of both regional teams and the entire business unit. Team members had to meet their individual performance goals to qualify for variable pay.[28]

Increase Employee Involvement

An old saying among compensation practitioners is: "Acceptability is the ultimate determinant of success in any compensation plan." When employees do not view a compensation program as legitimate, they will usually do whatever they can to subvert the system—from setting maximum production quotas for themselves to shunning coworkers who receive the highest rewards. The best way to increase acceptance is to have employees participate in the design of the pay plan.[29] Employee involvement will result in a greater understanding of the rationale behind the plan, greater commitment to the pay plan, and a better match between individual needs and pay-plan design.[30]

Employee participation in designing the plan is not the same as employee dispensation of the rewards. Managers should still control and allocate rewards because employees may not be able to separate self-interest from effective pay administration. Managers can, however, solicit employee input by instituting an appeal mechanism that allows workers to voice their complaints about how rewards have been distributed. Such a mechanism is likely to enhance the perceived fairness of the system, particularly if a disinterested third party acts as an arbitrator and is empowered to take corrective actions.[31]

Stress the Importance of Acting Ethically

Once a pay-for-performance system is in place, employees may be tempted to manipulate whatever criteria are being used to trigger incentives. Even the tightest monitoring systems may not be able to catch all transgressions. Hence, the organization is better off if employees can monitor themselves. To this end, ethics as a corporate value cannot be emphasized enough, and training programs providing examples of "gray" or unethical behaviors may help employees better decide when it is appropriate or inappropriate to act in a particular way in order to meet performance expectations.

Use Motivation and Nonfinancial Incentives

One of the most basic facts of motivation is that people are driven to obtain the things they need or want. Although pay is certainly a strong motivator, it is not an equally strong motivator for everyone. Some people are more interested in the nonfinancial aspects of their work.

Nonfinancial rewards include public and nonpublic praise, honorary titles, expanded job responsibilities, paid and unpaid sabbatical leaves, mentoring programs, and 100-percent tuition reimbursements.[32] Even if it is impossible to provide a financial reward for a job well done, many employees appreciate overt recognition of excellent performance. However, as discussed in Chapter 10, organizations need to be careful that employees do not come to see nonfinancial rewards as a ruse to justify compensation savings at their expense.

Types of Pay-for-Performance Plans

As Figure 11.1 shows, pay-for-performance plans can be designed to reward the performance of the individual, team, business unit or plant, entire organization, or any combination of these. All these plans have advantages and disadvantages, and each is more effective in some situations than in others. Most organizations are best served by using a variety of plans.

Individual-Based Plans

At the micro level, firms attempt to identify and reward the contributors of individual employees. *Individual-based pay plans* are the most widely used pay-for-performance plans in industry.[33]

Of the individual-based plans commonly used, merit pay is by far the most popular; its use is almost universal.[34] **Merit pay** consists of an increase in base pay, normally given once a year. Supervisors' ratings of employees' performance are typically used to determine the amount of merit pay granted. For instance, subordinates whose performance is rated "below expectations," "achieved expectations," "exceeded expectations," and "far exceeded expectations" may receive 0 percent, 3 percent, 6 percent, and 9 percent pay raises, respectively. Once a merit pay increase is given to an employee, it remains a part of that employee's base salary for the rest of his or her tenure with the firm (except under extreme conditions, such as a general wage cut or a demotion).

Individual **bonus programs** (sometimes called **lump-sum payments**) are similar to merit pay programs but differ in one important respect. Bonuses are given on a one-time basis and do not raise the employee's base pay permanently. Bonuses tend to be larger than merit pay increases because they involve lower risk to the employer (the employer is not making a permanent financial commitment). Bonuses can also be given outside the annual review cycle when employees achieve certain milestones (for example, every month that Continental ranks among the top five airlines in on-time arrivals, employees receive a check for at least $65) or offer a valuable cost-saving suggestion. A recent survey shows that 92 percent of firms offer special one-time spot awards, and 28 percent provide lump-sum payments to their employees. These types of bonuses often exceed 5 percent of annual salary.[35]

Merit pay
An increase in base pay, normally given once a year.

Bonus program or lump-sum payment
A financial incentive that is given on a one-time basis and does not raise the employee's base pay permanently.

Pay-for-Performance Programs

Figure 11.1

Unit of Analysis			
Micro Level		Macro Level	
Individual	Team	Business Unit/Plant	Organization
Merit pay	Bonuses	Gainsharing	Profit sharing
Bonuses	Awards	Bonuses	Stock plans
Awards		Awards	
Piece rate			

Awards, like bonuses, are one-time rewards but tend to be given in the form of a tangible prize, such as a paid vacation, a television set, or a dinner for two at a fancy restaurant.

Award
A one-time reward usually given in the form of a tangible prize.

Advantages of Individual-Based Pay-for-Performance Plans

Individual-based plans have four major advantages:

Expectancy theory
A theory of behavior holding that people tend to do those things that are rewarded.

- **Performance that is rewarded is likely to be repeated.** A widely accepted theory of motivation, known as **expectancy theory,** explains why higher pay leads to higher performance. People tend to do those things that are rewarded. Money is an important reward to most people, so individuals tend to improve their work performance when a strong performance-pay linkage exists.[36]
- **Individuals are goal oriented and financial incentives can shape an individual's goals over time.** A pay incentive plan can help make employees' behavior consistent with the organization's goals.[37] For instance, if an automobile dealer has a sales employee who sells a lot of cars, but whose customers rarely return to the dealership, the dealer might implement a pay incentive plan that gives a higher sales commission for cars sold to repeat buyers. This plan would encourage the sales staff to please the customer rather than just sell the car.
- **Assessing the performance of each employee individually helps the firm achieve individual equity.** An organization must provide rewards in proportion to individual efforts. Individual-based plans do exactly this. If individuals are not rewarded, high performers may leave the firm or reduce their performance level to make it consistent with the payment they are receiving.
- **Individual-based plans fit in with an individualistic culture.** National cultures vary in the emphasis they place on individual achievement versus group achievement (see Chapter 17). The United States is at the top of the list in valuing individualism, and U.S. workers expect to be rewarded for their personal accomplishments and contributions.

In contrast to U.S. firms, the Japanese do not tend to reward individual performance but economic pressures seem to be moving the Japanese toward a more "American" model. In a recent survey, 70 percent of Japanese leaders said they plan to cut wages and that only top performers may be able to keep (or exceed) their prior earnings.[38]

Disadvantages of Individual-Based Pay-for-Performance Plans

Many of the pitfalls of pay-for-performance programs are most evident at the individual level. Two particular dangers are that individual plans may (1) create competition and destroy cooperation among peers and (2) sour working relationships between subordinates and supervisors. And because many managers believe that below-average raises are demoralizing to employees and discourage better performance, they tend to equalize the percentage increases among employees, regardless of individual performance. This, of course, defeats the very purpose of an incentive plan.

Other disadvantages of individual-based plans include the following:

- **Tying pay to goals may promote single-mindedness.** Linking financial incentives to the achievement of goals may lead to a narrow focus and the avoidance of important tasks, either because goals are difficult to set for these tasks or because their accomplishment is difficult to measure at the individual level. For instance, if a grocery store sets a goal of happy and satisfied customers, it would be extremely difficult to link achievement of this goal to individual employees.
- **Many employees do not believe that pay and performance are linked.** Although practically all organizations claim to reward individual performance, it is difficult for employees to determine to what extent their companies really do so. So it should come as no surprise that many surveys over the past three decades have found that up to 80 percent of employees do not see a connection between personal contributions and pay raises.[39] The beliefs underlying this perception, many of which have proved to be very resistant to change, are summarized in Figure 11.2.
- **Individual pay plans may work against achieving quality goals.** Individuals rewarded for meeting production goals often sacrifice product quality. Individual-based plans also work

Figure 11.2

- Performance appraisal is inherently subjective, with supervisors evaluating subordinates according to their own preconceived biases.
- Regardless of the appraisal form used, supervisors tend to manipulate the ratings.
- Merit systems emphasize individual rather than group goals, and this may lead to dysfunctional conflict in the organization.
- To maintain an effective working relationship with all subordinates and prevent interpersonal conflict within the team, the supervisor may be reluctant to single out individuals for special recognition with pay.
- The use of a specified time period (normally one year) for the performance evaluation encourages a short-term orientation at the expense of long-term goals.
- Employees try to defend their ego by ignoring negative performance feedback, blaming the organization for their problems.
- Supervisors and employees seldom agree on the evaluation, leading to interpersonal confrontations.
- Supervisors often do not know how to justify a particular pay raise recommendation to an employee.
- Increments in financial rewards are spaced in such a way that their reinforcement value for work behaviors is questionable. For example, becoming twice as productive now has little perceived effect on pay when the employee must wait a whole year for a performance review.
- Individual merit pay systems are less appropriate for the service sector, where many people in the United States work. In knowledge-based jobs (such as "administrative assistant"), it is even difficult to specify what the desired product is.
- Supervisors typically control a rather limited amount of compensation, so merit pay differentials are normally quite small and, therefore, of questionable value.
- A number of bureaucratic factors that influence the size and frequency of merit pay (for example, position in salary range, pay relationships within the unit and between units, and budgetary limitations) have little to do with employee performance.
- Performance appraisals are designed for multiple purposes (training and development, selection, work planning, compensation, and so forth). When a system is used to accomplish so many objectives, it is questionable whether it can accomplish any of them well. It is difficult for the supervisor to play the role of counselor or adviser and evaluator at the same time.

Source: Updated (2006) from Balkin, D. B., and Gómez-Mejía, L. R. (Eds.). (1987). *New perspectives on compensation,* 159. Upper Saddle River, NJ: Prentice Hall.

against quality programs that emphasize teamwork because they generally do not reward employees for helping other workers or coordinating work with other departments.

- **Individual-based programs promote inflexibility in some organizations.** Because supervisors generally control the rewards, individual-based pay-for-performance plans promote dependence on supervisors. Thus, they prop up traditional organizational structures, which make them particularly ineffective for firms trying to take a team approach to work.

When Are Individual-Based Plans Most Likely to Succeed?

Despite the challenges they present to managers, rewards based on individual performance can be highly motivating, usually under the following conditions:

- **When the contributions of individual employees can be accurately isolated.** Identifying any one person's contributions is easier for some jobs than for others. For instance, a strong individual incentive system can work well with salespeople because it is relatively easy to measure their accomplishments. In contrast, research scientists in industry are generally not offered individual-based performance incentives because they typically work so closely together that individual contributions are hard to identify.
- **When the job demands autonomy.** The more independently employees work, the more it makes sense to assess and reward the performance of each individual. The performance of

managers of individual stores in a large retail chain like Gap can be rated fairly easily, whereas the performance of the HR director in a large company is much more difficult to assess.

■ **When cooperation is less critical to successful performance or when competition is to be encouraged.** Practically all jobs require some cooperation, but the less cooperation needed, the more successful an individual-based pay program will be. For example, less employee cooperation is expected of a stockbroker than of a pilot in an Air Force squadron.

Team-Based Plans

A growing number of firms are redesigning work to allow employees with unique skills and backgrounds to tackle projects or problems together. For instance, at Compaq Computer Corp., as many as 25 percent of the company's 16,000 employees are on teams that develop new products and bring them to market.[40] Employees in this new system are expected to cross job boundaries within their team and to contribute in areas in which they have not previously worked. Other companies that have implemented a team approach to job and work design are Clairol/Bristol-Myers Squibb, Hershey Chocolate (North America), Newsday/Times Mirror, Pratt & Whitney/United Technologies, General Motors, TRW, Digital Equipment, Shell Oil, and Honeywell.[41] A team-based compensation system can provide integral support for effective team arrangements.

Team-based pay plans normally reward all team members equally, based on group outcomes. These outcomes may be measured objectively (for example, completing a given number of team projects on time or meeting all deadlines for a group report) or subjectively (for example, using the collective assessment of a panel of managers). The criteria for defining a desirable outcome may be broad (for example, being able to work effectively with other teams) or narrow (for example, developing a patent with commercial applications). As with individual-based programs, payments to team members may be made in the form of a cash bonus or in the form of noncash awards such as trips, time off, or luxury items.

Some firms allow the team to decide how its bonus will be distributed within the group. Other companies couple team-based incentives with team-building exercises. Monsanto, for instance, made it onto *Fortune*'s 100 Best Companies in 2005 largely because of activities, such as snowshoe softball, intended to improve team cohesiveness. At several Monsanto sites, "people teams" of staffers are charged with designing employee bonding activities.[42]

A team of young managers at Yoplait Yogurt has built the company into a thriving business by setting tougher goals for themselves than the parent company, General Mills, set for them. When the team exceeded these goals, its managers collected bonuses of $30,000 to $50,000, about half their annual salaries.

Advantages of Team-Based Pay-for-Performance Plans

When properly designed, team-based incentives have two major advantages:

- **They foster group cohesiveness.** To the extent that team members have the same goals and objectives, work closely with one another, and depend on one another for the group's overall performance, team-based incentives can motivate group members to behave and think as a unit rather than as competing individuals. In this situation, each worker is more likely to act in a way that benefits the entire group.[43]
- **They aid performance measurement.** A number of studies have shown that performance can be measured more accurately and reliably for an entire team than for individuals.[44] This is true because less precise measurement is required when an individual's performance does not need to be identified and evaluated in relation to others in a group.

Disadvantages of Team-Based Pay-for-Performance Plans

Managers need to be aware of potential pitfalls with team-based plans. This may account for the limited adoption of these types of incentives, which are used by firms about a third as often as individual-based incentives.[45] The disadvantages are as follows:

- **Possible lack of fit with individualistic cultural values.** Because most U.S. workers expect to be recognized for their personal contributions, they may not react well to an incentive system in which individual efforts take a back seat to the group effort, with all team members rewarded equally. On the other side of the coin, individual incentives are likely to fail in societies with a collective orientation. In a striking display of cultural insensitivity, many U.S. companies have introduced high-risk individual incentives to their Japanese subsidiaries. These plans have generally failed.[46]
- **The free-riding effect.** In any group, some individuals put in more effort than others. In addition, ability levels differ from one person to the next. Those who contribute little to the team—either because of low effort or limited ability—are *free riders*.[47]

  When all team members (including free riders) are rewarded equally for a group outcome, there are likely to be complaints of unfairness. The result may be conflict rather than the cooperation the plan was intended to foster, with supervisors having to step in to judge who is contributing what.[48]

  To minimize the free-riding effect, some companies have been adjusting pay incentives to encourage individual performance within teams. W. L. Gore, the maker of Gore-Tex fabric, has its 4,000-plus employees evaluate fellow team members each year to individualize team-based incentives (each team member receives a payment according to his or her personal contributions as assessed by peers).[49]
- **Social pressures to limit performance.** Although group cohesiveness may motivate all team members to increase their effort and work to their full potential, it can also dampen team productivity. When commercial airline pilots want to express a grievance, for instance, they sometimes agree among themselves to fly "by the book." This means that they follow every rule without exception, leading to an overall work slowdown. Group dynamics may also encourage team members to try to beat the game—cheating to get the reward, for instance—as a way to get back at management.[50]
- **Difficulties in identifying meaningful groups.** Before they decide how to distribute rewards based on team performance, managers must define a *team*. Coming up with a definition can be tricky, because various groups may be highly interdependent, making it difficult to identify which ones did what. Also, a person may be a member of more than one team, and teams may change members frequently.
- **Intergroup competition leading to a decline in overall performance.** A team may become so focused on maximizing its own performance that it ends up competing with other teams. The results can be quite undesirable. For instance, the manufacturing group may produce more units than the marketing group can possibly sell, or the marketing group may make sales commitments that manufacturing is hard pressed to meet on schedule.[51]

Under Which Conditions Are Team-Based Plans Most Likely to Succeed?

Although managers need to be aware of the potential disadvantages of team-based plans, they should also be on the lookout for situations conducive to their successful use. Such plans are likely to be successful under the following circumstances:

■ **When work tasks are so intertwined that it is difficult to single out who did what.** This is often the case in research and development labs, where scientists and engineers work in teams. It is also the case with firefighter crews and police units, which often think of themselves as one indivisible entity.

■ **When the firm's organization facilitates the implementation of team-based incentives.** Team-based incentives are appropriate when:

   1. **There are few levels in the hierarchy, and teams of individuals at the same level are expected to complete most of their work with little dependence on supervisors or upper management.** Both public- and private-sector organizations that have had to lay off workers to maintain efficiency and profitability have found that teamwork becomes a necessity. For instance, when the city of Hampton, Virginia, underwent a massive downsizing and restructuring that resulted in the loss of several layers of supervision, it had to redesign its work. The city created self-managed teams and incorporated team-based pay into a multilayered pay-for-performance plan.[52]

   2. **Technology allows for the separation of work into relatively self-contained or independent groups.** This can be done more easily in a service unit (such as a telephone repair crew) than in a large manufacturing operation (such as a traditional automobile assembly line).

   3. **Employees are committed to their work and are intrinsically motivated.** Such workers are less likely to shirk responsibility at the expense of the group, so free riding is not a serious concern. Intrinsic motivation is often found in not-for-profit organizations, whose employees are emotionally committed to the organization's cause.

   4. **The organization needs to insist on group goals.** In some organizations this is a paramount need. For example, high-tech firms often find that their research scientists have their own research agendas and professional objectives—which are frequently incompatible with those of the firm or even their peers. Team-based incentives can focus such independent-minded employees' efforts on a common goal.[53]

   5. **Team-based incentives can help blend employees with diverse backgrounds and perspectives and focus their efforts on goals important to the organization.** See the case of Intel in the Manager's Notebook, "Linking Compensation to a Customer-Driven Strategy."

■ **When the objective is to foster entrepreneurship in self-managed work groups.** Sometimes, to encourage innovation and risk taking within employee groups, a firm will give certain groups extensive autonomy to perform their task or achieve certain objectives. This practice is often referred to as *intrapreneuring* (a term coined by Gifford Pinchot, who published a book with that title in 1985).[54] In an intrapreneuring environment, management often uses team-based incentives as a hands-off control mechanism that allows each group to assume the risk of success or failure, as entrepreneurs do.

Figure 11.3 summarizes the advantages and disadvantages of individual- and team-based pay-for-performance plans.

Plantwide Plans

Plantwide pay-for-performance plans reward all workers in a plant or business unit based on the performance of the entire plant or unit. Profits and stock prices are generally not meaningful performance measures for a plant or unit because they are the result of the entire corporation's performance. Most corporations have multiple plants or units, which make it difficult to attribute financial gains or losses to any single segment of the business. Therefore, the key performance indicator used to distribute rewards at the plant level is plant or business unit efficiency, which is normally measured in terms of labor or material cost savings compared to an earlier period.

Customer-Driven HR

Linking Compensation to a Customer-Driven Strategy

Paul S. Otellini was appointed Intel's CEO in 2005 with a mandate to change the company's culture. He's making it clear to employees that under his leadership Intel is entering a new era. Otellini is the first chief executive without an engineering degree at a company where technical types have reigned supreme. He believes that to keep Intel growing, employees should focus every idea and technical solution on meeting customers' needs. So rather than just relying on its engineering prowess, Intel reorganized in 2006 to bring together engineers, software writers, and marketers in five market-focused units: corporate computing, the digital home, mobile computing, health care, and channel products (that is, PCs for small manufacturers). "Customer-focused teamwork" is now the new mantra at Intel.

Long-dominant hardware engineers are learning to work more closely with marketers and software engineers, and their incentives are tied directly to how well they cooperate with each other. The new system will likely jolt the corporate culture. For decades, employees have been compensated for their own work. Now teams will be judged as a whole. Engineers, long the top dogs, may resist working with others. "It's like saying to a baseball player, 'Gee, we're deciding to play pro football,' " says Edward E. Lawler, a professor at the University of Southern California's Marshall School of Business. "All of a sudden, the rules of the game are very different."

Source: Adapted with permission from Edwards, C. (2005, January 31). Shaking up Intel's insides. *BusinessWeek*, 35–36.

Gainsharing
A plantwide pay-for-performance plan in which a portion of the company's cost savings is returned to workers, usually in the form of a lump-sum bonus.

Plantwide pay-for-performance programs are generally referred to as **gainsharing** programs because they return a portion of the company's cost savings to the workers, usually in the form of a lump-sum bonus. Three major types of gainsharing programs are used. The oldest is the *Scanlon Plan,* which dates back to the 1930s. It relies on committees of employees, union leaders, and top managers to generate and evaluate cost-saving ideas. If actual labor costs are lower than expected labor costs over an agreed-on period (normally one year), the difference is shared between the workers (who, as a group, usually receive 75% of the savings) and the firm (which usually receives 25% of the savings). A portion of the savings may also be set aside in a rainy day fund.

Advantages and Disadvantages of Individual- and Team-Based Pay-for-Performance Plans

Figure 11.3	Individual-Based Plans	Team-Based Plans
Advantages	■ Rewarded performance is likely to be repeated ■ Financial incentives can shape a person's goals ■ Can help the firm attain individual equity ■ Fit an individualistic culture	■ Fosters group cohesiveness ■ Aids performance measurement
Disadvantages	■ Can promote single-mindedness ■ Disbelief that pay and performance are linked ■ May work against achieving quality goals ■ May promote inflexibility	■ Possible lack of fit with individualistic culture ■ May lead to free-riding effect ■ Group may pressure members to limit performance ■ Hard to define a team ■ Intergroup competition

The second gainsharing program, the *Rucker Plan,* uses worker–management committees to solicit and screen ideas. These committees are less involved and simpler in structure than those used by the Scanlon Plan. But the cost-saving calculation in the Rucker Plan tends to be more complex because the formula encompasses not only labor costs but also other expenses involved in the production process.

The last type of gainsharing program, *Improshare* ("*Impro*ved *pro*ductivity through *shar*ing"), is a relatively new plan that has proved easy to administer and communicate. First, a standard is developed—based on either studies by an industrial engineering group or some set of base-period experience data—that identifies the expected number of hours required to produce an acceptable level of output. Any savings arising from production of this agreed-on output in fewer than the expected hours are shared between the firm and the workers.

Advantages of Plantwide Pay-for-Performance Plans

The primary rationale for gainsharing programs can be traced to the early work of Douglas McGregor,[55] a colleague and collaborator of Joseph Scanlon, founder of the Scanlon Plan. According to McGregor, a firm can be more productive if it follows a participative approach to management—that is, if it assumes that workers are intrinsically motivated, can show the company better ways of doing things if given the chance, and enjoy being team players.

In contrast to individual-based incentive plans, gainsharing does not embrace the idea that pay incentives motivate people to produce more. Rather, gainsharing suggests that cost savings result from treating employees better and involving them intimately in the firm's management. The underlying philosophy is that competition between individuals and teams should be avoided, that all workers should be encouraged to use their talents for the plant's common good, that employees are willing and able to contribute good ideas, and that the financial gains generated when those ideas are implemented should be shared with employees.

Gainsharing plans can provide a vehicle to elicit active employee input and improve the production process. They can also increase the level of cooperation across workers and teams by giving everyone a common goal. In addition, gainsharing plans are subject to fewer measurement difficulties than individual- or team-based incentives. Because gainsharing plans do not require managers to sort out the specific contributions of individuals or interdependent teams, it is easier both to formulate bonus calculations and to achieve worker acceptance of these plans.[56]

Disadvantages of Plantwide Pay-for-Performance Plans

Like all other pay-for-performance plans, plantwide gainsharing programs may suffer from a number of difficulties, among them:

- **Protection of low performers.** The free-rider problem can be very serious in plants where rewards are spread across a large number of employees. Because so many people work together in a plant, it is less likely that peer pressure will be used to bring low performers into the fold.
- **Problems with the criteria used to trigger rewards.** Although the formulas used to calculate bonuses in gainsharing plans are generally straightforward, four problems may arise. First, once the formula is determined, employees may expect it to remain the same forever. A too-rigid formula can become a management straitjacket, but managers may not want to risk employee unrest by changing it. Second, improving cost savings will not necessarily improve profitability, because the latter depends on many uncontrollable factors (such as consumer demand). For example, an automobile production facility can operate at high efficiency, but if it is producing a car that is in low demand, that plant's financial performance will not look good. Third, when gainsharing is first instituted, it is easier for inefficient than for efficient plants or business units to post a gain. This occurs because opportunities for dramatic labor-cost savings are much higher in the less-efficient units.[57] Thus, gainsharing programs may seem to penalize already efficient units, which can be demoralizing to those who work in them. Fourth, there may be only a few labor-saving opportunities in a plant. If these are quickly exhausted, further gains will be difficult to achieve.

- **Management–labor conflict.** Many managers feel threatened by the concept of employee participation. When the gainsharing program is installed, they may be reluctant to give up their authority to committees, thus creating conflict and jeopardizing the program's credibility. In addition, only hourly workers are included in many gainsharing plans. The exclusion of salaried employees may foster hard feelings among them.

Conditions Favoring Plantwide Plans

A number of factors affect the successful implementation of gainsharing programs.[58] These are:

- **Firm size.** Gainsharing is more likely to work well in small to midsize plants, where employees can see a connection between their efforts and the unit's performance.
- **Technology.** When technology limits improvements in efficiency, gainsharing is less likely to be successful.
- **Historical performance.** If the firm has multiple plants with varying levels of efficiency, the plan must take this variance into account so that efficient plants are not penalized and inefficient plants rewarded. It is difficult to do this where there are scanty historical records. In these cases, past data are insufficient for establishing reliable future performance standards making it difficult to implement a gainsharing program.
- **Corporate culture.** Gainsharing is less likely to be successful in firms with a traditional hierarchy of authority, heavy dependence on supervisors, and a value system that is antagonistic to employee participation. Gainsharing can be used effectively in a firm that is making the transition from a more autocratic to a more participative management style, but it probably cannot lead the charge as a stand-alone program.
- **Stability of the product market.** Gainsharing is most appropriate in situations where the demand for the firm's product or service is relatively stable. Under these circumstances, historical data may be used to forecast future sales reliably. When demand is unstable, the formulas used to calculate bonuses may prove unreliable and force management to change the formula, which is likely to lead to employee dissatisfaction.

Corporatewide Plans

Profit sharing
A corporatewide pay-for-performance plan that uses a formula to allocate a portion of declared profits to employees. Typically, profit distributions under a profit-sharing plan are used to fund employees' retirement plans.

The most macro type of incentive programs, *corporatewide pay-for-performance plans*, reward employees based on the entire corporation's performance. The most widely used program of this kind is **profit sharing**, which differs from gainsharing in several important ways:[59]

- In a profit-sharing program, no attempt is made to reward workers for productivity improvements. Many factors that affect profits (such as luck, regulatory changes, and economic conditions) have little to do with productivity, and the amount of money employees receive depends on all of these factors.
- Profit-sharing plans are very mechanistic. They make use of a formula that allocates a portion of declared profits to employees, normally on a quarterly or annual basis, and do not attempt to elicit worker participation.
- In the typical profit-sharing plan, profit distributions are used to fund employees' retirement plans. As a result, employees seldom receive profit distributions in cash. (This deferral of profit-sharing payments is commonly done for tax reasons.) Profit sharing that is distributed via a retirement plan is generally viewed as a benefit rather than an incentive. Some companies do have profit-sharing programs that are true incentives, however. A notable case is Andersen Corporation, the Minnesota-based manufacturer of windows and patio doors. Employees have received up to 84 percent of their annual salary in a lump-sum check at the end of the year from Andersen's profit-sharing pool.[60]

Employee stock ownership plan (ESOP)
A corporatewide pay-for-performance plan that rewards employees with company stocks, either as an outright grant or at a favorable price that may be below market value.

Like profit sharing, **employee stock ownership plans (ESOPs)** are based on the entire corporation's performance—in this case, as measured by the firm's stock price. ESOPs reward employees with company stock, either as an outright grant or at a favorable price that may be below market value.[61] Employers often use ESOPs as a low-cost retirement benefit for employees because stock contributions made by the company are nontaxable until the employee redeems the stock.[62] Under the right conditions, ESOPS may result in a bonanza for employees. For example, stocks of *Fortune's* 100 best companies beat the market by 300 percent from 1998 to 2005.[63] Employees whose retirement plans are based on ESOPs are exposed to risk, however, because the price of the company's stock may fluctuate as a result of general stock market activity or mismanagement of the firm.

Risk was not in the mind of most stock-owning employees as the stock market sky-rocketed during the 1990s. Examples of firms that offer ESOPs to all employees who saw at least a tripling of their original value during the 1990s include Amgen, Arrow Electronics, Autodesk, Hewlett-Packard, Intel, Lucent Technologies, Marriot International, Merck, Sun Microsystems, and Whole Foods Market.[64] However, many employees were shocked to find that during the recession from 2000 to 2003 the value of their stockholdings declined by a third or more within a year and, in some cases, in a matter of months.

Firms in the United States have led the world in ESOPs, particularly in industries such as high technology. Now, multinational firms and foreign firms are extending stock ownership opportunities to their employees at home and abroad. Companies offering stock options to employees include Siemens and SAP in Germany, Marconi and British Telecom in the United Kingdom, and Suez Lyonnaise des Eaux and Alcatel in France.[65] And many foreign governments are establishing the legal framework to permit such plans, which until recently were unknown outside the United States. (See the Manager's Notebook, "The Worldwide Growth of Employee Ownership Phenomenon.") Depending on the specific country, many U.S. companies are surprised to find that, contrary to U.S. practice:[66]

- Option gains may be included in mandatory severance payments.
- Suspending vesting during a maternity leave may not be legal.
- Excluding part-time employees from participating in the plan based solely on the criterion that they are part time may be impermissible.
- An employee's consent and/or notification to a government agency may be required before information necessary to determine an option grant is collected and transferred to a U.S. database.
- The company may have to provide stock options to all employees, regardless of their rank as employees or managers, and seniority may determine who gets how much.

As of fiscal year 2006, the Internal Revenue Services requires all firms to "expense" the cost of stock-based programs, which means that the firm must estimate the value of the stocks handed out to employees and executives even though the price of the stock (and hence its value) lies in the future (assuming stockholders have yet to convert their shares into cash). As you can see in the Manager's Notebook, "Stock Options Are No Longer "Free": How Will Companies Cope?" this is not a straightforward calculation, and it will probably take at least a decade before uniform conventional standards for expensing stock options emerge. Some analysts believe that stock option use, which has exploded over the past 15 years, is likely to decline in the United States as firms are forced to declare options as a cost, eliminating much of their appeal from an accounting perspective.[67] Recent data seems to support that prediction as the number of U.S. employees who received stock options declined from approximately 10 million in 2002 to 7 million in 2006.[68]

Global

MANAGER'S NOTEBOOK

The Worldwide Growth of Employee Ownership Phenomenon

Employers throughout the world are embracing various employee equity-based compensation plans and many foreign governments are changing their tax laws, securities laws, and other laws to facilitate—or at least reduce—impediments to these types of incentive programs:

- A high-level commission of the Chinese government has been charged with crafting a regulatory infrastructure for employee stock options.
- The U.K. government, as part of its stated policy goal of doubling the level of employee ownership, passed a law creating a new type of pretax employee share scheme dubbed the All

Employee Share Ownership Plan (AESOP). The United Kingdom also enacted a new program to encourage the use of stock options in entrepreneurial enterprises.

- India recently liberalized rules allowing information technology, pharmaceutical, and biotechnology companies to offer stock options to employees.
- South Korea passed a law actively encouraging stock-based incentives, which the government described as "an optimal tool to raise worker productivity because it aligns employee and employer goals."
- Taiwan's Securities and Futures Commission approved the use of employee stock options.
- Denmark, Switzerland, Australia, Ireland, Singapore, the Netherlands, Brazil, and Chile, among others, have all recently enacted similar changes in tax laws to facilitate, or encourage, the use of stock-based incentive plans.

Sources: Adapted with permission from Butler, M. J. (2001, 2nd Quarter). Worldwide growth of employee ownership phenomena. *Worldatwork Journal, 10*(2), 1–5; Burchman, S. (2005, April). LTI vehicles deployed globally. *Workspan,* 30.

MANAGER'S NOTEBOOK

Emerging Trends

Stock Options Are No Longer "Free": How Will Companies Cope?

As of 2006, U.S. firms are required to treat stock options as an expense. Yet the Securities and Exchange Commission (SEC) has given companies wide latitude in calculating the expense. The SEC recognizes that expensing stock options is not a simple process and that similar option plans, depending on the assumptions and formula used, may be valued at varying amounts. This will make it difficult to compare financial statements. The SEC openly recognizes that the next decade or so will be a period of experimenting with the expensing of stock options. Over time, however, "the staff anticipates that particular approaches may begin to emerge as best practices."[a] But as one analyst notes, "in the post-expensing world, accounting methods used to reduce option expenses will make it more difficult for investors to evaluate earnings quality. Comparing companies or industries will become tougher, as investors will have to plow through footnotes to figure out which companies boosted earnings by tweaking accounting assumptions for options, which didn't—and which changes were warranted."[b]

Companies may trim option expenses in a number of ways:[c]

- By predicting that their stocks will be more stable, which, according to financial theory, can cut the option's value
- By assuming that workers will exercise options earlier
- By allowing prior granted options to vest right away so that they don't have to be expensed under new rules
- By increasing the vesting period, companies can award options over a longer period of time and thus spread out their costs.

Sources: [a]Norris, F. (2005, March 31). Windfall never came, big tax bill did. *New York Times,* A-1; [b]Lavelle, L. (2005, January 17). Time to start weighing the options. *BusinessWeek,* 32–33. [c]Bartl, T.J. (2006, January). SEC chairman looks to revise disclosure rules. *Workspan,* 56–58.

Advantages of Corporatewide Pay-for-Performance Plans

Corporatewide pay-for-performance plans have distinct advantages, several of which are economic rather than motivational. These are:

- **Financial flexibility for the firm.** Both profit sharing and ESOPs are variable compensation plans: Their cost to the firm is automatically adjusted downward during economic downturns.

This feature allows the firm to retain a larger workforce during a recession. In addition, these plans allow employers to offer lower base compensation in exchange for company stock or a profit-sharing arrangement. This feature gives the firm "float," or flexibility to direct scarce cash where it is most needed. ESOPs may also be used to save a foundering company—one whose cash is running out or is facing a hostile takeover bid. Weirton Steel, Hyatt Clark, Polaroid, and Chevron have effectively used ESOPs for this purpose.[69]

- **Increased employee commitment.** Employees who are entitled to profit sharing and ESOPs are more likely to identify themselves with the business and increase their commitment to it. Many consider the sharing of profits between the firm's owners and workers as a just distribution of income in a capitalistic society.

- **Tax advantages.** Both profit sharing and ESOPs enjoy special tax privileges. In essence, they allow the firm to provide benefits (discussed in detail in Chapter 12) that are subsidized in part by the federal government. Although these types of plans are sometimes blamed for the loss of enormous amounts in tax revenues, it can be argued that they let firms that cannot afford to pay employees high salaries grow and prosper, thereby creating more jobs and tax revenues in the long run. Apple Computer, Sun Microsystems, Oracle Corporation, Quantum Corporation, and Microsoft might not be around today were it not for tax-subsidized ESOPs and profit-sharing plans.

Disadvantages of Corporatewide Pay-for-Performance Plans

Like all other pay-for-performance programs, corporatewide plans have their drawbacks:

- **Employees may be at considerable risk.** Under profit-sharing or ESOP plans, workers' financial well-being may be threatened by factors beyond their control. Often workers are not fully aware of how much risk they face because the factors affecting profits or stock prices can be very complex. The more reliant long-term employees are on these programs for savings (for their children's college tuition, their own retirement, or some other purpose), the more vulnerable they are to the firm's fate.

  Many employees of *Fortune* 500 firms saw their life savings take a huge fall after the bull market turned into a bear market late in 2000. As the Enron case and its aftermath traveled through the legal and legislative process, it became evident that employers can subject employees to great financial risk when they impose restrictions that prohibit them from selling or diversifying their company stock until a certain age or when they are allowed to bet 100 percent of their long-term savings on their company stock. Among entrepreneurial firms, the risk can be huge: Many of these firms do not survive past five years, so the stock employees own may not be worth the paper it is printed on.[70]

- **Limited effect on productivity.** Because the connection between individual goal achievement and firm performance is small and difficult to measure, corporatewide programs are not likely to improve productivity. However, they should reduce turnover if seniority strongly affects how much an employee is entitled to under the plan.

- **Long-run financial difficulties.** Both profit sharing and ESOPs often appear painless to the company in the short run, either because funds are not paid out to employees until retirement or because employees are paid in "paper" (company stock). As noted earlier, firms are now required to expense this "paper money," but they may still trim the option expenses in a number of ways. This illusion may induce managers to be more generous with these types of compensation than they should be, leaving future management generations with less cash available, lower profits to distribute to investors, and a firm that has decreased in value.

Conditions Favoring Corporatewide Plans

A number of factors influence the successful implementation of corporatewide pay-for-performance plans:

- **Firm size.** Although they may be used at firms of any size, profit sharing and ESOPs are the plans of choice for larger organizations, in which gainsharing is less appropriate.[71]
- **Interdependence of different parts of the business.** Corporations with multiple interdependent plants or business units often find corporatewide plans most suitable because it is difficult to isolate the financial performance of any given segment of the corporation.

Conditions That Favor Various Pay-for-Performance Plans

Figure 11.4	
Type of Plan	**Favorable Conditions**
Individual-Based Plans	■ The contributions of individual employees can be accurately isolated ■ The job demands autonomy ■ Successful performance does not depend on cooperation, or competition should be encouraged
Team-Based Plans	■ Work tasks are so intertwined that it is difficult to single out who did what ■ The firm's organization supports the implementation of team-based incentives ■ The firm's objective is to foster entrepreneurship in self-managed work groups
Plantwide Plans	■ Firm size is small to midsize ■ Technology does not limit efficiency improvements ■ Clear records of historical performance are available ■ Corporate culture supports participative management ■ A stable product market is present
Corporatewide Plans	■ Firm size is large ■ Different parts of the business are interdependent ■ A relatively unstable (cyclical) product market is present ■ Other incentives are present

■ **Market conditions.** Unlike gainsharing, which requires relatively stable sales levels, profit-sharing and ESOP programs are attractive to firms facing highly cyclical ups and downs in the demand for their product. The structuring of these incentives helps the firm cut costs during downturns. (This is why these programs are often called "shock absorbers.") Employees (except those who are closer to retirement) are not immediately affected by these fluctuations in short-term earnings because most profit-sharing benefits are deferred until retirement.

■ **The presence of other incentives.** Because corporatewide pay-for-performance plans are unlikely to have much motivational impact on individuals and teams within the firm, they should not be used on their own. When used in conjunction with other incentives (for example, individual and team bonuses), corporatewide programs can promote greater commitment to the organization by creating common goals and a sense of partnership among managers and workers.

Figure 11.4 summarizes the conditions that favor individual, team, plantwide, and corporatewide pay-for-performance plans.

Designing Pay-for-Performance Plans for Executives and Salespeople

Executives and salespeople are normally treated very differently than most other types of workers in pay-for-performance plans. Because pay incentives are an important component of these employees' total compensation, it is useful to examine their special compensation programs in some detail. It is also useful to examine how companies are rewarding excellence in customer service—a key source of competitive advantage today.

Executives

According to most recent figures, leaders of major corporations pocket a median annual compensation of $14 million, with some nearing the $90 million mark.[72] Approximately 43 percent of this amount is cash compensation (salary, bonus); the rest is stock-based compensation.

According to some estimates, each of the *Fortune* 500 CEOs could live to age 95 among the top 2 percent of Americans if he or she saved just one year's pay. At the higher end, some could have $1.2 million a year for life by saving one year's pay.[73] CEOs earn approximately 240 times what the average employee makes, up from 42 times in 1980, and far more than in any other industrialized nation both on absolute and relative grounds. That is, U.S. CEOs make more money than CEOs in other countries and they earn more compared to what the average worker does than CEOs from other nations earn. For instance, in Japan the CEO is paid 33 times what the average Japanese worker is paid.[74]

Until the most recent bear market, the trend has been for CEO pay to be less in the form of salary and more in the form of long-term income. Between 1995 and 1999, CEO salary as a proportion of total pay dropped by almost 20 percent while long-term income grew by almost 20 percent. This trend was the result of several forces, including favorable tax treatment for long-term income (for the CEO, stock gains are tax deferred and when stocks are cashed they are taxed at the capital gains rate, which is lower than the rate on salary and bonuses); stock grants not counted as an expense in the balance sheet (although this changed starting in 2006); a rapidly rising stock market; and investor calls for greater CEO accountability (unlike salary, long-term income is not assured and reflects growth in shareholder value).

Ironically the trend toward greater emphasis on long-term income to reward executives has had several unintended consequences. First, a bull market (as in the 1990s) can make CEO pay soar, fueling the belief that CEO pay is out of control. During the 1991–2001 decade, the nation's corporate elite saw their average pay increase by more than 550 percent, almost 20 times faster than raises to the typical worker.[75]

Second, because executives may decide at any time to cash the stock options they received years earlier, it is difficult to see the link between CEO pay and firm performance. For example, Lawrence J. Ellison, CEO of Oracle Corporation, received a "windfall" of $706 million in 2001, even though for Oracle that year had been a disaster (the total return to Oracle's shareholders declined 57% during 2001). The huge amount received by Ellison (which exceeds the gross domestic product of many countries) came from exercising long-held stock options, and his decision to cash them in in 2001 probably had nothing to do with Oracle's poor showing in 2001. In other words, it is difficult to see the chronological tie between stock-based pay and firm performance because of the time between receiving and cashing a stock option. Many complex methods have been devised by academics to estimate the true linkage of long-term income to firm performance, yet these are arcane, often controversial, and the results tend to be inconsistent.[76]

And, third, when the stock market changes from bull to bear, firms face the problem of what to do with executives whose stocks "are under water" (for instance, the current market price is below the price when they were provided to the executive, so the options have become worthless). Many firms believe that "underwater" options are demotivating to executives and could make those executives an attractive recruitment target by competitors. To deal with this possibility, firms might make new additional grants to compensate the executive for the loss of value of previously granted stocks, cancel and reissue stock options to ensure they are not under water, or buy underwater stock with cash.[77] This strategy may reinforce the notion that top executives incur little risk with their pay while employees are often asked to bear the brunt of employment and compensation risk because they are more likely to be laid off and see their bonus cut during a downturn.[78]

A large number of plans are used to link executives' pay to firm performance, but there is little agreement on which is best. The disagreement is only heightened by the huge sums of money involved and the weak or inconsistent correlation between executive earnings and firm performance.[79]

Salary and Short-Term Incentives

The amount of executives' base pay increases as firms get larger[80]—practically all CEOs of *Fortune* 500 firms earn a base of at least half a million dollars a year with an average of $2.1 million in cash compensation annually based on 2006 estimates.[81] Executives' bonuses are usually short-term incentives linked to the firm's specific annual goals. More than 90 percent of U.S. firms reward executives with year-end bonuses, but the criteria used to determine these bonuses vary widely.

Two major concerns are often expressed regarding executives' annual bonuses. First, because executives are likely to maximize whatever criteria are used to determine their bonuses, they may make decisions that have short-term payoffs at the expense of long-term performance. For instance, long-term investments in research and development may be crucial to the firm's success in introducing new products over time. Yet if bonus calculations treat such investments as costs that reduce net income, executives may be tempted to scale back R&D. Second, many bonus programs represent salary supplements that the CEO can expect to receive regardless of the firm's performance. For instance, an examination of the *Wall Street Journal's* executive pay survey in 2005 shows that during the previous year (characterized by relatively weak profits) approximately three-fourths of the CEOs in the survey received a substantial bonus. An earlier study in 2002 found that if we focus on companies with a drop of total shareholder return of 40 percent or more, we find that a surprising number of those CEOs received a bonus in excess of half a million dollars during the same period (including, for instance, Aplera, Crown Cork & Seal, Continental Airlines, and Boeing).[82]

The almost automatic payment of lavish bonuses to top executives has led to much resentment among middle managers. One vice president at a major bank expressed a common middle-management frustration: "It disturbs me when someone on high dictates that no matter how hard you work or what you do, you're only going to get a 6 percent increase, and if you don't like it, you can take a hike. Yet whatever they've negotiated for themselves—10 percent, 20 percent, or 30 percent—is a different issue from the rest of the staff."

Long-Term Incentives

Most executives also receive long-term incentives, either in the form of equity in the firm (stock-based programs) or a combination of cash awards and stock. A brief description of the most commonly used executive long-term incentive plans appears in Figure 11.5.

The primary criticism of long-term incentive plans is that they are not very closely linked with executive performance. There are three reasons for this. First, even executives themselves rarely know how much their equity in the firm is worth because its value depends on stock prices at redemption. Second, the executive is likely to have very little control over the value of a company's stock (and thus the worth of his or her own long-term income) because stock prices tend to be highly volatile. (As noted earlier, depending on the time period, this can benefit the executive as during the decade of the 1990s or hurt the executive as during the first half of the 2000s.) Third, designing long-term incentive plans involves many judgment calls, and these are not always addressed in a manner consistent with achieving the firm's long-term strategic objectives. The major questions that firms should address in designing executive long-term programs are listed in Figure 11.6 on page 360.

Perks

Perquisites ("perks")
Noncash incentives given to a firm's executives.

In addition to cash incentives, many executives receive a large number of **perquisites** or **"perks."** These may include a wide array of "special deals" such as physical exams, financial counseling, club memberships, company plane, airline VIP clubs, chauffer service, and concierge service, among other similar perquisites. These may keep the executive happy, but they are seldom linked to business objectives.[83] They are also an easy target of criticism for those who feel that executive compensation is already excessive and who believe that perks are a form of "stealth wealth," representing "a hidden way [for executives] to increase their compensation."[84] To make CEO pay more transparent, the Internal Revenue Service and the SEC passed new rulings to provide for better disclosure of CEO pay starting in 2007, including perks. "It's very tough to get your hands around what the whole compensation package is," SEC chairman William Donaldson said in a recent interview. "We're going to change what must be reported and the form in which it is reported so you don't have to be Sherlock Holmes or a CPA to see what the payments are."[85]

There are no easy answers to these criticisms. Executive compensation will probably always be more an art than a science because of all the factors that must be considered and each firm's unique conditions. Nonetheless, it is safe to say that an executive compensation plan is more likely to be effective if (1) it adequately balances rewarding short-term accomplishments with

Figure 11.5

Stock-Based Programs

Stock Options Allow the executive to acquire a predetermined amount of company stock within a stipulated time period (which may be as long as 10 years) at a favorable price.

Stock Purchase Plans Provide a very narrow time window (usually a month or two) during which the executive can elect to purchase the stocks at a cost that is either less than or equal to fair market value. (Stock purchase plans are commonly available to all employees of the firm.)

Restricted Stock Plans Provide the executive with a stock grant requiring little, if any, personal investment in return for remaining with the firm for a certain length of time (for example, four years). If the executive leaves before completing the specified minimum length of service, all rights to the stock are forfeited.

Stock Awards Provide the executive with "free" company stock, normally with no strings attached. Often used as a one-time-only "sign-on" bonus for recruitment purposes.

Formula-Based Stock Stock provided to the executive either as a grant or at a stipulated price. Unlike other stock-based programs, the value of the stock to the executive when he or she wishes to redeem it is not its market price but one calculated according to a predetermined formula (normally book value, which is assets minus liabilities divided by the number of outstanding shares). Used when the board believes that the market price of an organization's stock is affected by many variables outside the control of the top-management team.

Junior Stock Stock whose value is set at a lower price than common stock, so that the executive is required to spend less cash up front to acquire it. Unlike the owners of common stock, the owners of junior stock have limited voting and dividend rights. However, junior stock can be converted to common stock upon achievement of specific performance goals.

Discounted Stock Options Stock with a strike price lower than the market value of the stock at the date of the grant. Introduced during recent bear market (2001–2003) where there was a reasonable probability that the market value of the stock will rise slowly or may drop.

Tracking Stock Options A class of shares linked to the performance of a specific business or unit of the parent company rather than linked to the performance of the corporation as a whole.

Programs That Combine Cash Awards and Stocks

Stock Appreciation Rights (SARs) Provide the executive with the right to cash or stocks equal to the difference between the value of the stock at the time of the grant and the value of that same stock when the right is exercised. Thus, the executive is rewarded for any increase in the value of the stock, although no stock was actually granted by the firm. No investment on the executive's part is required. May be offered alone or mixed with stock options.

Performance Plan Units Under this plan, the value of each share is tied to a measure of financial performance such as earnings per share (EPS). For example, for every 5 percent increase in EPS, the firm may provide the executive with $1,000 for every share he or she owns. Therefore, if EPS increases by 15 percent the executive will receive $3,000 for each share owned. The payment may be made in cash or common stocks.

Performance Share Plans Offer the executive a number of stocks based on profitability figures using a predetermined formula. The actual compensation per share depends on the market price per share at the end of the performance or award period.

Phantom Stock Pays executives a bonus proportional to the change in prices of company stocks, rather than changes in profitability measures. A phantom stock is only a bookkeeping entry because the executive does not receive any stock per se. The executive is awarded a number of shares of phantom stock to track the cash reward that will be received upon attaining the performance objectives. The award may be equal to the appreciation or the value of the share of phantom stock.

Source: Updated version (2006) of chart appearing in Gómez-Mejía, L. R., and Balkin, D. B. (1992). *Compensation, organizational strategy, and firm performance,* 219, Cincinnati, OH: South-Western. Copyright 1992 by South-Western Publishing. All rights reserved. See also *www.watsonwyatt.com* (2006).

Commonly Used Long-Term Executive Incentive Plans

Figure 11.6

1. How long should the time horizon be for dispensing rewards?
2. Should length of service be considered in determining the amount of the award?
3. Should the executive be asked to share part of the costs and, therefore, increase his or her personal risk?
4. What criteria should be used to trigger the award?
5. Should there be a limit on how much executives can earn or a formula to prevent large unexpected gains?
6. How often should the awards be provided?
7. How easy should it be for the executive to convert the award into cash?

Sources: Makri, M., and Gómez-Mejía, L. R. (2007). Executive compensation: Something old, something new. In Werner, S. (ed.) *Current Issues in Human Resource Management.* London: Routledge. Grabke-Rundell, A., and Gómez-Mejía, L. R. (2002). Power as a determinant of executive compensation. *Human Resource Management Review, 12,* 3–23; and Deya-Tortella, B., Gómez-Mejía, L. R., De Castro, J., and Wiseman, R. (2005). Incentive alignment or perverse incentives? *Management Research,* 3(2), 109–120.

motivating the executive to consider the firm's long-term performance, (2) the incentives provided are linked to the firm's overall strategy (for example, fast growth and risky investments versus moderate growth and low business risks), (3) the board of directors can make informed judgments about how well the executive is fulfilling his or her role, and (4) the executive has some control over the factors used to calculate the incentive amount.[86]

Directors and Shareholders as Equity Partners

The board of directors is responsible for setting executive pay. Traditionally, the board members have been paid in cash. In recent years, however, the relative elements of director compensation have changed fundamentally, as we see a shift toward payment in stock and stock options to tie the financial interests of directors to those of the firm and thus increase their incentive to monitor the executives more closely. Close to 85 percent of firms include at least some stock as part of the annual compensation of directors, with $45,000 in stock on average per director.[87]

Although in theory this change in director compensation is a good idea, two well-known researchers warn us that it could be tantamount to the fox watching the chicken. In other words, boards may be tempted to act in a self-serving manner because in most cases the board sets its own compensation.[88] For instance, directors may set lower performance targets for the granting of stock options. And even if the board acts in good faith with the best interest of shareholders in mind, the appearance of a conflict of interest would always loom in the background.[89]

Historically, boards of directors have played mostly a ceremonial role, meeting a few hours a year and seldom challenging the CEO. The large number of corporate scandals during 2000–2006, the appearance of unjustifiably high CEO compensation, and passage of the Sarbanes-Oxley Act in 2002 (which outlines a set of accountability standards for public companies in the areas of financial reporting, disclosure, audits, conflict of interest, and governance) are forcing boards of directors to become active watchdogs.[90] In a 2005 cover story, *BusinessWeek* summarized this dramatic change: "Boards used to be hired as much for their golf handicaps as for any other expertise. They read reports from management, offered occasional bits of advice, and generally greenlit decisions the CEO had already made. These days, they are apt to become involved in key corporate functions, from strategies to succession to auditing. And if there is a difference with the CEO, they will lawyer up in a heartbeat."[91] Apparently, the United States is not alone in this respect. In Japan, for instance, after a decade of disappointing corporate results, "oversight of top decisions, from staffing to compensation is now handled by committees governed by a majority of outside directors."[92]

Salespeople

Sales professionals, working with the marketing staff, are responsible for bringing revenues into the company. There are several reasons why setting up a compensation program for salespeople is so much different from setting up compensation programs for other types of employees.[93]

- The spread in earnings between the lowest- and highest-paid salespeople is usually several times greater than the earnings spread in any other employee group within the company.
- The reward system for salespeople plays a supervisory role because these employees generally operate away from the office and may not report to the boss for weeks at a time.
- Perceptions of pay inequity are a lesser concern with this group than with others because few employees outside the company's marketing organization have knowledge of either sales achievement or rewards.
- Sales compensation is intimately tied to business objectives and strategies.
- The performance variation among salespeople tends to be quite large. Most organizations rely on relatively few stars to generate most of the sales.
- The salesperson generally works alone and is personally accountable for results.
- Accurate market data on pay practices and levels are extremely difficult to find for salespeople, and commercial salary surveys are usually unreliable.
- The positive motivational impact of compensation plan designs is based largely on the accuracy of sales goals and forecasts.[94]

Sales professionals may be paid in the form of *straight salary* (with no incentives), *straight commission* (in which all earnings are in the form of incentives), or a *combination plan* that mixes the two. Straight salary is most appropriate when maintaining good customer relations and servicing existing accounts are the key objectives, with increased sales a secondary goal. Straight commission is most appropriate when the key objective is to generate greater sales volume through new accounts. Only one-fourth of all firms use either a straight-salary or straight-commission method. Three-quarters use a combination of the two, though the relative proportion of salary versus incentives varies widely across firms. The trend has been to put more emphasis on commissions in a mixed plan.[95]

As Figure 11.7 shows, all three sales compensation methods have their pros and cons. The main criterion that should determine the type of plan chosen is overall marketing philosophy, which is derived from the firm's business strategies.[96] If increased sales is the major goal and these sales involve a one-time transaction with the customer and little expectation of a continuing relationship, then a greater proportion of incentives in the pay mix is appropriate. If customer service is crucial and the sales representative is expected to respond to clients' needs on a long-term basis, then greater reliance on straight salary is appropriate. For example, used car salespeople are often paid in the form of straight commission, whereas sales representatives for highly technical product lines (which often require extensive customer service) tend to be paid on straight salary.

Rewarding Excellence in Customer Service

More and more companies are using incentive systems to reward and encourage better customer service. A survey of 1,400 employers revealed that 35 percent of the respondents factor customer satisfaction into their formula for determining incentive payments. Another third are considering doing so. Common measures of customer satisfaction used to determine incentive payments are customer surveys, records of on-time delivery of products and services, and number of complaints received.[97]

Customer service rewards may be individual-, team-, or plant-based. For example, Storage Technology in Louisville, Colorado, uses customer service as part of its formula to distribute gainsharing monies to all employees covered by the plan. To ensure that sales representatives and managers do not shortchange the customer for the sake of increasing sales and short-term profits, IBM introduced a plan where 40 percent of incentive earnings are tied to customer satisfaction. IBM uses a survey to determine if buyers are happy with the local sales team.[98] AT&T Universal Card provides a $200 on-the-spot bonus for employees who deal effectively with customers' complaints on the phone; phone calls are randomly monitored for this purpose.[99]

Figure 11.7

Straight-Commission Sales Compensation Plan

Advantages	Disadvantages
■ Effective for generating new accounts ■ Sales force is highly motivated to sell the product ■ High performers' contributions are recognized with pay ■ Sales representatives become entrepreneurial and require minimal supervision ■ Selling costs are efficiently controlled ■ Fixed costs are kept to a minimum	■ Sales volume is emphasized over profits ■ Customer service may be neglected ■ Sales representative may overstock the customer ■ Offers less economic security to sales force ■ Provides less direct control over sales force ■ Plan administration is simple ■ Top-performing sales representatives may outearn other employees, including executives ■ Possible resistance to changes in sales territories ■ Possible focus on products that require the least effort to sell

Straight-Salary Sales Compensation Plan

Advantages	Disadvantages
■ Secure income ■ Sales force is willing to perform nonselling activities ■ Plan administration is simple ■ Sales force is less likely to overstock customers ■ Low resistance to change in sales territories ■ Low employee turnover rates ■ Sales force treated as salaried professional ■ More cooperation and less competition in sales force	■ Low motivational impact ■ Difficult to attract or retain top sales performers ■ More sales managers are needed to provide supervision ■ Sales representatives may focus on products that require least effort to sell

Combination Sales Compensation Plan

Advantages	Disadvantages
■ Incorporates advantages of both straight-salary and straight-commission plans ■ Recognizes both selling and nonselling activities with pay ■ Can offer both economic security and monetary incentives to sales representatives ■ Greater variety of marketing goals can be supported with plan	■ Plan is more complicated to design ■ Sales force may become confused and try to accomplish too many objectives ■ Plan is more difficult and costly to administer ■ Sales representatives may receive unanticipated windfall earnings

Source: Updated version (2006) of chart appearing in Gómez-Mejía, L. R., and Balkin, D. S. (1992). *Compensation, organizational strategy, and firm performance.* Cincinnati, OH: South-Western. Reproduced with the permission of South-Western College Publishing. Copyright 1992 by South-Western College Publishing. All rights reserved.

Salary? Commission? Or Both? A Guide to Compensating Salespeople

Summary and Conclusions

Pay-for-Performance: The Challenges

Pay-for-performance (incentive) programs can improve productivity, but managers need to consider several challenges in their design and implementation. Employees may be tempted to do only what they get paid for, ignoring those intangible aspects of the job that are not explicitly rewarded. Cooperation and teamwork may be damaged if individual merit pay is too strongly emphasized. Individual merit systems assume that the employee is in control of the primary factors affecting his or her work output, an assumption that may not be true. Individual performance is difficult to measure, and tying pay to inaccurate performance measures is likely to create problems. Pay incentive systems can be perceived as an employee right and can be difficult to adapt to the organization's changing needs. Many employees do not believe that good performance is rewarded (the credibility gap). Emphasizing merit pay can place employees under a great deal of stress and lead to job dissatisfaction. Finally, merit pay may decrease employees' intrinsic motivation.

Meeting the Challenges of Pay-for-Performance Systems

To avoid the problems sometimes associated with pay-for-performance systems, managers should (1) link pay and performance appropriately, (2) use pay for performance as part of a broader HRM system, (3) build employee trust, (4) promote the belief that performance makes a difference, (5) use multiple layers of rewards, (6) increase employee involvement, and (7) consider using nonfinancial incentives. Employee participation in the design of the plan can enhance its credibility and long-term success.

Types of Pay-for-Performance Plans

There are four types of incentive programs. At the level of individual employees, merit pay (which becomes part of base salary) and bonuses and awards (given on a one-time basis) determined via supervisory appraisals are most common. At the next level, team-based plans reward the performance of groups of employees who work together on joint projects or tasks, usually with bonuses and noncash awards. At the level of the plant or business unit, gainsharing is the program of choice. Gainsharing rewards workers based on cost savings, usually in the form of a lump-sum bonus. At the fourth and highest level of the organization—the entire corporation—profit sharing and employee stock option plans (ESOPs) are used to link the firm's performance with employees' financial rewards. Both plans are commonly used to fund retirement programs.

Designing Pay-for-Performance Plans for Executives and Salespeople

Two employee groups, top executives and sales personnel, are normally treated very differently than most other workers in pay-for-performance plans. Short-term annual bonuses, long-term incentives, and perks may be used to motivate executives to make decisions that help the firm meet its long-term strategic goals. Sales employees are revenue generators, and their compensation system is normally used to reinforce productive behavior. A reliance on straight salary for salespeople is most appropriate where maintaining customer relations and servicing existing accounts are the key objectives. A heavy reliance on straight commission is most appropriate if the firm is trying to increase sales. Most firms use a combination of the two plans. In today's globally competitive marketplace, many firms are also using incentive programs to reward customer service.

Key Terms

award, 345
bonus program or lump-sum payment, 344
employee stock ownership plan (ESOP), 352

expectancy theory, 345
gainsharing, 350
merit pay, 344
pay-for-performance system or incentive system, 338

perquisites ("perks"), 358
piece-rate system, 342
profit sharing, 352

Discussion Questions

1. This chapter identifies three assumptions underlying pay-for-performance plans. Do you believe these assumptions are valid?

2. How can a pay-for-performance system increase the motivation of individual employees and improve cooperation at the same time?

3. One observer notes that "the problem with using pay as an incentive is that it is such a powerful motivational weapon that management can easily lose control of the situation." Do you agree? Why or why not?

4. How can a company avoid the ethical problems associated with financial incentives as presented in the Manager's Notebook, "Perverse Incentives?"

5. Lou Gerstner, IBM's retired CEO, founded the Teaching Commission in 2005 to improve teacher quality. Gerstner is using his corporate reputation as a charismatic CEO to help link teachers' salaries to performance. To do so, he plans to tie teachers' pay to test scores. Do you think Gerstner's proposal is a good idea?

6. In his 2005 book *The World Is Flat,* Thomas Friedman argues that the world is flattening, meaning that it is becoming increasingly interconnected. According to Friedman, the long-term outlook for the United States isn't so great: "India's specialized technology institutes are turning out battalions of software wizards. China is producing armies of engineers and scientists. They are

all eager to work for wages that would violate labor standards in the United States but provide a nice middle-class income in their countries." He adds that technology is "making it a snap to send offshore the jobs of accountants, software writers, radiologists, illustrators and just anyone else whose work is knowledge-based." Do you agree with Friedman's assessment? Is there anything U.S. knowledge workers can do to maintain their standard of living in this "flattening" world?

7. A committee of top-level CEOs of the largest French firms made a recommendation that top executive pay should remain secret in France (unlike the United States where by law it must be disclosed for all publicly traded firms). Their rationale? French CEOs earn up to 50 percent less pay than their American and British counterparts for firms of similar size, in the same industry, and for similar performance levels. In a press conference, Marc Viénot, Honorary Chairman of Société Générale, remarked that "Revealing it would just help rivals lure French CEOs away with better pay packages . . . [Besides] Americans like bragging about their pay, and the French don't."[100] Do you agree with the committee's decision and its rationale? Explain.[102]

8. A customer survey for Landmark Company reports that people do not trust what sales representatives say about their firm's products. How might you use the compensation system to help change this negative image?

There is a variety of additional material available on the Web site that accompanies this text. You can access this information by visiting the Web site at **www.prenhall.com/gomez.**

YOU MANAGE IT!

Global Case 11.1

Does Money Motivate?

Consistent with several prior surveys, a 2005 poll in the United States by *Time* magazine found that when people were asked about their major source of happiness, money ranked 14th. Still, most people behave as though happiness is one wave of a credit card away. Too many Americans view expensive purchases as "shortcuts to well-being," says Martin Seligman, a psychologist at the University of Pennsylvania.[a]

Ample evidence suggests that being poor causes unhappiness. Studies by Ruut Veenhoven, a sociologist at Erasmus University in Rotterdam, found that the poor—those in Europe earning less than about $10,000 a year—are rendered unhappy by the relentless frustration and stress of poverty. However, Veenhoven found that money and happiness decouple and cease to have much to do with each other once a person's annual income exceeds $10,000. In contrast, according to *Time*'s poll, in the United States happiness tends to increase once annual income hits $50,000 a year. (The median annual U.S. household income in 2006 is around $43,000.) Additional income does not appear to have a dramatic effect on whether a person feels good about life. Edward Diener, a psychologist at the University of Illinois, interviewed members of the *Forbes* 400, the 400 richest Americans. He found that the *Forbes* 400 were only a tiny bit happier than the public as a whole. Because those with wealth often continue to feel jealousy about the possessions or prestige of other wealthy people, even large sums of money may fail to confer well-being.

One telling fact suggests that money never satisfies: Polls show that Americans believe that, whatever their income level, they need more to live well. Most Western Europeans, however, are satisfied with what they have once they reach a minimal income threshold. Even those Americans making large sums say that still larger sums are required. In fact, in 2005 a survey by the *New York Times* found that respondents indicated that an income of $200,000 was needed to live well, twice what it was a few years back, controlling for inflation.[b] As men and women move up the economic ladder, most almost immediately stop feeling grateful for their elevated circumstances and focus on what they still don't have. Suppose you lived in a two-bedroom house for years and dreamed of three bedrooms. You finally get that three-bedroom house. Will it bring you happiness? Not necessarily. Three bedrooms will become your new norm, and you'll begin to long for a four-bedroom abode.

Critical Thinking Questions

1. Why do you think most Americans rank money very low in importance for happiness yet act in ways that suggest just the opposite? Do you think people in other countries are much different than Americans in this regards? Explain.

2. One observer suggests that "we have never been so keen for green even though it often gives us more social anxiety than satisfaction." Do you agree or disagree? Explain.

3. The use of variable pay and financial incentives tied to performance measures has increased dramatically during the past 25 years or so. How does the importance of money to U.S. workers influence pay-for-performance plans in organizations? Relatedly, the use of pay-for-performance linkages is much higher in the United States than in most other countries. Why do you think this is the case?

Team Exercise

Class is divided into teams of five. Some teams are asked to defend the view that money is not an important motivator, whereas other teams are asked to defend a contrarian view; that is, that monetary incentives are important to most employees. Each pair of teams (pro and con) will debate for about 15 minutes, moderated by instructor. Debate is then opened to discussion for the entire class.

Experiential Exercise

Americans suffer from the stereotype that "they have made materialism and the cycle of work and spend their principal goals. Then they wonder why they don't feel happy." Some say that "Americans live to work while the rest of the world works to live." Interview any friends, acquaintances, relatives, coworkers, or others who come from (or have lived) in other countries. Ask their perceptions of whether this is an accurate stereotype. What are the implications of your research for a global firm that operates not only in United States, but also abroad? Exchange findings with classmates in an open class format, with the instructor serving as the mediator.

Sources: [a]Adapted with permission from Easterbrook, G. (2005, January 17). The real truth about money. *Time*, A32–34; [b]Reported in Williams, A. (2005, February 27). Six figures? Not enough! *New York Times*, C-9.

Discussion Case 11.2   YOU MANAGE IT!

Loafers at Lakeside Utility Company

Lakeside Utility Company provides electrical power to a county with 50,000 households. Pamela Johnson is the manager in charge of all repair and installation crews. Each crew consists of approximately seven employees who work closely together to respond to calls concerning power outages, fires caused by electrical malfunctions, and installation of new equipment or electric lines. Fourteen months ago Johnson decided to implement a team-based incentive system that will award an annual bonus to each crew that meets certain performance criteria. Performance measures include indicators such as average length of time needed to restore power, results of a customer satisfaction survey, and number of hours required to complete routine installation assignments successfully. At the end of the first year, five crews received an average cash bonus of $12,000 each, with the amount divided equally among all crew members.

Soon after Johnson announced the recipients of the cash bonus, she began to receive a large number of complaints. Some teams not chosen for the award voiced their unhappiness through their crew leader. The two most common complaints were that the teams working on the most difficult assignments were penalized (because it was harder to score higher on the evaluation) and that crews unwilling to help out other crews were being rewarded.

Ironically, members of the crews that received the awards also expressed dissatisfaction. A surprisingly large number of confidential employee letters from the winning teams reported that the system was unfair because the bonus money was split evenly among all crew members. Several letters named loafers who received "more than their share" because they were frequently late for work, took long lunches and frequent smoking breaks, and lacked initiative. Johnson is at a loss about what to do next.

Critical Thinking Questions

1. What major issues and problems concerning the design and implementation of pay-for-performance systems does this case illustrate? Explain.

2. Are team-based incentives appropriate for the type of work done by Johnson's crews?

3. Might it be desirable to use a combination of team-based and individual incentives at Lakeside Utility Company? How might such a plan be structured?

Team Exercises

Students form pairs. One student takes the role of Pamela Johnson; the other, the role of an HRM consultant Johnson has hired to help her decide what to do next. Role-play the meeting between the two. Johnson explains what has happened and the consultant reacts.

The class divides into groups of five students each. One of the students takes the role of a consultant hired by Pamela

Johnson to help her decide what to do. The remaining four students take the roles of line workers, each from a different crew. The consultant is gathering information from the crews about how they feel about the bonus system and what changes they would like to see.

Experiential Exercise

This experiential exercise involves a group of six students. One will be a manager and five will be part of a team that has worked closely together during the past year. A bonus of $12,000 is to be divided among the five team members. A peer evaluation based on a scale of 1 (low) to 5 (high) shows that Ana, Robert, Steve, Peter, and Tom received scores of 4.4, 4.1, 3.7, 3.2, and 3.0, respectively. The manager is responsible for allocating the bonus. The manager must explain to each team member the rationale for the pay amount decided upon.

YOU MANAGE IT!

Global Case 11.3

Are American CEOs That Much Better?

According to a study by a leading consulting firm, at companies with sales of at least $35 billion, on average, U.S. and European chiefs earn salaries and bonuses of $24 million. However, American CEOs receive far more in stock and stock options. The end result is that "in the U.S. the imperial CEO still takes the lion's share."[a] Another study presents more striking data that shows that compensation inequality between the CEO and the rest of the organization is far greater in the United States.[b] The authors of that study suggest that European companies tend to spread wealth more evenly among employees and that the pay differentials observed in the United States would not be "socially tolerated" in Europe. Figure 11.8 shows CEO pay as a ratio of average employee earnings in a number of different countries.

Critical Thinking Questions

1. Based on the data presented in the figure, how would you explain the large differential in CEO pay ratios between the United States and other countries? Are these differentials justified? Explain.

2. Some people argue that U.S. executives are paid more because the "going rate" in the U.S. marketplace is a lot higher than that in other countries. An American firm has little choice but to pay the domestic market rate to executives, otherwise the best executives would migrate to competitors. Furthermore, the key objective is not to attain greater compensation equality, but rather to maximize the profitability of the entire organization, which in the end benefits everyone. Do you agree or disagree? Explain.

3. Do you think that most employees care or even think about how much the firm's CEO makes? Considering that CEO pay is a tiny fraction of the total operating cost in most organizations, why is there so much fuss about CEO pay? Explain.

Team Exercise

Class is divided into teams of five. Some teams are asked to defend the position that CEOs receive what they deserve; other teams are asked to argue that CEOs are overpaid. After each team meets for approximately 15 minutes both sides will then discuss their respective position in class, with the instructor acting as a moderator.

Total CEO Pay in Large Firms as a Multiple of Average Hourly Paid Employees' Earnings in Large Firms: A Selected Country Comparison

Figure 11.8	
Country	CEO Pay as Ratio of Average Employee Earnings
United States	531
United Kingdom	25
Netherlands	22
Belgium	19
Italy	19
Spain	18
France	16
Germany	11

Experiential Exercise

Class is divided into teams of five. Each team is asked to take an annual issue of *BusinessWeek* that lists the compensation of each executive as well as firm performance during the prior year. Each team will analyze this data and develop a set of conclusions as to whether executives are rewarded based on firm performance. Different teams will present their conclusions to the entire class. Instructor will moderate discussion among various teams and provide his or her own views on the issue.

Sources: [a] Lavelle, L. (2005, January 17). Time to start weighing the options. *BusinessWeek*, 32–33; [b] Bruce, A., Buck, T., and Main, B.G. (in press). Top executives remuneration: A view from Europe. *Journal of Management Studies*, forthcoming.

Discussion Case 11.4 — YOU MANAGE IT!

Playing the Compensation Game

The following situations emerged in very different organizational settings after incentives were introduced to reward good employees:[a]

- After the discovery of insect parts in its pea packages, Green Giant designed a bonus plan to reward employees for removing insect parts from the vegetables. Green Giant abandoned the incentive plan when it learned that employees were bringing insect parts from home, putting them into the vegetables, and then removing them to get their bonuses.

- A software developer had problems with a different kind of bug: software program glitches. Like Green Giant, the company installed an incentive plan to reward programmers for finding and removing the bugs. Initially, the plan seemed successful. But, as in Green Giant's case, the developer's performance numbers hid the problem—employees were, in fact, creating the very bugs the incentive plan was paying them to remove.

- Sunbeam had hired Al Dunlap as CEO to restructure the company and turn around its performance, as he had done at Scott Paper in the mid-1990s. To support that objective, the company compensated Dunlap with a pay package rich in stock options. By late 1996, the new CEO had clearly met his goals: the stock value had returned more than 130 percent to the shareholders. Then in 1998 the SEC launched an investigation of Sunbeam's accounting practices coincident with a dramatic decline in stock value. By June 1998, the stock was selling at $3.75, down from a 1996 high of $53. Dunlap had met his goal of improving the short-run value of the company but was unable to find a buyer as he had done at Scott Paper. Sunbeam's board eventually fired him as CEO.

- In 1805, an army private deserted from the Lewis and Clark expedition on its trek across North America. Because desertion is serious business, one captain decided to offer a reward to ensure that the private was punished: $10 to anyone who brought the private back alive, or $20 for the private's scalp. The captain got exactly what he was willing to pay for: lots and lots of scalps.

Critical Thinking Questions

1. What is the common thread across the widely different examples of "pay for performance" given in this case?
2. What are some of the pros and cons of linking pay to objective criteria that are important to the organization such as quality control measures, profitability, and low turnover?
3. Alfie Kohn, a well-known management consultant and writer, argues that "the failure of any incentive program is due less to a glitch in that program than to the inadequacy of the psychological assumptions that ground all such plans."[b] Kohn believes that stock options, piece rates, commission, bonuses, and even rewards such as employee-of-the-month programs, vacations, and praise are bribes that can cause more harm than good. Do you agree? Explain.
4. How would you prevent the problems that arose at Green Giant, the software developer, and Sunbeam and still reward good performance? Explain.
5. Assuming you are a top executive at Green Giant and the software developer, would you punish the employees who engaged in those unethical acts, the managers that devised the incentive system, or both?
6. Some people believe that most employees will act ethically even though they have a chance to take advantage of an incentive system through inappropriate behaviors. Do you agree?

Team Exercise

Divide the class into groups of three to five students. One set of teams will defend the proposition that incentives can be beneficial to a firm by reinforcing desired behaviors. Another set of teams will defend the position that in most cases incentives promote a "let's beat the game" attitude among employees that leads to poor performance.

Experiential Exercise

In a Midwestern state prone to frequent and severe snowstorms, the head of the Department of Transportation (DOT) has introduced a proposal to provide an incentive to snowplow operators linked to the number of miles shown on the odometer during each shift. The incentive plan, scheduled on a trial basis for the winter seasons of 2007–2010, is intended to motivate the snowplow operators to cover more ground and to clean the roads quicker. One student will role-play a compensation consultant to advise the DOT on the proposal; another student will role-play the position of the head of the DOT. The role-play should last 10 to 15 minutes, after which the instructor will moderate an open class discussion on the issue.

Source: [a]Adapted with permission from Bloom, M. (1999). The art and context of the deal: A balanced view of executive incentives. *Compensation and Benefits Review, 31*(1), 25–31; [b]Kohn, A. (1993, September to October). Why incentive plans cannot work. *Harvard Business Review,* 54–63.

Designing and Administering

Benefits

After reading this chapter, you should be able to deal more effectively with the following challenges:

1 **Explain** the significance of employee benefits to both employers and employees.

2 **Design** a benefits package that supports the firm's overall compensation strategy and other HRM policies.

3 **Distinguish** between a defined benefit retirement plan and a defined contribution retirement plan and recognize the situations in which each is most appropriate.

4 **Discuss** how traditional health insurance plans and managed-care health insurance plans work and the advantages and disadvantages of each.

5 **Develop** cost-containment strategies for the different types of employee benefits.

6 **Understand** the administrative complexities of providing a full array of benefits to the workforce and suggest ways to deliver benefits effectively.

7 **Recognize** the HR department's key role in keeping accurate records of employee benefits and informing employees about their benefits.

Today's HR managers face a number of challenges that did not exist a decade ago. One of these challenges is managing the rapidly increasing costs of employee benefits. Although health-care costs have received the most attention, the costs of many other employee benefits are also increasing. At the same time, benefits have become crucial to attracting, retaining, and motivating employees. A report by the National Study of the Changing Work Force found that 43 percent of employees who changed jobs rated employee benefits as "very important" in their decision, while only 35 percent said the same for salary or wages.

The following examples give some idea of the many ways companies are managing employee benefits in difficult times. Some companies are:

■ **Cutting benefits costs wherever they can** IBM recently changed the basis of its pension from a traditional plan that uses a fixed formula for retirement income based on an employee's seniority and last five years of salary to a new type of pension called a "cash balance" plan. The cash balance plan sets aside the same amount of savings for an employee each year instead of accelerating the contributions toward the end of an employee's career as the traditional plans do. The new plan reduces the amount of resources needed to fund a pension and makes it more predictable for the company. It also makes it easier for employees to change jobs and take the full value of the retirement account with them, which was not the case with the traditional pension plan.

Although younger employees who are more likely to change jobs favored the cash balance plan, older IBM employees with 20 or more years of experience felt betrayed by the new plan design. Why? Their expected retirement income would be significantly less than their expected income under the traditional plan.[1] As a result, IBM faced its first serious union organization threat in many years. Disappointed employees with seniority considered organizing a union that could help them bargain with management to shift back to the original plan.[2]

■ **Providing cutting-edge benefits** By providing innovative, cutting-edge benefits that satisfy specific employee needs, a company is in a better position to attract and retain talented employees who are in scarce supply. Delta Air Lines recently offered to provide computers and Internet access at the homes of all of its 72,000 employees for $12 a month. Delta wanted to make it easier for its pilots and flight attendants to schedule their flights while away from their office.[3] Sun Microsystems provides concierge services that give personal assistance to busy employees. For a small fee the concierge service will pick up groceries, take the car for scheduled maintenance, provide dry cleaning and laundry pickup and delivery, order and deliver flowers, and provide other personal services for employees. Interlock Resources, a Clayton, Missouri, software company, provides complete meals so employees do not need to leave the company at meal times. President and CEO Wayne Haar noted: "Having food on site makes it easy for our staff to stay in for lunch or dinner. Our kitchen is stocked with our employees' favorite foods, snacks and beverages, which they select and order through a local grocery store's Internet site."[4] Wegmans, a grocery chain based in Rochester, New York, was ranked number one on *Fortune*'s list of "The 100 Best Companies to Work For" because of the caring way it treats its employees, which includes its use of employee benefits. Wegmans has provided over $50 million in college scholarships to 17,500 full- and part-time employees over the years.[5]

Offering benefits that give employees a sense of security and containing costs might seem to be mutually exclusive goals. The challenge is for managers and HR professionals to work together to (1) give employees meaningful benefit choices that match their needs, (2) keep the costs of these benefits under control, and (3) ensure that employees are fully informed of their benefit options.

THE MANAGERIAL PERSPECTIVE

In the United States, unlike most other developed countries, the employer provides most of an employee's benefits. The benefits, which are part of a group benefit plan, are designed to safeguard employees and their families against problems due to sickness, accidents, or retirement. More than almost any other issue addressed in this text, an organization's HR staff controls benefits programs. Still, managers must be familiar with benefits for several reasons:

■ **Benefits issues are important to employees** Managers must help employees understand and make the best use of their benefits. For instance, if an employee has a child who needs urgent medical attention, the employee's manager should be able to explain the company's medical benefits to ensure that the employee obtains all available coverage.

- **Benefits are a powerful recruiting tool** Managers at firms that offer enticing benefits can use this advantage to recruit high-quality applicants.

- **Benefits help retain talented employees** Firms that offer an attractive benefits package to employees give managers an advantage because the package often helps reduce turnover.

- **Certain benefits play a part in managerial decisions** Some benefits—such as vacations, family and medical leave, and sick days—give employees scheduling flexibility. Managers need to be aware of these benefits to effectively manage work schedules.

- **Benefits are important to managers** Managers need to be aware of their own benefit options. Some decisions, particularly those concerning retirement plans, have long-term consequences. Good decisions in this area made early in a career can affect quality of life at the end of and after a career.

However, understanding benefit plan designs is not an easy task. As we see in the chapter, cost-control measures, the need to offer benefits that attract and retain employees, and new laws and regulations have led to many changes in the design of benefit programs.

In this chapter, we explain benefits in detail. We begin with an overview of employee benefits and the relationship of benefits to the rest of the compensation package. We then examine strategies for designing benefits programs. Next, we describe the scope and significance of two categories of employee benefits programs: legally required benefits and voluntary benefits. Finally, we discuss some important issues in benefits administration.

An Overview of Benefits

Employee benefits are group membership rewards that provide security for employees and their family members. They are sometimes called **indirect compensation** because they are given to employees in the form of a plan (such as health insurance) rather than cash. A benefits package complements the base-compensation and pay-incentives components of total compensation. According to the U.S. Bureau of Labor Statistics, benefits cost U.S. companies about $13,380 per year for the average employee.[6] Figure 12.1 shows how the benefit dollar is divided in the average firm.

Employee benefits protect employees from risks that could jeopardize their health and financial security. They provide coverage for sickness, injury, unemployment, and old age and

Employee benefits or indirect compensation
Group membership rewards that provide security for employees and their family members.

How the Benefit Dollar Is Spent

Source: U.S. Bureau of Labor Statistics (2004). Employer costs for employee compensation.

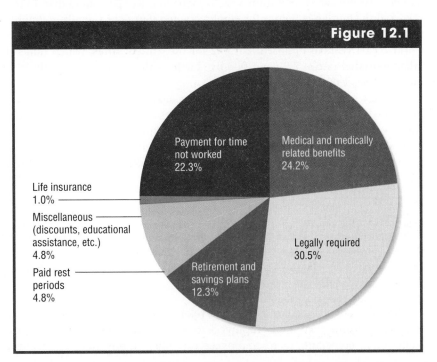

Figure 12.1

- Payment for time not worked 22.3%
- Medical and medically related benefits 24.2%
- Life insurance 1.0%
- Miscellaneous (discounts, educational assistance, etc.) 4.8%
- Paid rest periods 4.8%
- Retirement and savings plans 12.3%
- Legally required 30.5%

death. They may also provide services or facilities that many employees find valuable, such as child-care services or an exercise center.

In the United States, the employer is the primary source of benefits coverage. The situation is quite different in other countries, where many benefits are sponsored by the government and funded with taxes. For example, in the United States employers voluntarily provide their employees with health insurance, while in Canada health insurance is a right bestowed on all citizens by the country's national health system. For a brief summary of Canada's health-care policy, see Exhibit 12.1, "Benefits Across the Border: A Look at Canada's Health-Care System."

The benefits package offered by a firm can support management's efforts to attract employees. When a potential employee is choosing among multiple job offers with similar salaries, a firm offering an attractive benefits package will be ahead of the pack. For example, Swedish Medical Center, a hospital in Denver, Colorado, uses its on-site child-care center as a recruiting tool to attract high-quality staff.[7] It is one of only two hospitals in its region that offer this benefit.

EXHIBIT 12.1	**Benefits Across the Border: A Look at Canada's Health-Care System**

When Tommy Bettis from Arkansas broke his arm and cut his head while helping to repair the garage of his Ontario friend, Kristopher Goering, Bettis received emergency care at a Canadian hospital by presenting Goering's health card. Although this case involved an emergency occurring in Canada, thousands of Americans are routinely borrowing Canadian health cards to get medical care.

Why are ailing Americans going to another country and using illegal means to get health care there? Because in Canada health care is free. In the debate on U.S. health-care reform, the U.S. media have alternately portrayed Canada's national health-care system as a medical miracle or as a bureaucratic nightmare. The truth seems to be somewhere in between. Yet, from the vantage point of 45 million uninsured residents of the United States—many of whom are employed full- or part-time—Canada's system is more in the miracle category.

Canada's national system covers all residents' medical and hospital bills and is funded through income taxes (top bracket: 48% on income over $50,000) and through a payroll tax on employers. Doctors and hospitals are reimbursed directly by provincial governments according to a negotiated schedule of fees, while patients pay nothing—except higher taxes than U.S. citizens. (In fact, Americans take home the largest percentage of their gross pay among all industrialized nations.) Health-care expenditures are 40 percent lower per capita than in the United States, however, and the burden is lighter for employers, too. But does Canada get more out of its health system for less? Statistics seem to say so: Canada boasts the eighth-highest life expectancy in the world, 77.03 years as opposed to 75.22 for the United States, which ranks thirty-third. Canada's infant mortality rate of 7.9 per 1,000 live births is the tenth lowest in the world, whereas the U.S. rate of 10 per 1,000 is twenty-first.

Is there a catch in the Canadian system? Canadians sometimes have to wait for nonemergency procedures, but rarely for run-of-the-mill services. Also, in Canada, recession has cut into tax revenues, so the system is facing a financial crunch. But there is one rising cost Canada can do something about: the cost of Americans using the system illegally. Canadian officials are cracking down on health-care fraud, seizing the cards of ineligible users and making a bigger effort to collect for medical services provided to nonresidents.

Sources: Krauss, C. (2005, June 10). In blow to Canada's health system, Quebec law is voided. *New York Times*, A-3; Krauss, C. (2003, February 13). Long lines mar Canada's low-cost health care. *New York Times*, A-3; Farnsworth, C. H. (1993, December 20). Americans filching free health care in Canada. *New York Times*, A-1; Crossette, B. (2001, October 11). Canada's health care shows strains. *New York Times*, A-12.

Benefits can also help management retain employees. Benefits that are designed to increase in value over time encourage employees to remain with their employer. For instance, many companies make contributions to employees' retirement funds, but these funds are available only to employees who stay with the company for a certain number of years. For this reason, benefits are sometimes called "golden handcuffs." An excellent example of the power of benefits to retain employees is the U.S. military, which provides early retirement benefits to personnel who put in 20 years of service. This "20 years and out" retirement provision allows retired military people to start a second career at a fairly young age with the security of a lifelong retirement income to supplement their earnings. These generous benefits help the armed forces retain valuable officers and professionals who would otherwise be attracted to higher-paying civilian jobs.[8]

Basic Terminology

Before we proceed, let us define some basic terms that we will use throughout this chapter:

- **Contributions** All benefits are funded by contributions from the employer, the employee, or both. For example, vacations are an employer-provided benefit: The salary or wages paid to the employee during the vacation period come entirely from the employer. Premiums for health-care insurance are often paid partly by the employer and partly by the employee.
- **Coinsurance** Payments made to cover health-care expenses that are split between the employer's insurance company and the employee. For instance, under an 80/20 insurance plan, the employer's insurance company would pay 80 percent of the employee's health-care costs and the employee would pay the remaining 20 percent.
- **Copayment** A small payment that the employee pays, usually $5 to $15 dollars, for each office visit to a physician under the health plan. The health plan pays for additional medical expenses that exceed the copayment at no cost to the employee.

Contributions
Payments made for benefits coverage. Contributions for a specific benefit may come from the employer, employee, or both.

Coinsurance
Payments made to cover health-care expenses that are split between the employer's insurance company and the insured employee.

Copayment
A small payment made by the employee for each office visit to a physician under a health plan. The health plan pays for additional medical expenses that exceed the copayment at no cost to the employee.

Guerra DeBerry Coody, a full-service marketing firm based in San Antonio, Texas, offers on-site child care to its employees. Tess Coody, one of the partners, states that on-site child care helps attract and retain star performers to the firm and has contributed to a reduction in turnover.

■ **Deductible** An annual out-of-pocket expenditure that an insurance policyholder must make before the insurance plan makes any reimbursements. For instance, the 80/20 plan described previously may also have a $500 deductible, in which case the employee would be responsible for the first $500 of medical expenses before the insurance company makes its 80 percent coinsurance payment.

■ **Flexible benefit programs** A **flexible benefits program**, also called a **cafeteria benefits program**, allows employees to select the benefits they need most from a menu of choices. Unlike employers that try to design a one-size-fits-all benefits package, employers with a flexible benefits program recognize that their employees have diverse needs that require different benefits packages. A 30-year-old married female employee with a working spouse and small children is likely to need child-care benefits and may be willing to forgo extra paid vacation days in exchange for this benefit. A 50-year-old married male employee with grown children may prefer a larger employer contribution to his retirement plan.

The Cost of Benefits in the United States

The cost of employee benefits in the United States has increased dramatically over the decades as businesses have offered more and more benefits. The cost of employee benefits as a percentage of an employer's payroll increased from 3 percent in 1929 to about 29.6 percent in 2004.[9] This growth can be explained by a combination of factors, including federal tax policy, federal legislation, the influence of unions, and the cost savings of group plans.

Federal Tax Policy

Since the 1920s, the federal government has provided favorable tax treatment for group benefit plans that meet certain standards (discussed later in this chapter).[10] Employers who meet the tax policy guidelines receive tax deductions for their benefits expenditures.

Employees also receive favorable treatment under the tax policy because they receive many of their benefits on a *tax-free* basis. For example, employees receive their employer's contribution to a health insurance plan tax-free. In contrast, self-employed individuals have to pay for health insurance out of their taxable income. Other benefits are received on a *tax-deferred* basis. For example, employee contributions to a qualified retirement plan (up to a maximum amount) may be tax-deferred until the employee retires, at which time the person may be taxed at a lower rate. Federal tax policy on benefits has encouraged employees to demand additional benefits, because each additional dollar a company allocates for benefits has more value than a dollar allocated as cash compensation, which is taxed as ordinary income.

Federal Legislation

In 1935, federal legislation decreed that all employers must provide Social Security and unemployment insurance benefits to their employees. We take a closer look at these benefits later in this chapter. At this point, we only wish to make the point that federal law requires some benefits and that federal legislation will probably continue to cause significant growth in the cost of benefits.

Union Influence

Unions have been in the forefront of the movement to expand employee benefits for the last half century. In the 1940s, powerful unions such as the United Auto Workers and the United Mine Workers obtained pensions and health insurance plans from employers. In recent years, unions have been asking for dental-care coverage, extended vacation periods, and unemployment benefits beyond those required by federal law.

Once benefit patterns are established in unionized firms, these same benefits tend to spread to nonunionized companies, which often wish to avoid union organization drives.

Cost Savings of Group Plans

Employers can provide benefits for much less money than employees would pay to obtain them on their own. When insurance companies can spread risk over a large group of individuals, they can reduce the cost of benefits per person. This fact causes employees to put considerable pressure on their employers to provide certain benefits.

Types of Benefits

Benefits can be organized into six categories. These categories, which we examine in detail later in this chapter, are:

1. **Legally required benefits** U.S. law requires employers to give four benefits to all employees, with only a few exceptions: (1) Social Security, (2) workers' compensation, (3) unemployment insurance, and (4) family and medical leave. All other benefits are provided by employers voluntarily.
2. **Health insurance** Health insurance covers hospital costs, physician charges, and the costs of other medical services. Because of its importance, health insurance is usually considered separately from other types of insurance.
3. **Retirement** Retirement benefits provide income to employees after they retire.
4. **Insurance** Insurance plans protect employees or their dependents from financial difficulties that can arise as a result of disability or death.
5. **Paid time off** Time-off plans give employees time off with or without pay, depending on the plan.
6. **Employee services** Employee services are tax-free or tax-preferred services that enhance the quality of employees' work or personal life.

Figure 12.2 shows the percentage of full-time U.S. employers providing selected benefits plans. As the figure makes clear, large- and medium-sized private firms (those that employ more than 100 individuals) and state and local governments offer a wider variety of benefits than small businesses do.

The growth of benefits over the years, coupled with increased benefits costs, has encouraged employers to hire more part-time or temporary employees when their business grows. Companies often do not provide benefits to part-time employees and temporary employees.. However, both Starbucks and UPS discovered that it pays to offer good benefits even to part-time employees, as explained in the Manager's Notebook, "Starbucks and UPS Offer Generous Benefits to Part-Time Employees."

Figure 12.2 — Percentage of Employers Providing Selected Benefit Plans

	Medium and Large Private Firms*	Small Private Firms**	State and Local Governments
Health Insurance	76	64	86
Retirement Plans			
Defined Benefit Plans	50	15	90
Defined Contribution Plans	57	38	14
Insurance Plans			
Life Insurance	87	62	89
Long-Term Disability Insurance	43	22	34
Time-Off Plans			
Paid Vacations	95	86	67
Paid Holidays	89	80	73
Paid Sick Leave	56	50	96
Flexible Benefits Plans	13	4	5

*Firms employing 100 workers or more.

**Firms employing fewer than 100 workers.

Source: U.S. Department of Labor, Bureau of Labor Statistics (1999). *Employee benefit survey*; U.S. Department of Labor, Bureau of Labor Statistics (2000). *Employee benefits in state and local governments, 1998.*

Ethics

Starbucks and UPS Offer Generous Benefits to Part-Time Employees

Starbucks and UPS depend heavily on part-time employees to provide services to their customers. Each company offers a generous and broad array of employee benefits to its part-time employees, counter to the practices of most companies, which treat part-timers as second-class citizens. Both Starbucks and UPS recognize that it is a good business practice to treat part-time employees well when it comes to benefits. Here are some highlights of the benefits provided by these two companies:

Starbucks employs many part-time employees, called "baristas," at its ubiquitous coffee shops to serve customers during peak demand times. Part-time employees (those who work between 20 and 40 hours) receive the following benefits:

- Health-care benefits (medical, prescription drugs, dental, and vision care)
- Retirement savings plan
- Life insurance and disability insurance
- Adoption assistance
- Domestic partner benefits
- Referral programs and support resources for child and eldercare
- Discounted Starbucks merchandise
- Participation in stock program

UPS employs many part-time employees (and a large percentage of these part-timers are college students) to sort packages at its package-distribution centers. The shipping business alternates between bursts of activity and slack time throughout the day, which requires a high utilization of part-time employees. UPS part-time employees who work 15 or more hours per week have access to the following benefits:

- Comprehensive medical and life insurance for the employee and dependents
- 401(k) retirement plan
- $3,000 per year for tuition assistance
- $2,000 per year payback on UPS Earn & Learn Student Loans
- Paid vacations and holidays
- Discounted stock-purchase plan

Sources: Starbucks. (2005). "The starbucks experience." *www.starbucks.com/aboutus/jobcenter_thesbuxexperince.asp*; UPS. (2005). "UPS careers: Package operations." *ups.managehr.com/opportunities/parttime/main.html*; Clark, J. (2004, August). Steppingstone jobs for recent grads: These employers offer health insurance and more, even for part-timers. *Kiplinger's*, 107–108.

The Benefits Strategy

To design an effective benefits package, a company needs to align its benefits strategy with its overall compensation strategy. The benefits strategy requires making choices in three areas: (1) benefits mix, (2) benefits amount, and (3) flexibility of benefits. These choices provide a blueprint for the design of the benefits package.

Benefits mix
The complete package of benefits that a company offers its employees.

The Benefits Mix

The **benefits mix** is the complete package of benefits that a company offers its employees. There are at least three issues that should be considered when making decisions about the benefits mix: the total compensation strategy, organizational objectives, and the characteristics of the workforce.[11]

The total compensation strategy issue corresponds to the "below-market versus above-market compensation" decision we discussed in Chapter 10. The company must choose the market in which it wants to compete for employees and then provide a benefits package attractive to the people in that market. In other words, management tries to answer the question: Who are my competitors for employees and what kinds of benefits do they provide?

For example, a high-tech firm may want to attract people who are risk takers and innovators. The firm's management may decide not to offer retirement benefits because high-tech companies are usually considered desirable places to work by people in their 20s, and people this young are generally not concerned about retirement. As an upstart challenger to IBM, Apple Computer at first chose not to offer retirement benefits because management did not think this benefit would attract the entrepreneurial employees it wanted.[12] Later, when Apple's workforce became older, its employees expressed a need for retirement benefits, and Apple redesigned its benefits mix and offered retirement benefits in response to employees' needs.

The organization's objectives also influence the benefits mix. For instance, if the company philosophy is to minimize differences between low-level employees and top management, the benefits mix should be the same for all employees. If the organization is growing and needs to retain all its current personnel, it needs to ensure that it offers the benefits its workforce desires.

Finally, the characteristics of the workforce must be considered when choosing the benefits mix. If the firm's workforce consists largely of parents with young children, it is likely that child-care and other family-friendly benefits will be important. A professional workforce will probably want more say in decisions about its retirement funds. A unionized workforce is likely to demand a guaranteed retirement plan.

Benefits Amount

The choice of benefits amount governs the percentage of the total compensation package that will be allocated to benefits as opposed to the other components of the package (base salary and pay incentives). This choice corresponds to the "fixed versus variable pay" decision covered in Chapter 10. Once management determines the amount of money available for all benefits, it can establish a benefits budget and decide on the level of funding for each part of the benefits program. Management will then know how much it can contribute for each benefit and how much it will need to ask employees to pay toward that benefit. In larger companies, these calculations are usually performed by the benefits administrator; smaller companies often hire a benefits consultant to do the math.

A company that focuses on providing job security and long-term employment opportunities is likely to devote a large portion of its compensation dollars to benefits. One company that prides itself on its excellent employee benefits is Procter & Gamble (P&G). Its profit-sharing plan—the oldest such plan in continuous operation in the United States—was started in 1887. P&G was also one of the first companies to offer all its employees comprehensive sickness, disability, and life insurance programs.[13]

Flexibility of Benefits

The *flexibility of benefits choice* concerns the degree of freedom employees have to tailor the benefits package to their personal needs. This choice corresponds to the "centralization versus decentralization of pay" decision described in Chapter 10. Some organizations have a relatively standardized benefits package that gives employees few options. This system makes sense in organizations that have a fairly homogeneous workforce. In these firms, a standardized benefits package can be designed for a "typical" employee. However, because of the changing demographics of the U.S. workforce—more women working full-time, dual-career marriages, and single-parent families—there is now a greater variety of employee needs. In organizations that cannot develop a "typical" employee profile, a decentralized benefits package that emphasizes choice will probably be more effective. We discuss flexible benefits packages in detail at the end of this chapter.

A Question of Ethics

Most larger employers provide some sort of retirement fund for their employees. Do you think that companies are ethically bound to offer this benefit? Does the financial condition (good or poor) or size of the firm make any difference to your analysis?

Legally Required Benefits

With only a few exceptions, all U.S. employers are legally required to provide Social Security, workers' compensation, and unemployment insurance coverage for their employees—benefits that are designed to give the workforce a basic level of security. The employer pays a tax on an employee's earnings for each of these three required benefits. In the case of Social Security, the employee also pays a tax to fund the benefit. A fourth legally required benefit has been added in recent years: Employers must offer unpaid leave to employees in certain family and medical circumstances.

Social Security

Social Security

A government program that provides income for retirees, the disabled, and survivors of deceased workers, and health care for the aged through the Medicare program.

Social Security provides (1) income for retirees, the disabled, and survivors of deceased workers and (2) health care for the aged through the Medicare program. Established by the Social Security Act in 1935, Social Security is funded through a payroll tax paid in equal amounts by the employer and the employee. The Social Security tax in 2005 was 7.65 percent of an employee's annual earnings on the first $90,000 of income. This means that both the employer and employee pay a tax of 7.65 percent on the employee's earnings. The Social Security tax actually has two components: a tax of 6.2 percent to fund the retirement, disability, and survivor benefits, and a tax of 1.45 percent to fund Medicare. Employees who earn more than $90,000 are taxed at 1.45 percent of all their additional earnings. This 1.45 percent tax is also matched by the employer.

To be eligible for full Social Security benefits, a person must have worked 40 quarter-year periods (which equals 10 years of total employment) and have earned a minimum of $920 per quarter. Figure 12.3 spells out the provisions of the four Social Security benefits—retirement income, disability income, Medicare, and survivor benefits—and who is eligible to receive them.

Retirement Income

Social Security provides retirement income to people who retire at age 65. Workers who retire between ages 62 and 64 receive benefits reduced by as much as 20 percent.

Figure 12.3

Benefit	Eligibility	Provisions
Retirement income	■ Age 65–67 (full benefits) *or* ■ Age 62–64 (benefits reduced up to 20%)	Monthly payments for life beginning at retirement. Average benefit provides about 25 percent of earnings prior to retirement.
Disability income	■ Totally and continuously disabled for 5 months. ■ Disability should be expected to last at least 12 months or result in death.	Monthly payments comparable to retirement benefits as long as totally disabled. Provisions for payments to dependents.
Medicare	■ Age 65 *or* ■ Receiving Social Security disability payments for 24 months.	Covers hospital expenses, nursing home and home health agency expenses, subject to a deductible payment. Medical expenses are covered, subject to monthly premium.
Survivor benefits	■ Family members of the deceased person, including widow or widower age 60 or over, child or grandchild under age 18, or dependent parent age 62 or over.	Monthly payments related to the deceased worker's primary Social Security retirement benefit.

Source: Adapted from the 2005 Social Security online Web site *www.ssa.gov*.

Social Security Benefits

The retirement income provided by Social Security averages about 25 percent of one's earnings in the final year before retirement at age 65. This means that people need to develop other sources of postretirement income if they want to maintain a lifestyle similar to the one they enjoyed before retirement. These sources might include a company-provided pension plan, personal savings, or another job. According to the Social Security Administration, people who retired at age 65 in 2005 could expect a monthly Social Security check ranging from $579 to $1,939, depending on their preretirement earnings. In the future, the minimum age for receiving Social Security benefits will increase. For people born after 1950, the minimum retirement age for full benefits will be 66, and for individuals born in 1960 or later, it will be age 67. The average monthly retirement income provided by Social Security in 2005 was $955 for an individual and $1,574 for a retired married couple. The amount of Social Security retirement income for recipients is adjusted each year based on an automatic *cost of living adjustment* (COLA), computed by economists at the Social Security Administration in order to protect the standard of living of retirees (for additional information on COLAs, see Chapter 15).

Disability Income

For people who become disabled and cannot work for at least 12 months, Social Security provides a monthly income comparable to retirement benefits. Because the level of disability income averages only about 30 percent of one's earnings from the job, workers need to derive disability income from other sources. These sources include short- and long-term disability insurance and personal savings and investments. The average amount of Social Security disability income provided to beneficiaries in 2005 was $895 per month.

Medicare

Medicare provides health insurance coverage for people 65 and older. Medicare has two parts. Part A covers hospital costs. People who pay an annual deductible ($912 in 2005) receive up to 60 days of hospital expenses covered under Medicare. Part B, for which individuals pay a monthly fee ($78.20 in 2005), covers medical expenses such as doctors' fees and the cost of medical supplies. The deductibles and monthly fees for Medicare are adjusted periodically as the cost of medical care increases. Part C, called Medicare + Choice, is an alternative to the original program (Parts A and B) and provides health care from different options, such as managed care or private fee-for-service plans. Part D begins in 2006 and provides coverage for prescription drugs. The monthly premium for Part D coverage is $35 and a $250 deductible, after which Medicare pays 75 percent of drug costs, up to $2,250. After that, the beneficiary pays 100 percent of drug costs from $2,250 to $5,100. Finally, Medicare pays 95 percent of perscription drug costs above $5,100.[14]

Medicare
A part of the Social Security program that provides health insurance coverage for people aged 65 and over.

Survivor Benefits

A deceased employee's surviving family members may receive a monthly income if they qualify. Survivor benefits are related to the deceased worker's primary retirement benefit. Those eligible to receive survivor benefits are (1) widows and widowers age 60 and over, and (2) widows and widowers of any age who care for a child age 16 or younger, an unmarried child or grandchild younger than age 18, or a dependent parent age 62 or over.

Workers' Compensation

Workers' compensation provides medical care, income continuation, and rehabilitation expenses for people who sustain job-related injuries or sickness. "Workers' comp" also provides income to the survivors of an employee whose death is job related.

Workers' compensation is designed to provide a *no-fault remedy* to workers who are injured on the job. This means that even workers who were wholly at fault for their accidents can still receive a benefit. Employers who provide workers' compensation coverage cannot be sued by injured employees.

Workers' compensation is administered by state governments and is required by 48 of 50 states for all employees, including part-time workers. In Texas and New Jersey, workers' comp is elective. It is funded by a payroll tax, the proceeds of which go to a state workers' compensation

Workers' compensation
A legally required benefit that provides medical care, income continuation, and rehabilitation expenses for people who sustain job-related injuries or sickness. Also provides income to the survivors of an employee whose death is job related.

fund or to a private insurance company. Only the employer pays for workers' compensation. Although the average workers' compensation cost is only about 1 percent of total payroll expense, companies in accident-prone industries may pay more than 25 percent of their payroll in workers' compensation taxes.[15]

The rates that employers pay for workers' compensation are based on three factors: (1) the risk of injury for an occupation, (2) the frequency and severity of the injuries sustained by a company's workforce (called the company's injury *experience rating*), and (3) the level of benefits provided for specific injuries within the state where the company is located. Because the company's experience rating is based on its own safety record, managers have an incentive to design and promote a safe work environment: A better safety record leads directly to a lower payroll tax rate. Some states offer greater benefits to injured workers, which leads to higher workers' comp taxes assessed on employers in those states. States with the highest workers' compensation costs are California, Oklahoma, Louisiana, Rhode Island, Texas, and Florida.[16]

Small businesses in industries such as construction and food service have had great difficulty dealing with cost increases in workers' compensation taxes resulting from increasing claims. Consider the following examples:

■ Workers' compensation costs for William Solburg, the owner of a small construction company near Tallahassee, Florida, have skyrocketed. More than 25 percent of Solburg's total payroll costs go to cover workers' compensation insurance, and he foresees a significant increase in the near future. Solburg is uncertain whether his business can survive much longer with workers' compensation costs rising so quickly.[17]

■ At Olsten Corporation, a Westbury, New York, temporary employee service firm, workers' compensation costs tripled in a recent four-year period. Some of these cost increases came about because certain Olsten employees filed fraudulent claims for alleged long-term disabilities. When Olsten hired a detective agency to monitor a worker out on disability for a back injury, the camera caught him changing a tire on his car, a job that required bending over and heavy lifting.[18]

A Question of Ethics

One way for companies to lower their workers' compensation costs is to move from a state with a high workers' compensation tax rate to one with a lower rate. Is this a legitimate reason for moving a business? What other ethical issues should employers think about when trying to decrease workers' comp costs?

Some small companies are fighting back by banding together to form *self-insurance* pools. L.E. Mason Company, a Boston maker of lighting fixtures and other construction materials, joined a self-insurance group because its rates were 40 percent below Mason's alternatives. Here's how a self-insurance fund works: A fund's member companies, often in the same industry, band together and hire an administrator. The administrator contracts with actuaries, investment managers, health-care providers, and anyone else necessary to perform the functions of an insurance company. Fund members share one another's risk, paying losses out of premiums and investment returns. A typical fund member has between 60 and 100 employees and pays between $50,000 and $100,000 a year for coverage. By 2005, 49 states allowed self-insurance funds, with North Dakota the exception.

Self-insurance funds are not the answer for all companies. In firms that go it alone, HR staff can help managers control workers' compensation costs in several important ways:

■ The HR department should stress safe work procedures by impressing upon employees the importance of safety (see Chapter 16). Many accidents are caused by carelessness, ignorance of safe work practices, personal problems, or the use of alcohol or drugs. HR staff should train managers and supervisors to communicate and enforce the company's safety program. Employees who disregard safe work practices should be disciplined.[19]

■ The HR department should audit workers' compensation claims. Managers should challenge any claim they suspect is fraudulent or not job related. For example, a manager can ask an injured worker to submit to a drug test. A positive result from the drug test can be a reason for denying a claim. Or after a serious accident a safety specialist could conduct an investigation at the scene of the accident. Information gathered from the investigation may reveal inconsistencies in the story that may indicate the employee's claim is fraudulent.[20]

■ HR should manage how workers' comp benefits work with employers' health insurance benefits when workers sustain job-related injuries. HR should establish controls so that duplicate medical benefits are not paid out to employees.

■ HR staff should design jobs and work assignments so that there are fewer risks of injuries such as back strain and repetitive motion injuries. For example, employees can have their video display terminals adjusted daily to avoid strain on the arms and wrists.[21]

■ HR can encourage workers who are partially disabled to return to work under a *modified duty plan*. Under such a plan, a manager or HR staff member works with injured employees to develop modified tasks that they can perform until they are ready to handle their regular job. For instance, a maintenance worker with a back injury might be assigned to help schedule the work orders. Modified duty plans can save the company money on benefits that provide income continuation for employees who may be needlessly postponing the return to employment.

Unemployment Insurance

The Social Security Act of 1935 established **unemployment insurance** to provide temporary income for people during periods of involuntary unemployment. The program is part of a national wage stabilization policy designed to stabilize the economy during recessionary periods. The logic underlying this policy is fairly simple: If unemployed workers have enough income to maintain their consumption of basic goods and services, the demand for these products will be sustained, which ultimately will preserve the jobs of many people who might otherwise be added to the ranks of the unemployed.

> **Unemployment insurance**
> A program established by the Social Security Act of 1935 to provide temporary income for people during periods of involuntary unemployment.

Unemployment insurance is funded by a tax paid by employers on all employees' earnings. The tax averages 6.2 percent on the first $7,000 earned by each employee.[22] The proceeds of the tax are split between the state government and the federal government, which provide different services for the unemployed. The federal government levies a tax of 0.8 percent, a rate that does not change from employer to employer. In contrast, the state's assessment ranges from at or near zero to more than 10 percent (the average is about 5.4%). All the states give employers an experience rating comparing the employer's contributions to the unemployment insurance fund against the benefits drawn by the employer's workers from the fund over a period of time. This system allows the state to lower the unemployment tax rate for employers that discharge only a small number of employees, and raise it for those that discharge large numbers of employees for any reason (including layoffs).

To be eligible for unemployment insurance, employees must meet several qualifications. First, they must be available for and actively seeking employment. Second, they must have worked a minimum of four quarter-year periods out of the last five quarter-year periods and have earned at least $1,000 during those four quarter-year periods combined. Finally, they must have left their job involuntarily.

Employees may be disqualified for unemployment insurance benefits for several reasons. The following people are not eligible for unemployment insurance:

■ An employee who quits voluntarily.
■ An employee who is discharged for gross misconduct (for example, for failing a drug test).
■ An employee who refuses an offer of suitable work (that is, a job and pay level comparable to the employee's previous position).
■ An employee who participates in a strike (48 of 50 states deny benefits to strike participants).
■ A person who is self-employed.[23]

Unemployment benefits were designed to cover an employee's basic living expenses but not to be a disincentive against actively seeking employment. For this reason, unemployment benefits seldom cover more than 50 percent of lost earnings, and people discharged from high-paying jobs generally receive only a small fraction of their lost earnings. States have developed their own schedules for unemployment benefits and cap them at a maximum level that ranges from about $100 to $500 per week. Unemployment benefits last for 26 weeks, although in states with persistently high unemployment rates, extensions of benefits in 13-week periods may be given. In addition, some companies provide **supplemental unemployment benefits (SUB)** to their laid-off employees. These benefits are most often written into the union contract.

> **Supplemental unemployment benefits (SUB)**
> Benefits given by a company to laid-off employees over and above state unemployment benefits.

It is interesting to compare the level of replacement income and duration of benefits provided by unemployment insurance in the United States to the benefits provided to unemployed workers in other countries.[24]

■ United States: 50 percent of salary for 6 months
■ Italy: 80 percent of salary for 6 months

- Japan: 80 percent of salary for 10 months
- France: 75 percent of salary for 60 months
- Germany: 60 percent of salary for 12 months
- Sweden: 80 percent of salary for 15 months

The amount and duration of unemployment benefits in the United States are modest compared to benefits in other countries. In the United States, government policy is designed to encourage unemployed workers to actively seek employment, and it views generous benefits as suppressing an employee's motivation to search for a new job.

Containing the costs of unemployment insurance is an important priority for management. The HR department can make significant contributions here by establishing practices that lower the firm's experience rating. Here are some useful HR practices in this area:

- HR planning can tell management whether an increase in the company's workload is due to short or long-term causes. Short-term increases in the workload should be handled by hiring temporary employees or consultants rather than by creating full-time positions. Because neither temporary employees nor consultants can claim unemployment benefits, it costs the company nothing to let them go when the workload decreases. If the increased workload appears to be long-term, however, the company may decide to hire more full-time employees.
- The employee benefits administrator should audit all unemployment claims filed by former employees. Employers have the right to appeal these claims, and in about half the cases they win.[25]
- Managers or members of the HR department should conduct exit interviews with all discharged employees to (1) come to a mutual understanding on the reason for termination and (2) advise them that the company will fight unemployment claims not made for good reason. For example, if an employee discharged for theft makes a claim for unemployment benefits, the company will contest the claim.

Unpaid Leave

Family and Medical Leave Act of 1993 (FMLA)
A federal law that requires employers to provide up to 12 weeks' unpaid leave to eligible employees for the birth or adoption of a child; to care for a sick parent, child, or spouse; or to take care of health problems that interfere with job performance.

Employees occasionally need long periods of time off to take care of their families or their own health problems. Until recently, most employers refused to give workers unpaid leaves for any reason other than the birth of a child. The **Family and Medical Leave Act of 1993 (FMLA)**, enacted under the Clinton administration, now requires most employers to provide up to 12 weeks' unpaid leave to eligible employees for the following reasons:[26]

- The birth of a child
- The adoption of a child
- To care for a sick spouse, child, or parent
- To take care of the employee's own serious health problems that interfere with effective job performance

The FMLA applies only to businesses with 50 or more employees and to employers with multiple facilities that have 50 workers within a 75-mile radius. The law requires employers to give employees returning from FMLA leave the same job they held before taking the leave or an equivalent job. Employers must maintain coverage of health insurance and other employee benefits while the employee is on FMLA leave.[27] Employees are eligible to take FMLA leave after accumulating one year of service with their employer. "Highly compensated" employees—those at the top 10 percent of the pay scale and who tend to be the company's top managers—are not eligible for FMLA leave because it may be a hardship for the employer to replace them for a 12-week period.

The FMLA forces companies to develop contingency plans to keep their operations running with a minimum of disruption and added cost when employees are on leave. Managers may want to consider (1) cross-training some workers to cover for employees on leave or (2) hiring temporary workers.[28]

Mandatory unpaid leave also forces companies to confront some troublesome issues, such as:

- Can employees substitute accrued sick days for unpaid leave?
- What sort of illnesses are serious enough to justify a leave?[29]

The Family and Medical Leave Act of 1993 requires most employers to provide up to 12 weeks of unpaid leave to eligible employees who experience the birth or adoption of a child; need to care for a sick spouse, child, or parent; or who must take care of their own serious health problems that interfere with job performance.

■ How can FMLA leave be coordinated with other laws such as the Americans with Disabilities Act?

■ Just what constitutes an "equivalent" job when a leavetaker returns and finds his or her job filled?

The last question was the subject of a Wisconsin lawsuit filed well before the FMLA was passed. Elizabeth Marquardt returned from maternity leave to find that her Milwaukee-based employer, Kelley Company, had eliminated her job as credit manager during a restructuring. Kelley gave Marquardt a new job with the same pay and benefits. However, the new job involved supervising one employee instead of four, and unlike the old position, it included about 25 percent clerical work. Marquardt resigned the next day. Kelley claimed that the reassignment was intended to sidestep Marquardt's longstanding problems with customers. But a Wisconsin appeals court ruled that the jobs were not equivalent because Marquardt's "authority and responsibility were greatly reduced in the new position." HR professionals and line managers will have to work together to avoid such court challenges.[30] The Manager's Notebook, "What to Do When an Employee Returns from FMLA Leave," specifies an employer's duties and obligations.

Surveys that have examined how employees have used FMLA show that over 80 percent of the time it was used by workers recovering from an illness or caring for a sick family member. More than 14 percent of eligible workers use FMLA every year, and 35 percent of leavetakers were off more than once, according to a 2005 survey by the Employment Policy Foundation. The method employers were most likely to use to cover for an employee taking FMLA leave was to assign the work temporarily to other employees; the second-most prevalent method was to hire an outside temporary replacement to do the work.[31]

Emerging Trends

MANAGER'S NOTEBOOK

What to Do When an Employee Returns from FMLA Leave

Employers have both duties and rights when an employee returns from FMLA leave. Here are some key points to consider:

1. Although an employer is not required to hold an employee's specific position open for an indefinite period of time, the employee is entitled to an "equivalent" job when he or she returns. Under FMLA, an equivalent position is one that is virtually identical to the former position in terms of pay, benefits, and working conditions. The job must also have the same or substantially similar duties and responsibilities.

2. On returning from FMLA, the employee must receive any unconditional pay raises, such as cost-of-living increases, given to other employees during the leave period. The employee must also be given all benefits accrued at the time his or her leave began, such as paid vacation, sick leave, or personal leave, unless this has been substituted for FMLA leave.

3. An employer is not required to apply the time taken for FMLA to seniority or length of service schedules that are used to determine pay increases, promotions, or other rewards unless the employer's policy is to recognize all unpaid leave taken by employees as an input to seniority.

4. Employers are not required to provide an equivalent position to a returning employee who took FMLA leave if the employee is laid off during the leave period, or his or her work shift is eliminated. Similarly, if an employee would have been terminated because of misconduct or incompetence that occurred before the leave, the employer isn't required to reinstate the employee after the leave.

Source: Adapted from Flynn, G. (1999, April). What to do after an FMLA leave. *Workforce,* 104–107.

Voluntary Benefits

The benefits provided voluntarily by employers include health insurance, retirement benefits, other types of insurance plans, time off, and employee services. Future legislation may move some of these benefits from the voluntary category to the legally required category.

Health Insurance

Health insurance provides health-care coverage for both employees and their dependents, protecting them from financial disaster in the wake of a serious illness. Because the cost of individually obtained health insurance is much higher than that of an employer-sponsored group health plan, many people could not afford health insurance if it were not provided by their employer. As Figure 12.2 on page 375 shows, 76 percent of large- and medium-sized private businesses in the United States offer health insurance to their employees. However, only 64 percent of small firms (those with fewer than 100 employees) do so. It has been estimated that about 45 million people in the United States do not have any health insurance coverage.[32]

During the early 1990s, U.S. health-care costs increased at an astonishing 10 to 20 percent per year. By 2005 spending on health care accounted for about 15 percent of the U.S. gross domestic product (GDP). This is the highest percentage found in any country in the world. For example, per capita health spending in the United States exceeds that of Canada by 50 percent, of Germany by 39 percent, and of the United Kingdom by 104 percent. And unlike the United States, these countries provide health-care coverage for all their citizens. Figure 12.4 compares health-care expenditures across the 24 countries that were members of the Organization for Economic Cooperation and Development (OECD) in 2003.

Obviously, cost containment of health spending will be an important issue for companies and the nation for many years. The benefits specialist in the HR department can make an important contribution to the bottom line by keeping spending on health insurance under control. For example, many companies are now requiring employees to make larger contributions toward the cost of their health insurance.

The health insurance benefits that a company offers are significantly affected by the **Consolidated Omnibus Budget Reconciliation Act (COBRA) of 1985**, which gives employees the right to continue their health insurance coverage after their employment has terminated. Employees and their dependents are entitled to 18 to 36 months' additional coverage from the group health insurance plan after separation from the organization. Employees who quit or are discharged from an organization are entitled to 18 months of continued group health coverage under COBRA, whereas a divorced spouse of an employee or a survivor of a deceased employee can receive up to 36 months of continued coverage. The former employee (or relative of the employee) must pay the full cost of coverage at the group rate, plus a 2-percent administrative fee, which is still considerably less than the individual rate that could be purchased from a

Consolidated Omnibus Budget Reconciliation Act of 1985 (COBRA)
Legislation that gives employees the right to continue their health insurance coverage for 18 to 36 months after their employment has terminated.

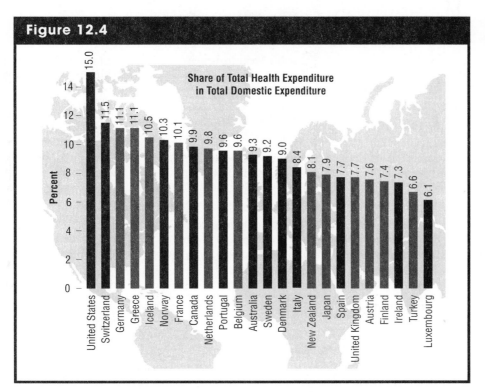

Figure 12.4

Share of Total Health Expenditure in Total Domestic Expenditure

Health Spending in Various Countries 2003

Source: OECD health data (2005), *www.oecd.org.*

health insurance company on the open market. All employees who are covered by an organization's health-care plan are also covered by COBRA provisions.

The ability of an employee to transfer between health insurance plans without a gap in coverage due to a preexisting condition is protected by a federal law enacted in 1996 called the **Health Insurance Portability and Accountability Act (HIPAA)**. A **preexisting condition** is a medical condition that was treated while the employee was covered under a former employer's health plan and requires further treatment under a new employer's different health plan. Under HIPAA, an employee earns a credit of coverage for every month he or she is covered by the former employer's health insurance plan. When an employee earns 12 months of credit with the former employer, he or she is immediately covered by the new employer's health plan and cannot be denied coverage due to a preexisting condition.[33] In 2004, new provisions were added to HIPAA that require employers to ensure protection of employees' privacy concerning health information so that it is not used in any employment-related decisions without an employee's consent. Employers are expected to erect a privacy shield around employees' personal health information, so that if an employee has been diagnosed with cancer, for example, this information is not disclosed to a manager without the employee's permission.[34]

There are three common types of employer-provided health insurance plans: (1) traditional health insurance, (2) health maintenance organizations (HMOs), and (3) preferred provider organizations (PPOs). Figure 12.5 summarizes the differences among these plans.

Health Insurance Portability and Accountability Act (HIPAA)
A federal law that protects an employee's ability to transfer between health insurance plans without a gap in coverage due to a preexisting condition.

Preexisting condition
A medical condition treated while an employee was covered under a former employer's health plan and requires treatment under a new employer's different health plan.

Traditional Health Insurance

Provided by an insurance company that acts as an intermediary between the patient and health-care provider, *traditional health insurance plans* (also called *fee-for-service plans*) develop a fee schedule based on the cost of medical services in a specific community. They then incorporate these fees into the costs of insurance coverage. The best-known examples of traditional health insurance plans are the Blue Cross and Blue Shield organizations. Traditional health insurance covers hospital and surgical expenses, physicians' care, and a substantial portion of expenses for serious illnesses. In 2004 traditional health plans were selected by 5 percent of employees who had health insurance coverage.[35]

Traditional health insurance plans have several important features. First, they include a deductible that a policyholder must meet before the plan makes any reimbursements. Second, they require a monthly group rate (also called a **premium**) paid to the insurance company. The premium is usually paid partially by the employer and partially by the employee. Third, they provide for coinsurance. The typical coinsurance allocation is 80/20 (80% of the cost is covered

Premium
The money paid to an insurance company for coverage.

Figure 12.5

Issue	Traditional Coverage	Health Maintenance Organization (HMO)	Preferred Provider Organization (PPO)
Where must the covered parties live?	May live anywhere.	May be required to live in an HMO-designated service area.	May live anywhere.
Who provides health care?	Doctor and health-care facility of patient's choice.	Must use doctors and facilities designated by HMO.	May use doctors and facilities associated with PPO. If not, may pay additional copayment/deductible.
How much coverage of routine/preventive medicine?	Does not cover regular checkups and other preventive services. Diagnostic tests may be covered in part or full.	Covers regular checkups, diagnostic tests, and other preventive services with low or no fee per visit.	Same as HMO if doctor and facility are on approved list. Copayment and deductibles are much higher for doctors and facilities not on list.
What hospital care costs are covered?	Covers doctors' and hospitals' bills.	Covers doctors' bills; covers bills of HMO-approved hospitals.	Covers bills of PPO-approved doctors and hospitals.

Source: Milkovich, G., and Newman, J. (2002). *Compensation* (7th ed.), 473. Homewood, IL: Irwin McGraw-Hill.

Employer-Provided Health Insurance Plans

by the insurance plan and 20% is picked up by the employee). The deductible, premium, and coinsurance can be adjusted, so the employer's and employee's costs of health-care insurance vary depending on how the parties agree to allocate the costs.

Traditional plans give employees the greatest amount of choice in selecting a physician and a hospital. However, these plans have several disadvantages. First, they often do not cover regular checkups and other preventive services. Second, calculating the deductible and coinsurance allocation requires a significant amount of paperwork. Each time they visit a physician, employees must fill out claims forms and obtain bills with long, itemized lists of services. This can be frustrating for patients and costly to physicians, who often need to hire clerical workers solely to process forms.

Health Maintenance Organizations (HMOs)

Health maintenance organization (HMO)
A health-care plan that provides comprehensive medical services for employees and their families at a flat annual fee.

A **health maintenance organization (HMO)** is a health-care plan that provides comprehensive medical services for employees and their families at a flat annual fee. People covered by an HMO have unlimited access to medical services, because the HMO is designed to encourage preventive health care to reduce ultimate costs. (The "stitch in time saves nine" analogy applies here.) HMO members pay a monthly premium, plus a small copayment or deductible. Some HMOs have no copayment or deductible. The HMOs' annual flat fee per member acts as a monetary disincentive to the HMOs' participatory doctors, who might otherwise be tempted to give patients unnecessary medical tests or casually refer them to expensive medical specialists. In 2004, HMOs were selected by 40 percent of employees who have health insurance coverage.[36]

HMOs have two major advantages. First, for a fixed fee, people covered by the HMO receive most of their medical services (including preventive care) without incurring coinsurance or deductibles or having to fill out claims forms. Second, HMOs encourage preventive health care and healthier lifestyles.

The major disadvantage of HMOs is that they restrict people's ability to select their physicians and the hospitals at which they receive medical services. The HMO may service a limited geographic area, which may restrict who can join the plan. People may be forced to leave their existing doctor and choose one from a list of those who belong to the HMO. In the case of serious illnesses, the specialists consulted must also belong to the HMO, even if there are doctors in the area with better reputations and stronger qualifications. In addition, some consumer groups have criticized HMOs for skimping on patient care to save money on medical costs.

To deal with the problem of patients being denied health-care services by administrators under an HMO, federal lawmakers have proposed a "Patient's Bill of Rights," which is intended to protect patients from abuses of cost-control policies. Although federal lawmakers continue to debate this issue, 38 states now have laws allowing patients to appeal medical decisions to external review boards that have independent experts. In addition, 10 states, led by Texas, have passed laws giving patients the right to sue HMOs, and 23 more are considering such legislation.[37]

Preferred Provider Organizations (PPOs)

A **preferred provider organization (PPO)** is a health-care plan in which an employer or insurance company establishes a network of doctors and hospitals to provide a broad set of medical services for an annual flat fee per participant. The fee is lower than that which doctors and hospitals normally charge their customers for the bundle of services, and the monthly premium is lower than that charged by a traditional plan for the same services. In return for charging a lower fee, the doctors and hospitals who join the PPO network expect to receive a larger volume of patients. Members of the PPO can use it for preventive health care (such as checkups) without paying a doctor's usual fee for the service. PPOs collect information on the utilization of their health services so that employers can periodically improve the plan's design and reduce costs. In 2004, PPOs were selected by 55 percent of employees who have health insurance coverage.[38]

PPOs combine some of the best features of HMOs (managed health care and a wide array of medical services for a fixed fee) with the flexibility of the traditional health insurance plan. They include provisions that allow their members to go outside the PPO network and use non-PPO doctors and medical facilities. People who select non-PPO doctors and hospitals pay additional fees in the form of deductibles and copayments determined by the PPO. Because PPOs have few of the disadvantages of traditional health insurance plans or HMOs, they are expected to continue growing rapidly.

Millions of employees have no health insurance coverage because they are self-employed or work for small businesses whose owners offer no health benefits to reduce costs. These persons who are uncovered by employer-sponsored health insurance plans will need to find their own health insurance coverage. The Manager's Notebook, "Tips for Obtaining Your Own Health Insurance," should provide some useful insights for those who are seeking health insurance coverage.

Preferred provider organization (PPO)
A health-care plan in which an employer or insurance company establishes a network of doctors and hospitals to provide a broad set of medical services for a flat fee per participant. In return for the lower fee, the doctors and hospitals who join the PPO network expect to receive a larger volume of patients.

Customer-Driven HR

MANAGER'S NOTEBOOK

Tips for Obtaining Your Own Health Insurance

Buying your own health insurance can be more expensive than having coverage with an employer-sponsored plan. That's because an employer can spread the risks of an illness or injury over a large group of employees so that the costs are more predictable than for an individual. Here are some ways an individual can find health insurance coverage at a reasonable cost when no employer-sponsored plan is provided.

- **Form your own small group.** Even for small groups, health insurance policies cost 20 to 50 percent less than individual policies. For example, in New Jersey two employees can form a group as long as each employee works a minimum of 25 hours per week. In the state of Washington, self-employed people can form a group of one and have a wider selection of policies with more competitive prices.
- **Join an association that has group coverage.** In some areas, such as Rochester, New York, the local chamber of commerce offers some of the best health insurance options for individuals without employer coverage.
- **Check out prices on the Web.** In most states, *eHealthInsurance.com* can give you immediate quotes from several companies, including many Blue Cross/Blue Shield plans, and will spell out what benefits you will get for the price.
- **Take advantage of COBRA provisions.** If you have left a company that provided health insurance benefits coverage, and your employer had more than 20 employees, the company is

required by law to let you continue your health insurance coverage for up to 18 months. In order to receive this health insurance coverage under the COBRA law, you need to pay the full cost of the health insurance plus an additional 2 percent in administrative expenses. COBRA coverage may be useful if you need to stay under the care of your current doctors. However, because company plans often have more features than an individual may need, you may find a better deal by shopping around for a health plan with only the basic features that you need.

Source: Adapted from Lankford, K. (2001, February). The best of health: Finding a policy you can afford when you're on your own. *Kiplinger's,* 82–86.

Health Insurance Coverage of Employees' Partners

Traditionally, health insurance benefits have been offered only to employees and their spouses or dependents. Today, however, employers are being asked to offer the same health insurance benefits to employees' domestic partners—that is, unmarried heterosexual or homosexual partners.

So far, only a handful of companies and municipalities allow employees to include domestic partners in their health insurance coverage, and most of these limit coverage to gay and lesbian employees. But among the firms that offer such benefits are some of the most prestigious names in U.S. business: Silicon Graphics, Microsoft, Viacom, Apple Computer, and Warner Bros. Companies that also cover unmarried heterosexual couples include Ben & Jerry's Homemade, Levi Strauss, and the Federal National Mortgage Association (Fannie Mae).

Most of corporate America, however, is resisting the pressure to extend health insurance benefits to domestic partners for a number of reasons. First, some companies fear that they will end up footing the bill for more AIDS-related expenses if they offer health benefits to gay partners. Second, companies fear that employees will abuse the domestic partner benefits by signing up a friend or a string of partners. Finally, companies worry about pitting gay and straight employees against each other, since most current plans offer benefits only to same-sex couples.

Most of these fears seem unfounded. Research shows that, in fact, health-care costs for gay partners and unmarried heterosexual couples are often lower than those for married couples. Moreover, many homosexual employees do not sign up for the benefits because they want to keep their sexual orientation private. Employers can protect themselves against abuse by asking eligible employees to file affidavits of "spousal equivalency" showing a history of living together and sharing assets. The question of pitting heterosexual employees against gay and lesbian employees may become moot because the growing threat of discrimination lawsuits may force employers to offer coverage to all domestic partners in the near future.[39]

Health Savings Accounts

Health Savings Account (HSA)
A qualified health plan with a high deductible that lets individuals save money for health-care expenses with pretax dollars and lets unspent money accumulate as a tax-free stash of money.

In 2004, a new type of medical plan, called a **health savings account (HSA)** became available to employees. An HSA lets individuals save money for health-care expenses with pretax dollars. Employers offer the accounts in conjuction with a qualified health plan that has a high deductible—at least $1,000 for single coverage and $2,000 for a family, to a maximum in 2005 of $2,650 for singles and $5,250 for families.[40] The account's earnings are not taxed, nor are withdrawls used to pay for qualified medical expenses. HSAs allow unspent money to be rolled over from one year to the next, potentially building up a tax-free stash of money. In exchange for higher deductibles, premiums on HSAs are lower than on other health insurance policies, making them attractive for relatively healthy families that do not need a lot of routine care and preventive services.

The theory behind the HSA concept is that the more of one's own money a customer of medical services spends, the more likely that person will make financially responsible decisions, such as skipping a visit to an emergency room for a minor problem or choosing a generic rather than a brand-name drug.[41]

Health-Care Cost Containment

A company's HR benefits manager can control health-care costs by designing (and modifying) health insurance plans carefully and developing programs that encourage employees to adopt healthier lifestyles. Specifically, HR staff can:

■ **Develop a self-funding arrangement for health insurance.** A company is self-funding when it puts the money it would otherwise pay in insurance premiums into a fund to pay employee health-care expenses. Under this type of plan, the employer has an incentive to assume some responsibility for employees' health. Self-funding plans can be designed to capture administrative efficiencies that translate into lower costs for the same services provided by a traditional health insurance plan.[42]

■ **Coordinate health insurance plans for families with two working spouses.** HR staff can encourage spouses who have duplicate coverage under two different insurance plans to establish a cost-sharing arrangement. Many companies, such as General Electric, require employees whose working spouses decline their own employers' health insurance to pay a significantly higher premium than nonworking spouses or those who cannot get insurance elsewhere.[43]

■ **Develop a wellness program for employees.** A *wellness program* assesses employees' risk of serious illness (for example, heart disease or cancer) and then teaches them how to reduce that risk by changing some of their habits (such as diet, exercise, and avoidance of harmful substances such as alcohol, tobacco, and caffeine).[44] Adolph Coors Company, the Colorado-based beer producer, has a wellness program composed of six areas: health hazard appraisal, exercise, smoking cessation, nutrition and weight loss, physical and cardiovascular rehabilitation, and stress and anger management. It has been estimated that Coors' wellness program returns $3.37 to the company for each dollar spent on it.[45]

Retirement Benefits

After retiring, people have three main sources of income: Social Security, personal savings, and retirement benefits. Because Social Security can be expected to provide only about one-fourth of preretirement earnings, retirees must rely on retirement benefits and personal savings to maintain their standard of living. Retirement benefits support an employee's long-term financial goal of achieving a planned level of retirement income.

An important service that the HR department can provide to employees nearing retirement is preretirement counseling. *Preretirement counseling* sessions give employees information about their retirement benefits so that they can plan their retirement years accordingly.[46] A benefits specialist can answer questions such as:

■ What will my total retirement income be when Social Security is added to it?
■ Would I be better off taking my retirement benefits in the form of a lump sum or as an annuity (a fixed amount of income each year)?
■ What would be the tax effects on my retirement benefits if I earn additional income from a part-time job?

Retirement benefit plans that are "qualified" by the Internal Revenue Service receive favorable tax treatment under the Internal Revenue Code. To qualify, the retirement plan must be available to broad classes of employees and must not favor highly compensated workers over lower-paid workers. Under a qualified retirement plan, employees pay no taxes on the contributions made to the plan until these funds are distributed at retirement. Also, the earnings on the fund's investments accumulate without being taxed each year. Employers may also take a tax deduction for the annual contributions they make to a qualified retirement plan.

ERISA

The major law governing the administration of retirement benefits in the United States is the **Employee Retirement Income Security Act (ERISA).** Passed in 1974, ERISA protects employees' retirement benefits from mismanagement.[47] The key provisions of ERISA cover who is eligible for retirement benefits, vesting, and funding requirements.

■ **Eligibility for retirement benefits.** ERISA requires that the minimum age for participation in a retirement plan cannot be greater than 21. However, employers may restrict participation in the retirement plan to employees who have completed one year of service with the company.

Employee Retirement Income Security Act (ERISA)
A federal law established in 1974 to protect employees' retirement benefits from mismanagement.

Vesting
A guarantee that accrued retirement benefits will be given to retirement plan participants when they retire or leave the employer.

Portable benefits
Employee benefits, usually retirement funds, that stay with the employee as he or she moves from one company to another.

Pension Benefit Guaranty Corporation (PBGC)
The government agency that provides plan termination insurance to employers with defined benefit retirement programs.

Defined benefit plan or pension
A retirement plan that promises to pay a fixed dollar amount of retirement income based on a formula that takes into account the average of the employee's last three to five years' earnings prior to retirement.

Defined contribution plan
A retirement plan in which the employer promises to contribute a specific amount of funds into the plan for each participant. The final value of each participant's retirement income depends on the success of the plan's investments.

■ **Vesting.** A guarantee that accrued retirement benefits will be given to retirement plan participants when they retire or leave the employer is called *vesting.* Under current ERISA rules, employee vesting rules must conform to one of two schedules: (1) full vesting after five years of service; or (2) 20 percent vesting after three years of service and a further 20 percent vesting each year thereafter, until the employee is fully vested at seven years of service. Employers are allowed to vest employees faster than this if they wish. Vesting pertains only to employer contributions to the retirement plan. Any contributions the employee has made to the plan are always the employee's property, along with any earnings that have accumulated on those contributions. These employee-provided funds, and any employer contributions that are vested, are said to be **portable**—that is, they stay with the employee as he or she moves from one company to another.

■ **Funding requirements and obligations.** In addition to establishing guidelines for a retirement plan's minimum funding requirements, ERISA requires that retirement plan administrators act prudently in making investments with participants' funds. Plans that do not meet ERISA funding standards are subject to financial penalties from the Internal Revenue Service.

To protect employees from an employer's possible failure to meet its retirement obligations, ERISA requires employers to pay for plan termination insurance, which guarantees the payment of retirement benefits to employees even if the plan terminates (either because of poor investment decisions or because the company has gone out of business) before they retire. Termination insurance for defined benefit plans (discussed next) is provided by the **Pension Benefit Guaranty Corporation (PBGC)**, a government agency.

Defined Benefit Plans

A **defined benefit plan**, also called a **pension**, is a retirement plan that promises to pay a fixed dollar amount of retirement income based on a formula that takes into account the average of the employee's last three to five years' earnings before retirement. The amount of annual income provided by defined benefit plans increases with the years of service to the employer. For example, based on a final five-year preretirement average salary of $50,000, Eastman Kodak's pension plan pays a retired employee with 30 years of service $20,523 per year at age 65. Merck, the pharmaceutical giant, pays an employee with the same salary and 30 years of service $24,000 per year at age 65.[48] Medium and large companies are more likely to provide a pension plan for their workers: 50 percent of these firms offer a defined contribution plan, compared to only 15 percent of small businesses (see Figure 12.2).

Under a defined benefit plan, the employer assumes all the risk of providing the promised income to the retiree and is likely to make all of the financial contributions to the plan. Defined benefit plans are most appropriate for firms that want to provide a secure and predictable retirement income for employees. Michigan-based Dow Chemical is one such company.[49] Such plans are less appropriate for firms that stress risk taking and want employees to share in the risk and responsibility of managing their retirement assets.

Most companies that use defined benefit plans for retirement provide the maximum retirement income only after an employee has spent an entire career of 30 to 35 years with the company. Those who change jobs by moving to different companies are penalized with much lower retirement incomes. Employees currently entering the labor market expect to change jobs and employers several times. Defined benefit plans are less attractive to these employees, because few will spend an entire career at one company. Consequently, there has been a decline in the number of companies offering defined benefit plans for their employees' retirement.[50]

Defined Contribution Plans

A **defined contribution plan** is a retirement plan in which the employer promises to contribute a specific amount of funds into the plan for each participant. For example, a defined contribution plan may require the employer to contribute 6 percent of the employee's salary into the plan each pay period. Some defined contribution plans also allow or require employees to make additional contributions to the plan. The retirement income that the participants receive depends on the success of the plan's investments and therefore cannot be known in advance.[51] Companies that value employee risk taking and participation are likely to offer defined contribution plans. Under these plans, employees and employers share both risk and responsibility for retirement

				Tax Break on
Plan	**Available to**	**Appropriate for**	**Maximum Contributions**	**Contributions Earnings**
401(k)	Employees of for-profit businesses	Everyone who qualifies	15 percent of salary up to $14,000 in 2005	Yes/Yes
IRA	Anyone with earned income	Those without company pension plans or who have put the maximum into their company plan	100 percent of salary up to $4,000, $8,000 if joint with spouse	Sometimes/Yes
SEP	The self-employed and employees of small businesses	Self-employed person who is a sole proprietor	25 percent of gross self-employment income or $41,000, whichever is less	Yes/Yes
Profit-Sharing Keogh	The self-employed and employees of unincorporated small businesses	Small-business owner who is funding a plan for self and employees	Same as SEP	Yes/Yes

Source: Internal Revenue Service Web site (2005). www.irs.gov

A Comparison of Defined Contribution Retirement Plans

benefits. Employees may need to decide how to allocate their retirement funds from different investment choices that represent various levels of risk. Because they require fewer obligations from employers than defined benefit plans, most of the new retirement plans established in recent years have been defined contribution plans.

There is a dark side to this trend toward defined contribution plans. Whereas highly educated and highly paid employees may benefit from such risk-taking arrangements, defined contribution plans are likely to be devastating for low-wage workers, according to a report by the Senate Labor and Human Resources Committee. By the year 2020, more than 50 million U.S. men and women will be of retirement age, but many will not be able to retire because as low-wage earners, they could not afford to invest in the defined contribution plans established by their employers. Many of these low-wage workers are women.[52]

Figure 12.6 summarizes the most common defined contribution retirement plans: the 401(k) plan, the individual retirement account (IRA), the simplified employee pension (SEP), and the profit-sharing Keogh. These plans all have tax benefits that can prove very valuable in the long run.

401(k) Plan. To understand the features and benefits of a *401(k) plan* (as well as other tax-deferred retirement plans), consider the following situation. Suppose you want to save $100 per month for your retirement, you are in the 28 percent federal income tax bracket, and the money you invest will earn 8 percent per year. If you save the money out of your salary and put it into a personal savings account, the $1,200 that you set aside each year would, in effect, be reduced to $864 because of taxes (Figure 12.7). With one year's interest, that $864 would grow to $891. Each year the investment earnings would also be taxed at the 28 percent rate. If you continue to set aside $1,200 each year in a personal account, your retirement fund would grow to $67,514 in 30 years.

With tax-deferred retirement plans like the 401(k), the money you save each month is not taxed. Therefore, each year you are saving the full $1,200 you put into your retirement account. In addition, the earnings on your investment are not taxed. After the first year, the value of your account would be $1,251 (compared to $864 under the personal account scenario). After 30 years, the value would grow to $141,761, more than twice the size of the personal account. When you retire and draw the funds, your withdrawals will be taxed at your retirement tax rate.

Personal Account versus Deferred Compensation Plan

Source: State of Tennessee. *Introduction to the deferred compensation programs.*

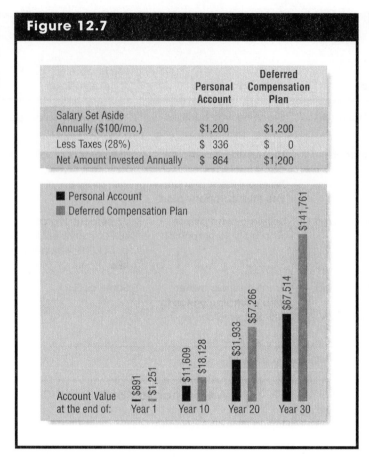

Figure 12.7

	Personal Account	Deferred Compensation Plan
Salary Set Aside Annually ($100/mo.)	$1,200	$1,200
Less Taxes (28%)	$ 336	$ 0
Net Amount Invested Annually	$ 864	$1,200

- ■ Personal Account
- ■ Deferred Compensation Plan

Account Value at the end of:	Year 1	Year 10	Year 20	Year 30
Personal Account	$891	$11,609	$31,933	$67,514
Deferred Compensation Plan	$1,251	$18,128	$57,266	$141,761

Anyone who works for a for-profit business is eligible to participate in a 401(k) plan.[53] Most companies that establish 401(k) plans will match 25 percent to 100 percent of employee contributions up to 6 percent of the employee's salary.[54] In 2005 the maximum employee annual contribution that could be made to a 401(k) plan was 15 percent of salary up to a limit of $14,000. Employees in not-for-profit companies can also save for retirement with a 403(b) retirement plan, which has the same features as the 401(k) plan. The 403(b) plan lets employees in not-for-profit organizations take advantage of the same retirement savings opportunities as those offered to employees in the for-profit sector who are eligible to participate with a 401(k) plan.

The 401(k) plan's matching feature makes it attractive to both employers and employees. Employees benefit by accumulating tax-deferred retirement funds; employers benefit by reducing their risk, because there is no payment required when the employee leaves or retires. Usually, employees are free to decide individually how they wish to invest their funds. The basic choice is between an investment strategy with a high potential return, but the risk of a low or even a negative return, and a strategy with low risk and a low to moderate return. Investing in the stock market is an example of the first investment strategy; investing in a savings account is an example of the second.

One controversial aspect of 401(k) plans is a practice that permits many large companies to provide their matching contribution to an employee's 401(k) contribution in the form of company stock. For example, Procter & Gamble, Pfizer, General Electric, and McDonald's use company stock for matching an employee's 401(k) contribution.[55] An employee who has a large portion of her retirement savings in the stock of one company puts her retirement investment at considerable risk. This risk became apparent in 2001 with the bankruptcy of Enron, a large energy company, and the subsequent collapse of its stock price that wiped out the retirement savings of thousands of Enron employees.[56] Even worse, Enron restricted employees from selling their stock until they were close to retirement age. If possible, employees should try to reallocate their 401(k) savings in company stock to other less risky investment choices when permitted to do so.

A recent development in the use of 401(k) plans is an automatic enrollment feature that has been adopted by 59 percent of companies that use the plans, according to Hewitt Associates, a benefits consulting firm. This feature is designed to increase enrollment among the 25 percent of employees who do not sign up for their company 401(k) plan because they may be overwhelmed with benefits decisions when they start their jobs. With automatic enrollment, employees are enrolled in a 401(k) plan at the time they are hired, and they are given an opt-out choice that they can use if they do not want to participate. When ALON USA, a Texas oil refiner, instituted automatic enrollment to its 401(k) plan, the employee participation level increased from 40 to 80 percent of the workforce.[57]

IRA. An *individual retirement account (IRA)* allows people in 2005 to contribute up to $4,000 per year tax free (or $8,000 per year into a joint account with a spouse). Unlike the other defined contribution plans, IRAs are personal savings plans—that is, employers do not contribute to them. As with the 401(k) plan, the interest on an IRA account is tax deferred until the employee cashes it in at retirement. This tax-free benefit is eliminated for employees who participate in a qualified retirement plan with their employer and/or employees who have an adjusted gross income of at least $55,000 (single people) or $75,000 (married people filing a joint return). However, there are no such restrictions on the IRA's tax-deferred earnings. IRAs are available to both those without company pension plans and those who have contributed the maximum to their company plan. The IRA contribution maximum for individuals is scheduled to increase to $5,000 in 2008.

In 1998, a new version of the IRA called the *Roth IRA* became available. The Roth IRA allows people to contribute up to $4,000 per year of after-tax income into a savings plan in which the accumulation of interest on the contributions is not taxed and the distributions of income are not taxed after retirement. The Roth IRA (similar to the regular IRA) requires a person to attain a minimum age of $59\frac{1}{2}$ before income can be taken out of the savings without a penalty. Roth IRAs are restricted to people with adjusted gross incomes of less than $110,000 as a single person or $160,000 for married people filing joint returns. The Roth IRA is advantageous for people who anticipate being in higher tax brackets in the future, because the tax savings possible under the traditional IRA would be more than offset by the tax-free distributions of retirement income taken when the person moves to a higher tax bracket.[58]

SEP. A *simplified employee pension (SEP)* is similar to an IRA, but while IRAs are available to people who also participate in a retirement fund through their employer (subject to the limits described earlier), SEPs are available only to people who are self-employed or who work for small businesses that do not have a retirement plan. Those who are eligible for an SEP can invest up to 25 percent of their annual income or $41,000 (whichever is less) on a tax-deferred basis.

Profit-Sharing Keogh Plan. A *profit-sharing Keogh plan* provides for the same maximum contribution as an SEP but allows the employer to contribute to an employee's retirement account on the basis of company performance as measured by profits. Profit-sharing Keogh plans allow employers to make smaller contributions when profits are modest and larger contributions when profits are high. Keogh plans have three main advantages. First, because they allow employees to share in the company's success, they foster a sense of teamwork. Second, they let employers make contributions to the retirement plan that reflect their ability to pay. Third, their tax benefits are similar to those of SEPs.

Hybrid Pension Plans. Several hybrid pension plans have sprung up to address the limitations of both defined benefit plans and defined contribution plans. Defined benefit plans reward long-term service in a world in which employees are more and more mobile. And although defined contribution plans offer greater portability than defined benefit plans, defined contribution plans are tied more to investment returns than to job performance. Thus, fast-trackers who move from job to job may end up with less retirement income than those who work in a company with a traditional pension plan. One of the most popular hybrid plans developed to bridge these two types of pensions is the *cash balance plan,* which works like this: Employees are credited with a certain amount of money for their tax-deferred retirement account each year, based on their annual pay. These contributions are compounded using an agreed-upon interest rate (such as the interest rate on five-year Treasury bills). The employees take the cash balances with them when they change jobs. One drawback of cash balance plans is the time-consuming and expensive recordkeeping required for individual accounts. Another problematic issue is the effect on employees when a company decides to convert from a traditional pension plan to a cash balance pension plan. In some cases the cash balance plan provides lower retirement income than traditional pensions for more senior employees. As described in the vignette at the start of this chapter, IBM made this switch without giving employees who were close to retirement age the chance to remain with the traditional plan. The affected employees protested strongly, threatening to organize a union to protect their interests.[59]

Despite these potential drawbacks, cash balance plans are becoming popular because they are effective for retaining younger employees. Duracell International and Bank of America are two companies that have cash balance plans.[60]

Insurance Plans

A wide variety of insurance plans can provide financial security for employees and their families. Two of the most valued company-provided insurance benefits are life insurance and long-term disability insurance.

Life Insurance
Basic *term life insurance* pays a benefit to the survivors of a deceased employee. The typical benefit is one or two times the employee's annual income. For example, both Citicorp and AT&T offer their employees life insurance that will pay one year's salary to their survivors. In most cases, company-provided term life insurance policies cover workers only while they are employed by the organization. Companies with a flexible benefits policy may allow employees to purchase insurance beyond the basic level. An employee with a nonworking spouse, for example, may need a benefit of three to five years' salary to provide for his or her survivors. Approximately 87 percent of medium and large businesses provide a life insurance benefit to full-time employees.

Long-Term Disability Insurance
Employees who experience a serious injury away from the job (for example, in an auto accident) may not be able to perform their job duties for a long period of time. These employees need replacement income to cover the earnings lost while they are recovering from the accident or, if they are permanently disabled, for the rest of their lives. Workers' compensation does not provide disability income for people who have had off-duty accidents, and Social Security provides only a modest level of disability income to cover the most basic needs.

Long-term disability insurance provides replacement income to disabled employees who cannot perform their essential job duties. An employee is eligible to receive disability benefits after being disabled for six months or more. These benefits range from 50 to 67 percent of the employee's salary.[61] For example, Xerox provides 60 percent replacement income under its long-term disability insurance plan, whereas IBM provides 67 percent.[62] Employees who are disabled for less than six months are likely to receive replacement income under a sick leave policy (discussed later in this chapter). Employees can also purchase short-term disability insurance, which provides coverage until the long-term coverage takes over.

With Social Security benefits added to long-term disability insurance benefits, an employee's total replacement income is likely to be 70 percent to 80 percent of his or her salary. Long-term disability insurance plans usually take Social Security into account and are designed so that disabled employees do not receive more than 80 percent of their salary from these combined sources—the theory being that a higher percentage might be a disincentive to return to work. Approximately 43 percent of medium and large companies offer long-term disability insurance benefits to their workers (see Figure 12.2).

Paid Time Off

Paid time off provides breaks from regularly scheduled work hours so that employees can pursue leisure activities or take care of personal or civic duties. Paid time off includes sick leave, vacations, severance pay, and holidays. Paid time off is one of the most expensive benefits for the employer. Paid time off costs U.S. employers 6.7 percent of total payroll.[63]

Sick Leave

Sick leave provides full pay for each day that an employee experiences a short-term illness or disability that interferes with his or her ability to perform the job. Employees are often rewarded with greater amounts of sick leave in return for long-term service to the company. According to the U.S. Bureau of Labor Statistics, employers with sick leave benefits provide an average of 15 days of sick leave for employees with one year of full-time service to the company. Many employers allow employees to accumulate unused sick leave over time. For example, an employee with ten years on the job may accumulate 150 sick days if he or she has not used any sick time (10 years × 15 days per year of sick leave = 150 days). This accumulated coverage would be more than enough to give the employee full replacement income for the first six months of a serious illness, after which long-term disability coverage takes over.

Some companies allow retiring employees to collect pay for accumulated unused sick leave and vacation time. For example, when John Young retired as the CEO of Hewlett-Packard, he collected $937,225 in lieu of unused sick pay and vacation leave accumulated during his 34 years with the company.[64]

An HR benefits specialist must monitor and control sick leave benefits to prevent employees from using sick leave to take care of personal business or to reward themselves with a "mental health day" off from work. The HR department should consider instituting the following guidelines:

- Set up a "wellness pay" incentive program that monetarily rewards employees who do not use any sick days. Wellness programs may also encourage employees to adopt healthier lifestyles and file for fewer health benefits. For example, Quaker Oats provides bonuses of as much as $500 for employees who exercise, shun smoking, and wear seat belts.[65]
- Establish flexible work hours so that employees can take care of some personal business during the week, thereby decreasing their need to use sick days for this reason.
- Reward employees with a lump sum that represents their unused sick days when they leave or retire from the organization. Alternatively, give employees the chance to accrue vacation days as a percentage of unused sick leave.
- Allow employees to take one or two personal days each year. This helps to discourage employees from regarding sick days as time off to which they are entitled even if they do not get sick.
- Establish a paid time off (PTO) bank, which is a policy that pools time off in a bank of days that employees use for vacation, sick leave, personal days, and floating holidays. PTO programs allow employees to choose how they will use their time off without feeling the pressure to justify their absence to the boss. With PTOs, employees can take time off for any reason as long as it is scheduled with supervisors. Time off can also be used for unplanned reasons such as sickness and emergencies.[66]

Vacations

Employers provide paid vacations to give their employees time away from the stresses and strains of the daily work routine. Vacation time allows employees to recharge themselves psychologically and emotionally and can lead to improved job performance.[67] Many companies reward long-term service to the company with more vacation time. For example, Hewlett-Packard employees with one year of service are eligible for 15 days' vacation; after 30 years of service, they are entitled to 30 days.

Figure 12.8 is an international comparison of the average annual number of paid vacation days that employees receive from their companies. U.S. employees average about 10 days (two weeks) of paid vacation. This is the same as in Japan, but far less than in most European Union nations. For example, French workers receive 30 days (six weeks) and British workers receive 25 days (five weeks) of paid vacation. Many European countries have laws stipulating the number of paid vacation days that workers must receive, but the United States has no such laws.

Some U.S. businesses are starting to offer employees *sabbatical leave,* which is an extended vacation with pay. Sabbaticals, which can be considered a vacation with a purpose, help employees

**Average Annual
Number of Vacation
Days in Various
Countries for
Employees**

Source: Galvan, S. (2004, July 6).
Wake up and smell the beach,
Americans. *Denver Post*, B-6.

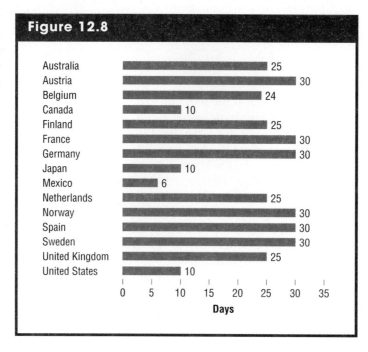

Figure 12.8

improve their skills or provide a service to the community. Sabbaticals are very common for college and university faculty, for whom they are a tradition. In the business world, where they are much newer, they are most likely to be found in the high-tech industries, where employee skills become obsolete rapidly and need to be renewed. At Intel, for example, engineers and technical employees who have worked for the company for seven years are entitled to an eight-week paid sabbatical in addition to their annual paid vacation. Employees have used these sabbaticals to continue their education, teach in public schools or colleges, or do volunteer work for nonprofit organizations.[68]

Severance Pay

While not typically thought of as a benefit, the severance pay given to laid-off employees is also a form of paid time off. The type of severance pay offered varies widely. Some organizations offer one month's pay for each year the employee has worked for them, often capped at one year's salary. Severance pay is provided to cushion the shock of termination and to finance the employee's search for a new position.

Holidays and Other Paid Time Off

Many employers give their employees paid holidays or pay extra to employees who are required or volunteer to work on holidays. In the United States, employers provide an average of 10 paid holidays per year to employees. Other countries provide similar or more paid holidays with an average of 10 paid holidays in the United Kingdom, 13 in Brazil, 14 in Japan, and 11 in France.[69] While they are not required to, many employers also provide paid leave for jury duty. In manufacturing environments where employees work on tight time schedules, many employers provide (either voluntarily or through a union contract) time for employees to eat, clean up, and get dressed. Some union contracts (particularly those in railroad and other transportation firms) also stipulate that employees will be paid if they are scheduled for work even though no work is available.

Employee Services

The last category of employee benefits is *employee services*, which employers provide on a tax-free or tax-preferred basis to enhance the quality of employees' work or personal life. Figure 12.9 lists some well-known employee services. These include child care, health club memberships, subsidized company cafeterias, parking privileges, and discounts on company products.

Companies are taking a fresh look at employee services and their value to employees. For years, employers offered services tentatively and experimentally, often as kind of a side dish to

	Figure 12.9
1. Charitable contributions	**13.** Transportation to and from work
2. Counseling	**14.** Travel expenses
■ Financial	■ Car reimbursement
■ Legal	■ Tolls and parking
■ Psychiatric/psychological	■ Food and entertainment
3. Tax preparation	reimbursement
4. Education subsidies	**15.** Clothing reimbursement/allowance
5. Child adoption	**16.** Tool reimbursement/allowance
6. Child care	**17.** Relocation expenses
7. Elder care	**18.** Emergency loans
8. Subsidized food service	**19.** Credit union
9. Discounts on merchandise	**20.** Housing
10. Physical awareness and fitness	**21.** Employee assistance programs
programs	**22.** On-site health services
11. Social and recreational opportunities	**23.** Credit unions
12. Parking	**24.** Concierge services

Source: HR Focus. (2000, June). What benefits are companies offering now? 5–7.

**Selected Tax-Free
or Tax-Preferred
Employee Benefits or
Services**

the main course of medical and health insurance and pension plans. But today companies are using a wide array of services to attract and retain employees, particularly if they cannot offer competitive salaries or raises. John Hancock Mutual Life Insurance of Boston recruits prospective employees with a heavy emphasis on its variety of benefits, including flexible scheduling, dependent-care services, fitness center, and take-home food from the company cafeteria.[70] Accenture, an IT consulting firm, provides concierge services as a benefit for its busy consultants who spend a lot of time away from home traveling on consulting projects. Concierge services take care of personal errands for employees such as car care, taking clothes to the cleaners, event planning, gift buying, and ticket purchasing. This support helps decrease employee stress by reducing the time busy employees spend on personal tasks.[71]

Some companies offer unconventional services. For example, one increasingly popular employee service is free self-defense classes. Model Muggings of Boston, a firm that specializes in teaching self-defense techniques, has seen considerable growth in the demand for its on-site classes. When book publisher Houghton Mifflin began offering Model Muggings classes at its Boston site, 210 of 800 workers signed on immediately.[72]

One of the most valued employee services today is child care.[73] Currently, about 5 percent of U.S. employers provide some child-care benefits, and this percentage is likely to increase because of the growing number of single parents and dual-career households with children.[74]

Companies that decide to offer child-care services have several options. The most expensive is an on-site child-care center. Other child-care options include subsidizing employee child-care costs at off-site child-care centers and establishing a child-care referral service for working parents.[75] Because child care is expensive employers usually subsidize 50 to 75 percent of the costs and require employees to pay the rest.[76]

Administering Benefits

We conclude this chapter by examining two critical issues in the administration of employee benefits: (1) the use of flexible benefits and (2) the importance of communicating benefits to employees. The HR department usually takes the lead in administering benefits, but managers need to help communicate options to employees, provide advice occasionally, keep records (vacation time, sick days), and be prepared to call on the HR department if disputes arise.

Flexible Benefits

Employees have different benefits needs, depending on a number of factors: age, marital status, whether the employee's spouse works and has duplicate benefits coverage, and the presence and ages of children in the household. A flexible benefits program allows employees to choose from a selection of employer-provided benefits such as vision care, dental care, health insurance coverage for dependents, additional life insurance coverage, long-term disability insurance, child care, elder care, more paid vacation days, legal services, and contributions to a 401(k) retirement plan.[77]

As Figure 12.2 shows, 13 percent of large- and medium-sized U.S. employers have a flexible benefits plan in place, among them TRW Systems, Educational Testing Services, DaimlerChrysler, and Bell Atlantic.[78] In the future, as the workforce becomes even more diverse, it is likely that more companies will implement flexible benefits plans.

Types of Flexible Benefits Plans

The three most popular flexible benefits plans are modular plans, core-plus options plans, and flexible spending accounts.[79]

Modular plans consist of a series of different bundles of benefits or different levels of benefits coverage designed for different employee groups. For example, Module A might be the basic package paid for entirely by employer contributions. It would include only the most essential benefits and would be designed for single employees. Module B might include everything in Module A plus additional benefits such as family coverage under the health insurance plan, dental care, and child care. This module might be designed for married employees with young children and could require both employer and employee contributions.

Core-plus options plans consist of a core of essential benefits and a wide array of other benefits options that employees can add to the core. The core is designed to provide minimum economic security for employees, and usually includes basic health insurance, life insurance, long-term disability insurance, retirement benefits, and vacation days. Core-plus options plans give employees "benefits credits" that entitle them to "purchase" the additional benefits that they want. In most cases, all employees receive the same number of credits and may use them either to purchase higher levels of coverage in the core benefits package or to purchase additional benefits such as dental care or child care.

Flexible spending accounts are individual employee accounts funded by the employer, the employee (with pretax dollars), or both. Employees "pay" for the combination of benefits from their accounts. The result can be added take-home pay because employees do not pay taxes on the dollars that they have spent on benefits from their flexible spending accounts. Employee benefits administrators must design flexible spending accounts that conform to the rules specified in Section 125 of the Internal Revenue Code, which governs which benefits are exempt from taxes and which are not. For example, educational benefits and van pooling cannot be included in a flexible spending account because they are taxable benefits.

Challenges with Flexible Benefits

Flexible benefits offer employees the opportunity to tailor a benefits package that is meaningful to them at a reasonable cost to the company. However, they do pose some challenges to benefits administrators. These are:

- **Adverse selection.** The *adverse selection* problem occurs when enough employees use a specific benefit more than the average employee does. Intensive use of a benefit can drive up the benefit's cost and force the employer either to increase spending on benefits or reduce the amount of coverage it provides. For example, employees who know they will need expensive dental work may select a dental-care option instead of some other benefit. Or employees who know they have a high probability of an early death (due to a health condition such as high blood pressure or even a terminal condition such as cancer) may choose extra life insurance coverage. In both cases, the cost of the insurance coverage will eventually be driven up.

  Benefits administrators can deal with the adverse selection problem by placing restrictions on benefits that are likely to result in adverse selection problems. For instance, the company might require those applying for higher life insurance coverage to successfully pass a physical examination. They can also bundle a broad package of benefits together into modules to ensure a more balanced use of each benefit.[80]

■ **Employees who make poor choices.** Sometimes employees make a poor choice of benefits and later regret it. For example, an employee who selects additional vacation days instead of long-term disability insurance is likely to regret his choice if he experiences a long-term illness that exceeds his accumulated amount of sick leave. Benefits administrators can manage this problem by (1) establishing core benefits that minimize an employee's risks and (2) communicating benefits choices effectively so that employees make appropriate choices.

■ **Administrative complexity.** A flexible benefits program is difficult to administer and control. Employees must be kept informed of changes in the cost of benefits, the coverage of benefits, and their utilization of benefits. They must also be given the opportunity to change their benefits selection periodically. In addition, the potential for errors in recordkeeping is high. Fortunately, computer software packages can help the HR department manage the recordkeeping aspect of benefits administration. Benefits consultants can assist HR staff in selecting and installing these software programs.

Benefits Communication

Benefits communication is a critical part of administering an employee benefits program. Many employees in companies with excellent benefits packages have never been informed of the value of these benefits and are therefore likely to underestimate their worth.[81] The two major obstacles to effective benefits communication are (1) the increasing complexity of benefits packages and (2) employers' reluctance to devote enough resources to explain these complex packages to employees.

Traditionally, benefits have been communicated via a group meeting during new-employee orientation or a benefits handbook that describes each benefit and its level of coverage. In today's dynamic world of employee benefits, however, more sophisticated communication media (such as videotape presentations and computer software that generates personalized benefits status reports for each employee) are needed. Here are a few of the approaches employers are taking to inform employees about additions to or changes in their benefits:

■ General Electric (GE) uses its benefits Web site to give its employees access to benefits information 24 hours a day. GE's benefits Web site has reduced the number of calls to its benefits department by 25,000 calls per month, resulting in substantial cost savings of $175,000 per month. GE reported that a telephone inquiry to the benefits department cost $8.00, whereas a Web site inquiry cost only $1.00.[82]

■ In its innovative $15\frac{1}{2}$ minute video, the Los Angeles County Employees Retirement Association (LACERA) uses a Sam Spade–type detective character to "crack the case" of confusing retirement plans. During the course of the video the animated detective discovers what confusing terms like *noncontributory* and *defined benefits* mean—and so do LACERA's 500 new hires each month.[83]

Figure 12.10 on page 400 lists some of the ways a company can keep its employees informed about their benefits or answer questions about coverage.

Summary and Conclusions

An Overview of Benefits

Benefits are group membership rewards that provide security for employees and their families. Benefits cost companies about $13,380 per year for the average employee. The cost of employee benefits has increased dramatically in recent years. Although benefits programs are usually centrally controlled in organizations, managers need to be familiar with them so they can counsel employees, recruit job applicants, and make effective managerial decisions.

The Benefits Strategy

The design of a benefits package should be aligned with the business's overall compensation strategy. The benefits strategy requires making choices in three areas: (1) benefits mix, (2) benefits amount, and (3) flexibility of benefits.

Legally Required Benefits

The four benefits that almost all employers must provide are Social Security, workers' compensation, unemployment

Selected Methods of Employee Benefits Communication

Figure 12.10

Benefits Web Sites
Lets employees access information about their benefits from home, a hotel, or anywhere with an Internet connection. Employees can also enroll in a different HMO health insurance plan, for example, on the Web site without having to go to the company benefits office and wait for an appointment with a benefits specialist.

Colorful Fliers or Newsletters
Can be mailed to employees' homes so they can read them at leisure.

Audio-Visual Presentations
Slides and videos that present concepts in an upbeat fashion can ensure that employees at different locations receive the same information.

Toll-Free Number
Lets employees call to enroll in a benefits program or hear automated information about these programs 24 hours a day.

Computer Software Package
Allows employees to play "what-if" scenarios with their benefits. For example, they can determine the amount that will be deducted from their paychecks if they enroll in medical plan A as opposed to plan B, or how much money they would save by age 60 if they contribute 6 percent a year to the 401(k) plan.

Sources: Wojcik, J. (2004, December 6). As workers' benefit needs change, so do methods of communication. *Business Insurance,* 10–11; and Cohen, A., and Cohen, S. (1998, November/December). Benefits Websites: Controlling costs while enhancing communication. *Journal of Compensation and Benefits,* 11–18.

insurance, and unpaid family and medical leave. These benefits form the core of an employee's benefits package. All other employer-provided benefits are designed to either complement or augment the legally required benefits.

Voluntary Benefits

Businesses often provide five types of voluntary benefits to their employees: (1) Health insurance provides health care for workers and their families. The major types of health insurance plans are traditional health insurance, health maintenance organizations (HMOs), and preferred provider organizations (PPOs). (2) Retirement benefits consist of deferred compensation set aside for an employee's retirement. Funds for retirement benefits can come from employer contributions, employee contributions, or a combination of the two. The Employee Retirement Income Security Act (ERISA) is the major law governing the management of retirement benefits. There are two main types of retirement benefit plans: defined benefit plans and defined contribution plans. In a defined benefit plan, the employer promises to provide a specified amount of retirement income to an employee. A defined contribution plan requires employees to share with their employer some of the risk of and responsibility for managing their retirement assets. The most popular defined contribution plans are 401(k) plans, individual retirement accounts (IRAs), simplified employee pension plans (SEPs), and profit-sharing Keogh plans. (3) Insurance plans protect employees or their survivors from financial disaster in the case of untimely death, accidents that result in disabilities, and serious illnesses. Two kinds of insurance likely to be included in a benefits package are life insurance and long-term disability insurance. (4) Paid time off, which gives employees a break to pursue leisure activities or take care of personal and civic duties, includes sick leave, vacations, severance pay, holidays, and other paid time off. (5) Employee services consist of a cluster of tax-free or tax-preferred services that employers provide to improve the quality of their employees' work or personal life. One of the most valued employee services is child-care benefits.

Administering Benefits

Two important issues involving benefits administration are the use of flexible benefits and communicating benefits to employees. Although the benefits administration is likely to be performed by an HR benefits specialist, managers need to understand their companies' benefits package well enough to help communicate benefits to their employees and keep records.

Key Terms

benefits mix, 376

coinsurance, 373

Consolidated Omnibus Budget
  Reconciliation Act of 1985
  (COBRA), 385

contributions, 373

copayment, 373

deductible, 374

defined benefit plan or pension, 390

defined contribution plan, 390

employee benefits or indirect
  compensation, 371

Employee Retirement Income Security
  Act (ERISA), 389

Family and Medical Leave Act of 1993
  (FMLA), 382

flexible or cafeteria benefits program,
  374

Health Insurance Portability and
  Accountability Act (HIPAA), 385

health maintenance organization
  (HMO), 386

health savings account (HSA) 388

Medicare, 379

Pension Benefit Guaranty Corporation
  (PBGC), 390

portable benefits, 390

preexisting condition, 385

preferred provider organization (PPO),
  387

premium, 386

Social Security, 378

supplemental unemployment benefits
  (SUB), 381

unemployment insurance, 381

vesting, 390

workers' compensation, 379

Discussion Questions

1. How might the increasing diversity of the workforce affect the design of employee benefits packages in large companies?

2. The United States mandates only four benefits, yet U.S. employers provide many other benefits—such as health insurance, retirement benefits, and paid vacations—voluntarily. Why do so many employers provide these benefits even though they are not legally required to do so?

3. What are the advantages and disadvantages of enacting a federal law that requires all employers to provide health insurance for their workers?

4. How do managed-care health insurance plans (HMOs and PPOs) differ from traditional fee-for-service health insurance plans? What are the costs and benefits of each to the employer? To the employee?

5. Why should younger employees (those in their 20s and 30s) care about retirement benefits?

6. Why is cost containment such an important issue in employee benefits programs?

7. Only a small percentage of part-time and temporary employees in the United States receive health insurance and retirement benefits compared to employees with full-time jobs. How serious a problem is this? Which people do you think are most likely to be affected by this lack of benefits coverage? What, if anything, can be done about this situation?

8. Some benefits experts claim that unemployment insurance and workers' compensation benefits create a disincentive to work. Why do you think they say this? Do you agree or disagree with this position?

There is a variety of additional material available on the Web site that accompanies this text. You can access this information by visiting the Web site at **www.prenhall.com/gomez.**

Emerging Trends Case 12.1   YOU MANAGE IT!

Employees Are Paying Increasingly Larger Shares of Their Health-Care Benefit Costs

Employees covered by employer-sponsored health-care plans in 2004 are paying over 50 percent more out of their own pockets than they did 4 years ago, according to a study sponsored by the Kaiser Family Foundation and Health Research and Educational Trust. In 2004, for the fourth consecutive year health insurance premium increases over the previous year exceeded 10 percent. The cost of employee health care is a high priority issue in labor negotiations. The automobile industry, which has an aging workforce, already pays $9,000 per year, per employee, for health insurance, about 50 percent more than the rest of corporate America. In addition, companies in the manufacturing sector, such as the automotive and steel industries, that have made promises to give health benefits to retired workers, are increasingly finding postretiree health benefits to be a huge cash drain that negatively effects firm performance.

Employees' monthly contributions to health insurance premiums for family coverage in 2004 averaged $222, a $21 increase over the previous year. The average monthly contribution for single coverage was $47, up $5 from the previous year. On an annual basis, average family and single coverage cost $2,664 and $564, respectively. Health-care economists say that rising costs reflect advances in drugs and health-care technology and a loosening of managed care cost restraints that were in force during the 1990s. Although employers are still paying most of employees' health-care costs, currently about 75 percent, most employers are in the process of shifting more costs to workers, in the hopes of lowering expenses by discouraging heavy use of doctors, hospitals, and prescription drugs. The following are some ways that companies are attempting to reduce health-care costs:

- Medtronic, a medical-device manufacturer, is paying up to $2,000 per worker into a "personal care account." Employees can spend the money as they choose, as long as it is on health care. The hope is that better information and greater personal responsibility will lead to better choices.
- In a pilot project, Ford gives bonuses to doctors who achieve treatment goals and rewards employees who agree to monitor health indicators such as blood glucose levels. It also tracks information on the quality of care given at 1,000 hospitals and feeds that information back to employees so they can use it to make better informed choices about where to go to get medical services.
- United Technologies requires that workers pick up 30 percent of the cost of using in-network services from managed care plans and 40 percent of out-of-network health services, until the costs reach caps as high as $10,000 per year.

Critical Thinking Questions

1. One of the key factors contributing to higher health-care costs is the age composition of the American workforce. For example, the average age of U.S. employees covered by employer-provided health-care plans is now 41 years, up from 38 in 2000. Why do you think the aging of the U.S. workforce increases health-care costs? Do you expect this trend to continue in the future? Explain.

2. Referring to the approach used by United Technologies to lower health insurance costs presented in the case, what would be the maximum amount of out-of-pocket health costs than an employee could be expected to experience during a given year? How does this maximum annual health-care expenditure at United Technologies compare to the average cost to employees of family health-care coverage for 2004 that was given in the case? What conclusions do you draw from this health-care-cost comparison?

Team Exercise

With a group of four or five students, evaluate the advantages and disadvantages of each of the three approaches used by specific U.S. companies to reduce health-care costs presented in the case. How are the approaches similar? How do they differ? Is one approach superior to the others? Identify some key factors that you expect to affect the choices that managers make when they select ways to reduce health-care costs. For example, would large companies (over 1,000 employees) select different methods to reduce health-care costs than small companies (under 100 employees)? If so, why? Be prepared to present your team findings to the class.

Experiential Exercise

This experiential exercise shows the importance of benefits communication between managers and employees. With a partner, decide who will enact one of two roles: (1) the role of a manager and (2) the role of an employee who is a subordinate in the manager's unit. In the role-play, the manager has called a meeting to inform the employee that in the upcoming year the employee share of the cost of the health insurance premium for family coverage will increase $25 per month. The employee has a family with a stay-at-home spouse and is upset that the company is asking each employee to bear more of the burden of paying health insurance premiums. Each person role-plays their assigned role to be consistent with the situation. The role-play should continue for about 5 minutes. What could the manager have done to improve benefits communication? How could the HR department have helped the manager? The role-play partners should be prepared to share their insights of effective benefits communication with other members of the class.

Sources: HR Focus. (2005, March). The latest benchmarks for health-care costs, 3–6; Freudenheim, M. (2003, September 10). Employees paying ever-bigger share for health care. *New York Times,* A-1, C-2; *The Economist.* (2003, September 20). Employers' liability: Paying for health care, 61; Symonds, W. (2003, October 20). Get used to the pain: Another round of double-diget hikes in health-care costs is in the mail. *BusinessWeek,* 42–43.

Ethics Case 12.2 — YOU MANAGE IT!

Employee Retirement Savings in 401(k) Plans Collapse at Enron

Marie Thibaut spent 15 years as an administrative assistant at Enron in Houston, Texas. During that time, she dutifully put 15 percent of her salary into a 401(k) retirement plan, investing the entire amount in the company's rapidly climbing stock. Enron then matched that investment with yet more company shares. By the winter of 2000, she had amassed close to $500,000 in stock, enough for the 61-year-old divorcée to begin contemplating retirement. "My children told me I should diversify," Thibaut said. "But all the mutual funds were going down, and I just kept going up." She's not going up any longer. In 2001 Enron declared bankruptcy and Thibaut was out of work, a victim of one of the worst corporate collapses in history. Her 401(k) is worth just $22,000.

That depressing story has been repeated thousands of times at Enron, Lucent, Nortel, and other technology companies whose stocks have retreated after the Internet bubble burst in 2000. But, despite the punishing market and calls for diversification, workers continue to pour a huge portion of their retirement money into their employer's shares of stock. Benefits consulting firm Hewitt Associates estimates that at the end of 2001 almost 30 percent of the $71 billion in assets in some 1.5 million 401(k) plans were invested in the stock of the sponsoring company. At some places the proportion is even higher. Microsoft employees keep 46 percent of their 401(k) funds in company stock. At Enron, the figure was 62 percent. At Coca-Cola 81 percent of employees' 401(k) funds are in company stock. To make matters worse, many of these retirement plans, like Enron's, restrict the sale of stock. For example, Enron employees were not able to sell their company stock until they reached 50 years of age.

As every undergraduate business student who has taken a basic course in finance knows, it is very risky to put a large percentage of a person's retirement funds into the stock of one company—doing that violates the basic financial principle of asset diversification. So why have millions of Americans made this mistake with their retirement funds?

First, many Americans have not taken a basic course in finance and are unaware of the risk of owning so much of a single stock, especially when it is the stock in a company that they believe they know—the company where they work.

Moreover, companies should be matching employees' 401(k) contributions in cash, not in stock. But stock matches are cheaper and many executives think it is fine for their employees to hold big stakes in the stock of their company. Many of these executives also hold large amounts of company stock, but they are far wealthier than ordinary employees and are better able than those employees to withstand the investment risk when the company stock plunges.

Unbalanced, one-stock 401(k) plans violate every safety-and-soundness principle of investing, according to New Jersey Governor Jon Corzine, who was formerly cochair of the investment firm Goldman Sachs. For example, defined benefit pension plans are not permitted to put more than 10 percent of their money into a single stock according to the regulations governing pension plans. Institutional investors, such as mutual funds and insurance firms, generally set a cap at 5 percent of their money in any one company stock.

These standards of prudence are backed by both academic studies and common sense, Corzine says. Employees counting on company stock may get lucky for a few years. But, over time, they run a higher and higher risk of major loss.

Critical Thinking Questions

1. Why do many employers of large companies such as Enron and Coca-Cola decide to give the matching contributions to their employees' 401(k) plans in the form of company stock instead of cash? Do you think this human resource practice is ethical? Explain your position.
2. Suppose your employer fully matched your contribution to your 401(k) plan in company stock. What can you do to reduce your investment risk? Would it be a good idea not to contribute any money to your company's 401(k) plan? Do you think it would be a good idea to diversify your savings between your company 401(k) plan and a personal IRA plan that you start? What other investment strategies might you want to explore?

Team Exercise

With a group of four or five students discuss the merits of making a government policy to regulate company 401(k) retirement plans to protect employees' retirement savings from disasters such as what happened to employees at Enron. Here are some possible regulations for you to discuss in your group: (1) regulation to require that companies have a ceiling of no more than 20 percent of company stock to be applied to any single employee's 401(k) retirement plan; and (2) a regulation permitting employees to be able to sell the company stock from their employer matching contribution after a one-year waiting period, so that an employee could use the sale of the stock to buy mutual funds or bonds that are less risky. Regulations of an employee benefit such as 401(k) plans unfortunately may lead to unexpected consequences. What unexpected consequences could occur as a result of legislation that regulates 401(k) plans? Finally, be prepared to let the class know if your group recommends in favor of 401(k) plan regulations to protect employee retirement plans or recommends in favor of rejecting any regulations. Give your reason for your group decision.

Experiential Exercise

In this experiential exercise, you will interview three financial experts on the following issues raised in the case: What should a person do as a prudent investor when the employer matches employee 401(k) contributions with company stock? Some types of people to select to interview include (1) a friend who is a finance major in business school and who is knowledgeable about investments; (2) an investment advisor or financial expert or someone who works at a financial services firm such as Charles Schwab, Merrill Lynch, or Dean Witter; or (3) a finance or accounting professor at your business school. Questions to ask during your interviews include (1) Is it worth investing in a 401(k) plan with an employer match of company stock, or should one allocate the money available for

the 401(k) plan in other opportunities outside the company (which would be made in after-tax income)? (2) Can one opt out of the company stock match in the 401(k) and ask for an equivalent amount of cash to be matched by the employer? (3) What benefits does the employer receive when it matches employee 401(k) contributions in company stock, rather than cash? Summarize your findings and be prepared to share the results with your classmates.

Sources: Adapted from Kahn, J. (2002, January 7). When 401(k)s are KO'd. *Fortune,* 104; Quinn, J. (2002, January 21). 401(k)s and the Enron mess. *Newsweek,* 25; *The Economist.* (2001, December 15). When labor and capital don't mix: Enron's demise unmasks conflicts in company pension plans, 60.

YOU MANAGE IT!   Ethics Case 12.3

Keeping Workers' Compensation Costs Under Control

Oregon Retirement Apartments is an apartment complex in Portland, Oregon, that provides housing, meals, and some assisted living services for its residents. Approximately 300 residents live in the facility. Fifty people work for the complex: a professional staff of administrators and social workers and an operations staff consisting of food service employees, housekeepers, building and maintenance workers, and night managers. Oregon Retirement Apartments tries to provide a rich social and cultural life for its residents (most of whom are in their 70s and 80s) so that they can live independently in a pleasant environment.

Barbara Spector, the facility's executive director, is very concerned about employees who abuse workers' compensation. This concern results from an incident involving Pat O'Toole, a housekeeping employee who filed a claim for workers' compensation benefits for a work-related back injury. Barbara suspected that Pat's injury did not occur on the job and therefore contested the claim. The investigation that followed showed that the claim was indeed false; Pat had sustained her back injury in a skiing accident, not during work hours. The investigation also revealed Pat's long history of filing workers' compensation claims with previous employers. According to files maintained by the state government, Pat has filed a total of 12 workers' compensation claims over her employment life.

After the incident with Pat, Barbara decided to establish a new hiring policy: People with a high likelihood of filing workers' compensation claims will not be hired. She justifies this policy change by citing her responsibility for containing the cost of workers' compensation insurance (which is adjusted according to the safety record of a company's workforce). The new policy requires Oregon Retirement's HR staff to examine the workers' compensation records of all job applicants at the

same time that their references are checked. The services of a local HR consulting firm are used to scan the workers' compensation database for evidence of an applicant's previous claims. Job applicants who have filed three or more workers' compensation claims are considered a "high risk" and dropped from the applicant pool.

Critical Thinking Questions

1. Is Barbara Spector's policy of rejecting job applicants who have filed three or more workers' compensation claims fair? Is it ethical?
2. What impact does the Americans with Disabilities Act (see Chapter 3) have on an employment practice that rejects applicants who have previously filed workers' compensation claims? Could this practice discriminate against people with disabilities?

Team Exercise

With a partner or a small group, develop some alternative employment practices to help Barbara Spector avoid hiring people who are likely to misuse workers' compensation benefits.

Discuss the following situation with your partner or group: During a job interview, an applicant reports that he has never applied for workers' compensation benefits. After hiring the applicant, the employer checks on this information and finds out that the employee lied. What should the company do?

Experiential Exercise

Find a partner and decide who will be assigned to each of the following roles: (1) Barbara Spector, the executive director, who is interviewing a food-service employee seeking employment and (2) Sarah Green, who is seeking a job as a food-service employee and being interviewed by Barbara. Sarah has filed a worker' compensation claim in the past. It is common in the food-service industry to have accidents during work hours. Barbara is in the middle of interviewing Sarah and wants to find out about her work history and determine whether she has filed any false workers' compensation claims. Each person in the role-play acts consistently with their role and the situation. The role-play should continue for about 5 minutes before

ending. The students in the role-play should attempt to answer the following questions: Did Barbara ask a question that violated Sarah's rights? If so, which rights were violated? Did Barbara ask any unethical questions? On what basis do you consider the question(s) unethical? Did Barbara obtain the workers' compensation information she was seeking in the interview? Why or why not? Be prepared to share the answers to these questions with other class members.

Customer-Driven HR Case 12.4 YOU MANAGE IT!

Managing Employee Benefits with Fair Procedures

One of the most important aspects of managing employee benefits is ensuring that the company uses fair procedures to apply the benefit to employees. The purpose of this exercise is to give you some practice in developing skills to handle some ethical or administrative challenges involving employee benefits that a manager or HR specialist could encounter. When determining if your proposed benefit procedure is fair, make sure you consider all the parties involved in the decision before you choose the best alternative. Read each of the following scenarios before answering the questions that follow:

Scenario 1

Sue is a 55-year-old employee at Company A. Her children are out of college and her parents are deceased. Company A offers a child-care program to all employees along with an elder-care program. However, Sue, like many other employees at Company A, currently has no need for these services and will not need them in the future. Should the firm retain these benefits programs or get rid of them? Should the company offer alternate benefits for employees who have no use for such services?

Scenario 2

Dan is the manager of employee benefits at Company B. He noticed that some employees use sick leave as a way to take care of personal business, such as caring for a sick child, having a dental appointment, or catching up on work at home. Currently each employee is entitled to one sick leave day per month. To improve efficiency, Dan eliminated the sick leave benefit and replaced it with six personal leave days that employees can take on a discretionary basis by notifying their supervisor in advance. Dan reasoned that under the former sick leave policy employees who play by the rules and only use leave when they are sick are penalized, whereas under the new personal leave benefit policy everybody has access to personal leave days to use for illnesses or other reasons for taking leave. Employees are not rewarded with days off for withholding the truth under this new benefit policy. Do you agree or disagree with Dan's decision?

Scenario 3

Frank works 25 hours per week at Company C, a mail-order firm, in the packaging department. He receives no benefits other than those required by the law. Frank does the same work as three other full-time employees who work in his department. These full-time employees qualify for pensions, health insurance, long-term disability, child-care, and vacations—none of which are provided to Frank. Is it ethical or fair to not provide benefits to part-time employees, even if they are doing the same work as full-time employees? Assume that Frank would like to work full-time, wants to receive the benefits, and feels frustrated because he is not eligible to receive them. Remember, too, that the firm is not legally required to pay Frank's or other part-time employees' benefits. The company justifies its position because it saves money on benefits costs by hiring part-time employees, including Frank.

Critical Thinking Questions

1. In each of the three scenarios determine what the benefits issues are. For example, in Scenario 1 does it make sense to get rid of a benefit that some employees use and others do not use? How important is this benefit? In Scenario 2, is it better to eliminate a benefit that a few abuse and replace it with a different one, or should a different tactic be employed? In scenario 3, do part-time employees deserve the same benefits as full-time employees or different ones?

2. Assume you are a manager in each of the three scenarios. How would you manage the benefits procedures in each situation? Assume you want to be as fair as possible to the employees in your unit. What would you do? How would you determine if the employees view your solution as a fair one?

Team Exercise

Work with a small group of three or four students to develop a fair benefits procedure or policy for each of the three scenarios. For scenario 1 develop a benefits procedure or policy for the situation when employees are not able to use a benefit that is provided by the employer. For scenario 2 develop a procedure or policy that addresses employee abuse of sick-leave benefits. For scenario 3 develop a procedure or policy for the situation when part-time employees receive reduced benefits compared to full-time employees. Note the areas of agreement and disagreement within your group discussion. How important do you think the manager's decision-making *process* for achieving the benefits procedure or policy is?

Experiential Exercise

Form a group of four to five students and ask each person to share a personal experience of using an employer's company benefits during a summer job, internship, or full-time job. If possible, each person should give both a good and a bad experience related to using their benefits. Try to explain which fac-

tors contributed to making the experience with benefits a good one or a bad one. Some possible benefits that could be discussed include health insurance, workers' compensation claims, unemployment benefits, vacation, sick leave, retirement benefits, or education benefits. After each person has spoken, the group should collaborate to develop two or three general rules about how managers can be more effective at administering employee benefits. Be prepared to share your group's findings with the class.

Source: Adapted from Nkomo, S. M., Fottler, M. D., and McAfee, R. B. (2000). *Applications in human resource management* (4th ed.), 216–219. Cincinnati, OH. South-Western.

Challenges

After reading this chapter, you should be able to deal more effectively with the following challenges:

1 **Outline** how good employee relations and communications can contribute to business goals.

2 **Describe** the three types of programs used to facilitate employee communications.

3 **Explain** the various appeals procedures through which employees can challenge management actions.

4 **Know** how employee assistance programs can help employees deal with personal problems that may interfere with job performance.

5 **Summarize** the technological innovations that allow managers to disseminate information quickly and explain how information dissemination influences an organization's employee relations.

Nancy is a customer service manager for a copier company. She started about four years ago as a customer service representative. In her job, she occasionally came into contact with customers who would "hit" on her or make suggestive comments, but she was always able to handle those situations. Usually, a diplomatic brush-off was enough. Now, however, she faces a situation that she does not know how to handle.

It all began six months ago when she was promoted to her current position of customer service manager. She really likes the job and the company, and hopes to be promoted further. The problem is her boss. Steve was largely responsible for her promotion, and Nancy feels indebted to him. But after about two months, she realized that his attention to her went beyond work. He began to tell her about his marital problems and commented that he found her very attractive. After all the help he had given her, Nancy hesitated to tell him directly that she was not interested in him romantically. But after he started sending flowers and asking her out, she finally asked him to stop.

That did not work. In fact, things got much worse. Steve's requests became more direct, and now they had threats attached. Specifically, he told her that if she did not begin a relationship with him, he would not only not recommend her for any further promotions, but he also would try to get her terminated. Nancy feels trapped. She knows that Steve is well liked by his colleagues, and she is afraid that if she complains about him, she will only lose her job sooner.

Then she read in the monthly newsletter about the company's employee relations program. One of the program's goals is to give employees confidential access to an employee relations specialist who can help them resolve interpersonal problems on the job. Nancy called the confidential hot line and set up an appointment with a counselor. She is looking forward to explaining her dilemma to someone who is impartial and in a position to help her.

THE MANAGERIAL PERSPECTIVE

Dealing successfully with a problem like Nancy's requires effective employee relations—the subject of this chapter. Companies with strong employee relations benefit because their employees are highly motivated to expend their best efforts. In exchange, the employees expect to be treated fairly and recognized for their achievements. To develop and sustain relations, employers must keep employees informed of company policies and strategies. That way, employees can learn new behaviors or skills as needed and understand the workings of the firm more fully. In addition, employers must have policies that allow employees to discuss problems with or communicate important information to company representatives who can respond effectively.

As a manager, you will play a key role in employee relations. You must listen to your employees' concerns and feelings, observe their experiences, and help keep employees informed about changes in the business and the effects of such changes.

HR specialists also play a crucial role in employee relations. If they develop communication policies and procedures that apply appropriate communication tools in a timely manner, employees can access more abundant, higher quality information and can communicate more effectively with management. Managers and HR specialists must work in partnership to ensure that the communication policies and procedures bolster employee relations.

In this chapter, we explore how managers and employee relations specialists can work together to coordinate an employee relations program. Next, we present a model of communication and explore specific policies that give employees access to important information. Finally, we examine some programs for recognizing employees' individual and team contributions to company goals.

The Roles of the Manager and the Employee Relations Specialist

Having good *employee relations* means providing fair and consistent treatment to all employees so that they will be committed to the organization. Companies with good employee relations are likely to have an HR strategy that places a high value on employees as stakeholders in the business. Employees who are treated as *stakeholders* have certain rights within the organization and can expect to be treated with dignity and respect. For example, Johnson & Johnson, a company known for its excellent employee relations, is committed to a philosophy of respect for the individual. To foster good employee relations, managers must listen to and understand what employees are saying and experiencing, keep them informed about what management plans to do with the business, and tell them how those plans may affect their jobs. They should also give employees the freedom to air grievances about management decisions. There may be good reasons for not changing the decision, but management should at least listen to the grievances.

Effective employee relations require cooperation between managers and **employee relations representatives**. These specialists are members of the HR department who act as internal consultants to the business. They try to ensure that company policies and procedures are followed and advise both supervisors and employees on specific employee relations problems. **Employee relations policies** provide channels to resolve such problems before they become serious.

For example, an employee whose supervisor has denied her request for two weeks' vacation (to which she is entitled according to the employee handbook) may ask the employee relations representative to speak to her supervisor and clarify why she is being denied her preferred vacation time. Or, a supervisor may request assistance because he suspects that one of his subordinates has an alcohol abuse problem that is affecting job performance. In both these cases, the employee relations representative will try to resolve the problem within the letter and spirit of the appropriate employment policy, while carefully balancing the interests of the supervisor, the employee, and the company.

Employee relations representatives may also develop new policies that help maintain fairness and efficiency in the workplace. The client in this situation may be a top manager who needs assistance in drafting a new policy on smoking in the workplace or the hiring of employees' spouses and other relatives.

Employee relations representative
A member of the HR department who ensures that company policies are followed and consults with both supervisors and employees on specific employee relations problems.

Employee relations policy
A policy designed to communicate management's thinking and practices concerning employee-related matters and prevent problems in the workplace from becoming serious.

Developing Employee Communications

Many companies have found that the key to a good employee relations program is a *communication channel* that gives employees access to important information and an opportunity to express their ideas and feelings. When supervisors are familiar with employment policies and employees are aware of their rights, there is less opportunity for misunderstandings to arise and productivity to drop.

Because corporations are very complex, they must develop numerous communication channels to move information up, down, and across the organizational structure. For instance, Intel provides many communication channels that allow employees and managers to speak with one another and share information. Managers communicate with their employees by walking around and talking to them informally, sponsoring newsletters, and providing a Web site with key employment policies. Employees give feedback to managers through e-mail, memos, meetings, and other forms of face-to-face communication. As today's organizations have delegated more responsibilities and decision-making authority to employees, the importance of making more information available to employees has increased substantially.[1]

Types of Information

Two forms of information are sent and received in communications: facts and feelings. *Facts* are pieces of information that can be objectively measured or described. Examples are the cost of a computer, the daily defect rate in a manufacturing plant, and the size of the deductible payment in the company-sponsored health insurance policy. Recent technological advances have made factual information more accessible to more employees than ever before. Facts can be stored in databases and widely distributed to employees by networks of personal computers.

Feelings are employees' emotional responses to the decisions made or actions taken by managers or other employees. Managers who implement decisions must be able to anticipate or respond to the feelings of the employees who are affected by those decisions. If they cannot or do not, the plan may fail. For example, a public university changed its health insurance coverage without consulting the employees affected by the change. When these employees learned of their diminished coverage, they responded so negatively that the manager of employee benefits resigned. (The health insurance policy was subsequently changed to be more favorable to the employees.)

A company must be especially careful of employees' feelings when it is restructuring or downsizing and laying off a considerable portion of its workforce. A production employee at a large East Coast manufacturing firm remembers how top management kept issuing memos that said, in effect, "we're doing fine, we're doing fine," and then suddenly announced layoffs. Survivors of the layoff were shocked and hurt and became highly distrustful of management.[2]

Organizations need to design communication channels that allow employees to communicate facts and feelings. In many cases, these channels must provide for face-to-face communication because many feelings are conveyed nonverbally.[3] Employees cannot write on a piece of paper or record on a computer database their complex emotional reactions to a decision that they fear will cost them their jobs.

How Communication Works

Figure 13.1 is a simple representation of the communications process within an organization. Communication starts with a *sender,* who has a message to send to the *receiver.* The sender must *encode* the message and select a *communication channel* that will deliver it to the receiver. In communicating facts, the message may be encoded with words, numbers, or digital symbols; in communicating feelings, it may be encoded as body language or tone of voice.

Some communication channels are more appropriate than others for sending certain messages. For example, memos are usually not very effective for sending information that has a lot of feeling in it. A more effective channel for conveying strong emotions is a meeting or other form of face-to-face communication.

Communication is not effective unless the receiver is able to *decode* the message and understand its true meaning. The receiver may misinterpret a message for many reasons. For example, the message may be filled with technical jargon that makes it difficult to decode, the receiver may misinterpret the sender's motives for sending the message, or the sender may send a message that lends itself to multiple interpretations.

Because of the strong possibility of miscommunication, important communications should include opportunities for *feedback* from the receiver. This way the sender can clarify the message if its true meaning is not received. In addition, noise in the sender's or receiver's environment may block or distort the message. *Noise* is anything that disrupts the message: inaccurate communication by the sender, fatigue or distraction on the part of the receiver, or actual noise that distorts the message (other people talking, traffic, telephone ringing). Very often noise takes the form of information overload. For example, if the receiver gets 100 e-mail messages in one day, she may not read the most important one carefully enough because she is overwhelmed by the barrage of information.

Communications that provide for feedback are called *two-way communications* because they allow the sender and receiver to interact with each other. Communications that provide no opportunity for feedback are one way. Although ideally all communications should be interactive, this is not always possible in large organizations, where large amounts of information must

The Communications Process Within an Organization

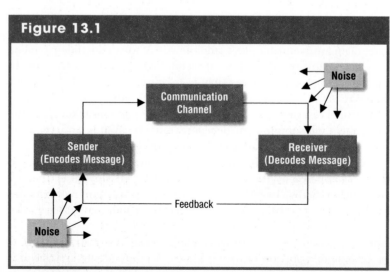

Figure 13.1

be distributed to many employees. For example, top executives at large companies do not usually have the time to speak to all the employees they need to inform about a new product about to be released. Instead, they may communicate with the employees via a memo, report, or e-mail. In contrast, top executives at small businesses have much less difficulty communicating with their employees. The Manager's Notebook, "How to Communicate Useful Feedback to Employees," offers tips for managers who want to improve the communication process of giving and receiving feedback. (Note additional information in Chapter 7 on giving feedback during performance appraisals.)

Customer-Driven HR

MANAGER'S NOTEBOOK

How to Communicate Useful Feedback to Employees

Here are some ways to communicate useful feedback to subordinates and other employees.

- **Focus on specific behaviors.** Provide feedback that lets employees know what specific behaviors are effective or need improvement. That way, they are able to sustain and intensify the desired behaviors and are motivated to change those that may be inappropriate. Avoid vague statements such as "you have a bad attitude." It is better to give more specific feedback such as "you ignored the customer when she tried to get your attention."
- **Keep the feedback impersonal.** Try to keep the feedback descriptive rather than judgmental or evaluative. To do this, focus on job-related behaviors rather than make value judgments about the employee's motivations. Rather than telling an employee "you are incompetent," it would be preferable to say, "I noticed some gaps in your product knowledge when you gave a presentation to the marketing group."
- **Give the feedback at the appropriate time and place.** The best time to give feedback is right after the person who should receive the feedback engages in the behavior at issue. A manager who waits months until the formal performance appraisal to give the feedback has lost an opportunity to coach and motivate an employee to improve at the time the behavior was observed. Similarly, the appropriate place to provide critical feedback is in private. Giving negative feedback publicly can humiliate the person being critiqued and is likely to provoke anger rather than the intended result of the message. Conversely, giving positive feedback in front of others can be motivational not only to the person who is being praised, but also to others who may learn from the good example set by the employee whose behaviors are positively recognized.
- **Focus negative feedback on behaviors that can be controlled by the employee.** When giving negative feedback to another employee, focus on behaviors that the employee can control. For example, it may be appropriate for a manager to criticize an employee who is late arriving at a team meeting. However, if the manager asked the employee to handle a customer service problem that took longer to solve than originally anticipated, the criticism about tardiness may be unfair.

Sources: Adapted from Gomez-Mejia, L., Balkin, D., and Cardy, R. (2005). *Management* (2nd ed.). Burr Ridge, IL: McGraw-Hill Irwin; Robbins, S. P. and Hunsaker P. L. (2006). *Training in Interpersonal Skills* (4th ed.). Upper Saddle River, NJ: Prentice Hall.

Downward and Upward Communication

Employee relations specialists help to maintain both downward communication and upward communication in an organization. **Downward communication** allows managers to implement their decisions and to influence employees lower in the organizational hierarchy. It can also be used to disperse information controlled by top managers. **Upward communication** allows employees at lower levels to communicate their ideas or feelings to higher-level decision makers. Unfortunately, many organizations erect serious barriers in their upward communication channels. For example, in many companies it is considered disloyal for an employee to go "over the head" of an immediate supervisor and communicate with a higher-level executive about a problem.

Downward communication
Communication that allows managers to implement their decisions and to influence employees lower in the organizational hierarchy.

Upward communication
Communication that allows employees at lower levels to communicate their ideas and feelings to higher-level decision makers.

One final but very important note concerning communication in general: The U.S. economy is shifting from an industrial base to an information base. This revolution is as significant as the move from an agrarian to an industrial economy over a century ago. In an industrial economy, production processes are the focus of concern. In an information economy, communication (the production and transmission of information) is the focus. How information is communicated, both internally and externally, is becoming more and more important to organizational success. A strong symbol of this transition is the rise of Microsoft, the software giant. Software is almost pure information; it has no tangible aspect. Yet the person who supplies most of the world's operating system software (the kind that controls a computer's operation and directs the processing of programs) and application software (the specific programs run on the computer)—Bill Gates, the founder and CEO of Microsoft—is reportedly the wealthiest person in the United States.

Encouraging Effective Communications

Working with supervisors and managers, employee relations representatives can aid effective communications by developing and maintaining three types of programs: information dissemination, employee feedback, and employee assistance.

Information Dissemination Programs

Knowledge worker
A worker who transforms information into a product or service.

Information is a source of power in organizations. In traditional top-down hierarchies, top managers zealously guard information as their special preserve. But the information age has forced many businesses to forge a new set of rules. Today, organizations depend more and more on knowledge workers to produce their product or service. **Knowledge workers** (for example, programmers, writers, educators) transform information into a product or service and need large amounts of information to do their jobs effectively. For these workers, the dissemination of information throughout the organization is critical to providing high-quality service and products to the organization's customers.

Information dissemination
The process of making information available to decision makers, wherever they are located.

Information dissemination involves making information available to decision makers, wherever they are located. Employees who have access to abundant information are more likely to feel empowered and are better able to participate in decision making. Information dissemination also helps managers adopt more participative leadership styles and work configurations, leading to greater employee involvement and, ultimately, to better employee relations.

The most important methods of disseminating information to employees are employee handbooks, written communications, audiovisual communications, electronic communications, meetings, retreats, and informal communications.

The Employee Handbook

A Question of Ethics

Some companies attempt to restrict the behavior of employees while they are off the job. The most common restriction is a prohibition against smoking. Less common is a prohibition against public drinking. Is it ethical for a company to try to control its employees' behavior while they are not on the job?

The *employee handbook* is probably the most important source of information that the HR department can provide. It sets the tone for the company's overall employee relations philosophy,[4] informing both employees and supervisors about company employment policies and procedures and communicating employees' rights and responsibilities. The handbook lets employees know that they can expect consistent and uniform treatment on issues that affect their job or status in the company. It also tells supervisors how to evaluate, reward, and discipline their employees. It can protect supervisors and the company from making uninformed and arbitrary decisions that may hurt the workforce's morale or lead to litigation from angry employees.

Employee handbooks cover issues such as employee benefits, performance evaluation, dress codes, employment of family members, smoking, probationary employment periods, drug-testing procedures, family leave policies, sexual harassment, discipline procedures, and safety rules.[5] Handbooks need to be updated annually to reflect the current legal environment and to remain consistent with the company's overall employee relations philosophy. Although employee handbooks are usually printed and distributed to employees, it is becoming more common for companies to put them online as electronic documents that can be updated easily. Online handbooks reduce printing costs, because employees can print only the pages they need.[6]

Although they are sometimes considered a tool for only large corporations, small businesses can also benefit from the use of employee handbooks. For example, a restaurant owner recently discharged an employee who did not pay for a meal, even though there was no written policy on meals and the owner had previously allowed some other employees to eat meals at the restaurant. The ex-employee took the owner to court over this misunderstanding. The owner spent over $7,000 in legal fees defending the decision to discharge the ex-employee. This dispute could have been avoided if an "employee meals" policy had been distributed in an employee handbook.[7]

Court decisions in some states have suggested that employee handbooks may constitute an implied contract between employer and employee that restricts the employer's freedom to discharge employees without just cause. To avoid such restrictive interpretations by the courts, employers should include at the end of their handbook a disclaimer stating that employees can be discharged for any reason or no reason and that the handbook does not constitute an employment contract, but rather it is a set of guidelines.[8] Some firms go even further to protect themselves: They ask all new employees to sign an employee handbook acknowledgment form stating they have received the handbook; will refer to it for company rules, regulations, and policies; and understand that it is in no way a contract. Figure 13.2 shows a sample employee handbook acknowledgment form.[9] Not surprisingly, such forms have been controversial because the legal protection they provide the employer also tends to undermine the goodwill the handbook was designed to foster.

Figure 13.2

Sample Employee Handbook Acknowledgment Form

Source: Reprinted, by permission of the publisher, from *Management Review*, June 1993. © 1993. American Management Association, New York. All rights reserved.

TJP INC. EMPLOYEE HANDBOOK ACKNOWLEDGMENT FORM

This employee handbook has been given to _____
on (date) _____
by _____ (title) _____
Employee's effective starting date _____
Employee's pay period _____
Employee's hours and workweek are _____
Welcome to TJP, Inc. Below is a list of your benefits with their effective date:

Benefit	**Effective Date**
Hospitalization _____	_____
Life insurance _____	_____
Retirement _____	_____
Vacation _____	_____
Sick leave _____	_____
Holidays _____	_____
Personal days _____	_____
Bereavement _____	_____
Workers' compensation _____	_____
Social Security _____	_____
Your first performance appraisal will be on _____	_____

I understand that my employee handbook is for informational purposes only and that I am to read and refer to the employee handbook for information on employment work rules and company policies. TJP, Inc. may modify, revoke, suspend or terminate any and all policies, rules, procedures, and benefits at any time without prior notice to company employees. This handbook and its statements do not create a contract between TJP, Inc. and its employees. This handbook and its statements do not affect in any way the employment-at-will relationship between TJP, Inc. and its employees.

(Employee's signature) _____
(Date) _____

Figure 13.3

Nepotism Policy

Section 1. Family Member Employment. The company considers it an unlawful employment practice regarding a member of an individual's family working or who has worked for the Company to:
a. Refuse to hire or employ that individual;
b. Bar or terminate from employment that individual; or
c. Discriminate against that individual in compensation or in terms, conditions, or privileges of employment.

Section 2. Conflict of Interest. The Company is not required to hire or continue in employment an individual if it:
a. Would place the individual in a position of exercising supervisory, appointment, or grievance adjustment authority over a member of the individual's family, or in a position of being subject to the authority that a member of the individual's family exercises; or
b. Would cause the Company to disregard a bona fide occupational requirement reasonably necessary to the normal operation of the Company's business.

Section 3. Member of an Individual's Family. Member of an individual's family includes wife, husband, son, daughter, mother, father, brother, brother-in-law, sister, sister-in-law, son-in-law, daughter-in-law, father-in-law, mother-in-law, aunt, uncle, niece, nephew, stepparent, or stepchild of the individual.

Source: Adapted from Decker, K. H. (1989). *A manager's guide to employee privacy: Policies and procedures*, 231–232. New York, Wiley.

Nepotism
The practice of favoring relatives over others in the workplace.

Still, employee handbooks can help prevent or solve problems in the workforce. Figure 13.3 shows how a firm might communicate an enlightened nepotism policy through its employee handbook. (**Nepotism** is the practice of favoring relatives over others in the workplace.) The policy communicated in Figure 13.3 protects the rights of family members but balances those rights with the company's need to avoid conflicts of interest that could affect the efficiency of its business.

In family-owned businesses in which owners often groom sons, daughters, or other family members to take over the company, nepotism is taken for granted. How much nepotism is okay? It is not uncommon for company owners to put their children in positions of power and grant them pay, titles, and privileges denied to more experienced or qualified company employees. Naturally, this antagonizes nonfamily employees. Family business consultants Craig E. Aronoff and John L. Ward recommend that family members meet the following three qualifications before making the family business a permanent career:

- Get an education appropriate for the job sought.
- Work three to five years outside the family business.
- Start in an existing, necessary job within the family business and honor precedents for pay and performance.[10]

Written Communications: Memos, Financial Statements, Newsletters, and Bulletin Boards

There are many other forms of written communication besides the employee handbook. *Memos* are useful for conveying changes in policies or procedures. For example, when there is a change in coverage of a specific type of medical procedure, the affected group of employees can be notified by written memo. In addition, the company should disseminate *financial reports* to make employees knowledgeable about the company's performance. Shareholders are routinely given this information, but employees should receive it, too, because it is an important source of feedback on their aggregate performance.[11]

One activity for which the HR department is likely to have direct responsibility is the production and distribution of an employee newsletter. The *newsletter* is usually a short monthly or quarterly publication designed to keep employees informed of important events, meetings, and transitions and to provide inspirational stories about employee and team contributions to the business.[12] Newsletters help foster community spirit in a company or unit. The advent of desktop publishing packages for personal computers has made newsletter production and distribution feasible for even the smallest of companies. Some managers use a simple *bulletin board* to post current team performance data and comparisons with outside competitors or other teams with the company. Moreover, a common feature of a company Web site is to have an *electronic bulletin board* that contains announcements of interest to employees that can be posted quickly and can be viewed by all the employees regardless of their location. For example, an employee who anticipates the start of a one-year international assignment may want to post an announcement on the electronic bulletin board that he is willing to sublease his home for a year.

Audiovisual Communications

New technologies have made it possible to disseminate information that goes beyond the printed word. Visual images and audio information are powerful communication tools. The widespread use of videocassette recorders (VCRs) in the home allows companies to distribute videotapes to employees when they need to convey important information. Managers at the Rocky Flats Nuclear Weapons Arsenal in Denver used prerecorded videotapes quite successfully to announce a downsizing (due to defense cuts) that would result in the layoff of several thousand employees. Each employee received a videotape containing a message from top executives explaining the reasons for the workforce reduction and the company's new mission. The tape also included a personal message from then-President George Bush explaining why the end of the Cold War meant a change in the U.S. government's spending priorities. In this case, audiovisual communication helped to maintain employee morale despite all the changes and uncertainty at the company.

Teleconferencing allows people with busy schedules to participate in meetings even when they are a great distance away from the conference location (or one another). Through video cameras and other sophisticated equipment, teleconferencing makes it possible for employees at remote locations to interact with one another as if they were all seated in the same conference room. One four-hour video conference that keeps five people off an airplane and out of hotels and restaurants could save a company at least $5,000.

With teleconferencing systems ranging in price from $10,000 to $40,000, however, the costs are still prohibitive for many companies. Fortunately, advances in computers and phone networks may soon make it possible to equip desktop computers with a camera and videoconferencing circuit board for as little as $1,000 to $1,500. Besides making videoconferencing more affordable, desktop systems promise to make the technology less intimidating to managers and employees.[13] Another way companies can teleconference affordably is to rent the equipment as needed. For instance, Kinko's rents rooms equipped with teleconferencing equipment in many of its locations.

Teleconferencing
The use of audio and video equipment to allow people to participate in meetings even when they are a great distance away from the conference location or one another.

Electronic Communications

Advances in electronic communications have made interactive communications possible even when the sender and receiver are separated by physical distance and busy schedules. With **voice mail**, an employee can avoid playing "telephone tag" with busy managers and instead leave a detailed voice message for them. The sender can also transmit a prerecorded voice mail message to some or all the people within the company's telephone network. For example, an executive can send a personalized greeting to a large group of employees. In addition, the receiver can leave different voice mail messages for different types of callers by creating a menu of messages.

Like any technology, voice mail has some drawbacks. Many people still dislike speaking to a machine. And this machine has plenty of potential for misuse. People often use it to screen calls, avoiding callers they do not want to talk to by pretending they are not there. This is fine in private life, but screening too many calls at the office can create problems. The following guidelines can help managers cut down on potential abuses of the voice mail system:[14]

Voice mail
A form of electronic communication that allows the sender to leave a detailed voice message for a receiver.

- **Limit message capacity.** To discourage long-winded voice mail messages, set the individual message capacity for 60 seconds.
- **Do not leave people in limbo.** Sometimes it is necessary to screen calls. However, screening does not mean not returning calls for five or six days. To prevent the screening habit, some

companies have a policy stipulating that answering machines cannot be turned on when employees are in their offices.

- **Do not allow voice mail to be used as a crutch.** Senders who are supposed to phone someone with unpleasant news should not wait until the person is out to lunch so they can leave the message on voice mail.
- **Make sure everyone understands the system.** This includes temporary employees, people from other departments, and new hires.
- **Respect the caller.** Employees who will be away from the office on business, or on vacation and not checking their messages, should leave a message for the callers telling them how to reach a colleague who is taking their calls.[15]

Electronic mail (e-mail)
A form of electronic communication that allows employees to communicate with each other via electronic messages sent through personal computer terminals linked by a network.

Electronic mail, or **e-mail**, allows employees to communicate with each other via written electronic messages sent through personal computer terminals linked by a network. In addition, e-mail allows employees to offer feedback to anyone in the organization, no matter what that person's rank. E-mail is a very fast way to convey important business results or critical events to a large number of employees.[16] It also permits the sharing of large information databases among employees and even members of different organizations. E-mail has made it possible for professors at different universities worldwide to collaborate on research studies, write manuscripts, and share data as quickly as if they were working next door to each other at the same university. Interorganizational electronic communication is likely to increase significantly in the coming years, thanks to the rise of the Internet.

Despite its many advantages, e-mail has created some problems for managers. One problem is that, through ease of use, e-mail contributes to information overload. "Fifty percent of e-mail is a complete waste of time," says the assistant director of fire and aviation at the U.S. Forestry Service. "People create mailing lists and send one document to 50 people when only five people need to see it." To combat this problem, the U.S. Forestry Service's system typically allows space for only 30 to 50 messages; senders often have their memos sent back to them if the receiver's mailbox is full. Another problem is people's tendency to print out every message they get, causing exactly the kind of paper blitz that e-mail is supposed to prevent.[17]

Firms that set up e-mail systems with the idea of boosting productivity are sometimes dismayed to find that they are actually *lowering* productivity. Ira Chaleff, president of International Business Technology U.S., a Washington, DC–based management consulting firm, recommends the following guidelines for using e-mail productively:

- Establish an e-mail improvement team to develop protocols and procedures for getting the most out of the system.
- Create electronic files for messages that need to be saved and organize them in subject folders for quick retrieval.
- Set up a common folder or electronic bulletin board to which senders can route reports and memos intended for general distribution. An electronic bulletin board can save considerable system space and time.[18]
- Shut off the computer beep that alerts the receiver to incoming messages to prevent constant interruptions of work.
- Assume that your e-mail from a company computer will be read by management. Use other communication channels for private or controversial messages.
- Protect sensitive documents with encryption software so that private information is not accessible to hackers or other unintended receivers.

A Question of Ethics

Should companies have the right to read and monitor their employees' e-mail?

The thorniest problem managers confront with e-mail requires consultation with HR professionals. This is the tendency of employees to view their e-mail messages as private property, immune to employer inspection. This assumption can lead them to use e-mail to communicate about off-hours activities or to spread rumors, misinformation, and complaints throughout the organization. Some managers have been shocked to find that disgruntled employees have developed grievance Web sites that encourage workers to use e-mail to sabotage managers' plans.[19] For these reasons, employers sometimes decide to monitor their employees' e-mail. Employees usually resent this, regarding it as an invasion of their privacy.[20] A survey taken in 2001 of 435 employers sponsored by the American Management Association found that about 62 percent of the employers exercise their legal right to monitor employees' e-mail.[21] For more information about grievance sites on the Web, see Exhibit 13.1.

How Managers Can Use Grievance Sites to Quell Dissent

EXHIBIT 13.1

Managers may be horrified by complaints posted on online grievance sites, yet if they can get past the angry tone of these messages there is valuable information embedded within them. Kyle Shannon, co-founder of e-commerce consultancy Agency.com, logged onto one of the grievance sites at Vault.com and read a slew of messages left by some of his employees who did not reveal their identities. One message, "I saw people cry at work regularly," was written by a woman who claims she quit after eight months with Agency. Another message stated, "I managed a team of five developers that, except for one person, were not capable of doing the work required of them. Upper management was clueless."

These grievance sites are a new phenomenon that allows tech-savvy employees to vent their anger and frustration with their company anonymously on the Internet and share this information with other employees. These forums range from message boards at Vault.com and Yahoo.com to company-specific sites like United.com (a site for peeved United Airlines employees and customers) and Walmartyrs.com (for employees who feel alienated by Wal-Mart employment policies). Management understandably is not enamored of all this airing of dirty company laundry in a display for all the world to see. Some firms such as Morgan Stanley, an investment bank, have gone as far as barring employees from accessing Vault.com at the workplace.

However, instead of banning the "gripe sites" managers would be better off logging on to them. If nothing else, "it's a free focus group," suggests Bob Rosner, founder of a grievance site called Working Wounded and author of a book by the same name. Rosner suggests not investing too much importance in individual postings but rather looking for themes that point to problems in the organization. He encourages managers to identify themselves and to "try to start a discussion and see what flows from these complaints."

Making even a small improvement from the grievance site can have a significant effect on the company's morale. Witness the impact of Kyle Shannon's visit to Vault.com. After perusing the angry messages, Shannon tapped out his response: "I can assure you that we take the messages on these boards very seriously." He apologized to workers who were having a "poor experience," acknowledged Agency's growing pains, and promised he would "listen to the issues and address them as quickly as possible." A few months later Shannon started his own discussion forum on Vault.com and encouraged Agency workers to use it. They did. Then Shannon hired a new "vice president of people management" to smooth relations with employees. Almost immediately the angry tone of the messages in Agency's grievance site at Vault.com began to taper off.

Source: Adapted from Simons, J. (2001, April 2). Stop moaning about gripe sites and log on. *Fortune*, 181–182.

For example, when setting up Epson America's e-mail system, e-mail administrator Alana Shoars reassured 700 nervous Epson employees that their e-mail would be private. When Shoars found out that her supervisor was copying and reading employees' e-mail messages, she complained—and lost her job. She filed suit, but the judge agreed with the company. Because state privacy statutes did not make specific reference to e-mail or the workplace, the judge said, the law did not protect electronic messages in the office. Epson has since notified employees that it cannot guarantee e-mail privacy, citing in part its need to protect itself from computer crime. Unless HR staff members develop e-mail policies that are explicit and reasonable, employee relations may suffer.[22] A company may violate employee privacy if it captures its employees' electronic profiles when they visit the company Web or intranet site and then sells those profiles to marketers. The marketers may in turn send unwanted marketing messages by e-mail, telephone, and junk mail to employees who match the target market profile.[23]

In many workplaces, e-mail reigns as the primary form of communication with colleagues, clients, and suppliers. Overdependence on e-mail can lead to misunderstandings that increase conflict and cause strained work relationships, due to the limits on e-mail's ability to transmit emotional content between the sender and receiver. By choosing e-mail communication over face-to-face communication, the sender is deprived of the opportunity to display nonverbal information such as tone of voice, facial expressions, body posture, and eye gaze, which receivers often depend on to figure out what someone really means.[24] Whenever a message has a high potential for emotional content from either the sender's or receiver's perspectives, it is advisable to deliver it face-to-face during a meeting or through management by walking around, both of which are discussed later in this chapter.

Multimedia technology—integrating voice, video, and text, all of which are encoded digitally and can be transported on fiber optic networks—make it possible to interact with video images of employees located across the country or around the world as if they were in the same room.

Multimedia technology has potential applications in many areas. One is in employee training programs (see Chapter 8). For example, pilots can develop aviation skills on a multimedia flight simulator without risking an accident to the plane. Many textbooks now offer multimedia disks that help students learn skills and apply the information they've learned from the text.[25] These multimedia programs include voice and video clips and ask the student to make a decision from a menu of possible choices. After making a decision, the student can see the outcome on video.

Another application of multimedia technology is in telecommuting, a trend that is already changing the face of companies across the nation.[26] More and more employees are working with company-equipped computer systems and faxes in their homes.[27] The Manager's Notebook, "Five Keys to Managing Telecommuters," addresses the managerial implications of this new workplace development.

Multimedia technology
A form of electronic communication that integrates voice, video, and text, all of which can be encoded digitally and transported on fiber optic networks.

MANAGER'S NOTEBOOK

Emerging Trends

Five Keys to Managing Telecommuters

Telecommuting must be planned carefully. The following suggestions can make managing telecommuters a little easier:

- Select telecommuters with care, considering the work habits of the employee and the type of work involved. People who are not very self-motivated may not be able to manage their time well at home.
- Maintain schedules and make sure telecommuters stick to deadlines. Although it is okay for telecommuters' to work off-hours, they should be available for consultation when the company needs them.
- Make sure the technology works. Without the right compatibility between employers' and telecommuters computer systems, there will be delays in communication and traffic tie-ups on the electronic highway.
- Have home-based workers come in to the office on a regular basis so they can attend meetings and interact with managers. Doing so not only keeps these employees in the flow but also helps combat their feelings of isolation.
- Develop a well-planned telecommuting contract that includes performance expectations with measurable results. Managers of telecommuters must develop new skills and learn to transition from managing with a focus on employees' behaviors and time to one with an emphasis on managing by results.

Sources: Based on Grensing Pophal, L. (1999, January). Training supervisors to manage teleworkers. *HRMagazine,* 67–72; Fisher, A. (2005, May 30). How telecommuters can stay connected. *Fortune,* 142. *HR Focus.* (2002, May). Time to take another look at telecommuting, 6–7.

Meetings

Formal meetings are opportunities for face-to-face communication between two or more employees and are guided by a specific agenda. Formal meetings facilitate dialogue and promote the nurturing of personal relationships, particularly among employees who may not interact frequently because they are separated by organizational or geographic barriers. Meetings are particularly useful in the formation of teams; team members can work out their interpersonal differences and build mutual trust in order to develop collaborative working relationships necessary for effective performance.

Meetings take place at different organizational levels. For example, staff meetings allow managers to coordinate activities with subordinates in their units.[28] Division or corporate meetings involve issues that have a larger impact and may include managers or employees from all divisions across the corporation. For instance, when a company like Microsoft decides to unveil a new product, organization-wide meetings are sometimes used to make sure that everyone in the organization is communicating the same message. Task force meetings may be called to discuss specific goals such as a change in marketing strategy or compensation policies.

It has been estimated that managers and executives spend as much as 75 percent of their time in meetings.[29] Poorly managed meetings can be a colossal waste of time that lower a company's productivity. Think about what it might cost for several highly paid executives to spend three hours at a meeting without accomplishing their objectives—and then multiply that amount by 260 workdays a year. However, meetings do not have to be a necessary evil. Here are some guidelines for making meetings more productive:

1. Decide whether it is even necessary to hold a meeting. If a matter can be handled by a phone call or memo, do not schedule a meeting.
2. Make meeting participation match the meeting's purpose. For instance, if a meeting is being held for the purpose of sharing information, a large group might be appropriate. For a problem-solving session, a smaller group is usually more productive.
3. Distribute a carefully planned agenda before the meeting. This will provide participants with purpose and direction and give them a chance to plan their own contributions.
4. Choose an appropriate meeting space and time. It is difficult for people to accomplish much when they are crowded into a small room with notepads balanced on their laps. Holding a meeting in a room that is too large may encourage participants to spread out and not develop the necessary cohesion. Timing is crucial, too. At meetings scheduled in the hour before lunch, attendees may be listening to their stomachs growl rather than to their colleagues. Some managers like to schedule meetings in the morning, when people are more alert. To encourage promptness, they set a time that is not exactly on the hour—such as 10:10 instead of 10:00 A.M.
5. In the case of a problem-solving or policy-setting meeting, close with an action plan and follow up with a memo outlining what happened at the meeting and what steps need to be taken.[30]

Skillful management of the dynamics among meeting participants is even more important than logistics. It is inevitable that some participants will attempt to dominate the proceedings with either helpful or negative contributions. Meeting leaders must strive to establish an atmosphere in which everyone feels at ease—one in which differences of opinion are encouraged and treated with respect.

Further clouding the air in the conference room are gender differences. Women often complain that they find it difficult to get, and hold, the floor in meetings with male colleagues. Sociolinguist Deborah Tannen has found that women and men have different communication

IBM's Joanna Dapkevich, a part-time manager who telecommutes, relies on multimedia technology to meet with her staff. The company made her telecommuting arrangements clear and workable. The results have been positive: Her team's morale is the highest in the division and its customer service ratings have improved significantly.

styles that lead to misunderstandings both at work and at home.[31] Cultural differences also crop up in the meeting room. In a U.S. business meeting, the focus tends to be on action. In contrast, the objective of Japanese business meetings is to gather information or to analyze data before planning action. In Italy, meetings are often a way for managers to demonstrate their authority and power.[32]

In addition to scheduled formal meetings with specific work-related goals, managers can use informal meetings to build personal relationships among employees. Friday social hours have become a regular part of business at high-technology companies, including Cisco Systems and Sun Microsystems. At these social hours, technical employees talk among themselves and with managers and marketing staff about projects and share information that may not be communicated through formal channels. This practice has spread to many other types of businesses.

Retreats

A *retreat* is an extended meeting in which the company takes employees to a relaxing location such as a mountain lodge or an oceanside resort, where they mix business with recreational activities like golf, tennis, or sailing. Some retreats are designed to develop creative ideas for long-term planning or for implementing changes in business practices. Others, such as the outdoor adventures organized by Outward Bound, encourage employees to develop interpersonal skills by involving them in such activities as mountain climbing or whitewater rafting, where they are forced to be interdependent. These intense shared experiences can foster mutual appreciation among coworkers. A retreat can also be an excellent way of improving employee relations. For example, one medium-sized law firm in the Denver area used a retreat to improve relations between partners and associates. All the firm's members spent two days at a mountain lodge talking in small groups about ways to improve their relationships with one another. These discussions brought into the open many touchy issues that had been simmering. In the retreat setting, the firm's members could deal with them constructively.

Many family businesses are discovering the value of retreats. Two brothers, Steve and Elliott Dean, bought all the stock in their father's company, Dean Lumber Company in Gilmer, Texas. Three years later Steve realized that he had been so busy with day-to-day affairs that he had not spoken with family members about his plans for the company's future. The solution: a family retreat at which all 15 members of the Dean clan gathered for two days to discuss Steve's vision for Dean Lumber, helped by a facilitator from the Family Business Institute at Baylor University in Waco, Texas. The retreat, which included a preretreat screening, facilities with meals, the facilitator, and guest speakers, cost the Deans $5,000.

Most family business consultants recommend using a nonfamily facilitator at the first retreat, to get the process going and keep emotions from running too high. Later on the role of facilitator can be rotated among family members. To help the Dean family get a grip on the issue of succession, for example, the facilitator asked the group to pretend that Steve and Elliott had been killed in a plane crash and asked what they would do. This proved a shocking exercise for the brothers because it made them realize how very little short- or long-term planning they had done.[33] In addition to using retreats to air important issues, many family businesses use them to set up a *family council,* an organizational and strategic planning group whose members regularly meet to decide values, policy, and direction.[34]

Informal Communications

Informal communications
Also called "the grapevine." Information exchanges without a planned agenda that occur informally among employees.

Sometimes called the "grapevine," **informal communications** consist of information exchanges without a planned agenda that occur informally among employees. Many informal communications take place among employees who form friendships or networks of mutual assistance at the water fountain or in the hallway, company cafeteria, offices, or parking lot. Informal communications pass along information that is usually not available through more formal communication channels—for example, the size of upcoming merit pay increases, who is in line for a big promotion, who has received an outside job offer, and who has gotten a low performance evaluation and is upset about it.

Informal communications can be the source of creative ideas. Qwest, a regional telecommunications company, has designed a new research facility to take advantage of the benefits of informal communication. The architect designed "breakout rooms" and hallways to optimize spontaneous interactions between technicians and scientists so that informal groups can brainstorm together to solve technical problems and generate ideas.

Managers and HR staff need to be aware of informal social groups among employees called *cliques,* which may disrupt the flow of information among employees by excluding those who are not part of the clique. Cliques often form among employees who are similar to each other, which results in the exclusion of those who are different on factors such as age, race, gender, or ethnicity. In one case, a top executive at Adams-Blake, a California software firm, noticed that within one of the company's software development teams, a clique had formed that prevented two team members from obtaining information from those on the team who were part of the clique. Team performance was negatively affected by the social tension between the clique and the excluded employees. The executive was able to improve team performance in the short run by threatening to discharge anyone in the clique who withheld information.[35] Better ways to deal with some of the harmful effects of cliques over the long term include rotating team members between different projects, allowing employees to form working relationships with diverse members of the organization. Company-sponsored social events also open new channels of communication so that more information is shared, thus reducing some of the harmful effects of cliques.

When organizations allow too much information to be communicated informally, there is a good chance that it will be distorted by rumor, gossip, and innuendo. The result may be poor employee morale and poor employee relations. To guard against this, the HR department and managers need to monitor informal communications and, when necessary, clarify them through more formal channels. One effective way to monitor informal communications is through **management by walking around (MBWA)**. MBWA, championed by Tom Peters and Robert Waterman in their wildly successful book *In Search of Excellence,* is a management technique in which the manager walks around the company so that employees at all levels have an opportunity to offer suggestions or voice grievances. This management style is used to build rapport with employees and monitor morale at IBM and many other companies.[36] Management behavior in the workplace can communicate trustworthiness to other employees. The Manager's Notebook, "Managerial Behaviors That Promote Interpersonal Trust," offers tips on behavior that communicates and builds trust with others.

Management by walking around (MBWA)
A technique in which managers walk around and talk to employees informally to monitor informal communications, listen to employee grievances and suggestions, and build rapport and morale.

MANAGER'S NOTEBOOK
Ethics

Managerial Behaviors That Promote Interpersonal Trust

The way managers behave in the workplace communicates their trustworthiness to other employees. Here are some examples of trustworthy behaviors that managers can engage in to build trust with others:

- **Act with discretion and keep secrets.** Keeping a secret means not exposing another employee's vulnerability. Divulging a confidence makes a person seem malevolent and unprofessional.
- **Be consistent between word and deed.** People who don't say one thing and do another are perceived as caring about others (i.e., they do not mislead) and being competent enough to follow through. Managers should set realistic expectations when committing to do something, and then deliver.
- **Engage in collaborative communication.** People are more willing to trust someone who shows a willingness to listen and share, to get involved and talk things through. In contrast, people are wary of someone who seems closed and will only answer clear-cut questions or discuss complete solutions. Thus, it is important for managers to be willing to work with people to improve on their partially formed ideas.
- **Ensure that decisions are fair and transparent.** People take their cues from the larger environment. As a result, the way management treats other people influences the way employees treat each other. Therefore, fair and transparent decisions, in which the decision process and outcomes are revealed to all, can translate into a more trusting environment for all employees.

Source: Adapted from Abrams, L., Cross, R., Lesser, E., and Levin, D. (2003, November). Nurturing interpersonal trust in knowledge-sharing networks. *Academy of Management Executive,* 67.

Employee Feedback Programs

Employee feedback program
A program designed to improve employee communications by giving employees a voice in policy formulation and making sure that they receive due process on any complaints they lodge against managers.

To provide upward communications channels between employees and management, many organizations offer **employee feedback programs.** These programs are designed to improve management-employee relations by (1) giving employees a voice in decision making and policy formulation and (2) making sure that employees receive due process on any complaints they lodge against managers. The HR department not only designs and maintains employee feedback programs, but is also expected to protect employee confidentiality in dealing with sensitive personal issues. HR personnel are also charged with ensuring that subordinates are not subject to retaliation from angry managers.

The most common employee feedback programs are employee attitude surveys, appeals procedures, and employee assistance programs. Here we discuss the first two kinds of programs, which are intended to resolve work-related problems. We discuss employee assistance programs (EAPs), which are designed to help employees resolve personal problems that are interfering with their job performance, later in this chapter.

Employee Attitude Surveys

Employee attitude survey
A formal anonymous survey designed to measure employee likes and dislikes of various aspects of their jobs.

Designed to measure workers' likes and dislikes of various aspects of their jobs, **employee attitude surveys** are typically formal and anonymous. They ask employees how they feel about the work they do, their supervisor, their work environment, their opportunities for advancement, the quality of the training they received, the company's treatment of women and minorities, and the fairness of the company's pay policies. An excerpt from an employee attitude survey is reproduced in Figure 13.4. The survey responses of various subgroups can be compared to those of the total employee population to help managers identify units or departments that are experiencing poor employee relations.

Making specific improvements in employee relations can avert acts of sabotage or labor unrest (such as strikes, absenteeism, and turnover) that are directly attributable to strains between subordinates and managers. For example, in analyzing attitude survey data, a chain of retail stores in the Midwest found that employees at one store had much lower levels of satisfaction

Excerpt from an Employee Attitude Survey

Figure 13.4

To What Extent Am I Satisfied With . . .

	Highly Satisfied		Satisfied		Highly Dissatisfied
1. my pay and bonus	1	2	3	4	5
2. my benefits—over all	1	2	3	4	5
3. my chance to get a promotion or a better job	1	2	3	4	5
4. having a sense of well-being on the job	1	2	3	4	5
5. the respect and recognition I receive from management	1	2	3	4	5
6. my job security	1	2	3	4	5
7. the morale of my division	1	2	3	4	5
8. the degree of responsibility and autonomy I have in doing my work	1	2	3	4	5
9. the opportunity to have my ideas adopted	1	2	3	4	5
10. working with highly talented and capable people	1	2	3	4	5
11. interdivisional cooperation and communication	1	2	3	4	5

Source: Goodrich & Sherwood Company, 521 Fifth Avenue, New York, NY 10175. Used with permission.

than the employees at any other store in the chain. The chain's top managers immediately realized this was the same store that had experienced several serious acts of sabotage. Instead of retaliating against employees, corporate management set out to solve the store's supervision problems with training and mediation.

To manage an employee attitude survey effectively, managers should follow three rules. First, they should tell employees what they plan to do with the information they collect and then inform them about the results of the survey. There is no point in surveying opinions unless the firm intends to act on them. Second, managers should use survey data ethically to monitor the state of employee relations, both throughout the company and within employee subgroups (such as women, accountants, or newly hired workers), and to make positive changes in the workplace. They should not use the information they collect to fire someone (for example, a supervisor whose workers are unhappy) or to take away privileges. Finally, to protect employee confidentiality and maintain the integrity of the data, the survey should be done by a third party, such as a consulting firm.

The application of the Internet with custom-designed software provides employee attitude survey feedback on a just-in-time basis. For example, eePulse, an Ann Arbor, Michigan, company, produces weekly reports of employee job satisfaction and other work attitude measures for its clients based on taking the pulse of various employee subgroups with an e-mail survey. The Web-based attitude survey lets managers identify the factors that cause declines in employee satisfaction more rapidly than is possible with traditional paper-and-pencil surveys.[37]

In which countries are workers the most satisfied with their jobs and their employers? According to a survey (Figure 13.5), Swiss workers are the happiest, whereas Japanese workers are the least happy. The United States falls in the middle range—at about the same level as Germany and Sweden, two countries known for their enlightened approaches to management.[38]

Appeals Procedures

Providing a mechanism for employees to voice their reactions to management practices and challenge management decisions will enhance employees' perception that the organization has fair employment policies. Organizations without an effective set of appeals procedures increase their risk of litigation, costly legal fees, and back-pay penalties to employees who use the courts to obtain justice.[39] Effective appeals procedures give individual employees some control over the decisions that affect them and help to identify managers who are ineffective or unfair.

Appeals procedure
A procedure that allows employees to voice their reactions to management practices and to challenge management decisions.

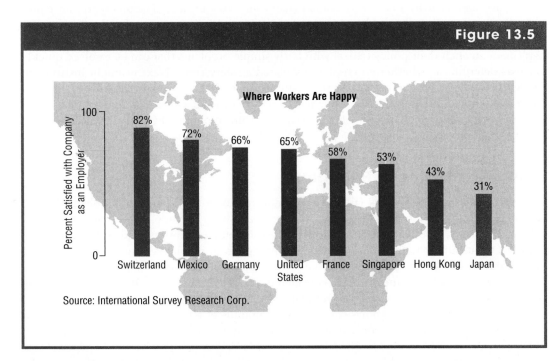

Figure 13.5

Where Workers Are Happy

Source: International Survey Research Corp.

International Comparisons of Employee Satisfaction

Source: Reprinted from June 24, 1996 issue of *BusinessWeek* by special permission, copyright © by The McGraw-Hill Companies, Inc.

Some of the most common management actions appealed by employees are:

- The allocation of overtime work
- Warnings for safety rule violations
- The size of merit pay increases
- The specification of job duties
- The employer's reimbursement for medical expense claims filed by employees
- Performance evaluations

Managers may choose from several different types of appeals procedures that vary in formality.[40] The most informal is an *open-door program*. Although the specifics of open-door programs vary from company to company, the common theme is that all employees have direct access to any manager or executive in the organization. Lucent Technologies' open-door policy has been much admired. A Lucent employee can walk into the office of any manager, up to and including the CEO, and ask for an opinion on a complaint or any other problem worrying the employee. The manager consulted must conduct a fair investigation into both sides of the issue and provide an answer within a specified period of time. For example, an employee who is dissatisfied with his or her performance evaluation may seek a second opinion from another manager. The open-door policy has two major benefits: It makes employees feel more secure and committed to Lucent, and it makes managers less likely to act arbitrarily.

Like the open-door policy, a *speak-up program* is informal and flexible. It differs in that it prescribes specific steps for the employee to take in bringing a work problem to management's attention. CIGNA, a financial services and insurance company, has a speak-up program called Speak Easy that guarantees employees access to higher levels of management, but only after they bring their problems to the attention of their immediate supervisor (Figure 13.6).

The grievance panel and the union grievance procedure are the most formal mechanisms used by organizations to handle employee complaints. *Grievance panels* are used in nonunion firms. They are composed of the complaining employee's peers and managers other than the employee's direct manager. The grievance panel conducts an investigation into the grievance brought before it. Grievance panels are typically the last step in the appeal process. For example, Honeywell's grievance panel, called the Management Appeals Committee, is asked to resolve a grievance only if solutions have not been found at earlier steps involving, first, the employee's supervisor and, second, an employee relations representative.

The *union grievance procedure* is the appeals procedure used by all employees working under a union contract. Like the grievance panel procedure, it entails multiple steps leading to a final and binding decision made by a neutral decision maker called an arbitrator. The union grievance procedure is an important feature of labor contracts, and we explain it in greater detail in Chapter 15.

Organizations should use a mix of appeals procedures. For instance, a company might implement an open-door policy to deal with fairly simple problems that can be resolved quickly (such as determining whether an employee violated a safety rule). Next, it might institute an employee assistance program to deal with sensitive problems that involve an employee's privacy (such as a terminal illness). Finally, it might set up a grievance panel to examine complex problems affecting employee relations within a group or organizational unit (such as the definition of a fair production quality standard).

Employee Assistance Programs

Employee assistance program (EAP)

A company-sponsored program that helps employees cope with personal problems that are interfering with their job performance.

Employee assistance programs (EAPs) help employees cope with personal problems that are interfering with their job performance. These problems may include alcohol or drug abuse, domestic violence, elder care, AIDS and other diseases, eating disorders, and compulsive gambling.[41] Organizations with EAPs publicize the programs to employees and assure them that their problems will be handled confidentially. When an employee's personal problem interferes with job performance, the individual is considered a *troubled employee*.[42] In a typical company about 10 percent of the total employee population at any given time is troubled.

Figure 13.7 on page 426 shows some of the symptoms of a troubled employee. A troubled employee generally behaves inconsistently in terms of attendance, quality of work, attention to

Figure 13.6

Speak Easy

Speak Easy is a special program which gives you the opportunity to talk to management about work-related concerns. Speak Easy, with the support of CIGNA Corporation management, ensures an open line of communication and guarantees a timely response.

Through the Speak Easy Program, you may want to:

- Comment on your treatment as an employee.
- Describe a specific situation that is affecting your performance or the way you feel about your job.

Management wants to hear what you have to say . . . so Speak Easy.

Here's how the program works:

Phase I This is the first and most direct way to raise issues about your job or work situation. Go to your supervisor or manager and ask to talk over problems or questions. He or she is committed to listen and give you a fair and honest answer.

But if your supervisor or manager disagrees, cannot correct the situation, or is unwilling to change an earlier decision, Phase I offers you another step.

At your request, your supervisor will arrange interview(s) with additional levels of your management, including the top company official of your department or location. You will be invited to present your concerns, and every effort will be made to resolve your issue.

Phase II Phase II has been designed for privately raising the matters not resolved in Phase I. You may be unhappy with the course of action taken or feel the matter is too touchy to go through your supervisor. Phase II will give you another audience— someone not directly involved in the situation. But it's important to note that this phase is normally **not a replacement for Phase I employee-management discussions.**

In Phase II of the program, your issues will be kept strictly confidential and reviewed impartially by the Speak Easy Coordinator. Only the coordinator will know your identity if you choose.

All you do is pick up a Speak Easy envelope located in holders throughout your office and fill in the pertinent information. . . . Then drop the completed form and envelope in the mail. You can expect a prompt response from the coordinator, so long as your signature, home address, and phone number are on the form. Otherwise, you cannot be contacted and advised of the results of the coordinator's review.

If, for some reason, the review cannot be continued without revealing your name, the coordinator will tell you. It will be your decision whether or not to continue.

Please remember the sole responsibility of the Speak Easy Coordinator is to make sure that your situation is dealt with fairly and equitably.

Phase III This is the final step if you still aren't completely satisfied with the decision. This phase gives you direct access to the Head of your Operating Group or Staff Organization.

If after using Phases I and II, you are not satisfied with the decision about your situation, you may send a Speak Easy form or a letter fully stating the issue to the Head of your Operating Group or Staff Organization with a copy to your Speak Easy Coordinator.

The situation will be immediately reviewed and you will be informed promptly of the final resolution of your appeal. If the review supports the previous opinions or decisions, these will be upheld; if not, the prior decision will be modified.

Source: Excerpt from CIGNA's "Speak Easy" Brochure. Reprinted with permission of the CIGNA Corporation.

Excerpt from CIGNA's Speak Easy Brochure

detail, and concern for personal appearance.[43] A great deal of the person's energy is devoted to coping with a personal crisis that he or she may want to keep secret from the company. Until this personal problem is resolved, the employee will be in emotional and/or physical pain and the company will be deprived of the full benefit of his or her skills. It is, therefore, in the interests of both the troubled employee and the employer to resolve the problem.

An EAP involves four steps (Figure 13.8):

1. The first step is identifying troubled employees and referring them for counseling. About half of all referrals are self-referrals by employees who realize they are in a crisis and need help, but want to keep their problem confidential. The other half are made by supervisors who observe some of the symptoms of a troubled employee. When job performance is deficient, the EAP referral is usually linked to the company's discipline procedure—it may be

**Symptoms of a
Troubled Employee**

Figure 13.7

1. Excessive absenteeism patterns: Mondays, Fridays, days before and after holidays
2. Unexcused absences
3. Frequent absences
4. Tardiness and early departures
5. Altercations with co-workers
6. Causing injuries to other employees through negligence
7. Poor judgment and bad decisions
8. Unusual on-the-job accidents
9. Increased spoilage and breaking of equipment through negligence
10. Involvements with the law—for example, a DWI (driving while intoxicated) conviction
11. Deteriorating personal appearance
12. Obsessive behavior such as inappropriate discussion of personal problems with customers

Source: Adapted from Filipowicz, C. A. (1979). The troubled employee: Whose responsibility? *Personnel Administrator, 24*(6), 8. Reprinted with the permission of *HRMagazine* (formerly *Personnel Administrator*) published by the Society for Human Resource Management. Alexandria, VA, and Wojcik, J. (1998, November 23). Signs may foreshadow workplace violence. *Business Insurance*, 41.

the last step taken before the employee is dismissed. Employees have the right to refuse to participate in the EAP, but refusal may mean termination if the problem has a significant negative impact on their work. In fact, though, many employees appreciate the company's willingness to help them through EAP counseling.

2. The second step after referral is a visit with an EAP counselor, who interviews the employee to help identify the problem. In the case of a complex personal problem like alcohol abuse, employees may strongly deny having a problem. The counselor, however, is trained to identify the problem and arrange for treatment. The location of an EAP can be at an on-site facility, with counselors available on the company premises, or an off-site facility. Off-site EAP facilities can provide counseling services to employees by the use of an 800 telephone line with counselors on call on a 24-hour per day basis. However, because EAPs are driven by relationships between counselors and employees, a recent survey by consulting firm EAP

Figure 13.8

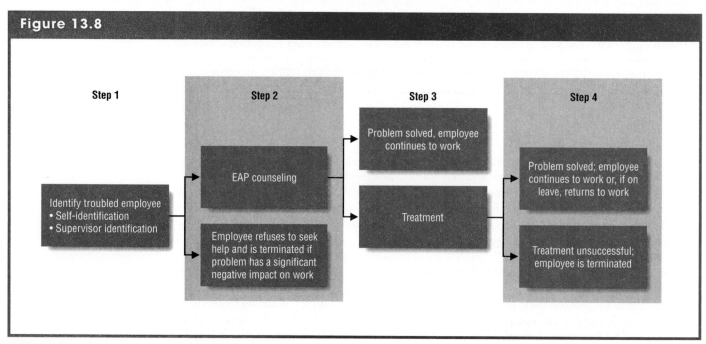

An Employee Assistance Program

Support Systems found that overall use of off-site EAP programs was one-third less than that of on-site EAP programs.[44]

3. The third step is to solve the problem. Sometimes the EAP counselor is able to help the employee do this in a short time (three sessions or fewer). For example, an employee in financial difficulty may need only short-term counseling in how to manage personal finances. Some problems, however, take longer to resolve. For these, the EAP counselor will send the troubled employee to an outside agency equipped to provide the necessary treatment. The counselor will try to find a service that best fits the employee's needs and is also cost-effective. For example, an EAP counselor who determines that an employee needs treatment for alcoholism must decide if the employee should receive inpatient residential treatment, receive outpatient treatment, or attend Alcoholics Anonymous (AA) meetings.[45] Inpatient residential treatment may require a 30-day hospitalization period that costs about $15,000. The other two alternatives cost much less.

4. The fourth and final step depends on the outcome of the treatment. If the employee has been placed on leave and the treatment is successful, the employee is allowed to return to work. In some cases, treatment does not require the employee to take a leave of absence; the employee remains on the job while being treated and continues after treatment has been successfully concluded. If the treatment is unsuccessful and the difficulty continues to disrupt the employee's work performance, the employer usually terminates the employee.

EAPs can help employees suffering from anxiety and stress due to restructurings or downsizings. The EAP at Rohm & Haas, a specialty chemical company headquartered in Philadelphia, played an important role in easing the effects of downsizing the company's production facility. When employment was cut from 800 to about 550, the company negotiated with its EAP vendor for an on-site psychologist who, in addition to maintaining office hours at the plant, sat in on management meetings and walked around the plant talking to employees. At GTE, EAPs are used to identify and provide support for managers who are dealing with people who are being let go or transferred.[46]

In the United States, there are more than 12,000 EAPs; 74 percent of large companies use them[47] to deal with a wide variety of problems. Gambling casinos in the Atlantic City, New Jersey, area have used EAPs to deal with the high incidence of alcohol- and drug-related performance problems that employees in the gambling industry experience. The EAP for the Association of Flight Attendants, which represents flight attendants from 19 airlines, has an unusually large number of individuals seeking help with weight loss.[48] At Harmon

Martha Rodriguez, left, discussed domestic violence with her supervisor Christine Lucas, resulting in counseling for the entire family facilitated by the EAP.

International Industries, a California manufacturing firm, the EAP for the company developed some special programs to help Harmon's employees deal with domestic violence, a problem that costs U.S. industry $700 million in lost productivity a year, according to the Family Violence Prevention Fund. The EAP provided awareness training to managers to show them how to detect warning signs of domestic violence and how to make referrals to the EAP counselor. The EAP helped one of Harmon's employees who reported domestic violence, Martha Rodriguez, to obtain a restraining order and obtain psychiatric care for her husband, herself, and her children.[49]

EAPs contribute to effective employee relations because they represent a good-faith attempt by management to support and retain employees who might otherwise be dismissed because of poor performance. The annual cost per employee of an EAP runs about $20 to $30.[50] However, employers gain financial benefits that outweigh their out-of-pocket EAP expenses in terms of savings on employee turnover, absenteeism, medical costs, unemployment insurance rates, workers' compensation rates, accident costs, and disability insurance costs. One study showed that the rate of problem resolution for EAPs is about 78 percent.[51] PricewaterhouseCoopers consultants estimate that each dollar invested in an EAP could return four to seven times that amount in cost reductions.[52]

Employee Recognition Programs

Employee recognition program
A program that rewards employees for their ideas and contributions.

Companies operating in global markets need employees who continuously improve the way they do their jobs to keep the company competitive. Employees are more likely to share their ideas for work improvements when managers give them credit for their contributions. **Employee recognition programs** can enhance employee relations by communicating that the organization cares about its employees' ideas and is willing to reward them for their efforts.[53] The HR department can help here by developing and maintaining formal employee recognition programs such as suggestion systems and recognition awards.

Suggestion Systems

A *suggestion system* is designed to solicit, evaluate, and implement suggestions from employees and then reward the employees for worthwhile ideas.[54] Although the reward is often monetary, it does not have to be. It might instead be public recognition, extra vacation time, a special parking spot, or some other benefit. Suggestion systems have been successfully implemented in such diverse organizations as hospitals, universities, the U.S. Postal Service and other branches of government, and private-sector companies such as BP Amoco, Eastman Kodak, Black & Decker, Simon & Schuster, and Lincoln Electric Company.[55] Firms that use suggestion systems in the United States average approximately 10 suggestions per 100 employees. Although this yield of suggestions appears modest, management experts indicate that many incremental workplace improvements are normally made outside of a formal suggestion system.[56]

Managers should adhere to some guidelines when designing a suggestion system. They should:

- Provide a simple, easy process for submitting suggestions.[57]
- Use a suggestion evaluation committee to evaluate each suggestion fairly and provide an explanation to employees why their suggestions have not been used.
- Implement accepted suggestions immediately and give credit to the suggestion's originator. The company newsletter can be used to publicly recognize employees whose suggestions have resulted in improvements.
- Make the value of the reward proportional to the suggestion's benefit to the company. For example, a loan manager at Bank of America who made a suggestion that saved the bank $363,520 a year received a cash award of $36,520 for her idea.[58] The average award that companies paid per employee suggestion was $235, according to a survey by the Employee

Involvement Association. The survey also reported that the value received by employers from these suggestions was about 10 times greater.[59]

■ Let the HR department track and manage the suggestion program by taking a coordinating role to ensure that employees buy into the program.[60]

Suggestion systems, long a part of U.S. business, have become more popular globally in recent years. For example, Japanese companies such as Toyota, Honda, and Mitsubishi have successfully gathered numerous suggestions from their employees resulting in significant improvements in their products (including automobiles). At Honda, employees who provide suggestions that result in quality improvements earn points that can be applied to prizes such as a new Honda Accord or two international airline tickets.[61]

Recognition Awards

Recognition awards give public credit to people or teams who make outstanding contributions to the organization. These people or teams may become role models for others by communicating what behaviors and accomplishments the company values. McDonald's Employee of the Month award consists of a notice posted in each restaurant for all employees and customers to see. IBM employees who make major contributions are recognized in a host of different ways, ranging from a simple thank-you letter from a division manager to a cash award of $150,000 (given to two company scientists who won the Nobel Prize in science).

The recognition of teams and people who make important quality contributions can be either monetary or nonmonetary. For example, FedEx allows supervisors to confer instant cash awards to employees for quality efforts.[62] FedEx has earned the Malcolm Baldrige National Quality Award, the highest recognition of quality that a U.S. company can receive.

An employee recognition award can be as simple as a thank you for a job well done. At KeySpan, a large U.S. distributor of natural gas, CEO Bob Catell sends a personal voice mail message of gratitude to employees who are selected as one of the company's "unsung heroes." Administrative assistant Elizabeth Kousidis indicated she was "surprised and happy" when CEO Catell recognized her as an unsung company hero.[63]

A recognition award can be initiated by a manager or by an internal customer of an individual or a team, with nominees evaluated by a recognition and awards committee. To emphasize that quality improvement should be continuous, there should be no limit on the number of times that a person or team can receive a recognition award.

A recognition award should be a celebration of the team or individual's success that encourages all organization members to work toward the organization's goals.[64] Recognition awards that focus attention on team or individual accomplishments include:

■ A company-paid picnic to which all team members and their families are invited.
■ T-shirts, coffee mugs, or baseball caps with a team insignia encouraging team commitment.
■ A company-paid night on the town (such as dinner at a nice restaurant or tickets to a concert or sports event) for an employee and his or her spouse.[65]
■ A plaque engraved with the names of individuals or teams that have made outstanding contributions.
■ A donation in the name of an employee to the charity of his or her choice.

Recognition programs can serve purposes other than providing positive feedback to employees.[66] A Phoenix area hotel rewarded employees who made outstanding contributions with a free night's stay at the hotel. Not only was this a valued prize, but it also gave employees the chance to view their organization from the customer's perspective. Management hoped that this experience would prompt new suggestions for improving customer service.

Although public recognition can be a powerful tool to sustain employee and team motivation, the Manager's Notebook, "Guidelines for Public Recognition Rewards," shows managers how to avoid pitfalls with public recognition awards. For example, when a reward appears to be motivated by favoritism or becomes a popularity contest rather than clear recognition of excellent performance, it can depress rather than improve company morale.[67]

Guidelines for Public Recognition Rewards

Public recognition rewards can have a high upside impact on employee and team levels of motivation if they are administered well. Most employees find it very rewarding to be recognized and honored in front of their peers. However, a public reward that is poorly administered due to favoritism or being perceived as a popularity contest can demotivate employees and embarrass the recipient of the reward. Here are some key points to keep in mind when administering public recognition rewards to employees.

■ **Have clear reward criteria.** Reward criteria that are clear, unambiguous, and well communicated to employees beforehand are likely to result in an employee perception of fairness and deservedness of the reward on the part of its recipient.

■ **Ensure that judges of the recognition reward are not personally related to the recipient.** The individuals on the committee who determine the winner of the public recognition reward should have an arm's-length relationship to the reward recipient. For example, if an employee's supervisor or coworker is on the rewards committee, this person may need to excuse himself or herself from the voting to avoid a perception of favoritism.

■ **The presentation of the reward should be given on a sincere basis.** The speaker who presents the reward to the recipient in front of peers should focus on giving a sincere message of appreciation to the employee being honored. The presenter should avoid engaging in theatrics and exaggerated gestures that make the recipient feel undeserving and embarrassed.

■ **Try to personalize the reward if possible.** Rewards that are personalized to the needs of the recipient have the greatest impact on motivation. An employee who loves sports will probably appreciate tickets to a baseball game more than tickets to hear an orchestra play classical music. A personalized plaque given in a public ceremony will have longer-lasting memory value than cash because the cash is soon spent whereas the plaque remains in an employee's office or in his or her home.

Sources: Adapted from Wiscombe, J. (2002, April). Rewards get results. *Workforce,* 42–48; Ginther, C. (2000, August). Incentive programs that really work. *HRMagazine,* 117–120.

Summary and Conclusions

The Roles of the Manager and the Employee Relations Specialist

Good employee relations involve providing fair and consistent treatment to all employees so that they will be committed to the organization. The backbone of an effective employee relations program is the manager, who is expected to evaluate, reward, and discipline employees in line with the company's employee relations philosophy. Employee relations representatives from the HR department ensure that employment policies are being fairly and consistently administered within the company. They often consult with both supervisors and employees on specific employee relations problems.

Developing Employee Communications

To develop effective employee relations, a company needs communication channels to move information up, down, and across the organization. Effective communications in an organization involve (1) a sender who encodes the message, (2) a communication channel that transmits the message, (3) a receiver who decodes the message, and (4) provisions for feedback because noise in the environment may distort the message's true meaning.

Facilitating Effective Communications

Working with supervisors and managers, employee relations representatives can facilitate effective communications by developing provisions for (1) information dissemination, (2) employee feedback, and (3) employee assistance programs.

Information dissemination involves making information available to decision makers, wherever they are located. Employee handbooks, written communications (memos, financial statements, newsletters, and bulletin boards), audiovisual communications, electronic communications (voice mail, e-mail, and multimedia applications), meetings, retreats, and informal communications are some of the choices available for disseminating information to employees.

Employee feedback programs are designed to improve communications by giving employees a voice in decision making and policy formulation and making sure they receive due process on any complaints they lodge against managers. Two programs that the HR department can establish to solicit employee feedback are (1) employee attitude surveys and (2) appeals procedures.

Employee assistance programs are designed to help employees whose emotional or psychological troubles are affecting their work performance. The employee is given the opportunity and resources to resolve the problem. Successful resolution of personal problems benefits both the employer and the employee.

Employee Recognition Programs

Employee recognition programs can enhance communications and employee relations by recognizing and rewarding employees who make important contributions to the organization's success. Recognition programs often use suggestion systems and recognition awards. The rewards given to individuals or teams may be monetary or nonmonetary.

Key Terms

appeals procedure, 423
downward communication, 411
electronic mail (e-mail), 416
employee assistance program (EAP), 424
employee attitude survey, 422
employee feedback program, 422
employee recognition program, 428

employee relations policy, 409
employee relations representative, 409
informal communications, 420
information dissemination, 412
knowledge worker, 412
management by walking around (MBWA), 421
multimedia technology, 418

nepotism, 414
teleconferencing, 415
upward communication, 411
voice mail, 415

Discussion Questions

1. List three ways the HR department can contribute to positive employee relations in a company.

2. Employee privacy has been called "today's most important workplace issue." What kinds of dilemmas have the new technologies created regarding employee privacy? What other kinds of problems have the new technologies created in employee relations and communications, and how might managers deal with them?

3. What are the advantages and disadvantages of telecommuting employees from the company's perspective?

4. Shelly Wexler tells her supervisor, Rob Levine, that having to care for her aging mother is forcing her to leave work early and is making her feel increasingly "stressed out." Rob refers her to the company's EAP, but he also tries to convince her to put her mother in a home for the aged and even gives her some information about nursing homes in the area. Do you think Rob is just showing ordinary concern for his employee, or do you think he is overstepping managerial boundaries? Discuss the supervisor's role in implementing an EAP. Should a supervisor try to diagnose an employee's personal problem? Why or why not?

5. Do you think most employees have reservations about using an appeals procedure such as an open-door policy? What can managers do to convince employees that the available procedures are fair and effective?

6. Some communication experts claim that men and women have different styles of communication that create barriers to decoding messages from a sender of the opposite sex. What do you think are the important differences between the way men and women communicate with each other in a work environment? What are the implications of these sex differences in communication from the perspective of effective employee relations?

7. Many managers receive over 100 e-mail messages each day from diverse senders such as the employees who are their subordinates, customers, managers who are peers, top executives at higher ranks, and various other parties. Be able to list at least three effective practices for managers to deal with this large flow of information. Are there ways to prioritize the importance of these messages so that the senders receive the information they are seeking? How can a manager reduce the number of e-mail messages that are received each day to a more manageable number?

8. A minority of employees are actually demotivated by being given public recognition in front of their co-workers. What might be a reason why some employees feel uncomfortable being recognized in a public ceremony? Do you think that this could be an issue related to diversity in the workplace? Assuming that you are a manager and you are aware that one of your employees does not respond well to public recognition, what can you do to recognize this employee's good performance as an individual or part of a team?

 There is a variety of additional material available on the Web site that accompanies this text. You can access this information by visiting the Web site at ***www.prenhall.com/gomez***.

Emerging Trends Case 13.1

Coping with the 24-Hour Service Economy at Wal-Mart

Some 1,400 Wal-Mart stores are now open 24 hours a day up from no more than 300 several years ago. Careful managers, with the aid of computer tracking, make sure that at any hour of the day a Wal-Mart has no more staff than is absolutely needed. Daytime shifts from 7 A.M. to 4 P.M., which are the most desirable ones, are allocated on the basis of employee seniority. The third shift is the nighttime one, and most new employees start to work at Wal-Mart on the third shift or the second shift, which runs through the late afternoon and evening. The night work schedule has slightly higher pay than the day schedule, but it has all the disadvantages of nighttime work. These drawbacks include the difficulty of learning to sleep during the day and being out of phase with the lifestyles of family and friends so that it is more difficult to spend time together. Moreover, new Wal-Mart employees assigned to an evening or night shift receive minimum contact with their supervisors and managers who usually work on a daytime schedule. Ironically, it is the new employees who have the greatest need for feedback from supervisors as they learn how to do their jobs and how to fit into the Wal-Mart culture, which places a high priority on giving excellent service to customers.

Wal-Mart stores traditionally have been located in smaller, rural cities not very different from Bentonville, Arkansas, where Wal-Mart headquarters is found. The company's progressive human resource policies, such as its "open-door" policy (empowering employees to bring their concerns to managers at any level), profit-sharing bonuses, retirement benefits funded with Wal-Mart stock, and time and a half pay on Sundays, were greatly appreciated by employees in these rural areas. For these employees, night shift work was tolerated because of the scarcity of alternative employers that provided the same benefits that Wal-Mart could give.

However, as Wal-Mart expanded to new markets, many stores opened in larger cities and urban areas such as Las Vegas and Dallas. For example, in the Las Vegas, Nevada, stores Wal-Mart is experiencing challenges it never faced in its stores in rural America. Wal-Mart in Las Vegas competes with hotels and gambling casinos for service workers, and the unionized casino pay is considerably more. Wal-Mart stores have suffered high turnover rates and have difficulty retaining employees who have attractive job alternatives not available to those who work in small town stores. Consequently, sometimes jobs remain unfilled in Las Vegas stores, making it difficult to provide the level of service expected by Wal-Mart customers. Furthermore, Wal-Mart has recently had to deal with union organizing drives in Las Vegas, which it never experienced in its rural markets. Wal-Mart management has always strived to avoid unions so that its special culture of informality and rural friendliness to the customers is preserved. Strikes and formal contracts, often associated with unions, pose a threat to this culture. This situation in Las Vegas and other urban stores is troubling to Wal-Mart managers because future planned expansion of the company is focused on serving other urban markets where the opportunities for growth reside.

Critical Thinking Questions

1. What impact does the Wal-Mart policy of keeping stores open 24 hours per day have on employee relations? Why is the effect of the 24-hour service policy on employee relations different in urban areas such as Las Vegas than it is in smaller towns in rural areas?
2. Some countries, such as Germany, actually restrict retail stores from being open on Sundays and regulate the weekday evening hours a store can remain open. The idea behind these laws is to protect employees' time with their families. Do you agree or disagree with this rationale? What is the basis of your agreement or disagreement?

Team Exercise

With a group of four or five other students assume you have been asked for advice by Wal-Mart management to recommend some changes in human resource policies for stores located in urban areas to achieve the following goals: (1) improve retention rates of Wal-Mart employees and (2) improve the employee relations climate in Wal-Mart stores. Assume that Wal-Mart wants to retain its 24-hour service policy in those stores. Be able to justify your recommendations. You may want to visit the Wal-Mart Web site at www.walmart.com for additional information about the culture, policies, and recent news about Wal-Mart.

Experiential Exercise

The purpose of this experiential exercise is to learn about nighttime work from people who have done it, because it is becoming more commonplace in the 24-hour service economy.

Find three people who have worked a nighttime job and are willing to discuss their work experience with you. You could interview friends, family members, or fellow students for this exercise. Ask each person who has worked a nighttime job what he or she considers to be the main advantages as well as disadvantages of working at night. Find out why each person decided to work the nighttime job. Did the interviewees experience any problems working at night, and, if so, what were

they? Summarize your findings and be prepared to share them with other members of your class. Now that you have learned about the experiences from others who have done nighttime work, would you consider accepting a job working at night? Explain your reasoning.

Source: Adapted from Gimein, M. (2002, March 18). Sam Walton made us a promise. *Fortune*, 121–130.

Ethics Case 13.2 YOU MANAGE IT!

Employers That Give Holiday Parties for Employees Are Exposed to Risks

A female employee at a company holiday party had too much to drink. In short, she was out of control in public, and her behavior repulsed those who witnessed it. When a female representative from human resources came to escort her to the women's restroom, she became belligerent and physically pushed her away. The employee was terminated the next day for inappropriate workplace conduct. Unfortunately, she couldn't remember what happened, but the HR representative was able to recount enough of the details to give her a pretty accurate picture. The employees response, interestingly enough, was defensive: "Why should I be terminated for my behavior at a company-sponsored event? After all, I never would have acted that way in the office. Besides, you provided the alcohol. When there's an open bar, I sometimes get carried away. I'll apologize to the appropriate people for my behavior, but I want my job back." Unfortunately, bad behavior at a company-sponsored event, even if she is a stellar performer, is still likely to lead to her termination as it did in this company.

As this worst-case scenario illustrates, once management becomes aware of the potential risks with holiday parties, it may decide to cancel the event. This reaction is happening with greater frequency. However, canceling may be an overreaction. HR can help management by providing some guidelines for organizing the party so that risks are minimized. Here are some areas of concern that should be anticipated in advance when organizing a company holiday party for employees.

One of the most common concerns at holiday parties is whether to serve alcohol. A legal liability is incurred when employees drive under the influence of alcohol and cause an accident that injures themselves or others. Unrestricted serving of alcohol also fuels the potential for outrageous employee behavior at the event, because some employees have difficulty controlling their drinking or are overly sensitive to the effects of alcohol. Finally, employers may be exposed to a risk if minors are served alcohol and the minors are involved in an accident.

Another important concern is whether to permit religious symbols and decorations to have a role related to the holiday party. For example, calling the event the "Office Christmas Party" may offend employees who practice non-Christian

religions or who are not religious. Putting religious decorations, such as an image of the three wise men adoring the baby Jesus, in common work areas in the company building can also offend persons of different religions whose religion is not represented in the decorations. However, forbidding employees to decorate their own offices with Christmas lights and other paraphernalia may also be viewed as a violation of an employee's right to religious expression. Employers generally need to find a way to be inclusive so it does not appear that one religion is favored over all the others.

A final concern is the issue of gift giving. Employees can become resentful or have their feelings hurt if they sense there is social pressure on them to exchange gifts with coworkers or their boss during the holiday season. Employees may also feel pressured into giving an overly expensive gift to a colleague so that an important working relationship is preserved. Furthermore, an employee may give an inappropriate gift to a co-worker at a company function that causes humiliation or a perception of sexual harassment.

Critical Thinking Questions

1. In dealing with the employer liability related to serving alcohol at holiday parties, do you think all alcoholic beverages should be forbidden? Is there a way to manage the distribution of alcoholic beverages so they are not abused? What factors should enter into this decision? Who should be involved in the decision?

2. Should an employer giving a holiday party permit religious symbols to be displayed at the holiday party or in personal or public work areas at the company? If so, what procedures should be used to permit employees to display religious symbols?

3. Should the employer permit or forbid the exchange of gifts among employees during the holidays? How can gifts be exchanged without causing some of the problems raised in this case?

Team Exercise

With a group of four or five students develop a policy for holiday parties that can be used at a company or organization that your group identifies. One possibility is to have a policy that discourages holiday parties. If this position is selected, have a well-thought-out reason for why this company should discourage the holiday party. If your group decides to have a policy that permits holiday parties, develop some general guidelines for dealing with some of the areas of risk discussed in the case, such as the serving of alcohol, the display of religious decorations, and the exchange of gifts between employees. You may be asked to present your holiday party policy to the class. Be prepared to answer questions they may have about your policy.

Experiential Exercise

Some university administrations have recently implemented policies that prohibit the use of university funds for the purchase of alcoholic drinks at campus-sponsored social events, as well as at professional activities, such as recruiting job candidates who are taken out for lunch or dinner where alcohol may be served. Students, faculty, and staff are all affected by these policies that prohibit the use of school funds for alcoholic beverages. One university administration implemented these policies after some students died from alcohol poisoning at campus-sponsored social organizations run by fraternities or sororities. In this exercise, you will select a few students and faculty members at your school and ask them to share their opinions about how they would react to a university policy that prohibits the use of university funds for alcoholic beverages at your campus. Would they be for or against such a policy? Why? Other questions to ask: What are the implications of such a policy for employee relations on campus ? What do you think the university hopes to accomplish by not paying for alcoholic beverages at social events or professional activities? Be prepared to share with the class a summary of the opinions of the people you talk to and also be willing to share your own opinions.

Sources: Adapted from Falcone, P. (2001, December). 'Tis the season. *HRMagazine*, 97–101; Segal, J. (2001, December). The most wonderful time of the year. *HRMagazine*, 103–108.

YOU MANAGE IT! | ## Customer-Driven HR Case 13.3

Casual Dress at Digital Devices

Digital Devices designs and manufactures custom integrated circuits for electronic consumer products such as pocket pagers, electronic calculators, and cellular phones. Based on the results of an employee attitude survey, the company's top executives decided to implement a casual dress-code policy for Digital employees. Management announced the casual dress policy in the employee newsletter and in an e-mail message sent to all employees. The policy stated simply that employees were encouraged to come to work in casual clothes except on days when they had meetings with clients (on those days, appropriate business attire is required).

Casual dress offers several advantages for both the company and employees. Casual dress improves employee morale by reducing status barriers that tend to separate managers (who are likely to wear suits and ties) from nonmanagement personnel. There is likely to be better communication and collaboration throughout the organization when status barriers are reduced. Casual dress is a good recruiting tool for top technical people, who tend to be young engineering graduates who want to work in a progressive company with a "fun" atmosphere. Employees also like the fact that casual dress is more comfortable and saves them money—they do not have to buy more expensive business clothes or use dry cleaning services to maintain the clothing.

Six months after the casual dress policy was announced, Sharon Greene, Digital's manager of human resources, noticed that it was a mixed blessing. Several unanticipated problems cropped up, including the following:

■ Some employees try to test the limits of casual dress. Computer programmers have come to work in T-shirts with references to drug use or sexual innuendoes that may offend other employees or clients.

■ Employees' behavior has become more casual, and in phone conversations with clients they often refer to customers or prospects as "buddies." This casual attitude has resulted in some complaints to the sales manager.

■ The HR department is now referred to as the "fashion police," because it is expected to uphold dress standards when employees wear inappropriate dress (tank tops, bicycle shorts, jeans with holes in them, and so on). This new role has undermined some of HR's credibility.

Greene is now contemplating ways to improve the casual dress policy at Digital Devices.

Critical Thinking Questions

1. Do you think Digital Devices should abandon its casual dress policy? Why or why not?
2. Suppose that Digital decides to revise its casual dress policy. Should the revised policy list approved types of clothing and unacceptable types of clothing so that employees know exactly what they can and cannot wear to work? Are there any potential problems with this approach?
3. How should the company communicate the revised casual dress policy to its employees?

Team Exercise

The class divides into groups of four or five students each. Each group develops a new casual dress code policy for Digital Devices. One representative of each group presents the group's recommended policy to the class. Other students and the instructor may ask questions or comment on the features of each group's policy.

Experiential Exercise

The purpose of this experiential exercise is to find out how people interpret casual dress policies. Find three to five people in your class or elsewhere and ask each one how they would dress if they worked for an employer that had a casual dress policy. What type of dress would they consider to be a violation of the policy? After you collect the information, do you have a better or worse idea of what a casual dress policy should be? Were there some agreements or disagreements among the people who spoke with you? What conclusions can you draw about a casual dress policy from this exercise? Be prepared to share your findings with the class.

Global Case 13.4   YOU MANAGE IT!

In Praise of Nepotism?

Nepotism is a global HR practice that gives preference in the workplace to relatives and friends of organization members in decisions such as hiring, promotions, and pay. In places such as China and Africa, nepotism has been used to favor members of one's kinship group or tribe over others. In Western Europe and the United States, nepotism has been used to favor members of one's family or social class.

Nepotism challenges some of the core values in the U.S. workplace, such as the principles of merit and equal opportunity. Yet nepotism is still applied in the United States in business, public life, and the creative arts. Bill Ford, great-grandson of founder Henry Ford, is the current CEO of Ford Motor Company, and his ascendency to the top job at Ford is related to the fact that there is a special class of voting shares owned by the Ford family that allows them to have a strong voice in the company's affairs. U.S. President John Kennedy chose his 34-year-old brother, Robert Kennedy, for Attorney General, and current U.S. President George W. Bush is son of former President George H. W. Bush. It is unlikely if either of these political leaders would have held their respective office without the assistance of their relative who was a U.S. President. Current Mayor Richard Daley of Chicago has the same job as his father with the same name, who was mayor from 1955 to 1976. In the movie industry, children or relatives of actors such as Goldie Hawn (daughter Kate Hudson), Kirk Douglas (son Michael Douglas), and Rosemary Clooney (nephew George Clooney) are presented opportunities to work in the entertainment business that are difficult to obtain for those without family connections.

Nepotism can be good or bad, according to Adam Bellow, author of *In Praise of Nepotism: A Natural History*. Bellow indicates that factors that affect the good or bad use of nepotism include merit and the distinction between private and public. Consider the following:

- In his bestselling book *Good to Great*, Jim Collins found that companies that markedly outperform their peers in terms of total shareholder return over extended periods of time are disproportionately led by CEOs who are the descendants of founders.

- In recent years, some highly publicized CEO failures occurred with descendents of company founders in firms such as Motorola (Chris Galvin) and Seagrams (Edgar Bronfman, Jr.).

- President Suharto of Indonesia excelled at nepotism and "crony capitalism" when he lavished business monopolies on his six children, whose wealth was estimated to exceed $40 billion. This blatant favoritism of family members had a major effect on influencing Indonesians to overthrow his government in 1998.

- In some of America's top universities, children of university alumni (called "legacies") are given preference in filling 10 to 15 percent of spots in the entering freshman class. For example, William Fitzsimmons, dean of admissions of Harvard College, admits that 40 percent of legacy student applications are accepted compared to only 11 percent of ordinary applicants. Even at good public universities such as the University of Virginia, legacy applicants are two to four times as more likely to be admitted than nonlegacy applicants.

Adam Bellow argues that nepotism can create family dynasties such as the Rothschilds (banking), Rockefellers (finance and philanthropy), and Hiltons (hotels) that become brands offering perceived value to customers when the family remains involved in the business. He argues that the family member who is hired in a dynastic organization is more likely to perform better and make greater sacrifices for the company than others in order to protect the reputation of the family name and the business, which are closely related.

Critical Thinking Questions

1. Why do you think people are more accepting of the application of nepotism in the workplace in a privately owned business than in one that is publicly owned by many shareholders? Why is there little tolerance for nepotism in the government, such as when the mayor of a city puts friends and family members on the government payroll?

2. Under what conditions could it be considered acceptable to hire a relative of an employee or executive in a public

organization, such as in federal government, or a publicly owned business, such as General Motors?

3. Do you agree or disagree with Bellow's argument that relatives of company owners have a greater motivation to perform well and make sacrifices for the business to protect the family reputation than do nonrelatives? Explain.

Team Exercise

Form a team with four or five of your classmates to learn why some organizations have implemented *antinepotism policies,* which are employment rules that restrict the hiring of relatives of employees in an organization. The team should find one or two examples of an antinepotism policy to share with the class. (For example, these policies are quite common in city government units such as police or firefighting departments.) For each antinepotism policy, indicate which relatives are not permitted to seek employment and which ones are (possibilities may include in-laws, step relations, or grandchildren). Develop a theory or explanation why you think each organization implemented its antinepotism policy. Do you agree or disagree that the organizations should use antinepotism policies?

Experiential Exercise

Find a partner in the class for this exercise and take turns sharing your opinions about the long-entrenched practice used by elite universities such as Harvard, Yale, and Princeton to reserve 10 to 15 percent of the spaces in the incoming freshman class for legacy students who are related to former alumni. Some critics of this practice call it "affirmative action for the wealthy." Is this a fair comment? Why do highly selective schools continue this form of nepotism? Would it make a difference if you learned that many selective schools that help children of alumni gain admission also give full financial scholarships to economically disadvantaged students who meet their admission standards? After both partners have shared their opinions, summarize the key points and be prepared to share your ideas with other members of the class.

Sources: Ciulla, J. (2005, January). In praise of nepotism? *Business Ethics Quarterly,* 153–160; *The Economist.* (2004, January 10). The curse of nepotism, 27; Bellow, A. (2003, August 5). When in doubt, hire your kin. *Wall Street Journal,* B-2.

Respecting Employee Rights and Managing Discipline

Challenges

After reading this chapter, you should be able to deal more effectively with the following challenges:

1 **Understand** the origins and the scope of employee rights and management rights.

2 **Explain** why the HR department must balance management's rights and employees' rights when designing employment policies.

3 **Describe** the employment-at-will doctrine.

4 **Distinguish** between progressive discipline procedures and positive discipline procedures.

5 **Apply** fair standards to a case of employee misconduct and justify the use of discipline.

6 **Manage** difficult people who challenge their supervisors with such problems as poor attendance, low performance, insubordination, and substance abuse.

7 **Avoid** disciplinary actions by taking a proactive and strategic approach to HRM.

All employees have rights that are based on laws, company employment policies, and traditions. Employers also have rights that support their authority and what they can expect from their employees. Sometimes these two sets of rights conflict. Consider the following situations:

■ Aligo, a Mountain View, California, producer of "mobile services," sells a product called Worktrack that enables employers to monitor employees electronically to see where they are and what they are doing at any time. Among the principal customers of Worktrack are employers in the heating and air conditioning business. Workers have cell phones equipped with a GPS (global positioning satellite) chip that transmits their locations to computers in the back office. The location coordinates can be compared to the location of the work site where the employee is expected to be. If an employee is not in the right area, he or she is considered to not be work-ing, and a notification will be sent to the employee's office. The system also tracks how fast the workers drive, so the employer can verify to insurance companies that no one is speeding. This monitoring is legal, because employers have the right to monitor their workers. However, when employees are constantly monitored by an employer, does this practice infringe on employees' rights to ethical treatment in the workplace?[1]

■ An American Management Association study in 2001 revealed that 62 percent of companies monitored their employees' Internet use. Discipline for misuse of electronic communications is increasing in frequency and severity. The New York Times Company in 1999 discharged 23 employees in its Norfolk, Virginia, processing center for disseminating sexually explicit pic-tures through its e-mail system. The Xerox Corporation in 2000 discharged 40 employees for spending excessive time visiting non-work-related or sexually oriented sites. Are employees' privacy rights being violated by employers who monitor their use of the Internet and e-mail communications?[2]

■ Workers for Weyco, a health-benefits administrator in Okemos, Michigan, can now be fired for smoking—on or off the job. The company randomly tests workers at least once a year for smok-ing. As a business that pays claims for health plans, "we see some of the devastating effects of smoking-related illnesses," says Gary Climes, vice president of finance. "We are trying to avoid it." Do such policies violate employees' rights to engage in legal activities (smoking) during nonwork hours?[3]

THE MANAGERIAL PERSPECTIVE

The three examples in the chapter opener suggest that the rights of both employees and employers should be clearly spelled out in every employment relationship. The HR department can help in several ways, such as:

■ Developing and enforcing policies that inform employees of their rights and responsibilities.
■ Making managers aware of employees' rights and managers' obligations to employees.
■ Acting as an employee advocate, especially in cases where a supervisor misunderstands or disregards discipline policy.

But it is the manager who can make a tremendous difference here. Managers who respect employees' rights are more likely to have employees with high levels of morale and job satisfaction than managers who ignore these rights. Respecting employees' rights also lessens the likelihood of a costly grievance procedure or lawsuit. As a result, managers need to learn what their employees' rights are, conduct thorough investigations on behalf of employees with a complaint, and learn to administer discipline as a way to correct a behavior or habit that is nonproductive—rather than as a form of punishment.

In this chapter, we examine employee rights and employee discipline. These two issues are closely related to the quality of employee relations (discussed in the preceding chapter). Organizations with effective employee relations ensure that their managers respect employees' rights and use fair and consistent discipline procedures.

First, we examine the concepts of employee rights, management rights, and the employment-at-will doctrine that governs many nonunion employers. Second, we explore some challenges that man-agers encounter in balancing employee rights with the rights of management. Next, we discuss employee discipline and offer some suggestions for managing difficult employees. We conclude by examining how the HR department can support managers with proactive policies that minimize the need for disciplinary procedures.

Employee Rights

A **right** is the ability to engage in conduct that is protected by law or social sanction, free from interference by another party (such as an employer). For example, employees have the legal right to form a union. It is illegal for an employer to discourage employees from exercising their right to form a union by withholding pay increases from those who support the union.

The scope of *employee rights* has broadened in the last 35 years as the federal and state governments have enacted laws giving employees specific protections. Additionally, in the last decade courts have been more willing to protect employees from wrongful discharge than they were in the past. Many believe that the courts have been more proactive in protecting employees' rights because of the shrinking proportion of the labor force that is protected by union contracts.

Figure 14.1 shows the three different categories of employee rights that managers must consider: (1) statutory rights, (2) contractual rights, and (3) other rights.

Right
The ability to engage in conduct that is protected by law or social sanction, free from interference by another party.

Statutory Rights

Employees' **statutory rights** are protected by specific laws enacted by government. Employees' key statutory right is protection from discrimination based on race, sex, religion, national origin, age, handicap, or other protected status under Title VII of the Civil Rights Act of 1964 and other equal employment opportunity laws (see Chapter 3). The *Equal Employment Opportunity Commission (EEOC)* regulates employer conduct to ensure that employees are not discriminated against.

Another important employee statutory right is protection from unsafe or unhealthy working conditions. The Occupational Safety and Health Act (OSHA) requires employers to provide safe working conditions for workers and has established the *Occupational Safety and Health Administration* to regulate health and safety practices at companies (see Chapter 16).

Employees also have the legal right to form unions and participate in union activities (see Chapter 15). The *National Labor Relations Board (NLRB)* regulates employer and employee conduct to ensure fair labor practices.

Statutory right
A right protected by specific laws.

Contractual Rights

Contractual rights are based on the law of contracts. A **contract** is a legally binding promise between two or more competent parties.[4] A breach of contract, in which one of the parties does not perform his or her promised duty to the other party, is subject to legal remedy.

Both employers and employees have rights and obligations to each other when they enter into a contract. An **employment contract** spells out explicitly the terms of the employment relationship for both employee and employer. In general, such contracts state that the employee is expected to work competently over a stipulated period of time and that the employer is expected to provide a mutually agreed upon amount of pay, as well as specific working conditions, over this time period.[5] Employees covered by employment contracts include nonunionized public school teachers, college football coaches, actors in film and television, top-level executives, and middle management.[6] Only a very small percentage of the labor force works under employment contracts.

Contractual rights
A right based on the law of contracts.

Contract
A legally binding promise between two or more competent parties.

Employment contract
A contract that spells out explicitly the terms of the employment relationship for both employee and employer.

Figure 14.1

Statutory Rights	Contractual Rights	Other Rights
■ Protection from discrimination	■ Employment contract	■ Ethical treatment
■ Safe working conditions	■ Union contract	■ Privacy (limited)
■ Right to form unions	■ Implied contracts/employment policies	■ Free speech (limited)

Categories of Employee Rights

The provisions of the employment contract give the employee job security and are, at least theoretically, negotiated individually. We say "theoretically" because there are cases in which contracts are so similar as to be standard. For instance, many public school teachers not covered by union contracts are hired on a year-to-year basis by the school district. In theory, each teacher negotiates his or her own contract. In practice, because of the volume of contracts that must be written, the vast majority of these contracts follow a standard pattern.

Some industries have standard contract provisions to protect their interests more fully. For instance, employers in competitive technology and service industries often have several employment contract provisions that forbid employees to (1) disclose trade secret information during or after their employment, (2) solicit business from former customers, or (3) attempt to hire former coworkers after leaving the company.[7] For some high-profile jobs, such as top-level executives, the contract will not follow the standard pattern and will, in fact, be negotiated individually.[8] An employee under contract may be fired for reasons other than nonperformance, but he or she is then entitled to compensation for the life of the contract.

A significant percentage of employees in the U.S. labor force (around 13%) are covered by *union contracts,* which protect groups of unionized workers. Union contracts do not provide as much job security as individually negotiated employment contracts do, but they do provide some job security through seniority and union grievance procedures. Seniority provisions protect the jobs of the most senior workers through the "last in, first out" layoff criterion that is commonly written into the union contract (see Chapter 6), Union grievance procedures subject all disciplinary actions (including discharge) to **due process**, which requires a fair investigation and a showing of just cause to discipline employees who have not performed according to expectations. An arbitrator who is empowered to decide discipline and rights cases can restore the job rights and back pay of an employee who has been wrongfully discharged. (**Wrongful discharge** is discharge for reasons that are either illegal or inappropriate, such as age or the refusal to engage in illegal activities.)

Sometimes employers and employees enter into a contract even though no formal contract exists. In this case, the employer and the employee are said to have entered into an *implied contract.* Certain employment policies and practices may unintentionally create an implied contract. The courts have interpreted statements made by an interviewer or manager such as "You will always have a job as long as you do your work" as a promise of job security.[9] Employees who lost their jobs because of layoffs have successfully obtained legal remedies when such promises were made.

Employee handbooks can be another source of implied employment contracts if they offer job security. Some courts have interpreted statements like "Employees will be dismissed only for just cause" as placing the burden of proof on the company for a termination decision.[10] In addition, when an employee handbook or employment policy makes a distinction between "probationary" and "permanent" employees, the courts have held that employers are promising continued employment to workers who successfully complete the probationary period and become permanent employees. To date, at least 30 state supreme courts have ruled that employee handbooks can be interpreted as enforceable contracts.[11]

Due process
Equal and fair application of a policy or law.

Wrongful discharge
Termination of an employee for reasons that are either illegal or inappropriate.

Other Rights

Employees often expect certain other rights in addition to statutory and contract rights. These include a right to ethical treatment and limited rights to free speech and privacy. These rights differ from the first two categories of rights in an important way: Although employees may expect these rights, they may have no legal recourse if they feel that these rights have been violated. Even though the law does not require employers to extend these other rights to employees, doing so is likely to result in more satisfied workers who are willing to go the extra mile for the organization.

Right to Ethical Treatment

Employees expect to be treated fairly and ethically in return for providing their employer with a fair and reasonable amount of work. This expectation is called the *psychological contract.*[12] Employers who uphold the psychological contract generally have more productive employees. In contrast, those who violate the psychological contract may cause employees to quit or to form a union. Because employee turnover is costly and unionization results in some loss of control over the business, managers should be aware of the importance of the psychological contract to employees.[13] One way of sealing the psychological contract is to develop and publicize a code of ethics.[14] HR can contribute to maintaining an ethical environment by integrating the code of ethics into employment policies, orientations for new employees, and formal training programs.[15] The excerpt from Starbucks' mission statement (Figure 14.2), which includes ethical standards, gives an example of how a company can publicize its ethical values.

Managers and supervisors can influence their companies' climate of fairness and ethical behavior by the tone they set for employees in their work units.[16] Specifically, managers and supervisors should:

- Take actions that develop trust, such as sharing useful information and making good on commitments.
- Act consistently so that employees are not surprised by unexpected management actions or decisions.
- Be truthful and avoid white lies and actions designed to manipulate others by giving a certain (false) impression.
- Demonstrate integrity by keeping confidences and showing concern for others.
- Meet with employees to discuss and define what is expected of them.
- Ensure that employees are treated equitably, giving equivalent rewards for similar performance and avoiding actual or apparent special treatment of favorites.
- Adhere to clear standards that are seen as just and reasonable—for example, neither praising accomplishments nor imposing penalties disproportionately.
- Demonstrate respect toward employees, showing openly that they care about employees and recognize their strengths and contributions.[17]

Limited Right to Privacy

The right to privacy protects people from unreasonable or unwarranted intrusions into their personal affairs. Although this right is not explicitly stated in the U.S. Constitution, the Supreme Court found in a 1965 ruling that it is implicit in the Constitution. For instance, the Constitution does explicitly prohibit unreasonable searches and seizures, and this prohibition is consistent with a more general right to privacy.

There are two additional legal bases for privacy rights. First, several state constitutions (including those of Arizona and California) contain an explicitly stated right to privacy. Second, several federal laws protect specific aspects of an employee's privacy. For instance, the Crime Control and Safe Streets Act of 1968 has a provision that prevents employers from viewing or listening to an employee's private communications without obtaining prior consent.

Because the U.S. and state constitutions limit the powers of the government, federal and state employees' privacy rights are protected, although not absolutely. For instance, under a program mandated by Congress, employees whose jobs in U.S. aviation are directly related to safety must undergo periodic blood alcohol testing.[18] However, the same constitutional protections do

Figure 14.2

Starbucks Mission Statement

Establish Starbucks as the premier purveyor of the finest coffee in the world while maintaining our uncompromising principles while we grow.

The following six guiding principles will help us measure the appropriateness of our decisions:

Provide a great work environment and treat each other with respect and dignity.

Embrace diversity as an essential component in the way we do business.

Apply the highest standards of excellence to the purchasing, roasting and fresh delivery of our coffee.

Develop enthusiastically satisfied customers all of the time.

Contribute positively to our communities and our environment.

Recognize that profitability is essential to our future success.

not apply to private employee arrangements. For instance, government employers are typically prohibited from searching their employees' personal work space (desks, lockers, etc.) unless they have reasonable cause, but private employers typically are not prohibited from this kind of activity. Still, because employees expect certain privacy rights, it is almost always good policy for an employer to respect employee privacy.

A sensitive issue involving employee privacy rights is the maintenance of personnel files. Each worker's **personnel file** contains the documentation of critical information, such as performance appraisals, salary history, disciplinary actions, and career milestones. Access to the personnel file should be denied to all people except managers who have a job-related "need to know" certain information. Employees should be able to review the information in their personnel file periodically to ensure its accuracy. If personnel files are stored in a human resource information system (HRIS), access to this sensitive information should be controlled by the use of passwords or special codes to protect employees' privacy rights.

Employees of the U.S. federal government have the privacy of their personnel files protected under the **Privacy Act of 1974**. The act requires federal agencies to permit employees to examine, copy, correct, or amend employee information in their personnel file. The act also includes provisions for an appeal procedure if there is a dispute over the accuracy of the information or what is to be included in the file.[19]

Limited Right to Free Speech

The First Amendment to the U.S. Constitution guarantees all U.S. citizens the right to free speech. This right is therefore more explicit than the right to privacy. However, it too is limited.[20] Again, government employees are more fully protected than those who work for private employers. For instance, an IRS agent who disagrees with the current president's tax policies is perfectly free to say so publicly without fear of official retribution. However, if a Sears store manager publicly disagrees with corporate pricing strategy, Sears is free to discipline or terminate that manager. Thus, managers in the private sector can legally discipline employees who say something damaging to the company or its reputation. Similarly, a company can and should discipline an employee for using demeaning language that insults a person based on his or her race or gender. Texaco did not discipline the managers who insulted African American employees on the basis of race, which resulted in an expensive discrimination lawsuit.[21] There are important exceptions to this situation, however. When employees reveal management misconduct to outsiders, they are engaging in whistleblowing, which is a legal right under federal and some state laws. We discuss whistleblowing in detail later in this chapter.

As with the right to privacy, managers should interfere as little as possible with employees' free speech because this right is so deeply ingrained in U.S. culture. Managers need to balance the costs and benefits of extending versus not extending privacy and speech rights. For instance, we saw in Chapter 13 that e-mail is becoming a very popular method of communication. Should companies establish a policy allowing managers to read all their employees' electronic communications? For example, an employer could have employees sign a consent form acknowledging the company's right to access e-mail messages.[22] Employees who know that managers are looking at their communications are likely to "censor" them to some degree, and the loss of candor may lead to less-than-optimal decisions. In addition, such a policy would injure the trust relationship between employees and their employer. Thus, any theoretical benefit a company might gain from such a policy—like guarding against criminal activity—would almost certainly be offset by work-related and psychological costs.

Management Rights

The rights of the employer, usually called **management rights**, can be summed up as the rights to run the business and to retain any profits that result. In the United States, management rights are supported by property laws, common law (a body of traditional legal principles, most of which originated in England), and the values of a capitalistic society that accepts the concepts of private enterprise and the profit motive.[23] The stockholders and owners who control a firm through their property rights delegate the authority to run the business to managers.

Personnel file
A file maintained for each employee, containing the documentation of critical HR-related information, such as performance appraisals, salary history, disciplinary actions, and career milestones.

Privacy Act of 1974
Guarantees the privacy of personnel files for employees of the U.S. federal government.

A Question of Ethics

A computer programming manager suspects that one of her programmers is sharing programming information with a competitor through electronic mail. Is it appropriate for the manager to examine her employee's e-mail files without the suspected programmer's permission?

Management rights
Management's rights to run the business and retain any profits that result.

Management rights include the right to manage the workforce and the rights to hire, promote, assign, discipline, and discharge employees. Management's right to direct the workforce is moderated by the right of employees (at least those who have not signed an employment contract) to quit their jobs at any time. Thus, it is in management's interest to treat employees fairly.

Management rights are influenced by the rights of groups who have an interest in decisions made in the workplace. For example, managers have the right to hire the employees they wish to hire, but this right is affected by EEOC laws that prevent the employer from discriminating on the basis of certain applicant characteristics (age, race, sex, and so on). Furthermore, managers have the right to set pay levels for their employees, but the presence of a union labor contract with a pay provision requires managers to pay employees according to the contract's terms.

Management rights are often termed *residual rights* because they pertain to the remaining rights that are not affected by contracts or laws that represent the interests of employees or other parties (such as a union).[24] According to the residual rights perspective, managers have the right to make decisions that affect the business and the workforce except where limited by laws or contract provisions.

One of the most important employer rights is employment at will.

Employment at Will

Employers have long used **employment at will**, a common-law rule, to assert their right to end their employment relationship with an employee at any time for any cause. U.S. courts adopted the rule in the nineteenth century to promote flexibility in the labor market by acknowledging the existence of a symmetrical relationship between employer and employee. Because workers were free to terminate their relationship with their employer for any reason, the courts deemed it fair for employers to be able to end their relationship with employees whenever they see fit to do so. Employment at will can be a particularly important management right in small business, where a low-performing employee can make the difference between a healthy profit and an unhealthy loss.

Although the courts originally assumed that employment at will would give both parties equal footing in the employment relationship, it is apparent that employment at will has stacked the deck in favor of employers. Because of the employment-at-will doctrine, many employees who are wrongfully discharged each year have no legal remedies.[25] One labor relations expert has estimated that approximately 150,000 employees are wrongfully discharged by their employers each year.[26] Virtually all these wrongful discharges occur in the 70 percent of the U.S. labor force that is not protected by either a union contract or *civil service rules,* which guarantee government employees the right of due process in termination procedures. Employment at will is not accepted in other parts of the world, including Japan and the nations of the European Union. These countries have enacted laws that make it difficult for employers to discharge a worker without good cause. In France, Belgium, and the United Kingdom, the only grounds for immediate dismissal are criminal behavior.[27]

Legal Limitations to Employment at Will

For the past 25 years or so, state courts have been ruling that employment at will is limited in certain situations.[28] Because these are state rather than federal cases, they have varied widely. In general, however, employment-at-will limitations can be grouped into three categories: public policy exceptions, implied contracts, and lack of good faith and fair dealing. In some states, plaintiffs have received sizable settlements for punitive damages as well as back pay. Although juries have given a median award of $205,000 to plaintiffs in wrongful discharge cases, in one recent case at a Wall Street investment bank a manager was awarded $1.9 million by his former employer to settle his claim.[29]

Public Policy Exceptions.   The courts have ruled that an employee may not be discharged for engaging in activities that are protected by law. Examples are filing a legitimate workers' compensation claim, exercising a legal duty, such as jury duty, refusing to violate a professional code of ethics, and refusing to lobby for a political candidate favored by the employer.[30]

Employment at will
A common-law rule used by employers to assert their right to end an employment relationship with an employee at any time for any cause.

Implied Contracts. As we saw earlier, the courts have determined that an implied contract may exist when an employer makes oral or written promises of job security. For instance, an implied contract may exist when an employee handbook promises job security for good performance, or when a manager who is unaware of this doctrine makes promises during the selection interview, such as "good performers will always have opportunities at our company." To prevent implied contract lawsuits, employers should carefully rewrite employee handbooks to eliminate any language that could be interpreted as an implied contract. In addition, employers must train managers to refrain from implying promises of job security in conversations with new and current workers.

Lack of Good Faith and Fair Dealing

Courts in some jurisdictions expect each party in the employment relationship to treat the other in good faith. If one party acts with malice or bad faith, the courts may be willing to provide a remedy to the injured party. For example, the courts may reason that firing a worker shortly before he or she becomes eligible for a retirement plan indicates bad faith. In this situation, the burden of proof may be on the employer to show that the discharge was for just cause.

The following case makes it plain how costly it can be for an employer to act in bad faith in discharging employees:

In 1987 two employees of a New Jersey real estate management firm took maternity leave. One was dismissed after she returned to work; the other was fired seven weeks before her planned return. Both women sued, and in 1992 a jury awarded them $210,000 and $225,000, respectively, in compensatory damages. They were awarded another $250,000 each in punitive damages, and on top of that the judge added another $374,000 in interest and legal fees. Total cost to the employer: $1.3 million.[31]

To minimize the risk of wrongful discharge lawsuits based on an implied contract, many employers have drawn up employment-at-will statements that all new employees must sign, acknowledging their understanding that the employer can terminate their employment at any time for any reason.[32]

Employee Rights Challenges: A Balancing Act

Four workplace issues are particularly challenging to HR professionals and managers because they require walking a thin line between the rights of employees and those of management: (1) random drug testing, (2) electronic monitoring, (3) whistle-blowing, and (4) office romance.

Random Drug Testing

The practice of random drug testing pits management's duty to protect the safety of its employees and customers against an employee's right to privacy. *Random drug testing* screens employees for the use of drugs randomly, without suspicion or cause. The test usually includes the analysis of a urine specimen provided by the employee.

Many employees consider random drug testing an unreasonable and illegal invasion of their privacy.[33] Although random drug testing is required by law for specific occupations where safety is critical, such as airline pilots and military personnel, it has been challenged in cases where the employer has other methods available to ensure a drug-free work environment. For example, the International Association of Fire Fighters will permit clauses in its labor contracts that allow drug testing based on "probable cause" but will not agree to random drug testing. Numerous employers also use preemployment drug testing as a condition of employment.[34]

Because no employee groups have succeeded in stopping drug testing under the U.S. Constitution, the legal battle between employee privacy and employer-mandated drug testing is being played out at the state level.[35] Not only do state constitutions vary widely in their protections of employee privacy—for example, New Jersey and California have added employee privacy provisions to their state constitutions, whereas Utah and Texas have not[36]—but the courts' interpretation of these protections has veered from one side to the other as well. For instance, the California Supreme Court dealt what was considered a death blow to random drug testing in that state when it ruled in 1990 that an employer must have a "compelling interest" to require employees not in safety-sensitive positions to submit to random drug tests.[37] Pro-employee groups cheered the ruling, but four years later the California Supreme Court allowed the National Collegiate Athletic Association to conduct random drug testing of student athletes. The court said that the private sector, like the government, must abide by the state constitution's right of privacy, but that the private sector can invade privacy for "legitimate" interests.[38]

Designing a random drug-testing policy poses numerous challenges. The HR staff can be helpful in counseling management on how to deal with some of the following issues:

- How should employees who have positive drug test results be treated? Should the manager discharge them or attempt to rehabilitate them?
- If an employee has a positive test for a legitimate reason, such as using a prescription drug or eating a poppy seed bagel (poppy seeds are the source of opium), how can the employer ensure that the employee is not charged with using illegal drugs? How can an employer protect employees from false-positive results in general?
- What can managers do to maintain security over urine specimens provided for the drug test so that they are free from adulteration designed to alter the results? Should managers require that employees be monitored while providing the urine sample to ensure its authenticity? Or does such monitoring violate the employee's privacy rights?

Motorola's random drug-testing policy was designed specifically to deal with these issues. It is administered by the company's HR department and is described in detail in Exhibit 14.1. Motorola decided to implement random drug testing after it estimated the cost of employees' drug use in terms of lost time, reduced productivity, and health-care and workers' compensation claims at $190 million annually. This amounted to 40 percent of the company's net profits.[39]

The jury is still out on whether the benefits of random drug testing outweigh the resentment and mistrust this policy often generates. A survey of workers at one of the nation's largest railroads found that only 57 out of 174 respondents expressed support for periodic drug testing—and all stipulated that it was justifiable only for safety reasons. Many commented that drug testing undermined their loyalty to the company. One worker wrote:

> I am a faithful and loyal employee. I felt like a common criminal, and I didn't even do anything wrong. . . . I happen to have bashful kidneys. The first time I took a drug test it took me almost three hours of drinking water and coffee before I could give a sample. Needless to say I was upset, angry, humiliated, defensive, etc. . . .[40]

Employees' anger and humiliation about random drug testing is compounded by the evidence that it does not help deter accidents: In 1991 a Federal Railroad Administration report found that only 3.2 percent of workers involved in railroad accidents tested positive for drugs.[41]

In order to avoid some of the disadvantages related to having employees submit to random drug-testing procedures, management in firms that are not involved with transportation or safety-sensitive jobs may decide to use either a preemployment drug test or a probable cause drug test.[42] A *preemployment drug test* is given to each job applicant as part of the hiring process. For example, the preemployment drug test may be taken as part of a physical examination that a job candidate must take before being given a job offer. Those who fail the test are not hired.[43] A *probable cause drug test* is given to employees who have accidents, engage in unsafe job behavior, or show behavioral signs of drug use, which may include having impaired judgment or slurred speech. Notice that neither the preemployment drug test nor the probable cause drug test is given on a random basis but instead is given either at a predetermined time (such as the time an employee is hired) or for a predetermined reason, such as having an accident or being reprimanded for unsafe conduct in the workplace. In a survey taken in 2001 by the American Management Association, 67 percent of U.S. firms reported using some form of drug testing.

Moreover, there is an alternative to drug testing that does not invade employee privacy and that is much more reliable for determining an employee's fitness for work: the performance test.

For example, there are computer-based performance tests that test workers' hand–eye coordination to measure their ability to do their jobs. Every morning at Silicon Valley's Ion Implant Services, Inc., delivery drivers line up in front of a computer console to "play" a short video game. Unless the machine spits out a receipt confirming they have passed the test, they cannot climb behind the wheel of their trucks. What happens to workers who fail their performance tests? Some companies refer them to a supervisor, others to an employee assistance program. Besides being both more reliable and less invasive of employees' privacy, performance testing has another advantage over random drug testing: It is cheaper. Performance tests cost from $0.60 to $1 per employee compared with the $10 per employee that the cheapest drug test costs.[44]

EXHIBIT 14.1

How Motorola's Random Drug-Testing Policy Works

Companies that wish to implement a random drug-screening process face many challenges. The following is a description of Motorola's drug-testing policy.[a]

Motorola's drug policy is stated simply. "No use of illegal drugs, no use of legal drugs illegally." To enforce the policy, the Illinois-based electronics manufacturer instituted a universal drug-testing program that HR administers. Here is how it works.

Every employee's name—including that of the chairperson and the contractors who remain on company premises for longer than 30 days—becomes part of a database. A specially designed computer program selects from each Motorola site employee names to be tested each day. The computer program ensures that every employee is selected at least once in three years for a drug test. It is possible, however, for some employees to be selected more than once during that period. This process is designed to prevent an employee's feeling safe from testing after taking one test. When the computer selects names of workers who are sick, on vacation, or away from the job site for any other legitimate reason, those names are put into a pool to be selected again randomly within 90 days.

After selecting the names of individuals to be tested on a particular day, an HR staff member informs the employees' supervisors, who are responsible for relaying the information to the employees. This serves two purposes. Not only does it get the information to the employees who will be tested, but it also allows the supervisors to prepare for those employees' brief absences. The employees whose names are selected must report at their designated times. Failure to do so results in disciplinary action.

The collection area prepares split samples for the Motorola employees, allowing for analyses from two different labs if the employees request it. If an employee's test results are positive, the company's medical review officer is contacted. The medical review officer discusses the situation with the employee to determine if there is a legitimate reason—such as a prescription drug that the employee forgot to mention—for a positive result. Except in security-sensitive positions, it is up to the employee to decide whether his or her supervisor should be notified of the results.

If it is determined that a drug abuse problem exists, the next step for the employee is to report to HR to set a meeting with an EAP adviser and plan a rehabilitation method. The company pays for the employee's rehabilitation. "We're trying to do as much as we can on the rehabilitation side, as opposed to the discipline or punitive side," says Motorola's assistant corporate director of employee relations.

All employees, except some in safety-sensitive or security clearance positions, continue working in their jobs during rehabilitation. (An exception is when the rehabilitation requires an extended stay at an in-patient treatment center.) The government requires that the organization report any positive tests of individuals who work in clearance-type operations. If the government deems it appropriate to suspend the employee's safety clearance, Motorola must remove the employee from that position. The company will try to place that employee in another position temporarily.

Similarly, if an employee who has positive test results works in a safety sensitive position, the organization will place the employee in another job during rehabilitation, if recommended by the EAP. Removal from the position is contingent on circumstances.

After employees complete their rehabilitation program, their names go into a special random pool. Motorola tests these employees once every 120 days for a one-year period.

If during this one-year period, an employee again has a positive test, the organization terminates him or her. If, however, all test results following rehabilitation are negative, the employee's name goes back into the three-year pool, and he or she begins the testing process again.

Although Motorola gives an employee who has a positive test an automatic chance for rehabilitation, other companies take a different approach.[b] Toyota Manufacturing of Kentucky uses a peer review committee for its hourly production workers who have positive drug tests. After a review of the employee's work record and listening to his or her side of the story, the committee votes on the employee's fate. In 60 percent of the cases the employee is discharged and 40 percent of the time is asked to return to work. Managers are not given a peer review and are automatically discharged for a positive drug test because they are held to a higher standard of performance.[c]

Employees who test positive for illegal drug use at Keystone RV Co., an Indiana manufacturer of recreational vehicles, are discharged. When management received information in 2005 from police and other sources that employees were using illegal drugs during lunch and breaks, the company shut down its operations for a day and gave drug tests to its entire production workforce. The result: One-fourth of the plant's workers (34 out of 120) tested positive and were discharged including 6 employees who resigned rather than submit to a mandatory drug test.[d]

Sources: [a]Gunsch, D. (1993, May). Training prepares workers for drug testing. *Personnel Journal*, 54. Copyright May 1993. Reprinted with the permission of *Personnel Journal*, ACC Communications Inc., Costa Mesa, CA: all rights reserved; [b]Gemignani, J. (1999, June). Substance abusers: Terminate or treat? *Business of Health*, 32–38; [c]Ibid.; [d]Gurchiek, K. (2005, June). Dozens who failed drug tests were fired, but RV plant keeps rolling. *HR Magazine*, 42–43.

Many employers justify random drug testing on the grounds that drug use is illegal. In recent years, however, some companies have also begun testing employees who engage in *legal* activities, such as smoking. Exhibit 14.2 examines the controversy surrounding employer policies that reject all applicants who smoke on or off the job.

Can an Employer Deny Jobs to People Who Smoke?

EXHIBIT 14.2

In one of the first court cases dealing with off-the-job smoking as part of the screening and selection process, the U.S. Supreme Court refused to hear the appeals of job applicants who were rejected from consideration for employment with the City of North Miami, Florida, because they are smokers. The denied appeal leaves in place an earlier Florida Supreme Court decision in favor of a city regulation requiring that all job applicants sign an affidavit stating that they have not used any tobacco products for one year before seeking a job with the city.[a]

Arlene Kurtz, a cigarette smoker who applied for a job as a clerk-typist, filed suit, claiming that the city's action interfered with her privacy rights to smoke during her time away from the job. Kurtz offered to comply with any reasonable on-the-job smoking restrictions but indicated that she had smoked for 30 years and had tried to quit smoking without success. The city argued that it established the policy because employees who use tobacco cost as much as $4,611 per year more than nonsmokers. The court noted that the regulation was the least intrusive way to accomplish the city's interest because it does not affect current employees, only job applicants.[b]

An even more restrictive employee smoking policy went into effect in 2005 at Weyco, an insurance benefits administrator in central Michigan, which alerted all incumbent employees that they will be randomly tested annually for smoking on or off the job.[c] See the chapter opener for details.

Other companies have taken a more moderate approach to controlling smoking behavior. They have enacted nonsmoking policies that restrict on-the-job smoking due to safety concerns and to protect nonsmoking employees from secondary smoke exposure. For example, FedEx has a nonsmoking policy that prohibits the use of tobacco products in all company buildings, facilities, vehicles, and aircraft but does not try to regulate employee's off-duty smoking behavior.[d]

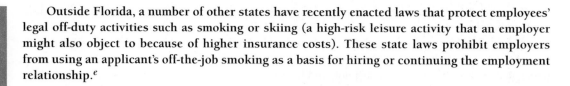

Outside Florida, a number of other states have recently enacted laws that protect employees' legal off-duty activities such as smoking or skiing (a high-risk leisure activity that an employer might also object to because of higher insurance costs). These state laws prohibit employers from using an applicant's off-the-job smoking as a basis for hiring or continuing the employment relationship.[e]

Sources: [a]Barlow, W., Hatch, D., and Murphy, B. (1996, April). Employer denies jobs to smoker applicants. *Personnel Journal*, 142; [b]*Ibid.*; [c]Peters, J. (2005, February 8). Company's smoking ban means off-hours, too. *New York Times*, C5; [d]Grensing-Pophal, L. (1999, May). Smokin' in the workplace. *Workforce*, 58–66; [e]Barlow et al., 1996.

Electronic Monitoring

Experts estimate that employee theft costs U.S. business over $400 billion a year.[45] "Theft" includes theft of merchandise, embezzlement, industrial espionage, computer crime, acts of sabotage, and misuse of time on the job. While the average annual loss a bank suffers from embezzlement is $42,000, the average computer crime costs around $400,000.[46] A retail store loses an average of $213 in a shoplifting incident (when a store customer steals merchandise) but loses an average of $10,587 for an employee theft incident.[47] Industrial spies who steal competitive trade secrets, such as software codes or plans for a microprocessor chip, may take property so valuable that its theft threatens the very existence of the business. Employees' theft of time from employers can also be costly. Employees steal time when they take long lunches, use the telephone for private conversations, misuse sick leave for extra vacation time, or surf the Internet for personal reasons.

Companies are attempting to fight these various forms of theft by using electronic surveillance devices to monitor employees.[48] In industries like telecommunications, banking, and insurance, as many as 80 percent of employees are subject to some form of electronic monitoring.[49] To eavesdrop on employees, companies use hidden microphones and transmitters attached to telephones and tiny fish-eye video lenses installed behind pinholes in walls and ceilings. In a survey published by *Macworld* magazine, more than 21 percent of respondents said they have "engaged in searches of employee computer files, voice mail, electronic mail or other networking communications." Most said they were monitoring work flow or investigating thefts or espionage.[50]

The increased sophistication of computer and telephone technology now makes it possible for employers to track employees' job performance electronically—for example, to count the number of keystrokes an employee makes on a computer terminal or determine how many reservations a travel agent books in a given time period.[51] As noted in the chapter opener, air conditioning service employees who drive to serve clients can be monitored by special cell phones containing chips that are tracked by global positioning satellites so that the employer knows the employees' location at any time and can compare it to where they are expected to be.[52] This use of electronic monitoring has raised concerns not only about employee privacy, but also about the dehumanizing effect such relentless monitoring can have on employees.[53] Many employees whose work is tracked electronically feel that monitoring takes the human element out of their work and causes too much stress. One study comparing monitored and nonmonitored clerical workers showed that 50 percent of monitored workers felt stressed, compared with 33 percent of nonmonitored workers; and that 34 percent of monitored workers lost work time because of stress-induced illness, compared with 20 percent of nonmonitored workers.[54] Some research suggests that there is a higher incidence of headaches, backaches, and wrist pains among monitored employees.[55]

Employees are most likely to see electronic monitoring as legitimate when management uses it to control theft. But even in this area some managers have exceeded reasonable standards. For example, experts estimated that in the year 2000 thirty million U.S. workers were subjected to secret electronic monitoring.[56] In one case, the nurses at Holy Cross Hospital in Silver Spring, Maryland, became quite upset after discovering that a silver box hanging on the locker room wall was a video camera monitored by the hospital security chief—who was a man.[57]

Some employers use electronic monitoring devices to control employee theft of time when they are on the company payroll. This wasted time is sometimes spent playing video games or

Electronic surveillance of employees' computer use is becoming more common, but it can cause friction between employees and employers. To maintain stronger employee relations, managers should notify employees of any surveillance in the workplace.

visiting pornographic Web sites. Employers monitor to eliminate such wastage. For example, Turner Broadcast Systems, a unit of Time Warner Inc., is planning to use software that can monitor every Web page a worker visits and help pinpoint anyone wasting company time online. The company started monitoring online activity when it noticed substantial increases in overtime pay expenditures because some employees were wasting time browsing Web sites with their computer. Turner will not pay overtime to employees who are caught surfing the Web on company time.[58]

To use electronic monitoring devices to control theft while not intimidating or invading the privacy of honest employees (who make up the majority of the workforce), managers should:

■ Avoid secret monitoring, except with specific individuals whom managers have reason to believe are stealing from the company. In those cases, management should obtain a court order to perform the secret surveillance.

■ If the company decides to monitor employees' e-mail and Internet use, then management should provide guidelines to employees for exchanging e-mail messages and accessing Web sites. The guidelines may also state that employees should not access Web sites that are related to gambling, chat rooms, online game playing, or sites with violent or sexually explicit images.[59]

■ Find positive uses for electronic monitoring devices that are beneficial to employees as well as to the employer. Avis Rent A Car, for example, has used monitoring devices to provide feedback on employee performance. This practice has been accepted as a valuable training tool.

■ Develop a systematic antitheft policy and other practices to discourage theft, such as reference checks, pencil-and-paper honesty or integrity tests that screen out employees who are likely to behave dishonestly, and internal controls that control the use of cash (accounting controls), merchandise (inventory controls), computers and databases (computer security controls), and company trade secrets (security badges and clearance procedures).

Whistle-Blowing

Whistle-blowing occurs when an employee discloses an employer's illegal, immoral, or illegitimate practices to persons or organizations that may be able to take corrective action.[60] Whistle-blowing

Whistle-blowing
Employee disclosure of an employer's illegal, immoral, or illegitimate practices to persons or organizations that may be able to take corrective action.

is risky because managers and other employees sometimes deal harshly with the whistle-blower.[61] Although whistle-blowers often have altruistic motives, they may be shunned, harassed, and even fired for their efforts.[62] For example:

A Question of Ethics

You discover that your supervisor has been billing the company for business trips that he never took. When you ask him about it, he says this is common practice throughout the company, the other department heads do the same thing, and corporate headquarters has set reimbursement rates so low that employees have to pad their expense accounts to be fairly reimbursed. What should you do?

- Jared Bowen, a Wal-Mart executive, gave the company information to investigate expense-account abuses and false invoices for as much as $500,000 made by vice chairman Thomas Coughlin that resulted in the board's asking for Coughlin's resignation from the company in 2005. Shortly afterwards, Wal-Mart also discharged Bowen, because it claimed he had tampered with his college transcripts by reporting an inflated grade point average and number of college credits. Bowen has filed a complaint with the U.S. Department of Labor claiming that Wal-Mart violated federal whistle-blower rules by firing him.[63]
- The CEO of a New Jersey bank suspected that several of the members of the bank's board of directors were making deposits as a way to launder Panamanian drug money, so he reported the transactions to the New Jersey Banking Commissioner. When board members discovered he had blown the whistle on their activities, they ordered his subordinates not to talk to him, began criticizing his decisions, told major customers he was on his way out, and later fired him.[64]
- Mark Whitacre, an executive at Archer Daniels & Midland (ADM), a U.S. agribusiness firm, spent three years helping an FBI probe into alleged price fixing conducted by the company's top executives. When ADM discovered Whitacre's connection to the FBI, it accused him of stealing $2.5 million and fired him.[65]

Dealing with whistle-blowing requires balancing employees' right to free speech with the employer's right to prevent employees from disregarding managers' authority or disclosing sensitive information to outsiders. Although whistle-blowers who work for the federal government and some state and local governments have certain legal protections, there is far less protection for private-sector employees, except in states that have enacted whistle-blower laws. Many times the whistle-blower is subject to the employment-at-will rule and may be discharged in retaliation for going public about an illegal or unethical company activity. A potential whistle-blower should have good documentation of the evidence of wrongdoing before disclosing it to others. The whistle-blower should also be prepared to deal with employer retaliation and have a contingency plan, which may include lining up another job in case the worst happens.

Despite all these risks, many employees have used whistle-blowing to call their employers to account. For example, in 2001 Enron executive Sherron Watkins wrote a blunt memo to Enron CEO Kenneth Lay warning him that the company might "implode in a wave of accounting scandals." Instead of thanking her, management factions tried to squelch the bad news and intimidate her for not being a team player. After the financial scandal broke and became a media event, Watkins was praised for her courage and became a positive role model for whistle-blowers.[66] For this reason, many companies have realized that it is in their best interests to establish a whistle-blowing policy that encourages people to reveal misconduct internally instead of exposing it externally. This way the company can avoid negative publicity and all the investigative, administrative, and legal actions associated with it.[67] Figure 14.3 lists some of the most important elements of an effective whistle-blowing policy. Probably the most important is support by top management, including the CEO. Other important elements of a whistle-blowing policy are provisions for the whistle-blower to remain anonymous initially and to be protected from retribution. Some companies that have effective whistle-blowing policies are Bank of America, Pacific Gas & Electric, McDonald's, and General Electric.[68]

The financial scandals at Enron and WorldCom prompted the passage of the Sarbanes-Oxley Act in 2002. The whistle-blower provision in Sarbanes-Oxley protects whistle-blowers from retaliation from the company or its employees and holds those who violate the law liable for both civil and criminal penalties.[69]

Restrictions on Office Romance

The office is an inviting place for romance. People fall in love at work because that is where they spend much of their time and meet people with similar interests. Some controversial high-profile office romances such as the affair between President Clinton and Monica Lewinsky, a young White House intern, have influenced many companies to view an office romance with a critical eye. The

Figure 14.3

1. Get input from top management as you develop the policy and obtain approval of the final version.

2. Develop a written policy that is communicated to employees through multiple media, such as the employee handbook, e-mail and the company intranet site, and at department meetings and training sessions. Communicating the written policy signals the company's commitment to exposing misconduct.

3. Make it possible for employees to submit their initial complaint anonymously.

4. Develop a streamlined process that makes it easy for employees to report misconduct. Designate a special representative to hear initial employee complaints so that employees do not have to report to their supervisor first.

5. Safeguard employees who report suspected misconduct in good faith against reprisals.

6. Develop a formal investigative process and communicate to employees exactly how their reports will be handled. Use this process consistently in all cases.

7. If the investigation reveals that the employee's allegations are accurate, take prompt action to correct the wrongdoing. Whatever the outcome of the investigation, communicate it quickly to the whistle-blower.

8. Establish an appeals process for employees dissatisfied with the outcome of the initial investigation. Provide an advocate (probably from the HR department) to assist the employee who wishes to appeal an unfavorable outcome.

9. To ensure the success of the whistle-blowing policy, the organization—from top management on down—must be committed to creating an ethical work environment.

Sources: Adapted from Dworkin, T., and Baucus, M. (1998). Internal vs. external whistleblowers: A comparison of whistleblowing processes. *Journal of Business Ethics, 17,* 1281–1298; and Barrett, T., and Cochran, D. (1991). Making room for the whistleblower. *HRMagazine, 36*(1), 59. Reprinted with permission of *HRMagazine* (formerly *Personnel Administrator*) published by the Society for Human Resource Management, Alexandria, VA.

Developing an Effective Whistle-Blowing Policy

challenge of dealing with an office romance forces management to balance the need to protect the company from its liability for preventing sexual harassment with the need to protect the privacy of employees during their off-duty hours so they feel free to develop romantic relationships with people of their choosing. The biggest danger occurs when a person in authority dates a subordinate. If the romance goes sour, the subordinate may claim that the boss forced the relationship, which opens the door for a sexual harassment case.[70] A recent survey conducted by the Society for Human Resource Management (SHRM) found that 24 percent of employer respondents reported having had a sexual harassment claim filed against them as a result of a workplace romance.[71]

How organizations deal with office romance depends on the goals and culture of the organization. The U.S. military restricts personal relationships between officers and enlisted personnel when the relationship compromises the chain of command. In the military the need for a highly disciplined, strongly bonded group of individuals is critical to a combat unit's success. A minority of companies has enacted *no-dating policies* that attempt to eliminate the presence of romantic relationships at the workplace between employees. Enforcing no-dating policies can be difficult. Recently, a senior executive at Staples, an office supply company that instituted a no-dating policy, was forced to resign when it was revealed he was having a consensual affair with his secretary. Staples lost a valued officer, and the manager forfeited his lucrative job for violating company rules, even though he committed no illegal act.[72]

Other companies view office romance more positively by recognizing the beneficial effect it may have on employee morale due to the fact that many office romances lead to marriage. For example, Microsoft CEO Bill Gates met his wife, Melinda French, at the company when she was a marketing executive. Representative of companies that do not interfere with office romance is Delta Airlines, which does not have any rule against dating between employees. Delta expects its employees to maintain a professional and businesslike approach to work, which includes all work-related relationships. The only exception it makes is that the company does not allow a spouse or romantic partner to supervise the other. If that were to happen, one of the partners would be transferred to another work unit.[73] Some companies go beyond tolerating office romance and condoned it. At Princeton Review, a well-known New York test-preparation company, 6 of the 10 top executives, including the CEO and president, are married to people on the payroll. More than 40 couples who met at the company have married. So far there have been no divorces and no lawsuits—though more than 20 children have been born from these marriages.[74] The employment trend of longer work hours in U.S. firms suggests that more employees will be tempted to develop a romantic relationship with a colleague at the workplace. A recent survey on employee attitudes about office romance by the American Management Association revealed that 67 percent of respondents said they approved of dating at the office, and 30 percent said they had done it themselves.[75] Management can be expected to look for guidance on how to deal with office romance from HR representatives as they struggle with balancing the privacy rights of employees with the company's liability to prevent sexual harassment.

Disciplining Employees

Employee discipline is a tool that managers rely on to communicate to employees that they need to change a behavior. For example, some employees are habitually late to work, ignore safety procedures, neglect the details required for their job, act rude to customers, or engage in unprofessional conduct with coworkers. Employee discipline entails communicating the unacceptability of such behavior along with a warning that specific actions will follow if the employee does not change the behavior.[76]

Employee discipline is usually performed by supervisors, but in self-managed work teams employee discipline may be a team responsibility. For instance, at Hannaford Bros., a food distribution center outside Albany, New York, the 120 warehouse employees are divided into 5 teams, each of which has a serious conduct committee. The committee handles employee discipline and makes recommendations to management, including counseling and even termination. Management usually adopts these recommendations. The committees generally come up with creative solutions for handling discipline problems. In fact, it has rarely proved necessary to terminate an employee.[77]

Employee and employer rights may come into conflict over the issue of employee discipline. Sometimes employees believe they are being disciplined unfairly. In such situations, a company's HR staff may help sort out disputed rights. This HR contribution is particularly valuable because it can enable the employee and the supervisor to maintain an effective working relationship.

Two different approaches to employee discipline are widely used: (1) progressive discipline and (2) positive discipline. In both these approaches, supervisors must discuss the behavior in question with their employees. Managers almost invariably find it difficult to confront an employee for disciplinary purposes. Reasons for their discomfort range from not wanting to be the bearer of bad news, to not knowing how to start the discussion, to a fear that the discussion will get out of control. The Manager's Notebook, "Five Steps for Effective Disciplinary Sessions," offers some guidelines that should make it easier for managers to handle an admittedly distasteful task.

MANAGER'S
NOTEBOOK   Ethics

Five Steps for Effective Disciplinary Sessions

1. **Determine whether discipline is called for.** Is the problem an isolated infraction or part of a pattern? Consult with HR experts and get some feedback before making a disciplinary decision.[a]
2. **Outline clear goals for the discussion in your opening remarks.** Do not rely on indirect communication or beat around the bush. The employee should gain a clear idea of your expectations for improvement.[b]
3. **Ensure two-way communication.** The most helpful disciplinary meeting is a discussion, not a lecture. The objective of the meeting, after all, is to devise a workable solution, not to berate the employee.[c]

4. Establish a follow-up plan. The agreement to a follow-up plan is crucial in both the progressive and positive disciplinary procedures. It is particularly important to establish the time frame in which the employee's behavior is to improve.[d]

5. End on a positive note. You may want to emphasize the employee's strengths so that he or she can leave the meeting believing that you—and the company—want the employee to succeed.[e]

Sources: [a]Cottringer, W. (2003, April). The abc's of employee discipline. *Supervision,* 5–7; [b]*Ibid.;* [c]Day, D. (1993, May). Training 101. Help for discipline dodgers. *Training & Development,* 19–22; [d]*Ibid.;* [e]*Ibid.*

Progressive Discipline

The most commonly used form of discipline, **progressive discipline**, consists of a series of management interventions that gives employees opportunities to correct their behavior before being discharged. Progressive discipline procedures are warning steps, each of which involves a punishment that increases in severity the longer the undesirable behaviors persist.[78] If the employee fails to respond to these progressive warnings, the employer is justified in discharging the individual.[79]

Progressive discipline systems usually have three to five steps, although a four-step system is the most common, as shown in Figure 14.4. Minor violations of company policy involve using all the steps in the progressive discipline procedure. Serious violations, sometimes referred to as *gross misconduct,* can result in the elimination of several steps and sometimes even begin at the last step, which is discharge. Examples of gross misconduct are assaulting a supervisor and falsifying employment records. However, most applications of discipline involve minor rule infractions like violating a dress code, smoking at an inappropriate time or place, or being habitually late. Figure 14.5 shows more examples of minor and serious violations.

A four-step progressive discipline procedure includes the following steps:[80]

1. **Verbal warning.** An employee who commits a minor violation receives a verbal warning from the supervisor and is told that if this problem continues within a specific time period, harsher punishment will follow. The supervisor provides clear expectations for improvement.

Progressive discipline
A series of management interventions that gives employees opportunities to correct undesirable behaviors before being discharged.

Figure 14.4

1. Verbal Warning
The employee has an unexcused absence from work. He or she receives a verbal warning from the supervisor and is told that if he or she takes another unexcused absence within the next month, harsher punishment will follow.

2. Written Warning
Two weeks after the verbal warning from his or her supervisor, the employee takes another unexcused absence. He or she now receives a written warning that if he or she fails to correct the absenteeism problem within the next two months, more severe treatment will follow. This warning goes into the employee's personnel file.

3. Suspension
Six weeks later the employee fails to show up for work for two consecutive days. This time he or she is suspended from work without pay for one week. He or she also receives a final warning from his or her supervisor that if there is another unexcused absence within three months after returning from suspension, he or she will be terminated.

4. Discharge
Two weeks after his or her return from suspension, the employee does not show up for work. Upon his or her return to work the following day, he or she is discharged.

Four Steps in a Progressive Discipline Procedure

Categories of Employee Misconduct

Figure 14.5

Minor Violations	Serious Violations
■ Absenteeism	■ Drug use at work
■ Dress code violation	■ Theft
■ Smoking rule violation	■ Dishonesty
■ Incompetence	■ Physical assault upon a supervisor
■ Safety rule violation	■ Sabotage of company operations
■ Sleeping on the job	
■ Horseplay	
■ Tardiness	

2. **Written warning.** The employee violates the same rule within the specified time period and now receives a written warning from the supervisor. This warning goes into the employee's records. The employee is told that failure to correct the violation within a certain time period will result in more severe treatment.
3. **Suspension.** The employee still fails to respond to warnings and again violates the work rule. The employee is now suspended from employment without pay for a specific amount of time. He or she receives a final warning from the supervisor, indicating that discharge will follow upon violating the rule within a specified time period.
4. **Discharge.** The employee violates the rule one more time within the specified time period and is discharged.

Figure 14.4 illustrates how an employer would use progressive discipline with an employee who has a pattern of unexcused absences from work.

For infractions that fall between the categories of minor violation and serious violation, one or two steps in the procedure are skipped. These infractions are usually handled by supervisors, who give the employees an opportunity to correct the behavior before discharging them. For example, two employees get into a fistfight at work, but there are mitigating circumstances (one employee verbally attacked the other). In this situation, both employees may be suspended without pay and warned that another such violation will result in discharge.

Positive Discipline

Positive discipline
A discipline procedure that encourages employees to monitor their own behaviors and assume responsibility for their actions.

The emphasis on punishment in progressive discipline may encourage employees to deceive their supervisor rather than correct their actions. To avoid this outcome, some companies have replaced progressive discipline with **positive discipline**, which encourages employees to monitor their own behaviors and assume responsibility for their actions.

Positive discipline is similar to progressive discipline in that it too uses a series of steps that increase in urgency and severity until the last step, which is discharge. However, positive discipline replaces the punishment used in progressive discipline with counseling sessions between employee and supervisor. These sessions focus on getting the employee to learn from past mistakes and initiate a plan to make a positive change in behavior.[81] Rather than depending on threats and punishments, the supervisor uses counseling skills to motivate the employee to change. Rather than placing blame on the employee, the supervisor emphasizes collaborative problem solving. In short, positive discipline alters the supervisor's role from adversary to counselor.

To ensure that supervisors are adequately prepared to counsel employees, companies that use positive discipline must see that they receive appropriate training either from the company's own HR department or from outside professional trainers. At Union Carbide, which began using positive discipline in the late 1970s, managers attend a two-day training program to gain familiarity with positive discipline policies and practices. Because Union Carbide had long used a progressive discipline approach, a key element of the training is helping managers abandon their tendency to respond to performance problems in a punitive way. Managers also receive training in documenting their discussions specifically, factually, and defensibly.[82]

A four-step positive discipline procedure starts with a first counseling session between employee and supervisor that ends with a verbal solution that is acceptable to both parties. If this solution does not work, the supervisor and employee meet again to discuss why it failed and to develop a new plan and timetable to solve the problem. At this second step, the new agreed-upon solution to the problem is written down.

If there is still no improvement in performance, the third step is a final warning that the employee is at risk of being discharged. Rather than suspend the employee without pay (as would happen under progressive discipline), this third step gives the employee some time to evaluate his or her situation and come up with a new solution. In doing so, the employee is encouraged to examine why earlier attempts to improve performance did not work. Some companies even give the employee a "decision-making day off" with pay to develop a plan for improved performance.[83]

Managers often resist this aspect of positive discipline because they feel that it rewards employees for poor performance. Some suspect that employees intentionally misbehave to get a free day off. According to the employee relations director of Union Carbide, which uses a paid decision-making day off as part of its disciplinary procedure, this is not so. The company believes a paid day off is more effective than the unpaid suspension used in progressive discipline procedures because (1) workers returning from an unpaid suspension often feel anger or apathy, which may lead to either reduced effectiveness on the job or subtle sabotage; (2) paying the employee for the decision-making day off avoids making the employee a martyr in the eyes of coworkers; and (3) paying for the decision-making day off underscores management's "good faith" toward the employee and probably reduces the chances that the employee will win a wrongful discharge suit if he or she is eventually terminated.[84]

Failure to improve performance after the final warning results in discharge, the fourth step of the positive discipline procedure. Incidents of gross misconduct (such as theft) are treated no differently under a positive discipline procedure than under a progressive discipline procedure. In both systems, theft will most likely result in immediate discharge.

In addition to the costs of training managers and supervisors in appropriate counseling skills and approaches, positive discipline has another drawback. Counseling sessions require a lot of time to be effective, and this is time that both the supervisor and employee are not working on other tasks. Nonetheless, positive discipline offers considerable benefits to both employees and managers. Employees prefer it because they like being treated with respect by their supervisors. Counseling generally results in a greater willingness to change undesirable behaviors than discipline does. Supervisors prefer it because it does not demand that they assume the role of disciplinarian. Counseling makes for better-quality working relationships with subordinates than discipline does. In addition, under a system of positive discipline, managers are much more likely to intervene early to correct a problem.

Finally, positive discipline can have positive effects on a company's bottom line, as evidenced at Union Carbide. Studies in five of the company's facilities have shown an average decline in absenteeism of 5.5 percent since the company switched from punitive to positive discipline procedures. Moreover, in one unionized facility at the company, disciplinary grievances went down from 36 in one year to 8 in the next. Since Union Carbide executives estimate that taking an employee complaint through all steps of the grievance procedure (short of arbitration) costs approximately $400 at this facility, the switch in discipline procedures saved the company over $11,000 per year.[85] Pennzoil, General Electric, and Procter & Gamble also have adopted the positive discipline procedure and have reported successful outcomes with it.[86] In addition, many city police forces and some universities use positive discipline. For example, one university used positive discipline with a professor who would yell at, criticize, and belittle students when they volunteered the wrong answers to his questions or avoided class participation. The department chair and the professor worked together to develop a plan to control his temper in the classroom. The department chair saw a positive change in the professor's classroom behavior that would not have occurred had the chair used a more confrontational form of discipline, such as the progressive discipline procedure.

Administering and Managing Discipline

Managers must ensure that employees who are disciplined receive due process. In the context of discipline, *due process* means fair and consistent treatment. If an employee challenges a disciplinary action under the EEO laws or a union grievance procedure, the employer must prove that the employee engaged in misconduct and was disciplined appropriately for it. Thus, supervisors should be properly trained in how to administer discipline.[87] Two important elements of due process that managers need to consider in this area are (1) the standards of discipline used to determine if the employee was treated fairly and (2) whether or not the employee has a right to appeal a disciplinary action.

Basic Standards of Discipline

Some basic standards of discipline should apply to all rule violations, whether major or minor. All disciplinary actions should include the following procedures at a minimum:

- **Communication of rules and performance criteria.** Employees should be aware of the company's rules and standards and the consequences of violating them. Every employee and supervisor should understand the company's disciplinary policies and procedures fully. Employees who violate a rule or do not meet performance criteria should be given the opportunity to correct their behavior.
- **Documentation of the facts.** Managers should gather a convincing amount of evidence to justify the discipline. This evidence should be carefully documented so that it is difficult to dispute. For example, time cards could be used to document tardiness; videotapes could document a case of employee theft; the written testimony of a witness could substantiate a charge of insubordination. Employees should have the opportunity to refute this evidence and provide documentation in self-defense.
- **Consistent response to rule violations.** It is important for employees to believe that discipline is administered consistently, predictably, and without discrimination or favoritism. If they perceive otherwise, they will be more likely to challenge discipline decisions. This does not mean that every violation should be treated exactly the same. For example, an employee with many years of seniority and an excellent work record who breaks a rule may be punished less harshly than a recently hired employee who breaks the same rule. However, two recently hired employees who break the same rule should receive the same punishment.

Hot-stove rule
A model of disciplinary action: Discipline should be immediate, provide ample warning, and be consistently applied to all.

The **hot-stove rule** provides a model of how a disciplinary action should be administered. The rule suggests that the disciplinary process is similar to touching a hot stove: (1) Touching a hot stove results in an immediate consequence, which is a burn. Discipline should also be an immediate consequence that follows a rule infraction. (2) The hot stove provides a warning that one will get burned if one touches it. Disciplinary rules should inform employees of the consequences of breaking the rules as well. (3) A hot stove is consistent in administering pain to anyone who touches it. Disciplinary rules should be consistently applied to all.[88]

The Just Cause Standard of Discipline

In cases of wrongful discharge that involve statutory rights or exceptions to employment at will, U.S. courts require the employer to prove that an employee was discharged for *just cause*. This exacting standard, which is written into union contracts and into some nonunion companies' employment policies and employee handbooks, consists of seven questions that must be answered in the affirmative for just cause to exist.[89] Failure to answer "yes" to one or more of these questions suggests that the discipline may have been arbitrary or unwarranted.

    1. Notification. Was the employee forewarned of the disciplinary consequences of his or her conduct? Unless the misconduct is very obvious (for example, theft or assault), the employer should make the employee aware, either verbally or in writing, that he or she has violated a rule.

2. **Reasonable rule.** Was the rule the employee violated reasonably related to safe and efficient operations? The rule should not jeopardize an employee's safety or integrity in any way.

3. **Investigation before the discipline.** Did managers conduct an investigation into the misconduct before administering discipline? If immediate action is required, the employee may be suspended pending the outcome of the investigation. If the investigation reveals no misconduct, all of the employee's rights should be restored.

4. **Fair investigation.** Was the investigation fair and impartial? Fair investigations allow the employee to defend himself or herself. An employee who is being interviewed as part of a disciplinary investigation has a right based on federal law to have another employee present to be his or her advocate, or to have someone to consult with, or simply to be a witness.[90]

5. **Proof of guilt.** Did the investigation provide substantial evidence or proof of guilt? Management may need a "preponderance of evidence" to prove serious charges of gross misconduct, and a less stringent (but still substantial) amount of evidence to prove minor violations.

6. **Absence of discrimination.** Were the rules, orders, and penalties of the disciplinary action applied evenhandedly and without discrimination? It is not acceptable for managers to go from lax enforcement of a rule to sudden rigorous enforcement of that rule without notifying employees that they intend to do so.

7. **Reasonable penalty.** Was the disciplinary penalty reasonably related to the seriousness of the rule violation? The employer should consider related facts, such as the employee's work record, when determining the severity of punishment. There might be a range of penalties for a given rule infraction that depend on the length and quality of the employee's service record.

Because the just cause standard is fairly stringent and can prove unwieldy in cases of minor infractions that require immediate supervisory attention, nonunion employers who believe that their employees work under employment at will may choose a less demanding discipline standard.[91]

The Right to Appeal Discipline

Sometimes employees believe they have been disciplined unfairly, either because their supervisors have abused their power or because their supervisors are biased in dealing with individuals whom they like or dislike. For a disciplinary system to be effective, employees must have access to an appeals procedure in which others (who are perceived to be free from bias) can examine the facts. As we discussed in Chapter 13, good employee relations requires establishing appeals procedures that employees can use to voice their disagreement with managers' actions. For challenging disciplinary actions, two of the most useful appeals procedures are the open-door policy and the use of employee relations representatives. These two methods are attractive because of their flexibility and their ability to reach quick resolutions. The Manager's Notebook, "Mistakes to Avoid When Administering Discipline," lists some common pitfalls that can occur when disciplining employees and ways to avoid them.

Managing Difficult Employees

So far we've focused on the challenges of administering discipline. We now turn to some common problems that managers are likely to encounter. All of the problems we discuss here—poor attendance, poor performance, insubordination, workplace bullying, and substance abuse—often lead to disciplinary actions. Managing the discipline of difficult employees requires good judgment and common sense.

Poor Attendance

The problem of poor attendance includes absenteeism and/or tardiness. Poor attendance can become a serious problem that leads to discharge for just cause. If poor attendance is not managed properly, employee productivity can decline and group morale can suffer as those with good attendance are forced to increase their efforts to compensate for people who shirk their responsibilities.

MANAGER'S NOTEBOOK

Customer-Driven HR

Mistakes to Avoid When Administering Discipline

1. **Losing your temper.** When you lose control of your temper, you may say things that damage your relationship with the employee and that you may later regret. Your loss of self-control may also encourage the employee to lose control and yell right back at you. It is preferable to step back and take a deep breath before you begin to speak to the employee who is misbehaving, no matter how angry you are feeling. Once you are calm you can have a more constructive conversation with the employee.

2. **Avoiding disciplinary action entirely.** Many supervisors avoid disciplinary action entirely because they associate it with punishment and fear harming the relationship with an employee. A supervisor needs to understand that the purpose of discipline is to correct behavior, not necessarily to punish an individual. Avoiding disciplinary action may actually harm an employee who is deprived of the chance to learn how to correct his or her behavior.

3. **Playing therapist.** Trying to get to the root causes and motives for a behavior may send the wrong message to an employee. Unless a supervisor is trained as a therapist, the employee may misinterpret the supervisor's personal questions as being nosy or overly analytical, which is unlikely to achieve the desired change in behavior. Employees respond more positively to a supervisor who is more decisive and points out the inappropriate behavior and communicates clearly what kind of performance is expected in its place.

4. **Making excuses for an employee.** It is common for employees to make excuses that explain their mistakes. Some employees become adept at creating sympathy for themselves by telling tales of woe involving their family or personal hardships. By falling for these excuses, supervisors deprive employees the chance to accept responsibility for their mistakes and instead enable them to continue rationalizing their performance deficiencies. If an employee truly has a serious personal problem that is affecting work performance, he or she should seek help with the EAP.

Sources: Adapted from Bielous, G. A. (1998, August). Five worst disciplinary mistakes (and how to avoid them). *Supervision,* 11–13; Lisoski, E. (1998, October). Nine common mistakes made when disciplining employees. *Supervision,* 12–14.

Sometimes employees are absent or tardy for legitimate reasons—for example, sickness, child-care problems, inclement weather, or religious beliefs. Managers should identify those employees who have legitimate reasons and treat them differently than they treat those who are chronically absent or tardy.

When disciplining an employee for poor attendance, managers need to consider several factors:

■ **Is the attendance rule reasonable?** Attendance rules should be flexible enough to allow for the emergencies or unforeseen circumstances that most employees experience from time to time, including religious or cultural holidays celebrated by a diverse workforce. Most companies deal with this issue by showing leniency when an employee gives notice that he or she is sick or experiencing an emergency.

- **Has the employee been warned of the consequences of poor attendance?** This could be particularly important when an employee is unaware of how much time flexibility is possible in reporting to the job.
- **Are there any mitigating circumstances that should be taken into consideration?** Sometimes special circumstances need to be considered. These circumstances include work history, length of service, reason for absence, and likelihood of improved attendance.[92]

Managers should be aware of patterns of poor attendance within a work unit. Employees may dread coming to work because coworkers are unpleasant, the job has become unchallenging, they are experiencing conflicting demands from job and family, or supervision is poor. A disciplinary approach is not the best way to deal with this type of absenteeism. Possible solutions to such job avoidance are redesigning jobs or, when the problem is widespread, restructuring the organization.

For employees whose absences are due to overwhelming family demands, flexible work schedules or permission to work at home (telecommuting) may be desirable. Flexible work schedules are gaining popularity at companies both large and small. Ten months into Xerox Corporation's experiment with flexible work schedules, absences had fallen by one-third, teamwork had improved, and worker surveys showed that morale had risen.[93]

Poor Performance

Every manager must deal with employees who perform poorly and who do not respond to coaching or feedback. In most cases, the performance appraisal (see Chapter 7) can be used to turn around poor performers by helping them develop an action plan for improvement. Sometimes, however, the poor performance is so serious that it requires immediate intervention. Consider the following situations:

- A restaurant manager receives daily complaints from angry customers about the quality of one waitress's service.
- A partner's poor interpersonal skills affect his working relationships with the other two partners in his firm. The firm is now failing to meet its goals because of the severe conflicts and disruptions instigated by this one person.

These examples suggest a glaring need for progressive or positive discipline procedures. If these employees failed to improve their performance after receiving some warnings or counseling, dismissal would be justified.

Companies and managers should follow three guidelines when applying discipline for poor performance:

1. The company's performance standards should be reasonable and communicated to all employees. Job descriptions can be used for this purpose.
2. Poor performance should be documented, and poor performers should be told how they are not meeting the expected standards. One source of documented evidence can be the pattern of the employee's performance appraisals over a period of time.
3. Managers should make a good-faith attempt to give employees an opportunity to improve their performance before disciplining them.

Sometimes poor performance is the result of factors beyond the employee's control. In these cases, managers should avoid using discipline except as a last resort. For example, an employee may be unable to perform at expected standards because of incompetence. An *incompetent employee* (one who is lacking in ability, not effort) may be given remedial training (see Chapter 8) or transferred to a less demanding job rather than be dismissed. An incompetent employee's poor performance may be the result of a flaw in the organization's selection system that caused a poor match between the employee's skills and the job requirements.

Some organizations use a *probationary employment period* (a period of time that allows the employer to discharge any employee at will) to weed out incompetent employees early.

Probationary employment periods typically last one to three months. In Europe, where permanent employment is the norm, many companies insist on a six-month trial period as part of the employment contract. However, this policy can present a problem when recruiting executives, who understandably want to be guaranteed a permanent position before leaving their current job.

It is not only inappropriate but also illegal to use discipline to correct poor performance when an employee has a physical or mental disability.[94] The Americans with Disabilities Act (ADA, see Chapter 3) requires employers to make reasonable accommodation for disabled employees who cannot perform the job as it is structured. Accommodation may include redesigning the job or modifying policies and procedures. For example, an employee who is diagnosed with a terminal illness may request a change from a full-time job to a part-time job or one with a more flexible work schedule. The EEOC, which regulates how employers respond to the needs of employees with disabilities, would probably consider this a reasonable request, so failure to make such an accommodation could lead to government sanctions.

Unfortunately, many myths hinder firms' compliance with the ADA. One myth is that reasonable accommodation always involves prohibitive expense. Actually, accommodation is not necessarily costly, and more often than not, the money spent to accommodate a disabled individual is minor compared with the cost of litigation. Samsonite Corporation, a luggage company located in Denver, has employed deaf production workers for years. The only accommodation necessary—beyond an accommodating attitude and the willingness of many employees to learn some sign language—has been the use of lights in the production area in addition to the standard beepers alerting employees to the presence of forklifts.[95]

Insubordination

The willingness of employees to carry out managers' directives is essential to a business's effective operations. For example, consider the case of a sales representative who refuses to submit the weekly activity reports requested by his manager.[96] How should the sales manager react to the sales representative's behavior?

Insubordination
Either refusal to obey a direct order from a supervisor or verbal abuse of a supervisor.

Insubordination, an employee's refusal to obey a direct order from a supervisor, is a direct challenge of management's right to run the company. Insubordination also occurs when an employee is verbally abusive to a supervisor. The discipline for insubordination usually varies according to the seriousness of the insubordination and the presence or absence of mitigating factors. Mitigating factors include the employee's work history and length of service and whether or not the employee was provoked by a supervisor's verbal abuse.

To justify disciplining an employee for insubordination, managers should document the following: (1) The supervisor gave a direct order to a subordinate, either in writing or orally; and (2) the employee refused to obey the order, either by indicating so verbally or by not doing what was asked. The discipline for a first insubordination offense ranges from applying the first step of the progressive discipline procedure to immediate suspension or discharge.

Two exceptions allow an employee to disobey a direct order: illegal activities and safety considerations. For instance, a California court found that an employer had violated public policy when it fired an employee who refused to commit perjury. Other illegal orders that employees can refuse with legal protection are participation in price-fixing and improper bookkeeping.[97] The whistle-blowing laws passed in some states provide further protection to employees who can prove they were discharged for refusing to break the law. The Occupational Safety and Health Administration protects the rights of employees who refuse to expose themselves to serious jeopardy. For insubordination to be acceptable, the employee should have "reasonable cause" to fear for his or her safety—for example, knowing that a truck the worker is ordered to drive has defective brakes.

Because the penalties for insubordination are severe, companies should create internal systems and cultures (open-door policies, appeal systems) that allow employees to appeal charges of insubordinate behavior. The legal and monetary penalties to companies for refusing to hear an employee's reasons for insubordination can be severe. Managers should be sure that insubordination charges are not being used to protect their own illegal or unethical behavior. For instance, a supervisor who charges an employee with insubordination may be attempting to force out someone who objects to the supervisor's illegal behavior. Companies that ignore such signs of trouble may find that a small problem has escalated into a very difficult and/or expensive situation.

Workplace Bullying

Employees have a right to be treated with dignity and respect in the workplace. Unfortunately, many are not. They wake up in the morning and go to work dreading that they will face another day of abuse.[98] Employees who feel this way likely experience **workplace bullying,** a form of harassment that results in employees experiencing mental distress, physical illness, loss of productivity, and a higher propensity to quit to avoid being in a toxic workplace. Workplace bullying consists of ". . . persistent, offensive, abusive, intimidating, malicious or insulting behavior, abuses of power or unfair penal sanctions, which makes the recipient feel upset, threatened, humiliated, or vulnerable, which undermines their self-confidence and which may cause them to suffer stress."[99] The bully could be a boss chewing out a subordinate in front of colleagues, a peer who spreads a damaging rumor that harms an employee's reputation, or a subordinate who withholds support to the boss during a crisis.

Although legal remedies are available for sexual harassment, other forms of antisocial behavior, such as workplace bullying, are not considered to be illegal, yet can be equally harmful to the employees who are being targeted. Therefore, it is up to the organization, with the assistance of the HR staff, to provide remedies to employees being bullied by abusive colleagues.

The media have focused attention on some high-profile situations in which individuals assumed it was permitted to treat employees harshly, and then found out the hard way that it is not:

> Staff sergeant Michael G. Rhoades, a drill sergeant at Fort Knox, Kentucky, used abusive methods to train soldiers, including calling them humiliating names such as "fat nasty," and punching a recruit in the stomach. Rhoades was court-martialed and found guilty of cruelty and dishonorably discharged for mistreating recruits.[100]
>
> In 2005, CEO Philip J. Purcell was asked by the board of directors to resign his job as CEO of Morgan Stanley, a financial services giant, after a stream of top-performing executives quit in recent years, adversely affecting company performance. Former employees indicated that CEO Purcell treated employees ruthlessly, and was intolerant of dissent or argument with his ideas. He pushed away and demeaned strong executives and preferred to surround himself with yes men and women.[101]

Some examples of bullying behaviors are listed in Figure 14.6. Although a single occurrence of one of the specified behaviors in Figure 14.6 is not likely to be perceived as a form of bullying, a persistent pattern of displaying one or more of these behaviors to a targeted employee has the cumulative effect of undermining an employee's self-confidence and morale to the point where the workplace becomes a stressful and toxic environment.

Workplace bullying
A form of harassment that consists of a persistent pattern of offensive, abusive, intimidating, malicious or insulting behavior focused at a target employee.

Figure 14.6

Examples of Bullying Behaviors in the Workplace

Swearing at an employee in a hostile manner	Threatening an employee to reveal private or embarassing information to others
Treating an employee in a rude and/or disrespectful manner	Subjecting an employee to temper tantrums when disagreeing
Subjecting an employee to obscene or hostile gestures	Criticizing an employee for his or her personal life and activities
Subjecting an employee to mean pranks	Subjecting an employee to unwanted terms of endearment
Subjecting an employee to derogatory name calling	Treating an employee in a condescending and insulting manner
Targeting an employee to rumors or gossip with intentions to harm	

Source: Neuman, J., and Keashly, L. (2005, August 9). Reducing aggression and bullying: A long-term intervention project in the U.S. Department of Veterans Affairs. In J. Raver (chair), *Workplace bullying: International perspectives on moving from research to practice.* Symposium conducted at the meeting of the Academy of Management, Honolulu, HI.

Unless an organization has a communication channel such as an open-door policy that encourages the reporting of workplace bullying behavior and provides remedies for it, employees will tolerate it, and targets of bullying will suffer in silence until they are able to quit. Two social scientists, Christine Pearson and Christine Porath, conducted a survey of employees who have been targeted by bullies to discover practices that reduce these incidents of uncivil conduct between employees. One of the recommendations from this study was for organizations to develop policies that promote zero tolerance for bullying and other forms of employee-to-employee incivility (rude conduct). Supporting this idea, organizations need value statements similar to that of AT&T, which states "we treat each other with respect and dignity."[102] Such statements set the tone for conduct that is acceptable and indicate that bullying behavior is not tolerated. Once there is a general consensus that employees need to be treated with dignity and respect, incidents of bullying can be treated as any other discipline problem.

Alcohol-Related Misconduct

Employees' use of alcohol presents two separate challenges to managers. First, there is the challenge of managing an employee who is an alcoholic. Second, there is the challenge of managing an employee who uses alcohol or is intoxicated on the job. Each of these employees should be disciplined differently.

Alcoholic employees are generally viewed sympathetically because alcoholism is an illness and medical treatment is the generally accepted remedy for it. However, as we mentioned in Chapter 13, some alcoholic employees have a strong denial mechanism that prevents them from admitting that they are alcoholics: Others may not view them as alcoholics either because alcoholism is often masked by behavioral symptoms such as poor attendance. Thus, a supervisor may perceive an alcoholic employee as someone who has an attendance or performance problem rather than an alcohol problem and discipline the employee accordingly. Organizations with EAPs give employees with performance problems the opportunity to visit a counselor as the last step in progressive discipline before discharge. This is where the alcoholism may finally be discovered and the employee referred to an alcohol rehabilitation facility.

Sometimes employees claim to be alcoholic to cover up their misconduct. If the EAP counselor determines that the individual is not an alcoholic, the discipline procedure is the appropriate managerial response to the problem.

Using alcohol on the job and coming to work intoxicated are both considered serious misconduct and can lead to harsh discipline. Organizations that have job-related reasons to restrict alcohol use at work or working "under the influence" should have clearly stated and reasonable policies. For example, it is reasonable to restrict the alcohol use, on or off the job, of heavy equipment operators at a construction site. It is more difficult to forbid a sales representative to drink alcohol when entertaining a prospective client at a lunch.

The best way to prove that an employee has come to work intoxicated is to administer a blood alcohol content test. A supervisor can ask an employee to submit to this test if there is a reasonable suspicion that the worker is intoxicated. Supervisors may suspect an individual is intoxicated if he or she engages in unusual behavior (talking particularly loud or using profanity), has slurred speech, or has alcohol on the breath.

A first intoxication offense may result in suspension or discharge because of the potential for damage that an alcohol-impaired employee can create. An extreme example of an alcohol-impaired employee's cost to an organization is the accident in which the Exxon *Valdez* oil tanker spilled oil off the coast of Alaska in March 1989. A blood alcohol test revealed that the ship's captain was intoxicated at the time of the oil spill, which cost Exxon over $1 billion to clean up.

Illegal Drug Use and Abuse

Drug use and abuse by employees also presents a serious challenge to managers. *Illegal drug use* refers to any use of prohibited substances such as marijuana, heroin, and cocaine as well as the illegal use of prescription drugs such as Valium. The problems associated with drug use are very similar to those associated with the use of alcohol. The key difference is that the use of illegal drugs is socially unacceptable, whereas the use of alcohol in moderation is socially acceptable.

We examined the specifics of drug-use detection systems earlier in this chapter, and we will address the health aspects of drug use in Chapter 16. Here we note only that illegal drug use is often masked by symptoms such as inattention and unexplained absences. Managers who suspect that drug use or addiction is the source of a performance problem should refer the employee to EAP counseling if the organization has such a program. Simultaneously, they should document performance problems and begin disciplinary procedures. These will prove valuable should it be necessary to terminate the employee because of failure to overcome the substance abuse problem after counseling and treatment. Managers who refer employees to an EAP program for problems that are not strictly related to performance may create some risk for the company, as we see in Chapter 16.

Preventing the Need for Discipline with Human Resource Management

By taking a strategic and proactive approach to the design of HRM systems, managers can eliminate the need for a substantial amount of employee discipline. HR programs designed to use employees' talents and skills effectively reduce the need to resort to discipline to shape employee behavior. In this section we briefly revisit some of the functional areas of HR we discussed in earlier chapters to show how each can be designed to prevent problem employees.[103]

Recruitment and Selection

By spending more time and resources on recruiting and selection, managers can make better matches between individuals and the organization.

■ Workers can be selected for fit in the organization as well as the job. Choosing applicants who have career potential in the company decreases the likelihood that employees will exhibit performance problems later.

■ Checking references and gathering background information on applicants' work habits and character are useful preliminaries to making a job offer.

■ Multiple interviews that involve diverse groups in the company can reduce biases that lead to poor hiring decisions. When women, minorities, peers, and subordinates, as well as senior people, are involved in the interviewing process, companies stand a better chance of obtaining an accurate portrait of the applicant.

Training and Development

Investing in employees' training and development now saves a company from having to deal with incompetents or workers whose skills are obsolete down the road.

■ An effective orientation program communicates to new employees the values important to the organization. It also teaches employees what is expected from them as members of the organization. These insights into the company can help employees manage their own behavior better. FedEx, for instance, has an extensive orientation program to communicate company values to employees.[104]

■ Training programs for new employees can reduce skill gaps and improve competencies.

■ Retraining programs can be used for continuing employees whose skills have become obsolete. For example, employees may need periodic retraining on word processing software as the technology changes and more powerful programs become available.

■ Training supervisors to coach and provide feedback to their subordinates encourages supervisors to intervene early in problem situations with counseling rather than discipline.

■ Career ladders can be developed to give employees incentives to develop a long-term commitment to the organization's goals. When employees know that the organization has a long-term use for their contributions, they are more likely to engage in acts of good citizenship with their coworkers and customers.

Human Resource Planning

Jobs, job families, and organizational units can be designed to motivate and challenge employees. Highly motivated workers seldom need to be disciplined for inadequate performance.

- Jobs should be designed to use the best talents of each employee. It may be necessary to build some flexibility into job designs to put an employee's strengths to best use. One way companies are creating greater job flexibility is through *job banding*. Discussed in Chapter 10, this system replaces traditional narrowly defined job descriptions with broader categories, or bands, of related jobs. By putting greater variety into jobs, job banding makes it less likely that employees will feel so underchallenged or bored that they start avoiding work through absences or tardiness. Job banding has been implemented successfully by companies such as Aetna, General Electric, and Harley Davidson.[105]
- Job descriptions and work plans should be developed to communicate effectively to employees the performance standards to which they will be held accountable.

Performance Appraisal

Many performance problems can be avoided by designing effective performance appraisal systems. An effective performance appraisal system lets people know what is expected of them, how well they are meeting those expectations, and what they can do to improve on their weaknesses.

- The performance appraisal criteria should set reasonable standards that employees understand and have some control over.
- Supervisors should be encouraged to provide continuous feedback to subordinates. Many problems can be avoided with early interventions.
- Performance evaluations for supervisors should place strong emphasis on their effectiveness at providing feedback and developing their subordinates.
- Employee appraisals should be documented properly to protect employers against wrongful discharge or discrimination suits.

Compensation

Employees who believe that rewards are allocated unfairly (perhaps on the basis of favoritism) are likely to lose respect for the organization. Worse, employees who believe that pay policies do not recognize the value of their contributions are more likely to withhold future contributions.

- Pay policies should be perceived as fair by all employees. Employees deserve rewards for their contributions. It is important to explain to them the procedures used to establish their compensation level.
- An appeal mechanism that gives employees the right to challenge a pay decision should be established. Employees who can voice their frustration with a pay decision through a legitimate channel are less likely to engage in angry exchanges with supervisors, coworkers, or customers.

Summary and Conclusions

Employee Rights

In the employment relationship, both employees and employers have rights. Employee rights fall into three categories: statutory rights (protection from discrimination, safe work conditions, the right to form unions), contractual rights (as provided by employment contracts, union contracts, and employment policies), and other rights (the rights to ethical treatment, privacy, and free speech).

Management Rights

Employers have the right to run their business and make a profit. These rights are supported by property laws, common law, and the values of a society that accepts the concepts of private enterprise and the profit motive. Management rights include the right to manage the workforce and to hire, promote, assign, discipline, and discharge employees. Another important management right is employment at will, which allows an employer to dismiss an employee at any time for any cause. There are three key exceptions to the employment-at-will doctrine: public policy exceptions, implied contracts, and lack of good faith and fair dealing.

Employee Rights Challenges: A Balancing Act

Sometimes the rights of the employer and employees are in conflict. For example, a random drug-testing policy can create a conflict between an employer's responsibility to provide a safe workplace and employees' rights to privacy. HR professionals need to balance the rights of the employee with those of the employer when designing policies that address workplace issues like random drug testing, electronic monitoring of employees, whistleblowing, and office romance.

Disciplining Employees

Managers rely on discipline procedures to communicate to employees the need to change a behavior. There are two approaches to discipline. The progressive discipline procedure relies on increasing levels of punishment leading to discharge. The positive discipline procedure uses counseling sessions between supervisor and subordinate to encourage the employee to monitor his or her own behavior. Both procedures are designed to deal with forms of misconduct that are correctable.

Administering and Managing Discipline

To avoid conflict and lawsuits, managers must administer discipline properly. This entails ensuring that disciplined employees receive due process. Managers need to be aware of the standards used to determine if an employee was treated fairly and whether or not the employee has a right to appeal disciplinary action. For a disciplinary system to be effective, an appeal mechanism must be in place.

Managing Difficult Employees

It is often necessary to discipline employees who exhibit poor attendance, poor performance, insubordination, workplace bullying, or substance abuse. Managing the discipline process in these situations requires a balance of good judgment and common sense. Discipline may not be the best solution in all cases.

Preventing the Need for Discipline with Human Resource Management

The need for discipline can often be avoided by a strategic and proactive approach to HRM. A company can avoid discipline by recruiting and selecting the right employees for current positions as well as future opportunities, by training and developing workers, by designing jobs and career paths that best utilize people's talents, by designing effective performance appraisal systems, and by compensating employees for their contributions.

Key Terms

contract, 439
contractual rights, 439
due process, 440
employment at will, 443
employment contract, 439
hot-stove rule, 456

insubordination, 460
management rights, 442
personnel file, 442
positive discipline, 454
Privacy Act of 1974, 442
progressive discipline, 453

right, 439
statutory right, 439
whistle-blowing, 449
workplace bullying, 461
wrongful discharge, 440

Discussion Questions

1. Why have managers needed to place greater emphasis on employee rights in recent years?
2. Do employers have rights? If so, what are these rights?
3. In a highly publicized court case in 1988, *Foley v. Interactive Data Corp.,* the plaintiff was fired two months after he told a company vice president that his supervisor, a recent hire, was under investigation by the FBI for embezzlement from his previous employer. (The supervisor pleaded guilty in court six months after Foley was fired.) In his more than six years of employment at Interactive Data, Foley had received a steady stream of raises, promotions, and superior performance reviews. Based on his performance reviews and the company's written termination policy (which prescribed a seven-step

termination procedure), Foley believed that Interactive Data could not dismiss him. He sued the company on the basis of three theories, or causes, of action. What do you think these three causes of action were? Could any of these be considered exceptions to employment at will?

4. National Medical Enterprises, Inc., a $4 billion operator of hospitals and psychiatric treatment centers, faced criminal probes for practices such as widespread overbilling and fraudulent diagnoses to extend patients' hospital stays. Investigators found that NME's top management urged hospital administrators to adopt "intake" goals designed to lure patients into hospitals for lengthy and unnecessary treatments. Hospital staffers were also urged to admit fully

half of all patients who came in for an evaluation. Suppose a hospital staffer at NME refused to admit patients for whom she felt treatment was unnecessary. Could her refusal be considered insubordination? If the same staffer considered exposing fraudulent diagnoses to an outside agency, what whistle-blowing precautions would she be wise to consider before going public with her case?

5. Compare and contrast the progressive and positive discipline procedures.

6. What are the advantages and disadvantages of letting the team administer discipline to a team member?

7. The administration of discipline usually occurs between a manager and a subordinate employee. How can HR staff contribute to the fairness of the administration of discipline? How can HR staff contribute to the reduction of the need to administer discipline to employees within a company?

8. Can you think of a job-related reason why a company would decide to restrict dating between employees and enforce a no-dating policy? Do you think employers have a right to restrict any or all of the following off-duty conduct of their employees: (1) smoking cigarettes, (2) engaging in high-risk leisure activities such as skiing, motocross racing, rock climbing, or sky diving, (3) actively supporting a radical political candidate in an election, (4) having a romantic affair outside of the marriage relationship, and (5) joining a religious cult that preaches hatred against minorities? Justify your answer.

There is a variety of additional material available on the Web site that accompanies this text. You can access this information by visiting the Web site at ***www.prenhall.com/gomez***.

YOU MANAGE IT! Emerging Trends Case 14.1

Do Religion and Business Mix?

The EEOC laws in the United States request that employers make accommodations for employees for religious observances outside the workplace. For example, an employer could reasonably accommodate an employee who seeks to take a few hours off work on Saturday morning to teach a Bible study class. However, technology, global competition, downsizing, and reengineering have created a workforce of employees seeking value, support, and meaning in their lives that finds expression not only at home but also on the job. This search for religious and spiritual meaning in the workplace is a departure from the more traditional business mentality. People who bring their religious practices to the workplace can create challenges for employers or other employees who want to maintain a secular business environment. When does an employee's right to practice a religion infringe on an employer's right to manage an enterprise? When does an employer's religious practice interfere with an employee's right to have a secular environment at the workplace? Consider the following situations and then answer the questions that follow.

■ Numerous employee groups meet regularly for religious study in restaurants, conference rooms, or in an employee's residence. About 10,000 small companies participate in ongoing Bible study and other religious activities. The Pittsburgh Experiment is a Christian workplace ministry with about 40 affiliated groups, some of which meet weekly at Christian prework breakfasts in prayer and support gatherings. In a Manhattan business community, a Jewish Theological Seminary rabbi discusses confronting life's daily ethical dilemmas with a monthly Old Testament Bible study group of 20 business leaders.

■ Corporate training courses are offered to employees on such topics as miracles, shamanic journeying, and yoga. Companies such as Xerox and Motorola offer workshops on meditation in order to let employees develop their spirituality.

■ Courts have held that the rights of nonreligious employees should be protected from discrimination. For example, the seniority rights that determine employee work schedules under a union contract should override the need to make a religious accommodation to an employee. Thus, a nonreligious employee with the greatest amount of seniority has the right to bid on a preferred work schedule over that of a religious employee with less seniority, even if the latter employee's claim on the work schedule is based on a religious accommodation.

■ A company attempted to control the customer greetings of employees with guidelines after customer complaints that food service employees greeted them with such phrases as "God bless you," and "Praise the Lord." The religious employees took their case to court, which settled in favor of letting the employees express themselves spontaneously. It reasoned that a brief greeting with a spiritual overtone does not mean the employees were trying to proselytize or impose their beliefs on customers, and there was no evidence of business lost as a result of employees' practices. Consequently, the employer did not have proof of undue hardship and the employees' religious freedom prevailed.

Critical Thinking Questions

1. Suppose that a religious Moslem employee in a U.S. company refuses to cooperate with a female supervisor because it violates his religion to take orders from a female boss. Should the employer at this company make a religious accommodation for the religious employee? Justify your answer. How should this situation be handled?

2. Several female tellers at a bank wear large and prominent Christian crucifixes that hang from a necklace. These tellers are born-again Christians and meet regularly to discuss the Bible. Some customers have complained to management that religious ornaments such as the large crucifix are not appropriate at the bank and have threatened to take their business elsewhere. Bank management does not want to lose these customers. Is there an accommodation that can be made to balance the employees' religious rights and the bank's need to serve customers efficiently?

Team Exercise

With a group of four or five students discuss the implications to employee rights when the CEO of a company is a devoutly religious person who brings his or her religious beliefs to the workplace. What are the advantages of having a devoutly religious CEO? What are the disadvantages? Would it make any difference if the CEO was a Christian, a Moslem, or a Jew? Would it make a difference when a CEO practices his or her religion at the workplace compared to the situation when any ordinary employee behaves in a similar fashion? Be prepared to share your ideas with other members of the class.

Experiential Exercise

Find a partner and have a five-minute conversation with that person where each of you take turns expressing your thoughts about the following four situations that mix business and religion. Decide which ones you deem to be appropriate and which ones (if any) you deem to be inappropriate or that make you feel uncomfortable. Are there any conclusions you can draw after examining these four situations? Repeat the exercise two more times with other people in the class. Be prepared to share your findings with the class when called on by your instructor.

1. Several employees in your department wear large, highly visible religious crucifixes at work.
2. Every time the manager of your unit calls a meeting with your coworkers, he begins the meeting with a prayer.
3. One of your coworkers always quotes Biblical scripture when engaging you in a work-related conversation.
4. The company where you work lets employees engage in solicitation of funds from other employees to support religious causes they want to promote, such as missionary work or religious schools.

Sources: Adapted from Cash, K., and Gray, G. (2000, August). A framework for accommodating religion and spirituality in the workplace. *Academy of Management Executive*, 124–134; Gunther, M. (2001, July 9). God & business. *Fortune*, 59–80.

Ethics Case 14.2 — YOU MANAGE IT!

Welcome to the World of a Whistle-Blower

Randy Robarge, a nuclear power plant supervisor, never intended to be a whistle-blower. To Robarge, raising concerns about the improper storage of radioactive material at Commonwealth Edison's Zion power plant on Lake Michigan was just part of doing a good job. The 20-year veteran was so respected when it came to safety issues that Commonwealth Edison used him to narrate the company's training video on safety, which is still used throughout the industry. So he never expected that speaking up would end his career.

At first the harassment was subtle. He says he was routinely denied days off and asked to cover for employees who were out. Coworkers kept their distance, and supervisors began criticizing his work. Three months later Robarge was out of a job. Over the next two years a federal investigation would prove that Zion's radiation containment procedures—the ones Robarge had complained about—were lax, and the plant was eventually shut down.

The Department of Labor also ordered the company to pay Robarge a small settlement for his improper treatment. In the eyes of the court, Robarge was vindicated. But six years after speaking up and hundreds of job applications later, Robarge still can't get a job in his industry. "It's a living hell," says Robarge, 49, who supports himself with savings and odd jobs. "This is my livelihood, what I love to do. But I'm off limits. No one wants to touch me. I was labeled as a whistle-blower."

Unfortunately, Robarge is not alone. About half of all whistle-blowers get fired, half of those fired will lose their homes, and most of those will then lose their families too, says C. Fred Alford, author of *Whistleblowers: Broken Lives and Organizational Power*. For every Sherron Watkins, who became a hero after she blew the whistle on Enron's shady financial deal making, there are about 200 whistle-blowers that people never hear about who fare poorly. Overall, 90 percent of whistle-blowers can expect some kind of reprisal—public humiliation, isolation, career freezing, firing, blacklisting—from their company.

Because coworkers, and even friends, rarely rally behind whistle-blowers, feelings of isolation and betrayal run high. "It is lonely," says Michael Lissack, the former Smith Barney banker who became a whistle-blower celebrity after exposing a municipal finance scam on Wall Street. "My wife said, 'Thank you for ruining both our lives,' and walked out the door." There is even an annual retreat for whistle-blowers headed by a psychologist, to help them deal with the stress and repercussions of speaking up.

Critical Thinking Questions

1. What motivates an employee to become a whistle-blower if the consequences to one's professional and personal life are so severe? Do you agree or disagree that more employees should be encouraged to become whistle-blowers? State your reasons. What can management do to encourage an employee to blow the whistle on illegal or unethical activities committed within the company?

2. What could Robarge have done in preparation for blowing the whistle on the company that could have reduced the painful consequences he experienced? For example, do you think Robarge should have first found another job with a different employer before blowing the whistle on his former employer? Explain. Do you think Robarge should have sought out an experienced counselor to discuss his intention to blow the whistle? Explain. What other ways could Robarge prepare for whistle-blowing?

Team Exercise

With a group of four or five students examine Figure 14.3 ("Developing an Effective Whistle-Blowing Policy") with

respect to Randy Robarge's experience with whistle-blowing. Was Randy somewhat naïve when he blew the whistle on his company? What mistakes do you think he made? Was the company partially at fault for the way Randy was treated? What could the company have done differently with respect to protecting the rights of whistle-blowers? What conclusions can you draw from Randy's experience with blowing the whistle on his company?

Experiential Exercise

Assume you notice that one of the students in your human resource management course is cheating during the final exam. Would you "blow the whistle" on this student and let the professor know that you saw the student cheating on the exam? What factors would you consider before deciding whether to blow the whistle on the cheating student? Do you think it would matter to you if your school had an honesty policy that provides strong sanctions to students who are found cheating? How do you think the other students would react to a whistle-blower who informs on a cheater? What could the school do to increase the rate of whistle-blowing so that more instances of cheating are reported?

Source: Adapted from Daniels, C. (2002, April 15). It's a living hell: Whistleblowing makes for great TV. But the aftereffects can be brutal. *Fortune,* 367–368.

YOU MANAGE IT! Emerging Trends Case 14.3

Stealing a Smoke, Losing a Job

Health Unlimited is a store in Jacksonville, Florida, that sells health foods to the general public. It offers organically grown produce, meat that is raised without chemical additives, vitamins, and a health-food restaurant with a salad and sandwich bar. As a condition of employment, each employee is required to sign a statement that he or she is a nonsmoker and will not smoke either at work or away from work. Smoking at any time is considered a violation of this no-smoker policy and is enforced with immediate discharge. The company justifies this policy by saying that smokers are generally less healthy than nonsmokers and raise the health insurance rates it must pay for all employees. Many of the store's customers and employees are as adamantly opposed to smoking as the company is.

Lisa DeMarco is the produce manager of Health Unlimited. She was an ex-smoker at the time of her initial employment. In recent months, though, because she is experiencing stress over

her separation from her husband, Lisa has started smoking again. She restricts her smoking to off-duty hours away from the market. However, one of Lisa's coworkers spotted her smoking in a local bar and informed the store's manager, Ellen Guidry.

The next day Ellen Guidry confronted Lisa, who admitted to smoking and explained her situation. Ellen said she was sorry, but the no-smoker policy had to be enforced. She had no recourse but to discharge Lisa immediately. Lisa felt that her discharge was not fair because she was honest with her boss and had a good work record. She also believed she deserved some consideration for the difficulties she was going through in her personal life.

Critical Thinking Questions

1. Is it legal for a business to institute a no-smoking policy that restricts smoking during off-duty hours as well as at work? If legal, is such a policy ethical?

2. Do you think Ellen treated Lisa fairly by discharging her for violating the no-smoker policy? Should the mitigating circumstances Lisa cited have entered into Ellen's decision? How would you have handled this case?

Team Exercise

In a small group, discuss why it is difficult to discipline employee off-duty conduct. Develop some general guidelines that managers should use to decide when and how to discipline employees' off-duty conduct.

Experiential Exercise

If an employer is able to prohibit employees from smoking during their nonwork hours, then it may follow that an employer may also decide to penalize employees by discharging them if they engage in one or more of the following off-duty activities. Each of these prohibited activities could be justified by employers who can claim that they must pay higher health insurance, life insurance, or other costs when employees engage in a prohibited activity:

- Skiing (Employer pays higher health insurance rates because skiing is a risky sport.)
- Motorcycling (Motorcycles have higher accident and mortality rates than cars or public transportation, raising health and life insurance rates.)
- Obesity (Obese employees are subject to more health problems.)
- Rock climbing (Rock climbers participate in a high-risk sport.)
- Radical politics (An employee's radical political views may harm a company's reputation, causing it to lose customers if they are offended by an employee's political beliefs.)

How would you like to work for an employer that prohibits all or some of these activities during one's leisure time? Do you think employers should be free to restrict what employees do in their free time if they can show the restricted activity negatively affects the cost of doing business? Be prepared to share your views with the class.

Global Case 14.4 — YOU MANAGE IT!

Illegal Immigrants in the Workforce: Opportunity or Challenge?

Illegal immigrant labor is a global HRM issue that arises from people from less developed countries (LDCs) illegally entering more affluent countries to seek employment. Illegal immigrants are likely to work for wages lower than those that are paid to citizens within a country. In addition, they are often paid in cash, and therefore avoid paying taxes on their earned income. This raises issues of unfairness by those who "play by the rules" and pay taxes or who wait their turn to enter the country legally.

Most of the income earned by illegal immigrants goes back to family members in their country of origin. This increases their family's living standards and contributes to the economic stability of their country of origin, reducing its need for foreign economic assistance. Illegal immigrants are often exploited by unscrupulous employers who may not provide safe working conditions or who may force them to work excessive hours beyond what is permitted by the host country's labor laws. Illegals may not have the same legal rights as the host country's citizens or they may be unaware of their rights; thus, they are easily taken advantage of.

Countries as diverse as Spain, Poland, Italy, and the United States have significant numbers of illegal immigrants in the workforce. In Spain, large numbers of Romanians, Moroccans, Ecuadorans, and Columbians work in the booming tourist and construction industries. Poland has tens of thousands of illegal immigrants, chiefly from Ukraine. Italy has many Albanians working illegally in its underground economy. Finally, the world's largest illegal immigrant workforce is in the United States, with estimates as high as 10 million illegals working within its borders in mainly low-wage jobs in industries such as farm labor, meat and poultry processing, lawn care, restaurant labor, and drywall and ceiling tile installation.

In the United States, the illegal immigrant population is so large that it has become an important market segment. Millions of illegal immigrants from Mexico have been issued *matricula* cards from the Mexican consulate, with the approval of the U.S. government, that entitles the card bearer to open bank accounts and to hold driving licenses. Wells Fargo Bank has opened bank accounts for *matricula* card holders, and U.S. Sprint Corp. accepts the card for cell phone contracts. Kraft has developed new drink products with the illegal immigrant consumer in mind. In some parts of the country, entire industries depend on the labor of illegal immigrants. The U.S. Department of Labor estimates that in California, the most important fruit and vegetable producer in the nation, 90 percent of farm labor consists of illegal immigrants. In Texas, restaurants depend heavily on illegals to clear tables and wash dishes.

With the exportation of millions of higher paying jobs to India and China through outsourcing arrangements and the presence of a large and growing illegal immigrant workforce for low-wage jobs, U.S. citizens are feeling more uncertain than ever about their own job security and the opportunities that will be available for their children. Depending on how it is framed, the illegal immigrant workforce can be viewed as either a new opportunity providing new markets to serve—or as a challenge that needs to be controlled so that citizens who follow the economic rules, pay their taxes, and obey the law do not feel they are being treated unfairly by their government.

Critical Thinking Questions

1. What do you consider to be the primary opportunities related to the issue of illegal immigrants in the workforce? State your reasoning.
2. What do you consider to be the main challenges related to the issue of illegal immigrants in the workforce? State your reasoning.
3. What makes it so difficult to find an acceptable solution for this issue, assuming that the status quo concerning illegal immigration needs to be changed?

Team Exercise

With a group of four or five students, determine which workplace rights or benefits illegal immigrant employees and regular employees share, and which ones employees who are citizens or legal residents have that are not available to illegals. Here are some examples of rights or benefits you can examine to answer this question: Social Security, worker's compensation, unemployment insurance, government safety standards, overtime pay, minimum wage, union membership, and job opportunities working for the U.S. government. What type of employer is most likely to hire illegal immigrants? Be prepared to share your group's findings with the class.

Experiential Exercise

This exercise asks you to explore your attitudes concerning illegal immigrants in the workplace.

- Would you work for an employer who makes it a point to hire illegal immigrants? Why or why not?
- Would you consume the products of a company that you know purposely hires illegal immigrants? Why or why not?
- If you worked in a restaurant and found out that some of the employees working there were illegal immigrants, would you inform the restaurant manager? Why or why not?
- If you were the owner of a restaurant and the only way you could fill the dishwashing jobs was to hire people you expected to be illegal immigrants would you hire these people? Why or why not?
- If you were a department manager and you discovered a prospective professional employee had an illegal immigrant providing babysitting services for her children, would you still extend a job offer to this person? Why or why not?

Be prepared to share your answers with other members of the class when called on by your instructor.

Sources: Grow, B. (2005, July 18). Embracing illegals. *BusinessWeek,* 42–49; Justich, R., and Ng, B. (2005). *The underground labor force is rising to the surface.* New York: Bear Stearns Asset Management Inc.; *The Economist.* (2005, September 10). The grapes of wrath, again, 50; Colvin, G. (2005, September 5). On immigration policy, we've got it backward. *Fortune,* 44.

Working with Organized Labor

Challenges

After reading this chapter, you should be able to deal more effectively with the following challenges:

1 **Understand** why employees join unions.

2 **Understand** the National Labor Relations (Wagner) Act and how the National Labor Relations Board regulates labor practices and union elections.

3 **Describe** labor relations in the United States and other parts of the world.

4 **Identify** labor relations strategies and describe how they affect operational and tactical labor relations decisions.

5 **Describe** the three phases of the labor relations process: union organizing, collective bargaining, and contract administration.

6 **Explain** how the union grievance procedure works and why the supervisor's role is critical in achieving sound labor relations with a union.

7 **Identify** the ways in which a union can affect a company's entire pattern of human resource management, including its staffing, employee development, compensation, and employee relations policies.

Few institutions illustrate the power of people banding together for a common cause more effectively than labor unions. Unions can change the policies and practices of management profoundly. Consider the following two situations.

The UPS Strike

One of the most significant labor relations events during the 1990s was a two-week strike that took place in August 1997 between the Teamsters Union and UPS. The opponents could not agree whether UPS would provide more full-time jobs for its workforce of 300,000 employees, 60 percent of whom are part-time workers. UPS settled the strike with the Teamsters after it cost the company about $700 million in lost revenues plus a decline in market share to rivals FedEx and the U.S. Postal Service.[1]

UPS agreed to create 10,000 new full-time jobs over a five-year period. Current part-time employees were eligible to apply for those jobs.[2] Some part-time employees had been working at UPS for as long as 10 years while waiting for the scarce full-time jobs that would become available. UPS full-time employees earned around $20 per hour, whereas part-time employees earned about $11 per hour. The benefits package (health insurance, pension, vacation days, and so on) is similar for both full- and part-time employees.[3]

In the aftermath of the strike, both union and management worked to improve their relationship. In 2002, UPS and the Teamsters Union successfully negotiated their next labor contract without a strike. The agreement included a wage increase of 22 percent over a six-year term. Health and retirement fund contributions were also improved. The labor contract was the result of negotiations that began six months earlier with an exchange of proposals over regularly held negotiating sessions that culminated in an agreement. Both the Teamsters Union and UPS management were more cooperative during the most recent bargaining sessions because they both wanted to avoid the losses they experienced during the 1997 strike.[4] However, in 2005 the peace at UPS was threatened with an impending strike by a different union, the Independent Pilots Union, representing 2,500 pilots who fly commercial aircraft for UPS's package and freight delivery service. The pilots and UPS management were far from agreement over the issue of pilot salaries, and both parties were working with mediators to avoid a work stoppage.[5]

Doctors Unionize

Many doctors are turning to unions to battle fee cuts and controls over treatment decisions that are championed by health maintenance organizations (HMOs). As of 2005, the ranks of unionized doctors had swelled to 50,000.[6] In fact, a union succeeded for the first time in organizing U.S. doctors at a for-profit managed-care company. The Federation of Physicians and Dentists organized the doctors at Thomas-Davis Medical Centers, one of the oldest and most prestigious clinics in Tucson, Arizona. Many more doctors are considering forming unions to protect their ability to practice medicine as they see fit, rather than letting managed care organizations dictate how they treat patients. Doctors hope unions will make the following improvements to current managed-care practices:

- **Reduce patient loads.** HMOs have increased doctors' patient loads, which reduces the amount of time a doctor can spend with each patient.
- **Reduce referral restrictions.** HMOs enforce complicated procedures for approving referrals to other physicians, which take a doctor's valuable time. Doctors also complain about the overall quality of the approved list of specialists to which patients can be referred.
- **Regain control of patient care decisions.** Doctors have to justify more of their professional decisions regarding patients, such as prescribing medication or types of treatment. Many HMOs require substantial paperwork to defend medical decisions and can override a doctor's decision.

Doctors hope that as union ranks grow, the balance of power in the medical field will shift away from health insurers back toward members of their profession.[7]

THE MANAGERIAL PERSPECTIVE

The relationship between managers and their employees changes in a unionized organization. The law requires managers to meet and confer with elected union representatives when making decisions that affect pay, hours of employment, or working conditions. When unionized employees are dissatisfied with pay or other job factors, the company faces the possibility of a strike or other form of collective action designed to pressure the firm to respond to employees' preferences. Managers, then, need to understand the basics of labor relations and labor law to handle day-to-day labor–management relations effectively.

The presence of a union increases managers' need for HR services. HR specialists in labor relations can help managers develop tactics and strategies to work constructively with the union and its representatives in areas such as negotiating the terms of new labor contracts, interpreting a labor contract, or responding to an employee grievance. Managers that grasp the basics of labor relations will know when to turn to HR specialists and what questions to ask.

In this chapter, we explore the labor-management relationship between companies and unions. We begin by examining why employees join unions and why some employers prefer the workplace not to be unionized. Second, we outline the major U.S. legislation that governs labor issues and describe the current labor-relations climate in the United States and in some other countries. Third, we investigate different labor relations strategies and explore the rules and procedures that govern union activities. Finally, we address the impact of unions on a variety of HR practices.

Why Do Employees Join Unions?

A **union** is an organization that represents employees' interests to management on issues such as wages, work hours, and working conditions. Employees participate in administering the union and support its activities with *union dues,* fees they pay for the union's services. The law protects employees' rights to join and participate in unions. The law also requires employers to bargain and confer with the union over certain employment issues that affect unionized employees.

Employees join unions for different reasons. For example, in Israel, employees join unions because many believe in the social justice the union represents.[8] Employees in the United States seek union representation when they (1) are dissatisfied with certain aspects of their job, (2) feel that they lack influence with management to make the needed changes, and (3) see unionization as a solution to their problems.[9] The union's best ally is bad management. If managers listen to employees, give them some say in the policies that affect their jobs, and treat them fairly, employees usually will not feel the need to organize. Managers who ignore their workers' interests and treat them inconsistently often end up having to deal with a union.

Union
An organization that represents employees' interests to management on such issues as wages, work hours, and working conditions.

Teamsters Union employees celebrate the end of the strike and a new contract with UPS.

Companies usually prefer a nonunion workforce. The primary reason is that wages are typically higher for union employees, which puts unionized companies at a competitive disadvantage if their competitors are not unionized. In addition, unions constrain what managers can and cannot do with a particular employee. For instance, a unionized employee who is doing a particularly good job usually cannot be given a merit raise or promoted over someone who has greater seniority. And many labor agreements spell out the specific work responsibilities of certain employees, which reduces flexibility in work assignments. Of course, many unionized companies flourish, and unions have some very positive social benefits. For example, a study reported that unions boosted productivity at hospitals by 16 percent compared to nonunion hospitals.[10] But given the choice, most managers would prefer a nonunion environment.

The Origins of U.S. Labor Unions

Unions, as we think of them today, were largely unprotected by law in the United States until 1935. The approach of the U.S. government to unions prior to 1935 was simple: In a free market economy, the employment relationship is essentially a private one, and both employee and employer are free to accept or reject this relationship if they find it unsatisfactory. (See the discussion of employment at will in Chapter 14.)

This thinking regards the employer and the employee as in similar positions of power: Employees who find their compensation unfair or working conditions unreasonable are free to find another job; employers who are unhappy with an employee's performance can fire that employee. In practice, of course, employers have considerably more power than individual employees. A large steel manufacturer does not miss one employee who quits because there is usually a ready supply of applicants to replace that person. However, a large employer can so dominate a neighborhood, city, or region that there are few or no other employment alternatives. The large steel mills in Pittsburgh, the auto manufacturers in Detroit, the coal mine operators in Appalachia, and the tire companies in Akron are examples of employers and industries that have dominated their respective regions.

In the Great Depression of the 1930s, millions of workers lost their jobs as employers came under tremendous pressure to cut production costs. These cutbacks put even more pressure on the working class. It was in this environment that union activity as we know it was legalized by the Wagner Act (1935), which attempted to equalize the power of employers and employees. In fact, this goal explains much of the governmental and societal response to union activity during the Depression and in the years following World War II. Unions were widely supported because of the public perception that working people had little power.

Toward the end of the twentieth century, however, public perception had changed. When President Reagan ordered the firing of striking air traffic controllers on August 5, 1981, two days after they began an illegal strike, the terminated employees received little sympathy from society at large, probably because unions were widely perceived to have become too powerful. This action took place in the middle of a period of dramatic decline in strikes in the United States: From a peak of 424 in 1974, strikes decreased to 17 in 2004.[11] However, as we saw in the opening vignette, unions are growing in some fields such as medicine. Furthermore, the public had a relatively positive perception of the UPS strikers in the fight to make more part-time employees full-time workers. As unions tackle new issues and represent workers in new professions, public perception of union activities is likely to change.

The Role of the Manager in Labor Relations

Labor relations specialist
Someone, often a member of the HR department, who is knowledgeable about labor relations and can represent management's interests to a union.

When a union represents a group of employees in a company, the company needs a staff of specialists who can represent management's interests to the union. These **labor relations specialists**, who are often members of the HR department, help resolve grievances, negotiate with the union over changes in the labor contract, and provide advice to top management on a labor relations strategy.

Still, it is managers who bear the major responsibility for day-to-day labor–management relations. Thus, it is important that they understand the workplace issues associated with unions. First, as we noted earlier, unions generally take hold only in firms where employees are dissatisfied with their jobs, and managers greatly influence how employees perceive their work environment. Second, where there is a union, managers are responsible for the day-to-day implementation of the terms of the labor agreement. The more effectively they carry out this responsibility, the less time the company will spend resolving labor conflicts. Third, managers need to have a basic understanding of labor law so that they do not unintentionally create a legal liability for the company. Finally, individual managers are often asked to serve on committees to hear grievances brought by union members against the company. A manager who understands general labor issues will be better prepared to hear and decide such cases.

Because the nature and function of unions are so dependent on legislation, we look at the specifics of that legislation next.

Labor Relations and the Legal Environment

The key labor relations legislation in the United States consists of three laws enacted between the 1930s and 1950s: the Wagner Act (1935), the Taft-Hartley Act (1947), and the Landrum-Griffin Act (1959). These laws regulate labor relations in the private sector. Public-sector labor relations are covered by federal or state laws that are patterned after these laws.

In the history of labor relations law in the United States, the government has tried to balance (1) employers' rights to operate their businesses free from unnecessary interference, (2) unions' rights to organize and bargain for their members, and (3) individual employees' right to choose their representatives or to decide that they do not want or need union representation. Before 1935, employer rights were essentially unchecked by federal legislation. After passage of the Wagner Act, however, many felt that union rights were too strongly protected, relative to both employer and individual employee rights. This sentiment led Congress to pass two laws—the Taft-Hartley Act and the Landrum-Griffin Act—in an attempt to achieve balance.

The Wagner Act

The **Wagner Act**, also known as the **National Labor Relations Act**, was passed during the Great Depression in 1935. It was designed to protect employees' rights to form and join unions and to engage in activities such as strikes, picketing, and collective bargaining. The Wagner Act created the **National Labor Relations Board (NLRB)**, an independent federal agency charged with administering U.S. labor law.

The NLRB's primary functions are (1) to administer *certification elections,* secret ballot elections that determine whether employees want to be represented by a union and (2) to prevent and remedy unlawful acts called *unfair labor practices.* The NLRB remedies an unfair labor practice by issuing a *cease and desist order,* which requires the guilty party to stop engaging in the unlawful labor practice. The Wagner Act identified five illegal labor practices that can be remedied by the National Labor Relations Board:

Wagner Act/National Labor Relations Act (1935)
A federal law designed to protect employees' rights to form and join unions and to engage in such activities as strikes, picketing, and collective bargaining.

National Labor Relations Board (NLRB)
The independent federal agency created by the Wagner Act to administer U.S. labor law.

1. Interfering with, restraining, or coercing employees to keep them from exercising their rights to form unions, bargain collectively, or engage in concerted activities for mutual protection.
2. Dominating or interfering with the formation or administration of a union or providing financial support for it.
3. Discriminating against an employee to discourage union membership. Discrimination can include not hiring a union supporter, or not promoting, firing, or denying a pay raise to an employee who is a union member or who favors union representation.
4. Discharging or otherwise discriminating against an employee who has filed charges or given testimony under the act's provisions.
5. Refusing to bargain collectively with the union that employees chose to represent them.

The Taft-Hartley Act

Taft-Hartley Act (1947)
A federal law designed to limit some of the power acquired by unions under the Wagner Act by adjusting the regulation of labor–management relations to ensure a level playing field for both parties.

The **Taft-Hartley Act**, enacted in 1947 shortly after the end of World War II, was designed to limit some of the power that unions acquired under the Wagner Act and to protect the rights of management and employees. Although the Taft-Hartley Act was basically favorable to management's interests, its goals were to adjust the regulation of labor–management relations to ensure a level playing field for both parties.

Taft-Hartley included remedies from the National Labor Relations Board for six unfair union labor practices:

1. Restraining or coercing employees in the exercise of their rights guaranteed under the act, and/or coercing an employer's choice of a representative in collective bargaining.
2. Causing or attempting to cause an employer to discriminate against an employee who is not a member of a labor union for any reason other than failure to pay the union dues and initiation fees uniformly required as a condition of acquiring or retaining membership in the union.
3. Refusing to bargain in good faith with an employer after a majority of the employees in a unit have elected the union as their representative.
4. Asking or requiring its members to boycott products made by a firm engaged in a labor dispute with another union (*secondary boycott*). However, a union can call a boycott of products produced by its own firm (*primary boycott*).

Union shop clause
A union arrangement that requires new employees to join the union 30 to 60 days after their date of hire.

5. Charging employees excessive or discriminatory union dues as a condition of membership in a union under a union shop clause. (A **union shop clause** requires employees to join the union 30 to 60 days after their date of hire.)
6. Causing an employer to pay for services that are not performed. This practice, often called *featherbedding,* is technically illegal, but the definition of unnecessary or unperformed work is often murky. For example, railroad unions continued to require the presence of firemen on engines long after their main duty (taking care of the fire on a steam engine) was eliminated by the advent of diesel engines.

Twelve years later, the Landrum-Griffin Act added a seventh unfair union labor practice: It is illegal for a union to picket an employer for the purpose of union recognition (a practice known as *recognitional picketing*).

Right-to-work law
A state law that makes it illegal within that state for a union to include a union shop clause in its contract.

Perhaps the most controversial provision of the Taft-Hartley Act is Section 14b, which gives permission to the states to enact right-to-work laws. A **right-to-work law** makes it illegal within a state for a union to include a union shop clause in its contract. Unions negotiate union shop clauses into their contracts to provide greater security to union employees and prevent nonunion employees from receiving union services without paying union dues. A less restrictive arrangement called the *agency shop clause* requires employees to pay a union service fee (about equal to union dues) but does not require them to join the union. Currently, 22 states have right-to-work laws, which make it more difficult to organize and sustain unions in those states.[12] Most of these states are located in the southern or western United States, away from major industrial centers.

Several other provisions of Taft-Hartley are noteworthy. First, the act made *closed shops,* which require an employee to be a union member as a condition of being hired, illegal. This provision was modified 12 years later by the Landrum-Griffin Act to allow a closed shop in the construction industry as the only exception. Second, Taft-Hartley allowed employees to get rid of a union they no longer want through a *decertification election* and charged the NLRB with regulating decertification elections. Finally, Taft-Hartley created a new agency, the *Federal Mediation and Conciliation Service,* to help mediate labor disputes so that economic disruptions due to strikes and other labor disturbances would be fewer and shorter.

The Landrum-Griffin Act

Landrum-Griffin Act (1959)
A law designed to protect union members and their participation in union affairs.

The **Landrum-Griffin Act** was enacted in 1959 to protect union members and their participation in union affairs. It allows the government, through the Department of Labor, to regulate union activities. The Landrum-Griffin Act includes the following key provisions:

1. Each union must have a bill of rights for union members to ensure minimum standards of internal union democracy.
2. Each union must adopt a constitution and provide copies of it to the Department of Labor.
3. Each union must report its financial activities and the financial interests of its leaders to the Department of Labor.
4. Union elections are regulated by the government, and union members have the right to participate in secret ballot elections.
5. Union leaders have a fiduciary responsibility to use union money and property for the benefit of the membership and not for their own personal gain. Members can sue and recover damages from union leaders who fail to exercise their fiduciary responsibilities.

Other laws that affect labor relations include the Railway Labor Act (1926, last amended in 1970), the Norris-LaGuardia Act (1932), and the Byrnes Antistrikebreaking Act (1938). Of course, the equal employment opportunity laws discussed in Chapter 3 also apply to unionized workers. Most noteworthy of these other labor laws is the **Railway Labor Act**, which regulates labor relations in the transportation industry. This law covers the railway, airlines, and trucking industries that are critical to sustain commerce. It provides dispute settlement procedures if the parties are unable to achieve a labor agreement. The Railway Labor Act has provisions for congressional and presidential intervention in a labor dispute that could be disruptive to interstate commerce. For example, the President intervened in a labor dispute in the airline industry when one of the major airlines forced the union to go on strike because of a breakdown in negotiations.[13]

Railway Labor Act
A law designed to regulate labor relations in the transportation industry.

Although much of U.S. labor relations law is more than four decades old, it would be a mistake to assume that nothing new is happening in this area. As this text was being written, Congress was considering the Teamwork for Employees and Management Act, which would amend the Wagner Act to ensure that employers are permitted to establish and maintain employee involvement programs.[14] Another set of amendments under consideration would eliminate an employer's right to use permanent replacements during an economic strike or work stoppage.[15] In Canada, several provinces have recently enacted laws that restrict employers from using replacement workers during strikes.[16] Clearly, the struggle to find the correct balance of employer, union, and employee rights is ongoing.

We now turn to a description of the current state of labor relations in the United States.

Labor Relations in the United States

Labor relations in the United States evolved from the philosophy of the U.S. labor movement, which accepted the country's capitalist economic structure and wanted to operate within it.[17] U.S. unions have avoided a permanent affiliation with a political party and have focused on improving their members' welfare through dealing directly with the companies that employ their members. The key factors that characterize labor relations in the United States are (1) business unionism, (2) unions structured by type of job, (3) a focus on collective bargaining, (4) labor contracts, (5) the adversarial nature of labor–management relations and shrinking union membership, and (6) the growth of unions in the public sector.

Business Unionism

Business unionism is unionism that focuses on "bread-and-butter" issues (such as wages, benefits, and job security) so that workers get a larger slice of the economic pie. U.S. unions, which practice business unionism, have traditionally avoided trying to influence the running of the company, and they provide little input to management on strategic decisions such as how to market a product or what types of new business to enter. It is rare to see U.S. union members on a company's board of directors.[18] U.S. labor laws reinforce this tendency by making wages, hours, and working conditions mandatory topics for bargaining. This means that management is obligated to bargain on these issues in good faith.

Business unionism
A form of unionism that focuses on improving workers' economic well-being.

Unions Structured by Type of Job

In contrast to unions in some other countries, U.S. unions tend to be organized by type of job. For instance, truck drivers are often members of the Teamsters Union, many public school teachers are members of the National Education Association, and most autoworkers belong to the United Auto Workers, no matter which automaker employs them. Because most unions represent employees from multiple employers, they are typically arranged into *locals* governed by a national body. Each local consists of the union members in a particular geographical location. The local has its own officers and is generally concerned with day-to-day labor practices and disputes. The national organization ties these locals together, governs how locals are organized and operated, and, most importantly, establishes policy for contract negotiations.

The *AFL-CIO*, formed by the merger of the old American Federation of Labor and the Congress of Industrial Organizations, is a confederation of many different unions. Because it represents so many workers (approximately 9 million), the AFL-CIO has a tremendous influence on federal labor policies.[19] It also provides support to individual national unions and mobilizes support for laws that are beneficial to working people. Finally, the AFL-CIO resolves disputes between national unions.[20]

In 2005, four large unions representing 4 million employees voted to disaffiliate from the AFL-CIO and become independent. The unions that left the AFL-CIO were the Service Employees International Union, the International Brotherhood of Teamsters, the United Food and Commercial Workers Union, and Unite Here, a union of apparel and hotel workers. These unions wanted the organized labor movement to spend more time and money recruiting new members.[21]

Focus on Collective Bargaining

Unions and management are the dominant players in the U.S. labor relations system. Generally, the U.S. government takes a neutral role, allowing the players to make the rules that govern their particular workplace. The mechanism of choice for developing these rules is collective bargaining. Under a **collective bargaining** system, unions and management negotiate with each other to develop the work rules under which union members will work for a stipulated period of time, usually two or three years. **Work rules** include any terms or conditions of employment, including pay, work breaks and lunch periods, vacation, work assignments, and grievance procedures.

Unions that are legally elected by workers in the United States act as the sole representative of those workers' concerns to management. Although unions may compete for recognition, once one is recognized, individual employees cannot choose to be represented by another union.

Labor Contracts

The product of collective bargaining is a **labor contract** that spells out the conditions of employment and work rules that affect employees in the unit represented by the union. Because both parties enter into the contract voluntarily, one party can use the legal system to enforce the terms of the contract if the other party does not fulfill its responsibilities.

Labor contracts are an important feature of the U.S. labor relations system. In many other countries, such as Germany and Sweden, working conditions and employee benefits are codified into labor laws, but in the United States labor and management have historically established workers' economic benefits without government interference. Increasingly, however, the United States is following the lead of other countries in this respect. The most recent example is the Family and Medical Leave Act of 1993 (see Chapter 3), which grants employees many protections that had previously been available only to employees covered by a union contract. Current health reform proposals also seek to mandate certain health insurance benefits that until now have been the subject of labor–management negotiation.

Collective bargaining
A system in which unions and management negotiate with each other to develop the work rules under which union members will work for a stipulated period of time.

Work rules
Any terms or conditions of employment, including pay, work breaks and lunch periods, vacation, work assignments, and grievance procedures.

Labor contract
A union contract that spells out the conditions of employment and work rules that affect employees in the unit represented by the union.

The Adversarial Nature of Labor–Management Relations and Shrinking Union Membership

U.S. labor laws view labor and management as natural adversaries who will disagree over the distribution of the firm's profits. For this reason, rules have been put in place so that the pie is distributed peacefully.

In a sense, the U.S. labor relations system is modeled on the U.S. court system. In a court, "justice" may be considered the result of the clash of adversaries, with the district attorney representing the plaintiff's interests and the defense attorney representing the defendant's interests. Similarly, "economic justice" may be considered the result of negotiations between the union (the advocate of the employees) and management (the advocate of the firm's owners). Although this adversarial model worked well for many years in the United States, it has recently become an obstacle to union–management cooperation, which has grown in importance as both labor markets and product markets have become more globally competitive.

As Figure 15.1 shows, 13 percent of the U.S. labor force is unionized.[22] This is down from a peak of about 35 percent in 1945. There are several reasons for this decline: the shrinking base of blue-collar industrial jobs (the traditional area of unionization) due to automation and foreign competition; the increase in employment legislation that provides workers with remedies that address their needs; and the aggressively hostile labor relations strategies of many companies, which have made it difficult for unions to organize workers. Other possible reasons for declining union membership are an increasingly educated workforce, as well as the highly publicized legal problems of some union leaders.

Despite shrinking union membership, unions continue to be an important part of the U.S. labor relations system because they establish wage and benefit patterns that influence nonunion employers. In this way, unions indirectly affect about 40 to 50 percent of the U.S. labor force. In fact, many employees of nonunion firms benefit from the upward adjustments in their wages and

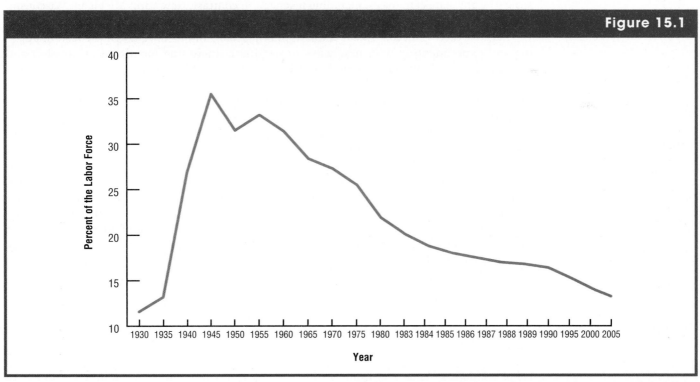

Figure 15.1

Union Membership in the United States, 1930–2005

Source: Bureau of Labor Statistics, Department of Labor.

benefits that their employers make to prevent a union from organizing their workers. Unions have also pioneered worker safety measures and antidiscriminatory labor practices. Unless the underlying causes that gave birth to unions are abolished—low wages, unsafe working conditions, health hazards, arbitrary firings, and layoffs—it is a safe bet that unions will not disappear.

The Growth of Unions in the Public Sector

As the percentage of unionized workers in the private sector has declined, the percentage of unionized workers in the public sector has increased substantially. This increase is due in part to the expansion of local government in the 1980s and in part to organizing efforts that have targeted both public-sector and service-sector employees.[23]

Unions in the public sector are in many ways a special case of labor relations because although public-sector employees are more likely to be organized than private-sector employees, public-sector workers tend to have less bargaining power. There are two main reasons for this difference.

First, governmental power is diffuse. The typical private-sector firm is hierarchically organized so that there is one individual at the top who is in charge. However, governmental bodies in the United States have been intentionally structured so that power is divided among the legislative, executive, and judicial branches. This makes it more difficult for public-sector unions to negotiate and bargain collectively, because the employer's representative often has only limited authority. For instance, a city employees' union may bargain with the mayor's office for higher pay, but the money for the higher salaries has to be appropriated by the city council, which may not concur with the mayor.

The second reason public-sector unions have less power is that many governmental entities severely restrict their employees' right to strike. The reasoning is that the government is a monopoly provider of essential services like police protection, garbage collection, and highway maintenance. If its employees were to go on strike, there would be no one else to provide these essential services. States differ in restrictiveness on this issue. For instance, Colorado forbids strikes by any state employees, including teachers. In contrast, New York, Michigan, Wisconsin, and some other states give some of their employees the right to strike in certain circumstances.

Because their right to strike is limited, public-sector unions have taken the lead in devising and experimenting with new ways to negotiate, including mandated arbitration and mediation. Their limited economic power has also made public-sector unions less likely than private-sector unions to put pay issues at the top of their agendas. For instance, teachers' unions often focus on such issues as class size, job security, and academic freedom rather than straight salary issues.

Although having government as an employer can present difficulties to unionized workers, it also brings certain advantages. One is that union members, by virtue of the fact that they are also voters, have some political power over their employer. Because voter participation in nonfederal elections is often low in the United States, a well-organized public-sector union can be a powerful force in local politics. In fact, even national candidates court public-sector union support. A second advantage stems from the very diffusion of power we discussed earlier. This makes it possible for the union to play one branch of government against the other in certain circumstances. For instance, a union may be able to achieve a bargaining victory because it has the support of a city council member whose vote the mayor needs on some unrelated issue.

Labor Relations in Other Countries

Labor relations systems vary from country to country because unions mean different things in different countries. In the United States, labor relations involves collective bargaining and labor contracts, but in Sweden and Denmark it involves national wage setting, in Japan it involves enterprise unions that cooperate with company management, in Great Britain it involves union affiliation with the Labor Party, and in Germany it involves union representation on the company's board of directors.[24] Moreover, the shrinking percentage of private-sector employees represented by unions in the United States is not a world trend. Unions not only represent a large portion of the labor force in most other industrialized countries, but are also important factors in the labor relations systems of many of those countries.

Figure 15.2 compares union membership as a percentage of the labor force in 13 industrialized countries, including the United States. Union membership as a percentage of the labor force is higher in most European countries, with Italy and Sweden having, respectively, 35 percent and 79 percent of their workers represented by unions in 2001. Although unionism declined in Great Britain in the 1980s, British unions still represented 29 percent of the workforce in 2001, double the percentage of U.S. workers. Even in Japan, whose firms seek to avoid unions when they locate factories in the United States, 20 percent of workers are unionized. This is significantly higher than the U.S. percentage.[25]

How Unions Differ Internationally

One analysis of unionism around the globe suggests that unions in different countries have different priorities.[26] As we have seen, U.S. unions place a very strong emphasis on economic issues, particularly pay, benefits, and job security. For example, in recent years outsourcing has become a major concern of U.S. unions, because the first jobs to be subcontracted tend to be blue-collar jobs, the union's mainstay.[27] Compared to unions in other countries, U.S. unions place much less emphasis on political issues. Political involvement is just another means to address economic concerns.

At the other end of the spectrum, unions in France tend to be much more politically involved and less concerned with economic issues. The two largest labor confederations in France have clear political orientations, and one is even religiously oriented. Strikes in France tend to focus on political change as the primary means of protecting or improving conditions for union members. Unions in Spain also use political tactics to carry out their goals. For example, in 2002 Spanish unions collaborated to organize a one-day general strike to convince the political leaders to reject the government proposal to lower the level of unemployment benefits for Spanish workers. A *general strike* is a work stoppage of all organized labor over a brief, predetermined time period that is designed to influence the government to support a particular political goal representing the interests of workers.[28]

In China, unions are low in both economic and political involvement, because of the pervasive control of the Chinese Communist Party over both political and economic affairs. A secondary reason is that the large majority of Chinese employees work for very small firms, which are notoriously difficult to organize. Finally, Swedish unions tend to have a high degree

---

Figure 15.2

Percent of Total Civilian Wage and Salary Employees Belonging to Unions

Year	United States	Canada	Austria	Australia	Japan	Denmark	France	Germany	Italy	Netherlands	Sweden	Switzerland	United Kingdom
1965	28	28	46	—	36	63	20	38	33	40	68	32	45
1970	30	31	43	—	35	64	22	37	43	38	75	31	50
1975	29	34	48	—	35	72	23	39	56	42	83	35	53
1980	25	35	47	—	31	86	19	40	62	41	88	35	56
1985	17	36	47	—	29	92	17	40	61	34	95	32	51
1990	16	36	43	34	25	88	—	—	—	28	95	31	46
1995	14	37	39	35	24	78	9	26	32	23	87	23	32
2001	13	30	40	28	20	88	9	30	35	27	79	24	29

Sources: European Foundation for the Improvement of Living and Working Conditions (2002); *The Economist.* (2003, June 7). Special report: Trade unions, 60; International Labor Organization (1997); and Chang, C., and Sorrentino, C. (1991, December). Union membership statistics in 12 countries. *Monthly Labor Review,* 48.

Union Membership in Selected Countries, 1965-2001

of economic and political involvement. Swedish trade unions are often represented on governmental commissions in addition to actively representing their workers in economic affairs.[29]

We now turn our attention to two labor relations systems that have achieved high productivity and cooperation between unions and management: those of Germany and Japan.

Labor Relations in Germany

German law requires that all corporations involve workers in decisions at both the plant and the corporate level. This system is sometimes called *industrial democracy*. As practiced in Germany, industrial democracy means workers are represented at the plant level in works councils and at the corporate level through codetermination.

Works councils are committees composed of both worker representatives and managers who have responsibility for governing the workplace. They participate in operational decisions, such as the allocation of overtime, the discipline and discharge of workers, the hiring of new workers, and training.[30] At the plant level, works councils make many decisions on which unions would bargain with management in the United States. German unions focus on bargaining across industries on such issues as wages, rather than on bargaining within an industry, as is typical in the United States. However, the unification of Germany's high-wage West and lower-wage East means that unions and employers need more wage flexibility in labor contracts. Currently, more wage agreements are occurring at the company level in Germany.[31] Works councils are also used in several other countries in addition to Germany. Austria, France, Belgium, the Netherlands, and Sweden have enacted laws that require that large companies organize works councils to represent the interests of employees.[32]

Codetermination brings worker representation to a corporation's board of directors. With one-third to one-half of their boards of directors representing workers, German companies are likely to give employees' needs a high priority.[33] (The other board members represent the shareholders.) Not surprisingly, codetermination has fostered a spirit of cooperation between workers and managers. For the German economy, the results have been fewer strikes and higher productivity. For workers, the results have been both greater responsibility and greater security. For example, IG Metall, Germany's largest union, has taken the lead on a number of important issues instead of merely reacting to company proposals. The union's group-work policies, the product of nearly two decades of research and activism, are designed to protect workers from layoff or transfer to lower-paying jobs.

Labor Relations in Japan

Japan has developed a successful labor relations system characterized by a high degree of cooperation between unions and management. A key factor in this success has been the Japanese enterprise union. The **enterprise union**, which represents Japanese workers in large corporations such as Toyota, Toshiba, and Hitachi, organizes the workers in only one company. This practice ensures that the union's loyalty will not be divided among different companies. The enterprise union negotiates with management with an eye on the company's long-term prosperity. This labor relations system was long reinforced by large Japanese corporations' offer of lifelong employment, which allowed Japanese workers to feel secure and unthreatened by changes in technology or job characteristics.[34]

The traditional lifelong employment policy has encouraged cooperation between the enterprise unions and management. Many Japanese executives started their careers as union members right out of school, advanced to a leadership position in the union, and then got promoted into management, all within the same company. Because the enterprise union's legitimacy is unchallenged by management, there is a degree of trust and respect between the union and management in Japan that would be unthinkable in the United States. This fact helps to explain the behavior of Japanese executives who cooperate with a union in Japan but try at all costs to avoid unionization in their U.S. plants.

Unfortunately, there are signs that the labor relations systems in both Germany and Japan are in danger. In Germany, high labor costs for the average factory worker ($33 per hour versus $20 per hour in the United States in 2005) and the economic costs of unification with East Germany are forcing companies to drive a harder bargain with unions. Competition in global markets has

---

Works councils
A committee composed of both worker representatives and managers who have responsibility for governing the workplace; used in Germany.

Codetermination
The representation of workers on a corporation's board of directors; used in Germany.

Enterprise union
A labor union that represents workers in only one large company rather than in a particular industry; used in Japan.

led to downsizings in some of Germany's largest companies and has strained labor relations. For example, Daimler-Benz (now called DaimlerChrysler), Germany's largest industrial company, reduced its workforce by 70,000 jobs and announced expansion of a new automobile plant in Alabama, where labor costs are much lower than in Germany.[35] And in Japan, a closer look at lifelong employment policies shows that they have always been restricted to the largest companies, applied only to men, and end at age 55. Moreover, downsizing in Japan has made it difficult to sustain lifelong employment policies. NTT, Japan's giant telecommunications company, reduced its workforce by 45,000 jobs, a quarter of its total number of employees. Nissan, the automaker, from 1999 to 2002 laid off 21,000 workers and closed five auto assembly plants.[36]

Labor Relations Strategy

A company's **labor relations strategy** is its management's overall plan for dealing with unions. As Figure 15.3 shows, a company's labor relations strategy sets a tone that can range from open conflict with the union to labor–management cooperation. The most important choice affecting a company's labor relations strategy is management's decision to accept or to avoid unions.[37]

Labor relations strategy
A company's overall plan for dealing with labor unions.

Union Acceptance Strategy

Under a **union acceptance strategy,** management chooses to view the union as its employees' legitimate representative and accepts collective bargaining as an appropriate mechanism for establishing workplace rules. Management tries to obtain the best possible labor contract with the union, and then governs employees according to the contract's terms. The labor relations policy shown in Figure 15.4 is an example of a union acceptance strategy.

A union acceptance strategy is likely to result in labor relations characterized by labor–management cooperation or working harmony. The relationship between General Motors and the UAW union at the Saturn auto plant in Tennessee is an example of such a strategy. The union negotiated a very flexible contract with management at this plant in exchange for union recognition and job security for its workers. Management can redesign jobs, change technology, and streamline work rules—a degree of flexibility unknown in other unionized General Motors auto plants.[38] In turn, labor is involved in decision making to a degree that is rare in unionized companies. Groups of 5 to 15 workers perform managerial tasks such as hiring. They also elect representatives to higher-level teams that make joint decisions with management on every aspect of the business, from car design to marketing to sticker price.[39] Another tactic used to create a climate of union–management cooperation is the establishment of a joint committee composed of union and management representatives who work to solve long-term problems in the workplace that have a high potential for conflict. At Xerox, management and representatives of the Amalgamated Clothing Workers Union formed joint committees and workplace teams whose collaborative efforts resulted in improved plant safety, work flow and production, reduced grievance rates, and the preservation of jobs that otherwise would have been eliminated.[40]

Unfortunately, the road to union–management cooperation can be rocky. Even at Saturn, which is often held up as a model of cooperative labor relations, there are signs of trouble: Recent hires are frequently less committed to the employee participation idea than those who have been at the plant from the beginning, and some distrust the union's close ties with management. In fact, worker distrust of union–management cooperation threatens to derail teamwork initiatives at an increasing number of companies, especially since the NLRB ruled that management-led employee teams can violate the Wagner Act.[41] For management guidelines in this area, see the Manager's Notebook, "When Is a Team Not a Team?"

Labor relations scholars have found that cooperative labor relations occur more often in industries with patterns of labor contract agreements that foster union–management collaboration like the automobile, telecommunications, steel, and construction industries.[42] An example of such a contract provision is one that establishes joint labor–management committees that

Union acceptance strategy
A labor relations strategy in which management chooses to view the union as its employees' legitimate representative and accepts collective bargaining as an appropriate mechanism for establishing workplace rules.

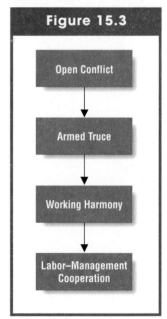

Figure 15.3

Open Conflict

↓

Armed Truce

↓

Working Harmony

↓

Labor–Management Cooperation

Types of Labor-Management Relations

Source: Mills, D. O. (1989). *Labor-management relations* (4th ed.), 222. New York: McGraw-Hill.

Figure 15.4

Our objective is to establish a labor policy that is consistent and fair. The purpose is to develop an agreeable working relationship with the union while retaining our full management rights. The rationale behind our labor relations policy is consistency, credibility, and fairness to union representatives and the workers who are in the union. In order to make our policy effective, the Company will:

- Accept union representation of employees in good faith, provided the union represents the majority of our employees;
- Maintain the right of management to manage;
- Adopt procedures by which top management continuously supports the positions of its representatives in implementing the firm's policies and practices in the area of industrial relations;
- Enforce disciplinary policies in a fair, firm, and consistent manner;
- See to it that union representatives follow all Company rules except those from which they are exempted under specific provisions of the labor contract;
- Handle all employee complaints fairly, firmly, and without discrimination;
- See that every representative of management exercises a maximum effort to follow Company policies fairly and consistently; and
- See to it that all decisions and agreements pertaining to the present contract are documented in writing.

Source: The company policy manual (1990), 332. New York Harper Business Division of HarperCollins Publishers.

Labor Relations Policy: Union Acceptance Strategy

meet on a regular basis and develop agreements over issues of mutual benefit such as (1) a drug-free workplace, (2) occupational safety rules, (3) gain-sharing plans, (4) equal opportunity for employees with disabilities, and (5) policies that prohibit any type of workplace harassment.[43]

MANAGER'S NOTEBOOK

Emerging Trends

When Is a Team Not a Team? Guidelines for Employee Involvement Committees

Two conditions determine whether a company's employee involvement (EI) group violates the Wagner Act. A group is illegal if it can be proved to be *both* "employer dominated" and a "labor organization" under the law.

- Determine whether the issues addressed by an EI team clearly constitute "conditions of employment." Until legal developments shed new light on the situation, experts say EI groups should be limited to addressing production, quality, and safety matters.[a]
- Employer domination can be construed if any group of employees is perceived as constituting a "select" group empowered to speak to management on behalf of all employees. Guard against such a charge by periodically rotating employee participants on EI teams.[b]
- Make sure that any such group functions in a way that is strictly independent of management influence. If disputes are settled by means of a negotiation process between employer and employee, employer dominance is often readily established. But if management delegates the authority to resolve grievances to the group and the group resolves such problems on its own, the group is likely to be seen as benign, despite the fact that management played a key role in establishing and encouraging it.[c]
- In a unionized setting, getting union participation in EI committees is virtually a surefire way to avoid litigation.[d] If the company is nonunion, the situation can be trickier. Get visible employee input and make the venture a cooperative and voluntary one.[e] An alternative would be to let peers nominate employees to participate rather than have management select them.[f]
- *Never* start an EI group during a union organizing campaign. Such activity can readily be seen as union busting.[g]

Sources: ^aAdapted by permission of the publisher, from *Management Review Forum*, February 1994, © 1994. American Management Association, New York. All rights reserved. ^b*Ibid.* ^c*Ibid.* ^d*Ibid.* ^e*Ibid.* ^fLeRoy, M. H. (1999) Are employers constrained in the use of employee participation groups by Section 8(a)(2) of the NLRA? *Journal of Labor Research* 22(1), 63–71; ^g*Management Review Forum,* 1994.

Although many small business owners work closely with their workers, they tend to regard such concepts as worker–management teams as a big company's game. According to the NLRB, two-thirds of unfair labor practice complaints are filed against employers with fewer than 100 workers. Because the great majority of small businesses are nonunionized, this record has encouraged unions to target small firms for membership expansion. In recent years, unions won certification at firms with fewer than 50 workers at twice their rate of success at companies employing more than 500 workers.[44] To avoid the loss of management control caused by unionization, many small companies have chosen to pursue a union avoidance strategy.

Union Avoidance Strategy

Management selects a **union avoidance strategy** when it fears the union will have a disruptive influence on its employees or fears losing control of its workers to a union. Companies that choose a union avoidance strategy are likely to be, at best, in an armed truce with unions and, at worst, in open conflict with them (see Figure 15.3). There are two different approaches to union avoidance: union substitution and union suppression.[45] Which approach a company pursues usually depends on the values of top management.

Union avoidance strategy
A labor relations strategy in which management tries to prevent its employees from joining a union, either by removing the incentive to unionize or by using hardball tactics.

Union Substitution

In the **union substitution** approach, also known as the **proactive human resource management approach**, management becomes so responsive to employees' needs that it removes the incentive for unionization. Using this approach, IBM, Hewlett-Packard, Eli Lilly, and Eastman Kodak avoided unionization and simultaneously developed a reputation as good places to work. Some of the policies that take the union substitution approach are:

Union substitution/proactive human resource management
A union avoidance strategy in which management becomes so responsive to employees' needs that it removes the incentives for unionization.

- Job security policies that protect the jobs of full-time workers. Among these is a policy that subcontracted, temporary, and part-time workers must be discharged before permanent employees can be laid off.
- Promoting-from-within policies that encourage the training and development of employees.
- Profit-sharing and employee stock ownership plans (see Chapter 11) that share the company's success with its employees.
- High-involvement management practices that solicit employee input into decisions.
- Open-door policies and grievance procedures that try to give workers the same sense of empowerment that they would have under a union contract.[46]

Union Suppression

Management uses the **union suppression** approach when it wants to avoid unionization at all costs and does not make any pretense of trying "to do the right thing" for its employees. Under this approach, management employs hardball tactics, which may be legal or illegal, to get rid of a union or to prevent the union from organizing its workers.[47]

Union suppression
A union avoidance strategy in which management uses hardball tactics to prevent a union from organizing its workers or to get rid of a union.

For example, in the mid-1980s, Continental Airlines' CEO Frank Lorenzo used the U.S. bankruptcy courts to reorganize Continental and escape the company's obligations to employees under its labor contracts with its unions. When the airline emerged from bankruptcy, it had a nonunion workforce with pay levels about 40 percent lower than had prevailed under the union contracts. In another case at about the same time, the *Chicago Tribune* bargained aggressively with its production unions and, when the union workers went out on strike, substituted permanent replacement workers. The result was a completely nonunionized workforce at the newspaper. More recently, in 2000 Wal-Mart used union suppression tactics to reduce its susceptibility to work with a union after the United Food & Commercial Workers union (UCFW) attempted to organize its meat cutters. Wal-Mart's response was to reorganize its supply chain and buy prepackaged meat for its U.S. stores and eliminate most of its meat counter jobs around the country.[48]

Sometimes the union suppression approach backfires and management reaps nothing but an angry union, bitter employees, and the worst kind of public relations. In 1990, management at the New York *Daily News,* which was then owned by the Chicago Tribune Company, tried to use replacement workers to intimidate its striking unions, but lost the battle because the media and the public sympathized with the union cause. J. P. Stevens, a textile manufacturer with plants in the southern United States, illegally tried to intimidate its workers by firing union organizers before a union certification election. The NLRB intervened on behalf of the union and ordered J. P. Stevens to recognize and bargain with the union.

In general, the union suppression approach is a higher-risk strategy than the union substitution approach and for this reason is used less frequently. Hardball tactics not only entail legal risks but can also come back to haunt management. Frank Lorenzo's use of the bankruptcy courts to break the company's unions looked like a great success at the time. However, in 1994 Lorenzo's bid to start a new low-fare airline was rejected by the Department of Transportation because of safety and regulatory compliance problems during Lorenzo's stewardship of Eastern and Continental Airlines. The DOT said that both of these airlines "experienced operational, maintenance, and labor-related problems that were among the most serious in the history of aviation."[49]

Managing the Labor Relations Process

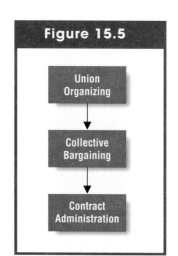

Figure 15.5

- Union Organizing
- Collective Bargaining
- Contract Administration

The Three Phases of the Labor Relations Process

Now that you have some grounding in the history of labor–management relations and relevant law, as well as a sense of the current state of labor relations and corporate strategies in this area, we can examine the specific components of the labor relations process. As Figure 15.5 shows, three phases of labor relations that managers and labor relations specialists must deal with are (1) union organizing, in which employees exercise their right to form a union; (2) collective bargaining, in which union and management representatives negotiate a labor contract; and (3) contract administration, in which the labor contract is applied to specific work situations on a daily basis.

Union Organizing

Union organizing takes place when employees work with a union to form themselves into a cohesive group. The key issues that managers confront in a union organizing campaign are union solicitation, preelection conduct, and the certification election.

Union Solicitation

Before it will order a union certification election, the NLRB requires a union to show that there is significant interest in unionization among a company's employees. To meet this requirement, a minimum of 30 percent of the employees in the relevant work unit must sign an authorization card indicating that they want to be represented by a specific union for collective bargaining purposes.

Unions often conduct the early stages of their solicitation effort in private homes or public facilities so that management will not be aware of the organizing drive until the required percentage of workers has signed authorization cards. However, sometimes the union finds it necessary to solicit on company property, which alerts management and gives it the opportunity to respond.

More than half of all unions have Web sites where they can communicate with current and potential members.[50] In a drive to organize IBM employees in Colorado, the Communication Workers of America (CWA) alerted employees to a special Web site designed to teach them how to form a union at IBM.[51] The AFL-CIO site (*www.aflcio.org*) discusses union organizing and other issues, such as the pay of the top executives in U.S. public corporations compared to average

A Question of Ethics

One strategy for suppressing union activity is to ask certain workers to report to management any union-organizing activities that are taking place at the company. Is this strategy legal? Is it ethical? If you answered yes to both questions, do you think it is a good management practice? Why or why not?

employee pay and work/family concerns. The Web site gives interested employees a way to turn to unions affiliated with the AFL-CIO to attain social and economic justice.

Management's choice of labor relations strategy guides a company's response to union solicitation. Companies with a union avoidance strategy usually have a "no-solicitation" policy that restricts all solicitations to nonwork areas (for example, solicitation may take place in lunch or break rooms, but not in offices) and nonwork times. A no-solicitation policy makes it more difficult for the union to influence workers' attitudes toward the union and persuade them to sign authorization cards. However, companies that have a no-solicitation policy must be careful to enforce it consistently so that *all* solicitations (including those for charitable causes) are restricted. Singling out union-organizing activities for restriction is an unfair labor practice that can result in an NLRB order to cease and desist the discriminatory policy.

Consistent enforcement of a no-solicitation policy was one of the key factors that led the Supreme Court to rule in favor of Lechmere, Inc., a Newington, Connecticut, store that had banned unions from its premises. The court found that Lechmere did not violate the Wagner Act, largely because it had consistently enforced its no-solicitation policy against all organizations, including the Girl Scouts and the Salvation Army. The court also found that the store's 200 workers were otherwise accessible to the union's nonemployee organizers.[52]

Preelection Conduct

If the union can show sufficient employee interest in forming a union, the NLRB will schedule a certification election. During the period before the election, management and union leaders should allow employees to freely exercise their right to vote for or against representation. It is the NLRB's policy to provide an environment in which employees can make an uncoerced choice in their selection of a bargaining agent—or, alternatively, an uncoerced choice not to be represented by any union.

During the preelection period, managers must avoid treating employees in a manner that could be interpreted as using their position to influence the outcome of the election. The NLRB "Notice to Employees" shown in Figure 15.6 indicates some types of conduct that are unacceptable before an election. Managers are prohibited from threatening employees with

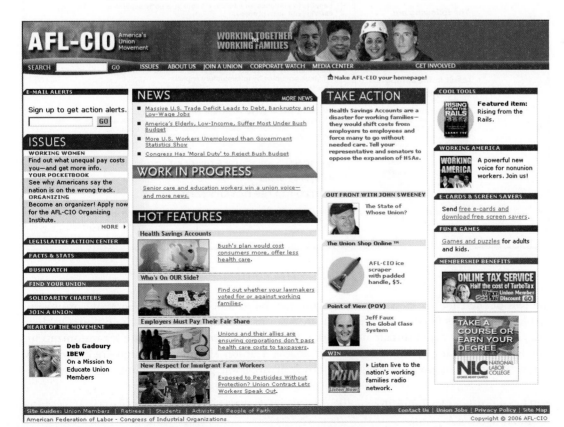

More than half of all unions have Web sites. The sites, such as this one, give employees who want to unionize the information they need quickly and efficiently.

**NLRB Representation
Election Notice to
Employees**

Source: National Labor Relations
Board.

Figure 15.6

NOTICE TO EMPLOYEES

FROM THE
National Labor Relations Board

A PETITION has been filed with this Federal agency seeking an election to determine whether certain employees want to be represented by a union.

The case is being investigated and NO DETERMINATION HAS BEEN MADE AT THIS TIME by the National Labor Relations Board. IF an election is held Notices of Election will be posted giving complete details for voting.

It was suggested that your employer post this notice so the National Labor Relations Board could inform you of your basic rights under the National Labor Relations Act.

**YOU HAVE
THE RIGHT
under
Federal Law**

- To self-organization
- To form, join, or assist labor organizations
- To bargain collectively through representatives of your own choosing
- To act together for the purposes of collective bargaining or other mutual aid or protection
- To refuse to do any or all of these things unless the union and employer, in a state where such agreements are permitted, enter into a lawful union-security agreement requiring employees to pay periodic dues and initiation fees. Nonmembers who inform the union that they object to the use of their payments for nonrepresentational purposes may be required to pay only their share of the union's costs of representational activities *(such as collective bargaining, contract administration, and grievance adjustments).*

It is possible that some of you will be voting in an employee representation election as a result of the request for an election having been filed. While NO DETERMINATION HAS BEEN MADE AT THIS TIME, in the event an election is held, the NATIONAL LABOR RELATIONS BOARD wants all eligible voters to be familiar with their rights under the law IF it holds an election.

The Board applies rules that are intended to keep its elections fair and honest and that result in a free choice. If agents of either unions or employers act in such a way as to interfere with your right to a free election, the election can be set aside by the Board. Where appropriate the Board provides other remedies, such as reinstatement for employees fired for exercising their rights, including backpay from the party responsible for their discharge.

NOTE:

**The following are
examples of conduct
that interfere with
the rights of
employees and may
result in the setting
aside of the election.**

- Threatening loss of jobs or benefits by an employer or a union
- Promising or granting promotions, pay raises, or other benefits to influence an employee's vote by a party capable of carrying out such promises
- An employer firing employees to discourage or encourage union activity or a union causing them to be fired to encourage union activity
- Making campaign speeches to assembled groups of employees on company time within the 24-hour period before the election
- Incitement by either an employer or a union of racial or religious prejudice by inflammatory appeals
- Threatening physical force or violence to employees by a union or an employer to influence their votes

Please be assured that IF AN ELECTION IS HELD every effort will be made to protect your right to a free choice under the law. Improper conduct will not be permitted. All parties are expected to cooperate fully with this Agency in maintaining basic principles of a fair election as required by law. The National Labor Relations Board, as an agency of the United States Government, does not endorse any choice in the election.

NATIONAL LABOR RELATIONS BOARD
an agency of the
UNITED STATES GOVERNMENT

THIS IS AN OFFICIAL GOVERNMENT NOTICE AND MUST NOT BE DEFACED BY ANYONE

FORM NLRB-666 (5-90)   ☆U.S. GOVERNMENT PRINTING OFFICE: 1991-312-471/51356

the loss of their jobs or benefits if they vote for the union. They must also avoid promising employees benefits (such as pay raises or promotions) if they vote against the union. On their side, unions must avoid threatening workers with harm if they do not vote for unionization. The NLRB's rules for permissible conduct during a union election campaign are exceedingly complex and constantly changing; here, however, are some general guidelines for managers:

- **Threats.** It is unlawful to threaten employees with theoretical dire consequences should the union win the election.

- **Intimidation.** Employers by law cannot intimidate or coerce employees to vote against the union.
- **Promises.** Management cannot promise employees benefits or rewards if they vote against the union.
- **Surveillance.** It is unlawful to secretly or overtly spy on organizing meetings.[53]

It *is* permissible for managers to try to persuade employees before a representation election that they would be better off without a union. Managers can legally do this by:[54]

- Making speeches to groups of employees emphasizing why they do not need a union (legal up to 24 hours before the election).
- Employing a labor relations consultant to assist with the antiunion strategy.
- Sending a personal letter to employees.
- Showing movies that view unions in an unfavorable light.
- Writing memos to employees that summarize all the good things that the employer has provided for them.

Firms in the United States can also hire consultants who specialize in helping management maintain a nonunion workforce. One study estimated that employers spent an average of $500 per employee on consultants in union election campaigns.[55]

Certification Election

The NLRB supervises the certification election, determining who is eligible to vote and counting the ballots. The voting is done by secret ballot, and the outcome is determined by the participating voters. If the union receives a majority of the votes, it becomes the certified bargaining agent for all of the unit's employees. This means that it becomes the exclusive agent for both union and nonunion employees in collective bargaining with the employer. The *bargaining unit* consists of all the employees who are represented by a union that engages in collective bargaining with the employer.

If the majority of voters vote against the union, NLRB policy states that no other representation election may be held for a 12-month period. In recent years, unions have won slightly over half of the representation elections held in the United States. In 2004, unions won 56 percent of the certification elections.[56] Exhibit 15.1, "Organizing Campaigns: A New Priority," gives some examples of successful attempts by U.S. unions to organize diverse groups of employees.

Collective Bargaining

If union organizing results in certification, the next step in the labor relations process is collective bargaining that results in a labor contract. Most labor contracts last for two to three years, after which they are subject to renegotiation.

Four of the most important issues related to collective bargaining are bargaining behavior, bargaining power, bargaining topics, and impasses in bargaining. In all of these areas, managers must monitor their behavior carefully.

Organizing Campaigns: A New Priority   **EXHIBIT 15.1**

In recent years, many unions have started to pour significant resources into their organizing campaigns. Here are some examples of recent successful union-organization activities:

- The UAW has recently won recognition to represent employees in several major nonunion auto parts companies, including Collins & Aikman, Dana, Lear, and Metaldyne, bringing tens of thousands of employees into the union. The parts companies agreed to recognize the UAW in exchange for the union's compromise to offer lower wage rates and provide more flexible work rules than were available in its contract with the Big Three automobile manufacturers.[a]
- Graduate students work long hours teaching courses, grading papers, and doing laboratory experiments and other important activities at universities for low salaries that average between $11,000 and $15,000 per year. At New York University, graduate students attempted to form a union that was challenged in the courts by the administration. University administration

argued that collective bargaining between the students and the university would be an infringement of academic freedom and justified the low wages paid to students by claiming that the graduate assistant work was part of their educational experience. The National Labor Relations Board disagreed with the administration's reasoning and decided to allow the graduate students to form a union organized by the United Auto Workers. Following in the footsteps of the graduate students at New York University, graduate students have begun union organizing drives at Columbia, Brandeis, and University of Pennsylvania.[b]

■ Winning the biggest unionization drive in more than half a century the Service Employees International Union gained the right to represent 74,000 Los Angeles County home-care workers who feed, bathe, and clean the elderly and disabled. Many said they voted to join a union because they wanted to fight to raise their wages of $5.75 per hour and to obtain two benefits long denied them: health insurance and paid vacations.[c]

Sources: [a]Welch, D. (2004, August 2). A breakthrough for labor. *BusinessWeek*, 86–87; [b]Greenhouse, S. (2001, May 15). Graduate students push for union membership. *New York Times*, A-19; [c]Greenhouse, S. (1999, February 26). In biggest drive since 1937, union gains a victory, *New York Times*, A-1, A-15.

Bargaining Behavior

Once the NLRB certifies a union as the bargaining agent for a unit of employees, both management and the union have a duty to bargain with each other in "good faith." Refusing to bargain

Workers at Blacksheep Technology in Seattle, Washington, meet at the Labor Temple in order to plan their union-organizing strategy.

in good faith can result in an NLRB cease-and-desist order that is enforced in the courts. The parties are showing good faith in collective bargaining when:

- Both parties are willing to meet and confer with each other at a reasonable time and place.
- Both parties are willing to negotiate over wages, hours, and conditions of employment (the mandatory bargaining topics).
- The parties sign a written contract that formalizes their agreement and binds them to it.
- Each party gives the other a 60-day notice of termination or modification of the labor agreement before it expires.

In general, *good-faith bargaining* means treating the other party reasonably even when disagreements arise. To show good faith, management should develop different proposals and suggestions for negotiating with the union instead of simply rejecting all union proposals. For example, in the early 1960s a negotiator for General Electric made a single proposal to the union on a take-it-or-leave-it basis, and then refused to negotiate on any of the union's counteroffers. The NLRB interpreted this inflexible approach to bargaining as an unfair labor practice that did not show good faith. For additional insights on how union and management representatives should behave in order to sustain good faith bargaining, see the Manager's Notebook, "Bargaining Etiquette."

> ### A Question of Ethics
>
> Suppose at a prebargaining meeting between the company's negotiating team and top management it is decided that the company will give up to a 4 percent raise. When negotiations start, however, the lead management negotiator states that the company cannot afford more than a 2 percent raise, and will go no higher. Is this ethical behavior? What if the situation were reversed and it was the union negotiator who stated an absolute minimum demand, knowing that the union leadership will accept less? Would that be ethical?

Ethics

MANAGER'S NOTEBOOK

Bargaining Etiquette

Here are some guidelines for management and union-bargaining teams to follow so that good faith can be maintained during collective bargaining sessions:

- **Show courtesy to the other bargaining team.** When the management team takes a caucus break to develop a response to a union proposal, the management team should notify the union team by telephone that they are ready to continue bargaining instead of walking in and interrupting a conversation between the union team members.
- **Set the tone by being friendly to the other bargaining team.** Team members should shake hands, make eye contact, and show interest in the members of the other bargaining team.
- **Maintain team solidarity.** Make it a point that all team members will arrive and leave the bargaining sessions at the same time. It is disruptive when team members arrive and leave while bargaining sessions are in progress.
- **Establish ground rules to deal with difficult bargaining issues.** Rules should cover when caucus breaks occur and for how long they last, the location where the bargaining sessions take place, and whether the bargaining meetings should occur at night. (It is better to avoid bargaining late into the night because when people are tired their behavior may be come less civil.)
- **Keep negative emotions under control.** If things get heated, take a caucus break, which allows the team members to regroup and calm down. Personal attacks on the opposing bargaining team members should be avoided. Negativity has no place at the bargaining table.

Source: Adapted from Tyler, K. (2005, January). Good-faith bargaining. *HRMagazine*, 49–53.

Bargaining Power

In collective bargaining sessions, both parties are likely to take opening positions that favor their goals but leave them some room to negotiate. For example, on the topic of pay raises, the union may initially ask for 8 percent but be willing to go as low as 5 percent. Management may initially offer the union 2 percent but be willing to go as high as 6 percent.

At which point will the parties reach agreement, 5 percent or 6 percent? The party that understands how to use its bargaining power will probably be able to achieve settlement closer to its initial bargaining position. *Bargaining power* is one party's ability to get the other party to agree to its terms. If management has greater bargaining power than the union, it is likely to get the union to agree to a 5 percent pay increase.

An important aspect of a party's bargaining power is how it is perceived by the other party. Each party can engage in behaviors that shape the other party's perceptions. Management that acts in a powerful and intimidating manner may influence the union to make additional concessions. However, aggressive posturing by management may backfire and cause union negotiators to make fewer concessions.

Parties in negotiations have several tactical alternatives. Two bargaining tactics are often used to increase bargaining power: distributive bargaining and integrative bargaining.[57]

Distributive bargaining

Bargaining that focuses on convincing the other party that the cost of disagreeing with the proposed terms would be very high.

Distributive Bargaining. **Distributive bargaining** focuses on convincing your counterpart in negotiations that the cost of disagreeing with your terms would be very high. In collective bargaining, the cost of disagreement is often a strike. Strikes usually occur in the United States when a labor contract expires without both sides reaching a new agreement. Distributive bargaining tactics tend to be used when the two sides are competing for very limited resources.

Labor uses distributive bargaining when it attempts to convince management that it is willing and able to sustain a long strike that will severely damage the company's profits and weaken the company's position against its competitors. For example, in its 1993 negotiations with UPS, the Teamsters Union presented the company with several key bargaining demands, including substantial pay and benefit increases, improved job security, conversion of part-time jobs to full-time jobs, and less stringent productivity standards. When UPS, after intense contract talks and contract extensions, presented the Teamsters with a contract that did not come close to meeting the union's demands, the Teamsters suspended negotiations and set a strike date. A national strike against UPS could have crippled the company at a time when it was facing stiff competition from nonunion rivals, such as FedEx and Roadway Package Services. Before this happened, however, Ron Carey, the Teamsters' reformist president, hammered out a contract that provided a good economic package and an end to some of the stringent work rules that had long irked union members.[58] Distributive bargaining tactics do not always avoid strikes. As the opening vignette shows, UPS and the Teamsters were not able to avoid a strike four years later when bargaining over terms of a new contract failed to reach a settlement before the old contract expired.

Management uses distributive bargaining when it tries to convince the union that it can sustain a long strike much better than union members, who will have to survive without their paychecks. For example, in 1975 management at the *Washington Post* tried to persuade the newspaper's unions that it could sustain a strike and still get the paper out because it had cross-trained managers to do the jobs of union workers. In this instance, management was able to pull it off.

Union leaders may also adopt distributive bargaining tactics when they believe union members are willing to accept the cost of a long strike that is likely to cause a vulnerable company severe economic damage. This situation occurred in 1998 when the UAW struck General Motors over the issue of preventing union jobs from being given to outsourcing firms. GM's motivation for outsourcing was to reduce its labor costs. A two-month strike ensued when there was a strong demand for but a short supply of new General Motors car models. The timing of the strike helped convince management to make concessions to the union after the strike cost GM $2.2 billion in losses.[59]

Integrative bargaining

Bargaining that focuses on convincing the other party that the benefits of agreeing with the proposed terms would be very high.

Integrative Bargaining. **Integrative bargaining** focuses on convincing your counterpart in negotiations that the benefits of agreeing with your terms would be very high. Integrative bargaining is similar to a problem-solving session in which both parties are seeking mutually beneficial alternatives. Goodyear Tire & Rubber Co. and the United Steelworkers Union (USW) negotiated an agreement that illustrates the benefits of integrative bargaining. Because of Goodyear's need to become globally competitive, Goodyear placed a high priority on reducing its operating expenses. In exchange for the union's willingness to slash labor costs by $1.15 billion over three years and to eliminate 3,000 jobs, Goodyear agreed to keep, and invest in, all but two of its U.S. factories and to limit imports from its factories in Brazil and Asia. The union accepted the company's terms in a contract in 2003 in the hopes of saving as many of the 19,000 union jobs at

Goodyear as possible.[60] The Manager's Notebook, "Guidelines for Integrative Bargaining," shows what both parties need to do to achieve integrative bargaining.

Customer-Driven HR

Guidelines for Integrative Bargaining

Integrative bargaining is the process of identifying a common, shared, or joint goal and developing a process to achieve it. An emphasis on integrative bargaining can lead to cooperation between union and management and the possibility of mutual gains for both. To achieve integrative bargaining, both parties should:

- **Attempt to understand the other negotiator's real needs and objectives.** The parties should engage in a dialogue in which both sides disclose preferences and priorities, rather than disguise or manipulate them.[a]
- **Create a free flow of information.** Negotiators must be willing to listen to the other negotiator carefully, and to accept a joint solution that incorporates both parties' needs.[b]
- **Emphasize the commonalities, and minimize the differences, between the parties.** Specific goals should be reframed to be considered part of a larger, collaborative goal. For example, a safe workplace may be a goal on which both the union and management agree, although they may differ on a specific approach to achieve this goal.[c]
- **Search for solutions that meet both parties' goals and objectives.** When parties are combative or competitive, they are more likely to focus only on their own objectives and ignore those of the other party. Integrative bargaining is successful only when both parties' needs are met.[d]
- **Develop flexible responses to the other negotiator's proposals.** Each negotiator should try to accommodate and adapt to the needs of the other party by modifying his or her proposals. Avoid getting stuck in one intractable position that does not provide room to make tactical trade-offs. By behaving flexibly, a negotiator can encourage the other party to reciprocate in a similar fashion and move toward a settlement with mutual gains.[e]

Sources: [a]Lewicki, R., Saunders, D., and Barry, B. (2006). *Negotiation* (5th ed.). Burr Ridge, IL: McGraw-Hill Irwin; [b]Ibid.; [c]Ibid.; [d]Ibid.; [e]Das, T. K., and Teng, B. (1998). Between trust and control: Developing confidence in partner cooperation and alliances. *Academy of Management Review, 23,* 491–512.

It is not unusual in collective bargaining for both sides to use both distributive and integrative bargaining tactics. However, the firm's overall labor relations strategy generally determines what type of bargaining it adopts.[61] Firms with a union acceptance strategy are more likely to mix integrative and distributive bargaining, while those with a union avoidance strategy are more likely to focus solely on distributive bargaining. In addition, the strategies selected by the union will influence a firm's bargaining strategies and tactics because collective bargaining is a dynamic process.

Bargaining Topics

The NLRB and courts classify bargaining topics into three categories: mandatory, permissive, and illegal. As mentioned earlier, *mandatory bargaining topics* are wages, hours, and employment conditions. These are the topics that both union and management consider fundamental to the organization's labor relations. Some examples of each of these mandatory topics are shown in Figure 15.7.

The NLRB and courts have interpreted wages, hours, and employment conditions fairly broadly. "Wages" can mean any type of compensation, including base pay rates, pay incentives, health insurance, and retirement benefits. "Hours" can mean anything to do with work scheduling, including the allocation of overtime and the amount of vacation time granted. "Employment

Mandatory Bargaining Topics

		Figure 15.7
Wages	**Hours**	**Employment Conditions**
Base pay rates	Overtime	Layoffs
Overtime pay rates	Holidays	Promotions
Retirement benefits	Vacation	Seniority provisions
Health benefits	Shifts	Safety rules
Travel pay	Flextime	Work rules
Pay incentives	Parental leave	Grievance procedures
		Union shop
		Job descriptions

conditions" can mean almost any work rule that affects the employees represented by the union. These include grievance procedures, safety rules, job descriptions, and the bases for promotions.

Permissive bargaining topics may be discussed during collective bargaining if both parties agree to do so, but neither party is obligated to bargain on these topics. Some permissive bargaining topics are provisions for union members to serve on the company's board of directors and benefits for retired union members. In the recessionary economy of the early 1990s, some unions swapped wage concessions for equity in the company and a stronger voice in how it is run. Management–labor agreements in the airline industry have incorporated some novel approaches to rescue faltering airlines and thousands of jobs. For instance:

■ Financially beleaguered Northwest Airlines and its three major unions—the Machinists, the Air Line Pilots Association, and the International Brotherhood of Teamsters—reached an agreement in 1993 on contract concessions to keep the carrier flying. The unions consented to more than $700 million worth of concessions in return for 30 percent of Northwest's preferred stock, three seats on the company's 15-member board, enhanced job security, and a significant voice in company operations.[62]

■ At United Airlines, the unions that represent pilots and machinists traded 15 percent in pay cuts for 55 percent of the company stock and three of 12 board seats in 1994. By 1996, United's stock price had more than doubled and the employee-owned airline was outperforming most of its rivals.[63] However, United Airlines stock plunged in 2001 after the terrorist attack on the United States when United grounded 31 percent of its flights and furloughed 20,000 of its employees. This reversal of company fortunes put a damper on the union's interest in taking additional pay cuts to help the company overcome its latest financial crisis.[64]

Illegal bargaining topics may not be discussed in collective bargaining. Examples of illegal topics are closed shop agreements, featherbedding, and discriminatory employment practices. The NLRB considers the discussion of illegal bargaining topics an unfair labor practice.

Impasses in Bargaining

A labor contract cannot be finalized until the bargaining representatives on both sides go back to their organizations and obtain approval of the contract. Union negotiators typically ask the members to vote on the contract. Most unions require a majority of union members to approve the contract. Management's negotiating team may need approval from the company's top executives. If the parties cannot agree on one or more mandatory issues, they have reached an *impasse* in bargaining. A party that insists on bargaining over a permissive topic to the point of impasse engages in an unfair labor practice.

If the impasse persists because the parties have taken rigid positions, a strike may result. Before a strike is called, either party may ask a mediator to help resolve the impasse. Mediators are trained in conflict resolution techniques and are sometimes able to improve communication so that the impasse is resolved. The Federal Mediation and Conciliation Service (FMCS), established by the Taft-Hartley Act, monitors labor disputes and (under certain circumstances) mediates disputes. In addition, the FMCS maintains a list of impartial mediators and arbitrators who are qualified to assist with contract disputes.

If the contract's expiration date approaches, and the parties are still at an impasse, the union may ask its members to vote on a strike. If members approve, the strike will start the day after the current labor contract expires. Striking union members withhold their labor from the employer and often publicize their dispute by picketing in front of the employer's buildings. A strike imposes costs on both parties. Striking union members receive no wages or benefits until they return to work, although they may draw some money from the union's strike fund, which is set up to give a small allowance to cover the striking members' basic expenses. However, a long strike may exhaust the strike fund, putting pressure on the union to make concessions in order to get its members back to work.

Workers on strike also face the risk of losing their jobs to permanent replacement workers. Caterpillar, Inc., the world's largest manufacturer of construction equipment, used the threat of hiring permanent replacement workers to win a heated dispute with the UAW. The company set a deadline and told striking workers, "Go back to work or lose your job." The strikers were scared off the picket line and returned to work on management's terms.[65] The use of permanent replacement workers is very controversial, and organized labor is trying to get Congress to pass legislation restricting it.[66] See Exhibit 15.2, "Permanent Replacement Workers: A Strike Against Labor or an Economic Necessity?" for more on this issue.

Sometimes unions are legally bound by their contracts to honor another union's picket line, which makes it more difficult for the company to hire replacement workers. For example, during a strike by the screenwriters at the three major U.S. television networks, all the other television production workers left their jobs in a *sympathy strike*. The solidarity of the unions forced the television studios to abandon all production work until they could reach a settlement with the screenwriters.

Permanent Replacement Workers: A Strike Against Labor or an Economic Necessity?

EXHIBIT 15.2

When over 6,300 drivers abandoned Greyhound buses during a bitter strike in 1989, the company had 700 new recruits on hand to drive the fleet and 900 more in training. And after the strike ended, most of the new hires remained on the job. Replacement workers also remained on the job after bitter protracted strikes at International Paper and Eastern and Continental Airlines.

Replacing striking workers has been a legal employer option for about 60 years, but it was not until 1981, when President Ronald Reagan fired striking air traffic controllers and kept the air traffic system going with replacements, that employers began using this tactic regularly.

To organized labor, the hiring of permanent replacement workers undermines the bargaining power granted to unions under the Wagner Act's guaranteed right to strike. Once the unions' trump card, the strike has become a card many unions are afraid to play in an era when strikers fear losing their jobs. Labor advocates argue that permanent replacement is the same as firing striking workers, which is illegal.

The current law on replacement workers derives from a 1938 case, *NLRB v. Mackay Radio & Telegraph Co.*, in which the court declared that while the company in this case (Mackay) was guilty of firing strikers, in other cases where management has committed no illegal practices, the company is not bound to discharge replacement workers and hire back strikers when they wish to return to work. Labor advocates insist that "not hired back" equals "fired." On their side, employers argue that the ability to hire permanent replacements is necessary to ensure the survival of companies. Jack Schwartz, the labor counsel for National Tea, a New Orleans–based company, echoed the views of many employers when he said that legislation banning permanent replacement workers will encourage companies to relocate to "Mexico or another country where they don't have to worry about that risk."

Sources: Singh, P., and Harish, J. (2001). Striker replacements in the United States and Mexico: A review of the law and empirical research. *Industrial Relations, 40,* 22–53; Budd, J. (1996). Canadian strike replacement legislation and collective bargaining: Lessons for the United States. *Industrial Relations, 3b,* 245–260; BNA's *Employee Relations Weekly.* (1994, January 24). Negotiators for management and labor gauge impact of striker replacements, *12*(4), 87–88. Bernstein, A. (1991, August 5). You can't bargain with a striker whose job is no more. *BusinessWeek,* 27; Kliborn, P. T. (1990, March 13). Replacement workers. Management's big gun. *New York Times.* A24.

Management also faces significant strike costs. A strike can force a company to shut down operations and lose customers. In a highly competitive market, such actions may plunge the company into bankruptcy. This is exactly what happened at Eastern Airlines when the International Association of Machinists and Aerospace Workers (IAM) struck the air carrier in a contract dispute in 1989. A strike also poses a threat to a company from a loss of market share to its rivals in highly competitive industries. This is what happened to Boeing in 2000 in the competitive commercial aircraft industry when it sustained a six-week strike of 18,000 engineers and technicians of the Society of Professional Engineering Employees in Aerospace (SPEEA) in the largest white-collar strike occurring in the United States. Eventually the company settled with a contract favorable to the union's demands. The union demanded and obtained in its contract provisions for the company to continue paying for all of the employees' health insurance benefits and to give employees a 5 percent annual pay increase over a three-year period.[67]

Despite the negative outcomes sometimes associated with strikes, they are an important feature of the collective bargaining process. The pressure of an impending strike deadline forces both union and management negotiators to make concessions and resolve their differences. In the United States less than 0.2 percent of total working time lost is lost because of strikes. Put another way, less working time is lost because of strikes than because of the common cold.[68]

The type of strike we have been discussing thus far, which takes place when an agreement is not reached during collective bargaining, is called an **economic strike**. Another type of strike, called the **wildcat strike**, is a spontaneous work stoppage that happens under a valid contract and is usually not supported by union leadership. Wildcat strikes generally occur when workers are angered by a disciplinary action taken by management against one of their colleagues. Some contracts forbid wildcat strikes and penalize workers who participate in them, sometimes by termination. The preferred method of resolving disputes between unionized workers and management is the grievance procedure. One tool that employers can use against workers is the lockout. A **lockout** occurs when the employer shuts down its operation before or during a labor dispute. Employers may use a lockout during a bargaining impasse to protect themselves from unusual economic hardship when the timing of a strike may ruin critical materials. For example, a brewer must bottle beer by a certain date or the entire batch can be ruined. Because employers have other alternatives to influence the union to make concessions, such as the use of replacement workers, lockouts are rarely used. A 10-month lockout occurred when National Hockey League (NHL) team owners and the Player's Association representing the hockey players failed to come to terms over owners' demand for a salary cap on each team's wage bill, citing losses of $273 million the previous year. The lockout resulted in the cancellation of the entire 2004–2005 NHL season. The Player's Association finally caved in and agreed to a deal with the owners that caps each team's total wage bill at $39 million and includes a 24-percent reduction in player salaries.[69]

Contract Administration

The last phase of labor relations is contract administration, which involves application and enforcement of the labor contract in the workplace. Disputes occasionally arise between labor and management over such issues as who should be promoted or whether an employee has abused sick leave privileges. The steps taken to resolve such disputes are spelled out in the labor contract.

The mechanism preferred by most unions and managements to settle disputes is the grievance procedure.[70] A **grievance procedure** is a systematic, step-by-step procedure designed to settle disputes regarding the interpretation of the labor contract.

Although employees may attempt to settle their grievances through such alternatives as an open-door policy or a meeting with an employee relations representative in the HR department (see Chapter 13), grievance procedures under union contracts have two significant advantages for employees that no other HRM program can provide:

1. The grievance procedure provides the employee with an advocate dedicated to representing the employee's case to management. This representative is called the **union steward**. Under any other system used to handle grievances, the employee is represented by someone who is either a manager or an agent of management. Such people obviously cannot be entirely dedicated to the employee's position.

Economic strike
A strike that takes place when an agreement is not reached during collective bargaining.

Wildcat strike
A spontaneous work stoppage that happens under a valid contract and is usually not supported by union leadership.

Lockout
Occurs when an employer shuts down its operations before or during a labor dispute.

Grievance procedure
A systematic step-by-step process designed to settle disputes regarding the interpretation of a labor contract.

Union steward
An advocate dedicated to representing an employee's case to management in a grievance procedure.

2. The last step in the grievance procedure is **arbitration**, a quasi-judicial process that is binding on both parties. The arbitrator is a neutral person selected from outside the firm and compensated by both the union and management (who split the fee). Unlike grievance panels, which are composed of people on the company payroll, the arbitrator has no personal stake in the outcome and can make a tough decision without worrying about how it will affect his or her career.[71]

Arbitration
The last step in a grievance procedure. The decision of the arbitrator, who is a neutral individual selected from outside the firm, is binding on both parties.

Steps in the Grievance Procedure

Most union grievance procedures have three or four steps leading up to arbitration, the final step. Figure 15.8 illustrates a four-step union grievance procedure. Usually a time limit is set for resolution of the grievance at each step. Later steps in the procedure require more time than earlier steps, and the degree of formality increases with each step. Because the grievance procedure is time consuming and distracts several people from their regular job duties, it is generally advantageous for the company to resolve disputes as early as possible.

The key to an effective grievance procedure is training supervisors to understand the labor contract and to work with union stewards to settle grievances at the first step. The labor relations staff in the HR department can make an important contribution here by training and consulting with supervisors.

The first step of the grievance procedure is taken when an employee tells the union steward about his or her grievance. In our example in Figure 15.8, the employee must make the dispute known to the steward and/or the supervisor within five working days of its occurrence. The steward refers to the labor contract to determine if the grievance is valid and, if it is, tries to work with the employee's supervisor to settle it. The grievance may or may not be put in writing. Most grievances (about 75%) are settled at this first step.

If the dispute cannot be resolved at this first step, the grievance is put into writing, and, in our example, the department or plant manager and a union official (such as the union's business

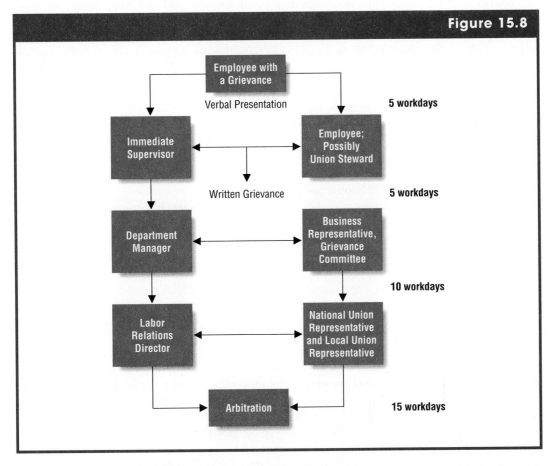

Figure 15.8

Employee with a Grievance

Verbal Presentation   5 workdays

Immediate Supervisor ↔ Employee; Possibly Union Steward

Written Grievance   5 workdays

Department Manager ↔ Business Representative, Grievance Committee

10 workdays

Labor Relations Director ↔ National Union Representative and Local Union Representative

Arbitration   15 workdays

A Union Grievance Procedure

Source: Adapted from Allen, R., and Keavany, T. (1988). *Contemporary labor solutions* (2nd ed.), 530. Reading, MA: Addison-Wesley. Reprinted by permission of Robert Allen.

representative) have an additional five working days to resolve the issue. At this second step, a formal meeting is usually held to discuss the grievance.

If the second step is unsuccessful at resolving the grievance, the parties move on to the third step. This step usually involves both a corporate manager (for example, the company's director of labor relations) and a local and national union representative. In our example, the labor agreement gives these people 10 days to respond to and resolve the grievance. Grievances that have the potential to set precedents affecting employment policy may get "kicked up" to this level because it is inappropriate for plant supervisors or managers to settle them. For example, a grievance concerning production standards may have widespread implications for all workers if a corporate-wide labor contract is in effect. Because the third step is the last step before arbitration, it is management's final opportunity to negotiate a settlement with the union. It is common for management to try to "cut a deal" with the union at this step.

The final step of the grievance procedure is arbitration. Only about 1 percent of grievances get as far as arbitration; the rest are settled at the earlier steps. Both parties select the arbitrator, before whom the union and management advocates present their case and evidence at a hearing with a quasi-judicial format. The arbitrator then examines the evidence and makes a ruling. Most arbitrators also write an opinion outlining their reasoning and the sections of the labor contract that influenced their decision. This opinion can serve as a guideline for dealing with similar disputes in the future. The arbitrator's decision is final and binding on both parties.

Types of Grievances

Employees initiate two types of grievances. The first is a *contract interpretation grievance* based on union members' rights under the labor contract. If the contract's language is ambiguous, this type of grievance may go to arbitration for clarification. For example, suppose that a labor contract allows workers two 10-minute coffee breaks per day. If management decides it would be more efficient to get rid of coffee breaks, employees may file a contract interpretation grievance to get this privilege restored.

The second type of grievance involves employee discipline. In such cases, the grievance procedure examines whether the employee in question was disciplined for just cause, and management has the burden of proof. An important aspect of these cases is determining whether the disciplined employee received due process. For minor infractions, management is expected to give employees the opportunity to correct their behavior via the progressive discipline procedure (verbal warning, written warning, suspension, discharge). For more serious charges (such as theft), management must provide strong evidence that the discipline was warranted.

Benefits of Union Grievance Procedures

Union grievance procedures provide benefits to both management and employees. Specifically:

- The grievance procedure protects union employees from arbitrary management decisions; it is the mechanism for organizational justice.
- The grievance procedure helps management quickly and efficiently settle conflicts that could otherwise end up in the courts or result in work stoppages.
- Management can use the grievance procedure as an upward communications channel to monitor and correct the sources of employee dissatisfaction with jobs or company policies.

The Impact of Unions on Human Resource Management

In the absence of a union, management is more likely to develop HRM policies based on the principle of efficiency. For example, a nonunion company is more likely to adopt a meet-the-market pay policy because the market wage is the most efficient way to allocate labor costs (see Chapter 10). But when a union enters the picture, management must develop policies that reflect the preferences of the majority of workers who are represented by the union.[72] In this section, we look at the changes in staffing, employee development, compensation, and employee relations practices that are likely under unionization.

Staffing

Under a labor contract, job opportunities are allocated to people on the basis of seniority. **Seniority** is the length of time a person works for an employer. In a unionized company, promotions, job assignments, and shift preferences are given to the employee with the most seniority in the unit.[73] Layoffs in unionized firms are also governed according to the last in, first out rule (see Chapter 6).[74]

    Work rules tend to be less flexible in a unionized workplace because they are likely to be formalized in the labor agreement. When labor relations are adversarial, labor contracts are more likely to have inflexible work rules written into them. When labor relations are more cooperative, work rule specifications may purposely be left out of the contract. In certain industries, this gives management the flexibility to adjust to the rapidly changing technological requirements of producing a product or service. For instance, under the terms of the 1999 contract between DaimlerChrysler and the UAW, the company agreed to give the union a rich economic pay package with a $1,350 signing bonus and a 3 percent pay increase in addition to pay adjustments for inflation. In return, DaimlerChrysler got the union to agree to allow the company to reduce the size of the workforce through attrition (that is, the company does not have to fill jobs vacated through quits and retirements). The reduction of the workforce gives the company the opportunity to decrease costs through increased productivity.[75]

    In the absence of a union, the employer is more likely to allocate job opportunities to employees on the basis of merit.[76] In most cases, merit is determined by a supervisor's judgment of the employee's performance. Supervisors in a nonunion workplace have more power and influence because of their authority to reward employees' efforts with promotions, attractive job assignments, and preferred work schedules. Layoff decisions in nonunion firms are more likely to take both merit and seniority into consideration. Finally, work rules are often more flexible in a nonunion firm because the employer is not tied to a contract and is, therefore, not required to justify to employees any changes made in the way work is done. In nonunion firms it is management alone that determines the most efficient way to produce a product or service and deliver it to the customer.

Employee Development

In unionized companies, the uses of performance appraisal are very limited because the appraisal data usually come from the supervisor, a source that many unions find problematic. Unions tend to balk at using performance appraisal as the basis for making pay and staffing decisions. If performance appraisal is done at all for union employees, it is used simply to provide some feedback on their performance. In a nonunion workplace, however, the performance appraisal is used to determine pay raises, promotions, job assignments, career planning, training needs, and layoff or discharge.[77]

    Unionized firms tend to retain their employees longer than nonunion firms do.[78] First, unionized employees are more likely to express their dissatisfaction through the grievance procedure, so this channel may become an alternative to quitting. Second, unionized firms on average pay their employees a higher wage, which may make it more difficult for them to find an equally high-paying job if they leave.

    Unions themselves have become far more interested in worker training and development in recent years. The 1990 contract between General Motors and the UAW, for instance, specified that the company will create Skills Centers (adult educational facilities) for union workers. So far, 36 GM plants in the United States have set up these centers. As unions have stepped up their organizing efforts, many have offered to fund worker training programs. In New York City, for instance, locals of the Amalgamated Labor and Textile Workers Unions, the International Ladies Garment Workers Union, and other major unions work with a Center for Worker Education to provide English as a second language and high school equivalency classes for their members and for worker groups they are trying to organize.[79]

Compensation

A company experiences an increase in total compensation costs when a union organizes its employees. On average, union employees earn 10 to 20 percent higher wages than comparable nonunionized employees.[80]

Seniority
The length of time a person works for an employer.

Cost-of-living adjustment (COLA)
Pay raises, usually made across the board, that are tied to such inflation indicators as the consumer price index.

The presence of a union also affects the company's policy on pay raises. Unionized firms avoid using merit pay plans and are likely to give across-the-board pay raises to employees based on market considerations.[81] Across-the-board pay plans are often based on **cost-of-living adjustments (COLAs)** that are tied to inflation indicators such as the consumer price index. About 23 percent of unionized U.S. workers received COLAs in 2002.[82] Unions prefer across-the-board pay raises to merit pay plans because they see the latter as undermining union solidarity by encouraging employees to compete against one another to win higher pay increases. Furthermore, unions are often skeptical of the fairness of merit pay increases because of the potential for favoritism on the part of supervisors (see Chapter 7). Unions apply this same logic to the use of individual pay incentives such as lump-sum bonuses. In contrast, nonunion firms tend to use merit pay and bonuses to encourage competition and recognize their top performers.

Unions are less likely to object to group pay incentives because group plans (such as gainsharing or profit sharing) tend to reinforce group cohesion. Each of the Big Three automakers in the United States has negotiated a profit-sharing plan with the UAW. It is not unusual to find gainsharing plans in both union and nonunion companies.[83] However, nonunion firms generally have more flexibility to use both individual and group pay incentives to reward different types of work outcomes.

Unions have generally influenced employers to offer a more valuable benefits package to each employee.[84] Through collective bargaining, they have been able to negotiate packages with a broader array of benefits than nonunion workers receive.

In unionized firms the employer pays for most benefits, while in nonunion firms employer and employee share the costs.[85] The result is better health benefits for unionized employees than for their nonunion counterparts. As U.S. health-care costs have soared over the last decade, nonunionized companies have begun asking their employees to pay a greater share of these costs through both higher monthly premiums and higher deductibles. Although unionized employers face the same rising health-care costs, unions have used collective bargaining to persuade many employers to pursue alternative cost-saving methods such as managed health care, second opinions, and audits.[86]

In terms of retirement benefits, unions have been able to provide more security for employees by influencing employers to adopt a defined benefit plan, which provides a fixed amount of income to employees upon retirement. Nonunion employers are more likely to adopt a defined contribution plan, which requires only that the employer set aside a fixed portion of the employee's income each month in a plan that meets the ERISA (Employee Retirement Income Security Act) standards for these plans. Under a defined contribution plan, employees do not know how much total income will be available for their retirement until they actually retire (see Chapter 12).

Unions can play an important role in monitoring and enforcing legally required benefits such as workers' compensation and unemployment insurance.[87] In a unionized firm, employees are more likely to receive workers' compensation and unemployment insurance benefits because union representatives give workers information on how to use them. Furthermore, unionized workers are less likely to be discouraged from filing claims for fear of being penalized or challenged by their employer.[88] In contrast, management in a nonunion firm is not as likely to make employees aware of their right to use these government-mandated benefits because a firm's payroll taxes to fund the benefit increase in proportion to the number of employees using the benefit (see Chapter 12).

Employee Relations

The union is an empowerment mechanism that gives employees a voice in the development of work rules that affect their jobs. The labor contract gives employees specific rights. For example, an employee overlooked for promotion may file a grievance and be reconsidered for the promotion if the contract stipulates that the employee has a right to that promotion.

Nonunion employers tend to document their employees' basic rights in an employee handbook (see Chapter 13). However, employee handbooks provide fewer employee rights than labor contracts do. In fact, many of them contain only general guidelines and specifically state that supervisors may need to make exceptions to the written policy from time to time.

The appeals mechanism that a nonunion employer is most likely to use is the open-door policy.[89] Unlike the grievance procedure, which is administered by both the union and management, the open-door policy is controlled by management. It gives management the opportunity to resolve an employee's complaint while balancing both parties' interests. The only recourse open to employees who are unhappy with the resolution of a complaint under the open-door policy is to find legal counsel and go to court to obtain justice—an option more employees are pursuing every year. Under the union grievance procedure, it is much less likely that an employee will take a case to court because judges are usually unwilling to challenge the results of arbitration.

When an employer is investigating a union employee for the purposes of imposing discipline, the employee has a right to have a union representative present during questioning. The right to have a union representative present during a disciplinary investigation is called a *Weingarten right* based on a 1975 Supreme Court case, *NLRB v. Weingarten,* which established this right from an interpretation of the National Labor Relations Act.[90] The union representative in the investigation is likely to be a union steward who is trained in conflict resolution methods and understands employee rights under the labor contract. In 2000, the National Labor Relations Board ruled that nonunion employees are also entitled to *Weingarten rights,* which permits them to have a coworker present when undergoing an investigatory interview that could lead to a disciplinary action. However, the coworker selected as an employee representative in the nonunion setting is likely to have fewer skills at resolving grievances or defusing conflict than a trained union steward.[91]

Summary and Conclusions

Why Do Employees Join Unions?
U.S. employees generally seek representation from a union because they (1) are dissatisfied with certain aspects of their job, (2) lack influence with management to make the needed changes, and (3) see the union as a solution to their problems.

Labor unions were largely unprotected by law in the United States until 1935. Economic conditions during the Great Depression led Congress to try to equalize the power of employers and employees. After several decades of widespread support, unions are today widely perceived as too powerful.

Managers strongly affect how employees perceive the work environment and thus whether they will be susceptible to unionization. Managers must possess enough knowledge of basic labor law to (1) avoid creating a legal liability for the company, (2) implement the terms of labor agreements fairly and impartially, and (3) hear and resolve employee grievances.

Labor Relations and the Legal Environment
The most important laws governing labor relations in the United States are the Wagner Act (1935), the Taft-Hartley Act (1947), and the Landrum-Griffin Act (1959). The Wagner Act created the National Labor Relations Board, which administers union certification elections and prevents and remedies unfair labor practices.

Labor Relations in the United States
Labor relations in the United States are characterized by (1) business unionism, (2) unions structured by type of job, (3) a focus on collective bargaining, (4) the use of labor contracts, (5) the adversarial nature of labor–management relations and shrinking union membership, and (6) the growth of unions in the public sector.

Labor Relations in Other Countries
The labor relations systems of two key global competitors of the United States, Germany and Japan, have achieved a greater degree of cooperation between unions and management than the U.S. system has. The German system uses works councils and codetermination to involve workers in decisions at all levels of the organization. In Japan, enterprise unions have worked closely with companies for the mutual benefit of both parties. Some believe that economic pressures are straining labor–management relations in these countries today.

Labor Relations Strategy
A labor relations strategy is a company's overall plan for dealing with unions. Companies that choose a union-acceptance strategy view unions as their employees' legitimate representatives and accept collective bargaining as an appropriate mechanism for establishing workplace rules. Companies that choose a union-avoidance strategy use either union substitution or union suppression to keep unions out of the workplace.

Managing the Labor Relations Process
The labor relations process has three phases: (1) union organizing, (2) collective bargaining, and (3) contract administration. In the union organizing phase, management must confront the issues involved with union solicitation, pre-election conduct, and the certification election. In the collective bargaining phase, union and management representatives negotiate workplace rules that are formalized in a labor contract. The contract administration phase starts after the labor contract is settled and deals with day-to-day administration of the workplace. A key feature of the contract administration phase is the grievance procedure, a step-by-step process for settling employee disputes about contract interpretations or disciplinary actions.

The Impact of Unions on Human Resource Management
The impact of a union on the way a company manages its human resources is significant. Management can expect that

the union will affect virtually every major area of HRM. In a unionized workplace, staffing decisions will be heavily influenced by seniority rather than by merit. Individually focused performance appraisals are severely curtailed, while training programs are emphasized. Unionized employees tend to receive larger compensation and benefit packages. Finally, employee relations processes in a union shop are by definition highly structured.

Key Terms

arbitration, 497
business unionism, 477
codetermination, 482
collective bargaining, 478
cost-of-living adjustment (COLA), 500
distributive bargaining, 492
economic strike, 496
enterprise union, 482
grievance procedure, 496
integrative bargaining, 492
labor contract, 478
labor relations specialist, 474

labor relations strategy, 483
Landrum-Griffin Act (1959), 476
lockout, 496
National Labor Relations Board (NLRB), 475
Railway Labor Act, 477
right-to-work law, 476
seniority, 499
Taft-Hartley Act (1947), 476
union, 473
union acceptance strategy, 483
union avoidance strategy, 485

union shop clause, 476
union steward, 496
union substitution/proactive human resource management, 485
union suppression, 485
Wagner Act/National Labor Relations Act (1935), 475
wildcat strike, 496
works councils, 482
work rules, 478

Discussion Questions

1. Why have labor and management tended to treat each other as adversaries in the U.S. labor relations system?

2. Suppose a goal of management is to reduce the number of grievances filed by union employees each year. What are some ways that the HRM staff can contribute to this goal?

3. How can management's collective bargaining tactics be influenced by the company's labor relations strategy? Provide examples.

4. What are some advantages and disadvantages of a strike from management's perspective? From the union's perspective?

5. What, in your opinion, is the most significant impact of a union on the management of human resources? Explain.

6. It is often said that "good pay and good management" are the keys to successful union avoidance. Spell out the kind of policies and practices companies should develop if they want to keep their workers from unionizing. Do you think the employee relations practices you've

mentioned are less costly or more costly than working with unionized labor?

7. The Teamsters strike with UPS in 1997 (see opening vignette) has been considered by labor relations experts to be one of the most important strikes in the United States in recent times. Do you agree or disagree with this assessment? What do you think were the issues that made this conflict between labor and management at UPS so noteworthy?

8. Some experts in the field of labor relations believe that when a union can pose a credible threat of a strike to management in the collective bargaining process, both parties—union and management—are motivated to move in the direction of a settlement and reach a labor agreement. They also claim that without a credible strike threat, the two parties are less likely to arrive at a joint agreement. What is the basis for this justification for giving the union the privilege of exercising its right to strike? Do you agree or disagree with this argument? Explain your reasoning.

There is a variety of additional material available on the Web site that accompanies this text. You can access this information by visiting the Web site at **www.prenhall.com/gomez**.

Ethics Case 15.1   YOU MANAGE IT!

Courts Affirm Nonunion Employee Rights Under Federal Labor Law

The federal labor laws were designed to protect the rights of employees to form unions, but they also apply to nonunion employees. In 2001, Loretta Williams, an insurance adjuster for the United Services Automobile Association (USAA), distributed 1,300 fliers in the workplace expressing dissatisfaction with a company reorganization that had resulted in layoffs of long-term employees. USAA advised managers that distribution of the materials violated company policy, and employees later were told that the fliers would be collected because of the company's no-distribution policy.

When Williams was questioned by a USAA human resources official, she denied that she had prepared or distributed the fliers during work hours and stated that she had not claimed any overtime hours for her activities. She was fired on the grounds that she lied about these activities.

The National Labor Relations Board concluded that the USAA management had violated federal labor law by coercively interrogating Williams and terminating her. It also ruled that the company's no-distribution policy was impermissibly broad and ordered the company to rescind that policy.

Upon appeal, the U.S. Court of Appeals for the District of Columbia Circuit upheld the decision. It explained that the company's questioning of Williams was illegal because its purpose was to find out who else was involved in preparing and distributing the fliers. Moreover, her alleged "dishonesty about her protected concerted activity did not constitute a lawful reason to discharge her." Also, the USAA's overly broad no-distribution policy was deemed to be invalid.

This case should remind employers that union and nonunion employee actions regarding wages and employment issues may be considered a "concerted activity" protected by federal labor law.

Critical Thinking Questions

1. On what basis did the courts overturn the company's no-distribution policy? Do you agree with the decision? Explain your reasoning.

2. What labor law protects the "concerted activity" of employees? Is it the Wagner, Taft-Hartley, or Landrum-Griffin Act?

Team Exercise

With four or five students develop a no-distribution policy that does not violate the rights of employees in the workplace. Why do companies such as USAA need a no-distribution policy? What factors should management take into consideration when implementing a no-distribution policy? What role should HR staff play in putting this policy into practice? Be prepared to share the answers to these questions with other members of your class.

Experiential Exercise

For a no-distribution policy to be upheld if challenged in court, managers must be consistent in how literature and other persuasive information is distributed within the company. This means that distribution of fliers that seek to inform employees about such activities as politics, charitable giving, religious events, Girl Scouts, and other non-work-related activities are prohibited while employees are working. Such restrictions can also prohibit the wearing of pins that tell people how to vote for a candidate or issue, the wearing of sweatshirts or T-shirts that have messages or codes, and the distribution of gifts such as pens or keychains with printed messages. If you became aware of the existence of a no-distribution policy at a company prior to seeking a job there, would such a policy affect your interest in the position? What assumptions would you make about how management treats its employees after learning about the existence of a no-distribution policy? Be prepared to share your thoughts with other members of the class.

Source: Hatch, D. (2005, March). Nonunion employee rights upheld. *Workforce Management,* 16.

Emerging Trends Case 15.2   YOU MANAGE IT!

High-Technology Employees Still Do Not March to the Union Beat—Yet!

As the labor movement sets its sights on the booming high-technology world, employees like Matt Shea, a 24-year-old

software developer, seem ripe for the picking. He often clocks 70-hour weeks, his managers sometimes push him to work past midnight, and he never receives overtime pay. But ask Matt whether he wants a union at his workplace, a thriving

Internet start-up called Go2Net, and his response is a puzzled expression that says: "Does not compute."

"As far as me personally, and for everyone else here, unions have never come up," said Shea, who says he loves his job, notwithstanding the sweatshop hours. "Everything I want is offered to me here."

The American labor movement has belatedly recognized that if it is to reverse the decades-long slide in the percentage of workers belonging to unions, it must make some headway in high technology, the economy's fastest-growing sector. To increase its numbers and its influence in politics and at the bargaining table, unions cannot afford to be shut out of the glamorous and powerful high-technology industry, which accounts for an ever-larger share of the workforce. Persuading technology workers to join unions will not be easy, though, because of all that is lavished on people like Mr. Shea. His job gives him valuable stock options, flexible hours, an excellent medical plan, a sense of family and, perhaps most important, the thrill of building something.

Labor leaders acknowledge that they face an uphill battle— only a small fraction of the nation's 2 million computer and software developers, programmers, and engineers belongs to labor unions. But organizers are far from packing their bags in Silicon Valley, convinced that many high-technology employees will eventually warm to labor's message that workers need a collective voice to stand up to management.

Although there are many contented high-tech workers such as Mr. Shea, there are also many discontented have-nots. Most have-nots come from the sea of long-term temporary employees who work at Microsoft and other high-tech companies. They often complain of being second-class citizens who receive bare-bones benefits and have no job security or stock options. Microsoft employs 20,500 regular workers domestically and 6,000 temps, who call themselves perma-temps because they work anywhere from six months to three years at the company, testing software, writing manuals, designing Web pages, and developing CD-ROMs. Industry experts estimate that at many companies, including Compaq Computer, Hewlett-Packard, and Intel, more than 10 percent of the workers are temps.

Critical Thinking Questions

1. Why do you think it is difficult to organize high-technology employees into unions?

2. Suppose you were trying to organize a union at a high-tech company such as Microsoft, which has a large group of disgruntled temporary employees who do not share in the success of the company with the full-time workers. How would you try to organize these employees into a union? What difficulties should you be prepared to overcome?

3. What possible threats do you think a union would pose for the management of a high-tech firm such as Microsoft?

Team Exercise

With a group of four or five students, assume that you have been hired as consultants to assist a union that wants to market its services to a group of high-technology employees in a large technology company similar to Microsoft or IBM. Work together to develop a list of five or six "selling points" that you could use to convince this group of high-technology employees that they could greatly benefit from union representation in their company. What objections might these employees have to one or more of your selling points? Be prepared to post your list of selling points on the blackboard or on an overhead transparency and be ready to explain your points to other members of the class.

Experiential Exercise

Assume that a union is attempting to organize the company where you currently work. What types of services can a union provide that would convince you to vote for the union? Are these services that unions traditionally provide to the membership as described in this chapter? How much would you be willing to pay in union dues on a monthly basis to cover the cost of these services? (Unions need to collect dues from the membership in order to pay for the costs of the member services.) Be prepared to share your answers to these questions with other class members.

Source: Adapted from Greenhouse, S. (1999, July 26). Unions need not apply: High-technology sector still unmoved by labor's song. *New York Times,* C-1, C-14.

YOU MANAGE IT!

Customer-Driven HR Case 15.3

When Is a Team a Union?

Amalgamated Tool, a nonunion manufacturer of auto parts in Michigan, suffered such significant financial losses in 2006 that it froze the pay of all its employees to conserve cash. The company also asked its employees to pay a larger share of their health insurance costs. The employees were extremely

upset by these actions, and both morale and productivity declined.

To improve morale, Amalgamated's management decided to form several problem-solving employee teams. After meeting to discuss the problems at Amalgamated, the teams presented management with suggestions on how to provide pay raises and health insurance to employees fairly and efficiently.

Each problem-solving team had a leader elected by the other team members to present the team's suggestions, but only about 20 percent of Amalgamated's employees were asked to serve on a team. The teams' suggestions were largely adopted by management, and morale and efficiency went up the next year.

On behalf of some dissatisfied Amalgamated employees, a local union filed an unfair labor practice claim stating that management had illegally used the problem-solving teams to form a management-dominated union, in violation of a provision of the Wagner Act that states: "It is an unfair labor practice for an employer to dominate or interfere with the formation of any labor organization or contribute financial support to it."

The National Labor Relations Board sustained the union's position and ordered Amalgamated to cease and desist using its problem-solving teams.

Critical Thinking Questions

1. Why did the local union object to the way Amalgamated's management used problem-solving teams?
2. What is the difference between a team and a union?
3. To avoid the NLRB's cease-and-desist order, what should Amalgamated's management have done differently in using problem-solving teams?

Team Exercise

Students form into groups of four to six members and role-play National Labor Relations Board members. Each group discusses whether Amalgamated violated the Wagner Act's prohibition of a company "dominating a union or providing financial support to it." Compare conclusions and arguments across groups.

Experiential Exercise

In the United States, company-dominated unions, called *company unions*, are prohibited under federal labor law. Until the 1930s, companies organized these unions to let employees experience belonging to a union, with the expectation that the employees would then not have a need for an independent union to represent them and make demands that management did not want to fulfill. As indicated in this chapter, company unions are the major form of union representation within Japan, and they function effectively within the context of the Japanese economic system. Do you think a company union could represent your interests to management in the same way an independent union could? Would it make sense for employees to have a choice between a company union and an independent union? Be prepared to share your answers to these questions with the class.

Ethics Case 15.4   YOU MANAGE IT!

Recognizing and Avoiding Unfair Labor Practices

Managers who supervise employees need to be able to recognize situations that could be considered to be an unfair labor practice and avoid them. If an alleged unfair labor practice is committed, the Department of Labor may order an investigation to determine if a penalty or other sanction is warranted. The purpose of this exercise is to develop skills for recognizing and avoiding unfair labor practices and finding ways to manage the workplace without violating government labor policy. Before starting this exercise, review the five unfair management labor practices listed under the Wagner Act that we discussed in this chapter. Now read the next three scenarios and answer the questions that follow.

Scenario 1

You are finishing up some paperwork at the end of a hard day. As the HR manager, you have been involved in the company's negotiations with the union regarding the truck drivers' new contract with your firm. The negotiations have not been going well, and all indications are that a strike will be called in a matter of days. As you are preparing to leave your office, three long-time truck drivers ask to have a word with you in private. They inform you that they are not happy with their union and

that a number of the other drivers feel the same way. They ask you to help them "get rid of the union." Should you act on this request?

Scenario 2

You are the store manager for a regional supermarket chain. Your store is nonunion. When a local union attempts to organize your employees, you receive orders from headquarters to discharge the employees from your store who have signed union authorization cards. Your regional manager also orders you to prepare termination slips for each of the fired employees detailing false reasons for their termination. How should you proceed?

Scenario 3

The negotiations between your company and the union representing the 110 production workers in your firm have reached a dead end. Union members have already voted to go on strike. At a meeting of the key managers involved in running the company, the production manager suggests using the remaining clerical, accounting, and managerial staff as replacements to keep the plant running. She also suggests contacting a temporary employment agency to help fill any remaining critical positions while the union members are on strike. As the HR manager, how would you respond to this suggestion?

Critical Thinking Questions

1. For each of the three scenarios, determine whether you think an unfair labor practice would be committed if you as a manager act on the request that is being given to you by management or employees. Which unfair labor practice(s) could be violated? In some situations, more than one unfair labor practice could occur.

2. Place yourself in the position of the manager in each of the scenarios and respond to each of the requests. If you decide to reject or accept the request, indicate the reason for your decision. Then develop a suggested plan of action that will deal with the issue that has been brought to your attention.

Team Exercise

With a group of four or five students, discuss and compare each of your responses to the three scenarios in the previous questions. Try to arrive at a consensus on how to handle these three cases. Then develop a policy or procedure to guide other managers for each case so that the company has a consistent approach to dealing with the union if these circumstances ever arise in the future.

Experiential Exercise

You have just been redeployed away from your job as an accountant to work in the loading dock area where you are expected to load and unload heavy packages onto and off of trucks, a job that used to be done by unionized employees who are out on strike. As you drive to work each morning, you must drive by picketing employees who are protesting their dispute with management. You recognize some of these striking workers whom you consider to be your friends. What will you be thinking as you drive by the picketing employees? How will you feel about doing their jobs while they are on strike and earning no income for their families? What will it be like when the strike is settled and you encounter these employees back at work in the company cafeteria? If the strike lasts a long time—some strikes can last for several months—do you think it will be difficult to catch up on your job as accountant after having been away from your job so long? How would you feel if your boss asks you to do your accounting job at night on an overtime basis after putting in a full eight-hour shift working at the loading dock? Be prepared to share your answers to these questions with the class.

Source: Adapted from Nkomo, S. M., Fottler, M. D., and McAfee, R. B. (2000). *Applications in human resource management* (4th ed.), 278–279. Cincinnati, OH: South-Western.

Managing Workplace Safety and Health

Challenges

16

After reading this chapter, you should be able to deal more effectively with the following challenges:

1 **Describe** the extent of the employer's responsibility to maintain a safe and healthy work environment.

2 **Explain** the reasons for safety and health laws and the costs and obligations they impose on employers.

3 **Identify** the basic provisions of workers' compensation laws and the Occupational Safety and Health Act.

4 **Develop** an awareness of contemporary health and safety issues, including AIDS, workplace violence, smoking in the workplace, cumulative trauma disorders, fetal protection, hazardous chemicals, and genetic testing.

5 **Describe** the features of safety programs and understand the reasons for and the effects of programs designed to enhance employee well-being.

On May 11, 1996, ValuJet Flight 592 crashed into the Everglades about 10 minutes after takeoff from Miami, Florida. The flight had erupted into a raging fire, and the flaming nose-dive crash took the lives of all 110 people aboard. Although the crash occurred years ago, its effects are still unfolding.

National Transportation Safety Board investigators concluded that the tragedy was the result of supervisory failures "all up and down the line, from federal regulators to airline executives in the board room to workers on the shop room floor."[1] The board found that the probable immediate or direct cause of the accident was hazardous oxygen containers that employees of SabreTech (a contractor for ValuJet) placed in the flight's cargo hold. However, safety board investigators found

34 violations by the airline, including delayed maintenance and failure to report jammed landing gear.[2] It also found that ValuJet knew of some problems for months but had not taken corrective action.

Some outcomes of the wake of the crash included:

- Replacement of the top leaders of the Federal Aviation Authority and the Department of Transportation
- The addition of hundreds of inspectors to the Federal Aviation authority
- ValuJet's struggle to rebuild its business (newly named American TransAir), which floundered after the crash

In July 1999, the state of Florida brought charges of 110 counts of third-degree murder against SabreTech, and a federal grand jury also indicted the company, two of its mechanics, and a maintenance director on charges of conspiring to cover up problems that led to the accident. More specifically, the federal grand jury charged that the maintenance director at SabreTech pressured employees to skip prescribed work steps and falsely sign paperwork to confirm the work had been done. The grand jury also charged SabreTech with failing to train personnel in proper handling of the hazardous oxygen canisters.[3]

Leading up to these charges, the safety board concluded that someone at SabreTech had loaded more than 100 armed oxygen generators into the cargo hold of Flight 592. Furthermore, these canisters had been mislabeled "empty" and did not have attached protective caps that could have prevented accidental discharge and a 500° chemical reaction.

Murder indictments against a company are rare in the United States, and this marked the first time in U.S. history that criminal charges were filed in the case of an airline crash. Although the jury acquitted the SabreTech employees, it found the company guilty of nine hazardous materials violations, including the failure to train its workers properly.[4]

THE MANAGERIAL PERSPECTIVE

The crash of ValuJet Flight 592 and its aftermath dramatically illustrate the devastating consequences of paying insufficient attention to safety concerns and social responsibility. Ensuring a safe working environment is legally mandated. More important, it is an obligation for any socially responsible manager. Safety and health must be a priority in all that you do.

An organizational culture that places a greater value on speed or saving money than on safety can result in workplace accidents—some that involve the loss of human life. To disregard safety and health issues can cause more than legal difficulty for an organization. It can sever the trust between workers and management, irretrievably damage employee commitment and performance, and ruin an organization's reputation. Managers, then, must understand safety and health issues and take steps to maintain a safe work environment with the help of HR staff.

In this chapter, we consider the contemporary context of the safety and health issue and how managers build and develop safe and healthy working conditions. First, we deal with the legal issues of workplace safety and health by exploring management's legal obligations to fund a workers' compensation system and to provide a safe and healthy workplace. Next we examine a variety of contemporary safety and health issues, including AIDS, violence in the workplace, cumulative trauma disorders, fetal protection, dangerous chemicals, and the use of genetic testing on employees. Finally, we describe and evaluate programs designed to maintain employee safety and health.

Workplace Safety and the Law

The most recent data from the Bureau of Labor statistics indicate that in 2003 more than 4.3 million people were injured on the job and 5,559 were killed.[5] Currently, the national average per 100 workers is 2.6 workplace injuries or illnesses that are serious enough to result in lost workdays.[6] The cost of occupational accidents was estimated to total $49.6 billion in 2002.[7]

All levels of government have passed numerous laws to regulate workplace safety. Many of these laws include detailed regulations dealing with work hazards in specific industries such as coal mining and railroads. However, two basic sets of workplace safety laws affect most workers: the various workers' compensation laws at the state level and the Occupational Safety and Health Act of 1970 (OSHA) at the federal level. The objectives, policies, and operations of these two sets of laws are very different.

Each state has its own workers' compensation law, so the provisions for funding and enforcing the law differ by state. As we discussed in Chapter 12, the main goal of the workers' compensation system is to provide compensation to workers who suffer job-related injuries or illnesses. Workers' compensation laws have no safety regulations or mandates, but they do require employers to pay for workers' compensation insurance. Because insurance costs are higher for employers with more workplace accidents and injuries, employers have a financial incentive to create and maintain a safe work environment.

In contrast, OSHA is a federal law designed to make the workplace safer by ensuring that the work environment is free from hazards. The act mandates numerous safety standards and enforces these standards through a system of inspections, citations, and fines. Unlike the workers' compensation laws, however, OSHA does not provide for the compensation of accident victims.[8]

Workers' Compensation

In the early 1800s, people injured on the job went without medical care unless they could afford to pay for it themselves and rarely received any income until they could return to work. Employees who sued their employers for negligence had little hope of winning, because under U.S. common law the courts habitually ruled that employees assumed the usual risks of a job in return for their pay. In addition, under the *doctrine of contributory negligence* employers were not liable for an employee's injuries when that employee's own negligence contributed to or caused the injury. And under the *fellow-servant rule,* employers were not responsible for an employee's injury when the negligence of another employee contributed to or caused the injury.

In the early years of the twentieth century—after a host of workplace disasters, including a 1911 fire in a New York shirt factory that killed more than 100 women—public opinion pressured several state legislatures to enact *workers' compensation* laws. The workers' compensation concept is based on the theory that work-related accidents and illnesses are costs of doing business that the employer should pay for and pass on to the consumer.[9] Since 1948, all states have had workers' compensation programs, although workers' compensation is mandatory in only 47 states. These state-administered and employer-funded programs are designed to provide financial and medical assistance to employees injured on the job.

The stated goals of the workers' compensation laws are:[10]

■ Providing prompt, sure, and reasonable medical care to victims and income to both victims and their dependents.
■ Providing a "no-fault" system in which injured workers can get quick relief without undertaking expensive litigation and suffering court delays.
■ Encouraging employers to invest in safety.
■ Promoting research on workplace safety.

To be eligible for an award from the workers' compensation system, an employee's injury must have occurred in the course of his or her employment. Sometimes serious accidents, even death, can occur in the workplace, but the accident may not be directly due to the performance of the job. Is the employer still liable for this unfortunate outcome? In many of today's workplaces, job descriptions are more ambiguous and broader than ever before. What is really inside or outside someone's job responsibilities is often not clear. This breadth and ambiguity can encourage flexibility and broad commitment in the workplace, but it may also have the unintended consequence of increasing an employer's exposure to liability for accidents that may occur. The Manager's Notebook, "Greater Ambiguity—Increased Liability," provides an example of an unfortunate death that occurred at work. The example illustrates the importance of defining job duties to limit liability for accidental injury or death.

The Benefits of Workers' Compensation

Workers' compensation benefits compensate employees for injuries or illnesses occurring on the job. These benefits are:[11]

- **Total disability benefits.** Partial replacement of income lost as the result of a work-related total disability.
- **Impairment benefits.** Benefits for temporary or permanent partial disability, based on the degree and duration of the impairment. Injuries are classified as scheduled or nonscheduled. Scheduled injuries are those in which a body part (such as an eye or a finger) is lost; there is a specific schedule of payments for these injuries. Unscheduled injuries are all other injuries (such as back injuries); these are dealt with on a case-by-case basis.
- **Survivor benefits.** In cases of work-related deaths, the worker's survivors receive a burial allowance and income benefits.
- **Medical expense benefits.** Workers' compensation provides medical coverage, normally without dollar or time limitations.
- **Rehabilitation benefits.** All states provide medical rehabilitation for injured workers, and many states provide vocational training for employees who can no longer work at their previous occupation as the result of a job-related injury or illness.

MANAGER'S NOTEBOOK

Emerging Trends

Greater Ambiguity—Increased Liability

Keith Marshall was a lifeguard at an aquatic center. His job duties included performing general pool maintenance and supervising swimmers. Keith told his boss that he was trying to increase the distance he could swim under water. A few weeks later, Keith was found dead—he had drowned in the swimming pool. There were no witnesses, and the autopsy concluded that the cause of death was drowning. Keith's mother sought workers' compensation benefits on behalf of Keith's child. A critical question in this unfortunate case is whether Keith Marshall died during his employment. If so, his child would be entitled to a workers' compensation award. A Virginia court concluded that the death occurred while at work and this decision was upheld by an appeals court.

We will never know exactly what led to Keith's death, but his statement about working on underwater endurance may be the best clue we have to go on. Although we can't be sure in this case, accidental drowning, particularly of an experienced swimmer working on increasing underwater distance, is most likely due to a phenomenon called shallow water blackout. This phenomenon can overcome victims without their ever realizing they are drowning. Shallow water blackout is most often associated with free diving, but it has also claimed victims in swimming pools.

Was underwater swimming endurance part of Keith's job? It certainly could be argued to at least be relevant to performance of the job of lifeguard. Even more pertinent to the question of workers' compensation benefits is that Keith's boss knew of the endurance training and didn't disallow it. His boss did not specify to Keith that his job was to be a lifeguard, not to be an underwater swimming champion. He did not tell Keith that the pool was not to be used for his personal goals. Key to the court's awarding the compensation benefits was that the employer had knowledge of the endurance training (what would be conjectured to be the probable cause of the drowning) and didn't prohibit it.

Here are the lessons to be learned from this story.

First, given that part of your goal as manager is to limit liability and workers' compensation insurance costs, you need to clearly and immediately tell employees to stop if you encounter them engaging in risky behavior outside of their normal job duties.

Second, courts rely on job descriptions to help make determinations of what is within the scope of employees' job duties. Ambiguity in these descriptions can lead to costly legal battles. Prohibited employee activities could be added to these job descriptions and posted in the workplace, resulting in decreased ambiguity and liability. Of course, you risk being labeled a spoilsport or worse. However, it's your choice as to whether you manage rationally and safely and risk being called spoilsport or risk liability for accidental injuries and possibly death.

And, third, on a personal note, if you or anyone you know swims, learn about shallow water blackout. It is a little-known phenomenon, but information about it is readily available on the Internet. One of us (Bob Cardy) has a daughter (Lara) who had an episode of shallow water blackout while doing underwater endurance during a synchronized swimming practice. Luckily, it looks like Lara is going to be fine, but the phenomenon has claimed many lives. As the saying goes, knowledge is power. Learn about this risk and protect yourself and others.

Source: Marshall, A. (2002). Some employee "heroics" need to be saved for off the job. *Hotel & Motel Management, 27,* 10.

The Costs of Workers' Compensation

The cost to employers of workers' compensation insurance is directly affected by accidents with premiums that can increase dramatically and stay high for years as a result of a single injury.[12] Workers' compensation insurance is based on payroll, but premiums paid are modified by an organization's safety record. Unfortunately, fraudulent claims occur, and the crime drives up the costs of workers' compensation.[13] To keep workers' compensation rates under control, companies are becoming more aware of fraud and many are contesting claims they believe to be fraudulent (see the Manager's Notebook, "Managing Fraud in Workers' Compensation Claims"). Some states have law enforcement units that focus on helping to combat workers' compensation fraud, but they operate with limited staff and budget.[14]

In another attempt to control and reduce workers' compensation costs, some employers are using on-site occupational health centers that provide immediate evaluation and treatment of injured workers. These on-site centers offer faster treatment of occupational injuries and can produce cost savings for employers.[15]

Other attempts to control costs focus on the causes of injuries and on their treatment. For example, overexertion is a top cause of workplace injuries.[16] Common examples of overexertion include heavy lifting, pushing, or pulling. Given the prevalence of overexertion injuries, and thus of worker compensation claims, it makes business sense to address issues, such as correct lifting techniques, that may reduce injury rates and costs. Overexertion is a common cause of injury across companies and industries, but the top causes of injury differ across companies. To effectively manage and control injuries and their costs, managers need to know the causes of injuries at their company and then address them.

Infrequent types of injuries can sometimes be more important than common ones. For example, repetitive motion injuries (such as carpal tunnel syndrome) can result in expensive and lengthy absences from work.[17] Thus, it is important for a manager to consider both frequency as well as costs when determining where to focus attention and resources.

In terms of treatment, the Hartford Financial Services Group has reported that 67 percent of increased workers' compensation costs can be attributed to the use of more costly drugs. For example, pain medications for back, knee, and shoulder problems are common for workers' compensation patients, but there has been a shift toward use of more costly medications for these problems. The use of, for instance, a time-release version of a medication may cost $3.00 per dose while a traditional pain-relieving medication may cost $1.50 per dose.[18] The Hartford analysis found that higher-priced drugs were often prescribed for conditions that could be treated with lower-priced drugs. Hartford recommends managing workers' compensation costs by providing information to workers and physicians about alternative medications and recommending generic drug substitutions whenever possible.

The Occupational Safety and Health Act (OSHA)

Changing political and social values during the 1960s added considerable momentum to the movement to regulate workplace safety. In 1969, the death of 78 coal miners in a mine explosion galvanized public opinion and led to the passage of the Coal Mine Health and Safety Act to regulate mine health and safety.[19] While no single event is responsible for the passage of the **Occupational Safety and Health Act of 1970 (OSHA)**, the dramatic increase in reported injury rates and workplace deaths during the 1960s (reflecting the inability of workers' compensation laws to give employers adequate incentives to maintain a safe work environment) was probably the major impetus.[20] During the latter part of that decade, the federal government reported that job-related accidents killed more than 14,000 workers and disabled nearly 2.5 million workers annually. In addition, an estimated 300,000 new cases of occupational diseases were being reported every year. OSHA was passed to address the staggering economic and human costs of workplace accidents and health hazards.[21]

OSHA's Provisions

OSHA is fairly straightforward. It imposes three major obligations on employers:

■ **To provide a safe and healthy work environment.** Each employer has a general duty to provide a place of employment free from recognized hazards that are likely to cause death or serious physical harm. This *general duty provision* recognizes that not all workplace hazards can be covered by a set of specific standards. The employer is obligated to identify and deal with safety and health hazards not covered by specific regulations.[22]

■ **To comply with specific occupational safety and health standards.** Each employer must become familiar with and comply with specific occupational standards (OSHA's rules deal with specific occupations rather than with industries), and must make certain that employees comply as well.

■ **To keep records of occupational injuries and illnesses.** Under OSHA, employers must record and report work-related accidents and injuries. Organizations with eight or more employees must keep records of any occupational injury or illness resulting in death, lost work time, or medical treatment and retain these records for five years. The injuries and illnesses must be recorded on OSHA forms and posted annually on an employee bulletin board for all to see. The records must also be made available to OSHA compliance officers, and annual summaries must be prepared.[23] Because record-keeping requirements have been unclear on some points, OSHA issued revised record-keeping standards that are meant to be more flexible and easier to follow.[24] You can view current online materials by visiting OSHA's Web site at *www.osha.gov*. You will also find there a Spanish version of the Web site, designed for Spanish-speaking employers and employees. The information in Spanish is meant to overcome the language barrier and inform the OSHA-estimated 10 million Spanish-speaking U.S. employers and employees of their safety rights, responsibilities, and resources.

MANAGER'S NOTEBOOK

Emerging Trends

Managing Fraud in Workers' Compensation Claims

Fraudulent workers' compensation claims add to the costs of doing business and need to be controlled. Here are suggestions for reducing abuse of the workers' compensation system and indicators for spotting potential fraud.

Managing to Limit Abuse of the Workers' Compensation System

■ *Make the work environment as safe and risk free as possible.* Job-specific safety training can reduce on-the-job injuries and help to develop a culture of safety in the organization.

Occupational Safety and Health Act of 1970 (OSHA)
A federal law that requires employers to provide a safe and healthy work environment, comply with specific occupational safety and health standards, and keep records of occupational injuries and illnesses.

- *Institute postoffer screening for job-related physical capacity.* For jobs that require physical work, consider screening applicants for job-related physical capacity. A screening program must comply with the Americans with Disabilities Act; the screening should be given only after an offer of employment has been made and it should be based on a job analysis. A preemployment screening can lower accident rates by ensuring that each worker has the capacity to perform the tasks. Furthermore, the screening can provide a baseline measure that could help guide rehabilitation efforts if an accident did occur.
- *Educate employees about the workers' compensation system.* False injury claims can be lessened when workers understand the workers' compensation system, why it exists, and how it works. Most important, false claims can be reduced when workers realize that, following a claim, their ability to perform the functions of the job will be objectively examined.
- *Offer temporary modified duty.* The goal is to get injured employees back to work as soon as they are medically able. However, the longer an employee is away from work, the greater the chances are that he or she will never return to work. An early-return-to-work program can ease workers back into the workplace by temporarily modifying their job functions to a nature and level that the employees are capable of performing. Modifying tasks to provide for an early return to work can result in a reduction in lost workdays and an increase in productivity in the organization.

Indicators of Potential Fraud

- Vague accident details
- No witnesses
- Minor accident but a major injury
- Extended length of time between occurrence of an accident and filing of a report
- Documentation by treating physician that doesn't support the type of injury claimed by the employee
- A pattern of "doctor hopping" in which an employee frequently changes physicians, perhaps looking for a health-care provider who is sympathetic to his or her claims
- A history of discipline or job dissatisfaction. Filing a workers' compensation claim can be a means for a worker to balance the scales of workplace justice

Source: Adapted from Sanna, M. (2002). Sick and wrong: An expert offers advice about how to spot fraudulent injuries and maintain a healthy bottom line. *Walls & Ceilings,* 65(3); *Payroll Manager's Report.* (2002). Beware: Down markets breed false workers' compensation claims. January Newsletter of the Institute of Management and Administration, 7–8.

Under the new standard, failure to keep either written or electronic records can result in fines and citations. For example, OSHA recently fined Weyerhaueser $77,000 for failing to record 38 injuries and illnesses at its Buchhanon, West Virginia, plant and General Motors $148,000 for willful record-keeping violations, such as failing to record work-related hearing losses, at its Massena, New York, plant.[25] Falsifying records can result in a fine and a six-month prison sentence. The revised standard also makes it clear that an accident that *could* have caused injury—not just one that *did* cause injury—should be recorded. In other words, close calls count under the OSHA standard.

In addition, the standard clarifies who is an employee under OSHA. For example, a temporary worker from an employment agency doing clerical work for an organization is considered an employee of that organization. However, an independent contractor is an employee only if the business hires and supervises the person. Thus, the Perfect Lawn landscaping crew is not likely to be considered a law firm's employees, but a software specialist the firm hires from an employment agency probably is. This distinction is important because an employer is responsible for keeping records on its employees.

Employees also have responsibilities under OSHA. Although they cannot be cited for violations, they must comply with the relevant safety and health standards. They should also report all hazardous conditions, injuries, or work-related illnesses to their employer. Employee rights under OSHA include the right to file safety or health grievances and complaints to the government, participate in OSHA inspections, and request information on safety and health hazards without fear of discrimination or retaliation by their employer.[26]

Under both OSHA and state *right-to-know regulations,* employers must provide employees with information about hazardous substances in the workplace.[27] OSHA's hazardous substance regulation, known as the *Hazard Communication Standard,* is explained in the pamphlet excerpt reproduced in Figure 16.1. OSHA has developed a Haz Com initiative to help employers and employees comply with the Hazard Communication Standard. You can see this initiative at *www.osha.gov/SLTC/hazardcommuications/index.html.* In addition, the U.S. Supreme Court has upheld an employee's right to refuse to work under conditions where the employee reasonably believes there is an immediate risk of injury or death.[28] If the hazard is of a chemical nature, another federal agency may also be relevant. The Chemical Safety and Hazard Investigation Board, funded by Congress in 1997, is charged with promoting safety and preventing incidents of chemical release.[29] The board works closely with OSHA and the Environmental Protection Agency. A hazard in the form of a chemical spill would result in an accident investigation by the Board. The focus of the board is to then make recommendations to companies and government agencies regarding changes in process or equipment that would prevent similar accidents.

Three agencies administer and enforce OSHA: the *Occupational Safety and Health Administration* (the OSH Administration, also known by the acronym *OSHA*), the *Occupational Safety and Health Review Commission (OSHRC),* and the *National Institute for Occupational Safety and Health (NIOSH).* States with federally approved safety plans have their own regulatory apparatus.

OSHA's Hazard Communication Standard

This excerpt from the OSHA Web site explains that employers must tell their employees how OSHA's hazardous communication standard is being put into effect in their workplace.

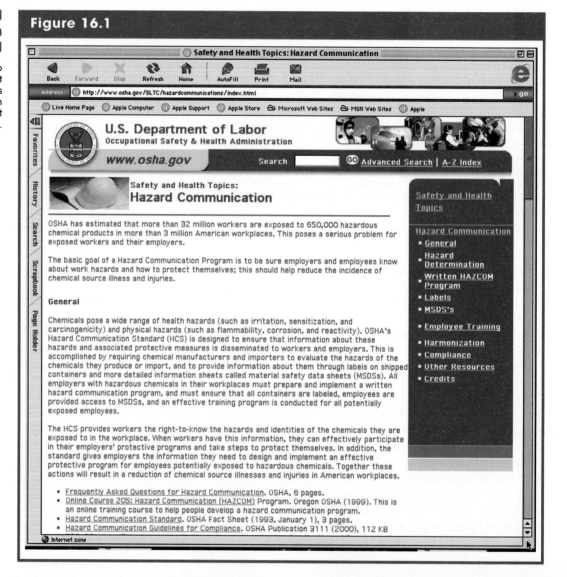

Figure 16.1

The Occupational Safety and Health Administration

The Occupational Safety and Health Administration has the primary responsibility for enforcing OSHA. It develops occupational standards, grants variances to employers, conducts workplace inspections, and issues citations and penalties.

■ **Occupational standards.** Occupational standards, which cover hazards ranging from tools and machinery safety to microscopic airborne matter, can be exceedingly complex and detailed. Although many standards are clearly reasonable and appropriate, OSHA has frequently been criticized for adopting infeasible standards or standards whose costs exceed their benefits. The courts, however, generally do not require OSHA to balance the costs and benefits of particular standards, only to demonstrate their feasibility.[30]

The development of occupational standards can begin with OSHA, NIOSH, state and local governments, or a variety of other sources, including industry groups and labor organizations. Proposed new standards are published in the *Federal Register,* the official legal news publication of the U.S. government. Comments from interested parties are sought, and hearings regarding the standards may be held. The full text of any adopted standard and the implementation date are then reported in the *Federal Register.*[31]

■ **Variances.** Employers may ask OSHA for a temporary (up to one year) variance from a standard when they cannot comply with a new standard by its effective date. The OSH Administration may grant a permanent variance from a particular standard when an employer can demonstrate that it has in place alternatives that protect employees as effectively as compliance with the standard would.[32]

■ **Workplace inspections.** OSHA has the power to conduct workplace inspections to make sure that organizations are complying with OSHA standards. Because it would be impossible to inspect each of the hundreds of thousands of affected workplaces each year, OSHA has established an inspection priority system that calls for inspections to be made in the following order:[33] (1) situations involving "imminent danger" in the workplace, (2) incidents resulting in fatalities or hospitalization of five or more employees, (3) follow-up of employee complaints of unsafe or unhealthful working conditions, and (4) "high-hazard" industries and occupations (for example, mining, farming, construction, and transport). For 2005, OSHA's goal was to conduct 37,700 inspections.[34]

OSHA inspectors have the right to enter an establishment without notice to examine work environment, materials, and equipment, and to question both employers and employees. However, this right conflicts with the employer's constitutional protection from warrantless searches. In a 1978 case involving a company's refusal to allow an OSHA inspection until the agency could produce a search warrant, the Supreme Court ruled that the employer does have a right to demand a search warrant before OSHA can make an inspection. Although OSHA can generally obtain a search warrant based on an employee complaint or on the agency's own inspection priority system, some argue that forfeiting the element of surprise makes inspection less effective because it gives employers a means to alter unsafe conditions or practices (for example, erratically using safety equipment) until after the inspection.[35]

■ **Citations and penalties.** OSHA may issue citations and impose penalties for any violations of OSHA standards. The exact penalty varies with the employer's good faith attempts to comply with OSHA regulations, its history of previous violations, the seriousness of the infraction, and the size of the business. These penalties may include criminal penalties as well as substantial fines. In fact, executives of firms that recklessly endanger workers are becoming increasingly likely to spend time in jail.[36] In 1987, five senior executives of Chicago Magnet Wire Company were prosecuted for causing workers' illnesses by allowing them to be exposed to hazardous chemicals. In 1989, a supervisor at Jackson Enterprises in Michigan was convicted of involuntary manslaughter in an employee's work-related death.[37]

Fines for violations of OSHA standards may range from no fine for minor violations to megafines of several million dollars for companies guilty of numerous, repeated, and willful infractions. However, companies can object to OSHA's proposed penalties and may be able to negotiate a lower fine. For example, OSHA proposed fines against newspaper operations totaling $101,850 in 2004 for various safety violations, but newspapers paid only $53,681 in penalties in 2004.[38] OSHA fined a BP plant in Augusta, Georgia, when three workers died in an explosion of molten plastic. OSHA accused BP of willfully violating safety rules and fined the company $141,000. BP negotiated a lower classification of violation and paid $119,000 in fines.[39] Critics contend that the negotiation process can yield lowered fines that don't provide companies with enough incentive to improve the safety levels of their operations. OSHA, however, contends that its primary focus is on improving workplaces to protect workers, not on punishing companies.

An important question is whether these fines have any meaningful impact on organizations. One approach to answering this question is to see whether the announcement of fines levied by the OSHA has any impact on the value of the firm's stock. If there is no such impact, top executives have little incentive to improve safety and health conditions and avoid future fines. Research suggests that the announcement of OSHA penalties does have a significant negative impact on the firm's stock.[40] However, the downturn in stock prices is a short-term effect that occurs only in the day or two after the announcement of the penalties. Furthermore, it appears that it is simply the announcement of a violation, not the amount of the fine, that has the impact on the company's stock price.

OSHA offers a free consultation service that works with businesses to help them identify potential workplace hazards and improve safety management systems. This service is especially useful for small businesses. It provides for a confidential inspection, completely separate from OSHA's inspection program, that does not result in penalties or fines. However, the employer is obligated to correct serious safety and health hazards found in the inspection.

The procedure works as follows:[41]

1. The employer must contact the OSHA consultant to get things started.
2. An opening conference is scheduled at the work site to discuss the consultant's role and the employer's obligations under the service.
3. Employer and consultant examine workplace conditions together. The consultant may talk to employees, discuss OSHA standards with them, and point out safety problems.
4. In a closing conference, the consultant reviews the findings of the inspection with the employer, detailing both what the employer is doing right and where improvement is needed.
5. After the closing conference, the consultant provides a written report explaining the findings and confirming proposed times within which the employer is to remedy hazards found in the inspection. (These are known as *abatement periods*.)

A Question of Ethics

Opponents of "Big Government" claim that excessive regulation of workplace safety hurts productivity and increases costs. They argue that in a free market, employees should be responsible for their own health and safety—that they should be free to choose between taking a wage premium for hazardous work and accepting lower pay for safer work. Would such a policy be ethical? What are its pros and cons?

The Occupational Safety and Health Review Commission (OSHRC)

OSHRC operates independently of OSHA, and reviews its citations. An employer can appeal an OSHA citation, an abatement period, or a penalty to OSHRC. Rulings made by this commission can be appealed only through the federal court system.[42]

The National Institute for Occupational Safety and Health (NIOSH)

NIOSH exists mainly to research safety and health problems and to assist the OSHA in the creation of new health and safety standards. Like OSHA, NIOSH may inspect the workplace and gather information from employers and employees about hazardous materials. In addition, NIOSH trains inspectors and others associated with the enforcement of OSHA.[43]

State Programs

OSHA permits states to create their own occupational safety and health programs, and many states have chosen to do so. OSHA will approve a state plan if the state shows that it is able to set and enforce standards, provide and train competent enforcement personnel, and give educational and technical assistance to business. Upon approval of a state program, OSHA funds 50 percent of that program's operating costs and passes primary enforcement responsibility to the state. OSHA continually monitors and evaluates state programs and may withdraw approval if it determines that a state is failing to maintain an effective program.[44]

The Effectiveness of OSHA

Has OSHA been an effective tool for creating a safer and healthier workplace? OSHA's critics suggest that its detailed and expansive regulations produce costs that exceed their benefits. However, many other people feel that while the OSHA-related costs borne by employers are direct and easy to measure, the benefits of an accident-free workplace are not. They point out that it is accident victims—employees—who bear the costs of an absence of health and safety regulations, not the employer.

Indeed, the costs of accidents and illness can be immense. For example, workplace accidents in the United States cost employers $49.6 billion in 2002.[45] The good news is that there is evidence that the regulations, penalties, and increased awareness brought about by OSHA have significantly improved workplace safety. Bureau of Labor Statistics data for 2002 and 2003 show that workplace fatalities are at their lowest levels since it started collecting workplace fatality data in 1992.[46] Nonetheless, some occupations remain dangerous. Figure 16.2 shows the death rate for the deadliest occupational areas in the United States.

Managing Contemporary Safety, Health, and Behavioral Issues

Effectively managing workplace safety and health requires far more than reducing the numbers of job-related accidents and injuries. In practice, managers must deal with a variety of practical, legal, and ethical issues, many of which involve a careful balancing of individual rights (particularly the right to privacy) with the needs of the organization (see Chapter 14). Because these issues often give rise to legal questions, HR professionals are frequently called upon to develop and implement policies to deal with them. Among the weightiest issues facing employers today are dealing with AIDS in the workplace, workplace violence, smoking in the workplace, cumulative trauma disorders, hearing impairment, fetal protection, hazardous chemicals, and genetic testing.

It is important to recognize that, in addition to these direct challenges, there is also the challenge of employee commitment to safety and health programs. Many organizations face the problem of employees ignoring and even being hostile to safety and health measures. The reason: Employees often view safety and health measures as intrusive and inefficient.

Top managers can generate commitment to safety and health programs by explaining to supervisors and others the rationale for the relevant safety and health practices. For example, it is important that everyone understand the cost of accidents to the organization. Furthermore, the costs (such as fines) for violating safety and health standards should be clearly explained to employees at all levels. Once people understand the link between safety measures and the business's bottom line, resistance to safety programs should largely disappear. Of course, removing human resistance to any kind of program can be a difficult and delicate process that requires time and commitment.

Recent research supports the value of taking a participative approach to the improvement of safety and empowering workers to manage and solve their own safety programs.[47] The research focused on cleaners at a 600-bed hospital. Safety teams consisting of employees, supervisors, and safety experts were formed. The employees were trained in the basics, such as hazard identification and control, and were charged with identifying and reducing safety risks. Some of the solutions identified and implemented by these teams included changing purchasing procedures so that floors would be easier to clean, purchasing safer equipment, and more frequent job rotation to minimize repetitive strain. After implementation of the safety teams, workers' compensation claim rates fell by 67 percent, claim costs by 73 percent, and injury duration by 43 percent. An empowered approach to safety would appear to be an effective means to improve safety.

Figure 16.2	
Farming, fishing, and forestry occupations	27.9
Transportation and material moving	16.9
Construction and extraction	12.7
Protection services	11.4

*Rates are annual deaths per 100,000 workers.

Source: Adapted from Bureau of Labor Statistics. (2004). National Census of Fatal Occupational Injuries in 2003. www.bls.gov/iif/oshcfoi1.htm.

Death Rates* for the Deadliest Occupations

AIDS

Dealing effectively with workplace concerns that arise when an employee contracts acquired immunodeficiency syndrome (AIDS) has become an important workplace health challenge. In the early 1980s, AIDS was scarcely known, but by 1996 the Centers for Disease Control and Prevention reported that two-thirds of organizations with more than 2,500 employees had already experienced an employee with this disease or HIV (the human immunodeficiency virus that leads to AIDS).[48] In 2003, 5 million people worldwide were infected with HIV and over 3 million died from AIDS.[49] In the United States, approximately 40,000 new cases of HIV infection emerge each year.[50]

Some companies may prefer to avoid or ignore the topic of AIDS, but there are federal guidelines regarding AIDS that require organizational compliance. The major sources of these guidelines are OSHA and the Americans with Disabilities Act (ADA).

OSHA

In 1992, OSHA issued the Bloodborne Pathogens Standards, which must be followed in all workplaces where employees can reasonably be expected to come in contact with blood or other body fluids. For example, people who are in the environmental health, safety, or emergency response professions, among others, fall under this standard. Since AIDS became a recognized diagnosis in the early 1980s, 52 instances of HIV infection in health-care workers have been documented as work related.[51] At least another 114 instances of HIV infections in health-care workers are suspected of being work related. OSHA requires all workers who may come into contact with infectious bodily fluids to be educated about bloodborne pathogens and trained in how to reduce the risks of infection. This preparation should help workers reduce their risks and employers' health-care costs. Figure 16.3 summarizes the key points of the OSHA standards.

ADA and the Manager's Role

According to ADA guidelines, having HIV infection or AIDS does not necessarily prevent people from performing the essential functions of most jobs.[52] Thus, organizations must make reasonable accommodations for infected employees. Reasonable accommodation might include adjustments to work schedules or workstation modifications. For example, one company gave a manager with AIDS a chair that converted into a sleeping recliner and allowed a 90-minute break in the afternoon.[53] The chair allowed the manager to deal with the drop in his energy level in the afternoon. The manager scheduled all meetings in the morning and came into work extra hours on evenings and weekends, if needed. This arrangement was reasonable and provided an important accommodation for the manager at minimal cost.

ADA guidelines also affect the hiring process. Employers cannot ask job candidates about their HIV or AIDS status or require job candidates to take an HIV test before making a job offer. Testing *can* be done and questions posed after a job offer is made. However, test results must be kept confidential. The job offer cannot be withdrawn on the basis of a positive HIV test unless the employer can demonstrate that the person would pose a direct threat to coworkers or customers

Key Components of OSHA's Bloodborne Pathogens Standards

Figure 16.3

- **Exposure Control Plan** Outline the procedures to identify workers at risk and specify methods for complying with standards.
- **Universal Precautions** Follow the Centers for Disease Control and Prevention's recommendations for handling all blood and body fluid as though they are contaminated.
- **Personal Protective Equipment** Provide all necessary personal protection equipment, such as gloves and masks.
- **Cleaning Protocols** Identify the methods of decontamination and the procedures for handling waste.
- **Hazard Communication** Use warning labels and signs to identify restricted areas.
- **Information and Training** Educate employees regarding AIDS and the OSHA standards.
- **Recordkeeping** Document efforts relating to the standards and keep the medical records of employees exposed to risk for the duration of their employment plus 30 years.

Source: Adapted from Oswald, E. M. (1996). No employer is immune: AIDS exposure in the workplace. *Risk Management, 43,* 18–21; and Hunter, S. (1998). Your infection control program. *Occupational Health and Safety, 67,* 76–80.

and that this threat could not be eliminated through reasonable accommodation. Such demonstration would be all but impossible in most jobs.

In addition to simply complying with the guidelines issued by federal agencies, organizations should proactively address the AIDS issue by developing an AIDS policy. The content of the policy should address all terms and conditions of employment, from hiring and job assignments to compensation and termination.[54] Such a policy sends a clear signal of the importance the company places on its human resources and the support it provides to AIDS victims.

An effective AIDS policy should not only outline the procedures to be followed when an employee contracts HIV infection, but also educate the workforce. Many employees fear that they can contract the disease by working alongside someone who has AIDS. Educational programs can eliminate these fears by providing accurate information about the disease and how it is transmitted.

What is the role of managers and supervisors in dealing with AIDS in the workplace? Managers should be able to answer employee questions about AIDS and effectively deal with any AIDS-related issues that arise. For this reason, the educational effort should involve familiarizing supervisors and managers with the organization's AIDS policy and training them in how to deal with AIDS issues.[55] An open approach to educating and discussing AIDS in the workplace is recommended. However, there are boundaries to discussion of AIDS-related issues. Specifically, the ADA includes strict confidentiality provisions in regard to employee medical information. Confidential medical information can be disclosed to supervisory personnel only if they need to know for purposes of providing reasonable accommodation or to safety personnel who might be required to provide emergency medical services to the employee.[56] An employer who discloses an employee's medical condition, such as AIDS, risks violating the employee's right of privacy and the right to work without discrimination as provided by the ADA. Open discussion of the issue of AIDS in the workplace can help create a positive and productive environment, but disclosure of an employee's AIDS status is legally prohibited.

Violence in the Workplace

Salavador Tapia worked for an auto parts supply company on the South Side of Chicago in 2003 until he was fired for tardiness and absenteeism. He had several phone conversations with his former boss at the Windy City Core Supply warehouse. Then on August 23, 2003, Tapia arrived at his former workplace early in the morning. He carried a semi-automatic pistol and shot and killed six of his former supervisors and coworkers. He then killed himself in a shootout with police. Tapia had an arrest record going back over 10 years that included gun violations, aggravated assault, and domestic battery.[57]

Too many other shootings across the country provide dramatic examples of violence in the workplace. Between 1994 and 2003, 164 workplace shootings occurred in the United States.[58] In 2004 alone 29 workplace shootings occurred, resulting in the deaths of 36 workers and injury to 15 others. Violence in the workplace, however, encompasses more than just the extreme example of homicide.

Violence in the workplace can take a variety of forms, including assaults, threats, and sabotage. According to U.S. Department of Labor figures, approximately 5,500 incidents of workplace violence occur every day and at least 3 people are murdered.[59] Approximately 13,000 women are assaulted, stalked, or murdered at work each year by a significant other. The cost of workplace violence in the United States has been estimated to be as high as $4.2 billion per year.[60]

Reducing Assaults and Threats

It would be reassuring to think that today's employers are proactively addressing the topic of workplace violence. Unfortunately, it appears that many companies avoid the issue. A recent survey of safety engineers found that only 1 percent of their employers have written policies on workplace violence.[61] But whether there is a policy or not, threats and assaults can occur in the workplace. An important source of this violence is domestic abuse.

Businesses lose an estimated $727.8 million in productivity and more than 7.9 million work days annually due to domestic violence.[62] Domestic violence can adversely affect an employee's performance though absenteeism, tardiness, poor performance, and mistakes on the job. A recent survey of *Fortune* 1000 companies found 47 percent of senior executives viewed domestic violence as a cause of decreased productivity.[63] Thus, there is hope that companies

The Limited has started a training and hot line program to prevent domestic abuse from spilling into the workplace.

will become more proactive in preventing workplace threats and assaults. At present, however, too few companies are actively addressing the issue. Some notable exceptions among companies taking positive approaches to manage domestic violence may spill over into the workplace.

Harmon International Industries, Inc., a manufacturer of audio electronics (such as Harmon/Kardon and JBL), provides mandatory domestic abuse training for its 3,000 employees. It has a domestic violence policy in place, prompted by the murder of one of its employees by her ex-husband, and has created a supportive environment for abuse victims to share their situations and difficulties. Another company using preventive management to reduce domestic violence is Liz Claiborne. The company trains its managers in how to spot and respond to domestic violence. It also maintains a domestic violence response team that deals with victims. In 2 years, the company handled more than 40 cases that required more action than simply a referral.

Implementing a workplace violence policy and taking a preventive approach should lower the risk of violence erupting at work. However, the threat can still arise. The Manager's Notebook, "Management Suggestions Regarding Domestic Violence," provides suggestions to help manage a workplace threat due to domestic violence.

MANAGER'S NOTEBOOK   Ethics

Management Suggestions Regarding Domestic Violence

Domestic violence can spill into the workplace, affecting the abuse victim and others. The following are some management suggestions when there is an identifiable domestic violence threat:

- Request that local law enforcement patrol the workplace, particularly at the beginning and end of an abuse victim's shift.
- Provide closer parking for the abuse victim so that he or she has a shorter walk into the building.

▓ If an escort for the employee to and from the parking lot seems like a good idea, provide someone who is a trained authority. An escort shouldn't just be the nice person in the office, unless he or she has security training.

▓ Use monitoring and detection devices, such as surveillance equipment. They can give immediate warning of a problem on site.

▓ Temporarily move the employee to another site or work station.

▓ In an extreme case, provide the employee time off through an administrative leave or sick leave.

Source: Adapted from Gurchiek, K. (2005). Study: Domestic violence spills over into the workplace. *HRMagazine,* *50*, 32, 38.

Reducing Threats from Sabotage

Another form of workplace violence is sabotage. Sabotage is not physical violence, but it is a violent act just the same. Acts of sabotage can be directed either at a person, such as attempts to damage someone's career, or at an organization, such as attempts to damage equipment or reputation. Most sabotage includes an aspect or motive of revenge. Angry and bitter employees have done everything from putting rodents into food products to needles in baby food and starting company fires and wiping out computer databases.[64]

Currently, no organizations keep track of acts of sabotage, so the frequency and prevalence of the problem is difficult to assess. However, experts suggest that sabotage is increasingly a problem for organizations. Many saboteurs are disgruntled former employees who, as the victims of downsizing or termination, feel underappreciated and unfairly treated by their former employers. Disgruntled employees who retaliate by doing damage to a computer system pose a major concern in organizations.

Although the frequency of sabotage is difficult to estimate, sabotage costs organizations dearly in the form of property damage and work stoppage. Experts estimate that losses from employee fraud and other forms of sabotage cost organizations $400 billion per year. Figure 16.4 offers tips on how to prevent sabotage.

Whatever form workplace violence may take, it is the legal and social responsibility of managers to deal with workplace violence proactively. Under **negligent hiring** laws, employers can be held responsible for their employees' violent acts on the job, particularly when the employer knows, or should know, that an employee has a history of violent behavior (see Chapter 5). In one California case, for example, a temporary help agency employed a man who subsequently stabbed a woman coworker to death. The man was a paroled murderer with a five-year gap in his résumé that the agency had failed to investigate. A state court ordered the temporary agency to pay the dead woman's relatives $5.5 million. Negligence is not limited to hiring. In 1999, a North Carolina jury awarded $7.9 million to two families in a case of two men killed on the job in 1995 by a violent former worker who had been terminated.[65] The jury found that the

Negligent hiring
Hiring an employee with a history of violent or illegal behavior without conducting background checks or taking proper precautions.

Figure 16.4

Managing the Threat of Sabotage

Here are some tips managers can take to prevent sabotage:

■ Make it explicit in organizational policy statements that acts of sabotage will not be tolerated and the expense of any damage to organizational property due to an employee's negligence or fault will be the responsibility of the employee.

■ Hire the best people for the jobs and treat them well. Sabotage is more likely to occur when a worker is frustrated and feels unfairly treated. Making sure that there is a good fit between the person and the job and that organizational treatment is fair can prevent sabotage.

■ Offer employees training in conflict management and ways to appropriately vent anger.

■ Consider offering a third party hotline for employees to report incidents of workplace sabotage.

Source: Adapted from Laabs, J. (1999). Employee sabotage: Don't be a target. *Workforce, 78,* 32–38.

company's management was negligent in failing to protect the workers. These types of cases are still uncommon, but their numbers appear to be increasing.[66]

Managers need to take responsibility for reducing or eliminating violence in the workplace. To this end, they must be sensitive to the causes of workplace violence. Many people feel pressured in their jobs and fear layoffs. Add to this stress level workplace events such as negative performance appraisals; personality conflicts with coworkers or managers; or personal problems, such as a divorce; and a potentially dangerous person may emerge.

Certainly, managers cannot eliminate all these pressures, which are realities of everyday life in modern organizations. However, they can make sure that employees are treated fairly. Treating employees as though they are expendable will not create commitment to the company and could be enough to trigger a violent reaction. Managers should deal with performance problems by focusing on the behavior and future improvement, rather than condemning the person for past performance problems (see Chapter 7 on performance appraisal). Managers should never discipline employees in front of coworkers; doing so can humiliate the person and incite a violent reaction.[67]

Managers should also take steps to reduce the possibility of hiring workers who might be prone to violence. For example, interviewers might ask job candidates to describe how they reacted to a past management decision they did not agree with and why.[68] The responses to this question and follow-up questions could be quite revealing. Also, interviewers should check for evidence of substance abuse or emotional problems, which might be indicated by careless driving or DWI (driving while intoxicated) entries on driving records. Unexplained gaps in a person's employment history should be carefully examined.

Smoking in the Workplace

In 1994, Melvin Simon and Associates, owner of 85 large shopping malls throughout the United States, announced that smoking would no longer be allowed in any of its facilities. This announcement closely followed decisions by two major fast-food chains, McDonald's and Arby's, to eliminate smoking in their restaurants.[69] Since these actions, many organizations have enacted smoking elimination policies.

The push to restrict workplace smoking has come largely in the last decade. As far back as 1964, the U.S. Surgeon General published the initial government report on the health consequences of smoking. By 1981, however, a Bureau of National Affairs survey revealed that only 8 percent of U.S. companies restricted smoking. In the mid-1980s a report from Surgeon General C. Everett Koop asserted that smokers create health risks for nonsmoking coworkers and customers.[70] By 1986, 36 percent of all organizations restricted smoking in the workplace.[71] A 1998 survey of 80,000 employees found that 65 percent were employed in workplaces wherein smoking is not allowed.[72] Smoke-free workplaces are rapidly becoming the norm in the United States.

An increasing number of companies ban smoking in the workplace, while a few, such as Union Pacific Corporation, are beginning to reject employment applications from smokers.[73] However, the decision of one Michigan company to terminate workers for smoking made national headlines. Weyco, a medical benefits administrator, decided it was going to be a no-smoking employer.[74] The president of the company, Howard Weyers, a former college football coach, is now in his 70s yet works out regularly and can squat-press 340 pounds. Weyers said that because employee lifestyle choices affect the bottom line, his company will not employ people who smoke, even on their own time. He announced the absolute ban on smoking to Weyco's 200 employees, who were given 15 months to quit along with smoking cessation classes and support groups. Approximately 20 Weyco workers quit smoking during that time period.

On January 1, 2005, four workers refused to take a nicotine test to demonstrate that they were smoke-free. At least some of these workers never had any intention of quitting and viewed the absolute smoking ban as an unacceptable personal intrusion. Those four workers were terminated. Some of the workers who quit smoking are happy with their healthier lifestyle. In addition, Weyco should benefit because smokers, as a group, tend to have higher absenteeism and lower productivity than nonsmokers.[75] Weyco should also enjoy lower health-care costs due to the workforce being nonsmokers.

Nonetheless, there is room to question how much an employer can control what a worker does outside the workplace, particularly when using a legal substance. The four former Weyco employees have not, as of this writing, filed a lawsuit over their terminations, but litigation is still possible.

While not taking as extreme a position as Weyco's, many cities and states have enacted regulations regarding smoking.[76] The state of New York has one of the most comprehensive laws protecting the rights of nonsmoking employees in the workplace. It requires each employer to adopt a written smoking policy, post the policy prominently in the workplace, and supply written copies to employees upon request. Requirements include:[77]

- A smoke-free work area for nonsmoking employees.
- A work area set aside for smoking if all working in the area agree.
- Contiguous nonsmoking areas in cafeterias and break rooms.
- A prohibition against smoking in auditoriums, gymnasiums, restrooms, elevators, hallways, and other common areas.
- A prohibition against smoking in company vehicles and meeting rooms unless all present agree that smoking is permitted.

In addition to New York, states with strict smoking laws include Connecticut, Maine, Delaware, and California. Rhode Island and Massachusetts have also recently passed workplace-smoking bans. A review of state laws on workplace smoking can be found at the Alexander Hamilton Institute Web site (*www.ahipubs.com*).

Limits on smoking are not unique to the United States. As presented in the Manager's Notebook, "Global Smoke Out," a number of countries limit smoking in the workplace.

Global | MANAGER'S NOTEBOOK

Global Smoke Out

Smoking tobacco might seem like a private matter that should have nothing to do with the workplace. However, a growing number of countries are taking steps to limit smoking in public places, including the workplace. Here are some of them.

- **United States.** California led the way with legislation banning smoking in the workplace. Ten years later, 90 percent of Californians support the measure. Seven states have passed smoke-free workplace legislation, and another nine are likely to soon join their ranks.
- **Cuba.** "Have a Havanna" used to be a common phrase that referred to smoking a Cuban cigar. This phrase is in danger of becoming obsolete, as Cuba has now banned smoking in public places, including workplaces. Fidel Castro gave up smoking 20 years ago. Even though half of adult Cubans are smokers, apparently Castro feels that stopping smoking is also a good policy for the country.
- **Canada.** Canada enjoys one of the lowest smoking levels in the world. A number of provinces (New Brunswick, Manitoba, Saskatchewan) and territories (Nunavet, Northwest Territories) are smoke free. Other districts (Quebec, Ontario) have plans to follow suit.
- **South America.** Brazil has some restriction on smoking in the workplace. Most other South American countries have few restrictions.
- **Indonesia.** Smoking in workplaces will be banned in Jakarta sometime in 2006.
- **Italy.** A quarter of Italians smoke, but the country has now banned smoking in workplaces.
- **Ireland.** Ireland has a ban on smoking in enclosed workplaces.
- **Australia.** Smoking in workplaces is banned in the "land down under."
- **European Union.** The European Union would like to ban workplace smoking, but as of the time of this writing, no legislation is yet in place.

Other countries that have restrictions on smoking in most public places and workplaces are Germany, Finland, The Netherlands, New Zealand, Norway, and Sweden. Limitations on smoking are a global phenomenon.

Source: Adapted with permission from Berry, M. (February 15, 2005). Cuba joins global effort to stub-out smoking in public. *Personnel Today,* 6–7.

Cumulative Trauma Disorders

Cumulative trauma disorder (CTD)
An occupational injury that occurs from repetitive physical movements, such as assembly-line work or data entry.

Cumulative trauma disorders (CTDs) are also called repetitive stress (or motion or strain) injuries (or illnesses or syndromes). CTDs refer not to one disorder, but rather to a wide array of maladies, from *carpal tunnel syndrome (CTS),* which often affects the wrists of computer keyboard users, to tennis elbow and forearm and shoulder complaints.[78] The number of workers with CTDs has risen dramatically in recent years. In 1983, there were fewer than 50,000 U.S. workers in whom CTDs were diagnosed. By 2003, the number had risen to 435,180, accounting for approximately one-third of workplace injuries and illnesses that resulted in days away from work.[79] In addition to prevalence, the costs associated with CTDs are impressive. The General Accounting Office stated that CTDs cost private employers more than $60 billion annually.

Although legal compliance may not be an issue right now, socially responsible organizations should be aware of CTDs and their likely causes. Managers should take steps to reduce CTDs by educating workers and altering the physical arrangement of the workplace if necessary. Figure 16.5 presents a set of do's and don'ts to help workers avoid CTDs. Managers should also remember that posting these tips prominently can decrease the likelihood that workers will develop a CTD.

Hearing Impairment

It is widely recognized that loud noise can lead to loss of hearing. However, consistent exposure to loud noise of 95 decibels has also been found to be related to elevated blood pressure and various digestive, respiratory, allergenic, and musculoskeletal disorders. Exposure to loud noise has also been found to lead to disorientation and reduction of eye focus, possibly leading to an increase in the rate of accidents and injuries.[80] Evidence regarding the potential negative health effects of loud noise led OSHA to develop the Occupational Noise Exposure standard. This standard requires organizations to provide hearing protectors free to employees who are exposed to an average of 85 decibels of noise or greater. Regardless of this standard, research findings indicate that, on average, fewer than 50 percent of employees who should wear hearing protectors actually wear them.[81] Furthermore, many employees who wear hearing protectors don't wear them correctly. Part of the problem in dealing with the prevention of hearing loss is getting employees to recognize and take seriously the threat that noise can pose to hearing acuity. The Manager's Notebook, "Say What? Management Steps to the Prevention of Hearing Loss," offers steps that can be taken to motivate employees to protect their hearing.

Avoiding CTDs: The Do's and Don'ts

Figure 16.5

Do:
- Take breaks (every 20 minutes).
- Stretch and relax at your work area (once per hour).
- Maintain and build your physical fitness.
- Maintain good posture when working at a computer/terminal:
  - Sit erect.
  - Feet flat on floor.
  - Bend elbows at a comfortable angle.
  - Sit about 18–28 inches from the screen.
  - Place documents at the same height and angle as the monitor.

Don't:
- Engage in a lot of repetitive motion with your hands and arms.
- Bend your wrists continuously.
- Grasp or pinch objects continuously.
- Work in an awkward position.
- Exert a lot of force with your arms and hands.

Source: Adapted from Worsnop, R. L. (1995). Repetitive stress injuries. *CQ Researcher, 5,* 537–560.

Efforts to prevent hearing loss should not be limited to getting employees to protect their hearing. Reducing the amount of noise in the work environment is a direct and primary way of preventing hearing loss. Although noise reduction isn't always possible, many organizations are finding that new machinery often offers the advantage of quieter operation.[82] Efforts to prevent hearing loss need to be broad-based and include consideration of both system (machinery) and person (employee) factors.

Fetal Protection, Hazardous Chemicals, and Genetic Testing

During the 1970s and 1980s, a handful of large U.S. firms developed workplace policies designed to prevent pregnant employees from exposure to hazardous chemicals that might damage the fetus. These policies were controversial because they tended to restrict women's access to some of industry's better-paying jobs. For example, in 1978 several women working for American Cyanamid underwent sterilization rather than risk losing highly paid jobs.

Customer-Driven HR

MANAGER'S NOTEBOOK

Say What? Management Steps to the Prevention of Hearing Loss

Motivating workers to take seriously threats to their hearing can be difficult. Hearing loss is something that can't be seen and isn't immediately perceived by the victim. Furthermore, hearing protection can be viewed as cumbersome. Here are some suggestions to help bring employees on board with a hearing loss prevention effort.

- *Show workers what hearing loss is like.* Knowing what it is like to have hearing loss can be an effective motivational technique. Demonstrations of hearing loss can be found at *www.aero. com/html/industrial/tech01.asp#audiodemo.*
- *Offer testimonials.* A former employee or someone in the industry who suffered work-related hearing loss can offer an effective and motivating presentation to employees. A testimonial can make the issue real to employees and make clear that it could happen to them.
- *Have them do their own demonstration.* If you have workers who resist wearing ear protection, even though it is needed, have them try this test: When arriving for work, turn down the car stereo so that it can barely be heard. Leaving it set at that volume, go to work. Returning to the car after a day's work, turn on the radio with the volume still as set in the morning. Can you hear the radio?
- *Offer incentives.* Offer incentives to supervisors or teams based on the percentage of workers who wear hearing protection devices.

Source: Adapted from Safety Director's Report (2002). Hearing protection strategies for any safety department budget. May Newsletter of the Institute of Management and Administration.

The fetal protection controversy came to national attention in 1982 when Johnson Controls, a battery manufacturer, prevented women of childbearing age from working in jobs involving contact with lead. The union sued Johnson Controls for sex discrimination because the company's policy restricted only female employees. The Supreme Court ruled against the company, finding it guilty of illegal sex bias.[83]

This decision caused great concern among companies like General Motors, DuPont, Olin, Monsanto, and others with fetal protection policies. These companies argue that their only alternative is to greatly reduce the use of certain substances. But reducing the use of these compounds, they claim, would be both difficult and costly. Critics counter that these companies should do more to protect *all* workers, not simply remove some from the workplace.[84]

Reproductive health concerns are an important workplace issue with the potential to affect thousands of employers and millions of workers. For example, one study of 1,600 pregnant women showed that those who use video display terminals (VDTs) heavily have a miscarriage rate double that of women who do not use monitors. A study of pregnant women at a Digital Equipment plant in Houston reached a similar conclusion. Clearly, the implications of this type of problem are substantial when one considers the number of VDTs currently in use.[85] The fetal health issue is compounded by the fact that only a handful of companies have comprehensive fetal health policies, and research about the effects of many industrial compounds on reproductive health is inconclusive or incomplete. Although some substances (for example, lead) represent clear health threats to fetuses, exposure to many other compounds may not cause problems. These compounds may also present significant reproductive hazards to *both* sexes, not just women.

Hazardous Chemicals

Many thousands of workplace accidents and injuries reported each year have been attributed to exposure to toxic chemicals. In the past, workers were often required to handle chemicals without being fully informed of the hazards involved. In 1983, however, OSHA's hazard communication standard gave employees the right to know about hazardous chemicals in the workplace (see Figure 16.1). The current standard requires manufacturers and users of hazardous chemicals to identify the chemicals, provide employees with information about them, and train employees in the dangers and handling of them.[86]

The Hazard Communications Standard is far-reaching, covering more than 35 million workers exposed to hazardous chemicals at more than 3.5 million sites.[87] Each year, companies lose thousands of dollars in fines for failing to make Material Safety Data Sheets (MSDS) available to employees. Part of the problem is the cumbersome paper-based MSDS system, which is difficult to keep up to date. To remedy the problem, many companies are putting MSDS information online to provide better access to information and easier compliance with the Hazard Communication Standard.

Genetic Testing

Genetic testing
A form of biological testing that identifies employees who are genetically susceptible to specific occupational substances.

A new and controversial tool used to deal with exposure to workplace substances is **genetic testing,** which identifies employees who are genetically susceptible to specific occupational substances. The goal is to avoid placing at-risk employees in dangerous jobs. Very few organizations use genetic testing at present (1% or fewer), but advances in genetic research may make this screening device more attractive in years to come. Critics question the predictive ability of genetic screening and criticize it from both legal and ethical perspectives because it has significant potential to discriminate. Indeed, heavy use of genetic screening may conflict with both Title VII of the Civil Rights Act and the ADA. In 1999, a U.S. Court of Appeals ruled that genetic tests conducted by a federal laboratory on its employees without the employees' permission may have violated the workers' civil rights and invaded their privacy.[88] An additional argument against genetic screening is similar to that raised against fetal protection policies: It is the work environment that is the problem, not the worker, and organizations should remove the hazard, not the person.[89]

The Burlington Northern Santa Fe Railroad began using genetic testing in March 2000. The company required employees who claimed a work-related CTD to provide blood samples as part of routine medical examinations used to evaluate employee injury claims. The blood samples were used to test for the presence of a genetic trait that might predispose someone to musculoskeletal disorders. The testing was brought to light when employees made complaints to their labor unions. The EEOC filed a lawsuit in February 2002 contending that the genetic testing violated the ADA. This is the first time that the EEOC challenged testing. In a mediated settlement reached in May 2002, the railroad agreed to pay 36 workers $2.2 million to resolve allegations that it conducted genetic testing without employee knowledge or consent.[90] The railroad contended that the genetic tests weren't used to screen out employees. However, the EEOC contends that the mere gathering of genetic information may violate the ADA. Currently, 22 states have banned the use of genetic screening for employment purposes.[91]

The U.S. Senate unanimously passed a bill in 2003 outlawing the denial of employment or health insurance based on genetic testing results. However, the bill never was brought to a vote by the House of Representatives due to funding concerns and the belief that genetic discrimination isn't a problem.[92] The Genetic Information Nondiscrimination Act of 2005 was again unanimously passed by the Senate and referred to the House Ways and Means Committee in March 2005. If passed by the House of Representatives, it would provide federal protection against genetic discrimination.

Safety and Health Programs

We have devoted most of the chapter thus far to discussing physical hazards in the workplace and their impact on both workers and the organization. However, other hazards have major effects on workers, including stress, unsafe behaviors, and poor health habits. To cope with both physical and other types of hazards, companies often design comprehensive safety and health programs.

Safety Programs

A safe working environment does not just happen; it has to be created. The organizations with the best reputations for safety have developed well-planned, thorough safety programs. Concern for safety should begin at the highest level within the organization, and managers and supervisors at all levels should be charged with demonstrating safety awareness, held responsible for safety training, and rewarded for maintaining a safe workplace. Although support for safety has to start at the top, no one knows the job, its risks, and what could be improved better than the employees. The input and participation of line workers is critical to an effective safety program.[93]

Effective safety programs share the following features:

- They include the formation of a safety committee and participation by all departments within the company. Employees participate in safety decisions and management carefully considers employee suggestions for improving safety.
- They communicate safety with a multimedia approach that includes safety lectures, films, posters, pamphlets, and computer presentations.
- They instruct supervisors in how to communicate, demonstrate, and require safety, and they train employees in the safe use of equipment.
- They use incentives, rewards, and positive reinforcement to encourage safe behavior. They reward employee complaints or suggestions about safety. They may also provide rewards (such as safe driving awards given to truck drivers) to employees with exceptional safety records.
- They communicate safety rules and enforce them. OSHA obligates employees to adhere to safety rules, and in good programs managers are willing to use the disciplinary system to penalize unsafe work behavior.
- They use safety directors and/or the safety committee to engage in regular self-inspection and accident research to identify potentially dangerous situations, and to understand why accidents occur and how to correct them.

Companies with comprehensive safety programs are likely to be rewarded with fewer accidents, fewer workers' compensation claims and lawsuits, and lower accident-related costs. Keep in mind that OSHA considers employee involvement a key feature of a successful safety program. Organizations often involve employees by establishing a safety committee. Although the specific details may vary, the overall purpose of a safety committee is to have employees and managers collaborate to promote workplace safety and health.[94] Safety committees typically evaluate the adequacy of safety procedures; monitor findings and trends; review accidents, illnesses, and safety suggestions; and recommend and evaluate hazard solutions. However, experts recommend that safety committees do not enforce the policies, or they risk being viewed as the "safety police." Instead, the committees should make recommendations that management should implement and enforce.

Involving employees on safety committees has been effective. Pennsylvania, for example, has found such a return on investment that it offers a 5 percent discount for five years on workers' compensation insurance premiums as an incentive for organizations to establish safety committees.[95] State level OSHAs in Oregon, Nevada, and Washington have such a positive assessment of the effectiveness of safety committees that they are required in most workplaces.

The creation of safety action teams at Alberto Culver provides an example of the potential that can be realized by including employees in the safety-improvement process.[96] Alberto Culver used safety committees but rarely consulted with employees closest to the work situation—forklift drivers, shipping clerks, and packers. That all changed when the company initiated its first safety action team in 1999. The team collaborated with frontline workers with the purpose of leveraging their knowledge to improve workplace safety. This first team operated in one plant, and within one year the recordable injury rate at the plant dropped by 44 percent and lost time decreased by 70 percent. The results were undeniable, and the safety action team at Alberto Culver has now been expanded to 46 global improvement teams involving 425 employees.

Employee Assistance Programs (EAPs)

As we saw in Chapter 13, *employee assistance programs (EAPs)* are programs designed to help employees whose job performance is suffering because of physical, mental, or emotional problems. EAPs address a variety of employee problems ranging from drug abuse to marital problems. Recent surveys indicate that EAPs are offered by most companies, but many workers, approximately 20 percent, do not know their companies offer them.[97] EAPs have the potential to provide effective assistance, but only if employers make their availability known to workers.

Many organizations create EAPs because they recognize their ethical and legal obligations to protect not only their workers' physical health but their mental health as well. The ethical obligation stems from the fact that the causes of organizational stress—climate, change, rules, work pace, management style, work group characteristics, and so forth—are also frequently the causes of behavioral, psychological, and physiological problems for employees.[98] Ethical obligation becomes legal obligation when employees sue the company or file workers' compensation claims for stress-related illnesses. In fact, much of the heightened concern about dealing with the consequences of workplace stress stems from the increasing incidence and severity of stress-related workers' compensation claims and their associated costs.[99] In Japan, work-related stress (*karoshi*) has come to be seen as a deadly national problem. Interestingly, a United Nations study released in September 1999 found Americans now work the longest hours in the industrialized world—surpassing even the Japanese.[100]

Burnout
A stress syndrome characterized by emotional exhaustion, depersonalization, and reduced personal accomplishment.

Stress often results in **burnout**, a syndrome characterized by emotional exhaustion, depersonalization, and reduced personal accomplishment.[101] People who experience burnout may dread returning to work for another day, treat coworkers and clients callously, withdraw from the organization, and feel less competent in their jobs. Some of the factors that may lead to burnout include ambiguity and conflict when dealing with various job-related issues and problems.[102] A lack of social support can aggravate these effects.

Burnout can lead to serious negative consequences for the individual and for the organization and can have a negative impact on mental and physical health.[103] Mental health problems resulting from burnout can include depression, irritability, lowered self-esteem, and anxiety. Physical problems can include fatigue, headaches, insomnia, gastrointestinal disturbances, and chest pains. Organizational outcomes associated with burnout include turnover, absenteeism, and a decrease in job performance.[104] In addition, sometimes burnout leads to increased drug and alcohol use.[105]

Depression is another topic that merits consideration in any discussion of EAP issues. Clinical depression is a serious mental illness and a bigger problem in the workplace than many people realize. Dr. Ronald Kessler, a health-care policy professor at Harvard Medical School, states that depressed workers report "having problems with time and motion, lifting things, and having accidents on the job."[106] Research studies are consistent with this observation and suggest that depressed workers may be more prone to accidents due to lack of concentration, fatigue, memory difficulties, and slower reaction time. In addition to possible accident proneness, depression has been linked to decreased productivity. It is estimated that as many as 15 to 20 million adult Americans experience depression each year, resulting in 200 million lost workdays and a total annual cost to the U.S. economy of $43.7 billion.[107]

Because of the pervasiveness of depression, mental health experts contend that managers have an obligation to learn about depression, to recognize its warning signs, such as substance abuse, decreased productivity, morale problems, absenteeism, and complaints about fatigue, and to become aware of sources of help. However, keep in mind that you should not play armchair psychiatrist. As a manager, you are there to focus on performance and discuss observable job-relevant behaviors, not to discuss medical problems. There are numerous causes of depression, including genetic, situational, biological, and cognitive factors. Depression can be treated with counseling and medication, but you should leave this treatment to professionals by referral to your EAP or other source for help.

Many organizations perceive EAPs as being cost-effective solutions to performance, stress, and burnout problems. In fact, although U.S. businesses spend as much as $750 million per year on EAPs, many see this as an investment rather than a cost. EAP professionals claim that for every dollar invested in EAP programs, employers recover three to five dollars.[108] The savings come from lower insurance costs, reduced sick time, and better job performance.

Despite these benefits a manager should refer an employee to an EAP solely on the basis of a performance problem and no other. The case of a manager at Lucky Stores grocery store illustrates this point.[109] The manager had been a star performer, but employees started complaining about his abusive and hostile manner. Company representatives asked whether he was having "problems" and offered him assistance. He denied having problems, and a transfer to another store did not improve the situation. He was then offered a leave of absence if he contacted the company's EAP. The EAP staff determined he was suffering from stress and diagnosed a mental illness. He was fired after six months of leave.

The store manager brought suit against the company and the court found that although he was not disabled, the company may have perceived him to be disabled. Therefore, the former manager may have had a claim under the ADA. The company and former manager reached an out-of-court settlement. The message of this and some similar cases is that referral to an EAP should be based on work-related performance issues, rather than on inferences or conclusions about the worker's mental or emotional well-being.

Wellness Programs

As health-care costs continue to skyrocket, organizations have become more interested in preventive programs. Recognizing that they can have an effect on their employees' behavior and lifestyle off the job, companies are encouraging employees to lead more healthy lives. They are also attempting to reduce health-care costs through formal employee wellness programs. Whereas EAPs focus on *treating* troubled employees, **wellness programs** focus on *preventing* health problems. A recent survey of employer coalitions found that 75 percent sponsored wellness programs.[110]

Wellness program
A company-sponsored program that focuses on preventing health problems in employees.

Staying Healthy, Staying Happy. American Airlines offers a variety of activities designed to help employees stay happy, healthy, and productive. Here, food-service workers take a lunchtime aerobics class.

A complete wellness program has three components:

1. It helps employees identify potential health risks through screening and testing.
2. It educates employees about health risks such as high blood pressure, smoking, poor diet, and stress.
3. It encourages employees to change their lifestyles through exercise, good nutrition, and health monitoring.

Wellness programs may be as simple and inexpensive as providing information about stop-smoking clinics and weight-loss programs or as comprehensive and expensive as providing professional health screening and multimillion-dollar fitness facilities.

The Rewards of Good Health Habits

Many organizations find that the employees who are involved in the company wellness plans are people who already are health conscious and have healthy habits. How can you get other employees, many of whom may benefit the most, involved in the wellness program? Some companies are finding that nothing motivates like incentives. For example, when Pfizer Inc. started a wellness plan for its 40,000 employees it included financial incentives to get things started.[111] The program starts with an online health assessment, and a $100 gift card is given to employees who complete a health assessment before the end of the year. As an additional incentive, employees who complete the health assessment by the end of September also earn a $100 deduction on their health-care premium for that year.

Note, however, that punishing employees for unhealthy behavior may be illegal.[112] Penalties are disallowed according to guidelines associated with the 1997 Health Insurance Portability and Accountability Act. For example, excluding certain employers from health insurance coverage or charging them more for health benefits would be discriminatory. Offering rewards is fine, but penalties relating to health insurance coverage or cost are not legally acceptable.

Wellness programs, if implemented effectively, can make a positive contribution to the bottom line in an organization. Although there are costs to starting and maintaining a wellness program, the return in terms of reduced health-care costs and absenteeism can greatly offset the investment. Consider the following benefits documented by employers:[113]

- DuPont experienced a 14-percent decline in absences due to illness at sites where it had implemented a wellness program, compared to a 5.8-percent decline at sites without one.
- Pacific Bell's FitWorks program decreased absenteeism by 0.8 percent, saving the company $2 million in one year. Employees participating in the program also spent 3.3 fewer days on short-term disability, saving an additional $4.7 million.
- Coca-Cola Co. found an average per-person reduction of $500 in annual health-care claims for employees participating in its fitness program.

These kinds of results indicate that wellness efforts can pay off in tangible ways. In addition, it may be difficult to measure, but people claim that they work better when they feel better and can often better solve problems and be more productive after an exercise break.

Summary and Conclusions

Workplace Safety and the Law

There are two sets of workplace safety laws: (1) workers' compensation, an employer-funded insurance system that operates at the state level, and (2) the Occupational Safety and Health Act (OSHA), a federal law that mandates safety standards in the workplace.

Workers' compensation—which consists of total disability, impairment, survivor, medical expense, and rehabilitation benefits—is intended to ensure prompt and reasonable medical care to employees injured on the job, as well as income

for them and their dependents or survivors. It also encourages employers to invest in workplace safety by requiring higher insurance premiums from employers with numerous workplace accidents and injuries.

OSHA compels employers to provide a safe and healthy work environment, to comply with specific occupational safety and health standards, and to keep records of occupational injuries and illnesses. Its safety standards are enforced through a system of inspections, citations, fines, and criminal penalties.

Managing Contemporary Safety, Health, and Behavioral Issues

The most significant safety, health, and behavioral issues for employers are AIDS, violence in the workplace, cumulative trauma disorders, fetal protection, hazardous chemicals, and genetic testing. In all of these areas, line managers must deal with a variety of practical, legal, and ethical questions that often demand a careful balancing of individual rights (especially privacy rights) with the needs of the organization.

Safety and Health Programs

Comprehensive safety programs are well-planned efforts in which management (1) involves employees and carefully considers their suggestions, (2) communicates safety rules to employees and enforces them, (3) invests in training supervisors to demonstrate and communicate safety on the job, (4) uses incentives to encourage safe behaviors and discipline to penalize unsafe behaviors, and (5) engages in regular self-inspection and accident research to identify and correct potentially dangerous situations.

Employee assistance programs (EAPs) are designed to help employees cope with physical, mental, or emotional problems (including stress) that are undermining their job performance.

Wellness programs are preventive efforts designed to help employees identify potential health risks and deal with them before they become problems.

Key Terms

burnout, 528

cumulative trauma disorder (CTD), 523

genetic testing, 525

negligent hiring, 520

Occupational Safety and Health Act of 1970 (OSHA), 512

wellness program, 529

Discussion Questions

1. What is the difference between the objectives of workers' compensation and the objectives of OSHA?
2. What kinds of policies do you think would work best to prevent workplace violence?
3. Do you think the approach taken by OSHA to improve ergonomic safety will be effective? Why or why not?
4. If a job is potentially hazardous to the fetus of a pregnant employee, should it be legal for the company to restrict the job to men?
5. How could genetic testing be used to discriminate?
6. How can managers use the organization's reward system to encourage workplace safety?
7. *Karoshi*, a term coined by the Japanese, means "death from overwork." *Karoshi* is now the second-leading cause of death, after cancer, among Japanese workers. Put yourself in the place of a Japanese manager. What could you do to reduce the risk of *karoshi* in your workers? Do you think *karoshi* will become a problem in the United States? Explain your answer.
8. It was argued in this chapter that an empowerment approach to improving safety could yield positive results. The operation of consultative safety teams including cleaning workers was used as an example. However, a participative approach to safety improvement means employee time away from other duties and decreased productivity. Do you think the trade-off may be worth it? Why or why not?

There is a variety of additional material available on the Web site that accompanies this text. You can access this information by visiting the Web site at **www.prenhall.com/gomez**.

Ethics Case 16.1 — YOU MANAGE IT!

Workplace Bullying

We all probably remember the spectre of the schoolyard bully—a person who would intimidate, criticize, belittle, and generally make life miserable for others. Unfortunately, bullying doesn't stop in the school playground; it can happen anywhere, including the workplace. So, just what is workplace bullying? Washington State's Workplace Bullying and Trauma Institute defines bullying as repeated, nonphysical, health-impairing psychological mistreatment that falls outside of discriminatory harassment.[a] The Institute does not have estimates of the financial impact of workplace bullying in the United States. However, it is estimated that in Europe bullying results in 80 million lost workdays per year, stress, and mental health problems. Further, bullying can reduce productivity and lead to increased turnover.[b] Australian researchers estimate that bullying costs $20,000 per case.[c]

Critical Thinking Questions

1. Is workplace bullying different from harassment? Explain.
2. One approach to managing workplace bullying is legislation.[d] Australia, for example, has legal standards that directly or indirectly address bullying. Norway, Britain, and France have similar legislation. Quebec is the first region in North America to have passed legislation, the Labor Standards Act, that addresses workplace bullying. The act defines psychological harassment at work as "vexatious behavior that manifests itself in the form of conduct, verbal comments, actions or gestures" that are repetitive, hostile, and unwanted.

   Is legislation an effective tool for managing workplace bullying? Why or why not? Do you think workplace bullying legislation should be passed in the United States? Explain.

Team Exercise

An old business adage states that if you can't measure it, you can't manage it. Applying this simple but powerful logic to workplace bullying suggests that workplace bullying needs to be measured in order to be effectively managed. Just what, however, can or should be measured? That question can best be addressed by considering examples of workplace bullying. The following list provides behavioral examples of workplace bullying. You can find more examples by going to *www.bullyonline.org.*

- Being constantly criticized over trivial matters
- Being humiliated, shouted at, or threatened, often in front of others
- Finding that your work and credit for it have been stolen

- Finding things that you say and do are twisted and misrepresented

As a team, address the issue of measuring bullying in the workplace. How should it be measured? What kind of measurement instrument should be used? How will the criteria be generated? Address these key issues and identify a process that your team would recommend to develop measures of workplace bullying.

If possible, generate an example of what a measure might look like. Would it be a rating scale, a checklist, or something else? Also, who would complete the measures?

Lastly, identify your plan for the resulting data. That is, what would you do with your results? Would you assess individuals with the data? Would you try to identify bullies? What utility would the measurements have?

Share your measurement approach and example with the rest of the class. Also describe your management plan with regard to the use of the data. Under the direction of the instructor, the class should select the best measurement approach and the best management plan.

Experiential Exercise

Workplace bullying can take a variety of forms (see the partial list in the team exercise). With your teammates, identify an episode representing workplace bullying and prepare to role-play this example. Each team presents their role-play example to the class. If needed, the team should explain how the action portrays bullying.

As a class, consider the role-play examples. For each role-play, address what should be done to prevent or eliminate such bullying. (The instructor can lead this class discussion following each role-play.) Also as a class, consider the possible utility of such role-plays. How could the role-play approach be used as part of a program to manage bullying in organizations?

Sources: [a] Gurchiek, K. (2005). Study: Domestic violence spills over into the workplace. *NRMagazine, 50,* 32, 38; [b] *Ibid.;* [c] Nood, S. B. (2004). Workplace bullying. *Canadian Business, 77,* 87–89; [d] *Ibid.*

YOU MANAGE IT!   Emerging Trends Case 16.2

On the Tip of a Beryllium Iceberg?

The Occupational Safety and Health Administration (OSHA) is the agency companies and workers count on, sometimes grudgingly, to make sure that the workplace is a safe as it can be. One of the principal means by which OSHA uses to ensure workplace safety is standards for work practices, acceptable levels of chemicals, and so on. Safety isn't just a matter of standards, however; managers and workers must act together to develop a

culture of safety so that safety is a guiding value rather than a matter of compliance. What happens, however, if the standards really aren't sufficient to keep people safe? It looks like this may be the case with the standard for exposure to beryllium, and some of the people affected include OSHA's own employees.

Beryllium is an impressive metal; it is lighter than aluminum, yet stiffer than steel. It is an ingredient in atomic bombs and is used in the dental, telecom, and aerospace industries. It shows up in cell phones, computers, cars, and golf clubs. Beryllium is also showing up in recycling operations.

The problem with beryllium is that its dust is toxic. Just a few millionths of a gram can fatally damage lungs and other organs. Exposure to smaller amounts can sensitize the immune system and lead to the development of a disease called *chronic beryllium disease*. Beryllium is increasingly being used in workplaces, but it appears that this use could be placing workers at risk. The National Jewish Medical and Research Center in Denver tests and treats people with chronic beryllium disease. Dr. Lee Newman, a leading expert who works at the Center, considers chronic beryllium disease an unrecognized epidemic whose full extent we have scarcely begun to understand.

A standard for exposure to beryllium exists, but it looks like it may be inadequate to ensure safety. That was the concern of Adam Finkel, an OSHA employee who told a reporter that he thought OSHA was not protecting its own workers from the danger of beryllium. Finkel pushed for tests for all OSHA inspectors. According to Finkel, OSHA's response was to attack and demote him. OSHA denied this charge, and Finkel filed a whistle-blower complaint and settled the case for an undisclosed sum. Perhaps most important, OSHA has since been testing its inspectors for sensitization to beryllium. Of the 271 inspectors tested at the time of this writing, 10 have been found to be sensitized to the metal and are at risk for developing a potentially fatal lung disease. However, as many as 1,000 current and former compliance officers may have been exposed. The largest producer of beryllium, BrushWellman Inc., considers OSHA's current standards to be inadequate. The company has adopted its own exposure standard for airborne beryllium that is one-tenth the level permitted by OSHA.

Critical Thinking Questions

1. The beryllium sensitization of OSHA's compliance officers has raised concerns for the thousands of industry workers who are exposed to beryllium. OSHA officers visit the workplaces only sporadically, while industry workers are exposed on a more regular basis. Do you think these workers should be tested for beryllium sensitization? Who should bear the cost of the testing?

2. OSHA has been criticized for its inadequate beryllium exposure standards. The agency did try to push through lower exposure limits in the 1970s, but companies stopped passage of the new standards by claiming they couldn't afford to meet the lower standard. Given this history, do you think the companies or OSHA are responsible for today's inadequate exposure standards?

3. OSHA could lose credibility with companies over other safety issues due to the beryllium exposure problems. If you were hired as a consultant by OSHA, what would you recommend to reduce the possible damage of the beryllium issue to the agency's reputation and effectiveness?

Team Exercise

As a team, place yourselves in the position of managers in a company that assesses beryllium. What standard for beryllium exposure would you recommend? Would you defer to OSHA standards, knowing that some of its officers have developed beryllium sensitivity? Or, would you recommend a lower standard? How could this new standard be determined? How should the company go about choosing a safe standard?

Many workers in your company may be concerned, even fearful, regarding their own exposure levels. What are your recommendations for dealing with the concerns of these workers?

As a team, present your recommendations regarding a standard in managing the concerns of the workers. With the guidance of the instructor, the class selects and compiles the best recommendations from the teams.

Experiential Exercise

It is ironic that OSHA's own officers were exposed to unsafe conditions. More than irony, some people are questioning not only the standards, but the safety culture within OSHA.

Select representatives to serve in the roles of OSHA advisory board members. These representatives are responsible for generating recommendations for OSHA to follow in reestablishing a strong safety culture within the organization. What are the drawbacks if these steps are not taken?

Sources: Adapted from Carey, J. (2005, May). The 'unrecognized epidemic': Beryllium can be toxic to the workers who handle it. Where has OSHA been? *BusinessWeek,* 40–42; Minter, S. G. (2005). Erring on the side of disaster. *Occupational Hazards,* 67, 6.

Global Case 16.3   YOU MANAGE IT!

Mental Health: A Global Concern

Hazards in the workplace can pose risks to mental health, just as they can pose risks to physical health. Unfortunately, poor mental health sometimes can have a negative connotation and is often not addressed. Fortunately, the importance of mental health in the work place is being recognized in multiple countries.

Mental health problems can influence how someone experiences life (including work), how engaged they are, and their effectiveness as an employee. It is estimated that each year one in four people will experience a mental health problem, with depression and anxiety being the most common problems.[a] Further, it is increasingly being recognized that mental health problems can be brought on or exacerbated by workplace conditions. A recent survey found that two-thirds of respondents believe that heavy workloads, unrealistic expectations, and overwork cause or exacerbate mental health problems.

In Europe, stress-related sick leave is estimated to total 91 million working days per year—an enormous loss to European business. Europeans are taking a proactive approach to the problem. In 2005, 52 countries endorsed a "Mental Health Plan for Europe" that highlights the importance of workplace interventions to improve mental health. According to the plan, employers need to recognize and accept mental health as a legitimate concern and take responsibility for minimizing workplace causes of mental health problems. European companies are being advised to conduct an audit or survey to identify workplace characteristics that may be problematic. European companies are also being encouraged to develop mental health policies, take steps to raise awareness and reduce stigma, and introduce preventive and rehabilitative steps.

The importance of mental health in the workplace is also being recognized in Canada. A recent Canadian survey of 100 organizations found that over three-quarters of the organizations believe mental health issues are a leading cause of short- and long-term disability claims.[b] Unfortunately, although recognizing the importance of mental health, few Canadian companies seem to be doing much about it. The problem isn't that companies don't want to do anything; they just don't know what actions should be taken to improve employees' mental health. A 10-year study is currently looking at practical workplace actions to deal with, delay, or prevent mental health problems in the Canadian workforce.

China also recognizes the importance of the mental health of employees. Chinese workers are facing increasing workloads and stress on their jobs, and depression and anxiety are increasing.[c] China recently announced that it will introduce a program to help employees improve their mental health. The program will apply models that have been effective in other countries, such as employee assistance programs, to improve the mental health of Chinese workers.

Critical Thinking Questions

1. Mental health problems often have a negative stigma. What, if anything, do you think companies can do to reduce this stigma?

2. Recognizing the importance of mental health in the workplace seems like the only moral thing to do. Yet, employers face difficulties in effectively dealing with this area. For example, mental health is less visible and apparent than physical health. How can an employer be protected from feigning and fraud if it takes a liberal approach to dealing with mental health?

3. Mental health problems can be caused by many factors outside of the workplace. For example, genetics and family life may predispose or cause mental health difficulties.

Nonetheless, these difficulties can show up in the workplace. Does the employer have some responsibility for dealing with these mental health problems? Explain.

Team Exercise

The European model includes an audit as well as actions to improve mental health. Place yourselves in the position of a mental health task force for a company. As a team, develop steps to address mental health in the workplace. Specifically, what would your team recommend for an audit? What should be measured and how? What actions would you recommend to reduce a negative stigma that can be associated with mental health problems? Finally, identify actions companies can take to improve mental health in the workplace.

Share your team's recommendations with the rest of the class. With the direction of the instructor, the class should put together a combined plan that puts together the best recommendations from the team presentations.

Experiential Exercise

The increasing importance of mental health in the workplace can be attributed to the characteristics of modern work. Technology has brought about increased efficiency, but also more rapid change and stress. Work must now be accomplished more quickly and often from remote sites. In addition, downsizing and outsourcing have increased pressure and uncertainty for workers. These work characteristics can take their toll on employees' mental health.

However, some experts question whether the workplace has really become more stressful.[d] Work is not meant to be a therapeutic environment. Further, the stress of today's work pales in comparison to working conditions in the past. Previous generations of your family probably worked for little pay, no pension, no health care, and under oppressive conditions. Claiming to be "stressed out" can just be an employee's excuse for time away from work.

Select representatives for two opposing teams reflecting the two positions just described. One team takes the position that mental health in the workplace is an important issue that calls for proactive employer actions. The other team takes the position that mental health is not the employer problem it is made out to be and that special employer actions are not needed. Each team should identify its assumptions and rationale.

As a class, determine whether there was a clear winner to the debate. Is there a consensus in the class on the workplace mental health issue?

Source: Adapted from [a] St. John, T. (2005, May). Mental health at work: The hard facts. *Training Journal,* 44–47; [b] Brown, D. (2005). Mental illness a top concern, but only gets band-aid treatment. *Canadian HR Reporter, 18,* 1–3; [c] Xinhua General News Service (2005, June 3). China to introduce special news program for employees' mental health; [d] Furedi, F. (2005, April 11). Have we become too feeble to cope with life? *The Express* (U.K.), 18.

Discussion Case 16.4

Refusing to Perform a Hazardous Task at Whirlpool

At the Whirlpool appliance plant in Marion, Ohio, overhead conveyors were used to transport appliance components from one area of the plant to another. To prevent workers from being harmed by falling parts, the company had installed a horizontal wire mesh screen secured to angle iron frames beneath the conveyor belts. The mesh was about 20 feet above the plant floor.

Part of regular maintenance at the plant included spending several hours each week removing parts from the screen and replacing paper used to catch grease that dropped from the conveyor. Maintenance employees had to stand on the angle frames, or on the mesh itself to perform the work.

In 1973, the company began to replace the mesh with a heavier mesh because of safety concerns. Several employees had fallen partway through the mesh, and one had even fallen to the floor below but had survived. When employees brought complaints about the unsafe conditions to the foreman, they were instructed to walk on the iron beams only, not the mesh.

In June 1974, a maintenance employee fell through the old mesh to his death. The next week two maintenance employees, Virgil Deemer and Thomas Cornwell, again complained about safety issues. Two days later, they asked the plant safety director to provide them with a phone number of the area OSHA office. They were told to think about what they were doing, but were given the number. They subsequently called an OSHA inspector.

The next day, the foreman instructed Deemer and Cornwell to walk on the mesh screen to perform regular maintenance. They refused to comply with the foreman's order, claiming that the work was unsafe. Both employees were told to go to the personnel office. They were then instructed to punch out for the remainder of the day and were subsequently given a written reprimand for insubordination.

This case eventually made its way to the U.S. Supreme Court. The Court upheld the rights of workers under the Occupational Safety and Health Act to choose not to perform their assigned task because of a reasonable apprehension of death or serious injury, when no other alternative is available to them.

Critical Thinking Questions

1. Was Deemer and Cornwell's refusal to perform their assigned tasks justified by a reasonable apprehension of death or injury?
2. The HR manager has the responsibility to protect employees, but at the same time it does not want to be perceived as undermining a supervisor's authority. Why is this balancing act so difficult in the type of situation discussed in this case?
3. What unanticipated and damaging results could an organization suffer if it forces workers to do what they perceive as dangerous work?
4. Place yourself in the position of safety director at Whirlpool. What would you say and/or do when the employees come to you asking about how to contact OSHA? Outline your plans.
5. Describe how you would approach safety so that the accident at Whirlpool might have been prevented. Design the type of system or policies that you think should be in place to maximize safety in that type of environment.

Team Exercise

Students form into groups of four or five. Each group should develop criteria for "reasonableness" by which to judge refusal to perform job tasks perceived as dangerous. The leader of each group should then present its set of criteria to the class.

Experiential Exercises

Identify people in the class who have worked on dangerous jobs and ask them how dangerous tasks are assigned. Has anyone ever refused to perform, or been in a situation where they have seen others refuse to perform, dangerous work? If so, what was the result of the refusal?

Students form into groups of three or four to discuss the effects on individuals of asking them to choose between their livelihood (their job) and their safety. Each group should elect a leader to present its conclusions to the class.

Source: Whirlpool Corp v. Marshall, 100 S.Ct. 883 [1980].

Customer-Driven HR Case 16.5

Desk Rage: Safe Office Environment or Explosive Reactions Waiting to Happen?

Costas worked long hours in cramped quarters at an Internet company in New York. He continually had to deal with rushed deadlines, but he kept a check on his frustration over the work demands and his work environment. One day his boss pushed him one time too many and Costas unloaded with an obscenity-laden tirade. He quit his job one week later commenting "sometimes you just snap."

Two engineers at an aerospace company in Connecticut had a disagreement over the proper procedure for filing paperwork regarding a faulty computer chip. The disagreement quickly escalated and the engineers had to be physically separated.

These two real-life workplace examples illustrate the explosion of tempers that can occur in the workplace. Such incidents led the *Wall Street Journal* to label the phenomenon "desk rage." The occurrence of desk rage is thought to be a function of various sources of stress. For example, lost tempers, shouting matches, and fistfights can be induced by overwork and crowding. As pointed out by Victor Scarano, director of occupational and forensic psychiatry at Baylor College of Medicine in Houston, "You can't run an engine at full throttle for 10 years and not expect it to crack." In addition to high work demands, many workers are finding themselves more cramped for space than ever before. Perhaps due to cost-containment efforts and the price of commercial real estate, the average number of employees per square foot is at a peak level in many office spaces. In addition, many employees commute long distances and by the time they reach their demanding and cramped work environments, they are already frustrated, if not irate, from battling traffic congestion. The problem of stress appears to be more of an issue in larger organizations with approximately a third of employees in organizations with more than 1,000 people reporting that they are "at least somewhat" stressed whereas 16 percent of employees in organizations with fewer than 100 people report this level of stress.

Although many organizations ignore the desk rage issue, there are some companies that have taken steps to manage the problem. General Motors Corporation, for example, offers meditation and tai chi at its workout facilities. At its tax center in Indianapolis, Ernst & Young has included golfing areas, fish tanks, and a recreation room where workers can nap.

Critical Thinking Questions

1. Do you think desk rage is a problem that should be dealt with in organizations? Why or why not?
2. What do you think should be done when people lose their tempers in the workplace? What disciplinary actions should be taken for episodes such as yelling and using obscenities, physical engagement, and hitting? Does one episode merit disciplinary action or would you wait for a pattern to develop? Why?
3. Given your judgments in response to item 2, construct a matrix made up of desk rage examples along one axis and possible disciplinary actions along the other. (You may want to consult Chapter 14 and consider including positive discipline as an option in the array of possible management actions.) Make checks in the cells of the matrix when each type of disciplinary action is appropriate for the various forms of desk rage. Explain your rationale for the discipline choices.

Team Exercise

The management of desk rage, if it occurs, seems to focus on relaxing people and helping them to deal with stress. However,

this approach can be viewed as addressing the symptom, not the causes. If desk rage is a problem, it would seem worthwhile to try to solve the problem rather than alleviate the symptom. In other words, a cure would seem more advisable than temporary improvement.

As a team, address two fundamental issues:

1. Is desk rage a problem?
2. What should be done about it?

Divide your team in half so that the two issues can be separately but simultaneously addressed. For the first issue, generate measures you think would indicate the extent to which desk rage may be a problem. For example, questionnaire items measuring the stress employees experience could be an important indicator. Also consider using measures that ask people about their intention or likelihood to, for example, throw items or yell at others in the workplace. You may also want to include measures of the occurrence of rage, asking, for example, if employees have observed or experienced someone acting out various forms of desk rage in the workplace. Finalize your set of measures.

The second issue of what to do to manage the problem leads to a consideration of causes. Specifically, what might be the major causes of desk rage? You might begin to structure sets of possible causes by categorizing causes as either person or system causes. Person causes would be factors that reside inside a worker, such as someone naturally being "hot-headed" or having little impulse control. Situational causes would be factors outside of the person that the employee experiences as stress. For each cause, identify whether it fits in the person or system category and brainstorm what, if anything, could be done to eliminate, reduce, or somehow improve the causal factor.

As one team, put together your measures with your model of causes and management actions. Are there causes that aren't being addressed in the measures of the extent to which desk rage is a problem? If so, can you add or refine the measures to include these causes? Finally, how could you determine the effectiveness of actions you might take to manage the causes of desk rage?

Experiential Exercise

Place yourself in the role of a consultant team. You have an assessment tool and a model of possible solutions if you find a problem. Sell your products and process to the rest of the class. What can you offer? Does every organization need to take action to manage desk rage? How will you know what to do and how can you tell if it will be effective? In sum, what will the rest of the class as a fictitious organization get if it invests in your consulting team?

Source: Adapted from Costello, D. (2001). Desk rage incidents erupt in more offices . . . Long hours produce some short fuses. *Asian Wall Street Journal,* January 18, N–1.

International HRM Challenge

Challenges

After reading this chapter, you should be able to deal more effectively with the following challenges:

1 **Specify** the HRM strategies that are most appropriate for firms at different stages of internationalization.

2 **Identify** the best mix of host-country and expatriate employees given the conditions facing a firm.

3 **Explain** why international assignments often fail and the steps a firm can take to ensure success in this area.

4 **Reintegrate** returning employees into the firm after they complete an international assignment.

5 **Develop** HRM policies and procedures that match the needs and values of different cultures.

6 **Consider** ethical implications of HRM policies and procedures on a global basis.

Nicaraguan-born Roberto Castillo has had a series of jobs at car dealerships—first Ford, then Pontiac, and eventually Hyundai. But two years ago he landed the job he really wanted: selling Toyotas. "Everyone knows the reputation (of Toyotas)," he says, "so you never have to sell (people) on the benefits." Nowadays, Castillo works at Longo Toyota in the Los Angeles suburb of El Monte. Last year he piled up commissions worth more than $80,000. "You can make good money with Toyota," he says.

From headquarters in Toyota City, 62 miles east of Nozoya, Japan, Toyota Chief Executive Fujio Cho has given Toyota's top executives this simply stated goal: "We must Americanize!"

That goal and its results are being achieved. Consider the following facts, including some statistics that scare Toyota's rivals in Detroit:

- Toyota sells more vehicles in the United States (2.10 million) than in Japan (1.73 million). Analysts figure that almost two-thirds of Toyota's operating profit comes from the United States. By 2006 Toyota is close to overtaking General Motors, Ford, and Chrysler in the domestic US market.
- Unions are joining hands with state government to woo Toyota to open plants in Michigan. They hope the company that has taken business away from the Big Three—G.M., Ford, and the Chrysler division of DaimlerChrysler—will hire those workers who have been laid off or who have seen their compensation and benefits curtailed (see Chapter 10).
- Toyota's U.S. factories directly employ more than 56,000 workers, but including those who work for local suppliers and dealerships dependent on Toyota's production, the total number of Americans who make a living from Toyota is approximately 160,000, far more than the number for Coca-Cola, Microsoft, and Oracle combined.[1]
- Toyota's top U.S. executives are increasingly U.S. hires. James Press, chief operating officer of Toyota Motor Sales USA Inc. in Torrance, California, says "Thirty years ago, we were more dependent on Japan."

Toyota has changed its strategy of localization, or establishing factories in major markets and building out supply chains around the world in order to create a single integrated production process with parts manufactured in one country designed for use in vehicles assembled in another.[2] This means that In the next several years, Toyota will stress the selection, training and development, performance appraisal, and appropriate incentives for a new cadre of "global employees" capable of implementing this universal strategy. As a start, Toyota has opened a new Global Production Center where 1,500 employees—half from overseas facilities in China, Malaysia, and Indonesia—are trained in integrated production processes. Most of these trainees will go back to their home country and assist in the effective execution of a global supply chain.[3]

THE MANAGERIAL PERSPECTIVE

As firms such as Toyota begin to dominate international markets, HRM practices must have a global perspective to give the company a competitive advantage. There are at least 58,000 multinational companies with 50,000 affiliates worldwide.[4] Managers must select, retain, promote, reward, and train employees to help them meet this global challenge. Even small firms trying to export their products or services via the Internet must cope with the challenges of international business. For the growing number of companies operating in various countries, the HRM system and practices must be successfully adapted to a variety of cultural, socioeconomic, and legal conditions.

Virtually every U.S. company now faces competition from abroad, and the fortunes of most U.S. firms, large and small, are inextricably bound to the global economy.[5] In this chapter, we demonstrate how managers can use HRM practices to enhance their firms' competitiveness in an era of international opportunities and challenges. First, we cover the stages of international involvement, the challenges of expatriate job assignments, and ways to make those assignments more effective. We then discuss the development of HRM policies in a global context and the specific HR concerns of exporting firms.

The Stages of International Involvement

As Figure 17.1 shows, firms progress through five stages as they internationalize their operations.[6] The higher the stage, the more the firm's HR practices must be adapted to diverse cultural, economic, political, and legal environments.

- In *Stage 1*, the firm's market is exclusively domestic. One firm at this stage today is Boulder Beer, which produces its ales in the Boulder, Colorado, area and seldom sells them outside the Mountain States region. Many other U.S. firms are still at this stage, but their number is diminishing, particularly in manufacturing. Staffing, training, and compensation for firms at Stage I are dictated primarily by local and/or national forces. The only sites considered for plant locations are in the United States, and only the national or regional market is considered in strategic business decisions about production and marketing issues.

- In *Stage 2*, the firm expands its market to include foreign countries but retains its production facilities within domestic borders. HRM practices at this stage should facilitate exporting of the firm's products through managerial incentives, appropriate training, and staffing strategies that focus on the demands of international customers.[7]

  An example of a Stage 2 firm is Turbo-Tek Enterprises, Inc., located in Los Angeles. It generates $50 million a year in revenues, 38 percent of which comes from overseas sales. The firm's single product is Turbo Wash, a water-spraying attachment for common household hoses. Turbo-Tek's entire manufacturing, packaging, and distribution system is designed with international markets in mind, and the firm's HRM practices play a crucial role in this system. Managerial bonuses are substantially based on foreign sales, and Turbo-Tek rewards its employees for developing innovative ideas to increase exports.

  Falling trade barriers are greatly increasing the number of U.S. firms that fall into Stage 2.[8] According to the World Trade Centers Association (WTCA), which has more than 287 licensed world trade affiliates in 88 countries and more than 750,000 companies and individuals, approximately 45 percent of companies with fewer than 500 employees exported products and

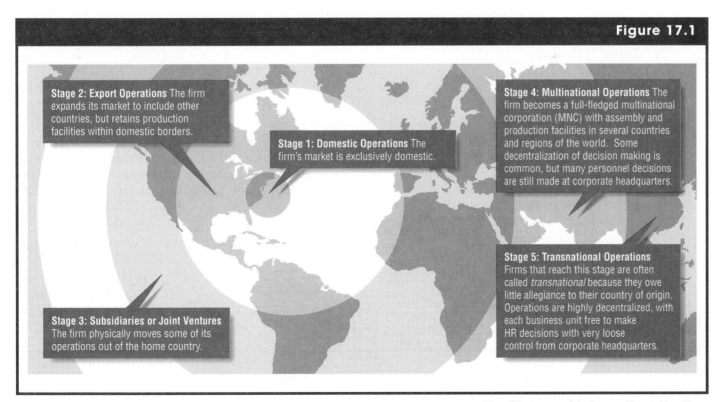

Figure 17.1

Stage 2: Export Operations The firm expands its market to include other countries, but retains production facilities within domestic borders.

Stage 1: Domestic Operations The firm's market is exclusively domestic.

Stage 4: Multinational Operations The firm becomes a full-fledged multinational corporation (MNC) with assembly and production facilities in several countries and regions of the world. Some decentralization of decision making is common, but many personnel decisions are still made at corporate headquarters.

Stage 5: Transnational Operations Firms that reach this stage are often called *transnational* because they owe little allegiance to their country of origin. Operations are highly decentralized, with each business unit free to make HR decisions with very loose control from corporate headquarters.

Stage 3: Subsidiaries or Joint Ventures The firm physically moves some of its operations out of the home country.

The Stages of Internationalization

services in 2006—more than three times the number of companies that did so in 1992. For instance, after NAFTA went into effect in 1993, Treatment Products Ltd. landed contracts with almost every major retail chain in Mexico. Shipments to Mexico have tripled to roughly $300,000, about 20 percent of the company's total current exports.[9]

- In *Stage 3,* the firm physically moves some of its operations out of the home country. These facilities are primarily used for parts assembly, although some limited manufacturing may take place. For instance, many U.S. apparel manufacturers have opened facilities throughout the Caribbean to assemble a wide variety of garments. The foreign branches or subsidiaries tend to be under close control of corporate headquarters at this stage, and a high proportion of top managers are **expatriates** (employees who are citizens of the corporation's home country). HRM practices at Stage 3 need to focus on the selection, training, and compensation of expatriates, as well as on the development of HR policies for local employees where the foreign facilities are located.

- In *Stage 4,* the firm becomes a full-fledged **multinational corporation (MNC)**, with assembly and production facilities in several countries and regions of the world. Strategic alliances between domestic and foreign firms, such as that between Ford Motor Company and Mazda Motor Corporation to build trucks in Thailand, are very common.[10] While there is usually some decentralization of decision making for firms at Stage 4, many personnel decisions affecting foreign branches are still made at corporate headquarters, typically by an international personnel department. In addition, foreign operations are still managed by expatriates. Amoco, IBM, Rockwell, General Motors, General Electric, and Xerox are all at Stage 4.

- In *Stage 5,* the most advanced stage of internationalization, firms are often called **transnational corporations** because they owe little allegiance to their country of origin and have weak ties to any given country. Operations are highly decentralized; each business unit is free to make personnel decisions with very loose control from corporate headquarters. The board of directors is often composed of people of different nationalities, and the firm tries hard to develop managers who see themselves as citizens of the world.

  HRM practices at Stage 5 companies are designed to blend individuals from diverse backgrounds to create a shared corporate (rather than national) identity and a common vision. For instance, Gillette conducts an extensive management training program for which local personnel offices in 48 countries search for the best young university graduates who are single and fluent in English. In the words of Gillette's international personnel director, "The person we are looking for is someone who says, 'Today, it's Manila. Tomorrow, it's the U.S. Four years from now, it's Peru or Pakistan.' . . . We really work hard at finding people who aren't parochial and who want international careers."[11]

Expatriate
A citizen of one country living and working in another country.

Multinational corporation (MNC)
A firm with assembly and production facilities in several countries and regions of the world.

Transnational corporation
A firm with operations in many countries and highly decentralized operations. The firm owes little allegiance to its country of origin and has weak ties to any given country.

A Question of Ethics

U.S. law does not prohibit selection decisions based on marital status, as long as they are applied equally to men and women. Why might a company have such a policy? Is it ethical? Is it in the best long-term interests of the company?

The Rise of Outsourcing

Firms in Stages 3 through 5 often outsource their production and services to countries where they find a competitive advantage in lower labor costs. Fewer and fewer firms can grow or even survive unless they engage in some form of outsourcing (see the Manager's Notebook, "Outsourcing Around the World Increases at Breakneck Speed"). While some believe that exporting jobs to less developed countries keeps salaries and benefits at home low, most international business experts believe that it is not realistic to turn the clock back when companies are free to locate where ever they want.[12] Further, consumers benefit from lower prices achieved by outsourcing, and countries that are the recipients of outsourcing use increased earnings to purchase goods and services from the United States. Political leaders are unlikely to push for restrictive legislation to curtail outsourcing in the foreseeable future.

MANAGER'S NOTEBOOK

Emerging Trends

Outsourcing Around the World Increases at Breakneck Speed

In a recent editorial, *BusinessWeek* warns that

outsourcing is proving to be a far greater challenge to America than anticipated. Not only are companies sending their low-cost production and services to Asia, but they are also shipping much more of their research and development overseas. What were once considered core competencies for high tech and other companies are now becoming inexpensive global commodities.[a]

A similar sentiment is becoming prevalent in Western Europe, where labor costs are even higher in several countries than in the United States.[b] Here are some instances of this emerging trend.

The Case of India[c]

When British prime minister Tony Blair went to India, he didn't visit the Taj Mahal; he visited the lavish corporate campus of Inform, one of the most successful players in the $12 billion market for offshore software coding and maintenance. The Nasdaq-listed company earned $131 million on $413 million in revenues.

India today earns more than $17 billion from corporations worldwide seeking low-cost overseas talent to do everything from writing software to collecting debts to designing semiconductors. A top software programmer in India with two to four years' experience makes about $10,000 a year, compared with $62,000 in the United States, according to Hewitt Associates LLC, a Lincolnshire, Illinois, consulting firm. U.S. firms are rushing in to take advantage of this opportunity. For instance, in addition to hiring at least 1,000 scientists, General Electric has hired 10,000 Indian employees in the last few years to handle accounting, claims processing, customer service, and credit evaluation.

The Case of China[d]

China, which sends one-third of its exports to the United States, accounts for 26 percent of the U.S. trade gap. Most of its exports to the United States are manufactured products, made by workers earning only 4.5 percent of the average U.S. factory wage. For instance, using 2005 figures, the *New York Times*[e] estimates that the hourly cost of wages and benefits in the Chinese auto sector is $1.96, compared with $49.60, $40.96, and $36.55 in Germany, Japan, and United States, respectively. As more U.S. companies try to cut costs, Chinese workers are increasingly competing for U.S. manufacturing jobs and putting downward pressure on pay. Approximately 75 percent of all garments sold in the United States, most with U.S. company labels, are manufactured in China. Likewise, the European Union has seen garment imports from China increase more than 10-fold after a 40-year quota system was lifted in 2005.[f] As Chinese industry becomes more sophisticated, more complex products are likely to follow. For example, the Chrysler unit of DaimlerChrysler is planning to start producing sedans in China by 2009 to import back to the United States.

The Case of Mexico[g]

Mexico's maquiladoras, U.S. owned assembly units south of the U.S.–Mexico border, employ approximately 1.2 million Mexican workers, producing $19 billion in foreign exchange for Mexico, surpassing contributions from oil exports or remittances from Mexicans working abroad. Among the sector's big labor gainers in recent years are so-called "service" maquiladoras, operations that do everything from sorting supermarket coupons to repairing home appliances returned to retailers under warranty by U.S. consumers. However, Mexico is losing ground to Asia in the competition for light-assembly jobs. According to Roberto Coronado (an El Paso economist), "Apparel has grown, but not as fast as it used to." Labor costs for unskilled labor in China are less than one-third of those in Mexico.

Sources: [a]*BusinessWeek* (2005, March 21). Getting an edge on innovation, 124; [b]Jacoby, M. (2005, March 4). EU won't allow crossing borders for health work. *Wall Street Journal*, A-13; [c]Adapted with permission from Salomon, J., and Kranhold, K. (2005, March 23). In India's outsourcing boom, GE played a starring role. *Wall Street Journal*, A-1; See also Lavin, D. (2002, February 1). Globalization goes upscale. *Wall Street Journal*, A-3; [d]Tyson, L. (2005, May 2). Stop scapegoating China before it is too late. *BusinessWeek*, 26; [e]*New York Times*. (2005, April 22). China looming as the next big auto exporter, C-5; [f]Medler, P. (2005, April 23). Rise in Chinese textile imports prompts inquiry in Europe. *New York Times*, B-2; [g]Adapted with permission from Millman, J. (2005, March 22). Maquiladora resumed hiring growth. *Wall Street Journal*, A-13.

The growth of outsourcing may be attributed to a large extent to the Internet. However, the Internet poses some serious challenges to outsourcing, because of problems with online security (see the Manager's Notebook, "Hiring and Training Employees to Control Cyberspace.") Rank-and-file employees are increasingly asked to play a role in fighting Internet-based threats. For instance, in India, which depends heavily on the Internet for much of the outsourcing it receives, there is widespread fear that well-publicized security threats could wreak havoc on the economy. Hence, Indian companies are trying to select workers who can be trusted and training all employees to be on the lookout for any suspicious activity.

As a case in point, two Indian employees who worked for MPhasis BFLTD, a Citibank subcontractor, logged on to Citi's online system and transferred at least $426,000 from U.S. customers to their own accounts. Because computer systems at Citibank subcontractors in India let local employees see sensitive information about U.S. customers (for example, Social Security number, credit history, and savings account number), the system was open to abuse. This kind of security risk is compounded by hasty selection and training, because attrition in the industry is about 60 percent.[13] But most Indian companies, including MPhasis, are channeling more resources into improving employee screening, reducing attrition, and training employees to spot and report potential security problems. Citibank has no plans to curtail outsourcing to India. "If the industry can keep improving security, it has little to fear in the long-term."[14]

MANAGER'S NOTEBOOK

Emerging Trends

Hiring and Training Employees to Control Cyberspace

No matter how security conscious a firm is, computer programs created anywhere on the planet can bend computers to serve the illicit purposes of the writer. The technology that has made the "global economy" possible has become, in the words of one analyst, "our Frankenputer."[a] In the next decade or so one of the biggest HR challenges on a global scale will be to train employees to combat this threat. This is no small task. The Internet is free of any jurisdiction, and attacks can come from just about any PC, from the jungles of the Phillipines to a small village in Nigeria. And what makes Internet technology easy to use is also what makes it vulnerable to attack.

Anonymous computer scanners from all five continents are rampaging across the Web, according to a new study by the German Honeynet project at Aachen University. At least 1 million computers are under cyber con artists' control worldwide. These computers are often linked together into powerful networks called *botnets* and rented to fellow scammers for as little as 2.5 cents per bot per week; some number 150,000 PCs. "Botnets are one of the most powerful weapons on the Internet," says Felix Freiling, professor of computer science at Aachen.[b]

Microsoft is particularly worried. The software giant recently trained 85 cybercrime fighters from 20 countries in techniques to combat the threat. After cybercriminals tried to steal $410 million from a large London bank, British banks began training tellers to recognize "computers infected by malicious software that turns them into zombies from which hackers can secretly send spam, launch viruses, or steal personal data."[c] The U.S. Postal Service is training its own employees as well as those of other organizations to recognize fraudulent postal money orders sent online from Nigeria, Ghana, and Eastern Europe. According to a USPS spokesperson, "The quality of what they are producing is very good. Ordinary consumers are not going to know what they are looking at."[d]

One country trying particularly hard to put limits on the Internet is China.[e] The Chinese have hired an army of 50,000 "Internet police" and plan to train twice as many in the future not only.

Sources: [a]Ross, P. E. (2005, March 14). Our Frankenputer. *Forbes,* 64; [b]Adapted with permission from *BusinessWeek.* (2005, May 2). Cybercriminals: Bots go Bonnie and Clyde, 14; [c]*Ibid.;* [d]Cited in Zeller, T. (2005, April 26). A common currency for online fraud. *New York Times,* C-1; [e]Adapted with permission from French, H. W. (2005, March 4). Chinese censors and Web users match wits. *New York Times,* B-2.

Determining the Mix of Host-Country and Expatriate Employees

Once a firm passes from the exporting stage (Stage 2) to the stage in which it opens a foreign branch (Stage 3)—either a **wholly owned subsidiary** (the foreign branch is fully owned by the home office) or a **joint venture** (part of the foreign branch is owned by a host-country entity: another company, a consortium of firms, an individual, or the government)—it must decide who will be responsible for managing the unit. A survey of 151 executives representing 138 large companies identified the choice of management for overseas units as one of their most crucial business decisions.[15]

There are three approaches to managing an international subsidiary: ethnocentric, polycentric, and geocentric.[16]

- In the **ethnocentric approach**, top management and other key positions are filled by people from the home country. For instance, Fluor Daniel, Inc., has 50 engineering and sales offices on five continents and construction projects in as many as 80 countries at any given time. The firm uses a large group of expatriate managers, including 500 international HRM professionals who are involved in recruitment, development, and compensation worldwide and who report directly to a corporate vice president.
- In the **polycentric approach**, international subsidiaries are managed and staffed by personnel from the host country. For instance, General Electric's Tungsram subsidiary in Hungary runs eight factories and employs 8,000 people, almost all of whom are Hungarian nationals.[17]
- In the **geocentric approach**, nationality is deliberately downplayed and the firm actively searches on a worldwide or regional basis for the best people to fill key positions.[18] Transnational firms (those in Stage 5) tend to follow this approach. For example, Electrolux has for many years attempted to recruit and develop a group of international managers from diverse countries. Rather than representing a particular country, they represent the organization wherever they are. Most important to Electrolux is the development of a common culture and an international perspective, and the expansion of its international networks.[19]

As Figure 17.2 shows, there are both advantages and disadvantages to using local nationals and expatriates in foreign subsidiaries. Most firms use expatriates only for key positions such as senior managers, high-level professionals, and technical specialists. Because expatriates tend to be very costly (approximately $85,000 to $280,000 per person per year, with some expatriates in Tokyo costing $500,000 a year in 2006 figures), it makes little financial sense to hire expatriates for positions that can be competently filled by foreign nationals. It has been estimated that an expatriate costs 2,000 to 4,000 percent more than a local employee.[20] In addition, many countries require that a certain percentage of the workforce be local citizens, with exceptions usually made for upper management.

In general, reliance on expatriates increases when:[21]

- **Sufficient local talent is not available.** This is most likely to occur in firms operating in developing countries. For instance, top managers of Falcombridge and Alcoa (both mining companies operating in Latin America and Africa) are almost always expatriates.
- **An important part of the firm's overall business strategy is the creation of a corporatewide global vision.** For example, Whirlpool Corporation, has operations in 40 countries and is deeply committed to the notion of one global company with one global vision. The company has a worldwide leadership program involving extensive use of expatriates, conferences that bring together top executives from different subsidiaries around the world, and global project teams that tackle common problems and facilitate a total international integration process.[22]
- **International units and domestic operations are highly interdependent.** For example, IBM, Hewlett-Packard, and Xerox have specialized manufacturing facilities in different parts of the United States and the world. The outputs of these different facilities (computer chips, software) must be closely monitored and integrated to produce highly sophisticated products such as computers, medical equipment, and photocopying machines. Linking production processes generally calls for greater reliance on expatriate managers and specialists, who can bridge the gaps and tie the units of the organization together.

Wholly owned subsidiary
In international business, a foreign branch owned fully by the home office.

Joint venture
In international business, a foreign branch owned partly by the home office and partly by an entity in the host country (a company, a consortium of firms, an individual, or the government).

Ethnocentric approach
An approach to managing international operations in which top management and other key positions are filled by people from the home country.

Polycentric approach
An approach to managing international operations in which subsidiaries are managed and staffed by personnel from the host country.

Geocentric approach
An approach to managing international operations in which nationality is downplayed and the firm actively searches on a worldwide or regional basis for the best people to fill key positions.

Figure 17.2

Locals

Advantages	Disadvantages
■ Lowers labor costs ■ Demonstrates trust in local citizenry ■ Increases acceptance of the company by the local community ■ Maximizes the number of options available in the local environment ■ Leads to recognition of the company as a legitimate participant in the local economy ■ Effectively represents local considerations and constraints in the decision-making process ■ Greater understanding of local conditions	■ Makes it difficult to balance local demands and global priorities ■ Leads to postponement of difficult local decisions (such as layoffs) until they are unavoidable, when they are more difficult, costly, and painful than they would have been if implemented earlier ■ May make it difficult to recruit qualified personnel ■ May reduce the amount of control exercised by headquarters

Expatriates

Advantages	Disadvantages
■ Cultural similarity with parent company ensures transfer of business/management practices ■ Permits closer control and coordination of international subsidiaries ■ Gives employees a multinational orientation through experience at parent company ■ Establishes a pool of internationally experienced executives ■ Local talent may not yet be able to deliver as much value as expatriates can ■ Provides broader global perspective	■ Creates problems of adaptability to foreign environment and culture ■ Increases the "foreignness" of the subsidiary ■ May involve high transfer, salary, and other costs ■ May result in personal and family problems ■ Has disincentive effect on local-management morale and motivation ■ May be subject to local government restrictions

Sources: Adapted from Hamil, J. (1989). Expatriate policies in British MNNs. *Journal of General Management, 14*(4), 20; Sheridan, W. R., and Hansen, P. T. (1996, Spring). Linking international business and expatriate compensation strategies. *ACA Journal,* 66–78; Hill, C. W. (2006). *International Business.* Chicago: Irwin McGraw-Hill.

Advantages and Disadvantages of Using Local and Expatriate Employees to Staff International Subsidiaries

Technology has dramatically reduced the need for expatriates to link the international units of the firm to the home office. For instance, a Wal-Mart outpost opens every week somewhere outside the United States, managed primarily by local employees. Wal-Mart can rely on local employees because it has 1,000 full-time information technology developers in the United States who develop systems that allow close monitoring of the stores from corporate headquarters in Bentonville, Arkansas.

■ **The political situation is unstable.** Corporations tend to rely on expatriates for top management positions when the risk of government intervention in the business is high, when actual or potential turmoil within the country is serious, when the threat of terrorism exists, and when there has been a recent history of social upheaval in the country. Although expatriate top managers may increase tensions between nationalistic groups and a foreign firm, they do provide some assurance to the home office that its interests are well represented locally. Expatriates are also less susceptible to the demands of local political forces.

■ **There are significant cultural differences between the host country and the home country.** The more dissimilar the cultures, the more important it is to appoint expatriates who can serve as interpreters or go-betweens. Because this boundary-spanning role demands much cross-cultural sensitivity, the MNC needs to select and carefully train individuals suitable for these positions. This may require considerable career planning.[23]

The Challenges of Expatriate Assignments

While the number of expatriates as a proportion of the total managerial and professional MNC workforce has declined over the years, their absolute number is on the rise in all regions.[24] A recent survey of 874 MNCs in 24 major industries shows that almost half of firms report an increase in the use of expatriates in the last few years. However, managing expatriates remains a challenge.

The failure of U.S. expatriates—that is, the percentage who return prematurely, without completing their assignment—is estimated to be in the 20 to 40 percent range, three to four times higher than the failure rates experienced by European and Asian companies. Perhaps this accounts for the fact that more and more U.S. firms prefer to send Europeans or Asians to foreign assignments, which usually last from one to three years.[25] One reason for the high U.S. failure rate: Two generations of economic dominance and a strong domestic market have contributed to the creation of a colonial mentality in many U.S. companies.[26]

Failures can be very expensive. Premature returnees cost $170,000 to $360,000 each in 2006, which translates into $4.0 billion per year in direct costs to U.S. firms. The intangible costs of failure include business disruptions, lost opportunities, and negative impact on the firm's reputation and leadership and are probably many times greater. In addition, the personal hardship on employees and their families, including diminished self-image, marital strife, uprooted children, lost income, and tarnished career reputation, can be substantial.[27]

Why International Assignments End in Failure

Six factors account for most failures, although their relative importance varies by firm.[28] These are career blockage, culture shock, lack of cross-cultural training, an overemphasis on technical qualifications, a tendency to use international assignments as a way to get rid of problem employees, and family problems.

Career Blockage

Initially, many employees see the opportunity to work and travel abroad as exciting. But once the initial rush wears off, many feel that the home office has forgotten them and that their career has been sidetracked while their counterparts at home are climbing the corporate ladder. Although U.S. companies give themselves high marks for career planning for their expatriate employees, most of their employees do not, according to a survey by the Society for Human Resources Management (SHRM) conducted in the 1990s. Only 14 percent of the 209 expatriate managers who completed the society's questionnaire said their firm's career planning for them was sufficient.[29] Fortunately, this situation may be changing for the better, although there is still a long way to go. A more recent survey this decade in which the SHRM also participated indicates that in comparing the careers of expatriates against employees with no international experience, 41 percent of respondents report that expatriates obtain new positions in the company more easily; 39 percent said that expatriates are promoted faster; and 27 percent say that the expatriate assignment helped them get a better job at another company.[30] A survey of 2,700 managers by Korn/Ferry International revealed that more than a third view an overseas assignment as positive for their career and that they would consider taking one.[31]

Culture Shock

Many people who take international assignments cannot adjust to a different cultural environment, a phenomenon called **culture shock**. Instead of learning to work within the new culture, the expatriate tries to impose the home office's or home country's values on the host country's employees. This practice may trigger cultural clashes and misunderstandings that escalate until the expatriate decides to return home to more familiar surroundings—perhaps leaving a mess behind.

Culture shock
The inability to adjust to a different cultural environment.

Lack of "cultural intelligence," or the inability to relate to people from different cultural backgrounds,[32] and being monolingual[33] are often cited as reasons for expatriate failure. Firms can help employees avoid culture shock by using selection tools to choose the employees with the highest degree of cultural sensitivity and who know the local language. Korn Ferry International found that 9 of 10 headhunters worldwide look for prospective expatriates who know at least one foreign language. These headhunters are becoming increasingly sophisticated in the use of a variety of methods (structured interviews, role-playing exercises, assessment centers, and such) to identify those who are "prepared to spot cultural differences, some of them startlingly subtle, that can trip the unwary."[34]

Lack of Predeparture Cross-Cultural Training

Surprisingly, only about one-third of MNCs provide *any* cross-cultural training to expatriates, and those that do tend to offer rather cursory programs.[35] Often the expatriate and his or her family literally pack their bags and travel to their destination with only a U.S. passport and whatever information they could cull from magazines, tourist brochures, and the library. This is a recipe for trouble, as the following example illustrates:

> I once attended a business meeting in Tokyo with a senior U.S. executive. The Japanese go through a very elaborate ritual when exchanging business cards, and the American didn't have a clue. She just tossed some of her business cards across the table at the stunned Japanese executives. One of them turned his back on her and walked out. Needless to say, the deal never went through.[36]

Overemphasis on Technical Qualifications

The person chosen to go abroad may have impressive credentials and an excellent reputation in the home office for getting things done. Unfortunately, the same traits that led to success at home can be disastrous in another country. Consider the experience of one executive from a large U.S. electronics firm who spent only three months of what was supposed to be a two-year assignment in Mexico:

> I just could not accept the fact that my staff meetings would always start at least a half hour late and that schedules were treated as flexible guidelines with much room to spare. Nobody seemed to care but me! I also could not understand how many of the first-line supervisors would hire their friends and relatives, regardless of competence. What I viewed as nepotism of the worst kind was seen by them as an honorable obligation to their extended families, and this included many adopted relatives or compadres who were not even related by blood.[37]

In a recent survey, 96 percent of respondents rated the technical requirements of a job as the most important selection criteria for international assignments, largely ignoring cultural sensitivity.[38] In more enlightened companies, such as Prudential Relocation (an arm of Prudential Insurance), nearly 35 percent of managers cite "cultural adaptability" as the most important trait for overseas success.[39]

Getting Rid of a Troublesome Employee

International assignments may seem to be a convenient way of dealing with managers who are having problems in the home office. By sending these managers abroad, the organization is able to resolve difficult interpersonal situations or political conflicts at the home office, but at a significant cost to its international operations. The following true story was told to one of the authors:

> Joe and Paul were both competing for promotion to divisional manager. The corporate vice president responsible for making the selection decision felt that Joe should get the promotion but also believed that Paul would never be able to accept the decision and would actively try to undermine Joe's authority. Paul also had much support from some of the old-timers, so the only way to avoid the dilemma was to find a different spot for Paul where he could not cause any trouble. The vice president came up with the idea of promoting Joe to divisional manager while appointing Paul as a senior executive at the Venezuelan subsidiary. Paul (who had seldom been out of the country and who had taken introductory Spanish in high school 20 years earlier) took the job. It soon became obvious that the appointment was a mistake. Two months into Paul's tenure, there was a major wildcat strike attributed to his heavy-handed style in dealing with the labor unions, and he had to be replaced.

Family Problems

More than half of all early returns can be attributed to family problems.[40] It is surprising that most firms do not anticipate these problems and develop programs to prevent them. Indeed, few companies consider the feelings of employees' families on international assignments.[41] One expatriate's wife comments:

> A husband who is racked by guilt over dragging his wife halfway around the world, or distracted because she is ill-equipped to handle a foreign assignment, is not a happy or productive employee. . . . Most women actually start out all right. The excitement quickly fades for a traveling wife, though, when her husband abandons her for a regional tour immediately upon arrival and she's left behind with the moving boxes and the responsibility of finding good schools. Or when she is left to hire servants to set up a household without knowing the language . . . [Often] they are asked to jump off their own career paths and abandon healthy salaries . . . just so that they can watch their self-esteem vanish somewhere over the international date line.[42]

The expectations of dual-career couples are another cause of failure in expatriate assignments. MNCs are increasingly confronted with couples who expect to work in the same foreign location—at no sacrifice to either's career. Yet one spouse usually has to sacrifice, and this often leads to dissatisfaction. When 10-year AT&T veteran Eric Phillips was asked to move to Brussels, his wife, Angelina, had to give up her well-paying job as a market researcher. Although the move represented a terrific career opportunity for Phillips, his wife found it very difficult to adjust.[43]

Difficulties on Return

The expatriates' return home may also be fraught with difficulties. Between 20 and 40 percent of returning expatriates, called *repatriates,* leave the organization shortly after returning home.[44] Some employers report that nearly half of employees leave the company within two years.[45] Four common problems confronting returning expatriates are their company's lack of respect for the skills they acquired while abroad, loss of status, poor planning for the expatriate's return, and reverse culture shock.[46] Figure 17.3 summarizes some of the practices companies can use to counter these problems. We discuss these in greater detail later in this chapter.

Lack of Respect for Acquired Skills

Most U.S. firms are still heavily oriented toward the domestic market, even those that have a long history of operating internationally. The expatriate who has gathered a wealth of information and

---

Figure 17.3　　**Communicate to Repatriate**

Companies that have relatively low repatriation failure rates attribute their success to intensive interactions with the individual and his or her family before, during, and after the international assignment. Here are some of the practices that increase organizational commitment among expatriate employees:

■ *Advance career planning helps expatriates know what to expect when they return to the United States.* Management needs to sit down with HR professionals and the employee to lay out a potential career path before the employee goes abroad.

■ *Mentors can make expatriates feel they are vital members of the organization.* At Nashville-based Northern Telecom, Inc., senior managers and vice presidents correspond regularly with expatriate employees and meet with them periodically either at the home office or on location.

■ *Opening global communication channels keeps expatriates up-to-date on organizational developments.* Newsletters, briefings, and, of course, telecommunications technology enable expatriates to stay in constant touch with the home office.

■ *Recognizing the contributions of repatriated employees eases their reentry.* Repatriated employees whose accomplishments abroad are acknowledged are more likely to stay with the company.

Source: Adapted from Shilling, M. (1993, September). How to win at repatriation. *Personnel Journal,* 40.

valuable skills on a foreign assignment may be frustrated by the lack of appreciation shown by peers and supervisors at corporate headquarters. According to a 2001 survey, only 12 percent of expatriates felt that their overseas assignment had enhanced their career development, and almost two-thirds reported that their firm did not take advantage of what they had learned overseas.[47]

However, given the rapid increase in outsourcing during the least few years this situation may be changing. A 2005 study from Duke University's Fuqua School of Business and Archstone Consulting says that American companies with offshore operations plan to ship out 81 percent more research jobs, 55 percent more engineering jobs, and 75 percent more HR jobs. Another 2005 study suggests that this is not just an American phenomena. In Europe, for instance, labor costs in the most expensive Western countries are over 10 times those in the least costly Eastern European countries.[48] Companies are on the lookout for seasoned managers with international experience to go abroad and run things. According to one analyst, "while an overseas stint used to be a ticket to oblivion, now if you want to rise far in almost any big corporation, you can't afford to ignore the new global order."[49]

Loss of Status

Returning expatriates often experience a substantial loss of prestige, power, independence, and authority. This *status reversal* affects as many as three-fourths of repatriated employees.[50] A recent survey shows that disappointment upon return is so profound that 77 percent of returning expatriates would prefer to accept an international position with another employer than a domestic position with their current company.[51] The following example illustrates:

> When I was in Chile, I had occasions to meet various ministers in the government and other high-ranking industry officials. Basically my word was the final one. I had a lot of latitude because the home office didn't really want to be bothered with what was happening in Chile and therefore was uninformed anyway. I made decisions in Chile that only our CEO would make for the domestic operation. When I returned, I felt as though all the training and experience I had gotten in Chile was totally useless. The position I had seemed about six levels down as far as I was concerned. I had to get approval for hiring. I had to get my boss's signature for purchases worth one-tenth of the values of ones I approved in Chile. To say I felt a letdown would be a significant understatement.[52]

Poor Planning for Return Position

Uncertainties regarding their new career assignment may provoke much anxiety in returning employees. One survey suggests that more than half of expatriates were unaware of what job awaited them at home.[53] The following story is typical:

> I received a letter from the home office three months prior to the expiration of my assignment in Hungary (where I was responsible for a team of engineers developing a computerized system for handling inventories in four new joint ventures). I was told that I would be assuming the position of Supervisor of Technical Services in corporate headquarters. It sounded impressive enough. I was astonished to find out upon return, however, that I was given the honorary title of supervisor with nobody under my command. It smelled like a dead rat to me so I jumped ship as soon as I could.[54]

Reverse Culture Shock

Living and working in another culture for a long time changes a person, especially if he or she has internalized some of the foreign country's norms and customs. Expatriates are usually unaware of how much psychological change they have undergone until they return home. As many as 80 percent of returning expatriates experience *reverse culture shock,* which sometimes leads to alienation, a sense of uprootedness, and even disciplinary problems.[55] One expatriate who had worked in Spain notes:

> I began to take for granted the intense camaraderie at work and after hours among male friends. Upon returning to the U.S. I realized for the first time in my life how American males are expected to maintain a high psychological distance from each other, and their extremely competitive nature in a work environment. My friendly overtures were often misperceived as underhanded maneuvers for personal gain.[56]

Despite all these difficulties, many managers today are lining up for international assignments as companies gradually realize that employees with international experience can be a

American businessman John Kuhn, chairman of New World Power and Professor Yu Zhian of China Chang Jiang Energy Corporation shake hands after signing a deal worth USD 30 million.

valuable asset.[57] Gerber Products has announced that from now on, international assignments will be emphasized as part of normal career development for company executives. As a result, Gerber's country manager in Poland feels he has an edge over many of his colleagues. "My overseas experience sets me apart from the rest of the M.B.A. bunch," he says. "I'm not just one of hundreds of thousands."[58]

Effectively Managing Expatriate Assignments with HRM Policies and Practices

Companies can minimize the chances of failure by creating a sensible set of HRM policies and practices that get to the root of the problems we have discussed. In this section, we look at how selection, training, career development, and compensation policies can help companies avoid these problems.

Selection

The choice of an employee for an international assignment is a critical decision. Because most expatriates work under minimal supervision in a distant location, mistakes in selection are likely to go unnoticed until it is too late. To choose the best employee for the job, management should:

- **Emphasize cultural sensitivity as a selection criterion.** Assess the candidate's ability to relate to people from different backgrounds. For instance, one large electronics manufacturing firm

Businesses such as CitiGroup, McKinsey & Co., and several Silicon Valley firms actively recruit students from the Indian Institutes of Technology. IIT has produced several star CEOs, including Sun Microsystems cofounder Vinod Khosla and US Airways CEO Rakesh Gangwal.

conducts in-depth interviews with the candidate's supervisors, peers, and subordinates, particularly those whose gender, race, and ethnic origin are different from the candidate's. Personal interviews with the candidate and written tests that measure social adjustment and adaptability should also be part of the selection process.

■ **Establish a selection board of expatriates.** Some HRM specialists strongly recommend that all international assignments be approved by a selection board consisting of managers who have worked as expatriates for a minimum of three to five years.[59] This kind of board should be better able to detect potential problems than managers with no international background.

■ **Require previous international experience.** Although not always feasible, it is highly desirable to choose candidates who have already spent some time in a different country. The major reason the state of Utah is in the forefront of international business is its large Mormon population, whose church requires them to spend a minimum of two years as missionaries in another country. Some schools (such as the American Graduate School of International Management in Phoenix, Arizona) and some MNCs offer overseas internships. In this way, candidates acquire some knowledge of a country's language and customs before taking on a full-blown expatriate assignment.

■ **Explore the possibility of hiring foreign-born employees who can serve as "expatriates" at a future date.** Japanese companies have been quite successful at hiring young foreign-born (non-Japanese) employees straight out of college to work in the home office in Japan. These recruits enter the firm with little experience and exposure to work in their host country and, thus, are blank slates on which the Japanese MNC can write its own philosophy and values.[60] Some U.S. companies, such as Coca-Cola, have been following a similar practice for years.

■ **Screen candidates' spouses and families.** Because the unhappiness of expatriates' family members plays such a large role in the failure of international assignments, some companies are screening candidates' spouses. For instance, Ford formally assesses spouses on qualities such as flexibility, patience, and adaptability, asking questions such as: "How do you feel about this assignment? Do you feel you can adjust?" Exxon, too, meets with spouses and children during the selection process.[61]

■ **Develop an effective selection program not only for expatriates, but also for those locals who will help the expatriate manager carry out his or her mission.** The international firm should generate a pool of needed human resources at the local level to help accomplish its objectives. The expatriate's job becomes easier if he or she can focus on broader issues while delegating other tasks to expert local staff.

Training

The assumption that people everywhere respond in similar fashion to the same images, symbols, and slogans has hurt U.S. companies offering their products in international markets. See the Manager's Notebook, "Avoiding Cultural Blunders in Reaching Your Customers."

Customer-Driven HR

Avoiding Cultural Blunders in Reaching Your Customers

The ad campaign left shoemaker Nike Inc. flatfooted. The company's "Chamber of Fear" spot featured LeBron James of the NBA's Cleveland Cavaliers battling—and defeating—a computer-generated Kung Fu master. It might not have raised eyebrows elsewhere, but Chinese consumers found the concept insulting, and Beijing banned the ad last December. China is now the third-largest ad market in the world, as the nation's 1.3 billion people gear up for the 2008 Beijing Olympics.

The potential to make cultural blunders in China is limitless. KFC Corp. found that Colonel Sanders didn't resonate with consumers, and Nike's "Just Do It" campaign didn't work because it emphasized individualistic youthful irreverence. Toyota had a similar experience with an ad featuring stone lions, a traditional symbol of power in China, bowing down to Toyota's Prado GX. Chinese consumers balked at the notion of bowing to anything—even a car—representing Japan.

To prevent these blunders, many foreign firms are sending their top executives and marketing expatriates in China to cross-cultural training programs. Expatriates are paired up with local Chinese mentors who advise them on what to do and what not to do and warn them of how a particular message or symbol may be interpreted. Ogilvy and Malter Worldwide has 1,000 local employees in four cities in China to help expatriates avoid cultural blunders.

Source: Adapted with permission from Balfour, F., and Kiley, D. (2005, April 25). China: Ad agencies unchained. *BusinessWeek,* 51.

Cross-cultural training sensitizes candidates for international assignment to the local culture, customs, language, tax laws, and government.[62] Ideally, the training process should begin nine to twelve months in advance of the international assignment.[63]

Although training can cost $1,500 and more per manager in 2007 estimates, many companies feel the expense is minor compared to the huge cost of failed expatriate stints. For instance, despite massive cost-cutting moves at General Motors, the auto giant still spends nearly $500,000 a year on cross-cultural training for about 150 Americans and their families headed abroad. GM's general director of international personnel attributes the very low (less than 1%) premature return rate of GM expatriates to this training. The experience of a Cortland, Ohio, family transferred to Kenya by GM is typical. The family members underwent three days of cross-cultural training that consisted of a crash course in African political history, business practices, social customs, and nonverbal gestures. The family's two teenagers, who were miserable about moving to Africa, sampled Indian food (popular in Kenya) and learned how to ride Nairobi public buses, speak a little Swahili, and even how to juggle.[64]

A recent survey indicates that 57 percent of companies provide one day's worth of cross-cultural preparation; 32 percent provide it for the expatriate employee's entire family; and 22 percent for only the expatriate employee and spouse. Surprisingly, only 41 percent of firms mandated participation in cross-cultural preparation.[65] Figure 17.4 shows three approaches to cross-cultural training. The least expensive type, the *information-giving approach,* lasts less than a week and merely provides indispensable briefings and a little language training. The *affective approach* (one to four weeks) focuses on providing the psychological and managerial skills the expatriate will need to perform effectively during a moderate-length assignment. The most extensive training, the *impression approach* (one to two months), prepares the manager for a long assignment with greater authority and responsibility by providing, for instance, field experiences and extended language training. Ideally, at least a portion of these training programs should be targeted to the expatriate's family. Although Figure 17.4 is concerned with predeparture training, it is also possible (indeed desirable) to use similar "decompression" training programs for returning expatriates to help them cope with reverse culture shock.

Perhaps the most critical part of expatriate training occurs "on the job" and takes place shortly after the expatriate's arrival. Local managers need to be prepared to train incoming

Figure 17.4

Length of Stay	Length and Level of Training	Cross-Cultural Training Approach
1–3 years	1–2 months + High	**Impression Approach** Assessment center Field experiences Simulations Sensitivity training Extensive language training
2–12 months	1–4 weeks Moderate	**Affective Approach** Language training Role-playing Critical incidents Cases Stress-reduction training Moderate language training
1 month or less	Less than a week Low	**Information-Giving Approach** Area briefings Cultural briefings Films/books Use of interpreters "Survival-level" language training

Source: Adapted from Mendenhall, M., and Oddou, G. (1986). Acculturation profiles of expatriate managers: Implications for cross-cultural training. *Columbia Journal of World Business,* 78. Copyright 1986. *Columbia Journal of World Business.* Reprinted with permission.

expatriates to ensure a smooth transition and to warn them of unexpected cultural pitfalls they may encounter. For instance, Dennis Ross, general manager of offshore operations at Convergys, a call-center company based in Cincinnati, works closely with Convergys' Indian Vice President Jaswinder Ghumman. When Convergys was building its company cafeteria in Gurgaon, a suburb of New Delhi, Ghumman was obliged to point out to Ross that Indian food must be served hot, and the cafeteria had to be able to support hot meal service. In addition, U.S. managers had to be educated on Indian food preferences and learn that cold sandwiches were not considered a meal item. According to Ross, "Who'd have though tuna on rye could be such a stumbling block? We've succeeded by fostering open communications with our local people by taking nothing for granted."[66]

Career Development

The expatriate's motivation to perform well on an international assignment, to remain in the post for the duration of the assignment, and to be a high performer upon returning to the home office will depend to a large extent on the career development opportunities offered by the employer. At a minimum, successful career planning for expatriates requires the firm to do three things:

■ **Position the international assignment as a step toward advancement within the firm.** The firm should explicitly define the job, the length of the assignment, and the expatriate's reentry position, level, and career track on return. Some companies are shortening the length of expatriates' assignments. Three-quarters of firms responding to a 2005 survey indicate that the typical expatriate assignment is less than 12 months.[67] One reason is to ensure that the expatriate does not become too far removed from the company's mainstream. A second is that in 79 percent of cases the family remains behind. One obvious drawback of this policy is that it may take a minimum of three to six months for an expatriate to feel comfortable with the local culture, just when it is time to return back home. Successful performance often depends on the establishment of internal and external social networks that take time to develop.

- **Provide support for expatriates.** Maintaining contact can be accomplished in a number of ways.[68] A popular method is the buddy system, in which a manager or mentor at the home office is appointed to keep in touch with the expatriate and to provide assistance wherever necessary. Another approach has the expatriate employee coming back to the home office occasionally or at specified intervals to foster a sense of belonging to the organization and to reduce reentry shock. Some firms will pay for the expatriate's family to return home with him or her during this time.

- **Provide career support for spouse.** If the spouse is giving up his or her job to move, it can reduce family income by an average of 28 percent.[69] A recent Merrill Lynch survey indicated that most expatriates now expect the company to provide dual career support.[70]

Compensation

Firms can use compensation packages to enhance the effectiveness of expatriate assignments. However, compensation policies can create conflict if locals compare their pay packages to the expatriate's and conclude that they are being treated unfairly. Planning compensation for expatriates requires management to follow three important guidelines:

- **Provide the expatriate with a disposable income that is equivalent to what he or she would receive at home.** This usually requires granting expatriate employees an allowance for price differences in housing, food, and other consumer goods. Allowances for children's schooling and the whole family's medical treatment may also be necessary. The best-known cost-of-living index for world locations is published by Corporate Resources Group, a Geneva-based consulting firm that surveys 97 cities worldwide twice a year.

    The U.S. State Department also maintains a current cost-of-living index for most major cities around the world. Some of the most expensive locations around the world—including Tokyo, Osaka, London, and most Scandinavian cities—cost at least 50 percent more to live in than New York City. For short-term stays, the Runzheimer Guide provides per diem costs for 1,000 international cities. This index is used by hundreds of organizations to approve, benchmark, and budget travel expenses.[71]

    Maintaining income equality with the home office is not an exact science (for example, finding housing in Japan comparable to that available in U.S. suburbs is nearly impossible), but as a general rule, it is better to err on the side of generosity. See Figure 17.5 for a comparison of living costs in various cities around the world.

- **Provide an explicit "add-on" incentive for accepting an international assignment.** The company may provide a sign-on bonus before departure. Or it may offer the employee a percentage increase over his or her home base salary; the standard increase is 15 percent of the base salary.[72] Or it may provide a lump-sum payment upon successful completion of the foreign assignment. Some firms offer a combination of these incentives. Generally, the greatest incentives are reserved for the least desirable locations. For instance, MNCs hoping to lure Western managers to Eastern Europe, where poor air quality, political instability, and a shortage of quality housing make assignments unattractive, often offer packages that include company-paid housing, subsidized shipment of scarce consumer goods, up to four trips home a year, and weekend getaways to Western Europe.[73] Oil companies operating in Colombia amid civil war face a constant threat of terrorism. Expatriates have been kidnapped and murdered. Occidental Petroleum alone has seen its pipeline bombed by rebels about 170 times a year.[74] In this situation, most expatriates receive hardship pay three to five times greater than the pay they would earn at home.

- **Avoid having expatriates fill the same jobs held by locals or lower-ranking jobs.** Local employees tend to compare their pay and living standards to those of expatriates, and feelings of unfairness are more likely to surface if an expatriate at the same or lower rank than the local is receiving greater pay. Unfortunately, it may be impossible to prevent those feelings of inequity, particularly if a U.S. firm sends one of its top executives overseas. Compared to

Figure 17.5

Cost-of-Living Index 2006

Seoul	149
Tokyo	140
Moscow	114
London	110
Singapore	98
New York	100
Beijing	85
Mexico City	78
Paris	80
Rio de Janeiro	58
Rome	79
Sydney	60
Bombay	56
Toronto	56

*For three-person U.S. family at $100,000 income level

Source: Estimated by authors from various resources

Living Costs Around the Globe

Western European countries, for instance, U.S. executives may earn as much as 20 times what a similar executive makes locally.

In some local labor markets, such as India, wages are increasing fast for certain occupations as outsourcing outfits scramble for talent. For instance, controlling for inflation, the salary of a project manager in India in 2006 was two and a half times what it was in 2000, and turnover in 2005 was running at 25 to 35 percent annually. As a result, companies in India and other places are starting to hire U.S. talent in order to fill a void at the local level as the cost of native skilled labor rises.[75]

Calculating compensation packages for expatriate employees is one of the most difficult tasks facing MNCs.[76] Compensation used to be a relatively simple issue: Low-level local hires got paid in the local currency, while expatriate managers' pay was pegged to U.S. salaries. However, in an era of dramatic corporate restructuring to cut costs, expatriate packages based on U.S. salaries are increasingly being considered too expensive. Moreover, as companies move into the later stages of internationalization, they work with a team of international employees operating out of the home office rather than just expatriates.

Still, some companies continue to compensate their expatriates generously. To avoid potential pay inequities when employees are transferred from one international post to another, 3M compares net salaries in both the old and the new country and provides the transferred employee whichever pay package is higher.[77] And Seagram Spirits and Wine Group has come up with an "international cadre policy" for those expatriates who work abroad permanently (as opposed to expatriates who will return to the United States in the future). The package features a standardized cost-of-living adjustment and a global standard employee housing contribution that is the same regardless of location. For temporary U.S. expatriates, Seagram maintains what it terms a "pure expatriate" package that keeps people up to par with U.S. compensation standards.[78]

One thing that makes these pay comparisons easier today is the availability of international pay and benefit surveys on the Web. For instance, Personnel Systems Associates offers a directory of 1,500 such surveys covering hundreds of job titles.[79]

Several other excellent sources that provide comprehensive global pay data include the Radford International Survey (*www.radford.com*), the Culpepper Global Compensation Survey (*www.culpepper.com*), the ERI Economic Research Institute Survey (*www.erieri.com*), and the Mellon Compensation Surveys (*www.mellonsurveys.com*).

One issue that continues to complicate compensation design for expatriates is fluctuating exchange rates. For instance, in 2000 each dollar was worth approximately 1.22 euros. By 2005, each dollar was worth .70 euros. Pay equity ratios between natives (paid in local currency) and expatriates (paid in dollars) can change very quickly. Firms usually handle this problem by adjusting the pay of employees who are "losing" (those whose currency is being devalued), but this needs to be done carefully because the value of the currency may change again.[80] Paying all employees (locals and expatriates) in U.S. dollars adds even more complexity to the pay equity issue. As recently noted by one analyst, "This has often resulted in distortion of several local pay markets as natives in countries with relatively weak currencies compared with the U.S. dollar (e.g., Africa, Asia-Pacific) who are paid in dollars received compensation of 200 percent to 300 percent more than local norms."[81]

Role of HR Department

A recent survey asked expatriates, "What advice would you have for HR departments about handling expatriates?" According to Professor Joyce Osland, who conducted the study, "What they want most from the HR department is to have unnecessary uncertainty eliminated. There is enough ambiguity overseas—they don't need any more from the HR department. Expatriates want HR to remove obstacles." According to one survey respondent, "The first thing that HR needs to do is to make sure it knows how to handle the logistics such as getting the furniture moved. Because you have all of these little . . . [problems] that take up all of your time when you are trying to deal with other things . . ."[82]

Another survey by Polak International Consultants, an international human resources consulting firm, confirms that most expatriates are unhappy with the services provided by their HR departments; the survey respondents considered the HR department unprepared to meet the requirements of a global workforce. This suggests that a priority in coming years is for multinational corporations' HR departments to be more aware and sensitive to the needs of an international workplace.[83] To achieve this requires not only better service to expatriates but also better tracking of HR trends overseas.

Women and International Assignments

Although in 2006 women represented almost half of all managers in the United States, only 14 percent of U.S. managers sent abroad are women. According to a study by Catalyst, an international consulting firm, there are three misconceptions about women's ability and willingness to handle international assignments: (1) Companies assume that women are not as internationally mobile as men, yet 80 percent of women have never turned down an expatriate assignment offered to them, whereas only 71 percent of men have never turned down expatriate assignments. (2) Companies assume that women encounter more work–life conflict working on a global schedule. However, nearly half of *both* women *and* men report they find work–life balance difficult. (3) Most companies believe clients outside the United States are not as comfortable doing business with women as they are with men. In fact, 76 percent of expatriate women said being a woman had a positive or neutral impact on their effectiveness overseas.[84]

Figure 17.6 addresses some of the ways women can overcome key barriers to getting selected for the global business arena.

		Figure 17.6
Strategies	**HR Tool, Method, or Intervention**	**Possible Problems/ Strategies for Implementation**
1. Select female expatriates who demonstrate the technical or managerial skills for the position. Don't send tokens.	Selection based on demonstrated competencies. Additional technical or managerial training prior to departure, if needed.	It may be difficult to find a person with every necessary credential who is willing to accept the assignment. The organization should identify every skill needed for a given global assignment.
2. Select female expatriates who possess a greater perceptual orientation (e.g., openness).	Select expatriates based on personality characteristics, such as openness and flexibility. Consider using the SAGE (Self-Assessment for Global Endeavors) or a similar instrument.	It may be difficult to find someone with the requisite personality characteristics who is willing to accept the assignment.
3. Train female expatriates on the norms, values, and traditions the host nationals possess regarding women.	Offer predeparture plus on-site, culture-specific training for female expatriates.	All of the difficult situations cannot possibly be anticipated.
4. To dispel the "token" image, MNCs should actively promote expatriate women as their "best-qualified" candidate.	Letters of introduction. In-person introduction by a senior executive. A statement of qualification. Any other culturally appropriate method for establishing credibility.	Some of these initiatives could be misinterpreted, depending on the cultural context. The intervention should be culture specific.

Strategies for Maximizing the Effectiveness of Women on Global Assignments

Figure 17.6 (Continued)

Strategies	HR Tool, Method, or Intervention	Possible Problems/ Strategies for Implementation
5. Provide female expatriates with an in-country support network or mentor.	Have a mentor back home and a method for communication.	Communication is more difficult from a great distance.
	Have an in-country mentor.	Provide specific communication media (e.g., videoconferencing, e-mail) plus training on their use and protocol.
6. Offer mechanisms to improve the likelihood the spouses of female expatriates will adjust well cross-culturally.	Cross-cultural training for spouses.	There is always a chance that the spouse's needs will not match what is being offered.
	Male-oriented social networks.	
	Language classes.	The spouse may choose not to use the services.
	Reemployment assistance.	
		The options may not be available in a given location.
	Money for professional or personal development.	
		To promote usage, try to match these services to the spouses' needs.
7. Offer mechanisms to improve the likelihood that the children of female expatriates will adjust well cross-culturally.	Day care.	Some services may not be available for expatriate children in a given location.
	Educational assistance.	
	Language classes.	Find the necessary services for expatriate children.
	Cross-cultural training.	
8. Western female expatriates should not attempt to "blend in" with host national women.	Train women on how to cope with being "different" from the host national women.	It may be difficult for the female expatriate to balance perceptions (i.e., not appear too masculine).
	Train women on the behaviors that could be required (e.g., serving tea in Japan).	Provide role models from which expatriate women can learn appropriate (and professional) behaviors.
9. Give host nationals greater exposure to successful women in the organization.	Have more professional women take short business trips to the host country to increase interactions between Western females and host nationals.	Provide pretrip training to professional women.
	Have host nationals take business trips to headquarters for the same purpose.	
10. Offer training to the host nationals who are going to be interacting with female expatriates.	Offer training to host nationals before the female expatriate arrives on location.	The host nationals may not participate in the training; and if they do, they may not change their behaviors toward women as a result of the training.
11. Ensure that female expatriates fill jobs with high position power.	Succession planning into high-level expatriate positions for women.	Can be a risky strategy if the person in the position did not have the competence for the job.

Source: Adapted with permission from Caliguiri, P., and Cascio, W. F. (2002). Sending women on global assignments. Challenges, myths, and solutions. *Worldatwork Journal, 9*(2), 1–8.

Developing HRM Policies in a Global Context

Firms operating in multiple countries need to worry not just about meeting the special needs of expatriate employees but also about the design and implementation of HRM programs in diverse cross-cultural settings. One company that is widely viewed as exceptional in its achievement of a unified global HRM program—even with two-thirds of its employees working overseas—is Coca-Cola.

In many countries reliance on U.S., or Western, managerial practices is likely to clash with deeply ingrained norms and values.[85] For instance, the open-door style of management, which works well in a culture that readily accepts questioning of authority, will probably not work in countries where such behavior is considered unacceptable—such as China.[86] Rather than simply transferring abroad HRM practices that are based on the home country's social and cultural standards, managers should mold these practices to the cultural environment in which a particular facility is located.[87]

National Culture, Organizational Characteristics, and HRM Practices

"Culture is important to HRM practices." This statement may seem obvious, but its relevance may be lost in a country like the United States, where many of the best-known theories of management practice are firmly rooted in Western culture. Geert Hofstede, a Dutch professor, has spent the better part of his professional life studying the similarities and differences among cultures. He has concluded that there are five major dimensions to culture:

1. **Power distance.** Extent to which individuals expect a hierarchical structure that emphasizes status differences between subordinates and superiors.
2. **Individualism.** Degree to which a society values personal goals, autonomy, and privacy over group loyalty, commitment to group norms, involvement in collective activities, social cohesiveness, and intense socialization.
3. **Uncertainty avoidance.** Extent to which a society places a high value on reducing risk and instability.
4. **Masculinity/femininity.** Degree to which a society views assertive or "masculine" behavior as important to success and encourages rigidly stereotyped gender roles.
5. **Long-term/short-term orientation.** Extent to which values are oriented toward the future (saving, persistence) as opposed to the past or present (respect for tradition, fulfilling social obligations).[88]

Although Hofstede's research has been criticized for being based largely on the experiences of employees working for only one company (IBM) and for downplaying the importance of cultural differences within countries, other evidence suggests that the five dimensions are a fair summary of cultural differences.[89] They provide clues regarding the general configuration of HRM strategies that are most likely to mesh with a particular culture's values. Figure 17.7 outlines the characteristics of cultures ranking high or low on each of Hofstede's dimensions, lists sample countries falling at each end of the spectrum, and summarizes the organizational features and HRM practices that work best at each end of the scale.

The information in Figure 17.7 has significant implications for international firms. As a general principle, *the more an HRM practice contradicts the prevailing societal norms, the more likely it will fail.*[90] For instance, Hofstede describes management by objectives (MBO) as "perhaps the single most popular management technique 'made in the U.S.A.'"[91] because it assumes (1) negotiation between the boss and employee, or a not-too-large power distance, (2) a willingness on the part of both parties to take risks, or weak uncertainty avoidance, and (3) both supervisors and subordinates seeing performance and its associated rewards as important. Because all three assumptions are prominent features of U.S. culture, MBO "fits" the United States. But in other countries—France, for example—MBO has generally run into problems because of cultural incompatibility:

> The high power distance to which the French are accustomed from childhood ultimately has thwarted the successful utilization of MBO as a truly participative process. . . . The problem is not necessarily with MBO per se but the French managers . . . who are unaware that they are trying to exert control through the implementation of the objectives of MBO almost by fiat.[92]

Figure 17.7

Power Distance: Organizational Characteristics and Selected HR Practices

Dominant Values	Sample Countries	Organizational Features	Reward Practices	Staffing/Appraisal Practices
Power Distance				
High				
■ Top-down communications ■ Class divisions seen as natural ■ Authoritarianism	■ Malaysia ■ Philippines ■ Mexico	■ Centralization and tall organizational structures ■ Traditional line of command	■ Hierarchical compensation system ■ Difference in pay and benefits reflect job and status differences; large differential between higher and lower-level jobs ■ Visible rewards that project power, such as a large office or company car	■ Limited search methods in recruitment; emphasis on connections and "whom you know" ■ Few formal mechanisms of selection ■ Superior makes selection choice for his or her sphere of influence
Low				
■ Egalitarianism ■ Status based on achievement ■ Joint decision making	■ The Netherlands ■ Australia ■ Switzerland	■ Flatter organizational structures ■ Decentralized control ■ Great degree of worker involvement	■ Egalitarian-based compensation systems ■ Small differences in pay and benefits between higher- and lower-level jobs ■ Participatory pay strategies (such as gainsharing) more prevalent	■ Multiple search methods; extensive advertisement ■ Formalized selection methods "to give everyone a fair chance" ■ Superior constrained in making selection choices ■ Selection based on merit; loyalty to superiors deemphasized

Cultural Characteristics and Dominant Values

EEO in the International Context

The globalization of industry raises numerous equal employment opportunity (EEO) issues, only some of which the U.S. courts have addressed. This is not a well-developed area of employment law.[93] However, the following principles seem clear:

■ U.S. companies are prohibited from basing employment decisions on employee characteristics such as race, sex, and age. This prohibition applies to international assignments, with the single exception that companies are not required to violate a host nation law. Thus, if a nation prohibits women from working in a specific business context, a U.S. company doing business in that nation is free to offer the particular international assignment covered by this host country law only to men. However, most countries that openly discriminate against their own female citizens are quite flexible in dealing with U.S. companies' female employees. Therefore, companies should not make exclusions automatically.

■ Foreign national employees of U.S. companies working in their own country or in some other foreign country are not covered by U.S. employment law. For instance, the U.S. Supreme Court ruled that a Saudi Arabian citizen working for an American oil company in Saudi Arabia could not sue his employer under Title VII.[94]

■ Under the Immigration Control and Reform Act of 1986, people who are not U.S. citizens but who are living and have legal work status in the United States may not be discriminated against.

Figure 17.7 (Continued)

Individualism: Organizational Characteristics and Selected HR Practices

Dominant Values	Sample Countries	Organizational Features	Reward Practices	Staffing/Appraisal Practices
Individualism				
High ■ Personal accomplishment ■ Belief in individual control and responsibility ■ Belief in creating one's own destiny	■ United States ■ Great Britain ■ Canada	■ Organizations not compelled to care for employees' total well-being ■ Employees look after their own individual interests ■ Explicit systems of control necessary to ensure compliance and prevent wide deviation from organizational norms	■ Performance-based pay ■ Individual achievement rewarded ■ External equity emphasized ■ Extrinsic rewards are important indicators of personal success ■ Attempts made to isolate individual contributions (i.e., who did what) ■ Emphasis on short-term objectives	■ Emphasis on credentials and visible performance outcomes attributed to individual ■ High turnover; commitment to organization for career reasons ■ Performance rather than seniority as criterion for advancement
Low ■ Team accomplishment ■ Sacrifice for others ■ Belief in group control and responsibility ■ Belief in the hand of fate	■ Singapore ■ South Korea ■ Indonesia	■ Organizations committed to high-level involvement in workers' personal lives ■ Loyalty to the firm is critical ■ Normative, rather than formal, systems of control to ensure compliance	■ Group-based performance is important criterion for rewards ■ Seniority-based pay utilized ■ Intrinsic rewards essential ■ Internal equity guides pay policies ■ Personal needs (such as number of children) affect pay received	■ Value of credentials and visible performance outcomes depends on perceived contributions to team efforts ■ Low turnover; commitment to organization as "family" ■ Seniority plays an important role in personnel decisions ■ "Fitting in" with work group crucial: belief that interpersonal relations are important performance dimension

Important Caveats

The effectiveness of an HRM practice depends on how well it matches a culture's value system. Even so, managers need to keep several caveats in mind.

■ **"National culture" may be an elusive concept.** For this reason, managers should be careful not to be guided by stereotypes that hold some truth but may not apply to very many people in a culture. Stereotyping is a great danger in large, heterogeneous countries such as the United States, where cultural differences are often huge, but it can also cause problems even in relatively homogeneous nations. For instance, Western German firms hiring Eastern German workers frequently found that the latter reacted negatively to incentive systems that

Figure 17.7 (Continued)

Uncertainty Avoidance: Organizational Characteristics and Selected HR Practices

Dominant Values	Sample Countries	Organizational Features	Reward Practices	Staffing/Appraisal Practices
Uncertainty Avoidance				
High ■ Fear of random events and the unknown ■ High value placed on stability and routine ■ Low tolerance for ambiguity	■ Greece ■ Portugal ■ Italy	■ Mechanistic structures ■ Written rules and policies guide the firm ■ Organizations strive to be predictable	■ Bureaucratic pay policies utilized ■ Compensation programs tend to be centralized ■ Fixed pay more important than variable pay	■ Bureaucratic rules/procedures to govern hiring and promotion ■ Seniority an important factor in hiring and promotions ■ Government/union regulations limit employer discretion in recruitment, promotion, and terminations
Low ■ Unexpected viewed as challenging and exciting ■ Stability and routine seen as boring ■ Ambiguity seen as providing opportunities	■ Singapore ■ Denmark ■ Sweden	■ Less-structured activities ■ Fewer written rules to cope with changing environmental forces ■ Managers are more adaptable and tend to make riskier decisions	■ Variable pay a key component in pay programs ■ External equity emphasized ■ Decentralized pay program is the norm	■ Fewer rules/procedures to govern hiring and promotions ■ Seniority deemphasized in personal decisions ■ Employer provided much latitude in recruitment, promotion, and terminations

A Question of Ethics

In some areas of the world business practices that are contrary to Western values—such as child labor, payment of bribes to government officials, and sex or race discrimination in hiring and promotion—are common. Should U.S. corporations and their expatriate representatives refuse to engage in such practices even if doing so would put the firm at a competitive disadvantage?

had been used successfully with their Western German counterparts—despite the fact that the two groups shared the same language, ethnicity, and cultural background. The Eastern Germans distrusted such incentive schemes, reported they felt manipulated by management, and shunned those workers who outproduced others.[95]

■ **Corporate headquarters sometimes blame international personnel problems on cultural factors without careful study.** Often personnel problems have little to do with cultural values and much to do with poor management. For example, a U.S. company introduced individual incentives for R&D employees at its English subsidiary. This policy created intense conflict, lack of cooperation, and declining performance. Top managers blamed the strong role of labor unions in England for these disappointing results. In fact, a large amount of evidence indicates that individual-based incentives are counterproductive when the nature of the task requires extensive teamwork (as is the case in R&D).[96]

■ **Hard data on the success or failure of different HRM practices as a function of national culture are practically nonexistent.** This means that judgment calls, gut feeling, and some trial and error based on a fine-tuned cultural sensitivity and open-mindedness are mandatory in international HRM.

■ **Different cultures often have very different notions of right and wrong.** In many cases, corporate headquarters may have to impose its own value system across multiple nations with conflicting value structures. For example, child labor is common in many Asian and African countries. The corporation may choose to avoid such practices on ethical grounds, but it must recognize that doing so can put it at a competitive disadvantage because local firms that have no qualms about using child labor will have lower labor costs. And,

Figure 17.7 (Continued)

Masculinity/Femininity: Organizational Characteristics and Selected HR Practices

Dominant Values	Sample Countries	Organizational Features	Reward Practices	Staffing/Appraisal Practices
Masculinity				
High ■ Material possessions important ■ Men given higher power and status than women ■ Rigid gender stereotypes	■ Mexico ■ Germany ■ United States	■ Some occupations labeled as "male," others as "female" ■ Fewer women in higher-level positions	■ Differential pay policies that allow for gender inequities ■ Tradition an acceptable basis for pay decisions ■ "Male" traits rewarded in promotions and other personnel decisions	■ De facto preferential treatment for men in hiring/promotion decisions into higher-level jobs (even if it is illegal) ■ "Glass ceiling" for women ■ Occupational segregation
Low ■ Quality of life valued more than material gain ■ Men not believed to be inherently superior ■ Minimal gender sterotyping	■ The Netherlands ■ Norway ■ Sweden ■ Finland	■ More flexibility in career choice for men and women ■ More women in higher-level jobs	■ Jobs evaluated without regard for gender of job holders ■ Focus on work content rather than tradition to assess value of different jobs ■ Well-developed "equity goals" for pay determination	■ Gender deemphasized in hiring/promotion decisions for any job ■ More women in upper-level positions ■ Occupational integration between the sexes

although members of the World Trade Organization and the United Nations have agreed to a set of "core labor standards" prohibiting employment discrimination, exploitive forms of child labor, and the use of forced labor such as prison labor, violations still occur in many countries, with at least 13 million children working in export industries, such as textiles.[97]

■ **The business laws of other countries often force companies to change their practices.** In some cases, if the firm wants to do business in another country, it must accept local regulations and practices even if these differ significantly from those in the home country.[98]

■ **Multinationals must find the right balance between tailor-made HR policies to fit particular cultures and the need to integrate global consistency with local adaptability.** The current trend in establishing international HR policies appears to be to strive toward integration rather than segmentation of HR policies. The reason for this trend toward integration, according to a recent survey, is that 85 percent of global companies are trying to establish a corporate culture in all locations consistent with the organization's goals and vision. However, 88 percent report that local culture and customs have a "moderate to great" influence on the way they conduct business in particular locations.[99] This requires that organizations try to balance the need for local adaptation with the trend toward global consistency of HR policies.

Although the discussion in this chapter has focused mainly on differences in HRM practices across different countries, global forces are exerting a great deal of influence to make them more similar. Financial investors and the stock market in general appear to favor certain organizational practices (such as pay for performance, promotion based on merit, and restructuring), regardless of nationality, and firms all over the world appear to be responding accordingly, as we see in Exhibit 17.1.

Figure 17.7 (Continued)

Long-Term/Short-Term Orientation: Organizational Characteristics and Selected HR Practices

Dominant Values	Sample Countries	Organizational Features	Reward Practices	Staffing/Appraisal Practices
		Long-Term/Short-Term Orientation		
High ■ Future-oriented ■ Delayed gratification ■ Long-term goals	■ Japan ■ Hong Kong ■ China	■ Stable organizations ■ Low employee turnover ■ Strong company culture	■ Long-term rewards ■ Seniority as basis for pay ■ Managers rewarded for multiyear accomplishments ■ No expectation of frequent pay adjustments	■ Slow promotions ■ Promotions from within ■ High employment security ■ High emphasis on saving employees' face ■ High emphasis on coaching versus evaluation ■ High investment in training and employee development
Low ■ Past- or present-oriented ■ Immediate gratification ■ Short-term goals	■ United States ■ Indonesia	■ Changing organization ■ High employee turnover ■ Weak company culture	■ Short-term rewards ■ Recent performance as a basis for pay ■ Managers rewarded for annual accomplishments ■ High expectation of frequent pay adjustments	■ Fast promotions ■ Internal and external hires ■ Low employment security ■ Low emphasis on saving employees' face ■ High emphasis on evaluation versus coaching ■ Low investment in training and employee development

Source: This is an updated and expanded version of an earlier chart appearing in Gómez-Mejía, L. R., and Welbourne, T. (1991). Compensation strategies in a global context. *Human Resource Planning, 14*(1), 38.

EXHIBIT 17.1

HRM Practices Becoming More Alike Around the Globe

Expectations for higher returns from the stock market and investment funds irrespective of national boundaries are forcing firms all over the world to adopt HRM practices that until recently were seen as American. These include low job security, performance-based pay, flatter organizations, frequent performance appraisals, promotions based on merit, global hiring, "scientific" selection programs, and teaming up with firms across frontiers in part to have access to a broader employee base and expertise. For example:

- When Sony Corp. announced plans to cut 17,000 jobs—10 percent of its workforce—in a sweeping restructuring, long-suffering investors finally had something to feel good about. Sony's American depository receipts (ADRs) promptly soared by more than one-third, to $104.
- Firms such as Toshiba and NEC review employee performance on a regular basis, and employees who do not meet certain objectives are put on probation or terminated. Traditionally, such firms would find makeshift jobs for low performers and keep them on payroll.
- In Mexico, two large firms have instituted HR practices to become more efficient. For instance, Grupo Televisa, the world's largest Spanish-language media company, and Empresas ICA, the country's biggest construction outfit, use batteries of selection devices to hire employees and avoid the traditional "amigismo" practices (hiring your friends) used by many Latin American firms.
- European conglomerates ranging from Germany's Veba to France's Lagardère Group are bringing in hot new talent from all over the world, a radical practice for European firms.
- Because stock options will be expensed in the United States after 2006 (see Chapter 11), making them less attractive from an accounting perspective, the proportion of compensation in the form of stock options is becoming more equal around the world (most countries already required stock options to be included as part of total operating costs).

Human Resources Management and Exporting Firms

Our discussion so far has focused on larger firms with international facilities (that is, those in Stages 3 to 5 of internationalization). However, the practices we have discussed are also relevant to smaller firms that are interested solely in exporting their products. It is estimated that only about 20 percent of U.S. firms with fewer than 500 employees have ever been active exporters, a percentage that lags way behind that found in most industrialized nations. At least 30,000 small firms in the United States have the potential to export competitively but do not do so.[100]

A number of studies have shown that the key impediments to exporting are (1) lack of knowledge of international markets, business practices, and competition and (2) lack of management commitment to generating international sales.[101] These impediments can be largely attributed to poor utilization of human resources within U.S. firms rather than to external factors. There is some evidence that a company that clearly reinforces international activities in its HRM practices is more likely to fare well in its export attempts.[102] Reinforcing international activities in HRM practices requires a company to:

- Explicitly consider international experience when making promotion and recruitment decisions, particularly to the senior management ranks.
- Provide developmental activities designed to equip employees with the skills and knowledge necessary to carry out their jobs in an international context. Developmental activities that enhance a firm's ability to compete globally include (1) programs designed to provide specific job skills and competencies in international business, (2) opportunities for development and growth in the international field, and (3) the use of appraisal processes that explicitly consider international activities as part of performance reviews.
- Create career ladders that take into account short- and long-term international strategies.
- Design a reward structure that motivates key organizational players to take full advantage of the company's export potential. Reinforcing desired export-related behaviors is likely to increase commitment to foreign sales as managers devote greater attention to skill development, information gathering, and scanning the environment for international opportunities.

The decision to export will require CEOs and senior marketing personnel to spend a significant time away from the office attending trade shows and developing relationships with distributors and companies abroad. Particularly in small companies, this means that the staff back home must be empowered to make decisions regarding the running of the business, with the traveling CEOs and executives keeping in touch via phone, fax, or e-mail.

The process of making the right export connections and establishing relationships used to be slow and painstaking, but the Web is changing all that, opening exports to firms of any size. For instance, net sales of clothing and accessories overseas by U.S. firms through the Internet are projected to soar to $40 billion by 2008 from $330 million in 1998. In the first year of its operation, New York-based Girlshop.com, for example, exported 2 million dollars worth of avant-garde merchandise and made $250,000 in operating profit.[103]

To succeed internationally on the Web, however, firms must provide HR practices such as selection and training programs. These services can help firms surmount language barriers, use cutting-edge technology to mix and match products to diverse customer needs, adapt products to different cultural tastes and preferences, engender customer trust, and the like. Although many of these issues also apply to the domestic market, they become more challenging overseas where the market is far more heterogeneous and segmented.[104]

Ethics and Social Responsibility

Globalization increases the possibility that managers, especially those sent to regions very different from their home country, will face ethical dilemmas. For instance, in many countries what would be considered a bribe in the United States would be considered a commission or an expected gift of reciprocity, part of doing business. Because competition is global, expatriates may feel that if they apply a stricter code of ethics than managers at other firms, the company may be put at a disadvantage, which would reflect poorly on their performance evaluations.

The U.S. Congress passed the Foreign Corruption Practices Act in 1977 as a result of United Brand's $2.5 million bribe to Honduran government official to reduce the banana tax. The law expressly forbids substantial payments by U.S. firms to foreign officials to influence decisions. The act does not appear to have had an adverse effect on U.S. firms operating overseas. It is even possible that the legislation improved the image of U.S. firms, counterbalancing any losses.[105] Yet despite the act, U.S. expatriates may still be tempted to take the risk of paying foreign bribes to generate more business. One company recently found guilty of illegal activities under the Foreign Corruption Practices Act is Titan Corporation (see Ethics Case 17.4, "When in Rome Do as the Romans Do?").

What is ethical and what is legal may differ, and the differences are probably more pronounced when HR practices are considered on a global basis. In many countries, for instance, child labor is not illegal and discrimination against women in employment is viewed as normal. Hence, the multinational firm, and more specifically the expatriates who are often in top management positions overseas, confront tough ethical choices even though legality is not the issue. Consider, for instance, the following story from the late 1990s. Kathie Lee Gifford tearfully confessed on her morning talk show that she had not known that her Wal-Mart outfits were made by Honduran girls paid 31 cents an hour. Made in the U.S.A., a lobbying group, informed consumers that Michael Jordan reportedly earned $20 million a year endorsing Nike sneakers— more than the total annual payroll for the thousands of Indonesians who made them.

The flaying of celebrities like Gifford and Jordan makes it easy to miss the point. As noted by one ethics writer:

> For years, children have been sold as slaves, blinded or maimed for crying or rebelling, or trying to return home, ill-fed, bone-weary, short-lived. They file the scissors blades, mix the gunpowder for the firecrackers, knot the carpets, stitch the soccer balls with needles longer than their fingers. Human-rights groups guess there may be 200 million children around the world, from China to South America, working full time—no play, no school, no chance. All of which raises the question, once the news lands on the front page: How much are we willing to sacrifice the children of other countries to give our children what they want? Americans search for bargains with enduring passion, but it is hard to find them—such as a handmade rug for only $7,000—without tiny fingerprints on them somewhere. If child-labor and safety laws were truly enforced, trade experts say, whole industries in many countries would collapse, at great cost to both developing and developed economies.[106]

These issues are still with us, although international firms are becoming much more concerned about self-regulation to prevent the worst abuses. Nike, for example, as described in the Managers' Notebook, "Just Do It: Nike Gets Revelatory," has done much to change the negative image it had a few years back for exploiting young children (often under the age of 10) in Indonesia by paying them a dime per hour. It was alleged that many of these children developed permanent disabilities after working in Nike's factories. Many firms and industry groups have developed or are developing their own voluntary code of conduct for foreign operations. For example, the American Apparel Manufacturers Association (AAMA), whose members include Sara Lee, Jockey International, and VF, requires members to pay the existing minimum wage, maintain certain minimum safety standards, and avoid the use of child labor.

MANAGER'S NOTEBOOK

Ethics

Just Do It: Nike Gets Revelatory

In a broad step toward workplace transparency by a company long hounded by sweatshop allegations, in 2005 Nike Inc. released a list of more than 700 contract factories around the world that manufacture its footwear, apparel, and equipment.

The disclosure, part of Nike's latest corporate-responsibility report, comes at a time when consumer awareness about issues such as labor rights and the environment is high, putting companies like Nike under pressure to reveal more detail about how they do business abroad. Nike was long seen as indifferent to workplace conditions, an image it has sought to reverse in recent years. The report spells out areas of continuing concern, including problems involving wages, union organization, and harassment at the factories it uses.

Although many apparel companies have adopted codes of conduct and taken other steps aimed at improving factory conditions, Nike says it is going further by actually naming its subcontractors, so that they are also under the spotlight if they engage in actions considered offensive in the West (such as hiring very young children to work long hours at low wages). This practice is in contrast to its actions a few years ago when Nike endured blistering criticism about working conditions at contract factories. At that time, Nike was the "poster child for abuse," says David Vogel, professor at the Haas School of Business at the University of California at Berkeley. "In the beginning, they were irresponsible and didn't seem to be acting in good faith," he says.

In the report, Nike Chairman Philip H. Knight acknowledges both the company's rocky past in dealing with the issue and its desire to do better. "Our goal in writing this report has been to be as accurate, complete and honest as we can be about how Nike performs," Mr. Knight wrote in the report's forward. He added that the company is intent on proving it is focused on improved working conditions after "a bumpy original response" to critics, "an error for which yours truly was responsible."

Source: Adapted with permission from Kang, S. (2005, April 13). Just do it: Nike gets revelatory. *Wall Street Journal,* B-11.

Summary and Conclusions

The Stages of International Involvement
Firms progress through five stages as they internationalize their operations: (1) domestic operations, (2) export operations, (3) subsidiaries or joint ventures, (4) multinational operations, and (5) transnational operations. The higher the stage, the more HR practices need to be adapted to diverse cultural, economic, political, and legal environments.

Determining the Mix of Host-Country and Expatriate Employees
In managing its overseas subsidiaries, a firm can choose an ethnocentric, polycentric, or geocentric approach. Firms tend to rely on expatriates more when sufficient local talent is unavailable, the firm is trying to create a corporatewide global vision, international and domestic units are highly interdependent, the political situation is unstable, and there are significant cultural differences between the host country and the home country.

The Challenges of Expatriate Assignments
An important part of international HRM is managing expatriate employees, both during their international assignments and when they return home. International assignments fail because of career blockage, culture shock, lack of predeparture cross-cultural training, an overemphasis on technical qualifications, the use of such assignments to get rid of troublesome employees, and family problems. Upon returning, expatriates may meet with a lack of respect for their acquired skills, a loss of status, poorly planned jobs, and reverse culture shock.

Enhancing the Effectiveness of Expatriate Assignments
In selecting people for international assignments, employers should emphasize cultural sensitivity, establish a selection board of expatriates, require previous international experience when possible, explore the possibility of hiring the foreign-born who can later serve as "expatriates," and screen candidates' spouses and families. Cross-cultural training programs of various lengths and levels of rigor can be implemented to prepare employees for their assignments. In terms of career development for expatriates, companies should position international assignments as a step toward advancement within the firm and provide support for expatriates. To avoid problems in the compensation area, companies should provide expatriates with enough disposable income and incentive bonuses and avoid having expatriates fill the same or lower-ranking jobs than locals hold in the international operation.

Developing HRM Policies in a Global Context
Managers should not simply transfer abroad HRM practices based on the home country's social and cultural standards. Rather, they should mold these practices to the cultural environments in which the international facilities are located. In general, the more an HRM practice contradicts prevailing societal norms, the more likely it will fail.

Human Resource Management and Exporting Firms
Many firms have the potential to export profitably. A company is more likely to fare better in its export attempts when it clearly reinforces international activities by (1) explicitly considering international experience in hiring decisions, (2) providing developmental activities to equip employees with international skills, (3) creating career ladders for internationally experienced employees, and (4) designing a reward structure that motivates employees to begin export activities.

Key Terms

culture shock, 545
ethnocentric approach, 543
expatriate, 540

geocentric approach, 543
joint venture, 543
multinational corporation (MNC), 540

polycentric approach, 543
transnational corporation, 540
wholly owned subsidiary, 543

Discussion Questions

1. According to a recent news story in *BusinessWeek,* "For years, American multinationals have been pilloried for shipping U.S. jobs overseas. Now, they're exporting something else: layoffs. Among the giants going abroad with their axes: Motorola, Goodyear, Procter & Gamble, Compaq Computer, JDS Uniphase, and Delphia Automotive. Each is cutting at least 2,500 overseas jobs. Sara Lee is cutting 1,300 jobs—not one in the U.S. All are at its Hanes clothing plants in Central and South America. Those were on top of 7,000 European layoffs at Hanes plants."[107] Many people abroad are shocked at how easily U.S. firms can throw long-term employees out of work, particularly when it is very difficult to find another job in a labor market where layoffs are uncommon. Do you think that U.S. companies should be more compassionate with displaced employees when local conditions in a foreign country make it very difficult for laid-off workers to find alternative employment opportunities?

2. How might an international firm trying to adapt HRM practices to the local culture produce worse results than it would produce by "exporting" HRM practices from the home office?

3. Under what specific conditions would you recommend an ethnocentric, a polycentric, and a geocentric approach to international staffing?

4. U.S. MNCs experience a much higher rate of early returns with their expatriate employees than European and Japanese MNCs do. What explains this difference? What HRM policies and procedures would you develop to reduce this problem?

5. According to Peter Tippet, a physician who invented the antivirus software now sold by Norton and who is now chief of technologists at computer firm Cybertrust, "it is hard to overestimate how poisonous an environment the global Internet is."[108] Do you agree? Apart from technical fixes, which to date have had limited success, what can a company do to combat viruses? Explain.

6. Some people believe that U.S. MNCs should serve as vehicles for cultural change in developing countries by introducing modern U.S. HRM practices and instilling values (such as punctuality and efficiency) in the workforce that are necessary for industrialization. Do you agree with this assertion? Explain your position.

7. Go back to the Manager's Notebook, "Outsourcing Around the World Increases at Breakneck Speed." (page 540). What can U.S. employees do to defend themselves against the possibility that their jobs may be taken over by foreign subcontractors who are willing to work at much lower wages? Do you agree with the argument that foreign subcontracting ultimately helps the U.S. economy, generating opportunities for everybody by making U.S. firms more competitive in global markets? Explain.

8. Go back to the Manager's Notebook, "Avoiding Cultural Blunders in Reaching Your Customers." (page 550). How do you think firms can better utilize HR practices or avoid the pitfalls illustrated in the notebook? Explain.

There is a variety of additional material available on the Web site that accompanies this text. You can access this information by visiting the Web site at ***www.prenhall.com/gomez.***

Discussion Case 17.1

Managing Human Resources in a European Context

Jerome Wirth and his business partner, Frederic Herbinet, launched the Internet start-up Beweb in 1997. Today, Beweb is a $2.5 million-a-year business providing software and services to e-commerce companies. It has operations in France and Britain and plans to expand across Europe.

But Beweb is saying "au revoir" to its Paris operations and moving them to London, where payroll taxes will be less than one-fourth of the 45 percent that the company pays in Paris. The coup de grace for Beweb, though, was a French law cutting the maximum workweek from 39 to 35 hours. Introduced in 2000 for major employers, it was extended in 2002 to businesses with under 20 workers (although in 2003 the law changed again to allow for more flexibility). Hiring extra staff to make up the lost work hours is impractical for Beweb, which has 15 employees. "It's impossible," says Wirth. "I love France, but I am very pessimistic for my country."

To the 76 million tourists who visit each year, France looks as desirable as ever. The Centre Pompidou and the Paris Opéra boast expensive face-lifts. On spring afternoons, parks and cafés are filled with people, thanks to the 35-hour workweek. That's because the country's corporations are laying off and aren't hiring. To avoid rigid antilayoff laws, big companies such as tire maker Michelin and building materials giant St. Gobain are moving manufacturing abroad. Others, such as carmakers Renault and PSA Peugeot Citroën, have relied on improved productivity to limit hiring. For most young people, the best places to get a job are with small businesses, which accounted for nearly 90 percent of the jobs created in France during the past decade. But taxes and rules are making it ever harder for these businesses to compete.

At the same time, an alarming number of France's brightest young people are leaving the country. Since 1995, the number of French citizens living outside the country has risen 30 percent, to nearly 2 million, including 240,000 in Silicon Valley. Almost all are in their twenties and thirties. An additional 200,000 or so have fled to Britain. Even worse, young people living in France are about to get socked with the pension bill for the baby boomers. France has the most generous retirement system in Europe, allowing workers to leave their jobs at age 60 with full benefits. In the meantime, joblessness for those under 25 is around 21 percent.

Germany, another key player in the European Union, is also having big problems. According to Paul Johnson, eminent British historian and author;

> An object lesson for us all is the present deplorable state of Germany . . . it shows what happens when a society opts for security at any price. Today, the German economy is a model—especially for the rapidly expanding nations

of the Third World, such as China and India—for what not to do. Stagnant production, static or falling productivity and appalling levels of unemployment are the salient factors. German unions insist on short hours, high wages, immense social security benefits and conditions of work that make productivity increases virtually impossible. Germany has one of the world's lowest birthrates, a rapidly aging population and a calamitously expensive social security system, all of which combine to project a dark and dangerous future.

Critical Thinking Questions

1. According to Gary Becker, Nobel laureate in economics, "The European pattern of high unemployment rates, long average duration of unemployment, early retirement of older workers, and very slow growth in employment . . . are the result of high social security and other labor taxes, laws that make it difficult to lay off employees, generous payments to the unemployed, and, in France, high minimum-wage laws. I advocate easing the cost to companies when they hire and fire workers, lowering labor taxes, lowering minimum wages, and raising retirement ages." Do you agree? Explain.

2. According to a European commentator, "HR practices in the U.S. often reflect the inhumane, cutthroat capitalism underlying American society." Europeans boast about their superior quality of life and how they avoid the stress of the U.S. work environment. Americans see European HR practices as too inflexible, paternalistic, with government-mandated regulations (such as the 35-hour workweek, which was largely rescinded in 2005) as too inhospitable to productivity, competition, and entrepreneurship. What is your assessment of these two starkly different views? Explain.

3. To get around its restrictive labor laws, Spain has significantly extended the percentage of workers who could be on temporary contracts. In 2006 at least one-third of Spanish workers have temporary contracts. In the United States, approximately 40 percent of employees work under such contracts, meaning they are hired for a fixed time and at the end of that time the company decides whether to renew the contract for another specified time. Do you think that this is a good policy and that more companies should use it? Justify your answer.

Team Exercise

A U.S. automobile company is trying to decide whether or not to expand its operations in France. One consideration in this decision is whether the HR practices in France would make it cumbersome for the company to manage its workers. Students divide up into groups of five to role-play a situation in which they provide advice to top management as to what decision to make.

Experiential Exercise

A committee of five HR experts has been established to advise the governments of France and Germany as to how to redesign their HR policies. Each committee will consist of five students who will assume the following roles: a compensation expert, a labor relations expert, a staffing expert, a performance appraisal expert, and a training and development expert. Each

expert will provide recommendations in a role-playing exercise in front of the entire class, followed by an open class discussion moderated by the instructor.

Sources: Adapted with permission from Matlack, C. and Rossant, J. (2002, April 22). France: Who speaks for youth? *BusinessWeek,* 48–50; Johnson, P. (2005, January 31). Germany's dismal future. *Forbes,* 37. Updated information provided by Gómez-Mejía, L. R., Balkin, D. B., and Cardy, R. L.

YOU MANAGE IT! Emerging Trends Case 17.2

Western Management Experts Descend on an Eager China

The crowded auditorium began to take on the feel of a rock concert. At the urging of the speaker, people stood up and, to the pulsing strains of a recording by the group Barenaked Ladies, thrust their fists in the air and shouted, "Yes! Yes! Yes!"

After the speaker finished, a middle-aged woman, who had been lucky enough to catch one of the souvenir furry carrots tossed into the crowd, dashed toward the podium like a wild teenager, seeking another one. Then a larger throng of people scrambled toward the dais in search of autographs.

Something similar happened a few days earlier at the prestigious Tsinghua University in Beijing when a group of students and faculty members pushed one another trying to reach the speaker: a tall, Western business icon. Several students crashed to the floor in the mayhem. Everyone wanted to meet Chester Elton. Mr. Elton, the 46-year-old author of a 105-page management handbook entitled "The 24-Carrot Manager," is practically unknown in the United States. But in China, where Western business and management gurus are suddenly all the rage, he is a big celebrity.

According to Mr. Elton, "I feel like a rock star here." Mr. Elton is actually just one of many popular management gurus; experts say the country has a severe shortage of skilled business managers and a growing cadre of people who want to be the next Bill Gates.

So Western management experts—teaching everything from how to reward employees to how to foster innovation— are flocking to China, trying to capitalize on the capitalist frenzy. Big names are coming, such as John F. Welch, Jr.; Stephen R. Covey; and Michael E. Porter, a Harvard Business School specialist on competition. But so are the lesser known. They are conducting management training seminars, hawking their books, making television appearances, and soaking up the adoration. Many of them, like Mr. Elton, have even been hired by Communist Party officials, who are eager to transform China's struggling, money-losing state-owned companies into lean, mean capitalist machines.

"There's a huge demand for management training in this country," says Juan A. Fernandez, a professor of management at the China Europe International Business School in Shanghai. America's leading universities are now offering high-priced executive M.B.A. programs in China. Major consulting firms are also rushing into China to help train managers.

Critical Thinking Questions

1. What are the benefits and potential pitfalls to a country such as China of having Western instructors train local managers? Explain.

2. How should a Chinese firm decide who should be hired from the West to provide management training? How can the firm differentiate a truly knowledgeable person from one who "looks good" but may not really have the appropriate credentials to provide such training? Explain.

3. Training Chinese managers to motivate workers is a popular topic in China. Why do you think this is the case? Motivation is a very complex issue in the United States, and many theories have been developed over the years to try to explain it (see Chapter 2). Do you think this type of training in China is legitimate or a gimmick to drum up business by the people and/or organizations doing the training? Explain.

Team Exercise

Students form teams of five. Each team will create a proposal for a Chinese firm that is trying to teach managers how to apply good HR practices. Each team will present its recommendations in front of the whole class, to be followed by open class discussion moderated by the instructor.

Experiential Exercise

One student is asked to role-play a management training instructor employed by a large American consulting firm trying to sell its services to a Chinese firm. The consulting firm specializes in motivational training. Another student will role-play a Chinese manager who is responsible for the firm's training programs. Role-play will last for approximately 15 minutes, to be followed by open class discussion moderated by the instructor.

Source: Adapted with permission from Barboza, D. (2005, February 19). Seven habits of highly effective cadres. *New York Times,* B-1.

Discussion Case 17.3   YOU MANAGE IT!

Two Sides to Every Story

Four years ago, Pressman Company, a U.S.-based firm, entered into a joint venture with a Polish firm to manufacture a variety of plumbing supplies, both for the internal Polish market and for export to neighboring countries. Last week Pressman received the resignation of Jonathan Smith, an expatriate from the home office who nine months ago was appointed general manager of the Polish subsidiary for a four-year term. In the previous 39 months, two other expatriate general managers had also decided to call it quits long before their foreign assignments expired. In addition, 13 of the 28 U.S. technicians sent to work in the Polish facility returned home early. George Stevens, a senior vice president in corporate headquarters, estimates that these expatriates' resignations and early returns have cost the company at least $4 million in direct expenses and probably three times as much in lost production and delayed schedules.

When he heard rumors of widespread discontent in the workforce and a threatened strike, Stevens decided to travel to the Polish facility to find out what was happening. In the course of interviewing five local supervisors and 10 workers with the help of a translator, he repeatedly heard three complaints: first, the American managers and technicians thought they "knew it all" and treated their Polish counterparts with contempt; second, the American employees had unrealistic expectations of what could be accomplished within the stipulated deadlines established at corporate headquarters; and third, American employees were making three times more money than their Polish counterparts and enjoyed looking down their noses at locals by driving fancy cars, living in expensive homes, and hiring an army of maids and helpers.

When he arrived back in the States, Stevens also interviewed Jonathan Smith and five of the technicians who returned early. Some common reasons for their early resignations emerged from these interviews. First, they described their Polish colleagues as "lazy" and "just doing the minimum to get by while keeping a close eye on the clock for breaks, lunches, and go-home time." Pushing them to work harder only provoked anger. Second, they indicated that the Polish workers and managers had a sense of entitlement with little intrinsic motivation and initiative. Third, they complained of loneliness and their inability to communicate in Polish. Finally, most reported that their spouses and children were homesick and longing to return to the States after the first month or so. As he sits in his office, George Stevens is staring blankly out the window, trying to decide what to do.

Critical Thinking Questions

1. Based on what you have learned in this chapter, what do you think are the underlying problems in the Polish subsidiary of Pressman Company?
2. How would you account for the sharp differences in the perceptions of the Polish locals and U.S. expatriates?
3. If you were hired as a consultant by Pressman Company, what steps would you recommend that Stevens take?

Team Exercise

Students form pairs. One student plays Stevens, the other an HRM consultant. Role-play the initial meeting between these two, with Stevens explaining the problems at the Polish plant and the consultant identifying the additional information that will be needed to get to the root of the difficulties, and how this information might be collected.

Students form into groups of four or five. Each group's task is to make suggestions for the content of a training program for the next group of employees to be sent to Pressman's Polish plant. Besides information from this chapter, use principles you learned from Chapters 4, "Managing Diversity," and 8, "Training the Workforce," to develop these programs. When the task is finished (approximately 20 minutes), a member from each group should present the group's recommendations to the class. How similar or dissimilar are the groups' recommendations? Why? Which recommendations are likely to be most effective?

Experiential Exercise

One student will role-play a Polish employee while another role-plays a U.S. expatriate. Each will present his or her perspective to the HR director of Pressman Company (role-played by another student) who will try to understand and bridge the differences between the two. Role-play should last for approximately 10 to 15 minutes, followed by an open class discussion moderated by the instructor.

Ethics Case 17.4

When in Rome Do as the Romans Do? The Case of Foreign Bribes

Titan Corporation, based in San Diego, California, has about 12,000 employees dispersed across 60 countries. In 2005, it was found guilty of bribing the president of Benin. The combined penalties of $28.5 million are the largest imposed on a company in the history of the Foreign Corrupt Practices Act. Titan, with $2 billion in annual sales, mainly from military, intelligence, and homeland security contracts with the U.S. government, pleaded guilty to three felonies before a federal judge in San Diego. According to the Securities and Exchange Commission (SEC), Titan's misconduct was global. Though Titan does business in more than 60 countries, the company has no policy on overseas bribery and failed to monitor its 120 international agents. The SEC said Titan underreported commission payments in its business dealings in France, Japan, Nepal, Bangladesh, and Sri Lanka.

Paul R. Berger, an associate director at the SEC's enforcement division, said that the evidence in the case showed "the virtually complete lack of internal controls" at Titan, along with the company's inability to operate with policies and procedures that would help them detect and deter such problems.

Critical Thinking Questions

1. Do you think that Titan is an isolated example or that many companies engage in similar behaviors overseas but are never caught? Do you think it is acceptable for a firm to take the risk and pay a bribe if the firm believes that the chances of getting caught are small and that in the worst-case scenario the fine imposed will be an insignificant fraction of total operating costs? Explain.

2. Shortly after Titan pleaded guilty to the bribery charges, it hired Daniel W. Danjczek under a new position title of "vice president for compliance and ethics." Danjczek's job is to "instill ethical behavior at the company." Do you think this is a wise and sincere attempt to redress the company's ethical problems or a public relations gimmick? What would you do to ensure that such an appointment is not perceived by employees as a superficial "quick fix" to improve the firm's ethical reputation? Explain.

3. When a company operates in many different countries with widely diverse legal systems and ethical standards, how can it develop and enforce a global set of criteria as to what is right and wrong? Explain.

Team Exercise

Class is divided into groups of five. Each team will provide Mr. Danjczek with a set of recommendations as to what he should do in his new job to improve the ethical climate at Titan. Depending on class size, each team will present its recommendations to the entire class for approximately 10 minutes, to be followed by open class discussion moderated by the instructor.

Experiential Exercise

One student will role-play Mr. Danjczek; five other students will role-play international agents of Titan at five different locations (Brazil, Bermuda, Saudi Arabia, Nigeria, and Rumania). Mr. Danjczek is trying to convey the message that the company is serious about its ethical turnaround and that "the old chapter in the company's history of laxed ethical standards has come to a close." Local agents believe that this is a wonderful thing to say from a public relations perspective, but that Titan cannot be competitive against other foreign firms that have no qualms about doing whatever they have to do to secure contracts. Role-play should last for about 15 to 20 minutes, after which the instructor will moderate open class discussion of the issues raised.

Discussion Case 17.5

Are Culture-Specific HR Policies a Good Idea?

Over the past 10 years, East Computer Company has grown from a domestic producer of IBM clones in Boston to a multinational company with assembly plants in four foreign locations. The company's personnel policies were developed five years ago, before East Computer's international expansion, by a task force headed by the vice president for HRM in Boston. The company's CEO has just appointed a new task force to

examine the extent to which current domestic personnel policies can be "exported" to East's new international locations. The essential elements of these policies are the following:

1. All job openings are posted to allow any employee to apply for a position.
2. Selection is based on merit. Appropriate selection devices (for example, tests, structured interviews, and the like) are used to ensure proper implementation of this policy.

3. Nepotism is expressly forbidden.

4. Promotion from within is the norm whenever feasible.

5. Equal employment opportunities are available to all, regardless of sex, race, national origin, or religion.

6. Pay for various positions is established through a rational process that includes both job evaluation and market survey data.

7. There is equal pay for equal work, regardless of sex, race, national origin, or religion.

8. Goals are jointly set by supervisor and subordinate, with an annual formal appraisal session at which both parties have the chance to discuss progress toward goal achievement. The appraisal is used both to provide performance feedback to the employee and as a basis for merit pay decisions.

As a first step in evaluating these policies, the vice president for HRM classified the countries where East's facilities are located according to Hofstede's dimensions. She came up with the matrix shown below.

You have been hired by East Computer Company to help management develop personnel policies for each of the four international facilities. Ideally, management would prefer to use the same policies that it uses in the United States to maintain consistency and reduce administrative problems. However, the vice president for HRM has made a strong case for "tailor-made" personnel policies that are suitable to each facility's cultural environment.

Critical Thinking Questions

1. Given East Computer Company's present personnel policies, what problems is the company likely to face in each facility if it transports its domestic policies abroad?

2. How would you change or adapt each of the company's current personnel policies to better fit the cultural environment of each international facility?

3. What set of management recommendations would you provide for keeping, changing, or adapting East Computer Company's HR policies for the United States, Australia, Mexico, England, and Norway? In your recommendations, be sure to mention any risks associated with implementing your recommendations.

Team Exercises

Students break into groups of five. One student role-plays a consultant who is conducting an exercise to uncover possible problems in uniform application of the company's current policy. Each of the other four students takes the role of advocate for one of the four international locations. Each advocate should make an argument for or against keeping specific parts of East's existing HR policies.

Students form groups of four students, with each group acting as the advocate for one of the four international locations. After deciding which policies to keep and which to change, a representative from each group presents the group's recommendations to the class. After these brief presentations, the class discusses the costs and benefits of culture-specific HR policies.

Experiential Exercise

Find some individuals (other students, friends, or relatives) who were either raised in and/or are familiar with a foreign country. Interview them and ask their opinions about how they perceive that country in terms of five of Hofsteade's dimensions. On which dimensions is the country high? Low? Based on the interviewee's assessment, is the culture of that country reflected in any human resource practices such as hiring procedures, compensation, performance appraisal and the like? Several student will be asked to present their finding to entire class (about 5 to 10 minutes each) to be followed by open class discussion moderated by the instructor.

Cultural Dimensions					
Facility Location	Power Distance	Individualism	Uncertainty Avoidance	Masculinity	Long-Term Orientation
Australia	Low	High	Medium	Medium	Low
Mexico	High	Low	High	High	Medium
England	Low	High	Low	High	Low
Norway	Low	Medium	Medium	Low	High

HRM and Business Periodicals

The following is an annotated listing of general business publications and specialized HRM publications. Many of these resources may prove helpful to you, not only in your study of HRM but also in your own career development. As we noted in the text, more and more companies are shifting career development responsibilities onto their employees, while providing them with tools for career planning. These tools can be the first in your career-planning toolkit.

General Business Periodicals

Across the Board. Conference Board. 845 Third Avenue, New York, NY 10022. Provides articles that present business topics in nontechnical terms. Articles range from discussions of general business issues to examinations of specific companies and industries.

Black Enterprise. Earl G. Graves Publishing Co. 130 Fifth Avenue, New York, NY 10011. *Black Enterprise* focuses on business, jobs, career potential, and financial opportunities as they relate to African, Caribbean, and African-American consciousness. Its annual list of the nation's top black businesses and financial institutions is considered an invaluable accounting of African-American business enterprises.

BusinessWeek. McGraw-Hill, Inc. 1221 Avenue of the Americas, New York, NY 10020. The leading general business magazine, *BusinessWeek* offers comprehensive coverage of the news and developments affecting the business world. It includes information on computers, finance, labor, industry, marketing, science, and technology.

Fast Company. P.O. Box 52760, Boulder, CO 80321-2760. Fairly new on the scene, *Fast Company* focuses on a wide variety of business topics and is geared toward giving companies an edge in a very competitive marketplace. The magazine's subtitle is "How smart business works."

Forbes. Forbes, Inc. 60 Fifth Avenue, New York, NY 10011. A general business magazine that celebrates capitalism. Short articles report on company activities, industry developments, economic trends, and investment tips.

Fortune. Time, Inc. Time & Life Building, Rockefeller Center, New York, NY 10020. *Fortune* reports on companies and industries, developments and trends. Its articles tend to be longer than those in other business magazines, and its frequent use of sidebars allows readers to learn more about corollary issues.

Harvard Business Review. Graduate School of Business Administration, Harvard University. Boston, MA 02163. This well-known product of Harvard Business School publishes articles in the areas of business and management. Topics include planning, manufacturing, and innovation. Each issue includes a case study.

Hispanic Business. P.O. Box 469038, Escondido, CA 92046-9038. A general business magazine focusing on a variety of business issues (including career opportunities, entrepreneurial ventures, and legislation) as they relate to Latino workers and Latino-owned businesses in the United States.

Inc.: The Magazine for Growing Companies. Goldhirsch Group, Inc. 38 Commercial Wharf, Boston, MA 02110. Inc. is targeted to the person involved in managing new, small, or growing companies. Articles focus on entrepreneurial ventures, general business topics, and profiles of successful managers.

Journal of Business Ethics. Kluwar Academic Publishers. 101 Philip Dr., Norwell, MA 02061. This journal publishes scholarly articles dealing with the ethical issues confronted in business. It is clearly written, free of technical jargon, and contains articles on such topics as ethics and business schools, competitor intelligence, corporate executives, and disasters.

Management Review. American Management Association. 135 West 50th St., New York, NY 10020. This monthly publication describes management trends, techniques, and issues for middle- and upper-level managers in the corporate and public sector.

Nation's Business: U.S. Chamber of Commerce. 1615 H St. N.W., Washington, DC 20062. *Nation's Business* reports on current business activities and topics such as quality, entrepreneurship, and going public. It is directed mainly to entrepreneurs and small business owners and managers. Each issue contains a feature on issues affecting family businesses.

Small Business Reports. American Management Association. 135 West 50th St., New York, NY 10020. Articles in this monthly magazine tend to offer practical advice for small business owners and managers. However, topics are of interest to all business managers.

The Wall Street Journal. Dow Jones & Co., Inc. 200 Liberty St., New York, NY 10281. With a greater circulation than either The *New York Times* or *USA Today*, this comprehensive national newspaper offers in-depth coverage of national and international finance and business. A must for anyone interested in the business of business.

Working Woman. Working Woman, Inc. 230 Park Avenue, New York, NY 10169. Geared toward the white-collar career woman interested in advancing in her field. Articles focus on career advancement, management, communicaiton skills, money management, and investment information. Features items on new technology, changing demographics, and profiles of successful businesswomen. Of special interest is the annual "Hottest Careers" issue featuring listings of up-and-coming occupations.

HRM Periodicals

Workspan. WorldatWork Association, 14040 N. Northsight Blvd., Scottsdale, AZ 58260. Published monthly, this newsletter includes articles of interest to HR practitioners. It also reports on the resources available to practitioners, as well as positions available in the field.

Academy of Management Perspectives. Pace University, P.O. Box 3020, Briarcliff Manor, NY 10510. Published quarterly and geared toward executives and students of business, this journal presents straightforward practical articles, many of them written by leading management scholars.

WorldatWork Journal. WorldatWork Association, 14040 N. Northsight Blvd., Scottsdale, AZ 85260. The *WorldatWork Journal* is a specialized publication of the WorldatWork Association. Issues appear quarterly and feature six to eight articles on such compensation-related topics as pay for performance, compensation strategy, tax considerations, executive pay, and benefits.

Compensation & Benefits Review. American Management Association. 135 West 50th St., New York, NY 10020. A specialized publication of the American Management Association, this journal contains four to six articles in each issue, covering compensation management and strategy and such diverse topics as job evaluation as a barrier to excellence and compensating overseas executives. One invaluable feature is its condensations of noteworthy articles appearing in other business publications.

CompFlash. WorldatWork Association, 14040 N. Northsight Blvd., Scottsdale, AZ 58260. Published monthly, this newsletter includes short articles and information on the latest trends/statistics useful for compensation management, including the most recent surveys.

Employee Relations Law Journal. Executive Enterprises, Inc. 22 West 21st St., New York, NY 10010. Although geared toward attorneys specializing in employment law, in-house counsel, and HR executives, this journal contains practical advice that is not highly technical. Articles deal with such topics as personnel management techniques, legal compliance, and court cases, and such issues as sex discrimination, privacy in the workplace, and drug testing. Features up-to-date coverage of federal regulatory agency actions.

Employee Relations Weekly. Bureau of National Affairs. 1231 25th Street, N.W. Washington, DC 20037. This government publication covers such workplace issues as EEO developments, health and safety, pay and benefits, and policy and practices. Recent articles have touched on employee committees, domestic partner benefits, and sexual harassment. Useful for discussions of court cases relevant to employee relations.

HRMagazine. Society for Human Resource Management. 606 N. Washington St., Alexandria, VA 22314. Formerly called *Personnel Administrator*, this magazine offers in-depth coverage of all areas of HRM.

International Journal of Human Resource Management. Routledge Journals, 11 New Fetter Lane, London EC4P 4EE. Published monthly, this journal covers research on international HRM issues and trends.

Labor Notes. Labor and Education Research Project. 7435 Michigan Avenue, Detroit, MI 48210. This workers' magazine is as critical of big labor as it is of management. It features nationwide coverage of such issues as contracts, ongoing negotiation, boycotts, working conditions, and problems confronting women and minority workers. Useful for its "shop-floor" view and as counterbalance to the management perspective.

Monthly Labor Review. Bureau of Labor Statistics. U.S. Department of Labor, Washington, DC 20402. The source for U.S. labor statistics. Each issue carries four in-depth articles on labor-related topics.

Organizational Dynamics. American Management Association. 135 West 50th St., New York, NY 10020. Articles deal with appraisal systems and management systems in general, as well as with other relevant aspects of systems administration.

Personnel Journal. 245 Fischer Ave. B-2, Costa Mesa, CA 92626. *Personnel Journal* covers the full range of issues in human resources. There is extensive coverage of current HR policies and practices at actual companies, and each article contains company vital statistics. *Personnel Journal* also sponsors the annual Optimas Awards, which spotlight companies with excellent HR initiatives in a variety of categories.

Public Personnel Management. Personnel Management Association. 1617 Duke St., Alexandria, VA 22314. Research articles useful to personnel administrators in public-sector personnel management. Typical subjects are recruiting, interviewing, training, sick leave, and home-based employment.

Supervisory Management. American Management Association, 135 West 50th St., New York, NY 10020. Within its concise 12-page format, this magazine contains numerous brief articles offering practical advice on such topics as building quality awareness, handling problem employees, and conducting effective meetings.

Training & Development. American Society for Training & Development. 1640 King St., Alexandria, VA 22313. The official magazine of ASTD, *Training & Development* is directed toward HR professionals and other managers. It covers both practical issues and trends in training and development, including such topics as how to make a training video, how to train workers to write more clearly, and the ins and outs of successful diversity training.

Ability Competence in performing a job. (81)

Absolute judgment An appraisal format that asks supervisors to make judgments about an employee's performance based solely on performance standards. (212)

Adverse impact Discrimination that occurs when the equal application of an employment standard has an unequal effect on one or more protected classes. Also called *disparate impact*. (90)

Affirmative action A strategy intended to achieve fair employment by urging employers to hire certain groups of people who were discriminated against in the past. (87)

Age Discrimination in Employment Act (1967) The law prohibiting discrimination against people who are 40 or older. (98)

Americans with Disabilities Act (1990) The law forbidding employment discrimination against people with disabilities who are able to perform the essential functions of the job with or without reasonable accommodation. (98)

Appeals procedure A procedure that allows employees to voice their reactions to management practices and to challenge management decisions. (423)

Apprenticeship A program in which promising prospective employees are groomed before they are actually hired on a permanent basis. (138)

Arbitration The last step in a grievance procedure. The decision of the arbitrator, who is a neutral individual selected from outside the firm, is binding on both parties. (496)

Assessment center A set of simulated tasks or exercises that candidates (usually for managerial positions) are asked to perform. (170)

Attrition An employment policy designed to reduce the company's workforce by not refilling job vacancies that are created by turnover. (192)

Award A one-time reward usually given in the form of a tangible prize. (345)

Base compensation The fixed pay an employee receives on a regular basis, either in the form of a salary or as an hourly wage. (301)

Behavioral appraisal instrument An appraisal tool that asks managers to assess a worker's behaviors. (214)

Benchmark or key jobs A job that is similar or comparable in content across firms. (321)

Benefits mix The complete package of benefits that a company offers its employees. (378)

Bona fide occupational qualification (BFOQ) A characteristic that must be present in all employees for a particular job. (91)

Bonus program or lump-sum payment A financial incentive that is given on a one-time basis and does not raise the employee's base pay permanently. (344)

Boundaryless organizational structure An organizational structure that enables an organization to form relationships with customers, suppliers, and/or competitors, either to pool organizational resources for mutual benefit or to encourage cooperation in an uncertain environment. (48)

Brain drain The loss of high-talent key personnel to competitors or start-up ventures. (19)

Brainstorming A creativity training technique in which participants are given the opportunity to generate ideas openly, without fear of judgment. (257)

Bureaucratic organizational structure A pyramid-shaped organizational structure that consists of hierarchies with many levels of management. (46)

Burnout A stress syndrome characterized by emotional exhaustion, depersonalization, and reduced personal accomplishment. (528)

Business process reengineering (BPR) A fundamental rethinking and radical redesign of business processes to achieve dramatic improvements in cost, quality, service, and speed. (50)

Business unionism A form of unionism that focuses on improving workers' economic well-being. (477)

Business unit strategy The formulation and implementation of strategies by a firm that is relatively autonomous, even if it is part of a larger corporation. (28)

Career development An ongoing and formalized effort that focuses on developing enriched and more capable workers. (273)

Career path A chart showing the possible directions and career opportunities available in an organization; it presents the steps in a possible career and a plausible timetable for accomplishing them. (285)

Career resource center A collection of career development materials such as workbooks, tapes, and texts. (286)

Codetermination The representation of workers on a corporation's board of directors; used in Germany. (482)

Coinsurance Payments made to cover health-care expenses that are split between the employer's insurance company and the insured employee. (373)

Collective bargaining A system in which unions and management negotiate with each other to develop the work rules under which union members will work for a stipulated period of time. (478)

Comparability In performance ratings, the degree to which the performance ratings given by various supervisors in an organization are similar. (220)

Comparable worth A pay concept or doctrine that calls for comparable pay for jobs that require comparable skills, effort, and responsibility and have comparable working conditions, even if the job content is different. (327)

Compensable factors Work-related criteria that an organization considers most important in assessing the relative value of different jobs. (318)

Compensatory damages Fines awarded to a plaintiff to compensate for the financial or psychological harm the plaintiff has suffered. (97)

Competencies Characteristics associated with successful performance. (210)

Competency model Set of competencies associated with a job. (210)

Conciliation An attempt to reach a negotiated settlement between the employer and an employee or applicant in an EEO case. (102)

Consolidated Omnibus Budget Reconciliation Act of 1985 (COBRA) Legislation that gives employees the right to continue their health insurance coverage for 18 to 36 months after their employment has terminated. (385)

Contingent workers Workers hired to deal with temporary increases in an organization's workload or to do work that is not part of its core set of capabilities. (68)

Contract A legally binding promise between two or more competent parties. (439)

Contractual rights A right based on the law of contracts. (439)

Contributions Payments made for benefits coverage. Contributions for a specific benefit may come from the employer, employee, or both. (373)

Copayment A small payment made by the employee for each office visit to a physician under a health plan. The health plan pays for additional medical expenses that exceed the copayment at no cost to the employee. (373)

Core time Time when all employees are expected to be at work. Part of a flexible work hours arrangement. (73)

Core workers An organization's full-time employees. (68)

Corporate strategy The mix of businesses a corporation decides to hold and the flow of resources among those businesses. (28)

Cost-of-living adjustment (COLA) Pay raises, usually made across the board, that are tied to such inflation indicators as the consumer price index. (599)

Cross-functional training Training employees to perform operations in areas other than their assigned job. (256)

Cultural determinism The idea that one can successfully infer an individual's motivations, interests, values, and behavioral traits based on that individual's group memberships. (139)

Cultural relativity concept of management The management concept holding that management practices should be molded to the different sets of values, beliefs, attitudes, and behaviors exhibited by a diverse workforce. (124)

Culture shock The inability to adjust to a different cultural environment. (545)

Cumulative trauma disorder (CTD) An occupational injury that occurs from repetitive physical movements, such as assembly-line work or data entry. (523)

Decentralization Transferring responsibility and decision-making authority from a central office to people and locations closer to the situation that demands attention. (11)

Deductible An annual out-of-pocket expenditure that an insurance policyholder must make before the insurance plan makes any reimbursements. (374)

Defined benefit plan or pension A retirement plan that promises to pay a fixed dollar amount of retirement income based on a formula that takes into account the average of the employee's last three to five years' earnings prior to retirement. (390)

Defined contribution plan A retirement plan in which the employer promises to contribute a specific amount of funds into the plan for each participant. The final value of each participant's retirement income depends on the success of the plan's investments. (390)

Development An effort to provide employees with the abilities the organization will need in the future. (240)

Dimension An aspect of performance that determines effective job performance. (210)

Discrimination The making of distinctions. In HR context, the making of distinctions among people. (89)

Disparate treatment Discrimination that occurs when individuals are treated differently because of their membership in a protected class. (89)

Distinctive competencies The characteristics that give a firm a competitive edge. (34)

Distributive bargaining Bargaining that focuses on convincing the other party that the cost of disagreeing with the proposed terms would be very high. (491)

Diversity Human characteristics that make people different from one another. (119)

Diversity audit A review of the effectiveness of an organization's diversity management program. (138)

Diversity training programs Programs that provide diversity awareness training and educate employees on specific cultural and sex differences and how to respond to these in the workplace. (135)

Downsizing A company strategy to reduce the scale (size) and scope of its business in order to improve the company's financial performance. (190)

Downward communication Communication that allows managers to implement their decisions and to influence employees lower in the organizational hierarchy. (411)

Dual-career couple A couple whose members both have occupational responsibilities and career issues at stake. (277)

Due process Equal and fair application of a policy or law. (440)

Economic strike A strike that takes place when an agreement is not reached during collective bargaining. (496)

Egalitarian pay system A pay plan in which most employees are part of the same compensation system. (308)

Electronic mail (e-mail) A form of electronic communication that allows employees to communicate with each other via electronic messages sent through personal computer terminals linked by a network. (416)

Elitist pay system A pay plan in which different compensation systems are established for employees or groups at different organizational levels. (308)

Employee assistance program (EAP) A company-sponsored program that helps employees cope with personal problems that are interfering with their job performance. (424)

Employee attitude survey A formal anonymous survey designed to measure employee likes and dislikes of various aspects of their jobs. (422)

Employee benefits or indirect compensation Group membership rewards that provide security for employees and their family members. (371)

Employee feedback program A program designed to improve employee communications by giving employees a voice in policy formulation and making sure that they receive due process on any complaints they lodge against managers. (422)

Employee recognition program A program that rewards employees for their ideas and contributions. (428)

Employee relations policy A policy designed to communicate management's thinking and practices concerning employee-related matters and prevent problems in the workplace from becoming serious. (409)

Employee relations representative A member of the HR department who ensures that company policies are followed and consults with both supervisors and employees on specific employee relations problems. (409)

Employee Retirement Income Security Act (ERISA) A federal law established in 1974 to protect employees' retirement benefits from mismanagement. (389)

Employee separation The termination of an employee's membership in an organization. (183)

Employee stock ownership plan (ESOP) A corporatewide pay-for-performance plan that rewards employees with company stocks, either as an outright grant or at a favorable price that may be below market value. (352)

Employment at will A common-law rule used by employers to assert their right to end an employment relationship with an employee at any time for any cause. (443)

Employment contract A contract that spells out explicitly the terms of the employment relationship for both employee and employer. (439)

Empowerment Providing workers with the skills and authority to make decisions that would traditionally be made by managers. (19)

Enterprise union A labor union that represents workers in only one large company rather than in a particular industry; used in Japan. (482)

Environmental challenges Forces external to a firm that affect the firm's performance but are beyond the control of management. (4)

Equal Employment Opportunity Commission (EEOC) The federal agency responsible for enforcing EEO laws. (102)

Equal Pay Act (1963) The law that requires the same pay for men and women who do the same job in the same organization. (88)

Essential functions Job duties that each person in a certain position must do or must be able to do to be an effective employee. (99)

Ethnocentric approach An approach to managing international operations in which top management and other key positions are filled by people from the home country. (543)

Executive order A presidential directive that has the force of law. In HR context, a policy with which all federal agencies and organizations doing business with the federal government must comply. (97)

Exempt employee An employee who is not covered by the provisions of the Fair Labor Standards Act. Most professional, administrative, executive, and outside sales jobs fall into this category. (326)

Exit interview An employee's final interview following separation. The purpose of the interview is to find out the reasons why the employee is leaving (if the separation is voluntary) or to provide counseling and/or assistance in finding a new job. (186)

Expatriate A citizen of one country living and working in another country. (540)

Expectancy theory A theory of behavior holding that people tend to do those things that are rewarded. (345)

Extended leave A benefit that allows an employee to take a long-term leave from the office, while retaining benefits and the guarantee of a comparable job on return. (137)

External equity The perceived fairness in pay relative to what other employers are paying for the same type of labor. (302)

Fair employment The goal of EEO legislation and regulation: a situation in which employment decisions are not affected by illegal discrimination. (87)

Fair Labor Standards Act (FLSA) The fundamental compensation law in the United States. Requires employers to record earnings and hours worked by all covered employees and to report this information to the U.S. Department of Labor. Defines two categories of employees: exempt and nonexempt. (326)

Family and Medical Leave Act of 1993 (FMLA) A federal law that requires employers to provide up to 12 weeks' unpaid leave to eligible employees for the birth or adoption of a child; to care for a sick parent, child, or spouse; or to take care of health problems that interfere with job performance. (382)

Flat organizational structure An organizational structure that has only a few levels of management and emphasizes decentralization. (48)

Flexible or cafeteria benefits program A benefits program that allows employees to select the benefits they need most from a menu of choices. (374)

Flexible work hours A work arrangement that gives employees control over the starting and ending times of their daily work schedules. (73)

Flextime Time during which employees can choose not to be at work. Part of a flexible work hours arrangement. (73)

Four-fifths rule An EEOC provision for establishing a prima facie case that an HR practice is discriminatory and has an adverse impact. A practice has an adverse impact if the hiring rate of a protected class is less than four-fifths the hiring rate of a majority group. (91)

Frame-of-reference (FOR) training A type of training that presents supervisors with fictitious examples of worker performance (either in writing or on videotape), asks the supervisors to evaluate the workers in the examples, and then tells them what their ratings should have been. (220)

Gainsharing A plantwide pay-for-performance plan in which a portion of the company's cost savings is returned to workers, usually in the form of a lump-sum bonus. (350)

Genetic testing A form of biological testing that identifies employees who are genetically susceptible to specific occupational substances. (525)

Geocentric approach An approach to managing international operations in which nationality is downplayed and the firm actively searches on a worldwide or

regional basis for the best people to fill key positions. (543)

Glass ceiling The intangible barrier in an organization that prevents female and minority employees from rising to positions above a certain level. (125)

Grievance procedure A systematic step-by-step process designed to settle disputes regarding the interpretation of a labor contract. (496)

Health Insurance Portability and Accountability Act (HIPAA) A federal law that protects an employee's ability to transfer between health insurance plans without a gap in coverage due to a preexisting condition. (385)

Health maintenance organization (HMO) A health-care plan that provides comprehensive medical services for employees and their families at a flat annual fee. (386)

Hiring freeze An employment policy designed to reduce the company's workforce by not hiring any new employees into the company. (193)

Hostile work environment sexual harassment Harassment that occurs when the behavior of anyone in the work setting is sexual in nature and is perceived by an employee as offensive and undesirable. (93)

Hot-stove rule A model of disciplinary action: Discipline should be immediate, provide ample warning, and be consistently applied to all. (456)

HR audit A periodic review of the effectiveness with which a company uses its human resources. Frequently includes an evaluation of the HR department itself. (37)

Human resource information system (HRIS) A system used to collect, record, store, analyze, and retrieve data concerning an organization's human resources. (75)

Human resource planning (HRP) The process an organization uses to ensure that it has the right amount and the right kind of people to deliver a particular level of output or services in the future. (148)

Human resource strategy A firm's deliberate use of human resources to help it gain or maintain an edge against its competitors in the marketplace. The grand plan or general approach an organization adopts to ensure that it effectively uses its people to accomplish its mission. (3)

Human resources (HR) People who work in an organization. Also called *personnel*. (3)

Human resource tactic A particular HR policy or program that helps to advance a firm's strategic goal. (3)

Individual challenges Human resource issues that address the decisions most pertinent to individual employees. (16)

Individual equity The perceived fairness of individual pay decisions. (304)

Individuals with disabilities Persons who have a physical or mental impairment that substantially affects one or more major life activities. (98)

Informal communications Also called "the grapevine." Information exchanges without a planned agenda that occur informally among employees. (420)

Information dissemination The process of making information available to decision makers, wherever they are located. (412)

Insubordination Either refusal to obey a direct order from a supervisor or verbal abuse of a supervisor. (460)

Integrative bargaining Bargaining that focuses on convincing the other party that the benefits of agreeing with the proposed terms would be very high. (492)

Internal equity The perceived fairness of the pay structure within a firm. (302)

Internal Revenue Code (IRC) The code of tax laws that affects how much of their earnings employees can keep and how benefits are treated for tax purposes. (329)

Involuntary separation A separation that occurs when an employer decides to terminate its relationship with an employee due to (1) economic necessity or (2) a poor fit between the employee and the organization. (188)

Job aids External sources of information, such as pamphlets and reference guides, that workers can access quickly when they need help in making a decision or performing a specific task. (255)

Job analysis The systematic process of collecting information used to make decisions about jobs. Job analysis identifies the tasks, duties, and responsibilities of a particular job. (58)

Job banding The practice of replacing narrowly defined job descriptions with broader categories (bands) of related jobs. (324)

Job description A written document that identifies, describes, and defines a job in terms of its duties, responsibilities, working conditions, and specifications. (65)

Job design The process of organizing work into the tasks required to perform a specific job. (57)

Job enlargement The process of expanding a job's duties. (57)

Job enrichment The process of putting specialized tasks back together so that one person is responsible for producing a whole product or an entire service. (58)

Job evaluation The process of evaluating the relative value or contribution of different jobs to an organization. (315)

Job hierarchy A listing of jobs in order of their importance to the organization, from highest to lowest. (319)

Job rotation The process of rotating workers among different narrowly defined tasks without disrupting the flow of work. (57)

Job sharing A work arrangement in which two or more employees divide a job's responsibilities, hours, and benefits among themselves. (70)

Job specifications The worker characteristics needed to perform a job successfully. (68)

Job-posting system A system in which an organization announces job openings to all employees on a bulletin board, in a company newsletter, or through a phone recording or computer system. (285)

Joint venture In international business, a foreign branch owned partly by the home office and partly by an entity in the host country (a company, a consortium of firms, an individual, or the government). (543)

Knowledge worker A worker who transforms information into a product or service. (412)

Knowledge, skills, and abilities (KSAs) The knowledge, skills, and abilities needed to perform a job successfully. (60)

Knowledge-based pay or skill-based pay A pay system in which employees are paid on the basis of the jobs they can do or talents they have that can be successfully applied to a variety of tasks and situations. (307)

Labor contract A union contract that spells out the conditions of employment and work rules that affect employees in the unit represented by the union. (478)

Labor demand How many workers the organization will need in the future. (147)

Labor relations specialist Someone, often a member of the HR department, who is knowledgeable about labor relations and can represent management's interests to a union. (474)

Labor relations strategy A company's overall plan for dealing with labor unions. (483)

Labor supply The availability of workers with the required skills to meet the firm's labor demand. (147)

Landrum-Griffin Act (1959) A law designed to protect union members and their participation in union affairs. (476)

Line employee An employee involved directly in producing the company's good(s) or delivering the service(s). (3)

Literacy The mastery of basic skills (reading, writing, arithmetic, and their uses in problem solving). (258)

Lockout Occurs when an employer shuts down its operations before or during a labor dispute. (496)

Management by objectives (MBO) A goal-directed approach to performance appraisal in which workers and their supervisors set goals together for the upcoming evaluation period. (216)

Management by walking around (MBWA) A technique in which managers walk around and talk to employees informally to monitor informal communications, listen to employee grievances and suggestions, and build rapport and morale. (421)

Management of diversity The set of activities involved in integrating nontraditional employees (women and minorities) into the workforce and using their diversity to the firm's competitive advantage. (120)

Management rights Management's rights to run the business and retain any profits that result. (442)

Manager A person who is in charge of others and is responsible for the timely and correct execution of actions that promote his or her unit's success. (3)

Medicare A part of the Social Security program that provides health insurance coverage for people aged 65 and over. (479)

Mentoring A developmentally oriented relationship between senior and junior colleagues or peers that involves advising, role modeling, sharing contacts, and giving general support. (288)

Merit pay An increase in base pay, normally given once a year. (344)

Motivation A person's desire to do the best possible job or to exert the maximum effort to perform assigned tasks. (18)

Motivation That which energizes, directs, and sustains human behavior. In HRM, a person's desire to do the best possible job or to exert the maximum effort to perform assigned tasks. (54)

Multimedia technology A form of electronic communication that integrates voice, video, and text, all of which can be encoded digitally and transported on fiber optic networks. (418)

Multinational corporation (MNC) A firm with assembly and production facilities in several countries and regions of the world. (540)

National Labor Relations Board (NLRB) The independent federal agency created by the Wagner Act to administer U.S. labor law. (575)

Negligent hiring Hiring an employee with a history of violent or illegal behavior without conducting background checks or taking proper precautions. (520)

Nepotism The practice of favoring relatives over others in the workplace. (414)

Nonexempt employee An employee who is covered by the provisions of the Fair Labor Standards Act. (326)

Occupational Safety and Health Act of 1970 (OSHA) A federal law that requires employers to provide a safe and healthy work environment, comply with specific occupational safety and health standards, and keep records of occupational injuries and illnesses. (512)

Office of Federal Contract Compliance Programs (OFCCP) The federal agency responsible for monitoring and enforcing the laws and executive orders that apply to the federal government and its contractors. (103)

Old boys' network An informal social and business network of high-level male executives that typically excludes women and minorities. Access to the old boys' network is often an important factor in career advancement. (134)

Organizational challenges Concerns or problems internal to a firm; often a by-product of environmental forces. (10)

Organizational culture The basic assumptions and beliefs shared by members of an organization. These beliefs operate unconsciously and define in a basic taken-for-granted fashion an organization's view of itself and its environment. (12)

Organizational structure The formal or informal relationships between people in an organization. (45)

Orientation The process of informing new employees about what is expected of them in the job and helping them cope with the stresses of transition. (263)

Outcome appraisal instrument An appraisal tool that asks managers to assess the results achieved by workers. (216)

Outplacement assistance A program in which companies help their departing employees find jobs more rapidly by providing them with training in job-search skills. (186)

Outsourcing Subcontracting work to an outside company that specializes in and is more efficient at doing that kind of work. (15)

Pay grades Groups of jobs that are paid within the same pay range. (315)

Pay incentive A program designed to reward employees for good performance. (301)

Pay policy A firm's decision to pay above, below, or at the market rate for its jobs. (322)

Pay-for-performance system or incentive system A system that rewards employees on the assumptions that (1) individual employees and work teams differ in how much they contribute to the firm; (2) the firm's overall performance depends to a large degree on the performance of individuals and groups within the firm; and (3) to attract, retain, and motivate high performers and to be fair to all employees, the firm needs to reward employees on the basis of their relative performance. (338)

Peer review A performance appraisal system in which workers at the same level in the organization rate one another. (217)

Peer trainers High-performing workers who double as internal on-the-job trainers. (256)

Pension Benefit Guaranty Corporation (PBGC) The government agency that provides plan termination insurance to employers with defined benefit retirement programs. (390)

Performance appraisal The identification, measurement, and management of human performance in organizations. (208)

Perquisites ("perks") Noncash incentives given to a firm's executives. (358)

Personnel file A file maintained for each employee, containing the documentation of critical HR-related information, such as performance appraisals, salary history, disciplinary actions, and career milestones. (442)

Piece-rate system A compensation system in which employees are paid per unit produced. (342)

Polycentric approach An approach to managing international operations in which subsidiaries are managed and staffed by personnel from the host country. (543)

Portable benefits Employee benefits, usually retirement funds, that stay with the employee as he or she moves from one company to another. (390)

Positive discipline A discipline procedure that encourages employees to monitor their own behaviors and assume responsibility for their actions. (454)

Preexisting condition A medical condition treated while an employee was covered under a former employer's health plan and requires treatment under a new employer's different health plan. (385)

Preferred provider organization (PPO) A health-care plan in which an employer or insurance company establishes a network of doctors and hospitals to provide a broad set of medical services for a flat fee per participant. In return for the lower fee, the doctors and hospitals who join the PPO network expect to receive a larger volume of patients. (387)

Premium The money paid to an insurance company for coverage. (386)

Privacy Act of 1974 Guarantees the privacy of personnel files for employees of the U.S. federal government. (442)

Problem-solving team A team consisting of volunteers from a unit or department who meet one or two hours per week to discuss quality improvement, cost reduction, or improvement in the work environment. (52)

Productivity A measure of how much value individual employees add to the goods or services that the organization produces. (17)

Profit sharing A corporatewide pay-for-performance plan that uses a formula to allocate a portion of declared profits to employees. Typically, profit distributions under a profit-sharing plan are used to fund employees' retirement plans. (352)

Progressive discipline A series of management interventions that gives employees opportunities to correct undesirable behaviors before being discharged. (453)

Promotability forecast A career development activity in which managers make decisions regarding the advancement potential of subordinates. (282)

Protected class A group of people who suffered discrimination in the past and who are given special protection by the judicial system. (89)

Punitive damages Fines awarded to a plaintiff in order to punish the defendant. (97)

Quality of work life A measure of how safe and satisfied employees feel with their jobs. (18)

Quid pro quo sexual harassment Harassment that occurs when sexual activity is required in return for getting or keeping a job or job-related benefit. (93)

Quotas Employer adjustments of hiring decisions to ensure that a certain number of people from a certain protected class are hired. (97)

Railway Labor Act A law designed to regulate labor relations in the transportation industry. (477)

Rater error An error in performance appraisals that reflects consistent biases on the part of the rater. (219)

Realistic job preview (RJP) Realistic information about the demands of the job, the organization's expectations of the job holder, and the work environment. (263)

Reasonable accommodation An action taken to accommodate the known disabilities of applicants or employees so that disabled persons enjoy equal employment opportunity. (100)

Recruitment The process of generating a pool of qualified candidates for a particular job; the first step in the hiring process. (152)

Relative judgment An appraisal format that asks supervisors to compare an employee's performance to the performance of other employees doing the same job. (211)

Reliability Consistency of measurement, usually across time but also across judges. (162)

Reverse discrimination Discrimination against a nonprotected-class member resulting from attempts to recruit and hire members of protected classes. (104)

Right The ability to engage in conduct that is protected by law or social sanction, free from interference by another party. (439)

Right-to-work law A state law that makes it illegal within that state for a union to include a union shop clause in its contract. (476)

Rightsizing The process of reorganizing a company's employees to improve their efficiency. (190)

Selection The process of making a "hire" or "no hire" decision regarding each applicant for a job; the second step in the hiring process. (152)

Self-managed team (SMT) A team responsible for producing an entire product, a component, or an ongoing service. (51)

Self-review A performance appraisal system in which workers rate themselves. (217)

Senior mentoring program A support program in which senior managers identify promising women and minority employees and play an important role in nurturing their career progress. (137)

Seniority The length of time a person works for an employer. (548)

Simulation A device or situation that replicates job demands at an off-the-job site. (250)

Situational factors or system factors A wide array of organizational characteristics that can positively or negatively influence performance. (227)

Skills inventory A company-maintained record of employees' abilities, skills, knowledge, and education. (285)

Social Security A government program that provides income for retirees, the disabled, and survivors of deceased workers, and health care for the aged through the Medicare program. (378)

Socialization The process of orienting new employees to the organization or the unit in which they will be working; the third step in the hiring process. (152)

Special-purpose team A team or task force consisting of workers who span functional or organizational boundaries and whose purpose is to examine complex issues. (52)

Staff employee An employee who supports line employees. (4)

Statutory right A right protected by specific laws. (439)

Strategic HR choices The options available to a firm in designing its human resources system. (24)

Strategic human resource (HR) planning The process of formulating HR strategies and establishing programs or tactics to implement them. (20)

Structured interview Job interview based on a thorough job analysis, applying job-related questions with predetermined answers consistently across all interviews for a job. (168)

Subordinate review A performance appraisal system in which workers review their supervisors. (217)

Succession planning A career development activity that focuses on preparing people to fill executive positions. (382)

Supplemental unemployment benefits (SUB) Benefits given by a company to laid-off employees over and above state unemployment benefits. (381)

Support group A group established by an employer to provide a nurturing climate for employees who would otherwise feel isolated or alienated. (136)

Taft-Hartley Act (1947) A federal law designed to limit some of the power acquired by unions under the Wagner Act by adjusting the regulation of labor–management relations to ensure a level playing field for both parties. (475)

Team A small number of people with complementary skills who work toward common goals for which they hold themselves mutually accountable. (51)

Telecommuting A work arrangement that allows employees to work in their homes full-time, maintaining their connection to the office through phone, fax, and computer. (73)

Teleconferencing The use of audio and video equipment to allow people to participate in meetings even when they

are a great distance away from the conference location or one another. (415)

360° feedback The combination of peer, subordinate, and self-review. (218)

Title VII Section of the Civil Rights Act of 1964 that applies to employment decisions; mandates that employment decisions not be based on race, color, religion, sex, or national origin. (89)

Total compensation The package of quantifiable rewards an employee receives for his or her labors. Includes three components: base compensation, pay incentives, and indirect compensation/benefits. (301)

Total quality management (TQM) An organizationwide approach to improving the quality of all the processes that lead to a final product or service. (10)

Training The process of providing employees with specific skills or helping them correct deficiencies in their performance. (240)

Trait appraisal instrument An appraisal tool that asks a supervisor to make judgments about worker characteristics that tend to be consistent and enduring. (213)

Transnational corporation A firm with operations in many countries and highly decentralized operations. The firm owes little allegiance to its country of origin and has weak ties to any given country. (540)

Turnover rate The rate of employee separations in an organization. (183)

Unemployment insurance A program established by the Social Security Act of 1935 to provide temporary income for people during periods of involuntary unemployment. (381)

Union An organization that represents employees' interests to management on such issues as wages, work hours, and working conditions. (473)

Union acceptance strategy A labor relations strategy in which management chooses to view the union as its employees' legitimate representative and accepts collective bargaining as an appropriate mechanism for establishing workplace rules. (483)

Union avoidance strategy A labor relations strategy in which management tries to prevent its employees from joining a union, either by removing the incentive to unionize or by using hardball tactics. (485)

Union shop clause A union arrangement that requires new employees to join the union 30 to 60 days after their date of hire. (476)

Union steward An advocate dedicated to representing an employee's case to management in a grievance procedure. (496)

Union substitution/proactive human resource management A union avoidance strategy in which management becomes so responsive to employees' needs that it removes the incentives for unionization. (485)

Union suppression A union avoidance strategy in which management uses hardball tactics to prevent a union from organizing its workers or to get rid of a union. (485)

Universal concept of management The management concept holding that all management practices should be standardized. (124)

Upward communication Communication that allows employees at lower levels to communicate their ideas and feelings to higher-level decision makers. (411)

Validity The extent to which the technique measures the intended knowledge, skill, or ability. In the selection context, it is the extent to which scores on a test or interview correspond to actual job performance. (163)

Vesting A guarantee that accrued retirement benefits will be given to retirement plan participants when they retire or leave the employer. (390)

Virtual reality (VR) The use of a number of technologies to replicate the entire real-life working environment in real time. (252)

Virtual team A team that relies on interactive technology to work together when separated by physical distance. (53)

Voice mail A form of electronic communication that allows the sender to leave a detailed voice message for a receiver. (415)

Voluntary separation A separation that occurs when an employee decides, for personal or professional reasons, to end the relationship with the employer. (187)

Wagner Act/National Labor Relations Act (1935) A federal law designed to protect employees' rights to form and join unions and to engage in such activities as strikes, picketing, and collective bargaining. (475)

Wellness program A company-sponsored program that focuses on preventing health problems in employees. (529)

Whistle-blowing Employee disclosure of an employer's illegal, immoral, or illegitimate practices to persons or organizations that may be able to take corrective action. (449)

Wholly owned subsidiary In international business, a foreign branch owned fully by the home office. (543)

Wildcat strike A spontaneous work stoppage that happens under a valid contract and is usually not supported by union leadership. (596)

Work flow The way work is organized to meet the organization's production or service goals. (45)

Work flow analysis The process of examining how work creates or adds value to the ongoing processes in a business. (49)

Work rules Any terms or conditions of employment, including pay, work breaks and lunch periods, vacation, work assignments, and grievance procedures. (478)

Worker Adjustment and Retraining Notification Act (WARN) of 1988 A federal law requiring U.S. employers with 100 or more employees to give 60 days' advance notice to employees who will be laid off as a result of a plant closing or a mass separation of 50 or more workers. (195)

Workers' compensation A legally required benefit that provides medical care, income continuation, and rehabilitation expenses for people who sustain job-related injuries or sickness. Also provides income to the survivors of an employee whose death is job related. (379)

Works councils A committee composed of both worker representatives and managers who have responsibility for governing the workplace; used in Germany. (482)

Wrongful discharge Termination of an employee for reasons that are either illegal or inappropriate. (440)

Notes

Chapter 1

1. Porter, E. (2005, October 22). Reinventing the mill. *New York Times*, B-1.
2. *Ibid.*
3. Barlett, D. L., and Steel, J. B. (2005, October 31). The broken promise. *Time*, 31–47; Greenhouse, S., and Barbaro, M. (2005, October 26). Wal-Mart memo suggests ways to cut employee benefit costs. *New York Times*, C-1.
4. *Infoworld.* (2005, September 6). The myth of job security. www.inforworld.com.
5. Darlin, D. (2005, October 29). No brainer health care is passé. *New York Times*, B-1.
6. Monster.com (2005, October 18). No rest if you want a decent raise. content.salary.monster.com; *Newsline.* (2005, September 19). Funding for annual bonuses up, but more difficult to earn. www.worldatwork.com.
7. Coy, P. (2002, February 11). Enron. How good an energy trader? *BusinessWeek*, 42–44.
8. Dalin, S. (2005, October 22). Latinos said to fill more business. *Arizona Republic*, D-3.
9. White, E. (2005, February 22). The jungle. *Wall Street Journal*, B-8.
10. Butler, J. E., Ferns, G. R., and Napier, N. K. (1991). *Strategy and human resources management.* Cincinnati, OH: South-Western; McDonald, D. (2002). Radical change: Breaking ground for e-HR implementation. *Workspan, 45*(2), 5–10.
11. Golden, K., and Ramanujan, V. (1985). Between a dream and a nightmare: On the integration of the human resource function and the strategic business planning process. *Human Resource Management, 24*, 429–451; Gagne, K. (2002). One day at a time: Using performance management to translate strategy into results. *Workspan, 45*(2), 20–26. See also Huselid, M.A. (1995). The impact of human resource management on turnover, productivity, and corporate financial performance. *Academy of Management Journal, 38*, 635–672.
12. Zingheim, P., and Schuster, J. (2002, February 12). Creating a workplace business brand. *HR.com*, www.hr.com/hrcom.
13. Gunther, M. (2000, January 10). Publish or perish? *Fortune*, 141–160.
14. Ante, S. E., and Sager, I. (2002, February 11). IBM's new boss. *BusinessWeek*, 66–72.
15. SHRM Special Expertise Panels: Trends Report. (2005). Alexandria, VA: Society for Human Resource Management.
16. Mandel, M. (2005, October 3). The real reasons you are working so hard. *BusinessWeek*, 60–73; Merritt, J. (2005, March 14). MBA family values. *BusinessWeek*, 104–105; Saranow, J. (2005, January 24). Anybody want to take a nap? *Wall Street Journal*, R-5.
17. Cited in Useem, J. (2000, January 10). Welcome to the new company. *Fortune*, 63.
18. Saranow, J. (2005, January 24). Anybody want to take a nap? *Wall Street Journal*, R-5.
19. *Ibid.*
20. Tejada, C. (2002, March 5). Home office: Millions don't leave work at home. *Wall Street Journal*, A-1.
21. Bond, J. T., Galinsky, E., and Hill, J. E. (2005). Flexibility: A critical ingredient in creating an effective workplace. *Workspan*, 17–20; Kronos, S. (2005, October). Insight into an innovative workplace wellness program. *Workspan*, 55–63; Kronos, S. (2005, October). Wellness at work. *Workspan*, 55–63; Maher, K. (2005, July 4). Popular but cheap. *Wall Street Journal*, R-4; Merritt, J. (2005, March 14). MBA family values. *BusinessWeek*, 104–105; *Newsline.* (2005, October 7). Study shows offsite workers feel less connected with employers. www.worldatwork.com; Rosenbaum, D. E. (2005, October 16). Study ranks Homeland Security Dept. lowest in morale. *New York Times*, C-17; *Workspan.* (2005, February 5). Underworked employees are least happy—balance is preferred. www.worldatwork.com.
22. Fisher, A. (2005, February 21). How to prevent violence at work. *Fortune.*
23. Chessher, M. (2005, October). Cubicle Karma. *Southwest Airlines Spirit*, 66–69; Cropper, C. M. (2005, January 17). Keeping your job when you are ill. *BusinessWeek*, 80–82; Rosenbaum, D. E. (2005, October 16). Study ranks Homeland Security Dept. lowest in morale. *New York Times*, C-17.
24. *Newsline.* (2005, October 12). Workloads and sustained stress have employees' just getting by. www.worldatwork.com.
25. Caminiti, S. (2005, January 24). A new health-care prescription. *Fortune*, 52–55; Chessher, M. (2005, October). Cubicle Karma. *Southwest Airlines Spirit*, 66–69; Drummond, M. (2005, October 22). Conventional cubicles stretching boundaries. *Arizona Republic*, A-1; Fisher, A. (2005, February 21). How to prevent violence at work. *Fortune*; Fuhrmans, V. (2005, February 11). One cure for high health costs: In-house clinics at companies. *Wall Street Journal*, A-1; Offutt, S. (2005, October 5). Best workplaces for commuters. *Workspan*, 45–47; Tejada, C. (2002, March 5). Home office: Millions don't leave work at home. *Wall Street Journal*, A-1; Thottam, J. (2005, January 17). Thank God, it is Monday. *Time*, A-58–A-62; *Workspan.* (2005, February 5). Underworked employees are least happy—balance is preferred. www.worldatwork.com.
26. See, for instance, stories appearing in Port, O. (2002, March 4). Web. *BusinessWeek*, 97; Green, H., and Hof, R. D. (2002, April 22). Lessons from the cyber survivors. *BusinessWeek*, 42; Nusbaum, A. (2000, January 5). Web cuts an entire order of middlemen. *Financial Times*, 14; Bulkeley, W. M. (2000, January 6). Virtual utilities peddle power over the Web. *Wall Street Journal*, B-1; Aeppel, T. (2000, January 5). A Web auctioneer soils the rust belt. *Wall Street Journal*, B-1; Ramstad, E. (2000, January 5). Hot e-products from small fry jolt tech giants. *Wall Street Journal*, B-1.
27. Dreazen, Y. J. (2002, February 4). U.S. says Web use has risen to 54% of the population. *Wall Street Journal*, B-4; *Newsline* (2001, July 18). U.S. corporations losing millions through poor e-mail control. Available from http://resourcepro.worldatwork.org.
28. *Business 2.0* (2000, January). Who uses the Internet, 36.
29. *BusinessWeek* (2000, January 17). The top technological blunders of the century, 8.
30. *Newsline* (2001, June 14).
31. *Newsline* (2001, July 19). E-mail not a time saver. resourcepro.worldatwork.org.

32. Lublin, J. (1999, October 26). To find CEOs, Web firms rev-up search engines. *Wall Street Journal,* B-1; Lublin, J. S. (1999b, November 9). An e-company CEO is also the recruitment chief. *Wall Street Journal,* B-1.

33. Needleman, S. E. (2005, October 4). Moving your resume to level "titanium." *Wall Street Journal,* A-22.

34. Tedeschi, B. (2005, March 28). E-commerce report. *New York Times,* D-3.

35. Symonds, W. C. (2000, January 10). Log on for company training. *BusinessWeek,* 138–139.

36. Fisher, A. (2005, February 7). Find online training that pays off. *Fortune,* 34.

37. Richards, B. (1999, November 15). Automating human-resources operations used to be a luxury only big companies could afford. Not any longer. *Wall Street Journal,* R-18; McDonald, D. (2002). Radical change: Breaking ground for e-HR implementation. *Workspan, 45*(2), 5–10.

38. *Ibid.*

39. Bureau of Labor Statistics (2006). Labor force characteristics. www.bls.gov.

40. *Ibid.*

41. National Bureau of Economic Research study by David Card, John Dinardo, and Eugena Estes, summarized in Koretz, G. (2000, January 17). Hazardous to your career. *BusinessWeek,* 26; Pew Hispanic Center. (2005). Hispanics: A people in motion. www.pewhispanic.org.

42. Zachary, P. G. (2000, January 1). A mixed future. *Wall Street Journal,* R-41.

43. *Ibid.*

44. Conlin, M., and Zellner, W. (1999, November 22). The CEO still wears wingtips. *BusinessWeek,* 83; *BusinessWeek* (2000, January 10). The best managers: What it takes, 158; Henderson, N. (2005, Oct.) Disabled and willing. *Southwest Airlines Spirit,* 56–59; Hymowitz, C. (2005, October 24). Too many women full of stereotype of selves, study says. *Wall Street Journal,* B-1; Vitelo, P. (2005, October 25). Home Depot settles with mentally disabled ex-worker. *New York Times,* A-25.

45. Hagerty, B. (1993, June 14). Trainers help expatriate employees. *Wall Street Journal,* B-1, B-3.

46. *Newsline.* (2005, October 14). Race for talent seen as top potential risk for technology companies. www.worldatwork.com; Reinhardt, A., and Vitzhun, C. (2005, September 5). Cafes, beaches, and call centers. *BusinessWeek,* 51.

47. Dodge, S. (2002, February 12). Using? on recruitment. *HR.com.* www4.hr.com/hrcom, 2.

48. Kripalani, M. (2005, November 7). India's skills crunch. *BusinessWeek,* 54–57.

49. *BusinessWeek* (2005, October 31). Upfront: An Indian labor shortage? 10.

50. *The Economist.* (2005, October 1). The great job switch, 13.

51. Greenhouse, S. (2005, February 26). At a small shop in Colorado, Wal-Mart beats a union once more. *New York Times,* A-7.

52. Walker, J. (1992). *Human resource strategy.* New York: McGraw-Hill.

53. Newman, B. (1999, December 9). In Canada, the point of immigration is still unsentimental. *Wall Street Journal,* A-1.

54. Conlin, M., Coy, P., Palmer, A., and Saveri, G. (1999, December 6). The wild new workforce. *BusinessWeek,* 35–46; and Tejada, C. (2002, March 5). Home office: Millions don't leave work at home. *Wall Street Journal,* A-1.

55. Flynn, J. (1999, October 25). E-mail, cellphones, and frequent-flier miles let virtual expats work abroad but live at home. *Wall Street Journal,* A-26.

56. Gómez-Mejía, L. R. (1994). *Fostering a strategic partnership between operations and human resources.* Scarsdale, NY: Work in America Institute.

57. Ledvinka, J., and Scarpello, V. G. (1991). *Federal regulation of personnel and human resource management.* Boston: Kent.

58. *Working Mother.* (2005, December–January) Hearing more from women of color. 55.

59. Tahmincioglu, E. (2005, March 31). Compete with caution against past employer. *New York Times,* C-7.

60. Barrett, P. M. (2000, January 4). Why Americans look to the courts to cure the nation's social ills. *Wall Street Journal,* A-1.

61. Levering, R., and Moskowitz, M. (2002, February 4). The best in the worst of times. *Fortune,* 60–68.

62. Bureau of Labor Statistics Web page (2006). www.stats.bls.gov/empind/htm.

63. Albergotti, R., Bennett, A., Efrati, A., Whelan, C., and Windham, C. (2005, February 18). America's A list internships. *Wall Street Journal,* W-1; Lublin, J. S. (2005, March 1). Winning a new position with employer requires trying harder. *Wall Street Journal,* B-1.

64. Perry, N. (1988, November 7). Saving the schools: How business can help. *Fortune,* 42–52.

65. Nussbaum, B. (1988, September 19). Needed: Human capital. *BusinessWeek,* 100–103.

66. Miller, W. H. (1988, July 4). Employers wrestle with "dumb" kids. *Industry Week,* 4.

67. Salwen, K. G., and Thomas, P. (1993, December 16). Job programs flunk at training but keep Washington at work. *Wall Street Journal,* A-1.

68. Saulny, S. (2005, Jan. 29). New York plans test to affirm fitness for basic jobs. *New York Times,* B-12.

69. *Newsline.* (2005, October 12). Many employees displaced by Katrina to take on payrolls indefinitely. www.worldatwork.com.

70. *Ibid.*

71. *Workspan.* (2005, October 5). Quickguide: Disaster belief. www.worldatwork.com.

72. *Ibid.*

73. Schmid, R. E. (2005, October 22). Bird flu will spread, U.S. secretary says. *Arizona Republic,* A-25.

74. Denney, W. (2002, February 12). Ford takes a wrong turn and ends up in a ditch. *HR.com.* www4.hr.com/hrcom, 2.

75. Doeringer, P. B., and Piore, M. J. (1971). Theories of low-wage labor workers. In L. G. Reynolds, S. H. Masters, and C. H. Moser (Eds.), *Readings in labor economics and labor relations,* 15–31. Upper Saddle River, NJ: Prentice Hall; Pinfield, L. T., and Berner, M. F. (1994). Employment systems: Toward a coherent conceptualization of internal labor markets. In G. Ferris (Ed.), *Research in Personnel and Human Resources Management,* 12, 50–81.

76. Gumbel, P., and Wartzman, R. (2000, January 5). E-covery. *Wall Street Journal,* A-1; Dreazen, Y. J. (2002, February 4). U.S. says Web use has risen to 54% of the population. *Wall Street Journal,* B-4.

77. Lublin, J. S. (1994b, February 9). Before you take that great job, get it in writing. *Wall Street Journal,* B-1; Nussbaum, B. (2002, January 28). Can you trust anybody anymore? *BusinessWeek,* 31–35.

78. Singer, M. (2005, September 22). Tough choices ahead for Sony. http://news.com.com.

79. Matlock, C. (2001, November 5). The high cost of France's aversion to layoffs. *BusinessWeek,* 58; Lavelle, L. (2002, February 11). Swing that ax with care. *BusinessWeek,* 78; Colvin, G. (2002, February 4). You are on your own. *Fortune,* 42; Fairlamb, D. (2002, January 21). Wiggle room for euro bosses. *BusinessWeek,* 20.

80. Landler, M. (2005, October 26). German labor's new reality. *New York Times,* C-1.

81. *Ibid.*

82. Ireland, D. R., and Hitt, M. A. (1999, February). Achieving and maintaining strategic competitiveness in the 21st century. *Academy of Management Executive, 13*(1), 43–57; Deogun, N., and

Lipin, S. (1999, December 8). Some hot mergers come undone for a variety of reasons. *Wall Street Journal,* C-1.

83. Boglarski, C. A. (2005, February). Steps to successful mergers and acquisitions. *Workspan,* 50–52.

84. McCartney, S. (March, 2005). Tight airline staffing leaves little room for error. *Wall Street Journal,* D-3.

85. Manz, C. C. (1992). *Mastering self-leadership: Empowering yourself for personal excellence.* Upper Saddle River, NJ: Prentice Hall.

86. Manz, C. C., and Sims, H. P., Jr. (1993). *Business without bosses: How self-managing teams are building high-performance companies.* New York: Wiley.

87. *Ibid.*

88. U.S. Small Business Administration. (n.d.). SBA Loan Programs. Washington, DC: U.S. Small Business Administration.

89. Bounds, G. (2005, March 22). SBA reconsiders what "small" should mean. *Wall Street Journal,* B-3.

90. Fry, F. L. (1993). *Entrepreneurship: A planning approach.* St. Paul, MN: West.

91. Gómez-Mejía, L. R., Larraza, M., and Makri, M. (2003). Determinants of executive compensation in family owned firms. *Academy of Management Journal,* 42(2) 130–141.

92. Dalin, S. (2005, October 22). Latinos said to fill more business. *Arizona Republic,* D-3.

93. *Ibid.*

94. Adapted from Schein, E. H. (1986). *Organizational culture and leadership.* San Francisco, CA: Jossey Bass.

95. *Ibid.*

96. Khermouch, G. (2002, January 21). There goes the creative juices. *BusinessWeek,* 52.

97. Lavelle, L. (2005, February 28). Three simple rules Carly ignored. *BusinessWeek,* 46.

98. Stewart, T. (2000, January 10). How Teledyne solved the innovator's dilemma. *Fortune,* 188–189.

99. *Newsline.* (2005, October 7). Study shows offsite workers feel less connected with employers. www.worldatwork.com.

100. Simpson, G. R. (2000, January 6). E-commerce firms start to rethink opposition to privacy regulation as abuses, anger rise. *Wall Street Journal,* A-24.

101. *Harper's Magazine* (2000, January 1). Special issue on the Internet, 57.

102. Rothfeder, J. (1994, January). Dangerous things strangers know about you. *McCall's,* 88–94.

103. Baker, S., and Grow, B. (2005, March 21). A painful lesson: E-mail is forever. *BusinessWeek,* 36.

104. *Ibid.*

105. *Ibid.*

106. Pepper, T. (2005, February 21). Inside the head of an applicant. *Newsweek,* E24–E26.

107. Wilke, J. R. (1993, December 9). Computer links erode hierarchical nature of workplace culture. *Wall Street Journal,* A-10.

108. *Ibid.*

109. Lavelle, L. (2002, January 14). First, kill the consultants. *BusinessWeek,* 122.

110. Geller, A. (2005, March 6). Stores now selling background checks. *Arizona Republic,* A-1.

111. Burger, T., and Bennett, B. (2005, February 7). The Russians are coming. *Time,* 48; Puliyenthuruthel, J., and Kripalani, M. (2005, March 28). A whiff of terror in Bangalore. *BusinessWeek,* 52.

112. Green, H. (2001, April 23). Your right to privacy going, going . . . *BusinessWeek,* 32–33.

113. Armour, S. (2002b, June 19). Security checks worry workers. *USA Today,* A-1.

114. Zeller, T. (2005, November 1). Data security laws seem likely. *New York Times,* B-3.

115. Dash, E. (2005, October 27). Carleton Fiorina joins the board of a big data security company. *New York Times,* C-4.

116. Forelli, C. (2005, March 15). Crack in computer security code raises red flag. *Wall Street Journal,* A-1; Foust, D. (2005, March 28). Keeping a grip on identity. *BusinessWeek,* 34–35; Guth, R. A., and Bank, D. (2005, February 16). Microsoft makes push of security. *Wall Street Journal,* B-5; *Newsline.* (2005, February 14). FBI computers: You don't have mails. www.worldatwork.com; Perez, E., and Brooks, R. (2005, March 7). Choice point breach, stock sales, are both under federal scrutiny. *New York Times,* A-2; Zeller, T. (2005, February 24). Breach points up flaws in privacy laws. *New York Times,* C-1; Zeller, T. (2005, February 25). Senator says data services has lax rules for security. *New York Times,* C-4; Zeller, T. (2005, March 10). Another data broker reports a breach. *New York Times,* C-1; Zeller, T. (2005, March 21). Investigators argue for access to private data. *New York Times,* C-6.

117. Lancaster, H. (1995, September 12). Saving your career when your position has been outsourced. *Wall Street Journal,* B-1

118. *Workspan.* (2005, March). Compensation among least outsourced functions. 16.

119. *Ibid.*

120. Tejada, C. (2002, March 5). Home office: Millions don't leave work at home. *Wall Street Journal,* A-1.

121. Melcher, R. A. (1996, January 8). Who says you can't find good help? *BusinessWeek,* 107.

122. Gupta, A. K., and Govindarajan, V. (1984). Business unit strategy, managerial characteristics, and business unit effectiveness at strategy implementation. *Academy of Management Journal,* 27, 25–41.

123. Anderson, J. (2005, April 29). Insurer admits bad accounting in several areas. *New York Times,* A-1; Dugan, I. J., and Francis, T. (2005, March 12). How a hot insurance product burned AIG. *Wall Street Journal,* C-1.

124. Eic henwald, K. (2005, March 16). When the top seat is the hot seat. *New York Times,* C-1.

125. *Ibid.*

126. *Ibid.*

127. Pasztor, A. (2005, February 22). Boeing ex-officer gets prison term over hiring talks. *New York Times,* A-4.

128. Perez, E., and Brooks, R. (2005, March 7). Choice point breach, stock sales, are both under federal scrutiny. *New York Times,* A-2.

129. Songtag, D. (2005, February 7). Abuses imperiled veterans in cancer experiments. *New York Times,* A-25.

130. Slackman, M. (2005, February 25). Officials dodge ethics cases by leaving their posts. *New York Times,* A-21.

131. McDowell, J. (2005, October 17). Case of looted relics. *Time,* 80.

132. *New York Times.* (2005, October 22). C-3.

133. Zaun, T. (2005, March 31). Mitsubishi motors seek damages from ex-officials. *New York Times,* C-6.

134. Zagorin, A. (2005, November 7). Oil for food: Sadam and Company. *Time,* 18.

135. Dilenschneider, R. L. (2005, March 15). When CEOs roamed the earth. *Wall Street Journal,* B-2; Latour, A., and Young, S. (2005, March 1). Ebbers denies he knew about Worldcom's fraud. *Wall Street Journal,* A-14; Lundegaard, K. (2005, March 7). Delphi discloses accounting problems. *Wall Street Journal,* A-1; Morse, D. (2005, March 1). HealthSouth ex-finance chief says Scrushy knew of fraud. *Wall Street Journal,* C-5; Rivlin, G., and Markoff, J. (2005, February 14). Tossing out a chief executive. *New York Times,* C-1.

136. Armour, S. (2002a, February 4). Employees' motto: Trust no one. *USA Today,* 5-A.

137. Noe, R., Hollenbeck, J. R. Gerhart, G., and Wright, P. M. (1994). *Human resource management: Gaining a competitive advantage.* Homewood, IL: Austen.

138. Dilenschneider, R. L. (2005, March 15). When CEOs roamed the earth. *Wall Street Journal,* B-2; Latour, A., and Young, S. (2005, March 1). Ebbers denies he knew about Worldcom's fraud. *Wall Street Journal,* A-14.

139. Mathieu, J. E., and Zajac, D. M. (1990). A review and meta-analysis of the antecedents, correlates, and consequences of organizational commitment. *Psychological Bulletin, 108,* 171–194.

140. McCarthy, M. J. (1999b, October 21). How one firm tracks ethics electronically. *Wall Street Journal,* B-1.

141. Eichenwald, K. (2005, March 16). When the top seat is the hot seat. *New York Times,* C-1.

142. *Ibid.*

143. O'Connell, V. (2005, October 27). Rx how Malboro man. *Wall Street Journal,* A-1.

144. Berstein, A. (2001, February 26). Low skilled jobs: Do they have to move? *BusinessWeek,* 94–96.

145. White, J. B. (2000, January 1). Corporation aren't going to disappear but they are going to look a lot different. *Wall Street Journal,* R-36

146. Kelly, L. (2000, January 2). Preparation by applicant key to successful interview. *Arizona Republic,* C-1.

147. Hom, P., and Griffeth, R. (1994). *Employee turnover.* Cincinnati, OH: South-Western.

148. Campion, M. A., and McClelland, C. L. (1991). Interdisciplinary examination of the costs and benefits of enlarged jobs. *Journal of Applied Psychology, 76,* 186–198.

149. Cited in Hymowitz, C. (2000, January 4). How can a manager encourage employees to take bold risks? *Wall Street Journal,* B-1.

150. *Ibid.*

151. Petzinger, T. (2000, January 1). There is a new economy out there. *Wall Street Journal,* R-31; White, J. B. (2000, January 1). Corporations aren't going to disappear but they are going to look a lot different. *Wall Street Journal,* R-36.

152. National Academy of Engineering, www.nae.edu.

153. Kripalani, M. (2005, November 7). India's skills crunch. *BusinessWeek,* 54–57.

154. Conlin, M., and Salkever, A. (2001, July 30). Revenge of the downsized nerds. *BusinessWeek,* 40.

155. Dempsey, J., and Siebenhaar, M. (2002). Bankruptcy blues: retaining key employees during a financial crisis. *Workspan, 45*(2) 1–5.

156. Arndt, M. (2002, January 21). 3M: A lab for growth? *Business Week,* 50–52.

157. Drucker, P. (1993, October 21). The five deadly business sins. *Wall Street Journal,* R-2.

158. Arndt, M. (2002, January 21). 3M: A lab for growth? *BusinessWeek,* 50–52.

159. Butler, J. E., Ferris, G. R., and Napier, N. K. (1991). *Strategy and human resources management.* Cincinnati, OH: South-Western.

160. Mintzberg, H. (1990). The design school: Reconsidering the basic premises of strategic management. *Strategic Management Journal, 11,* 171–196; Walker, J. (1992). *Human resource management strategy,* Chapter 1. New York: McGraw-Hill.

161. *Ibid.*

162. SHRM Special Expertise Panels: Trends Report. (2005). Alexandria, VA: Society for Human Resource Management.

163. Brockner, J. (1992). The escalation of commitment to a failing course of action: Toward theoretical progress. *Academy of Management Review, 17*(1), 39–61; Staw, B. (1976). Knee-deep in Big Muddy: A study of escalating commitment to a chosen course of action. *Organizational Behavior and Human Performance, 16,* 27–44.

164. See the following reviews: Dyer, L., and Holder, G. W. (1988). A strategic perspective of human resource management. In L. Dyer (Ed.), *Human resource management: Evolving roles and responsibilities.* Washington, DC: Bureau of National Affairs; Gómez-Mejía, L. R., and Balkin, D. B. (1992). *Compensation, organizational strategy, and firm performance.* Cincinnati, OH: South-Western.

165. Bulkeley, W. M. (2000, January 6). Virtual utilities peddle power over the Web. *Wall Street Journal,* B-1.

166. Warren, S. (2002, February 5). DuPont cajoles independent units to talk to one another. *Wall Street Journal,* B-4.

167. Kerr, J. (1985). Diversification strategies and managerial rewards: An empirical study. *Academy of Management Journal, 28,* 155–179; Leontiades, M. (1980). Strategies for diversification and change. Boston: Little, Brown; Pitts, R. A. (1974, May). Incentive compensation and organization design. *Personnel Journal, 20*(5), 338–344.

168. Gómez-Mejía, L. R. (1992). Structure and process of diversification, compensation strategy and firm performance. *Strategic Management Journal, 13,* 381–397; Kerr, J. (1985). Diversification strategies and managerial rewards: An empirical study. *Academy of Management Journal, 28,* 155–179.

169. Farnam, A. (1994, February 7). Corporate reputations. *Fortune,* 50–54.

170. Porter, M. E. (1980). *Competitive strategy.* New York: Free Press; Porter, M. E. (1985). *Competitive advantage.* New York: Free Press; Porter, M. E. (1990). *The competitive advantage of nations.* Boston: Free Press.

171. Miles, R. E., and Snow, C. C. (1978). *Organizational strategy, structure, and process.* New York: McGrawHill; Miles, R. E., and Snow, C. C. (1984). Designing strategic human resources systems. *Organizational Dynamics, 13*(1), 36–52.

172. Montemayor, E. F. (1994). Pay policies that fit organizational strategy: Evidence from high-performing firms. Unpublished paper. East Lansing, MI: School of Industrial and Labor Relations, Michigan State University.

173. Porter, M. E. (1980). *Competitive strategy.* New York: Free Press.

174. *Ibid.*

175. Byrne, H. S. (1992, November 16). Illinois Tool Works: Satisfying customers . . . and investors. *Barron's,* 51–52.

176. Miles, R. E., and Snow, C. C. (1978). *Organizational strategy, structure, and process.* New York: McGraw-Hill; Miles, R. E., and Snow, C. C. (1984). Designing strategic human resources systems. *Organizational Dynamics, 13*(1), 36–52.

177. Miles, R. E., Snow, C. C., Meyer, A. D., and Coleman, H. J. (1978). Organizational strategy, structure, and process. *Academy of Management Review, 3,* 546–562.

178. Gómez-Mejía, L. R., and Balkin, D. B. (1992). *Compensation, organizational strategy, and firm performance,* 125. Cincinnati, OH: South-Western; Gagne, K. (2002). One day at a time: Using performance management to translate strategy into results. *Workspan, 45*(2), 20–26.

179. For another example, see Corden, R., Elmer, M., Knudsen, J., Mountain, R., Rider, M., and Ross, W. (1994, March–April). When a new pay plan fails: The case of Beta Corporation. *Compensation & Benefits Review,* 26–32.

180. Fulmer, I. S., Gerhart, B., and Scott, M. S. (2003). Are the 100 best better? An empirical investigation of the relationship between being a great place to work and firm performance. *Personnel Psychology, 56,* 383–404; Guthrie, J. P., Spell, C. S., Nyamori, R. O. (2002). Correlates and consequences of high involvement work practices: The role of competitive strategy. *International Journal of Human Resource Management, 13,* 183–197; Huselid, M. A. (1995). The impact of human resource practices on turnover, productivity, and corporate financial performance. *Academy of Management Journal, 38,* 635–672.

181. Wright, P. M., Gardner, T. M., Moynihan, L. M., and Allen, M. R. (2005). The relationship between HR practices and firm performance: Examining causal order. *Personnel Psychology, 58,* 409–446.

182. Zingheim, P., and Schuster, J. (2002, February 12). Creating a workplace business brand. *HR.com,* www.hr.com/hrcom; McDonald, D. (2001). HR—earning its place at the table. *Worldatwork Journal, 10*(1), 1–6.

183. For more information, see Wiley, C. (1992, August). The certified HR professional. *HRMagazine, 37*(8), 77–79, 82–84; Wiley, C., and Goff, E. F. (1994). *Trends, strategies, objectives, linkages, and*

professionalism. Compensation guide. New York: Warren Gorham and Lamont.

184. www.eri-salary-survey.com.

185. Springer, K. (2005, February 7). Smoking light up and you may let go. *BusinessWeek*, 41.

186. Quoted in Conlin, M., Coy, P., Palmer, A., and Saveri, G. (1999, December 6). The wild new workforce. *BusinessWeek*, 35–46.

Chapter 2

1. Gimbel, B. (2005, May 16). Southwest's new flight plan. *Fortune*, 93–98.

2. Keenan, F., and Ante, S. (2002, February 18). The new teamwork. *BusinessWeek e.biz*, 12–16.

3. Gogoi, P. (2003, July 28). Thinking outside the cereal box. *BusinessWeek*, 74.

4. Hitt, M., Ireland, R., and Hoskisson, R. (2005). *Strategic management* (6th ed.). Mason, OH: Southwestern.

5. Smart, T. (1996, October 28). Jack Welch's encore. *BusinessWeek*, 155–160.

6. Ante, S. (2003, June 23). Savings tip: Don't do it yourself: Human resources and accounting are but two cost centers ripe for outsourcing. *BusinessWeek*, 78–79.

7. Lawler, E. (1992). *The ultimate advantage.* San Francisco, CA: Jossey-Bass.

8. Johnson & Johnson Web site (2005). www.jnj.com.

9. Hof, R. D. (1999, January 18). Is the center of the computing universe shifting? Sun power. *BusinessWeek*, 64–72; Sager, I., and Yang, C. (1998, December 7). A new cyber order. *BusinessWeek*, 27–31.

10. Dobriansky, J. (2004, June). Business process reengineering: The cornerstone of successful entreprise IT systems implementation. *Contract Management*, 44, 28–30.

11. Hammer, M., and Champy, J. (1993). *Reengineering the corporation.* New York: HarperCollins.

12. *Ibid.*

13. Greengard, S. (1993, December). Reengineering: Out of the rubble. *Personnel Journal*, 48B–48O; Verity, J. (1993, June 21). Getting work to go with the flow. *BusinessWeek*, 156–161.

14. Hammer, M., and Champy, J. (1993). *Reengineering the corporation.* New York: HarperCollins.

15. *Ibid.*

16. Hammer, M. (1995, May 15). Beating the risks of reengineering. *Fortune*, 105–114.

17. *The Economist.* (1994, July 2). Re-engineering reviewed, 66.

18. Katzenback, J., and Smith, D. (1993, March–April). The discipline of teams. *Harvard Business Review*, 111–120.

19. Orsburn, J., Moran, L., Musselwhite, E., and Zenger, J. (1990). *Self-directed work teams.* Homewood, IL: Business One Irwin.

20. Kuipers, B., and de Witte, M. (2005, February). Teamwork: A case study on development and performance. *International Journal of Human Resource Management*, 18, 185–201.

21. Jassawalla, A. R., and Sashittal, H. C. (1999). Building collaborative cross-functional new product teams. *Academy of Management Executive*, 13(3), 50–63.

22. Hoerr, J. (1989, July 10). The payoff from teamwork. *BusinessWeek*, 56–62.

23. Caudron, S. (1993, December). Are self-directed teams right for your company? *Personnel Journal*, 76–84.

24. Bassin, M. (1996, January). From team to partnerships. *HRMagazine*, 86–92.

25. Balkin, D., and Montemayor, E. (2000). Explaining team-based pay: A contingency perspective based on the organizational life cycle, team design, and organizational learning literatures. *Human Resource Management Review*, 10, 249–269.

26. Kirsner, S. (1998, April). Four lessons on teamwork from SEI investments. *Fast Company*, 132.

27. Orsburn, J., Moran, L., Musselwhite, E., and Zenger, J. (1990). *Self-directed work teams.* Homewood, IL: Business One Irwin.

28. *Ibid.*

29. Dumaine, B. (1994, September 5). The trouble with teams. *Fortune*, 86–92.

30. Caramanica, L., Ferris, S., and Little, J. (2001, December). Self-directed teams: Use with caution. *Nursing Management*, 77.

31. Orsburn, J., Moran, L., Musselwhite, E., and Zenger, J. (1990). *Self-directed work teams.* Homewood, IL: Business One Irwin.

32. Chatman, J., and Flynn, F. (2001). The influence of dempgraphic hetereogeneity on the emergence and consequences of cooperative norms in work teams. *Academy of Management Journal*, 44, 956–974.

33. Hoerr, J. (1989, July 10). The payoff from teamwork. *BusinessWeek*, 56–62.

34. Greene, J. (2004, May 3). Why the world's hottest tech company will struggle to keep its edge. *BusinessWeek*, 82–90.

35. Lawler, E. (1992). *The ultimate advantage.* San Francisco, CA: Jossey-Bass.

36. Hertel, G., Geister, S., and Konradt, U. (2005). Managing vertual teams: A review of current empirical research. *Human Resource Management Review*, 15, 69–95.

37. Kostner, J. (2001, October). Bionic eTeamwork. *Executive Excellence*, 78.

38. Majchrzak, A., Malhotra, A., Stamps, J., and Lipnack, J. (2004, May). Can absence make a team grow stronger? *Harvard Business Review*, 131–137.

39. *Ibid.*

40. Steers, R. (1984). *Introduction to organizational behavior* (2nd ed.). Glenview, IL: Scott, Foresman.

41. Herzberg, F. (1968, January–February). One more time: How do you motivate employees? *Harvard Business Review*, 52–62.

42. Lofquist, L., and Dawis, R. (1969). *Adjustment to work: A psychological view of man's problems in a work-oriented society.* Upper Saddle River, NJ: Prentice Hall.

43. Locke, E. (1968). Toward a theory of task motives and incentives. *Organizational Behavior and Human Performance*, 3, 157–189.

44. Pinder, C. (1984). *Work motivation.* Glenview, IL: Scott, Foresman.

45. Hackman, J., and Oldham, G. (1976). Motivation through the design of work: Test of a theory. *Organizational Behavior and Human Performance*, 16, 250–279.

46. Nadler, D. A., Hackman, J. R., and Lawler, E. E. (1979). *Managing organizational behavior.* Boston: Little, Brown.

47. *Ibid.*

48. Behson, S., Eddy, E., and Lorenzet, S. (2000). The importance of critical psychological states in the job characteristics model: A meta-analytic and structural equations modeling examination. *Current Research in Social Psychology*, 5(12), 170–189.

49. Hackman, J. (1976). Work design. In Hackman, J., and Suttle, J. (Eds.). *Improving life at work*, 96–162. Santa Monica, CA: Goodyear.

50. Denton, D. K. (1992, August). Redesigning a job by simplifying every task and responsibility. *Industrial Engineering*, 46–48.

51. Szilagyi, A., and Wallace, M. (1980). *Organizational behavior and performance* (2nd ed.). Santa Monica, CA: Goodyear.

52. Lawler, E. (1986). *High involvement management.* San Francisco, CA: Jossey-Bass.

53. *Ibid.*

54. Steers, R. (1984). *Introduction to organizational behavior* (2nd ed.). Glenview, IL: Scott, Foresman.

55. Drach-Zahavy, A. (2004). The proficiency trap: How to balance enriched job designs and the team's need for support. *Journal of Organizational Behavior*, 25, 979–996.

56. Campion, M. A., and Higgs, A. C. (1995, October). Design work teams to increase productivity and satisfaction. *HRMagazine*, 101–107.

57. Lawler, E. (1992). *The ultimate advantage.* San Francisco, CA: Jossey-Bass.

58. Taylor, A. (2004, December 13). GM's Saturn problem: After losing billions, GM junks the "different kind of company" plan and tries again. *Fortune*, 119–130.

59. Drauden, G. M. (1988). Task inventory analysis in industry and the public sector. In S. Gael (Ed.), *The job analysis handbook for business, industry, and government*, 105–171. New York: Wiley and Sons.

60. Flanagan, J. C. (1954). The critical incident technique. *Psychological Bulletin, 51*, 327–358.

61. McCormick, E., and Jeannerette, R. (1988). The position analysis questionnaire. In S. Gael (Ed.), *The job analysis handbook for business, industry, and government*, 880–901. New York: John Wiley and Sons.

62. Fine, S. A. (1992). *Functional job analysis: A desk aid.* Milwaukee, WI: Sidney A. Fine.

63. Harvey, R. (2002). Functional job analysis. *Personnel Psychology, 55*, 202–205.

64. U.S. Department of Labor. (1991). *Dictionary of occupational titles* (4th ed.). Washington, DC: U.S. Government Printing Office.

65. Chatman, J. A. (1989). Improving interaction organizational research: A model of person–organization fit. *Academy of Management Review, 14*, 333–349.

66. Cardy, R. L., and Dobbins, G. H. (1994). *Performance appraisal: Alternative perspectives.* Cincinnati, OH: South-Western.

67. Leonard, S. (2000, August). The demise of the job description. *HRMagazine*, 184.

68. Johnson, C. (2001, January). Refocusing job descriptions. *HRMagazine*, 66–72.

69. Cardy, R. L. and Dobbins, G. H. (2000, January). Jobs disappear when work becomes more important. *Workforce*, 30–32.

70. Cardy, R., and Dobbins, G. (1992, Fall). Job analysis in a dynamic environment. *Human Resources Division News*, 4–6.

71. Ibid.

72. Jones, M. (1984, May). Job descriptions made easy. *Personnel Journal*, 31–34.

73. Fierman, J. (1994, January 24). The contingent work force. *Fortune*, 30–36.

74. Hershey, R. D. (1995, August 19). Survey finds 6 million, fewer than thought, in impermanent jobs. *New York Times*, 1, 17; Melcher, R. A. (1996, June 10). Manpower upgrades its résumé. *BusinessWeek*, 81+.

75. Stewart, T. A. (1995, March 20). World without managers. *Fortune, 72*.

76. Uchitelle, L., and Kleinfield, N. R. (1996, March 3). The downsizing of America. *New York Times*, special report.

77. Flynn, G. (1999, September). Temp staffing carries legal risk. *Workforce*, 56–62; Bernstein A. (1999, May 31). Now temp workers are a full-time headache. *BusinessWeek*, 46.

78. The Economist. (2000, June 10). Western Europe's job-seekers limber up, 53–54.

79. Rogers, B. (1992, May). Companies develop benefits for part timers. *HRMagazine*, 89–90.

80. Hewlett, S., and Luce, C. (2005, March). Off-ramps and on-ramps: Keeping talented women on the road to success. *Harvard Business Review*, 43–54; Huff, C. (2005, May). With flextime, less can be more. *Workforce Management*, 65–68.

81. McClenahen, J. (2005, May). Outsourcing reconsidered. *Industry Week*, 14; The Economist (2004, November 13). A world of work: A survey of outsourcing, 1–20.

82. Wahlgren, E. (2004, April). The outsourcing dilemma. *Inc. Magazine*, 41–42.

83. Klaas, B., McClendon, K., and Gainey, T. (2001, Summer). Outsourcing HR: The impact of organizational characteristics. *Human Resource Management*, 125–138.

84. Bates, S. (2002, April). Fishing bigger: HR outsourcing firms are forming partnerships and acquiring resource in a bid to get contracts from big business. *HRMagazine*, 38–42.

85. James, G. (1997, November). Tipping the scales your way. *Datamation*, 48–53.

86. Sunoo, B. P., and Laabs, J. J. (1994, March). Winning strategies for outsourcing contracts. *Personnel Journal*, 69–78.

87. The Economist. (1994, April 23). Benetton: The next era, 68.

88. For information on a new twist on outsourcing, see Semler, R. (1993). *Maverick.* New York: Warner Books.

89. Doh, J. (2005). Offshore outsourcing: Implications for international business and strategic management theory and practice. *Journal of Management Studies, 42*, 695–704.

90. The Economist (2003, December 13). Special report offshoring: Relocating the back office, 67–69.

91. Levy, D. (2005). Offshoring in the new global political economy. *Journal of Management Studies, 42*, 685–694.

92. Ante, S. (2004, January 12). Shifting work offshore? Outsourcer beware. *BusinessWeek*, 36–37; Kripalani, M., and Engardio, P. (2003, December 8). The rise of India. *BusinessWeek*, 66–76.

93. Pearce, J. (1993). Toward an organizational behavior of contract laborers: Their psychological involvement and effects on employee co-workers. *Academy of Management Journal, 36*, 1082–1096.

94. Albrecht, D. G. (1998, April). New heights: Today's contract workers are highly promotable. *Workforce*, 43–48.

95. Brewster, M. (2004, December). The freelance conundrum. *Inc. Magazine*, 39.

96. Mullich, J. (2004, July). Giving employees something they can't buy with a bonus check. *Workforce Management*, 66–67.

97. Cunningham, C., and Murray, S. (2005, February). Two executives, one career. *Harvard Business Review*, 125–132.

98. Denton, D. (1993, January–February). Using flextime to create a competitive workplace. *Industrial Management*, 29–31.

99. Pierce, J., and Dunham, R. (1992). The 12-hour work day: A 48-hour, eight-day week. *Academy of Management Journal*, 1086–1098.

100. Sunoo, B. P. (1996, January). How to manage compressed workweeks. *Personnel Journal*, 110.

101. Fisher, A. (2005, May 30). How telecommuters can stay connected. *Fortune*, 142; Greengard, S. (2005, March). Sun's shining example. *Workforce Management*, 48–49.

102. Garvey, C. (2001, August). Teleworking HR. *HRMagazine*, 56–60.

103. Kavanaugh, M., Guetal, H., and Tannenbaum, S. (1990). *Human resource information systems: Development and application.* Boston, MA: PWS-Kent.

104. Dzamba, A. (2001, January). What are your peers doing to boost HRIS performance? *HR Focus*, 56.

105. Turnbull, I. (2005, April 25). Many reasons to track time. *Canadian HR Reporter*, 14.

106. Leonard, B. (1991, July). Open and shut HRIS. *Personnel Journal*, 59–62.

107. Ibid.

Chapter 3

1. Takahashi, D. (2005, May 27). Sex-harassment suit filed against Sun Microsystems, former exec. *San Jose Mercury News*, 3E.

2. Long, S. (1999, April). Quick reactions by employer prevents sexual harassment liability. *HR Focus*, 3.

3. Hall, F. S., and Hall, E. L. (1994). The ADA: Going beyond the law. *Academy of Management Executive, 8*, 17–26.

4. Coie, P. (2001, December). Ninth circuit affirms $1.03 million jury verdict in race discrimination suit. *Washington Employment Law Letter*, 1.

5. Faircloth, A. (1998, August 3). Guess who's coming to Denny's? *Fortune*, 108–110.

6. Denny's Web site. (2005). www.dennys.com/en/cms/diversity/.

7. Serwer, A. (2005, April 18). Bruised in Bentonville. *Fortune*, 84–89; Daniels, C. (2003, July 21). Women vs. Wal-Mart. *Fortune*, 78–82.

8. *Griggs v. Duke Power Co.*, 401 U.S. 424 (1971).

9. *Wards Cove v. Antonio*, 109 S.Ct. 2115, 49 FEP CASES 1523 (1989).

10. Hall, F. S., and Hall, E. L. (1994). The ADA: Going beyond the law. *Academy of Management Executive, 8*, 17–26.

11. Sites, J. (2005, May). Equal pay for the sexes. *HR Magazine*, 65–69.

12. Bernstein, A. (2004, June 14). Women's pay: Why the gap remains a chasm. *BusinessWeek*, 58–59.

13. Strout, E. (2001, July). Tough sell. *Sales & Marketing Management*, 50–55.

14. Ledvinka, J., and Scarpello, V. G. (1991). *Federal regulation of personnel and human resource management* (2nd ed.). Boston: PWS-Kent; Twomey, D. P. (1990). *Equal employment opportunity* (2nd ed.). Cincinnati, OH: South-Western.

15. *BNA's Employee Relations Weekly*. (1993, September 13). EEOC meets new, higher burden of proof in race bias case in California court. *11*, 1991.

16. *Griggs v. Duke Power Co.*, 401 U.S. 424 (1971).

17. *HR News*. (1994, February). No beard rule found to have disparate impact, 17.

18. *Albemarle Paper Co. v. Moody*, 422 U.S. 405 (1975).

19. *McDonnell Douglas Corp. v. Green*, 411 U.S. 792 (1973).

20. Equal Employment Opportunity Commission. (1978). *Uniform Guidelines on Employee Selection Procedures*, 29 Code of Federal Regulations, Part 1607, Sec. 6.A.

21. EEOC Web site. (2005). www.eeoc.gov/facts/fs-nator.html.

22. Uheling, A. (2002, April 29). Pregnancy Discrimination Act set clear management limits. *Federal Human Resources Week*, 1.

23. *Ibid.*

24. *HR Reporter*. (2001, June 4). City settles discrimination charge by pregnant police officer, 1.

25. Fitzgerald, L. F., Drasgow, F., Hulin, C., Gelfond, M., and Magley, V. J. (1997). Antecedents and consequences of sexual harassment in organizations: A test of an integrated model. *Journal of Applied Psychology, 82*, 578–589.

26. Gruber, J. E. (1998). The impact of male work environments and organizational policies on women's experiences of sexual harassment. *Gender & Society, 12*, 301–321.

27. Hendrix, W. H. (1998). Sexual harassment and gender differences. *Journal of Social Behavior and Personality, 13*, 135–253.

28. *BNA's Employee Relations Weekly*. (1994, January 31). Medical center employee awarded $1 million in Massachusetts suit, *12*, 111–112.

29. Shepela, S. T., and Levesque, L. L. (1998). Poisoned waters: Sexual harassment and the college climate. *Sex Roles, 8*, 589–611; Shelton, N. J., and Chavous, T. M. (1999). Black and white college women's perceptions of sexual harassment. *Sex Roles, 40*, 593–615.

30. *Harris v. Forklift Systems, Inc.* 114 S. Ct. 367 (1993).

31. Cole, J. (1999, March). Sexual harassment: New rules, new behavior. *HR Focus*, 1–15.

32. Muller, J. (1999, November 15). Ford: The high cost of harassment. *BusinessWeek*, 94–96.

33. Aronson, P. (2002, April 29). Mitsubishi comes back from disaster of 1998. *National Law Review*, A23.

34. Lewis, N. A. (1999, July 30). New penalty of Clinton in Jones case. *New York Times*, A15.

35. The U.S. Equal Employment Commission. (2005). www.eeoc.gov/stats/harass.html

36. *Human Resource Management Ideas and Trends*. (1996, February 14). Sexual harassment complaints no longer limited to women, 30.

37. *The Economist*. (1998, July 4). Men, women, work and law, 21–22.

38. *BNA's Employee Relations Weekly*. (1994, April 4). Survey finds 31 percent of women report having been harassed at work, *12*, 367.

39. Luthar, H., and Pastille, C. (2000). Modeling subordinate perceptions of sexual harassment: The role of superior–subordinate social-sexual interaction. *Human Resource Management Review, 10*, 211–244.

40. Flynn, G. (1999, May). Sexual harassment interpretations give cause for new concerns. *Workforce*, 105–106; Garland, S. B. (1998, July 13). Finally, a corporate tip sheet on sexual harassment *BusinessWeek*, 39.

41. O'Leary-Kelly, A., and Bowes-Sperry, L. (2001). Sexual harassment as unethical behavior: The role of moral intensity. *Human Resource Management Review, 11*, 73–92.

42. Slade, M. (1998, July 19). A hint of clarity in harassment case law. *New York Times*, www.nytimes.com.

43. *Wards Cove Packing Co. v. Antonio*, 409 U.S. 642 (1989).

44. Bureau of National Affairs. (1991, November 11). Civil rights act of 1991. *Employee Relations Weekly* (special supplement).

45. Carson, K. P. (1991, November 22). New civil rights law shoots itself in the foot. *Wall Street Journal*, A10.

46. Geyelin, M. (1993, December 17). Age-bias cases found to bring big jury awards. *Wall Street Journal*, B1.

47. Harper, L. (1994, April 5). Labor letter. *Wall Street Journal*, A1.

48. Milkovich, G. T., and Newman, J. M. (1996). *Compensation* (5th ed.). Chicago: Irwin.

49. Sharpe, R. (1994, April 19). Labor letter. *Wall Street Journal*, A1.

50. EEOC. (1992, January). *A technical assistance manual on the employment provisions of the Americans with Disabilities Act.*

51. Stevens, M. (2002, April 29). "Toyota" may be seen as a reasonable balancing act. *The National Law Journal*, A34.

52. Hall, J. E., and Hatch, D. D. (1999, August). Supreme Court decisions require ADA revision. *Workforce*, 60–67.

53. Hatch, D., Hall, J., and Kobata, M. (2005, March). EEOC guidance on dealing with intellectual disabilities. *Workforce Management*, 16; EEOC Web site. (2005). www.eeoc.gov/facts/intellectual_ disabilities.html

54. Petesch, P. J. (1999, June). Are the newest ADA guidelines "reasonable"? *HRMagazine*, 54–58.

55. *The Economist*. (1998, April 18). The halt, the blind, the dyslexic, 25–26.

56. Martinez, M. N. (1990, November). Creative ways to employ people with disabilities. *HRMagazine*, 40–44, 101.

57. EEOC. (1992, January). *A technical assistance manual on the employment provisions of the Americans with Disabilities Act.*

58. Wells, S. (2001, April). Is the ADA working? *HRMagazine*, 38–46.

59. EEOC Web site. (2005). www.eeoc.gov.

60. The U.S. Equal Employment Opportunity Commission. (2002, February 22). EEOC issues fiscal 2001 enforcement data. www.eeoc.gov/press.

61. *Johnson v. Santa Clara County, Transportation Agency, Santa Clara County*, 107 S.Ct. 1442, 43 FEP Cases 411 (1987); Nazario, S. L. (1989, June 27); Many minorities feel torn by experience of affirmative action. *Wall Street Journal*, A1; Roberts, S. V. (1995, February 13). Affirmative action on the edge. *U.S. News & World Report*, 32–38.

62. *Regents of the University of California v. Bakke*, 438 U.S. 265 (1978).

63. *The Economist*. (1995, April 15). A question of colour, 13–14.

64. Wynter, L. (1996, February 7). Business and race. *Wall Street Journal*, B1.

65. Sovereign, K. L. (1994). *Personnel Law* (2nd ed.). Upper Saddle River, NJ: Prentice Hall.

66. Ledvinka, J., and Scarpello, V. G. (1991). *Federal regulation of personnel and human resource management* (2nd ed.). Boston: PWS-Kent.
67. *BNA's Employee Relations Weekly.* (1994, March 28). Testing programs deter abuse, are cost effective, report says, *12,* 349.
68. *HR News.* (1994, March). Washington scorecard, *13,* 4.
69. Hall, F. S., and Hall, E. L. (1994). The ADA: Going beyond the law. *Academy of Management Executive, 8,* 17–26.
70. *HR News.* (1994, March). Legal report, 18.
71. Miclat, C. (2000, January). Recognition policies protect from potential discrimination. *Workforce,* 72–73.

Chapter 4

1. Edwards, A. (1991, January). The enlightened manager. *Working Woman,* 45–51.
2. Allport, G. W., and Odbert, H. S. (1933). Trait-names: A psycho-lexical study. *Psychological Monographs, 47,* 171–220.
3. Loden, M., and Rosener, J. B. (1991). *Workforce America, 18.* Homewood, IL: Irwin; Society for Human Resource Management (SHRM). (2006). What are employee networks and should they be a part of our diversity initiative? www.shrm.org/ diversity.
4. Rosen, R. H. (2000). *Global literacies.* New York: Simon & Schuster; Lynnes, K. S. (2002). Finding the key to the executive suite: Challenges for women and people of color. In R. Sitzer (Ed.). *The 21st Century Executive,* 229–274. San Francisco: Jossey-Bass.
5. *Fortune* (2003). Best companies for Asian, Black, and Hispanic employees. www.fortune.com.
6. *Ibid.*
7. Society for Human Resource Management (SHRM). (2006). Diversity training. www.shrm.org/diversity.
8. Dass, P., and Parker, B. (1999). Strategies for managing human resource diversity: From resistance to learning. *The Academy of Management Executive, 13*(2), 68–80, White, J. E. (1999, August 23). Affirmative action's Alamo. *Time,* 48; Society for Human Resource Management (SHRM). (2006). How is a diversity initiative different from my organization's affirmative action plan? www.shrm.org/diversity.
9. Society for Human Resource Management (SHRM). (2006). Where HR meets the world: How should my organization define diversity? www.shrm.org/diversity.
10. Bureau of Labor Statistics, Economic Surveys (2005). Data and reports. www.lib.gsu.edu.
11. Johnson, R. S. (1998, August 3). The 50 best companies for blacks and Hispanics. *Fortune,* 94–112.
12. *Fortune* (2003).
13. IBM. (2006). IBM valuing diversity: Awards and Recognition. www.ibm.com/employment/US/diverse/awards.
14. Weaver, V. (2001, September 10). Winning with diversity. *BusinessWeek,* special section.
15. Dass, P., and Parker, B. (1999). Strategies for managing human resource diversity: From resistance to learning. *The Academy of Management Executive, 13*(2), 68–80; Society for Human Resource Management (SHRM). (2006). How can the results of our initiative be measured? www.shrm.org/ diversity.
16. Kanter, R. M. (1983). *The change masters, 52.* New York: Simon & Schuster.
17. Author's files.
18. Sheppard, C. R. (1964). *Small groups, 118.* San Francisco: Chandler; Gómez-Mejía, L. R., and Balkin, D. B. (2007). *Management.* New York: Irwin/McGraw-Hill.
19. Gomez-Mejia, L. R., and Balkin, D. B. (2007). Management. New York: Irwin/McGraw-Hill.
20. *Ibid.*
21. Ely, R. (2004). A field study of group diversity, participation in diversity education programs, and performance. *Journal of Organizational Behavior, 25,* 755–780.
22. Author's files.
23. Study results reported in McDonough, D. C. (1999, April 26). A fair workplace? Not everywhere. *BusinessWeek,* 6.
24. Fine, M. C., Johnson, P. L., and Regan, S. M. (1990). Cultural diversity in the workplace. *Public Personnel Management, 19*(3), 305–319 (p. 307). See also Society for Human Resource Management (SHRM). (2006). How is a diversity initiative different from my organization's affirmative action plan? www.shrm.org/diversity.
25. Harrison, D. A., Price, K. H., and Bell, M. P. (1998). Beyond relational demography: Time and the effects of surface- and deep-level diversity on work group cohesion. *Academy of Management Journal, 41*(1), 96–107.
26. Fine, M. C., Johnson, P. L., and Regan, S. M. (1990). Cultural diversity in the workplace. *Public Personnel Management, 19*(3), 305–319 (p. 307).
27. Merritt, J. (2002, March 11). Guess who's pushing a bold plan for diversity? Big business. *BusinessWeek,* 56–58.
28. Morris, K. (1998, November 23). You've come a short way, baby. *BusinessWeek,* 82–86; *The Economist.* (2002, March 2). Women in suits, 60–61.
29. Dwyer, P., and Cuneo, A. (1991, July 8). The "other minorities" demand their due. *BusinessWeek,* 60; Pimentel, R. O. (2002, January 1). For Latinos, 2001 played tag with issues, emotions. *Arizona Republic,* A-18.
30. Kasindorf, M. (1999, September 10). Hispanics and blacks find their futures entangled. *USA Today,* 21-A; Pimentel, R. O. (2002, February 19). Latino assimilation: A median point or a melting pot? *Arizona Republic,* B-1; and Pimentel, R. O. (2002, February 26). Latino question insults Latino politicians. *Arizona Republic,* B-7.
31. Roberts, S. (2005, February 21). More Africans enter U.S. than in the days of slavery. *New York Times,* A-1.
32. Hamilton, A., and Bailey, P. (2005, January 17). Recharging the mission. *Time,* 5–51.
33. Paltrow, S. J. (2002, January 9). Life of Georgia nears settlement over race bias. *Wall Street Journal,* C-1; Crockett, R. V. (2005, February 21). How the NAACP could get its clout back. *BusinessWeek,* 18.
34. Berstein, A. (2002, February 25). The time bomb in the workforce: Illiteracy. *BusinessWeek,* 122.
35. *Wall Street Journal.* (2002, April 8). The good news on race, A-26; Koretz, G. (2001, September 3). Giant strides for U.S. blacks, *BusinessWeek,* 28; Hamilton, A., and Bailey, P. (2005, January 17). Recharging the mission. *Time,* 5–51.
36. Society for Human Resource Management (SHRM). (2006). How is a diversity initiative different from my organization's affirmative action plan? www.shrm.org/diversity.
37. Roberts, S. (2005, February 21). More Africans enter U.S. than in the days of slavery. *New York Times,* A-1.
38. Marosi, R. (2002, March 11). Study finds deadly spike in racial violence against Asian Americans. *Arizona Republic,* A-18.
39. Loden, M., and Rosener, J. B. (1991). *Workforce America, 18.* Homewood, ILs Irwin; Lynnes, K. S. (2002). Finding the key to the executive suite: Challenges for women and people of color. In R. Sitzer (Ed.). *The 21st Century Executive,* 229–274. San Francisco: Jossey-Bass.
40. L H Research national phone poll. (1994, March 4). *Chattanooga Times,* 1.
41. Colvin, J. (1999, July 19). The 50 best companies for Asians, blacks, and Hispanics. *Fortune,* 53–57.
42. Wong, J. (1996, February 9). Asian women migrant workers suffering abuse. *Wall Street Journal,* A-7.

43. Marosi, R. (2002, March 11). Study finds deadly spike in racial violence against Asian Americans. *Arizona Republic,* A-18. For related stories, see Simmons, M. (2005, February 27). More Dutch plan to emigrate as Muslim influx tips scales. *New York Times,* 46; Lyall, S. (2005, March 3). British court says banning Muslim gown violates student's rights. *New York Times,* A-13.

44. Weber, J. (1988, June 6). Social issues: The disabled. *Business Week,* 140; Savage, D. G. (2002, March). Wordaday rulings. *ABA Journal,* 34–35.

45. Koss-Feder, L. (1999, January 25). Able to work. *Time,* 25–30; Savage, D. G. (2002, March). Wordaday rulings. *ABA Journal,* 34–35.

46. Weber, J. (1988, June 6). Social issues: The disabled. *BusinessWeek,* 140; Greenhouse, L. (2005, March 1). Disabled cruise passengers ask for justices' protection. *New York Times,* A-15.

47. Perry, N. J. (1991, June 10). The workers of the future. *Fortune,* 51–58; Barlett, D. L., and Steele, J. B. (2004, September 20). Who left the door open? *Time,* 51–63.

48. Briefs. (1993, February 22). *Workforce Strategies,* 4(2), WS-12; Society for Human Resource Management (SHRM). (2006). How can the results of our initiative be measured? www.shrm.org/diversity.

49. Koss-Feder, L. (1999, January 25). Able to work. *Time,* 25–30.

50. Savage, D. G. (2002, March). Wordaday rulings. *ABA Journal,* 34–35.

51. Greenhouse, L. (2005, March 1). Disabled cruise passengers ask for justices' protection. *New York Times,* A-15.

52. *Wall Street Journal.* (2002, February 13). Economic focus: Immigrants, B-13; Greenberg, P. (2005, February 3). Illegal aliens! *Wall Street Journal,* A-17; Barlett, D. L., and Steele, J. B. (2004, September 20). Who left the door open? *Time,* 51–63.

53. Moore, S. (1999). Study results cited in Shaffer, M. (1999, September 3). Importing poverty. *Arizona Republic,* A-1; *Time.* (2002, January 7). Immigration: The home front, 130; Bernstein, N. (2005, March 3). New study paints clearer picture of Mexicans in New York City. *New York Times,* A-23; Barlett, D. L., and Steele, J. B. (2004, September 20). Who left the door open? *Time,* 51–63.

54. Golden, D. (2002, April 2). Some community colleges fudge facts to attract foreign students. *Wall Street Journal,* B-1.

55. McKinley, J. C. (2005, March 22). Mexican pride and death in U.S. service. *New York Times,* A-6.

56. Bernstein, N. (2005, February 17). Caught between parents and the law. *New York Times,* A-24.

57. Hawley, C. (2005, March 22). Undocumented coming to stay. *Arizona Republic,* A-1.

58. Greenhouse, S. (2005, March 11). Wal-Mart to pay U.S. $11 million in lawsuit on immigrant workers. *New York Times,* A-1; Kirkpatrick, D. D. (2005, February 11). House passes tightening of laws on immigration. *New York Times,* A-11; Kornblut, A. (2005, March 24). Bush cites political hurdles in plan for guest workers. *New York Times,* A-6; Lee, K. A. (2005, February 14). State department relaxes visa rules for some scientists and students. *Wall Street Journal,* A-1.

59. *BusinessWeek.* (2005, February 28), 15.

60. For a critical discussion of the higher figure, see Muir, J. G. (1993, March 31). Homosexuals and the 10% fallacy. *Wall Street Journal,* A13.

61. Divito, N. (2005, March 7). I kept quiet, and lost my job anyway. *Newsweek,* 18.

62. Lyall, A. (2005, February 22). New course by Roya Royal Navy: A campaign to recruit gays. *New York Times,* A-1.

63. Portes, A., and Truelove, L. (1987). Making sense of diversity: Recent research on Hispanic minorities in the U.S. *American Review of Sociology, 13,* 359–385 (p. 360); Pimentel, R. O. (2002, February 19). Latino assimilation: A median point or a melting

pot? *Arizona Republic,* B-1; Pew Hispanic Center. (2005). Hispanics: A people in motion. www.pewhispanic.org.

64. Porter, E. (2002a, April 19). Hispanic targeted advertising outpaces overall adgrowth. *Wall Street Journal,* A-1.

65. Pew Hispanic Center. (2005). Hispanics: A people in motion. www.pewhispanic.org.

66. *Ibid.*

67. Porter, E. (2002b, February 13). Quirky English course evolves into fixture of Latino pop culture. *Wall Street Journal,* A-1; Pew Hispanic Center. (2005). Latinos see race as a measure of belonging. www.pewhispanic.org/diversity.

68. Romero, C. C. (2002, January 19). Hard time for Hispanics. *Arizona Republic,* D-1; Porter, E. (2002b, February 13). Quirky English course evolves into fixture of Latino pop culture. *Wall Street Journal,* A-1; Pew Hispanic Center. (2005). Latinos see race as a measure of belonging. www.pewhispanic.org/diversity.

69. Doyle, R. (2002, February). Assembling the future. *Scientific American,* 30; Society for Human Resource Management (SHRM). (2006). How is a diversity initiative different from my organization's affirmative action plan? www.shrm.org/diversity.

70. Russel, J. (1995, September). Trading with the world. *Hispanic Business,* 26–27; Porter, E. (2002a, April 19). Hispanic targeted advertising outpaces overall ad growth. *Wall Street Journal,* A-17.

71. Kaufman, J. (2002, January 10). Whites and Hispanics fall out over quest for suburban dream. *Wall Street Journal,* A-1; Pimentel, R. O. (2002, January 1). For Latinos, 2001 played tag with issues, emotions. *Arizona Republic,* A-18; Pimentel, R. O. Untold story: Hispanic middle class blazing new trails. *Arizona Republic,* B-9; Pimentel, R. O. (2002, February 19). Latino assimilation: A median point or a melting pot? *Arizona Republic,* B-1; Wingett, Y. (2005, January 21). More Latinos opting out of barrios. *Arizona Republic,* A-2.

72. Pew Hispanic Center. (2005). Hispanics: A people in motion. www.pewhispanic.org; Pew Hispanic Center. (2005). A look at where Latinos live. www.pewhispanic.org.

73. Wingett, Y. (2005, January 21). More Latinos opting out of barrios. *Arizona Republic,* A-2; Pew Hispanic Center. (2005). A look at where Latinos live. www.pewhispanic.org

74. Munk, N. (1999, February 1). Finished at forty. *Fortune,* 50–64; Goldberg, B. (2000). *Age works.* New York: The Free Press; Quinn, J. B., (2005, February 4). Your retirement: How to land on your feet. *Newsweek,* 47–52; Alster, N. (2005, January 30). When gray heads roll, is age bias at work? *New York Times,* B-3; Engardio, P., Matlock, C. Edmondson, G., Rowley, I. Barraclough, C., and Smith, E. (2005, January 31). Global aging: Now, the geezer glut. *BusinessWeek,* 214–217.

75. Chen, K. (2002, February 25). Age discrimination complaints rose 8.7% in 2001 amid overall increase in claims. *Wall Street Journal,* B-13; Quinn, J. B., (2005, February 4). Your retirement: How to land on your feet. *Newsweek,* 47–52; Gardner, M. (2005, January 22). Younger boss, older employees learn new ropes. *Arizona Republic,* D-3.

76. Bravin, J. (2005, March 31). Court expands age bias claims for workforce. *Wall Street Journal,* A-8.

77. Loden, M., and Rosener, J. B. (1991). *Workforce America, 18.* Homewood, IL: Irwin. 65.

78. Levin, D. P. (1994, February 20). The graying factory. *New York Times,* C-16; Trilich, T. (2002, Winter). Young or old are about equally dedicated to their jobs. *Gallup Management Journal,* 32; Freudenheim, M. (2005, March 23). Help wanted: Older workers please apply. *New York Times,* A-1; Richards, M. (2005, March 5). Betting on the baby boomers. *New York Times,* A-11.

79. Bureau of Labor Statistics; Employment and Earnings. (1999, January). Tables 44 and 45.

80. Trilch, T. (2002, Winter). Young or old are about equally dedicated to their jobs. *Gallup Management Journal,* 32.

81. Fellows, D. S. (2001). Striking gold in a silver mine: Leveraging senior workers as knowledge champions. *Worldatwork Journal,* 10(4), 112; Freudenheim, M. (2005, March 23). Help wanted: Older workers please apply. *New York Times,* A-1; Fisher, G. (2005, March 21). How to battle the coming brain drain. *Fortune,* 121–128.

82. McNamee, M. (1998, August 17). First hired, first fired? *BusinessWeek,* 22; Society for Human Resource Management (SHRM). (2006). How can the results of our initiative be measured? www.shrm.org/diversity; Society for Human Resource Management (SHRM). (2006). What are employee networks and why should they be part of our diversity initiative? www.shrm.org/diversity; Society for Human Resource Management (SHRM). (2006). Diversity training. www.shrm.org/ diversity; Society for Human Resource Management (SHRM). (2006). What are the components of a successful diversity initiative? www.shrm.org/diversity.

83. Gomez, Meija L. R., Balkin D. B., Cardy R. L. (2007). Management. New York: Irwin/McGraw Hill.

84. *New York Times.* (2005, March 9). Census report details lives of U.S. Arabs, A-6; Lyall, S. (2005, March 3). British court says banning Muslim gown violates student's rights. *New York Times,* A-13; Rauf, F. A. (2004, October 18). Bringing Muslim nations into the global century. *Fortune,* 80–81; Simmons, M. (2005, February 27). More Dutch plan to emigrate as Muslim influx tips scales. *New York Times,* C-16; *The Economist.* (2003, October 25). Islam in France, 32–33.

85. *New York Times.* (2005, March 9). Census report details lives of U.S. Arabs, A-6.

86. *Ibid.*

87. Simmons, M. (2005, February 27). More Dutch plan to emigrate as Muslim influx tips scales. *New York Times,* C-16; Lyall, S. (2005, March 3). British court says banning Muslim gown violates student's rights. *New York Times,* A-13.

88. Bureau of Labor Statistics, 2006, stats.bls.gov.

89. Highlights of Women's Earnings. (2005). Bureau of Labor Statistics, stats.bls.gov.

90. Morris, K. (1998, November 23). You've come a short way, baby. *BusinessWeek,* 82–86; *The Economist.* (2002, March 2). Women in suits, 60–61; Deutsch, R. H. (2005, February 27). Are women responsible for their own low pay? *New York Times,* B-7.

91. *BusinessWeek.* (2002, January 14). The top 25 managers of the year, 52–71; Berman, D. K. (2002, January 7). Lucent veteran Russo to return as CEO. *Wall Street Journal,* A-3.

92. Shellenbarger, S. (1995, May 11). Women indicate satisfaction with role of breadwinner. *Wall Street Journal,* B6–B7; Conlin, M. (2003, January 27). Look who is bringing home the bacon. *BusinessWeek,* 85; Tyson, L. D. (2005, March 28). What Larry Summers got right. *BusinessWeek,* 24.

93. Blass, F. D. (1998, March). The well-being of American women: 1970–1995. *Journal of Economic Literature,* 36(1), 112–165; Lynnes, K. S. (2002). Finding the key to the executive suite: Challenges for women and people of color. In R. Sitzer (Ed.). *The 21st Century Executive,* 229–274. San Francisco: Jossey-Bass; Tyson, L. D. (2005, March 28). What Larry Summers got right. *BusinessWeek,* 24.

94. Baird, J. E., Jr., and Bradley, P. H. (1979, June). Styles of management and communication: A comparative study of men and women. *Communication Monographs,* 46, 101–110.

95. DePalma, A. (1991, November 12). Women can be hindered by lack of "boys" network. *Boulder Daily Camera,* Business Plus Section, 9; Society for Human Resource Management (SHRM). (2006). What are employee networks and should they be part of our diversity initiative? www.shrm.org/diversity.

96. *The Economist.* (2002, March 2). Women in suits, 60–61; Carlson, M. (1999, September 20). Sexual harassment, Chapter 999. *BusinessWeek,* 94–95; Morris, B. (1999, May 10). Addicted to sex. *Fortune,* 65–70; Deutsch, R. H. (2005, February 27). Are women responsible for their own low pay? *New York Times,* B-7.

97. Conlin, M., and Zellner, W. (2001, July 16). Is Wal-Mart hostile to women? *BusinessWeek,* 58–60; Berstein, N. (2005, March 21). Wal-Mart vs. class action. *BusinessWeek,* 73–74.

98. *The Economist.* (2002, March 2). Women in suits, 60–61.

99. *Ibid.*

100. *Fortune,* www.fortune.com (2005).

101. Weaver, V. (2001, September 10). Winning with diversity. *BusinessWeek,* special section.

102. Society for Human Resource Management (SHRM). (2006). What if your diversity training is successful? www.shrm.org/ diversity.

103. Wheeler, M. L. (1998, December 14).

104. Stewart, T. A. (1991, December 10). Gay in corporate America, *Fortune,* 42–50 (43); Divito, N. (2005, March 7). I kept quiet, and lost my job anyway. *Newsweek,* 18; Lyall, S. (2005, February 22). New course by Royal Navy. A campaign to recruit gays. *New York Times,* A-1.

105. Thomas, R. F (1990, March–April). From affirmative action to affirming diversity. *Harvard Business Review,* 107–119; and Society for Human Resource Management (SHRM). (2006). Where HR meets the world: How should my organization define diversity? www.shrm.org/diversity.

106. Society for Human Resource Management (SHRM). (2006). Diversity training. www.shrm.org/diversity.

107. Society for Human Resource Management (SHRM). (2006). What if your diversity training is successful? www.shrm.org/ diversity.

108. *Ibid.*

109. *Comp/flash.* (1994, January). Benefits flash. *American Management Association,* 5; Zinsmeister, K. (2005). Problem with day care. The American Enterprise online. www.taemag.com.

110. Ashton, A. (2002, February). Around-the-clock child care. *Working Woman,* 14.

111. Conlin, M. (1999, September 20). 9 to 5 isn't working anymore. *BusinessWeek,* 94–95; Bond, J. T., Galinsky, E., and Hill, E. J. (2005, February). Flexibility: A key ingredient in creating an effective work place. *Workspan,* 17–22.

112. Newman, A. M. (2002, February). Fair shares. *Working Woman,* 64–71.

113. Goodstein, J. D. (1994). Institutional pressures and strategic responsiveness: Employer involvement in work–family issues. *Academy of Management Journal,* 37(2), 350–383; Society for Human Resource Management (SHRM). (2006). How can the results of our initiative be measured? www.shrm.org/ diversity.

114. Fisher, A. (1998, October 12). Women need at least one mentor and one pantsuit. *Fortune,* 208.

115. Hymowitz, C. (1995, April 24). How a dedicated mentor gave momentum to a woman's career. *Wall Street Journal,* B1.

116. Glater, J. D. (2005, April 1). Sex discrimination lawsuit filed against Smith Barney. *New York Times,* C-3.

117. Wartzman, R. (1992, May 4). A Whirlpool factory raises productivity and pay of workers. *Wall Street Journal,* A1.

118. Scott, R. S. (2002, April 15). Hooray Halle! *U.S. News and World Report,* 8–12; Pimentel, R. O. (2002, February 26). Latino question insults Latino politicians. *Arizona Republic,* B-7; *Time.* (2002, January 7). Immigration: The home front, 130; Kornblut, A. (2005, March 24). Bush cites political hurdles in plan for guest workers. *New York Times,* A-6.

119. Barlett, D. L., and Steele, J. B. (2004, September 20). Who left the door open? *Time*, 51–63.

120. Tyson, L. D. (2005, March 28). What Larry Summers got right. *BusinessWeek*, 24.

Chapter 5

1. Hand, T. (2002). Choosing the right recruiter. *Network World*, 19, 41.

2. *The Controller's Report*. (2002, March). Working alternatives to job cuts: The latest strategies for preserving human capital.

3. *Managing HR Information Systems*. (2002). Three companies reveal how they use employ! to cut hiring paperwork. January Newsletter, 1, 12–14.

4. *Managing HR Information Systems*. (2001). Automating recruitment: How to select and implement the best new recruiting app. December Newsletter, 1, 11–14.

5. See, for example, Rothwell, W. J., and Kazanis, H. C. (1988). *Strategic human resources planning and management*. Upper Saddle River, NJ: Prentice Hall; Bartholomew, D. J., and Forbes, A. F. (1979). *Statistical techniques for manpower planning*. Chichester, England: Wiley-Interscience; Heneman, H. G., III, and Sandver, M. G. (1977). Markov analysis in human resource administration: Applications and limitations. *Academy of Management Review*, 2(4), 535–542; Burack, E. H., and Mathys, N. J. (1987). *Human resource planning: A pragmatic approach to manpower staffing and development*. Lake Forest, IL: Brace-Park.

6. Cardy, R. L., and Carson, K. P. (1996). Total quality and the abandonment of performance appraisal: Taking a good thing too far? *Journal of Quality Management*, 1, 193–206.

7. Adler, L. (2005). The 2X factor: The real cost of bad hiring. *China Staff*, 11, 27.

8. Frazier, M. 2005. *Help wanted: The crucial game of recruitment and retention, Chain Store*, Age, 81, 37.

9. Hinkin, T. R., and Tracey, J. B. (2000). The cost of turnover: Putting a price on the learning curve. *Cornell Hotel and Restaurant Administration Quarterly*, 41, 14–21.

10. Adapted with permission from Hinkin, T. R., and Tracey, J. B. (2000). The cost of turnover: Putting a price on the learning curve. *Cornell Hotel and Restaurant Administration Quarterly*, 41, 14–21.

11. Halliman, E. R. (2005). Managing employee costs: Getting to the meat of the matter. *Reeves Journal*, 85, 14.

12. *Ibid*.

13. O'Reilly, C. A., and Chatman, J. (1994). Working smarter and harder: A longitudinal study of managerial success. *Administrative Science Quarterly*, 39, 603–627.

14. Rynes, S. L. (1991). Recruitment, job choice, and posthire consequences: A call for new research directions. In M. D. Dunnette and L. M. Hough (Eds.), *Handbook of industrial and organizational psychology* (2nd ed.), Vol. 2, 399–444. Palo Alto, CA: Consulting Psychologists.

15. *Ibid*.

16. Pont, J. (2005, May 1). Companies are getting smarter about how to use the Web, strengthening employee referral programs and sharpening their focus on attracting workers with the right skills—even if they are not looking for a new job. *Workforce Management*, 49.

17. Kreimer, S. (2005, April 24). Hospitals paying big for referrals: Hiring workers' friends proves beneficial for all. *The Washington Post*, K1.

18. *Human Resource Department Management Report*. (2002). What's your department's policy on rehiring laid-off employees? Institute of Management and Administration February Newsletter, 1, 13–14.

19. Gallagher, J., and Burns, A. (2005, May 23). Hiring temps can be good for business. *The Augusta Chronicle*.

20. Business Wire (2005, March 14). New labor forecast predicts robust growth in demand for temporary workers in 2005 second quarter.

21. Institute of Management & Administration (2005). Need short-term workers? How about hiring employees' teens? *HRFocus*, 82, 9.

22. Kever, J. (2002, January 27). Life as a temp. *Houston Chronicle*, Texas Magazine section, 6.

23. Perry, P. (2002). Battle for the best: What works today in recruiting top technical talent. *Research Technology Management*, 45, 17(5).

24. Posner, B. G. (1990). Putting customers to work. *Inc.*, 12, 111–112.

25. Kanter, R. M. (2002). Strategy as improvisational theater: Companies that want to outpace the competition throw out the script and improvise their way to new strategies. *MIT Sloan Management Review*, 43, 76.

26. PRNewswire. (2005, May 3). Small businesses face tough competition attracting top talent according to Wells Fargo/Gallup small business index.

27. Sackett, P. R., and Arvey, R. D. (1993). Selection in small settings. In N. Schmitt, W. C. Borman (Eds.). *Personnel selection in organizations*. San Francisco: Jossey-Bass.

28. Wanous, J. P. (1992). *Organizational entry* (2nd ed.). Reading, MA: Addison-Wesley.

29. Grossman, R. J. (2005). The truth about the coming labor shortage: Confusing predictions and data are clouding the real picture of tomorrow's labor supply. *HR Magazine*, 50, 46.

30. Overman, S. (1999). Put overlooked labor pools on your recruiting list. *HRMagazine*, 44, 86–90.

31. O'Donnell, A. (2001). Reaching out for diversity. *Insurance and Technology*, 26, 65.

32. Evans, T. (2005). Companies walk a fine line in recruiting minorities. *The Houston Chronicle*, Business section, 1.

33. Laab, J. J. (1991, May). Affirmative outreach. *Personnel Journal*, 86–93.

34. Weber, H. R. (2005). Home Deport woos Hispanics. *The Arizona Republic*, D8.

35. Walker, J. W. (1990, December). Human resource planning, 1990s style. *Human Resource Planning*, 229–230.

36. Hunter, J. E., and Hunter, R. F. (1984). Validity and utility of alternative predictors of job performance. *Psychological Bulletin*, 96, 72–98.

37. Heneman, H. G., III, Heneman, R. L., and Judge, T. A. (1997). *Staffing organizations*. Middleton, WI: Mendota House/Irwin.

38. Kleiman, L. S., and Faley, R. H. (1985). The implications of professional and legal guidelines for court decisions involving criterion-related validity: A review and analysis. *Personnel Psychology*, 38, 803–833.

39. Heneman et al., 1997.

40. *Ibid*.

41. Muchinsky, P. M. (1979). The use of reference reports in personnel selection: A review and evaluation. *Journal of Occupational Psychology*, 52, 287–297.

42. Aamodt, M. G., Bryan, D. A., and Whitcomb, A. J. (1993). Predicting performance with letters of recommendation. *Public Personnel Management*, 22, 81–90.

43. Peres, S. H., and Garcia, J. R. (1962). Validity and dimensions of descriptive adjectives used in reference letters for engineering applicants. *Personnel Psychology*, 15, 279–296.

44. Taylor, P. (1999). Providing structure to interviews and reference checks. *Workforce Tools* (supplement to *Workforce*), 7, 10.

45. Russell, C. J., Mattson, J., Devlin, S. F., and Atwater, D. (1990). Predictive validity of biodata items generated from retrospective life experience essays. *Journal of Applied Psychology*, 75, 569–580.

46. Hunter, J. E. (1986). Cognitive ability, cognitive aptitudes, job knowledge, and job performance. *Journal of Vocational Behavior, 29*, 340–362.

47. Bounds, G. M., Dobbins, G. H., and Fowler, O. S. (1995). *Management: A total quality perspective.* Cincinnati, OH: South-Western.

48. Marelli, A. F. (2005). The performance technologist's toolbox: Work samples. *Performance Improvement, 44*, 4.

49. Harville, D. L. (1996). Ability test equity in predicting job performance work samples. *Educational and Psychological Measurement, 56*, 344–348.

50. Hogan, J., and Quigley, A. (1994). Effects of preparing for physical ability tests. *Public Personnel Management, 23*, 85–104.

51. Landy, F. J. (2005). Some historical and scienfic issues related to research on emotional intelligence. *Journal of Organizational Behavior, 26*, 411–424.

52. Daus, C. S., and Ashkanasy, N. M. (2005). The case for the ability-based model of emotional intelligence in organizational behavior. *Journal of Organizational Behavior, 26*, 453–466.

53. Conte, J. M. (2005). A review and critique of emotional intelligence measures. *Journal of Organizational Behavior, 26*, 433–440.

54. *Ibid.*

55. Guion, R. M., and Gottier, R. F. (1965). Validity of personality measures in personnel selection. *Personnel Psychology, 18*, 135–163.

56. Bernardin, H. J., and Beatty, R. W. (1984). *Performance appraisal: Assessing human behavior at work.* Boston: Kent.

57. Landy, F. J. (1989). *The psychology of work behavior* (4th ed.). Pacific Grove, CA: Brooks/Cole.

58. Guion, R. M., and Gottier, R. F. (1965). Validity of personality measures in personnel selection. *Personnel Psychology, 18*, 135–163.

59. Kleiman, L. S., and Faley, R. H. (1985). The implications of professional and legal guidelines for court decisions involving criterion-related validity: A review and analysis. *Personnel Psychology, 38*, 803–833.

60. Safford, D. (2005, May 31). Heads-up hiring. *The Kansas City Star,* D1.

61. Funder, D. C., and Dobroth, J. M. (1987). Difference between traits: Properties associated with inter-judge agreement. *Journal of Personality and Social Psychology, 52*, 409–418.

62. Digman, J. M. (1990). Personality structure: Emergence of the five-factor model. *Annual Review of Psychology, 41*, 417–440; Goldberg, L. R. (1993). The structure of phenotypic personality traits. *American Psychologist, 48*, 26–34.

63. Barrick, M. R., and Mount, M. K. (1991). The big five personality dimensions and job performance: A meta analysis. *Personnel Psychology, 41*, 1–26; Digman, J. M. (1990). Personality structure: Emergence of the five-factor model. *Annual Review of Psychology, 41*, 417–440; Hogan, R. (1991). Personality and personality measurement. In M. D. Dunnette and L. M. Hough (Eds.), *Handbook of industrial and organizational psychology* (2nd ed.), Vol. I. Palo Alto, CA: Consulting Psychologists.

64. Barrick, M. R., and Mount, M. K. (1991). The big five personality dimensions and job performance: A meta analysis. *Personnel Psychology, 41*, 1–26.

65. Haaland, D. E. (2005). Who's the safest bet for the job? Find out why the fun guy in the next cubicle may be the next accident waiting to happen. *Security Management, 49*, 51.

66. House, R. J., Shane, S. A., and Herold, D. M. (1996). Rumors of the death of dispositional research are vastly exaggerated. *Academy of Management Review, 21*, 203–224.

67. Dunn, W., Mount, M. K., Barrick, M. R., and Ones, D. S. (1995). Relative importance of personality and general mental ability in managers' judgments of applicant qualifications. *Journal of Applied Psychology, 80*, 500–509.

68. Wolfe, R. N., and Johnson, S. D. (1995). Personality as a predictor of college performance. *Educational and Psychological Measurement, 55*, 177–185.

69. Whitaker, B. (2005, February 23). Employee theft can do you in. *New York Times,* G2.

70. Shuster, W. G. (2005). Winning the battle against internal theft: Employee theft is the biggest cause of retail shrinkage—here's how to deter it. *Jewelers Circle Keystone,* 98.

71. Terris, W., and Jones, J. W. (1982). Psychological factors elating to employees' theft in the convenience store industry. *Psychological Reports, 51*, 1219–1238.

72. Bernardin, H. J., and Cooke, D. K. (1993). Validity of an honesty test in predicting theft among convenience store employees. *Academy of Management Journal, 36*, 1097–1108.

73. Arnold, D. W., and Jones, J. W. (2002). Who the devil's applying now? Companies can use tests to screen out dangerous job candidates. *Security Management, 46*, 85.

74. Budman, M. (1993, November–December). The honesty business. *Across the Board,* 34–37.

75. Arvey, R. D., and Campion, J. E. (1982). The employment interview: A summary and review of recent research. *Personnel Psychology, 35*, 281–322; and Harris, M. M. (1989). Reconsidering the employment interview: A review of recent literature and suggestions for future research. *Personnel Psychology, 42*, 691–726.

76. Springbett, B. M. (1958). Factors affecting the final decision in the employment interview. *Canadian Journal of Psychology, 12*, 13–22.

77. Buckley, M. R., and Eder, R. W. (1988). B. M. Springbett and the notion of the "snap decision" in the interview. *Journal of Management, 14*, 59–67.

78. Campion, M. A., Pursell, F. D., and Brown, B. K. (1988). Structured interviewing: Raising the psychometric properties of the employment interview. *Personnel Psychology, 41*, 252.

79. Pursell, E. D., Campion, M. A., and Gaylord, S. R. (1980). Structured interviewing: Avoiding selection problems. *Personnel Journal, 59*, 907–912.

80. Wright, P. M., Licthenfels, P. A., and Pursell, E. D. (1989). The structured interview: Additional studies and a meta-analysis. *Journal of Occupational Psychology, 62*, 191–199.

81. See Pulakos, E. D., and Schmitt, N. (1995). Experience-based and situational interview questions: Studies of validity. *Personnel Psychology, 48*, 289–308.

82. Hunter, J. E., and Hunter, R. F. (1984). Validity and utility of alternative predictors of job performance. *Psychological Bulletin, 96*, 72–98.

83. Warmke, D. L., and Weston, D. J. (1992, April). Success dispels myths about panel interviewing. *Personnel Journal,* 120–126.

84. Harris, M. M. (1989). Reconsidering the employment interview: A review of recent literature and suggestions for future research. *Personnel Psychology, 42*, 691–726.

85. Chatman, J. A. (1989). Improving interaction organizational research: A model of person–organization fit. *Academy of Management Review, 14*, 333–349.

86. Pouliot, J. S. (1992, July). Topics to avoid with applicants. *Nation's Business,* 57–59.

87. Corning, B. (1999). Seek and you may find. *Accountancy, 123*, 46–47.

88. Boyle, S., Fullerton, J., and Yapp, M. (1993). The rise of the assessment centre: A survey of AC usage in the UK. *Selection and Development Review, 9*, 14.

89. McEvoy, G. M., and Beatty, R. W. (1989). Assessment centers and subordinate appraisals of managers: A seven-year study of predictive validity. *Personnel Psychology, 42*, 37–52.

90. Brownell, J. (2005). Predicting leadership: The assessment center's extended role. *International Journal of Contemporary Hospital Management, 17,* 7–21.

91. Coulton, G. F., and Feild, H. S. (1995). Using assessment centers in selecting entry-level police officers: Extravagance or justified expense? *Public Personnel Management, 24,* 223–254.

92. Argetsinger, A. (1998, May 21). Principles for principals: Written exam replaces role-playing for applicants. *Washington Post,* M1.

93. Bender, J. M. (1973). What is "typical" of assessment centers? *Personnel, 50,* 50–57; Carrick, P., and Williams, R. (1999). Development centres—A review of assumptions. *Human Resource Management Journal, 9,* 77–92.

94. Gill, a. (2005). Expert's view: Alison Gill on Assessment Centres. *Personnel Today,* October 5, p. 35.

95. Lopez, J. A. (1993, October 6). Firms force job seekers to jump through hoops. *Wall Street Journal,* B1, B6.

96. Cowan, T. R. (1987). Drugs and the workplace: to drug test or not to test? *Public Personnel Management, 16,* 313–322.

97. Workplace Substance Abuse Advisor. (2005, May 26). Workplace amphetamine abuse increasing: Overall positivity rate unchanged, *19*(13).

98. Workplace Substance Abuse Advisor. (2005, April 28). Survey finds drug-testing in decline, industry experts surprised, *19*(11).

99. Wessel, D. (1989, September 7). Evidence is skimpy that drug testing works, but employers embrace practice. *Wall Street Journal,* B1, B9.

100. Brown, M. (1991, December). Reference checking: The law is on your side. *Human Resource Measurements* (a supplement to *Personnel Journal*), 4–5.

101. Hernan, P. (2002). Looking for trouble: Employee's backgrounds face closer scrutiny in the wake of September 11. *Industry Week, 251,* 15(3).

102. Steen, M. (2002, March 25). Under security. *San Jose Mercury News,* E1.

103. Fowler, A. (1991). An even-handed approach to graphology. *Personnel Management, 23,* 40–43.

104. Rafaeli, A., and Klimoski, R. J. (1983). Predicting sales success through handwriting analysis: An evaluation of the effects of training and handwriting sample content. *Journal of Applied Psychology, 68,* 212–217.

105. Cox, A., and Tapsell, J. (1991). Graphology and its validity in personnel assessment. Paper presented at the British Psychological Society.

106. Bianchi, A. (1996, February). The character-revealing handwriting analysis. *Inc.,* 77–79.

107. Kleinmutz, B. (1990). Why we still use our heads instead of formulas: Toward an integrative approach. *Psychological Bulletin, 107,* 296–310.

108. For a review, see Gatewood, R. D., and Feild, H. S. (1994). *Human resource selection.* Orlando, FL: Harcourt, Brace.

109. Cardy, R. L., and Stewart, G. (1998). Quality and teams: Implications for HRM theory and research. In S. Ghosh and D. B. Fedor (Eds.), *Advances in the management of organization quality,* Vol. 3, Greenwich, CT: JAI Press.

110. Kristof, A. L. (1996). Person–organization fit: An integrative review of the conceptualizations, measurement, and implications. *Personnel Psychology, 49,* 1–49; Barrett, R. S. (1995). Employee selection with the performance priority survey. *Personnel Psychology, 48,* 653–662.

111. Rynes, S. L. (1991). Recruitment, job choice, and posthire consequences: A call for new research directions. In M. D. Dunnette and L. M. Hough (Eds.), *Handbook of industrial and organizational psychology* (2nd ed.), Vol. 2, 399–444. Palo Alto, CA: Consulting Psychologists.

112. Macan, T. H., Avedon, M. J., Paese, M., and Smith, D. (1994). The effects of applicants' reactions to cognitive ability tests and an assessment center. *Personnel Psychology, 47,* 715–738.

113. Heneman, H. G., Huett, D. L., Lavigna, R. J., and Oston, D. (1995). Assessing managers' satisfaction with staffing service. *Personnel Psychology, 48,* 163–172.

114. Cook, S. H. (1988, November). Playing it safe: How to avoid liability for negligent hiring. *Personnel,* 32–36.

115. *Ibid.*

Chapter 6

1. Polsky, D. (1999). Changing consequences of job separation in the United States. *Industrial and Labor Relations Review, 52,* 565–580.

2. Cascio, W. F. (1991). *Costing human resources: The financial impact of behavior in organizations.* Boston: PWS-Kent.

3. Schiesel, S. (1998, February 8). AT&T: A leaner company without a crash diet. *New York Times.* www.nytimes.com/library/financial/Sunday/archive/.

4. Retention management and metrics. (2002). Available at www.nobscot.com/sales/retention.cfm.

5. Bliss, W. G. (2002). Fair treatment in firings avoids suits. *National Underwriter Property & Casualty, 106,* 20(3).

6. Alexander, S. (1999, March 3). No cure in sight. *Computerworld.* www.computerworld.com/home/print.nsf/all/9903299EA.

7. *Report on Salary Surveys.* (2002). How companies now structure severance and separation benefits. April Newsletter of the Institute of Management and Administration.

8. Lewis, D. E. (2005, January 2). Online exit interviews reveal more honesty. *Boston Globe,* Boston Works section, G2.

9. Taylor, J. (1999, April). Avoid avoidable turnover. *Workforce,* 6.

10. Mobley, W. H. (1982). *Employee turnover: Causes, consequences, and control.* Reading, MA: Addison-Wesley.

11. Connolly, A. (2005, March 31). About 30 NASA Langley workers take buyout offer. *Virginian-Pilot.*

12. Associated Press (2005, April 5). Ford offers buyout packages to around 1,000 employees.

13. *The Economist.* (1999, September 4). Aging workers: A full life, 65–68.

14. Munk, N. (1999, February 1). Finished at forty. *Fortune,* 50–54.

15. Watson, M. (2005, June 8). UAW skeptical of GM's plan to shrink: Automaker expects $2.5 billion in savings. *The Commercial Appeal* (Memphis, TN), A-1.

16. Hakim, D. (2005, June 9). GM cuts are deep, but analysts wonder if more are coming. *New York Times,* 13.

17. Richards, D. (1999, July 5). Petrochemical manufacturers lay off thousands. *Chemical Market Reporter, 5,* 40.

18. Plety, J., and Plohetski, T. (2002, February 18). Job cuts forever changed Dell Computer, workers, Austin, Texas, are firm. *Austin American-Statesman.*

19. *Ibid.*

20. Fedor, L. (2005, May 22). Lost horizons. *Star Tribune* (Minneapolis, MN), A-1.

21. Robbins, D. K., and Pearce, J. A. (1992). Turnaround: Retrenchment and recovery. *Strategic Management Journal, 13,* 287–309.

22. Laabs, J. (1999, April). Has downsizing missed its mark? *Workforce,* 30–38.

23. Kuczynski, S. (1999, June). Help! I shrunk the company. *HRMagazine,* 40–45.

24. Messmer, M. (1991, October). Right-sizing reshapes staffing strategies. *HRMagazine,* 60–62.

25. Ellis, M., and McCracken, J. (2005, June 8). GM plans to close more U.S. factories. *Detroit Free Press.*

26. Balkin, D. B. (1992). Managing employee separations with the reward system. *Academy of Management Executive, 6*(4), 64–71.

27. Byrne, J. (1994, May 9). The pain of downsizing. *BusinessWeek,* 60–68.

28. Hill, R. E., and Dwyer, P. C. (1990, September). Grooming workers for early retirement. *HRMagazine,* 59–63.

29. Grant, P. B. (1991). The "open window"—Special early retirement plans in transition. *Employee Benefits Journal, 16*(1), 10–16.

30. Lopez, J. A. (1993, October 25). Out in the cold: Many early retirees find the good deals not so good after all. *Wall Street Journal,* B1. Tomasko, R. (1991). Downsizing: Layoffs and alternatives to layoffs. *Compensation and Benefits Review, 23*(4), 19–32.

31. Murauski, J. (2005, April 20). Hundreds to make up for buyouts. *The News & Observer* (Raleigh, NC), D-1.

32. Beck, M. (1991, December 9). Old enough to get fired. *Newsweek,* 64.

33. Johnson, P. B. (2002, February 24). FedEx finds ways to fight tough times in High Point, NC, area. *High Point Enterprise.*

34. *HR Focus.* (2002, February). How employers are handling layoffs and their aftermath, 79, 8; *HR Focus.* (2002, January). If you must lay off workers: Consider the long-term consequences, 79, 8.

35. Greenhouse, S. (1999, September 23). In the U.A.W. deal, something for almost everyone? *New York Times.* www.nytimes.com/library/financial.

36. Stucke, J. (2005, April 6). Sacred Heart layoffs fewer than expected: More patients, hiring freeze cited for better outlook. *Spokesman Review* (Spokane, WA), A-8.

37. McGarvey, R. (2002). Solving the personnel puzzle: Finding the right number of employees is only part of the staffing picture—the pieces also need to fit together. *Electronic Business, 28,* 62(5).

38. Nolan, J. (2005, March 2). Comair pilots approve pay-freeze request by airline. Associated Press State & Local Wire.

39. Ehrenberg, R. G., and Jakubson, G. H. (1989). Advance notification of plant closing: Does it matter? *Industrial Relations, 28,* 60–71.

40. Brockner, J., Grover, S., Reed, T. F., and DeWitt, R. L. (1992). Layoffs, job insecurity, and survivors' work effort: Evidence of an inverted-U relationship. *Academy of Management Journal, 35,* 413–425.

41. Ehrenberg, R. G., and Jakubson, G. H. (1988). *Advance notice provisions in plant closing legislation.* Kalamazoo, MI: W.E. Upjohn Institute for Employment Research.

42. Reingold J. (1999, September 20). Brain drain. *BusinessWeek,* 112–126.

43. Eisman, R. (1992, May). Remaking a corporate giant. *Incentive,* 57–63.

44. Bayer, R. (2000, January). Firing: Letting people go with dignity is good for business. *HR Focus,* 10.

45. Bunning, R. L. (1990). The dynamics of downsizing. *Personnel Journal, 69*(9), 69–75.

46. Thibodeau, P. (1998, February 19). Computer security woes come from outside as well as within. *Computerworld.* www.computerworld.com/home/onine9697.nsf/all/980218computer1CEBA; Fabis, P. (1998, June 15). Safe exits. *CIO,* Sect. 1, 32.

47. Brockner, J. (1992). Managing the effects of layoffs on survivors. *California Management Review, 34*(2), 9–28.

48. *Pay for Performance Report.* (2002, March). One key to success after layoffs.

49. Enright, E. (2002). After the fall: How to cope in a downsized workplace. *Meetings & Conventions, 37,* 47.

50. *Ibid.*

51. Sweet, D. H. (1989). Outplacement. In W. Cascio (Ed.), *Human resource planning, employment and placement.* Washington, DC: Bureau of National Affairs.

52. Newman, L. (1988). Goodbye is not enough. *Personnel Administrator, 33*(2), 84–86.

53. Naumann, S. E., Bennett, N., Bies, R. J., and Martin, C. L. (1999). Laid off, but still loyal: The influence of perceived justice and organizational support. *International Journal of Conflict Management, 9,* 356–368.

54. Sweet, D. H. (1989). Outplacement. In W. Cascio (Ed.), *Human resource planning, employment and placement.* Washington, DC: Bureau of National Affairs.

55. Gibson, V. M. (1991). The ins and outs of outplacement. *Management Review, 80*(10), 59–61.

56. Burdett, J. O. (1988). Easing the way out. *Personnel Administrator, 33*(6), 157–166.

57. Crofts, P. (1991). Helping people face up to redundancy. *Personnel Management, 23*(12), 24–27.

58. Rudolph, B. (1986, December 8). The sun also sets. *BusinessWeek,* 60–61.

Chapter 7

1. Carroll, S. J., and Schneir, C. E. (1982). *Performance appraisal and review systems: The identification, measurement, and development of performance in organizations.* Glenview, IL: Scott, Foresman.

2. Banks, C. G., and Roberson, L. (1985). Performance appraisers as test developers. *Academy of Management Review, 10,* 128–142.

3. Cleveland, J. N., Murphy, K. R., and Williams, R. E. (1989). Multiple uses of performance appraisals: Prevalence and correlates. *Journal of Applied Psychology, 74,* 130–135.

4. Institute of Management and Administration (2005). Getting to the most productive results. *HRFocus, 82,* 6.

5. Osterman, R. (2005, February 21). Repeat performance: A growing number of companies think they can improve worker evaluations by doing more of them. *Sacramento Bee,* D1.

6. *Ibid.*

7. Yemm, G. (2005). Getting the most from appraisals—from both sides of the desk. *Management Services, 49,* 36.

8. Mayo, A. (2005, February). Goodbye appraisals? *Training Journal,* 64.

9. Scholtes, P. R. (1999). Review of performance appraisal: State of the art in practice. *Personnel Psychology, 52,* 177–181.

10. Gray, G. (2002). Performance appraisals don't work. *Industrial Management, 44,* 15.

11. Deming, W. E. (1986). *Out of the crisis.* Cambridge, MA: Center for Advanced Engineering Study, Massachusetts Institute of Technology.

12. Heffes, E. M. (2002). Measure like you mean it: Q&A with Michael Hammer. *Financial Executive, 18,* 46(3).

13. Gillespie, G. (2002). Do employees make the grade? *Health Data Management, 10,* 60.

14. Rath, T. (2005). Good competencies, bad competencies: Does your organization's program pass the test? *Gallup Management Journal,* http://gmj.gallup.com.

15. Nunnally, J. C. (1978). *Psychometric theory.* New York: McGraw-Hill.

16. Bernardin, H. J., and Beatty, R. W. (1984). *Performance appraisal: Assessing human behavior at work.* Boston, MA: Kent; Latham, G. P., and Wexley, K. N. (1981). *Increasing productivity through performance appraisal.* Reading, MA: Addison-Wesley; Miner, J. B. (1988). Development and application of the rated ranking technique in performance appraisal. *Journal of Occupational Psychology, 6,* 291–305.

17. Miner, J. B. (1988). Development and application of the rated ranking technique in performance appraisal. *Journal of Occupational Psychology, 6,* 291–305.

18. Bernardin, H. J., Kane, J. S., Ross, S., Spina, J. D., and Johnson, D. L. (1995). Performance appraisal design, development, and implementation. In G. R. Ferris, S. D. Rosen, and D. T. Barnum (Eds.), *Handbook of human resources management.* Cambridge, MA: Blackwell.

19. Cardy, R. L., and Sutton, C. L. (1993). *Accounting for halo-accuracy paradox: Individual differences.* Paper presented at the Annual Conference of the Society for Industrial and Organizational Psychology, 1993, San Francisco.

20. Bernardin, H. J., and Beatty, R. W. (1984). *Performance appraisal: Assessing human behavior at work.* Boston, MA: Kent.

21. *Ibid.*

22. Latham, G. P., and Wexley, K. N. (1981). *Increasing productivity through performance appraisal.* Reading, MA: Addison-Wesley.

23. Blood, M. R. (1973). Spin-offs from behavioral expectation scale procedures. *Journal of Applied Psychology, 59,* 513–515.

24. Harris, C. (1988). A comparison of employee attitudes toward two performance appraisal systems. *Public Personnel Management, 17,* 443–456.

25. Drucker, P. F. (1954). *The practice of management.* New York: Harper.

26. Gillespie, G. (2002). Do employees make the grade? *Health Data Management, 10,* 60.

27. Cardy, R. L., and Krzystofiak, F. J. (1991). Interfacing high technology operations with blue collar workers: Selection and appraisal in a computerized manufacturing setting. *Journal of High Technology Management Research, 2,* 193–210.

28. Bernardin, H. J., and Beatty, R. W. (1984). *Performance appraisal: Assessing human behavior at work.* Boston, MA: Kent.

29. See, for example, Smith, R. W. (1992, Fall). Moving managers to a higher plane of performance. *Business Forum, 17,* 5–6.

30. Cardy, R. L., and Dobbins, G. H. (1994a). *Performance appraisal: Alternative perspectives.* Cincinnati, OH: South-Western.

31. Borman, W. C. (1979). Individual difference correlates of rating accuracy using behavior scales. *Applied Psychological Measurement, 3,* 103–115.

32. Cardy, R. L., and Kehoe, J. F. (1984). Rater selective attention ability and appraisal effectiveness: The effect of a cognitive style on the accuracy of differentiation among ratees. *Journal of Applied Psychology, 69,* 589–594.

33. Cardy, R. L., and Dobbins, G. H. (1994a). *Performance appraisal: Alternative perspectives.* Cincinnati, OH: South-Western.

34. Thorndike, E. L. (1920). A constant error in psychological ratings. *Journal of Applied Psychology, 4,* 25–29.

35. Cooper, W. H. (1981). Ubiquitous halo. *Psychological Bulletin, 90,* 218–244.

36. Haunstein, N. M. H. (1998). Training raters to increase the accuracy of appraisals and the usefulness of feedback. In J. W. Smither (Ed). *Performance appraisal: State of the art in practice.* San Francisco: Jossey-Bass.

37. Rosen, D. I. (1992, November). Appraisals can make—or break—your court case. *Personnel Journal,* 113–116.

38. Edwards, M. R., Wolfe, M. E., and Sproull, J. R. (1983). Improving comparability in performance appraisal. *Business Horizons, 26,* 75–83.

39. Bernardin, H. J., and Buckley, M. R. (1981). Strategies in rater training. *Academy of Management Review, 6,* 205–212.

40. Institute of Management and Administration (2005). Getting to the most productive results. *HRFocus, 82,* 6.

41. Bernardin, H. J., and Pence, E. C. (1980). Rater training: Creating new response sets and decreasing accuracy. *Journal of Applied Psychology, 65,* 60–66; Cardy, R. L., and Keefe, T. J. (1994). Observational purpose and valuative articulation in frame-of-reference training: The effects of alternative processing models on rating accuracy. *Organizational Behavior and Human Decision Processes, 57,* 338–357.

42. Cardy, R. L., and Dobbins, G. H. (1994b). Performance appraisal: The influence of liking on cognition. *Advances in Managerial Cognition and Organizational Information Processing, 5,* 115–140.

43. Cardy, R. L., and Dobbins, G. H. (1994a). *Performance appraisal: Alternative perspectives.* Cincinnati, OH: South-Western.

44. Cardy, R. L., and Dobbins, G. H. (1986). Affect and appraisal: Liking as an integral dimension in evaluating performance. *Journal of Applied Psychology, 71,* 672–678.

45. Cardy, R. L., and Dobbins, G. H. (1994a). *Performance appraisal: Alternative perspectives.* Cincinnati, OH: South-Western.

46. Bernardin, H. J., and Walter, C. S. (1977). Effects of rater training and diary keeping on psychometric error in ratings. *Journal of Applied Psychology, 62,* 64–69; Flanagan, J. C. (1954). The critical incident technique. *Psychological Bulletin, 51,* 327–358.

47. Painter, C. N. (1999). Ten steps for improved appraisals. *Supervision, 60,* 11–13.

48. Flanagan, J. C., and Burns, R. K. (1955, September–October). The employee performance record: A new appraisal and development tool. *Harvard Business Review,* 95–102.

49. Bookman, R. (1999). Tools for cultivating constructive feedback. *Association Management, 51,* 73–79.

50. Jacobs, H. (1993, October). The rating game. *Small Business Reports,* 21–25.

51. Ferris, G. R., and Judge, T. A. (1991). Personnel/human resources management: A political influence perspective. *Journal of Management, 17,* 1–42.

52. Murphy, K. R., and Cleveland, J. N. (1991). *Performance appraisal: An organizational perspective.* Boston: Allyn & Bacon.

53. Adapted from C. O. Longenecker, H. P. Sims, Jr., and D. A. Gioia. Behind the mask: The politics of employee appraisal. Copyright © by the Academy of Management. Reprinted by permission of the publisher. *Academy of Management Executive, 1*(3), August 1987, 183–193.

54. Ferris, G. R., and Judge, T. A. (1991). Personnel/human resources management: A political influence perspective. *Journal of Management, 17,* 1–42; Ferris, G. R., Judge, T. A., Rowland, K. M., and Fitzgibbons, D. E. (1993). Subordinate influence and the performance evaluation process: Test of a model. *Organizational Behavior and Human Decision Processes, 58,* 101–135.

55. Kozlowski, S. W., Chao, G. T., and Morrison, R. F. (1998). Games raters play: Politics, strategies, and impression management in performance appraisal. In J. W. Smither (Ed.), *Performance appraisal: State of the art in practice.* San Francisco: Jossey-Bass.

56. Banks, C. G., and Roberson, L. (1985). Performance appraisers as test developers. *Academy of Management Review, 10,* 128–142.

57. Cardy, R. L., and Dobbins, G. H. (1994a). *Performance appraisal: Alternative perspectives.* Cincinnati, OH: South-Western.

58. *Ibid.*

59. Poon, J. M. L. (2004). Effects of performance appraisal politics on job satisfaction and turnover intention. *Personnel Review, 33,* 3.

60. Reilly, R. R., and McGourty, J. (1998). Performance appraisal in team settings. In J. W. Smither (Ed.), *Performance appraisal: State of the art in practice.* San Francisco: Jossey-Bass.

61. Dominick, P. G., Reilly, R. R., and McGourty, J. W. (1997). The effects of peer feedback on team member behavior. *Group and Organization Management, 22,* 508–520.

62. Reilly, R. R., and McGourty, J. (1998). Performance appraisal in team settings. In J. W. Smither (Ed.), *Performance appraisal: State of the art in practice.* San Francisco: Jossey-Bass.

63. Denton, K. D. (2001). Better decisions with less information. *Industrial Management, 43,* 21.

64. Cardy, R. L., and Stewart, G. L. (1997). Quality and teams: Implications for HRM theory and research. In D.B. Fedor (Ed.), *Advances in the management of organization quality,* Vol. 2, Greenwich, CT: JAI Press.

65. *Ibid.*

66. Barrett, G. V., and Kernan, M. C. (1987). Performance appraisal and terminations: A review of court decisions since *Brito v. Zia* with implications for personnel practices. *Personnel Psychology, 40,* 489–503.

67. Werner, J. M., and Bolino, M. C. (1997). Explaining U.S. courts of appeals decisions involving performance appraisal: Accuracy, fairness, and validation. *Personnel Psychology, 50,* 1–24.

68. Meyer, H. H., Kay, E., and French, J. R. P., Jr. (1965, March). Split roles in performance appraisal. *Harvard Business Review,* 9–10.

69. Prince, J. B., and Lawler, E. E. (1986). Does salary discussion hurt the development appraisal? *Organizational Behavior and Human Decision Processes, 37,* 357–375.

70. *Report on Salary Surveys.* (2002). Annual reviews are standard at most companies. April Newsletter of the Institute of Management and Administration.

71. Bernardin, H. J., and Beatty, R. W. (1984). *Performance appraisal: Assessing human behavior at work.* Boston, MA: Kent.

72. Dobbins, G. H., Cardy, R. L., and Carson, K. P. (1991). Perspectives on human resource management: A contrast of person and system approaches. In G. R. Ferris and K. M. Rowland (Eds.), *Research in personnel and human resources management,* Vol. 9. Greenwich, CT: JAI Press; Ilgen, D. R., Fisher, C. D., and Taylor, S. M. (1979). Consequences of individual feedback on behavior in organizations. *Journal of Applied Psychology, 64,* 347–371.

73. Carson, K. P., Cardy, R. L., and Dobbins, G. H. (1991). Performance appraisal as effective management or deadly management disease: Two initial empirical investigations. *Group and Organization Studies, 16,* 143–159.

74. Kelly, H. H. (1973). The processes of causal attribution. *American Psychologist, 28,* 107–128.

75. Cascio, W. F. (1998). *Applied psychology in human resource management* (5th ed.). Upper Saddle River, NJ: Prentice Hall.

76. Blumberg, M., and Pringle, C. D. (1982). The missing opportunity in organizational research: Some implications for a theory of work performance. *Academy of Management Review, 7,* 560–569; Carson, K. P., Cardy, R. L., and Dobbins, G. H. (1991). Performance appraisal as effective management or deadly management disease: Two initial empirical investigations. *Group and Organization Studies, 16,* 143–159; Schermerhorn, J. R., Jr., Gardner, W. L., and Martin, T. N. (1990). Management dialogues: Turning on the marginal performers. *Organizational Dynamics, 18,* 47–59.

77. Blumberg, M., and Pringle, C. D. (1982). The missing opportunity in organizational research: Some implications for a theory of work performance. *Academy of Management Review, 7, 560–569;* Rummler, G. A. (1972). Human performance problems and their solutions. *Human Resource Management, 19,* 2–10.

78. Bernardin, H. J., Hagan, C. M., Kane, J. S., and Villanova, P. (1998). Effective performance management: A focus on precision customers, and situational constraints. In J. W. Smither (Ed.), *Performance appraisal: State of the art in practice.* San Francisco: Jossey-Bass.

79. Rummler, G. A. (1972). Human performance problems and their solutions. *Human Resource Management, 19,* 2–10.

80. Schermerhorn, J. R., Jr., Gardner, W. L., and Martin, T. N. (1990). Management dialogues: Turning on the marginal performers. *Organizational Dynamics, 18,* 47–59.

81. Cardy, R. L. (1997). Process and outcomes: A performance-management paradox? *News: Human Resources Division, 21,* 12–14.

Chapter 8

1. Fitzgerald, W. (1992). Training versus development. *Training & Development, 46,* 81–84.

2. Bartz, D. E., Schwandt, D. R., and Hillman, L. W. (1989). Differences between "T" and "D." *Personnel Administrator, 34,* 164–170.

3. Sullivan, J. (1998, July 20). Why training doesn't work . . . and what operators better do about it. *Nation's Restaurant News, 32,* 54, 138.

4. Bernardin, H. J., Hagan, C. M., Kane, J. S., and Villanova, P. (1998). Effective performance management: A focus on precision, customers, and situational constraints. In J. W. Smither (Ed.), *Performance appraisal: State of the art in practice.* San Francisco: Jossey-Bass. Evans, S. (2005, May). Stopping the training drain. *Training Journal,* 36–39.

5. Calvacca, L. (1999). The value of employee training. *Folio: The Magazine for Magazine Management, 27,* 186–187.

6. *Ibid.*

7. Tyler, K. (2005). Do the right thing. *HR Magazine, 50,* 2.

8. Carlson, L. (2005, February 1). Spending on employee training remains stable. *Employee Benefit News.*

9. *HR Focus.* (2002, May). Training investments climb despite recession and layoffs. *Newsletter of the Institute of Management and Administration.*

10. *Graphic Arts Monthly.* (2005, February). Education and training linked to profitability, 59.

11. Galligano, M. L. (2002, April 12). Employer's failure to train managers is "extraordinary mistake." Warrants double damages in age discrimination case. *Monday Business Briefing,* Report of Mondag Ltd.

12. Tyler, K. (2005). Do the right thing. *HR Magazine, 50,* 2.

13. American Society for Training and Development (2004). State of the industry report. www.astd.org.

14. Salopek (2002). Think of the economic turndown as a pit stop: The race will still run. *T&D, 56,* 68–71.

15. Galvin, T. (2002). The 2002 Training Top 100. *Training, 39,* 20(6).

16. Earnest, L. (2005, February 23). Retailers suit up for the latest tailored book. *Los Angeles Times,* C-1.

17. Pfeffer, J. (1999). Seven practices of successful organizations: Part 2. *Health Forum Journal, 42,* 55–57.

18. Cook, S. (2005, February). Learning needs analysis part 2: Linking learning needs analysis to business. *Training Journal,* 50.

19. Goldstein, I. L. (1986). *Training in organizations: Needs assessment, development, and evaluation* (2nd ed.). Monterey, CA: Brooks-Cole.

20. Mager, R. F., and Pipe, P. (1984). *Analyzing performance problems: Or, you really oughta wanna.* Belmont, CA: Lake and Rummler, 1972.

21. Nowack, K. M. (1991). A true training needs analysis. *Training & Development, 45,* 69–73; Phillips, J. J. (1983, May). Training programs: A results-oriented model for managing the development of human resources. *Personnel,* 11–18.

22. Galvin, T. (2002). The 2002 Training Top 100. *Training, 39,* 20(6).

23. Shalo, S. (2005, May). What does it take to be a global leader in training? *Pharmaceutical Executive,* 42–47.

24. Nowack, K. M. (1991). A true training needs analysis. *Training & Development, 45,* 69–73; Phillips, J. J. (1983, May). Training programs: A results-oriented model for managing the development of human resources. *Personnel,* 11–18.

25. *Wood Technology.* (1999). Industry asked to help create skills standards, *126,* 16.

26. *Ibid.*

27. Gupta, U. (1996, January 3). TV seminars and CD-ROMs train workers. *Wall Street Journal,* B-1, B-8.

28. Leibs, S. (2002). Class struggle: E-learning technology may be poised to go mainstream. *CFO: The Magazine for Senior Executives, 18,* 31(2).

29. Brown, J., Eager, R., and Lawrence, P. (2005). BP refines leadership. *Training & Development, 59,* 3.

30. Bartholomew, D. (2005). Taking the e-train. *Industry Week, 254,* 34–37.

31. Brown, M. V., and Galli, A. L. (2005). E-learning goes mainstream. *Power, 149,* 30.

32. Raisglid, M. (2004, November). Shell's speedy remedy. *Training & Development, 58,* 59–61.

33. Carlson, L. (2005, February 1). Spending on employee training remains stable. *Employee Benefit News,*

34. For more on CD-ROM training, see Murphy, K. (1996, May 6). Pitfalls vs. promise in training by CD-ROM. *New York Times,* D-3.

35. Agry, B. W. (1999). Class is out. *US Banker, 109,* 52–55.

36. Major, M. (2002). E-learning becomes essential: New and enhanced computer-based training programs have become a high priority for aggressive retailers. *Progressive Grocer, 81,* 35(2).

37. Bartholomew, D. (2005). Taking the e-train. *Industry Week, 254,* 34–37.

38. Business Wire (2005, June 21). FATS, Inc. and CMT Solutions launch regional training center for military, law enforcement, and security forces.

39. Business Wire (2005, January 12). Immersion medical upgrades CathSim Accutouch system.

40. Geber, B. (1990). Simulating reality. *Training, 27,* 41–46.

41. Kaplan, A. (2005, April 1). Virtually possible: Treating and preventing psychiatric wounds of war. *Psychiatric Times,* 1.

42. *Ibid.*

43. Haitsuka, A. (1997, July 31). Virtual-reality training idea puts Mesa firm in demand. *Arizona Republic,* E-1.

44. Orenstein, D. (1999). Virtual reality saves on training. *Computerworld, 33,* 44.

45. *Heart Disease Weekly.* (2005, January 23). Medical training: Virtual reality training is wave of the future for cardiovascular medicine, 117.

46. Agry, B. W. (1999). Class is out. *US Banker, 109,* 52–55.

47. Estabrooke, R. M., and Foy, N. F. (1992). Answering the call of "tailored training." *Training, 29,* 85–88.

48. Patterson, P. A. (1991). Job aids: Quick and effective training. *Personnel, 68,* 13.

49. Overman, S. (1993, October). Retraining our work force. *HRMagazine,* 40–44.

50. Simmons, D. L. (1995). Retraining dislocated workers in the community college: Identifying factors for persistence. *Community College Review, 23,* 47–58.

51. Nilson, C. (1990). How to use peer training. *Supervisory Management, 35,* 8.

52. Messmer, M. (1992). Cross-discipline training: A strategic method to do more with less. *Management Review, 81,* 26–28.

53. Fyock, C. D. (1991). Teaching older workers new tricks. *Training & Development, 45,* 21–24.

54. Purdum, T. (2005, May). Teaming, take 2. *Industry Week,* 41.

55. *Ibid.*

56. *Ibid.*

57. Burns, G. (1995). The secrets of team facilitation. *Training & Development, 49,* 46–52.

58. Phillips, S. N. (1996). Team training puts fizz in Coke plant's future. *Personnel Journal, 75,* 87–92.

59. Goldstein, I. L. (1993). *Training in organizations* (3rd ed.). Pacific Grove, CA: Brooks-Cole.

60. Amer, S. (2005). Bam! Teambuilding exercises heat up as groups head into the kitchen. *Successful Meetings, 54,* 52.

61. Wise, R. (1991). The boom in creativity training. *Across the Board, 28,* 38–42.

62. Solomon, C. M. (1990). Creativity training. *Personnel Journal, 69,* 65–71.

63. Hequet, M. (1992, February). Creativity training gets creative. *Training,* 41–46.

64. Shane, C. (1999). The fine arts of corporate management. *Across the Board, 36,* 7–8.

65. Birdi, K. S. (2005). No idea? Evaluating the effectiveness of creativity training. *Journal of European Industrial Training, 29,* 102–112.

66. Koretz, G. (1996, May 20). A crash course in the 3R's? *BusinessWeek,* 26; Educational Testing Service (1990). *From school to work.* Princeton, NJ: Educational Testing Service.

67. *Training & Development.* (2005, May). Good writing is good business. *59,* 22.

68. Mingail, S. (2004, November 22). Tackling workplace literacy is a no-brainer. *Canadian HR Reporter, 17,* G3–G4.

69. Hays, S. (1999). Basic skills training 101. *Workforce, 78,* 76–82.

70. Anfuso, D. (1998). I would like to go as far as I can go. *Workforce, 77,* 112.

71. Lund, L., and McGuire, E. P. (1990). *Literacy in the work force.* New York: The Conference Board.

72. Gillian, F. (1999). White males see diversity's other side. *Workforce, 78,* 52–55.

73. Gordon, J. (2005). Diversity as a business driver. *Training, 42,* 24–29.

74. Prince, C. J. (2005). Doing diversity. *Chief Executive, 207,* 46–49.

75. Bensimon, H. F. (1994). Crisis and disaster management: Violence in the workplace. *Training & Development, 48,* 27–32.

76. Elan, E. (2005). Industry vets, educators say training an answer to poor-service problem. *Nation's Restaurant News, 39,* 6–7.

77. Institute of Management and Administration. (2005, March). Employers spend the most on customer service training. *Managing Training & Development, 5,* 8.

78. Berta, D. (2002). Operators strive to include all in the family: Claim progress toward diversity amid new rash of bias suits. *Nation's Restaurant News, 36,* 1(4).

79. Kirkpatrick, D. (1998). Evaluating training programs. Berrett-Koehler Publishers: San Francisco.

80. Densford, L. E. (1999, February). Motorola University: The next 20 years. *Corporate University Review.*

81. Edwards, M. R. (1999, February). Measurement as a catalyst for learning. *HR Focus,* S9–S10.

82. Wanous, J. P., Reichers, A. E., and Matik, S. D. (1984). Organizational socialization and group development: Toward an integrative perspective. *Academy of Management Review, 9,* 670–683.

83. Breaugh, J. A. (1983). Realistic job previews: A critical appraisal and future research directions. *Academy of Management Review, 8,* 612–623.

84. Philips, J. M. (1998). Effects of realistic job previews on multiple organizational outcomes: A meta-analysis. *Academy of Management Journal, 41,* 673–690.

85. Bragg, A. (1989, September). Is a mentor program in your future? *Sales & Marketing Management,* 54–63.

86. Little, P. J. (1998 July/August). Selection of the fittest. *Management Review,* 43–47.

87. Winkler, K., and Janger, I. (1998). You're hired! *Across the Board, 35,* 16–23.

88. *Ibid.*

Chapter 9

1. Leibowitz, Z. B. (1987). Designing career development systems: Principles and practices. *Human Resource Planning, 10,* 195–207.

2. Gutteridge, T. G., Leibowitz, Z. B., and Shore, J. E. (1993). *Organizational career development: Benchmarks for building a world-class workforce.* San Francisco: Jossey-Bass; London, M., Larsen, H. H., and Thisted, L. N. (1999). Relationships between feedback and self-development. *Group and Organization Management, 24,* 5–27.

3. Murphy, D. (1999, July 18). New attitude for employees: "Emergent" workers think job, not career. *Arizona Republic,* AZ-11.

4. Taylor, M. A., and Walsh, K. (2005). Retaining management talent: What hospitality professionals want from their jobs. Report

produced by the Center for Hospitality Research at Cornell University, Ithaca, NY.

5. Weber, P. F. (1998). Getting a grip on employee growth. *Training & Development, 53,* 87–91.

6. Morgan, D. C. (1977). Career development programs. *Personnel, 54,* 23–27.

7. Gutteridge, T., and Otte, F. (1983). Organizational career development: What's going on out there? *Training & Development, 37,* 22–26; Hall, D. T. (1986). An overview of current career development, theory, research, and practice. In D. T. Hall et al. (Eds.), *Career development in organizations,* 1–20, San Francisco: Jossey-Bass; Leibowitz, Z. B., and Schlossberg, N. K. (1981). Designing career development programs in organizations: A systems approach. In D. H. Montross and C. J. Shinkman (Eds.), *Career development in the 1980s,* 277–291, Springfield, IL: Charles C Thomas.

8. Russell, J. E. A. (1991). Career development interventions in organizations. *Journal of Vocational Behavior, 38,* 237–287.

9. Koonce, R. (1991, January–February). Management development: An investment in people. *Credit Magazine,* 16–19.

10. Steele, B., Bratkovich, J. R., and Rollins, T. (1990). Implementing strategic redirection through the career management system. *Human Resource Planning, 13,* 241–263.

11. Feldman, D. C., and Weitz, B. A. (1991). From the invisible hand to the gladhand: Understanding a careerist orientation to work. *Human Resource Management, 30,* 237–257.

12. Aryee, S., Wyatt, T., and Stone, R. (1996). Early career outcomes of graduate employees: The effect of mentoring and ingratiation. *Journal of Management Studies, 33,* 95–118.

13. Kalish, B. B. (1992, March). Dismantling the glass ceiling. *Management Review, 64;* Hawkins, B. (1991, September 8). Career-limiting bias found at low job levels. *Los Angeles Times Magazine,* 33.

14. Galvin, K. (1999, January 7). Texaco settlement with female staff to cost $3 million. *Arizona Republic,* D-1.

15. Deogun, N. (1999, May 20). Coca-Cola report addressed race in '95. *Wall Street Journal,* Brussels, A-5.

16. Mazier, E. E. (2002). Insurance women still hit "glass ceiling." *National Underwriter Property & Casualty, 106,* 23.

17. *BusinessWeek.* (2005, February 25). Engendering female entrepreneurs. *Business week online.*

18. Jones, D. (1999, July 20). What glass ceiling? *USA Today,* B-1, B-2.

19. Applebaum, S. (2002). A real operator. *Multichannel News, 23,* 8.

20. Kelly, J. (2002). Does health care still have a glass ceiling? *H & HN, 76,* 30.

21. Segal, J. A. (2005). Shatter the glass ceiling, dodge the shards. *HR Magazine, 50,* 121–126.

22. Kelly, J. (2002). Does health care still have a glass ceiling? *H & HN, 76,* 30.

23. Barnett, R. C., and Rivers, C. (1999, May 10). Family values go to work. *Washington Post,* A-23.

24. Bourne, K. (1992). Companies offer career management for couples. *Journal of Compensation and Benefits, 7,* 32–36.

25. *Ibid.*

26. Harvey, M., and Wiese, D. (1998). Global dual-career couple mentoring: A phase model approach. *Human Resource Planning, 21,* 33–48.

27. Frazee, V. (1999). Expert help for dual-career spouses. *Workforce, 4,* 18–20.

28. Bures, A. L., Henderson, D., Mayfield, J., Mayfield, M., and Worley, J. (1995). The effects of spousal support and gender on workers' stress and job satisfaction: A cross national investigation of dual career couples. *Journal of Applied Business Research, 12,* 52–58.

29. Barnett, R. C., and Rivers, C. (1999, May 10). Family values go to work. *Washington Post,* A-23.

30. Gordon, J. (1998). The new paternalism. *Forbes, 162,* 68–70.

31. Haskell, J. R. (1993, February). Getting employees to take charge of their careers. *Training & Development,* 51–54.

32. Anastasi, A. (1976). *Psychological testing* (4th ed.). New York: Macmillan.

33. Burn, A. (1998, November/December). Testing times. *British Journal of Administrative Management,* 16–17.

34. Fleischer, J. (2005). Lessons for leaders. *Call Center Magazine, 18,* 8–10.

35. Scarpello, V. G., and Ledvinka, J. (1988). *Personnel/human resource management: Environment and functions.* Boston: PWS-Kent; and Russell, 1991.

36. Mayo, A. (2004, July). One more time—how do we manage performance? *Training Journal,* 80.

37. Morgan, M. A., Hall, D. T., and Martier, A. (1979). Career development strategies in industry—Where are we and where should we be? *Personnel, 56,* 13–30.

38. Villeneure, K. (1999). Thought about succession? You should. *Discount Store News, 38,* 16.

39. Wailgum, T. (2005, May 1). Nothing succeeds like succession. *CIO Magazine.*

40. Judge, T. A., Cable, D. M., Boudreau, J. W., and Bretz, R. D. (1995). An empirical investigation of the predictors of executive career success. *Personnel Psychology, 48,* 485–519.

41. Baehr, M. E., and Orban, J. A. (1989). The role of intellectual abilities and personality characteristics in determining success in higher-level positions. *Journal of Vocational Behavior, 35,* 270–287.

42. Seibert, S. E., and Kraimer, M. L. (1999). The five-factor model of personality and its relationship with career success. Paper presented at the Annual Meeting of the Academy of Management, Chicago.

43. Weber, P. F. (1998). Getting a grip on employee growth. *Training & Development, 53,* 87–91.

44. Russell, J. E. A. (1991). Career development interventions in organizations. *Journal of Vocational Behavior, 38,* 237–287.

45. Gutteridge, T. (1986). Organizational career development systems: The state of the practice. In D. T. Hall et al., *Career development in organizations,* 50–94. San Francisco: Jossey-Bass.

46. *Ibid.*

47. Russell, J. E. A. (1991). Career development interventions in organizations. *Journal of Vocational Behavior, 38,* 237–287.

48. Noe, R. A. (1988). An investigation of the determinants of successful assigned mentoring relationships. *Personnel Psychology, 41,* 457–479.

49. Hill, S. K., and Bahniuk, M. H. (1998). Promoting career success through mentoring. *Review of Business, 19,* 4–7.

50. Starcevich, M., and Friend, F. (1999, July). Effective mentoring relationships from the mentee's perspective. *Workforce,* Extra Supplement, 2–3.

51. Institute of Management & Administration (2005 March). How two companies make mentoring matter, from the bottom to the top. *Managing Training & Development Newsletter, 5,* 2.

52. Jenkins, M. (2005). Why you need a mentor. *Black Enterprise, 35,* 80–86.

53. Barbian, J. (2002). The road best traveled. *Training, 39,* 38(4).

54. Dansky, K. H. (1996). The effect of group mentoring on career outcomes. *Group & Organization Management, 21,* 5–21.

55. Cramm, S. (2005). A team starts with two: The best way to develop employees is one-on-one coaching, yet too few executives seem interested in making the effort. *CIO, 18,* 1.

56. Stephenson, S. (2002). And wind up better off: Join the team! *Food Service Director, 15,* 80.

57. Morrisey, G. L. (1992, November). Your personal mission statement: A foundation for your future. *Training & Development,* 71–74.

58. Matejka, K., and Dunsing, R. (1993). Enhancing your advancement in the 1990s. *Management Decision, 31,* 52–54.

Chapter 10

1. Milkovich, G. T., and Newman, J. M. (2005). *Compensation* (6th ed.). Homewood, IL: McGraw-Hill/Irwin; Freudenheim, M. (2005, March 23). Fewer employers totally cover health premiums. *New York Times*, A-1; Giancola, F. (2005, February). Need a new system for evaluating management positions? *Workspan*, 29–32; Hovy, M. (2005, February). Future global remuneration strategies. *Workspan*, 35–39.

2. Brenan, J. (1999). Group legal insurance: An effective recruitment and retaining tool. *Compensation and Benefits Review, 31*(3), 46–53; *HR Focus* (2002, February); Hovy, M. (2005, February). Future global remuneration strategies. *Workspan*, 35–39; Masternak, R., and Camuso, M. A. (2005, First Quarter). Gainsharing and six sigma perfect together. *Worldatwork*, 42–49.

3. Gómez-Mejía, L. R., and Balkin, D. B. (1992a). The determinants of faculty pay: An agency theory perspective. *Academy of Management Journal, 35*(5), 921–955; Lee, J. (2002, April). Finding the sweet spots: Optimal executive compensation. *Workspan*, 40–46; Zingheim, P. K., and Schuster, J. R. (2005, First Quarter). Revisiting effective incentive design. *Worldatwork Journal*, 50–58.

4. *Workspan*. (2005, March). Employer generous with benefits despite rising costs, 70.

5. *Newsline*. (2005, February 22). Biggest barrier to retirement saving may be lack of motivation. www.worldatwork.com; *Newsline*. (2005, March 1). Majority of U.S. workers greatly underestimate how much their employer contributes to their medical insurance. www.worldatwork.com.

6. Hawkins, L. (2005, March 21). GM plans to cut salaried staff. *Wall Street Journal*, A-1.

7. Hakim, D. (2005, March 17). GM sees a loss near 1 billion; stock falls 14 percent. *New York Times*, A-1.

8. *Newsline*. (2005, January 3). Talent management among top five priorities in 2005. www.worldatwork.com.

9. Melcher, R. A., Cohn, L., and Symonds, W. C. (1999, July 19). You can go home again—with a raise. *BusinessWeek*, 44–45; Gorman, C. (1999, February 8). Black days for doctors. *Time*, 53; *HR Focus a.* (2002); Richlet, M. (2005, March 9). Changing rules of the game. *New York Times*, C-1; Longnecker, B., and Crawford, L. (2005, March). A new day, a new definition. *Workspan*, 44–48.

10. Delves, D. (1999). Practical lessons for designing an economic value incentive plan. *Compensation and Benefits Review, 31*(2), 61–70; Ray, H. H., and Altmansberger, H. N. (1999). Introducing goal sharing in a public sector organization. *Compensation and Benefits Review, 31*(3), 40–45; Jaross, J., Byrnes, R., and Mercer, W. (2002, April). Mastering the share plan circus. *Workspan*, 55–64; Abernathy, W. B. (2005, First Quarter). Behavior systems technology: Reengineering closed behavior systems. *Worldatwork Journal*, 71–76; Bradley, G. (2005, First Quarter). Procter & Gamble's balanced approach to long-term incentives. *Worldatwork Journal*, 6–14.

11. Heneman, R. L., and Dixon, K. E. (2001, November–December). Reward and organizational systems alignment: An expert system. *Compensation and Benefits Review*, 18–27; Ledeler, J., and Weinberg, L. R. (1999). Setting executive compensation: Does the industry you are in really matter? *Compensation and Benefits Review, 31*(1), 13–24; Bloom, M. (1999). The art and context of the deal: A balanced view of executive incentives. *Compensation and Benefits Review, 31*(1), 25–31; Bout, A. (2005, April). The changing landscape of equity compensation. *Workspan*, 16–21; Cairns, A. (2005, February 22). Next Health South CEO . . . Richard Scrushy? *Wall Street Journal*, C-1; Hymowitz, C. (2005, March 8). When meeting targets become the strategy, CEO is on wrong path. *Wall Street Journal*, B-1.

12. Milkovich, G. T., and Newman, J. M. (2005). *Compensation* (6th ed.). Homewood, IL: McGraw-Hill/Irwin.

13. Zingheim, P. K., and Schuster, J. (2001, November–December). Creating a powerful customized workplace reward brand. *Compensation and Benefits Review, 33*(6), 30–34; Wolf, M. G. (2000). Compensation: An overview. In Berger, L. A., and Berger, D. R. (Eds.), *The compensation handbook* (4th ed.). New York: McGraw-Hill.

14. Hovy, M. (2005, February). Future global remuneration strategies. *Workspan*, 35–39.

15. Gómez-Mejía, L. R., and Balkin, D. B. (1992a). The determinants of faculty pay: An agency theory perspective. *Academy of Management Journal, 35*(5), 921–955; Werner, S., Tosi, H., & Gomez-Mejia, L.R. (2005, April). Ownership structure and employee pay. *Strategic Management Journal*, 35–44.

16. Balkin, D. B., and Gómez-Mejía, L. R. (2000). Is CEO pay related to innovation in high-technology firms? *Academy of Management Journal, 43*(6), 30–41.

17. Aeppel, T. (2005, February 22). Economists gain star power. *Wall Street Journal*, A-2.

18. Gómez-Mejía, L. R., and Welbourne, T. M. (1988). Compensation strategy: An overview and future steps. *Human Resource Planning, 11*(3), 173–189; Heneman, R. L., and Dixon, K. E. (2001, November–December). Reward and organizational systems alignment: An expert system. *Compensation and Benefits Review*, 18–27; Fisher, A. (2004, November 1). A strategic way to calculate pay. *Fortune*, 62; *Workspan*. (2005, February). Poll results: How often does your organization adjust its compensation structure using market data? 6.

19. Dunham, K. J. (2002, February 5). The jungle: Focus on recruitment, pay, and getting ahead. *Wall Street Journal*, B-8; O'Neal, S. (2005, Jan.). Total rewards and the future of work. *Workspan*, 19–25.

20. *Arizona Republic*. (2002, February 19). Retention bonuses under fire, D-15; O'Neal, S. (2005, Jan.). Total rewards and the future of work. *Workspan*, 19–25.

21. Scott, D., McMullen, T. D., and Nolan, J. (2005, First Quarter). Taking control of your counteroffer environment. *Worldatwork Journal*, 25–30.

22. *WorldWork* (2006). Cash bonuses: Four ways to attract, retain and motivate employees. Scottsdale, Az: WorldatWork Association. Barton, G. M. (2006). Recognition at work: Crafting a value added rewards program. Scottsdale, Az: WorldatWork Association.

23. Desmond, E. W. (1996, April 22). The failed miracle. *Time*, 61–64; Longnecker, B. M., Petersen, B., and Hitt, R. (1999). Long-term incentives: How private companies can compete with public companies. *Compensation and Benefits Review, 31*(1), 44–53; Bradley, G. (2005, First Quarter). Procter & Gamble's balanced approach to long-term incentives. *Worldatwork Journal*, 6–14.

24. Gilles, P. L. (1999). A fresh look at incentive plans. *Compensation and Benefits Review, 31*(1), 61–72; Saura, M. D., and Gómez-Mejía, L. R. (1997). The effectiveness of organization-wide compensation strategies in technology intensive firms. *Journal of High Technology Management Research, 8*(2), 301–317; Bradley, G. (2005, First Quarter). Procter & Gamble's balanced approach to long-term incentives. *Worldatwork Journal*, 6–14; Bout, A. (2005, April). The changing landscape of equity compensation. *Workspan*, 16–21; Doubleday, D., Eichen, S., and Laarman, L. (2005, March). Fas 123 (R). *Workspan*, 20–26; Ehrenfeld, T., Penner, S., and Tinkham, R. (2005, April). Broad-based equity. *Workspan*, 22–28.

25. Levering, R., and Moskowitz, M. (2005, January). The 100 best companies to work for. *Fortune*, 61–91.

26. *Ibid.*

27. Blumestien, R., Solomon, D., and Chen, K. (2002, February 21). As global crossing crashed, executives got loan relief pension payouts. *Wall Street Journal*, B-1; Schultz, E. E. (2002, January 16).

"Lockdowns" of 401(k) plans draw scrutiny. *Wall Street Journal*, C-1; Schultz, E. E., and Francis, T. (2002, January 23). Enron pensions had more room at the top. *Wall Street Journal*, A-4; Davis, A. (2005, February 21). Street's top dogs get top dollars. *Wall Street Journal*, C-1; Cairns, A. (2005, February 22). Next Health South CEO . . . Richard Scrushy? *Wall Street Journal*, C-1; Craig, S., and Dugan, J. I. (2005, February 4). At the big board, Grasso's secretary made big bucks, too. *Wall Street Journal*, A-1; Deutsch, C. H. (2005, February 15). Top executive of Office Max leaves post amid inquiry. *New York Times*, A-1; Eisinger, J. (2005, February 16). Follow the CEO's money. *Wall Street Journal*, C-1; Enishwitler, J. R. (2005, March 3). CitiGroup discloses relatives of executives were on payroll. *Wall Street Journal*, C-4; Forelle, C., and Maremont, M. (2005, February 3). Gillette CEO payday may be richer. *Wall Street Journal*, B-2; Glater, J. (2005, March 13). Sorry, I am keeping the bonus anyway. *New York Times*, B-1; Hechinger, J., and Sidel, R. (2005, February 18). American Express's advisory unit faces fraud charges. *Wall Street Journal*, C-13; Jaffe, M. (2005, March 14). Pay perks draw warning. *Arizona Republic*, D-1.

28. Norris, F. (2005, March 31). Windfall never came, big tax bill did. *New York Times*, A-1.

29. Bloomberg News (2005, February 1). Cut is forced on mechanics at United Air. *New York Times*, C-3; *Newsline*. (2005, January 3). Talent management among top five priorities in 2005. www.worldatwork.com.

30. Levering, R., and Moskowitz, M. (2005, January). The 100 best companies to work for. *Fortune*, 61–91.

31. *Workspan*. (2002b, February). Financial awards produce better results, 12; Swinford, D. N. (1999). Don't pay for executive failure. *Compensation and Benefits Review*, 31(1), 54–60.

32. *Worldatwork*. (2002a, February 13). Topic briefing: Skill-based pay. See customerrelations@worldatwork.org.

33. *Newsline*. (2005, January 3). Talent management among top five priorities in 2005. www.worldatwork.com.

34. Hovy, M. (2005, February). Future global remuneration strategies. *Workspan*, 35–39.

35. Milkovich, G. T., and Newman, J. M. (2005). *Compensation* (6th ed.). Homewood, IL: McGraw-Hill/Irwin.

36. Tosi, H., and Tosi, L. (1986). What managers need to know about knowledge-based pay. *Organizational Dynamics*, 14(3), 52–64; Ledford, G. E., and Heneman, R. L. (2000). Pay for skills, knowledge, and competencies. In Berger, L. A., and Berger, D. R. (Eds.), *The compensation handbook* (4th ed.). New York: McGraw-Hill.

37. Ledford, G. E., and Heneman, R. L. (2000). Pay for skills, knowledge, and competencies. In Berger, L. A., and Berger, D. R. (Eds.), *The compensation handbook* (4th ed.). New York: McGraw-Hill; Brown, D. (2000). Relating competencies to pay: A desirable or dangerous practice. In Berger, L. A., and Berger, D. R. (Eds.), *The compensation handbook* (4th ed.). New York: McGraw-Hill.

38. Gómez-Mejía, L. R., and Balkin, D. B. (1992b). *Compensation, organizational strategy, and firm performance*. Cincinnati, OH: South-Western; Milkovich, G. T., and Newman, J. M. (2005). *Compensation* (6th ed.). Homewood, IL: McGraw-Hill/Irwin.

39. Caudron, S. (1993, June). Master the compensation maze. *Personnel Journal*, 64B–64O.

40. Gilles, P. L. (1999). A fresh look at incentive plans. *Compensation and Benefits Review*, 31(1), 61–72; O'Neal, S. (2005, Jan.). Total rewards and the future of work. *Workspan*, 19–25; Bout, A. (2005, April). The changing landscape of equity compensation. *Workspan*, 16–21; Bradley, G. (2005, First Quarter). Procter & Gamble's balanced approach to long-term incentives. *Worldatwork Journal*, 6–14.

41. Levering, R., and Moskowitz, M. (2005, January). The 100 best companies to work for. *Fortune*, 61–91;

42. Eisenberg, D. (1999, August 16). We are for hire, just click. *Time*, 46–50.

43. Levering, R., and Moskowitz, M. (2005, January). The 100 best companies to work for. *Fortune*, 61–91.

44. Milkovich, G. T., and Newman, J. M. (2002). *Compensation* (6th ed.). Homewood, IL: McGraw-Hill/Irwin; Ingster, B. (2000). Methods of job evaluation. In Berger, L. A., and Berger, D. R. (Eds.), *The compensation handbook* (4th ed.). New York: McGraw-Hill; Giancola, F. (2005, February). Need a new system for evaluating management positions? *Workspan*, 29–32.

45. Levering, R., and Moskowitz, M. (2005, January). The 100 best companies to work for. *Fortune*, 61–91.

46. Bureau of Labor Statistics (2006). *Business Economics and Financial Statistics*. www.lib.gsu.edu/collections/govdocs/stats.htm; Jarrel, S. B., and Staley, T. D. (1990). A meta-analysis of the union–nonunion wage gap. *Industrial and Labor Relations Review*, 44(1), 54–67.

47. *Workspan*. (2005, February). Poll results: How often does your organization adjust its compensation structure using market data? 6.

48. Hambrick, D. C., and Snow, C. C. (1989). Strategic reward systems. In C. C. Snow (Ed.), *Strategy, organization design, and human resources management*. Greenwich. CT: JAI Press; Gilles, P. L. (1999). A fresh look at incentive plans. *Compensation and Benefits Review*, 31(1), 61–72; Heneman, R. L., and Dixon, K. E. (2001, November–December). Reward and organizational systems alignment: An expert system. *Compensation and Benefits Review*, 18–27; Files, J. (2005, March 20). A prescription for getting rich. *New York Times*, B-1; *Workspan*. (2005, February). Poll results: How often does your organization adjust its compensation structure using market data? 6.

49. Associated Press. (1991, April 4). What matters to Americans, *Arizona Republic*, AZ; Easterbrook, G. (2005, January 17). The real truth about money. *Time*, 32–34.

50. Seidman, W. L., and Skancke, S. L. (1989). *Competitiveness: The executive's guide to success*. New York: M.E. Sharpe.

51. Levering, R., and Moskowitz, M. (2005, January). The 100 best companies to work for. *Fortune*, 61–91.

52. Stewart, T. A. (1998, June 8). Can even heroes get paid too much? *Fortune*, 289–290; Poster, C. Z. (2002, January–February). Retaining key people in troubled companies. *Compensation and Benefits Review*, 34(1), 7–12; Zingheim, P. K., and Schuster, J. R. (2005, First Quarter). Revisiting effective incentive design. *Worldatwork Journal*, 50–58.

53. *Newsline*. (2005, March 3). Cash still king. www.worldatwork.com.

54. Lawler, E. E., III. (1990). *Strategic pay*. San Francisco: Jossey-Bass; Files, J. (2005, March 20). A prescription for getting rich. *New York Times*, B-1; *Workspan*. (2005, February). Poll results: How often does your organization adjust its compensation structure using market data? 6.

55. Gómez-Mejía, L. R., and Balkin, D. B. (1992a). The determinants of faculty pay: An agency theory perspective. *Academy of Management Journal*, 35(5), 921–955; Milkovich, G. T., and Newman, J. M. (2005). *Compensation* (6th ed.). Homewood, IL: McGraw-Hill/Irwin.

56. Balkin, D. B., and Gómez-Mejía, L. R. (1990). Matching compensation and organizational strategies. *Strategic Management Journal*, 11, 153–169; Heneman, R. L., and Dixon, K. E. (2001, November–December). Reward and organizational systems alignment: An expert system. *Compensation and Benefits Review*, 18–27; Lee, J. (2002, April). Finding the sweet spots: Optimal executive compensation. *Workspan*, 40–46; Abernathy, W. B. (2005, First Quarter). Behavior systems technology: Reengineering closed behavior systems. *Worldatwork Journal*, 71–76.

57. Cantoni, C. J. (1995, May 15). A waste of human resources. *Wall Street Journal,* B-1; Berstein, A. (1999, June 14). Stock options bite back. *BusinessWeek,* 50–51; Bout, A. (2005, April). The changing landscape of equity compensation. *Workspan,* 16–21.

58. Milkovich, G. T., and Newman, J. M. (2005). *Compensation* (6th ed.). Homewood, IL: McGraw-Hill/Irwin.

59. *Ibid.*

60. *Ibid.*

61. *Ibid.*

62. Additional information on the criteria, contentions, interpretation, and application of the MAA (NMTA) plan can be obtained by contacting the nearest MAA association office: AAIM Management Association, St. Louis, MO; AAIM, The Management Association, North Haven, CT; American Society of Employers, Southfield, MI; Capital Associated Industries, Inc., Raleigh, NC; CMEA The Employers Association, Worcester, MA; Employers Association, Inc., Minneapolis, MN; Employers Association of Western Massachusetts, Inc., Ludlow, MA; TEA-The Employers Association, Inc., Braintree, MA; The Employers Association, Lincoln, RI; Employers Resource Council, Seven Hills, OH; IMA Management Association, Inc., Clifton, NJ; IMC-Industrial Management Council, Rochester, NY; The Management Association of Illinois, Broadview, IL; MidAtlantic Employers' Association, Valley Forge, PA; MRA-The Management Association, Inc., Brookfield, WI.

63. NMTA Associates. (1992). National position evaluation plan, 3. Clifton, NJ.

64. Werner, S., Konopaske, R., and Touchey, C. (1999). Ten questions to ask yourself about compensation surveys. *Compensation and Benefits Review, 31*(3); 54–59; Drizin, M. (2005, April). Benchmarks help employers drive results. *Workspan,* 46–52.

65. Dunlop, J. T. (1957). The task of contemporary wage theory. In G. W. Taylor and F. C. Pierson (Eds.), *New concepts in wage determination.* New York: McGraw-Hill; Gerhart, B., and Milkovich, G. T. (1993). Employee compensation: Research and practice. In M. D. Dunnette and L. M. Hough (Eds.), *Handbook of industrial and organizational psychology,* Vol. 3. Palo Alto, CA: Consulting Psychologists Press; Treiman, D. J., and Hartmann, H. I. (Eds.). (1981). *Women, work, and wages: Equal pay for jobs of equal value.* Washington, DC: National Academy Press; Berstein, A. (1999, June 14). Stock options bite back. *BusinessWeek,* 50–51.

66. LeBlanc, P. V., and Ellis, G. M. (1995, Winter). The many faces of banding. *ACA Journal,* 52–62; *ACA Journal.* (1995, Autumn). Clark refining and marketing broadbands: Annual pay rates, 57.

67. Haslett, S. (1995, November/December). Broadbanding: A strategic tool for organizational change. *Compensation and Benefits Review,* 40–43; Worldatwork. (2002b, February 12). Topic briefings: Broadbanding. Customerrelations@worldatwork.org/ topicbriefings.

68. Ledford, G. E., and Heneman, R. L. (2000). Pay for skills, knowledge, and competencies. In Berger, L. A., and Berger, D. R. (Eds.), *The compensation handbook* (4th ed.). New York: McGraw-Hill; Worldatwork. (2002a, February 13). Topic briefing: Skill-based pay. See customerrelations@worldatwork.org.

69. *Workspan* (2003, March). The work experience, 16; Varca, P.E. (2005, First Quarter). The case for emotionally intelligent workers. *Worldatwork Journal,* 35–57; O'Neal, S. (2005, Jan.). Total rewards and the future of work. *Workspan,* 19–25.

70. Barton, P. (1996, February). Team-based pay. *ACA Journal, 5*(1), 15–30; Watson Wyatt Data Services (1996). The 1995–1996 ECS surveys of middle management and office personnel compensation. Rochelle Park, NJ; Gross, S. E. (2000). Team based pay. In Berger, L. A., and Berger, D. R. (Eds.), *The compensation handbook* (4th ed.). New York: McGraw-Hill; Welbourne, T., and Gómez-Mejía, L. R. (2000). Optimizing team based incentives. In Berger, L. A., and Berger, D. R. (Eds.), *The compensation handbook*

(4th ed.). New York: McGraw-Hill; Edwards, C. (2005, January 31). Shaking up Intel's insides. *BusinessWeek,* 35–36.

71. Gupta, N., Ledford, G. E., Jenkins, G. D., and Doty, D. (1992). Survey-based prescriptions for skill-based pay. *American Compensation Association Journal, 1*(1), 48–59; Ledford, G. E., and Heneman, R. L. (2000). Pay for skills, knowledge, and competencies. In Berger, L. A., and Berger, D. R. (Eds.), *The compensation handbook* (4th ed.). New York: McGraw-Hill; Tosi, H., and Tosi, L. (1986). What managers need to know about knowledge-based pay. *Organizational Dynamics, 14*(3), 52–64.

72. Barton, P. (1996, February). Team-based pay. *ACA Journal, 5*(1), 15–30;

73. Alpert, D. E., and Gerard, D. (2005, April). Fair labor standards act update. *Workspan,* 38–41; Deibel, M. (2004, August 21). Overtime changes debut. *Rocky Mountain News,* C-5.

74. Aaron, H. J., and Lougy, C. M. (1986). *The comparable worth controversy,* 3–4. Washington, D.C.: The Brookings Institution; Rhoads, S. E. (1993, July–August). Pay equity won't go away. *Across the Board,* 37–41; Stillson, C. A., and Mohler, K. M. (2001). History still in the making—the continuing struggle for equal pay. *Worldatwork Journal, 10*(1), 1–8.

75. *Workspan* (2005, March). Systematic guidelines to avoid wage discrimination, 560.

76. Greenhous, S. (2005, April 6). Wal-Mart's chief calls its critics unrealistic. New York Times, C-11.

Chapter 11

1. *HR Focus.* (2001, April). Incentive pay plans: Which ones work . . . and why, 3–5; Poster, C. Z. (2002, January–February). Retaining key people in troubled companies. *Compensation and Benefits Review, 34*(1), 7–12; Gilles, P. L. (1999). A fresh look at incentive plans for privately held companies. *Compensation and Benefits Review, 31*(1), 61–72; Watson Wyatt Data Services. (2006). Domestic compensation survey references. Rochelle Park, N.J.

2. Branch, S. (1999, January 11). The 100 best companies to work for in America. *Fortune,* 118; Levering, R., and Moskowitz, M. (2005, January). The 100 best companies to work for. *Fortune,* 61–91.

3. Levering, R., and Moskowitz, M. (2005, January). The 100 best companies to work for. *Fortune,* 61–91.

4. Milkovich, G. T., and Newman, J. (2005). *Compensation* (8th ed.). New York: McGraw-Hill; Drizin, M. (2005, April). Benchmarks help employers drive results. *Workspan,* 46–52.

5. Ray, H. H., and Altmansberger, H. N. (1999, May/June). Introducing goalsharing in a public sector organization. *Compensation and Benefits Review, 31*(3), 40–45; Gómez-Mejía, L. R., Welbourne, T., and Wiseman, R. (2000). Gainsharing and employee risk takings. *Academy of Management Review, 25*(3), 492–509; Bradley, G. (2005, First Quarter). Procter & Gamble's balanced approach to long-term incentives. *Worldatwork Journal,* 6–14; Easterbrook, G. (2005, January 17). The real truth about money. *Time,* A32-A34.

6. Bloom, M. (1999). The art and context of the deal: A balanced view of executive incentives. *Compensation and Benefits Review, 31*(1), 25–31; Tully, S. (1999, April 26). The earnings illusion. *Fortune,* 206–210; Byrne, J. A. (2002, April 15). Pay-related wealth: Winners and losers. *BusinessWeek,* 83; Makri, M., and Gómez-Mejía, L. R. (2002). Rewarding executives. In R. Silzer (Ed.), *The 21st Century Executive* (pp. 200–228). San Francisco: Jossey-Bass; Abernathy, W. B. (2005, First Quarter). Behavior systems technology: Reengineering closed behavior systems. *Worldatwork Journal,* 71–76; Fisher, A. (2004, November 1). A

strategic way to calculate pay. *Fortune,* 62; Hovy, M. (2005, February). Future global remuneration strategies. *Workspan,* 35–39; Hymowitz, C. (2005, March 8). When meeting targets become the strategy, CEO is on wrong path. *Wall Street Journal,* B-1; Kleiner, A. (2004, Winter). Recombinant innovation: Best product ideas are hatched by collaborators, not soloists. *Strategy and Business,* 30–37; Zingheim, P. K., and Schuster, J. R. (2005, First Quarter). Revisiting effective incentive design. *Worldatwork Journal,* 50–58.

7. *Boston Globe.* (1992, October 16). Teaching to the test shortchanges pupils. *Arizona Republic,* A-4; Symonds, W. C. (2001, March 19). How to fix American schools. *BusinessWeek,* 68–73.

8. Byrnes, N., McNamee, M., Grover, L., Muller, J., and Park, A. (2002, April 8). Auditing here, consulting over there. *BusinessWeek,* 34–36; Kahn, J. (2002, April 29). Deloitte restates its case. *Fortune,* 64–74.

9. Drizin, M. (2005, April). Benchmarks help employers drive results. *Workspan,* 46–52.

10. Saura, M. D. and Gómez-Mejía, L. R. (1997). The effectiveness of organization-wide compensation strategies in technology intensive firms. *Journal of High Technology Management Research,* 8(2), 301–317; Nofsinger, G. A. (2000). Performance measures: An overview. In L. Berger and D. R. Berger (Eds.) *The compensation handbook.* New York: McGraw-Hill; Rich, J. T. (2002, February). The solution to employee performance mismanagement. *Workspan,* 45(2), 1–6.

11. Gómez-Mejía, L. R., Balkin, D. B., and Cardy R. L. (2007). *Management.* New York: Irwin/McGraw-Hill.

12. Gorman, C. (1999, February 8). Bleak days for doctors. *Time,* 53.

13. *Ibid.*

14. Bloom, M. (1999). The art and context of the deal: A balanced view of executive incentives. *Compensation and Benefits Review,* 31(1), 25–31; Edwards, M., and Ewen, A. J. (1995, Winter). Moving multisource assessment beyond development. *ACA Journal,* 5(1), 82–87; Bors, K. K., Clark, A. W., Power, V., Seltz, J. C., Schwartz, R. B., and Turbidy, G. S. (1996, Spring). Multiple perspectives: Essays on implementing performance measures. *ACA Journal,* 5(1), 40–45; Milkovich, G. T., and Newman, J. M. (2005). *Compensation* (8th ed.), New York: McGraw-Hill.

15. Lawler, E. E., III, and Cohen, S. G. (1992). Designing a pay system for teams. *American Compensation Association Journal,* 1(1), 6–19; Abernathy, W. B. (2005, First Quarter). Behavior systems technology: Reengineering closed behavior systems. *Worldatwork Journal,* 71–76.

16. Heneman, R. L., and Dixon, K. E. (2001, November–December). Reward and organizational systems alignment: An expert system. *Compensation and Benefits Review,* 18–27.

17. Hills, F. S., Scott, D. K., Markham, S. E., and Vest, M. J. (1987). Merit pay: Just or unjust desserts? *Personnel Administrator,* 32(9), 53–64; Hughes, C. L. (1986). The demerit of merit. *Personnel Administrator,* 31(6), 40; Berstein, A. (1999, June 14). Stock options bite back. *BusinessWeek,* 50–51; Drizin, M. (2005, April). Benchmarks help employers drive results. *Workspan,* 46–52.

18. Rich, J. T. (2002, February). The solution to employee performance mismanagement. *Workspan,* 45(2), 1–6; Drizin, M. (2005, April). Benchmarks help employers drive results. *Workspan,* 46–52.

19. Walters, S. (1999, September 19). Fury over Blunkett's huge wage rises for teachers. *The Mail on Sunday,* 5; Symonds, W. C. (2001, March 19). How to fix American schools. *BusinessWeek,* 68–73; Pollock, R. L. (2001, August 20). The truth about the teacher "shortage." *Wall Street Journal,* A-5.

20. Schwab, D. P. (1974). Conflicting impacts of pay on employee motivation and satisfaction. *Personnel Journal,* 53(3), 190–206.

21. Makri, M., and Gómez-Mejía, L. R. (2002). Rewarding executives. In R. Silzer (Ed.), *The 21st Century Executive* (pp. 200–228). San Francisco: Jossey-Bass; *Newsline.* (2005, March 15). Working while sick continues to pervade U.S. workplace. www.worldatwork.com.

22. Deci, E. L. (1972). The effects of contingent and non-contingent rewards and controls on intrinsic motivation. *Organizational Behavior and Human Performance, 8,* 15–31. See related discussion in Bloom, M. (1999). The art and context of the deal: A balanced view of executive incentives. *Compensation and Benefits Review,* 31(1), 25–31; Kohn, A. (1993, September–October). Why incentive plans cannot work. *Harvard Business Review,* 54–63.

23. Levering, R., and Moskowitz, M. (2005, January). The 100 best companies to work for. *Fortune,* 61–91.

24. *Academy of Management Review.* (1998, August). Special issue on trust; Drizin, M. (2005, April). Benchmarks help employers drive results. *Workspan,* 46–52.

25. *Profit-Building Strategies for Business Owners.* (1992, December), 22(12), 23–24.

26. Rich, J. T. (2002, February). The solution to employee performance mismanagement. *Workspan,* 45(2), 1–6; Parks, T. (2002). Uphill battle: Motivating a sales force in tough times. *Workspan,* 4(2), 65–67; and *HR Focus.* (2001, April). Incentive pay plans: Which ones work . . . and why, 3–5.

27. Gómez-Mejía, L. R., and Balkin, D. B. (1992). *Compensation, organizational strategy, and firm performance.* Cincinnati, OH: South-Western; Varca, P. E. (2005, First Quarter). The case for emotionally intelligent workers. *Worldatwork Journal,* 35–57.

28. *Work in America Institute.* (1991, October). AT&T credit: Continuous improvement as a way of life, 16(10), 2.

29. Gómez-Mejía, L. R., Page, R. C., and Tornow, W. (1982). A comparison of the practical utility of traditional, statistical, and hybrid job evaluation approaches. *Academy of Management Journal, 25,* 790–809; Varca, P. E. (2005, First Quarter). The case for emotionally intelligent workers. *Worldatwork Journal,* 35–57.

30. Rich, J. T. (2002, February). The solution to employee performance mismanagement. *Workspan,* 45(2), 1–6.

31. Greenberg, J. (1990). Looking fair vs. being fair: Managing impressions of organizational justice. In L. Cummings and B. M. Staw (Eds.), *Research in organizational behavior,* Vol. 2. Greenwich, CT: JAI Press.

32. *Fortune.* (2002). Fortune's best companies to work for. www.fortune.com/lists/bestcompanies/snap_502.html.

33. Milkovich, G. T., and Newman, J. M. (2005). *Compensation* (8th ed.), Plano, TX: B.P.I.

34. Gómez-Mejía, L. R., and Balkin, D. B. (1989). Effectiveness of individual and aggregate compensation strategies. *Industrial Relations, 28,* 431–445; Balkin, D. B., and Gómez-Mejía, L. R. (2000). Is CEO pay related to innovation in high technology firms? *Academy of Management Journal,* 43(6), 30–41.

35. *HR Focus.* (2001, April). Incentive pay plans: Which ones work . . . and why, 3–5; Watson Wyatt Data Services. (2006). Domestic compensation survey references. Rochelle Park, N.J.

36. Weiss, T. B. (2000). Performance management. In L. Berger and D. R. Berger (Eds.), *The compensation handbook.* New York: McGraw-Hill; Miller, J. S., Wiseman, R. M., and Gómez-Mejía, L. R. (2002). The fit between CEO compensation design and firm risk. *Academy of Management Journal,* 45(5), 90–99.

37. Locke, E. A., Shaw, K., Saari, L. M., and Latham, G. P. (1981). Goal setting and task performance: 1969–1980. *Psychological Bulletin, 90,* 125–152.

38. Larimer, T., and Dickerson, J. F. (2002, February 18). Time for hardball. *Time,* 42–44; Gomez-Mejia, L. R., Balkin, D. B., and Cardy, R. (2007). *Management.* Chicago: Irwin/McGraw-Hill.

39. Gómez-Mejía, L. R., and Balkin, D. B. (1992). *Compensation, organizational strategy, and firm performance.* Cincinnati, OH:

South-Western; Makri, M., and Gómez-Mejía, L. R. (2002). Rewarding executives. In R. Silzer (Ed.), *The 21st Century Executive* (pp. 200–228). San Francisco: Jossey-Bass; Drizin, M. (2005, April). Benchmarks help employers drive results. *Workspan*, 46–52.

40. Hewitt Associates, Lincolnshire, IL, reported in *Wall Street Journal* (1995, November 28), A-1.

41. Welbourne, T. M., and Gómez-Mejía, L. R. (2000). Team incentives in the workplace. In L. Berger (Ed.), *Handbook of wage and salary administration* (2nd ed., pp. 240–245). New York: McGraw-Hill; *HR Focus*. (2001, April). Incentive pay plans: Which ones work . . . and why, 3–5; Levering, R., and Moskowitz, M. (2005, January). The 100 best companies to work for. *Fortune*, 61–91.

42. Levering, R., and Moskowitz, M. (2005, January). The 100 best companies to work for. *Fortune*, 61–91.

43. Gross, S., and Blair, J. (1995, September/October). Reinforcing team effectiveness through pay. *Compensation and Benefits Review*, 34–36; Zigon, J. (1996). How to measure the results of work teams. Zigon Performance Group, Media, PA; Welbourne, T. M., and Gómez-Mejía, L. R. (2000). Team incentives in the workplace. In L. Berger (Ed.), *Handbook of wage and salary administration* (2nd ed., pp. 240–245). New York: McGraw-Hill.

44. Liden, R. C., and Mitchell, T. R. (1983). The effects of group interdependence on supervisor performance evaluations. *Personnel Psychology, 36*, 289–299.

45. *HR Focus*. (2001, April). Incentive pay plans: Which ones work . . . and why, 3–5.

46. Butler, M. J. (2001, 2nd Quarter). Worldwide growth of employee ownership phenomena. *Worldatwork Journal, 10*(2), 1–5.

47. Heneman, F., and Von Hippel, C. Interview appearing in *Wall Street Journal* (1995, November 28), A-1.

48. Albanese, R., and VanFleet, D. D. (1985). Rational behavior in groups: The free-riding tendency. *Academy of Management Review, 10*, 244–255.

49. Levering, R., and Moskowitz, M. (2005, January). The 100 best companies to work for. *Fortune*, 61–91.

50. Gordon, D. M., Edwards, R., and Reich, M. (1982). *Segmented work, divided workers: The historical transformation of labor in the United States*. London: Cambridge University Press.

51. Mohrman, A. M., Mohrman, S. A., and Lawler, E. E. (1992). *Performance measurement, evaluation and incentives*. Boston: Harvard Business School.

52. Milkovich, G. T., and Newman, J. M. (2005). *Compensation* (8th ed.), New York: McGraw-Hill.

53. Miller, J. S., Wiseman, R. M., and Gómez-Mejía, L. R. (2002). The fit between CEO compensation design and firm risk. *Academy of Management Journal, 45*(5), 90–99; Makri, M., and Gómez-Mejía, L. R. (2002). Rewarding executives. In R. Silzer (Ed.), *The 21st Century Executive* (pp. 200–228). San Francisco: Jossey-Bass.

54. Pinchot, G. (1985). *Intrapreneuring*. New York: Harper & Row.

55. McGregor, D. (1960). *The human side of enterprise*. New York: McGraw-Hill.

56. Gómez-Mejía, L. R., Welbourne, T., and Wiseman, R. (2000). Gainsharing and employee risk takings. *Academy of Management Review, 25*(3), 492–509; Masternak, R., and Camuso, M. A. (2005, First Quarter). Gainsharing and six sigma perfect together. *Worldatwork*, 42–49.

57. Gómez-Mejía, L. R., Welbourne, T., and Wiseman, R. (2000). Gainsharing and employee risk takings. *Academy of Management Review, 25*(3), 492–509.

58. Welbourne, T., and Gómez-Mejía, L. R. (1995). Gainsharing: A critical review. *Journal of Management, 21*(3), 559–609; Welbourne, T., Balkin, D., and Gómez-Mejía, L. R. (1995). Gainsharing and mutual monitoring. *Academy of Management Journal, 38*(3), 818–834; Gómez-Mejía, L. R., Welbourne, T., and Wiseman, R. (2000). Gainsharing and employee risk takings. *Academy of Management Review, 25*(3), 492–509.

59. Florkowski, G. W. (1987). The organizational impact of profit sharing. *Academy of Management Review, 12*, 622–636; Berner, R. (2002, March 18). Keeping a lid on unemployment: No bonus may mean fewer layoffs. *BusinessWeek*, 18.

60. *Time*. (1988, February 1), 13.

61. Jaross, J., Byrnes, R., and Mercer, W. (2002, April). Mastering the share plan circus. *Workspan*, 55–64; Lee, J. (2002, April). Finding the sweet spots: Optimal executive compensation. *Workspan*, 40–46.

62. Kaplan, J., and Granados, L. (2002, April). Tax law changes affect ESOPs. *Workspan*, 46–50.

63. *Newsline*. (2005, March 18). Stocks of best companies to work for beat the market by 300%. www.worldatwork.com.

64. Branch, S. (1999, January 11). The 100 best companies to work for in America. *Fortune*, 118.

65. Butler, M. J. (2001, 2nd Quarter). Worldwide growth of employee ownership phenomena. *Worldatwork Journal, 10*(2), 1–5.

66. Burmeister, E. D. (2001). The top mistakes in implementing a global stock plan. *Worldatwork Journal, 10*(2), 3.

67. Bout, A. (2005, April). The changing landscape of equity compensation. *Workspan*, 16–21; Ehrenfeld, T., Penner, S., and Tinkham, R. (2005, April). Broad-based equity. *Workspan*, 22–28.

68. Gimein, M. (2006, April 3). The bottom line on options. BusinessWeek, 32–36.

69. *HR Focus*. (2001, April). Incentive pay plans: Which ones work . . . and why, 3–5; Conlin, M., and Berner, R. (2002, February 18). A little less in the envelope. *BusinessWeek*, 64–66; Lavelle, L. (2002, March 4). The danger of deferred compensation. *BusinessWeek*, 110.

70. Gómez-Mejía, L. R., Balkin, D. B., and Cardy R. L. (2007). *Management*. New York: Irwin/McGraw-Hill.

71. Cheadle, A. (1989). Explaining patterns of profit sharing activity. *Industrial Relations, 28*, 387–401.

72. Lublin, J. (2005, February 26). Bonuses soar for CEOs bad and good. *Wall Street Journal*, D-1; Strauss, G., and Hansen, B. (2005, March 30). Special report: CEO pay is business as usual. *USA Today*, A-1.

73. Stewart, T. A. (1998, June 8). Can even heroes get paid too much? *Fortune*, 289–300; Poster, C. Z. (2002, January–February). Retaining key people in troubled companies. *Compensation and Benefits Review, 34*(1), 7–12.

74. Lublin, J. (2002a, April 11). Executive pay under radar. *Wall Street Journal*, B-7; Lublin, J. (2002b, April 11). The hot seat. *Wall Street Journal*, B-10.

75. *BusinessWeek*, (2002, April 15), Round UP, 15.

76. Rundell, A. G., and Gómez-Mejía, L. R. (2002). Power as a determinant of exective pay. *Human Resource Management Review, 12*(3), 3–23.

77. Thompson, M. A. (2001). Managing stock options in down market conditions. *Worldatwork Journal, 10*(2), 1–6; Bryniski, T., and Harsen, B. (2002, January–February). The cancel and regrant: A roadmap for addressing underwater options. *Compensation and Benefits Review, 34*(1), 28–33; Fox, R. D., and Hauder, E. A. (2001). Sending out an SOS—Methods for companies to resuscitate underwater stock options. *Worldatwork Journal, 10*(2), 7–12.

78. Kahn, J. (2002, January 7). When 401(k)s are KO'd. *Fortune*, 104; Hymowitz, C. (2003, February 24). How to fix a broken system. *Wall Street Journal*, R–1.

79. Hyman, J. S. (2000). Long-term incentives. In L. Berger and D. R. Berger (Eds.), *The compensation handbook*. New York: McGraw-Hill; Gómez-Mejía, L. R., and Wiseman, R. (1997). Reframing executive compensation: An assessment and outlook. *Journal of Management, 23*(3), 291–374; Mazer, M. A. and Larre, E. C.

(2000). Executive compensation strategy. In L. Berger and D. R. Berger (Eds.), *The compensation handbook*. New York: McGraw-Hill; Lublin, J. (2002a, April 11). Executive pay under radar. *Wall Street Journal*, B-7; Lublin, J. (2002b, April 11). The hot seat. *Wall Street Journal*, B-10.

80. Tosi, H., Katz, J., Werner, S., and Gómez-Mejía, L. R. (2000). A meta-analysis of executive compensation studies. *Journal of Management, 26*(2), 1–39.

81. Lublin, J. (2002a, April 11). Executive pay under radar. *Wall Street Journal*, B-7; Strauss, G., and Hansen, B. (2005, March 30). Special report: CEO pay is business as usual. *USA Today*, A-1.

82. *Wall Street Journal*. (2002, April 11). The boss's pay, B-15–B-19.

83. *Wall Street Journal News Roundup*. (1995, March 7). In a cost-cutting era, many CEOs enjoy imperial perks, B-1.

84. Lublin, J. (2002a, April 11). Executive pay under radar. *Wall Street Journal*, B-7; Strauss, G., and Hansen, B. (2005, March 30). Special report: CEO pay is business as usual. *USA Today*, A-1.

85. Jaffe, M. (2005, March 14). Pay perks draw warning. *Arizona Republic*, D-1.

86. Gómez-Mejía, L. R., and Wiseman, R. (1997). Reframing executive compensation: An assessment and outlook. *Journal of Management, 23*(3), 291–374; Wiseman, R., and Gómez-Mejía, L. R. (1998). A behavioral agency model. *Academy of Management Review, 23*(1), 150–196.

87. Dalton, D. R., and Daily, C. M. (1999). Directors and shareholders as equity partners? *Compensation and Benefits Review, 31*(1), 73–79.

88. *Ibid*.

89. Creswell, J. (1999, April 4). More companies are linking directors' pay to performance. *Wall Street Journal*, R-6; McNamee, M. (2002, April 22). Turn up the heat on board cronyism. *BusinessWeek*, 36;

90. Lublin, J. S. (2005, April 11). Goodbye to pay for no performance. *Wall Street Journal*, A-1; Raghavan, A. (2005, January 28). More CEOs say 'no thanks' to board seats. *Wall Street Journal*, B-1; Todd, P., and Barrett, A (2005, First Quarter). Director pay: Current trend and practices. *Worldatwork Journal*, 15–24.

91. Henry, D., France, M., and Lavelle, L. (2005, April 25). The boss on the sidelines. *BusinessWeek*, 86–96.

92. Sapsford, J., and Fackler, M. (2005). Director's role shift in Japan. *Wall Street Journal*, A-15.

93. Makri, M., and Gómez-Mejía, L. R. (2002). Rewarding executives. In R. Silzer (Ed.), *The 21st century executive* (pp. 200–228). San Francisco: Jossey-Bass; Johnson, A. M. (2000). Designing and implementing total executive compensation programs. In L. Berger and D. R. Berger (Eds.), *The compensation handbook*. New York: McGraw-Hill; Parks, T. (2002). Uphill battle: Motivating a sales force in tough times. *Workspan, 4*(2), 65–67; Knight, T. G. (2005, January). Sales compensation plans for a recovering economy. *Workspan*, 63–66.

94. Knight, T. G. (2005, January). Sales compensation plans for a recovering economy. *Workspan*, 63–66.

95. *Ibid.*; Watson Wyatt Data Services, (1996). *The 1995–1996 sales and marketing personnel report*. New York, New York.

96. Parks, T. (2002). Uphill battle: Motivating a sales force in tough times. *Workspan, 4*(2), 65–67.

97. *HR Focus*. (2001, April). Incentive pay plans: Which ones work . . . and why, 3–5.

98. Sager, I., McWilliams, G., and Hof, D. (1994, February 7). IBM leans on its salesforce. *BusinessWeek*, 110.

99. *Forbes*. (1994, February 28), 15–20.

100. Edmonson, G. (1999, August 9). France: A CEO's pay secret shouldn't be a secret. *BusinessWeek*, 47.

101. Lavelle, L. (2005, January 17). Time to start weighing the options. *BusinessWeek*, 32–33.

Chapter 12

1. McNamee, M. (1999, October 4). Good pensions, bad sales pitch. *BusinessWeek*, 44.

2. Sager, I. (1999, October 11). Look for the union label—at IBM. *BusinessWeek*, 46.

3. Kerwin, K. (2000, February 21). Employee benefits: Workers of the world, log on. *BusinessWeek*, 52.

4. DeYoung, P. (2000, October). High-tech talent perks are ripe for the picking. *Workspan*, 28–33.

5. Boyle, M. (2005, January 24). The Wegmans way. *Fortune*, 62–68.

6. U.S. Bureau of Labor Statistics. (2004, June). *Employer costs for employee compensation*, 1–4.

7. Lieb, J. (1990, March 19). Day-care demand creates new perk. *Denver Post*, 1-C, 5-C.

8. Gómez-Mejía, L. R., and Balkin, D. B. (1992). *Compensation, organizational strategy and firm performance*. Cincinnati, OH: South-Western.

9. Mulvey, J. (2005, March 31). Rising benefits costs crowd out wage growth. *Employee Benefits Factsheet*, 1.

10. Martocchio, J. (2003). *Employee benefits*. Burr Ridge, IL: McGraw-Hill Irwin.

11. McCaffery, R. M. (1989). Employee benefits and services. In L. R. Gómez-Mejía (Ed.), *Compensation and benefits*. Washington, DC: The Bureau of National Affairs.

12. Lawler, E. E. III. (1990). *Strategic pay*. San Francisco: Jossey-Bass.

13. Levering, R., Moskowitz, M., and Katz, M. (1984). *The 100 best companies to work for in America*. Reading, MA: Addison-Wesley.

14. Lankford, K. (2004). The new medicare: Prescription drug coverage. *Kiplinger's Retirement Planning 2004*, 91–92.

15. U.S. Chamber of Commerce. (1991). *Employee benefits 1990*. Washington, DC: U.S. Chamber of Commerce.

16. Treaster, J. (2003, June 23). Cost of insurance for work injuries soars across U.S. *New York Times*, A-1, A-18; Hansen, F. (1999, May–June). Workers compensation: Hard times ahead. *Compensation and Benefits Review*, 15–20; Cenicernos R. (2005, July 4). California gaining self-insurers. *Business Insurance*, 4–5; Martocchio, J. (2003). *Employee benefits*. Burr Ridge, IL: McGraw-Hill Irwin.

17. Thompson, R. (1990, March). Fighting the high cost of workers' compensation. *Nation's Business*, 20–29.

18. Light, L. (1992, October 5). When injured employees act anything but. *BusinessWeek*, 120.

19. Lorenz, C. (1995, May–June). Nine practical suggestions for streamlining workers' compensation costs. *Compensation and Benefits Review*, 40–44.

20. *Occupational Safety Hazards*. (2002, February). A checklist for managing workers' comp claims, 24.

21. Fefer, M. D. (1994, October 3). Taking control of your workers' comp costs. *Fortune*, 131–136.

22. Milkovich, G. T., and Newman, J. M. (2005). *Compensation* (8th ed.). Homewood, IL: Irwin, McGraw-Hill.

23. Richman, L. S. (1995, April 17). Getting past economic insecurity. *Fortune*, 161–168.

24. Preston, H. (2002, March 16). Walking papers: How to make the best of losing a job. *International Herald Tribune*, 13.

25. Grossman, R. (2004, November). The UI blues. *HRMagazine*, 55–59.

26. Snarr, B. (1993, May–June). The Family and Medical Leave Act of 1993. *Compensation and Benefits Review*, 6–9.

27. Crampton, S. M., and Mishra, J. M. (1995). Family and medical leave legislation: Organizational policies and strategies. *Public Personnel Management, 24*(3), 271–289.

28. Gunsch, D. (1993, September). The Family Leave Act: A financial burden? *Personnel Journal*, 48–57.

29. Paltell, E. (1999, September). FMLA: After six years, a bit more clarity. *HRMagazine*, 144–150.

30. McNamee, M. (1993, August 9). Sure, "unpaid leave" sounds simple, but. . . . *BusinessWeek*, 32–33.

31. Bernstein. A. (2005, June 13). The fight brewing over family leave. *BusinessWeek*, 62–63; Hansen, F. (2001, March–April). Seven years after the FMLA. *Compensation and Benefits Review*, 22–30.

32. Grow, B. (2004, September 13). It's enough to make you sick. *BusinessWeek*, 58–61.

33. Sunoo, B. P. (1998, November). Carrying the weight of the HIPAA-potamus. *Workforce*, 58–64.

34. Brislin, J. (2003, March). HIPPA privacy rules and compliance with federal and state employment laws: The participant authorization form. *Employee Benefits Journal*, 51–63; Wellner, A. (2003, November). The privacy time bomb: Comply with HIPPA now or risk big fines later. *Inc.*, 34.

35. Kaiser Family Foundation. (2004). www.kff.org.

36. *Ibid.*

37. Benko, L. (2004, June 28). New call for patients' bill of rights. *Modern Healthcare*, 12.

38. Kaiser Family Foundation. (2004). www.kff.org.

39. Jefferson, D. J. (1994, March 8). Family matters: Gay employees win benefits for partners at more corporations. *Wall Street Journal*, A-1, A-6; Jenner, L. (1994, January), Domestic partner update: Awareness and resistance. *HR Focus*, 10.

40. Farrell, C. (2005, June 13). This could keep you in the pink: Health savings accounts may be just the ticket for entrepreneurs. *BusinessWeek*, 88–89; Lankford, K. (2005, June). In search of health coverage. *Kiplinger's*, 83–85.

41. Weisser, C. (2005, January). Five ways to cut your healthcare costs. *Money*, 90–95; Franklin, M., and Lankford, K. (2004, November). A new way to save on premiums, *Kiplinger's*, 87–89.

42. Newton, C. (2002, February). Branching out with self-funded health care. *Workspan*, 45–47.

43. Bernstein, A. (1991, August 19). Playing "Pin the insurance on the other guy." *BusinessWeek*, 104–105.

44. Reese, A. (1999, August). Setting the pace. *Business & Health*, 17–18.

45. Bunch, D. K. (1992, March). Coors Wellness Center—Helping the bottom line. *Employee Benefits Journal*, 14–18.

46. Wiley, J. L. (1993, August). Preretirement education: Benefits outweigh liability. *HR Focus*, 11.

47. Johnson, R. (1998, Autumn). Dispelling the fables of ERISA. *ACA Journal*, 19–27.

48. *Money.* (1993, May). The best benefits, 130–131.

49. Murray, K. A. (1993, July). For some companies, portable pensions aren't practical. *Personnel Journal*, 38–39.

50. Milkovich, G. T., and Newman, J. M. (2005). *Compensation* (8th ed.). Homewood, IL: Irwin, McGraw-Hill.

51. Rotello, P., and Cornwell, R. (1994, February). Is it time to rethink your retirement program? *HR Focus*, 4–5.

52. Dimeo, J. (1992, October). Women receive the short end when it comes to their retirement pension incomes. *Pension World*, 28, 30.

53. Poterba, J. M., Venti, S. F., and Wise, D. A. (1998). 401(k) plans and future patterns of retirement saving. *American Economic Review*, 88, 179–184.

54. Hogan, M. C. (1992, December). Educating the 401(k) investor. *Employee Benefits Journal*, 18–22.

55. *The Economist.* (2001, December 15). American company pensions: When labor and capital don't mix, 60.

56. Quinn, J. (2002, January 21). 401(k)s and the Enron mess. *Newsweek*, 25.

57. Gleckman, H. (2005, April 25). A nest egg that's a no-brainer. *BusinessWeek*, 108–110.

58. Foran, N., and Bryant, J. (1999, September). Roth IRA regs. offer clarity and guidance. *Tax Advisor*, 654–663.

59. McNamee, M. (1999, October 4). Good pensions, bad sales pitch. *BusinessWeek*, 44.

60. Murray, K. A. (1993, July). How HR is making pensions portable. *Personnel Journal*, 36–46; Tobin, V. M. (1992). Beyond defined contribution or defined benefit pension plans. In *The Conference Board report 1004: Controlling the costs of employee benefits*. New York: The Conference Board; Snell, N. W. (1992). Pension plan modifications. In *The Conference Board report 1004: Controlling the costs of employee benefits*. New York: The Conference Board.

61. DeCenzo, D. A., and Holoviak, S. J. (1990). *Employee benefits*. Upper Saddle River, NJ: Prentice Hall.

62. *Money.* (1993, May). The best benefits, 130–131.

63. U.S. Bureau of Labor Statistics. (2004, February 26). Employer costs for employee compensation. Washington, D.C.: United States Department of Labor.

64. Eckhouse, J. (1993, March 24). Retired exec at HP received $937,225 for unused sick leave. *San Francisco Chronicle*, C-1, C-40.

65. Tully, S. (1995, June 12). America's healthiest companies. *Fortune*, 98–106.

66. Reinberg, J. (2002, February). It's about time: PTOs gain popularity. *Workspan*, 53–55.

67. Matthes, K. (1992, May). In pursuit of leisure: Employees want more time off. *HR Focus*, 1.

68. Gómez-Mejía, L. R., Balkin, D. B., and Milkovich, G. T. (1990). Rethinking your rewards for technical employees. *Organizational Dynamics*, 1(1), 62–75.

69. Briscoe, D., and Schuler R. (2004). *International human resource management* (2nd ed.). New York: Routledge.

70. Fuchsberg, G. (1992, April 22). What is pay, anyway? *Wall Street Journal*, R-3.

71. Huang, A. (1999, July). Concierge services free employees from distractions. *HR Focus*, 6.

72. BNA. (1994, January 31). Self-defense classes for employees becoming popular. *Workforce Strategies* (published with *BNA's Employee Relations Weekly*), 5, 3.

73. Symonds, W. (2002, June 10). Providing the killer perk: Companies say on-site day care pays off in higher productivity and reduced turnover. *BusinessWeek*, 101.

74. Dex, S., and Schneibel, F. (1999, Summer). Business performance and family-friendly policies. *Journal of General Management*, 22–37.

75. *The Conference Board.* (1995). Child care services, 5(4), 3–12.

76. Henderson, R. (1989). *Compensation management* (5th ed.). Upper Saddle River, NJ: Prentice Hall.

77. Barringer, M. W., and Milkovich, G. T. (1998). A theoretical exploration of the adoption and design of flexible benefit plans: A case of human resource innovation. *Academy of Management Review*, 23, 305–324.

78. Alderman, L., and Kim S. (1996, January). Get the most from your company benefits. *Money*, 102–106.

79. DeCenzo, D. A., and Holoviak, S. J. (1990). *Employee benefits*. Upper Saddle River, NJ: Prentice Hall.

80. McCaffery, R. M. (1992). *Employee benefit programs: A total compensation perspective* (2nd ed.). Boston: PWS-Kent.

81. Black, A. (2005). *Effective benefit communication trends, techniques and technology*. Brookfield, WIS: International Foundation of Employee Benefit Plans; Wilson, M., Northcraft, G., and Neale, M. (1985). The perceived value of fringe benefits. *Personnel Psychology*, 38, 309–320.

82. Cohen, A., and Cohen, S. (1998, November/December). Benefits Websites: Controlling costs while enhancing communication. *Journal of Compensation and Benefits*, 11–18.

83. Shalowitz, D. (1992, October 12). Cracking the case of the confusing retirement plan. *Business Insurance,* 22.

Chapter 13

1. Roberts, K. (2002, May). Honest communications. *Executive Excellence,* 20.
2. Noer, D. M. (1993). *Healing the wounds: Overcoming the trauma of layoffs and revitalizing downsized organizations,* 103–104. San Francisco: Jossey-Bass.
3. Jay, J. (2005, January). On communicating well. *HRMagazine,* 87–90.
4. Johnson, P. R., and Gardner, S. (1989). Legal pitfalls of employee handbooks. *SAM Advanced Management Journal,* 54(2), 42–46.
5. Felsberg, E. (2004, Summer). Composing effective employee handbooks. *Employment Relations Today,* 117–118.
6. Wojcik, J. (2004, December 6). Toshiba employee handbook goes online. *Business Insurance,* 18.
7. Farr, J. (1999, January). Put your rules in writing. *Restaurant Hospitality,* 38.
8. Sosnin, B. (2001, July). Package your policies: To be effective, employee handbooks must be well-structured, carefully drafted in plain language and reflective of your practices and culture. *HRMagazine,* 67–72.
9. Brady, T. (1993, June). Employee handbooks: Contracts or empty promises? *Management Review,* 33–35.
10. Aronoff, C. E., and Ward, J. L. (1993, January). Rules for nepotism. *Nation's Business,* 64–65.
11. Prasad, A. (2002, January). Digging deep for meaning: A critical hermeneutic analysis of CEO letters to shareholders in the oil industry. *The Journal of Business Communication,* 92–116.
12. Sosnin, B. (1996, June). Corporate newsletters improve employee morale. *HRMagazine,* 106–110.
13. Flanagan, P. (1994, February). Videoconferencing changes the corporate meeting. *Management Review,* 7; Bhargava, S. W., and Coy, P. (1991, November 12). Video-screen meetings: Still out of sight. *BusinessWeek,* 162E.
14. *Information Management Forum.* (1993, January). Voice mail or voice pony express, insert into *Management Review,* 3.
15. Weeks, D. (1995, February). Voice mail: Blessing or curse? *World Traveler,* 51–54.
16. Leonard, A. (1999, September 20). We've got mail—always. *Newsweek,* 58–61.
17. Pearl, J. A. (1993, July). The e-mail quandary. *Management Review,* 48–51.
18. *Ibid.*
19. France, M. (1999, April 2). A site for soreheads. *BusinessWeek,* 86–90.
20. Brady, R. (1995, October). Electronic mail: Drafting a policy. *HR Focus,* 19; Daniel, T. (1995, Summer). Electronic and voice mail monitoring of employees: A practical approach. *Employee Relations Today,* 1–10; Weiss, B. (1996, January). Four black holes in cyberspace. *Management Review,* 30–32.
21. *Information Management Journal.* (2002, January/February). Company e-mail: To monitor or not to monitor, 8.
22. *Information Management Forum.* (1993, July). Who's reading your e-mail? An insert into *Management Review,* 1, 4; Casarez, N. B. (1993, Summer), Electronic mail and employee relations: Why privacy must be considered. *Public Relations Quarterly,* 37–39.
23. Baig, E., Stepnek, M., and Gross, N. (1999, April 5). Privacy: The Internet wants your personal information. *BusinessWeek,* 84–90; McGrath, P. (1999, March 29). Knowing you too well. *Newsweek,* 48–50.
24. Wellner, A. (2005, September). Lost in translation. *Inc.,* 37–38.
25. *The Economist.* (1996, April 20). Textbooks on CD-ROM, 11.
26. *HR Focus.* (2002, May). Time to take another look at telecommuting, 6–7.
27. Kugelmass, J. (1995). *Telecommuting.* New York: Lexington Books.
28. Falcone, P. (1998, October). Communication breakdown. *HR Focus,* 8.
29. *The Economist.* (2003, October 25). Think before you meet: Too many meetings are a waste of time, 17.
30. Michaels, E. A. (1989, February). Business meetings. *Small Business Reports,* 82–88.
31. Interview of Deborah Tannen by L. A. Lusardi (1990, July). Power talk. *Working Woman,* 92–94.
32. Elashmawi, F. (1991, November). Multicultural business meetings and presentations. *Tokyo Business Today,* 59(11), 66–68.
33. Montgomery, E. (1993, October). A family affair. *Small Business Reports,* 10–14; Jaffe, D. T. (1992, June). How to create a family council. *Nation's Business,* 54–55. For more on succession planning, see *Inc.* (1996, July). Three ways to plan ahead, 96.
34. Meyer, A. (2005, August 22). Retreats help strengthen ties for family-owned firms. *Chicago Tribune,* 3–4.
35. Wellner, A. (2005, January). Playing well with others: Office cliques sap morale and kill productivity—does your firm have them? *Inc.,* 29–31
36. McCune, J. C. (1998, July/August). That elusive thing called trust. *Management Review,* 10–16.
37. *Business 2.0.* (2002, May). eePulse Inc. helps hospital save thousands and improve productivity. www.business2.com.
38. Mandel, M. J. (1996, June 24). Satisfaction at work. *BusinessWeek,* 28.
39. Gómez-Mejía, L. R., and Balkin, D. B. (1992). *Compensation, organizational strategy, and firm performance.* Cincinnati, OH: South-Western.
40. Aram, J. D., and Salipante, P. F., Jr. (1981). An evaluation of organizational due process in the resolution of employee/employer conflict. *Academy of Management Review,* 16, 197–204.
41. Strazewski, L. (2005, July). Investing in EAPs—employee assistance programs. *Rough Notes,* 52–53.
42. Filipowicz, C. A. (1979). The troubled employee: Whose responsibility? *Personnel Administrator,* 24(6), 5–10.
43. Bahls, J. (1999, March). Handle with care. *HRMagazine,* 60–66.
44. Lee, K. (2000). Bringing home benefits. *Employee Benefit News,* 13(4), 1–3.
45. Carson, K. D., and Balkin, D. B. (1992). An employee assistance model of health care management for employees with alcohol-related problems. *Journal of Employment Counseling,* 29, 146–156.
46. Wise, D. (1993, April). Employee assistance programs expand to fit companies' needs. *Business & Health,* 40–45.
47. Strazewski, L. (2005, July). Investing in EAPs—employee assistance programs. *Rough Notes,* 52–53.
48. Fisher, C., Schoenfeldt, L., and Shaw, J. (1996). *Human resource management* (3rd ed.). Boston, MA: Houghton Mifflin.
49. Karamally, L. (2004, September). Companies try to bring domestic violence issues into the open. *Workforce Management,* 60–63.
50. Cascio, W. (2000). *Costing human resouces* (4th ed.). Cincinnati, OH: Southwestern College Publishing.
51. Luthans, F., and Waldersee, R. (1989). What do we really know about EAPs? *Human Resource Management,* 28, 385–401.
52. *Risk Management.* (1999, May). Working assistance, 8.
53. Deal, T. E., and Key, M. K. (1998). *Corporate celebration.* San Francisco: Barrett-Koehler.
54. Meyers, D. W. (1986). *Human resources management.* Chicago: Commerce Clearing House.
55. Nelson, B. (1994). *1001 ways to reward employees.* New York: Workman Publishing.

56. Arthur, J., and Aiman-Smith, L. (2001). Gainsharing and organizational learning: An analysis of employee suggestions over time. *Academy of Management Journal, 44,* 737–754.

57. Wells, S. (2005, February). From ideas to results: To get the most from your company's suggestion system, move ideas up the ladder through a formal process. *HRMagazine,* 55–58.

58. Trunko, M. E. (1993). Open to suggestions. *HRMagazine, 38*(2), 85–89.

59. Wells, S. (2005, February). From ideas to results: To get the most from your company's suggestion system, move ideas up the ladder through a formal process. *HRMagazine,* 55–58.

60. *Ibid.*

61. Oldering, S. R. (1998, May/June). Mitsubishi and Honda on competition and quality circles. *Journal for Quality & Participation,* 55–59.

62. Knouse, S. (1995). *The reward and recognition process.* Milwaukee, WI: ASQC Quality Press.

63. Gilbert, M. (2004, November). A culture that recognizes the contributions made by unsung heroes. *Workforce Management,* 82–84.

64. Orsburn, J. D., Moran, L., Musselwhite, E., and Zenger, J. H. (1990). *Self-directed work teams.* Homewood, IL: Business One Irwin.

65. Flynn, G. (1998, July). Is your recognition program understood? *Workforce,* 30–35.

66. Ruffalo, N. (2000, January). HR 101: Recognition. *Workforce,* 62–63.

67. Wiscombe, J. (2002, April). Rewards get results. *Workforce,* 42–48.

Chapter 14

1. Levy, S. (2004, June 7). A future with nowhere to hide? *Newsweek,* 76.

2. Lewis, J. (2002, January). I know what you e-mailed last summer. *Security Management,* 93–99; Zimmerman, E. (2002, February). HR must know when employee surveillance crosses the line. *Workforce,* 38–45.

3. Springen, K. (2005, February 7). Smoking: Light up and you may be let go. *Newsweek,* 14.

4. Cheeseman, H. (1997). *Contemporary business law* (2nd ed.). Upper Saddle River, NJ: Prentice Hall.

5. Egler, T. (1996, May). A manager's guide to employment contracts. *HRMagazine,* 28–33.

6. Flynn, G. (1999, February). Employment contracts gain ground in corporate America. *Workforce,* 99–101.

7. *Ibid.*

8. LaVan, H. (2000). A logit model to predict the enforceability of noncompete agreements. *Employee Responsibilities and Rights Journal, 12,* 219–235.

9. Gullett, C. R., and Greenwade, G. D. (1988). Employment at will: The no fault alternative. *Labor Law Journal, 39*(6), 372–378.

10. *Ibid.*

11. *Defense Counsel Journal.* (2005, April). Conning the IADC newsletters, 203–206; McWhiter, D. (1989). *Your rights at work.* New York: Wiley.

12. Ho, V. (2005). Social influence on evaluations of psychological contract fulfillment. *Academy of Management Review, 30,* 113–128; Ho, V., and Levesque, L. (2005). With a little help from my friends (and substitutes): Social referents and influence in psychological contract fulfillment. *Organization Science, 16,* 275–290.

13. Rousseau, D. (1995). *Psychological contracts in organizations.* Thousand Oaks, CA: Sage.

14. Weaver, G. R., Trevino, L. K., and Cochran, P. L. (1999). Corporate ethics programs as control systems: Influence of executive commitment and environmental factors. *Academy of Management Journal, 42,* 41–57.

15. Weaver, G., and Trevino, L. (2001). The role of human resources in ethics/compliance management: A fairness perspective. *Human Resource Management Review, 11,* 113–134.

16. Driscoll, D. (1998, March). Business ethics and compliance: What management is doing and why. *Business and Society Review,* 33–51.

17. Sashkin, M., and Kiser, K. J. (1993). *Putting total quality management to work.* San Francisco: Berrett-Koehler.

18. Otto, J. (1993, January 11). Random alcohol test proposed. *Aviation Week & Space Technology, 138*(2), 33.

19. Sovereign, K. (1994). *Personnel law* (3rd ed.). Upper Saddle River, NJ: Prentice Hall.

20. Hays, S. (1999, September). Censured! "Free" speech at work. *Workforce,* 34–37.

21. Labich, K. (1999, September 6). No more crude at Texaco. *Fortune,* 205–212.

22. Anton, G., and Ward, J. (1998, March). Every breath you take: Employee privacy rights in the workplace—An Orwellian prophecy come true? *Labor Law Journal,* 897–911.

23. Holley, W. H., and Jennings, K. M. (1991). *The labor relations process* (4th ed.). Chicago, IL: Dryden.

24. Elkouri, F., and Elkouri, E. A. (1973). *How arbitration works* (3rd ed.). Washington, DC: Bureau of National Affairs.

25. Brown, D. R., and Gray, G. R. (1988, Summer). A positive alternative to employment at will. *SAM Advanced Management Journal, 53,* 13–16.

26. Maltby, L. L. (1990). The decline of employment at will—a quantitative analysis. *Labor Law Journal, 41*(1), 51–54.

27. Utroska, D. R. (1992, November). Management in Europe. *Management Review,* 21–24.

28. Seligman, D. (2003, November 10). The right to fire. *Forbes,* 126.

29. Smith, R. (1999, September 14). Saloman former manager is awarded $1.9 million in wrongful discharge case. *Wall Street Journal,* 1; Jones, D. (1998, April 2). Fired workers fight back . . . and win. *USA Today,* 1-B.

30. Janove, J. (2005, May). Keep 'em at will, treat 'em for cause. *HRMagazine,* 111–117; Roehlilng, M. (2003, October). The employment at will doctrine: Second level ethical issues and analysis. *Journal of Business Ethics,* 115–124.

31. Bordwin, M. (1993 November). Timing is everything. *Small Business Reports,* 43–51.

32. Flynn, G. (2000, July). How do you treat the at-will employment relationship? *Workforce,* 178–179.

33. Rosse, J., Miller, J., and Ringer, R. (1996, Summer). The deterrent value of drug and integrity testing. *Journal of Business and Psychology, 10,* 477–485.

34. Flynn, G. (1999, January). How to prescribe drug testing. *Workforce,* 107–109.

35. Zigarelli, M. (1995). Drug testing litigation: Trends and outcomes. *Human Resource Management Review, 5,* 245–265; Flynn, G. (1996, April). Will drug testing pass or fail in court? *Personnel Journal,* 141–144.

36. Green, W. E. (1989, November 21). Drug testing becomes corporate mine field. *Wall Street Journal,* B-1, B-8.

37. Verespoj, M. A. (1990, July 2). Death blow for random testing. *Industry Week,* 47–48.

38. *Wall Street Journal.* (1994, February 8). Drug testing gets big boost from the California Supreme Court, A-1.

39. Gunsch, D. (1993, May). Training prepares workers for drug testing. *Personnel Journal,* 52–59.

40. Hanson, A. (1990, July). What employees say about drug testing. *Personnel,* 32–36.

41. Maltby, L. (1990, July). Put performance to the test. *Personnel,* 30–31.

42. Griffin, S., Keller, A., and Cohn, A. (2001, Winter). Developing a drug testing policy at a public university: Participant perspectives. *Public Personnel Management,* 467–481.

43. Nadell, B. (2001, August). Is your corporate culture on drugs? *Occupational Health & Safety,* 28–31.

44. Hamilton, J. O. (1991, June 3). A video game that tells if employees are fit for work. *BusinessWeek,* 36; Maltby, L. (1990, July). Put performance to the test. *Personnel,* 30–31.

45. Eisenberg, B., and Johnson, L. (2001, December). Being honest about being dishonest. Society for Human Resources Management. www.shrm.org/whitepapers/.

46. Willis, R. (1986, January). White collar crime. *Management Review,* 75, 22–30.

47. Payne, M. (2001, April 8). Sticky fingers. *Boulder Daily Camera,* 6-F.

48. Vaught, B., Taylor, R., and Vaught, S. (2000, January). The attitudes of managers regarding the electronic monitoring of employee behavior: Procedural and ethical considerations. *American Business Review, 18,* 107–114.

49. DeTienne, K., and Flint, R. (1996, Spring). The boss's eyes and ears: A case study of electronic monitoring and the privacy for consumers and workers act. *Labor Lawyer,* 93–115.

50. *USA Today.* (1993, May 24). Bosses peak at e-mail, B1:2.

51. *BusinessWeek.* (1990, January 15). Is your boss spying on you? 74–75.

52. Levy, S. (2004, June 7). A future with nowhere to hide? *Newsweek,* 76.

53. Alder, S., and Ambrose, M. (2005). Towards understanding fairness judgements associated with computer performance monitoring: An integration of the feedback, justice, and monitoring research. *Human Resource Management Review,* 15, 43–67.

54. See Garson, B. (1988). *The electronic sweatshop: How computers are transforming the office of the future into the factory of the past.* New York: Penguin Books; Piturro, M. (1989, May). Employee performance monitoring . . . or meddling? *Management Review,* 31–33.

55. DeTienne, K., and Flint, R. (1996, Spring). The boss's eyes and ears: A case study of electronic monitoring and the privacy for consumers and workers act. *Labor Lawyer,* 93–115.

56. Bates, R., and Holton, E. (1995). Computerized performance monitoring: A review of human resource issues. *Human Resource Management Review,* 5, 267–288.

57. *BusinessWeek.* (1990, January 15). Is your boss spying on you? 74–75.

58. McCarthy, M. J. (1999, October 21). Now the boss knows when you're clicking. *Wall Street Journal,* B-1.

59. Zimmerman, E. (2002, February). HR must know when employee surveillance crosses the line. *Workforce,* 38–45.

60. Near, J., and Miceli, M. (1985). Organizational dissidence: The case of whistleblowing. *Journal of Business Ethics, 4,* 1–16.

61. Near, J., and Miceli, M. (1995). Effective whistle-blowing. *Academy of Management Review,* 20, 679–708.

62. Felsberg, E. (2005, Spring). Understanding retaliation and whistleblowing claims. *Employment Relations Today,* 91–96.

63. Zimmerman, A., and Bandler, J. (2005, May 24). Wal-Mart ex-worker files complaint. *Wall Street Journal,* B-5; Zimmerman, A. (2005, July 11). Wal-Mart takes shot at credibilit of fired executive. *Wall Street Journal,* B-5.

64. Dworkin, T. M., and Baucas, M. S. (1998). Internal vs. external whistleblowers: A comparison of whistleblower processes. *Journal of Business Ethics,* 17, 1281–1298.

65. *The Economist.* (1995, August 19). The uncommon good, 55–56.

66. Wiscombe, J. (2002, July). Don't fear whistleblowers. *Workforce,* 26–32; Zellner, W. (2002, January 28). A hero—and a smoking gun letter. *BusinessWeek,* 34–35.

67. Boyle, R. D. (1990). A review of whistle-blower protection and suggestions for change. *Labor Law Journal, 41*(12), 821–828.

68. Miceli, M., and Near, J. (1994). Whistle-blowing: Reaping the benefits. *Academy of Management Executive, 8*(3), 65–72.

69. Steinberg, M., and Kaufman, S. (2005, Spring). Minimizing corporate liability exposure when the whistle blows in the post Sarbanes-Oxley era. *Journal of Corporation Law,* 445–463; Sraeel, H. (2005, August). With the whistleblower provision, no one wins. *USBanker,* 8.

70. Overman, S. (1998, November). Relationships: When labor leads to love. *HR Focus, 1,* 14.

71. Greenwald, J. (2000, February 14). Office romances may court trouble. *Business Insurance,* 3–4.

72. Stanton, M. (1998, October). Courting disaster: The perils of office romance. *Government Executive,* 35–39.

73. Overman, S. (1998, November). Relationships: When labor leads to love. *HR Focus, 1,* 14.

74. Gossage, B. (2005, February). Fishing off the company pier. *Inc.,* 17–19.

75. Todorova, A. (2005, February 27). Romancing a colleague. *Wall Street Journal Sunday,* 4.

76. Cottringer, W. (2003, April). The abc's of employee discipline. *Supervision,* 5–7.

77. Weinstein, S. (1992, September). Teams without managers. *Progressive Grocer,* 101–104.

78. Redeker, J. R. (1989). *Employee discipline.* Washington, DC: Bureau of National Affairs.

79. Firing and disciplining employees. (2005). www.hrzone.com/topics/firing.html.

80. Ramsey, R. D. (1998, February). Guidelines for the progressive discipline of employees. *Supervision,* 10–12.

81. King, K. (2003, Summer). Employee-proposed discipline: How well is it working? *Public Personnel Management,* 197–209.

82. Osigweh, C., Yg, A. B., and Hutchison, W. R. (1989, Fall). Positive discipline. *Human Resource Management, 28*(3), 367–383.

83. Grote, D. (2001, September/October). Discipline without punishment. *Across the Board,* 52–57.

84. Osigweh, C., Yg, A. B., and Hutchison, W. R. (1989, Fall). Positive discipline. *Human Resource Management, 28*(3), 367–383.

85. *Ibid.*

86. Harvey, E. L. (1987, March). Discipline vs. punishment. *Management Review, 76,* 25–29.

87. Falcone, P. (1998, November). Adopt a formal approach to progressive discipline. *HRMagazine,* 55–59.

88. Sherman, C. V. (1987). *From losers to winners.* New York: American Management Association.

89. Bureau of National Affairs. (1987). *Grievance guide* (7th ed.). Washington, DC: Bureau of National Affairs.

90. Flynn, G. (2000, September). Does a new right make a wrong? *Workforce,* 122–123.

91. Hindera, J. L., and Josephson, J. L. (1998). Reinventing the public employer–employee relationship. The just cause standard. *Public Administration Quarterly, 22,* 98–113.

92. Redeker, J. R. (1989). *Employee discipline.* Washington, DC: Bureau of National Affairs.

93. Shellenbarger, S. (1994, January 13). More companies experiment with workers' schedules. *Wall Street Journal,* B1-3.

94. Segal, J. (1997, July). Looking for trouble? When it comes to the Americans with Disabilities Act, what you know about your employees can hurt you. *HRMagazine,* 76–83.

95. Breuer, N. L. (1993, September). Resources can relieve ADA fears. *Personnel Journal,* 131–142.

96. Mamis, R. (1995, January). Employees from hell. *Inc.,* 50–57.

97. Sculnick, M. W. (1990, Spring). Key court cases. *Employee Relations Today, 17*(1), 53–59.

98. Peyton, P. (2003). *Dignity at work: Eliminate bullying and create a positive working environment.* New York: Brunner-Routledge.

99. *Ibid.*

100. Eckholm, E. (2005, July 26). As recruiting suffers, military reins in abuses at boot camp. *New York Times,* A-1, A-14.

101. Nocera, J. (2005, June 18). In business, tough guys finish last. *New York Times,* B-1, B-4.

102. Pearson, C., and Porath, C. (2005, February). On the nature, consequences and remedies of workplace incivility: NO time for "nice"? Think again. *Academy of Management Executive,* 7–18.

103. Sherman, C. V. (1987). *From losers to winners.* New York: American Management Association.

104. Denton, D. K. (1992, Summer). Keeping employees: The Federal Express approach. *SAM Advanced Management Journal, 57*(3), 10–13.

105. Leblanc, P. V., and McInerney, M. (1994, January). Need a change? Jump on the banding wagon. *Personnel Journal,* 72–78.

Chapter 15

1. Harris, N. (1997, October 27). UPS puts its back into it. *BusinessWeek,* 50.

2. Rocks, D. (1999, November 15). UPS: Will this IPO deliver? *BusinessWeek,* 41.

3. Bernstein, A. (1997, August 25). This package is a heavy one for the Teamsters. *BusinessWeek,* 40–41.

4. Blake, N. (2002, July 16). UPS, Teamsters reach agreement on new six-year contract. www.pressroom.ups.com.

5. Brooks, R. (2005, March 25). UPS pilots union to vote on strike after long talks. *Wall Street Journal,* A-2.

6. Federation of Physicians and Dentists. (2005). www.fpdunion.org; American College of Osteopathic Family Physicians. (2005). www.acofp.org; Bernstein, A. (1999, June 28). The Amalgamated Doctors of America? *BusinessWeek,* 36.

7. Adelson, A. (1997, April 5). Physician, unionize thyself. *New York Times,* A-21–A-22.

8. Haberfeld, Y. (1995). Why do workers join unions? The case of Israel. *Industrial and Labor Relations Review, 48,* 656–670.

9. Brett, J. M. (1980). Why employees want unions. *Organizational Dynamics, 9,* 316–332.

10. Bernstein, A. (1994, May 23). Why America needs unions. *BusinessWeek,* 70–82.

11. U.S. Bureau of Labor Statistics. (2005, April 8). Work stoppages involving 1,000 or more workers, 1947–2004. www.bls.gov.

12. Greer, S., and Baird, C. (2004, Spring). The phony case against Taft-Hartley and the real one. *Labor Law Journal,* 25–37.

13. Moorman, R. (2000, March). Throwing down the gauntlet. *Air Transport World,* 49–51.

14. Flynn, G. (1996, February). TEAM Act: What it is and what it can do for you. *Personnel Journal,* 85–87.

15. *HR News.* (1994, February). Washington scorecard. *13*(2), 5.

16. Budd, J. (1996). Canadian strike replacement legislation and collective bargaining: Lessons for the United States. *Industrial Relations, 35,* 245–260.

17. Holley, W. H., and Jennings, K. M. (1991). *The labor relations process.* Chicago: Dryden.

18. Hunter, L. W. (1998). Can strategic participation be institutionalized? Union representation on American corporate boards. *Industrial and Labor Relations Review, 51,* 557–578.

19. *Management Report.* (2005, October). Big unions disaffiliate from AFL-CIO, 1.

20. Fossum, J. (1995). *Labor relations* (6th ed.). Chicago: Irwin.

21. Maher, K. (2005, September 13). AFL-CIO stands to shrink further; United Here, representing about 450,000 workers, may be next union to split. *Wall Street Journal,* D-7; Maher, K. (2005,

September 26). Breakaway unions to organize themselves first. *Wall Street Journal,* A6.

22. *The Economist.* (2005, May 14). The labor movement: Brothers at arms, 32–36.

23. Overman, S. (1991, December). The union pitch has changed. *HRMagazine,* 44–46.

24. Freeman, R. B. (1989). The changing status of unionism around the world. In W. C. Huang (Ed.), *Organized labor at the crossroads.* Kalamazoo, MI: W. E. Upjohn Institute for Employee Research.

25. European Foundation for the Improvement of Living and Working Conditions. (2002); *The Economist.* (2003, June 7). Special report: Trade unions, 60.

26. Ofori-Dankwa, J. (1993). Murray and Reshef revisited: Toward a typology/theory of paradigms of national trade union movements. *Academy of Management Review, 18,* 269–292.

27. Husain, I. (1995, January). Fresh start: Laid off workers need somewhere to turn. *Entrepreneur,* 306.

28. *The Economist.* (2002, May 25). Europe: A general strike looms; Spanish labor law, 50.

29. Ofori-Dankwa, J. (1993). Murray and Reshef revisited: Toward a typology/theory of paradigms of national trade union movements. *Academy of Management Review, 18,* 269–292.

30. Mills, D. Q. (1989). *Labor–management relations.* New York: McGraw-Hill.

31. *The Economist.* (2004, February 21). German industrial relations: Slowly losing chains, 49.

32. *The Economist.* (2001, April 14). You're fired, 45–46.

33. Wilpert, B. (1975). Research in industrial democracy and the German case. *Industrial Relations Journal, 6*(1), 53–64.

34. Marsland, S. E., and Beer, M. (1985). Note on Japanese management and employment systems. In M. Beer and B. Spector (Eds.), *Readings in human resource management.* New York: The Free Press.

35. *The Economist.* (1996, February 10). Stakeholder capitalism: Unhappy families, 23–25.

36. Thornton, E. (1999, November 15). Remaking Nissan. *Business Week,* 70–76.

37. Delaney, J. T. (1991). Unions and human resource policies. In K. Rowland and G. Ferris (Eds.), *Research in personnel and human resources management.* Greenwich, CT: JAI Press.

38. Lawler and Mohrman, 1987. Lawler, E. E, and Mohrman, S. A. unions and the new management. *Academy of Management Executive, 1,* 293–300.

39. Bernstein, A. (1993, January 25). Making teamwork work—and appeasing Uncle Sam. *BusinessWeek,* 101.

40. Lewin, D. (2001, Winter). IR and HR perspectives on workplace conflict: What can they learn from each other? *Human Resource Management Review,* 453–485.

41. Woodruff, D. (1993, February 8). Saturn: Labor's love lost? *BusinessWeek,* 122, 124.

42. McHugh, P. P., and Yim, S. G. (1999, Fall). Developments in labor–management cooperation: The codification of cooperative mechanisms. *Labor Law Journal,* 230–236.

43. Gray, G. R., Meyers, D. W., and Meyers, P. S. (1999, January). Cooperative provisions in labor agreements: A new paradigm? *Monthly Labor Review,* 29–45.

44. Farber, H. (2001, January). Union success in representation elections: Why does unit size matter? *Industrial and Labor Relations Review,* 329–348.

45. Kochan, T. A., and Katz, H. C. (1988). *Collective bargaining and industrial relations.* Homewood, IL: Irwin.

46. *The Economist.* (1999, October 2). Wal-Mart wins again, 33.

47. Bernstein, A. (1999, July 19). All's not fair in labor wars. *BusinessWeek*, 43.

48. Zellner, W. (2000, March 13). Up against the Wal-Mart. *BusinessWeek*, 76–78.

49. Bryant, A. (1994, April 6). Lorenzo plan for airline rejected. *New York Times*, D-53.

50. Olafson, C. (1999, May). Cyber unions. *The Futurist*, 70.

51. Romero, C. L. (1999, November 11). Union makes pitch to local IBMers. *Boulder Daily Camera*, 3A.

52. *Small Business Reports*. (1933, March). Unions vs. private property, 25.

53. Spognardi, M. A. (1998), Conducting a successful union-free campaign. A primer (Part II). *Employee Relations Law Journal, 24* (3), 31–53.

54. Spognardi, M. A. (1998). Conducting a successful union-free campaign: A primer (Part II). *Employee Relations Law Journal*, 24(3), 31–53.

55. Kleiner, M. (2001, Summer). Intensity of management resistance: Understanding the decline of unionization in the private sector. *Journal of Labor Research*, 519–540.

56. Union elections: Certifcation elections. (2005). www.laborresearch.org.

57. Walton, B., and McKersie, R. (1965). *A behavioral theory of labor negotiations*. New York: McGraw-Hill.

58. Cimini, M. H., Behrmann, S. L., and Johnson, E. M. (1994, January). Labor–management bargaining in 1993. *Monthly Labor Review*, 20–35.

59. McGinn, D. (1998, August 10). GM still has miles to go: The settlement doesn't fix its deep problems. *Newsweek*, 46.

60. Welch, D. (2003, October 20). What Goodyear got from its union. *BusinessWeek*, 148–149.

61. Voos, P. (2001, Winter). As IR perspective on collective bargaining. *Human Resource Management Review*, 487–503.

62. *Ibid*; Kelly, K. (1993, August 2). Labor deals that offer a break from "us vs. them." *BusinessWeek*, 30.

63. Bernstein, A. (1995, March 18). United we own. *BusinessWeek*, 96–102.

64. Arndt, M. (2001, November 12). To-do list for United's Mr. Fix-It. *BusinessWeek*, 62.

65. Cook, M. (Ed.). (1993). *The human resources yearbook: 1993/1994 edition*, 162. Upper Saddle River, NJ: Prentice Hall.

66. BLS Reports. (1994, February 14). Record low number of strikes continues into 1993. *BNA's Employee Relations Weekly*, 12(7), 167.

67. Greenhouse, S. (2000, March 21). Unions predict gain from Boeing strike. *New York Times*, A-11; *The Economist*. (2000, March 18). The slow death of Boeing man, 29–30.

68. Freeman, R. B., and Medoff, J. L. (1984). *What do unions do?* New York: Basic Books.

69. Adams, R. (2005, July 14). NHL, players carve out accord. *Wall Street Journal*, 1; *The Economist*. (2005, July 23). Lessons from a lock-out, 51.

70. Lewin, D. (2001, Winter). IR and HR perspectives on workplace conflict: What can they learn from each other? *Human Resource Management Review*, 453–485.

71. Holley, W., and Jennings, K. (1994). *The labor relations process* (5th ed.). Fort Worth, TX: The Dryden Press; Fossum, J. (1995). *Labor relations* (6th ed.). Chicago: Irwin.

72. Freeman, R. B., and Medoff, J. L. (1979). The two faces of unionism. *The Public Interest, 57*, 69–93.

73. Abraham, K. G., and Medoff, J. L. (1985). Length of service and promotions in union and nonunion work groups. *Industrial and Labor Relations Review, 38*, 408–420.

74. Abraham, K. G., and Medoff, J. L. (1984). Length of service and layoffs in union and nonunion work groups. *Industrial and Labor Relations Review, 38*, 87–97.

75. Greenhouse, S. (1999, September 23). In the UAW deal, something for almost everyone? *New York Times*, retrieved online at www.nytimes.com/library/financial; Meredith, R. (1999, September 17). DaimlerChrysler and the UAW reach tentative pack, *New York Times*, retrieved online at www.nytimes.com/html.

76. Foulkes, F. (1980). *Personnel policies in large nonunion companies*. Upper Saddle River, NJ: Prentice Hall.

77. Bernardin, J., and Beatty, R. (1984). *Performance appraisal: Assessing human behavior at work*. Boston: Kent.

78. Abraham, K. G., and Farber, H. S. (1988). Returns to seniority in union and nonunion jobs: A new look at evidence. *Industrial and Labor Relations Review, 42*, 3–19; Freeman, R. B., and Medoff, J. L. (1984). *What do unions do?* New York: Basic Books.

79. Gunsch, D. (1993, March). On-site schools are required by a UAW contract. *Personnel Journal*, 43.

80. Grossman, R. (2005, May). Unions follow suit. *HRMagazine*, 47–51; Foster, A. (2003). Differences in union and nonunion earnings in blue-collar and service occupations. *Compensation and Working Conditions Online*. www.bls.gov; Stevens, C. (1995). The social cost of rent seeking by labor unions in the United States. *Industrial Relations, 34*, 190–202; Jarrel, S., and Stanley, T. (1990). A meta-analysis of the union–nonunion wage gap. *Industrial and Labor Relations Review, 44*, 54–67; Freeman, R. (1982). Union wage practices and wage dispersion within establishments. *Industrial and Labor Relations Review, 36*, 3–21.

81. Freeman, R. B. (1982). Union wage practices and wage dispersion within establishments. *Industrial and Labor Relations Review, 36*, 3–21.

82. U.S. Bureau of Labor Statistics. (2002). Collective bargaining statistics descriptive data. www.bls.gov.

83. Driscoll, J. W. (1979). Working creatively with a union: Lessons from the Scanlon plan. *Organizational Dynamics, 8*, 61–80.

84. Freeman, R. B. (1981). The effect of unionism on fringe benefits. *Industrial and Labor Relations Review, 34*, 489–509.

85. Fosu, A. G. (1984). Unions and fringe benefits: Additional evidence. *Journal of Labor Research, 5*, 247, 254.

86. Gómez-Mejía, L. R., and Balkin, D. B. (1992). *Compensation, organizational strategy and firm performance*. Cincinnati: South-Western.

87. Budd, J. W., and McCall, B. P. (1997). The effect of unions on the receipt of unemployment insurance benefits. *Industrial and Labor Relations Review, 50*, 478–492.

88. Hirsch, B. T., MacPherson, D. A., and Dumond, M. (1997). Workers' compensation recipiency in union and nonunion workplaces. *Industrial and Labor Relations Review, 50*, 213–236.

89. Foulkes, F. (1980). *Personnel policies in large nonunion companies*. Upper Saddle River, NJ: Prentice Hall.

90. Flynn, G. (2000, September). Does a new right make a wrong? *Workforce*, 122–123.

91. Morgan, J., Owens, J., and Gomes, G. (2002, Winter). Union rules in nonunion settings: The NLRB and workplace investigations. *SAM Advanced Management Journal*, 22–32; Hodges, A., Coke, C., and Trumble, R. (2002, Summer). *Weingarten* in the nonunion workplace: Looking in the funhouse mirror. *Labor Law Journal*, 89–97.

Chapter 16

1. *Washington Post* (1997, August 21). ValuJet: The alarming truth, 18.

2. Schmid, R. E. (1997, August 18). Planes still have no cargo fire detectors, extinguishers might have averted '96 ValuJet crash, safety official says. *Arizona Republic*, A-2.

3. Phillips, D. (1999, July 14). Murder charged in ValuJet crash: Rare indictment names repair firm. *Washington Post*, A-1.

4. ABC News. (1999, December 7). ValuJet verdict: No conspiracy. ABCNEWS.com, retrieved online at more.abcnews.go.con/sections/ us/dailynews/valujetverdict 991207.html.

5. Bureau of Labor Statistics. (2005, June 29). Current injury, illness, and fatality data. www.bls.gov/iif/home.htm.

6. *Ibid.*

7. Lyon, B. K., and Hollcroft, B. (2005). Health and safety management systems: Focus on management. *Occupational Hazards, 67*, 45–48.

8. Ledvinka, J., and Scarpello, V. G. (1991). *Federal regulation of personnel and human resource management* (2nd ed.), 209. Boston: PWS-Kent.

9. Sherman, A. W., and Bohlander, G. W. (1996). *Managing human resources* (10th ed.). Cincinnati, OH: South-Western.

10. McCaffery, R. M. (1992). *Employee benefit programs: A total compensation perspective*, 57–58. Boston: PWS-Kent.

11. *Ibid.*, 59–60.

12. Bauer, T. F. (2002). Safety: A profit opportunity? Companies that consider safety more than a nuisance might profit from it. *C & D Recycler, 4*, 26(3).

13. Colburn, L. E. (1995). Defending against workers' compensation fraud. *Industrial Management, 37*, 1–2.

14. Hays, D. (2005). Comp fraud battle hits some hurdles, study finds. *National Underwriter P & C, 109*, 55.

15. Wilkerson, M. (1999). Healthy savings. *Strategic Finance, 80*, 42–46.

16. Borges, R. (2005, February). Getting the facts behind workplace injuries. *Presstime*, Workforce section, 38.

17. Nash, J. L. (2005). Report: Repetitive motion injuries are still No. 1. *Occupational Hazards, 67*, 13.

18. Hays, D. (2002). Costly prescription drugs are jacking up WC bills. *National Underwriter Life & Health, 106*, 36(2).

19. French, W. L. (1994). *Human resources management* (3rd ed.), 529. Boston: Houghton Mifflin.

20. Ashford, N. A. (1976). *Crisis in the workplace: Occupational disease and injury*, 3, Cambridge, MA: MIT Press.

21. U.S. Department of Labor, Occupational Safety and Health Administration. (1985). *All about OSHA* (rev. ed.), 1. Washington, DC: U.S. Government Printing Office.

22. Ledvinka, J., and Scarpello, V. G. (1991). *Federal regulation of personnel and human resource management* (2nd ed.), 215. Boston: PWS-Kent.

23. Anthony, W. P., Perrewe, P. L., and Kacmar, K. M. (1993). *Strategic human resource management*, 514. Fort Worth, TX: Dryden; Cascio, W. F. (1989). *Managing human resources: Productivity, quality of work life, profits* (2nd ed.), 554–556. New York: McGraw-Hill.

24. *HR Focus*. (2002). OSHA delays enforcing revised record-keeping rules until late April, *79*, 2.

25. Nash, J. L. (2004). OSHA fines General Motors Corp. $160,000 for record-keeping, safety violations. *Occupational Hazards, 66*, 8.

26. U.S. Department of Labor, Occupational Safety and Health Administration. (1985). *All about OSHA* (rev. ed.), 43–46. Washington, DC: U.S. Government Printing Office.

27. May, B. D. (1986, August). Hazardous substances: OSHA mandates the right to know. *Personnel Journal, 65*, 128.

28. See *Whirlpool Corporation v. Marshall*, 445 U.S. 1, 10–12 (1980).

29. Ellis, T. (1999). The governments' new response. *Occupational Health and Safety, 68*, 77–79.

30. Ledvinka, J., and Scarpello, V. G. (1991). *Federal regulation of personnel and human resource management* (2nd ed.), 221–224. Boston: PWS-Kent.

31. U.S. Department of Labor, Occupational Safety and Health Administration. (1985). *All about OSHA* (rev. ed.), 8. Washington, DC: U.S. Government Printing Office.

32. U.S. Department of Labor, Occupational Safety and Health Administration. (1985). *All about OSHA* (rev. ed.), 10. Washington, DC: U.S. Government Printing Office.

33. *Ibid.*, 19–22.

34. *Occupational Hazards*. (2005). OSHA touts "aggressive" 2005 goals, 2, 2.

35. Ledvinka, J., and Scarpello, V. G. (1991). *Federal regulation of personnel and human resource management* (2nd ed.), 224. Boston: PWS-Kent; *Marshall v. Barlow's, Inc.*, 436 U.S. 307 (1978).

36. Garland, S. B. (1989, February 20). This safety ruling could be hazardous to employer's health. *BusinessWeek*, 34.

37. *Ibid.*; Bureau of National Affairs. (1989, July 24). Michigan Supreme Court rules OSH Act does not preempt state proceedings. *BNA's Employee Relations Weekly*, 945.

38. Eng, D. (2005). OSHA penalties on the rise. *Presstime*, Workforce section, 54.

39. Ivanovich, D. (2005, March 28). OSHA accused of caving on penalties to get safety fixes made. *The Houston Chronicle*.

40. Courntey, T. K., and Clancy, E. A. (1998). A descriptive study of U.S. OSHA penalties and inspection frequency for musculoskeletal disorders in the workplace. *American Industrial Hygiene Association Journal, 59*, 563–571.

41. U.S. Department of Labor. (1989). *Fact sheet no. OSHA 89–04*. Washington, DC: U.S. Government Printing Office.

42. U.S. Department of Labor, Occupational Safety and Health Administration. (1985). *All about OSHA* (rev. ed.), 31–32. Washington, DC: U.S. Government Printing Office.

43. *Ibid.*, 8; Ledvinka, J., and Scarpello, V. G. (1991). *Federal regulation of personnel and human resource management* (2nd ed.), 220. Boston: PWS-Kent.

44. U.S. Department of Labor, Occupational Safety and Health Administration. (1985). *All about OSHA* (rev. ed.), 33–34. Washington, DC: U.S. Government Printing Office.

45. Lyon, B. K., and Hollcroft, B. (2005). Health and safety management systems: Focus on management. *Occupational Hazards, 67*, 45–48.

46. Bureau of Labor Statistics. (2004). National census of fatal occupational injuries in 2003. www.bls.gov/iif/oshefoi1.htm.

47. Safety Director's Report. (2002). Hearing protection strategies for any safety department budget. May Newsletter of the Institute of Management and Administration.

48. Oswald, E. M. (1996). No employer is immune: AIDS in the workplace. *Risk Management, 43*, 18–21.

49. Gerstle, D. J. (2005). The true cost of aids. *Journal of International Affairs, 58*, 293–296.

50. Davis, M. (2005). Is AIDS awareness of paradox? *Black Enterprise, 35*, 46.

51. Hunter, S. (1998). Your infection control program. *Occupational Health and Safety, 67*, 76–80.

52. Oswald, E. M. (1996). No employer is immune: AIDS in the workplace. *Risk Management, 43*, 18–21.

53. *Ibid.*

54. Mello, J. A. (1999). Ethics in employment law: The Americans with Disabilities Act and the employee with HIV. *Journal of Business Ethics, 20*, 67–83.

55. Oswald, E. M. (1996). No employer is immune: AIDS in the workplace. *Risk Management, 43*, 18–21.

56. Bee, L., and Maatman, G. L. (2002). Workers with AIDS have legal rights. *National Underwriter Property & Casualty, 106*, 32(3).

57. Wade, J. (2004). Reducing the threat. *Risk Management, 51*, 10–18.

58. *HR Focus.* (2005, April). How to predict and prevent workplace violence, *82*, 10–11.

59. Viollis, P. (2005). Most workplace violence avoidable. *Business Insurance, 39*, 10.

60. Barron, D. L. (2004). The best defense. *Best's Review, 105*, 80.

61. Viollis, P. (2005). Most workplace violence avoidable. *Business Insurance 39*, 10.

62. Gurchiek, K. (2005). Study: Domestic violence spills over into the workplace. *HRMagazine, 50*, 32, 38.

63. Shreve, M. (2004). Employer response important in dealing with domestic abuse. *Business Insurance, 38*, 4–5.

64. Laabs, J. (1999). Employee sabotage: Don't be a target. *Workforce, 78*, 32–38.

65. Jackson, M. (1999, August 2). No ignoring workplace violence. *Arizona Republic*, A-1.

66. Bureau of National Affairs. (1993, April 26). Preventing workplace violence: Legal imperatives can clash. *Employee Relations Weekly, 11*(17), 451–452.

67. Missouri Capitol Police. (1996, June 6). Violence in the workplace . . ., 1–6. www.dps.state.mo.us/DPS/MCP/STUDY/WKVIOLNC.HTM.

68. *Ibid.*

69. Boddenhausen, K. G. (1994, March 3). It's . . . becoming a fact of life. *Springfield News-Leader,* B-3.

70. Rudolph, B. (1987, May 18). Thou shalt not smoke. *Time, 129*, 58–59.

71. Prewitt, E. (1986, September 15). The drive to kick smoking at work. *Fortune, 114*, 42–43.

72. Joyce, A. (1998, November 15). Smoke-free workplaces spreading like wildfire: Sharp rise in number of employers that ban cigarettes is good news for advocates, and a burden for those who enjoy a puff. *Washington Post*, H-4.

73. Hoffman, K. B. (2005, February 9). No butts about it: Four fired for not giving up smoking. *The Arizona Republic*, D-1, D-4.

74. *Ibid.*

75. Rudner, S. (2005). Firing an employer for being a smoker. *Canadian HR Reporter, 18*, 23.

76. Litvan, L. M. (1994). A smoke-free workplace? *Nation's Business, 82*, 65.

77. New York Public Health Law, Section 1399 (Consol. 1993).

78. Worsnop, R. L. (1995). Repetitive stress injuries. *CQ Researcher, 5*, 539–556.

79. Nash, J. L. (2005). Report: Repetitive motion injuries are still No. 1. *Occupational Hazards, 67*, 13.

80. Whalen, J. (2001). Silence is golden. *Warehousing Management, 8*, 29.

81. Safety Director's Report. (2002). Hearing protection strategies for any safety department budget. May Newsletter of the Institute of Management and Administration.

82. Whalen, J. (2001). Silence is golden. *Warehousing Management, 8*, 29.

83. Wermiel, S. (1991, March 21). Justices bar "fetal protection" policies. *Wall Street Journal*, B-1, B-5.

84. Trost, C. (1990, October 8). Business and women anxiously watch suit on "fetal protection." *Wall Street Journal*, 1.

85. Altman, L. E. (1988, June 5). Pregnant women's use of VDT's is scrutinized. *New York Times*, 22; Meier, B. (1987, February 5). Companies wrestle with threats to reproductive health. *Wall Street Journal*, 23.

86. Jacob, S. L. (1988, November 22). Small business slowly wakes to OSHA hazard rule. *Wall Street Journal*, B-2; Myers, D. W. (1992).

Human resource management (2nd ed.), 717. Chicago: Commerce Clearing House.

87. Pirtle, L. (1999). Chemical safety goes online. *Occupational Hazards, 61*, 59–60.

88. *Employee Benefit Plan Review.* (1999). Genetic testing: "Minefield" of potential legal liability for employers, *53*, 41–42.

89. Bureau of National Affairs (1991, November 18). Value of genetic testing said minimal for gauging workplace risks. *BNA's Employee Relations Weekly*, 1235; Draper, E. (1991). *Risky business: Genetic testing and exclusionary practices in the hazardous workplace.* Cambridge, England: Cambridge University Press; Olian, J. D. (1984). Genetic screening for employment purposes. *Personnel Psychology, 37*, 423–438; Schuler, R. S., and Huber, V. L. (1993). *Personnel and human resource management* (5th ed.), 251. Minneapolis: West.

90. *Medicine & Health.* (2002). Government, railroad settle genetic testing case, *56*, 5.

91. *Occupational Hazards.* (2001). Railroad halts genetic testing, *63*, 34.

92. Begley, S. (2004, February 6). Bill seeking to ban DNA discrimination isn't really necessary. *Wall Street Journal*, B-1.

93. Petersen, D. (2005). Safety improvement. *Professional Safety, 50*, 45–49.

94. Cullen, L. (1999). Safety committees: A smart business decision. *Occupational Hazards, 61*, 99–104.

95. *Ibid.*

96. Kaletta, J. P., and Jolley, M. (2005). Safety improvement: Sparks organizational change at Alberto Culver. *Occupational Hazards, 67*, 54–56.

97. Employee Benefit News. (2005, June 1). Employers should promote EAPs to maximize ROI.

98. Fisher, C. C., Schoenfeldt, L. F., and Shaw, J. B. (1996). *Human resource management* (3rd ed.). Boston: Houghton Mifflin; Schuler, R. S., and Huber, V. L. (1993). *Personnel and human resource management* (5th ed.), 667–669. Minneapolis: West.

99. Thompson, R. (1990). Fighting the high cost of workers' comp. *Nation's Business, 78*(3), 28.

100. Moulson, G. (1999, September 6). The longest workday: It's in the U.S. *Arizona Republic*, A-1.

101. Maslach, C., and Jackson, S. E. (1981). The measurement of experienced burnout. *Journal of Occupational Behavior, 2*, 99–113.

102. Cordes, C. L., and Dougherty, T. W. (1993). A review and integration of research on job burnout. *Academy of Management Review, 18*, 621–656.

103. Kahill, S. (1988). Symptoms of professional burnout: A review of the empirical evidence. *Canadian Psychology, 29*, 284–297.

104. Cordes, C. L., and Dougherty, T. W. (1993). A review and integration of research on job burnout. *Academy of Management Review, 18*, 621–656.

105. Jackson, S. E., and Maslach, C. (1982). After effects of job-related stress: Families as victims. *Journal of Occupational Behavior, 3*, 63–77.

106. Nighswonger, T. (2002). Depression: The unseen safety risk. *Occupational Hazards, 64*, 38(3).

107. *Ibid.*

108. Kirrane, D. (1990, January). EAPs: Dawning of a new age. *HRMagazine*, 34.

109. Bahls, J. E. (1999). Handle with care. *HRMagazine, 44*, 60–66.

110. Helmer, D. C., Dunn, L. M., Eaton, K., Macedonio, C., and Lubritz, L. (1995). Implementing corporate wellness programs. *AAOHN Journal, 43*, 558–563.

111. Merx, K. (2005, June 22). Pfizer promotes wellness plan to cut health costs. Knight-Ridder Tribune Business News.

112. Brotherton, P. (1998). Paybacks are healthy. *HRMagazine, 43*, F2–F6.

113. Woodward, N. H. (2005). Exercise options. *HRMagazine, 50,* 78–84.

Chapter 17

1. Hakim, D. (2005, March 3). Taking down the 'no foreign cars' sign in Michigan. *New York Times,* C-1; www.toyota.com; Maynard, M. (2005, January 27). GM posts worst loss since 1992. New York Times, C-1.

2. Chandler, C. (2005, February 7). Full speed ahead. *Fortune,* 78–84.

3. *Ibid.*

4. Wellins, R., and Rioux, S. (2001, February). Solving the global HR puzzle. *Workspan, 44*(2), 1–14; Chandler, C. (2005, February 7). Full speed ahead. *Fortune,* 78–84; *Newsline.* (2005, January 11). Canadian employers moving to total rewards to compensation. www.worldatwork.com; *Newsline.* (2005, February 28). U.S. multinationals dramatically revising stock option awards for non-U.S. executives. www.worldatwork.com.

5. Kahn, J. (1999, June 7). Wal-Mart goes shopping in Europe. *Fortune,* 105–110; Guyon, J. (1999, February 15). Europe's new capitalists. *Fortune,* 104–110; Oyama, D. I. (1999, June 1). World watch. *Wall Street Journal,* A-16; Mandel, M. J. (2002, March 6). How companies can marry well. *BusinessWeek,* 28; D'Amico, M. L. (2005, March 9). Executive MBA is casing Germany. *Wall Street Journal,* B-3; Jacoby, M. (2005, March 4). EU won't allow crossing borders for health work. *Wall Street Journal,* A-13; Johnson, P. (2005, January 31). Germany's dismal future. *Forbes,* 37; Postret, V. (2005, January 21). Economic scene. *New York Times,* C-2.

6. Wild, J. J., Wild, K. L., and Han, J. C. Y. (2003). *International business.* Upper Saddle River, NJ: Prentice Hall; 6. Hill, C. W. (2006). *International business.* New York: McGraw-Hill/Irwin.

7. Collins, S. M. (1998). *Export, imports, and the American worker.* Washington, DC: Brooking Institute; Fisher, A. (2005, January 24). Offshoring could boost your career. *Fortune,* 36; Engardio, P., and Einhorn, B. (2005, March 21). Special report on outsourcing. *BusinessWeek,* 84–91; Kripalani, M., Hamm, S., Ante, S. E., and Reinhardt, A. (2004, January 26). Scrambling to stem India's onslaught. *BusinessWeek,* 81.

8. World Trade Organization, International Trade Trends and Statistics, 2003; Dickson, M. (1998, October 16). All those expectations aside, many firms are finding the Internet invaluable in pursuing international trade. *Los Angeles Times,* 10; Millman, J. (2002a, January 23). Mexico attracts U.S. aerospace industry. *Wall Street Journal,* A-1; Millman, J. (2002b, February 13). Visions of sugar plums south of the border. *Wall Street Journal,* A-15; World Trade Centers Association. (2006). www.wtedw.com.

9. Mandel, M. J. (2002, March 6). How companies can marry well. *BusinessWeek,* 28; Cooper, J. C., and Madigan, K. C. (1999, October 4). So much for that safety valve. *BusinessWeek,* 31–32; Smith, G., and Malkin, E. (1998, December 21). Mexican makeover. *BusinessWeek,* 50–52; Bellman, E. (2005, April 11). India senses patent appeal. *Wall Street Journal,* A-1; Millman, J. (2005, March 22). Maquiladora resumed hiring growth in 2004. *Wall Street Journal,* A-13.

10. Millman, J. (2002a, January 23). Mexico attracts U.S. aerospace industry. *Wall Street Journal,* A-1; Millman, J. (2002b, February 13). Visions of sugar plums south of the border. *Wall Street Journal,* A-15; Khanna, T., Gulati, R., and Nohria, N. (1998). The dynamics of learning alliances: Competition, cooperation, and relative scope. *Strategic Management Journal, 19,* 193–210; Vitzhum, C. (1999, July 20). Global strategy powers Endesa's power moves. *Wall Street Journal Europe,* 4–6; Millman, J. (2005, March 22). Maquiladora resumed hiring growth in 2004. *Wall Street Journal,* A-13;

McWilliams, G. (2005, March 10). In electronics, U.S. companies seize momentum from Japan. *Wall Street Journal,* A-1.

11. Prasso, S. (2002, April 22). To get an MNA is glorious. *BusinessWeek,* 14; Oster, P. (1993, November 1). The fast track leads overseas. *BusinessWeek,* 64–68; Murray, S. (1999, June 22). Europe's MBA programs attract Americans—Demand for global view gets students across Atlantic. *Wall Street Journal Europe,* 4–5; D'Amico, M. L. (2005, March 9). Executive MBA is casing Germany. *Wall Street Journal,* B-3; Yvan, L. (2005,. March 9). China's powerful hit the book. *Wall Street Journal,* A-18; Barboza, D. (2005, February 19). Seven habits of highly effective cadres. *New York Times,* B-1.

12. Hill, C. W. (2006). *International business.* New York: McGraw-Hill/Irwin.

13. Puliyenthuruthel, J., and Rocks, D. (2005, April 25). India: The soft underbelly of offshoring. *BusinessWeek,* 52.

14. *Ibid.*

15. *ACA News.* (1996, June). International, 32.

16. Heher, E. C. (2001). Helping expatriates get ready for a healthy assignment. *Innovations in International HR, 27*(3), 5–10; Schindler, K. P. (2001). Strategies for compensating married assignees. *Innovations in International HR, 27*(3), 11–20; Withercup, M. B. (2001). Location evaluation reports: An overview of troubled spots. *Innovations in International HR, 27*(3), 1–12; *Newsline.* (2005, February 25). Overseas assignments becoming more enticing to executives. www.worldatwork.com; *Newsline.* (2005, February 7). Expatriates on the rise. www.worldatwork.com.

17. Beck, E. (1995, May 1). Foreign companies in Hungary concerned about wage increase. *Wall Street Journal,* B-13(1).

18. Perkins, S. J. (2002). The people dimension: A European perspective on globalization. *Workspan, 43*(10), 15–25; Medler, P. (2005, April 23). Rise in Chinese textile imports prompts inquiry in Europe. *New York Times,* B-2; Medller, P. (2005, April 23). Rise in Chinese textile imports prompts inquiry in Europe. *New York Times,* B-2.

19. Carrico-Kahn, J., and Brahy, S. (2000). A meeting of minds: The importance of culture awareness in cross-border virtual teams. *Innovations in International HR, 26*(3), 1–11.

20. De La Torre, J., Doz, Y., and Devinney T. (2000). *Managing the global corporation.* New York: Irwin/McGraw-Hill; Sheridan, W. R., and Hansen, P. T. (1996, Spring). Linking international business and expatriate compensation strategies. *ACA Journal,* 66–78; Greenburg, L. (2001). Long distance care giving: Providing for elderly parents while living abroad. *Expatriate Observer, 24*(2), 9–11; Rogers, M. J. (2001). Effective tax rates: How much do you really pay? *Expatriate Observer, 24*(2), 1–3; Hill, C. W. (2006). *International business.* New York: McGraw-Hill/Irwin.

21. Boyacigiller, N. (1990). Role of expatriates in the management of interdependence, complexity, and risk of MNNs. *Journal of International Business Studies,* 3rd quarter, 357–378; Hill, C. W. (2006). *International business.* Chicago: Irwin.

22. Dunn, E. (1991, January). Global outlook; Whirlpool Corporation. *Personnel Journal,* 52.

23. Palich, L. E., and Gómez-Mejía, L. R. (1999). A theory of global strategy and firm efficiencies: Considering the effects of cultural diversity. *Journal of Management, 25*(4), 587–606.

24. *Newsline.* (2005, February 7). Expatriates on the rise. www.worldatwork.com.

25. Runzheimer Report on Relocation. (2002). U.S. companies impact high level employees. Available at www.runzheimer.com.

26. *Fortune.* (1995, October 16). From the front, 225.

27. Wilson, M. L. (1999, July 16). She got the last laugh when colleagues bet she would fail in Japan. *Wall Street Journal,* B-1; Frisbie, P. E. (2000). Expatriate policy and practices: Heading into

the 21st century. *International HR, 26*(2), 1–11; Hill, C. W. (2006). *International business.* New York: McGraw-Hill/Irwin.

28. Gómez-Mejía, L. R., and Balkin, D. B. (1987). The determinants of managerial satisfaction with the expatriation and repatriation process. *Journal of Management Development, 6,* 7–18; Cigna Corporation. (2002). Employers missing ROI when expatriating employees. Available at www.cigna.com; and Osland, J. (2002). What do expatriates want from HR departments? *HR.com.* Available at www.hr.com; Newsline (2005, March 9). Multinational firms favor global approach to compensation management. www.worldatwork.com.

29. Rowland, M. (1993, December 5). Thriving in a foreign environment. *New York Times,* Sect. 3, 17; Ossorio, S. (2002). Misconceptions about women in international area limit numbers. Available at www.catlystwomen.org.

30. *Newsline.* (2002, February 14). Expatriate activity expands but at a slower rate than expected. Available at www.windhamworld. com; *Newsline.* (2005, February 25). Overseas assignments becoming more enticing to executives. www.worldatwork.com. 17–44.

31. *Newsline.* (2005, February 7). Expatriates on the rise. www.worldatwork.com.

32. Swaak, R. (1995, November—December). Expatriate failures: Too many, too much cost, too little planning. *Compensation and Benefits Review,* 17–75.

33. Fisher, A. (2005, January 24). Offshoring could boost your career. *Fortune,* 36.

34. *Ibid.*

35. De La Torre, J., Doz, Y., and Devinney T. (2000). *Managing the global corporation.* New York: Irwin/McGraw-Hill; Wild, J. J., Wild, K. L., and Han, J. C. Y. (2003). *International business.* Upper Saddle River, NJ: Prentice Hall; Austin, J. W. (2001). Miscommunication: The most challenging issue for expatriate managers. *Expatriate Observer, 24*(2), 1–10; Hill, C. W. (2006). *International business.* New York: McGraw-Hill/Irwin.

36. *Fortune,* 1995.

37. Personal interview conducted by authors.

38. Swaak, R. (1995, November–December). Expatriate failures: Too many, too much cost, too little planning. *Compensation and Benefits Review,* 47–75; Hovy, M. (2005, February). Future global remuneration strategies. *Workspan,* 35–39; Newsline (2005, March 9). Multinational firms favor global approach to compensation management. www.worldatwork.com.

39. Dallas, S. (1995, May 15). Working overseas: Rule no. 1: Don't diss the locals. *BusinessWeek,* 8.

40. Tung, R. (1988). *The new expatriates: Managing human resources abroad.* Cambridge, MA: Bellinger.

41. Swaak, R. (1995, November–December). Expatriate failures: Too many, too much cost, too little planning. *Compensation and Benefits Review,* 47–75.

42. Pascoe, R. (1992, March 2). Employers ignore expatriate wives at their own peril. *Wall Street Journal,* A-10; Osland, J. (2002). What do expatriates want from HR departments? *HR.com.* Available at www.hr.com.

43. Oster, P. (1993, November 1). The fast track leads overseas. *BusinessWeek,* 64–68; *Newsline.* (2002, February 14). Expatriate activity expands but at a slower rate than expected. Available at www.windhamworld.com.

44. Oddou, G. R., and Mendenhall, M. E. (1991, January–February). Succession planning for the 21st century: How well are we grooming our future business leaders? *Business Horizons,* 26–35; Fulkerson, J. R. (2002). Growing global executives. In R. Silzer (Ed.), *The 21st Century Executive,* 300–335.

45. Cigna Corporation. (2002). Employers missing ROI when expatriating employees. Available at www.cigna.com.

46. Grant, L. (1997, April 14). That overseas job could derail your career. *Fortune,* 166; Fulkerson, J. R. (2002). Growing global

executives. In R. Silzer (Ed.), *The 21st Century Executive,* 300–335; *Newsline.* (2005, February 25). Overseas assignments becoming more enticing to executives. www.worldatwork.com; Fisher, A. (2005, January 24). Offshoring could boost your career. *Fortune,* 36.

47. Oddou, G. R., and Mendenhall, M. E. (1991, January–February). Succession planning for the 21st century: How well are we grooming our future business leaders? *Business Horizons,* 26–35.

48. Newsline (2005, April 14). Western Europe costs employers more. www.worldatwork.com.

49. Fisher, A. (2005, January 24). Offshoring could boost your career. *Fortune,* 36.

50. Gómez-Mejía, L. R., and Balkin, D. B. (1987). The determinants of managerial satisfaction with the expatriation and repatriation process. *Journal of Management Development, 6,* 7–18; Tanski, A. (2001). Going home again: A checklist for easy repatriation. *Expatriate Observer, 24*(1), 1–3.

51. Handel, J. (2001). Out of sight, out of mind—opinions differ on assignment success. *Workspan, 44*(6), 1–8.

52. Oddou, G. R., and Mendenhall, M. E. (1991, January–February). Succession planning for the 21st century: How well are we grooming our future business leaders? *Business Horizons,* 29.

53. Gómez-Mejía, L. R., and Balkin, D. B. (1987). The determinants of managerial satisfaction with the expatriation and repatriation process. *Journal of Management Development, 6,* 7–18; Wellins, R., and Rioux, S. (2001, February). Solving the global HR puzzle. *Workspan, 44*(2), 1–14.

54. Personal interview conducted by authors.

55. Gómez-Mejía, L. R., and Balkin, D. B. (1987). The determinants of managerial satisfaction with the expatriation and repatriation process. *Journal of Management Development, 6,* 7–18; Wellins, R., and Rioux, S. (2001, February). Solving the global HR puzzle. *Workspan, 44*(2), 1–14.

56. Personal interview conducted by authors.

57. *Newsline.* (2005, February 7). Expatriates on the rise. www.worldatwork.com.

58. Oster, P. (1993, November 1). The fast track leads overseas. *BusinessWeek,* 64–68.

59. Hixon, A. L. (1986, March). Why corporations make haphazard overseas staffing decisions. *Personnel Administrator,* 91–94.

60. Bird, A., and Makuda, M. (1989). Expatriates in their own home: A new twist in the human resource management strategies of Japanese MNCs. *Human Resource Management, 28*(4), 437–453.

61. Shellenbarger, S. (1991, September 6). Spouses must pass test before global transfers. *Wall Street Journal,* B-1.

62. Hill, C. W. (2006). *International business.* Chicago: Irwin; Wild, J. J., Wild, K. L., and Han, J. C. Y. (2006). *International business.* Upper Saddle River, NJ: Prentice Hall; De La Torre, J., Doz, Y., and Devinney T. (2000). *Managing the global corporation.* New York: Irwin/McGraw-Hill.

63. Osland, J. (2002). What do expatriates want from HR departments? *HR.com.* Available at www.hr.com.

64. Lublin, J. S. (1992, August 4). Companies use cross-cultural training to help their employees adjust abroad. *Wall Street Journal,* B-1, B-3.

65. *Newsline.* (2002, February 14). Expatriate activity expands but at a slower rate than expected. Available at www.windhamworld. com; *Newsline.* (2005, February 7). Expatriates on the rise. www.worldatwork.com.

66. Frost, L. (2005, March 25). With mixed feelings, France dismantles its 35-hour week. *Wall Street Journal,* A-13.

67. *Newsline.* (2005, February 7). Expatriates on the rise. www.worldatwork.com.

68. Grant, L. (1997, April 14). That overseas job could derail your career. *Fortune,* 166; Handel, J. (2001). Out of sight, out of mind—opinions differ on assignment success. *Workspan, 44*(6), 1–8; Fisher, A. (2005, January 24). Offshoring could boost your

career. *Fortune,* 36; *Newsline.* (2005, February 7). Expatriates on the rise. www.worldatwork.com.

69. Runzheimer Report on Relocation. (2000). Circle of chaos often develops during family relocation process. Available at www.runzheimer.com.

70. Cafaro, D. (2001, February). A passport to productivity in the new global economy. *Workspan, 44*(2), 1–8.

71. *Ibid.*

72. Fuchsberg, G. (1992, January 9). As costs of overseas assignments climb, firms select expatriates more carefully. *Wall Street Journal,* B-1.

73. Lublin, J. S. (1993, March 12). Jobs in Eastern Europe demand more goodies. *Wall Street Journal,* B-1.

74. Barrionuevo, A., and Herrick, T. (2002, February 7). Wages of terror: For oil companies defense abroad is the order of the day. *Wall Street Journal,* A-1.

75. Salomon, J. (2005, February 22). India poaches U.S. executives for tech jobs. *Wall Street Journal,* B-1.

76. Herod, R. (2001). The cardinal sins of expatriate policies. *International HR, 27*(4), 1–5.

77. Bennett, A. (1993, April 21). What's an expatriate? *Wall Street Journal,* R-5.

78. Cook, M. (Ed.). (1993). *The human resources yearbook, 1993–1994 edition,* 3.14–3.16.

79. Survey Sources for U.S. and International Pay and Benefits Survey. (2006). Available at resource.worldatwork.org.

80. Lyons, J. (2005, March 8). Squeezed by dolarization. *Wall Street Journal,* A-17; Wines, M. (2005, March 12). Dollar's fall ? Africa's garment factories. *New York Times,* A-1.

81. Hovy, M. (2005, February). Future global remuneration strategies. *Workspan,* 35–39.

82. Osland, J. (2002). What do expatriates want from HR departments? *HR.com.* Available at www.hr.com.

83. Polak International Consultants. (2002). International HR practices lay behind workplace trends. www.polak.net; Wallin, M. (2005, February 8). Among Islamic banks, a shortage of scholars. *New York Times,* C-8.

84. Ossorio, S. (2002). Misconceptions about women in international area limit numbers. Available at www.catlystwomen.org.

85. *BusinessWeek.* (1990, May 14). The stateless corporation, 98–105.

86. Chang, L. (1999, May 7). A dream project turned nightmare. *Wall Street Journal Europe,* 10.

87. Burg, J. H., Siscovick, I., and Brock, D. (2000). Aligning performance and reward practices in multinational subsidiaries. *Worldatwork Journal, 9*(3), 10–20; Bhagat, R. S., Kedia, B. L. Harveston, P. D., and Triandis, H. C. (2002). Cultural variations in the cross-border transfer of organizational knowledge. *Academy of Management Review, 27*(2), 204–222; Hovy, M. (2005, February). Future global remuneration strategies. *Workspan,* 35–39; McWilliams, G. (2005, March 10). In electronics, U.S. companies seize momentum from Japan. *Wall Street Journal,* A-1; Lavelle, L. (2005, March 21). Expats: Your options are going native. *BusinessWeek,* B-14; Hovy, M. (2005, February). Future global remuneration strategies. *Workspan,* 35–39; Sapsford, J., and Fackler, M. (2005, March 10). Directors' role shift in Japan. *Wall Street Journal,* A-15; *Wall Street Journal.* (2005, March 6). China regulators to consider caps on executive pay, A-17.

88. Hofstede, G. (1980). *Culture's consequences.* Beverly Hills, CA: Sage; *Academy of Management Executive.* (1993). Cultural constraints in management theories, 7, 81–94.

89. Jaeger, A. (1986). Organization development and national culture: Where's the fit? *Academy of Management Review, 11*(1), 178–190; and Bhagat, R. S., Kedia, B. L. Harveston, P. D., and Triandis, H. C. (2002). Cultural variations in the cross-border transfer of organizational knowledge. *Academy of Management Review, 27*(2), 204–222.

90. Palich, L. E., and Gómez-Mejía, L. R. (1999). A theory of global strategy and firm efficiencies: Considering the effects of cultural diversity. *Journal of Management, 25*(4), 587–606.

91. Hofstede, G. (1980). *Culture's consequences.* Beverly Hills, CA: Sage; *Academy of Management Executive.* (1993). Cultural constraints in management theories, 7, 58.

92. Jaeger, A. (1986). Organization development and national culture: Where's the fit? *Academy of Management Review, 11*(1), 180.

93. Player, M. A. (1991). *Federal law of employment discrimination.* St. Paul, MN: West Publishing; Twomey, D. P. (1994). *Equal employment opportunity* (3rd ed.). Cincinnati, OH: South-Western; Ledvinka, J., and Scarpello, V. G. (1991). *Federal regulation of personnel and human resource management* (2nd ed.). Boston: PWS-Kent.

94. Player, M. A. (1991). *Federal law of employment discrimination,* 28. St. Paul, MN: West Publishing.

95. Gómez-Mejía, L. R., and Welbourne, T. (1991). Compensation strategies in a global context. *Human Resource Planning, 14*(1), 38; Woodruff, D., and Widman, M. (1996, June 17). East Germany is still a mess—$580 billion later. *BusinessWeek,* 58.

96. Gómez-Mejía, L. R., and Welbourne, T. (1991). Compensation strategies in a global context. *Human Resource Planning, 14*(1), 38.

97. Bureau of National Affairs. (2001). Economic report calls for regulation of core labor standards. Available at www.bna.com.

98. Landsburg, S. (2002, February 11). Highway robbery. *Wall Street Journal,* B-2; Tran, K. T. L., and Johnson, K. (1999, September 30). Nike barred by Spanish court from use of name on sports apparel sold there. *Wall Street Journal,* B-24; Magnuson, P. (2005, January 24). A milestone for human rights. *BusinessWeek,* 63; Barboza, D. (2005, March 21). Wave of corruption tarnishes China's extraordinary growth. *New York Times,* C-1.

99. Wellins, R., and Rioux, S. (2001, February). Solving the global HR puzzle. *Workspan, 44*(2), 1–14.

100. Barrett, A. (1995, April 17). It is a small business world. *BusinessWeek,* 96–97.

101. Cavusgil, T. S. (1984). Organizational characteristics associated with export activity. *Journal of Management Studies, 24*(1), 3–21; Hill, C. W. (2003). *International business.* Chicago: Irwin.

102. Gómez-Mejía, L. R. (1988). The role of human resources strategy in export performance: A longitudinal study. *Strategic Management Journal, 9*(3), 493–505.

103. Echikson, W. (1999, October 11). Designers climb onto the virtual catwalk. *BusinessWeek,* 164–165.

104. *Ibid.*

105. Gomez-Mejia, L. R., Balkin, D. B., and Cardy, R. (2007). *Management.* New York: McGraw-Hill/Irwin.

106. Gomez-Mejia, L. R., Balkin, D. B., and Cardy, R. (2001). *Managing human resources* (3rd ed.). Upper Saddle River, NJ: Prentice Hall.

107. Prasso, S. (2002, April 22). To get an MNA is glorious. *BusinessWeek,* 10.

108. Hardy, Q. (2005, March 14). Technology, saving software from itself. *Forbes,* 60.

Photo Credits

Company, Name, and Product Index